INTERNATIONAL AND COMPARATIVE PATENT LAW

GRAEME B. DINWOODIE

Professor of Law & Norman and Edna Freehling Scholar
Director, Program in Intellectual Property Law
Chicago-Kent College of Law

WILLIAM O. HENNESSEY

Professor of Law
Franklin Pierce Law Center

SHIRA PERLMUTTER

Vice President and Associate General Counsel,
Intellectual Property Policy, AOL Time Warner, Inc.

Former Associate Register for Policy and International Affairs,
U.S. Copyright Office

Former Consultant on Copyright and Electronic Commerce,
World Intellectual Property Organization

LexisNexis™
Matthew Bender®

Library of Congress Cataloging-in-Publication Data

Dinwoodie, Graeme B.
 International and comparative patent law / Graeme B. Dinwoodie, William O.
Hennessey, Shira Perlmutter.
  p. cm.
 Includes index.
 ISBN 0-8205-5468-5 (soft bound)
 1. Patent laws and legislation. 2. Patents (International law) I. Hennessey, William O.
II. Perlmutter, Shira. III. Title.

K1505 .D56 2002
341.7'586—dc21   2002067275

Editorial Offices
744 Broad Street, Newark, NJ 07102 (973) 820-2000
201 Mission St., San Francisco, CA 94105-1831 (415) 908-3200
701 East Water Street, Charlottesville, VA 22902-7587 (804) 972-7600
www.lexis.com

(Pub.3154)

For our parents,

David and Isa
Graeme

Bill and Molly
Bill

Dan and Felice
Shira

PREFACE

Last year, we published our casebook on *International Intellectual Property Law and Policy*. We structured that book in a modular way that facilitates its use for separate discussion of copyright, trademark, or patent issues within the international intellectual property system. This book is in large part the materials from *International Intellectual Property Law and Policy* that pertain to patent and trade secret law and protection of industrial designs, although we have taken advantage of the later publication date to update some of those materials to reflect intervening developments.

More importantly, however, we have added a chapter (Chapter 2) focusing on comparative patent and related law. In that chapter, we explore (before consideration of the international patent system) the differences in national patent laws. This will both permit more extensive examination of how different countries deal with similar problems, and thus offer students an additional perspective from which to evaluate the content of domestic law. Moreover, national patent laws comprise the raw material for any consideration of international patent law. The differences among, and limits and effects of, national laws dictate the priorities of international institutions and laws. Thus, we hope that this set of materials on International and Comparative Patent Law will enable instructors to provide, and students to enjoy, an even more detailed analysis of the patent and trade secret issues with which we must now contend in a global environment.

We have retained some materials on topics that we view as common to all forms of intellectual property law, whether copyright, patent, or trademark. It is important, we believe, to place international patent law in the broader context of the international intellectual property system as a whole. Thus, although Bill was primarily responsible for the materials on patent and trade secret law, this book reflects our collective vision as first reflected in *International Intellectual Property Law and Policy*.

We have adopted the same editing practices as in *International Intellectual Property Law and Policy*. And we remain indebted to the several colleagues mentioned in the Preface to *International Intellectual Property Law and Policy*. To these, we wish to add our thanks to Rochelle Dreyfuss and our research assistant, Joseph Rearden.

GRAEME B. DINWOODIE
WILLIAM O. HENNESSEY
SHIRA PERLMUTTER

October 28, 2002

Preface to *International Intellectual Property Law and Policy (2001)*

We have each been teaching courses in international intellectual property law for several years. This book builds upon the materials that we have used in those courses, albeit with considerable expansion and refinement. The evolution of our materials reflects not only the experience of teaching but also the transformation of the subject. From a "niche" course taught at only a few law schools in the early to mid-1990s, international intellectual property law is fast becoming a staple of the intellectual property curriculum.

Perhaps this should not be surprising. The social, economic and technological changes of the late twentieth century have highlighted the importance of international intellectual property law and policy. One no longer can think or write about, or understand, intellectual property law without considering its international dimension; international developments often drive the content and direction of domestic intellectual property law. Nor, increasingly, can the development of international law and international relations be studied without attention to intellectual property law and policy.

The last couple of years, in particular, have witnessed an explosion of interest in the subject. That interest is the product of several forces, including the incorporation of intellectual property commitments within the primary international trade regime, the development of digital communication technologies which inevitably transcend national borders, the increasing exploitation of products in global markets, and greater public awareness of the role of intellectual property in shaping the conditions in which we live.

Heightened interest in the subject mirrors the frenetic pace of international lawmaking activity in many different fora. Our casebook reflects the causes and consequences of this activity. The very creation of the book embodies the internationalized flavor of modern life. The most substantial work on the project has been undertaken during the last three years, during which time the authors were variously based in Cincinnati, Philadelphia, Chicago, Beijing, Concord, Washington, Geneva and New York. The casebook also reflects the variety of ways in which one can now conceive of a course in international intellectual property law: as a traditional public international law course, as a specialty focus in modern international economic regulation, or as an important case study in international civil litigation.

A word about our approach to selection and editing of materials. We each teach somewhat different courses in international intellectual property law and policy. The book is consciously designed to permit variation (or concentration) tailored to the interests of the particular instructor and students. Thus, we generally group together materials pertaining separately to each of copyright, patent and trademark. But it is important to recognize and discuss the themes that transcend particular intellectual property regimes. Similarly, we largely discuss mechanisms for the acquisition and enforcement of intellectual property rights by private rightholders separately from the development of principles of public international intellectual property law among states. But it is our common preference to expose students to both the public and private aspects of the discipline. An understanding of the interaction between state-to-state relations and private enforcement of rights is crucial to appreciate fully the dynamic underlying the development of this body of law. Our approach to the materials has thus been infused by constant revisiting of integrated and core questions of international intellectual property policy that pervade the subject.

The casebook includes many materials that a student of U.S. intellectual property law might not have encountered. Reading foreign cases and reports of international dispute settlement tribunals is not the equivalent of reading U.S. case reports; and treaty provisions differ in style and structure from statutory text. While we have edited foreign and international materials to improve their use as teaching instruments, we believe that some part of the learning experience involves exposure to these primary materials. We have thus endeavored to retain the style of the original whenever possible. We have also included more articles than typically found in a casebook, especially in discussing the negotiation of treaty provisions. Again, we made a conscious decision that an understanding of this subject requires an appreciation of the more varied sources of thought that distinguish this discipline.

The book, in sum, reflects our collective vision of the system of international intellectual property law. Principal responsibility for the subject matter was, however, divided as follows: Graeme authored the materials on trademark and unfair competition law, geographical indications, and designs; Bill authored the materials on patent and trade secrets; and Shira authored the materials on copyright and related rights. Graeme also was primarily responsible for the materials on private enforcement of rights and state-to-state dispute resolution. Although we did not attempt to compromise our individual styles, we have sought to present a unified book that is both versatile and integrated.

The materials in the book are drawn from a wide variety of sources, and we are grateful to every one of the authors and publishers who graciously permitted our reproduction of their work. Several sources are, however, essential to any study of this subject, and we acknowledge them here both to express our gratitude and as a pointer to students pursuing research. The World Intellectual Property Organization makes available a wealth of information; we visit the WIPO web site (www.wipo.int) on a daily basis.

The Max Planck Institute for Foreign and International Patent, Copyright and Competition Law (based in Munich, Germany) publishes many important works, most notably (for our purposes) the International Review of Industrial Property and Copyright Law (which contains English translations of many foreign materials, particularly case law). The annual Fordham Conference on International Intellectual Property Law and Policy, organized by Hugh Hansen, is a place of pilgrimage for anyone interested in this subject, and the published conference proceedings are a rich source of topical information. More recently, the Journal of World Intellectual Property, and the European Trade Mark Reports and the European Copyright and Design Reports, the latter two of which are edited by Jeremy Phillips, have emerged as indispensable reading. The European Intellectual Property Review offers perspectives on world intellectual property law that belie the geographic limitations of its title. To make the volume of materials manageable, we have of course edited the work of others. This is indicated by ellipses. Deletions of citations are indicated by the bracketed word [cit.] Most footnotes have been omitted without indication; those that remain retain their original numbering.

This book would not have been possible without the support and assistance of many people. Foremost among these is Richard Wilder, with whom we conceived the book before he assumed responsibilities at WIPO that precluded his further involvement in achieving our common conception. Nonetheless, his intellectual fingerprints are manifest through the final product and we are indebted to Richard for his continuing generous assistance. We also benefitted greatly from comments received from the fifteen intellectual property professors who used the materials at different stages between conception and final product, as well as those colleagues and policymakers who offered comments or suggestions on draft sections. In particular, we thank Winifried Arnold, Homer Blair, Chris Blank, Francois Curchod, Christine Farley, Tom Field, Christine Galbraith, Jane Ginsburg, Hans Goldrian, Hugh Hansen, Larry Helfer, Craig Jepson, Karl Jorda, Lydia Loren, Dean Marks, Maria Martin-Prat, Mike Meller, Victor Nabhan, Joseph Straus, Michael Van Alstine and David Welkowitz. Brian Havel not only offered comments based upon his teaching of the materials, but also reviewed the entire manuscript in almost final form. We are immensely grateful.

Students in our classes at several schools offered helpful comments, and various deans supported our project in different but always important ways, including Jim Duggan, Dick Hesse, John Hutson, Chuck Mooney, Eric Neisser, Hank Perritt, Ralph Rohner, Joe Tomain and Robert Viles. We were fortunate to have splendid research assistance from Kevin Bowman, Marc Browning, Michelle Escola, Megan Gervase, J. Mike Hurst, David Lafkas, Eric Moran, Brad McPeek, Jason Otto, Abhijat Parikh, Susan Street, and Sheng Wu.

We are very grateful for the secretarial and publishing support provided by Silvana Burgese, Teresa Burgin, Betty Burks, Ellen Bosman, Julie

Colleluori, Olga Lizunova and Connie Miller. Finally, thanks to our publishers, particularly Heather Dean, Adriana Sciortino, and Lee Freudberg, for validating and encouraging our conception of how to present materials in international intellectual property law and policy. We hope and trust that the final product justifies their faith.

During the course of writing this book, we have been associated with a variety of institutions. Our colleagues in each institution have contributed immeasurably to the development of our views on international intellectual property law and policy. The views expressed in this book are, however, solely those of the authors and do not necessarily reflect the views of any of the institutions, whether academic, governmental, intergovernmental, or business, with which we have been, or currently are, affiliated.

GRAEME B. DINWOODIE
WILLIAM O. HENNESSEY
SHIRA PERLMUTTER

July 1, 2001

SUMMARY TABLE OF CONTENTS

TABLE OF CONTENTS

Page

PART III. PRINCIPLES OF INTERNATIONAL PROTECTION

Chapter 3. International Law and Institutions

**PART IV: ACQUISITION AND ENFORCEMENT OF
RIGHTS INTERNATIONALLY**

**Chapter 6. Mechanisms for the Acquisition of Patent and
Design Rights**

PART V. ISSUES IN INTERNATIONAL INTELLECTUAL PROPERTY LAW AND POLICY LOOKING FORWARD

Chapter 8. Issues in International Property Law and Policy Looking Forward

PART I

OVERVIEW AND INTRODUCTION

Chapter 1

OVERVIEW AND INTRODUCTION

§ 1.01 Overview

Increasingly, intellectual property in general and patents in particular are becoming the subject of significant public international law, that is, part of the web of rights and obligations that exist among sovereign countries. We devote Part III of the book (consisting of Chapters 3–5) to this topic. After introducing (in Chapter 3) some of the basic principles and institutions of public international law upon which public international intellectual property law is founded, we address the development and substantive content of public international patent law in Chapters 4–5. Chapter 4 covers the range of international patent law instruments, and Chapter 5 considers the means and institutions through which states resolve disputes regarding compliance with their international obligations.

Like all intellectual property rights, however, patent rights are territorial in nature. Classically, and still typically, this means that those rights are national in scope. There is, as yet, no such thing as a global patent (or global copyright or global trademark, for that matter). Public international intellectual property laws necessarily build and are dependent upon *national* laws and *private* rights. Countries have a responsibility to implement their international obligations in national intellectual property laws. Thus, whether countries are complying with their international obligations in the field of intellectual property law is largely determined by analysis of their national laws. Countries are motivated to engage in public international lawmaking by the demands of national concerns and by the limitations of national solutions to multinational problems. And although countries construct and administer systems of intellectual property (through administrative agencies and court systems), intellectual property laws are to a great extent used and enforced by private actors. The acquisition, transfer and exploitation of rights is also largely a matter of private arrangement.

This is not to say that international intellectual property law is devoid of public interests. To the contrary, public concerns do (and should) permeate the development of this field. Intellectual property law implements and furthers significant social, cultural, and economic values; and those values are placed front and center in the international context. But it does mean that an understanding of the international intellectual property system requires an appreciation of the means of private enforcement of rights (largely at a national level). Thus, Part IV of the book addresses matters of private international patent law. Chapter 6 focuses on the mechanisms established by international agreement to facilitate multinational acquisition of patent rights. And Chapter 7 looks at private enforcement of rights in an international setting. We conclude in Part V by considering the future directions of international patent law.

This book includes materials drawn both from the United States and elsewhere. U.S. patent laws often differ from those found in other countries, although many basic principles of most national patent laws are similar (and becoming more so with every passing year). We hew to the view that comparative analysis—an examination of how others deal with similar problems—is instructive in and of itself. Such analysis offers an additional perspective from which to evaluate the content of domestic law. But the reasons are even more practical in the study of international patent law. First, the national laws of many countries (or regional groupings of countries, such as the European Union) will be relevant to any transaction involving a foreign or multinational component. And transactions that involve foreign or multinational aspects—whether the persons involved or the conduct at issue—are increasing daily. The subject matter of intellectual property, as well as its role in the development of electronic commerce, places it at the vortex of globalization. Second, the national laws of individual countries throughout the world comprise the raw material for any consideration of public international intellectual property laws. The differences among, and limits and effects of, national laws dictate the priorities of international intellectual property institutions and laws.

Thus, in this book, we precede our discussion of international patent law with a selection of materials (Part II, Chapter 2) exploring patent law from a comparative perspective. These materials, which permit us to address the basic principles of patent law found in different national systems, focus on new technologies—particularly computer technology and biotechnology. Special attention is paid in this Chapter to a comparison of laws in the United States and in Europe, although mention is also made of the laws of other countries and regions.

It is important to understand the differences that exist between the different forms of intellectual property (principally, copyright, trademark, and patent). This is as true in studying international intellectual property law as it is in understanding domestic law. As international intellectual property law has developed and matured, however, many of the institutions that help to shape its content—and many of the basic substantive principles of which it is comprised—transcend particular intellectual property regimes. Thus, we constantly seek to place international patent law in the broader context of the international intellectual property system as a whole. The chapters addressing introductory themes (Chapter 1), general public international law and institutions (Chapter 3), and state-to-state dispute resolution (Chapter 5) in particular exemplify this approach. It is, however, an important question whether such an integrated approach to the field is appropriate; our editorial decision should prompt rather than preclude your continual consideration of that question.

§ 1.02 Introductory Themes

This introductory chapter contains materials that raise some of the basic themes that we will encounter throughout our study of international and comparative patent law. As you read these materials, consider how recent social, economic and political changes have altered the importance of intellectual property, the nature of intellectual property lawmaking, the character of scholarly and public policy debates, and the role and practice of lawyers. Consider also whether some of the concerns and arguments raised appear more or less applicable to different forms of intellectual property, and to patents in particular.

GEORGE KOUMANTOS, REFLECTIONS ON THE CONCEPT OF INTELLECTUAL PROPERTY [*]

Intellectual Property and Information Law: Essays in Honor of Herman Cohen Jehoram 39–45 (1998)

Terminology

Historical research gives us an indication of when the term "intellectual property" first appeared in the sense in which it is used today. Its first official use goes back to the 1950s, when the two International Bureaux set up under the Paris Convention for the Protection of Industrial Property (1883) and the Berne Convention for the Protection of Literary and Artistic Works (1886) to administer the two Conventions—the two bureaux were amalgamated in 1893—were named "Bureaux Internationaux Réunis pour la Propriété Intellectuelle" (BIRPI). These were the forerunners of the "Organisation Mondiale de la Propriété Intellectuelle" [in English, the World Intellectual Property Organization, or "WIPO"] founded in 1967 in Stockholm.

This first official use of the term determines its purport, which coincides with that of the two jointly administered Conventions . . . To begin with, the concept of intellectual property covered literary and artistic property (subsequently more commonly known as "droit d'auteur" ("author's rights") or "copyright" in common law countries—dealt with by the Berne Convention), patents (. . . dealt with by the Paris Convention) and trademarks (. . . also dealt with by the Paris Convention). Another matter dealt with by the [Paris] Convention, the law of unfair competition, could also be regarded as an aspect of intellectual property, but there are some doubts on this point . . . Intellectual property, like most concepts, has with time experienced several shifts in its meaning. . . .

. . . .

Meaning of the Concept

As already indicated, the concept of intellectual property was originally designed to cover ownership of literary and artistic works, inventions (patents) and trademarks. What these three objects of intellectual property have in common is their intangibility. . . . The object of the rights constituting intellectual property is not the tangible support incorporating a literary or artistic work, invention or trademark, but rather the form of the work, the invention, the relationship between a symbol and a business, as such.

This shared characteristic allows for the subsequent enlargement of the concept of intellectual property. This enlargement extends the concept to (a) rights which already existed but were not systematically categorized and (b) rights newly recognized as a result of technological development—where the object of a right transcends tangible support, that right is (or should be) included in the concept of intellectual property.

Thus the concept now covers the following, in addition to patents, trademarks and literary and artistic works:

a. designs and models, which are regulated in part both by the two Conventions cited—Paris and Berne—and the domestic laws of many countries;

b. commercial names, mentioned in the Paris Convention as an object of industrial property and recognized as such . . . by the domestic laws of several countries . . .

c. neighbouring rights, regulated internationally by the Rome Convention of 1961 on the protection of performing artists, producers of gramophone records and broadcasting organizations, and nationally by special provisions, often included in the laws on copyright, and often extending the protection to other categories;

d. plant production rights, which are the subject of an international Convention signed in Paris (in 1961 "for the protection of plant production rights") and revised at Geneva (1978 and 1991), and the domestic laws of the 32 countries that ratified the Convention;

e. the topographies of semiconductor products, which are protected by a Treaty signed at Washington (1989, "on intellectual property regarding integrated circuits," not in force) and European Union Directive 87/54 "on the legal protection of topographies of semiconductor products", which has been incorporated in the domestic law of the EU countries;

f. databases, when protected by a sui generis right—but this new area of intellectual property requires more detailed explanation.

The system adopted by the European Union for databases, [cit], provides two types of protection for this modern form of collection, which is both a work of the mind and a product of investment: copyright protection . . . and protection by a sui generis right (provided the database involves a major investment). This right . . . is in the nature of a neighbouring right and should therefore fall under the heading of intellectual property. But even leaving aside its resemblance to neighbouring rights, the sui generis right over databases should be considered as falling under the heading of intellectual property because of the intangible nature of its object.

. . . .

It remains to be seen whether the list should end here or whether it should be extended to include other objects. The Paris Convention already includes rules on unfair competition in the concept of industrial property. The TRIPS Agreement includes in its list of objects of intellectual property (Article 1 paragraph 2) geographical indications (Articles 22–24) and trade secrets (industrial and commercial, Article 39), in addition to those already mentioned . . . What can we say about this position adopted by two major international agreements?

It should be noted, first of all, that the two additional objects included in the TRIPS Agreement lists merely constitute specific cases of protection against unfair competition. This is stated explicitly in the case of secrets ("to provide effective protection against unfair competition", Article 39 paragraph 1), but the same holds true of [laws permitting the use of] geographical indications [of origin by only producers from the geographical area in question]: it would not be possible to conceive of a subjective right of ownership to a connection between a product and a territorial area, since a right of this kind would belong to all the producers acting in the territorial area and could not be transferred, inherited etc.

The question, then, is whether the rules on unfair competition give rise to objects of intellectual property. From the historical point of view, it should be easy to answer in the affirmative: given that unfair competition is one of the matters regulated by the Paris Convention and the administration of this Convention was one of the factors that led to the first official use of the term "intellectual property" . . . it would seem that this term obviously includes unfair competition. But things are more complicated . . .

Intellectual property, like any other kind of property, is a subjective right relating to an object—in the case of intellectual property a work, invention, trademark etc. At first sight the rules on unfair competition do not give rise to a subjective right and consequently do not relate to an object; they merely forbid certain acts, and interested parties can cite them when applying for the prohibition to be enforced. At the heart of the rules on unfair competition is not an object to be protected but an act to be prevented. This cannot therefore be referred to as property nor, in consequence, as intellectual property.

There is an objection that could be made to this conclusion, however. We have seen that the rules on unfair competition, by forbidding certain acts, aim to protect a specific object, a business as a structured entity consisting of goods, legal relationships and market status (goodwill); the rules on unfair competition would thus give rise to a subjective right and would protect an object. If we accept this principle, the right over the business, created indirectly by the rules on unfair competition, should partake of the nature of intellectual property, since its object, the actual structure of the business, is of the intangible nature required.

. . . .

Different Rules

[T]here are . . . differences in the legal regulation of each of the rights that constitute intellectual property. Thus the rules concerning the object and the extent of the right, as well as the extent of the protection, differ.

First, the object: copyright protects the form or other original aspects of personal intellectual creation in science or art; trademark law protects the connection between a word (or several words) or a picture and the business from which a product or service emanates; and patent law protects invention, i.e., a new solution to a technical problem which can be applied industrially. Here we have three different objects, the first of which is a creation of the mind, the second of commerce and the third of industry or craft.

Then we have the manner of acquisition: copyright is acquired by the mere fact of intellectual creation, without any formalities, in every country in the world (except the United States, to some extent); a trademark on the other hand, is acquired by recording it in the register of trademarks once it has been checked as complying with the conditions—although the mere fact of using it can give rise to certain restricted rights; and the right to use an invention is acquired by the issue of a patent once the formal conditions and basic conditions have been checked (this latter check is cursory in some countries).

Lastly, we have the extent of the protection: first the duration, which, in the case of copyright, varies depending on the domestic laws, with a minimum of fifty years laid down by the Berne Convention, which has now become seventy years in the European Union; in the case of trademarks it lasts ten years and can be renewed indefinitely; patents last twenty years and are non-renewable. Then [sanctions and remedies for infringement] differ as between the three types of right . . .

Monopolies?

The list of differences in the legal regime governing the various rights which constitute intellectual property is a long one. To this we need to add the major differences based on the economic, social and cultural functions of each of them. It is sometimes argued that the rights that constitute intellectual property create monopoly situations . . .

The idea that monopolies are the consequence of exclusive rights that constitute intellectual property is based on the hypothesis that all the objects of these rights are unique. But we need to remember that, in very many cases, the objects of intellectual property are interchangeable: if the right holder of the right to an object lays down exorbitant terms for a licence the user may substitute a different object—such competition breaks the monopoly.

But that is not all: it would be wrong to equate the different categories of rights covered by the concept of intellectual property with regard to the economic, social or cultural weight any monopoly situations created by them could have. After all, there is a big difference between preventing the use of a medicine by virtue of a monopoly and preventing the use of a song or novel. This is why the introduction of non-voluntary licences is often advocated in some areas. Given that the needs differ in intensity, non-voluntary licences (or any other restriction of intellectual property) should be a last resort, and their acceptability and terms and conditions should be examined on a case-by-case basis. To give the same treatment to the different objects of intellectual property goes against a sense of justice.

Is the Concept Justified?

[There are, therefore,] a large number of differences between the various rights covered by the concept of intellectual property—differences relating to the legal basis (national and international) for their protection, the solutions to certain problems which are common to all of them, their legal regulation, and their economic, social and cultural functions. We have even seen that including these rights in a single concept could result in their being given the same or similar treatment (notably in relation to non-voluntary licences and restrictions), failing to appreciate the need to differentiate. Are there enough common factors to justify the mere existence of the concept of intellectual property?

The need for a common administration for the various international Conventions on the specific rights covered by intellectual property cannot be regarded as an adequate raison d'être—albeit this may lie at the root of the concept. What would seem to justify its existence is the fact, already mentioned, that all the rights it covers have an essential common feature: the intangible nature of their respective objects and the consequences of this.

But this is not all: the objects of the rights covered by the concept of intellectual property are manifestations of human creativity. The purpose of regulating these rights is to protect this creativity and the creations emanating from it: literary, artistic and scientific works in the case of copyright, technical innovations in the case of patents, and business enterprise in the case of trademarks. It is this idea of protecting creativity that is the most important common factor in all these rights and the main justification for the concept of intellectual property.

Professor Koumantos references several landmark intellectual property treaties, which we will examine in detail at different parts of the book. The Paris Convention for the Protection of Industrial Property is a multinational agreement to which 162 countries are now party. The Berne Convention for the Protection of Literary and Artistic Works was concluded three years after the Paris Convention and now has 148 signatory parties. These two agreements were the principal international intellectual property agreements for over 100 years, and were revised at successive diplomatic conferences throughout the twentieth century (the most recent being the revision of the Berne Convention in Paris in 1971). The last decade of the twentieth century saw a flurry of activity on other fronts. Professor Koumantos mentions two intellectual property laws of the European Union (EU). The EU has become a powerful influence on the direction and content of international intellectual property laws, in part through its promulgation of "regional" intellectual property laws applicable throughout the territories of its increasingly numerous member states (now fifteen). And, in 1994, when the Uruguay Round of the General Agreement on Tariffs and Trade (GATT) was successfully completed, this hugely significant trade agreement included within it the Agreement on Trade Related Aspects of Intellectual Property (TRIPS). The content and revision of these and other leading agreements, as well as the role of the World Intellectual Property Organization (which administers the Paris and Berne Conventions), the EU, and the World Trade Organization (under whose auspices the TRIPS Agreement is monitored and enforced), are dealt with in detail in Part III *infra*.

ANDREW SULLIVAN, DOT-COMMUNIST MANIFESTO [*]
New York Times Magazine, June 11, 2000 at 30

A sharp, unexpected twang of conscience hit me the other day. It occurred to me as I was merrily downloading the umpteenth Pet Shop Boys B side from another Napster user's hard drive. Was this theft? Nobody, I rationalized, was going to be without the Extended Rollo Mix of "New York City Boy" because of my actions. All Napster is, after all, is a huge database of MP3 files, a musical commune dreamed up by a college-freshman geek. And sharing a database isn't theft. If you agree to join the Napster "community," you agree to share every MP3 you have with any other Napsterite who is online at the same time you are. . . .

So whom was I hurting by copying one lousy song? Sure, I'd avoided paying a record company a royalty—but it was rich enough already. Likewise the Pet Shop Boys. And it wasn't as if I'd smuggled a disc out of Tower Records in a knapsack. It wasn't even in any meaningful sense "mine," since other Napster users could now download it from me without my even noticing. Neither had it been in any meaningful sense "theirs"— once they agreed to pool their own MP3 collection with those of other Napsterites.

What exactly was going on here? The only workable definition is communism. . . . By turning physical property into endlessly duplicable e-property, the ancient human problem of "mine-thine" has been essentially solved. . . .

---

[*] Copyright 2000, New York Times.

J. THOMAS MCCARTHY, INTELLECTUAL PROPERTY— AMERICA'S OVERLOOKED EXPORT[*]
20 U. DAYTON L. REV. 809, 809–819 (1995)

I. INTRODUCTION: THE CHANGING FACE OF AMERICAN INDUSTRY

As we rush through each busy day, we often have to take no more than a hurried glance at the newspaper or at the news on television to see what's going on in the world. Sometimes we see an item that seems trivial on its face, but we subliminally recognize: "That's an amazing development! Things are changing faster than I thought."

A few years ago I saw one of those seemingly trivial facts noted in the business page and realized: "This is an important signal that the America I grew up with had irrevocably changed." What I saw in the newspaper was that the people who run the Dow Jones Index—a list of thirty industrial stocks representing a cross section of American commerce—dropped U.S. Steel from the list and replaced it with the Walt Disney Company. While the announcement may sound inconsequential, the fact that a steel giant was replaced by an entertainment empire is a symbol which keynotes the subject of this Essay.

Chicago Tribune columnist Bob Greene headlined his column on the subject: "A Mouse Replaces Men of Steel." Greene noted that the Dow Jones Index has always been the paramount financial symbol of U.S. business and industry. The Dow Jones industrial average was what American business was all about. It symbolized the source of America's strength and prosperity—or at least a dream of prosperity. A dream that has driven millions of people around the world to get to America at all costs—no matter what the odds—from countries as diverse as China, Russia, and Cuba.

Growing up in the 1940s and 1950s, I lived in what was then America's biggest factory town—Detroit, Michigan. I was taught that America was a great place to live and a robust and strong nation because it made millions of things that people all around the world wanted. Documentaries boosting American industry always seemed to include a shot of the Ford River Rouge plant (complete with smokestacks belching smoke) or a shot of white hot steel being rolled in a Pittsburgh foundry. Needless to say, U.S. Steel was a major part of that view of industrial America.

U.S. Steel stood shoulder to shoulder on the Dow Jones Index with manufacturing companies like Caterpillar, Chevron Oil, General Electric, Goodyear, and Union Carbide. What is a company whose major asset is Mickey Mouse doing with these brawny types?

The face of American business is changing, and changing fast. What America makes and what the rest of the world wants to buy is also changing. In ten years, Disney has grown "from an ailing $2 billion Hollywood also-ran into a $22 billion empire." . . .

Disney sells entertainment through movies, videos, television programs, theme parks, books and records. But what exactly is the basis of the Disney empire? We knew that the heart of U.S. Steel was property—those huge mills spewing sparks, belching smoke and turning out rolled steel twenty-four hours a day. But what is the property that is at the heart of a company like Disney? It is a new kind of property. We call it intellectual property. Intellectual, only because it is a property right in the products of the intellect—a product of the human mind, as opposed to real estate or tangible objects.

I know that I am oversimplifying to make my point. Of course, U.S. Steel had intellectual property in know how and engineering innovations. Disney, of course, owns a substantial amount of highly valuable real estate. But I want to focus on the heart of the fundamental differences between these two companies in order to illustrate how this simple substitution of one company for the other on the Dow Jones Index symbolizes the new era we are entering. Some call it the information age.

II. WHAT IS INTELLECTUAL PROPERTY?

Basically, the subject of all kinds of intellectual property is information. The job of intellectual property law is to create property rights in newly created information. We are continually told that we are entering a post-industrial information age. An age in which by far the most valuable thing to own and control is information—technological information, business information, political information and information about people. . . .

One of the wealthiest and most influential people in America today is Bill Gates, founder of Microsoft. Gates does not get the media coverage of a politician, but I think he is just as influential. And what product does Microsoft make? Nothing tangible, really. . . .

. . . .

III. INTELLECTUAL PROPERTY AND EXPORTS

Intellectual property has become one of the few bright spots in the otherwise dreary U.S. balance-of-trade picture. The rest of the world does not want to buy American cars or steel in the quantities purchased in years past. The world does want, however, to buy our computer programs, our movie and television entertainment and our high-tech information.

The United States enjoys a remarkable seventy-five percent of the international market for prepackaged computer software and a whopping sixty percent of the world market for software-related services. With the exception of agriculture, intellectual property producers make a larger positive contribution to the U.S. trade balance than any other U.S. industry. Although the statistics are largely guesses, U.S. exports of intellectual property have purportedly doubled in recent years and have been estimated to constitute as much as twenty-five percent of U.S. exports. Foreign sales in the copyright industry—publishing, computer programs, film making and the like—are larger than those of paper, plastics, rubber, lumber, pharmaceuticals, textiles and telephone equipment combined.

IV. PRESSURE ON OTHER NATIONS

A great deal of media coverage recently has been devoted to international economic agreements like the North American Free Trade Agreement (NAFTA) and the General Agreement on Tariffs and Trade (GATT). Each have significant intellectual property components built into them. The U.S. government is also conducting bilateral negotiations with several nations, including Japan and the People's Republic of China, seeking changes in their intellectual property laws. Why all this effort by our government, especially in the GATT negotiations, to include intellectual property as a key element of international trade agreements and treaty organizations?

Periodically, on the business page, we read that the U.S. Trade Representative threatens trade sanctions against a foreign nation under so-called "Special 301" or "Super 301" powers. In 1988, Congress created "Special 301," a power given to the U.S. Trade Representative to investigate and identify foreign nations that unjustifiably restrict U.S. commerce. For example, Special 301 gives the U.S. Trade Representative the power to ensure that foreign nations are adequately protecting U.S. intellectual property.

The Trade Representative can start a long, involved process that could eventually result in the imposition of trade sanctions by the President. These sanctions might include placing confiscatory duties on certain goods imported into the United States from the offending nation. Such sanctions are almost like a nuclear deterrent in the world trade war. To my knowledge, the United States has never actually imposed sanctions for failure to give adequate protection for intellectual property, although it has threatened to do so against the People's Republic of China on more than one occasion.

. . . .

Our government seeks to put pressure on other governments, especially those in Asia, to raise the level of their intellectual property protection and enforcement. But why should Americans care whether the People's Republic of China winks at piracy of computer programs and compact discs?

We care because if no intellectual property protection exists regarding technical and entertainment information, then we have little to sell to the rest of the world. In the old days of selling cars, steel, and aluminum to the rest of the world, the kind of patent, trademark and copyright laws implemented by other nations did not make a lot of difference. Their intellectual property laws were their business. Now it is our business.

American businesses suffer the most when an Asian government tolerates the widespread pirating of computer programs and CDS and the Asian market becomes flooded with pirated products. This occurs because America supplies the bulk of the world's software and music, as well as video tapes. While the Asian nations produce most of the hardware used in the entertainment and computer industries, such as televisions, CD players, and PC clones, America supplies the content for that hardware—the shows, songs, and software that makes the hardware valuable. If foreign nations do not recognize or enforce intellectual property laws, then America has nothing to sell . . .

If an American company sells only a few copies of a computer program or video because social customs permit widespread reproduction, then much less incentive exists to produce the product in the first place. Fewer copies will be produced and fewer Americans will be hired to produce those copies. In the information age, ineffective intellectual property protection and enforcement results in less protectable material produced. This phenomenon bodes poorly for the future of the United States, because we cannot compete in a world market for producing steel or clothes or VCRs when manufacturers in developing nations can pay what we would regard as a less than living wage. That leads to cries for protectionist legislation like trade barriers and tariffs.

. . . .

VI. DEMANDS OF FOREIGN TRADE DRIVE CHANGES IN UNITED STATES LAW

A new phenomenon in U.S. intellectual property law is that changes in our domestic law are being driven by the needs of world trade. For the first 200 years of our nation's history, we very loosely based our intellectual property laws on those of Great Britain. As the years went by, however, our laws became more and more idiosyncratic. Our intellectual property laws developed so differently from those of the rest of the world that they became a real impediment to free trade.

For example, we are still the only nation in the world to have a "first to invent" rule in our patent system to resolve situations in which more than one person claims to have created the same patentable invention. In the United States, the inventor who was first to invent the invention—not the first to file a patent application—is the owner of the patent. This rule requires an elaborate procedure called an "interference." The purpose of interference proceedings is to reveal who was first to conceive of and reduce the invention to practice. Interference proceedings will become even more elaborate now that GATT has been implemented in U.S. law. Among other changes, GATT expands the range of possible locations in which inventive activity counts towards priority to include activity that occurs within any of the World Trade Organization member countries.

In 1989, the United States changed to an intent to use trademark application system because we were the only nation in the world clinging to the notion that you had to use your trademark before you could apply to register it. We changed to a trademark registration system in which the merchant had an option and could choose to file the old way or the new way—via an "intent to use statement" prior to any use whatsoever of the designation intended to be used in the future as a trademark. Today, nearly half of all trademark applications are filed under the new intent to use system.

Similarly, until 1989, the United States was almost the only nation in the world to require that all distributed copies of software be marked with a copyright notice—the name, date and an encircled "c." If this technicality was not observed, the author or computer programmer lost the copyright. This highly technical requirement was not removed until 1989 when the United States became the last developed nation to join the Berne Union, the premier international copyright treaty organization.

Several recent changes in U.S. law were also required by the NAFTA and GATT agreements. All of these changes were driven by the need for harmonizing the United States' laws with those of our trading partners. No major trading nation in today's world can enjoy the indulgence of having intellectual property laws significantly different from those of the world community. In one sense, unusual intellectual property laws are a tariff and an unnatural barrier to world trade.

VII. INTELLECTUAL PROPERTY LAWS TRY TO KEEP UP TO DATE

Our present intellectual property laws are having trouble keeping up with the accelerating pace of innovation. . . .

In the trademark area, technology makes counterfeiting easier than ever, making the war on trademark counterfeiting harder than ever. It is estimated that world-wide losses to U.S. firms from counterfeiting are approaching $75 billion. Counterfeiting of status marks for luxury items, like fake Rolex watches, is not the real problem. The real counterfeiting problem is fake drugs and defective industrial parts.[20] Almost nine out of every ten fasteners, such as bolts and screws, used in the United States are imported, and it is estimated that more than six of every ten fasteners are counterfeit. Even more threatening are the counterfeit and ineffective drugs and pharmaceuticals that have caused hundreds of deaths in developing nations.

Looming on the horizon in the copyright field is the impact of the much discussed information superhighway. What will be its effect on the ability to charge for reproduction and display of copyrighted works? Millions of people are plugging into electronic networks such as the Internet, which connects your personal computer with any other computer in the world. This means that you can send any computer program, anything in print, or any picture, on the "net." The item can be put on an electronic bulletin

---

[20] *See Boeing Probes "Bogus" Parts Claims,* S.F. CHRON., Aug. 27, 1988, at A4 ("Some Boeing 737, 747, and 757 jet airliners manufactured since mid-1986 were fitted with more than 2000 allegedly counterfeit ball bearings that an engineer said could 'pose serious hazards'. . . ").

board, where anyone, anywhere in the world, can download it. How can you charge for the use of such copying and how can you even know copying has taken place? This puts copyright law right in the middle of cyberspace.

As computers plug into the global net and so-called cyberspace, the physical containers in which we are used to seeing information bottled up—like floppy disks and CD-ROMs—may become obsolete. Once that happens, all products of the information age, from books to films to computer programs, will exist as speeding electrons dancing around the world on the computer net. Where do we put the copyright turnstile on the global computer network in order to charge users and copiers?

. . .

VIII. CONCLUSION

Now the United States prepares to enter the information age and the twenty-first century, where intellectual property will be more important than property in land, buildings or objects. This will be an age in which the most important exports of the United States will be information and the means to control it, store it, and access it.

This will be an age in which all information will be broken into digital bits and sent back and forth around the world to be read on computer screens from Singapore to Chicago to Moscow. But who will thrive and prosper from this torrent of information zipping around the world? Like every other age throughout history, this will be an age of "haves" and "have nots." There will be those who have the knowledge and ability to control and access data and those who do not. There will still be plenty of piecework and manufacturing jobs, but they may be low-paying and located mainly in whatever nation is just emerging from its feudal, pre-industrial state of development.

As we read in the newspapers every day, it seems that while half the world is rushing to embrace the post-industrial information age, the other half seems to be sliding back into a medieval horror of cruel despotic governments, bloody ethnic civil war, widespread famine and killer epidemics. In part, it is a result of the information age that we are made so much aware of what happened this morning in Somalia or Rwanda or Bosnia. With hand-held videocameras, ubiquitous satellite disks and CNN, visual images appear almost instantaneously. Will the information age help or hurt efforts to solve age-old problems such as war and famine? . . .

As we enter the information age, both we and the world intellectual property system will have to change and adjust to new realities. Paradoxically, the world is getting bigger and smaller at the same time. The world is getting bigger because its population, now almost 5.7 billion, is growing at a record pace of more than ninety million persons a year.

At the same time, the world is getting smaller as global communications via computer networks make it easier to communicate and swap huge amounts of information. There is no doubt that in this new world, intellectual property must, and will, grow in importance. Intellectual property is the law's recognition that information is property—and we all know that property is power.

GRAEME B. DINWOODIE, THE INTEGRATION OF DOMESTIC AND INTERNATIONAL INTELLECTUAL PROPERTY LAWMAKING *
23 COLUM.-V.L.A. J.L. & ARTS 307, 307–08 (1999)

It is increasingly impossible to analyze intellectual property law and policy without reference to international lawmaking. That is not, however, merely because several recent domestic reforms have been prompted by international developments. [1] Indeed, because of significant U.S. influence in the formation of contemporary intellectual property treaties, U.S. law has undergone less change than most in order to comply with newly-assumed international obligations. Nor is it merely because, in an era of global trade and technological advances, a state is unable effectively to regulate economic activity on its own. Rather, the need for a broader awareness flows most directly from the integration of the international and domestic lawmaking processes.

Consider this historical example. As nations met in Berlin in 1908 to revise the Berne Convention, the United States received an invitation to attend "with full freedom of action." Instead, however, the Register of Copyrights attended only as an observer. The reason might now seem unduly quaint.

> [T]he Register of Copyrights explained to the Conference that the United States found it impractical to send a delegate authorized to commit it to actual adhesion to the Berne Convention since some of the questions to be discussed there were pending before the Congress and premature action at the Convention might embarrass the legislative branch of the Government. [2]

Today, in contrast, there is a conscious blending of domestic and international lawmaking. International lawmaking demands attention to Washington; and domestic lawmaking cannot be conducted without regard for what is going on in Brussels, Geneva, Tokyo and elsewhere. Indeed, in some areas of intellectual property, we may be moving toward a single lawmaking

---

[1] *See, e.g.*, Sonny Bono Copyright Term Extension Act, Pub. L. No. 105-298, tit. I, 112 Stat. 2827 (1998) (extending term of copyright partly in response to EU Term Directive); Digital Millennium Copyright Act, Pub. L. No. 105-304, 112 Stat. 2860 (1998) Tit. I (implementing WIPO Copyright Treaty); Uruguay Round Agreements Act, Pub. L. No. 103-465, 108 Stat. 4809 (1994), Tit. V (implementing TRIPS Agreement); Trademark Law Treaty Implementation Act, Pub. L. No. 105-330, 112 Stat. 3064 (1998), Tit. I (implementing Trademark Law Treaty).

[2] Barbara Ringer, *The Role of the United States in International Copyright—Past, Present and Future,* 56 GEO. L.J. 1050, 1057 (1968).

process that embodies a series of complex relations among national, regional and global institutions and laws.

Within the United States, this biplay between national and international fora—in particular, between executive branch activity at the international level, and legislative activity in Congress—has been treated by some with a certain suspicion. This interaction is, however, essential in a global age. And it should not be disconcerting. The Constitution sets out a process for concluding and ratifying treaties, and a separate process for enacting legislation. Each mechanism has its own limits. It would be somewhat surprising if each branch of government did not use the leverage with which it is endowed by the constitutional scheme. In any event, this blending or integration of lawmaking is a political reality of which we must take account in our assessment of how intellectual property law is made.

RUTH L. GANA, HAS CREATIVITY DIED IN THE THIRD WORLD? SOME IMPLICATIONS OF THE INTERNATIONALIZATION OF INTELLECTUAL PROPERTY[*]
24 DENV. J. INT'L L. & POL. 109, 112–16 & 141–42 (1995)

[A]ll forms of creative expression—mechanical, literary, or artistic—are value driven. The nature and variety of goods produced in any society is, initially, a function of needs as the popular adage "necessity is the mother of invention" attests. More important, however, the laws which protect these inventions—laws which define what is to be protected and how that protection is to be effected—reflect the underlying values of a society. Intellectual property law, like other law "is more than just another opinion; not because it embodies all right values, or because the values it does embody tend from time to time to reflect those of a majority or plurality, but because it is the value of values. Law is the principle institution through which a society can assert its values."

Further, the selection of what goods to protect and the nature of such protection is shaped by values and needs in accordance with a society's perceptions of what constitutes "the good life." Nowhere is this more reflected than in the Anglo-American philosophy of copyright protection which seeks to balance private reward and encouragement of creative activity with public benefit of access to a goodly supply of literary works. In Macauley's celebrated 1841 speech in the English House of Commons, the need for copyright was expressed as a matter of value and perceptions of what is needed for a good life. . . .In the United States, Thomas Jefferson's famed letter to Isaac McPherson on the protection of intellectual property reveals a similar understanding of the incidents of the good life and society. . . .

The idea that copyright, as well as other forms of exclusive privileges, was a necessary part of the good society reflects values such as liberty,

---

property, private enterprise, accumulation of capital and rapid consumption; in a word, values that nurture capitalism. . . .

. . . .

The modern debate over intellectual property protection in developing countries has failed to take account of cultural differences which affect the understanding of what constitutes property or what may rightfully be the subject of private ownership. . . . [I]t is important for the modern debate to link intellectual property laws to the social realities of societies in developing countries. Not only may this yield more effective approaches to securing enforcement of intellectual property rights in developing countries, it also presents the possibility that western based intellectual property laws may have some real impact on industrial innovative activity in these countries, thus contributing to the economic welfare of the Third World. However, . . . culture may influence what is created but it is those values, rooted in a conception of a good society, that determine how and what kind of intellectual property laws societies enact.

. . . .

SOME IMPLICATIONS

It is quite clear that one of the central motivations behind the TRIPS agreement was to target enforceability of foreign intellectual property rights in developing countries. As such, the global model of intellectual property protection imposed by the agreement is not a reflection of the need to encourage creativity or to promote the public welfare. Rather, the chief aim of the agreement is to secure from these countries and societies the full monopoly benefits that western intellectual property laws offer. The implications of these strategic moves are many . . .

. . . .

The need to maintain incentives to encourage creative activity is limited, in many respects, to western market democracies. These democracies revolve, in large part, around individual autonomy and liberty, notwithstanding the greater social loss of nonmaterial value that individualism tends to breed. The successful commodification of intellectual goods can only be achieved in a society which embraces this sort of rugged individualism. Until indigenous societies reach this point, the international community may have to come to terms with a persistent level of piracy in international trade. Piracy, however, cannot simply be explained mechanically in economic terms based on the reasoning that poverty necessitates the availability of cheap products. For many of these societies, the difficulty in introducing western copyright principles is that these principles attempt to overturn social values which are centuries old. The laws protecting intellectual goods in these societies simply reflect fundamental notions of what the society considers to be the appropriate subject of exclusive ownership. The duplication of literary work is thus, for example, not perceived as stealing but as making a good thing accessible to the general public. Knowledge in many indigenous societies is not perceived as something that can be commodified or objectified through law. It is impossible to ignore such fundamental conceptions in these communities.

In addition to responding to a persistent level of piracy, the internationalization of intellectual property also suggests that there is some way to objectively measure protection of intellectual property. By not taking into account the possibility of alternative forms of protection, the TRIPS agreement, as did its predecessor treaties, presupposes that "all civilized nations" will and must recognize this global model of intellectual property protection. By mandating this model, governments in developing countries are faced with the difficult job of destroying, or at least attempting to destroy, native conceptions about life and living and about what constitutes an ordered society. The allocation of material value to goods, and the way in which this value is expressed, is grounded firmly in the history of the evolution of a people. The internationalization of intellectual property threatens to undermine, if not totally destroy, the values that indigenous systems ascribe to intellectual property and the manner in which they allocate rights to intellectual goods.

What the internationalization of intellectual property implies, ultimately, is that there is only one way to participate in the international economy and that is by playing in accordance with prescribed rules, regardless of its impact on a group of peoples. It is a message that is not unfamiliar in the history of world affairs, and yet it is a message which, so history informs us, has caused devastation of unimagined proportions to human society. The next few years will reveal just how far native peoples, indigenous groups, and developing countries will fare in the preservation of their cultural patrimony and in their ability to determine the identity of their group in an increasingly hostile international economic environment.

P. JOHN KOZYRIS, COMPARATIVE LAW FOR THE TWENTY-FIRST CENTURY: NEW HORIZONS AND NEW TECHNOLOGIES[*]
69 TUL. L. REV. 165, 167–178 (1994)

COMPARATIVE LAW HERE AND NOW

Before gazing at the crystal ball, I will articulate three noncontroversial propositions about the here and now of comparative law; and before investigating the new horizons of comparative law, I will review the impact of new technologies.

My first proposition is that the utility of the comparative method is beyond dispute. Comparative law not only provides alternative solutions to be used in legal reform but also gives us a better understanding of our existing law. In short, it is an indispensable tool of legal science. In addition,

---

[*] Reprinted with permission of the Tulane Law Review Association, which holds the copyright. All rights reserved.

the internationalization of transactions and the increasing applicability of foreign law make comparative law an indispensable tool of the legal practitioner.

In 1951, Professor Ferdinand Stone told a story which rings true now more than ever. The story was about a man who traveled "from place to place upon the earth."

> [W]herever he went he would pick up bricks and compare them carefully one with another. His conduct excited comment. One man said, "he must be seeking the most perfect of all bricks." Another said, "he must be seeking to describe the qualities inherent in all bricks." Still another of a practical turn of mind said, "he is probably seeking a brick of just the right shape and color to fit into his wall." And still another said, "it is possible that he is not interested in the bricks as such but in their composition. Perhaps, he would set up a kiln of his own for making bricks."[15]

My comment is that these are all valid descriptions of the use of the comparative method today.

Any science, theoretical or applied, that would limit itself to one nation would be laughable.[16] Nevertheless, confused by the historical school and cowed by legal positivism, we have developed too parochial a view of legal science. We have lost sight of the fact that law is a universal phenomenon, and not just the temporal product of the lawmaker in a particular society. Common denominators in the human social condition demand a unified legal science. To be sure, a lawyer normally practices within one country and thus must acquire specialized, practical knowledge of local laws.[17] But a lawyer, even in the most mundane practice, will be impoverished if he wears the blinders of his own jurisdiction.

The great reliance on the comparative method in the world today testifies to its validity. In both the contexts of the conglomeration of states, such as the European Economic Community, now the European Union, which has become a vibrant comparative law lab, and of the disintegration of empires, as in the East where massive law reform is taking place, comparative law has proved vital.

In the United States, the best evidence of our recognition of the value of comparative law is that we teach even domestic law by the comparative method. No self-respecting law school teaches merely the laws of its own state. The Brandeisian idea of the states as law labs is deeply ingrained. Why do we teach in this manner even when many of the students are likely to practice in-state? The comparative method is a natural in America because we typically teach through fact patterns and cases, not statutes.

---

[15] Ferdinand F. Stone, *The End to Be Served by Comparative Law*, 25 Tul. L. Rev. 325 (1951).

[16] For example, imagine the sciences of medicine or horticulture confining themselves only to American medicine or American horticulture.

[17] Similarly, an American horticulturist may not typically specialize in jungle flora, or an American doctor may not become an expert on amoebiasis or yellow fever.

We reward students not so much for right answers as for seeing as many angles as possible and for arguing in every plausible policy direction, which necessitates transcending the boundaries of any one jurisdiction.

The main reason why we do not use much truly foreign law rather than sister-state law in our teaching is logistical, not conceptual. We face serious linguistic and cultural obstacles. Besides, there already exists too much material to cover from the United States materials alone. Yet, we are missing an important dimension by just keeping to one nation, however big and diverse it may be.

My second, and rather obvious point, is that you cannot truly pursue the comparative method through the study of formal legal texts alone. It is necessary to get to know what is behind the texts and also, even more important, how they function. This requires understanding the legal culture that produced the laws, and more broadly, the social and economic structures and the ethical and political values that support them. Laws cannot be grasped in an idealized form outside the context of the society that created them. Before a legal model can be transplanted, the conditions in the two societies—the one from which it comes and the one to which it goes—must be taken into account. To be sure, the more similar the societies, the less the need to engage in elaborate socio-legal studies. Eventually, the global village created under industrialization, urbanization, and the homogenizing influence of the global mass media may reduce such need even further. But we still have a long way to go before we can assume compatibility.

My third and final point on the here and now of comparative law is that, in the last half century or so, comparative law has exhibited remarkable stability within the United States and abroad. . . . [W]ith one apparent and one real exception, . . . the fundamentals of comparative law have not changed much in our times.

The apparent change relates to the growing literature from outside the United States and Western Europe, especially from Asia and Africa, as well as from some formerly communist nations. It would thus appear that comparative law is moving from eurocentric to global. There is some truth to this perception, but it is important to see it in the proper light. For example, close to half of the space in the first two issues of this year's American Journal of Comparative Law is devoted to judicial review in Korea and Poland, the Korean press law, the notion of legal personality in China, and legal thinking in Micronesia. Yet, with the exception of the last piece, the discourse is conducted with the traditional tools of the western legal tradition. Even the Micronesian article represents an exercise in western legal realism. What has happened, I believe, and this is starkly evident in Eastern Europe, is that the western legal tradition has spread all over the developed and developing world under the rubric of modernization. In the process, the western tradition has undoubtedly been enriched by other legal cultures. However, it remains dominant and, if anything, is becoming universal.

The real change relates to the shift of the center of gravity from private law and formal criminal law to public and regulatory law. The reasons why modern comparative law originally focused on private themes are rather clear. The great Roman law tradition, systematized and refined by legal science over the centuries, exploded into an array of comprehensive private law codes. These codes were not only detailed and stable but also traced their pedigree to reason, making them ideally suited to textual comparison and to the pursuit of erudite distinctions and penumbral nuances. By contrast, public and regulatory law was seen not only as more rough, raw, and untidy, but also as more positive, expressing the will of the sovereign, and more temporal, connected to the volksgeist of particular places and periods.

The centrality of public and regulatory law, however, has never been questioned. As the nations of the world, especially after World War II, were seeking their way in constitutionalism and liberal democracy, comparative constitutional law, starting with judicial review and expanding into political, civil, and human rights, attracted a lot of attention. With both the formation and disintegration of composite states, such as the European Union and the Soviet Union, comparative federalism has become a hot, complex, and fascinating topic. In the economic sphere, antitrust and, more recently, environmental law have also claimed their place under the sun of comparison.

In fact, comparative work in public law is more difficult because it requires not only technical expertise but also the ability to delve into policy issues in diverse social contexts. But the more that the conditions in the world become homogenized, the more the organization of power within societies falls into typical patterns, and the easier it becomes to control the variables necessary to use the comparative method fruitfully.

. . . .

NEW TECHNOLOGIES

In switching the discussion from the here and now of comparative law to new horizons for the twenty-first century, let me say a few words about the implications of new technologies. Printed materials on foreign law, especially in the English language, have become available at a fast pace. . . .

The most remarkable revolution in technology, however, has occurred in electronics. We all know how Lexis and Westlaw have dramatically changed the modes and speed of domestic legal research. In the comparative field, together with the Internet, Lexis and Westlaw are also doing quite a lot. First, they provide instant access to foreign materials in English, which are otherwise difficult, if not impossible, to find, especially in updated form. Second, Lexis has crossed the language barrier, giving us numerous materials in French. Other languages, at least those using the Latin alphabet, could easily be added. Third, the Internet not only provides access to specialized library catalogues but also enables faculty and other law professionals to communicate, form discussion groups, and share their ideas all over the world. And this is only the beginning. Before the end of the twentieth century, let alone the next century, these services will grow exponentially and their cost will decline. Foreign law information will be at every lawyer's fingertips, and most of it will be in the new lingua franca, English.

It is also very important to note that Lexis and Westlaw are not merely opening doors to information. As they become dominant worldwide, they set the standards for law retrieval along the patterns of the common law system, especially the American one, which relies heavily on key words and factual similarities rather than on statutory texts or conceptual analysis. As lawyers in other nations learn to use these services, they are bound to be influenced by the subtle shift in legal method from civilian deduction to common law induction.

NEW HORIZONS

. . . .

Let me conclude by briefly outlining my main points. Comparative law is now technologically easier, has crossed over from the private into the public domain, and is needed now more than ever because of the expansion of international transactions; the globalization of legal culture; and the movements for unification, federation, and law reform around the world. . . . In the twenty-first century, the United States would be well served if it were to make a public commitment to promote the scientific study of law, not only for the sake of study, but also to insulate our laws from the influence of special interests and to make them more systematic, consistent, and technically expert. . . .

WILLIAM L. KEEFAUVER, THE NEED FOR INTERNATIONAL THINKING IN INTELLECTUAL PROPERTY LAW *
37 IDEA 181 (1996)

In the late 1930s, Senator Arthur Vandenberg of Michigan was one of the leading isolationists in the U.S. Senate. But toward the end of the decade, as events in Europe were beginning to overtake us, he made a sudden conversion and became an internationalist. Because Senator Vandenberg was highly respected in foreign policy, I naively thought that this marked the end of isolationism. I was obviously a little premature, however, because even today we continue to hear proponents of isolationism, including a recent candidate for President of the United States.

---

* Copyright 1996, Franklin Pierce Law Center. IDEA is the intellectual property law journal at Franklin Pierce Law Center.

My focus here, however, is intellectual property, not politics. Intellectual property specialists from long before Senator Vandenberg have had to practice in the international field, making it essential for them to understand the laws and practices of many countries. But in those days, intellectual property specialists were what I would call "multinational" lawyers rather than international lawyers due to the lack of congruency between the laws of the different countries.

In the 1970s, a strong trend toward globalization of markets began. This trend was stimulated not only by advances in telecommunications, but also by the desires of suppliers to seek additional sources of revenue beyond their borders. Others found it necessary to counterattack by entering the home markets of these new foreign competitors. Simultaneously, the sometimes significant differences around the world in intellectual property protection began colliding with each other as companies formed business ventures across national lines. It then became important to see whether these friction points could be reduced.

. . . .

[I]t is market forces, not intellectual property lawyers, which have globalized the practice, and it is up to us as practitioners to make globalization work for our clients. With a focus on our clients, we must work to reduce some of the friction points by working for beneficial changes in conflicting laws and by becoming sufficiently knowledgeable of the laws and practices of other countries.

. . . .

Like many U.S. companies, my company, AT&T, had a domestic patent attorney group which focused on the United States and a foreign group to deal with other countries. However, it was during the period since the 1970s that I became aware of the globalization trend. I was also convinced that in order to represent client interests adequately, it was no longer sufficient for lawyers working in the United States to think of themselves solely as U.S. practitioners. So I announced a new paradigm for AT&T: henceforth, there would be no such dichotomy; every lawyer would be a global lawyer and have to become sufficiently knowledgeable to deal with the patent laws of all countries in which the corporation was interested.

This new paradigm meant worldwide patent prosecution responsibility. Also, when helping clients develop intellectual property strategies, the new global lawyer would do so from a worldwide perspective. Although I felt I was announcing a "sea of change," it met with little resistance. It had become obvious that we could no longer live on our own little island of U.S. law and claim to be providing adequate client representation. We simply had to know what was happening throughout the world.

Much of AT&T's globalization was driven by joint venture activity. Like many other companies, AT&T found that the only way to enter certain foreign markets was through joint ventures with local firms. If you have ever negotiated or looked at a joint venture agreement, you know that a major component is often the intellectual property piece which usually covers patents, trademarks, copyrights, software, and technical information. Quite often, a joint venture agreement has rights flowing to and from many countries. It takes a lot of creativity to reach agreement and usually involves negotiations by lawyers and businesspeople from several countries.

The intellectual property lawyers almost inevitably get involved in the business aspects of the deal since the allocation of rights often depends on the structuring of the work agreement and vice versa. Significantly, these negotiations are truly negotiations and are quite different from those of previous decades when a U.S. company could simply dictate the terms. All of this has not only been instructive, but also very helpful in broadening the perspectives of practitioners accustomed to thinking only of U.S. law.

Some of our U.S. colleagues continue to feel that to think internationally or to talk about compromise and change in U.S. law is to somehow put the United States in second place. My view is very clearly the opposite. Thinking internationally does not put the U.S. in second place. Rather, you have to think internationally to put the United States and your company or client in first place.

Certainly, all aspects of intellectual property now have a global dimension. Fortunately, we have been able to harmonize some of the more serious differences in copyright law as well as trademark law, and to some extent, patent law. These harmonization efforts, taken with the TRIPS agreement, should make it even more natural to think of intellectual property in international terms. Lawyers who do not think in these terms simply are not fulfilling their duties to their clients.

In a global market place there is little room for isolationism, and it is clear that our clients are thinking in international terms. We, as intellectual property lawyers, must have the same frame of reference as our clients to adequately and ethically support them.

NOTES AND QUESTIONS

(1) **The Changing U.S. Economy.** The development that begins Professor McCarthy's essay has since been repeated. On October 26, 1999, the editors of the *Wall Street Journal* (who select the stocks that comprise the Dow Jones Index) announced that in order to make the Dow Jones Index "even more representative of the evolving U.S. economy," the Index would no longer include the oil company Chevron, the retail chain Sears Roebuck, the chemical company Union Carbide, and Goodyear Tire and Rubber Co., but instead would include Intel, Microsoft, Home Depot (the specialty retailer), and SBC Communications, one of the regional Bell phone companies. *See* Floyd Norris, *Dow Takes On a New, High-Technology Look*, Oct. 27, 1999, N.Y. TIMES at C1 (noting that "until 1997, the Dow had just one large computer technology company, IBM. Then it added Hewlett-Packard,

and now it is adding Microsoft, the dominant personal computer software company, and Intel, the leading maker of semiconductor chips for such computers.").

(2) **Globalization.** The term "globalization" is frequently used to describe some of the contemporary phenomena discussed in the preceding excerpts. What does this (probably over-used) term mean? What is causing these changes in legal practice, economic priorities, lawmaking, and scholarly inquiry? Do the descriptions of social, political and economic change offered in these excerpts capture all the causes of globalization? Do they consider all the effects? To what extent should we critique the reasons for these changes, or should we simply address their consequences? What is the role of intellectual property law, or intellectual property lawyers or policy-makers, in the midst of these changes? Are you persuaded by Keefauver's distinction between intellectual property law and politics? Is it the role of lawyers "to make globalization work for our clients"?

(3) **The Significance of Intellectual Property in a Global Economy.** What characteristics of intellectual property explain its social, economic and political significance? Professor McCarthy suggests that Microsoft founder Bill Gates may be "one of the most influential people in America today." Why might that be the case? To what extent does ownership of intellectual property confer more influence or power in modern society than ownership of tangible property? Which of its characteristics have forced policymakers to address intellectual property law on the international stage? Are there considerations other than the inherent characteristics of intellectual property that have driven efforts to address intellectual prop-erty internationally? What might those external forces be? Do you agree with Professor McCarthy's assessment that "if foreign nations do not recognize or enforce intellectual property laws, then America has nothing to sell"?

(4) **The Costs and Benefits of Different National Laws.** What are the costs and benefits of intellectual property laws differing from country to country? Does this depend upon the nature of the differences? Which differences are likely to produce net gains, and which ones are likely to produce net costs? Are there circumstances in which possibly divergent national approaches might be necessary, or even desirable? In which circumstances is internationalization most warranted or most necessary? Who benefits from international standards of intellectual property law?

(5) **The Values Underlying Intellectual Property Laws.** What are the consequences of calling products of creativity "property?" How universal are the concerns articulated by McCarthy and Keefauver? What are the premises upon which these writers found their vision of intellectual property? A noted economist who is a wholesale critic of the intellectual property system argues that:

> [T]he idea that people should be paid to be creative is a point of view that stems from the Judeo-Christian and Muslim belief in a God who created humankind in His image. It has no analogue in

Hindu, Buddhist, or Confucian societies. There are real differences
in beliefs about what should be freely available in the public domain
and what should be for sale in the private marketplace.

Lester Thurow, *Needed: A New System of Intellectual Property Rights*,
HARV. BUS. REV., Sept. 1997, at 95, 100; *see also* DAVID F. NOBLE, THE
RELIGION OF TECHNOLOGY (1999). Is establishment of a strong intellectual
property system in a country which has a non-Western cultural and
religious heritage necessarily an indication that it is becoming Westernized,
or becoming "modernized"? Are there any differences between moderniza-
tion and Westernization? Is the Western paradigm becoming universal, as
Professor Kozyris suggests?

(6) **Thinking Internationally**. What does Keefauver mean by "thinking
internationally"? Is that what Professors McCarthy, Dinwoodie, Kozyris
and Gana are doing? What would be the consequences of American "isolationism" in the field of intellectual property law? Political commentators
have noted that there are two different forms of isolationism: one "rests
partly on a fearful assessment of America's ability to compete in a global
economy. The other derives not from . . . insecurities . . . but, conversely,
from a supreme self-confidence that America can go it alone, that its wealth
and military power make international treaties unnecessary." *Isolationism's Return*, N.Y. TIMES, Oct. 31, 1999, at WK14. To what extent does
either of these isolationist philosophies carry weight in determining the
policy that the United States should adopt toward international intellectual
property relations? Are there dangers in too effusive an embrace of international lawmaking? Two prominent scholars have noted that:

> [H]ow radically the world intellectual property policymaking arena
> has changed in the last several years. In this climate, it is literally
> possible for an as yet unimplemented legislative initiative of one
> government to become an international minimum standard for
> other governments before most people affected by it . . . even know
> that proposals for new intellectual property rights have been put
> on the table.

J.H. Reichman & Pamela Samuelson, *Intellectual Property Rights in Data?*,
50 VAND. L. REV. 51, 76 (1997).

Several U.S. academic commentators have bemoaned the extent to which
national legislatures in developed countries have been captured by industries seeking higher levels of intellectual property protection. Even before
we consider the international lawmaking institutions in detail, would you
expect special interests to have more or less influence in an enlarged and
more multifaceted lawmaking process (involving, as we will see, foreign
legislatures, international intellectual property institutions such as the World
Intellectual Property Organization, treaty negotiators, trade representatives, and dispute panels convened under the aegis of the World Trade
Organization) than before the U.S. Congress? What information would you
want to know to answer this question?

(7) **Civil Law Systems.** Civil law systems are generally founded on extensive statutory statements (normally, codifications) of the law, and these form the basis for judicial analysis. Civil law systems thus do not generally use a system of case law precedent where courts are *bound* to follow rules announced in certain earlier decisions. Courts in civil law countries are, however, generally influenced by prior decisions. Although earlier cases are not formally a "source of law," they naturally form part of the legal debate regarding the appropriate resolution of similar disputes. Courts in civil law countries aim to decide like cases alike, and they recognize the reality of the parties' appealing to higher courts that may have rendered the earlier decisions. Moreover, some civil law systems adhere to a philosophy of *jurisprudence constante*, under which a pattern of similar like decisions justifies the application of a constant rule. This philosophy requires a series of decisions before the reasoning underlying those decisions holds sway with later courts; a common law system of binding precedent gives greater weight to single decisions of courts of a particular level. But opinions in civilian systems are framed less formally by the need to consider prior decisions. This should be borne in mind in reading certain non-U.S. cases. (Decisions of courts in common law countries other than the United States may also be structured differently, for other reasons.) The concept of binding precedent develops most easily in legal systems where significant case law develops, and where there is routinized and accessible reporting of that case law. What other requirements are essential in order to employ a system of binding precedent? In what ways, other than contributing toward a system of binding precedent, might decided case law be used to further important public policy objectives?

A leading twentieth century Scottish judge, Lord Cooper, whose position on the highest Scottish court exposed him to a traditionally civilian system with a modern (English) common law influence, described the methodological differences between the civilian and common law systems thus:

> A civilian system differs from a common law system much as rationalism differs from empiricism or deduction from induction. The civilian naturally reasons from principles to instances, the common lawyer from instances to principles. The civilian puts faith in syllogisms, the common lawyer in precedents; the first silently asking himself as each new problem arises, "What should we do this time" and the second asking aloud in the same situation, "What did we do last time?" . . .The instinct of a civilian is to systematise. The working rule of the common lawyer is *solvitur ambulando*.

Thomas Mackay Cooper, *The Common Law and The Civil Law—A Scot's View*, 63 HARV. L. REV. 468, 470–71 (1950). Is one of these methodologies inherently more suited to the demands of an international environment? Do you agree with Professor Kozyris that technological developments will result in an international shift toward the common law methodology of induction? Do any of the developments described in these materials suggest countervailing tendencies?

§ 1.03 Territoriality of Patent Rights

As we will see, over the past century and a quarter a vast body of international intellectual property law has been developed. But it is a fundamental (if paradoxical) principle of international intellectual property law that, with very few exceptions, intellectual property rights are national in nature. And the nature of those national rights is determined largely by national laws (even if the national laws of a particular country are significantly shaped by the obligations of that country under international intellectual property law). We will periodically discuss the extent to which recent developments derogate from this principle of territoriality. The principle is, however, the starting point for any study of international patent law: patent laws operate territorially, and patent rights are thus national in scope.

A basic premise of the patent right has always been the principle of territoriality. In the United States, for example, 35 U.S.C. § 261 establishes that patents have the attributes of personal property and that "[t]he applicant, patentee, or his assigns or legal representatives may. . . convey an exclusive right under his application for patent, or patents, *to the whole or any specified part of the United States.*" Likewise, § 271(a) establishes that "whoever without authority makes, uses, offers to sell, or sells any patented invention, *within the United States* or imports *into the United States* any patented invention during the term of the patent therefor, infringes the patent." Section 154(a)(1) of the Patent Act mandates that the contents of the patent must make the territorial provisions of the patent grant explicit:

> (a)(1) Contents. Every patent shall contain a short title of the invention and a grant to the patentee, his heirs or assigns, of the right to exclude others from making, using, offering for sale, or selling the invention *throughout the United States* or importing the invention *into the United States*, and, if the invention is a process, of the right to exclude others from using, offering for sale or selling *throughout the United States, or importing into the United States*, products made by that process, referring to the specification for the particulars thereof.

One authority has recently observed that "of the three principal forms of intellectual property, patent rights are the most explicitly territorial." Donald S. Chisum, *Normative and Empirical Territoriality in Intellectual Property: Lessons from Patent Law*, 37 VA. J. INT'L L. 603, 605 (1997). "Patents are considered territorial, having legal effect only in the territory of the issuing state. Accordingly, the United States has no jurisdiction to apply its law to validate or invalidate a foreign patent, regardless of the origin of the invention, or the nationality, residence, or principal place of business of the holder of the patent or of any licensee." RESTATEMENT (THIRD) OF THE FOREIGN RELATIONS LAW OF THE UNITED STATES, § 415, comment i. Americans are sensitive to imposition of foreign standards on U.S. patent law, stressing the uniqueness and long history of U.S. patent traditions.

Although international patent law encompasses national treatment and minimum standards, territoriality is a core governing principle of patent protection, and (as we shall see in Chapters 2 and 4) the concept of international patent rights is still incipient if not inchoate.

But inchoate concepts can take or be given more concrete form with great rapidity under the proper historical circumstances. Technological advances do not recognize national boundaries. The following case discusses term and territorial limits on a U.S. patent owner's right to exclude a competitor from activities within the bounds of a claimed invention covered by a U.S. patent.

JOHNS HOPKINS UNIVERSITY v. CELLPRO, INC.
152 F.3d 1342 (Fed. Cir. 1998)

LOURIE, CIRCUIT JUDGE:

. . . .

E. The Repatriation Order

CellPro's final argument is that the court exceeded the scope of its power when it ordered the repatriation and destruction of the six vials that it exported to its business partner, Biomira, in Canada, as well as cloned vials and antibodies produced therefrom. CellPro contends that it has not committed an infringing act with respect to the exported vials. CellPro summarizes its activities as follows: it produced approximately 100 vials of 12.8 hybridoma to create a United States master cell bank prior to the issuance of the '204 patent, it exported six of those vials to Canada after issuance, and it used those vials in Canada to supply markets outside of the United States. CellPro asserts that none of these acts—pre-issuance manufacture, export, or use outside of the United States—constitutes infringement under 35 U.S.C. § 271, and accordingly that such acts are beyond the scope of the court's equitable powers.

Hopkins responds that the district court's order was properly predicated on the determination that CellPro used (i.e., by cloning or testing) other vials from its United States cell bank in the United States after the issuance of the patent and thereby infringed with respect to the United States cell bank "as a whole." Hopkins asserts that the injunctive power of the district courts is not limited to the prohibition of those activities that constitute patent infringement, but also extends to prohibitions necessary in order to fashion a meaningful remedy for past infringement. Hopkins argues that repatriation in this case is such a meaningful remedy and will prevent CellPro from unfairly capitalizing upon its infringement.

Section 283 of the Patent Code empowers the courts to "grant injunctions in accordance with the principles of equity to prevent the violation of any right secured by patent, on such terms as the court deems reasonable." 35 U.S.C. § 283 (1994). In accordance with the clear wording of this section, "an injunction is only proper to the extent it is 'to prevent the violation of any right secured by patent.' " A "necessary predicate" for the issuance of a permanent injunction is therefore a determination of infringement. *Id.* When deciding whether a district court abused the discretion provided by Section 283, we are mindful of the fact that the district courts are in the best position to fashion an injunction. *See* Joy Techs., Inc. v. Flakt, Inc., 6 F.3d 770, 777 (Fed. Cir. 1993) (citation omitted). However, judicial restraint of lawful noninfringing activities must be avoided. *See id.* (citing Deepsouth Packing Co. v. Laitram Corp., 406 U.S. 518, 529–31(1972)).

We agree with CellPro that the district court abused its discretion in ordering the repatriation and destruction of the exported vials. The repatriation aspect of the order does not enjoin activities that either have infringed the '204 patent or are likely to do so and thus does not prevent infringement—the proper purpose of an injunction under Section 283. It is clear that the six vials standing alone have not infringed the '204 patent. Mere possession of a product which becomes covered by a subsequently issued patent does not constitute an infringement of that patent until the product is used, sold, or offered for sale in the United States during the term of the patent. *See* Cohen v. United States, 487 F.2d 525 (1973); Columbia & N.R.R. Co. v. Chandler, 241 F. 261 (9th Cir. 1917) (holding that, while the patentee could not recover damages for the manufacture of infringing trucks prior to the issuance of the patent, it did not follow "that the trucks were set free from the monopoly of the patent, and could thereafter be used, without liability to the inventor"); *see also* Hoover Group, Inc. v. Custom Metalcraft, Inc., 66 F.3d 299, 304 (Fed. Cir. 1995) ("[The patentee] may of course obtain damages only for acts of infringement after the issuance of the patent."). Likewise, neither export from the United States nor use in a foreign country of a product covered by a United States patent constitutes infringement. *See* 35 U.S.C. § 271(a) (1994) ("[W]hoever without authority makes, uses, offers to sell, or sells any patented invention, within the United States or imports into the United States any patented invention during the term of the patent therefor, infringes the patent."); *see also* Paper Converting Mach. Co. v. Magna-Graphics Corp., 745 F.2d 11, 16 (Fed. Cir. 1984) ("[B]y the terms of the patent grant, no activity other than the unauthorized making, using, or selling of the claimed invention can constitute direct infringement of a patent, *no matter* how great the adverse impact of that activity on the economic value of a patent.") (emphasis in original).

That CellPro used other vials from the cell bank in an infringing manner in the United States does not taint the six exported vials with infringement.[31] The exported vials were not "guilty by association." One may consider the pre-issuance manufacture of two machines, one of which is

---

[31] We do not suggest, and neither party argues, that the court had no injunctive power with respect to those vials which were not exported but which were also not used in the United States. That these vials, like the exported vials, did not infringe does not free them from the court's equitable power under Section 283. Because CellPro had used some of its vials in the United States, a clear act of infringement, its propensity to infringe has been sufficiently established such that the court could conclude that enjoining the use of United States-based vials was necessary to prevent infringement.

used after the patent is issued and the other of which is exported. An injunction requiring return of the exported machine, which was never made, used, or sold during the term of the patent in the United States, is beyond the scope of Section 283 and hence an abuse of discretion. The same principle applies here to the vials exported to Canada. Accordingly, the court's conclusion that use of some of the vials of the cell bank constituted a use of the cell bank "as a whole" as a means of justifying its repatriation order was an abuse of discretion.

Moreover, there is also no evidentiary basis for concluding that the district court's order was necessary to prevent CellPro from committing further infringing activities. An injunction under Section 283 can reach extraterritorial activities such as those at issue here, even if these activities do not themselves constitute infringement. It is necessary however that the injunction prevent infringement of a United States patent. For example, in Spindelfabrik Suessen-Schurr v. Schubert & Salzer, 903 F.2d 1568 (Fed. Cir. 1990), the infringer argued that the district court's injunction "impermissibly extend[ed] the reach of American patent law beyond the boundaries of the United States" because it prohibited the infringer from making, in Germany, machines "for use in the United States" and machines "destined for delivery to the United States." This court held that the injunction was "a reasonable and permissible endeavor to prevent infringement in the United States and not a prohibited extra-territorial application of American patent law. They were well within the district court's authority." *Id*. at 1578.

The record in this case does not, as in *Spindelfabrik*, suggest that the exported vials will be used in a manner which will infringe the patent. CellPro has stipulated, and Hopkins does not refute, that Biomira intended to produce antibodies for CellPro in Canada "for use in products to be sold outside of the United States." CellPro's Opening Brief at 40 ("At no time has CellPro imported back into the United States the 12.8 monoclonal antibodies manufactured by Biomira in Canada or the cell suspension derived from using the 12.8 monoclonal antibodies."). Because the record is devoid of evidence upon which the district court could have concluded that its order would prevent further infringement, there was no basis for the court to order the exported hybridomas and its byproducts to be shipped to the United States.

We also do not find persuasive Hopkins' argument that the scope of the district court's order can be justified because it is necessary to fashion a meaningful remedy for CellPro's past infringement. Section 283 does not provide remedies for past infringement; it only provides for injunctive relief to prevent future infringement. The section under which a litigant must seek compensation for past infringement is Section 284. *See* 35 U.S.C. § 284, para. 1 (1994) ("Upon finding for the claimant the court shall award the claimant damages adequate to compensate for the infringement."). We do not understand Hopkins to seriously dispute that it has not received adequate compensation for CellPro's infringement. However, to the extent that Hopkins complains that CellPro's infringement has damaged its ability to service foreign markets, Hopkins must rely on foreign patent protection. *See Deepsouth*, 406 U.S. at 531 ("Our patent system makes no claim to extraterritorial effect. . . . To the degree that the inventor needs protection in markets other than those of this country, the wording of 35 U.S.C. §§ 154 and 271 reveals a congressional intent to have him seek it abroad through patents secured in countries where his goods are being used.") (citations and quotation omitted). Such a complaint cannot be remedied by the imposition of an injunction under Section 283.

Hopkins further argues, mimicking the district court's "as a whole" rationale, that it would be fair under the circumstances to order repatriation and destruction because CellPro has committed other clear acts of infringement with respect to other vials in the United States cell bank. We do not agree. As we have already stated, we disagree that this rationale provides a sufficient premise for the court's order given the facts of this case. Moreover, premising the order on this rationale amounts to punishment of CellPro for its infringement. This is not the proper purpose of injunctive relief under Section 283. [cit]. Those portions of the district court's permanent injunction order that ordered repatriation and destruction of vials exported by CellPro to Biomira and byproducts produced thereby are not consistent with the stated purpose of Section 283—to prevent infringement. Thus, the court abused its discretion, and those portions of the order are vacated.

Notes and Questions

(1) **Section 271(f).** The *CellPro* court referred to *Deepsouth Packing Co. v. Laitram Corp.*, 406 U.S. 518, 529–31 (1972) for the proposition that "judicial restraint of lawful noninfringing activities must be avoided." In that case, export of unassembled components of a patented shrimp-deveining machine (to be easily assembled abroad) was held not to be an infringement of a U.S. patent because the machine itself was not "made" under the U.S. patent law. Subsequently, Congress took the hint and in 1984 added section 271(f) to the patent law, subsection 1 of which states that

> [w]hoever without authority supplies or causes to be supplied in or from the United States all or a substantial portion of the components of a patented invention, where such components are uncombined in whole or in part, in such manner as to actively induce the combination of such components outside the United States in a manner that would infringe the patent if such combination occurred within the United States, shall be liable as an infringer.

Can Congress similarly close the loophole that allows CellPro to use outside the United States the vials which were exported from the United States prior to issuance of the patent? Assume you are a Congressional staff member and have been asked to draft such a provision. What would it look like? Would any such provision be an extraterritorial application of U.S. law? *Compare* RESTATEMENT (THIRD) OF THE FOREIGN RELATIONS LAW OF THE UNITED STATES § 415(3) cmt. i & Reporters' note 6. Does the *Cellpro* court's reference to the "intent of Congress" in its interpretation of section 154 bear upon your answer?

(2) **Offers to Sell.** In *Rotec Industries Inc. v. Mitsubishi Corp.,* 215 F.3d 1246 (Fed. Cir. 2000), the Federal Circuit affirmed a summary judgment that Mitsubishi did not infringe Rotec's patent for a conveyor system for carrying concrete over long distances. Mitsubishi sold a system for the Three Gorges Dam project on the Yangtze River in China. The central issue was whether Mitsubishi's "offer to sell," as that term is used in the 1994 patent code amendment, occurred in the United States or in China. The Federal Circuit decided that the phrase "offer to sell" should be interpreted according to its ordinary meaning in contract law, and the evidence did not show that an offer to sell within that meaning occurred in the United States. Judge Newman concurred on the ground that because no components of the equipment were made in the United States, and thus the sale did not infringe, the offer to sell could not infringe.

(3) **Serial National Litigation.** The need for an intellectual property owner in a multinational dispute to pursue separate national litigation for separate violations of separate national intellectual property rights is a common occurrence. *See, e.g., Improver Corp. and Sicommerce v. Remington Prods.,* 24 I.I.C. 838 (Dusseldorf Ct. App. 1991) (Germany) (action in Germany for infringement of patent on Epilady shaver); *Improver Corp. and Others v. Remington Consumer Prods. Ltd.,* 1990 F.S.R. 181 (Ch. D. 1989) (UK) (action in the UK for infringement of patent on same invention). The *Improver* cases, and some of the devices currently used, and being proposed, to mitigate the inefficiencies of serial national litigation are discussed in detail in Part IV *infra*.

PART II

COMPARATIVE PATENT LAW

Chapter 2

Comparative Principles of Patent Law

§ 2.01 Historical Overview

[A] Europe

VENETIAN PATENT LAW OF THE 19TH MARCH 1474

There are in this city, and also there come temporarily by reason of its greatness and goodness, men from different places and most clever minds, capable of devising and inventing all manner of ingenious contrivances. And should it be provided, that the works and contrivances invented by them, others having seen them could not make them and take their honour, men of such kind would exert their minds, invent and make things which would be of no small utility and benefit to our State.

Therefore, decision will be passed that, by authority of this Council, each person who will make in this city any new and ingenious contrivance, not made heretofore in our dominion, as soon as it is reduced to perfection, so that it can be used and exercised, shall give notice of the same to the office of our Provisioners of Common. It being forbidden to any other in any territory and place of ours to make any other contrivance in the form and resemblance thereof, without the consent and licence of the author up to ten years.

And, however, should anybody make it, the aforesaid author and inventor will have the liberty to cite him before any office of this city, by which office the aforesaid who shall infringe be forced to pay him the sum of one hundred ducates and the contrivance be immediately destroyed. Being then in liberty of our Government at his will to take and use in his need any of said contrivances and instruments, with this condition, however, that no others than the authors shall exercise them.

STATUTE OF MONOPOLIES 1623 (ENG.)
21 James I, ch. 3, quoted in 1 Robinson on Patents 13 (1890)

An Act concerning monopolies and dispensations of penal laws and the forfeiture thereof:

I. Whereas your majesty, in the year 1610, published a book declaring that all grants of monopolies, and of the benefit of penal laws, and of the power of dispensing with law, and of compounding penalties, are contrary to law; and whereas your majesty then expressly commanded that no suitor should every apply for such grants; and whereas, nevertheless, such grants have been applied for and allowed; Therefore to make void all these, and to prevent the like in time to come, may it please your majesty that it be declared and enacted by authority of this present parliament "that all monopolies and all commissions, grants, licenses, charters, and letters-patent, heretofore made or granted, or hereafter to be made or granted, to any person or persons . . . whatsoever, of or for the sole buying, selling, making, working, or using of anything, within this realm or the dominions of Wales, or of any other monopolies" and all licenses to do anything contrary to law, or to confer authority on others so to do . . . "are altogether contrary to the laws of this realm, and so are and shall be utterly void, and of none effect, and in no wise to be put in use or execution."

. . . .

VI. Provided also, and be it declared and enacted: That any declaration before mentioned shall not extend to any letters-patent and grants of privilege, of the term of fourteen years or under, hereafter to be made, of the sole working or making of any manner of new manufactures, within this realm, to the true and first inventor and inventors of such manufactures, which others, at the time of making such letters-patent and grant, shall not use, so as also they be not contrary to the law, nor mischievous to the state, by raising prices of commodities at home, or hurt of trade, or generally inconvenient; The said fourteen years to be accounted from the date of the first letters-patent or grant of such privilege, hereafter to be made; but that the same shall be of such force as they should be, if this act had never been made and of none other.

. . . .

ERICH KAUFER, THE ECONOMICS OF THE PATENT SYSTEM 2–8 (1989) *

The practice of granting property rights in what we now call inventions had its historical roots in mining law. During the Middle Ages, the term "invention" had a meaning much closer to what we would now call "discovery," *e.g.*, of new ore resources, than the meaning accepted under modern patent law. In medieval Latin, *"invenire"* meant (accidental) discovery, while *"ars"* was used to connote derived technological know-how. Medieval orders in the archives of Innsbruck Austria consistently refer to *"Perkwerks Erfyndung,"* that is, to the "invention" of mining sites. The Alps were an ore mining area from at least the time of the Celtic settlement. In such mining areas, there was a long common laws tradition concerning the mining, timber use, and water use property rights of those who were first to "invent" an ore site. As new ore locations were found in Saxony, Silesia, and Bohemia, the miners brought their unwritten common law with them. The law then became incorporated into the decisions of specialized mining courts and into the *"Constitutiones Juris Metallici"* promulgated by King Wenceslaus II in the year 1300. . . .

---

* Reprinted with permission.

In 1409, Venice granted the German Henricus von Heslingen a privilege to exploit an ore mine and use needed water and timber according to the common law prevailing in Germany. In the following decades, Venetian ore mining grew rapidly, necessitating a more formalized legal statute. In 1488 the Venetian Senate promulgated the *Statuto Mineraria*.

. . .

Meanwhile, institutions were also evolving to deal with "inventions"—often called *"edificium et ingenium"* in the Latin texts—of a more specifically technological character. They took two rather different forms. One important example was the privilege granted by the Venetian Senate in 1460 to a young German, Jacobus de Valperga, who had devised a new type of water pump. The grant stated that as long as Jacobus lived, no one could make the pump without an express license from Jacobus. Violation carried a penalty of 1,000 ducats and destruction of the offending machinery. However, Jacobus was obliged to grant licenses if reasonable royalties were offered. Thus, the focus was on preventing imitation of Jacobus' machine *without his permission*, and the privilege was limited by what we would now call a compulsory licensing provision. In contrast, another privilege granted in the same year to master engineer Guilielmus Lombardus reserved to Guilielmus exclusive monopoly rights in making certain furnaces, with no provision for "compulsory" licenses. The Venetian administrative practice distinguished between an invention privilege and a trade privilege. Jacobus asked for protection guaranteeing him license revenues from all who used his invention. Guilielmus, on the other hand, received a guarantee that no one could compete with him in selling the product that incorporated his invention.

Monopoly privileges, with or without licensing provisions, were not the only way Venice sought to foster technical advance. Venice's large and important naval weapons factory, the Arsenale, is not known to have conferred them. As the precursor of today's nationalized enterprise, the Arsenale instead attracted technically skilled persons by offering high salaries and benefits such as free housing.

As the 15th century progressed, Venice experienced a period of severe financial difficulties, partly because of its wars to extend its claims on the Italian Terra Firma and partly because of threats from the Turks. It therefore placed increasing emphasis on monopoly privileges as a substitute for government subsidies. In 1474, only a year after the Senate decided to build the Arsenale Novissimo, a formal patent code was promulgated. . . .

The code specified that the subject invention had to be proven workable and useful, if only by means of a model. . . . Also, no imitation was permitted for ten years without express permission from the inventor. However, the Republic retained the right to use the invention for its own purposes. An otherwise unauthorized use carried a penalty of one hundred ducats and destruction of the offending device. But the administrative practice that followed also included provisions for compulsory licensing and the revocation of patents not used commercially. Thus, the patent code, based in large part upon the decision in the matter of Jacobus de Valperga, must be seen as an instrument designed to attract engineers to the Republic. It was not an instrument to stimulate artisan production by granting monopolistic trade privileges . . . like the one issued to Guilielmus Lombardus.

As the grant of patents spread northward, and with the emergence of absolutist governments, tension mounted between grants with licensing provisions and those that conferred unconditional monopoly privileges, with or without some element of invention or innovation. Under the reign of Queen Elizabeth I in England, patent grants were used increasingly to implement mercantilist policy, and especially to benefit royal favorites. Parliament and the Crown clashed over who had, or ought to have, the prerogative of granting monopoly privileges. In 1623, Parliament prevailed decisively, passing the *Statute of Monopolies*. Among other privileges, patents were declared illegal, except for grants to the true and first inventor or inventors of a new manufacture. Newness had no international meaning; it was sufficient if the manufacture was new to England. The duration was to be fourteen years. This term was chosen because it encompassed the time it took to train two successive generations of apprentices, each serving a term of seven years. Thus, Parliament expressed its desire to protect the know-how accumulated by masters in implementing an invention.

In France, systematic use of patents as an instrument of mercantilist policy began in the middle of the 16th century. For the most part, privileges were granted only after a careful review of the benefits from encouraging a new trade. The monopoly restrictions were usually limited to a geographic boundary of ten miles, but narrower or wider territorial boundaries were sometimes set. In the first decades of the 18th century, such restrictions came increasingly to be used to protect established trades and manufacturers. Even before the Revolution, public opinion gravitated toward rejecting patents as contrary to the freedom of trade. To underline the break with the past brought about by the Revolution, the patent law of 1791 spoke only of "brevets d'inventions" and declared that the inventor had a natural property right to his invention. In this, the previous view of patents as a grant of royal privilege was replaced by a justification rooted in the rights of the citizen.

In the "Constituante" debate over French patent law, the British patent system, as it had evolved from the Statute of Monopolies, was referred to as a model case. It also became a model for British colonies in North America. Massachusetts passed a similar law in 1641. Connecticut followed suit in 1672. South Carolina (1691) was the first to speak of patents not as sovereign grants, but as a fulfillment of the rights of the inventor.

More than one hundred years passed before there were significant new developments. Then, in 1789, the American Constitution gave Congress the power:

> . . . to promote the progress of science and useful arts, by securing for limited times to authors and inventors the exclusive right to their respective writings and discoveries.

In 1790 the first U.S. federal patent law was promulgated. Like its predecessor in South Carolina, it rested in the premise that the inventor had a right to claim a patent on what he had invented. Furthermore, in order to ensure that patents were granted only for "new and useful" inventions, an official examination prior to the patent's issuance was required. In 1793, this prior examination was replaced by mere notification to the Secretary of State (initially, Thomas Jefferson). But in 1836, it was reinstituted, and it has been a part of the U.S. patent system, like most modern patent systems, ever since.

. . . .

[B]   United States

FRANK W. DAHN, COLONIAL PATENTS IN THE UNITED STATES OF AMERICA
3 J. Pat. Off. Soc'y 342 (1921)

The earliest patent in the United States appears to be the one granted by the General Court of the Massachusetts Bay Colony in October 1641, to Samuel Winslow for a process of manufacturing salt. This patent recited that he was to have the privilege for ten years, on condition that works were established within one year and prohibited all others "from making this article (during that period) except in a manner different from his." . . . In 1655, a patent was awarded to Joseph Jencks (or Jenks) for an engine for cutting grass. This "engine" was a scythe, and it is interesting to note that his invention which substituted for the short, thick straight blade of the old country a long thin blade with a stiffened back, was not merely a prototype of but almost the same device, still in common use.

. . . .

JAMES MADISON, FEDERALIST PAPER NO. 43

The utility of this power will scarcely be questioned. The copyright of authors has been solemnly adjudged in Great Britain to be a right at common law. The right to useful inventions seems with equal reason to belong to the inventors. The public good fully coincides in both claims with the claims of individuals. The states cannot separately make effectual provision for either of the cases, and most of them have anticipated the decision of this point, by laws passed at the instance of Congress.

FRANK D. PRAGER, PROPOSALS FOR THE PATENT ACT OF 1790[*]

36 J. PAT. OFF. SOC'Y, 157–167 (1954)

Starting in 1782 Noah Webster conducted a one-man campaign for the enactment of general copyright laws by the individual States. He was then a struggling young Connecticut schoolmaster and lawyer and itinerant journalist. His campaign was nationwide and had nationwide success. However, he desired further security for his and other authors' exclusive rights.

On April 16 and 17, 1789, Noah Webster wrote what he called a "federal copyright bill." It was in fact a combined patent and copyright bill. The draft is lost but its spirit can be gathered from other sources. In 1788 Webster wrote:

> The authors of useful inventions are among the benefactors of the public and are entitled to some peculiar advantages for their ingenuity and labor. The productions of genius and the imagination are if possible more really and exclusively property than houses and land and are equally entitled to legal security. The want of some regulation for this purpose may be numbered among the defects of the American Government.

In previous years he had caused the insertion of similar declarations in several of the State copyright acts.

It seems that Webster's argument was fairly successful again. On Monday, April 20, 1789, Congress appointed a House Committee for the purpose of bringing in a federal patent and copyright bill. It is conceivable that Congress had received other drafts; so much seems certain that official action started with the receipt of Webster's draft.

The public interest was then absorbed by the question of basic, natural rights, to be secured by a federal Bill of Rights. The movement for such a Bill probably gave support to the intellectual property idea of Webster and thereby to the early enactment of a federal patent and copyright act. It must not be assumed that the public was particularly agitated about any kind of basic property right, or that the problems of basic rights were very clearly understood. In fact, Webster was among those who opposed large parts of the Bill of Rights. Nevertheless, a popular movement was here. It favored the broad recognition of basic rights, including property rights; and there was a specific demand for basic property rights of inventors. These trends supported one another.

II.

In addition, entirely different ideas were at work. One of them was represented by James Rumsey, steamboat builder, rival of the now better

---

[*] Reprinted with permission.

known John Fitch. On June 6, 1789, James Rumsey, then staying in London, wrote a letter to Thomas Jefferson, who then was American ambassador in Paris and, in effect, Rumsey's patent attorney in France. Rumsey informed Jefferson that he had heard about the appointment of a committee to bring in a federal patent bill. He briefly discussed the English patent system, also the patent interferences between Rumsey and Fitch before the American state legislatures and the fact that Rumsey had substantially lost those interferences. He then made a legislative proposal in favor of:

The French method of having new inventions examined by a committee of philosophical characters before a grant can be obtained.

With obvious reference to Fitch, Rumsey remarked that such examination "has a tendency to prevent many simple projectors from ruining themselves by the too long pursuit of projects that they know little about."

The clear implication was that Jefferson should apply influence in connection with the bill in Congress in order to incorporate the system of "philosophical" examination therein. . . .

Rumsey's own idea, as stated by him, originated in France. This was the only country of importance, at that time, which had a system of "philosophical" or scientific patent examination. Some other countries had an examination of utility by fiscal or administrative officers. In most of those systems the examination was secret. The instruction of the public, if it occurred at all, resulted from the actual use of the invention, not from any published disclosures. In this respect the examination system envisaged by Rumsey differed materially from that which is now considered as self-evident. Its philosophy was far removed from that of the intellectual property idea of Webster which of course was based on an inventor's public claim and announcement of the metes and bounds of his discovery. Webster had proclaimed the inventor's property, based on his creative act and bounded only by his correct delineation of the new area; Rumsey suggested to subject it to preventive scrutiny and independent definition by state philosophers. . . . The manner in which Rumsey became familiar with the French tradition is not hard to detect. He had made the acquaintance and gained the support of Benjamin Franklin, member of various European scientific societies, president of the American Philosophical Society and chairman of what was known as the Rumseyan Society. Franklin had met and rejected Fitch late in 1785 and had attracted competition for Fitch, first by Arthur Donaldson in 1786 and then by Rumsey, whose open conflict with Fitch started in 1787.

III.

A federal copyright and patent bill was brought in on June 23, 1789 as House Bill 10. That bill as well as Webster's draft is lost. It was a printed document of 11 pages; that is considerably longer than the most detailed copyright or patent laws previously enacted anywhere. The size of the lost bill may indicate that Webster's draft was amplified and modified, in the interval between April 20 and June 23, 1789. The details are unknown. . . .

It seems that at least major parts if not all of the pertinent considerations were concerned with the intellectual property principle identifiable with Webster and the scientific preexamination principle identifiable with Franklin. Otherwise the debate, if any, probably related to such matters as the lawyers in Congress usually considered: the selection of tribunals and procedures and similar details.

IV.

Shortly before the formal presentation of House Bill 10, Fitch learned of this bill. Like Rumsey, he had filed a patent application of is own in Congress; in fact he had asked Congress for "encouragement" already in 1785 and for a patent in 1786 and again in the early part of 1789, always specifying the broad generic idea of steamboats as the subject matter of his claim. By contrast, Rumsey and his supporters had petitioned Congress for "encouragement" of a system of hydraulic actuation of pole boats, starting in 1783, and had publicly announced a steamboat plan only in the early part of 1788.

On June 18, 1789 a young friend of Fitch wrote him a letter from New York, informing him that Congress would not dispose of individual applications but would enact a general bill. Thereupon Fitch inquired of a Senator whom he knew remotely "Who the committee are who are appointed to form a general system of exclusive rights."

By letters or verbal information—the details are unknown—Fitch must have obtained fuller details. He quoted from the federal bill then "proposed," in a long brief that he filed in his interference with Rumsey before the Pennsylvania Legislature and Judges' Committee, September 11, 1789; and he prepared a printed version of this brief as one of his frequent public announcements. This particular paper, a broadside or hand bill, has four columns of fine print. Near the top of the second column it contained the following quotation from the "proposed law of Congress:"

> And if, upon such specification, the inventions or discoveries afore-said, claimed by two or more parties, shall appear to be substantially the same, both in principle and execution, then the said . . . shall enquire into the priority of said inventions or discoveries, and if either of the said parties shall so request, they shall issue their precept to the sheriff of . . . directed, commanding him to cause to come before them twelve good and lawful men of . . . who shall be indifferent and unconnected with the parties or either of them, as well as the subject matter in dispute, in which for the determination thereof, they shall have no immediate interest, and upon oath or affirmation of the said twelve men, shall enquire which of the said parties claiming the said inventions or discoveries, was the first and true inventor or discoverer thereof, and shall take their verdict and certify the same together with the names of the jurors; and the said petition or petitions, and the

specifications to the said, . . . who (is or are) hereby required to cause a patent to him or them who shall be so found to be the first true inventor or inventors, discoverer or discoverers, to be made out, proceeded upon and perfected in manner aforesaid.

A few months later a new federal draft was formally entered as House Bill 41, for the first time presenting the patent law alone, separate from the copyright law and superseding House Bill 10. It is not entirely clear whether Fitch's quotation stems from the original House Bill 10 or from a draft of the later House Bill 41. This latter bill, like so many other pertinent papers, seems to be lost. No pertinent papers have so far been found in the Fitch and Rumsey papers other than those cited above, and none in the papers of their respective supporters.

Fitch's handbill gave full approval to the jury provision for priority contents. Fitch like Webster and unlike Franklin and Rumsey wanted a patent system based on plain intellectual property, without other consideration of public policy, philosophical or otherwise. One of Fitch's typical statements was addressed to Jefferson in 1791:

> Inventions are something brought from Nature. . . . My ideas of inventions and exclusive rights as I have lived in a narrow sphere of life perhaps may be rude, but such as they be I beg leave to give them. I expect that the field of inventions is as free to every individual as air, or the rays of light, and whatever is collected from it becomes the most serious and real property of the inventor, as much as if he had gathered an acorn out of a common, and more so.

V.

As to the reactions of friends and neighbors, more is known of Fitch than of the secretive Rumsey. One of the principal shareholders in Fitch's steamboat company was William Thornton, who a few years later became the first Commissioner of Patents. He accepted the intellectual property idea wholeheartedly, together with other, partly less meritorious principles.

In Congress, the examination proposal of Franklin-Rumsey was apparently active, with or without Jefferson's support. It prevailed gradually over the plain intellectual property idea of Webster, Fitch and Thornton; but not immediately. For the moment a bill without official examination was approved.

On March 10, 1790 the House passed bill 41 in a form representing the first federal patent bill known in full detail. It provided for a patenting procedure entirely based on opposition proceedings— a basic thought far removed from any system of official preexamination. Both *ex parte* and interference proceedings were intrusted to arbitrators or so-called referees, to be chosen by the parties and if necessary by the Chief Justice of the Supreme Court. This system would have enabled an opposer to show cause why letters patent should not issue to an *ex parte* petitioner, or to either party in a contested case. In addition the bill provided for a repeal procedure. Within one year after a grant, a repeal suit could be based on the allegation, among others, that the patentee was not the "first and true" inventor.

Fitch protested at once against the elimination of the jury trial of priority issues; he claimed that the property character of inventions cannot be secured without such trial.

This protest of Fitch, like the preceding arguments for intellectual property, is very interesting; but the argument for jury trial of interferences was weak. Inventions may be and should be classifiable as property, and protected by the privilege of jury trial in cases at law. However, they need not and practically cannot be protected by a jury incident to procedures of Congress or its delegated authority in ascertaining the priority or scope of federal protection for an invention.

Whether the merits or demerits of the jury system received consideration in Congress is unknown. There was opposition to Fitch by "southern men"— probably supporters of Rumsey—and Fitch was "defeated" on March 30, 1790.

This time, even the intermediate or compromise idea of interference trials by referees was dropped. The patent act, as approved on April 10, 1790, adopted a system quite close to that advocated by Franklin and Rumsey: it authorized three high officers, including one who was known for scientific talent, to issue a patent "if they shall deem the invention or discovery sufficiently useful and important." No yard stick was handed to these officers by Congress other than the undefined concept of "invention or discovery" and their own opinion as to what is "sufficiently useful and important." Even novelty was required only for improvements, not for arts, machines, etc.

VI.

It may appear that the first American examination system, in effect between 1790 and 1793, represented a full victory of Franklin and Rumsey over Webster, Fitch and Thornton. However this impression would be incorrect. At least to some extent, Fitch prevailed in the Act of 1790. He prevailed mainly as to the requirement of "a specification" and the public disclosure thereof.

This requirement was one of the principal points constantly urged by Fitch against Rumsey. Rumsey's concept of a philosophical examination was surrounded by connotations of secrecy and political expediency. In Fitch's writings, on the other hand, we find frequent expressions such as these:

> If we have recourse to the enlightened nations of Europe and more especially to England . . . . we shall find that their laws imply that . . . the inventor can claim no benefit from his thought or inventions before he makes a public declaration of such invention in some place of record established for such purposes.

or:

> I conceive of it as a man taking up a piece of vacant land in a
> wilderness . . . he must clearly designate its boundaries.

The time factor was particularly important, and particularly controversial. According to Fitch the inventor can "claim no benefit . . . before he makes a public declaration." Rumsey, on the other hand, argued that it is sufficient to deliver and publish a specification at the end of the patent term; his philosophical examiners were conceived as instruments of public authority rather than public information.

The bill quoted in Fitch's broadside, as quoted above, implied clearly that patent petitioners had to file their specifications before the grant, and before any interference proceedings. The House version of March 10, 1790 was similar; it provided that the specification is due at the time of granting the patent and that the referees could ask for it at any time.

The principle of filing and perfecting the specification prior to the start of the patent term was enacted in the statute of 1790; and from here it has spread over the entire civilized world. This part of modern institutions of society seems traceable to the surveyor Fitch, while the principle of scientific examination seems creditable to his opponent Rumsey.

§ 2.02   The Purposes of Patent Protection

Patent laws are intended to encourage the introduction of new technology and the public disclosure of new technological information by giving the owner of the patent a limited right to exclude others from making, using, selling, or importing a product covered by the patent, in exchange for the patent owner disclosing the invention to the world. (Our discussion of patents will focus almost exclusively on patents for inventions, called utility patents in the United States, although we will occasionally mention other kinds of patents, such as patents for utility model—sometimes called petty patents—plant patents, and patents on ornamental designs.) Underpinning the patent law is an unquestioned belief in the extrinsic value of innovation and the intrinsic value of social progress. Proponents of a strong patent system accept as received wisdom that the production of new technological innovation and information is socially beneficial. (This thesis is not universally accepted, and is expressly rejected by some groups that venerate traditional cultural values and beliefs and/or, perhaps less kindly, others whose members are in a position to derive personal benefit from maintenance of the *status quo*.) But even assuming that technological progress is inherently beneficial to all present human societies, and that in any event we cannot turn back the clock to a pastoral age, answers to the questions of whether and, if so, to what extent the legal grant of a right to exclude others from practicing a patented technology actually *does* encourage the production of technological innovation within a particular human society with its own particular value system at a particular level of economic and technological development are fraught with complication and controversy.

The incentive theory of patent law is multifaceted: *from the standpoint of the patent owner*, the limited right to exclude is both an incentive to *invent* and an incentive to *invest*. The complex interaction of invention and investment underpinning the patent law is easily illustrated in the careers of a cavalcade of 19th and 20th century inventor-entrepreneurs such as Thomas Edison, Alfred Nobel, Chester Carlson, and Edwin Land, who built great commercial enterprises on the success of their patented inventions. The most prolific American inventor and patentee, Edison, who had only three months of formal schooling, produced his first major invention, a stock ticker for printing stock-exchange quotations in brokers' offices, at the age of 21 in 1870. With the $40,000 he was paid for improvements in stock tickers, he established a manufacturing shop and a small laboratory in Newark, N.J. He later moved to a more extensive laboratory (perhaps the world's first "research park") in Menlo Park, N.J., where he hired a cadre of researchers to work under his direction to develop new technologies systematically. In 1878 he invented the first commercially practical incandescent electric lamp and that same year established the eponymous Edison Electric Light Company. In 1882, his company designed and built the first central electric light-power station in New York City, the success of which led to a series of similar installations culminating in the formation of the General Electric Company in 1892. Along the way, he also developed the phonograph and the first motion picture projector using flexible celluloid film, among over 1,000 patented inventions attributed to him. What drives such a person to become the quintessential inventor-entrepreneur? Fame, fortune, or something else?

The growth of organized research exemplified by Menlo Park prompted Alfred North Whitehead to observe that "the greatest invention of the 19th century was the invention of the method of invention." But many inventor-industrialists continued to toil in solitude. Carlson was a 28 year old patent lawyer when he began looking for a fast way to make copies of line drawings and texts of patents, which led him to his invention of the xerographic printing process. Land, first interested in polarized light for sunglasses and cameras, was 28 years old when he started the Polaroid Corporation. Alfred Nobel was 29 in 1864 when an explosion in his father's nitroglycerin factory in Stockholm killed five people, including his younger brother, Emil. This "accident waiting to happen" sent him on a crusade to find a less volatile alternative. In 1867, he patented his mixture under the name dynamite and made a fortune, earning 355 patents in his lifetime. In 1901, five years after his death, the first (again eponymous) Nobel Prizes were to be awarded to those who, each year, are found to have conferred "the greatest benefit on mankind."

At one point on the private incentive continuum from the first technical application of a basic scientific discovery to commercial empire is the lone scientist problem-solver of lore, for whom financial incentives in the form of patent royalties may be utterly meaningless, but for whom a well-equipped laboratory is heaven on earth. At another is the modern technological firm, for which innovation through commercialization of new inventions is primarily a source of shareholder confidence sustaining thousands or tens of thousands of well-paying jobs, but within whose research departments and laboratories Nobel Prize winners are generally few and far between. (The Nobel Prize-winning invention of the transistor by Bardeen, Brattain, and Shockley at Bell Laboratories is a notable exception.) Quiet civic contribution by industrial firms not explicitly or implicitly promoting their own interests may be ubiquitous (and certainly should be encouraged!), but it is not at the center of what drives financial backers to invest in a firm or what drives the firm to channel that investment into R&D; return-on-investment, market entry, and expansion of market share are the keys to corporate behavior. Where ownership rights are clear, investors are confident. Most users of the patent systems of the world—from "knowledge workers" in labs and garages, in university spin-off companies, to executives in medium-size technology firms and multinational corporations—inhabit the complex zone of private interest calculus between the extremes of personal achievement and uncompensated fame on the one hand, and faceless but comfortable (or even luxurious) fortune on the other.

Beyond "supply-side," "new growth," and other private incentive economic theories are other public policy perspectives favoring a patent law. Government sponsorship of basic research must compete with many other budget priorities. The value of public disclosure of new technological information is rarely questioned. With dwindling government funds to support research, where is new information to be found? (It is estimated that 85–90 percent of all publicly available technical information appears only in the patent literature.) Competitors gain access to valuable technical information which would otherwise remain secret—information which they can then use to invent around a patent, creating more technical information in the process. Full disclosure of the patented invention provides certainty as to what is or is not excluded. But these direct public benefits must be weighed against the negative effects of excluding competitors from free competition in the patented technology itself. A race of duplicative research to reach the same technical goal for the purpose of excluding the losers ("rent-seeking") can be wasteful. Much depends upon the foreseeability of the goal. Patents have been called not just monopolies but an "embarrassment" (Jefferson's term, quoted in *Graham v. Deere* below). This view is correct, but incomplete. A patent contains within its terms the right to exclude all others from engaging in free competition, which is the foundation of the free market economy. As mentioned above, a patent is a legal monopoly. Yet this legal monopoly right is fundamentally different from most monopoly rights in the economic sense. As stated by the U.S. Supreme Court:

> monopolists have the sole right to buy, sell, or make and others are deprived of a preexisting right to buy, sell, or make. The patent grant gives the patentee only the right to exclude others; his own right to practice the invention may be subservient to another patent. Moreover, since novelty is a requisite of patentability, the grant does not exclude the public from a pre-existing right.

Standard Oil v. The United States, 221 US (1911).

Likewise, in *United States v. Dubilier*, 289 U.S. 178 (1933), the Court stated:

> [t]hough often so characterized, a patent is not, accurately speaking, a monopoly. . . . [t]he term monopoly connotes the giving of an exclusive privilege for buying, selling, working or using a thing which the public freely enjoyed prior to the grant. Thus a monopoly takes something from the people. An inventor deprives the public of nothing which it enjoyed before his discovery, but gives something of value to the community by adding to the sum of human knowledge. . . . He may keep his invention secret and reap its fruits indefinitely.

Patents may be implicated in anti-competitive behavior, such as in an arrangement to fix prices or to control availability of a product. But competition laws and patent laws go hand-in-hand, and rarely collide with one another within a single jurisdiction. As the Federal Circuit said in *Atari Games Corp. v. Nintendo of America, Inc.*, 897 F.2d 1572, 1576 (Fed. Cir. 1990):

> [T]he two bodies of law are actually complementary, as both are aimed at encouraging innovation, industry and competition . . . There may on occasion exist . . . a fine line between actions protecting the legitimate interests of a patent owner and antitrust law violations. On the one hand, the patent owner must be allowed to protect the property right given to him under the patent laws. On the other hand, a patent owner may not take the property right granted by a patent and use it to extend his power in the marketplace improperly, i.e. beyond the limits of what Congress intended to give in the patent laws. The fact that a patent is obtained does not wholly insulate the patent owner from the antitrust laws.

"The patent is a 'shield' to protect an invention," said the court, "not a 'sword' to eviscerate competition unfairly." The range and locale of competitor activities covered by a patent's limited right to exclude and thereby affecting the "legitimate interests of the patent owner" will be further examined below in our discussion of the "scope of patent rights."

A simple "yes/no" test for an invalid patent (where the winner takes all) might look like the following: "Does the patent in any way prevent a third party in a free market society from making, using, selling something it would have, but for the patent (and the invention therein), been able to make, use, or sell?" On balance, the trend of legislatures and courts in developed nations over the past three decades has been favorable to stronger intellectual property protection in general and stronger patent protection in particular. Rapid growth in the global scale and sophistication of access to and ability to exploit technological information has played a role in this phenomenon. In the Information Society, the patent system is envisioned as an engine driving the production of new technological information and indeed, completely new categories of such information, creating for the benefit of all an "infrastructure of innovation" underpinning a global technology-based economic system.

The implicit assumption of a patent system is that the patents to which it gives legal effect in fact meet the legal standards of patentability prescribed by the legislator. In modern examination systems, patent examiners are under tremendous pressure to dispose of patent applications quickly. Automation of patent information has helped ameliorate the problem of searching but exacerbated the problem of information overload. The patent offices of the developed world are inundated with applications— approaching half a million a year in Japan, forcing some offices (such as the EPO), to cut back on international cooperation because of the workload. Examiners may not be able to adequately search for prior art when faced with lengthy applications and dockets requiring them to reach a result on half a dozen or more elaborate applications in a single week. Bad patents do issue after examination. And they carry with them a legal presumption of validity. (See, for example, 35 U.S.C. Section 282). The alleged infringer must prove that the issued patent is invalid. Inability of patent examiners to search an art effectively creates the conditions for extortion if business competitors cannot afford to defend themselves in expensive patent litigation suits. It also leads to calls for exclusion from patent protection for some inventions as a better public policy alternative rather than leaving competitors to the mercy of well-heeled but unscrupulous patentees who threaten to sue on dubious patents and get to have their "day in court" before untutored juries with no technical training.

A final query to be posed in discussing the purposes of patent protection is whether a broad—even universal—international patent system spanning developed and developing nations of the globe alike (perhaps prefigured in the TRIPS Agreement) is in the offing. This is a question for the new century to answer, but might be posed in the following way: "Do the people of a developing nation need to participate in the global technological revolution in order to benefit from it? If so, how and at what cost?"

§ 2.03 How Does One Acquire Patent Rights?

Patent rights are acquired by application to an organ of the state (usually a Patent Office, Bureau of Standards, or Registrar of Companies) requesting the grant of a patent. The application is generally required to contain a request for a patent, a description of the invention (sometimes called a "disclosure" or a "specification"), a drawing (where appropriate), and until recently at least, one or more legal claims to "patentable subject matter." The applicant must also pay a fee. Applications that do not meet the formal requirements and inventions that do not meet the substantive requirements have no legal effect. In the United States, additional requirements include the signature of the true inventor or inventors and an explanation of what the applicant thinks is the "best mode" for practicing the invention at the time of application.

As introduced above, once a patent application has been filed, it may be examined and approved by a competent technical body of the granting organ prior to grant to ensure that the legally mandated standards of patentability, including full disclosure of the invention in the description, have been met as of the time of the application. This is referred to as an examination system. Or, alternatively, upon completion of application formalities, the patent may simply be registered by the granting authority, with substantive examination only conducted in a judicial proceeding by a court enforcing the patent if and when the "right to exclude" of the patent is asserted against another party. This is referred to as a registration system. The registration system has the putative benefits of simplicity and administrative economy. (The United States had a registration system for patents from 1793 until 1836.) Conversely, by weeding out substandard patents prior to granting them, the examination system reduces the risk of competitors being forced to defend against dubious patents in expensive, frivolous court proceedings. It also provides the necessary conditions for the establishment of a technically competent standing body to serve the nation as conservator of a vast repository of patent documentation in an official language of the nation granting the patent. As will be discussed in the context of patent harmonization, the native language requirement serves an important public policy objective, the elimination of which has proven to be an overwhelming and seemingly insurmountable hurdle for small nations (such as the EU states) seeking to unify their patent systems. And recently, proponents (usually English-speaking) of a cost-effective world patent in a single language (usually English) have downplayed the importance of the requirement for a patent application to be made in the language of the receiving state.

The modern trend in patent acquisition systems is toward grant of a patent only after substantive examination has taken place. With considerable variation between the jurisprudential practices in the courts of different countries, a level of legal deference is given by national courts to substantive examination prior to the grant of the patent conducted by the national patent office of that state. In addition, practically speaking, *de facto* deference may even be given to substantive examination completed by the patent office of one state or of an international organization by examiners in patent offices of other states or other international organizations where a counterpart patent application has already been filed, and applicants for a patent in one state may be required to disclose to patent authorities any disposition of a counterpart patent application in another state. Concerted efforts are underway to increase cooperation between patent examiners in national patent offices and international organizations (so-called "work-sharing") to avoid duplication of efforts. All (or in the case of the United States, all internationally filed) patent applications are placed open to the public after a period of time (usually no more than 18 months from filing), after which third parties may challenge the grant of a patent to the applicant in an *inter partes* action known as an "opposition" proceeding (or, in the United States, in a post-grant "reexamination" proceeding which can be initiated by a third party.) An opposition proceeding may occur before or after the grant of the patent, depending on the law of the granting state; however, the modern trend is toward expedited, pre-grant opposition proceedings. In the United States, where in contrast to the entire rest of the world the date of first application is not conclusive of the priority right to a patent, a different proceeding known as an "interference" may be conducted by the Board of Patent Appeals and Interferences of the Patent and Trademark Office. At an interference proceeding, the applicant and one or more third parties may assert and present evidence of their priority right to ownership of the disputed patent based upon earlier conception and reduction to practice. The U.S. "first-to-invent" system and the "first-to-file" system used everywhere else will be discussed further below in considering the substantive patentability requirement of novelty.

Notes and Questions

(1) **Patents and "Brain Drain."** The Venetian statute of 1474 proclaims that "there come temporarily by reason of its greatness and goodness, men from different places and most clever minds, capable of devising and inventing all manner of ingenious contrivances." It was designed, Kaufer states, "to attract engineers to the Republic. It was not an instrument to stimulate artisan production by granting monopolistic trade privileges." Given the mobility of contemporary world society, to what extent is a strong patent system a competitive advantage in world trade today owing purely to its ability to attract inventive individuals to the country which adopts it? Does a strong patent system (such as that in the United States) foster "brain-drain" from countries with weak patent laws?

(2) **Patents as Monopolies.** Notwithstanding the fact that patents for inventions are not in and of themselves economic monopolies (they are, rather, "legal monopolies"), the term "patent monopoly" is sometimes used rhetorically even by sophisticated modern writers. This is probably due to the fact that patents of invention were carved out as an exception to the Statute of Monopolies of 1623, which in turn was a curb on the prerogatives of the Crown. A contrarian author states, "This Statute abolished monopolies, but made an exception for patents on inventions. Thus, the patent system was born in contradiction." THOMAS A. MANDEVILLE, UNDERSTANDING NOVELTY: INFORMATION, TECHNOLOGICAL CHANGE AND THE PATENT SYSTEM 13 (1996). Another commentator observes: "Early seventeenth-century English reformers reacted to the perversion of the patent and copyright into royal monopolies by codifying into law that these were rights bestowed by government to stimulate innovation and expression." MICHAEL P. RYAN, KNOWLEDGE DIPLOMACY 6 (1998). Compare the plight of policy-makers in contemporary developing countries to the situation in Elizabethan England. "The practice of giving incentives to industry is particularly prevalent in developing countries. Concessions, rights, franchises, tax holidays, or bribes

secure valuable rights to manufacture, or to develop mineral, lumber and other natural resources, including gambling concessions. This . . . is a reversion to the situation in the early days of monopoly grants, which were abolished except for patents for new inventions. The right of the crown to grant monopolies in those days was [similarly] abused." G.E. Maybee, *A Philosophic Approach to the Patent System*, 53 J. PAT. & TM. OFF. SOC'Y 307, 324 (1971).

(3) **Patents of Invention, of Introduction, and of Importation.** The English statute speaks of "letters patents and [grants] of privilege . . . of the sole working or making of any manner of new manufactures within this *realm* to the true and first inventor." [emphasis added] "Patent of introduction" refers to privileges designed to encourage commercialization of foreign technology within "the realm." In its earliest formulation, in Elizabethan England the grant of exclusive privileges to inventors was linked to working requirements—an obligation to practice what one is privileged to do:

> In return for the grant, the crown had some rather defined expectations that, although they varied from grant to grant, were nonetheless consonant with the basic premise of developing new trade and industry within the realm. The most basic of these expectations was that the grantee would in fact undertake not only to introduce the new art, trade or industry into England but also to practice or "work" it within the country. That is to say, the crown sought not only to have it introduced but also established in England. . . . The first and most straightforward placed a temporal limitation on the patentee requiring introduction of the new industry within a fixed time. This varied typically from as short a time as two months to as long as three years. Failure to work the new art or industry in England within the period stipulated served as a basis for avoidance or withdrawal of the grant. There is some reason to believe that it was customary to bind aliens in this way.
>
> A second pragmatic requirement placed on a number of the grants obligated the patentee to employ and train native artisans to practice the art covered by the grant. This type of requirement generally applied only to foreigners and was for the purpose of assuring the establishment of the industry should the patentee withdraw when, or before, the term of his monopoly expired. It clearly was intended to accomplish the same result as the alternative "working" requirement. A variation on the theme was a limitation on the number of aliens that the patentee might have as partners or as employees. Again, the purpose was obviously to obligate the patentee to use English apprentices and artisans at least to a certain degree. . . .

Edward C. Walterscheid, *The Early Evolution Of The United States Patent Law: Antecedents (Part 2)*, 76 J. PAT. & TRADE. OFF. SOC'Y 849, 856–8 (1994). More recently, the same author has noted that the Patent Bill in the Second Session of the First U.S. Congress of 1790 [H.R. 41] included a provision recognizing patents of introduction at the behest of President Washington. That explicit provision was deleted by the House prior to passage, allegedly due to the belief by Madison that it was unconstitutional. *See* Edward C. Walterscheid, *Charting a Novel Course: The Creation of the Patent Act of 1790*, 25 AIPLA Q.J. 445, 503 (1997). Madison never explained why patents of introduction would be unconstitutional. Is there an explanation? Suppose the party introducing the invention was not the "true and first inventor?" *See* Notes 7 and 8 below.

(4) **Modern Viability of Patents of Introduction.** According to one commentator, "[t]he appeal of patent systems to countries that are set to catch up in the race for technology is a continuing one that makes the international aspects of patents, if anything, more important than domestic considerations." WILLIAM CORNISH, INTELLECTUAL PROPERTY: PATENTS, COPYRIGHT, TRADE MARKS AND ALLIED RIGHTS 67 (2d ed. 1989). According to the English 1691 case of *Edgeberry v. Stephens*, the English statute did not prevent a party from obtaining a patent in England on an invention derived from a foreign inventor, notwithstanding that the importer was not the true inventor. Related to patents of introduction are patents of importation, which allow a foreign patentee to receive a domestic patent covering the same invention claimed in a foreign patent for the term of the foreign patent in exchange for importing and working the patented technology, notwithstanding lack of novelty at the time of the application. Are the policies behind patents of introduction suitable for developing countries hoping to attract foreign technology today? *See* Ruth L. Gana, *Prospects For Developing Countries Under The TRIPS Agreement*, 29 VAND. J. TRANSNAT'L L. 735, 758 (1996). Article 5 of the Venezuelan patent law provides for such patents. *See* Mark Greenberg, Comment: *Recent Developments In Latin American Intellectual Property Law: The Venezuelan Response To Andean Pact Decision 313*, U. MIAMI INTER-AM. L. REV. 131, 147 (1993). For most developing countries attempting to modernize, was it the intrinsic benefits of a stronger patent system or the blandishments of greater market access in Europe, North America, and Japan which coaxed them into including intellectual property in the Uruguay Round agreement in 1994? *See* Judith C. Chin and Gene M. Grossman, *Intellectual Property Rights and North-South Trade*, Discussion Paper No. 143 WILSON PAPERS IN ECONOMICS, (Princeton 1988). This question will be explored further below.

(5) **The Competence of the State (Its Agencies or Its Courts) to Grant Compulsory Licenses.** H.R. 41 in the First Congress also had a Senate amendment which allowed for compulsory licenses in the event that "the Grantee of such Patent shall neglect to offer for sale within the United States a sufficient number of such manufacture . . . or shall sell the same at a price beyond what may be judged an adequate compensation." This provision was also deleted before the enactment of the bill and the United States has never had a compulsory licensing provision in its patent statute. *See* Edward C. Walterscheid, *Charting a Novel Course: The Creation of the Patent Act of 1790,* 25 AIPLA Q.J. 445, 522–24 (1997). Walterscheid

observes: "It appears that the House was not enamored of 'investing the judges of the Supreme Court with a power to determine the compensation which persons shall receive for their inventions.'" The scope of the exclusive right of a patent vis-a-vis "working requirements" and rights of third parties will be discussed further below in the context of Article 5 of the Paris Convention.

(6) **Patent Legislation and Patent Codification.** "The difference between the legal effect of a patent in the early part of the seventeenth century and of a patent at the close of the eighteenth and beginning of the nineteenth century are very great. They may be summarized briefly as follows: In the early period, the consideration for the grant was the introduction and establishment of a new industry, no formal written disclosure was required, patents for improvements were of doubtful validity, and the patent was invalid if a prior use could be shown. In the later period, the consideration for the grant was a written description which disclosed the invention to the public, actual establishment of the industry or working of the invention was not necessary, patents for improvements were good at law and the patent was invalid if it was not novel. The most remarkable fact, however, is that all these changes were made by a gradual development through judicial interpretation and not at all by statute. The Statute of Monopolies remained the only statute on patents in England until a period far into the nineteenth century." P.J.Federico, *Origin and Early History of Patents I*, 11 J. PAT. OFF. SOC'Y 292, 305 (1929). Many of the provisions of the U.S. Patent Act of 1952 (such as the concept of nonobviousness), originated in, and were codified from court cases. Some economic legislation, including the antitrust law and (until recently) trademark law, are based upon simply worded statutes fleshed out in numerous court decisions. Others, such as the exceptions to the exclusive rights of copyright law, are elaborate schemes of minutely drafted industry-specific legislation which are granted great deference by judges. Should the making of patent law be more like the making of traditional antitrust and trademark law on the one hand, or of copyright law on the other? Is the Congress (criticized for the influence of its well-paid lobbyists) or are the courts (faced with real-life economic competitors but lacking policy guidance) better situated to implement patent policy in the first instance? Put another way, is judicial activism subject to subsequent legislative response preferable to *a priori* legislation and a docile judiciary backed only by constitutional thresholds? (This will be discussed in the following section on what constitutes patentable subject matter.)

(7) **"Inventor's Rights."** What does Prager mean by "plain intellectual property, without other consideration of public policy, philosophical or otherwise" as the legal objective sought by surveyor Fitch in proposing his patent bill? Of the two positions, that of Webster-Fitch and that of Franklin-Rumsey-Thornton, which has more relevance to the U.S. patent law today? Does the fact that the Fitch-Rumsey debate was engendered by a set of interferences say something about the pervasiveness of the "inventor's rights" attitude, at least in some quarters of American inventors?

(8) **Abolishing the Patent System.** It is sometimes asserted that if the United States were to switch to a first-to-file system, it would deprive "inventors" of their rights. What, if anything, is to be made of the language in Article I, Section 8, Clause 8 of the U.S. Constitution: " . . . by *securing* to inventors . . . "? Is there a difference between Congress having the power to *secure* rights to inventors and having the power to *grant* such rights? The Patent Act of 1793 stated that the applicant must express "a desire for *obtaining* an exclusive property right." MICHAEL P. RYAN, KNOWLEDGE DIPLOMACY 26 (1998). In an early copyright case, the Supreme Court interpreted the clause, saying, "It refers to inventors as well as authors, and it has never been pretended by anyone, either in this country or in England, that an inventor has a perpetual right, at common law, to sell the thing invented." *Wheaton v. Peters*, 33 U.S. (8 Peters) 591 (1834). Even granting that, does the Constitutional language empower the Congress to *deny* patent protection altogether? In a famous opinion, the late Judge Giles Sutherland Rich of the U.S. Court of Appeals for the Federal Circuit said, "the Constitutional clause under consideration neither gave to nor preserved in inventors (or authors) any rights and set no standards for the patentability of individual inventions; it merely empowered Congress, if it elected to do so, to secure to inventors an 'exclusive right' for an unstated 'limited' time for the stated purpose of promoting useful arts." *In re Bergy*, 596 F.2d 952, 959 (1979).

(9) **The U.S. Patent System: Model Development Strategy or Exceptionalist?** The relationship between economic development and strong intellectual property protection is an ongoing problematic. The Austrian Premier, Count Andrassy, observed in 1873 that the countries with the strongest patent systems, Great Britain and the United States, also had the strongest economic development, and concluded that the former was the cause of the latter. Do patent systems become stronger as countries develop economically, or do countries develop economically because (at least in part) they first strengthen their patent systems? *See* Robert M. Sherwood, *The TRIPS Agreement: Implications For Developing Countries*, 37 IDEA 491 (1997)

(10) **Innovation Policy Without Patents.** States may subsidize research and development through the public purse if they so choose. Do government subsidies also promote economic development through commercialization of innovation? One view states that "[c]onventional patent theory seems to ignore the possibility and role of other incentives to innovate . . . that may exist in the absence of strong patent protection. These can include trade secrets, quick market penetration, oligopolistic cooperation, competitive product leadership, and various natural imitation lags including the high costs of reverse engineering complex technologies. *See* THOMAS A. MANDEVILLE, UNDERSTANDING NOVELTY: INFORMATION, TECHNOLOGICAL CHANGE AND THE PATENT SYSTEM 20 (1996). Is it likely that developing countries which do not have wealthy public coffers or strong patent protection would be able to benefit from any of these alternatives?

§ 2.04 What Kinds of Inventions Can Be Patented?

Worldwide standards for patentable inventions, which went into effect at the beginning of the year 2000 in all of the member countries of the World Trade Organization, are straightforward in principle: that the invention be "new," involve an "inventive step" and be "capable of industrial application." *See* TRIPS, art. 27. What is meant by "capable of industrial application" is examined below in two areas of modern technology where the issues are likely to be most hotly contested in the twenty-first century in the international arena, namely life forms and information technology. Following that, we will turn our attention to the requirements of novelty and inventive step.

[A] Patentable Subject Matter: Life Forms

[1] United States

DIAMOND v. CHAKRABARTY
447 U.S. 303 (1980)

MR. CHIEF JUSTICE BURGER delivered the opinion of the Court.

The Constitution grants Congress broad power to legislate to "promote the Progress of Science and useful Arts, by securing for limited Times to Authors and Inventors the exclusive Right to their respective Writings and Discoveries." Art. I, § 8, cl. 8. The patent laws promote this progress by offering inventors exclusive rights for a limited period as an incentive for their inventiveness and research efforts. The authority of Congress is exercised in the hope that "[the] productive effort thereby fostered will have a positive effect on society through the introduction of new products and processes of manufacture into the economy, and the emanations by way of increased employment and better lives for our citizens."

The question before us in this case is a narrow one of statutory interpretation requiring us to construe 35 U.S.C. § 101, which provides:

> Whoever invents or discovers any new and useful process, machine, manufacture, or composition of matter, or any new and useful improvement thereof, may obtain a patent therefor, subject to the conditions and requirements of this title.

Specifically, we must determine whether respondent's micro-organism constitutes a "manufacture" or "composition of matter" within the meaning of the statute. . . .

. . .

III(A)

In cases of statutory construction we begin, of course, with the language of the statute. And "unless otherwise defined, words will be interpreted as taking their ordinary, contemporary, common meaning." We have also cautioned that courts "should not read into the patent laws limitations and conditions which the legislature has not expressed."

Guided by these canons of construction, this Court has read the term "manufacture" in § 101 in accordance with its dictionary definition to mean "the production of articles for use from raw or prepared materials by giving to these materials new forms, qualities, properties, or combinations, whether by hand-labor or by machinery." Similarly, "composition of matter" has been construed consistent with its common usage to include "all compositions of two or more substances and . . . all composite articles, whether they be the results of chemical union, or of mechanical mixture, or whether they be gases, fluids, powders or solids." In choosing such expansive terms as "manufacture" and "composition of matter," modified by the comprehensive "any," Congress plainly contemplated that the patent laws would be given wide scope.

The relevant legislative history also supports a broad construction. The Patent Act of 1793, authored by Thomas Jefferson, defined statutory subject matter as "any new and useful art, machine, manufacture, or composition of matter, or any new or useful improvement [thereof]." Act of Feb. 21, 1793, § 1, 1 Stat. 319. The Act embodied Jefferson's philosophy that "ingenuity should receive a liberal encouragement." Subsequent patent statutes in 1836, 1870, and 1874 employed this same broad language. In 1952, when the patent laws were recodified, Congress replaced the word "art" with "process," but otherwise left Jefferson's language intact. The Committee Reports accompanying the 1952 Act inform us that Congress intended statutory subject matter to "include anything under the sun that is made by man."

This is not to suggest that § 101 has no limits or that it embraces every discovery. The laws of nature, physical phenomena, and abstract ideas have been held not patentable. Thus, a new mineral discovered in the earth or a new plant found in the wild is not patentable subject matter. Likewise, Einstein could not patent his celebrated law that $E = mc^2$; nor could Newton have patented the law of gravity. Such discoveries are "manifestations of . . . nature, free to all men and reserved exclusively to none."

Judged in this light, respondent's micro-organism plainly qualifies as patentable subject matter. His claim is not to a hitherto unknown natural phenomenon, but to a nonnaturally occurring manufacture or composition of matter—a product of human ingenuity "having a distinctive name, character [and] use.". . .

(B)

The petitioner's second argument is that micro-organisms cannot qualify as patentable subject matter until Congress expressly authorizes such protection. His position rests on the fact that genetic technology was unforeseen when Congress enacted § 101. From this it is argued that resolution of the patentability of inventions such as respondent's should be left to

Congress. The legislative process, the petitioner argues, is best equipped to weigh the competing economic, social, and scientific considerations involved, and to determine whether living organisms produced by genetic engineering should receive patent protection. . . . It is, of course, correct that Congress, not the courts, must define the limits of patentability; but it is equally true that once Congress has spoken it is "the province and duty of the judicial department to say what the law is." Congress has performed its constitutional role in defining patentable subject matter in § 101; we perform ours in construing the language Congress has employed. In so doing, our obligation is to take statutes as we find them, guided, if ambiguity appears, by the legislative history and statutory purpose. Here, we perceive no ambiguity. The subject-matter provisions of the patent law have been cast in broad terms to fulfill the constitutional and statutory goal of promoting "the Progress of Science and the useful Arts" with all that means for the social and economic benefits envisioned by Jefferson. Broad general language is not necessarily ambiguous when congressional objectives require broad terms. . . . This is especially true in the field of patent law. A rule that unanticipated inventions are without protection would conflict with the core concept of the patent law that anticipation undermines patentability. Congress employed broad general language in drafting § 101 precisely because such inventions are often unforeseeable.

To buttress his argument, the petitioner, with the support of amicus, points to grave risks that may be generated by research endeavors such as respondent's. The briefs present a gruesome parade of horribles. Scientists, among them Nobel laureates, are quoted suggesting that genetic research may pose a serious threat to the human race, or, at the very least, that the dangers are far too substantial to permit such research to proceed apace at this time. We are told that genetic research and related technological developments may spread pollution and disease, that it may result in a loss of genetic diversity, and that its practice may tend to depreciate the value of human life. These arguments are forcefully, even passionately, presented; they remind us that, at times, human ingenuity seems unable to control fully the forces it creates—that, with Hamlet, it is sometimes better "to bear those ills we have than fly to others that we know not of."

It is argued that this Court should weigh these potential hazards in considering whether respondent's invention is patentable subject matter under § 101. We disagree. The grant or denial of patents on microorganisms is not likely to put an end to genetic research or to its attendant risks. The large amount of research that has already occurred when no researcher had sure knowledge that patent protection would be available suggests that legislative or judicial fiat as to patentability will not deter the scientific mind from probing into the unknown any more than Canute could command the tides. Whether respondent's claims are patentable may determine whether research efforts are accelerated by the hope of reward or slowed by want of incentives, but that is all.

What is more important is that we are without competence to entertain these arguments—either to brush them aside as fantasies generated by fear of the unknown, or to act on them. The choice we are urged to make is a matter of high policy for resolution within the legislative process after the kind of investigation, examination, and study that legislative bodies can provide and courts cannot. That process involves the balancing of competing values and interests, which in our democratic system is the business of elected representatives. Whatever their validity, the contentions now pressed on us should be addressed to the political branches of the Government, the Congress and the Executive, and not to the courts. . . . Congress is free to amend § 101 so as to exclude from patent protection organisms produced by genetic engineering. *Cf.* 42 U. S. C. § 2181(a) (exempting from patent protection inventions "useful solely in the utilization of special nuclear material or atomic energy in an atomic weapon.") Or it may choose to craft a statute specifically designed for such living things. But, until Congress takes such action, this Court must construe the language of § 101 as it is. The language of that section fairly embraces respondent's invention.

Accordingly, the judgment of the Court of Customs and Patent Appeals is

Affirmed.

[2] European Patent Convention

NOTE: THE MUNICH (EUROPEAN PATENT) CONVENTION AND EUROPEAN PATENT OFFICE

The European Patent Convention [EPC] was signed on 5 October 1973 in Munich. It created a single granting system under the administration of a new organization, the European Patent Organization [EPO], supervised by an Administrative Council consisting of representatives of the member States (usually national patent office officials.) The EPC is a special agreement under the Paris Convention (EPC Preamble) which provides free accessibility and national treatment and right of priority (EPC Articles 87–89) in compliance with Article 4 of the Paris Convention.

The European Patent Organization is an autonomous and self-supporting intergovernmental organization which is completely independent of the European Union. Article 18 EPC establishes that a European patent application is to be examined by three examiners. Article 15 EPC establishes the Boards of Appeal and an Enlarged Board of Appeal. Article 21.3 EPC sets forth that for appeals from a decision of an Examining Division, a Technical Board of Appeal consisting of at least two technically qualified members and one legally qualified member shall review the rejection. The European patent system will be covered in further detail in later chapters.

Reporting of EPO Boards of Appeal Opinions

A most valuable resource for international intellectual property lawyers is the English-language scholarly journal International Review of Industrial Property and Copyright Law [IIC], published by the Federal Republic of Germany's Max-Planck Institute for Foreign and international Patent, Copyright, and Competition Law in Munich, from which several of the following cases are excerpted. One of the many research institutes which the Max-Planck Society comprises, the Institute for Foreign and International Patent, Copyright, and Competition Law was founded in 1952 by Professor Dr. Eduard Reimer, at that time President of the German Patent Office, to engage in systematic study and analysis of sources of law and legal decisions on industrial property and copyright law. IIC began publication in 1970, expanding the scope of publication of the national and international editions of the German-language journal Gewerblicher Rechtsschutz Und Urheberrecht [GRUR] published since 1896 by the German Association for the Protection of Industrial Property and Copyright. Case reports in IIC include headnotes and abstracts prepared by researchers at the institute, as well as the text of judicial opinions. EPO Boards of Appeal opinions in PDF format can also be found at the EPO website at <www.european-patent-office.org/epo/pubs/oj_index_e.htm>.

EUROPEAN PATENT CONVENTION, ARTICLE 53

European patents shall not be granted in respect of:

(a) inventions the publication or exploitation of which would be contrary to "ordre public" or morality, provided that the exploitation shall not be deemed to be so contrary merely because it is prohibited by law or regulation in some or all of the Contracting States;

(b) plant or animal varieties or essentially biological processes for the production of plants or animals; this provision does not apply to microbiological processes or the products thereof.

IN RE PRESIDENT AND FELLOWS OF HARVARD COLLEGE
(ONCO-MOUSE)
Technical Board of Appeal 3.3.2 of the European Patent Office
(Oct. 3. 1990) Reported at 22 IIC 74–84 (1991)

I. The exception to patentability under Article 53(b) EPC applies to certain categories of animals but not to animals as such.

II. In particular in the case of genetic manipulation of animals involving, as in this case, the insertion of an activated oncogene, there are compelling reasons to consider the provisions of Article 53(a) EPC in relation to the question of patentability.

FROM THE FACTS

I. European patent application No. 85 304 490.7, published as No. 0 169 672, was refused by the Examining Division in its decision of 14 July 1989 [cit]. The application as refused had 19 claims, Claims 1, 17 and 18 reading as follows:

1. A method for producing a transgenic non-human mammalian animal having an increased probability of developing neoplasms, said method comprising introducing an activated oncogene sequence into a non-human mammalian animal at a stage no later than the 8-cell stage.

17. A transgenic non-human mammalian animal whose germ cells and somatic cells contain an activated oncogene sequence introduced into said animal, or an ancestor of said animal, at a stage no later than the 8-cell stage, said oncogene optionally being further defined according to any one of Claims 3 to 10.

18. An animal as claimed in Claim 17 which is a rodent.

II. The grounds given for refusal were that the application did not meet the requirements of Articles 53(b) and 83 EPC. The relevance of Article 53(a) EPC was also discussed. The main arguments were as follows:

. . . .

(b) In interpreting Article 53(b) EPC it had to be borne in mind that its text was drawn virtually word for word from the Strasbourg Convention. This dated from 1963, when the question of patenting transgenic animals was scarcely conceivable. In interpreting the article. however, it was necessary to consider what the legislators' intentions had been at that time. The Strasbourg Convention enables the Contracting States to exclude animal varieties from patent protection. According to the Examining Division, the idea behind this exclusion was that animal varieties were not appropriate subject-matter for patent protection. This view was supported by the fact that the animal exclusion under Article 53(b) EPC used different taxonomic terms in the three languages: "animal varieties", "races animales" and "Tierarten." The Division then considered the applicability of the Article 53(b) EPC exclusion of "essentially biological processes" from patentability, concluding that in the light of decision T 320/87 (OJ EPO 1990. 71 [21 IIC 361 (1990)—Hybrid Plants]) it was to be construed narrowly and judged on the basis of the essence of the invention. The essence of the present process invention was the introduction of an oncogene into an animal by technical means such as micro-injection. As this was clearly not "essentially biological," no objection to the process claims was raised under Article 53(b), 1st half-sentence, EPC. With product Claims 17 and 18, however, the question arose as to whether they came under the exclusion provision of Article 53(b), 2nd half-sentence, EPC. The answer was that they contained two different process steps, namely the non-biological step already mentioned and a purely breeding step. The two steps resulted in two different products. Animals which had been genetically manipulated themselves were products of an essentially non-biological process, whereas further generations were the product of sexual and thus exclusively biological reproduction. The latter were therefore non-patentable under Article 53(b), 1st half-sentence, EPC. Even accepting the appellants' argument that the process as a whole was essentially non-biological. this would not make the product claims allowable; only products of microbiological processes within the meaning of Article 53(b), 2nd half-sentence, EPC were patentable. However, the second half-sentence had to be seen in conjunction with the first; if the product of a process was manifestly excluded under the first part of the article, the second part could not be interpreted in such a way as to set aside the first.

(c) The Division also felt that it should consider Article 53(a) EPC, which excluded patents for inventions whose publication or exploitation would be contrary to *"ordre public"* or morality; in the United States, for example, the patenting of higher organisms had encountered severe criticism for ethical reasons. In this connection it sought to address the following specific issues:

—Might it not be better to perform cancer tests of this kind on non-animal models?

—The purpose of the present invention was not to improve particular features but to produce tumors in the test animals.

—Animals were regarded as objects.

—Descendants of the transgenic animals might escape into the environment and spread malignant foreign genes through mating.

—Was evolution not being drastically interfered with?

The Division concluded that patent law was not the right legislative tool for resolving the potential problems.

III. The appellants appealed against the decision to refuse their application.

IV. With the statement of grounds the appellants filed four sets of claims: a main request and three auxiliary requests. Claims 1 and 19 of the main and first auxiliary requests read as follows:

Main request:

> 1. A method for producing a transgenic non-human mammalian animal having an increased probability of developing neoplasms, said method comprising chromosomally incorporating an activated oncogene sequence into the genome of a non-human mammalian animal.
>
> . . .
>
> 19. A transgenic non-human mammalian animal whose germ cells and somatic cells contain an activated oncogene sequence as a result of chromosomal incorporation into the animal genome, or into the genome of an ancestor of said animal. said oncogene optionally being further defined according to any one of claims 3 to 10.

1st auxiliary request:

> 1. A method for producing a transgenic non-human mammalian animal having an increased probability of developing neoplasms, said method comprising introducing an activated oncogene

sequence into a non-human mammalian animal at an embryonic stage.

. . .

19. A transgenic non-human mammalian animal whose germ cells and somatic cells contain an activated oncogene sequence introduced into said animal, or an ancestor of said animal, at an embryonic stage. Said oncogene optionally being further defined according to any one of claims 3 to 10.

The sets of claims under the third and fourth auxiliary requests correspond to those in the main and auxiliary requests refused by the Examining Division.

The appellants' arguments may be summarized as follows:

. . . .

(b) Turning to the Examining Division's basis for refusing the application—Article 53(b) EPC—the appellants argued that Board of Appeal case law had consistently been that patents should be granted for any invention meeting the general requirements of the EPC; wherever the law was not clear and admitted interpretation the Boards had taken the line that exceptions to patentability should be construed narrowly. . . . The present application provided an opportunity to develop this case law, as the meaning of Article 53(b) EPC was uncertain. The contested decision departed from this principle by placing a wide construction on the exclusion under Article 53(b) EPC. This ran counter in particular to decision T 49/83 [cit], which held that no general exclusion of inventions in the sphere of animate nature could be inferred from the European Patent Convention.

Above all, the Division erred in concluding that the different terms used in the three official languages to refer to the non-patentable subject-matter clearly showed that the Legislators' intention had been to exclude animals generally. Had this been the case, they could clearly have said so in unambiguous terms. The entire process defined in the newly filed claims was essentially non-biological. The Examining Division had already accepted this for that part of the process involving micro-injection of oncogene sequences into the embryo at various stages of development. However, this technical operation was so central to the invention itself, and to its effect in descendants of the first genetically manipulated animals, that the entire process concealed in the product claims was not to be regarded as "essentially biological" within the meaning of Article 53(b) EPC.

The invention was in any case clearly a "microbiological process." The dominant feature of both process and product was genetic manipulation, which was unquestionably of a microbiological and technical nature.

Lastly, the Examining Division's view that one exclusion provision could not be countermanded by another was wrong in law. It could not be right for subject-matter expressly declared patentable under Article 53(b) EPC— microbiological processes and their products—to be refused protection nonetheless on the basis that the products in question were excluded elsewhere in that provision.

The appellants requested that the following question be referred to the Enlarged Board of Appeal: "Insofar as the exclusion of Article 53(b) first part EPC relates to 'animal,' to what extent is animal protection possible under Article 53(b) EPC (if at all)?"

V. A large number of observations by third parties, most of them expressing serious concern about genetic manipulation of animals, have been filed under Article 115(1) EPC, showing considerable interest by the public in the present case.

VI. The appellants request that the application be remitted to the Examining Division for further prosecution on the basis of any of the sets of claims submitted in the appeal proceedings.

FROM THE OPINION

1. The appeal is admissible.

. . . .

4. Exceptions to patentability under Article 53(b) EPC.

4.1 The present patent application concerns, inter alia, genetically manipulated non-human mammals. The first half-sentence of Article 53(b) EPC reads as follows in English, French and German:

European patents shall not be granted in respect of:

(a) . . .

(b) plant or animal varieties or essentially biological processes for the production of plants or animals;

Les brevets europiens ne vient pas délivrés pour:

(a) . . .

(b) les variétés végétales ou les races animales ainsi que les procédés essentiellement biologiques d'obtention de végétaux ou d'animaux;

Europäische Patente werden nicht erteilt für:

(a) . . .

(b) Pflanzensorten oder Tierarten sowie für im wesentlichen biologische Verfahren zur Züchtung con Pflanzen oder Tieren

4.2 As pointed out by the Examining Division, the three texts of Article 53(b) EPC differ in terminology as to the non-patentable area. In particular, the German term *"Tierarten"* is broader than the English "animal varieties" and the French *"races animales"*.

4.3 Article 177(1) EPC lays down that the English, French and German texts of the EPC are all equally authentic. In the present case, there is obviously a need to establish their common meaning through interpretation of the Convention in order to determine to what extent animals are excluded from patentability under Article 53(b), first half-sentence, EPC.

4.4 In the decision under appeal the Examining Division interpreted Article 53(b) EPC as excluding not only certain groups of animals from patentability but, in fact, animals as such. The Board is unable to accept this interpretation.

4.5 Firstly, the Examining Division did not take duly into account that Article 53(b) EPC is an exception for certain kinds of inventions, to the general rule under Article 52(1) EPC that European patents "shall be" granted for all inventions which are susceptible of industrial application, which are new and which involve an inventive step. Any such exception must, as repeatedly pointed out by the Boards of Appeal, be narrowly construed. The Examining Division has given no convincing reasons for deviating in this particular case from this principle of interpretation, nor are any such reasons apparent to the Board.

4.6 The possibility that the reference to certain categories of animals rather than to animals as such was simply a mistake by the legislators can be ruled out. Nothing in the legislative history of either the EPC or the Strasbourg Convention of 27 November 1963 on the Unification of Certain Points of Substantive Law on Patents for Invention, whose Article 2(b) was taken over and incorporated into Article 53(b) EPC, supports such an assumption. On the contrary, a clear indication that the terms "animal varieties," "*races animales*" and "*Tierarten*" were not intended to cover animals as such is the wording of Article 53(b) EPC itself. The very same provision also contains, as appears from paragraph 4.1 above, a reference to "animals" (in general). In using the different terms 'animal varieties' ("*races animales*," "*Tierarten*") and "animals" ("animaux," "*Tiere*") in this way, the legislators cannot have meant "animals" in both cases.

4.7 In contrast to the exclusion of "plant varieties" from patentability under Article 53(b) EPC, the preparatory documents to this provision are completely silent as to the purpose of excluding "animal varieties" from patentability. However, the purpose of a law (*ratio legis*) is not merely a matter of the actual intention of the legislators at the time when the law was adopted, but also of their presumed intention in the light of changes in circumstances which have taken place since then. It is now the task of the European Patent Office to find a solution to the problem of the interpretation of Article 53(b) EPC with regard to the concept of "animal varieties," providing a proper balance between the interest of inventors in this field in obtaining reasonable protection for their efforts and society's interest in excluding certain categories of animals from patent protection. In this context it should, *inter alia*, be borne in mind that for animals— unlike plant varieties—no other industrial property right is available for the time being.

4.8 To sum up, the Board concludes that the Examining Division was wrong in refusing the present application on the ground that Article 53(b) EPC excludes the patenting of animals as such. The proper issue to be considered is, therefore, whether or not the subject-matter of the application is an "animal variety" ("*race animale*", "*Tierart*") within the meaning of Article 53(b) EPC. On this point the contested decision is for obvious reasons entirely silent. In view of the importance of this matter and the desirability of having it considered by at least two instances, the Board will exercise its powers under Article 111(1) EPC to remit the case to the department of first instance for further prosecution. It should also be noted that a number of questions outlined below and not yet dealt with by the Examining Division now need to be considered.

In its resumed examination with regard to Article 53(b) EPC, the Examining Division must, as indicated above, first consider whether the subject-matter of the present application constitutes an "animal variety," "*race animale*" or "*Tierart*" within the meaning of that provision. If it comes to the conclusion that the subject-matter is not covered by any of these three terms, then Article 53(b) EPC constitutes no bar to patentability. If, however, it considers that any of these terms applies, then refusal of the application would only be justified if that specific term represents the proper interpretation of Article 53(b) (see point 4.3 above). This would also presuppose that Article 53(b) EPC can be applied at all in respect of animals which are genetically manipulated, given that neither the drafters of the Strasbourg Convention nor those of the EPC could envisage this possibility.

4.9 Essentially biological processes (Article 53(b), 1st half-sentence, 2nd alternative, EPC)

4.9.1 Process claims

Under Article 53(b), 1st half-sentence, EPC, European patents are not granted for essentially biological processes for the production of animals. The present invention contains process claims for the production of transgenic, non-human mammals with an increased propensity to develop neoplasms through chromosomal incorporation of an activated oncogene sequence into the genome of the non-human mammal. The oncogene is inserted by technical means into a vector (*e.g.* a plasmid), which is then micro-injected at an early embryonic stage. In the Board's view. the Examining Division correctly concluded that this is not an "essentially biological process" within the meaning of Article 53(b) EPC.

4.9.2 Product claims

Claim 19 under the main request relates to a transgenic non-human mammalian animal whose germ cells and somatic cells contain an activated oncogene sequence as a result of chromosomal incorporation into the genome of the animal itself or into the genome of one of its ancestors. It thus covers both transgenic animals produced according to the process claims, making use of micro-injection, and the descendants of such animals. While the former are the result of a non-biological process, their descendants can be the outcome of a biological process based on sexual reproduction.

The Examining Division took the view that by artificially combining a non-biological and a breeding process the applicant was seeking to circumvent the exclusion under Article 53(b),1st half-sentence EPC, particularly since the two processes would give rise to two different products. The Board doubts whether the latter point is legally correct as the products of the two processes, at least from the point of view of patent law, cannot be distinguished from each other in respect of the transferred gene. However. this question may be left open for the time being since the basic assertion in the contested decision—that Claim 19 circumvents Article 53(b) EPC, and thus precludes the grant of a patent—is wrong in any case. As the Examining Division has noted. Claim 19 is a product claim. In the absence of any other definition, the product claimed is defined in terms of the process by which it is produced. Claim 19 is thus a "product-by-process" claim. But a product-by-process claim remains a product claim irrespective of the process it refers to. So a successful Claim 19 would result in a product patent, not a process patent. Since, however, Article 53(b) EPC excludes only processes for the production of animals, with which Claim 19 is not concerned, this provision per se is no bar to patenting the product. It may also be added that a reproductive process could conceivably be other than sexual, *i.e.* other than essentially biological. for example if an animal which has received the oncogene sequence by the first process were then to be cloned by asexual, technical means.

4.10 Microbiological processes and the products thereof (Art. 53(b), 2nd half sentence, EPC)

Article 53(b), 2nd half-sentence, EPC provides that Article 53(b), 1st half-sentence, EPC does not apply to microbiological processes or the products thereof. The Examining Division did not decide whether the present invention involves a microbiological process, taking the view that Article 53(b), 2nd half-sentence, EPC does not apply if the product (in this case the animal) is excluded under the 1st half-sentence on the grounds that the second part of the provision cannot be interpreted in a manner which would set aside the first part. The Board does not share this view. As indicated above, Article 53(b), 1st half-sentence, EPC is an exception to the general principle of patentability contained in Article 52(1) EPC. The second half-sentence is an exception to this exception. ensuring that the patentability bar does not cover microbiological processes or the products thereof. In other words, the general principle of patentability under Article 52(1) EPC is restored for inventions involving microbiological processes and the products of such processes. Consequently, patents are grantable for animals produced by a microbiological process. The Examining Division must therefore consider, should the case arise, whether the claimed processes constitute microbiological processes within the meaning of Article 53(b) EPC.

5. Exception to patentability under Article 53(a) EPC

Under the heading "Considerations under Article 53(a) EPC" in the contested decision, the Examining Division argued that patent law is not the right legislative tool for regulating problems arising in connection with genetic manipulation of animals. The Board considers, however, that precisely in a case of this kind there are compelling reasons to consider the implications of Article 53(a) EPC in relation to the question of patentability. The genetic manipulation of mammalian animals is undeniably problematical in various respects, particularly where activated oncogenes are inserted to make an animal abnormally sensitive to carcinogenic substances and stimuli and consequently prone to develop tumors, which necessarily cause suffering. There is also a danger that genetically manipulated animals, if released into the environment, might entail unforeseeable and irreversible adverse effects. Misgivings and fears of this kind have been expressed by a number of persons who have filed observations with the Board under Article 115 EPC. Considerations of precisely this kind have also led a number of Contracting States to impose legislative control on genetic engineering. The decision as to whether or not Article 53(a) EPC is a bar to patenting the present invention would seem to depend mainly on a careful weighing up of the suffering of animals and possible risks to the environment on the one hand, and the invention's usefulness to mankind on the other. It is the task of the department of first instance to consider these matters in the context of its resumed examination of the case.

GREENPEACE LTD. v. PLANT GENETIC SYSTEMS N.V., ET AL.

Case No. T 356/93 (Board of Appeals, European Patent Office, Feb. 21, 1995) reported at 28 IIC 75 (1997)

[A European patent was granted for a process of controlling a plant's physiology by adding a DNA sequence to the plant to express a protein which suppresses an inhibitor of glutamate synthetase, or GSI (to allow for resistance to a GSI herbicide), for the process of making the plant and its "reproductive material," for plant cells incorporating the heterologous DNA, and for the plant itself. Greenpeace filed an opposition on the grounds that the grant of a patent for plant life forms and the exploitation of the patent were contrary to morality and/ or ordre public" under EPC Article 53(a), that the claims relating to plants and to processes for their production were not patentable under EPC Article 53(b), and that plant products from any generation beyond the first one did not constitute an invention under Article 52 EPC. When Greenpeace's opposition was rejected, it appealed to the Board of Appeals.]

FROM THE OPINION

1. The appeal is admissible.

Questions at Issue

2. Two main questions are at issue in the present case, namely:

(a) whether any of the claimed subject-matter constitutes an exception to patentability under the provisions of Article 53(a) EPC; and

(b) whether any of the claimed subject-matter constitutes an exception to patentability under the provisions of Article 53(b) EPC.

Concepts of "Ordre Public" and "Morality" Under Article 53(a) EPC

3. Article 53(a) EPC excludes from patentability "inventions the publication or exploitation of which would be contrary to 'ordre public' or morality, provided that the exploitation shall not be deemed to be so contrary merely because it is prohibited by law or regulation in some or all of the Contracting States."

4. As is apparent from the historical documentation, the EPC Working Party recognized that "there was no European definition of morality". Its members were, therefore, unanimously of the opinion that the "interpretation of the concept of morality should be a matter for European institutions" The same applies to the concept of "ordre public." Thus, prior to any assessment of the patentability of the claimed subject-matter under Article 53(a) EPC, the meaning of these concepts must be defined by way of interpretation.

5. It is generally accepted that the concept of "ordre public" covers the protection of public security and the physical integrity of individuals as part of society. This concept encompasses also the protection of the environment. Accordingly, under Article 53(a) EPC, inventions the exploitation of which is likely to breach public peace or social order (for example, through acts of terrorism) or to seriously prejudice the environment are to be excluded from patentability as being contrary to "ordre public".

6. The concept of morality is related to the belief that some behavior is right and acceptable whereas other behavior is wrong, this belief being founded on the totality of the accepted norms which are deeply rooted in a particular culture. For the purposes of the EPC, the culture in question is the culture inherent in European society and civilisation. Accordingly, under Article 53(a) EPC, inventions the exploitation of which is not in conformity with the conventionally-accepted standards of conduct pertaining to this culture are to be excluded from patentability as being contrary to morality.

. . .

8. From the historical documentation relating to the EPC it appears that the view according to which "the concept of patentability in the European patent law must be as wide as possible" predominated. Accordingly, the exceptions to patentability have been narrowly construed, in particular in respect of plant and animal varieties. In the Board's view, this approach applies equally in respect of the provisions of Article 53(a) EPC.

. . .

10. The Board notes that both the historical documentation and the above quoted case law recognize that, in principle, patents may be granted in

respect of inventions concerning plants or animals (excluding plant or animal varieties) as well as inventions relating to processes of a technical nature for their production. Thus, in the Board's judgement, it can be inferred from the above that seeds and plants per se shall not constitute an exception to patentability under Article 53(a) EPC merely because they represent "living" matter or, as submitted by the appellants, on the ground that plant genetic resources should remain the "common heritage of mankind". In respect of the latter point, the Board observes that the patenting of wild-type plant resources which may be used as starting material is not at issue in the present case. That such resources should belong to the "common heritage of mankind" is therefore not in jeopardy.

11. Thus, under Article 53(a) EPC, the relevant question is not whether living organisms are excluded as such, but rather whether or not the publication or exploitation of an invention related to a particular living organism is to be considered contrary to "ordre public" or morality.

Assessment of Patentability with Regard to the Requirements of Article 53(a) EPC

12. Although it may be difficult to judge whether or not a claimed subject matter is contrary to "ordre public" or morality, the provisions of Article 53(a) EPC may not be disregarded by the EPO when assessing patentability.

. . .

14. In the present case, it has to be decided whether the exploitation of any of the subject-matter claimed in the patent in suit is either likely to seriously prejudice the environment or contrary to the conventionally accepted standards of conduct of European culture.

. . .

16. In essence, the appellants submit that the exploitation of the claimed subject-matter (particular reference was made to the subject-matter of Claims 24 to 36 as granted) would damage the environment. This objection is raised with respect to both the issue of "ordre public," due to the alleged environmental consequences, and the issue of "morality," owing to concerns about the dominion gained by man over the natural world. These issues will be dealt with separately hereinafter by the Board taking into account the meaning of the concepts of "ordre public" and morality as previously defined.

17. With regard to the morality issue, the Board's considerations are as follows.

17.1 The appellants have expressed concern about the dominion that was sought to be exercised by man over the natural world by the use of plant genetic engineering techniques. In this respect, it has to be considered that plant biotechnology is a technology which aims at accomplishing practical improvements or advances in the area of plants by using modern scientific knowledge. The development of this technology inevitably allows a better understanding and control of the natural phenomena linked to plants. However, in the Board's view, this does not render activities in this technical field intrinsically wrong. Indeed, in the Board's judgement, plant biotechnology per se cannot be regarded as being more contrary to morality than traditional selective breeding because both traditional breeders and molecular biologists are guided by the same motivation, namely to change the property of a plant by introducing novel genetic material into it in order to obtain a new and, possibly, improved plant. However, compared with traditional breeding techniques, genetic engineering techniques applied to plants allow a more powerful and accurate control of genetic modifications. Plant biotechnology allows punctual gene modifications as well as the introduction into a given plant of genetic material from unrelated species of plants and from organisms other than plants. These techniques are an important tool to assist in plant breeding, which enables the performance of manipulations that would simply not be feasible by means of traditional breeding techniques. The impressive potential of these techniques is at the origin of the concerns and apprehensions expressed by public opinion and generates considerable disagreement and controversy. This factual situation forms the basis of the appellants objection to the dominion gained by man over the natural world. These concerns are understandable because the power of science for good and evil has always troubled man's mind. Like any other tool, plant genetic engineering techniques can be used for constructive or destructive purposes. It would undoubtedly be against "ordre public" or morality to propose a misuse or a destructive use of these techniques. Thus, under Article 53(a) EPC, no patent may be granted in respect of an invention directed to such a use. Consequently, it has to be established in the present case whether or not the claimed subject-matter relates to a misuse or to a destructive use of plant biotechnology.

17.2 The aim of the present invention is essentially to develop plants and seeds which are resistant to a particular class of herbicides, namely glutamine synthetase inhibitors (GSIs), and which are thereby selectively protected against weeds and fungal diseases. It should be noted that GSI-resistant plants or seeds could also be obtained by traditional plant selection methods, since some plants may be naturally resistant or may develop such a resistance. The patent in suit discloses the use of modern biotechnological techniques for the production of GSI-resistant plants and seeds which contain, integrated into their genome in a stable manner, heterologous DNA encoding a protein capable of inactivating or neutralising the above-mentioned herbicides. In that way, a new trait is added to the genetic material of a plant of interest, which allows the plant to grow in the presence of GSIs.

17.3 In the Board's judgement, none of the claims of the patent in suit refer to subject-matter which relates to a misuse or destructive use of plant biotechnological techniques because they concern activities (production of plants and seeds, protection of plants from weeds or fungal diseases) and products (plant cells, plants, seeds) which cannot be considered to be wrong as such in the light of conventionally accepted standards of conduct of European culture. Alleged environmental consequences due to these activities will have to be considered against the background of the "ordre public" issue (*cf.* point 18 *infra*).

18. With regard to the issue of "ordre public," the Board, as already stated (*cf.* point 5 *supra*), takes the view that Article 53(a) EPC constitutes a bar to patentability for inventions the exploitation of which is likely to seriously prejudice the environment. Thus, careful consideration must be given to the objections and evidence put forward by the appellants in this respect.

18.1 Before going into a detailed examination of the specific points raised by the appellants, some general remarks need to be made about the rights conferred by a patent on its owner(s) and the function of patent offices.

. . .

18.5 In the Board's judgement, the revocation of a European patent under Article 53(a) EPC on the grounds that the exploitation of the invention for which the patent has been granted would seriously prejudice the environment presupposes that the threat to the environment be sufficiently substantiated at the time the decision to revoke the patent is taken by the EPO. This view is consistent with the requirement that the exceptions to patentability under Article 53(a) EPC have to be narrowly construed, irrespective of whether or not the exploitation of the invention for which a European patent has been granted is prohibited by law(s) or regulation(s) in some or all of the Contracting States (*cf.* points 7 and 8 *supra*).

18.6 In the present case, no conclusive evidence has been presented by the appellants showing that the exploitation of the claimed subject-matter is likely to seriously prejudice the environment. In fact, most of the appellants arguments are based on the possibility that some undesired, destructive events (*e.g.* the transformation of crops into weeds, spreading of the herbicide-resistance gene to other plants, damage to the ecosystem) might occur. Of course, such events may occur to some extent. This fact has even been admitted by the respondents. However, in the Board's judgement, the documentary evidence submitted on this subject is not sufficient to substantiate the existence of a threat to the environment such as to represent a bar to patentability under Article 53(a) EPC. . . .

18.7 These documents provide fundamental evidence of possible hazards from the application of genetic engineering techniques to plants, in particular regarding the production of herbicide-resistant plants. . . .

18.8 In the present case, since no sufficient evidence of actual disadvantages has been adduced, the assessment of patentability with regard to Article 53(a) EPC may not be based on the so-called "balancing exercise" of benefits and disadvantages, as submitted by the appellants. The Board observes that such a "balancing exercise" is not the only way of assessing patentability with regard to Article 53(a) EPC, but just one possible way, perhaps useful in situations in which an actual damage and/or disadvantage (*e.g.* suffering of animals as in the case of decision T 19/90 *supra*) exists.

19. To sum up, the Board is of the opinion that, in the present case, Article 53(a) EPC does not constitute a bar to patentability because none of the claims of the patent in suit comprises subject-matter the exploitation of which would be contrary to "ordre public" or morality within the meaning of that article.

The Concept of "Plant Varieties" Under Article 53(b) EPC

20. Article 53(b) EPC, first half-sentence, excludes "plant varieties" from patentability. Decisions T 49/83 and T 320/87 (*supra*) were already concerned with the exclusion from patentability of "plant varieties" under this provision. Both decisions took into consideration the legal history of Article 53(b) EPC as well as the definition given to the concept of "plant varieties" in the UPOV Convention.

21. According to decision T 49/83 (*supra*), the concept of "plant varieties" stands for "a multiplicity of plants which are largely the same in their characteristics and remain the same within specific tolerances after every propagation or every propagation cycle", as reflected in the then valid UPOV Convention, and thus, covers "all cultivated varieties, clones, lines, strains and hybrids which can be grown in such a way that they are clearly distinguishable from other varieties, sufficiently homogeneous, and stable in their essential characteristics . . . " (*cf.* point 2 of the reasons). The then competent Board held that "the legislator did not wish to afford patent protection under the European Patent Convention to plant varieties of this kind, whether in the form of propagating material or of the plant itself and concluded that "Article 53(b) EPC prohibits only the patenting of plants or their propagating material in the genetically fixed form of the plant variety (*cf.* point 3 of the reasons). It was further stated that "the very wording of Article 53(b) EPC before the semi-colon precludes the equation of plants and plant varieties . . . ' (*cf.* point 4 of the reasons). The claims underlying decision T 49/83 were directed to propagating material (seeds) of cultivated plants treated with an oxime derivative. It was held that the claimed innovation did not lie within the sphere of plant breeding, which was concerned with the genetic modification of plants. The parameter "treated with an oxime derivative" was not considered to be a criterion characteristic of a plant variety because the treatment could also be carried out on propagating material which did not meet the essential criteria of homogeneity or stability characteristic of a plant variety. Thus, Article 53(b) EPC was not considered an obstacle to the patenting of the claimed propagating material.

22. Decision T 320/87 (*supra*) confirmed the findings of T 49/83 (*supra*) in respect of the significance of the exclusion from patentability of "plant varieties" under Article 53(b) EPC. The claims underlying decision T 320/87 were directed to hybrid seeds or plants which were not stable and thus could not be defined as "varieties." In fact, the invention relied on going back repeatedly to the parent plants for further propagation by cloning because the hybrids resulting from the crossing of the parent plants, one of which

was heterozygous, did not provide plants, which, when further sexually propagated, remained stable with respect to the desired features. The then competent Board expressed the view that single individual plants were not to be so construed as being embraced within the subject-matter of the product claim. For these reasons, it was decided that the exception to patentability under Article 53(b) EPC did not apply to the claimed subject-matter.

23. Thus, in the Board's judgement, the concept of "plant varieties" under Article 53(b) EPC, first half-sentence, refers to any plant grouping within a single botanical taxon of the lowest-known rank which, irrespective of whether it would be eligible for protection under the UPOV Convention, is characterised by at least one single transmissible characteristic distinguishing it from other plant groupings and which is sufficiently homogeneous and stable in its relevant characteristics (cf. points 21 and 22 *supra*; Article 1, item (vi) of the revised UPOV Convention, Geneva 1991). Plant cells as such, which modern technology allows to culture much like bacteria and yeasts, cannot be considered to fall under the definition of a plant or of a plant variety. In this respect, it is further noted that plant cells are considered to be "microbiological products" in the broad sense under the current practice of the EPO (*cf.* points 34 and 35 *infra*).

24. A product claim which embraces within its subject-matter "plant varieties" as just defined (*cf.* point 23 *supra*) is not patentable under Article 53(b) EPC, first half-sentence (*cf.* point 20 *supra*).

The Concept of "Essentially Biological Processes for the Production of Plants" Under Article 53(b) EPC

25. Article 53(b) EPC further excludes "essentially biological processes for the production of plants . . . " from patentability. The historical documentation shows that, when drafting Article 53(b) EPC, the EPC Working Party recognised that even if protection of new plant varieties and processes for producing new plants was to be excluded under European patent law, European patents still had to be granted for processes which, while applicable to plants, were of a technical nature (*cf.* Document IV/2071/61-E, page 6, first paragraph).

Processes for producing new plants by irradiation of the plants themselves or the seed with isotopes were cited as an example of such processes (*ibid.*, loc. cit.). The Board observes that the example given is one in which plants or seeds undergo genetic modifications due to irradiation.

26. In order to provide a distinction between inventions resulting from nontechnical processes for the production of plants (*e.g.* essentially biological processes such as selective breeding), which were to be excluded, and inventions resulting from technical processes for the production of plants, which were considered patentable, the legislator introduced in Article 53(b) EPC, first half sentence, the exclusion from patentability of "essentially biological processes for the production of plants. . . ." As is derivable from

the example given in the quoted document of the EPC Working Party (*cf.* point 25 *supra*), this provision gives rise to the legal consequence that processes of a technical nature for producing plants, including processes involving genetic modification of plants, are patentable. By virtue of Article 64(2) EPC, the protection conferred by a European patent to a process extends also to the products (*e.g.* plants) directly obtained by such a process.

27. As regards the interpretation of the concept of "essentially biological processes for the production of plants . . . ," it is pointed out in Decision T 320/87 (*supra*) that whether or not a (non-microbiological) process is to be considered as essentially biological" within the meaning of Article 53(b) EPC "has to be judged on the basis of the essence of the invention taking into account the totality of human intervention and its impact on the result achieved" (*cf.* point 6 of the reasons). The then competent Board considered that the claimed processes for the preparation of hybrid plants represented an essential modification of known biological and classical breeders' processes which had a decisive impact on the desired resulting hybrid population. Accordingly, it was held that the said processes could not be considered "essentially biological" within the meaning of Article 53(b) EPC and that, therefore, the exclusion from patentability did not apply.

28. Based on the above considerations, it follows that a process for the production of plants comprising at least one essential technical step, which cannot be carried out without human intervention and which has a decisive impact on the final result (*cf.* points 25 to 27 *supra*), does not fall under the exceptions to patentability under Article 53(b) EPC, first half-sentence.

The Concepts of "Microbiological Processes" and "the Products Thereof" Under Article 53(b) EPC

29. Finally, Article 53(b) EPC, in its second half-sentence, disposes that the provision under Article 53(b) EPC, first half-sentence, concerning exceptions to patentability "does not apply to microbiological processes or the products thereof." In the light of the historical documentation, the inclusion of a specific exception to said provision for microbiological processes or the products thereof may be explained by the legislator's intention to make it absolutely clear that the EPC must provide patent protection for industrially applicable processes involving microorganisms and for their products. This clarification was most certainly considered useful in order to prevent the exclusion from patentability from being extended to processes using eucaryotic microorganisms which could be fitted into the pattern of the plant or animal kingdoms (*e.g.* some fungi, plant cells, animal cells).

30. In Decision T 19/90 [Harvard Onco-Mouse] (*supra, cf.* point 4.10 of the reasons), it is pointed out that the second half-sentence of Article 53(b) EPC is an exception to the exception to patentability provided for by the first half-sentence of this provision. Accordingly it is held that the second half-sentence restores the general principle of patentability laid down in Article 52(1) EPC for inventions involving microbiological processes and the

products thereof. Thus, from this decision it follows that animal varieties are patentable if they are the product of a microbiological process within the meaning of Article 53(b) EPC, second half-sentence. In the Board's judgement, this principle applies mutatis mutandis to plant varieties.

31. The Board observes that the EPC does not provide a definition of the concepts of "microbiological processes" and "the products thereof." Nor can a definition of these concepts or any relevant indication in this respect be found in the historical documentation relating to the EPC. As a matter of fact, the EPC Working Party stated that "it seemed preferable to leave the question . . . to the courts without laying down any express rules since there was a risk of any express rule distorting the sense of the provision by introducing an a contrario argument." Different views have been expressed in this context by the parties to the present appeal proceedings:

— The appellants maintained that a literal interpretation had to be given to the concepts in question. In their submissions, the second half-sentence of Article 53(b) EPC was limited to processes (e.g. production of antibiotics bv fermentation) involving microorganisms in the traditional sense, i.e. bacteria yeasts and the like. Consequently, in the appellants' view, the concept "microbiological" should not be construed as meaning technical.

—The respondents submitted that a technical process involving a microbiological step acquired a microbiological character and, consequently, its products had to be regarded as products of a microbiological process.

Both viewpoints find support in the specialized literature. . . .

32. The Board is satisfied that the proper course of action, in view of the recent important developments in the field of microbiology, is to interpret Article 53(b) EPC, second half-sentence, according to objective teleological criteria and that this way of interpreting is consistent with the legislative intent underlying this provision. Among these criteria, the principle of equal treatment of what is of the same kind or similar is of great importance. Such interpretation may give rise to subject-matter being regulated by this provision which could not possibly have been anticipated by the historical legislator.

33. Traditional microbiology was primarily concerned with the production, by means of fermentation processes, of primary and secondary metabolites (e.g. acetic acid or antibiotics), and with biotransformations (production of biomass, enzymatic reactions). Modern microbiology combines the traditional techniques with the genetic engineering techniques and makes use of experimental approaches which are widely applicable to human, animal and plant cells that can be maintained and grown in culture much like bacteria and yeasts.

34. According to the current practice of the EPO, the term "microorganism" includes not only bacteria and yeasts, but also fungi, algae, protozoa and human, animal and plant cells, i.e. all generally unicellular organisms with dimensions beneath the limit of vision which can be propagated and

manipulated in a laboratory. Plasmids and viruses are also considered to fall under this definition. This practice is consistent with the objective teleological interpretation of Article 53(b) EPC, second half sentence, in particular with the principle of equal treatment (*cf.* paragraph 32 *supra*), and is, therefore, fully acceptable. Furthermore, this practice takes clearly into account the developments of modern industrial microbiology . . . , fulfilling thereby an objective purpose of Article 53(b) EPC, second half-sentence.

35. Accordingly the term "microbiological" is interpreted as qualifying technical activities in which direct use is made of microorganisms as defined above. These include not only traditional fermentation and biotransformation processes, but also the manipulation of microorganisms by genetic engineering or fusion techniques. The production or modification of products in recombinant systems, etc. *i.e.*, briefly, all activities in which an integrated use is made of biochemical and microbiological techniques, including genetic and chemical engineering techniques in order to exploit the capacities of microbes and cultured cells. . . . Therefore, as an example, genetic engineering processes carried out on vegetable cells may be defined as "microbiological processes" and their products, namely genetically-modified vegetable cells and their cultures, may be defined as "the products thereof".

36. In the Board's judgement, the concept of "microbiological processes" under Article 53(b) EPC, second half-sentence, refers to processes in which microorganisms as defined above (*cf.* point 34 *supra*), or their parts, are used to make or to modify products or in which new microorganisms are developed for specific uses. Consequently, the concept of "the products thereof" under Article 53(b) EPC, second half-sentence, encompasses products which are made or modified by microorganisms as well as new microorganisms as such.

37. As modern biotechnology often uses or develops multistep processes for producing plants which include at least one microbiological process step (*e.g.* the transformation of cells with recombinant DNA), it has to be decided whether such processes as a whole can be considered to represent "microbiological processes within the meaning of Article 53(b) EPC, second half-sentence, and whether, owing to this, the products of such processes (*e.g.* plants) may be regarded as being "the products thereof" for the purposes of this provision.

38. In the Board's judgement, microbiological processes as defined above and technical processes comprising a succession of steps, herein at least one essential step is of a microbiological nature, may not be considered to be of the same kind or similar so that the principle of equal treatment would apply with respect thereto (cf. point 32 *supra*). Consequently, the concept of microbiological processes" under Article 53(b) EPC, second half-sentence, interpreted according to objective teleological criteria (*cf.* point 32 *supra*) may not be extended to include all the steps of such technical processes, neither are there scientific reasons to include them. Furthermore, the

second half-sentence of Article 53(b) EPC refers merely to "microbiological processes," and not to "essentially microbiological processes." In the Board's view, this indicates that the historical legislator did not want the concept of "microbiological processes" under Article 53(b) EPC, second half-sentence, to be extended to include such technical processes either. Besides, in principle, Article 53(b) EPC, first half-sentence, does not exclude from patentability modern multi-step processes for producing plants involving genetic engineering techniques. In fact, whenever such processes are shown to be of a technical nature, they are patentable under the EPC without limitation. In the Board's opinion, had the historical legislator been aware of such processes, it would have considered them to be further examples of technical processes applicable in particular to plants for which European patents had to be granted.

39. In conclusion, the Board is of the opinion that "technical processes including a microbiological step" may not simply be equated with microbiological processes." Nor can the resulting final products of such technical processes (*e.g.* plant varieties) be defined as "products of microbiological processes within the meaning of Article 53(b) EPC, second half-sentence (*cf.* points 23. 35 and 36 *supra*, and point 40.9 *infra*).

Assessment of Patentability with Regard to the Requirements of Article 53(b)

40. The examination of the main request (Claims 1 to 44 as granted) gives rise to the following considerations:

40.1 As regards the process according to Claim 7, the Board cannot share the appellants' view that, notwithstanding the human, technical intervention in the first step of the process in which, as a random event, plant cells or tissue are transformed with a recombinant DNA, the subsequent steps of regenerating and replicating the plants or seeds confer an overall biological character on the process and that, regarding the subject-matter of this claim, the exclusion from patentability under Article 53(b) EPC, first half-sentence, should therefore apply. On the contrary, Claim 7 does not relate to a process which is "essentially biological" within the meaning of this provision (*cf.* points 27 and 28 *supra*) because the step of transforming the plant cells or tissue with a recombinant DNA, regardless of whether its performance is dependent on chance or not, is an essential technical step which has a decisive impact on the desired final result. If it is not successfully performed, plants or seeds could most probably still be regenerated from the plant cells or tissue and they could replicate, but they would not display the desired distinctive characteristic of having the heterologous DNA integrated in their genome in a stable manner. Therefore, although the subsequent steps of regenerating and replicating the plants or seeds make use of the "natural" machinery, the decisive step, namely the insertion of the relevant DNA sequence into the genome of the plant, could not occur without human intervention. In this respect, it is also noted that the regeneration step is not entirely biological, but rather agrotechnical, since some degree of technical intervention is required in the selection of the proper working conditions. Therefore, the process of Claim 7 as a whole is not "essentially biological" and, thus, not excluded from patentability under Article 53(b) EPC, first half-sentence.

40.2 As for Claim 14, which relates to plant cells, the Board cannot agree with the appellants' submission that this claim covers de facto plant varieties and that, for this reason, it is not allowable under Article 53(b) EPC, because, as already stated (*cf.* point 23 *supra*), plant cells as such may not be considered to fall under the definition of a plant or plant variety. Thus, the subject-matter of Claim 14 does not represent an exception to patentability under Article 53(b) EPC.

40.3 As regards Claim 21, it is noted that this claim is not drafted in terms of a variety description because there is no reference to a single botanical taxon of the lowest-known rank (*cf.* point 23 *supra*). Rather this claim is in general directed to a plant which possesses, integrated in its genome in a stable manner, a heterologous DNA containing a foreign nucleotide sequence encoding a protein having a non-variety specific enzymatic activity capable of neutralizing or inactivating a glutamine synthetase inhibitor under the control of a promoter recognized by the polymerases of the plant cells. The reference to a "non-variety specific' enzymatic activity intends to emphasize that it is not characteristic of specific plant genes or species.

40.4 The subject-matter of Claim 21 differs decisively from the subject-matter dealt with in Decisions T 49/83 and T 320/87 (*cf.* points 21 and 22 *supra*) in that it relates to genetically modified plants which remain stable in their modified characteristic(s). The stated characterizing feature of the claimed plant is, in fact, transmitted in a stable manner in the plants and seeds throughout succeeding generations (cf. specification of the patent in suit, page 7, lines 59 to 61). The working examples in the patent in suit relate to the production of transformed plants from known varieties (*e.g.* Nicotiana tabacum cv. Petit Havana SRI, Solanum tuberosum cv. Berolina or cv. Desiree, Lycopersicum esculentum cv. Lucullus). It is shown with tobacco plants that the plants transformed in this way display normal fertility and that the second generation seedlings are homozygous for the resistance gene. Thus, the transformed plants or seeds of the working examples, irrespective of whether they would meet the conditions for the grant of a breeder's right, are plant varieties as they comply with the definition of the concept of plant varieties" (*cf.* points 21 to 23 *supra*), being distinguishable, uniform and stable in their relevant characteristics. As a matter of fact, these exemplified varieties may be construed as "essentially derived varieties", being obtained from known varieties by transformation by genetic engineering techniques [cf. Article 14(5), in particular item (c) of the revised UPOV Convention, Geneva 1991].

40.5 Claim 21 defines plants which regardless of whether or not they belong to any particular variety, are distinguished from all other plants by the stated specific characteristic which is transmitted in a stable manner to the progeny. While Claim 21 defines the distinctive feature common to all plants covered by this claim, the working examples of the patent in suit show that the practical forms of realisation of the invention according to Claim 21 are "genetically transformed" plant varieties. Consequently, the subject-matter of Claim 21 encompasses genetically transformed plant varieties showing said single distinctive feature, even though this claim is not drafted in terms of a variety description. This reasoning is in keeping with the general principle laid down in the established practice of the Boards of Appeal, according to which the provision in Article 69(1) EPC, stipulating that the description and drawings (if any) be used to interpret the claims, also applies when an objective assessment of the content of a claim has to be made. . . .

40.6 The respondents admit that the said working examples were carried out on existing varieties. Moreover, they do not deny that Claim 21 encompasses also plant varieties. Since the respondents cannot see any possibility of introducing an appropriate disclaimer, they submit that finding a specific plant variety which falls under Claim 21 may be compared to a selection invention in chemistry, the specific plant variety representing a selection among the broad class of plants claimed. The Board cannot accept this submission because plant varieties, regardless of whether or not they may represent a selection invention, are excluded from patentability by virtue of Article 53(b) EPC, first half-sentence, unless the exception under Article 53(b) EPC, second half-sentence, applies.

40.7 A claim is not allowable if the grant of a patent in respect of the invention defined in said claim is conducive to an evasion of a provision of the EPC establishing an exception to patentability. Accordingly, it has, for example, already been decided that a claim falls under the prohibition of Article 52(4) EPC if the invention claimed therein is not solely directed to a cosmetic effect, but is also necessarily defining a treatment of the human body by therapy (*cf.* T 290/86)

40.8 Given the fact that Claim 21 encompasses plant varieties (*cf.* point 40.5 *supra*), it follows, therefore, that Claim 21 is only allowable, if the exception to patentability under Article 53(b) EPC, first half-sentence, concerning plant varieties does not apply, because the subject-matter of this claim is to be regarded as the product of a microbiological process (*cf.* points 30 and 40.6 *supra*).

40.9 The plant according to Claim 21 is produced by a multi-step process (*cf.* process according to Claim 7) which, in addition to the initial microbiological process step of transforming plant cells or tissue with recombinant DNA, comprises the step of regenerating plants from the transformed plant cells or tissue and the step of reproducing the plant material. The initial microbiological process step undeniably has a decisive impact on the final result because by virtue of this step the plant acquires its characterizing feature that is transmitted throughout generations (*cf.* point 40.4 *supra*). However, the Board observes that the subsequent steps of regenerating and reproducing the plants have an important added value and contribute, although in a different manner, to the final result as well. These two process steps involve complex phenomena and events such as cell differentiation, morphogenesis and reproduction and may, therefore, not be equated to the much simpler process step of multiplying and propagating transformed plant cells or tissue in culture, which is a typical microbiological process. In fact, in a cell or tissue culture process plant cells proliferate in a rather disorganised manner either in suspension or by producing a mass of relatively undifferentiated cells which all look much alike (callus). In contrast to that, a process of regenerating a whole plant from plant cells or tissue, which takes advantage of the totipotency [sic] of many plant cells, comprises a series of important events and phases, such as the formation of shoot and then root meristems, the coordinated division, expansion and differentiation of cells, which require the careful selection of the appropriate working conditions, e.g. the manipulation of nutrients and growth regulators. Furthermore, a subsequent biological process step of replicating the regenerated plant involves a further series of relevant phenomena and events such as fertilization, germination, growth and development. It is the controlled performance and/or successful occurrence of all these phases and events which will then allow the "imprinted" plant cells or tissue to develop into a whole plant. Such a plant is not identical to the initial starting product (the transformed plant cells or tissue) in spite of the fact that it contains the same characterizing genetic information. A whole plant cannot be assimilated to a plant cell or tissue for the sole reason that it has acquired its characterizing feature during the initial "microbiological" step of transforming the plant cell or tissue. The plant according to Claim 21 is thus not merely the result of said initial step, but also of the subsequent series of relevant agrotechnical and biological steps.

40.10 It ensues that, regardless of the decisive impact that the microbiological process step has on the final result the multi-step process whereby the plant according to Claim 21 is produced is not a microbiological process within the meaning of Article 53(b) EPC, second half-sentence, (*cf.* points 38 and 39 *supra*). Accordingly, such a plant may not be considered to be "the product of a microbiological process".

40.11 This means that the exception to patentability under Article 53(b) EPC first half-sentence, concerning plant varieties does apply in respect of the invention as defined in Claim 21. Consequently, Claim 21, which encompasses plant varieties, is not allowable (*cf.* points 40.5 to 40.8 *supra*). Thus, the main request, of which Claim 21 is part, has to be rejected.

. . .

42. Claim 20 of the second auxiliary request, which is drawn up as a claim dependent upon Claims 14 to 17, is directed to plant cells "which are contained in a plant." It is noted that plant cells contained in a plant are differentiated cells which are morphologically and functionally organized to constitute the plant. In the Board's judgement, this is the inevitable understanding of the skilled person. Consequently, the dependency of Claim 20 upon Claim 14 is rather misleading, because the latter claim is in general

directed to transformed plant cells. Thus the subject-matter of Claim 20, irrespective of the way the latter is drafted, is nothing but a plant, and this claim does not exclude from its scope plant varieties for the same reasons as Claim 21 of the main request (*cf.* point 40.5 *supra*). Furthermore, like the plants according to Claim 21 of the main request, such plants may not be considered to be the product of a microbiological process (*cf.* points 40.9 to 40.11 *supra*). Thus, Claim 20 is not allowable for the same reasons given with respect to Claim 21 of the main request (*cf.* points 40.7 to 40.11 *supra*), and the second auxiliary request, of which Claim 20 is part, has equally to be rejected.

43. . . . As already discussed above (*cf.* points 40.1 and 40.2 *supra*), Claim 7 and Claim 14 of this request are not excluded from patentability under the provisions of Article 53(b) EPC. As for the remaining claims, none of them relate to subject matter which falls under the exclusion from patentability of that article. . . .

———

NOTES AND QUESTIONS

(1) **Statutory Exclusions in U.S. Patent and Trademark Law.** The U.S. Supreme Court in *Chakrabarty* states that Congress intended statutory patent subject matter to "include anything under the sun that is made by man." Unlike the patent law, the U.S. trademark law includes an exception to protection for marks which are "immoral . . . or scandalous." 15 U.S.C. § 1152(a). Since there is no express exclusion for patents and assuming that the Supreme Court is correct, does the U.S. Congress find certain trademarks expressly unregisterable for immorality and hold patentable inventions to a different standard? If so, why?

(2) **Law and Morality.** What is *"ordre public"*? In May, 1997, the Coordinating Body for Indigenous Organizations of the Amazon Basin (COICA) declared a citizen of the United States, Loren Miller, an "enemy of indigenous people" for allegedly patenting in the United States a variety of Ayahuasca or Yage (*Banisteriopsis caapi*), a plant with hallucinogenic properties considered sacred for the majority of the 400 indigenous groups in the nine countries that constitute COICA. Should the U.S. adopt a provision in its patent law similar to the EPC's Article 53 *"ordre public"* exception to patentability, if for no other reason to assuage such concerns?

(3) **Defining "Variety."** Is an "animal variety" fundamentally different from a "plant variety"? In *Onco-Mouse*, the Technical Board of Appeal makes much of the fact that Article 53(b) EPC uses the term "animal varieties"and the term "animals" in the same half-sentence, and that, thus, the term "animal varieties" cannot mean "animals as such." This provides it with a justification for looking beyond the text to the purpose of the law, i.e., "providing a proper balance between the interests of inventors in this field in obtaining reasonable protection for their efforts and society's

interest in excluding certain categories of animals from patent protection." Is a "category" of animals the same as an "animal variety?" How about an animal and its "offspring?" The Board later states that claim 19 "covers both transgenic animals produced according to the process claims. . . .*and the descendants* of such animals." It continues that the former is the result of a non-biological process and the latter are the "outcome" of a biological process, but if the animals are cloned rather than allowed to reproduce sexually, then the latter process is non-biological. Given that the case was decided "pre-Dolly" (the cloned sheep case), was the Technical Board making a mere hypothetical argument? By contrast, the Board found Claim 21 of the plant patent application to be directed to "genetically modified plants which remain stable in their modified characteristics." (Para. 40.4 above) It goes further to state that "a claim is not allowable if [it is] conducive to an evasion of a provision of the EPC establishing an exception to patentability." (Para. 40.7) What distinguishes the applicability of Article 53(b) first half-sentence in *Onco-Mouse* from its applicability in *Plant Genetic Systems?*

(4) **Interpreting Exceptions.** In terms of statutory interpretation, how solid is the *Onco-Mouse* Board's assertion that second half-sentence is an exception to an exception, thereby "ensuring that the patentability bar does not cover microbiological processes or the products thereof." When is an exception to an exception to be read to nullify the original exception and when should it be read more narrowly? If an exception is to be read narrowly, is an exception to that exception to be read even more narrowly?

(5) **Dominion Arguments.** In *Plant Genetic Systems,* the opposer pointed to the legislative history of Article 53(a) of the European Patent Convention and "expressed concern about the dominion that was sought to be exercised by man over the natural world by the use of plant genetic engineering techniques." The Board rejected the argument. By contrast in *Onco-mouse*, the EPO Board stated that it is considerations of animal suffering which must be taken into account for purposes of Article 53(a)'s morality exception. In the era of animal cloning and perhaps soon-to-be human cloning, is the "dominion" argument for excluding animal inventions from patent protection any more persuasive? We will look at attempts by the European Parliament to regulate patents on life forms below.

(6) *Sui Generis* **Protection.** Breeders of new plant varieties (but not animal varieties) in many countries may acquire legal protection under *sui generis* regimes outside the patent system. Should the fact that plant varieties may be protected by sui generis protection and animal varieties may not affect the protectability of such life forms by patent law? *See, e.g.,* Darrell G. Dotson, *The European Controversy over Genetic-Engineered Patents*, 19 Hou. J. Intl L. 919 (1997). An excellent comparison of U.S. and European law on patent protection for plants is found in Feertrui van Overwalle, *Patent Protection for Plants: A comparison of American and European Approaches*, 39 IDEA 143 (1999). International protection for plant varieties will be introduced in greater detail below.

(7) **Environmental Concerns.** The EPO Board refers both to Article 53(a)'s *ordre public* and immorality exceptions with regard to the possibility of serious environmental harm which could be caused by the release of genetically engineered plants. From a policy perspective, is there good reason why the U.S. Patent Office should expend time and effort to create incentives for inventions which may lead to animal suffering or cause damage to the environment?

(8) **Boundary Between Patent and *Sui Generis* Protection for Plants in Europe.** A more recent case report in the International Review of Industrial Property and Copyright Law, *see* 31 IIC 242 (2000), reported that on 20 December 1999 in the case of *In re Novartis*:

> The Enlarged Board of Appeal has decided that a claim wherein specific plant varieties are not identified is not excluded from patentability under Art. 53(b) of the EPC, even though it may embrace plant varieties. The Enlarged Board took the view that Art. 53(b) EPC defined the borderline between patent protection and plant variety protection. The extent of the exclusion for patents was the obverse of the availability of plant variety rights. Since plant variety rights were only granted for specific plant varieties and not for technical teachings which could be implemented in an indefinite number of plant varieties, it was not sufficient for the exclusion from patent protection in Art. 53(b) EPC to apply that one or more plant varieties were embraced or might be embraced by the claims of the patent application.

International protection for plant varieties (so-called "breeders' rights") will be addressed below.

(9) **Boundary Between Patent and *Sui Generis* Protection in the United States.** In *J.E.M. AG Supply, Inc. v. Pioneer Hi-Bred Int'l, Inc.*, 60 U.S.P.Q.2d 1865 (2001), the U.S. Supreme Court, citing *Chakrabarty*, held that utility protection for plants under Section 101 was not precluded by the existence of the Plant Patent Act of 1930, because of the "forward-looking perspective" of Section 101. Further, the Plant Variety Protection Act of 1970 does not expressly exclude utility patent protection for plants. Even though the PVPA created a comprehensive statutory scheme for plant varieties that are new, distinct, uniform, and stable, nowhere does it restrict the scope of patentable subject matter under Section 101. How close is the teleological approach found in Article 53(b) by the Board in *Plant Genetic Systems* to the forward-looking perspective found in Section 101 by the U.S. Supreme Court in *Pioneer*?

(10) **Stray Bulls and Sowed Oats.** In *Monsanto v. Percy Schmeiser*, 2001 FCT 256, a Canadian court considered the case of whether a farmer in Saskatchewan had infringed Monsanto's Canadian patent on "Roundup Ready" genetically modified [GM] canola seed. According to the plaintiff Monsanto, the defendant asserted that "the alleged invention is a life form intended for human consumption and is not the proper subject matter for

a patent; it is self-propagating and can spread without human intervention." Schmeiser, who had never purchased any of Monsanto's proprietary GM seed, discovered plants on the margin of one of his fields abutting a Monsanto licensee which apparently survived Roundup herbicide treatment in 1997 and replanted the seed produced from them in 1998. The farmer alleged that he used Roundup to prepare the soil and did not apply it to growing plants. Apparently, at least some of the seeds had been carried onto the farmer's lands by the wind. The defendant alleged that he had not planted the GM seed deliberately. The defendant argued, *inter alia*, that "the patent was obtained for an illicit purpose of creating a noxious plant that would spread by natural means to the lands of innocent parties so as to entrap them with nuisance patent infringement claims." The defendant asserted further that a farmer whose field contains seed or plants originating from seed spilled into them, or blown as seed from a neighbor's land, did not own the plants which emerged, analogizing to the common law "stray bull" rule, that the progeny of stray bulls impregnating cows of another belong to that other. Rejecting the defendant's arguments, the court noted that the defendant had actually tested the plants for resistance to the Roundup herbicide before selecting its progeny as seed for planting the next year. The court issued an injunction and awarded both damages and an accounting.

[B] Patentable Subject Matter: Computer Programs

STATE STREET BANK & TRUST CO. v. SIGNATURE FINANCIAL GROUP, INC.
149 F.3d 1368 (Fed. Cir. 1998)

RICH, CIRCUIT JUDGE

Signature Financial Group, Inc. (Signature) appeals from the decision of the United States District Court for the District of Massachusetts granting a motion for summary judgment in favor of State Street Bank & Trust Co. (State Street), finding U.S. Patent No. 5,193,056 (the '056 patent) invalid on the ground that the claimed subject matter is not encompassed by 35 U.S.C. 101 (1994). . . . We reverse and remand because we conclude that the patent claims are directed to statutory subject matter.

BACKGROUND

. . . The '056 patent is generally directed to a data processing system (the system) for implementing an investment structure which was developed for use in Signature's business as an administrator and accounting agent for mutual funds. In essence, the system, identified by the proprietary name Hub and Spoke®, facilitates a structure whereby mutual funds (Spokes) pool their assets in an investment portfolio (Hub) organized as a partnership. This investment configuration provides the administrator of a mutual fund with the advantageous combination of economies of scale in administering investments coupled with the tax advantages of a partnership.

State Street and Signature are both in the business of acting as custodians and accounting agents for multi-tiered partnership fund financial services. State Street negotiated with Signature for a license to use its patented data processing system described and claimed in the '056 patent. When negotiations broke down, State Street brought a declaratory judgment action asserting invalidity, unenforceability, and noninfringement in Massachusetts district court, and then filed a motion for partial summary judgment of patent invalidity for failure to claim statutory subject matter under § 101. The motion was granted and this appeal followed.

DISCUSSION

. . . The substantive issue at hand, whether the '056 patent is invalid for failure to claim statutory subject matter under [Section] 101, is a matter of both claim construction and statutory construction. "[W]e review claim construction de novo including any allegedly fact-based questions relating to claim construction." We also review statutory construction de novo. [cit]. We hold that declaratory judgment plaintiff State Street was not entitled to the grant of summary judgment of invalidity of the '056 patent under [Section]101 as a matter of law, because the patent claims are directed to statutory subject matter.

. . . The patented invention relates generally to a system that allows an administrator to monitor and record the financial information flow and make all calculations necessary for maintaining a partner fund financial services configuration. As previously mentioned, a partner fund financial services configuration essentially allows several mutual funds, or "Spokes," to pool their investment funds into a single portfolio, or "Hub," allowing for consolidation of, inter alia, the costs of administering the fund combined with the tax advantages of a partnership. In particular, this system provides means for a daily allocation of assets for two or more Spokes that are invested in the same Hub. The system determines the percentage share that each Spoke maintains in the Hub, while taking into consideration daily changes both in the value of the Hub's investment securities and in the concomitant amount of each Spoke's assets.

In determining daily changes, the system also allows for the allocation among the Spokes of the Hub's daily income, expenses, and net realized and unrealized gain or loss, calculating each day's total investments based on the concept of a book capital account. This enables the determination of a true asset value of each Spoke and accurate calculation of allocation ratios between or among the Spokes. The system additionally tracks all the relevant data determined on a daily basis for the Hub and each Spoke, so that aggregate year end income, expenses, and capital gain or loss can be determined for accounting and for tax purposes for the Hub and, as a result, for each publicly traded Spoke.

It is essential that these calculations are quickly and accurately performed. In large part this is required because each Spoke sells shares to the public and the price of those shares is substantially based on the Spoke's percentage interest in the portfolio. In some instances, a mutual fund administrator is required to calculate the value of the shares to the nearest penny within as little as an hour and a half after the market closes. Given the complexity of the calculations, a computer or equivalent device is a virtual necessity to perform the task.

The '056 patent application was filed 11 March 1991. It initially contained six "machine" claims, which incorporated means-plus-function clauses, and six method claims. According to Signature, during prosecution the examiner contemplated a 101 rejection for failure to claim statutory subject matter. However, upon cancellation of the six method claims, the examiner issued a notice of allowance for the remaining present six claims on appeal. Only claim 1 is an independent claim.

. . . The district court began its analysis by construing the claims to be directed to a process, with each "means" clause merely representing a step in that process. However, "machine" claims having "means" clauses may only be reasonably viewed as process claims if there is no supporting structure in the written description that corresponds to the claimed "means" elements. See In re Alappat, 33 F.3d 1526, 1540–41 (Fed.Cir.1994) (in banc). This is not the case now before us.

When independent claim 1 is properly construed in accordance with [35 U.S.C.§ 112, ¶ 6] it is directed to a machine, as demonstrated below, where representative claim 1 is set forth, the subject matter in brackets stating the structure the written description discloses as corresponding to the respective "means" recited in the claims.

1. A data processing system for managing a financial services configuration of a portfolio established as a partnership, each partner being one of a plurality of funds, comprising:

(a) computer processor means [a personal computer including a CPU] for processing data;

(b) storage means [a data disk] for storing data on a storage medium;

(c) first means [an arithmetic logic circuit configured to prepare the data disk to magnetically store selected data] for initializing the storage medium;

(d) second means [an arithmetic logic circuit configured to retrieve information from a specific file, calculate incremental increases or decreases based on specific input, allocate the results on a percentage basis, and store the output in a separate file] for processing data regarding assets in the portfolio and each of the funds from a previous day and data regarding increases or decreases in each of the funds, [sic, funds'] assets and for allocating the percentage share that each fund holds in the portfolio;

(e) third means [an arithmetic logic circuit configured to retrieve information from a specific file, calculate incremental increases and decreases based on specific input, allocate the results on a percentage basis and store the output in a separate file] for processing data regarding daily incremental income, expenses, and net realized gain or loss for the portfolio and for allocating such data among each fund;

(f) fourth means [an arithmetic logic circuit configured to retrieve information from a specific file, calculate incremental increases and decreases based on specific input, allocate the results on a percentage basis and store the output in a separate file] for processing data regarding daily net unrealized gain or loss for the portfolio and for allocating such data among each fund; and

(g) fifth means [an arithmetic logic circuit configured to retrieve information from specific files, calculate that information on an aggregate basis and store the output in a separate file] for processing data regarding aggregate year-end income, expenses, and capital gain or loss for the portfolio and each of the funds.

Each claim component, recited as a "means" plus its function, is to be read, of course, pursuant to § 112,¶ 6, as inclusive of the "equivalents" of the structures disclosed in the written description portion of the specification. Thus, claim 1, properly construed, claims a machine, namely, a data processing system for managing a financial services configuration of a portfolio established as a partnership, which machine is made up of, at the very least, the specific structures disclosed in the written description and corresponding to the means-plus-function elements (a)–(g) recited in the claim. A "machine" is proper statutory subject matter under § 101. We note that, for the purposes of a § 101 analysis, it is of little relevance whether claim 1 is directed to a "machine" or a "process," as long as it falls within at least one of the four enumerated categories of patentable subject matter, "machine" and "process" being such categories.

This does not end our analysis, however, because the court concluded that the claimed subject matter fell into one of two alternative judicially-created exceptions to statutory subject matter.[1] The court refers to the first exception as the "mathematical algorithm" exception and the second exception as the "business method" exception. Section 101 reads:

Whoever invents or discovers any new and useful process, machine, manufacture, or composition of matter, or any new and useful improvement thereof, may obtain a patent therefor, subject to the conditions and requirements of this title.

The plain and unambiguous meaning of § 101 is that any invention falling within one of the four stated categories of statutory subject matter may

---

[1] Indeed, although we do not make this determination here, the judicially created exceptions, *i.e.*, abstract ideas, laws of nature, etc., should be applicable to all categories of statutory subject matter, as our own precedent suggests. *See Alappat*, 33 F.3d at 1542; *see also* In re Johnston, 502 F.2d 765 (CCPA 1974) (Rich, J., dissenting).

be patented, provided it meets the other requirements for patentability set forth in Title 35, *i.e.*, those found in § 102, § 103, and § 112, ¶ 2.[2]

The repetitive use of the expansive term "any" in § 101 shows Congress's intent not to place any restrictions on the subject matter for which a patent may be obtained beyond those specifically recited in § 101. Indeed, the Supreme Court has acknowledged that Congress intended § 101 to extend to "anything under the sun that is made by man." Diamond v. Chakrabarty, 447 U.S. 303, 309 (1980); *see also* Diamond v. Diehr, 450 U.S. 175, 182 (1981).[3] Thus, it is improper to read limitations into [Sect.] 101 on the subject matter that may be patented where the legislative history indicates that Congress clearly did not intend such limitations. *See Chakrabarty*, 447 U.S. at 308 ("We have also cautioned that courts 'should not read into the patent laws limitations and conditions which the legislature has not expressed.'" (citations omitted)).

THE "MATHEMATICAL ALGORITHM" EXCEPTION

The Supreme Court has identified three categories of subject matter that are unpatentable, namely "laws of nature, natural phenomena, and abstract ideas." *Diehr*, 450 U.S. at 185. Of particular relevance to this case, the Court has held that mathematical algorithms are not patentable subject matter to the extent that they are merely abstract ideas. *See Diehr*, 450 U.S. 175; Parker v. Flook, 437 U.S. 584 (1978); Gottschalk v. Benson, 409 U.S. 63 (1972). In *Diehr*, the Court explained that certain types of mathematical subject matter, standing alone, represent nothing more than abstract ideas until reduced to some type of practical application, *i.e.*, "a useful, concrete and tangible result." *Alappat*, 33 F.3d at 1544.[4]

---

[2] As explained in In re Bergy, 596 F.2d 952, 960 (CCPA 1979) (emphases and footnote omitted):

The first door which must be opened on the difficult path to patentability is § 101. . . . The person approaching that door is an inventor, whether his invention is patentable or not. . . . Being an inventor or having an invention, however, is no guarantee of opening even the first door. What kind of an invention or discovery is it? In dealing with the question of kind, as distinguished from the qualitative conditions which make the invention patentable, § 101 is broad and general; its language is: "any . . . process, machine, manufacture, or composition of matter, or any . . . improvement thereof." Section 100(b) further expands "process" to include "art or method, and . . . a new use of a known process, machine, manufacture, composition of matter, or material." If the invention, as the inventor defines it in his claims (pursuant to § 112, second paragraph), falls into any one of the named categories, he is allowed to pass through to the second door, which is § 102; "novelty and loss of right to patent" is the sign on it. Notwithstanding the words "new and useful" in § 101, the invention is not examined under that statute for novelty because that is not the statutory scheme of things or the long-established administrative practice.

[3] The Committee Reports accompanying the 1952 Act inform us that Congress intended statutory subject matter to "include anything under the sun that is made by man." S.Rep. No. 82-1979 at 5 (1952); H.R.Rep. No. 82-1923 at 6 (1952).

[4] This has come to be known as the mathematical algorithm exception. . . . By keeping in mind that the mathematical algorithm is unpatentable only to the extent that it represents an abstract idea, this confusion may be ameliorated.

Unpatentable mathematical algorithms are identifiable by showing they are merely abstract ideas constituting disembodied concepts or truths that are not "useful." From a practical standpoint, this means that to be patentable an algorithm must be applied in a "useful" way. . . .

Today, we hold that the transformation of data, representing discrete dollar amounts, by a machine through a series of mathematical calculations into a final share price, constitutes a practical application of a mathematical algorithm, formula, or calculation, because it produces "a useful, concrete and tangible result"—a final share price momentarily fixed for recording and reporting purposes and even accepted and relied upon by regulatory authorities and in subsequent trades. . . .

[W]hen a claim containing a mathematical formula implements or applies that formula in a structure or process which, when considered as a whole, is performing a function which the patent laws were designed to protect (e.g., transforming or reducing an article to a different state or thing), then the claim satisfies the requirements of 101. . . . The dispositive inquiry is whether the claim as a whole is directed to statutory subject matter. It is irrelevant that a claim may contain, as part of the whole, subject matter which would not be patentable by itself. "A claim drawn to subject matter otherwise statutory does not become nonstatutory simply because it uses a mathematical formula, computer program or digital computer."

The question of whether a claim encompasses statutory subject matter should not focus on which of the four categories of subject matter a claim is directed to[9] —process, machine, manufacture, or composition of matter— but rather on the essential characteristics of the subject matter, in particular, its practical utility. Section 101 specifies that statutory subject matter must also satisfy the other "conditions and requirements" of Title 35, including novelty, nonobviousness, and adequacy of disclosure and notice. For purpose of our analysis, as noted above, claim 1 is directed to a machine programmed with the Hub and Spoke software and admittedly produces a "useful, concrete, and tangible result." *Alappat*, 33 F.3d at 1544. This renders it statutory subject matter, even if the useful result is expressed in numbers, such as price, profit, percentage, cost, or loss.

The Business Method Exception

As an alternative ground for invalidating the '056 patent under Section 101, the court relied on the judicially-created, so-called "business method" exception to statutory subject matter. We take this opportunity to lay this ill-conceived exception to rest. Since its inception, the "business method" exception has merely represented the application of some general, but no longer applicable legal principle, perhaps arising out of the "requirement for invention"—which was eliminated by Section 103. Since the 1952 Patent Act, business methods have been, and should have been, subject to the same

---

[9] Of course, the subject matter must fall into at least one category of statutory subject matter.

legal requirements for patentability as applied to any other process or method.[10]

The business method exception has never been invoked by this court, or the CCPA, to deem an invention unpatentable. . . . The district court announced the precepts of the business method exception as set forth in several treatises, but noted as its primary reason for finding the patent invalid under the business method exception as follows:

> If Signature's invention were patentable, any financial institution desirous of implementing a multi-tiered funding complex modeled (sic) on a Hub and Spoke configuration would be required to seek Signature's permission before embarking on such a project. This is so because the '056 patent is claimed (sic) sufficiently broadly to foreclose virtually any computer-implemented accounting method necessary to manage this type of financial structure.

Whether the patent's claims are too broad to be patentable is not to be judged under § 101, but rather under § 102, § 103 and § 112. Assuming the above statement to be correct, it has nothing to do with whether what is claimed is statutory subject matter. . . .

Reversed and Remanded

AT&T CORP. v. EXCEL COMMUNICATIONS, INC.
50 U.S.P.Q.2d 1447, 1451 (Fed. Cir. 1999)

PLAGER, CIRCUIT JUDGE

[AT&T had a patent (the '184 patent) on a method for indicating a telephone call recipient's primary interexchange carrier (PIC) as a data field in standard message record. Excel contended that the subject matter of the invention was nonstatutory and the District Court had granted summary judgment for the defendant.]

. . . Excel argues that method claims containing mathematical algorithms are patentable subject matter only if there is a "physical transformation" or conversion of subject matter from one state into another. The physical transformation language appears in *Diehr*. ("That respondents' claims involve the transformation of an article, in this case raw, uncured synthetic rubber, into a different state or thing cannot be disputed."), and has been echoed by this court in *Schrader*. ("Therefore, we do not find in the claim any kind of data transformation.") The notion of "physical transformation" can be misunderstood. In the first place, it is not an invariable requirement,

---

[10] As Judge Newman has previously stated, [The business method exception] is . . . an unwarranted encumbrance to the definition of statutory subject matter in section 101, that [should] be discarded as error-prone, redundant, and obsolete. It merits retirement from the glossary of section 101. . . . All of the "doing business" cases could have been decided using the clearer concepts of Title 35. Patentability does not turn on whether the claimed method does "business" instead of something else, but on whether the method, viewed as a whole, meets the requirements of patentability as set forth in Sections 102, 103, and 112 of the Patent Act. In re Schrader, 22 F.3d 290, 298 (Fed. Cir.1994) (Newman, J., dissenting).

but merely one example of how a mathematical algorithm may bring about a useful application. As the Supreme Court itself noted, "when [a claimed invention] is performing a function which the patent laws were designed to protect (*e.g.*, transforming or reducing an article to a different state or thing), then the claim satisfies the requirements of § 101." [*emphasis added*] The "e.g." signal denotes an example, not an exclusive requirement. . .

Excel also contends that because the process claims at issue lack physical limitations set forth in the patent, the claims are not patentable subject matter. This argument reflects a misunderstanding of our case law. The cases cited by Excel for this proposition involved machine claims written in means-plus-function language. *See, e.g.*, *State Street*. Apparatus claims written in this manner require supporting structure in the written description that corresponds to the claimed "means" elements. *See* 35 U.S.C. § 112, para. 6. Since the claims at issue in this case are directed to a process in the first instance, a structural inquiry is unnecessary.

[In *Alappat*] . . . we then pointed out that "the ultimate issue always has been whether the claim as a whole is drawn to statutory subject matter." . . . [T]he mere fact that a claimed invention involves inputting numbers, calculating numbers, outputting numbers, and storing numbers, in and of itself, would not render it nonstatutory subject matter, unless, of course, its operation does not produce a 'useful, concrete and tangible result." . . . [O]ur inquiry here focuses on whether the mathematical algorithm is applied in a practical manner to produce a useful result.

. . . .

D.

In his dissent in *Diehr*, Justice Stevens noted two concerns regarding the § 101 issue, and to which, in his view, federal judges have a duty to respond: First, the cases considering the patentability of program-related inventions do not establish rules that enable a conscientious patent lawyer to determine with a fair degree of accuracy which, if any, program-related inventions will be patentable. Second, the inclusion of the ambiguous concept of an "algorithm" within the "law of nature" category of unpatentable subject matter has given rise to the concern that almost any process might be so described and therefore held unpatentable.

Despite the almost twenty years since Justice Stevens wrote, these concerns remain important. His solution was to declare all computer-based programming unpatentable. That has not been the course the law has taken. Rather, it is now clear that computer-based programming constitutes patentable subject matter so long as the basic requirements of § 101 are met. Justice Stevens's concerns can be addressed within that framework. His first concern, that the rules are not sufficiently clear to enable reasonable prediction of outcomes, should be less of a concern today in light of the refocusing of the § 101 issue that *Alappat* and *State Street* have provided. His second concern, that the ambiguous concept of "algorithm" could be used to make any process unpatentable, can be laid to rest once the focus is understood to be not on whether there is a mathematical algorithm at work, but on whether the algorithm-containing invention, as a whole, produces a tangible, useful, result.

In light of the above, and consistent with the clearer understanding that our more recent cases have provided, we conclude that the district court did not apply the proper analysis to the method claims at issue. Furthermore, had the court applied the proper analysis to the stated claims, the court would have concluded that all the claims asserted fall comfortably within the broad scope of patentable subject matter under § 101. Accordingly, we hold as a matter of law that Excel was not entitled to the grant of summary judgment of invalidity of the '184 patent under § 101.

Since the case must be returned to the trial court for further proceedings, and to avoid any possible misunderstandings as to the scope of our decision, we note that the ultimate validity of these claims depends upon their satisfying the other requirements for patentability such as those set forth in 35 U.S.C. §§ 102, 103, and 112. Thus, on remand, those questions, as well as any others the parties may properly raise, remain for disposition.

CONCLUSION

The district court's summary judgment of invalidity is reversed, and the case is remanded for further proceedings consistent with this opinion.

Reversed and Remanded

EUROPEAN PATENT CONVENTION, ARTICLE 52

1. European patents shall be granted for any inventions which are susceptible of industrial application, which are new and which involve an inventive step.

2. The following in particular shall not be regarded as inventions within the meaning of paragraph 1:

(a) discoveries, scientific theories and mathematical methods;

(b) aesthetic creations;

(c) schemes, rules and methods for performing mental acts, playing games or doing business, and programs for computers;

(d) presentations of information.

3. The provisions of paragraph 2 shall exclude patentability of the subject-matter or activities referred to in that provision only to the extent to which a European patent application or European patent relates to such subject-matter or activities as such.

4. Methods for treatment of the human or animal body by surgery or therapy and diagnostic methods practised on the human or animal body shall not be regarded as inventions which are susceptible of industrial

application within the meaning of paragraph 1. This provision shall not apply to products, in particular substances or compositions, for use in any of these methods.

APPLICANT: VICOM SYSTEMS INC.
Decision of the Technical Board of Appeal 3.5.1 (15 July 1986)
Case T 208/84, Official Text, 1 O.J.E.P.O. 14–23 (1987)

SUMMARY OF FACTS AND SUBMISSIONS

[A U.S. applicant's European patent application was refused by a decision of the Examining Division rejecting Claims 1–12 stating that independent method Claims 1, 3, 5, 12 related to a mathematical method which is not patentable by virtue of Article 52(2)(a) and (3) EPC, that the dependent method Claims 2, 4, 6, 7 did not add technical features as required by Rule 29(1) EPC and that the apparatus Claims 8–11 in the absence of supporting disclosure of novel apparatus were unacceptable in view of Article 52(1) and 54 EPC. Furthermore, the Examining Division considered that the normal implementation of the claimed methods by a program run on a known computer could not be regarded as an invention in view of Article 52(2)(c) and (3) EPC. The applicant appealed to the Technical Board of Appeal.]

IV. In the statement of grounds the appellants argued essentially as follows:

The Examining Division appears to have reasoned that the disclosure is talking about mathematical operations which can be carried out on a conventional general purpose computer and since there is no detailed discussion of the circuitry of special purpose hardware, there is no basis for claiming the apparatus as being anything other than a suitably pro-grammed conventional computer. The disclosure, however, relates to special purpose hardware which is to be put into practice by the skilled man design-ing circuitry which can perform the specific operations detailed in the specification. These operations are precisely defined there by mathematical expressions; there is no basis for an objection of lack of support on this point as it is entirely conventional to define filters in terms of mathematical operations since it is one of the expected skills of a filter designer to be able to "reduce" a mathematically specified filter to its circuit form. For purposes of convenience, and as is conventional in this complex area of technology, the description of the point operator and the mask circuits are given mathematically, which is then understood by those skilled in this art to refer to a series of logic circuits which can perform the function specified by the mathematical description. Thus, the mathematics is merely a shorthand by which to describe a technical function and not the totality of the invention. In the claims the process steps might be said to be defined in terms of a novel algorithm. The Examining Division appears to take the view that something defined in terms of an algorithm is inherently unpa-tentable. The appellants consider that although an algorithm per se might be excluded by Article 52(2) EPC, a process carried out in accordance with an algorithm is clearly not excluded by Article 52(2) EPC. A definition in terms of an algorithm is no different in principle from any other sort of technical definition of a process and Article 52(2) EPC provides no basis for discriminating between algorithmically based definitions and others, particularly in view of Article 52(3)EPC. What should determine patentability is the substance of what is being claimed, not its manner of definition.

Under Article 52(1) EPC, patents shall be granted for inventions which are (a) susceptible of industrial application, (b) are new and (c) involve an inventive step. The appellants sell a product covered by the claims of the application, and this clearly demonstrates that the present invention is susceptible of industrial application.

In the section on "Mathematical Methods" of the Guidelines for Examination it is stated:

> A mathematical method for designing electrical filters is not patent-able; nevertheless filters designed according to this method could be patentable provided they had a novel technical feature to which a product claim can be directed.

A novel technical feature clearly exists in not only the hardware, but also in the method recited in the claims presented by this appeal. The invention furthermore confers a technical benefit namely a substantial increase in processing speed compared with the prior art.

Digital filtering in general and digital image processing in particular are "real world" activities that start in the real world (with a picture) and end in the real world (with a picture). What goes on in between is not an abstract process, but the physical manipulation of electrical signals representing the picture in accordance with the procedures defined in the claims. There is no basis in the EPC for treating digital filters differently from analogue filters.

The appellants have thus made a new and valuable contribution to the stock of human knowledge and patent protection for this contribution cannot be denied merely on the basis that the manner in which the invention is defined would appear to bring it within the exclusions of Article 52(3) EPC.

The invention contemplates and adequately discloses to those skilled in the art the use of novel special hardware and method steps, and those technical features are found in the claims.

V. In a communication of 30.09.85, the Rapporteur of the Board informed the appellants that it they were to amend their method claims so that these would relate to the digital processing of images in the form of a two dimensional data array, the grant of a patent was conceivable. At the same time, it was indicated that the Board would probably remit the case to the Examining Division to deal with any requirements of the EPC which might not be met other than the allowability of the claims under Article 52(2) and 52(3) EPC.

VI. The appellants thereupon filed amended Claims 1–12 on 11.11.85 and requested the grant of a European patent on the basis of these claims. Claims 1 and 8 of which read as follows:

1. A method of digitally processing images in the form of a two-dimensional data array having elements arranged in rows and columns in which an operator matrix of a size substantially smaller than the size of the data array is convolved with the data array, including sequentially scanning the elements of the data array with the operator matrix characterized in that the method includes repeated cycles of sequentially scanning the entire data array with a small generating kernel operator matrix to generate a convolved array and then replacing the data array as a new data array; the small generating kernel remaining the same for any single scan of the entire data array and although comprising at least a multiplicity of elements, nevertheless being of a size substantially smaller than is required of a conventional operator matrix in which the operator matrix is convolved with the data array only once, and the cycle being repeated for each previous new data array by selecting the small generating kernel operator matrices and the number of cycles according to conventional error minimization techniques until the last new data array generated is substantially the required convolution of the original data array with the conventional operator matrix.

8. Apparatus for carrying out the method in Claim 1 including data input means (10) for receiving said data array, and said data array to generate an operator matrix for scanning said data array to generate the required convolution of the operator matrix and the data array, characterized in that there are provided feedback means (50) for transferring the output of the mask means (20) to the data input means, and control means (30) for causing the scanning and transferring of the output of the mask means (20) the data input means to be repeated a predetermined number of times.

REASONS FOR THE DECISION

. . .

2. In the decision under appeal the Examining Division has held that the method of digitally filtering a two-dimensional data array (representing a stored image) according to Claim 1 which was submitted to the Examining Division was a mathematical method because at least the characterizing part of the claim would only add a different mathematical concept and would not define new technical subject-matter in terms of technical features. It was further considered that such claims concerned only a mathematical way of approximation of the transfer function of a two-dimensional finite impulse response (FIR) filter implemented by direct or conventional convolution. Finally, the Examining Division considered the digital image

processing as such was just a calculation carried out on two-dimensional arrays of numbers (representing points of an image) using certain algorithms for smoothing or sharpening the contrast between neighboring data elements in an array. Digital filtering had therefore to be considered as a mathematical operation.

3. Although the question as to whether a method for image processing is susceptible of industrial application (Article 57 EPC) has not been explicitly raised in the procedure before the Examining Division it seems desirable to consider this issue first before addressing the point of allowability of the claims under Articles 52 (2) and (3) EPC.

The Board's present view is that the question should be answered affirmatively.

Clearly a method for obtaining and/or reproducing an image of a physical object or even an image of a simulated object (as in computer-aided design/ computer-aided manufacturing (CAD/CAM) systems) may be used e.g. in investigating properties of the object or designing an industrial article and is therefore susceptible of industrial application. Similarly, a method for enhancing or restoring such an image, without adding to its informational content, has to be considered as susceptible of industrial application within the meaning of Article 57 EPC.

However, the appellants' argument that the fact that they sell a computer incorporating some new hardware and/or software is proof of industrial applicability cannot be accepted insofar as the process carried out under the control of such hard or software is concerned. Even though a computer is an industrial product it does not inevitably follow that a process carried out under its control is industrially applicable. It might, *e.g.*, relate exclusively to a game.

4. The now effective method Claims 1–7 and 12 are directed to methods for digitally processing images. One basic issue to be decided in the present appeal is, therefore, whether or not such a method is excluded from patentability under Article 52(2) and (3) EPC on the ground that it is a mathematical method as such.

5. There can be little doubt that any processing operation on an electric signal can be described in mathematical terms. The characteristic of a filter, for example, can be expressed in terms of a mathematical formula. A basic difference between a mathematical method and a technical process can be seen however, in the fact that a mathematical method or a mathematical algorithm is carried out on numbers (whatever these numbers may represent) and provides a result also in numerical form, the mathematical method or algorithm being only an abstract concept prescribing how to operate on the numbers. No direct technical result is produced by the method as such. In contrast thereto, if a mathematical method is used in a technical process, that process is carried out on a physical entity (which may be a material object but equally an image stored as an electric signal) by some technical means implementing the method and provides as its result a

certain change in that entity. The technical means might include a computer comprising suitable hardware or an appropriately programmed general purpose computer.

6. The Board, therefore, is of the opinion that even if the idea underlying an invention may be considered to reside in a mathematical method a claim directed to a technical process in which the method is used does not seek protection for the mathematical method as such.

7. In contrast, a "method for digitally filtering data" remains an abstract notion not distinguished from a mathematical method so long as it is not specified what physical entity is represented by the data and forms the subject of a technical process[,] *i.e.* a process which is susceptible of industrial application.

. . .

9. For all these reasons, the Board has come to the conclusion that the subject matter of Claim 1 (and similarly that of the other method Claims 2–7 and 12) is not barred from protection by Articles 52(2)(a) and (3) EPC.

10. The Board will now consider the Examining Division's argument that the implementation of the claimed methods for image processing by a program run on a computer could not be regarded as an invention under Article 52(2)(c) and (3) EPC which seems tantamount to saying that a claim directed to such subject-matter would seek protection for a computer program as such.

11. The appellants have stressed that the application discloses new hardware for carrying out the claimed methods but admit on the other hand that at least in principle it is possible to implement the method and apparatus according to the application by a suitably programmed conventional computer although such a computer may not be optimized for carrying out digital image processing. [cit].

12. The Board is of the opinion that a claim directed to a technical process which process is carried out under the control of a program (be this implemented in hardware or in software, cannot be regarded as relating to a computer program as such within the meaning of Article 52(3) EPC, as it is the application of the program for determining the sequence of steps in the process for which in effect protection is sought. Consequently, such a claim is allowable under Article 52(2)(c) and (3) EPC.

13. Concerning the apparatus Claim 8, the Examining Division has held that it is not acceptable because a new apparatus is not clearly disclosed. According to the decision under appeal, the claim when interpreted in the light of the description and the drawings seems to imply only the use of a conventional computer which could not provide the basis of an acceptable product claim in view of Articles 52(1) and 54 EPC. The Board understands this as meaning that the Examining Division was of the opinion that a conventional computer programmed so as to carry out a method according to one or more of the method claims is not novel.

14. In the view of the Board, however, Article 54 EPC leaves no room for such an interpretation. A computer of known type set up to operate according to a new program cannot be considered as forming part of the state of the art as defined by Article 54(2) EPC.

This is particularly apparent in the present case as Claims 8–11 clearly embrace also the use of special hardware, for which some indications are given in the description and also mixed solutions combining some special hardware with an appropriate program.

15. In view of certain considerations by the Examining Division which appear to apply to the apparatus claims as well (*cf.* paragraph 10 above) it remains to be examined if the present apparatus Claim 8 would be objectionable under Article 52(2)(c) as qualified by (3) EPC. For reasons analogous to these given in paragraph 12 above, the Board holds that this is not the case and the same applies to the other apparatus Claims 9–11. Generally claims which can be considered as being directed to a computer set up to operate in accordance with a specified program (whether by means of hardware or software) for controlling or carrying out a technical process cannot be regarded as relating to a computer program as such and thus are not objectionable under Article 52(2)(c) and (3) EPC.

16. In arriving at this conclusion the Board has additionally considered that making a distinction between embodiments of the same invention carried out in hardware or in software is inappropriate as it can fairly be said that the choice between these two possibilities is not of an essential nature but is based on technical and economical considerations which bear no relationship to the inventive concept as such.

Generally speaking, an invention which would be patentable in accordance with conventional patentability criteria should not be excluded from protection by the mere fact that for its implementation modern technical means in the form of a computer program are used. Decisive is what technical contribution the invention as defined in the claim when considered as a whole makes to the known art.

Finally, it would seem illogical to grant protection for a technical process controlled by a suitably programmed computer but not for the computer itself when set up to execute the control. . . .

MERRILL LYNCH'S APPLICATION
[1989] RPC 561 (Court of Appeal) (UK)

INTRODUCTION

This was an appeal by Merrill Lynch, Pierce, Fenner and Smith Inc. to the Court of Appeal from a decision of Falconer J in the Patents Court dismissing an appeal from a decision dated 14 September 1986 by Mr. MF Pilgrim, principal examiner acting for the Comptroller, that application No 8527346 did not relate to a patentable invention. . . .

Fox LJ: This is an appeal by the applicant from a decision of Falconer J, upholding the determination of the examiner and the principal examiner that the subject matter of the application was unpatentable by virtue of the provisions of Section 1(2)(c) of the Patents Act 1977. The case concerns computer-program-related inventions.

The principal examiner held that claim 1 as filed, did not define a patentable invention, nor did the first amended claim 1. However, he allowed the application to proceed on the basis that it might be possible to draft valid claims. The present appeal relates to the refusal of the original claim 1.

The application describes the invention as follows:

> This invention relates to business systems and, more specifically, to an improved data processing based system for implementing an automated trading market for one or more securities. The system retrieves and stores the best current bid and asked prices; qualifies customers buy/sell orders for execution; executes the orders; and reports the trade particulars to customers and to national stock price reporting systems. The system apparatus also determines and monitors stock inventory and profit for the market maker.

As regards the objects of the invention, the application states:

> It is an object of the present invention to provide an improved data processing apparatus for making an automated market for one or more securities.

> More specifically, it is an object of the present invention to provide an automated market making system for qualifying and executing orders for securities transactions.

> It is a further object of the present invention to provide automated market making program controlled apparatus which monitors the securities position of the market maker, and which develops and provides information characterizing the market maker's trading profits.

The specification then goes on to state:

> The above and other objects of the present invention are realized in specific, illustrative data processing based apparatus which makes an automated trading market for one or more securities.

Claim 1 is in the following terms:

> In combination in a data processing system for making a trading market in at least one security in which the system proprietor is acting, as principal; said system including means for receiving trade orders for said at least one security from system customers, said trade orders including fields identifying the stock to be traded and characterization of the trade as a customer purchase or sale, and the number of shares for the transaction; means for retrieving and

for storing operative bid and asked prices for said at least one security; means for entering and for storing order qualification parameters, said parameters and said stored prices determining which received orders and qualified for execution; means for storing data characterizing position, cost and profit for said at least one security; qualifying means responsive to said received trade orders and said stored prices and order qualification parameters for qualifying a trade order for execution when the received trade order fields do not violate the stored prices and qualification parameters; means for executing each trade order qualified by said qualification means; and post-execution updating means for updating said position and at least one of said stored parameters upon execution of a trade order.

The system can be implemented by any data-processing equipment of the kind familiar to those skilled in the art.

I come to the statutory provisions. They are in section 1 subsections (1) and (2) of the Patents Act 1977, and are as follows:

(1)A patent may be granted for an invention in respect of which the following conditions are satisfied, that is to say—

(a) the invention is new;

(b) it involves an inventive step;

(c) it is capable of industrial application;

(d) the grant of a patent for it is not excluded by subsections (2) and (3) below; and references in this Act to a patentable invention shall be construed accordingly.

(2) It is hereby declared that the following (among other things) are not inventions for the purposes of this Act, that is to say, anything which consists of—

(a) a discovery, scientific theory or mathematical method;

(b) a literary, dramatic, musical or artistic work or any other aesthetic creation whatsoever;

(c) a scheme, rule or method for performing a mental act, playing a game or doing business, or a program for a computer;

(d) the presentation of information; but the foregoing provision shall prevent anything from being treated as an invention for the purposes of this Act only to the extent that a patent or application for a patent relates to that thing as such.

I should also refer to the European Patent Convention, Article 52, [which the court then quoted in full].

The issue is whether the present case falls within the prohibition in section 1(2)(c) of the Patents Act 1977.

The view of the principal examiner was that the effect of section 1 of the Patents Act 1977 was that anything which was an excluded category was not to be treated as an invention and consequently its inclusion could not be considered to contribute to the required novelty and inventive step. That did not mean that matter which fell within an excluded category should be wholly disregarded, but that the mere presence of such matter could not contribute to the requirements of novelty and inventiveness. Thus, taking the example of a machine tool controlled by a program, the principal examiner said that if the physical components were wholly conventional and the system as a whole worked conventionally, any distinction from the prior art would have to be found in the program itself and this excluded the whole from patentability. His conclusion, in the present case, was as follows:

> I consider that the 'means' specified in claim 1 relate to features which either would be present in a conventional computer system or define essential functions required for the performance of the business method. Consequently this claim contains nothing which could be considered to constitute a new technical structure or to produce a technical effect in the sense in which this term is used in the Guidelines.

The Guidelines there referred to are the Guidelines for Examination in the European Patent Office. These Guidelines (which have no binding effect in law) provide, inter alia, in part C, Chapter IV, as follows:

> 2.2 In considering whether the subject-matter of an application is an invention within the meaning of Article 52, paragraph 1, there are two general points the examiner must bear in mind. Firstly, any exclusion from patentability under Article 52, paragraph 2, applies *only to the extent to which the application relates to the excluded subject-matter as such*. Secondly, the examiner should disregard the form or kind of claim and concentrate on its content in order to identify the real contribution which the subject-matter claimed, considered as a whole, adds to the known art. If this contribution is not of a technical character, there is no invention within the meaning of Article 52, paragraph 1. Thus, for example, if the claim is for a known manufactured article having a painted design or certain written information on its surface, the contribution to the art is as a general rule merely an aesthetic creation or presentation of information. Similarly, if a computer program is claimed in the form of a physical record, *e.g.* on a conventional tape or disc, the contribution to the art is still no more than a computer program. In these instances the claim relates to excluded subject-matter as such as is therefore not allowable. If, on the other hand, a computer program in combination with a computer causes the computer to operate in a different way from a technical point of view, the combination might be patentable.

The case for the applicant before the judge was that the words "as such" in section 1(2) excluded the specified matter and nothing else. Thus, if an application involves a program for a computer, section 1(2) only operates to exclude a claim for the computer program as such. But it was said a claim to apparatus operating in accordance with the requirements of the program is not a claim to the program "as such." The judge rejected that. He said that having regard to the words "to the extent that," the excluding effect of section 1(2) was wider than the mere exclusion of an application relative only to one of the specified matters.

The judge said[,] "It seems to me that the words 'to the extent that' contemplate that the subsection is also to be applicable to cases where the invention involves one of the excluding matters (specified in paragraphs (a), (b), (c) and (d)), but does not relate to it only. Using the exemplification of an invention involving a computer program, Mr[.] Thorley submitted that the wording 'only to the extent that' means that there cannot be a patentable invention in so far as the invention resides in the computer program itself, but if some practical (*i.e.* technical) effect is achieved by the computer or machine operating according to the instructions contained in the program and such effect is novel and inventive (*i.e.* not obvious), a claim directed to that practical effect will be patentable, notwithstanding it is defined by that computer program. In my judgment, Mr[.] Thorley was right in that submission."

In the result the judge endorsed the view of the principal examiner that on the determination of the question whether or not the application relates to an excluded matter it is necessary to take into account whether the non-excluded features are already known and obvious. And he decided that the principal examiner correctly concluded that claim 1 was not patentable. He therefore dismissed the appeal.

In *Genentech Inc.'s Patent*, [1987] RPC 553, Whitford J—who was apparently not referred to the judgment of Falconer J in the present case—came to a different conclusion from that of Falconer J. He held that the prohibition in section 1(2) was limited to inventions which related to the matters there specified in paragraphs (a) to (d), and did not include modes of using these matters either in a process or in relation to an artefact.

In the Court of Appeal in the *Genentech case*, [1989] RPC 147, the majority of the court (Purchas and Dillon LJJ) were of the opinion that the reasoning of Falconer J in the present case was erroneous.

Purchas LJ having expressed doubt [cit] whether there was any inventive step at all in the present case, said at page 207 line 36:

> 12.08. With great respect of Falconer J I have come to the conclusion that, while the decision in the *Merrill Lynch Application* was probably correct for the reason already indicated earlier, the broad expressions of policy were neither necessary for the decision nor can they be reconciled with the judgments of [earlier cases]. In rejecting the submission of Mr[.] Pumfrey as to the meaning of the word 'as such' which were in line with the opinions expressed by the Technical Board of Appeal in *Vicom Systems Inc.'s Application* (Decision T208/84), [1987] Official Journal EPO 14 and preferring the submission of Mr[.] Thorley, for the Comptroller, as to the meaning of the

words 'only to the extent that' as they are found in section 1(2), Falconer J placed an undue emphasis upon those words which effectively distorted the general meaning of the section itself.

12.09. In my judgment the plain and ordinary interpretation to be given to the words 'only to the extent that' in conjunction with 'relates to that thing as such' is derived from taking the two phrases together as meaning that any of the matters listed in sub-paragraphs (a) to (d) shall not be an invention for the purposes of the Act. Semble, otherwise they would have constituted inventions and shall only to the extent that the application or patent relates to that step as such be disqualified.

Dillon LJ (at page 239 line 40) said that Falconer J's conclusion was summed up by his acceptance of the submission that the wording 'only to the extent' means that there cannot be a patentable invention in so far as the invention resides in the computer program itself, but if some practical (*i.e.* technical) effect is produced by the computer operating according to the instructions in the program *and such effect is novel and inventive* (that is to say, not obvious), a claim directed to that technical end will be patentable even though it is defined by a computer program.

As to that Dillon LJ said (at page 239 line 49):

Such a conclusion, when applied to a discovery, would seem to mean that the application of the discovery is only patentable if the application is itself novel and not obvious, altogether apart from the novelty of the discovery. That would have a very drastic effect on the patenting of new drugs and medicinal or microbiological processes.

Dillon LJ, after citing the observations of Whitford J to the effect that while you cannot patent a discovery, if on the basis of that discovery you can tell people how it can be usefully employed, then a patentable invention may result, even though the mode of use is obvious enough [cit] stated that he preferred the opinion of Whitford J to the reasoning of Falconer J in the present case.

Dillon LJ, however, added [cit] that while he disagreed with the reasoning of Falconer J in the present case:

. . . it does not in the least follow that I disagree with the result of that case. It would be nonsense for the Act to forbid the patenting of a computer program, and yet permit the patenting of a floppy disc containing a computer program, or an ordinary computer when programmed with the program; it can well be said, as it seems to me, that a patent for a computer when programmed or for the disc containing the program is no more than a patent for the program as such.

Mustill LJ [cit] said that, having regard to the conclusions reach by Purchas and Dillon LJJ, he would say only that, if the logic of the principal examiner and Falconer J in the present case were to be overturned, the only available means was to emphasise the words "which consists of" in section 1(2).

On this appeal Mr[.] Thorley, for the Comptroller, accepts that, having regard to the decision of the majority of the Court of Appeal in the *Genentech* case, the reasoning of the principal examiner and Falconer J must be regarded as erroneous. The Comptroller, however, reserves his right, if the present case goes further, to contend that the reasoning was correct.

The contention of the applicant (appellant) in the present appeal is that the question to be addressed is: "Is the subject matter of the claim a computer program?" If it is, then it is not patentable. If it is not, then the invention is not excluded from patentability by section 1(2) provided, of course, that the requirements of section 1(1) are satisfied. Thus it is said that a piece of machinery (a computer) which follows the instructions of a novel computer program is patentable although the program itself would be excluded from patentability by section 1(2).

Section 1(2), it is said, only excludes the specified matters "as such." A computer program is a text which, when loaded into a computer, directs the matter in which the computer is to operate. A computer when programmed with a novel program is itself a novel piece of apparatus which, directed by the program, operates in a new way. The view of Falconer J was that if the novelty of the claim was in matter excluded by section 1(2), then you ignore that and look only at what is left, i[.]e[.], a conventional computer which is not patentable. That approach was held to be wrong in *Genentech* and the present claim (it is said) can properly be regarded as a claim to a novel piece of apparatus or machinery which is patentable.

I should now refer to the decision, dated 5 July 1986, of the Technical Board of Appeal of the European Patents Office in the case of *Vicom Systems Inc.'s Application* (Decision T208/84), [1987] Official Journal EPO 14. The decision of the Board is a matter of which we are required, by section 91(1) of the Patents Act 1977, to take "judicial notice". In *Vicom* it appears [cit], that the Examining Division regarded the claim as being concerned with mathematical operations which would be carried out on a conventional general-purpose computer, and, since there was no detailed discussion of the circuitry of special-purpose hardware, there was no basis for claiming the apparatus as being anything other than a suitably programmed conventional computer. The appellants asserted, however, that the claim related to special-purpose hardware which was to be put into practice by the skilled man designing circuitry which would perform specific operations detailed in the specification.

As I have already indicated, Article 53 of the Convention, like section 1(2), excludes from patentability mathematical methods as such. The Board held (paragraph 6) that even if the idea underlying an invention is considered to reside in a mathematical method, a claim directed to a technical process in which the method is used does not seek protection for the mathematical method as such.

The Board went on to consider the Examining Division's argument that the implementation of the claimed methods for image processing by a program run on a computer could not be regarded as an invention under Article 52(2)(c) and (3) of the Convention. In paragraph 12 the Board stated:

> The Board of Appeal is of the opinion that a claim directed to a technical process which process is carried out under the control of a program (be this implemented in hardware or in software) cannot be regarded as relating to a computer program as such within the meaning of Article 52(3) EPC, as it is the application of the program for determining the sequence of steps in the process for which in effect protection is sought. Consequently, such a claim is allowable under Article 52(2)(c) and (3) EPC.

And in paragraph 15 the Board states:

> In view of certain considerations by the Examining Division which appear to apply to the apparatus claims as well (cf paragraph 10 above) it remains to be examined if the present apparatus claim 8 would be objectionable under Article 52(2)(c) as qualified by Article 52(3) EPC. For reasons analogous to these given in paragraph 12 above, the Board of Appeal holds that this is not the case and the same applies to the other apparatus claims 9 to 11. Generally, claims which can be considered as being directed to a computer set up to operate in accordance with a specified program (whether by means of hardware or software) for controlling or carrying out a technical process cannot be regarded as relating to a computer program as such and thus are not objectionable under Article 52(2)(c) and (3) EPC.

Finally, the Board expressed the view, in paragraph 16, that:

> Generally speaking, an invention which would be patentable in accordance with conventional patentability criteria should not be excluded from protection by the mere fact that, for its implementation, modern technical means in the form of a computer program are used. Decisive is what technical contribution the invention as defined in the claim when considered as a whole makes to the known art.

The position seems to me to be this. *Genentech* decides that the reasoning of Falconer J is wrong. On the other hand, it seems to me to be clear, for the reasons indicated by Dillon LJ, that it cannot be permissible to patent an item excluded by section 1(2) under the guise of an article which contains that item — that is to say, in the case of a computer program, the patenting of a conventional computer containing that program. Something further is necessary. The nature of that addition is, I think, to be found in the *Vicom* case where it is stated: "Decisive is what technical contribution the invention makes to the known art." There must, I think, be some technical advance on the prior art in the form of a new result (*e.g.*, a substantial increase in processing speed as in *Vicom*).

Now let it be supposed that claim 1 can be regarded as producing a new result in the form of a technical contribution to the prior art. That result, whatever the technical advance may be, is simply the production of a trading system. It is a data-processing system for doing a specific business, that is to say, making a trading market in securities. The end result, therefore, is simply "a method . . . of doing business," and is excluded by section 1(2)(c). The fact that the method of doing business may be an improvement on previous methods of doing business does not seem to me to be material. The prohibition in section 1(2)(c) is generic; qualitative considerations do not enter into the matter. The section draws no distinction between the method by which the mode of doing business is achieved. If what is produced in the end is itself an item excluded from patentability by section 1(2), the matter can go no further. Claim 1, after all, is directed to "a data processing system for making a trading market." That is simply a method of doing business. A data processing system operating to produce a novel technical result would normally be patentable. But it cannot, it seems to me, be patentable if the result itself is a prohibited item under section 1(2). In the present case it is such a prohibited item. . . .

In the end, therefore, for the reasons which I have indicated, I reach the same result as Falconer J, namely that there is not a patentable invention here. I would dismiss the appeal.

DISPOSITION

Appeal dismissed with costs. Leave to appeal to the House of Lords refused.

PATENTABILITY OF SOFTWARE-RELATED INVENTIONS UNDER THE EUROPEAN PATENT CONVENTION
Anton S. Holzworth, Dir. 2201
European Patent Office, Munich

General Line of Current EPO Practice

Although computer programs as such are explicitly excluded from patentability, the current interpretation of Article 52(2) and (3) as laid down in the Guidelines and confirmed by a considerable number of decisions of the EPO Boards of Appeal allows patentability of subject-matter which makes a *technical contribution to the known art*, even if computer programs are involved.

The Guidelines and Board of Appeal Decisions give some basic examination rules:

1. A computer program claimed by itself or as a record on a carrier is not patentable, irrespective of its content.

2. The situation is not normally changed when the computer program is loaded into a known computer.

3. If, however, the subject-matter claimed makes a technical contribution to the known are, patentability should not be denied merely because a computer program is involved in its implementation.

4. For instance, a technical contribution can normally be assumed if the subject-matter claimed concerns treatment or manipulation of coded and stored representations of real physical entities, e.g., image processing, computer simulation of technical structures or processes, computer simulation of neural networks.

5. Indications of a technical contribution can further be seen, if analogies to real technical products or methods are identifiable, e.g.,

— an improvement concerning the man-machine interface of a computer system used as a working tool would be an analogy to an improvement of any mechanical tool like a hammer;

— training of a neural net can be seen as an analogy to calibration of an electronic device or of a measurement means;

— a set of weights in relation to the structure of a neural net used, e.g., for pattern recognition would be an analogy to a formula representing an optical structure or system;

— an improvement in the organization of data representing knowledge in a rule based system resulting in more efficient processing or faster access could be seen as an analogy to an improvement in the organisation of a mechanical or chemical process resulting in a higher efficiency ratio.

Examining Procedure

In practice, the following approach has turned out useful when examining whether there is a technical contribution.

In cases where subject-matter as defined in Article 52(2) EPC is explicitly claimed as such, an objection under Article 52(2) and (3) EPC should be raised. However, if possible with respect to the substance of the application as a whole, amendments which are suitable to overcome said objection should be considered and suggested.

Otherwise, identify the *closest piece of prior art* in the form of a prepublished document or as mentioned in the description or as common knowledge.

Identify the *difference* between the subject-matter claimed, considered as a whole, and said piece of prior art.

Identify the *effect* of said difference within the subject-matter considered as a whole.

Deduce the *objective problem* from said effect.

Identify the *field* in which said objective problem resides, whereby the following steps appear helpful:

Analyse the objective problem and its solution and identify the *skills* necessary to understand *what* is realised and *how* it is realised;

Verify if said *skills* lie *exclusively in non-technical fields*, like mathematics, aesthetic arts, linguistics, or pure programming.

In such cases formulate the arguments which show that the objective problem lies in a *non-technical field*.

If there are convincing arguments for the conclusion that said objective problem lies in a *non-technical field* raise the objection:

"The claimed subject-matter, considered as a whole, does not provide any contribution to the art in a field not excluded from patentability under Article 52(2) EPC, i.e., the present application relates to non-patentable subject matter as such, see Article 52(3) EPC."

Otherwise, go on as usual with inventive step examination.

NOTES AND QUESTIONS

(1) **U.K. Procedure.** There is no appeal of right from the Court of Appeals to the House of Lords. Although there are no special divisions in the Courts of Appeal, the Lord Chancellor's department, which is responsible for allocating individual judges to individual cases, does its best to match expertise with the issue to be heard. This applies at all levels— including the House of Lords. So, for example, although the House of Lords almost always comprises five judges, the actual composition in terms of personnel will vary according to the nature of the case being heard. Applicants in the U.K. have no choice as to which court to apply to, nor the composition of that court.

(2) **Judicial Notice and *Stare Decisis*.** The U.K. Court of Appeal was required under Section 91(1) of the Patents Act of 1977 to take judicial notice of the European Patent Convention, any bulletin, journal, or gazette published thereunder, and any decision of, or expression of, opinion by the EPO Boards of Appeals. The effect of "[this] is to give statutory force to certain provisions relating to the EPC." CIPA, HANDBOOK TO THE PATENTS ACT 406 (2d. ed. 1984). To what extent, if any, is judicial notice in *Merrill Lynch's Application* by the U.K. Court of Appeal giving "statutory force" to Article 52 EPC as interpreted by the EPO Board of Appeals in *VICOM* different from legally binding precedent (*stare decisis*)? Is the Board a "court?" (This will be discussed further in a later chapter in *Lenzing's case*.)

(3) **Rationale of the Lower Court in *Merrill Lynch's Application*.** Why was the reasoning of the lower court incorrect, according to the Court of Appeals (although the decision was correct)?

(4) **Interpreting Article 52 EPC.** What is the relationship between EPC Articles 52(1) and 52(2). Which section does the *VICOM* Board look to first and why?

(5) **The EPO *Versus* Europe.** Attempts to cope with the subject matter constraints of Article 52 in the context of computer software are discussed in Jurgen Betten, *Patentability of Software in Europe: The German Perspective (Parts I and II)*, 13 COMPUTER LAWYER 1 (Aug. & Sept. 1996); Sean J. Hackett, *Patent Protection In Europe For Software Invention*, 479 PLI/ PAT 889 (1997); and Jonathan Newman, *The Patentability Of Computer-Related Inventions In Europe,* 19 EUR. INTELL. PROP. REV. 701 (1997). Opposition to revising Article 52 or for broadening patent protection for computer software in Europe is driven largely by the "open source" movement, among many other groups. *See, e.g.,* www.eurolinux.org; www.parti-socialiste.fr/tic/ ps-tic_2002.php (This movement should be distinguished from the "free software" movement, www.gnu.org/philosophy/free-software-for-freedom.html#relationship).

(6) **Conflating Utility and Patentable Subject Matter.** In *State Street*, the Federal Circuit says "[t]he question of whether a claim encompasses statutory subject matter should not focus on which of the four categories of subject matter a claim is directed to—process, machine, manufacture, or composition of matter—but rather on the essential characteristics of the subject matter, in particular, its practical utility." In *Excel Communications*, it says "our inquiry focuses on whether the mathematical algorithm is applied in a practical manner to produce a useful result." Has the court conflated the "utility" and the "statutory subject matter requirements" for patentability? If so, is this permissible under the U.S. Constitution? *See* Robert A. Kreiss, *Patent Protection for Computer Programs and Mathematical Algorithms: The Constitutional Limitations on Patentable Subject Matter*, 29 N. MEX. L. REV. 31 (1999).

(7) **Computer Program Patents and Business-Method Related Patents.** Is *State Street* about a computer program or about a business method, or both? What about *Merrill Lynch's Application*? Are the two cases distinguishable on the facts, the law, or is the difference in the outcome of the two cases a matter of judicial attitudes toward "artful drafting" of a patent claim? Do either of the inventions sub judice make a "technical contribution to the known art?" Which court demonstrates the better judicial response to artful drafting? *See* John R. Thomas, *The Patenting of the Liberal Professions*, 40 B.U.L. REV. 1139, 1182 (1999). What about international public policy as expressed in the TRIPS Agreement? *See* Daniele Schiuma, *TRIPS and Exclusion of Software "as Such" from Patentability*, 31 IIC 36 (2000).

(8) **Proposed EU Directive on Software Patentability.** The European Commission has proposed a directive under Article 95 of the EC Treaty which would harmonize the conditions for patentability of computer programs under the laws of the member states of the EU, and thus effectively revise the exclusion of computer programs from patentability under Article 52 of the EPC. The Commission proposal notes that the German Federal Patent Court's jurisprudence does not appear to exclude the possibility that business methods can be patentable even if the only

contribution that the invention makes is non-technical. *See, e.g., Automatic Sales Control* [1999] GRUR 1078 and *Speech Analysis Apparatus* [2000] GRUR 930. This initiative has been criticized as a "rubber stamp" of the EPO approach drafted by the Business Software Alliance. *See* swpat.ffii.org/vreji/papri/eukonsult00/indexen.html#hist. The Commission has revised its proposal. *See* europa.eu.int/comm/internal_market/en/indprop/comp/02-32.htm.

(9) **Pension Benefit Systems.** In *Pension Benefit Systems Partnerships*, T931/95 (2000), the EPO Technical Board of Appeals, finding claims for a concrete apparatus suitable for performing an economic activity are not mentioned in the exclusions of Article 52(2) EPC, said "the formal category of such a claim does in fact imply physical features of the claimed subject-matter which may qualify as technical features of the invention concerned and thus be relevant for its patentability." *Id.* at ¶ 5. A commentator in the U.K. commenting that "technical effect" in the U.K. is not, as in the EPO, the be-all and end-all of subject matter patentability, observes that, "if the bar for patenting abstract business methods is the 'technicality' requirement, then this [*Pension Benefits*] decision may have eliminated the single most important tool excluding business methods from patentability. This decision brings European patent law closer to the law of the United States and may signal the opening of the floodgates for patents for methods of doing business, just as *State Street* did in the United States." Michal Likhovski, *Fighting Patent Wars*, 23 EUR. INTELL. PROP. REV. 267, 270 (2001). Is the United Kingdom, where the inquiry is into the subject matter to which the claim is directed rather than merely to whether the claimed invention has a "technical effect," likely to lead Europe, or to follow it, toward the U.S. case law?

§ 2.05   Novelty and Priority of Invention

In order to be patentable, an invention must be new. Novelty is determined by comparing the invention with technological information previously "known." According to popular usage, the body of such previously "known" and "disclosed" information is termed "prior art." An invention that is identically and publicly disclosed in the prior art is unpatentable for lack of novelty ("anticipation"). But standards for determining what is meant by the terms "known" and "disclosed" vary considerably from country to country. Even under the most recent international agreements, it is up to each country to determine under its own law what the terms "novelty" or "new" means. Does "known" mean "known within the country" or "known anywhere in the world?" In early English patent law, "known" meant "known in England" only, and as discussed above, a person who brought old knowledge from a foreign land into England for the first time was entitled to a patent, known as a patent of introduction. What does it mean "to disclose?" What kinds of printed publications or other disclosures are "public?" Earlier in this century, the German Patent Act (§ 2) limited prior art with respect to printed publications to what had been disclosed during the 100 years preceding the patent application. (Wouldn't a publication 101 years earlier be "known?") In the British patent law prior to 1977, patents more than 50 years old were not considered prior art. In the United States, patents and printed publications are treated more strictly than other forms of knowledge for purposes of determining novelty. Knowledge that is not in the form of a patent or printed publication must "exist" within the United States in order to affect the novelty of an invention for purposes of acquiring patent protection. Changes in information technology and international commerce are challenging the notion of novelty in the limited sense in which it has been used in the patent laws of many countries. One significant focus of recent attempts to harmonize patent laws of different countries has been to develop an international standard for assessing novelty.

A further distinction as to what is "known" occurs because some countries, for practical and policy reasons, allow an inventor a grace period by statute between the time an invention is conceived and the time a patent application is filed during which a public disclosure by the inventor will not destroy novelty, while other countries do not. Countries that prohibit any disclosure of an invention prior to the filing of a patent application are called "absolute novelty" countries. Member States of the European Patent Convention (among many other countries) are "absolute novelty" countries that have adopted a very broad standard of what constitutes "the state of the art" and which therefore cannot be the subject of a patent. Other countries (including Australia, Canada, Japan, and the United States) offer inventors a grace period in which to file an application after a public disclosure for a period of months under certain circumstances.

A second question related to the novelty requirement concerns what is called "priority of invention" between two applicants for a patent. A party is not entitled to a patent on an invention if a second party has priority of invention. In virtually all countries that have a patent system, priority of invention is a legal fiction: the first person to file a patent application is entitled to the right of priority of invention unless they derived the invention from another. In most of the world, then, priority of invention means merely priority of *application*. The only exception is the United States. While it is presumed in the U.S. that the first person to file a patent application is entitled to priority of invention against another who files an application claiming the same invention later, the ultimate question of who is entitled to the right of priority where there are conflicting claims will be determined in an arcane proceeding in the Patent Office called an "interference" (35 U.S.C. §§ 102(g) and 135) to determine who was the prior inventor. The U.S. is the last so-called "first-to-invent" country. The rest of the patenting countries of the world have implemented a "first-to-file" system for determining priority. (The Philippines, the last other country which had a "first-to-invent" system, changed to a first-to-file system on January 1, 1998.) Here, we introduce the general principles of novelty and grace periods.

GERALD J. MOSSINGHOFF & VIVIAN S. KUO, WORLD PATENT SYSTEM CIRCA 20XX, A.D[*]

38 IDEA 529, 548–549 (1998)

As between two true inventors-as contrasted with copiers-every nation in the world, except the United States, provides a patent to the inventor who first undertakes to use the patent system to disclose his/her invention to the public and gain protection. In shorthand, this is called a first-to-file system of priority. For reasons that perhaps made sense historically, the United States has a so-called first-to-invent system of priority that is intended to provide the patent to the first "inventor," i.e., the first person to "conceive" and/or "reduce the invention to practice" under an arcane and burdensome complex of substantive and procedural rules and regulations. In the United States, as one might expect, there are clear exceptions to the first-to-invent rule. For example, if a first inventor uses the invention commercially but secretly for more than a year prior to filing a patent application, he or she is barred from getting a patent, but a second inventor, not knowing of the secret commercial use, can obtain a valid U.S. patent. As early as 1965, a major Presidential Commission studying the United States patent system strongly recommended that the United States adopt the otherwise universal first-to-file system. Given the increasing use of low-cost and easily filed provisional applications and a personal defense of prior user rights, such a system would be of significant benefit to independent inventors and small businesses.

Except for the cloud now hanging over every patentee's head that someone else will later claim to be a "first inventor," the United States now has a virtual first-to-file system. The U.S. Patent and Trademark Office receives more than 220,000 patent applications each year. Historically, about 200 to 225 of these-or 0.1%-end up in interferences. And of those, the "junior party," the second to file, prevails in fewer than one-third of the cases.

An argument is often made that adopting the universal first-to-file rule would somehow disadvantage independent inventors and small businesses-two classes of extremely important and productive users of the U.S. patent system. But the reality is exactly the opposite. Forcing a small-entity inventor into an interference proceeding with a large and determined company that filed a patent application after the small entity could cost the small entity from $500,000 to $1,000,000 (including court appeals), according to current estimates, to prevail. More importantly, small entities by their very nature can move more quickly than larger bureaucracies. And here is where the United States provisional application comes into play. By filing a complete technical disclosure of the invention, a small entity can readily secure priority rights in a first-to-file system without a major expenditure of resources. This then gives the small inventor a year in which to file a professionally prepared patent application.

PRIOR ART: 35 U.S.C. § 102

A person shall be entitled to a patent unless—

(a) the invention was known or used by others in this country, or patented or described in a printed publication in this or a foreign country, before the invention thereof by the applicant for patent, or

(b) the invention was patented or described in a printed publication in this or a foreign country or in public use or on sale in this country, more than one year prior to the date of the application for patent in the United States,

. . . .

(e) the invention was described in a prior filed U.S. application for a patent of another which has become public by grant];

(f) he did not himself invent the subject matter sought to be patented. . . .

(g) [the invention was previously made in the U.S. by another inventor, that is either public or will likely become public in the sense that it has not been abandoned, suppressed, or concealed.

ODDZON PRODS, INC. v. JUST TOYS, INC.
122 F.3d 1396 (Fed. Cir. 1997)

Lourie, Circuit Judge

[OddzOn Products, Inc. was the owner of design patent No. 346,001 on the "Vortex" tossing ball, a foam football-shaped ball with a tail fin structure. The district court determined that two confidential designs that had been disclosed to the inventor qualified as subject matter encompassed within the meaning of 35 U.S.C. § 102(f) and concluded that these designs could be combined with other prior art designs for purposes of a challenge to the validity of the patent under 35 U.S.C. § 103.]

Section 102(f) provides that a person shall be entitled to a patent unless "he did not himself invent the subject matter sought to be patented." This is a derivation provision, which provides that one may not obtain a patent on that which is obtained from someone else whose possession of the subject matter is inherently "prior." It does not pertain only to public knowledge, but also applies to private communications between the inventor and another which may never become public. Subsections (a), (b), (e), and (g), on the other hand, are clearly prior art provisions. They relate to knowledge manifested by acts that are essentially public. Subsections (a) and (b) relate to public knowledge or use, or prior patents and printed publications; subsection (e) relates to prior filed applications for patents of others which have become public by grant; and subsection (g) relates to prior inventions of others that are either public or will likely become public in the sense that they have not been abandoned, suppressed, or concealed. Subsections (c) and (d) are loss-of-right provisions. Section 102(c) precludes the obtaining of a patent by inventors who have abandoned their invention. Section

102(d) causes an inventor to lose the right to a patent by delaying the filing of a patent application too long after having filed a corresponding patent application in a foreign country. Subsections (c) and (d) are therefore not prior art provisions.

In In re Bass, 59 C.C.P.A. 1342 (1973), the principal opinion of the Court of Customs and Patent Appeals . . . noted that the provisions of Section 102 deal with two types of issues, those of novelty and loss-of-right. It explained: "Three of [the subsections,] (a), (e), and (g), deal with events prior to applicant's *invention* date and the other, (b), with events more than one year prior to the U.S. *application* date. These are the 'prior art' subsections." Id. (emphasis in original). The principal opinion added, in dictum (Section 102(f) not being at issue), that "[o]f course, (c), (d), and (f) have no relation to Section 103 and no relevancy to what is 'prior art' under Section 103." Id. There is substantial logic to that conclusion. After all, the other prior art provisions all relate to subject matter that is, or eventually becomes, public. Even the "secret prior art" of Section 102(e) is ultimately public in the form of an issued patent before it attains prior art status.

Thus, the patent laws have not generally recognized as prior art that which is not accessible to the public. It has been a basic principle of patent law, subject to minor exceptions, that prior art is technology already available to the public. It is available, in legal theory at least, when it is described in the world's accessible literature, including patents, or has been publicly known or in . . . public use or on sale "in this country." That is the real meaning of "prior art" in legal theory— it is knowledge that is available, including what would be obvious from it, at a given time, to a person of ordinary skill in the art.

Moreover, as between an earlier inventor who has not given the public the benefit of the invention, e.g., because the invention has been abandoned without public disclosure, suppressed, or concealed, and a subsequent inventor who obtains a patent, the policy of the law is for the subsequent inventor to prevail. See W.L. Gore & Assocs., Inc. v. Garlock, Inc., 721 F.2d 1540, 1550 (Fed. Cir. 1983) ("Early public disclosure is a linchpin of the patent system. As between a prior inventor [who does not disclose] and a later inventor who promptly files a patent application . . . , the law favors the latter."). Likewise, when the possessor of secret art (art that has been abandoned, suppressed, or concealed) that predates the critical date is faced with a later-filed patent, the later-filed patent should not be invalidated in the face of this "prior" art, which has not been made available to the public. Thus, prior, but non-public, inventors yield to later inventors who utilize the patent system. . .

[The court went on to hold that changes in the patent law in 1984 were such that Section 102(f) also created a type of prior art for purposes of Section 103 illustrating as follows: "An invention, A', that is obvious in view of subject matter A, derived from another, is also unpatentable. The obvious invention, A', may not be unpatentable to the inventor of A, and it may not be unpatentable to a third party who did not receive the disclosure of A, but it is unpatentable to the party who did receive the disclosure."]

EUROPEAN PATENT CONVENTION, ARTICLE 54

1.An invention shall be considered to be new if it does not form part of the state of the art.

2. The state of the art shall be held to comprise everything made available to the public by means of a written or oral description, by use, *or in any other way*, before the date of filing of the European patent application. [Emphasis added]

JAPANESE PATENT ACT, ARTICLE 39

"First-to-File Rule"

(1) Where two or more patent applications relating to the same invention are filed on different dates, only the first applicant may obtain a patent for the invention.

(2) Where two or more patent applications relating to the same invention are filed on the same date, only one such applicant, agreed upon after mutual consultation among all the applicants, may obtain a patent for the invention. If no agreement is reached or no consultation is possible, none of the applicants shall obtain a patent for the invention.

. . . .

(5) Where a patent application . . . is abandoned, withdrawn or dismissed, or where an examiner's decision or trial decision that a patent application is to be refused has become final and conclusive, such application shall . . . be deemed never to have been made.

PROGRESS REPORT ON THE STATUS OF TRADITIONAL KNOWLEDGE AS PRIOR ART
WIPO Doc. No. GRTKF/IC/2/6 (July 1, 2001)

IV. Definitions of Prior Art and Their Relationship to Traditional Knowledge

. . . .

C. European Patent Convention

The European Patent Convention (EPC) defines prior art as follows:

> The state of the art shall be held to comprise everything made available to the public by means of a written or oral description, by use, or in any other way, before the filing of the European patent application.

With reference to this provision of the EPC, the *Guidelines for Examination in the European Patent Office* (EPO) emphasize that "[t]he width of this definition should be noted. There are no restrictions whatever as to the geographical location where, or the language or manner in which the relevant information was made available to the public; also no age limit is stipulated for the documents or other sources of the information. However certain specific exclusions exist. . . . " All traditional knowledge comprised in this wide definition of the state of the art is recognized as prior art by the EPO, for the purposes of Article 54(2), EPC.

The EPO has taken significant steps to improve its coverage of, and access to, sources of non-patent literature (NPL). The availability of NPL to examiners has been improved to allow searching in more NPL publications and to allow faster access to NPL. This activity includes loading of copies of commercial databases in-house at the EPO (INSPEC, ELSEVIER, BIOSIS, COMPENDEX, etc.) and an annual subscription to 1,400 journals from which 120,000 articles are copied and added yearly to the classified collection. Other examples include the cooperation within Europe by the EPO and some of its Member States to forge consortium contracts with publication houses/commercial hosts for access to their NPL databases.

D. Japan

Section 29 of the Japanese Patent Law (JPL) provides for absolute novelty as in the case of the EPC. This means that (i) inventions which were publicly known, (ii) inventions which were publicly worked, and (iii) inventions which were described in a distributed publication or made available to the public through telecommunication lines in Japan or elsewhere prior to the filing date or priority date constitute prior art. In particular, the JPL provides that any person who has made an invention which is industrially applicable may obtain a patent for the invention, with the exception, *inter alia*, of "inventions which have been described in a publication distributed in Japan or elsewhere or inventions which became available to the general public through telecommunication lines in such places prior to the filing of patent applications."

On December 10, 1999, the Japanese Patent Office (JPO) released 'Operational Guidelines on Treatment of Technical Information Disclosed on the Internet as Prior Art' which offer guidance on the treatment as prior art of "inventions which became available to the general public through telecommunication lines prior to the filing of patent applications." . . . The Guidelines define the term "general public" as meaning "unspecified persons in general." The Guidelines provide that "available to the general public" means that information is in a state where it can be seen by unspecified persons, and does not necessarily imply that it has actually been accessed.

Information of an online traditional knowledge database would be considered as being available to the general public if it is linked with any other site on the Internet, registered with any search engine, or the URL of the site is published in a means providing information to the general public (for example, a widely-known newspaper or magazine), and if, at the same time, public access to the site is not restricted. The online traditional knowledge database would be considered as accessible by unspecified persons even if access requires a password, if anybody can access it by acquiring a password through a set of non-discriminating procedures (regardless of whether there is a charge for the acquisition of a password). An online database that is accessible by the mere payment of a fee is considered as a website accessible by unspecified persons.

The Guidelines further provide that, in principle, information without an indication of the time of publication is not to be cited by the examiners. There are certain exceptions of cases where citation can be made (see Art. 3.1.1.(3) of the Guidelines) and normally the time of posting on the Internet is considered the time of publication. Therefore, if certain traditional knowledge is uploaded onto the Internet on date X, that would be the date of publication. If the holders of the traditional knowledge wish to argue that the knowledge had been publicly available prior to that date, they would have to prove this availability separately. This may have implications for traditional knowledge as prior art and should be taken into account when designing initiatives to establish traditional knowledge databases and digital libraries . . . For technical information disclosed on the Internet, it is specified that the question of whether the information became available before the filing of the patent application is judged based on the time of publication indicated in the cited electronic technical information. Finally, the Guidelines specify that electronic technical information retrieved from the Internet etc. must be cited in compliance with WIPO Standard ST.14.

E. United States of America

Section 102 of the U.S. Patent Act does not state a general definition of the term "prior art," but establishes a statutory bar against the grant of a patent in certain specified conditions. Specifically, 35 United States Code (U.S.C.) Section 102(a), (b) and (f), provide[. . .] a rule-bound method of determining which material will defeat a patent application describing an identical invention or render obvious an application that claims only a small advance over this prior art. Prior foreign activity anticipates a U.S. patent only if the foreign activity is described in a printed form, including a patent or patent application. However, prior foreign knowledge, use and invention are excluded from the prior art relevant to a U.S. patent application.

The Code of Federal Regulations provides that, on taking up an application for examination, the examiner "shall make a thorough investigation of the *available* prior art relating to the subject matter of the claimed invention." A primary condition for the consideration of foreign prior art under Section 102 is therefore its "availability" to the examining officer. To aid the officers in the discharge of this and other duties, the Commissioner maintains a library of scientific and other works and periodicals, both foreign and domestic, in the Patent and Trademark Office.

The technical literature, foreign patent documents, and reference and online search services which are available there "provide material which must be known or searched to determine whether claims of applications are directly anticipated and therefore unpatentable under the provisions of 35 U.S.C. 102."

Nevertheless, in certain cases examiners were not able to ascertain at the time when patents for traditional knowledge-related inventions were granted that there existed traditional knowledge-related non-patent literature which taught the use of the invention. In order to address this issue and prevent the patenting of traditionally used remedies, the USPTO has suggested to "address the need of creating more easily accessible non-patent literature databases that deal with traditional knowledge. . . . With the help of the developing countries, traditional knowledge can be documented, captured electronically, and placed in the appropriate classification systems so that it can be more easily searched and retrieved." This would provide a framework to integrate traditional knowledge databases into patent information systems which are seamlessly searchable for patent examination purposes.

Additionally, Section 1.104 of Chapter 37 of the Code of Federal Regulations provides that "[a]n international-type search will be made in all national applications filed on and after June 1, 1978." This provides that also national applications shall be subject to an international search, with the objective to discover "everything which has been made available to the public anywhere in the world by means of written disclosure (including drawings and other illustrations) and which is capable of being of assistance in determining that the claimed invention is or is not new and that it does or does not involve an inventive step (i.e., that it is or is not obvious), provided that the making available to the public occurred prior to the international filing date."

A. JOSE CORTINA, WHEN IS ABSOLUTE NOVELTY NOT ABSOLUTE NOVELTY? *
4 Intellectual Property Today 30–31 (Nov. 1997)

U.S. patent attorneys who secure patent protection in the United States and abroad for their clients have labored for years under the assumption that if there is a disclosure of an invention by publication or use in the United States, or anywhere else in the world, before the filing date of a U.S. application or before the priority date of an application filed elsewhere, with the exception of the United States and selected other countries, the filing of patent applications in most countries throughout the world is barred. This is known as an "absolute novelty" requirement. Thus, when U.S. patent attorneys have become aware of such facts, they often make the decision to not pursue filings in countries throughout the world beyond the United States. This is an erroneous assumption which can lead to unnecessary loss of rights for a client because there are a number of major country exceptions which allow such protection to be obtained notwithstanding a

---

* Reprinted with permission.

prior disclosure of the invention. Thus, although many countries appear to require "absolute novelty" to allow patenting of an invention, because of a number of individual country exceptions to the requirement, it is often a myth. These exceptions arise out of distinctions made between, for example, an inventor's actions, actions of others, actual use or publication of the invention and disclosure at official exhibitions.

Under the European Patent Convention, although the general rule is that absolute novelty is required, there are exceptions. Absolute novelty under the Convention is generally defined as being anything in the prior art which is made available to the public by means of written or oral description, by use, or other means before the filing or priority date of the application on the invention sought to be patented. However, an exception applies in that an earlier disclosure is not prejudiced if it occurred not earlier than six (6) months preceding the filing of the European patent application and was due to an evident abuse in relation to the applicant, or as a result of a display at an officially recognized exhibition. Effectively, this provision provides a six (6) month grace period under certain circumstances within which to file the European patent application.

Clear examples of the types of disclosures which would give rise to this exception include an applicant attending an official trade show and display-ing the invention as part of the applicant's exhibit, but making no other disclosure of the invention. Similarly, a disclosure by another party under obligations of confidentiality to the applicant, and in breach of such obligations of confidentiality, would also give rise to such an exception.

While the requirements for the national applications in the various European countries in the past differed from each other, each country which is a member of the European Patent Convention has now amended their laws for their national application filings to be in conformance with the requirements concerning absolute novelty for European patents under the European Patent Convention. The exception thus also applies for direct national filings in the European Patent Convention member countries.

A survey of the laws of various countries in Asia also reveals that the absolute novelty requirement is not necessarily violated by an earlier disclosure. For example, in Japan an invention is considered novel if it is not publicly known or "worked" in Japan, or not described in a publication published in Japan or in a foreign country. This may give rise to the situa-tion in which if the invention was known in another country or used in the other country, but not known or used in Japan, and not the subject of a publication, it will still be possible to secure patent protection in Japan. Similarly, in China novelty is maintained if no identical invention is dis-closed in publications in China or abroad, or publicly used or made known to the public by other means in China. Public knowledge and use in other countries absent a description in a publication in China or abroad would not serve to bar a filing in China.

Turning to Latin America, while Brazil has a novelty requirement, and the novelty would be defeated by any disclosure, an applicant may apply for guarantee of priority within which an application may be filed, and may obtain a grace period of up to one (1) year after the guarantee is granted. The guarantee allows disclosure at official exhibitions, experimental use and scientific publication of the invention before filing of the application. In Argentina novelty is not defeated even thought the invention may have been published if it is considered to have "not sufficiently" been published in books, pamphlets or periodicals in Argentina or abroad to enable it to be worked in Argentina, so long as it has not been worked in Argentina prior to the filing date. Similarly, Colombia appears to provide that novelty is lost if the invention is part of the state of the art which was published, exploited or patented prior to filing, or prior to the filing date of Andean group priority filing. However, novelty is not lost if the invention was disclosed up to one (1) year prior to such filings or the priority date, if the disclosure comes from the inventor or its successor, a national office contravening its duty of confidentiality, a third party who obtains the information from the inventor or the successor, or the information was used in detriment to the applicant or exhibited in an official exhibition in an Andean group country.

A survey of Africa reveals varying requirements. In Egypt absolute novelty is required. However, the events that are described as defeating novelty are 1) public use in Egypt or 2) a publication or a patent in Egypt dated no more than fifty (50) years prior to the filing of the application. This suggests that if there is no public use in Egypt and no such publications exist, that filing would still be possible. South Africa, on the other hand, appears to have a complete absolute novelty requirement with no exceptions. South Africa provides that novelty is negated by public knowledge, which is created by written or oral disclosure or patenting of the invention anywhere. Even a "secret" use in a commercial sale in South Africa will also serve to defeat novelty.

Finally, concluding this general survey, Australia initially also appears fairly strict and provides that an invention meets the requirements of novelty if it is not known anywhere in the world or through any use of the invention in Australia before the priority date of the Australian claims. However, Australia also provides a grace period during which applications on inventions allegedly disclosed and known may be filed.

As may be appreciated from the above discussion, just because a disclosure has been made prior to the filing of a priority application which will serve as the basis for later filings in other countries does not necessarily mean that the ability to file in those countries has been defeated. Disclosure may occur in a number of ways, but generally primarily through use, or publication. In many countries while one form of disclosure may constitute an act destroying absolute novelty, another may not. To assume that absolute novelty has been destroyed may be providing a disservice to a client because although an event has occurred which may appear to be destroying of novelty, exceptions may exist in the countries of interest which may still permit the filing to take place.

Further, not knowing or investigating these exceptions may defeat a client's claims against another party when action is not taken to preserve rights notwithstanding the other party's wrongful conduct. For example, if a wrongful disclosure is made by another party under obligations of confidentiality to the prospective applicant, ordinarily one would think there would be a claim for damages for loss of rights in countries in which applicant desired to seek protection. However, if the countries in which the applicant desired to seek protection are those countries which provide exceptions, for example, by providing a six (6) month grace period during which an application may be filed in the event of wrongful disclosure, and the applicant takes no action to mitigate the damage when he could have done so, this may be sufficient to defeat any claim of damages the applicant may have against the party who wrongfully disclosed the invention because no proximate cause of the damage can be established.

Similarly, the distinctions between use and knowledge as contrasted to publication of the invention must be recognized. As already pointed out, it is possible that the invention may have been in use and known in another country but not the subject of a publication. As explained above it may still be possible to file in countries such as Japan and China since use and knowledge defeating of novelty has to have occurred in those respective countries, and not in another country. There having been no publication of the invention, novelty would still have been preserved. The important thing to recognize is that assumptions concerning loss of rights in other countries cannot be made in the event of disclosures occurring prior to the priority filing dates. Instead, it is incumbent upon each patent attorney practicing in the international arena to recognize that these exceptions exist, and to investigate the laws of the countries of interest prior to reaching any final conclusions concerning the barring of the filing of any patent application as a result of a presumed loss of novelty.

UNITED STATES DEPARTMENT OF COMMERCE PATENT HARMONIZATION ADVISORY COMMISSION, GRACE PERIOD (1993) *

Long and firmly established traditions in the United States scientific community encourage open and free communication through early publication and dissemination of the results of scientific research. Yet, prior public disclosure of the substance of an invention serves as the most fundamental bar to the ability of an inventor to obtain patent protection. The U.S. patent laws provide a compromise to these two opposing principles through a grace period—an explicit right of an inventor to prevent the patent defeating effect of an earlier publication or public disclosure of the invention for a one-year period following the disclosure. If an inventor publishes details of the invention, and then later decides to file a patent application, that publication will not be a bar to obtaining a patent in the United States,

---

* This is excerpted from HAROLD WEGNER, PATENT HARMONIZATION _____-_____ (1993). Copyright 1993, Harold C. Wegner.

so long as the patent application is filed within one year of the publication. If a third party publishes the same invention within one year of the filing date, the publication will not be a bar to obtaining a patent in the U.S. so long as the inventor provides an adequate affidavit establishing that the date of invention was prior to the disclosure. The grace period is, therefore, of critical importance to the scientific community in facilitating early dissemination of research results, while preserving the patenting opportunity of the academic inventor for a reasonable period.

The grace period also is essential to protect entities which have limited financial resources for speculative patent application filing and prosecution. Such entities must have some time after a publication or other public disclosure to validate the commercial viability of an innovation, often by finding a prospective licensee as a precondition to making any significant financial commitment toward obtaining patent protection for that innovation. The U.S. grace period helps to ensure equal access for such entities to the benefits of U.S. patent protection, and protects against inadvertent loss of U.S. patent rights during the initial period of testing or promotional activities.

The protection offered by the U.S. grace period, however, are limited. Specifically, the U.S. grace period protects the inventor only against pre-filing publication or other public disclosure with respect to U.S. patent rights. The patent laws of most other countries do not provide inventors with a grace period. This means that pre-filing publication or public disclosure of the invention will defeat the inventor's attempt to obtain foreign patent protection for the disclosed invention. Thus, foreign patent offices will use the inventor's earlier publication as a basis for denial of the patent grant.

INTERVIEW WITH NIELS REIMERS, 1997
"Stanford's Office of Technology Licensing and the Cohen/Boyer Cloning Patents", Berkeley Program in the History of the Biological Sciences and Biotechnology
http://sunsite.berkeley.edu:2020/dynaweb/teiproj/oh/science/reimers/ @Generic__BookTextView/1;pt = 102

. . .

A Possibility of Premature Disclosure

HUGHES: Well, I'm back to challenges to the validity of the patent after it issued in 1980. The *Biotechnology Newswatch* in 1982 reported that an article by Edward Ziff in the *New Scientist* in October '73 might count as premature disclosure. Why was this an issue in 1982 when the process patent had already issued?

REIMERS: What they're saying is that there was that summer [1973] Gordon conference where Boyer first disclosed what he and Stan had done. You know there's a time lag before publication, so the publication hadn't occurred. The Gordon conference was supposed be an open exchange, and you're not to take advantage of someone else's discovery, in terms of beating them to publication. Each Gordon conference focuses on a narrow field. They're usually held at a prep school back in New England, and it's just an open discussion. So one of the attendees may have told something to Ziff. But there's a question of what Ziff put in his October article as to what is called "enablement" in patent terms. I don't even remember this, by the way. If he mentioned what Boyer presented at the Gordon conference, the question is whether the Ziff article was really an enabling disclosure. If it were, he would have screwed us. Obviously, it wasn't, or somebody would have picked it up.

HUGHES: Why was this being debated in 1982?

REIMERS: I don't know if it was being debated, but they probably thought that that meant the patent was invalid. And if it was invalid, you can bet your boots the pharmaceutical companies that were paying royalties would have ceased immediately.

NOTES AND QUESTIONS

(1) **First-to-File Versus First-to-Invent.** Consider the following observation:

> The Patent Clause is centered around the inventor. . . . "The engine that drives innovative new industries in the U.S. has repeatedly been the individual inventor." The United States patent system is designed to offer protection to those inventors. One of the major supporting factors for this proposition is the fact that the United States patent system, unlike patent systems in most of the world, is based upon the "first-to-invent" principle. Despite its apparent complexity, this system allows those who lack sufficient resources to have more time to collect all the information needed for the difficult process of filing a patent application.

Note, *To Thine Own Claim Be True: The Federal Circuit Disaster In Exxon Chemical Patents, Inc. v. Lubrizol Corp.*, 21 CARD. L. REV. 1335, 1369–70 (2000).

Is the advantage of the first-to-invent system touted by this commentator worth its apparent complexity? How readily are true believers in the first-to-invent system to be persuaded to change their mind by arguments that a first-to-file system is more efficient, less costly, or that the U.S., for virtually all intents and purposes, has a first-to-file system already? *See, e.g.,* www.ipcreators.org/congress/104cong/articles104/letsarts104.htm. We will return to this question in subsequent chapters with reference to the continued unwillingness of the United States to change to a first-to-file system to harmonize its patent laws with those of the rest of the world, even in exchange for a worldwide grace period.

(2) **Absolute Obscurity.** Why should a one-page reference in a single copy of a thousand-page book written in an exotic language in a faraway country destroy the novelty of an invention? What policy favors such a rigid construction of patent law? *Compare* EPC Article 54 *with* 35 U.S.C. Section 102(a). Why does the European definition of the non-patentable state of the art include oral disclosures anywhere in the world, while the parallel U.S. exclusion mention only non-published information "known or used by others in [the U.S.]?" Is the uninhibited internationalism of the European patent system a logical consequence of the international character of the European Community itself? At least in the U.K., the knowledge must have been made available to at least some persons from British industry. *See* WILLIAM R. CORNISH, INTELLECTUAL PROPERTY: PATENTS, COPYRIGHT, TRADE MARKS AND ALLIED RIGHTS 151 (3d ed. 1996).

(3) **Toward a Grace Period in Europe?** The general approach to novelty in Europe and other absolute novelty jurisdictions is discussed by the Presiding Judge of the German Federal Supreme Court in Rüdiger Rogge, *The Concept of Novelty and European Patent Law*, 28 IIC 443 (1997). For a more general discussion of grace periods, see William Lesser, *Grace Periods in First-to-File Countries*, 9 EUR. INTELL. PROP REV. 81 (1987). In February 2002, the U.K. Patent Office announced official consultations on the adoption of a grace period in Europe, suggesting that it be considered only as part of a "balanced package" requiring the U.S. to adopt a first-to-file system. *See* www.patent.gov.uk/about/consultations/grace/index.htm

(4) **Patenting Traditional Knowledge.** Conversely, should acupuncture methods that have been used in China but never written about be patentable in the United States? *See* Shayana Kadidal, *Subject-Matter Imperialism? Biodiversity, Foreign Prior Art And The Neem Patent Controversy*, 37 IDEA 371 (1997); HAROLD C. WEGNER, PATENT HARMONIZATION § 851 (1993). The WIPO excerpt above refers to the prior art effect of "traditional knowledge" which may have been in use in other countries for generations. (Other parts of the report discusses efforts to make traditional knowledge more accessible to patent searchers.) In 1995, the USPTO granted a patent to two Indian-born physicians for the use of turmeric as a healing powder. In a reexamination proceeding in the USPTO, India's Council of Scientific and Industrial Research [CSIR] cited 32 references against the patent, including an authorized translation of an ancient Sanskrit text that spoke of the medical use of turmeric. The Patent Office revoked the patent, rejecting all of its claims for lack of novelty. Suppose this traditional knowledge had been oral instead of written? Should knowledge have been imputed to the Indian inventors who had heard of an old wives' tale that turmeric had a medical effect? Suppose the inventors were not born in India but in Indianapolis? Should oral testimony of traditional knowledge be admissible to void the novelty of such a new use for an old product? *See India Applauds U.S. Patent Reversal*, 277 SCIENCE 1429 (Sept. 5, 1995).

(5) **Selection Patents.** Definitions of novelty must sometimes adapt to particular industries. Thus in the chemical industry, one member of a previously known class of products may be separately patentable as a "selection

patent" if it possesses some special advantage for a particular purpose or has a new use, even if the result would keep a competitor from using one of its named alternatives. "If from such a class of related or homologous products or processes a property, quality or use is discovered which could not have been predicted by anyone ordinarily skilled in the art in question, that discovery may be an invention giving rise to a valid selection patent." *EI Du Pont de Nemours & Co. v. AKZO NV (Witsiepe's Application)* [1982 F.S.R.] 303 (H.L.). If the new use had not been made available to the public, there may be a patentable invention, and the substance or subclass itself may be patentable—not just the use. Is that fair to competitors who knew about the substance earlier? Should the new patent be limited in its scope to the new use? The answer varies from country to country. *See* CORNISH, *supra*, at 159–161, esp. 160, n.82; Reinhard Spangenberg, *The Novelty of 'Selection' Invention,* 28 IIC 808 (1997). Also, in the U.K., there is what is called the Gillette defense (from the case of *Gillette Safety Razor v. Anglo-American Trading Company Ltd.* (1913) R.P.C. 465 (H.L.) *viz.*, "I do not care what is in your patent. If it does not cover what I do, I win because I do not infringe. If it does cover what I do, it is bad because what I do has been done before." *See* Robin Jacob, *Novelty of Use Claim,* 27 IIC 170 (1996). This has been called by one commentator a "common law prior user right." Gregor Binkley, *Prior User Rights and the Canadian Patent Act,* 18 C.I.P.R. 207, 210 (2001).

(7) **Geography and Section 102(b).** Suppose an inventor in Buffalo, New York uses her invention publicly in Canada for many years and then files an application for a patent in the United States? What result? *See* William LaMarca, *Reevaluating the Geographical Limitation of 35 U.S.C. § 102(b); Policies Considered,* 22 U. DAYTON L. REV. 25 (1996).

(8) **The Caveat System.** The U.S. at one time had a caveat system. A caveat was a formal written notice given to the officers of the Patent Office, requiring them to refuse letters patent on a particular invention or device to any other person, until the party filing the caveat (called the "caveator") had an opportunity to establish his claim to priority of invention. The practice was abolished by Act of June 25, 1910 c. 414 § 3, 36 Stat. 843.

§ 2.06   Inventive Step/Nonobviousness

[A]   United States

GRAHAM ET AL. v. JOHN DEERE CO. ET AL.
383 U.S. 1 (1966)

MR. JUSTICE CLARK delivered the opinion of the Court.

After a lapse of 15 years, the Court again focuses its attention on the patentability of inventions under the standard of Art. I, § 8, cl.8, of the Constitution and under the conditions prescribed by the laws of the United

States. Since our last expression on patent validity, the Congress has for the first time expressly added a third statutory dimension to the two requirements of novelty and utility that had been the sole statutory test since the Patent Act of 1793. This is the test of obviousness, *i.e.*, whether "the subject matter sought to be patented and the prior art are such that the subject matter as a whole would have been obvious at the time the invention was made to a person having ordinary skill in the art to which said subject matter pertains. Patentability shall not be negatived by the manner in which the invention was made." § 103 of the Patent Act of 1952, 35 U.S.C. § 103 (1964 ed.).

The questions, involved in each of the companion cases before us, are what effect the 1952 Act had upon traditional statutory and judicial tests of patentability and what definitive tests are now required. We have concluded that the 1952 Act was intended to codify judicial precedents embracing the principle long ago announced by this Court in Hotchkiss v. Greenwood, 11 How. 248 (1851), and that, while the clear language of § 103 places emphasis on an inquiry into obviousness, the general level of innovation necessary to sustain patentability remains the same. . . .

Manifestly, the validity of each of these patents turns on the facts. The basic problems, however, are the same in each case and require initially a discussion of the constitutional and statutory provisions covering the patentability of the inventions.

II.

At the outset it must be remembered that the federal patent power stems from a specific constitutional provision which authorizes the Congress "To promote the Progress of . . . useful Arts, by securing for limited Times to . . . Inventors the exclusive Right to their . . . Discoveries." Art. I, § 8, cl. 8. The clause is both a grant of power and a limitation. This qualified authority, unlike the power often exercised in the sixteenth and seventeenth centuries by the English Crown, is limited to the promotion of advances in the "useful arts." It was written against the backdrop of the practices—eventually curtailed by the Statute of Monopolies—of the Crown in granting monopolies to court favorites in goods or businesses which had long before been enjoyed by the public. The Congress in the exercise of the patent power may not overreach the restraints imposed by the stated constitutional purpose. Nor may it enlarge the patent monopoly without regard to the innovation, advancement or social benefit gained thereby. Moreover, Congress may not authorize the issuance of patents whose effects are to remove existent knowledge from the public domain, or to restrict free access to materials already available. Innovation, advancement, and things which add to the sum of useful knowledge are inherent requisites in a patent system which by constitutional command must "promote the Progress of . . . useful Arts." This is the standard expressed in the Constitution and it may not be ignored. And it is in this light that patent validity "requires reference to a standard written into the Constitution."

Within the limits of the constitutional grant, the Congress may, of course, implement the stated purpose of the Framers by selecting the policy which in its judgment best effectuates the constitutional aim. This is but a corollary to the grant to Congress of any Article I power. Within the scope established by the Constitution, Congress may set out conditions and tests for patentability. It is the duty of the Commissioner of Patents and of the courts in the administration of the patent system to give effect to the constitutional standard by appropriate application, in each case, of the statutory scheme of the Congress.

Congress quickly responded to the bidding of the Constitution by enacting the Patent Act of 1790 during the second session of the First Congress. It created an agency in the Department of State headed by the Secretary of State, the Secretary of the Department of War and the Attorney General, any two of whom could issue a patent for a period not exceeding 14 years to any petitioner that "hath . . . invented or discovered any useful art, manufacture, . . . or device, or any improvement therein not before known or used" if the board found that "the invention or discovery [was] sufficiently useful and important. . . ." 1 Stat. 110. This group, whose members administered the patent system along with their other public duties, was known by its own designation as "Commissioners for the Promotion of Useful Arts."

Thomas Jefferson, who as Secretary of State was a member of the group, was its moving spirit and might well be called the "first administrator of our patent system." He was not only an administrator of the patent system under the 1790 Act, but was also the author of the 1793 Patent Act. In addition, Jefferson was himself an inventor of great note. His unpatented improvements on plows, to mention but one line of his inventions, won acclaim and recognition on both sides of the Atlantic. Because of his active interest and influence in the early development of the patent system, Jefferson's views on the general nature of the limited patent monopoly under the Constitution, as well as his conclusions as to conditions for patentability under the statutory scheme, are worthy of note.

Jefferson, like other Americans, had an instinctive aversion to monopolies. It was a monopoly on tea that sparked the Revolution and Jefferson certainly did not favor an equivalent form of monopoly under the new government. His abhorrence of monopoly extended initially to patents as well. From France, he wrote to Madison (July 1788) urging a Bill of Rights provision restricting monopoly, and as against the argument that monopoly might serve to incite "ingenuity," he argued forcefully that "the benefit even of limited monopolies is too doubtful to be opposed to that of their general suppression," V Writings of Thomas Jefferson, at 47 (Ford ed., 1895).

His views ripened, however, and in another letter to Madison (Aug. 1789) after the drafting of the Bill of Rights, Jefferson stated that he would have been pleased by an express provision in this form:

> Art. 9. Monopolies may be allowed to persons for their own productions in literature & their own inventions in the arts, for a term not exceeding—years but for no longer term & no other purpose.

Id., at 113. And he later wrote:

> Certainly an inventor ought to be allowed a right to the benefit of his invention for some certain time. . . . Nobody wishes more than I do that ingenuity should receive a liberal encouragement.

Letter to Oliver Evans (May 1807), V Writings of Thomas Jefferson, at 75–76 (Washington ed.).

Jefferson's philosophy on the nature and purpose of the patent monopoly is expressed in a letter to Isaac McPherson (Aug. 1813), a portion of which we set out in the margin.[2] He rejected a natural-rights theory in intellectual property rights and clearly recognized the social and economic rationale of the patent system. The patent monopoly was not designed to secure to the inventor his natural right in his discoveries. Rather, it was a reward, an inducement, to bring forth new knowledge. The grant of an exclusive right to an invention was the creation of society—at odds with the inherent free nature of disclosed ideas—and was not to be freely given. Only inventions and discoveries which furthered human knowledge, and were new and useful, justified the special inducement of a limited private monopoly. Jefferson did not believe in granting patents for small details, obvious improvements, or frivolous devices. His writings evidence his insistence upon a high level of patentability.

As a member of the patent board for several years, Jefferson saw clearly the difficulty in "drawing a line between the things which are worth to the public the embarrassment of an exclusive patent, and those which are not." The board on which he served sought to draw such a line and formulated several rules which are preserved in Jefferson's correspondence.[3] Despite

---

[2] Stable ownership is the gift of social law, and is given late in the progress of society. It would be curious then, if an idea, the fugitive fermentation of an individual brain, could, of natural right, be claimed in exclusive and stable property. If nature has made any one thing less susceptible than all others of exclusive property, it is the action of the thinking power called an idea, which an individual may exclusively possess as long as he keeps it to himself; but the moment it is divulged, it forces itself into the possession of every one, and the receiver cannot dispossess himself of it. Its peculiar character, too, is that no one possesses the less, because every other possesses the whole of it. He who receives an idea from me, receives instruction himself without lessening mine; as he who lights his taper at mine, receives light without darkening me. That ideas should freely spread from one to another over the globe, for the moral and mutual instruction of man, and improvement of his condition, seems to have been peculiarly and benevolently designed by nature, when she made them, like fire, expansible over all space, without lessening their density in any point, and like the air in which we breathe, move, and have our physical being, incapable of confinement or exclusive appropriation. Inventions then cannot, in nature, be a subject of property. Society may give an exclusive right to the profits arising from them, as an encouragement to men to pursue ideas which may produce utility, but this may or may not be done, according to the will and convenience of the society, without claim or complaint from any body." VI Writings of Thomas Jefferson, at 180–181 (Washington ed.).

[3] "[A] machine of which we are possessed, might be applied by every man to any use of which it is susceptible." Letter to Isaac McPherson, *supra*, at 181.

"[A] change of material should not give title to a patent. As the making a ploughshare of cast rather than of wrought iron; a comb of iron instead of horn or of ivory. . . ." *Ibid.*

the board's efforts, Jefferson saw "with what slow progress a system of general rules could be matured." Because of the "abundance" of cases and the fact that the investigations occupied "more time of the members of the board than they could spare from higher duties, the whole was turned over to the judiciary, to be matured into a system, under which every one might know when his actions were safe and lawful." Letter to McPherson, *supra*, at 181, 182. Apparently Congress agreed with Jefferson and the board that the courts should develop additional conditions for patentability. Although the Patent Act was amended, revised or codified some 50 times between 1790 and 1950, Congress steered clear of a statutory set of requirements other than the bare novelty and utility tests reformulated in Jefferson's draft of the 1793 Patent Act.

<h1 style="text-align:center">III</h1>

The difficulty of formulating conditions for patentability was heightened by the generality of the constitutional grant and the statutes implementing it, together with the underlying policy of the patent system that "the things which are worth to the public the embarrassment of an exclusive patent," as Jefferson put it, must outweigh the restrictive effect of the limited patent monopoly. The inherent problem was to develop some means of weeding out those inventions which would not be disclosed or devised but for the inducement of a patent.

This Court formulated a general condition of patentability in 1851 in Hotchkiss v. Greenwood, 11 How. 248. The patent involved a mere substitution of materials—porcelain or clay for wood or metal in doorknobs—and the Court condemned it, holding:

> Unless more ingenuity and skill . . . were required . . . than were possessed by an ordinary mechanic acquainted with the business, there was an absence of that degree of skill and ingenuity which constitute essential elements of every invention. In other words, the improvement is the work of the skillful mechanic, not that of the inventor.

Hotchkiss, by positing the condition that a patentable invention evidence more ingenuity and skill than that possessed by an ordinary mechanic acquainted with the business, merely distinguished between new and useful innovations that were capable of sustaining a patent and those that were not. The *Hotchkiss* test laid the cornerstone of the judicial evolution suggested by Jefferson and left to the courts by Congress. The language in the case, and in those which followed, gave birth to "invention" as a word

---

"[A] mere change of form should give no right to a patent, as a high-quartered shoe instead of a low one; a round hat instead of a three-square; or a square bucket instead of a round one." *Id.*, at 181–182.

"[A combined use of old implements.] A man has a right to use a saw, an axe, a plane separately; may he not combine their uses on the same piece of wood?" Letter to Oliver Evans (Jan. 1814), VI Writings of Thomas Jefferson.

of legal art signifying patentable inventions. Yet, as this Court has observed, "the truth is the word ['invention'] cannot be defined in such manner as to afford any substantial aid in determining whether a particular device involves an exercise of the inventive faculty or not." Its use as a label brought about a large variety of opinions as to its meaning both in the Patent Office, in the courts, and at the bar. The *Hotchkiss* formulation, however, lies not in any label, but in its functional approach to questions of patentability. In practice, *Hotchkiss* has required a comparison between the subject matter of the patent, or patent application, and the background skill of the calling. It has been from this comparison that patentability was in each case determined.

IV

The 1952 Patent Act

The Act sets out the conditions of patentability in three sections. An analysis of the structure of these three sections indicates that patentability is dependent upon three explicit conditions: novelty and utility as articulated and defined in § 101 and § 102, and nonobviousness, the new statutory formulation, as set out in § 103. The first two sections, which trace closely the 1874 codification, express the "new and useful" tests which have always existed in the statutory scheme and, for our purposes here, need no clarification. The pivotal section around which the present controversy centers is § 103. It provides:

> § 103. Conditions for patentability; non-obvious subject matter
>
> A patent may not be obtained though the invention is not identically disclosed or described as set forth in section 102 of this title, if the differences between the subject matter sought to be patented and the prior art are such that the subject matter as a whole would have been obvious at the time the invention was made to a person having ordinary skill in the art to which said subject matter pertains. Patentability shall not be negatived by the manner in which the invention was made.

The section is cast in relatively unambiguous terms. Patentability is to depend, in addition to novelty and utility, upon the "non-obvious" nature of the "subject matter sought to be patented" to a person having ordinary skill in the pertinent art.

The first sentence of this section is strongly reminiscent of the language in *Hotchkiss*. Both formulations place emphasis on the pertinent art existing at the time the invention was made and both are implicitly tied to advances in that art. The major distinction is that Congress has emphasized "nonobviousness" as the operative test of the section, rather than the less definite "invention" language of *Hotchkiss* that Congress thought had led to "a large variety" of expressions in decisions and writings. In the title itself the Congress used the phrase "Conditions for patentability; *non-obvious* subject matter" ([emphasis] added), thus focusing upon "non-obviousness" rather than "invention." The Senate and House Reports, S. Rep. No. 1979, 82d Cong., 2d Sess. (1952); H.R. Rep. No. 1923, 82d Cong., 2d Sess. (1952), reflect this emphasis in these terms:

> Section 103, for the first time in our statute, provides a condition which exists in the law and has existed for more than 100 years, but only by reason of decisions of the courts. An invention which has been made, and which is new in the sense that the same thing has not been made before, may still not be patentable if the difference between the new thing and what was known before is not considered sufficiently great to warrant a patent. That has been expressed in a large variety of ways in decisions of the courts and in writings. Section 103 states this requirement in the title. It refers to the difference between the subject matter sought to be patented and the prior art, meaning what was known before as described in section 102. If this difference is such that the subject matter as a whole would have been obvious at the time to a person skilled in the art, then the subject matter cannot be patented.
>
> That provision paraphrases language which has often been used in decisions of the courts, and the section is added to the statute for uniformity and definiteness. This section should have a stabilizing effect and minimize great departures which have appeared in some cases.

H. R. Rep., *supra*, at 7; S. Rep., *supra*, at 6.

It is undisputed that this section was, for the first time, a statutory expression of an additional requirement for patentability, originally expressed in Hotchkiss. It also seems apparent that Congress intended by the last sentence of § 103 to abolish the test it believed this Court announced in the controversial phrase "flash of creative genius," used in Cuno Corp. v. Automatic Devices Corp., 314 U.S. 84 (1941).

It is contended, however, by some of the parties and by several of the amici that the first sentence of § 103 was intended to sweep away judicial precedents and to lower the level of patentability. Others contend that the Congress intended to codify the essential purpose reflected in existing judicial precedents—the rejection of insignificant variations and innovations of a commonplace sort—and also to focus inquiries under § 103 upon nonobviousness, rather than upon "invention," as a means of achieving more stability and predictability in determining patentability and validity.

The Reviser's Note to this section, with apparent reference to *Hotchkiss*, recognizes that judicial requirements as to "lack of patentable novelty [have] been followed since at least as early as 1850." The note indicates that the section was inserted because it "may have some stabilizing effect, and also to serve as a basis for the addition at a later time of some criteria which may be worked out." To this same effect are the reports of both

Houses, *supra*, which state that the first sentence of the section "paraphrases language which has often been used in decisions of the courts, and the section is added to the statute for uniformity and definiteness."

We believe that this legislative history, as well as other sources, shows that the revision was not intended by Congress to change the general level of patentable invention. We conclude that the section was intended merely as a codification of judicial precedents embracing the *Hotchkiss* condition, with congressional directions that inquiries into the obviousness of the subject matter sought to be patented are a prerequisite to patentability.

V

Approached in this light, the § 103 additional condition, when followed realistically, will permit a more practical test of patentability. The emphasis on nonobviousness is one of inquiry, not quality, and, as such, comports with the constitutional strictures.

While the ultimate question of patent validity is one of law, the § 103 condition, which is but one of three conditions, each of which must be satisfied, lends itself to several basic factual inquiries. Under § 103, the scope and content of the prior art are to be determined; differences between the prior art and the claims at issue are to be ascertained; and the level of ordinary skill in the pertinent art resolved. Against this background, the obviousness or nonobviousness of the subject matter is determined. Such secondary considerations as commercial success, long felt but unsolved needs, failure of others, etc., might be utilized to give light to the circumstances surrounding the origin of the subject matter sought to be patented. As indicia of obviousness or nonobviousness, these inquiries may have relevancy. . . .

This is not to say, however, that there will not be difficulties in applying the nonobviousness test. What is obvious is not a question upon which there is likely to be uniformity of thought in every given factual context. The difficulties, however, are comparable to those encountered daily by the courts in such frames of reference as negligence and scienter, and should be amendable to a case-by-case development. We believe that strict observance of the requirements laid down here will result in that uniformity and definiteness which Congress called for in the 1952 Act.

While we have focused attention on the appropriate standard to be applied by the courts, it must be remembered that the primary responsibility for sifting out unpatentable material lies in the Patent Office. To await litigation is—for all practical purposes—to debilitate the patent system. We have observed a notorious difference between the standards applied by the Patent Office and by the courts. While many reasons can be adduced to explain the discrepancy, one may well be the free rein often exercised by Examiners in their use of the concept of "invention." In this connection we note that the Patent Office is confronted with a most difficult task. Almost 100,000 applications for patents are filed each year. Of these, about 50,000 are granted and the backlog now runs well over 200,000. 1965 Annual Report of the Commissioner of Patents 13–14. This is itself a compelling reason for the Commissioner to strictly adhere to the 1952 Act as interpreted here. This would, we believe, not only expedite disposition but bring about a closer concurrence between administrative and judicial precedent.

Although we conclude here that the inquiry which the Patent Office and the courts must make as to patentability must be beamed with greater intensity on the requirements of § 103, it bears repeating that we find no change in the general strictness with which the overall test is to be applied. We have been urged to find in § 103 a relaxed standard, supposedly a congressional reaction to the "increased standard" applied by this Court in its decisions over the last 20 or 30 years. The standard has remained invariable in this Court. Technology, however, has advanced—and with remarkable rapidity in the last 50 years. Moreover, the ambit of applicable art in given fields of science has widened by disciplines unheard of a half century ago. It is but an evenhanded application to require that those persons granted the benefit of a patent monopoly be charged with an awareness of these changed conditions. The same is true of the less technical, but still useful arts. He who seeks to build a better mousetrap today has a long path to tread before reaching the Patent Office.

NOTES AND QUESTIONS

(1) **"Better" or "Different"?** Does an invention have to be "better" or only "different" in order to meet the standards of patentability? In an early U.S. case prior to the articulation of the standard of nonobviousness in *Hotchkiss*, Justice Story said:

> All that the law requires is, that the invention should not be frivolous or injurious to the well-being, good policy, or sound morals of society. The word "useful" therefore, is incorporated into the act in contradistinction to mischievous or immoral. For instance, a new invention to poison people, or to promote debauchery, or to facilitate private assassination, is not a patentable invention. But if the invention steers wide of these objections, whether it be more or less useful is a circumstance very material to the interests of the patentee, but of no importance to the public. If it not be extensively useful, it will silently sink into contempt and disregard. Lowell v. Lewis F. Cas. 1018 (Circuit Ct. Mass. 1817).

(2) **Articulating the Standard.** The Supreme Court spends a great deal of time and effort in *Deere* probing the constitutional limits of patent legislation. But does the *Deere* decision set a standard? *Compare Application of Bergy*, 596 F.2d 952 (C.C.P.A.), which was affirmed by the Supreme Court in *Chakrabarty*, in which Judge Rich says:

It is to be observed that the Constitutional clause under consideration neither gave to nor preserved in inventors (or authors) any rights and set no standards for the patentability of individual inventions; it merely empowered Congress, if it elected to do so, to secure to inventors an "exclusive right" for an unstated "limited" time for the stated purpose of promoting useful arts. We have previously pointed out that the present day equivalent of the term "useful arts" employed by the Founding Fathers is "technological arts."

Does that mean that Congress can define inventor for purposes of the patent law to mean "introducer of foreign technology" if it so chooses? Can Congress define a patent term of one year for pharmaceuticals or define the "true and first inventor" as the first inventor to file a patent application? If Congress cannot *over*reach, as the Supreme Court says, can it *under*reach some constitutional standard?

(3) **Fiction in the Making.** What is Justice Burger's authority for the putative role Jefferson played in the development of the U.S. patent system, later reiterated in *Chakrabarty*? *See* Edward C. Walterscheid, *The Use and Abuse of History: The Supreme Court's Interpretation of Thomas Jefferson's Influence on the Patent Law,* 39 IDEA 195 (1999).

[B]   Inventive Step in the European Patent Application: Technical Problem and Solution

EUROPEAN PATENT CONVENTION, ARTICLE 56

An invention shall be considered as involving an inventive step if, having regard to the state of the art, it is not obvious to a person skilled in the art. If the state of the art also includes documents within the meaning of Article 54, paragraph 3, these documents are not to be considered in deciding whether there has been an inventive step.

EUROPEAN PATENT OFFICE Rule 27(1)

The description shall:

(a) specify the technical field to which the invention relates;

(b) indicate the background art which, as far as known to the applicant, can be regarded as useful for understanding the invention, for drawing up the European search report and for the examination, and, preferably, cite the documents reflecting such are;

(c) disclose the invention, as claimed, in such terms that the technical problem (even if not expressly stated as such) and its solution can be understood, and state any advantageous effects of the invention with reference to the background art. . . .

ROMUALD SINGER, PROBLEM AND SOLUTION [*]

An advantage of the problem and solution approach is that [it] helps to avoid findings of obviousness based upon combinations of different teachings which would not have been made in real life. Even if it be true that part of an alleged invention is disclosed in one document and another part in another document, the problem and solution approach prevents the combination of those two teachings being used as a bases for finding obviousness, unless the skilled worker, starting from the problem identified in relation to one document identified as being the closest prior are, would, if given a second document, find in that second document a solution to *that problem*.

Another important advantage is that all the positive benefits brought about by an alleged invention can be taken into account before deciding whether it is inventive or not, avoiding the possible pitfall of disregarding an advance in the art on the ground that it is a mere side effect.

Although problem and solution analysis has some proponents, like any other analytical tool its use requires some caution. As its starting point is the prior art which has been found with actual knowledge of the invention, from the outset it is tainted with hindsight. In contrast, Article 56 is implicitly based on the premise that the skilled worker lacks actual knowledge of the invention and is confronted with the whole of the prior art, including teachings in the direction of and away from the invention, not the selected items which the invention has found to give the answer to the problem. . . . In general, the solution of a problem is an essential prerequisite of patentability. . . . Sometimes an invention can reside in the appreciation of the existence of a problem, rather than its solution.

. . . .

NOTES AND QUESTIONS

(1) **"Problem and Solution" Approach.** The problem and solution approach to determining inventive step is described as "Germanic" in the British patent agents' guide. *See* CIPA, GUIDE TO THE PATENTS ACTS ¶ 3.21 (4th ed., 1995). Attempts to push the Europeans in a more American direction can be found in two articles by Jochen Pagenberg, *The Evaluation of the 'Inventive Step' in the European Patent System—More Objective Standards Needed, Part I, 9 IIC 3 (1978) and Examination for Nonobviousness—A Critical Comment on German Patent Practice,* 12 IIC 1 (1981) (arguing for simultaneous appraisal of technical and factual considerations.) A distinguished commentator and former Chairman of one of the EPO Boards of Appeal states that "the need for consistency was considered

---

[*] Excerpted from RONALD SINGER, THE EUROPEAN PATENT CONVENTION 186–188 (rev. Eng. edition London 1995).

more important than any advantages of pragmatism," contrasting the American "quasi-logical" approach set out as the *Graham* test above. *See* George Szabo, *The Problem and Solution Approach in the European Patent Office*, 26 IIC 457, 459 (1995). An excellent commentary explains that the problem and solution method is mandatory in the EPO and that the "skilled technical assessment" of the patent examining corps is more persuasive than circumstantial evidence. *See* Paul Cole, *Inventive Step: Meaning of the EPO Problem and Solution Approach, and Implications for the United Kingdom*, 20 EUR. INTELL. PROP. REV. 214, 216 (1998). Both articles discuss the history of the development of the European view toward inventive step in detail. *See also* David Rickard, *Are You Skilled in the Art*, 44 IP WORLD 21 (1997).

(2) **A Step in Which Direction?** The debate over whether "progress in the useful arts" requires a certain standard of nonobviousness was very lively at the time the European Patent Convention was taking shape. The dynamic of the debate is well laid out in a 1983 article by the late Managing Director of the Max-Planck Institute for Foreign and International Patent, Copyright and Competition Law in Munich. *See* Friedrich-Karl Beier, *The Inventive Step in Its Historical Development*, 17 IIC 301 (1983). Another good example of the comparative law approach is Hans Ullrich, *Standards of Patentability for European Inventions: Should an Inventive Step Advance the Art?*, 1 IIC STUDIES (1977). The next reading looks at the "technical expertise" approach in detail. Attention should be paid to who makes or should make the final decision as to whether an invention makes a contribution to the state of the art: examiner, judge, or jury?

USPTO—EPO—JPO, A COMPARISON OF U.S., EUROPEAN, AND JAPANESE LAW ON INVENTIVE STEP
1990 PROJECT 12.4

I. Determining inventive step

A. Judicial, legislative or administrative criteria or guidelines for determining inventive step.

. . .

3. Background and purpose of the provision relating to inventive step

The import of all three Offices is identical, though each differs in expression. That means, in essence, the purpose of the provisions for inventive step is "to exclude from granting exclusive rights (Patent rights) inventions that could be made easily by a person skilled in the art, recognizing that to do so would hinder development of technology." EPO is taking steps to narrow the gaps among member countries with regards the standards for inventive step.

B. Claim interpretation criteria

The practices of all three Offices agree in points that the claim(s) is considered to consist of independent and dependent claims, and that inventive step is determined for each claim. Japanese patent law 36(4) requires the claims to state only the indispensable constituent features of the invention described in the detailed explanation of the invention, and this means that the applicant should define in the scope of claims the invention for which protection by patent is sought and which is disclosed in the detailed explanation of the invention. Hence, there is no difference among the three offices in requiring description of the extent of protection sought

1. Application of prior art to a claim with a Preamble stating features necessary, for definition of claimed subject matter followed by a characterizing Portion stating those technical features to be protected.

The practices of three Offices coincide in that Jepson type claims, as in the case of improvement, are encouraged but not compulsory, and that the matter stated in the preamble of the claim is taken into consideration when determining inventive step. However, difference exists in practice as the statement of prior art mentioned in the preamble of the claim can be used as a basis of refusal in EPO and USPTO, but generally not in JPO.

2. Determination of claimed scope and content

All three Offices follow the same practice in interpreting the claims by taking into account the specification and drawings, and assessing inventive step on the basis of the claims.

3. Dependent claim interpretation

All three Offices interpret the dependent claims as including all limitations in the cited claim. However, EPO's report mentions that a claim referring to another claim does not necessarily imply that the claim containing the reference is in fact a dependent one. For example, this would not be so if the claim referred to were in a different category or related to a co-operating part (e.g. plug/socket). It further states that if an independent claim is new and non-obvious, there is no need to investigate whether any claim dependent thereon involves an inventive step.

C. Basic approach applied in assessing inventive step, e.g., test for non-obviousness, avoidance of ex post facto reasoning, and considering what the skilled man would have done starting from a given Problem.

The approach applied by three Offices coincides in that the assessment of inventive step is made by comparing the invention with prior art and recognizing the difference between them. Based on the "Time of application (or the date of priority, if priority is claimed)" in JPO and EPO where the first-to-file principle is adopted, it is based on the "time the invention was made" in USPTO where the first-to-invent principle is adopted. JPO consciously grasps three elements, namely the purpose, constitution and effect of the invention as viewpoints when comparing the invention with prior art and makes comparison for each viewpoint (cf. JPO national report pages 4–5). Deriving from this fact, JPO applies, in principles, three typical methods dependent on the nature of invention as practical methods in the assessment of inventive step: 1) method of observing the predictability of each of the three elements; 2) method of placing emphasis in observation of the difference in "effect"; 3) method of placing emphasis in observation of the difference in "constitution." In EPO practice, the approach generally applied (the so-called problem-solution approach) may be summarized as follows: 1) comparing the claimed invention with the closest prior art in order to determine the differences, 2) establishing objectively, in the light of that closest prior art, the problem that is actually solved by the invention, and 3) determining whether a person skilled in the art, starting from the closest prior art and the problem so established, would arrive at the invention claimed on the basis of the whole prior art and/or common general knowledge.

In USPTO, a judicial precedent (*Graham* test) accounts for much in the assessment of inventive step.

D. Criteria for determining the ability to apply prior art from non-analogous technical fields.

The practices of three Offices coincide in that the application of prior arts is not limited in the technical field to which the invention pertains.

E. Criteria for determining the differences between the prior art and the claims

1. Combinations of prior art

a. Requirements, if any, of a teaching or suggestion to combine features.

There is no difference among the three Offices on the following two points: (1) The examiner will reject an invention as not having an inventive step, if the invention is mere juxtaposition of publicly known arts and not producing any new effect other than the arithmetic sum of the combined features. (2) The examiner must logically give reasons as to why a person skilled in the art would have combined the features cited in the documents.

b. Restrictions, if any, on the ability to modify a prior art teaching e.g., the number of prior art teachings that can be combined

The practices of three offices coincide in that there is no specific limitation on the number of prior arts that can be combined. EPO has pointed out that "the more teachings which are being combined, the more likely it is that ex post facto analysis or lack of proper reasoning is involved."

2. Problem of common general knowledge *i.e.* the question as to whether the examiner, if he is reasonably certain that a given feature is common General knowledge but cannot prove it (because there is no supporting document), is entitled to refuse a claim

a. On the basis of that knowledge alone

There is no difference among the three Offices in that the examiner can refuse a claim on grounds of his/her personal knowledge without producing a concrete citation when an appropriate citation is difficult to be presented.

However a difference does exist among the three Offices both as to the definition of "common general knowledge" and as to the conditions under which it can substantiate objections to a claim. JPO takes the "knowledge" as "a widely known art or a widely worked art in the technical field to which the invention pertains," while EPO as well as USPTO consider it as "the examiner's personal knowledge".

JPO's report states that the examiner should point out when refusing a claim that it is a widely known art or a widely worked art. EPO's report mentions that "the examiner is obliged to prove the grounds of his contention when the applicant objects to the refusal." USPTO's report describes that, when refusing a claim on the ground of the examiner's personal knowledge, the examiner may provide an affidavit and once it has been provided, it establishes his personal knowledge as admitted prior art, if the applicant fails to seasonably challenge such assertions. When the applicant objects to the refusal, the practice of each Office is as follows: Under JPO practice, the examiner cites a reference to support his position, however, final refusal without citing a reference to support the examiner's position as to general knowledge or widely known matters is not considered illegal merely for that reason.

Under EPO and USPTO practices, the examiner should cite a reference in support of his/her position. USPTO's report states that failure of the applicant to challenge the examiner's assertions establishes them as admitted prior art. In such cases the examiner may make a final rejection on the basis of common general knowledge without documentary proof to support the rejection.

b. On the basis of that knowledge combined with one or more published pieces of prior art

The same applies as for a. above.

3. Criteria for evaluating differences between the prior art and the invention in regard to:

a. Temperature or other ranges

The practices of the three Offices coincide on the following two points:

(1) No Office recognizes an inventive step if the invention constitutes a change in temperature or other ranges of prior art which could have easily been made by a person skilled in the art and which does not produce but a normally expected result.

(2) All Offices recognize inventive step when the new feature produces an unexpected effect and the choice of the new feature enables the conventional technical expectation to be surpassed.

b. Shapes or configurations

The practices of the three Offices coincides on the following two points:

(1) No Office recognizes an inventive step if the invention constitute a change in shape or configuration of prior art which could have easily been made by a person skilled in the art and which does not produce but a normally expected result.

(2) All three Offices recognize inventive step when the new feature produces an unexpected effect and the choice of the new feature enables the conventional technical expectancy to be surpassed.

c. Materials or Parts

The practices of the three Offices coincide on the following two points:

(1) No Office recognizes an inventive step if the invention constitutes a partial change or limitation of materials or parts of prior art which could have easily been made by a person skilled in the art and which does not produce but a normally expected effect.

(2) All three Offices recognize inventive step when the new feature produces an unexpected effect and the choice of the new feature enables the conventional technical expectancy to be surpasses.

d. Sizes, ratio or amounts

The practices of the three Offices coincide on the following two points:

(1) No Office recognizes an inventive step if the invention constitutes a change or a numerical limitation of sizes, ratios or amounts of prior art which could have easily been made by a person skilled in the art and which does not produce but a normally expected effect.

(2) All three Offices recognize inventive step when the new feature produces an unexpected effect and the choice of the new feature enables the conventional technical expectancy to be surpassed.

e. Reversed elements or parts

The practices of the three Offices coincide on the following two points:

(1) No Office recognizes an inventive step For an invention obtained by reversing elements or parts of prior art for elements or parts of another prior art, which could have easily been made by a person skilled in the art and which does not produce but a normally expected effect.

(2) All three Offices recognize inventive step when the new feature produces an unexpected effect and the choice of the new feature enables the conventional technical expectancy to be surpassed.

f. Omitted elements or parts

The practices of the three Offices coincide on the following two points:

(1) No Office recognizes an inventive step if the invention constitutes an omission of elements or parts and its corresponding loss in function.

(2) All three Offices recognize inventive step when the omission produces an unexpected effect. EPO, however, has commented an its assessment of the effect of omission that "No inventive step is seen if the omission is to reduce the price of product with consequent loss of quality. On the contrary, if the omission results surprisingly in an equal or even better quality, or, successfully goes totally against current technical opinion, then this is taken as a positive indication for there being an inventive step."

g. Change or limitation of use

The practices of the three Offices coincide on the following two points:

(1) No Office recognizes an inventive step if the invention constitutes a change or limitation of the use of prior art which could have easily been made by a person skilled in the art and which does not produce but a normally expected effect.

(2) All three Offices recognize inventive step when the new feature produces an unexpected effect and the choice of the new feature enables the conventional technical expectancy to be surpassed. EPO, however, has commented that "In the case of known chemical substances or compositions which are for the first time proposed for use in surgery, therapy or diagnostic methods, a product claim limited to that use may be granted provided the use is novel and inventive."

h. Selection invention

All three Offices follow the same practice in recognizing inventive step to an invention consisted of particular subordinate ideas contained in prior art if it shows a significant and unexpected result. . . .

4. Indication of Problem to be solved

All three Offices apply the same criterion for the judgement of inventive step by determining whether the problem to be solved could be expected or not from viewpoint of the technical level at the time of filing the application (JPO and EPO) or at the time invention was made (USPTO), by comparing the invention comprehensively against prior art. EPO, in addition, states that "If the problem (to be solved by the invention) itself is judged to be novel and to involve an inventive step, the solution to the problem as expressed in the claims is then deemed to involve an inventive step." On the other hand, USPTO has commented that "The problem to be solved is one item of secondary considerations that must be evaluated, and assigned its appropriate weight. The inventive step can reside in the discovery of the problem, the solution of which employs a combination of old elements.

5. Indication of advantage of claimed invention

All three Offices take the same view in that whether or not the advantage could be expected in view of the technical level at the tome of filing the application (JPO and EPO) or at the time the invention was made (USPTO), is one of criteria in judging the inventive step. USPTO has commented that USPTO does not require "advantage", it is a secondary consideration. Besides, in the EPO's view an advantageous effect is not mandatory and in any case it may be notified later on to the Examiner during the examination procedure.

6. Comparative test

The result of the comparative test between the invention and prior arts to clarify the difference in effect is employed as one of criteria in judging an inventive step by all three Offices. EPO, however, has pointed out that The comparative tests should only be called for when absolutely necessary."

USPTO also has Commented that the comparative tests are usually submitted as rebuttal evidence once the USPTO has established a case of prima facie obviousness in view of the prior art

7. Unexpected result

a. Cases where an unexpected result is an essential criterion for unobviousness (selection inventions and inventions and comprising the combination of known elements)

All three Offices follow the same practice in recognizing inventive step in the claimed invention, if it produces an unexpected result.

b. Cases where it is merely one of a number of relevant secondary criteria

Both EPO and USPTO consider "unexpected results" as just one factor that has to be taken into secondary consideration when determining inventive step, whereas JPO's report states that the judgement of the inventive step is carried out by comparing comprehensively the purpose, constitution and effect (result) of the invention with those of the prior art.

c. Does an unexpected effect (result) have to be advantageous to constitute an inventive step?

Under the three Offices' practice, an unexpected result is not required to be advantageous. . . .

F. Resolving the level of ordinary skill

1. A person skilled in the art, an average expert

a. Amount of knowledge and skill expected

Basically, there is no difference of opinion among the three Offices regarding the amount of knowledge and skill expected of the person skilled in the art, or an average expert. In other words, all Offices consider that the knowledge and skill expected of a person skilled in the technical field or an average expert means, in general, and ordinary knowledge and skill at the time of filing the application (JPO and EPO) or at the time the invention was made (USPTO), in the technical field to which the invention pertains, and in a broad relevant technical fields or in the closely related technical fields.

In addition, EPO's report states that "the person skilled in the art is not presumed to have access to or knowledge of every prior art as a whole" and that "with increasing specialization in technology, the person skilled in the art may possess the knowledge of a specialist in the specific technological area." USPTO's report also states that "the knowledge and skill required for an average expert would vary from case to case." The above two observations apply to all three Offices.

b. Ordinary practitioner/average expert

There is no essential difference among the three offices with respect to the definition of ordinary practitioner/average expert. In fact, an ordinary practitioner/average expert is considered to be a person aware of the common technical knowledge in the relevant are, with ordinary ability to solve the problem by applying such technical knowledge, but not endowed with special creativity or inventive flair.

c. A team of persons skilled in the art

EPO's report states that there may be instances where it is more appropriate to think in terms of a group of persons rather than a single person. On the other hand, both JPO and USPTO have no provision for "a team of persons skilled in the art".

2. Long-felt but unsolved needs

All three Offices take it as one of positive factors in judging the inventive step, if the applicant can show that the invention would satisfy a long-felt but unsolved needs.

3. Prior art teaching away from the claim (technical prejudice)

All three Offices take prior art teaching away from the claim (technical prejudice) into account as a positive factor in judging the inventive step. JPO's report states that the contents of prior art teaching away from the claim will be grasped objectively and taken into account considering the technical level in that technical field at the time of filing the application. EPO and USPTO state in their reports that then is as a general rule, inventive step when prior art leads a person skilled in the art away from the claim. The same applies to JPO also.

4. Showing of failure of others

All three offices consider the failure of others as a factor in judging inventive step. The USPTO sets forth the following criteria:

—the defect must have been a recognized and persistent one in fact;

—the failure of others must have been in the context of the "same state of the art"; and

—the inventor's solution in fact reached a superior result to prior solutions.

5. Showing the invention lies in a very active or crowded art

Both JPO and EPO take into consideration the fact that an invention lies in a very active or crowded art while examining the present state (peculiarity) of the technical field in question, and that the inventive step is judged together with other tests. EPO's report, in addition, states that the fact that an invention lies in a very active or crowded art may lead to cases where even a smaller step might be considered sufficient to constitute inventive step, if the state of the art is such as to leave limited room for further advances. On the contrary, USPTO's report states that the fact an invention lies in a very active or a crowded art does not mean that smaller steps forward would therefore constitute an inventive step.

6. Development of brand-new technical field

JPO and EPO take the fact of developing a brand-new technical field into consideration in judging the inventive step as relevant to the technical level of the time of filing the application. EPO's report states that where the technology involved in fact concerns a brand-new field, inventive step may be more likely to be present if there is no relevant prior art, or if the closest prior art is fairly distant from the invention at hand. The above matters apply commonly to JPO as well. USPTO states that there is no special consideration or different standards of obviousness given in evaluating the inventive step for an invention directed to brand-new technical field. Pioneering inventions by their very nature will receive claims of broader scope than claims of inventions directed to established fields and crowded arts.

7. Commercial Success

All three Offices do not consider the commercial success alone as indicative of inventive step, but take it into account in judging the inventive step only when the success is derived from the technical features of the claimed invention.

8. Complexity of the technology

JPO and EPO do not give a definite role to the complexity of the technology in judging the inventive step, but consider it in the current situation (peculiarity) of the technical field in question, and make judgment in combination with other tests. USPTO's report states that there is no special consideration or different standards of obviousness given in evaluating the inventive step because of the complexity of the technology.

9. Other criteria

The EPO report mentions the following other criteria which may be considered in judging the inventive step:

—unexpected technical advance (often the most important criterion, especially for certain types of invention such as selection and combination inventions),

—a surprising combination effect,

—the presence of a series of steps to proceed from the known art to the invention,

—avoidance of economic disadvantages,

—a stroke of luck in view of a statistical improbability of arriving at the solution proposed by the invention, and

—an inactive state of the art.

II. Special consideration applicable to chemical practice

A. Criteria used to determine the inventive step based upon

1.a. Unexpected or superior properties of a chemical

There is no difference in practice among the three Offices with respect to recognizing inventive step when a substance having a similar chemical structure to a known chemical possesses an unexpected property, i.e. a new property, or a superior effect with regard to the same property. The reasoning of each Office is as follows:

JPO: In the above case, the chemical is considered as having an inventive step because there is no analogical possibility in the combination of its chemical structure and properties.

EPO: The level of predictability is much lower for chemicals than it is for inventive features in other fields.

USPTO: The compound cannot be separated from its properties.

b. Determination of inventive step between chemical substances of similar structure.

Is a newly discovered property of the novel chemical compound having similar structure to a known chemical compound, which property is inherent to the known chemical compound, but not disclosed in the prior art, favorably taken into account when determining inventive step of the novel chemical compounds? Under USPTO practice, the mere discovery of a property lacks inventive step, where the property is inherent in a structurally similar chemical compound known in the art, even though the property is not disclosed in the known prior art compound. The JPO has not adopted the examination practice that the newly discovered property is always favorably considered. Under EPO practice, if the compounds of the prior art were described as having a different effect, unrelated to the one exhibited by the new compounds, or no effect at all, inventive step will be acknowledged by the examiner provided he is satisfied that the effect of the new compounds is unexpected in view of what the prior art teaches.

2. Evidence required to evaluate therapeutic properties

(1) There is a difference in the extent of data required between JPO and USPTO which require in principle clinical tests as evidence of pharmacological effect, and EPO which considers tests conducted on animals or in vitro to be sufficient except in cases where, owing to the content of the invention, only clinical (human) tests could prove the invention's therapeutic properties. However, as both JPO and USPTO have made mention of accepting animal experiments or in vitro tests in place of clinical tests depending on the contents of the invention, it seems that after all the three Offices apply the same principles in their practice.

(2) As for toxicity test, JPO requires a description of at least the result of acute toxicity test, but EPO and USPTO do not put forth such requirement.

3. Intermediates

All three Offices give the same definition of intermediate. The term "intermediate" as used here means intermediate or starting products which are, according to the patent application, described for their ability to be used to produce final products through a reaction in which the intermediate loses its identity. In addition, EPO distinguishes between two categories of possibly patentable intermediates (a) intermediates for a known end-product as a step in an inventive process and (b) intermediates for an inventive end-product through an obvious process. Requirements for inventive step are set accordingly in each of the two cases. JPO takes a similar practice but USPTO's practice is unknown.

4. Inventive step of invention defined by parameters (*e.g.* numerical formula)

There is no difference in practice between JPO and EPO with respect to the application of parameters, as each office allows their use only when the invention cannot be adequately defined with other methods.

The USPTO does not allow the use of an invention defined by parameters only when the invention can not be adequately defined by other methods. In judging inventive step, each Office requires consideration not only of the parameters but also of other matters described in the claim.

5. Other criteria

a. Characteristic of manufacturing method of a chemical substance and an inventive step as an invention of chemical substance

There is no difference in practice between JPO and EPO as regards a chemical substance defined by its process of manufacture as neither Office recognizes inventive step by the process of manufacture alone. In the USPTO it is the patentability of the product, not recited process steps, that must be evaluated in product-by-process type claims.

B. Criteria to evaluate compositions or structures

1. Chemical Product patentable per se

EPO states that a chemical product may be considered as having inventive step simply based on structural non-obviousness if it is structurally very different from any known compounds and there is no similar known compounds. On the other hand, JPO recognizes inventive step for a chemical product on condition that it has a usefulness.

In the USPTO, chemical products are patentable, per se, as compositions of matter, if they satisfy the utility, novelty and unobviousness requirements of patent statute. However, there is no substantial difference among three Offices as to a chemical product patentable per se, because there is a tendency in EPO also to refuse patentability of a product which exhibits no usefulness.

2. Structural obviousness in chemical cases

All three Offices share common practice in determining the inventive step of a chemical product, with emphasis on chemical structure, and properties (qualitative and/or quantitative). The question in determining inventive step of a chemical product from the viewpoint of its chemical structure, is whether the relation between the chemical structure and its properties is predictable (expected) or not. In short, if one property is unexpected, the chemical product will be considered as being inventive even if its chemical structure is similar to that of a known chemical product.

3. Purer form of known product

All three Offices share the view that inventive step cannot be recognized for purer form unless it possesses some unexpected property from corresponding known product (simple improvement in purity is not sufficient).

4. Novel physical forms; e.g. new crystalline structure

There is no difference in practice among the three Offices, as every Office treats products with novel physical forms as not having inventive step unless they show unexpected properties which was not known for the previously disclosed other physical forms.

5. Products of nature

All three Offices follow the same practice of not granting a patent to products of nature. However, all three Offices state that they may recognize inventive step on chemical substances isolated from nature if they show unexpected properties.

6. Effects of components of a mixture

There is no fundamental difference among the three Offices with respect to the judgement criterion for inventive step of mixtures. In short, all offices do not recognize inventive step for a mixture that exhibits only an effect in the extent expected from the effects of each component (the arithmetic sum of effects).

7. Various chemical forms of a compound; e.g., isomers

All three Offices basically share the same view as to the inventive step for isomers. In brief, the judgement depends upon whether or not the isomer in question possesses an unexpected property compared to corresponding chemical compounds, and corresponding isomers.

JPO's report further states that it considers in its approach the obviousness of existence of a stereoisomer as one of viewpoints (the obviousness referred to here corresponds to cases where, for instance, the existence of optical isomer is obvious due to the existence of asymmetric carbon atom as in the case of a simple optical isomer). There was no reference made on this point in the reports of EPO and USPTO.

C. Criteria for chemical processes; e.g. process producing known chemical product, old process using new starting materials, etc.

The practice applied by the JPO and EPO coincide in that a process claim based on a known reaction is considered as being inventive when, (1) the product obtained therefrom satisfies the requirements of patentability (expression used by each Office: JPO-chemical structure and properties; EPO-novelty and inventive step), or (2) The process itself, due to the specific means or conditions applied, produces an unexpected result. The USPTO practice is limited to the situation described in (2), above. That is, the process itself must be patentable and may not merely rely upon the recitation of a patentable product for patentability.

D. Other considerations to determine the inventive step in chemical practice

1. Secondary tests (subtests) of non-obviousness

All three Offices do not employ any secondary tests or subtests different from those applied in other technical fields in judging inventive step in the chemical field.

2. Extent to which comparative tests are required

All three Offices include comparative tests as a measure in judgement of inventive step.

[(a)] Requirement of comparative test

Comparative tests are required when the difference in effect between the invention and known art must be clarified, such as in the case of an improvement invention (JPO's report), or when the difference in effect from known art must be clarified and no other evidence is available to support the existence of inventive step (EPO's report). Although USPTO's report mentions that there are no requirements to submit comparative tests, there is no substantial difference among the three Offices, considering another USPTO mention that comparative tests are usually submitted as rebuttal evidence.

[(b)]Art to be compared

The reports of EPO and USPTO state that the claimed invention should be compared against the closest prior art. The same applies to JPO also. . . .

§ 2.07 Scope of Rights

Patent law confers on the owner of the patent a limited right to exclude others from making, using, offering for sale, selling, or importing a product or process covered by the patent, in exchange for the patent owner disclosing the invention to the world. The grant of the patent right to exclude is limited in time, place, and manner. The Patent and Copyright Clause of the U.S. Constitution, explicitly establishes that the grant of the "exclusive right" be "for limited times." Until recently, there was no international standard, either by agreement or custom, on the term of a patent. (The U.S. adopted a term of 17 years, apocryphally explained as a compromise between two terms (14 years) and three terms (21 years) of an apprenticeship. Costa Rica had a term of 1 year on patents for pharmaceuticals!). But since the enactment of the TRIPS Agreement, "the term of patent protection available shall not end before the expiration of a period of twenty years counted from the filing date" for all WTO Members. See TRIPS Agreement, Art. 33. Trees and vines are protected under the most recent breeder's rights protection agreement for 25 years. See International Convention For The Protection Of New Varieties Of Plants [UPOV] (1991 Act), art. 20. As noted above, the Australian "innovation patent" is protected for eight years. But disputes over patent term have not totally vanished. The Appellate Body of the WTO dispute settlement body issued a report in September 2000 finding Canada in violation of its TRIPS obligation by failing to make available a minimum of 20 years of protection for patents filed before October, 1989. *See Canada-Patent Protection Term, infra* § 4.04.

NOTE: INFRINGEMENT: LITERAL AND UNDER THE DOCTRINE OF EQUIVALENTS

As discussed above, full disclosure of the patented invention requires claims "particularly pointing out and distinctly claiming the subject matter which the applicant regards as his invention," (35 U.S.C. § 112, para. 2) to provide the competitor with certainty as to what is or is not excluded from the purview of its making, using (usually a process), selling and importing activities. The following reading discusses the scope of patent protection under the doctrine of equivalents, where a competitor may be found to infringe even where its activities lie outside the language of the claims.

DONALD S. CHISUM, THE SCOPE OF PROTECTION FOR PATENTS AFTER THE SUPREME COURT'S WARNER-JENKINSON DECISION: THE FAIR PROTECTION—CERTAINTY CONUNDRUM *
14 SANTA CLARA COMP. & HIGH TECH. L.J. 1, 3 (1998)

The Supreme Court's March 3, 1997 decision in Warner-Jenkinson Co., Inc. v. Hilton Davis Chemical Co. is a major step forward in bring greater certainty to the difficult process of determining the proper scope of protection for patents. Unlike prior landmark decisions on this subject, *Warner-Jenkinson* was a unanimous decision, which enhances its potential for stabilizing the law. However, the decision not only fails to solve all existing problems within the law of patent infringement, but also raises some new questions that only subsequent developments in case law can answer.

Recognizing the interest of existing patent owners in a fair scope of protection, the Supreme Court declined to "speak the death" of the "doctrine of equivalents," which has been applied by the courts since 1853, and confirmed by the Court in the 1950 *Graver Tank* decision. Under the doctrine, a "product or process that does not literally infringe upon the express terms of a patent claim may nonetheless be found to infringe if there is 'equivalence' between the elements of the accused product or process and the claimed elements of the patented invention." Abolishing the doctrine or limiting it severely by confining it to equivalents known at the time a patent issues, or by confining it to cases of intentional infringement, or by applying a rigid rule of estoppel whenever the patentee amended a claim might provide "brighter lines" in determining infringement, but would "change so substantially the rules of the game" as to "subvert" the various balances the PTO [Patent and Trademark Office] sought to strike when issuing the numerous patents which have not yet

---

* Reprinted with permission.

expired. . . . " Instead, the Court adopted an objective test of equivalency that is applied to each claim element, leaving to the Federal Circuit the task of developing the linguistic framework of equivalency.

On the other hand, the Supreme Court acknowledged concerns that the doctrine of equivalents "has taken on a life of its own" and "when applied, broadly conflicts with the definitional and public-notice functions of the statutory claiming requirement." To address these concerns, the Court adopted an element-by-element approach to the doctrine of equivalents as opposed to the overall approach previously administered by the Court. The decision emphasized that courts should exercise "a special vigilance against allowing the concept of equivalence to eliminate completely any such elements." *Warner-Jenkinson* also confirmed "prosecution history estoppel" as a limitation on equivalency. Although estoppel is not governed by a rigid rule precluding equivalency, whenever a claim is amended during prosecution there is a presumption that the amendment was made because an issue related to patentability existed. This presumption is rebutted if a patentee shows "an appropriate reason for a required amendment.

The *Warner-Jenkinson* decision does not resolve the issue regarding the role of juries in determining equivalency. The Supreme Court merely notes that there is ample authority supporting the Federal Circuit decision which states that disputed fact issues on equivalency are for resolution by a jury. But the Court does offer guidance on how to reduce concerns about unreviewability due to "black box jury verdicts." First and foremost, the limitations on equivalency, including prosecution history estoppel and whether the patentee's theory of equivalency would vitiate a claim element, are for resolution by the court presiding over the case. However, the Supreme Court encourages the Federal Circuit to "implement procedural improvements to promote certainty, consistency, and reviewability to this area of the law." Procedures for sifting out unsupported or inappropriate charges of infringement under the doctrine of equivalents should work in tandem with the procedures already being developed in the district courts to implement the Supreme Court's earlier decision in *Markman*, which held that patent claim construction is a question of law for resolution by a judge, not a jury.

. . .

The most important issue in intellectual property is the scope of protection: given that an intellectual property right exists, to what does it extend? This is true for all the species of intellectual property, including copyright, trademark, trade secret, and patent. For example, granted that there is a trademark property interest in the mark "McDonald's" for fast food restaurant services, what marks fall within the scope of right: McDonnell for fast food? McDevitt? Donald? If there were a current copyright on the play Romeo and Juliet, what dramatic works would fall within its scope: all plays that involve young lovers from warring families regardless of historical epoch, including West Side Story?

In addressing the preeminently important scope of protection issue, patent law is unique among intellectual rights in that it has long required the inventor to set forth a precise, fixed verbal definition of the patented invention, the definition taking the form of a "claim."

In the United States, patent infringement is defined by statute as the making, using, selling, offering for sale, or importing of a patented invention in the United States during the term of the patent without authority of the patent owner. Though the statute does not expressly so state, the "patented invention" is determined by reference to the claims of the patent. This is a natural inference from the statutory requirement that the specification of the patent "conclude with one or more claims particularly pointing out and distinctly claiming the subject matter which the applicant regards as his invention."

That the claims should be clear and should control the determination of infringement has been emphasized by the Supreme Court for over a century. In an 1877 decision, for example, the Court stressed that "nothing can be more just and fair both to the patentee and to the public, than that the former should understand and correctly describe just what he has invented and for what he claims a patent."

Although the courts have consistently recognized the importance of clear claiming, they have also been unwilling to confine patentees to the strict literal wording of their claims and have found infringement under some circumstances when an accused infringer has adopted an equivalent structure of process. This willingness to extend the scope of a patent beyond the literal language of the patent claims is known as the doctrine of equivalents. Judge Learned Hand referred to the doctrine as an anomaly:

> [A]fter all aids to interpretation have been exhausted, and the scope of the claims has been enlarged as far as the words can be stretched, on proper occasions courts make them cover more than their meaning will bear. If they applied the law with inexorable rigidity, they would never do this, but would remit the patentee to his remedy of re-issue, and that is exactly what they frequently do. Not always, however, for at times they resort to the "doctrine of equivalents" to temper unsparing logic and prevent an infringer from stealing the benefit of the invention. No doubt, this is, strictly speaking, an anomaly; but it is one which courts have frankly faced and accepted almost from the beginning.

Underlying the anomalous doctrine and the related doctrine of prosecution history estoppel is a policy dilemma. To coin a phrase, this dilemma can be termed as the "Fair Protection-Certainty Conundrum," which is inherent in any patent system that requires a fixed, written description of the invention (i.e., a "claim"). There is clearly an interest in providing a clear definition of the scope of the patent right; lack of clarity can impede legitimate investment in technology-based products and services. On the other hand, strict and literal adherence to the written claim in determining the scope of protection can invite subversion of a valuable right and substantially diminish the economic value of patents. Claims are often written by people with limited resources and time, imperfect expression skills, and incomplete understandings of the invention, the prior art that determines its patentability, and the forms in which it may later be cast.

The Conundrum was most clearly and directly confronted in Europe in the 1970s during the process of harmonizing the patent laws of the European nations. Traditionally, the United Kingdom focused heavily on claim language while Germany emphasized the nature of the underlying invention. Reconciling these views was a considerable problem in drafting the European Patent Convention. Article 69 of the Convention provides that the "extent of the protection conferred by a European patent . . . shall be determined by the terms of the claims" and that "[n]evertheless, the description and drawings shall be used to interpret the claims." The parties adopted a "Protocol on the Interpretation of Article 69 of the Convention," which states the following:

> Article 69 should not be interpreted in the sense that the extent of the protection conferred by a European patent is to be understood as that defined by the strict literal meaning of the wording used in the claim, the description and drawings being employed only for the purpose of resolving an ambiguity found in the claims. Neither should it be interpreted in the sense that the claims serve only as a guideline and that the actual protection conferred may extend to what, from a consideration of the description and drawings by a person skilled in the art, the patentee has contemplated. On the contrary, it is to be interpreted as divining a position between these extremes which combines a fair protection for the patentee with a reasonable degree of certainty for third parties" is the same goal the better-reasoned court decisions in the United States have sought to achieve. . . .

FESTO CORP. v. SHOKETSU KINZOKU KOGYO KABUSHIKI CO., LTD., ET AL.
122 S.Ct. 1831 (2002)

JUSTICE KENNEDY delivered the opinion of the Court.

This case requires us to address once again the relation between two patent law concepts, the doctrine of equivalents and the rule of prosecution history estoppel. The Court considered the same concepts in Warner-Jenkinson Co. v. Hilton Davis Chemical Co., 520 U.S. 17 (1997), and reaffirmed that a patent protects its holder against efforts of copyists to evade liability for infringement by making only insubstantial changes to a patented invention. At the same time, we appreciated that by extending protection beyond the literal terms in a patent the doctrine of equivalents can create substantial uncertainty about where the patent monopoly ends.

[cit.] If the range of equivalents is unclear, competitors may be unable to determine what is a permitted alternative to a patented invention and what is an infringing equivalent.

To reduce the uncertainty, *Warner-Jenkinson* acknowledged that competitors may rely on the prosecution history, the public record of the patent proceedings. In some cases the Patent and Trademark Office (PTO) may have rejected an earlier version of the patent application on the ground that a claim does not meet a statutory requirement for patentability. . . .When the patentee responds to the rejection by narrowing his claims, this prosecution history estops him from later arguing that the subject matter covered by the original, broader claim was nothing more than an equivalent. Competitors may rely on the estoppel to ensure that their own devices will not be found to infringe by equivalence.

In the decision now under review the Court of Appeals for the Federal Circuit held that by narrowing a claim to obtain a patent, the patentee surrenders all equivalents to the amended claim element. Petitioner asserts this holding departs from past precedent in two respects. First, it applies estoppel to every amendment made to satisfy the requirements of the Patent Act and not just to amendments made to avoid pre-emption by an earlier invention, i.e., the prior art. Second, it holds that when estoppel arises, it bars suit against every equivalent to the amended claim element. The Court of Appeals acknowledged that this holding departed from its own cases, which applied a flexible bar when considering what claims of equivalence were estopped by the prosecution history. Petitioner argues that by replacing the flexible bar with a complete bar the Court of Appeals cast doubt on many existing patents that were amended during the application process when the law, as it then stood, did not apply so rigorous a standard.

We granted certiorari to consider these questions. . . .

II

The patent laws "promote the Progress of Science and useful Arts" by rewarding innovation with a temporary monopoly. U.S. Const., Art. I, § 8, cl. 8. The monopoly is a property right; and like any property right, its boundaries should be clear. This clarity is essential to promote progress, because it enables efficient investment in innovation. A patent holder should know what he owns, and the public should know what he does not. For this reason, the patent laws require inventors to describe their work in "full, clear, concise, and exact terms," 35 U.S.C. § 112, as part of the delicate balance the law attempts to maintain between inventors, who rely on the promise of the law to bring the invention forth, and the public, which should be encouraged to pursue innovations, creations, and new ideas beyond the inventor's exclusive rights. [cit.]

Unfortunately, the nature of language makes it impossible to capture the essence of a thing in a patent application. The inventor who chooses to patent an invention and disclose it to the public, rather than exploit it in secret, bears the risk that others will devote their efforts toward exploiting the limits of the patent's language:

> "An invention exists most importantly as a tangible structure or a series of drawings. A verbal portrayal is usually an afterthought written to satisfy the requirements of patent law. This conversion of machine to words allows for unintended idea gaps which cannot be satisfactorily filled. Often the invention is novel and words do not exist to describe it. The dictionary does not always keep abreast of the inventor. It cannot. Things are not made for the sake of words, but words for things." Autogiro Co. of America v. United States, 181 Ct.Cl. 55, 384 F.2d 391, 397 (1967).

The language in the patent claims may not capture every nuance of the invention or describe with complete precision the range of its novelty. If patents were always interpreted by their literal terms, their value would be greatly diminished. Unimportant and insubstantial substitutes for certain elements could defeat the patent, and its value to inventors could be destroyed by simple acts of copying. For this reason, the clearest rule of patent interpretation, literalism, may conserve judicial resources but is not necessarily the most efficient rule. The scope of a patent is not limited to its literal terms but instead embraces all equivalents to the claims described. See Winans v. Denmead, 56 U.S. (15 How.) 330, 347, 14 L.Ed. 717 (1854).

It is true that the doctrine of equivalents renders the scope of patents less certain. It may be difficult to determine what is, or is not, an equivalent to a particular element of an invention. If competitors cannot be certain about a patent's extent, they may be deterred from engaging in legitimate manufactures outside its limits, or they may invest by mistake in competing products that the patent secures. In addition the uncertainty may lead to wasteful litigation between competitors, suits that a rule of literalism might avoid. These concerns with the doctrine of equivalents, however, are not new. Each time the Court has considered the doctrine, it has acknowledged this uncertainty as the price of ensuring the appropriate incentives for innovation, and it has affirmed the doctrine over dissents that urged a more certain rule. When the Court in *Winans* . . . first adopted what has become the doctrine of equivalents, it stated that "[t]he exclusive right to the thing patented is not secured, if the public are at liberty to make substantial copies of it, varying its form or proportions." . . .

The debate continued in Graver Tank & Mfg. Co. v. Linde Air Products Co., 339 U.S. 605 (1950), where the Court . . . held that patent claims must protect the inventor not only from those who produce devices falling within the literal claims of the patent but also from copyists who "make unimportant and insubstantial changes and substitutions in the patent which, though adding nothing, would be enough to take the copied matter outside the claim, and hence outside the reach of law." . . . Justice Black, in dissent, objected that under the doctrine of equivalents a competitor "cannot rely on what the language of a patent claims. He must be able, at the peril of heavy infringement damages, to forecast how far a court relatively unversed in a particular technological field will expand the claim's language . . . " [cit.]

Most recently, in *Warner-Jenkinson*, the Court reaffirmed that equivalents remain a firmly entrenched part of the settled rights protected by the patent. A unanimous opinion concluded that if the doctrine is to be discarded, it is Congress and not the Court that should do so:

> "[T]he lengthy history of the doctrine of equivalents strongly supports adherence to our refusal in *Graver Tank* to find that the Patent Act conflicts with that doctrine. Congress can legislate the doctrine of equivalents out of existence any time it chooses. The various policy arguments now made by both sides are thus best addressed to Congress, not this Court." [cit.]

III

. . . The doctrine of equivalents allows the patentee to claim those insubstantial alterations that were not captured in drafting the original patent claim but which could be created through trivial changes. When, however, the patentee originally claimed the subject matter alleged to infringe but then narrowed the claim in response to a rejection, he may not argue that the surrendered territory comprised unforeseen subject matter that should be deemed equivalent to the literal claims of the issued patent. On the contrary, "[b]y the amendment [the patentee] recognized and emphasized the difference between the two phrases[,] . . . and [t]he difference which [the patentee] thus disclaimed must be regarded as material." [cit.] . . .

Prosecution history estoppel ensures that the doctrine of equivalents remains tied to its underlying purpose. Where the original application once embraced the purported equivalent but the patentee narrowed his claims to obtain the patent or to protect its validity, the patentee cannot assert that he lacked the words to describe the subject matter in question. The doctrine of equivalents is premised on language's inability to capture the essence of innovation, but a prior application describing the precise element at issue undercuts that premise. In that instance the prosecution history has established that the inventor turned his attention to the subject matter in question, knew the words for both the broader and narrower claim, and affirmatively chose the latter.

A

The first question in this case concerns the kinds of amendments that may give rise to estoppel. Petitioner argues that estoppel should arise when amendments are intended to narrow the subject matter of the patented invention, for instance, amendments to avoid prior art, but not when the amendments are made to comply with requirements concerning the form of the patent application. . . . Petitioner is correct that estoppel has been discussed most often in the context of amendments made to avoid the prior art. . . . It does not follow, however, that amendments for other purposes will not give rise to estoppel. Prosecution history may rebut the inference that a thing not described was indescribable. That rationale does not cease simply because the narrowing amendment, submitted to secure a patent, was for some purpose other than avoiding prior art.

We agree with the Court of Appeals that a narrowing amendment made to satisfy any requirement of the Patent Act may give rise to an estoppel. As that court explained, a number of statutory requirements must be satisfied before a patent can issue. The claimed subject matter must be useful, novel, and not obvious. 35 U.S.C. §§ 101-103 In addition, the patent application must describe, enable, and set forth the best mode of carrying out the invention. § 112 . . . What is claimed by the patent application must be the same as what is disclosed in the specification; otherwise the patent should not issue. The patent also should not issue if the other requirements of § 112 are not satisfied, and an applicant's failure to meet these requirements could lead to the issued patent being held invalid in later litigation. . . .

B

. . . Our conclusion that prosecution history estoppel arises when a claim is narrowed to comply with § 112 gives rise to the second question presented: Does the estoppel bar the inventor from asserting infringement against any equivalent to the narrowed element or might some equivalents still infringe? . . . Though prosecution history estoppel can bar challenges to a wide range of equivalents, its reach requires an examination of the subject matter surrendered by the narrowing amendment. The complete bar avoids this inquiry by establishing a per se rule; but that approach is inconsistent with the purpose of applying the estoppel in the first place—to hold the inventor to the representations made during the application process and to the inferences that may reasonably be drawn from the amendment. By amending the application, the inventor is deemed to concede that the patent does not extend as far as the original claim. It does not follow, however, that the amended claim becomes so perfect in its description that no one could devise an equivalent. After amendment, as before, language remains an imperfect fit for invention. The narrowing amendment may demonstrate what the claim is not; but it may still fail to capture precisely what the claim is. There is no reason why a narrowing amendment should be deemed to relinquish equivalents unforeseeable at the time of the amendment and beyond a fair interpretation of what was surrendered. Nor is there any call to foreclose claims of equivalence for aspects of the invention that have only a peripheral relation to the reason the amendment was submitted. The amendment does not show that the inventor suddenly had more foresight in the drafting of claims than an inventor whose application was granted without amendments having been submitted. It shows only that he was familiar with the broader text and with the difference between the two. As a result, there is no more reason for holding the patentee to the literal terms of an amended claim than there is for abolishing the doctrine of equivalents altogether and holding every patentee to the literal terms of the patent.

This view of prosecution history estoppel is consistent with our precedents and respectful of the real practice before the PTO. . . . The Court of Appeals ignored the guidance of *Warner-Jenkinson*, which instructed that courts must be cautious before adopting changes that disrupt the settled expectations of the inventing community. [cit.] [T]he doctrine of equivalents and the rule of prosecution history estoppel are settled law. The responsibility for changing them rests with Congress. Fundamental alterations in these rules risk destroying the legitimate expectations of inventors in their property. . . . As *Warner-Jenkinson* recognized, patent prosecution occurs in the light of our case law. Inventors who amended their claims under the previous regime had no reason to believe they were conceding all equivalents. If they had known, they might have appealed the rejection instead. There is no justification for applying a new and more robust estoppel to those who relied on prior doctrine.

In *Warner-Jenkinson* we struck the appropriate balance by placing the burden on the patentee to show that an amendment was not for purposes of patentability:

> "Where no explanation is established, however, the court should presume that the patent application had a substantial reason related to patentability for including the limiting element added by amendment. In those circumstances, prosecution history estoppel would bar the application of the doctrine of equivalents as to that element."[cit.]

. . . Just as *Warner-Jenkinson* held that the patentee bears the burden of proving that an amendment was not made for a reason that would give rise to estoppel, we hold here that the patentee should bear the burden of showing that the amendment does not surrender the particular equivalent in question. . . . The patentee, as the author of the claim language, may be expected to draft claims encompassing readily known equivalents. A patentee's decision to narrow his claims through amendment may be presumed to be a general disclaimer of the territory between the original claim and the amended claim. . . . There are some cases, however, where the amendment cannot reasonably be viewed as surrendering a particular equivalent. The equivalent may have been unforeseeable at the time of the application; the rationale underlying the amendment may bear no more than a tangential relation to the equivalent in question; or there may be some other reason suggesting that the patentee could not reasonably be expected to have described the insubstantial substitute in question. In those cases the patentee can overcome the presumption that prosecution history estoppel bars a finding of equivalence.

This presumption is not, then, just the complete bar by another name. Rather, it reflects the fact that the interpretation of the patent must begin with its literal claims, and the prosecution history is relevant to construing those claims. When the patentee has chosen to narrow a claim, courts may presume the amended text was composed with awareness of this rule and that the territory surrendered is not an equivalent of the territory claimed. In those instances, however, the patentee still might rebut the presumption that estoppel bars a claim of equivalence. The patentee must show that at the time of the amendment one skilled in the art could not reasonably be expected to have drafted a claim that would have literally encompassed the alleged equivalent. . . .

The judgment of the Federal Circuit is vacated, and the case is remanded for further proceedings consistent with this opinion.

NOTES AND QUESTIONS

(1) *Festo* **Changes the Rules, Somewhat. . .** The Federal Circuit, in its *Festo* opinion, had opted (in the parlance of Chisum's conundrum) strongly for the "certainty" rule. The Supreme Court agreed that every claim-narrowing amendment designed to comply with any provision of the Patent Act automatically created prosecution history estoppel regardless of the reason for the amendment, but stopping short of a complete bar, continued, "There is no reason why a narrowing amendment should be deemed to relinquish equivalents unforeseeable at the time of the amendment and beyond a fair interpretation of what was surrendered. Nor is there any call to foreclose claims of equivalence for aspects of the invention that have only a peripheral relation to the reason the amendment was submitted." In a concurring opinion in *Johnson & Johnston Assocs., v. R.E.Serv. Co.*, 285 F.3d 1046 (Fed. Cir. 2002), an *en banc* decision issued two month's prior to the Supreme Court's May 28, 2002 decision, Judge Rader had offered the following "reconciling principle":

> This reconciling principle is simple: the doctrine of equivalents does not capture subject matter that the patent drafter could have foreseen during the application process and included in the claims. This principle enhances the notice function of claims by making them the sole definition of invention scope in all foreseeable circumstances. This principle also protects patentees against copyists who employ insubstantial variations to expropriate the claimed invention in some unforeseeable circumstances. . . . Foreseeability relegates non-textual infringement to its appropriate exceptional place in patent policy.

The scope of the doctrine of equivalents and "non-textual infringement" are considered further in Chapter 7 in the context of enforcing a European Patent.

(2) **Doctrine of Equivalents in International Perspective.** An excellent survey of the international scene on the doctrine of equivalents is found in the symposium volume, INTERNATIONAL PERSPECTIVES ON INTELLECTUAL PROPERTY: THE DOCTRINE OF EQUIVALENTS 1-166 (Kraig Hill and Toshiko Takenaka eds. 1997).

§ 2.08   Utility Models

REPORT ON THE INTRODUCTION OF NEW AND HARMONIZATION OF THE EXISTING UTILITY MODEL PROTECTION SYSTEMS
AIPPI Committee 117 Report 100–106

At the meeting of the Executive Committee in Rio in 1985 and at the London Congress in 1986, under the reference Question Q 83, AIPPI had declared itself in favour of the institution of a utility model system, arguing strongly in support of its position, and had laid down the different conditions under which that title could be granted, in comparison with patents.

This title should be granted quickly, without examination, at lower cost, and should have limited duration relative to the life of a patent. However, the London Congress had not been able to express views on the criteria relating to a utility model in comparison with a patent.

It is this study that the meeting of the executive committee in Copenhagen in 1994 undertook, on the basis of 23 reports from the National Groups. The discussion in Copenhagen showed up [sic] major divergences and the draft resolution from the Working committee was not adopted.

It was decided that the work should be continued at the Montreal Congress, and an additional working guidelines document was sent to the Groups. The Reporter General received 21 reports from the Groups from: Australia, Austria, Belgium, Canada, Denmark, Egypt, Finland, France, Germany, Great Britain [sic], Hungary, Ireland, Italy, Japan, Mexico, Netherlands, Norway, Spain, Sweden, Switzerland, and the United States. . . .

1. The question is not to express a view on the institution of a utility model in the different countries. Nowadays the utility model is a legal reality. It is a title whose existence is established and recognised by virtue of Article 1, paragraph 2 of the Paris Convention. It has been in existence for a century in a number of industrial countries and many countries have recently adopted it or modified the rules thereof. Finally, in 1985 and 1986, AIPPI stated that it was in favour of the institution of the utility model. It is to be noted that the Group from the United States and the French Group are markedly hostile to the adoption of the utility model system in their respective countries. In their view, such a system would give rise to the risk of weakening the system of protection by means of patents. As regards the British Group, while acknowledging that in London in 1986,

they were in favour of the utility model, this Group is now indicating that it has changed its view and it does not consider that the adoption of such a system is desirable.

I. Inventions which can be protected by a utility model.

1. A minority of Groups which however argued strongly in support of their position take the view that utility models should be applied only to three-dimensional articles and not to chemical and pharmaceutical products and processes. This is the opinion held by the Egyptian, Italian, Swedish, and Swiss Groups, for different reasons. In the report presented in Copenhagen, the Spanish Group had expressed the same view.

Reference may be made in particular to the reports from the Swedish and Swiss Groups which set out very clearly the reasons for refusing to apply utility models to inventions covered by long and complex claims which are therefore difficult to understand. A utility model should be reserved for inventions which are easy to understand and which in particular can be clearly set forth by drawings. Moreover the very expression "model" shows that this involves a three-dimensional article.

2. On the other hand, the majority of Groups take the view that there is no justification for such discrimination between inventions, and that all inventions which are capable of being patented should enjoy the benefit of protection by means of a utility model if it were set up. . . . Those Groups (on the whole) consider that some mechanical inventions can be very complicated and that in any case the informed public to which the utility model is addressed must be capable of understanding its scope, irrespective of the nature of the invention. Broadly speaking, there would not be any decisive reasons for refusing the benefit of this title to some industries such as the chemical and pharmaceutical industries.

In some areas, even those involving high technology, small improvements can be made and should also be able to enjoy the benefit of utility model protection. The Japanese Group recalls that, for historical reasons in Japan, only external features and shapes can be protected by a utility model and that no need has been found in Japan for that protection to be extended to all categories of inventions. If such an extension were to occur, it would then be appropriate to change the actual name of utility "model" which evokes a three-dimensional article.

The German Group gives a historical account of the institution of a utility model in Germany and then the modifications thereto; in 1891 the utility model was effectively set up to fill the gap between patents and ornamental models and to protect functional inventions which are easy to understand by means of a drawing, that is to say three-dimensional articles; a century later, in 1990, utility model protection was extended to all products including chemical and pharmaceutical products, but it does not permit protection for processes; incidentally, the German Group is critical of that exclusion and wants to see the utility model applied to all areas.

The Netherlands Group notes that the reply depends on the aim sought to be attained by the institution of the utility model. If a utility model is subject to the same conditions as a patent and if its sole aim is to obtain quick and economical protection, there would then not be any reason to refuse the application thereof to all inventions. If however, the conditions relating to protection by means of a utility model are pitched lower than the criteria required for patentability, then the institution of such a title could turn out to be dangerous, in particular in certain areas such as the chemical or pharmaceutical industries, be establishing unjustified monopolies. It is noteworthy that on this point the view of the Netherlands Group lies with that of the Italian Group which is in principle against extending utility models to inventions which do not constitute three-dimensional articles.

II. Are the criteria for inventions covered by utility models to differ from the criteria for a patentable invention?

The reflections from the Netherlands Group raise the question of whether the ultimate aim of a utility model is to cover inventions corresponding to the criteria required in respect of a patent, but by way of a title which is granted quickly and economically; or, on the contrary, whether a utility model is to be such as to cover inventions which would not comply with the criteria of patentability. The Canadian Group points out that, if the level of validity of a utility model is too high, there is no attraction in setting up such a title in addition to a patent. This appears to be the opinion of the other Groups who, generally speaking, agree that a criterion different to that of a patent should be sought for a utility model.

III. The validity criteria of a utility model.

1. Generally speaking, the Groups confirm that they are in favour of the criterion of absolute novelty, except for the Australian and British Groups who want simple use abroad not to be taken into consideration in relation to novelty. After having pointed out that in Germany use abroad is not relied upon as destroying novelty, the German Group expressed the view that nowadays the appropriate course is to adopt the criterion of absolute novelty, combined with a grace period.

2. However, all of the Groups except for the Mexican Group consider that simple novelty would not be sufficient and that an additional condition is to be required. It is about the formulation of the additional condition that the Executive Committee meeting in Copenhagen was divided.

   a).   The Swiss and Austrian Groups proposed as the relevant criterion a non-trivial technical effect. The Italian Group proposed a non-trivial objective advance. . . . As for the Belgian Group, it considers that the criterion is to be that of inventive activity as is required in relation to a patent.

  b).   The Australian, British, Irish and Japanese Groups accept the
         criterion of reduced obviousness; an invention covered by a utility
         model is not to be clearly obvious.

  c).   However, the majority of Groups oppose the adoption of a crite-
         rion of reduced obviousness, often for very strongly argued
         reasons, on grounds which are both intellectual and practical.

First of all, they consider that there could not be several degrees of
obviousness: an invention either is or is not within the capability of the
man skilled in the art.

On the other hand, the adoption of such a criterion gives rise to the risk
of having an effect on application of the idea of obviousness in relation to
patents and in particular increasing the level of requirement in relation
to patentability; now in regard to patents, inventive activity is already
difficult to assess and the institution of two degrees of obviousness runs
the risk of further complicating the question of determining inventive
activity.

The Canadian, Egyptian, Danish, Finnish, French, Netherlands, Norwegian and Swedish Groups are in favour of a criterion which does not refer
to the idea of obviousness. In general, and except for minor editorial
differences, they approve the objective criterion proposed by the working
guidelines, which draws inspiration incidentally from a proposal put
forward by the Canadian Group in Copenhagen:

    "Any novel technical innovation which has significant differences
    in relation to the state of the art and which affords a practical
    advantage can be protected by a utility model."

This definition combines two objective criteria:

Firstly there must be a certain distance between the prior art and the
invention, but there will not be any reason to assess whether the invention
does or does not result from an intellectual effort or merit. Thus, the Court
will not have to consider how the inventor could have been led to make
the invention, but only has to ascertain the significant difference between
the prior art and the invention;

In addition the Court will have to consider if that difference it finds
affords an advantage.

The Netherlands Group pertinently observes that this advantage may
be not only of a technical nature but also of an economic or commercial
nature.

IV. Transformation of a patent into a utility model and vice-versa:

Numerous Groups have indicated that an inventor should be allowed to
choose the title by means of which he intends to protect his invention.
However, the question which then arises is whether he can transform a
patent application into a utility model and vice-versa.

1. All the Groups which replied to the question agree with the option of transformation of a patent application into a utility model, up to grant of the patent.

2. However, the Groups are totally divided on the option of transforming a utility model application into a patent. . . .

V. On the coexistence of the two titles for the same invention:

Some Groups finally considered the question of coexistence of the two titles, patent of invention and utility model, for the same invention. The question moreover gives rise to two problems:

1. Can an inventor make application for the two titles, utility model and patent, for the same invention, insofar as the invention complies with the criteria of a patent?

2. If the two titles are granted, can the proprietor enjoy the benefit of the combined protection? Or in contrast, can that combination exist only up to definitive grant of the patent? The Committee will be able to study this additional point and also propose a solution.

NOTES AND QUESTIONS

(1) **Inventiveness in Utility Patent Law.** One authority notes: "Amongst the countries now collaborating in the EPC, a particularly stringent test of 'inventiveness' seems previously to have prevailed in the Netherlands and Switzerland; while in West Germany talk of a 'level of invention' together with the separate protection of utility models (a form of petty patent) that in theory at least need not reach the same inventive level, creates an impression that there, too, rather more has been required. The EPO has indicated that it aims for a middle level (roughly equivalent to that of German practice), rather than adopt the particularly favorable attitude toward applicants that has characterised British pre-grant procedure under the 1949 Act." CORNISH, *supra* at 128. A critical discussion both of the interrelationships between standards of patentability and kinds of patents available (utility patents, utility models, petty patents, and design patents, *inter alia*) and of recent proposals appears in Mark D. Janis, *Second Tier Patent Protection*, 40 HARV. J. INT'L L. 151 (1999).

(2) **The Purpose of Utility Model Protection.** Does utility model protection promote "progress?" Utility models are sometimes called "petty patents." Do some of the controversies over the nature and purpose of utility model protection mentioned in the AIPPI report have to do with the problem the U.S. Supreme Court addressed in *Graham v. Deere*? If so, would that make the lack of enthusiasm for utility models in the United States more understandable? Are utility models merely "watered down" patents? In some countries, such as Japan, many more utility model applications are

filed than patents for invention (which are confusingly called "utility patents" in the United States). Are they merely a means for an inventor who cannot meet the standards of patents for invention to acquire recognition in *some* form (and coincidentally, allow patent solicitors and patent offices to collect fees)? Or does protection for utility models serve a more valuable public purpose? *See generally* Mark D. Janis, *Second Tier Patent Protection*, 40 HARV. J. INT'L L. 151 (1999).

(3) **What are "Innovation Patents?"** In May, 2001, the Australian Innovation Patents Act came into effect, replacing the existing "petty patent" system. The term of protection is eight years. Applications are examined for compliance with formalities only. Innovation patents may not be enforced until they have been examined. The object of the innovation patent is to "stimulate innovation activity" by protecting incremental inventions. The new innovation patent has been criticized for possibly bringing more confusion over what is and what is not protected and for encouraging inventors to apply simultaneously for standard and innovation patents. Is then, an innovation patent, or rather the *idea* of an innovation patent, likely to serve the stated policy purpose? *See* Patent Amendment Act Will Enter Into Force in May, 15 W.I.P.R. 3 (Feb. 2001).

§ 2.09   Trade Secrets

The basic principles of the law of confidence, as it is known in the United Kingdom based upon the fiduciary duty of employees, or the law of trade secrets as the term is used in the U.S. to refer to intellectual property, vary greatly between jurisdictions. The passage of the Uniform Trade Secrets Act in most of the states of the United States has gone some way to reducing similar disparities within the United States. The first reading sets forth the modern view of trade secrets in the United States as established by the United States Supreme Court.

KEWANEE OIL v. BICRON
416 U.S. 470 (1974)

MR. CHIEF JUSTICE BURGER delivered the opinion of the Court.

[The plaintiff developed a process used in the growth of extremely large crystals. Employees of the plaintiff, having previously executed as a condition of employment at least one agreement each requiring them not to disclose confidential information or trade secrets obtained as employees of the plaintiff, left to join a competing firm. Within several months, the competing firm had produced a crystal of the same size as had been developed by the plaintiff. The plaintiff brought in action in federal district court under Ohio trade secret law. The court granted a permanent injunction against the disclosure or use by the employees of many of the claimed trade secrets until such time as the trade secrets had been released to the public, had otherwise generally become available to the public, or had been obtained by respondents from sources having the legal right to convey the information. The Court of Appeals for the Sixth Circuit held that the findings of fact by the District Court were not clearly erroneous, and that it was evident from the record that the employees appropriated to the benefit of the competing firm secret information on processes obtained while they were employees at the plaintiff. Further, the Court of Appeals held that the District Court properly applied Ohio law relating to trade secrets. Nevertheless, the Court of Appeals reversed the District Court, finding Ohio's trade secret law to be in conflict with the patent laws of the United States. The Court of Appeals reasoned that Ohio could not grant monopoly protection to processes and manufacturing techniques that were appropriate subjects for consideration under 35 U.S.C. § 101 for a federal patent but which had been in commercial use for over one year and so were no longer eligible for patent protection under 35 U.S.C. § 102(b). The U.S. Supreme Court thus considered the question of whether Ohio trade secret law should be preempted under the Supremacy Clause. This required the Court to consider whether the trade secret law of Ohio stood as an obstacle to the accomplishment and execution of the full purposes and objectives of Congress. The Court concluded that it did not, and reversed the Sixth Circuit.]

II

Ohio has adopted the widely relied-upon definition of a trade secret found at Restatement of Torts Section 757, Comment b (1939). . . . According to the Restatement

> (a) a trade secret may consist of any formula, pattern, device, or compilation of information which is used in one's business, and which gives him an opportunity to obtain an advantage over competitors who do not know or use it. It may be a formula for a chemical compound, a process of manufacturing, treating or preserving materials, a pattern for a machine or other device, or a list of customers.

The subject of a trade secret must be secret, and must not be of public knowledge or of a general knowledge in the trade secret or business. . . . This necessary element of secrecy is not lost, however, if the holder of the trade secret reveals the trade secret to another "in confidence, and under an implied obligation not to use or disclose it." . . . These others may include those of the holder's "employees to whom it is necessary to confide it, in order to apply it to the uses for which it is intended.". . . . Often the recipient of confidential knowledge of the subject of a trade secret is a licensee of its holder. . . .

The protection accorded the trade secret holder is against the disclosure or unauthorized use of the trade secret by those to whom the secret has been confided under the express or implied restriction of nondisclosure or nonuse. The law also protects the holder of a trade secret against disclosure or use when the knowledge is gained, not by the owner's volition, but by some "improper means," Restatement Section 757(a), which may include theft, wiretapping, or even aerial reconnaissance. A trade secret law, however, does not offer protection against discovery by fair and honest means, such as by independent invention, accidental disclosure, or by so-called reverse engineering, that is by starting with the known product and working backward to divine the process which aided in its development or manufacture.

Novelty, in the patent law sense, is not required for a trade secret. . . . "Quite clearly discovery is something less than invention." . . . However, some novelty will be required if merely because that which does not possess novelty is usually known; secrecy, in the context of trade secrets, thus implies at least minimal novelty.

The subject matter of a patent is limited to a "process, machine, manufacture, or composition of matter, or . . . improvement thereof," 35 U.S.C. § 101, which fulfills the three conditions of novelty and utility as articulated and defined in 35 U.S.C. §§ 101 and 102, and nonobviousness, as set out in 35 U.S.C. § 103. If an invention meets the rigorous statutory tests for the issuance of a patent, the patent is granted, for a period of 17 years, giving what has been described as the "right of exclusion." . . . This protection goes not only to copying the subject matter, which is forbidden under the Copyright Act, 17 U.S.C. §§ 101 et seq., but also to independent creation.

. . .

IV

. . .

The stated objective of the Constitution in granting the power to Congress to legislate in the area of intellectual property is to "promote the Progress of Science and useful Arts." The patent laws promote this progress by offering a right of exclusion for a limited period as an incentive to inventors to risk the often enormous costs in terms of time, research, and development. The productive effort thereby fostered will have a positive effect on society though the introduction of new products and processes of manufacture into the economy, and the emanations by way of increased employment and better lives for our citizens. In return for the right of exclusion—this "reward for inventions," . . . —the patent laws impose upon the inventor a requirement of disclosure. To insure adequate and full disclosure so that upon the expiration of the 17-year period "the knowledge of the invention enures to the people, who are thus enabled without restriction to practice it and profit by its use," . . . , the patent laws require that the patent application shall include a full and clear description of the invention and "of the manner and process of making and using it" so that any person skilled in the art may make and use the invention. 35 U.S.C. § 112. When a patent is granted and the information contained in it is circulated to the general public and those especially skilled in the trade, such additions to the general store of knowledge are of such importance to the public weal that the Federal Government is willing to pay the high price of 17 years of exclusive use for its disclosure, which disclosure, it is assumed, will stimulate ideas and the eventual development of further significant advances in the art. The Court has also articulated another policy of the patent law: that which is in the public domain cannot be removed therefrom by action of the states. . .

The maintenance of standards of commercial ethics and the encouragement of invention are the broadly stated policies behind trade secret law. "The necessity of good faith and honest, fair dealing, is the very life and spirit of the commercial world." . . . In A.O.Smith v. Petroleum Iron Works Co., 73 F.2d, at 539, the Court emphasized that even though a discovery may not be patentable, that does not

> destroy the value of the discovery to one who makes it, or advantage the competitor who by unfair means, or as the beneficiary of a broken faith, obtains the desired knowledge without himself paying the price in labor, money, or machines expended by the discoverer.

In Wexler v. Greenberg, 399 Pa. 569, 578–579 (1960), the Pennsylvania Supreme Court noted the importance of trade secret protection to the subsidization of research and development and to increased economic efficiency within large companies through the dispersion of responsibilities for creative developments.

Having now in mind the objectives of both the patent and trade secret law, we turn to an examination of the interaction of these systems of protection of intellectual property—one established by the Congress and the other by a State . . .

Certainly the patent policy of encouraging invention is not disturbed by the existence of another form of incentive to invention. In this respect the two systems are not and never would be in conflict. Similarly, the policy that matter once in the public domain must remain in the public domain is not incompatible with the existence of trade secret protection. By definition a trade secret has not been placed in the public domain. . . .

As to trade secret known not to meet the standards of patentability, very little in the way of disclosure would be accomplished by abolishing trade secret protection. With trade secrets of nonpatentable subject matter, the patent alternative would not reasonably be available to the inventor. . .

Nothing in the patent law requires that States refrain from action to prevent industrial espionage. In addition to the increased costs for protection from burglary, wire-tapping, bribery, and the other means used to misappropriate trade secrets, there is the inevitable cost to the basic decency of society when one firm steals from another. A most fundamental human right, that of privacy, is threatened when industrial espionage is condoned or is made profitable; the state interest in denying profit to such illegal ventures is unchallengeable.

The next category of patentable subject matter to deal with is the invention whose holder has a legitimate doubt as to its patentability. The risk of eventual patent invalidity by the courts and the costs associated with that risk may well impel some with a good-faith doubt as to patentability not to take the trouble to seek to obtain and defend patent protection for their discoveries, regardless of the existence of trade secret protection. Trade secret protection would assist those inventors in the more efficient exploitation of their discoveries and not conflict with the patent law . . . [T]hose who might be encouraged to file for patents by the absence of trade secret law will include inventors possessing the chaff as well as the wheat. Some of the chaff—the nonpatentable discoveries—will be thrown out by the Patent Office, but in the meantime society will have been deprived of use of those discoveries through trade secret-protected licensing. Some of the chaff may not be thrown out . . . More of those invalid patents would likely issue if trade secret law were abolished. Eliminating trade secret law for the doubtfully patentable invention is thus likely to have deleterious effects on society and patent policy which we cannot say are balanced out by the speculative gain which might result from the encouragement of some inventors with doubtfully patentable inventions which deserve patent protection to come forward and apply for patents. There is no conflict, then, between trade secret law and the patent law policy of disclosure, at least insofar as the first two categories of patentable subject matter are concerned.

The final category of patentable subject matter to deal with is the clearly patentable invention, i.e., that invention which the owner believes to meet the standards of patentability. It is here that the federal interest in disclosure is at its peak; these inventions, novel, useful and nonobvious, are "the things which are worth to the public the embarrassment of an exclusive patent." *Graham v. John Deere Co., supra.* (quoting Thomas Jefferson). The interest of the public is that the bargain of 17 years of exclusive use in return for disclosure be accepted. If a State, through a system of protection, were to cause a substantial risk that holders of patentable inventions would not seek patents, but rather would rely on the state protection, we would be compelled to hold that such a system could not constitutionally continue to exist. In the case of trade secret law no reasonable risk of deterrence from patent application by those who can reasonable expect to be granted patents exists.

Trade secret law provides far weaker protection in many respects than the patent law. While trade secret law does not forbid the discovery of the trade secret by fair and honest means, e.g., independent creation or reverse engineering, patent law operates "against the world," forbidding any use of the invention for whatever purpose for a significant length of time. The holder of a trade secret also takes a substantial risk that the secret will be passed on to his competitors, by theft or by breach of a confidential relationship, in a manner not easily susceptible of discovery or proof . . . Where patent law acts as a barrier, trade secret law functions relatively as a sieve. The possibility that an inventor who believes his invention meets the standards of patentability will sit back, rely on trade secret law, and after one year of use forfeit any right to patent protection, 35 U.S.C. Section 102(b) is remote indeed.

. . .

Trade secret law and patent law have co-existed in this country for over one hundred years. Each has its particular role to play, and the operation of one does not take away from the need for the other. Trade secret law encourages the development and exploitation of those items of lesser or different invention than might be accorded protection under the patent laws, but which items still have an important part to play in the technological and scientific advancement of the Nation. Trade secret law promotes the sharing of knowledge, and the efficient operation of industry; it permits the individual inventor to reap the rewards of his labor by contracting with a company large enough to develop and exploit it. Congress, by its silence over these many years, has seen the wisdom of allowing the States to enforce trade secret protection Until Congress takes affirmative action to the contrary, States should be free to grant protection to trade secrets.

. . .

KARL F. JORDA, THE PATENT/TRADE SECRET INTERFACE*
Germeshausen Center Newsletter Nos. 1–2 (1999)

[L]et me dispel . . . deep-seated misconceptions about the relationship between patents and trade secrets and level a lance in defense of trade secrets, the stepchild, the orphan in the IP family or the black sheep in the IP barnyard. Trade secrets are maligned as flying in the face of the patent system, the essence of which is disclosure of inventions to the public. Keeping inventions secret is, therefore, supposed to be reprehensible. One noted IP professor went even so far as to say "Trade secrets are the cesspool of the patent system."

Nothing could be further from the truth. Patents are but the tips of icebergs in a sea of trade secrets. Over 90% of all new technology is covered by trade secrets and over 80% of all license and technology transfer agreements cover proprietary know-how, i.e. trade secrets, or constitute hybrid agreements relating to patents and trade secrets. As a practical matter, licenses under patents without access to associated know-how are often not enough to use the patented technology. Bob Sherwood calls trade secrets the "workhorse of technology transfer." The quiet role they play in IP protection is thus deceiving.

Trade secrets are the first-line defense: they come before patents, go with patents, and follow patents. Patents and trade secrets are not mutually exclusive but actually highly complementary and mutually reinforcing; in fact, they dovetail. In this context, it should be kept in mind that our Supreme Court [in *Kewanee*] has recognized trade secrets as perfectly viable

---

* Reprinted with permission.

alternatives to patents: "the extension of trade secret protection to clearly patentable inventions does not conflict with the patent policy of disclosure") and further strengthened the bases for trade secret reliance in subsequent decisions (Aronson v. Quick Point Pencil (1979) and Bonito Boats v. Thunder Craft Boats (1989)). Interestingly, in his concurring opinion in the *Kewanee Oil* decision, Justice Marshall was "persuaded" that "Congress, in enacting the patent laws, intended merely to offer inventors a limited monopoly (*sic*) in exchange for disclosure of their inventions (rather than) to exert pressure on inventors to enter into this exchange by withdrawing any alternative possibility of legal protection for their inventions." Thus, it is clear that patents and trade secrets cannot only coexist, but are in harmony rather than in conflict with each other.

In the past — and even today — if trade secret maintenance was contemplated at all, e.g. for manufacturing process technology, which can be secreted unlike gadgets or machinery which upon sale can be reverse-engineered, the question always was phrased in the alternative (e.g., titles of articles discussing the matter read "Trade Secret vs. Patent Protection", "To patent or not to patent?", "Trade Secret or Patent?", etc.) I submit that it is not necessary and, in fact, shortsighted to choose one over the other. To me the question is not so much whether to patent or to padlock but rather what to patent and what to keep a trade secret and whether it is best to patent as well as to padlock, i.e. integrate patents and trade secrets for optimal protection of innovation.

Let me explain. It is true that patents and trade secrets are polar extremes on the issue of disclosure. Information that is disclosed in a patent is no longer a trade secret. As pointed out above, however, patents and trade secrets are indeed complementary, especially under the following circumstances:

Firstly, in the critical R&D stage and before any applications are filed and also before patents issue, trade secret law particularly "dovetails" with patent law (see *Bonito Boats*).

Secondly, provided that an invention has been enabled and the best mode described, as is requisite in a patent application, all associated know-how not disclosed can and should be retained as a trade secret. That the "written description" and "best mode" requirements apply only to the claimed invention, should be kept in mind in this context.

Thirdly, all the mass of R&D data, including data pertaining to better modes, developed after filing, whether or not inventive, can and should also be maintained as trade secrets, to the extent the data are not disclosed in separate applications.

Fourthly and especially with respect to complex technologies consisting of many patentable inventions and volumes of associated know-how, complementary patenting and secreting is tantamount to having the best of both worlds. In this regard, GE's industrial diamond process technology, which is partially patented and partially under trade secret protection, comes to mind as an excellent illustration of the synergistic integration of patents and trade secrets to secure invulnerable exclusivity. Was GE's policy to rely on trade secrets in this manner, or, for that matter, Coca-Cola's decision to keep their formula secret rather than patent, it which could have been done, damnable? I think not.

[The above] discussion obviously leaves open an analysis of the respective rights of a first inventor who elects to hold and use patentable subject matter as a trade secret (trade secret owner) and the second independent inventor who seeks and obtains a patent thereon (patentee). [An] impetus for writing this sequel is the threat by a noted patent attorney in hearings in the U.S. Patent & Trademark Office earlier this year about bills pending in Congress, that, inasmuch as prior user rights would be "unconstitutional, because they undermine the notion of 'exclusive rights' inherent in the patent grant," he is "prepared to sue to test it." Such a proposition is simply not tenable. This goes also for the common, baldly-stated misconception that the trade secret owner infringes the second-inventor's patent and hence can be enjoined.

First of all, the modifier "exclusive" doesn't mean "exclusive, exclusive". No right is ever totally exclusive and regarding patents, there are several areas where something akin or tantamount to a prior user right already exists. Angelo Notaro lists a veritable litany of statutory-or decisionally-created "co-uses", "forced sharing of inventions", "estoppels", "implied licenses", "intervening rights", "judicial recognition of prior user rights", etc. as, for example, shoprights, temporary uses of inventions on vessels or aircrafts, intervening rights in reissue and reexamination cases, co-uses in supplier/customer, manufacturer/distributor, contractor/contractee relationships, public interest situations where injunctive relief if denied, certain uses by government or uses under the Clean Air and Atomic Energy acts, compulsory licenses as a remedy for antitrust violations, etc. We also have an experimental use exception. And the patent right is a negative right and a patentee may be blocked by a dominant patent.

And as regards the respective rights, I contend that the trade secret owner has a *de facto* prior user right to continue the practice of his trade secret. I do so on the basis [*inter alia*] the fact that it has never happened that a trade secret owner was enjoined by the later patentee.

Such a right, which is very prevalent outside the U.S. and has existed in some countries for over 100 years, has also been posited in the literature as a kind of "in personam right", "shopright," "intervening right," "right of co-use," "right of personal possession" and "personal easement on the invention."

In his classic treatise on Trade Secrets, Ellis concluded: "To give a patent to a subsequent inventor without barring him from suing the first inventor and secret user of the invention, would be to offer, as a reward to anyone who could discover the invention by independent research, the economic scalp of the first inventor and secret user." A similar sentiment resides in the cogent maxim: "A Constitutional award to one inventor does not mandate a Constitutional penalty to another." (Bennett, The Trade Secret Owner Versus the Patentee, JPOS, 1975).

In the literature, referred to above, it is also emphasized that an in personam right or a prior user right:

- is a first inventor's common law right,
- is required by principles of equity and due process and
- not granting it, amounts to taking property without compensation.

The contrary position, espoused by patent advocates, holds that when the choice is made to forego a patent and to rely instead on trade secret protection, the trade secret owner assumes the risk of being enjoined by the patentee. Also clearly an untenable position! How can there be such an assumed risk when the Supreme Court recognized trade secrets as viable and compatible alternatives to patents [in the cases cited above] and when "no court has ever decided a case in which the issue was even raised." (Bennett).

The Gore v. Garlock (CAFC, 1983) decision has mistakenly been interpreted as putting an end to this debate by resolving the perceived conflict in favor of the patentee. Far from it! This case held that trade secrets of a third party are not prior art, but such a holding is an entirely different proposition from a holding that the trade secret owner is an infringer vis-à-vis the patentee.

Maintaining secrecy is a *sine qua non* in trade secret law and is not to be equated with "concealment" in patent law, which means in a Sec. 102(g) context only too long a delay in filing a patent application in relation to another applicant, i.e. in a situation where both resort to the patent system. This is to be clearly distinguished from a situation where one party relies on the trade secret system and is outside the patent system altogether.

Thus, it is abundantly clear that the patentee does not have superior rights vis-à-vis the trade secret owner, and the reason the later patentee leaves the trade secret owner alone is the former's concern that putting the patent on the block is risky, knowing he/she was not the first to invent and the patent may be invalid for a number of Sec. 102 and/or Sec. 102/103 grounds due to the activities of the trade secret owner. Consequently, an accommodation between the two serves them best because patent coverage continues and other competition is shut out. In light of the above argumentation, my advice, when such a respective rights issue came up in my corporate practice—a not infrequent occurrence— was to ignore the patents of the "Johnny-come-lately" inventor. No boomerang ever; after all, we do have a de facto prior user right system. . . .

What is needed is a true prior user rights provision that would cover commercial use of an invention or effective and serious preparations for such use, prior to the filing date of the later patent, such rights being of limited alienability (personal rights transferable only with the entire enterprise), limited territoriality (the territory of the patent), limited scope (continuation of existing prior use) and limited recognition of prior acts (good-faith use without derivation or theft).

As a final credo, it is submitted that such a strong prior user right, which is absolutely essential in a first-to-file system, is equally important in our first-to-invent system, as a better alternative to our archaic, costly and inadequate interference practice and as a better way for protection of trade secrets in view of their transcending importance.

Twenty-two years after the Supreme Court issued its landmark decision in *Kewanee v. Bicron*, Congress created a federal trade secret protection statute called the Economic Espionage Act of 1996. Despite the name, which conjures up images of post-Cold War James Bond sleuthing, in addition to a prohibition of international trade secret espionage (§ 1831), the Act also creates a federal cause of action with heavy fines for any theft of trade secret in interstate commerce (§ 1832). Furthermore, § 1838 of the Act makes explicit that federal trade secret protection does not preempt state trade secret protection laws. Major provisions of the Act are excerpted below.

ECONOMIC ESPIONAGE ACT OF 1996, 18 U.S.C. §§ 1831–39

§ 1831. Economic espionage

(a) *In general*. Whoever, intending or knowing that the offense will benefit any foreign government, foreign instrumentality, or foreign agent, knowingly—

(1) steals, or without authorization appropriates, takes, carries away, or conceals, or by fraud, artifice, or deception obtains a trade secret;

(2) without authorization copies, duplicates, sketches, draws, photographs, downloads, uploads, alters, destroys, photocopies, replicates, transmits, delivers, sends, mails, communicates, or conveys a trade secret;

(3) receives, buys, or possesses a trade secret, knowing the same to have been stolen or appropriated, obtained, or converted without authorization;

(4) attempts to commit any offense described in any of paragraphs (1) through (3); or

(5) conspires with one or more other persons to commit any offense described in any of paragraphs (1) through (3), and one or more of such persons do any act to effect the object of the conspiracy,

shall, except as provided in subsection (b), be fined not more than $ 500,000 or imprisoned not more than 15 years, or both.

(b) *Organizations*. Any organization that commits any offense described in subsection (a) shall be fined not more than $ 10,000,000.

§ 1832. Theft of trade secrets

(a) Whoever, with intent to convert a trade secret, that is related to or included in a product that is produced for or placed in interstate or foreign commerce, to the economic benefit of anyone other than the owner thereof, and intending or knowing that the offense will, injure any owner of that trade secret, knowingly—

(1) steals, or without authorization appropriates, takes, carries away, or conceals, or by fraud, artifice, or deception obtains such information;

(2) without authorization copies, duplicates, sketches, draws, photographs, downloads, uploads, alters, destroys, photocopies, replicates, transmits, delivers, sends, mails, communicates, or conveys such information;

(3) receives, buys, or possesses such information, knowing the same to have been stolen or appropriated, obtained, or converted without authorization;

(4) attempts to commit any offense described in paragraphs (1) through (3); or

(5) conspires with one or more other persons to commit any offense described in paragraphs (1) through (3), and one or more of such persons do any act to effect the object of the conspiracy,

shall, except as provided in subsection (b), be fined under this title or imprisoned not more than 10 years, or both.

(b) Any organization that commits any offense described in subsection (a) shall be fined not more than $ 5,000,000.

§ 1833. Exceptions to prohibitions

This chapter does not prohibit—

(1) any otherwise lawful activity conducted by a governmental entity of the United States, a State, or a political subdivision of a State; or

(2) the reporting of a suspected violation of law to any governmental entity of the United States, a State, or a political subdivision of a State, if such entity has lawful authority with respect to that violation.

§ 1834. Criminal forfeiture

(a) The court, in imposing sentence on a person for a violation of this chapter, shall order, in addition to any other sentence imposed, that the person forfeit to the United States—

(1) any property constituting, or derived from, any proceeds the person obtained, directly or indirectly, as the result of such violation; and

(2) any of the person's property used, or intended to be used, in any manner or part, to commit or facilitate the commission of such violation, if the court in its discretion so determines, taking into consideration the nature, scope, and proportionality of the use of the property in the offense.

(b) Property subject to forfeiture under this section, any seizure and disposition thereof, and any administrative or judicial proceeding in relation thereto, shall be governed by section 413 of the Comprehensive Drug Abuse Prevention and Control Act of 1970 (21 U.S.C. § 853), except for subsections (d) and (j) of such section, which shall not apply to forfeitures under this section.

§ 1835. Orders to preserve confidentiality

In any prosecution or other proceeding under this chapter [18 USC§§ 1831 et seq.], the court shall enter such orders and take such other action as may be necessary and appropriate to preserve the confidentiality of trade secrets, consistent with the requirements of the Federal Rules of Criminal and Civil Procedure, the Federal Rules of Evidence, and all other applicable laws. An interlocutory appeal by the United States shall lie from a decision or order of a district court authorizing or directing the disclosure of any trade secret.

§ 1836. Civil proceedings to enjoin violations

(a) The Attorney General may, in a civil action, obtain appropriate injunctive relief against any violation of this section.

(b) The district courts of the United States shall have exclusive original jurisdiction of civil actions under this subsection.

§ 1837. Applicability to conduct outside the United States

This chapter also applies to conduct occurring outside the United States if—

(1) the offender is a natural person who is a citizen or permanent resident alien of the United States, or an organization organized under the laws of the United States or a State or political subdivision thereof; or

(2) an act in furtherance of the offense was committed in the United States.

§ 1838. Construction with other laws

This chapter shall not be construed to preempt or displace any other remedies, whether civil or criminal, provided by United States Federal, State, commonwealth, possession, or territory law for the misappropriation of a trade secret, or to affect the otherwise lawful disclosure of information by any Government employee under section 552 of title 5 (commonly known as the Freedom of Information Act).

§ 1839. Definitions

As used in this chapter [18 USCS §§ 1831 et seq.]—

(1) the term "foreign instrumentality" means any agency, bureau, ministry, component, institution, association, or any legal, commercial, or business organization, corporation, firm, or entity that is substantially owned, controlled, sponsored, commanded, managed, or dominated by a foreign government;

(2) the term "foreign agent" means any officer, employee, proxy, servant, delegate, or representative of a foreign government;

(3) the term "trade secret" means all forms and types of financial, business, scientific, technical, economic, or engineering information, including patterns, plans, compilations, program devices, formulas, designs, prototypes, methods, techniques, processes, procedures, programs, or codes, whether tangible or intangible, and whether or how stored, compiled, or memorialized physically, electronically, graphically, photographically, or in writing if—

(A) the owner thereof has taken reasonable measures to keep such information secret; and

(B) the information derives independent economic value, actual or potential, from not being generally known to, and not being readily ascertainable through proper means by, the public; and

(4) the term "owner", with respect to a trade secret, means the person or entity in whom or in which rightful legal or equitable title to, or license in, the trade secret is reposed.

NOTES AND QUESTIONS

(1) **Trade Secrets as Property.** In his dissent in *Kewanee* (not excerpted above), Justice Douglas with whom Justice Brennan concurred, quoted Justice Holmes in *DuPont de Nemours Powder Co. v. Masland*, 244 U.S. 100, 102, for the proposition that "a trade secret, unlike a patent, has no property dimensions." Is a trade secret "property?" *See* Andrew Mitchell, *The Jurisdictional Basis of Trade Secret Actions: Economic and Doctrinal Actions*, 8 AUSTRAL. INT. PROP. J. 134 (1997). If so, why? In the U.K., trade secrets cannot be "stolen" because they do not constitute "property" for purposes of the Theft Act of 1968. According to a recent comment by one member of the U.K. Law Commission, "this is a country where the theft of the boardroom table is punished far more severely than the theft of the boardroom secrets." *See* Stephen Silber, *Secrets of Success Stay in the Boardroom*, THE TIMES, Nov. 25, 1997 (proposing criminal sanctions for misuse of trade secrets in the U.K.).

(2) **Staying in the World of Trade Secrets.** Professor Jorda stresses (indeed touts) the benefits of trade secret protection and the lack of conflict

between the policy of disclosure which underpins the patent system and the rights of the trade secret owner to maintain unpatented information under "padlock." How persuasive is his argument that the user of the trade secret is not similarly situated to a party who "suppresses or conceals" an invention under 35 U.S.C.section § 102(g)? In the recent decision, *Dow Chemical v. Astro-Valcour*, 267 F.3d 1334 (Fed. Cir. 2001), the Federal Circuit upheld the invalidation of Dow patents for plastic foam, because Astro-Valcour employees had made the "inventions" earlier than Dow, even though those employees did not apply for patents, and even though they did not understand that they had produced patentable inventions. The district court had concluded that AVI's production of foam in 1984 using isobutane as a blowing agent and GMS as a stability control agent anticipated the claims of the Dow patent. There was no question of anticipation under Section 102(a). The court stated, "Because the foam made by AVI would infringe the [Dow] patents if made after the [Dow] invention, it anticipates in fact the relevant claims of the Park patents, since it was made before Park's invention." AVI had "appreciated" the existence of its process, and whether it knew it was a patentable invention was immaterial. Because AVI had not "actively abandoned, suppressed or concealed," nor had it "unreasonably delayed" in making the invention known, AVI made a "public disclosure" of its invention by "commercializing" its isobutane-blown foam.

(3) **Statutory Prior User Rights.** The defense of "earlier inventor" was added to the U.S. patent law through the enactment of the American Inventors Protection Act of 1999, and is now codified in 35 U.S.C § 273. The statute limits the defense to methods of doing or conducting business. 35 U.S.C. § 273(a)(3). The person asserting the defense has the burden of establishing the defense by clear and convincing evidence. 35 U.S.C. § 273(b)(4). A patent is not to be deemed invalid under section 102 or 103 "solely because a defense is raised or established under this section." 35 U.S.C. § 273(b)(9). Does the existence of the "first inventor defense" by statute for users of business methods imply that such a defense is unavailable to the "first inventor" in a different field of technology?

(4) **State-Sponsored Espionage.** Is "state-sponsored" industrial espionage lawful? Is there a legal difference between industrial espionage by private parties and government-sponsored "economic espionage?" Note section 1831's reference to benefit to a *foreign* government and section 1833's exception from liability for "*otherwise lawful* activity by a government entity of the United States" in light of the following:

> In 1993 James Woolsey, then CIA director, publicly announced that economic intelligence was a big new priority for the CIA. The French had been particularly aggressive in spying on American executives, bugging and stealing from hotel rooms. CIA officers in Paris were instructed to gather information on French trade negotiations, the agency's inspector-general reported. Last week an American security official said: The agency (CIA) is all over Brussels. We have always believed that when Mickey Kantor (the US trade

representative) meets with Leon Brittan he has what Brittan is going to say in his back pocket.

American spies hack into Euro computers to steal trade secrets, THE TIMES, Aug. 4, 1996.

Is economic espionage meeting all the definitions of the Espionage Act but conducted by an agency of the U.S. government or a U.S. citizen in its employ outside the territory of the United States *lawful* under U.S. law? Should it be? Assuming the truth of such reports, should the U.K. or other European states enact similar statutes to reach such "American spies?"

(5) **Weighted Words.** Is there a difference between trade secret "misappropriation" and "economic espionage?" If so, what is the difference? Why might this terminology matter? How far beyond parties in a confidential (and contractual) relationship does the common law of trade secrets extend? *See Dupont v. Christopher*, 431 F.2d 1012 (5th Cir. 1970).

(6) **Criminal Enforcement.** Cases reported in the first year of passage of the Economic Espionage Act are discussed in Gerald J. Mossinghoff, J. Derek Mason, and David A. Oblon, *The Economic Espionage Act: A Prosecution Update*, 80 J. PAT. OFF. SOC'Y 360 (1998). Six criminal actions and two convictions had been reported.

> In United States v. Worthing, Patrick and Daniel Worthing were indicted for allegedly stealing confidential fiberglass manufacturing technology, valued at $20 million, from the Pittsburgh-based PPG Industries. Patrick Worthing worked at PPG under a contract with Affiliated Building Services as the supervisor of a maintenance crew at one of PPG's research and development facilities. With access to every office, he surreptitiously collected PPG's proprietary information, including diskettes, blueprints and other confidential research materials relating to fiberglass. . . . The indictment was based on an FBI sting operation prompted by a letter to Owens-Corning Fiberglass indicating that confidential PPG information could be made available to them. Both defendants pleaded guilty, with Daniel Worthing, who cooperated with the government, being sentenced to five years' probation, six months of home confinement and 100 hours of community service, and Patrick Worthing now serving a 15-month prison sentence, to be followed by three years' probation.

Id. A more recent and comprehensive summary of cases is Chris Carr, Jack Morton and Jerry Furniss, *The Economic Espionage Act: Bear Trap or Mousetrap*, 8 TEX. INT. PROP. L.J. 159 (2000).

(7) **Limits of Confidentiality.** Assume that a defendant alleges that what she is accused of stealing is not a trade secret. Could 18 U.S.C. § 1835 possibly obstruct her Sixth Amendment right to cross-examine or effectively defend herself? In *U.S. v. Kai-Lo Hsu et al.*, 982 F. Supp. 1026 (E.D. Pa. 1997), the defendants argued that they needed the very documents they were accused of conspiring and attempting to steal in their entirety in order

to establish that the government had failed to prove an essential element of its case: proof of the existence of a trade secret. They asserted a legal impossibility defense, contending that as a matter of law they could not be convicted of attempting and conspiring to steal a trade secret if the documents they were shown by the government during the sting operation did not contain trade secrets. The government argued that section 1835 of the EEA required the trade secret itself be placed under a protective order and that because the defendants were charged only with attempt and conspiracy and not theft, the question was not what the trade secret was but what the defendants thought it was. The District Court ordered the plaintiffs to hand over unredacted documents. The Third Circuit affirmed on the legal impossibility question. *See* 155 F.3d 189 (3d Cir. 1998).

MELVIN JAGER, A COMPARISON OF TRADE SECRET LAWS IN ASIA
XXXII Les Nouvelles, 54–59 (June 1997)

[T]he treatment of trade secrets in licensing agreements depends on the nature and scope of protection afforded by the laws of the relevant nation. Most nations will enforce the specific terms of a licensing contract if the agreement conforms with the law. An important consideration is the extent to which the laws protect trade secrets before or after a license agreement.

Comprehensive knowledge of various nations' trade secret protection is important when information is used or licensed internationally. An understanding of the comparison of the trade secret laws of the United States and the major Asian nations will avoid premature loss of rights and aid in maximizing a return on the information. . . .

General Trade Secret Protection

Determining the source of various nations' trade secret laws is the first step to defining the type of information that can be licensed as a trade secret. The increasing importance of trade secret protection is shown by the fact that many Asian nations have recently enacted trade secret laws. China enacted a trade secret law in 1993. Japan's new trade secrets law came into effect on June 15, 1991. In Korea, the Unfair Competition Prevention Act was modified to include trade secret protection on December 15, 1992.

Further, trade secrets protection in Asia will continue to change. In 1996, Taiwan enacted its first trade secret statute. The recent and continuing creation of trade secrets laws demonstrate the importance Asian nations now attach to the protection and licensing of information.

Hong Kong, Malaysia and Singapore rely on the common law for the protection of trade secrets. Reliance on the common law by these countries is a result of their common British heritage. Britain, like its former colonies, relies on the common law to protect trade secrets.

Some Asian nations have not yet realized the importance of comprehensive trade secret protection. As of 1994, laws in the Philippines did not exist that specifically protected trade secrets. In the Philippines, contract and fiduciary relationship laws provided some protection for secret information. Taiwan's contract and fiduciary laws also provided some protection for secret information. Additionally, Taiwan's antitrust laws do specifically prohibit acquiring technical secrets by coercion, bribery or improper means. However, the antitrust statute does not define technical secrets. Technology owners and licensors should examine the laws of the relevant countries very closely before entering into a licensing agreement.

. . .

Specific Trade Secret Provisions

Common Provisions

. . .

Due to their common heritage, the common law that has developed in Hong Kong, Malaysia and Singapore is very similar. Until recently, Malaysian final appeals were to a court in the United Kingdom. Hong Kong law is in a state of change. In the past, final appeals in Hong Kong were to a court in the United Kingdom. Additionally, Malaysia statutorily enacted the 1956 United Kingdom common law as Malaysian common law. Except for a few statutes not directly dealing with trade secrets, the common law of Singapore is the same as for Malaysia. Therefore, the trade secrets law in Hong Kong, Malaysia and Singapore are generally interchangeable.

Regardless of heritage, many trade secret provisions are common for all nations. An owner of information does not have to be the first person to possess that information to have a trade secret. Therefore, novelty is not required by the Asian nations [discussed here].

The nations with trade secrets commonly require relative secrecy, but not absolute secrecy. The information cannot be "generally" known in the applicable field. Both NAFTA and GATT explicitly follow this common trade secrets provision.

Furthermore, the trade secrets laws of these Asian countries protect technical information like blueprints, processes of manufacture and formulations. However the protection of business information is not uniform.

Additionally, Asian nations' trade secrets laws commonly provide for protection of either patentable or non-patentable information. Unlike patent protection, trade secret laws commonly provide that trade secrets may exist for an unlimited time. Only disclosure to the public will end the life of a trade secret. Furthermore, unlike patent protection, trade secrets do not protect against another person's development of the same information. Reverse engineering, dismantling a product to determine how it was built, is allowed by Asian nations with trade secret laws.

As an alternative to trade secrets law or as an additional form of information protection, all the Asian nations under consideration enforce contracts. Some Asian nations have specific legislation relating to technology transfer. Any technology license should address the requirements created by the related technology transfer legislation. Additionally, certain limitations on contract rights vary from nation to nation and should be understood before a license agreement is completed.

Provisions That Vary by Nation

Understanding the differences in trade secret protection between various nations will aid in preparing the proper license. Some trade secret provisions apply in some Asian nations and not in others. Trade secret definitions, misappropriation, remedies, contract and criminal provisions vary from nation to nation. Therefore, trade secret laws in any nation should be closely examined.

In the case of the definition of trade secrets, only protection of business information varies substantially from nation to nation. Protecting business information as a trade secret has also received varied degrees of acceptance in the United States. Generally, the nations that have recently enacted trade secrets statutes, China, Japan, Korea and Taiwan, provide for protection of business information such as mailing lists, discount lists and methods of doing business. The scope of Korea's protection of business information may be different from the other Asian nations. Korean trade secrets law protects "managerial" information used in business activities. To cover business information, China protects "operational" information as a trade secret. Additionally, Taiwan's antitrust statute protects trade secrets concerning production and/or "sales" information.

However, Malaysia, Singapore and Hong Kong do not protect business information under trade secret law. The law of "confidences" must be used to protect business information in these nations. The common law of confidences protects business information from disclosure by employees like the United States's fiduciary laws.

Concerning misappropriation of trade secrets, protection against third-party use or disclosure also receives varied protection. Where a third party obtains a trade secret from a misappropriator and uses or discloses the trade secret, nations use different levels of third-party intent to hold the third party guilty of trade secret misappropriation. Nations also place different emphasis on the intent necessary to hold a third party liable after good faith acquisition upon notice of a prior misappropriation.

Many states in the United States will hold a third party liable even if the initial trade secret use or disclosure was innocent. The third party becomes liable for misappropriation if he or she knew or should have known that the subsequent use of technology violated trade secret rights. Like those states, Malaysia, Singapore and Hong Kong similarly protect trade secret owners from innocent third-party misappropriation.

However, some nations require a higher degree of culpability by a third party. Japan, Taiwan and Korea require a third party to be grossly negligent in not knowing the information used or disclosed is a trade secret of another. A third party must have unreasonably not known of the prior misappropriation. This higher level of culpability is used to prevent the trade secret laws from discouraging beneficial transactions exchanging information. Misappropriation will occur if the information is used or disclosed in violation of a contractual obligation.

Both NAFTA and GATT-TRIPS explicitly deal with the acquisition of a trade secret by a third party. The third party will be liable if grossly negligent in not knowing the trade secret was improperly acquired. However, neither treaty addresses the situation where a trade secret was acquired in good faith, but then the acquirer is notified of a prior improper acquisition.

China takes a mid-ground approach. China allows a third party liability if the third party was negligent in not knowing of a prior improper appropriation or negligent in not learning of improper appropriation after acquisition of the trade secret.

In both Korea and Japan, trade secret protection against third party use or disclosure is greatly limited by an exception. If a third party is not grossly negligent in not knowing about a prior misappropriation while acquiring a trade secret in a transaction, then the third party can use and disclose the trade secret according to the rights acquired in the transactions. In other words, if a third party acquires a trade secret in good faith in a transaction, the third party may continue to use the trade secret according to the rights granted by the transaction. The exception virtually defeats the rule preventing use and disclosure of a trade secret where the third party is grossly negligent in not knowing subsequent to acquiring the trade secret about a prior misappropriation. Notice of misappropriation to a third party user may have little impact. The only limitation in the exception is that a "transaction" must have occurred, which includes licensing or sale of trade secret rights. However, a transaction does not include the hiring of another's employee. The purpose of this post acquisition third party use exception is to preserve the validity and stability of transactions involving technical or business information.

Contractual rights also vary between different Asian nations. Specifically, some nations allow royalty payments for the use of trade secrets to continue contractually after the trade secret information becomes public. Some states in the United States and Hong Kong both allow continuing royalties.

In China, statutes dictate that obligations of confidentiality cease once information is publically disclosed. The rules do not state whether royalties must continue to be paid. However, the Ministry of Foreign Trade and Economic Cooperation interprets the law to require continued royalty payments under a contract after public disclosure of a secret.

Under Japan's antitrust laws, a trade secret license royalty provision that lasts beyond public disclosure of the trade secret is highly likely to be considered an unfair business practiced. However, as long as the trade secret entered the public domain through no fault of the licensee, the royalties may continue for a short period of time past public disclosure. Therefore, the royalty payment schedule should receive heightened consideration when licensing in Japan.

Varying Trade Secret Remedies

Another broad area of trade secret protection variance is remedies. The availability of injunction, of actual damages, punitive damages and attorney's fees varies from nation to nation. Injunctions are the only remedy for violation of trade secret rights common to the nations [covered in this article]. Most nations will permanently enjoin a party from using or disclosing another's trade secret rights. . .

Actual damages are allowed by most Asian nations. If a trade secret is improperly taken, then the damages resulting from the taking are collectable by the owner of the trade secret. Generally, in Asia, damages are based on the market value of the information. If a trade secret owner would not have licensed the information, then the owner's lost profits provide compensation. However, if compensation from market value or lost profits cannot be proven, then the owner may receive an accounting of the misappropriator's profits. The trade secret owner is also entitled to have his business credit restored.

Malaysia and Singapore do not allow a trade secret owner to collect damages. Equity courts are responsible for the protection of trade secrets in these two nations. These equity courts rely on British common law at a date prior to the United Kingdom's statutory damages Lord Cairn's Act. Therefore, the equity courts of Malaysia and Singapore do not have jurisdiction to grant damages. However, like other Asian nations, damages are available under a breach of contract or tort theory of recovery.

Current Hong Kong law varies from that of Singapore and Malaysia, in this case. Hong Kong adopted more recent British laws allowing the collection of actual damages for trade secret misappropriation.

Besides actual damages, Asian nations also vary from the law in most states in the United States by not allowing punitive damages. The majority of states within the United States allow punitive damages, but others do not. Further, the United States' Uniform Trade Secrets Act, now law in 42 states in some form, statutorily allows punitive damages for willful and malicious misappropriation. Up to two times compensatory damages may be awarded. Additionally, some other states that have not enacted the Uniform Trade Secrets Act award punitive damages. However, China, Japan and Korea do not allow punitive damages.

Additionally, some states in the United States and Asian nations may allow punitive damages based on breach of fiduciary duty or breach of contract in conjunction with a tort violation. The laws of any jurisdiction should be examined closely to maximize protection and collection of damages for misappropriation or breach of a license agreement.

Taiwan's Trade Secret Act allows punitive damages up to three times actual damages.

Attorneys Fees Awards

Attorney fees as a form of damages also receives varied protection. Malaysia, Singapore and current Hong Kong law allow recovery of attorney fees under the traditional "British" rule. Some states in the United States grant attorney fees awards. The United States' Uniform Trade Secrets Act grants attorney fees for willful and malicious misappropriation or for a bad-faith claim of trade secret misappropriation. . . .

The law in China is silent on whether a winning party should be awarded attorney fees. The general practice is that each party bears its own attorney fees regardless of a lawsuit's outcome. However, in some recent intellectual property cases, the courts have ordered infringers to pay the plaintiff's attorney fees. Therefore, attorney fees might be collectable in China.

Japan allows collection of reasonable attorney fees for an injury in tort. Injuries from trade secret misappropriation are recoverable based on tort. However, the "reasonable" amount awarded by the courts is not necessarily linked to the attorney fees incurred by the injured party. Attorney fee calculations are normally 10% of the misappropriation damages. It is often the case that the attorney fees awarded by the court are far less than the fees actually paid by the injured party.

Criminal Law Provisions

Some Asian nations provide trade secret misappropriation protection through the criminal laws while others do not. Many states within the United States have statutes making it a crime to misappropriate a trade secret. In addition, the Economic Espionage Act of 1996 became the first federal law in the U.S. to make it a crime to steal trade secrets. The Espionage Act also makes it a crime to assist non-U.S. governments or agencies to steal trade secrets. Additionally, theft-of-property statutes will often provide governmental protection from trade secret misappropriation. Anyone found guilty will face possible jail time and substantial fines.

China specifically outlaws trade secrets misappropriation in the new Law for Countering Unfair Competition. Article 25 empowers the relevant authorities to impose fines and to order a misappropriator to desist from any violation of the law. Additionally, the law allows a trade secret owner to request government investigation and resolution. A trade secret owner is even allowed to request an appeal of the government's resolution with eventual resort to a civil court.

Moving down the spectrum of criminal protection, Korea has criminal sanctions for the theft of trade secrets. Only "special production technology" disclosed for the purposes of unjust enrichment or to cause harm to the trade secret owner are protected by the government. Imprisonment of three years or less and a fine are provided for misappropriation.

Taiwan provides limited criminal protection. Under Article 317 of the Taiwan Criminal Code, a person required by law or contract to keep information secret that he knows due to his occupation, may not disclose the secret. The punishment for violation of the criminal law is less than a year in jail or a fine.

The Philippines law also provides limited criminal protection. Also like Taiwan, the Philippines made it illegal for an employee to disclose the secrets of an employer.

Japan, Malaysia and Singapore laws do not protect trade secrets through criminal penalties. . . .

Understanding criminal and civil trade secret protection on a general level is important, but complete knowledge about a nation's trade secrets laws will further aid in the use and licensing of technology. Therefore, close attention should be paid to all the relevant laws of a nation before undertaking any licensing activities in that nation.

Variations in the Treatment of Technology Licenses

Relevant laws governing the licensing of technology vary from country to country. By way of example, many nations require government approval of certain trade secret licenses. Licenses in Korea will be examined by the Fair Trade Commission. The U.S. common law rules of contract are used to interpret Korean licenses. Usually, subject matter, the amount of royalties, or the duration of the license determine whether government approval is necessary.

While no specific trade secrets law exists in the Philippines, laws regulating the transfer of technology do exist. Royalties for technology use may not last beyond a 10 year period, and no automatic renewal provision is allowed. Therefore, the laws of the Philippines should be examined closely before licensing a trade secret on a long-term basis.

Korean "Guidelines and Types of Unfair Trade Acts in International Contracts" sets forth some limitations in technology licensing that are not accepted by advanced countries.

In China, a number of licensing regulations may have a potentially costly impact. Article 8 of the Regulations on Administration of Technology-Introduction Contracts provides that, unless specially approved by the government, the term of a license shall not exceed 10 years. Article 9 provides that a contract shall not contain, without special approval, a clause that prohibits the use of licensed technology after expiration of the contracts. Chinese law also dictates that confidentiality obligations cease on expiration unless special approval is obtained. Therefore, protection of secret information by contract in China may result in eventual public disclosure and a license free to use the information without royalty payments. However, due to complaints by many foreign trade secret potential licensors, the regulations may have been amended.

Korean law once limited the term of trade secret license agreements to 10 years. In 1991, the law was changed to remove government authority to require limited durations. However, in practice, the government agencies involved may still seek to enforce a duration limit.

A former regulation in Korea allows any licensee to use trade secrets after expiration of the license. Only patents or copyright rights protected the information. However, the new Korean Guidelines allow restrictions on the use of trade secrets after the license unless the know-how is already available to the public.

A significant problem for protecting trade secrets exists in Japan. Trials and hearings regarding trade secrets are held in courtrooms open to the public. There is no procedure for sealing the records or issuing protective orders. Therefore, trade secret litigation in Japan may disclose to the world the very secrets which need protection.

Korea and Taiwan also have public trade secrets trails, allowing public disclosure of a trade secret. While trade secret rights exist in these countries, the possibility of disclosure during a suit drastically reduces the use of legal actions to enforce trade secrets.

. . .

Conclusion

The laws governing the protection and licensing of trade secrets varies from nation to nation. Many Asian nations provide comprehensive protection for technical and even business information. Usually, the protection provided is comparable to the protection provided in the United States.

There are some Asian nations which do not provide any comprehensive protection for trade secrets. Information licensed in these nations must be carefully guarded and protected by contract.

Even in nations providing comprehensive protection, minor variations from nation to nation exist. Additionally, the practical consequences of any actions in a foreign nation based on cultural differences must always be considered. Therefore, licenses subject to an Asian nation's laws must be drafted and handled with a proper understanding of the nation's relevant laws and practical differences.

Due to the increasing importance of technology and licensing, many Asian nations are seeking to protect rights in technology through new trade secrets laws. The above-noted recent changes allowing more but varied protection of trade secrets makes it vital to know about the laws concerning the protection and licensing of trade secrets in various nations. Specific nations' provisions must always be examined to maximize protection of the licensed technology.

QUESTION

Your client, a chemical company using proprietary industrial processes requiring the intervention of catalysts that cannot be reverse engineered from the final product, is interested in licensing the technology as a way to enter significant Asian markets. At the same time, disclosure of the identity of any of its catalysts would have a severe impact on the company's business worldwide. Significant potential competitors exist in mainland China, Korea, Taiwan, Malaysia, and Singapore. What advice would you give? What licensing provisions need to be considered in certain jurisdictions?

§ 2.10 Industrial Designs

Although no international agreement defines authoritatively what is meant by the term "industrial design," traditionally, for legal scholars, it embodied the notion of ornamentation or features designed to appeal to the eye. *See, e.g.*, Registered Designs Act 1949 § 1(1) (U.K.) (defining "designs" for purposes of the Registered Designs Act, as "features of shape, configuration, pattern or ornament applied to an article by any industrial process, being features which in the finished article appeal to or are judged by the eye . . . "). Functional features, if protected at all, were dealt with by other intellectual property regimes. For manufacturers, however, industrial design has long encompassed more than ornamentation. In the early twentieth century, following the Bauhaus emphasis upon form following function, industrial design evolved to include the consideration and application of aesthetic design features as an integral part of the overall product development process. Industrial design in this modern sense—which might, with some over-generalization, be called "functionalist" design—began to figure prominently in the priorities of management in Europe by the late 1950s and thereafter in the United States. Modern industrial design is an efficient and fully integrated blend of form and function. The recently enacted EU Design Directive thus provides a good definition upon which to base modern legal debate: a design is "the appearance of the whole or a part of a product resulting from the features of, in particular, the lines, contours, colours, shape, texture and/or materials of the product itself and/or its ornamentation." Directive 98/71/EC of the European Parliament and of the Council of 13 October 1998 on The Legal Protection of Design, O.J. (L 289) (Oct. 28, 1998), art. 1(a). Industrial designs are applied to a wide range of industrial and consumer goods, such as technical instruments, sports equipment, furniture, kitchen products, jewelry, electrical appliances, children's toys, and office equipment, to name but a few products.

As the focus of the developed world moves (rightly or wrongly) from the provision of necessities to the incremental betterment of a society already in a state of some economic well-being, producers are devoting a significantly larger portion of their development resources to product design. Design has thus become crucial to commercial success. A study conducted by the Gallup Organization in 1985 revealed that senior U.S. business executives attributed 60% of the success of a new product to industrial design. *See* Hearings on S. 791 Before the Subcomm. on Patents, Copyrights and Trademarks of the Senate Comm. on the Judiciary, 100th Cong. 1st Sess. (1987) (statement of Cooper C. Woodring, Chairman of the Board, Industrial Designers Society of America, Mar. 26, 1987) at 32. The commercial significance (and necessity) of good design is likely only to grow, for several reasons linked to the nature of contemporary society. The integration of the world consumer product market presents the consumer with a larger array of relatively standardized products, and discrimination among these similar products will often depend upon design innovation. Appearance is also likely to assume a greater role in the differentiation of products as society becomes more visual. This latter influence is heightened by increasing global homogeneity; producers might seek to circumvent linguistic differences within broader target markets by the use of visual symbols (such as designs) that carry universal meaning. For these reasons, design is central to the new global economic climate—indeed, one British scholar has suggested that the entire body of intellectual property law can be constructed around analysis of the creative process of design. *See* Uma Suthersanen, *Breaking Down The Intellectual Property Barriers*, 2 INTELL. PROP. Q. 267 (1998).

As we will see in Chapter 4, however, international intellectual property law has made only minimal provision for designs, in part because of the conceptually ubiquitous nature of design. A product's design is art; it may embody a functional invention; and increasingly it may act as a product's source-identifier. The shape of a Volkswagen beetle car may at once be an artistic work of authorship, embody a safety advance that prevents the car from crumpling upon impact, and serve to inform consumers that the car is made by Volkswagen. Design may thus fit within traditional theories of copyright protection, patent protection or trademark protection, without the need for a separate form of intellectual property protection. Accordingly, different countries accommodate design in different parts of their overall intellectual property scheme, which may include not only these three primary regimes but also *sui generis* design codes, so-called utility model or petty patent systems, and varying laws of unfair competition. This has made international consensus difficult to achieve.

As a starting point for considering how design protection might be addressed internationally, therefore, in this Chapter we introduce some of the different national approaches to design protection. (The recently enacted

EU reforms are dealt with in greater detail in Chapters 4 and 6, *infra*.) A study of these divergent approaches reveals several issues central to the debate. As a preliminary matter, should design protection be dealt with under the primary intellectual property regimes, or should it be available under a special or *sui generis* design code? If the latter, should the design code be the exclusive form of protection for designs? If a separate design code is to be enacted, other issues arise: (1) which universe of designs should be protected, and should this universe extend beyond those designs intended to appeal solely to the eye (aesthetic designs) or should it also include designs that incorporate functional considerations; (2) should the threshold for protection be closer to copyright's standard of originality, or should protection be conditioned upon the design being wholly or substantially different from earlier designs; (3) should protection be available without registration and, if registration is required, should the application undergo substantive examination prior to the grant of rights; (4) should the rights received by the design owner be limited to protection against copying, or should the rights approximate that accorded by a patent right and enable the designer to prevent others from using or selling similar designs regardless of copying?

[A]   Cumulation

J.H. REICHMAN, THE INTRACTABLE PROBLEM OF CUMULATION [*]

The legal history of industrial art in the twentieth century may be viewed as a continuing effort to establish special regimes of design protection without unduly derogating from the general principles of copyright law. The difficulty of this task becomes apparent when it is recalled that, within the Berne Union, works of art original in the copyright sense[124] obtain long-term protection without formalities, whereas under special design laws, only short-term protection is normally available for novel and qualitatively original designs deposited or registered prior to divulgation. Even the most technically refined design laws can govern only those designs that fall within their jurisdictional sweep. The harder a country makes it to obtain copyright protection for industrial art, the more that country's special design law may determine the scope of the design protection actually available within that system. If a country makes it easy for industrial art to qualify for copyright protection as applied art, designers will have less incentive to make use of a special design law and design protection will increasingly be characterized by the copyright approach. The true scope and

---

[*] Excerpted from Design Protection in Domestic and Foreign Copyright Law: from the Berne Revision of 1948 to the Copyright Act of 1976, 1983 DUKE L.J. 1143, 1167-1171 (1983). Reprinted with permission.

[124] Normally, this means independent creation. [cit]. But in the case of designs protected as "applied art," states may require a degree of creativity that surpasses mere independent creation. [cit].

effectiveness of any given design law will therefore depend on the extent to which the scope of protection it affords, and the conditions it imposes, are undermined by the concurrent availability of copyright protection for industrial art. At the same time, measures needed to limit concurrent protection are likely to derogate from general principles of copyright law.

Hindsight suggests that the reform of sui generis design laws after 1958 was thwarted by the decisions made at [the Brussels revision of the Berne Convention] in 1948, which hardened the preexisting attitudes toward applied art and converted cumulation into "the biggest problem of all for the protection of designs and models." Cumulation means that concurrent protection is available for ornamental designs of useful articles in copyright and special design law. When concurrent protection is always possible, as in the French regime of absolute cumulation, special design laws serve as optional methods of augmenting manufacturers' rights, without forfeiting protection against copying under the law of artistic property. When, as in the Italian regime of noncumulation, there is virtually no possibility of concurrent protection for ornamental designs and models, short-term protection in a special design law becomes the only safe route regardless of the degree of artistic content. Italian manufacturers locked into the design law can lose all protection if they fail to meet its formal and substantive prerequisites, which reflect a modified patent-law paradigm. When partial cumulation is practiced, as in the Federal Republic of Germany, the Benelux countries, and the Scandinavian countries, manufacturers occasionally obtain copyright protection for designs and models that manifest exceptional creativity. As a rule, however, systems that allow partial cumulation attempt to relegate most industrial art to special design laws despite general principles of copyright law that prohibit legal discrimination on the basis of artistic merit.

Three options—cumulation, noncumulation and partial cumulation—have thus continued to exist in the Berne Union's intellectual property law system after the Brussels Conference of 1948. Some countries have shifted allegiance over the course of time, notably the United Kingdom[132] and the Benelux group. The choices among these options made by different countries reflect more than domestic self-interest; they also reflect fundamental differences of principle concerning both the nature of art and the proper

---

[132] . . . Prior to 1968, the United Kingdom adhered to a system of noncumulation . . . This aligned the United Kingdom with Italy's position, except that the United Kingdom adopted a purpose or destination test that tended to exclude designs reproduced in more than 50 single articles from copyright protection. Excluded designs were protectible, if at all, under the Registered Designs Act of 1949 or its predecessors, which follow the patent law paradigm. [cit]. . . . [However], the lines between copyright law, patent law, sui generis design law and utility models (not officially protected) have [since then] become blurred and, indeed, hopelessly confused as the result of "a series of mistakes and oversights on the part of legislative draftsmen." . . . [Ed. Note: In 1988, the United Kingdom enacted a significant revision of its design laws, reaffirming and strengthening provisions intended to exclude copyright protection proper to industrial designs, but supplementing its system of registered design protection with an anti-copying protection called the unregistered design right that protects both aesthetic and functional designs). *See* Copyright, Designs and Patents Act 1988, §§ 51, 213 et seq.]

limits of protection for intellectual property, which differences are exacerbated by the hybrid nature of industrial art. Until they are resolved or tempered by compromise, no international system of design protection can fulfill its goals, despite continuing efforts at harmonization and reform.

BRANDIR INT'L, INC. v. CASCADE PACIFIC LUMBER CO.
834 F.2d 1142 (2d Cir. 1987)

OAKES, CIRCUIT JUDGE:

In passing the Copyright Act of 1976 Congress attempted to distinguish between protectable "works of applied art" and "industrial designs not subject to copyright protection." See H.R. Rep. No. 1476, 94th Cong., 2d Sess. 54 (hereinafter H.R. Rep. No. 1476). The courts, however, have had difficulty framing tests by which the fine line establishing what is and what is not copyrightable can be drawn. Once again we are called upon to draw such a line, this time in a case involving the "RIBBON Rack," a bicycle rack made of bent tubing that is said to have originated from a wire sculpture. (A photograph of the rack is contained in the appendix to this opinion.) We are also called upon to determine whether there is any trademark protection available to the manufacturer of the bicycle rack, appellant Brandir International, Inc. The Register of Copyright . . . denied copyrightability. In the subsequent suit brought in the United States District Court for the Southern District of New York, Charles S. Haight, Jr., Judge, the district court granted summary judgment on both the copyright and trademark claims to defendant Cascade Pacific Lumber Co., d/b/a Columbia Cascade Co., manufacturer of a similar bicycle rack. We affirm as to the copyright claim, but reverse and remand as to the trademark claim.

Against the history of copyright protection well set out in the majority opinion in *Carol Barnhart Inc. v. Economy Cover Corp.*, 773 F.2d 411, 415-18 (2d Cir. 1985), and in Denicola, *Applied Art and Industrial Design: A Suggested Approach to Copyright in Useful Articles*, 67 Minn. L. Rev. 707, 709-17 (1983), Congress adopted the Copyright Act of 1976. The "works of art" classification of the Copyright Act of 1909 was omitted and replaced by reference to "pictorial, graphic, and sculptural works," 17 U.S.C. § 102(a)(5). According to the House Report, the new category was intended to supply "as clear a line as possible between copyrightable works of applied art and uncopyrighted works of industrial design." [cit]. The statutory definition of "pictorial, graphic, and sculptural works" states that "the design of a useful article, as defined in this section, shall be considered a pictorial, graphic, or sculptural work only if, and only to the extent that, such design incorporates pictorial, graphic, or sculptural features that can be identified separately from, and are capable of existing independently of, the utilitarian aspects of the article." 17 U.S.C. § 101.[1] The legislative

---

[1] The statute also defines "useful article" as one "having an intrinsic utilitarian function that is not merely to portray the appearance of the article or to convey information. An article that is normally a part of a useful article is considered a 'useful article.'" 17 U.S.C. § 101

history added gloss on the criteria of separate identity and independent existence in saying:

> On the other hand, although the shape of an industrial product may be aesthetically satisfying and valuable, the Committee's intention is not to offer it copyright protection under the bill. Unless the shape of an automobile, airplane, ladies' dress, food processor, television set, or any other industrial product contains some element that, physically or conceptually, can be identified as separable from the utilitarian aspects of that article, the design would not be copyrighted under the bill.

As courts and commentators have come to realize, however, the line Congress attempted to draw between copyrightable art and noncopyrightable design "was neither clear nor new." [cit]. One aspect of the distinction that has drawn considerable attention is the reference in the House Report to "physically *or conceptually*" (emphasis added) separable elements. The District of Columbia Circuit in *Esquire, Inc. v. Ringer*, 591 F.2d 796, 803-04 (D.C. Cir. 1978) (holding outdoor lighting fixtures ineligible for copyright), cert. denied, 440 U.S. 908 (1979), called this an "isolated reference" and gave it no significance. Professor Nimmer, however seemed to favor the observations of Judge Harold Leventhal in his concurrence in *Esquire*, who stated that "the overall legislative policy . . . sustains the Copyright Office in its effort to distinguish between the instances where the aesthetic element is conceptually severable and the instances where the aesthetic element is inextricably interwoven with the utilitarian aspect of the article." 591 F.2d at 807; *see* 1 Nimmer on Copyright § 2.08[B] at 2-93 to 2-96.2 (1986); [cit]. Looking to the section 101 definition of works of artistic craftsmanship requiring that artistic features be "capable of existing independently of the utilitarian aspects," Professor Nimmer queries whether that requires physical as distinguished from conceptual separability, but answers his query by saying "there is reason to conclude that it does not." See 1 Nimmer on Copyright § 2.08[B] at 2-96.1. In any event, in *Kieselstein-Cord v. Accessories by Pearl, Inc.*, 632 F.2d 989, 993 (2d Cir. 1980), this court accepted the idea that copyrightability can adhere in the "conceptual" separation of an artistic element. Indeed, the court went on to find such conceptual separation in reference to ornate belt buckles that could be and were worn separately as jewelry. *Kieselstein-Cord* was followed in *Norris Industries, Inc. v. International Telephone & Telegraph Corp.*, 696 F.2d 918, 923-24 (11th Cir.), cert. denied, 464 U.S. 818 (1983), although there the court upheld the Register's refusal to register automobile wire wheel covers, finding no "conceptually separable" work of art. *See also Transworld Mfg. Corp. v. Al Nyman & Sons, Inc.*, 95 F.R.D. 95 (D. Del. 1982) (finding conceptual separability sufficient to support copyright in denying summary judgment on copyrightability of eyeglass display cases).

In *Carol Barnhart Inc. v. Economy Cover Corp.*, 773 F.2d 411 (2d Cir. 1985), a divided panel of this circuit affirmed a district court grant of summary judgment of noncopyrightability of four life-sized, anatomically correct human torso forms. *Carol Barnhart* distinguished *Kieselstein-Cord*, but it surely did not overrule it. The distinction made was that the ornamented surfaces of the *Kieselstein-Cord* belt buckles "were not in any respect required by their utilitarian functions," but the features claimed to be aesthetic or artistic in the Carol Barnhart forms were "inextricably intertwined with the utilitarian feature, the display of clothes." [cit]. As Judge Newman's dissent made clear, the Carol Barnhart majority did not dispute "that 'conceptual separability' is distinct from 'physical separability' and, when present, entitles the creator of a useful article to a copyright on its design." [cit].

"Conceptual separability" is thus alive and well, at least in this circuit. The problem, however, is determining exactly what it is and how it is to be applied. Judge Newman's illuminating discussion in dissent in *Carol Barnhart*, see 773 F.2d at 419-24, proposed a test that aesthetic features are conceptually separable if "the article . . . stimulate[s] in the mind of the beholder a concept that is separate from the concept evoked by its utilitarian function." Id. at 422. This approach has received favorable endorsement by at least one commentator, W. Patry, Latman's The Copyright Law 43-45 (6th ed. 1986), who calls Judge Newman's test the "temporal displacement" test. It is to be distinguished from other possible ways in which conceptual separability can be tested, including whether the primary use is as a utilitarian article as opposed to an artistic work, whether the aesthetic aspects of the work can be said to be "primary," and whether the article is marketable as art, none of which is very satisfactory. But Judge Newman's test was rejected outright by the majority as "a standard so ethereal as to amount to a 'nontest' that would be extremely difficult, if not impossible, to administer or apply." 773 F.2d at 419 n.5.

Perhaps the differences between the majority and the dissent in *Carol Barnhart* might have been resolved had they had before them the Denicola article, *supra*. [cit]. There, Professor Denicola points out that although the Copyright Act of 1976 was an effort " 'to draw as clear a line as possible,' " in truth "there is no line, but merely a spectrum of forms and shapes responsive in varying degrees to utilitarian concerns." 67 Minn. L. Rev. at 741. Denicola argues that "the statutory directive requires a distinction between works of industrial design and works whose origins lie outside the design process, despite the utilitarian environment in which they appear." He views the statutory limitation of copyrightability as "an attempt to identify elements whose form and appearance reflect the unconstrained perspective of the artist," such features not being the product of industrial design. Id. at 742. "Copyrightability, therefore, should turn on the relationship between the proffered work and the process of industrial design." Id. at 741. He suggests that "the dominant characteristic of industrial design is the influence of nonaesthetic, utilitarian concerns" and hence concludes that copyrightability "ultimately should depend on the extent to which the work reflects artistic expression uninhibited by functional considerations."[2] Id. To state the Denicola test in the language of conceptual separability, if design elements reflect a merger of aesthetic and functional considerations, the artistic aspects of a work cannot be said to be conceptually separable from the utilitarian elements. Conversely, where design elements can be identified as reflecting the designer's artistic judgment exercised independently of functional influences, conceptual separability exists.

We believe that Professor Denicola's approach provides the best test for conceptual separability and, accordingly, adopt it here for several reasons. First, the approach is consistent with the holdings of our previous cases. In *Kieselstein-Cord*, for example, the artistic aspects of the belt buckles reflected purely aesthetic choices, independent of the buckles' function, while in *Carol Barnhart* the distinctive features of the torsos–the accurate anatomical design and the sculpted shirts and collars–showed clearly the influence of functional concerns. Though the torsos bore artistic features, it was evident that the designer incorporated those features to further the usefulness of the torsos as mannequins. Second, the test's emphasis on the influence of utilitarian concerns in the design process may help, as Denicola notes, to "alleviate the de facto discrimination against nonrepresentational art that has regrettably accompanied much of the current analysis."[3] Id. at 745. Finally, and perhaps most importantly, we think Denicola's test will not be too difficult to administer in practice. The work itself will continue to give "mute testimony" of its origins. In addition, the parties will be required to present evidence relating to the design process and the nature of the work, with the trier of fact making the determination whether the aesthetic design elements are significantly influenced by functional considerations. Turning now to the facts of this case, we note first that Brandir contends, and its chief owner David Levine testified, that the original design of the RIBBON Rack stemmed from wire sculptures that Levine had created, each formed from one continuous undulating piece of wire. These sculptures were, he said, created and displayed in his home as a means

---

[2] Professor Denicola rejects the exclusion of all works created with some utilitarian application in view, for that would not only overturn Mazer v. Stein, 347 U.S. 201 (1954), on which much of the legislation is based, but also "a host of other eminently sensible decisions, in favor of an intractable factual inquiry of questionable relevance." 67 Minn. L. Rev. at 741. He adds that "any such categorical approach would also undermine the legislative determination to preserve an artist's ability to exploit utilitarian markets." Id. (citing 17 U.S.C. § 113(a) (1976)).

[3] We are reminded not only by Judge Gesell in the district court in Esquire, 414 F. Supp. 939, 941 (D.D.C. 1976), but by Holmes in Bleistein v. Donaldson Lithographing Co., 188 U.S. 239, 251-52 (1903), by Mazer v. Stein, 347 U.S. at 214, and by numerous other opinions, that we judges should not let our own view of styles of art interfere with the decisionmaking process in this area. Denicola suggests that the shape of a Mickey Mouse telephone is copyrightable because its form is independent of function, and "[a] telephone shape owing more to Arp, Brancusi, or Moore than Disney may be equally divorced from utilitarian influence." 67 Minn. L. Rev. at 746. This is true, of course, of the artist Christo's "Running Fence," approved (following Professor Nimmer) as an example of conceptual separability in Keiselstein-Cord, 632 F.2d at 993.

of personal expression, but apparently were never sold or displayed elsewhere. He also created a wire sculpture in the shape of a bicycle and states that he did not give any thought to the utilitarian application of any of his sculptures until he accidentally juxtaposed the bicycle sculpture with one of the self-standing wire sculptures. It was not until November 1978 that Levine seriously began pursuing the utilitarian application of his sculptures, when a friend, G. Duff Bailey, a bicycle buff and author of numerous articles about urban cycling, was at Levine's home and informed him that the sculptures would make excellent bicycle racks, permitting bicycles to be parked under the overloops as well as on top of the underloops. Following this meeting, Levine met several times with Bailey and others, completing the designs for the RIBBON Rack by the use of a vacuum cleaner hose, and submitting his drawings to a fabricator complete with dimensions. The Brandir RIBBON Rack began being nationally advertised and promoted for sale in September 1979.

Turning now to the facts of this case, we note first that Brandir contends, and its chief owner David Levine testified, that the original design of the RIBBON Rack stemmed from wire sculptures that Levine had created, each formed from one continuous undulating piece of wire. These sculptures were, he said, created and displayed in his home as a means of personal expression, but apparently were never sold or displayed elsewhere. He also created a wire sculpture in the shape of a bicycle and states that he did not give any thought to the utilitarian application of any of his sculptures until he accidentally juxtaposed the bicycle sculpture with one of the self-standing wire sculptures. It was not until November 1978 that Levine seriously began pursuing the utilitarian application of his sculptures, when a friend, G. Duff Bailey, a bicycle buff and author of numerous articles about urban cycling, was at Levine's home and informed him that the sculptures would make excellent bicycle racks, permitting bicycles to be parked under the overloops as well as on top of the underloops. Following this meeting, Levine met several times with Bailey and others, completing the designs for the RIBBON Rack by the use of a vacuum cleaner hose, and submitting his drawings to a fabricator complete with dimensions. The Brandir RIBBON Rack began being nationally advertised and promoted for sale in September 1979.

In November 1982 Levine discovered that another company, Cascade Pacific Lumber Co., was selling a similar product. Thereafter, beginning in December 1982, a copyright notice was placed on all RIBBON Racks before shipment and on December 10, 1982, five copyright applications for registration were submitted to the Copyright Office. The Copyright Office refused registration by letter, stating that the RIBBON Rack did not contain any element that was "capable of independent existence as a copyrightable pictorial, graphic or sculptural work apart from the shape of the useful article." An appeal to the Copyright Office was denied by letter dated March 23, 1983, refusing registration on the above ground and alternatively on the ground that the design lacked originality, consisting of "nothing more than a familiar public domain symbol." In February 1984, after the denial of the second appeal of the examiner's decision, Brandir sent letters to customers enclosing copyright notices to be placed on racks sold prior to December 1982.

Between September 1979 and August 1982 Brandir spent some $38,500 for advertising and promoting the RIBBON Rack, including some 85,000 pieces of promotional literature to architects and landscape architects. Additionally, since October 1982 Brandir has spent some $66,000, including full-, half-, and quarter-page advertisements in architectural magazines such as Landscape Architecture, Progressive Architecture, and Architectural Record, indeed winning an advertising award from Progressive Architecture in January 1983. The RIBBON Rack has been featured in Popular Science, Art and Architecture, and Design 384 magazines, and it won an Industrial Designers Society of America design award in the spring of 1980. In the spring of 1984 the RIBBON Rack was selected from 200 designs to be included among 77 of the designs exhibited at the Katonah Gallery in an exhibition entitled "The Product of Design: An Exploration of the Industrial Design Process," an exhibition that was written up in the New York Times.

Sales of the RIBBON Rack from September 1979 through January 1985 were in excess of $1,367,000. Prior to the time Cascade Pacific began offering for sale its bicycle rack in August 1982, Brandir's sales were $436,000. The price of the RIBBON Rack ranges from $395 up to $2,025 for a stainless steel model and generally depends on the size of the rack, one of the most popular being the RB-7, selling for $485.

Applying Professor Denicola's test to the RIBBON Rack, we find that the rack is not copyrightable. It seems clear that the form of the rack is influenced in significant measure by utilitarian concerns and thus any aesthetic elements cannot be said to be conceptually separable from the utilitarian elements. This is true even though the sculptures which inspired the RIBBON Rack may well have been—the issue of originality aside—copyrightable.

Brandir argues correctly that a copyrighted work of art does not lose its protected status merely because it subsequently is put to a functional use. The Supreme Court so held in Mazer v. Stein, 347 U.S. 201 (1954), and Congress specifically intended to accept and codify Mazer in section 101 of the Copyright Act of 1976. [cit]. The district court thus erred in ruling that, whatever the RIBBON Rack's origins, Brandir's commercialization of the rack disposed of the issue of its copyrightability.

Had Brandir merely adopted one of the existing sculptures as a bicycle rack, neither the application to a utilitarian end nor commercialization of that use would have caused the object to forfeit its copyrighted status. Comparison of the RIBBON Rack with the earlier sculptures, however, reveals that while the rack may have been derived in part from one of more "works of art," it is in its final form essentially a product of industrial design. In creating the RIBBON Rack, the designer has clearly adapted the original aesthetic elements to accommodate and further a utilitarian purpose. These altered design features of the RIBBON Rack, including the spacesaving, open design achieved by widening the upper loops to permit parking under as well as over the rack's curves, the straightened vertical elements that allow in-and above-ground installation of the rack, the ability to fit all types of bicycles and mopeds, and the heavy-gauged tubular construction of rustproof galvanized steel, are all features that combine to make for a safe, secure, and maintenance-free system of parking bicycles and mopeds. Its undulating shape is said in Progressive Architecture, January 1982, to permit double the storage of conventional bicycle racks. Moreover, the rack is manufactured from 2 3/8-inch standard steam pipe that is bent into form, the six-inch radius of the bends evidently resulting from bending the pipe according to a standard formula that yields bends having a radius equal to three times the nominal internal diameter of the pipe.

Brandir argues that its RIBBON Rack can and should be characterized as a sculptural work of art within the minimalist art movement. Minimalist sculpture's most outstanding feature is said to be its clarity and simplicity, in that it often takes the form of geometric shapes, lines, and forms that are pure and free of ornamentation and void of association. As Brandir's expert put it, "The meaning is to be found in, within, around and outside the work of art, allowing the artistic sensation to be experienced as well as intellectualized." People who use Foley Square in New York City see in the form of minimalist art the "Tilted Arc," which is on the plaza at 26 Federal Plaza. Numerous museums have had exhibitions of such art, and the school of minimalist art has many admirers.

It is unnecessary to determine whether to the art would the RIBBON Rack properly would be considered an example of minimalist sculpture. The result under the copyright statute is not changed. Using the test we have adopted, it is not enough that, to paraphrase Judge Newman, the rack may stimulate in the mind of the reasonable observer a concept separate from the bicycle rack concept. While the RIBBON Rack may be worthy of admiration for its aesthetic qualities alone, it remains nonetheless the product of industrial design. Form and function are inextricably intertwined in the rack, its ultimate design being as much the result of utilitarian pressures as aesthetic choices. Indeed, the visually pleasing proportions and symmetricality of the rack represent design changes made in response to functional concerns. Judging from the awards the rack has received, it would seem in fact that Brandir has achieved with the RIBBON Rack the highest goal of modern industrial design, that is, the harmonious fusion of function and aesthetics. Thus there remains no artistic element of the RIBBON Rack that can be identified as separate and "capable of existing independently of, the utilitarian aspects of the article." Accordingly, we must affirm on the copyright claim.

As to whether the configuration of Brandir's bicycle rack can be protected under either section 43(a) of the Lanham Act, or New York State unfair competition law, we are reminded that the design of a product itself may function as its packaging or protectable trade dress. [cit]. The district court dismissed Brandir's claims, saying that its analysis of the copyright issue was sufficient to dispose of the Lanham Act and common law claims. The court stated "the design feature of the Ribbon Racks is clearly dictated by the function to be performed, namely, holding up bicycles. If the steam pipes were not bent into the design, but instead remained flat, the bicycles would not stand up, they would fall down." But as Judge Newman noted in his dissent in Carol Barnhart, 773 F.2d at 420 n. 1, the principle of conceptual separability of functional design elements in copyright law is different from the somewhat similar principle of functionality as developed in trademark law. . . .

Here, the district court limited its inquiry to determining whether portions of the RIBBON Rack performed the function of a bicycle rack. But the fact that a design feature performs a function does not make it essential to the performance of that function; it is instead the absence of alternative constructions performing the same function that renders the feature functional. Thus, the true test of functionality is not whether the feature in question performs a function, but whether the feature "is dictated by the functions to be performed," [cit] as evidenced by available alternative constructions. See Metro Kane Imports, Ltd. v. Rowoco, Inc., 618 F. Supp. 273, 275-76 (S.D.N.Y. 1985), aff'd mem., 800 F.2d 1128 (2d Cir. 1986) (finding high-tech design of orange juice squeezer not dictated by function to be performed as there was no evidence that design permitted juicer to be manufactured at lower price or with altered performance). There are numerous alternative bicycle rack constructions. The nature, price, and utility of these constructions are material issues of fact not suitable for determination by summary judgment. For example, while it is true that the materials used by Brandir are standard-size pipes, we have no way of knowing whether the particular size and weight of the pipes used is the best, the most economical, or the only available size and weight pipe in the marketplace. We would rather think the opposite might be the case. So, too, with the dimension of the bends being dictated by a standard formula corresponding to the pipe size; it could be that there are many standard radii and that the particular radius of Brandir's RIBBON Rack actually required new tooling. This issue of functionality on remand should be viewed in terms of bicycle racks generally and not one-piece undulating bicycle racks specifically. [cit]. We reverse and remand as to the trademark and unfair competition claims . . .

WINTER, CIRCUIT JUDGE, concurring in part and dissenting in part:

Although I concur in the reversal of the district court's grant of summary judgment on the trademark and unfair competition claims, I respectfully dissent from the majority's discussion and disposition of the copyright claim.

. . . The grounds of my disagreement are that: (1) my colleagues' adaptation of Professor Denicola's test diminishes the statutory concept of "conceptual separability" to the vanishing point; and (2) their focus on the process or sequence followed by the particular designer makes copyright protection depend upon largely fortuitous circumstances concerning the creation of the design in issue.

With regard to "conceptual separability," my colleagues deserve considerable credit for their efforts to reconcile [*Carol Barnhart*] with [*Kieselstein-Cord*]. In my view, these cases are not reconcilable. . . .

My colleagues' adaptation of the Denicola test tracks the *Carol Barnhart* approach, whereas I would adopt that taken in *Kieselstein-Cord*, which allows for the copyrightability of the aesthetic elements of useful articles even if those elements simultaneously perform utilitarian functions. The latter approach received its fullest elaboration in Judge Newman's dissent in *Carol Barnhart*, where he explained that "for the [artistic] design features to be 'conceptually separate' from the utilitarian aspects of the useful article that embodies the design, the article must stimulate in the mind of the beholder a concept that is separate from the concept evoked by its utilitarian function." 773 F.2d at 422 (Newman, J., dissenting).

In other words, the relevant question is whether the design of a useful article, however intertwined with the article's utilitarian aspects, causes an ordinary reasonable observer to perceive an aesthetic concept not related to the article's use. The answer to this question is clear in the instant case because any reasonable observer would easily view the Ribbon Rack as an ornamental sculpture. Indeed, there is evidence of actual confusion over whether it is strictly ornamental in the refusal of a building manager to accept delivery until assured by the buyer that the Ribbon Rack was in fact a bicycle rack. Moreover, Brandir has received a request to use the Ribbon Rack as environmental sculpture, and has offered testimony of art experts who claim that the Ribbon Rack may be valued solely for its artistic features. As one of those experts observed: "If one were to place a Ribbon Rack on an island without access, or in a park and surround the work with a barrier, . . . its status as a work of art would be beyond dispute."

My colleagues also allow too much to turn upon the process or sequence of design followed by the designer of the Ribbon Rack. They thus suggest that copyright protection would have been accorded "had Brandir merely adopted . . . as a bicycle rack" an enlarged version of one of David Levine's original sculptures rather than one that had wider upper loops and straightened vertical elements. I cannot agree that copyright protection for the Ribbon Rack turns on whether Levine serendipitously chose the final design of the Ribbon Rack during his initial sculptural musings or whether the original design had to be slightly modified to accommodate bicycles. Copyright protection, which is intended to generate incentives for designers by according property rights in their creations, should not turn on purely fortuitous events. For that reason, the Copyright Act expressly states that the legal test is how the final article is perceived, not how it was developed through various stages. It thus states in pertinent part:

> the design of a useful article . . . shall be considered a . . . sculptural work only if, and only to the extent that, such

design incorporates . . . sculptural features that can be identified separately from, and are capable of existing independently of, the utilitarian aspects of the article.

17 U.S.C. § 101 (1982) (emphasis added).

I therefore dissent from the decision so far as it relates to copyrightability but concur in its discussion and holding as to the trademark and unfair competition claims.

APPENDIX

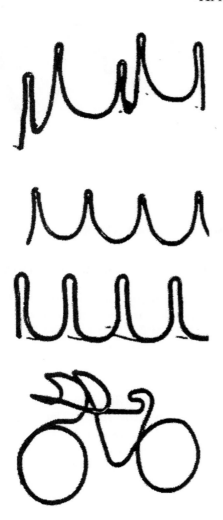

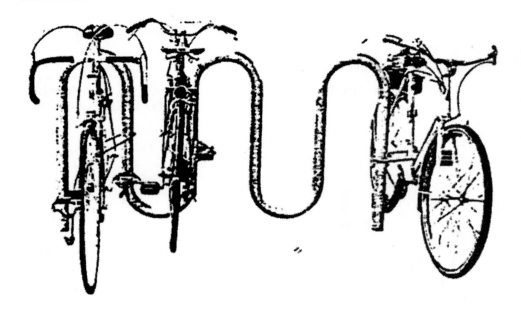

RE COCA-COLA CO'S APPLICATIONS
[1986] 2 All ER 274 (H.L. 1986) (UK)

LORD TEMPLEMAN.

My Lords, this is another attempt to expand on the boundaries of intellectual property and to convert a protective law into a source of monopoly. The attempt to use the Copyright Act 1956 for this purpose failed recently in British Leyland Motor Corp[.] Ltd[.] v[.] Armstrong Patents Co[.] Ltd[.] [1986] 1 All ER 850. The present attempt is based on the Trade Marks Act 1938.

Since the early 1920s the appellant, the Coca-Cola Co., has sold in the United Kingdom a non-alcoholic beverage under the name 'Coca-Cola' contained in bottles of a distinctive shape. The Patents Act 1977 and its predecessors conferred on the inventor of a registered novel product the right for a period, now 20 years, to control the use of the invention. The Coca-Cola bottle is not a novel product. The Copyright Act 1956 and its predecessors conferred on the author of an original artistic work the right for the life of the author and 50 years thereafter to control the reproduction of the work. The Coca-Cola bottle is not an artistic work. The Registered Designs Act 1949 and its predecessor, the Patents and Designs Act 1907, conferred on the author of a registered design the right for 15 years to control the use of the design. By section 1(3) of the 1949 Act "design" means:

features of shape, configuration, pattern or ornament applied to an article by any industrial process or means, being features which in the finished article appeal to and are judged solely by the eye . . .

The shape of the Coca-Cola bottle was accepted as a design and was registered under the 1907 Act. The effect of this registration expired in 1940 since when any rival manufacturer has been free to use the design of the Coca-Cola bottle.

The Coca-Cola Co. now claims that during and since the period of protection for the Coca-Cola bottle under the 1907 Act the Coca-Cola Co. has been entitled to a monopoly in the Coca-Cola bottle as a trade mark. The application of the Coca-Cola Co. to register the Coca-Cola bottle as a trade mark has been rejected by the hearing officer, by Falconer J, and by the Court of Appeal. [cit]. The Coca-Cola Co., undeterred by this formidable display of judicial unanimity, now appeals with the leave of the House.

The 1938 Act confers on the proprietor of a registered trade mark the exclusive right in perpetuity, subject to payment of fees and the observance of certain conditions not here relevant, to the use of a trade mark which is distinctive. . . . I assume, without deciding, that the Coca-Cola bottle is distinctive of a bottle containing the Coca-Cola beverage purveyed by the Coca-Cola Co. The application by the Coca-Cola Co. is for the registration of the Coca-Cola bottle with its distinctive shape as a trade mark in respect of non-alcoholic beverages.

It is not sufficient for the Coca-Cola bottle to be distinctive. The Coca-Cola Co. must succeed in the startling proposition that the bottle is a trade mark. If so, then any other container or any article of a distinctive shape is capable of being a trade mark. This raises the spectre of a total and perpetual monopoly in containers and articles achieved by means of the 1938 Act. Once the container or article has become associated with the manufacturer and distinctiveness has been established, with or without the help of the monopolies created by the Patents Act, the Registered Designs Act or the Copyright Act, the perpetual trade mark monopoly in the container or article can be achieved. In my opinion the 1938 Act was not intended to confer on the manufacturer of a container or on the manufacturer of an article a statutory monopoly on the ground that the manufacturer has in the eyes of the public established a connection between the shape of the container or article and the manufacturer. A rival manufacturer must be free to sell any container or article of similar shape provided the container or article is labelled or packaged in a manner which avoids confusion as to the origin of the goods in the container or the origin of the article. The Registrar of Trade Marks has always taken the view that the function of trade mark legislation is to protect the mark but not the article which is marked. I agree . . . The word "mark" both in its normal meaning and in its statutory definition is apt only to describe something which distinguishes goods rather that the goods themselves. A bottle is a container not a mark.

. . .

NOTES AND QUESTIONS

(1) **Unity of Art.** France is the prime example of a country following the philosophy of unity of art. "French law considers that any creation of form bearing an adequate mark of its author's personality, whatever its purpose or usefulness, comes necessarily under [copyright law and specific design legislation]. The said Unity of Art Theory results in a rejection of any criterion of aesthetic creation which could allow industrial art to be separated from real art." Marie-Angèle Pérot-Morel, *Specific Protection of Designs and its Relation to Protection by Copyright in French Law in* DESIGN PROTECTION 45, 47 (H. Cohen Jehoram ed. 1976). In what ways might copyright law be affected by permitting the copyright protection of relatively mundane industrial objects? *See* Graeme B. Dinwoodie, *Federalized Functionalism: The Future of Design Protection in the European Union*, 24 AM. INTELL. PROP. L. ASS'N Q.J. 611, 664 n.145 (1996) (discussing effect of expanding protectable subject-matter); ALAIN STROWEL, DROIT D'AUTEUR ET COPYRIGHT: DIVERGENCES ET CONVERGENCES 407-408 (1993) (discussing effect of unity of art doctrine on content of copyright law).

Although French law permits cumulative protection under copyright and design law, it does preclude the protection under those regimes of designs that are patentable and inseparable from the desired technical effect of the invention. *See* Specific Law on Designs, of July 14, 1909, art. 2; *Thermopac v. Seprosy*, (Cour de Cassation, 28 Mar. 1995), *reported at* 165 R.I.D.A. 326 (1995) (confirming scope of article 2). What justifications can be offered for permitting cumulation of copyright and design protection but not design and utility patent protection?

(2) **Limiting Cumulation.** In what ways are "measures needed to limit concurrent protection [under copyright law] likely to derogate from general principles of copyright law," as Professor Reichman suggests? Is it necessary to make it a distinction between industrial design and applied art? Why is it difficult to find a statutory formula that implements that distinction? Might a different line be easier to draw and equally effective? Review your answers to these questions, and consider which of the three positions on cumulation described by Professor Reichman seems most appropriate and why? Which position is endorsed by the Second Circuit in *Brandir*?

(3) **Trade Dress Protection for Designs.** In recent years, protection of designs in the United States has been achieved most effectively under trademark and unfair competition law. The first recognition of this development at the federal appellate level came in 1976. Twelve years before that, the U.S. Supreme Court made it more difficult for individual states to offer this form of protection under state unfair competition laws, *see Sears, Roebuck & Co. v. Stiffel Co.*, 376 U.S. 225 (1964); *Compco Corp. v. Day-Brite Lighting, Inc.*, 376 U.S. 234 (1964), but those decisions have been circumvented by the use of federal protection, and the permissible boundaries of such federal protection has not yet been fully tested before the U.S. Supreme Court. In the following two decades, courts have protected under

the rubric of "trade dress" the design features of an extensive range of products including kitchen appliances, sporting equipment, candies, bathroom fittings, sports cars, furniture, hardware items, fashion accessories, lamps, and even golf holes. For discussion of these developments, see generally Margreth Barrett, *Trade Dress Protection for Product Configurations and the Federal Right to Copy*, 20 HAST. COMM./ENT. L.J. 471 (1998); Graeme B. Dinwoodie, *The Death of Ontology: A Teleological Approach to Trademark Law*, 84 IOWA L. REV. 611 (1999); Graeme B. Dinwoodie, *Reconceptualizing the Inherent Distinctiveness of Product Design Trade Dress*, 75 NORTH CAROLINA L. REV. 471 (1997); J.H. Reichman, *Design Protection and the New Technologies: The United States Experience in a Transnational Perspective*, 19 U. BALT. L. REV. 6 (1989).

The EU Trademark Directive now requires EU member states to provide registered trademark protection for product shapes under national law. *See* Trademark Directive, art. 2. Why might the cumulation of trademark and design protection be more acceptable than cumulation of copyright and design protection? Or is Lord Templeman correct that trademark protection for shapes raises the specter of monopolies in useful articles? *See* Thomas F. Cotter, *Is This Conflict Really Necessary? Resolving An Ostensible Conflict Between Patent Law and Federal Trademark Law*, 3 MARQ. INTELL. PROP. L. REV. 25 (1999); Jay Dratler, Jr., *Trade Dress Protection For Product Configurations: Is There a Conflict with Patent Policy?*, 24 AM. INTELL. PROP. L. ASS'N Q.J. 427, 430-31 (1996). Lord Templeman's decision in *Coca-Cola* has been reversed in the U.K. by legislation implementing the EU Trademark Directive; indeed, the first shape-based registration applications under the new United Kingdom law included the Coca Cola bottle. Applications have also been made to register the design of products, such as the shape of the classic Morgan sports car. The shape of the Coca-Cola bottle has long been registered in the U.S. as a trademark for the carbonated soft drink produced by the Coca Cola Co.

[B] Specialized Design Protection Regimes

Although many countries have specialized design protection regimes, the substantive content, procedural formality, and practical reach of these regimes can vary widely. Moreover, the importance of specialized regimes in ensuring effective design protection in any country is in large part dependent upon the limits (both intended and unintended) of protection afforded designs under existing systems of intellectual property. The EU Design Directive, adopted in 2000, sought to harmonize the collection of specialized registered design laws then prevailing in the member countries of the Union. That Directive, which was to be implemented in member states by October 28, 2001, is discussed in detail *infra* Chapter 4. A study of the pre-Directive design laws in the countries of the EU illustrates, however, the points of divergence that one still finds among different national laws.

GRAEME B. DINWOODIE, FEDERALIZED FUNCTIONALISM: THE FUTURE OF DESIGN PROTECTION IN THE EUROPEAN UNION[*]

24 AM. INTELL. PROP. L. ASS'N Q.J. 611, 619-625 (1996)

Consider the following hypothetical involving a multinational producer of kitchen appliances. Our putative producer seeks to design a coffee-maker and market it throughout Europe. The design of the coffee-maker embodies the highest ideals of modern functionalism, reflecting (without clear demarcation) aesthetic, functional, ergonomic, safety, cultural and other concerns. Patent law might protect any technical advance made by the coffee-maker that is truly novel and inventive. But what protection do the laws . . . in place in the countries of the EU [prior to implementation of the EU Design Directive] offer to this paradigm of functionalism against imitation of its appearance by second-comers?

The cheapest form of protection to obtain is copyright, which is available without the need to comply with formalities. In some countries of the EU— most notably France and the Benelux countries—the design of the coffee-maker might be protectable by copyright (against unauthorized reproduction) for a relatively long period of time. Sole reliance on copyright would, however, provide incomplete protection elsewhere in Europe. Italian law would provide protection for the full term of copyright if the design passed the dissociability test of Italian law; but this is unlikely given the intentional blending of form and function. German and Spanish law might offer copyright protection, but only if the design displays a "marked artistic character"—a requirement that operates in practice to exclude most functionalist designs from copyright. And since 1988, U.K. law limits the application of copyright proper to industrially marketed designs. Thus, although copyright protection is cheap to obtain, and slow to expire, our producer seeking truly European-wide protection must look to other forms of protection.

Most of the countries of the EU, including those in which copyright might be available, also offer some form of special design law that might protect the design of the producer's coffee-maker. Indeed, although these protections typically last for a shorter period of time than copyright and impose the cost of depositing or registering the design, they confer (in most countries) broader monopoly-type rights.[26] The costs of registration might thus appear worthwhile; perhaps, even the cost of a separate (but similar) application in each Member State might be justified. The producer should not be too optimistic, however. Although nearly all the countries of the EU have enacted design laws of some sort, the elements of those systems diverge widely (even where those elements are similarly labeled).

---

[*] Copyright 1996, Graeme B. Dinwoodie.

[26] *See* Alison Firth, *Aspects of Design Protection in Europe*, 15 EUR. INTELL. PROP. REV. 42, 43 (1993) ("In most jurisdictions an absolute monopoly is conferred [by special design protection] . . . but in Germany and France, the [protection offered] . . . is against imitation [of the design]."); . . .

The variation in the requirement that a design be "novel," nominally common to all member states, illustrates graphically how terminology may mask significant differences. Novelty is far from a unitary concept. Some Member States judge the novelty of a design quite subjectively, affording it a meaning almost analogous to copyright originality; others conduct more objective measurements. Different Member States will cast their scrutiny of prior designs more or less broadly in time and space in determining whether the design in question is novel. [28] Indeed, marketing of the coffee-maker in one country in reliance upon the copyright protection available there might destroy the novelty required for design protection in other Member States.

Moreover, some Member States impose additional requirements above novelty that purport, in their own unique ways, to determine whether the design is sufficiently different from what has preceded it to warrant protection. Further discrepancies occur with respect to the duration of rights obtained, and the nature of the examination to which designs seeking this protection are subjected. [32] Finally, because our coffee-maker reflects the purest ideal of functionalism, and blends form imperceptibly with function, it may be denied protection in some Member States under an "ornamentality" or "eye-appeal" requirement. The United Kingdom, for example, offers registered design protection only to designs that "appeal to the eye," effectively excluding functional designs from protection. [33]

In short, our producer's coffee-maker might be novel in some countries, but not others; in some Member States, novelty might be insufficient to warrant protection; its functionalist pedigree may thwart claims of protection in many countries; and the applications to be filed in each country are by no means uniform, and may be subjected to different levels of scrutiny. Complexity and inconsistency are the hallmarks of design protection in Europe. And this brief description does not even address the additional options of trademark protection, unfair competition actions, and utility model

---

[28] Hugh Griffiths has summarized the problems of determining the appropriate prior art as follows:

> In Ireland, Benelux and the United Kingdom, there are limitations in space; the design has to be new in the State concerned. In Denmark and Portugal, there is a time criterion; the design is deemed to be new if no identical form has been used or protected since a certain point in the past. In Benelux and Germany, a design is not new if it is known to the national circles specialized in the relevant sector . . . "

Hugh Griffiths, *Overview of Developments in Europe on Industrial Design Protection*, 4 FORDHAM INTELL. PROP., MEDIA & ENT. J. 359, 362 (1993).

[32] Some countries impose no substantive examination (for example, the Benelux, Italy, Germany and Spain). Others, such as France, will examine as to certain grounds but conduct no search for prior art. Finally, the U.K. conducts a substantive examination prior to the grant of a registered design.

[33] *See* Registered Designs Act 1949 § 1(1) (U.K.). Countries other than the U.K. impose standards of ornamentality. *See* Firth, *supra*, at 45-46 (listing Germany and Spain as imposing ornamental requirement). In contrast, Sweden, for example, extends its registered design protection to all designs, whether aesthetic or functional. [cit].

protection that—again in varying ways in different Member States—might affect the protectability of the design of the coffee-maker.

L.A. GEAR, INC. v. THOM McAN SHOE CO.
988 F.2d 1117 (Fed. Cir. 1993)

NEWMAN, CIRCUIT JUDGE

Thom McAn Shoe Company, the Melville Corporation, and Pagoda Trading Company, Inc. (together "Appellants") appeal the decision of the United States District Court for the Southern District of New York, holding Melville and its division Thom McAn (together "Melville") liable for design patent infringement, and holding Appellants liable for unfair competition based on trade dress infringement in terms of § 43(a) of the Lanham Act and the New York State unfair competition law. The district court enjoined further infringement and awarded damages under the Lanham Act. The court declined to award enhanced damages or attorney fees.

We affirm the ruling of liability for patent infringement as to four shoe models, and reverse the ruling that infringement was not willful. We reverse the finding of liability under § 43(a) of the Lanham Act as to six shoe models.

Background

In 1987 L.A. Gear designed a line of women's and girls' athletic shoes identified as the L.A. Gear's "Hot Shots" shoes. United States Design Patent No 299,081 was granted on December 27, 1988 ("the '081 patent"). Figure 4 of the patent is shown:

Although color is not part of the patented design, the colors used on these shoes and their placement are part of the trade dress for which L.A. Gear claims protection from unfair competition.

In the summer and fall or 1987 L.A. Gear exhibited the Hot Shots line of shoes to retailers at trade shows, and announced that these shoes had been selected as L.A. Gear's "hero" or featured shoe line, on which major promotion and advertising would be focused for the ensuing year. . . . A L.A. Gear Hot Shots shoe is pictured:

This line of shoes was a commercial success, with four million pairs sold by February, 1989. The sales volume was significantly higher than for any of L.A. Gear's other styles. The shoes were sold primarily in department stores, sporting goods stores, and athletic shoe stores, at a retail price ranging from $35 to $60.

L.A. Gear testified that it had a policy against sale of its shoes in discount stores. Melville Corporation sells shoes in discount stores, through its divisions Thom McAn and Meldisco. Thom McAn sells shoes in its own stores, and Meldisco sells shoes in K Mart stores. The Pagoda Trading Company arranges for the manufacture of shoes in the Far East and their importation into the United States.

The district court found that in early 1988 the Appellants, observing the success of L.A. Gear's Hot Shots design, decided to copy it. Designers employed by the Appellants used the L.A. Gear shoes as models for the shoes accused of infringement: a women's high top shoe sold in Thom McAn stores with the trademark BALLOONS; high and low top women's and girls' models sold in K Mart stores with the trademark AEROBIX; and a women's low top shoe sold in K Mart stores with the trademark MacGREGOR. (Additional models carrying the marks JUST KIDDING and SHOOTERS were stated to have been discovered after trial, and are not included in our decision.) All of the trademarks are displayed in the same location on the shoe, in the same color-coordinated style, as the L.A. GEAR trademark. Acknowledging the presence of these trademarks, the district court found that six models of Appellants' shoes were "strikingly similar" to L.A. Gear's Hot Shots design, and that the conditions of unfair competition were met. These and related issues are raised on this appeal.

I. THE DESIGN PATENT

35 U.S.C. § 171 provides that a patent may be obtained for the ornamental design of an article of manufacture.

> 35 U.S.C. § 171. Whoever invents any new, original and ornamental design for an article of manufacture may obtain a patent therefor, subject to the conditions and requirements of this title.

A patented design is ordinarily claimed "as shown", that is, by its drawing.

> 37 C.F.R. § 1.153(a). The title of the design must designate the particular article. No description, other than a reference to the drawing, is ordinarily required. The claim shall be in formal terms to the ornamental design for the article (specifying name) as shown, or as shown and described. More than one claim is neither required nor permitted.

L.A. Gear charged only Melville with patent infringement, since Pagoda had ceased importation before the issuance of the '081 patent. Melville was held liable for patent infringement with respect to four models of shoes: a women's high top BALLOONS shoe (model no. 78191); a women's high top AEROBIX shoe (model no. 78505); and two girls' high top AEROBIX shoes (models no. 71878 and 76878).

Melville raised defenses of patent invalidity and non-infringement, on the following premises:

Functionality

Melville asserted at trial, and argues on appeal, that the design of the '081 patent is "functional" and that the patent is therefore invalid. Invalidity due to functionality is an affirmative defense to a claim of infringement of a design patent, and must be proved by the party asserting the defense. Applying the presumption of validity, [cit], invalidity of a design patent must be established by clear and convincing evidence.

A design patent is directed to the appearance of an article of manufacture. An article of manufacture necessarily serves a utilitarian purpose, and the design of a useful article is deemed to be functional when the appearance of the claimed design is "dictated by" the use or purpose of the article. [cit]. If the particular design is essential to the use of the article, it can not be the subject of a design patent.

Melville argues that each element comprising the '081 design has a utilitarian purpose: that is, the delta wing provides support for the foot and reinforces the shoelace eyelets; the mesh on the side of the shoe also provides support; the moustache at the back of the shoe provides cushioning for the Achilles tendon and reinforcement for the rear of the shoe; and the position of each of these elements on the shoe is due to its function. However, the utility of each of the various elements that comprise the design is not the relevant inquiry with respect to a design patent. In determining whether a design is primarily functional or primarily ornamental the claimed design is viewed in its entirety, for the ultimate question is not the functional or decorative aspect of each separate feature, but the overall appearance of the article, in determining whether the claimed design is dictated by the utilitarian purpose of the article. [cit].

That elements of the '081 design, such as the delta wing or the side mesh, also provide support for the foot does not mean that the specific design of each element, and the combination of these elements into the patented design, is dictated by primarily functional considerations. The elements of the design may indeed serve a utilitarian purpose, but it is the ornamental aspect that is the basis of the design patent. [cit].

The district court remarked on the existence of a myriad of athletic shoe designs in which each of the functions identified by Melville as performed by the '081 design elements was achieved in a way other than by the design of the '081 patent. When there are several ways to achieve the function of an article of manufacture, the design of the article is more likely to serve a primarily ornamental purpose. *See Avia Group International, Inc. v. L.A. Gear California, Inc.*, 853 F.2d 1557, 1563 (Fed. Cir. 1988). It was not disputed that there were other ways of designing athletic shoes to perform the functions of the elements of the '081 design. In today's marketplace, the primacy of appearance in the design of shoes can not be ignored when analyzing functionality.

The district court found that the '081 design was primarily ornamental, and that the patent was not invalid on the ground of functionality. Clear error has not been shown in this ruling, which is affirmed.

Obviousness

A patented design must meet the substantive criteria of patentability, including non-obviousness in accordance with the law of 35 U.S.C. § 103. *See* 35 U.S.C. § 171 ("The provisions of this title relating to patents for inventions shall apply to patents for designs, except as otherwise provided.").

In applying the law of § 103 to the particular facts pertinent to the patented design, obviousness vel non is reviewed from the viewpoint of a designer of ordinary skill or capability in the field to which the design pertains. *In re Nalbandian*, 661 F.2d 1214, 1216 (CCPA 1981). As with utility patents, obviousness is not determined as if the designer had hindsight knowledge of the patented design.

When the patented design is a combination of selected elements in the prior art, a holding of obviousness requires that there be some teaching or suggestion whereby it would have been obvious to a designer of ordinary skill to make the particular selection and combination made by the patentee. [cit]. The first step in the analysis, when the subject is design, is whether there is "a reference to something in existence, the design characteristics of which are basically the same as the claimed design, in order to support a holding of obviousness" [cit]. Thus not only the individual elements, but the ornamental quality of the combination must be suggested in the prior art. [cit].

Melville offered twenty-two references that were asserted to show or suggest various features of the '081 design, and argues that the '081 design is readily reconstructed from elements found in the prior art. The district court found that all of the elements of the design of the '081 patent were known, but that these particular elements had not previously been combined in a single shoe design. A reconstruction of known elements does not invalidate a design patent, absent some basis whereby a designer of ordinary skill would be led to create this particular design. The district court concluded that there was no teaching or suggestion in the prior art of the appearance of the claimed design as a visual whole. We discern no error in this conclusion or the premises on which it rests. The undisputed commercial success of the patented design, and Appellants' copying thereof, are also relevant to analysis of the obviousness of a design. [cit].

The district court's holding that the '081 design patent is not invalid under 35 U.S.C. § 103 is affirmed.

Infringement

In 35 U.S.C. § 289 infringement is defined as unauthorized manufacture or sale of "the patented design, or any colorable imitation thereof". Design patent infringement is a question of fact, to be proven by a preponderance of the evidence. [cit].

Design patent infringement requires a showing that the accused design is substantially the same as the claimed design. The criterion is deception of the ordinary observer, such that one design would be confused with the other:

> We hold, therefore, that if, in the eye of an ordinary observer, giving such attention as a purchaser usually gives, two designs are substantially the same, if the resemblance is such as to deceive such an observer, inducing him to purchase one supposing it to be the other, the first one patented is infringed by the other.

Gorham v. White, 81 U.S. (14 Wall.) at 528; [cit].

In conducting such analysis the patented design is viewed in its entirety, as it is claimed. As for other patented inventions, reference is made to the prior art and the prosecution history in order to give appropriate weight to the factors that contributed to patentability. [cit]. While the accused design must appropriate the novelty that distinguished the patented design from the prior art, *see Litton Systems, Inc. v. Whirlpool Corp.*, 728 F.2d 1423, 1444 (Fed. Cir. 1984), the ultimate question requires determining whether "the effect of the whole design [is] substantially the same". *Gorham v. White*, 81 U.S. at 530. *See Shelcore, Inc. v. Durham Industries, Inc.*, 745 F.2d 621, 628 n.16 (Fed. Cir. 1984) (the requirements of *Gorham v. White* and *Litton v. Whirlpool* are conjunctive).

The district court found that the designs of four models of Melville's accused shoes were "almost a direct copy" of the '081 design. Pictured is the BALLOONS model no. 78191:

Substantial similarity is not disputed; indeed, copying is admitted. However, Melville complains that the district court's treatment of the issue of patent infringement was "cursory", in that the court referred, in the part of its opinion relating to patent infringement, to its findings on likelihood of confusion relative to the trade dress issue.

In discussing trade dress, the district court had found that the L.A. Gear shoes and the accused shoes were substantially similar in design, such that the ordinary observer would confuse one with the other. Although design patent analysis requires comparison of the claimed design with the accused articles, Melville has not argued that the patent drawing differs from the embodiment in the L.A. Gear shoe, and has offered no reason why the finding of substantial similarity between the actual shoes was not applicable to the infringement analysis. When the patented design and the design of the article sold by the patentee are substantially the same, it is not error to compare the patentee's and the accused articles directly; indeed, such comparison may facilitate application of the Gorham criterion of whether an ordinary purchaser would be deceived into thinking that one were the other. It was in this context that the district court analyzed likelihood of confusion. No methodological error has been shown in this analysis.

Design patent infringement relates solely to the patented design, and does not require proof of unfair competition in the marketplace or allow of avoidance of infringement by labeling. The district court did not confuse the criteria relevant to these causes of action. Although Melville argues specific differences in features of the four models that were found to infringe the '081 patent, the district court found that "the placement of all the major design elements is the same, creating the same distinctive overall look", and recognized that the novelty resided in the overall appearance of the combination. The court found, in the terms of *Gorham v. White*, that the four infringing models were confusingly similar to the patented design, as viewed by an ordinary observer.

Reversible error has not been shown. The district court's holding of design patent infringement is affirmed.

[The Court reversed the district court's finding on wilfulness, and concluded that 43(a) of the Lanham Act had not been violated because the conspicuous and permanent placement of the plaintiff's and defendant's trademarks on the shoes prevented the likelihood of confusion].

NOTES AND QUESTIONS

(1) **The Inadequacies of Design Patent Protection.** The *L.A. Gear* decision represents a rare victory at the appellate level for a design patent owner alleging infringement. The dismal record of design patent owners before the courts (particularly prior to 1982) dissuaded many producers from seeking this form of protection. *See* David Goldenberg, *The Long And Winding Road: A History of The Fight Over Industrial Design Protection In The United States*, 45 J. COPR. SOC'Y 21, 22-24 (1997) (describing history of difficulties). From your understanding of the nature of modern industrial design, which aspects of the design patent law described in *L.A. Gear* would you expect to cause problems for producers seeking effective design protection?

(2) **The Elements of Design Patent Protection.** In what ways is the protection offered by a design patent in the United States different from that offered by U.S. trade dress law or copyright law? What explains those differences?

(3) **Japanese Law.** Japan protects designs under a *sui generis* design code, but does so only after the design application has undergone a

substantive examination. In 1993, in response to claims that (like the U.S. design patent system), the system was not offering effective protection to designs, Japan amended its unfair competition laws to offer protection against slavish imitation of products within three years after first marketing. *See* Kozo Yabe, *Protection of Configuration of Goods Under Unfair Competition Prevention Regulations in Japan*, 2 MODERN TRENDS IN INTELL. PROP. 65, 76-82 (1998); *see also* Shinto Teramoto, *Copyrightability and Scope of protection for Works of Utilitarian Nature Under Japanese Law*, 28 I.I.C. 51 (1997).

(4) **Protection of Incremental Innovation.** Design is not typically thought of as involving radical groundbreaking discoveries and inventions. It is more consciously a process of tinkering, of problem-solving. Professor Reichman has aptly described it as a form of "incremental innovation." J.H. Reichman, *Legal Hybrids Between the Patent and Copyright Paradigms*, 94 COLUM. L. REV. 2432 (1994). How does this observation affect the nature and extent of protection that should be offered industrial designs?

THE U.K. UNREGISTERED DESIGN RIGHT

Since 1988, U.K. law has limited the application of copyright proper to industrially marketed designs. *See* Copyright, Designs & Patents Act 1988, § 51. In this, the United Kingdom is not unlike Italy or the United States. And, like Japan and the United States, the United Kingdom subjects applications for registered design protection to a substantive examination of novelty. However, one aspect of the reforms enacted in the United Kingdom in 1988 was (at the time) unique: a new form of protection called "unregistered design right." The unregistered design right differs from the U.K. registered design right in several important ways. First, it is not contingent on the design "appealing to the eye" and is thus available to both aesthetic and functional designs. *Compare* Registered Designs Act, § 1(3); Copyright, Designs & Patents Act 1988 § 213(2) (designs defined without reference to aesthetic appeal). Second, it is available without registration; instead it subsists upon the design being recorded in a design document or an article being made to the design. *See id.* § 213(6). Third, protection is available to designs satisfying an arguably lower threshold: to obtain unregistered design protection, designs must merely be "original." *See id.* § 213(1). However, for the purposes of unregistered design right protection, a "design is not original if it is commonplace in the design field" in question. *See id.* § 213(4). Effectively, this imposes a threshold that is slightly more strenuous than copyright originality. Although in the first case to address the issue the provision was interpreted by the U.K. courts as imposing a requirement of objective novelty (similar to the test of registered design protection), *see C&H Engineering v. F. Klucznik & Sons*, 19 F.S.R. 421, 428 (Ch. D. 1992), this decision was criticized and later courts have not insisted upon that higher standard. *See* Lionel Bently & Alan Coulthard, *From the*

Commonplace to the Interface: Five Cases on Unregistered Design Right, 19 EUR. INTELL. PROP. REV. 401 (1997). Fourth, whereas a design registration confers the "exclusive right to make, sell or offer for sale articles in respect of which the design is registered," Registered Designs Act 1949, § 7, the unregistered design right provides protection only against copying. *See* Copyright Designs & Patents Act 1988, § 226; CHRISTINE FELLNER, INDUSTRIAL DESIGN LAW 203 (1995) ("there can be no design right infringement where the design has been independently created"). Finally, the unregistered design right is shorter in duration: ten years from the end of the calendar year in which the articles made to the design are first made available for sale or hire, with an additional five years remuneration rights, as opposed to twenty-five years protection accorded by registration. To which policy concerns does the creation of the unregistered right appear targeted? *See* FELLNER, *supra*, at 104-105. To what extent do the different characteristics of the right listed above assist in addressing those concerns?

Because the unregistered design right grants protection to functional designs on conditions intentionally less exacting than imposed on a utility patent applicant, the legislation introduced a series of exceptions to restrict protection of subpatentable designs with significant functional ramifications. Protection is not available to so-called "must-fit" designs. *See* Copyright, Designs & Patents Act, 1988, § 213(3)(b)(i) (design right does not subsist in "features of shape or configuration of an article which enable the article to be connected to, or placed in, around or against, another article so that either article may perform its function."). For example, the door seal of a washing machine must be the same shape as the opening that it is intended to seal or it will be of no use: such a shape cannot be the subject of protection. And "must-match" designs, such as body panels of cars that must match the appearance of the rest of the car, are also denied protection. These are "features of shape or configuration of an article which . . . are dependent upon the appearance of another article of which the article is intended by the designer to form an integral part." *Id.* § 213(3)(b)(ii). (Both of these exclusions also apply—expressly in the case of must-match designs, and effectively through a combination of other provisions as regards must-fit designs—to registered design protection.) What other types of design might fit the definition of "must-fit" and "must-match" designs? Does the need to exclude protection for door seals and body panels reveal anything about the nature of this new form of design protection?

THE VESSEL HULL DESIGN PROTECTION ACT

As the *Brandir* court noted, the separability requirement (consciously modeled on Italian law) was intended to preclude copyright protection for industrial designs. Until not long before passage of the 1976 Copyright Act, however, the bill being considered used the separability requirement not to prevent protection, but rather to force industrial designs to seek protection under a proposed Title II, which would have created short-term design rights for original ornamental designs. But at the last minute Title II was deleted, in large part because of opposition from the powerful Chair of the congressional subcommittee responsible for copyright. Efforts to enact design protection have been made almost every year since then, but with no success until the 1998 passage of the Vessel Hull Design Protection Act.

The Vessel Hull Design Protection Act, Title V of the Digital Millennium Copyright Act, Pub. L. No. 105-304, 112 Stat. 2860 (1998), codified at 17 U.S.C. § 1300 *et seq.*, gives ten years of anti-copying protection to the designers of original designs of the hulls (including the decks) of boats of less than 200 feet in length. Unlike the main body of the Copyright Act, the Vessel Hull Act defines the threshold requirement of originality, and does so in terms that resemble the standard used by courts in determining the originality of derivative works for copyright purposes. *See* 17 U.S.C. § 1301(b)(1) (a design is original if "it is the result of the designer's creative endeavor that provides a distinguishable variation over prior work pertaining to similar articles which is more than merely trivial and has not been copied from another source"). This standard is significantly lower than that required by the design patent statute, and appears well tailored to reflect the incremental nature of design innovation. Protection is, however, limited to designs "which make the article attractive or distinctive in appearance to the purchasing or using public," *id.* § 1301(a)(1), which appears similar to the "eye-appeal" requirement of U.K. registered design law. How well is this requirement tailored to the nature of modern design? How should this provision be interpreted? Should courts refer to case law on the "ornamentality" requirement in design patent law? (Under what head of analysis was that requirement effectively considered in the *L.A. Gear* opinion?) Should U.S. courts look to interpretation of the "eye appeal" concept in U.K. registered design law?

Even if the Vessel Hull Design Protection Act is liberally interpreted to reach functional designs, the statute (like the U.K. unregistered design right which consciously protects functional designs) carefully circumscribes protection to prevent over-protection of both subpatentable functional features and common design variants in the industry. The principal exclusions contained in the Vessel Hull Act are of designs that are "staple or commonplace" (or different from such a design in only "insignificant details or in elements commonly used in the relevant trades") or "dictated solely by a utilitarian function of the article that embodies it.". *See* 17 U.S.C. § 1302. To what extent do these differ from the functionality exclusions found in design patent law or trade dress law?

Protection under this new title subsists from the date that the design is made public by the public exhibition, distribution, offer for sale or sale to the public of the useful article embodying the design (or when the registration of the design is published, if that is earlier). *See* 17 U.S.C. §§ 1304, 1310(b). Application for registration must, however, be made by filing an application with the Copyright Office within two years of the boat hull embodying the design being made public by the design owner. *See id.* §§ 1310(a), 1302(5). And, as in copyright infringement actions, registration is a prerequisite to suit. *See id.* § 1321(a). The review by the Copyright Office will be restricted to determination of whether "the application relates to a design which on its face appears to be subject to protection." *Id.* § 1313. (The Office recently issued interim regulations governing the filing of applications. *See* Federal Register 36576 (July 7, 1999).) Although the rights of the owner are cast in terms that mirror those of a patentee, *see id.* § 1308, the rights are effectively anti-copying rights by virtue of defenses that are recognized in persons acting without knowledge. *See id.* § 1309(c). In many respects, therefore, as reflected perhaps by the allocation of institutional responsibilities, this is a copyright-inspired form of protection. Is copyright protection an appropriate model for the protection of functional designs? If so, why does U.S. law resist the unity of art philosophy found in French law? Why did Congress create a separate chapter, and a self-contained regime, in the copyright title of the U.S. Code?

The Vessel Hull Act would appear to be a potential model for more broad-based design protection legislation. The current provisions have been drafted in a way that would, with extremely minimal legislative effort, be converted into a broad-based regime. For example, the central provision of the legislation (Section 1301(a)(1)) states that:

> The designer or other owner of an original design of a useful article which makes the article attractive or distinctive in appearance to the purchasing or using public may secure the protection provided by this Chapter upon complying therewith.

The scope of the regime is thus established by the definition of "useful article." For the most part, that definition follows that currently found in the body of the Copyright statute: an article with "an intrinsic utilitarian function that is not merely to portray the appearance of the article or to convey information." However, the definition of "useful article" for the purposes of this chapter is preceded by this language: "a useful article is a vessel hull, including a plug or mold, which in normal use has . . . " With this preceding language, the design law is restricted to the appearance of the hull of boats; without it, the Act is a turnkey design law of general application. If you were a member of the U.S. Senate, would you support the minimal amendment necessary to convert the current statute into a broad-based design regime? The protection under this Chapter will be terminated upon the issuance of a design patent, *see id.* § 1329, but may be cumulated with trademark rights. *See id.* § 1330(2). If a broad-based design regime were enacted along the lines of the Vessel Hull Act, should cumulation be permitted? If not, should the design patent statute be repealed? Would it be appropriate also to restrict product design trade dress protection (either by complete denial of protection, or by prohibiting cumulation)?

PART III

PRINCIPLES OF INTERNATIONAL PROTECTION

Chapter 3

INTERNATIONAL LAW AND INSTITUTIONS

§ 3.01   The Nature and Sources of International Law

The system of nation states as we know it grew slowly over a period of centuries, crystallizing in Western Europe in the mid-seventeenth century with the Peace of Westphalia of 1648, then spread to North and South America first, and to Africa and Asia only later. The term "international law" was coined by Jeremy Bentham in 1789 in his *Introduction to the Principles of Morals and Legislation*. An older term, the "law of nations," from Roman times had referred to a universal law (*jus gentium*), an ethically determined "law of peoples" or even "law of tribes." Bentham's international law, by contrast, refers to the rules of engagement among nation states, distinguishable from the internal law of any of those states. In common parlance, the internal law of a nation-state is referred to as "municipal" or "local" law. Although the term "law of nations" is used less frequently today, the basic concept remains embodied in part in the term "customary international law."

Few nation states had significantly developed intellectual property laws in place at the beginning of the nineteenth century. The history of international intellectual property cooperation is much more recent, beginning in earnest only during the last three decades of the nineteenth century in the form of written international agreements. By that era, the modern view of international law espoused by Bentham had become the predominant one. In the milieu of the nineteenth century international system, positive international law gained its readiest expression in the form of treaties between nation states; and the expository jurisprudence of the period placed the explicit agreements between nation states in a hierarchy above empirical observations as to customary law between them or logically or ethically derived principles by which nation states should behave. Consequently, at least until very recently, few would have argued that intellectual property rights were determined by principles of customary international law. It is doubtful that most states today would accept any assertion that they were obliged to protect intellectual property rights of citizens of other states other than by express agreement in the form of a treaty or statute. But an understanding of the broader structure of international law is essential to an appreciation of the ways in which contemporary international intellectual property law and policy may be breaking new ground.

RESTATEMENT OF THE LAW (THIRD), FOREIGN RELATIONS LAW OF THE UNITED STATES, § 102*

Sources of International Law

(1) A rule of international law is one that has been accepted as such by the international community of states

  (a) in the form of customary law;

  (b) by international agreement; or

  (c) by derivation from general principles common to the major legal systems of the world.

(2) Customary international law results from a general and consistent practice of states followed by them from a sense of legal obligation.

(3) International agreements create law for the states parties thereto and may lead to the creation of customary international law when such agreements are intended for adherence by states generally and are in fact widely accepted.

(4) General principles common to the major legal systems, even if not incorporated or reflected in customary law or international agreement, may be invoked as supplementary rules of international law where appropriate.

Comments and Illustrations

. . . .

b. *Practice as customary law.* "Practice of states," Subsection (2), includes diplomatic acts and instructions as well as public measures and other governmental acts and official statements of policy, whether they are unilateral or undertaken in cooperation with other states, for example in organizations such as the Organization for Economic Cooperation and Development (OECD). Inaction may constitute state practice, as when a state acquiesces in acts of another state that affect its legal rights. The practice necessary to create customary law may be of comparatively short duration, but under Subsection (2) it must be "general and consistent." A practice can be general even if it is not universally followed; there is no precise formula to indicate how widespread a practice must be, but it should reflect wide acceptance among the states particularly involved in the relevant activity. Failure of a significant number of important states to adopt a practice can prevent a principle from becoming general customary law though it might become "particular customary law" for the participating states. [cit]. A principle of customary law is not binding on a state that declares its dissent from the principle during its development. [cit].

---

c. *Opinio juris*. For a practice of states to become a rule of customary international law it must appear that the states follow the practice from a sense of legal obligation (*opinio juris sive necessitatis*); a practice that is generally followed but which states feel legally free to disregard does not contribute to customary law. A practice initially followed by states as a matter of courtesy or habit may become law when states generally come to believe that they are under a legal obligation to comply with it. It is often difficult to determine when that transformation into law has taken place. Explicit evidence of a sense of legal obligation (e.g., by official statements) is not necessary; *opinio juris* may be inferred from acts or omissions.

d. *Dissenting views and new states*. Although customary law may be built by the acquiescence as well as by the actions of states (Comment b) and become generally binding on all states, in principle a state that indicates its dissent from a practice while the law is still in the process of development is not bound by that rule even after it matures. . . . As to the possibility of dissent from peremptory norms (*jus cogens*), a state that enters the international system after a practice has ripened into a rule of international law is bound by that rule.

e. *General and special custom*. The practice of states in a regional or other special grouping may create "regional," "special," or "particular" customary law for those states inter se. . . .

f. *International agreement as source of law*. An international agreement creates obligations binding between the parties under international law. [cit]. Ordinarily, an agreement between states is a source of law only in the sense that a private contract may be said to make law for the parties under the domestic law of contracts. Multilateral agreements open to all states, however, are increasingly used for general legislation, whether to make new law, as in human rights . . . or for codifying and developing customary law, as in the Vienna Convention on the Law of Treaties. . . . International agreements may contribute to customary law.

g. *Binding resolutions of international organizations*. Some international agreements that are constitutions or charters of international organizations confer power on those organizations to impose binding obligations on their members by resolution, usually by qualified majorities. Such obligations derive their authority from the international agreement constituting the organization, and resolutions so adopted by the organization can be seen as "secondary sources" of international law for its members.

. . . .

i. *International agreements codifying or contributing to customary law*. International agreements constitute practice of states and as such can contribute to the growth of customary law under Subsection (2). [cit]. Some multilateral agreements may come to be law for non-parties that do not actively dissent. That may be the effect where a multilateral agreement is designed for adherence by states generally, is widely accepted, and is not rejected by a significant number of important states. A wide network of similar bilateral arrangements on a subject may constitute practice and also result in customary law. . . .

j. *Conflict between international agreement and customary law.* Customary law and law made by international agreement have equal authority as international law. Unless the parties evince a contrary intention, a rule established by agreement supersedes for them a prior inconsistent rule of customary international law. However, an agreement will not supersede a prior rule of customary law that is a peremptory norm of international law; and an agreement will not supersede customary law if the agreement is invalid because it violates such a peremptory norm. *See* Comment k. A new rule of customary law will supersede inconsistent obligations created by earlier agreement if the parties so intend and the intention is clearly manifested. . . .

k. *Peremptory norms of international law (jus cogens).* Some rules of international law are recognized by the international community of states as peremptory, permitting no derogation. These rules prevail over and invalidate international agreements and other rules of international law in conflict with them. Such a peremptory norm is subject to modification only by a subsequent norm of international law having the same character. It is generally accepted that the principles of the United Nations Charter prohibiting the use of force [cit] have the character of *jus cogens*. . .

l. *General principles as secondary source of law.* Much of international law, whether customary or constituted by agreement, reflects principles analogous to those found in the major legal systems of the world, and historically may derive from them or from a more remote common origin. [cit]. General principles common to systems of national law may be resorted to as an independent source of law. That source of law may be important when there has not been practice by states sufficient to give the particular principle status as customary law and the principle has not been legislated by general international agreement. . . .

Reporters' Notes

. . . .

2. *Customary law.* No definition of customary law has received universal agreement, but the essence of Subsection (2) has wide acceptance. [cit]. Each element in attempted definitions has raised difficulties. There have been philosophical debates about the very basis of the definition: how can practice build law? Most troublesome conceptually has been the circularity in the suggestion that law is built by practice based on a sense of legal obligation: how, it is asked, can there be a sense of legal obligation before the law from which the legal obligation derives has matured? Such conceptual difficulties, however, have not prevented acceptance of customary law essentially as here defined. . . .

Earlier definitions implied that establishment of custom required that the practice of states continue over an extended period of time. That requirement began to lose its force after the Second World War, perhaps because improved communication made the practice of states widely and quickly known, at least where there is broad acceptance and no or little objection. . . .

The practice of states that builds customary law takes many forms and includes what states do in or through international organizations. [cit]. The United Nations General Assembly in particular has adopted resolutions, declarations, and other statements of principles that in some circumstances contribute to the process of making customary law, insofar as statements and votes of governments are kinds of state practice, [cit], and may be expressions of *opinio juris*. [cit]. The contributions of such resolutions and of the statements and votes supporting them to the lawmaking process will differ widely, depending on factors such as the subject of the resolution, whether it purports to reflect legal principles, how large a majority it commands and how numerous and important are the dissenting states, whether it is widely supported (including in particular the states principally affected), and whether it is later confirmed by other practice.

. . . .

Resolutions that may contribute to customary law are to be distinguished from resolutions that are legally binding on members [cit]. The latter, too, may reflect state practice or *opinio juris*, but they derive their authority from the charter of the organization, an international agreement in which states parties agreed to be bound by some of its acts. International conferences, especially those engaged in codifying customary law, provide occasions for expressions by states as to the law on particular questions. General consensus as to the law at such a conference confirms customary law or contributes to its creation.

The development of customary law has been described as part of a "process of continuous interaction, of continuous demand and response," among decision-makers of different states. These "create expectations that effective power will be restrained and exercised in certain uniformities of pattern. . . . The reciprocal tolerances . . . create the expectations of patterns and uniformity in decision, of practice in accord with rule, commonly regarded as law." [cit].

That a rule of customary law is not binding on any state indicating its dissent during the development of the rule (Comment d) is an accepted application of the traditional principle that international law essentially depends on the consent of states. [cit]. Refusal of states to adopt or acquiesce in a practice has often prevented its development into a principle of customary law, but instances of dissent and exemption from practice that developed into principles of general customary law have been few. . . .

Interpretation of treaties is central to an understanding of international intellectual property law. An intellectual property treaty creates obligations that bind the signatory states notwithstanding that the internal law of the signatory differs from that state's international obligations. The customary law of treaties is now codified in the Vienna Convention on the Law of Treaties of 1969. Although the United States has not yet ratified the Vienna Convention, it takes the position that the interpretive provisions of the Convention are largely consistent with the interpretive principles of customary international law.

VIENNA CONVENTION ON THE LAW OF TREATIES
May 23, 1969, 1155 U.N.T.S. 331

Article 26

Every treaty in force is binding upon the parties to it and must be performed by them in good faith.

Article 27

A party may not invoke the provisions of its internal law as justification for its failure to perform a treaty. . . .

Article 31

(1) A treaty shall be interpreted in good faith in accordance with the ordinary meaning to be given to the terms of the treaty in their context and in the light of its object and purpose.

(2) The context for the purpose of the interpretation of a treaty shall comprise, in addition to the text, including its preamble and annexes:

    (a)   any agreement relating to the treaty which was made between all the parties in connexion with the conclusion of the treaty;

    (b)   any instrument which was made by one or more parties in connexion with the conclusion of the treaty and accepted by the other parties as an instrument related to the treaty.

(3) There shall be taken into account, together with the context:

    (a)   any subsequent agreement between the parties regarding the interpretation of the treaty or the application of its provisions;

    (b)   any subsequent practice in the application of the treaty which establishes the agreement of the parties regarding its interpretation;

    (c)   any relevant rules of international law applicable in the relations between the parties.

. . . .

Article 32

Recourse may be had to supplementary means of interpretation, including the preparatory work of the treaty and the circumstances of its conclusion, in order to confirm the meaning resulting from the application of article 31, or to determine the meaning when the interpretation according to article 31:

    (a)   leaves the meaning ambiguous or obscure; or

    (b)   leads to a result which is manifestly absurd or unreasonable.

———

NOTES AND QUESTIONS

(1) **The Objects of Rights and Obligations Under International Law.** Who should be bound by international law in the sense used by Bentham? What premises underlie the Benthamite notion of international law as merely a set of rules agreed among states to regulate their relations *inter se*? What are the consequences of a philosophy of international law that treats states as the only legitimate actors? Who has rights under such a vision of international law? Who should be bound by an "ethically-derived" set of laws, by the "law of nations" or "customary international law"? Are there circumstances where private actors should be bound by norms of international law? *See Kadic v. Karadzic*, 70 F.3d 232, 239 (2d Cir. 1995).

(2) **State Practice and International Law**. How would you answer the question posed by the Reporters to the Restatement: how and why can practice build law? Is there a reason why practice may play a larger role in the identification of international, as opposed to internal national, law? How should the normative force of such "law" differ, if at all, from provisions of international treaties?

(3) **International Obligations and National Sovereignty.** Why would it be in a state's best interest voluntarily to enter into agreements and assume international legal obligations? To what extent is the acceptance of obligations under international law a derogation from national sovereignty?

§ 3.02   International Intellectual Property Instruments

The earliest efforts to move beyond purely national protection of intellectual property involved bilateral agreements between two countries. In response to some of the deficiencies of bilateral agreements, the late nineteenth century saw the development of multilateral agreements. These multilateral intellectual property treaties established unions of member countries that reached agreement on a number of common principles. They did not supplant national legislation; rather, they imposed upon member countries certain obligations as to how they will treat each other's products.

As noted in Chapter 1, the two most important of these treaties were originally negotiated in the late nineteenth century. They have been updated periodically, and are still in force.* They are the Berne Convention for the Protection of Literary and Artistic Works and the Paris Convention for the Protection of Industrial Property. A number of other multilateral intellectual property treaties, narrower in coverage and in membership than the Berne and Paris Conventions, have been concluded since then.

In the late twentieth century, different types of multilateral instruments governing intellectual property began to emerge. They were the outgrowth of a recognition that intellectual property had become important not only in itself but as a major component of global commerce. As a result, countries negotiating agreements on general commercial issues, such as trade and investment, began to incorporate provisions dealing with intellectual property. Some of these agreements are open to any country to join; others are regional agreements concluded among closed groups of countries with geographical ties. Similarly, when the European Union ("EU") was created in order to achieve a common market, intellectual property laws were identified as a potential barrier to trade. As a result, the EU has taken a number of initiatives intended to facilitate the acquisition and exploitation of intellectual property community-wide.

The most important trade agreement incorporating intellectual property provisions is the Agreement on Trade-Related Aspects of Intellectual Property Rights, known as the TRIPS Agreement. The TRIPS Agreement is an annex to the agreement creating the World Trade Organization, which itself was an outgrowth of the Uruguay Round of the General Agreement on Tariffs and Trade. TRIPS was negotiated over the course of five years, and concluded as part of the Uruguay Round in 1994. It contains provisions relating to copyrights (and related rights, in the terminology of many countries), patents, trademarks, trade secrets, and semiconductor chips. It incorporates most of the substantive obligations of the Berne and Paris Conventions.

All of these types of instruments co-exist today. Accordingly, an entity that seeks to exploit intellectual property outside the borders of its own country, or a lawyer advising such an entity, should be aware of the existence and coverage of a range of treaties: those relating to intellectual property specifically, to trade, and to investment; bilateral and multilateral agreements; and directives that harmonize the laws of the EU member states. All are described in this book, and many are reproduced in the Documentary Supplement.

---

* To complicate matters further, the different revisions are known as Acts, for example the 1971 Paris Act of the Berne Convention. Each new Act requires a new accession in order for a country to be bound by the new standards it contains. This means that different countries that are all party to Berne or Paris may be bound by different requirements. As a practical matter, however, because the TRIPS Agreement requires the application of the most recent Act of Berne and Paris, this latest version will be applied by virtually all Berne and Paris members.

Each of these multilateral treaties is administered by one or more international intergovernmental body. These organizations arrange and host meetings of their member countries to discuss, apply or update the relevant treaty, may assist in interpreting the treaty's provisions, and in the case of treaties which establish some sort of procedural mechanism like a filing system, actually operate the system. *See infra* Chapter 6. Their budgets are overseen by the governments of their member states. Depending on the organization, operating funds are provided by a combination of government contributions and/or by private sector fees for services. Each organization has an administrative staff, known as the International Bureau or Secretariat, which includes professionals from a variety of different member states.

The multilateral intellectual property treaties, including the Berne Convention and the Paris Convention, are administered by the World Intellectual Property Organization ("WIPO") (known in French as the *Organisation Mondiale de la Propriété Intellectuelle* ("OMPI")). Some are administered in conjunction with other organizations, such as UNESCO and the International Labor Organization ("ILO"). The TRIPS Agreement, as an annex to the World Trade Organization Agreement, is administered by the TRIPS Council of the World Trade Organization ("WTO"). These institutions are described in more detail below. *See infra* § 3.03.

Eligibility to join a treaty depends on the terms of the treaty itself. The TRIPS Agreement requires membership in the WTO; admission to the WTO requires agreement by the member states, upon satisfaction of a number of criteria relating to all of the trade issues covered by the WTO Agreement itself, not simply intellectual property. Regional agreements are limited to countries within the defined region. As a general matter, countries are expected or required to bring their laws into compliance with treaty obligations before joining.

As a practical matter, willingness to adhere to the multilateral intellectual property treaties has often been determined by balance of trade considerations: the country's status as primarily an exporter or an importer of the relevant form of intellectual property. The first signatories to the Berne Convention were primarily European countries, and the convention's rules were modeled on European *droit d'auteur* systems. Historically, developing countries have been reluctant to accede, at various times demanding special rules and concessions before they would do so. It was not until the late nineteenth century, for example, that the United States was ready to protect any foreign works within its borders, and not until nearly 100 years later that it joined the Berne Convention. Today, as the leading exporter of intellectual property in the world, the United States is a strong advocate for treaty membership and implementation.

The specific inclusion of intellectual property on the trade agenda in the 1980s, however, tipped the balance further toward widespread treaty membership. The advantages of various trade partnerships gave countries additional incentives, apart from an interest in protecting their own intellectual property exports. Joining the WTO, for example, provides many trade benefits, such as most favored nation status, that have been viewed by many countries as outweighing any detriment from providing protection to foreign intellectual property. Today, membership in the major multilateral conventions is quite high. Few countries that are substantial exporters or importers of intellectual property have not yet been brought into the international intellectual property community. Full compliance, of course, is another story, which will be discussed in Chapters 4-5.

§ 3.03 Leading International Institutions and Actors

As suggested above, the development of international intellectual property is undertaken by an increasingly broad range of institutions. These institutions include intergovernmental organizations, regional groupings of nation-states, international trade bodies, and private international law reform bodies. As intellectual property assumes a place of greater significance in social and economic policy, the number of relevant institutions multiplies. What follows is a description of the primary institutional "players" involved in the process of developing international intellectual property law and policy.

[A] The World Intellectual Property Organization

The World Intellectual Property Organization ("WIPO") was established in 1967, succeeding to the role of the Bureaux for the Protection of Intellectual Property (which was best known by its French acronym "BIRPI"), and is charged with "promoting the protection of intellectual property throughout the world through cooperation among states and, where appropriate, in collaboration with any other international organization." Convention Establishing the World Intellectual Property Organization signed at Stockholm, July 14, 1967 and as amended on September 28, 1979, art. 3(i). WIPO is an intergovernmental organization of 179 member nations with an International Bureau based in Geneva, and is a specialized agency of the United Nations. Prior to the TRIPS Agreement, WIPO was the dominant multilateral forum in which international intellectual property law was developed, and it remains one of the two leading fora along with the WTO (the latter including both the TRIPS Council and WTO Dispute Settlement Body).

Most of the major multinational intellectual property agreements establish unions consisting of all states that have adhered to the treaty in question. (Thus, for example, the international body responsible for the Paris Convention is referred to as the Paris Union.) The union in question is governed by an Assembly, consisting of the adherent countries, and by an Executive Committee. Since 1967, the WIPO has, as noted above, been the administrator of most major unions and treaties, with the principal exception of the TRIPS Agreement. (And, as we will see below, the WTO and the WIPO have concluded an agreement, envisaged by Article 68 of TRIPS, that gives WIPO an important role in the TRIPS system.)

WIPO thus remains a forum (arguably still the primary forum) for the drafting, discussion, revision and conclusion of new intellectual property treaties, as well as the development of intellectual property norms through less formal lawmaking processes (such as the adoption of resolutions or the promulgation of model laws). In addition, WIPO offers significant specialized expertise to countries seeking to develop or improve their intellectual property laws. Indeed, this "technical" or "education" function is becoming a bigger part of WIPO's role. In recent years, WIPO has also established an Arbitration Center for administration of private (i.e., involving individuals rather than states) international intellectual property disputes. Although this center was underused at first, the adjudication of disputes between trademark owners and domain name holders has since late 1999 been a boon to the center.

[B]   The World Trade Organization

One of the most significant developments in modern international intellectual property law has been the conclusion of the TRIPS Agreement. The TRIPS Agreement augmented the minimum standards of intellectual property protection found in previous international agreements, which is notable in and of itself. But perhaps more importantly, the TRIPS Agreement, which is an Annex to the Agreement Establishing the World Trade Organization (the WTO), brought intellectual property within the institutional infrastructure of the world's multilateral trading system. This was important not only because it provided certain countries non-intellectual property related incentives to join the community of intellectual property respecting nations, but also because disputes regarding compliance with TRIPS were subsumed within the dispute settlement system of the WTO. We will study the WTO dispute settlement system (involving both dispute settlement panels and a standing Appellate Body) in detail in Chapter 5. For present purposes, it should be noted only that decisions rendered under the WTO dispute settlement system are backed up by effective enforcement mechanisms; member states found to be in violation of TRIPS provisions must revise their laws under pain of penalties that include the imposition of trade sanctions.

Pre-TRIPS, the position was quite different. Proposals to amend the Paris Convention to submit disputes to the Permanent Court of International Justice, the predecessor to the International Court of Justice, were made as far back as 1925. But the United States vehemently opposed the proposal, and it was not until the 1967 revision that the Paris Convention contained the possibility of referring disputes between states to the International Court of Justice. *See* Paris Convention art. 28. Article 28 has, however, never been invoked; neither has Article 33 of the Berne Convention, which contains a similar provision. Of itself, the incorporation of international intellectual property obligations within an effective dispute settlement mechanism thus makes the WTO an important part of the modern international intellectual property system. The dispute settlement system is, however, only part of the WTO apparatus that contributes to the ongoing development of international intellectual property law: another important body is the TRIPS Council.

THE TRIPS COUNCIL *

The Council for TRIPS is the body, open to all Members of the WTO, that has responsibility for the administration of the [TRIPS] Agreement, in particular monitoring the operation of the agreement. The council also constitutes a forum for consultations on any problems relating to TRIPS arising between countries as well as for clarifying and interpreting provisions of the agreement. The aim is, whenever possible, to resolve differences between countries without the need for formal recourse to dispute settlement. The council meets in Geneva formally some five times a year as well as informally as necessary.

One of the characteristics of the former GATT and now of the WTO is the detailed and continuous follow-up of the implementation of obligations and the monitoring of compliance with them. The underlying belief is that unless there is detailed monitoring of compliance with international commitments, those commitments will be worth much less. Monitoring of compliance in the council is done in two main ways.

First, the TRIPS Council is a body in which any member can raise any issue relating to compliance by other parties. This has happened on a number of occasions, either in relation to the practices of a specific country or the application of a specific provision.

The second approach to monitoring compliance is a systematic examination of each member's national implementing legislation by the other members, involving the notification and review of the legislation of members.

Article 63.2 of the TRIPS Agreement requires members to notify the laws and regulations made effective by that member pertaining to the subject matter of the agreement to the Council for TRIPS in order to assist the Council in its review of the operation of the agreement. Laws and regulations should be notified promptly as of the time that the corresponding substantive obligation starts to apply. Given the difficulty of examining legislation relevant to many of the enforcement obligations in the agreement, members have undertaken, in addition to notifying legislative texts, to provide information on how they are meeting these obligations by responding to a checklist of twenty-five questions.

These notifications are the basis for reviews of implementing legislation carried out by the council. The council completed in the year 1997 its first review exercise that focused on those WTO members who no longer benefitted from a transition period, i.e. the developed countries. The council continued in the first part of 1998 [with] the review of six members whose

---

* This discussion of the TRIPS Council is excerpted from Matthijs Geuze & Hannu Wager, *WTO Dispute Settlement Practice Relating to the TRIPS Agreement*, J. INT'L ECON. L. 347, 382–84 (1999). Copyright 1999, Oxford University Press. Reprinted with permission.

legislation had already been subject to the 1996/97 review exercise but for whom the review had not been completed by the end of 1997. Including the questions of the Checklist of Issues on Enforcement, the review of the legislation of the thirty-three members taken up in the period between 1996 and the first part of 1998 generated responses to some 5,000 questions recorded in some 3,000 pages of documentation. Furthermore, the council reviewed in the autumn of 1998 the legislation of three members who had negotiated their accession to the WTO and, while applying a TRIPS transition period, had not yet been subject to the review.

One of the benefits of the review mechanism is that it is seen as an important vehicle for resolving issues that might otherwise become the subject of formal dispute settlement proceedings. Some of the more specific benefits include the *ex ante* effect of greater care in drafting legislation from the knowledge that new legislation will be reviewed, and the clearing up of misunderstandings about a country's legislation.

The review process also provides an opportunity to identify deficiencies in notified laws and regulations, as well as differences in interpretation. In a significant number of instances, the country whose legislation was under review has been willing to accept that it still has further work to do in order to make its laws conform fully with the WTO's rules. Some of the differences in interpretation will be discussed bilaterally. If they are not resolved in that way, they could eventually turn into formal disputes under the WTO dispute settlement proceedings.

A number of issues that have been subject to the invocation of the dispute settlement procedure have also been the focus of attention in the review process. For example, in the review of legislation on copyright and related rights, all members that were reviewed were asked to explain how they provide protection to pre-existing works, performances and phonograms. Similarly, in the review of legislation on enforcement, most members were asked to provide additional information on the way provisional measures could be ordered *inaudita altera parte*. Certain issues that were initially raised in the review of a given country were subsequently taken up in the dispute settlement proceedings.[98]

Consequently, in addition to panel and Appellate Body reports and notified mutually agreed solutions, useful information relevant to questions of interpretation of TRIPS provisions may also be obtained from the questions raised on the floor of the TRIPS Council and the answers given by members.

---

[98] It should be noted that the review does not, either explicitly or implicitly, lead to the granting of a "clean bill of health" to a member's legislation. The fact that a matter was not raised or, if raised, not pursued in the follow-up to the review does not in any way prejudice other members' right to raise the matter subsequently and, ultimately, have recourse to dispute settlement.

[C] The European Union

[1] Background to the European Union

The European Union ("EU") is presently comprised of fifteen member states: Austria, Belgium, Denmark, Finland, France, Germany, Greece, Ireland, Italy, Luxembourg, The Netherlands, Portugal, Spain, Sweden and the United Kingdom. The EU, and the intellectual property law that it develops, has over the past decade become a significant variable in the intellectual property lawmaking process internationally. The imprint of EU legislation can be found not only on the intellectual property laws in the member states of the union; EU legislation has also influenced the shape of national intellectual property laws outside the EU, as well as multinational intellectual property agreements. This influence arises in various ways. Non-EU countries that are within the European Economic Area ("EEA")—which is comprised of the EU countries plus Iceland, Norway and Lichtenstein—must also comply with various laws of the EU including its intellectual property laws. The proposed enlargement of the EU to accept new members, principally from Central and Eastern Europe, is not too distant, and other countries in the area have thus felt a need to align their laws with those of the EU. *See* Thomas Helbling, *Shapes as Trade Marks?— The Struggle to Register Three-Dimensional Signs: A Comparative Study of United Kingdom and Swiss Law*, 1997 INTELL. PROP. Q. 413, 417 (discussing reform of Swiss trademark law). Finally, the intensive legislative activity of the EU in recent years means that the EU has developed a series of laws which serve as useful models for countries seeking to introduce or modernize their own intellectual property laws.

Recent legislative developments involving intellectual property law in the EU have also found an echo in the United States. To cite only a couple of recent examples, the EU Database Directive adopted in 1996 has framed the discussion of database protection both on the multinational level and within the United States. Similarly, the Term Directive, which extended the term of copyright protection within Europe to life of the author plus seventy years, is in large part what motivated the parallel Sonny Bono Copyright Term Extension Act in the United States. Indeed, the extent of this influence led one scholar to write that there was a need for independent congressional investigation of the limits of cultural policy so as "to free U.S. innovation law from the grip of unelected foreign bureaucrats who have surrendered to sectoral protectionist demands." J.H. Reichman, *The Duration of Copyright and the Limits of Cultural Policy*, 14 CARD. ARTS & ENT. L.J. 625, 653 (1996).

Although the European Economic Community (and with it the collective grouping called the European Communities) was established in 1957 by the Treaty of Rome, an international agreement concluded among six countries, the entity that we now call the EU was only established in 1991 by the Treaty on European Union (the Maastricht Treaty). The union rests on three so-called "pillars":

(1) the European Communities (i.e., the former European Economic Community now renamed the "European Community" or "EC", the European Coal and Steel Community and the European Atomic Energy Community);

(2) the process of formal intergovernmental cooperation in the fields of foreign and security policy; and

(3) the process of formal intergovernmental cooperation in justice and home affairs (such as asylum policy, police co-operation).

Strictly speaking, intellectual property legislation is pursued through the legislative workings of the EC. The articles of the Treaty of Rome, the foundational document of the European Communities in 1957, have undergone successive revision over the course of the last forty-four years and are now codified in the EC Treaty. In 1998, these revisions were systematically consolidated, causing extensive renumbering of the treaty's articles. If we have edited pre-1998 EU materials (such as pre-98 court opinions) to reflect the new numbering, this editing is indicated through the customary use of square brackets; references to "ex-Article _____" are references to the number of the relevant article in the older text.

[2]   The Institutions of the European Union

The European Commission is central to the European project, and is essentially the administrative branch of the EU. The Council and the European Parliament require a proposal from the Commission before adopting legislation. The Commission is also central to the enforcement of EU law, by ensuring that member states are complying with their obligations under that law. Finally, the Commission has responsibility for negotiating and monitoring the union's international trade relationships. The Commission is based in Brussels, has twenty members, two each from the big five countries (France, Germany, Italy, Spain and the United Kingdom) and one from each of the other ten member states. Each commissioner serves a five year term. The appointed nature of the Commission has led to claims of a "democracy deficit" in the EU. Recent institutional reforms have attempted to remedy that by ensuring greater oversight by the elected body, the Parliament. The full Commission has to be approved by Parliament before its members can take office, and they can (as seen by the political maneuvering in 1999) be required to resign en bloc by a parliamentary vote of censure. Until recently, the Commission was divided into twenty-six numbered directorates-general ("DG"s). As of October 1, 1999, under a new organizational structure implemented by Commission President Romano Prodi, the DGs are now referred to by title rather than by number. Each DG is headed by a director-general, reporting to a commissioner who has the political and administrative responsibility for the work of the DG. Responsibility for intellectual property law is assigned to the DG with primary responsibility for the internal market (formerly called DG XV) and additional relevant activity can be found in the Information Society DG.

The Council of the European Communities is comprised of fifteen members, one from each member state government. The precise membership of the Council depends upon the subject matter before it. If the matter relates to finance, the fifteen governments will send their finance ministers; if the matter relates to transport, the fifteen governments will send their transport ministers. There are twenty-five of these different "subject-matters," with intellectual property being dealt with at the Internal Market Council meetings. The Presidency of the Council rotates among the fifteen member states, changing every six months. Voting in the Council is weighted, with the big four countries (Germany, France, the U.K. and Italy) receiving ten votes, Spain eight votes and the smaller countries receiving lesser numbers reflecting their different sizes.

The European Parliament sits in Strasbourg, France, but its committees also meet frequently in Brussels for ease of access to the Commission. The role of the European Parliament in the lawmaking process has increased as the EU has matured, partly because of the Parliament's status as the only directly elected body involved in the legislative process. The numbers of MEPs from each country corresponds approximately with that country's population, although the MEPs sit and act by political grouping rather than by nationality.

The European Court of Justice is discussed separately below.

[3] Legislative Instruments

The legislation of the EU may take two primary forms. A *Regulation* has general application, is binding in its entirety and is directly applicable in all member states. It does not require national implementing legislation to become effective in member states. It is essentially a federal law of Europe. A *Directive*, in contrast, is not directly applicable in the member states. Its provisions normally require positive implementation (called "transposition") in the domestic laws of the member states.* Article 249 (ex-Article 189) provides that "A Directive shall be binding as to the result to be achieved . . . but shall leave to the national authorities the choice of form and methods". A directive is not unlike a model state law, but one that states are obliged to enact (with some minor room for tailoring to the specialities of their own system). Directives must be given effect by a stated date by each of the member states. If the member state fails to transpose the directive by that date, the Commission may bring an action against the member state before the Court of Justice.

[4] Legislative Process

The European Commission initiates all legislation of the EC. Without the Commission, there is no legislation. The degree of involvement of the

---

* The European Court of Justice has held that certain provisions of directives may be treated as directly creating rights in member states, notwithstanding lack of adequate transposition by the member state in question, under the doctrine of "direct effect." This doctrine should not be confused with the question of direct applicability.

Council and the Parliament varies depending upon which provision of the Treaty of Rome the Commission rests its authority to propose the legislation. Different provisions implicate different legislative procedures. The precise legislative procedure involved is set out in great detail in the relevant authorizing provision, but there are two basic paradigms.

Under *the consultation procedure,* the opinion of Parliament must be obtained by the Council before acting on and adopting a legislative proposal of the Commission. But that is the sum of the Parliament's formal involvement. The Parliament thus has little ability to affect legislation that is pursued under this procedure; unanimous approval by the Council is, however, required. This procedure is followed, for example, where legislation rests upon the authority of Article 308 (ex-Article 235) of the EC Treaty, which might be viewed as the "Necessary and Proper" clause of the Treaty of Rome. Article 308 authorizes appropriate Community measures if necessary to attain the objectives of the Community even if the Treaty has not provided the necessary powers. This authority has been used to enact Community-level intellectual property regulations creating unitary EU-wide rights. *See infra* Chapter 6.

However, the bulk of the intellectual property legislation enacted or considered by the EU has taken the form of harmonization directives. Harmonization of the laws of member states is essential if the territorial nature of intellectual property rights is not to frustrate the free movement of goods, an objective which lies at the heart of the EU. The harmonization of intellectual property laws among the member states has typically been attempted by the Commission pursuant to Article 95 (ex-Article 100a) of the EC Treaty, which provides authority to enact legislation necessary to complete the internal market. Legislation proposed under that Article involves the *codecision* (or *joint legislative) procedure.* This procedure, which enhanced the role of the Parliament in the making of legislation, was introduced by the Maastricht Treaty in 1992. With respect to legislation proposed under this procedure, Parliament has a veto: if it rejects the so-called "common position" of the Council, the Council cannot adopt the legislation. Although Parliament has a greater ability to influence and halt legislation under this procedure, the Council is able to act by a qualified majority (i.e., with the support of states possessing a defined number of votes in the Council). Although Parliament has the power, by an absolute majority of votes cast, to veto legislation considered under the codecision procedure, it has exercised that prerogative only rarely. It *has* used the power, however. In 1995, Parliament used its power under the codecision procedure to block enactment of the first effort at a Biotechnology Patent Directive. *See infra* Chapter 4.

[5]   The Judicial Process

The European Court of Justice ("ECJ"), which sits in Luxembourg, is comprised of fifteen judges (one from each state), appointed for six year terms. The president of the court is selected by the members of the court themselves, and he or she will serve in that capacity for a renewable term of three years. In 1989, *the Court of First Instance* ("CFI") was created to help the ECJ deal with an increasingly busy workload, but there is no established system of inferior EU "federal" courts. The composition of the Court of First Instance is likewise fifteen judges appointed for six year terms, and again the president is chosen by the judges themselves. The court (and the Court of First Instance) sits in chambers of three or five, but can sit in plenary session when a member state or community institution (i.e., the Commission, Council or Parliament) that is party to the case requests that, or if the case is particularly complex. It was announced in December 1999 that the European Parliament is to consider interim measures to lessen the workload of the ECJ by increasing the responsibility of the Court of First Instance. Proposals are being considered to increase the number of CFI judges from fifteen to twenty-one, to assist mainly with intellectual property cases.

In the early stages of the case, the president assigns one judge as rapporteur, and an advocate-general is assigned to the case. There are eight advocates-general. The advocates-general listen to the argument along with the judges, and then deliver their opinions on the case in advance of the court issuing a decision. The opinion of the advocate-general is often extremely influential (and typically more lengthy than the judgement issued by the Court). The decisions of the Court are reached by majority vote, but no dissenting opinions are issued and judgments are signed by all the judges who participated in the case. The judgments of the Court tend to be more cryptic and more sparsely reasoned than U.S. opinions. The court does not adhere to stare decisis, but it does follow the continental European philosophy of *jurisprudence constante* in seeking to have some uniformity in the application of the law.

The Court of Justice has jurisdiction to hear a variety of types of cases, the most important of which are:

(1) *Enforcement Actions.* An action may be brought under Article 226 (ex-Article 169) against a member state for failure to fulfil an obligation under Community law. *See, e.g.,* Case C-213/98, *Commission v. Ireland*, Eur. Cur. L. 36, Nov. 1999 (E.C.J. Oct. 12, 1999) (upholding Commission action against Ireland under Article 169 for failure to implement Rental Rights Directive and rejecting Irish defense that implementation was awaiting full-scale review of Irish copyright legislation.) This will normally be brought by the Commission, but may also be brought (under ex-Article 170) by another member state. The remedy is to require compliance or, if that does not occur, to impose fines.

(2) *Preliminary Reference Procedure.* Perhaps the most important jurisdiction of the Court of Justice for the purpose of intellectual property law has been its "preliminary reference" jurisdiction under Article 234 (ex-Article 177). * Issues of EU law arise with increasing frequency in litigation in EU

---

* The jurisdiction of the Court of First Instance is more limited; most importantly it does not include the preliminary reference procedure.

member states. In order to prevent divergent national court decisions from leading to conflicting interpretations of Community law, if an issue of Community law arises before a national court that national court may, and in some cases must, seek a preliminary ruling from the Court of Justice on the relevant question. Although the reference is made by the national court, the private litigants in the national proceedings may appear before the Court of Justice when it hears the reference. Article 234 does not establish the Court of Justice as a court of final appeal above the national court systems (at least not conceptually); this is a reference procedure common in many jurisdictions. The national court will frame a question to be answered by the Court of Justice; the Court of Justice will apply the law and provide a ruling in the form of an answer to that question; and the national court will then apply the relevant law to the case at hand taking into account the answer of the Court.

[6] The Relationship Between National and Union Law

One of the most important early decisions of the Court of Justice was to declare the supremacy of Community law. If there is a conflict between applicable Community law and a provision of national law, the national law will be subordinated to Community law. These decisions, in the formative years of the Community, essentially wove a Supremacy Clause into the constitutional fabric of the Union. And it is through this principle that the European Court of Justice developed case law on intellectual property law. The Court strictly has no jurisdiction to interpret or rule on matters of national law absent harmonization of those laws by Community legislation or a conflict between those national laws and the laws of the EC. In the early years, before EU harmonization of national intellectual property laws, the Court reached intellectual property issues primarily in the context of analyzing their consonance with the competition law principles found in Articles 81–82 (ex-Articles 85–86) of the EC Treaty or with the free movement principles found in Articles 28 & 30 (ex-Articles 30 & 36). The latter relation—with free trade principles—took the Court on variety of detours before developing its current exhaustion jurisprudence. Perhaps because this was the context in which the early case law arose— whether intellectual property rights interfered with higher Community objectives—the Court was seen as suspicious of broad intellectual property rights. The Court's case load tended to place it in the role of preventing the assertion of national intellectual property rights in such a way as to partition the EU market. The Court still considers intellectual property issues in that context,* but in the last few years, an increasingly large part of the Court's intellectual property caseload has been generated by the need

---

* The Court has also considered the concordance of national intellectual property laws with other provisions of the EC Treaty. *See, e.g., Phil Collins v. Imtrat,* 1994 F.S.R. 166 (E.C.J. 1993) (holding that because discrimination on grounds of nationality is prohibited under the EC Treaty, the application of reciprocity requirements to deny protection to citizens of other EU states under multinational intellectual property treaties was a violation of EU law).

to assist national courts in interpreting the various intellectual property harmonization directives as they are given effect in national law.

[7] The Evolution of EU Attitudes to Intellectual Property Rights

The foundations of the EU are built on principles of free trade and a common market. As noted above, the initial attention to intellectual property law by the EU was thus prompted by a concern that the territorially-founded intellectual property laws of the different member states did not operate to restrict or impede the free flow of goods or the functioning of an efficient market. From that early perspective, reform of intellectual property law has assumed a more affirmative place on the EU agenda. As the political objectives of the Union have widened to include (more explicitly) such matters as industry competitiveness, the ability of intellectual property protection to encourage innovative activity in Europe has received a greater prominence, particularly on the legislative side of the ledger. In the late 1980s and the 1990s, therefore, the activity in the EU in connection with intellectual property reform was quite hectic. And the legislative developments since 1988 have all, for the most part, resulted in greater and more consistent protection of intellectual property rights in the EU.

As noted above, the largest part of the legislative agenda in the field of intellectual property law has been harmonization directives. These directives were brought forward by the Commission as part of efforts to complete the "internal market" by 1992. The harmonization that has been effected by these instruments has tended to be partial or fragmentary in nature. Thus, for example, the Trademark Directive harmonized registered trademark laws, but left untouched unregistered trademark or unfair competition laws. Similarly, the early reforms of copyright law were sector-specific, targeted harmonization; the Commission only rarely included so-called "horizontal provisions," which would apply to all copyrighted works, in harmonization directives. For example, the software directive establishes levels of copyright protection for software; the database directive does the same for databases.

In the case of industrial property rights, which are largely based upon registration, the Commission has sought to go further and enact unitary Community-wide rights. The alternative of harmonizing member states' laws (which had been used in eradicating differences in national protection accorded computer software, databases and semiconductor topographies) would be inadequate in this context. Harmonization in itself would not preclude the partitioning of markets that territorial protection creates; and where registered rights are involved, unlike the rights by which databases or software were protected, harmonization would not substantially reduce the costs involved in applying for rights separately in each country. The introduction of a single, autonomous law obviates the problems wrought by territorial protection. The first of these "unitary Community-wide laws" was created in 1994, when the EU enacted the Trademark Regulation, which created the Community Trade Mark, and a recent Regulation (which is still being implemented) created EU-wide design rights. Applications for a Community Trademark registration are determined by the Office for Harmonization in the Internal Market ("OHIM") which was set up in Alicante, Spain. And in June 1997, the Commission issued a Green Paper on reform of the patent system that asked whether it was time to introduce a unitary Community patent. *See infra* § 6.02[A][4].

[8]   The Status of the EU in International Intellectual Property Law

The EU may sign international agreements along with the member states. The Commission has responsibility for negotiating and monitoring the Union's international trade relationships. In *Opinion 1/94 on the Agreement Establishing the World Trade Organization*, [1995] 1 C.M.L.R. 205 (E.C.J. 1995), the European Court of Justice was asked to determine who had the competence to conclude and sign various agreements incorporated into or annexed to the World Trade Organization Agreement, including TRIPS. The Commission argued that the negotiation and ratification of TRIPS fell exclusively within the competence of the Community because of internal Community harmonization in the services sector, and that consequently the individual member states should not have co-signed the TRIPS agreement. The Court concluded that because there had only been partial harmonization achieved in the field of intellectual property, the Community and the member states were jointly competent to conclude TRIPS. Accordingly, the Commission (on behalf of the EU) and the member states each signed the agreements.

The incomplete federal status of the EU has raised problems in determining whether it has a right to a separate vote in international intellectual property assemblies. The newly formed Standing Committee on the Law of Trademarks, Industrial Designs and Geographical Indications decided at its first session in Geneva in July 1998 that membership in the Standing Committee would also be extended to the EU, provided that it shall not have the right to vote. Different solutions have been adopted in different contexts, such as in the negotiation of the Madrid Protocol (a trademark treaty) and the WIPO Copyright Treaty.

[D]   UNESCO

The United Nations Educational, Scientific and Cultural Organization ("UNESCO") came into being at the conclusion of the Second World War and currently has 188 member states. The principal goal of UNESCO is to contribute to peace and security in the world by promoting collaboration among nations through education, science, culture and communication. The founding documents of the Organization declare that:

> Since wars begin in the minds of men, it is in the minds of men that the defences of peace must be constructed . . . A peace based

exclusively upon the political and economic arrangements of governments would not be a peace which could secure the unanimous, lasting and sincere support of the peoples of the world, and the peace must therefore be founded, if it is not to fail, upon the intellectual and moral solidarity of mankind.

In addition to acting as a forum for discussion of these issues, which inevitably impinge upon matters of intellectual property law and policy, UNESCO provides technical assistance to member states and prepares the way for the adoption of international instruments pertaining to matters within its remit. The Organization also serves as administrator of the Universal Copyright Convention.

UNESCO is served by a Secretariat based in Paris and in sixty different offices scattered throughout the world; the Secretariat implements decisions taken by the member states in setting the Organization's agenda. UNESCO serves as an important link to a large number of non-governmental organizations with which it has official relations (and other NGOs with which it has informal relations).

[E]   OECD

The Organisation for Economic Co-operation and Development ("OECD") consists of twenty-nine member countries, largely from the developed world. The OECD provides a forum for member governments to discuss economic and social policy, including issues relating to intellectual property protection and ecommerce. Its role is as much to provide the opportunity for policy discussion as to produce formal international agreements. Although member states tend to be wealthier nations, membership in the OECD is conditioned only upon a country's commitment to a market economy and a pluralistic democracy. The original membership has expanded from Europe and North America, and now includes Japan, Australia, New Zealand, Finland, Mexico, the Czech Republic, Hungary, Poland and Korea.

The work of the organization and its constituent governments is supported by a Secretariat based in Paris. The work of the OECD Secretariat is financed by the member countries, with contributions calculated according to the weight of the member state's economy. (The United States is the biggest contributor followed by Japan.) The Secretariat, which is comprised of economists, scientists, lawyers and other professional staff, produces a wide range of data and research reports for use by the governments in the formulation of economic policies. Member countries meet and exchange information in committees; countries are represented either by government ministers or by personnel from the member's permanent delegation to the OECD. The principal (and decision-making) organ of the OECD is the Council, which meets at ministerial level annually. (A representative of the European Commission now attends these meetings along with a representative from each member state.)

As intellectual property becomes a more significant part of economic policy, the OECD has afforded the topic greater attention. At present, the question of ecommerce in particular is the subject of OECD study and thus the policies and decisions of the Organization, consisting as it does of extremely influential and powerful countries, will help to shape the principles of intellectual property law at the heart of the digital revolution.

[F] The Hague Conference on Private International Law

The first session of the Hague Conference on private international law was convened in 1893 by the Netherlands government. The Conference entered into a new era in 1955 with the entry into force of a statute which made the Conference a permanent intergovernmental organization. Since 1956, regular plenary sessions have been held every four years, the nineteenth of which met in 2001. The purpose of the Hague Conference is "to work for the progressive unification of the rules of private international law", primarily by the negotiation and drafting of multilateral treaties in various aspects of private international law. Thus, the Conference has addressed matters of international judicial and administrative co-operation (such as service of process or taking of evidence abroad), conflict of laws, and jurisdiction and enforcement of foreign judgments. This last topic is currently under heated discussion, and a draft convention under consideration contains provisions targeted particularly at international intellectual property litigation. *See infra* Chapter 7.

The initial research work of the Conference is undertaken by a permanent Secretariat based in the Hague, with the early drafts of proposed conventions prepared by special commissions made up of governmental experts. The drafts are then discussed and adopted at a plenary session of the Hague Conference, which is a diplomatic conference. The texts adopted are brought together in a Final Act that is signed by the delegations. Under the rules of procedure of the plenary sessions each member state has one vote. Decisions are taken by a majority of the votes cast by the delegations of member states which are present at the vote.

Formally, the Netherlands standing government committee on private international law sets the agenda for the plenary sessions, but in practice the special commissions of governmental experts meeting between sessions make recommendations to the plenary sessions which are considered and acted on by the plenary sessions.

The Hague Conference maintains continuing contacts with a number of international organizations involved in private international lawmaking, including the United Nations Commission on International Trade Law ("UNCITRAL") and the International Institute for the Unification of Private Law ("UNIDROIT").

§ 3.04 The Negotiation of Intellectual Property Treaties

The treaty negotiation process itself is an interesting and important part of the landscape of international intellectual property law. Bilateral negotiations are relatively simple, involving two countries working together each to gain certain benefits. As might be expected, the multilateral version becomes more complex both procedurally and substantively, as a greater number of diverse approaches and viewpoints must be heard and accommodated.

Bilateral agreements come about when two countries each sees something to be gained from making mutual promises. Some bilateral agreements relate specifically to one or more forms of intellectual property, such as the copyright agreement recently concluded between the United States and Vietnam. Others are agreements on trade or investment issues, which include aspects of intellectual property rights. Some developed countries prepare model agreements covering particular subjects, which are then adapted to the circumstances of the negotiating partner. With any of these bilateral agreements, representatives from the two countries' governments work together informally over an undefined period of time until they reach agreement.

Regional agreements almost by definition are trade agreements. Typically, contiguous or neighboring countries in a particular geographic region decide to work out the terms and conditions to remove market barriers between them. Often these terms include agreements on how to treat each other's intellectual property. The negotiation process is similar to the process for bilateral agreements, with representatives of several countries' governments working together in a closed, informal process.

Multilateral agreements, in contrast, are more institutionalized. They take place on the premises, and with the technical and administrative support, of intergovernmental organizations. Such agreements in essence establish an international framework or system that the negotiating countries agree is appropriate, and then those and other countries have the option of choosing whether to be bound by the obligations set out in the agreement.

The negotiating process for a multilateral agreement varies, depending primarily on which intergovernmental organization is involved. In any such negotiation, there are certain constants: formal negotiations take place with the help of simultaneous interpreters, translating statements into all of the official languages recognized by that intergovernmental organization. Informal but official negotiations also take place, sometimes with interpreters and sometimes without. Interspersed throughout are constant unofficial bilateral and smaller group discussions, in hallways, offices, meeting rooms and even coffee bars or restaurants. Many politically or theoretically difficult points may be resolved in these private talks, to be adopted by the larger group.

It is important to the dynamic of negotiations that each country, no matter what its size or the level of its economic interest in the issue under discussion, has only one vote. Accordingly, no single country can unilaterally determine a result. Nevertheless, a country or group of countries whose participation is critical to the success of the treaty may have great influence in the process, either by persuading others to follow its lead, or by threatening to withdraw from negotiations. Moreover, votes are rarely taken. Decisions are generally made by consensus, with voting only as a last resort on particularly controversial issues. Indeed, arguments have been made that treaty provisions or agreed statements adopted by less than consensus should be deemed less authoritative.

One of the hallmarks of multilateral negotiations is the formation of groups of countries with some type of common interest, that work together to develop a unified strategic position. Such groups may be comprised of highly industrialized countries, sharing an economic stake in strong protection for the intellectual property that they export. Or they may be developing countries from a particular region of the world, perhaps sharing a legal system or cultural concerns. These groups range from formally recognized U.N. groupings to informal and ad hoc alliances. In recent years, for example, the developing country members of WIPO have formed regional groups, respectively covering Latin America and the Caribbean, Africa, and Asia. The Arab countries and countries in Central and Eastern Europe also work cooperatively to make their collective voices heard. At meetings and conferences discussing or negotiating potential treaty language, a significant amount of time is spent determining the geographic and economic distribution of positions as officers presiding over the proceedings—the chair and vice-chairs of various committees.

While there are a number of international bodies that have sponsored treaty negotiations of various types, the major multilateral treaties today that deal with intellectual property have been sponsored by the WIPO and WTO. The WIPO process is markedly different from the WTO process in a number of respects. First, and most notably, the private sector plays a significant role at WIPO negotiations. Nongovernmental organizations ("NGOs") that have been accredited by the Secretariat are permitted to attend most preparatory meetings as well as the formal negotiating sessions. Such NGOs may be trade associations of commercial entities, or groups representing consumers, environmentalists, or other nonprofit interests. Not only do they observe, they also participate, making "interventions" to explain to governments their positions on the issues. The WTO process is less open. Not only is the private sector excluded from meetings and negotiating sessions, but WTO documents submitted or drafted by governments or the Secretariat are restricted in their distribution, and may only be made available to member governments unless and until they are specifically de-restricted.

Second, the process in the two organizations proceeds at a different rhythm and pace. The typical WIPO process is as follows: the Secretariat will identify a subject area that merits attention, organize one or more symposia and conferences in different locations to bring interested parties, academics and government policy-makers together to discuss it, and then place the subject on the organization's agenda. From then on, it will be a topic of discussion in ongoing meetings of a Committee of Experts, composed of government delegations representing WIPO member countries, usually taking place a few months apart over a period of several years.* Once the relevant Committee determines that the subject is ripe for consideration and negotiation of a treaty, it will recommend to the Governing Bodies (officials from member countries) that a Diplomatic Conference be convened, along with a schedule for preparatory work for the Conference. A Diplomatic Conference may take place in Geneva or in a member state that extends an invitation and typically continues for a set time period lasting several weeks. The treaty must be concluded within that time period; negotiations will normally not continue if they are not successful at that point. (It is theoretically possible to extend a diplomatic conference over several sessions, although this is rarely done and even more rarely successful.)

In the WTO, the negotiation of intellectual property provisions is part of a bigger and more extended series of negotiations, known as a "round." A new round is scheduled whenever member countries decide that there are sufficient outstanding trade issues on which further agreement would be useful. In the past, this has generally occurred at intervals of approximately five years. Preparatory work for a round is done through a combination of informal contacts and ministerial summit meetings, in which issues and concerns are identified and parameters established. Negotiations themselves take place over a lengthy period of time, with delegations convening to negotiate for a week every month or so over a period of years. Different members of the delegation will negotiate the details of particular issues within their competence, proceeding simultaneously. Final negotiations are concluded at a high political level, where trade-offs may be made among unrelated legal subjects. Deadlines are imposed at various stages, but are often extended.

NOTES AND QUESTIONS

(1) **Bilateral Agreements.** What are the deficiencies of bilateral agreements between two countries under which each agrees to offer intellectual property protection to the nationals of the other? What advantages do multilateral agreements offer? Are there any advantages to bilateral negotiation?

----

* In the past, separate Committees of Experts have been convened to deal with separate topics—for example, a Committee of Experts on the issue of database protection, and a separate Committee of Experts on the issue of audiovisual performers' rights. In reality, however, the membership of the committees was almost identical. As of the fall of 1998, WIPO has instead convened Standing Committees, each addressing a broad area of intellectual property. Thus, one standing committee deals with copyright and related rights, one with patents, and a third with trademark and unfair competition. The work of the standing committees, and the new forms of international intellectual property lawmaking that they represent, is discussed below in the context of specific proposals.

(2) **The Effect of Treaties on the Content of International Intellectual Property Law.** From the discussion of the recent history of international intellectual property treaties, what (possible) changes can you identify in the nature and sources of contemporary international intellectual property law?

(3) **Institutional Comparisons**. Compare the structures and objectives of the various institutions of international intellectual property lawmaking discussed in §§ 3.02–04. How are they different? In light of those differences, how would you expect the international lawmaking process (broadly construed) within each institution to differ, and how would you expect the outcomes of those processes to vary? What are the strengths and weaknesses of each institution as an instrument of international intellectual property lawmaking?

(4) **The EU as a Model for Global Unions**. The EU has become a hugely significant force in international intellectual property lawmaking. It is often claimed that the EU is a microcosm of the global economy and should thus be a model for a broader global union of states. What would it take to replicate the EU at a global level? In what ways would the operating premises of international law require modification? What hurdles would such a project face? Why were the EU member states able to overcome them? In April 2001, leaders from thirty-four countries agreed to establish a Free Trade Area of the Americas by 2005. Will the development of regional institutions that address intellectual property issues make it easier or harder to achieve broader global solutions?

(5) **The Role of National Law**. Note that national intellectual property laws are not automatically (or even typically) supplanted by international agreements. A review of national laws—as is conducted by the TRIPS Council and by the European Commission, to name but two institutions—is thus a crucial measure of the success of international law. In what ways is the review of the TRIPS Council different from that of the European Commission? In what ways does the TRIPS Council activities contribute to the development of international intellectual property law? International agreements clearly shape the content of national intellectual property laws. To what extent and in what ways might national law shape international intellectual property laws?

(6) **Inter-National Alliances**. Which groupings of countries would you expect to coalesce in the negotiation of intellectual property treaties? Is the fault line between developed and developing countries the only one that matters? Can you see others that might be relevant in the future?

§ 3.05   Treaties Under United States Law

The term "treaty" means something different in U.S. law than it does in international law. As used in the Vienna Convention on the Law of Treaties, a "treaty" means any "international agreement concluded between two States in written form and governed by international law." Vienna

Convention art. 2(1)(a). Note that the Restatement uses the term "international agreements" to describe the compacts that are a source of international law. As used in the U.S. Constitution, Art. II, § 2, the word "treaty" has a special meaning related to how one kind of international agreement becomes law within the United States: it is an agreement that is made "by and with the advice and consent of the Senate."

TREATIES AND OTHER INTERNATIONAL AGREEMENTS: THE ROLE OF THE UNITED STATES SENATE
S-Prt. 103-53, Study Prepared for the Committee On Foreign Relations, U.S. Senate (1993)

Treaties under International Law

Under international law an international agreement is generally considered to be a treaty and binding on the parties if it meets four criteria:

(1) The parties intend the agreement to be legally binding and the agreement is subject to international law;

(2) The agreement deals with significant matters;

(3) The agreement clearly and specifically describes the legal obligations of the parties;

(4) The form indicates an intention to conclude a treaty, although the substance of the agreement rather than the form is the governing factor.

International law makes no distinction between treaties and executive agreements. Executive agreements, especially if significant enough to be reported to Congress under the Case-Zablocki Act, are to all intents and purposes binding treaties under international law.

On the other hand, many international undertakings and foreign policy statements, such as unilateral statements of intent, joint communiqués, and final acts of conferences, are not intended to be legally binding and are not considered treaties.

Treaties under United States Law

Under the Constitution, a treaty, like a Federal statute, is part of the "supreme Law of the Land." Self-executing treaties, . . . which do not require implementing legislation, automatically become effective as domestic law immediately upon entry into force. Other treaties do not become effective as domestic law until implementing legislation is enacted, and then technically it is the legislation, not the treaty unless incorporated into the legislation, that is the law of the land.

Sometimes it is not clear on the face of a treaty whether it is self-executing or requires implementing legislation. Some treaties expressly call for implementing legislation or deal with subjects clearly requiring congressional action, such as the appropriation of funds or enactment of domestic penal provisions. The question of whether or not a treaty requires implementing legislation or is self-executing is a matter of interpretation largely by the executive branch or, less frequently, by the courts. On occasion, the Senate includes an understanding in the resolution of ratification that certain provisions are not self-executing or that the President is to exchange or deposit the instrument of ratification only after implementation legislation has been enacted.

When a treaty is deemed self-executing, it overrides any conflicting provision of the law of an individual state. If a treaty is in irreconcilable conflict with a Federal law, the one later in time prevails, although courts generally try to harmonize domestic and international obligations whenever possible.

EXECUTIVE AGREEMENTS UNDER U.S. LAW

The status in domestic law of executive agreements, that is, international agreements made by the executive branch but not submitted to the Senate for its advice and consent, is less clear. Executive agreements may validly coexist with treaties, but it is not clear that all subjects dealt with by treaty may also be dealt with by executive agreement, especially if the agreement is concluded on the sole authority of the President. Three types of executive agreements and their domestic legal status are discussed below.

(1) Congressional-Executive Agreements

Most executive agreements are either explicitly or implicitly authorized in advance by Congress or submitted to Congress for approval. Some areas in which Congress has authorized the conclusion of international agreements are postal conventions, foreign trade, foreign military assistance, foreign economic assistance, atomic energy cooperation, and international fishery rights. Sometimes Congress has authorized conclusion of agreements but required the executive branch to submit the agreements to Congress for approval by legislation or for a specified waiting period before taking effect. Congress has also sometimes approved by joint resolution international agreements involving matters that are frequently handled by treaty, including such subjects as participation in international organizations, arms control measures, and acquisition of territory. The constitutionality of this type of agreement seems well established and Congress has authorized or approved them frequently.

(2) Agreements Pursuant to Treaties

Some executive agreements are expressly authorized by treaty or an authorization for them may be reasonably inferred from the provisions of a prior treaty. Examples include arrangements and understandings under the North Atlantic Treaty and other security treaties. The President's authority to conclude agreements pursuant to treaties seems well established, although controversy occasionally arises over whether particular agreements were within the purview of an existing treaty.

(3) Presidential or Sole Executive Agreements

Some executive agreements are concluded solely on the basis of the President's independent constitutional authority and do not have an underlying explicit or implied authorization by treaty or statute. Authorities which Presidents claim as a basis for such agreements include:

— The President's general executive authority in Article II, section 1, of the Constitution;

— His power as Commander in Chief of the Army and Navy in Article II, section 2, clause 1;

— The treaty clause itself for agreements which might be part of the process of negotiating a treaty, Article II, section 2, clause 2;

— His authority to receive Ambassadors and other public Ministers, Article II, section 3;

— His duty to "take care that the laws be faithfully executed," Article II, section 3.

Courts have indicated that executive agreements based solely on the President's independent constitutional authority can supersede conflicting provisions of State law, but opinions differ regarding the extent to which they can supersede a prior act of Congress. What judicial authority exists seems to indicate that they cannot.

. . . .

THE HOUSE ROLE IN TREATIES

Because treaties become part of the law of the land, concern is sometimes expressed that the House of Representatives does not share in the treaty power. The Framers confined the treaty-making power to the President and the Senate in the belief that the latter's smaller size would enable it to be a confidential partner in the negotiations. The need for maintaining secrecy during negotiations and acting with speed were also cited as justifications for not including the House. In addition, by making the treaty power a national power and requiring the advice and consent of the Senate, the Framers gave expression to their desire to form a strong central government while affording the States ample safeguards.

The Supreme Court, in *INS v. Chadha*, cited the Senate's power to advise and consent to treaties negotiated by the President "as one of only four provisions in the Constitution, explicit and unambiguous, by which one House may act alone with the unreviewable force of law, not subject to the President's veto." In 1945 the House adopted a resolution to amend the Constitution to require the advice and consent of both Houses for treaties, but the Senate did not act on the measure.

The House from the beginning has played a role in treaties that require implementing legislation. On occasion, as in 1796 with the Jay Treaty, problems have arisen when Presidents have completed ratification of treaties and then called upon Congress to pass implementing legislation to prevent the United States from defaulting on its international obligations. Or treaties approved by the Senate have remained unfulfilled for long periods because implementing legislation was not passed.

The increasing use of statutory agreements has also equalized to some extent the role of the House vis-à-vis the Senate in the making of international agreements. Executive agreements authorized or approved by legislation give a majority in the House and Senate the power analogous to the Senate's advice and consent by a two-thirds majority.

. . . .

INCREASING USE OF EXECUTIVE AGREEMENTS

As the United States became more involved in world affairs, international agreements multiplied. Most of the growth was in executive agreements. . . . In the 1980s, the United States entered into three or four hundred executive agreements per year, compared to 8 to 26 treaties per year.

The executive branch found it was much easier to conclude an executive agreement than a treaty because it was not submitted to the Senate. . . . The Senate, too, accepted executive agreements as an alternate method of making many international agreements, since submitting all agreements to the Senate as treaties would either overwhelm the Senate with work or force approval to become perfunctory.

Of most concern to the Senate were executive agreements concluded solely on the President's own authority, without any authority from Congress. In other executive agreements, the Senate played a role anyway. In the case of executive agreements concluded under the authority of a treaty, the Senate consented to the original treaty. In the case of congressional-executive agreements, both Houses passed the legislation that authorized, required scrutiny of, or approved the agreements.

NOTES AND QUESTIONS

(1) **Trade Agreements as Executive or Congressional-Executive Agreements**. The Constitution grants the President the power "by and with the Advice and Consent of the Senate to make Treaties," U.S. CONST. ART II, § 2, but grants Congress the power "to lay and collect Taxes, Duties, Imposts and Excises. . . " U.S. CONST. ART I, § 8, CL.1. Thus, all agreements that affect import duties (tariffs) must be in the form of legislation passed by both houses of Congress rather than in the form of a treaty submitted to the Senate for its "Advice and Consent." Both the North

American Free Trade Agreement Implementation Act of 1993, Pub. L. 103-182, and the Uruguay Round Agreements Act of 1994, Pub. L. 103-465, originated as bills in the House of Representatives.

(2) **The Increase in Executive Agreements**. Why might the use of executive agreements be increasing as of late? What are the advantages of using such agreements? *See* Sol Picciotto, *Networks in International Economic Integration: Fragmented States and the Dilemmas of Neo-Liberalism*, 17 Nw. J. INT'L L. & BUS. 1014, 1050 (1997). Are there any dangers in Presidents making extensive use of executive agreements? For an example of a pure executive agreement negotiated by the U.S. Trade Representative not involving Congress in any direct way, see *China-United States: Agreement Regarding Intellectual Property Rights*, 34 I.L.M. 881 (1995) (a so-called "Memorandum of Understanding"). Are such administrative arrangements, which do not involve Congress in any way, subject to any constitutional limits? Does the fact that the China-U.S. agreement concerns obligations imposed only on China affect your analysis?

(3) **Fast-Track Authority**. Both the NAFTA Implementation Act and Uruguay Round Agreements Act were passed under the so-called "fast track" procedure. Section 151 of the Trade Act of 1974 (19 U.S.C.§ 2191) set forth specific procedures giving the President the ability to negotiate trade agreements with the understanding that Congress will either pass or reject the agreement without modification within ninety days. Section 161 (19 U.S.C. § 2211) required the U.S. Trade Representative to keep members of Congress informed on the status of trade agreement negotiations and to consult on a continuing basis with the House Ways and Means Committee and the Senate Finance Committee. Although the President's fast-track authority has since expired, Congress renewed the President's fast track authority (albeit under the different name of "trade promotion authority") by enacting the Trade Promotion Act of 2002 in August of that year. Why would the legislative branch continue to give the President this type of deference? One critic of the system of trade agreement approval has said:

> The international trade system operates contrary to every principle of democracy and government accountability embedded in U.S. domestic policymaking. Secrecy pervades the entire system. Trade officials operate behind closed doors with no public record of their activities when they negotiate or implement trade agreements or when they resolve disputes arising under them. As a result, there are no mechanisms for the public to monitor the development or implementation of international trade policy. To compound matters, trade decision-makers owe their allegiances to the trade regime and make no attempt to invite or incorporate other views. There are no avenues for public participation to ensure that other perspectives are taken into account. Thus, in the coming era of "government by trade agreements," domestic prerogatives will be foreclosed or made more costly by trade bureaucrats secretly negotiating agreements and adjudicating disputes thousands of miles away.

Patti Goldman, *Symposium: The Democratization of the Development of United States Trade Policy*, 27 CORNELL INT'L L.J. 631, 633 (1994).

Assuming such criticism is valid, does the opaqueness of the process of negotiation of trade agreements provide any benefits to the political branches of government? Do these benefits justify fast track treatment? Is legislation enacted pursuant to fast-track authority constitutional? Can it be argued that the procedure circumvents Article II, Section 2's treaty power, and that that provision represents the sole constitutional means of making an international agreement? *See Made in the USA Foundation v. United States*, 56 F. Supp.2d 1226 (N.D. Ala. 1999) (holding that the Treaty Clause did not constitute the exclusive means of enacting international commercial agreements, given Congress's plenary powers to regulate foreign commerce and the President's inherent authority under Article II to manage the nation's affairs), *aff'd*, 242 F.2d 1300 (11th Cir. 2001) (affirming because whether NAFTA was a treaty requiring Senate ratification pursuant to the Treaty Clause was a nonjusticiable political question).

ROBERTSON v. GENERAL ELECTRIC CO.
32 F.2d 495 (4th Cir. 1929)

PARKER, CIRCUIT JUDGE:

[The Paris Convention requires signatory states to recognize so-called "rights of priority," under which a patent applicant in one country is afforded twelve months in which to apply for a patent on the invention in another signatory country without the first patent acting to bar the grant of the patent in the second country. Both the United States and Germany had implemented such rights of priority in their national laws. Stoffregen, a German, filed a German patent application on October 11, 1915. Because of World War I, however, it was impossible for nationals of the combatants to file patent applications in enemy countries. Accordingly, Section 308 of the Treaty of Peace of Versailles provided that rights of priority available under international conventions shall be extended until "six months after the coming into force" of the Versailles Treaty. The Senate never ratified the Versailles Treaty; subsequently, the U.S. Congress enacted the Nolan Act of March 3, 1921, which specifically extended the time for filing patent applications for six months, until September 3, 1921. On November 2, 1921, the treaty of peace between the United States and Germany, known as the Treaty of Berlin, was ratified; and on November 11, 1921, it took effect upon the exchange of ratifications. Without specifically mentioning Section 308, the Treaty of Berlin stated that "the periods of time . . . of the Treaty of Versailles shall run, with respect to any act or election on the part of the United States, from the date of the coming into force of the present treaty." Stoffregen delayed filing an application for a patent with the U.S. Patent Office until May 10, 1922. It was rejected by the Patent Office Examiner on the ground that it had been filed more than twelve months after the filing of the foreign application, which decision was affirmed by the Court of Appeals for the District of Columbia. Appellees then filed a bill in the district court under R.S. 4915 (current 35 U.S.C. § 145) arguing that the Treaty of Berlin extended the effect of Section 308 for six months from the entry into force of the Treaty of Berlin. The district court agreed. The Fourth Circuit here reverses that decision.]

Th[is] bring[s] us to the second ground upon which we think that the prayer of complainants must be denied, viz.: That, even if the Treaty of Berlin is to be construed as incorporating Section 308 of the Versailles Treaty . . . complainants are not entitled to the patent applied for, because the section is not self-executing and no legislation has been enacted to carry it into effect. Assuming that a treaty provision affecting patents may be made self-executing, so that no supporting legislation is necessary under the Constitution to give rise to individual rights thereunder, we are satisfied that section 308 was not intended to be, and is not, such a self-executing provision.

The rule as to whether a treaty is self-executing or not is clearly stated by Chief Justice Marshall in Foster & Elam v. Neilson, 2 Pet. 253, 313 as follows:

> A treaty is, in its nature, a contract between two nations, not a legislative act. It does not generally effect, of itself, the object to be accomplished, especially so far as its operation is infraterritorial, but is carried into execution by the sovereign power of the respective parties to the instrument. In the United States, a different principle is established. Our Constitution declares a treaty to be the law of the land. It is, consequently, to be regarded in courts of justice as equivalent to an act of the Legislature, whenever it operates of itself, without the aid of any legislative provision. *But when the terms of the stipulation import a contract—when either of the parties engages to perform a particular act, the treaty addresses itself to the political, not the judicial department; and the Legislature must execute the contract, before it can become a rule for the court.* (Italics ours.)

The language of section 308 is that "the rights of priority . . . shall be extended by each of the high contracting parties," etc. This not only uses language of futurity, "shall be extended," as to a matter operating as to each nation infraterritorially, and not between nations, but it also provides that the extension shall be made, not by the instrument itself, but "by each of the high contracting parties." In other words, to use the language of Chief Justice Marshall, each of the parties "engages to perform a particular act," and therefore "the treaty addresses itself to the political, not the judicial, department, and the Legislature must execute the contract before it can become a rule for the court."

It was the opinion of Attorney General Miller (19 Op. Attys. Gen. 273) that, as Congress alone was given by the Constitution the power "to promote the progress of science and useful arts by securing for limited times to authors and inventors the exclusive right to their respective writings and discoveries," treaty provisions relating to patent rights must be deemed dependent upon legislation in aid thereof. And this seems to have been the view also of Judge Lowell in United Shoe Machinery Co. v. Duplessis Shoe Machinery Co. (C.C.) 148 F. 31, and there is much to be said in its favor. Patent rights differ from many other rights which are the subject of treaties, in that they are created by and dependent upon statutes which only Congress has power to enact. Furthermore, the right under a patent is not one which extends across national boundaries, and is therefore necessarily a matter for regulation by treaty, but is one which must be enjoyed within the territory of the nation. We think, however, that the better view is that a treaty affecting patent rights may be so drawn as to be self-executing. *See* United Shoe Machinery Co. v. Duplessis Shoe Mach. Co. (C.C.A. 1st) 155 F. 842. [cit]. But the reasons which led to the doubt as to whether a treaty could be so drawn as to effect patent rights, without supporting legislation by Congress, are matters which must be considered in the interpretation of treaties affecting patents; and they require that such treaties be held not self-executing, unless their language compels a different interpretation.

Patent rights are valid, of course, only within the country granting the patent. They are created by statute, and complicated administrative machinery is provided for the application of the statutory provisions. Treaties are drafted ordinarily to accomplish certain general results, and in the nature of things cannot regulate details and ought not to interfere with the domestic machinery which the several countries have provided for the regulation of patents. For these reasons, unless a contrary intention is clearly indicated, they should be construed, not as of themselves making changes in the patent laws, but as contemplating that the various parties signatory will enact appropriate legislation and promulgate proper rules to effectuate the ends which they are designed to accomplish.

This rule of construction has been uniformly followed in this country, and treaties affecting patent rights have been held to be not self-effectuating, where the purpose that they should be carried out by supporting legislation was not by any means so clearly indicated as in the section of the treaty under consideration. Thus article II of the [Paris] Convention of March 20, 1883, provided:

> The subjects or citizens of each of the contracting States shall enjoy, in all the other states of the Union, so far as concerns patents for inventions, trade or commercial marks, and the commercial name, the advantages that the respective laws thereof at present accord, or shall afterwards accord to subjects or citizens. In consequence they shall have the same protection as these latter, and the same legal recourse against all infringements of their rights, under reserve of complying with the formalities and conditions imposed upon subjects or citizens by the domestic legislation of each state.

In the opinion of Attorney General Miller, referred to above, this article was held not to be self-executing, but to require the support of legislation before it became a rule for the courts to follow. While the constitutional question to which we have adverted was discussed, the opinion was finally based upon the proposition that the treaty was a contract operating in the future intraterritorially. The Attorney General said:

> It is not necessary to the decision of the question submitted to me in the matter under consideration to determine whether all the provisions of treaties, whose execution requires the exercise of powers submitted to Congress, must be so submitted before they become law to the courts and executive departments, for the treaty under consideration is a reciprocal one; each party to it covenants to grant in the future to the subjects and citizens of the other parties certain special rights in consideration of the granting of like special rights to its subjects or citizens. It is a contract operative in the future infraterritorially. It is therefore not self-executing, but requires legislation to render it effective for the modification of existing laws.

In Rousseau v. Brown, 21 App.D.C. 73, a citizen of France based his claim upon the provisions of the Convention of March 20, 1883. In denying his claim, the court said:

> The convention is in the nature of a contract between the parties thereto, and is not self-executing. It requires the action of Congress to give it full force and effect. *This is the construction that has been placed upon it by most of the parties to it,* and they have adopted legislation giving effect to it. . . . But without regard to the action of other states, *the uniform construction of that convention by the Patent Office officials, and by the courts of this country, has been that the convention is not self-executing,* but requires the aid of an act of Congress. (Italics ours.) . . .

The Convention of Brussels of December 14, 1900, changed the priority period for patents to twelve months and inserted in the prior convention a section known as article "4bis," as follows:

> Patents applied for in the different contracting States by persons admitted to the benefit of the convention under the terms of articles 2 and 3 shall be independent of the patents obtained for the same invention in the other states adherents or nonadherents to the Union.

There was some controversy in the lower courts as to whether this was a self-executing provision or not, but the Supreme Court, in Cameron Septic Tank Co. v. Knoxville, 227 U.S. 39, set these controversies at rest by showing that it was the sense of Congress that the treaty required legislation to become effective, that this was the understanding of other nations also, and that the act of 1903 was passed to carry it into effect. The court said:

The act of 1903 was then enacted, and if there could be any doubt that it expressed the sense of Congress and those concerned with the treaty that it required legislation to become effective, such doubt would be entirely removed by the legislative action of other states. It appears from the report of the committee on patents of the Senate and of the House of Representatives on the proposed legislation that 13 countries had adopted legislation giving full force and effect to the provisions of the additional act either in the form of a general law or by specific amendment to other laws providing for carrying into force the provisions of the additional act as regards the extension of the 'delay and priority' to twelve months. Other countries were mentioned as being expected to do so. In explaining the object of the bill the member in charge of it in the House of Representatives said that it was to carry into effect the additional act of the convention held at Brussels in December, 1900. . . . If it [the treaty] be not self-executing, as it is certainly the sense of Congress that it was not and seems also to be the sense of some of the other contracting nations, and as the act of 1903 did not make effective article 4*bis*, the provisions of section 4887 apply to the Cameron patent and caused it to expire with the British patent for the same invention.

In the light of these decisions, relating to treaties the language of which does not negative the idea of self-execution near so plainly as does that of section 308 of the Treaty of Versailles, it is clear that that section cannot reasonably be construed as self-executing. As no legislation has been passed in aid of it, except the Nolan Act, the time limit of which had expired before complainants filed their application, it follows that there is nothing upon which they can base the extension of priority rights for which they contend.

. . . .

Reversed.

GENERAL MOTORS CORP. v. IGNACIO LOPEZ DE ARRIORTUA
948 F. Supp. 684 (E.D.Mich. 1996)

EDMUNDS, DISTRICT JUDGE.

Plaintiffs, General Motors Corporation ("GM") and Adam Opel AG ("Opel"), brought suit against Defendants alleging theft of trade secrets and conspiracy. GM is an American corporation and Opel is a German corporation wholly owned by GM. Defendants include:

1. Volkswagen AG, a German corporation ("VW")

2. Volkswagen of America, Inc., wholly owned by Volkswagen AG ("VWOA")

3. The "Lopez Group," including . . . Jose Ignacio Lopez, a former executive at GM Espana, Opel, and GM (Europe) AG. On February 1, 1993 he became group vice president of GM. Subsequently,

on March 10, 1993, he resigned from GM and moved to Germany. On March 16, he joined VW and was appointed to its management board. . . . .

Plaintiffs allege that while Lopez was a high level GM executive, he secretly communicated with VW representatives and agreed to leave GM and join VW. He agreed to bring confidential business plans and trade secret information with him. Lopez worked with the other Lopez Group Defendants to secretly collect confidential information. In March of 1993, the Lopez Group Defendants left GM and Opel to join VW where they were paid significantly higher salaries. They allegedly took over 20 cartons of stolen documents with them. Plaintiffs allege that Defendants copied the documents and entered them into VW computers, and then proceeded to shred the documents and cover up the theft.

On March 7, 1996, Plaintiffs filed this suit. Counts 3 and 4 of their complaint allege that Defendants violated the Lanham Act, 15 U.S.C. § 1126, and that Defendants violated the Copyright Act. [cit]. The complaint further alleges that VW has used and continues to use the trade secret information to reduce its costs and to increase its market share. Defendants moved to dismiss count 3 (Lanham Act) and count 4 (Copyright Act). For the reasons set forth below, Defendants' motions are denied.

. . . .

All Defendants (except those who have not been served) have moved to dismiss count 3 of the complaint. Count 3 alleges that Defendants violated the substantive terms of the Paris Convention, an international agreement incorporated into section 44 of the Lanham Act. [cit]. Defendants contend that the Lanham Act does not incorporate any substantive provisions of the Paris Convention, and thus that Plaintiffs have failed to state a viable claim for relief. They argue that the Paris Convention only required that signatory nations provide the same trademark protection to foreign citizens that they provide to their own citizens. Courts are split on the issue of whether section 44(b) of the Lanham Act incorporates substantive rights set forth in the Paris Convention.

Generally, the Lanham Act prohibits two types of unfair competition: trademark infringement (15 U.S.C. § 1114) and false designation of origin or "passing off" (15 U.S.C. § 1125). In addition, the Lanham Act provides rights stipulated by international conventions respecting unfair competition. Section 1127 provides:

> The intent of this chapter is . . . to provide rights and remedies stipulated by treaties and conventions respecting trade-marks, trade names, and unfair competition entered into between the United States and foreign nations.

This purpose is implemented in sections 44(b), (h), and (i). Section 44(b) provides:

> Any person whose country of origin is a party to any convention or treaty relating to trademarks . . . to which the United States

is also a party . . . shall be entitled to the benefits of this section under the conditions expressed herein *to the extent necessary to give effect to any provision of such convention [or] treaty . . . in addition to the rights to which any owner of a mark is otherwise entitled* by this chapter.

15 U.S.C. § 1126(b) (emphasis added). Under section 44(h), foreign citizens are entitled to protection against unfair competition as follows:

Any person designated in subsection (b) of this section as entitled to the benefits and subject to the provisions of this chapter shall be entitled to effective protection against unfair competition, and the remedies provided in this chapter for infringement of marks shall be available so far as they may be appropriate in repressing acts of unfair competition.

15 U.S.C. § 1126(h). The Act specifically provides under section 44(i) that United States citizens shall have the same rights as foreigners. "Citizens or residents of the United States shall have the same benefits as are granted by this section to persons described in subsection (b) of this section." 15 U.S.C. 1126(i).

One treaty incorporated by this section is the International Convention for the Protection of Industrial Property, the Paris Convention. 24 U.S.T. 2140 (July 14, 1967). The Paris Convention requires signatory nations to prohibit unfair competition.

(1) The countries of the Union are bound to assure to nationals of such countries effective protection against unfair competition. [3]

(2) Any act of competition contrary to honest practices in industrial or commercial matters constitutes an act of unfair competition.

Paris Convention, article 10*bis*. The broad concept of unfair competition set forth in the Paris Convention has been described as follows:

Article 10*bis* is not premised upon the narrow meaning of "unfair competition" as it was understood in American common law, but adopts the more liberal construction of the European countries such as France, Germany and Switzerland . . . The statement that unfair competition is competition "contrary to honest practice" is not a definition; it merely expresses the concept that a particular act of competition is to be condemned as unfair because it is inconsistent with currently accepted standards of honest practice. It impliedly affirms that unfair competition is too broad a concept to be limited to any narrow definition such as for instance, passing off.

4A Rudolf Callmann, *The Law of Unfair Competition, Trademarks and Monopolies*, § 2610 (4th ed. 1994). The United States and Germany are both signatories to the Paris Convention.

---

[3] Article 10*ter* of the Paris Convention also requires signatory nations to provide for legal remedies to enforce Article 10 *bis*. . .

Defendants concede that the Lanham Act incorporates the Paris Convention. However, they contend that the Paris Convention does not provide substantive rights, and that it only requires "national treatment." One authority on trademark law explained this interpretation of the Convention:

> The Paris Convention is essentially a compact between the various member countries to accord in their own countries to citizens of the other contracting parties' trademark and other rights comparable to those accorded their own citizens by their domestic law. *The underlying principle is that foreign nationals should be given the same treatment in each of the member countries as that country makes available to its own citizens ["national treatment"].* The Convention is not premised upon the idea that the trademark laws of each member nation shall be given extraterritorial application, but on exactly the converse principle that each nation's law shall have only territorial application.

In re Compagnie Generale Maritime, 993 F.2d 841, 850 (Fed. Cir.1993) (Nies, J., dissenting) (quoting 1 McCarthy, *Trademarks and Unfair Competition*, § 19:24, at 927 (2d ed. 1984) (emphasis added)).

Agreeing with the "national treatment" analysis, in Vanity Fair Mills, Inc. v. T. Eaton Co. 234 F.2d 633, 644 (2d Cir. 1956), the Second Circuit interpreted the Paris Convention and the Lanham Act as providing only limited protection from acts of unfair competition. In that case, plaintiff was an American company who brought suit against a Canadian company, alleging that the defendant violated plaintiff's trademark when it sold goods in Canada using plaintiff's "Vanity Fair" label. The court held that the Paris Convention was premised on the concept of national treatment and that the laws of the signatory nations should not have extraterritorial application. Thus, plaintiff could not hold the defendant Canadian corporation liable under American law for a trademark violation that occurred in Canada. *See also* Majorica S.A. v. Majorca International, Ltd., 687 F.Supp. 92 (S.D.N.Y.1988) (following *Vanity Fair*, court held that where Spanish Company sued American Company, Spanish law was not entitled to application in U.S. under Paris Convention). . . .

Contrary to *Vanity Fair*, other courts have held that the Lanham Act incorporates international agreements. In Toho Co. v. Sears, Roebuck & Co., 645 F.2d 788, 792 (9th Cir.1981), a Japanese company brought suit against Sears, an American company, alleging unfair competition. The court explained that sections 44(b) and (h) incorporated the provisions of a treaty between the United States and Japan. "The federal right created by subsection 44(h) is coextensive with the substantive provisions of the treaty involved. . . . [S]ubsections (b) and (h) work together to provide federal rights and remedies implementing federal unfair competition treaties." *Toho*, 645 F.2d at 792. The U.S.-Japan treaty only required national treatment. Thus, the court reasoned that the Japanese company was entitled to bring the same claims as an American company would be entitled to bring: both claims for trademark infringement and false designation of origin under the Lanham Act as well as a claim for unfair competition under state law.

. . . .

Still other courts have taken *Toho* one step further and have held that the Lanham Act incorporates the substantive provisions of the Paris Convention and thus creates a federal law of unfair competition applicable in international disputes. In Maison Lazard et Compagnie v. Manfra, Tordella & Brooks, Inc., 585 F.Supp. 1286, 1289 (S.D.N.Y.1984), a French company brought suit against an American company, alleging that the American company sold commemorative Olympic coins overseas in violation of the plaintiff's exclusive right to make such sales. In essence, the French company claimed that the defendant misappropriated an exclusive right and that this constituted unfair competition under the Paris Convention. The court followed *Toho*, holding that the Lanham Act incorporated the Convention. Because the Paris Convention provides broad protection from unfair competition, the court held that the plaintiff had a valid federal claim for misappropriation of an exclusive right. [cit].

The court is persuaded that *Toho* and *Maison Lazard* properly interpret the Lanham Act as incorporating the substantive provisions of the Paris Convention. The express purpose of the Lanham Act dictates this result. "The intent of this chapter is . . . to provide rights and remedies stipulated by treaties and conventions. . . ." 15 U.S.C. § 1127. The Paris Convention provides that signatory countries must protect individuals from unfair competition. Article 10*bis*. Subsection (b) of the Lanham Act implements this concept by providing that foreigners are entitled to benefits "to the extent necessary to give effect to any provision" of a convention. Subsection (h) specifies that foreigners are entitled "to protection against unfair competition."

The intent of Congress to incorporate substantive rights is further manifested in subsection (i), which provides that United States citizens shall be entitled to the same rights as foreign citizens. It was necessary to enact subsection (i) to make it clear that United States citizens were entitled to *additional* rights provided by the treaties incorporated. If the incorporation of the treaty did not incorporate additional rights, it would have been unnecessary to enact section 44(i). Interpreting section 44(b) as merely requiring "national treatment" renders section 44(i) superfluous. Courts must interpret statutes so as to give effect to every word and to avoid rendering certain language superfluous. . . .

The legislative history also reveals Congressional intent to incorporate additional rights and to provide such rights both to foreigners and to citizens. Congress expressed its concern that Americans be given the same protection from unfair competition as foreigners.

> We have the curious anomaly of this Government giving by treaty and by law with respect to trade-marks and unfair competition to

nationals of foreign governments greater rights than it gives its own citizens. . . . This [subsection 44(i) in the final draft] is an attempt to put the citizen on an equality with the foreigner. . . .

Hearings on H.R. 4744 Before the Subcomm. on Trademarks of the House Comm. on Patents, 76th Cong., 1st Sess. (1939), p. 164. Congress also explained that the Paris Convention prohibited unfair competition more broadly than did the Lanham Act. "The European Convention [meaning the Paris Convention] however, goes much farther than that and prohibits commercial bribery among other things. . . ." *Id.* at 168.[4]

The legislative history also reveals that Congress specifically considered whether it should broadly prohibit unfair competition. A prior draft of section 44 included the following as subsection (g):

All acts of unfair competition in commerce are declared to be unlawful and the provisions of section 32 to 35 inclusive shall be applicable thereto.

Id. at 163. One Congressman pointed out that the term "unfair competition" included all types of artificial interference with trade, including disparagement, trade bribery, and the like. [cit]. This draft of the statute provided the rights that the United States was obligated to provide by the Paris Convention. [cit]. At the subcommittee hearing, the legislators decided that the term "unfair competition" as used in subsection (g) was "dangerously broad," *id.* at 167, and that subsection (g) should be deleted. [cit]. The legislators did not acknowledge that by deleting subsection (g), the statute failed to fully incorporate the Paris Convention.

However, the legislators reversed this position. The final version of the statute contains language substantially similar to the deleted subsection (g). As discussed above, section 44(h) provides foreigners with "effective protection against unfair competition." The inclusion of this language is consistent with Congress' concern that it fully implement the Paris Convention, including the Convention's broad prohibition of unfair competition.

Opel seeks the right to sue for unfair competition pursuant to 44(h), and GM seeks to enforce the same rights pursuant to section 44(i). Because the Lanham Act incorporates the Paris Convention's broad prohibition against unfair competition, Plaintiffs have stated a claim.[5]

---

[4] Defendants also contend that if the Paris Convention provides substantive rights it is not clear what those rights are. While the precise nature of these rights is not clear at this juncture, it is clear that the rights provided by the Paris Convention include protection from commercial bribery. It also should be noted that because Plaintiffs seek the enforcement of foreign law, it is their obligation to inform the court of the content of that law. Rolnick v. El Al Israel Airlines, Ltd., 551 F.Supp. 261 (E.D.N.Y.1982).

[5] Defendants also argue that interpreting section 44 as incorporating the Paris Convention would eliminate diversity jurisdiction in all actions involving unfair competition. This is overstated. The court's holding is limited to the circumstances of this case. The Lanham Act incorporates the substantive provisions of the Paris Convention and thus creates a federal law of unfair competition applicable in international disputes. Diversity jurisdiction would still apply in a domestic dispute. It should also be noted that this issue is not before the court. The court has proper federal question jurisdiction in this case.

Defendants also claim that the Lanham Act does not reach extraterritorial acts. This is incorrect. Congress has the power to regulate even entirely foreign commerce where it has a substantial effect on commerce between the states or between the United States and foreign countries. *Vanity Fair*, 234 F.2d at 641. Accord Consolidated Gold Fields PLC v. Minorco, S.A., 871 F.2d 252, 261–62 (2d Cir.1989) (federal statutes apply if underlying conduct occurred within U.S. or if conduct which occurred abroad has substantial effects within U.S.). "Particularly is this true when a conspiracy is alleged with acts in furtherance of that conspiracy taking place in both the United States and foreign countries."*Id. See also* Steele v. Bulova Watch Co., 344 U.S. 280 (1952) (holding U.S. citizen who sold infringing watches only in foreign countries liable under Lanham Act).

. . .

Defendants' joint motion to dismiss counts 3 and 4 is *denied*.

NOTES AND QUESTIONS

(1) **Self-Execution Generally**. The *Robertson* court proceeds on the assumption that patent treaties may be self-executing. Are there any reasons why we should be cautious before treating intellectual property treaties (or treaties affecting certain types of intellectual property) as self-executing? What are the advantages of treating a treaty as self-executing? What difficulties are caused national courts or administrative officials if the United States relies on treaty self-execution rather than implementing legislation as a means of fulfilling its treaty obligations?

(2) **Alternatives to Self-Execution**. In what ways, if any, is the holding of the *Lopez* court different from treating Article 10*bis* of the Paris Convention as self-executing? How would you describe what Congress has done in the provisions of Section 44 of the Lanham Act quoted in *Lopez*? In what other ways could U.S. compliance with Article 10*bis* have been achieved? In certain circumstances, principles of EU directives may be treated as directly effective in member state law notwithstanding the lack of legislative transposition into national law. *See supra* § 3.03[C]. In what ways is giving direct effect to directives different from treating a treaty as self-executing?

(3) **The Paris Convention and Self-Execution.** It has never been clear whether the leading multilateral trademark treaties (including the Paris Convention) were self-executing in the United States. The U.S. Supreme Court held that the Inter-American Trademark Convention was self-executing, *see* Bacardi Corp. *of Am. v. Domenech*, 311 U.S. 150, 159 (1940), but (as the *Robertson* court noted) the U.S. Attorney-General issued an opinion in 1889 declaring that the Paris Convention of 1883 was not self-executing. *See* 19 Op. Att'y Gen. 273 (1889). Courts have been split on the latter question. *See generally* John B. Pegram, *Trademark Law Revision:*

Section 44, 78 TRADEMARK REP. 141, 158–162 (1988). Although most courts have rejected claims that the Paris Convention is self-executing, *see, e.g., French Republic v. Saratoga Vichy Spring Co.,* 191 U.S. 427, 438 (1903), lower courts appear to be more receptive to the argument of late. *See, e.g., Laboratories Roldan C. v. Tex Int'l,* 902 F. Supp. 1555, 1568 (S.D. Fla. 1995) (recognizing claim under Article 10*bis* of the Paris Convention); *Benard Indus. v. Bayer,* 38 U.S.P.Q.2d 1422, 1426 (S.D. Fla. 1996) (permitting claim under Paris Convention to proceed). The arguments in favor of self-execution are probably stronger with respect to some texts of the Convention than others. *See* Pegram, *supra,* at 161-162 (noting arguments that "whatever the effect of the London text, the likelihood that the Lisbon text is not self-executing has been recognized"). Compare the following provisions:

> The carrying out of the reciprocal obligations contained in the present Convention is subject, as far as necessary, to the observance of the formalities and rules established by the constitutional laws of those of the countries of the Union which are bound to procure the application, which they undertake to do with as little delay as possible.

London Text (1934), art. 17

> It is understood that at the time an instrument of ratification or accession is deposited on behalf of a country, such country will be in a position under its domestic law to give effect to the provisions of this Convention.

Lisbon Text (1958), art. 17

> (1) Any country party to this Convention undertakes to adopt, in accordance with its constitution, the measures necessary to ensure the application of this Convention.
>
> (2) It is understood that, at the time a country deposits its instrument of ratification or accession, it will be in a position under its domestic law to give effect to the provisions of this Convention.

Stockholm text (1967), art. 25.

(4) **The Berne Convention and Self-Execution.** Congress has made clear that the principal copyright treaty is not self-executing in the United States. Section 104(c) of the Copyright Act of 1976, as amended by the Berne Convention Implementation Act of 1988, Pub. L. No. 100-568, 102 Stat. 2853 (1988), provides that:

> No right or interest in a work eligible for protection under this title may be claimed by virtue of, or in reliance upon, the provisions of the Berne Convention, or the adherence of the United States thereto. Any rights in a work eligible for protection under this title that derive from this title, other Federal or State statutes, or the common law, shall not be expanded or reduced by virtue of, or in

reliance upon, the provisions of the Berne Convention, or the adherence of the United States thereto.

The declarations of Congress in Section 2 of the Berne Implementation Act similarly expressly prohibit any direct incorporation of the Berne Convention standards into U.S. copyright law:

> The Congress makes the following declarations:
>
> (1) The Convention for the Protection of Literary and Artistic Works, Signed at Berne, Switzerland, on September 9, 1886, and all acts, protocols, and revisions thereto (hereafter referred to as the "Berne Convention") are not self-executing under the Constitution and laws of the United States.
>
> (2) The obligations of the United States under the Berne Convention may be performed only pursuant to appropriate domestic law.
>
> (3) The amendments made by this Act, together with the law as it exists on the date of the enactment of this Act, satisfy the obligations of the United States in adhering to the Berne Convention and no further rights or interests shall be recognized or created for that purpose.

No similar provision has been enacted into either the Lanham Act of 1946 or the Patent Act of 1952. Why is Congress apparently more sensitive about self-execution of the Berne copyright convention than of the Paris industrial property convention?

§ 3.06   National Treatment and Unconditional Most-Favored Nation [MFN] Treatment

Bilateral intellectual property agreements were generally based on the principle of *reciprocity*. In essence, each country would agree to protect intellectual property from the other country under its own legal system, but only to the same extent that the other country extended protection to the first country's intellectual property. But by the late nineteenth century, it became clear that reciprocity had certain negative aspects: it was burdensome to apply, since it required determining the contents of the other country's laws; it discriminated against foreign right holders relative to national right holders; and the scope of protection for the same type of intellectual property could be quite different within the same country, depending on which country was its source.

In contrast, the general approach of the leading multilateral treaties concluded at the end of the nineteenth century was to replace the principle of reciprocity of protection with that of *national treatment*: member countries were required to give nationals of other member countries the same protection that they give their own nationals. National treatment has been the cornerstone of both the Paris Convention (Article 2) and the Berne Convention (Article 5), for over a century. It is also found in the intellectual property provisions of recent trade agreements: Article 1703 of the NAFTA and Article 3 of TRIPS require the states party to those agreements to observe the principle of national treatment. National treatment thus substitutes a rule of non-discrimination for the principle of reciprocity. To accept the principle of national treatment is implicitly to accept the proposition that states may differ in their substantive laws, but that international cooperation between states on important matters is itself valuable consideration, over and above any special benefits that may accrue in exchange for reciprocal benefits from that state. * In order to avoid substantial discrepancies in levels of protection in different countries, these national treatment-based treaties typically also require certain minimum rights to be granted to nationals of other member countries.

International trade agreements embody two concepts that can be grouped under the general heading of a principle of non-discrimination: national treatment, as discussed above, and *most favored nation* ("MFN") treatment. MFN requires that, if a state that is a party to the trade system grants benefits or bounties to other states, then such benefits will be accorded all states within the multilateral system. Unconditional MFN treatment is the cornerstone of the modern multilateral trading system which began with the establishment of the GATT in 1948. Article I of the GATT requires member states to accord "any advantage, favour, privilege, or immunity [granted to the products of one state] immediately and unconditionally" to all other contracting parties.

In the early development of the world trading system prior to 1986, intellectual property rights were not directly included in GATT's unconditional MFN obligations. GATT Article XX(d) states:

> Subject to the requirement that such measures are not applied in a manner which would constitute a means of arbitrary or unjustifiable discrimination between countries where the same conditions prevail, or a disguised restriction on international trade, nothing in this Agreement shall be construed to prevent the adoption or enforcement by any contracting party of measures:
>
> . . . .
>
> (d) necessary to secure compliance with laws or regulations which are not inconsistent with the provisions of this Agreement, including those relating to . . . the protection of patents, trade marks and copyrights, and the prevention of deceptive practices.

The MFN principles of GATT were, however, incorporated into the international intellectual property system in the TRIPS Agreement in 1994. *See* TRIPS Agreement art. 4.

---

* Some states (and international agreements) go even further. The European Patent Convention, for example, goes beyond national treatment and provides access to all applicants without consideration of nationality, residence, membership in a treaty system, or other status.

J.H. REICHMAN, UNIVERSAL MINIMUM STANDARDS OF INTELLECTUAL PROPERTY PROTECTION UNDER THE TRIPS COMPONENT OF THE WTO AGREEMENT [*]
29 INT. LAW. 345, 347-51 (1995)

Perhaps the most important "basic principle" that applies virtually across the board is that of national treatment of (that is, nondiscrimination against) foreign rights holders.[15] This principle of equal treatment under the domestic laws is then carried over to relations between states in the most-favored-nation (MFN) provisions of article 4. The latter article ostensibly prevents one member country from offering a better intellectual property deal than is required by international law[17] to nationals of a second member country and then denying similar advantages to the nationals of other member countries.

Taken together, the national treatment and MFN provisions attempt to rectify the damage that some states recently inflicted on the international intellectual property system by unilaterally asserting claims of material reciprocity with respect to hybrid legal regimes falling in the penumbra between the Paris and Berne Conventions. In practice, however, certain express limitations could diminish the effectiveness of these basic requirements. For example, while the national treatment and MFN clauses both apply "with regard to the protection of intellectual property," it turns out that, for purposes of the TRIPS Agreement, the term "intellectual property" refers only to seven of the eight subject-matter categories enumerated in sections 1 through 7 of Part II. These include (1) copyrights and related rights; (2) trademarks and (3) geographical indications; (4) industrial designs; (5) patents; (6) integrated circuit designs; and (7) trade secrets or confidential information. As regards neighboring rights covered by the International Convention for the Protection of Performers, Producers of Phonograms and Broadcasting Organizations (Rome Convention), national treatment and the MFN clause apply only to those rights that the TRIPS Agreement selectively provides, but not to rights generally flowing from that Convention.

The precise mesh of these provisions remains to be seen, but the following overall framework seems plausible. First, international intellectual property treaties existing at the time that the TRIPS Agreement takes effect are generally immunized from the MFN clause (but not the national treatment clause except as expressly provided) under a grandfather provision within the TRIPS Agreement, which only this Agreement can

---

[*] Copyright 1995, American Bar Association; J.H. Reichman. Reprinted with permission.

[15] *See* TRIPS, art. 3(1) . . . However, the requirement of national treatment is expressly subject to exceptions already provided in the Paris and Berne Conventions, and to exceptions recognized in both the [Rome Convention and in the IPIC Treaty]. *See* TRIPS Agreement, arts. 1(3) n.1, 3(1).

[17] *Cf. id.* art. 1(1) (allowing member states to "implement in their [domestic] law more extensive protection than is required by this Agreement").

override.[24] Second, existing and future agreements establishing "customs unions and free-trade areas" of a regional character may, to varying degrees, be immunized from applying MFN treatment, and possibly national treatment, to some non-TRIPS-mandated intellectual property measures affecting intra-regional adherents, at least insofar as past practice under article XXIV of the [GATT] is carried over to the WTO Agreement and applied to intellectual property rights. Third, states otherwise contemplating unilateral measures to protect intellectual property rights in the future must generally weigh the costs and benefits of nonreciprocity with respect to other WTO member countries, unless the measures contemplated fall outside the seven categories of "intellectual property" recognized by the TRIPS Agreement[27] and outside the residual national treatment clauses of the Paris and Berne Conventions.[28]

Whether any specific measures that were arguably not cognizable under existing conventions, such as the European Union's . . . regime to protect electronic data bases or certain levies for private copying of audio and visual recordings like those implemented in France, may escape the MFN and national treatment clauses of the TRIPS Agreement will thus depend on a variety of factors. These include evolving state practice with respect to regional trade agreements and the extent to which decision makers interpret "intellectual property" as narrowly defining the seven categories of subject matter to be protected or as broadly defining certain modalities of protection. It may also depend on who interprets these clauses, given the uncertain jurisdictional and substantive powers of the WTO panels to be established under binding dispute-resolution procedures set out in the TRIPS Agreement. In any event, the drafters seem to have built in some incentives for states contemplating new protectionist measures to seek to address their needs within the framework of ongoing multilateral discussions affecting barriers to trade in general.

Beyond these equal-treatment obligations, states must accord to the nationals of other member states those international minimum standards of intellectual property protection that are comprised within "the treatment provided for in this [TRIPS] Agreement." One component of this "TRIPS treatment" consists of the basic substantive provisions of the Paris Convention . . . , of the Berne Convention . . . , and of the Treaty on Intellectual

---

[24] See TRIPS Agreement, art. 4(d) (with the proviso that immunized measures "not constitute an arbitrary or unjustifiable discrimination against nationals of other members"); see also id. art. 4(b) (exempting inconsistent provisions of Berne Convention and Rome Convention).

[27] On this reading, the TRIPS Agreement would appear to override unilateral claims to material reciprocity like those incorporated into the United Kingdom's unregistered design right of 1988 . . . and into the United States' Semiconductor Chip Protection Act of 1984 . . . This follows because industrial designs and integrated circuit designs fall within the operative definition of intellectual property. In practice, the need for reciprocity under the SCPA was obviated by TRIPS Agreement arts. 35–38, which harmonize the protection of integrated circuit designs.

[28] See TRIPS Agreement, arts. 2(1) and 9(1), respectively incorporating by reference Paris Convention, art. 2(1), and Berne Convention, art. 5(1).

Property in Respect of Integrated Circuits (IPIC Treaty). The other component consists of minimum standards that the TRIPS Agreement applies irrespective of preexisting international norms and sometimes at the expense of those norms.[37] In either case, the relevant standards "are integral parts of this WTO Agreement, binding on all members."[38]

The Appellate Body of the WTO Dispute Settlement Body recently published a report containing its first analysis of the national treatment and most-favored-nation provisions of the TRIPS Agreement. The report in question concerned a provision of U.S. law (Section 211 of the Omnibus Appropriations Act of 1998) which, ironically, is not found in any of the U.S. intellectual property statutes. But the provision did affect the trademark rights that could be asserted and enforced in the United States, as was illustrated graphically by the decision of the Court of Appeals for the Second Circuit in *Havana Club Holding, S.A. v. Galleon S.A.*, 203 F.3d 116 (2d Cir. 2000). In *Havana Club Holding*, the Second Circuit refused to grant relief to a party claiming to own the mark HAVANA CLUB for rum because in 1960 that mark and the business in connection with which it was then used had been expropriated by the Cuban government without compensation to its owners (and, under Section 211, that fact made the trademark claim difficult to sustain).

The European Union's complaint before the WTO Dispute Settlement Body challenged the TRIPS-consistency of Section 211 and did *not* address the decision of the Second Circuit in the *Havana Club Holding* litigation. But the presence of the domestic private litigation in the background means that the WTO Appellate Body report is sometimes referred to as the *Havana Club* opinion rather than the *Section 211* opinion.

The European Union challenged Section 211 under several different provisions of TRIPS. The report's analysis of Section 211 under trademark- and trade name-specific provisions of TRIPS (and the Paris Convention, incorporated in TRIPS) is excerpted in our companion casebooks, *International Intellectual Property Law and Policy* and *International and Comparative Trademark and Unfair Competition Law*. The excerpt below addresses the generally-applicable national treatment and most favored nation provisions, and the scope of the TRIPS Agreement. In Chapter 5, we excerpt yet other parts of the report analyzing Section 211 under Article 42 of the TRIPS Agreement (relating to enforcement of rights).

[37] *See, e.g.*, TRIPS Agreement, arts. 1(3) (TRIPS treatment), 9(1) (mandating compliance with substantive provisions of Berne Convention, except for art. 6*bis* concerning moral rights).

[38] WTO Agreement, art. II(2) (distinguishing "Multilateral Trade Agreements," including TRIPS, that are binding on all members from "Plurilateral Trade Agreements," *see id.* art. II(3), which create obligations only for members that have accepted them).

UNITED STATES—SECTION 211 OMNIBUS APPROPRIATIONS ACT OF 1998
Report of the Appellate Body, WT/DS176/AB/R (WTO 2002)

I. Introduction

The European Communities and the United States appeal from certain issues of law and legal interpretations in the Panel Report, *United States— Section 211 Omnibus Appropriations Act of 1998* (the "Panel Report"). The Panel was established on 26 September 2000 to consider a complaint by the European Communities with respect to Section 211 of the United States Omnibus Appropriations Act of 1998 ("Section 211"). The European Communities alleged that Section 211 is inconsistent with certain obligations of the United States under the Agreement on Trade-Related Aspects of Intellectual Property Rights (the "TRIPS Agreement"), as read with the relevant provisions of the Paris Convention for the Protection of Industrial Property, as amended by the Stockholm Act of 1967 (the "Paris Convention (1967)"), which are incorporated by reference into the TRIPS Agreement.

. . .

The complaint by the European Communities relates to Section 211, which was signed into law on 21 October 1998. Section 211 states as follows:

(a) (1) Notwithstanding any other provision of law, no transaction or payment shall be authorized or approved pursuant to section 515.527 of title 31, Code of Federal Regulations, as in effect on September 9, 1998, with respect to a mark, trade name, or commercial name that is the same as or substantially similar to a mark, trade name, or commercial name that was used in connection with a business or assets that were confiscated unless the original owner of the mark, trade name, or commercial name, or the bona fide successor-in-interest has expressly consented.

[a] (2) No U.S. court shall recognize, enforce or otherwise validate any assertion of rights by a designated national based on common law rights or registration obtained under such section 515.527 of such a confiscated mark, trade name, or commercial name.

(b) No U.S. court shall recognize, enforce or otherwise validate any assertion of treaty rights by a designated national or its successor-in-interest under sections 44 (b) or (e) of the Trademark Act of 1946 (15 U.S.C. 1126 (b) or (e)) for a mark, trade name, or commercial name that is the same as or substantially similar to a mark, trade name, or commercial name that was used in connection with a business or assets that were confiscated unless the original owner of such mark, trade name, or commercial name, or the bona fide successor-in-interest has expressly consented.

(c) The Secretary of the Treasury shall promulgate such rules and regulations as are necessary to carry out the provisions of this section.

(d) In this section:

(1) The term "designated national" has the meaning given such term in section 515.305 of title 31, Code of Federal Regulations, as in effect on September 9, 1998, and includes a national of any foreign country who is a successor-in-interest to a designated national.

(2) The term "confiscated" has the meaning given such term in section 515.336 of title 31, Code of Federal Regulations, as in effect on September 9, 1998.

Section 211 applies to a defined category of trademarks, trade names and commercial names, specifically to those trademarks, trade names and commercial names that are "the same as or substantially similar to a mark, trade name, or commercial name that was used in connection with a business or assets that were confiscated" by the Cuban Government on or after 1 January 1959. Section 211(d) states that the term "designated national" as used in Section 211 has the meaning given to that term in Section 515.305 of Title 31, Code of Federal Regulations ("CFR"), and that it includes "a national of any foreign country who is a successor-in-interest to a designated national." The term "confiscated" is defined as having the meaning given that term in Section 515.336 of Title 31 CFR. Part 515 of Title 31 CFR sets out the Cuban Assets Control Regulations (the "CACR"), which were enacted on 8 July 1963 under the Trading with the Enemy Act of 1917. Under these regulations, "designated national" is defined as Cuba, a national of Cuba or a specially designated national. "Confiscated" is defined as nationalized or expropriated by the Cuban Government on or after 1 January 1959 without payment of adequate and effective compensation.

Section 211(a)(1) relates to licensing regulations contained in the CACR. The CACR are administered by the Office of Foreign Assets Control ("OFAC"), an agency of the United States Department of the Treasury. Under United States law, all transactions involving property under United States jurisdiction, in which a Cuban national has an interest, require a licence from OFAC. [31 C.F.R. § 515.201]. OFAC has the authority to grant either of two categories of licences, namely general licences and specific licences. A general licence is a general authorization for certain types of transactions set out in OFAC regulations. Such a licence is, in effect, a standing authorization for the types of transactions that are specified in the CACR. A specific licence, by contrast, is one whose precise terms are not set out in the regulations, so that a person wishing to engage in a transaction for which a general licence is not available must apply to OFAC for a specific licence.

Section 211 refers to Section 515.527 of Title 31 CFR. Prior to the entry into force of Section 211, a general licence was available under Section 515.527 for the registration and renewal of trademarks previously owned by Cuban nationals irrespective of whether such trademarks had been confiscated by the Cuban Government. . . . .

On 10 May 1999, some six months after the entry into force of Section 211, the CACR were amended by adding a new subparagraph (a)(2) to § 515.527, which effectively prohibits registration and renewal of trademarks and trade names used in connection with a business or assets that were confiscated without the consent of the original owner or *bona fide* successor-in-interest.

. . .

The effect of Section 211, as read with the relevant provisions of the CACR, is to make inapplicable to a defined category of trademarks and trade names certain aspects of trademark and trade name protection that are otherwise guaranteed in the trademark and trade name law of the United States. In the United States, trademark and trade name protection is effected through the common law as well as through statutes. The common law provides for trademark and trade name creation through use. The Trademark Act of 1946 (the "Lanham Act") stipulates substantive and procedural rights in trademarks as well as trade names and governs unfair competition.

[In the Panel Report circulated on August 6, 2001, the Panel ruled that trade names are not a category of intellectual property covered by the TRIPS Agreement, and accordingly limited its review to an examination of Section 211 as it relates to trademarks. The Panel rejected the European Communities' challenge on all grounds except that it found that Section 211(a)(2) was inconsistent with Article 42 of TRIPS, and thus it recommended that the Dispute Settlement Body (DSB) request the United States to bring its measures into conformity with its obligations under the TRIPS Agreement. Both the European Communities and the United States filed an appeal.]

. . . .

IX. Article 2(1) of the Paris Convention (1967) and Article 3.1 of the TRIPS Agreement

We turn now to the issue of national treatment. In this appeal we have been asked to address, for the first time, this fundamental principle of the world trading system as it relates to intellectual property. There are two separate national treatment provisions that cover trademarks as well as other intellectual property rights covered by the TRIPS Agreement. The European Communities claims, on appeal, that Sections 211(a)(2) and (b) violate both.

One national treatment provision at issue in this appeal is Article 2(1) of the Paris Convention (1967), which states:

> Nationals of any country of the Union shall, as regards the protection of industrial property, enjoy in all the other countries of the Union the advantages that their respective laws now grant, or may

hereafter grant, to nationals; all without prejudice to the rights specially provided for by this Convention. Consequently, they shall have the same protection as the latter, and the same legal remedy against any infringement of their rights, provided that the conditions and formalities imposed upon nationals are complied with.

[T]he Stockholm Act of the Paris Convention, dated 14 July 1967, is but the most recent version of that important international intellectual property convention. Article 2(1) was part of the Paris Convention in 1883. Since that time, it has remained a treaty obligation of all the countries that have been party to the Paris Convention.

The parties to this dispute are not unacquainted with the national treatment obligation and other protections for trademarks and other forms of industrial property provided by the Paris Convention. Every one of the fifteen Member States of the European Union has long been a country of the Paris Union. Most of the current Member States of the European Union became party to the Paris Convention in the 1880's. The most recent did so in 1925—seventy-seven years ago.

Likewise, the United States has, from almost the very beginning, been a country of the Paris Union. The United States became a country of the Paris Union on 30 May 1887—one hundred and fifteen years ago.

Thus, the national treatment obligation is a longstanding obligation under international law for all the countries directly involved in this dispute, as well as for many more countries of the Paris Union that, like the parties to this dispute, are also Members of the WTO. If there were no TRIPS Agreement, if there were no WTO, the parties to this dispute would be bound, nevertheless, under Article 2(1) of the Paris Convention (1967), to accord national treatment to other countries of the Paris Union.

[W]hat *is* new is that, as a consequence of the Uruguay Round, Article 2(1) of the Paris Convention (1967) was made part of the WTO Agreement. And . . . by virtue of Article 2.1 of the TRIPS Agreement, Article 2(1) of the Paris Convention (1967), as well as certain other specified provisions of the Paris Convention (1967), have been incorporated into the TRIPS Agreement and, thus, the WTO Agreement. Consequently, these obligations of countries of the Paris Union under the Paris Convention (1967) are also now obligations of all WTO Members, whether they are countries of the Paris Union or not, under the WTO Agreement, and, thus, are enforceable under the [Dispute Settlement Understanding (DSU)].

In addition to Article 2(1) of the Paris Convention (1967), there is also another national treatment provision in the TRIPS Agreement. The other national treatment provision at issue in this appeal is Article 3.1 of the TRIPS Agreement, which states in relevant part:

Each Member shall accord to the nationals of other Members treatment no less favourable than that it accords to its own nationals with regard to the protection [footnote 3] of intellectual property, subject to the exceptions already provided in, respectively, the Paris

Convention (1967), the Berne Convention (1971), the Rome Convention or the Treaty on Intellectual Property in Respect of Integrated Circuits.

Footnote 3: For the purposes of Articles 3 and 4, "protection" shall include matters affecting the availability, acquisition, scope, maintenance and enforcement of intellectual property rights as well as those matters affecting the use of intellectual property rights specifically addressed in this Agreement.

Thus, in drafting the TRIPS Agreement, the framers of the WTO Agreement saw fit to include an additional provision on national treatment. Clearly, this emphasizes the fundamental significance of the obligation of national treatment to their purposes in the TRIPS Agreement.

Indeed, the significance of the national treatment obligation can hardly be overstated. Not only has the national treatment obligation long been a cornerstone of the Paris Convention and other international intellectual property conventions.[168] So, too, has the national treatment obligation long been a cornerstone of the world trading system that is served by the WTO.

As we see it, the national treatment obligation is a fundamental principle underlying the TRIPS Agreement, just as it has been in what is now the GATT 1994. The Panel was correct in concluding that, as the language of Article 3.1 of the TRIPS Agreement, in particular, is similar to that of Article III:4 of the GATT 1994, the jurisprudence on Article III:4 of the GATT 1994 may be useful in interpreting the national treatment obligation in the TRIPS Agreement.

. . . .

The European Communities claims that Sections 211(a)(2) and (b) violate the national treatment obligation in both Article 2(1) of the Paris Convention (1967) and Article 3.1 of the TRIPS Agreement by treating non-United States nationals less favourably than United States nationals in two different situations to which the measure applies: first, that of successors-in-interest or bona fide successors-in-interest to original owners; and, second, that of original owners. The European Communities contends that this discrimination occurs in different ways in these two different situations, but, in each situation, they see a violation of the fundamental obligation of national treatment.

We examine first the European Communities' claims relating to the alleged discrimination among successors-in-interest under Sections 211(a)(2) and (b).

Before the Panel, the European Communities argued that Section 211(a)(2) applies only to Cuban nationals and to other foreign (that is,

---

[168] For example, see Article 2 of the International Convention for the Protection of Performers, Producers of Phonograms and Broadcasting Organizations ("Rome Convention (1961)"), adopted at Rome on 26 October 1961; and also Article 5 of the Treaty on Intellectual Property in Respect of Integrated Circuits ("IPIC Treaty"), adopted at Washington on 26 May 1989.

non-United States) successors-in-interest. The European Communities argued that this violates the national treatment obligation in Article 2(1) of the Paris Convention (1967) and Article 3.1 of the TRIPS Agreement because it imposes restrictions on Cubans and other foreign nationals that it does not impose on United States nationals.

In response to the claim by the European Communities that Section 211(a)(2) violates the national treatment obligation of the United States with respect to successors-in-interest, the Panel reasoned as follows:

> Section 211(a)(2) provides that no US courts are to recognize, enforce or validate any rights by a "designated national" based on registration of trademarks obtained through a licence from OFAC. We note that the term "designated national" is defined in Section 211(d)(1) to include (1) Cuba, (2) any Cuban national, (3) "a specially designated national" or (4) "a national of any foreign country who is a successor-in-interest to a designated national." We consider that the term "designated national" must be read as a whole and cannot be segregated into two tiers. We note that "designated national" is defined to include "[a] national of *any foreign country* who is a successor-in-interest to a designated national" and does not include US nationals. *Thus, it is plausible that while a foreign national who is a successor-in-interest to a designated national may not have its rights to the underlying mark recognized, enforced or validated, a US national who is a successor-in-interest to a designated national can have US courts recognize, enforce or validate rights in respect of the underlying mark that was registered pursuant to a specific licence granted by OFAC. Such differential treatment in respect of intellectual property right protection could be considered to provide a less favourable treatment to nationals of other Members as it denies effective equality of opportunities to non-US nationals in the United States.*[170] (emphasis added)

Thus, with respect to successors-in-interest, the Panel stated that Section 211(a)(2), in and of itself, "could be considered" to provide less favourable treatment to non-United States nationals than to United States nationals. Yet, the Panel refrained from making, at that stage, findings with respect to Article 2(1) of the Paris Convention (1967) and Article 3.1 of the TRIPS Agreement. Instead, the Panel went on to examine the argument of the United States that any more favourable treatment that might arise under Section 211(a)(2) for United States nationals was offset[171] by OFAC's practice under Section 515.201 of the CACR of not issuing specific licences to United States nationals to become successors-in-interest to "designated nationals". As the Panel summarized it, the United States argued that:

---

[170] . . . Like the Panel, we note that Section 211(d)(1) broadened the definition of "designated national" to include, in addition to Cuba and any Cuban national, nationals of any foreign country (that is, non-United States nationals) who are successors-in-interest to a designated national . . .

[171] For purposes of this appeal, we use the term "offset" to describe a situation in which an action counterbalances, counteracts or neutralizes the effect of a contrary action.

Section 211(a)(2) is not inconsistent with Article 3.1 on the basis that US nationals, although not specifically set out in the measure, cannot become successors-in-interest to designated nationals because Section 515.201 of 31 CFR prohibits US nationals from becoming successors-in-interest without obtaining a specific licence from OFAC. The United States submitted that OFAC has never issued a specific licence to a US national for the purpose of becoming a successor-in-interest to trademarks that were used in connection with confiscated assets. The United States asserted that a law is only WTO-inconsistent on its face if it mandates WTO-inconsistent actions and that if the law allows the national authority to act in [sic] manner consistent with the WTO Agreement, panels should not assume that a Member will use its discretion in a manner contrary to its international obligations.

Thus, before the Panel, the United States argued that Section 211(a)(2) does not apply to United States nationals because, under the CACR, United States nationals are prohibited from owning or having an interest in property that was confiscated by the Cuban Government and, therefore, cannot become successors-in-interest. . . . OFAC has the discretion administratively to authorize specific licences with respect to certain transactions that would enable United States nationals to deal with such property. . . . [But, based on the report of the panel in United States Measures Affecting the Importation, Internal Sale and Use of Tobacco ("US—Tobacco") (1994) and on the Report of the Appellate Body in United States—Anti-Dumping Act of 1916 ("US—1916 Act") (Appellate Body 2000)], the Panel concluded that, where discretionary authority is vested in the executive branch of a WTO Member, it cannot be assumed that that Member will exercise that authority in violation of its obligations under any of the covered agreements.

The Panel found, as a matter of fact, that OFAC has never granted a specific licence to allow any United States national to become a successor-in-interest to a "designated national". Further, the Panel found that the European Communities had not demonstrated that, in exercising its discretionary authority, OFAC had acted in a manner that was inconsistent with the national treatment obligation in Article 2(1) of the Paris Convention (1967) and Article 3.1 of the TRIPS Agreement.

In view of this, the Panel concluded that:

Because US nationals are unable to obtain licences so as to become a successor-in-interest and OFAC has not granted any such licence for such purpose and in light of our conclusion that Section 211(a)(2) does not accord a treatment less favourable to foreign original owners than it accords to original owners who are US nationals, we find that Section 211(a)(2) is not inconsistent with Article 3.1 of the TRIPS Agreement and Article 2.1 of the TRIPS Agreement in conjunction with Article 2(1) of the Paris Convention (1967).

The European Communities appeals these findings [and] argues that the offsetting effect of this admittedly longstanding OFAC practice does not cure the discrimination in Section 211(a)(2) with respect to successors-in-interest who are *not* United States nationals.

According to the European Communities, the discriminatory treatment in favour of successors-in-interest who are United States nationals and against successors-in-interest who are *not* United States nationals continues to exist because of what the European Communities sees as an "extra hurdle" that non-United States nationals face procedurally under United States law.

That "extra hurdle" is this. United States nationals who are successors-in-interest must go successfully only through the OFAC procedure. In the circumstances addressed by Section 211, they are not subject to the constraints imposed by Section 211(a)(2). In contrast, non-United States successors-in-interest not only must go successfully through the OFAC procedure, but also find themselves *additionally* exposed to the "extra hurdle" of an additional proceeding under Section 211(a)(2). In sum, United States nationals face only one proceeding, while non-United States nationals face *two*. It is on this basis that the European Communities claims on appeal that Section 211(a)(2), as it relates to successors-in-interest, violates the national treatment obligation in the TRIPS Agreement and the Paris Convention (1967).

At the oral hearing in this appeal, the United States reiterated that it is very unlikely that a United States national would ever be licensed to become a successor-in-interest to a "designated national"; therefore, the United States argues that it does not matter "what happens to such a successor-in-interest when he gets to the enforcement level". In any event, the United States continues, if a United States national were ever granted a specific licence, the United States courts would apply the "longstanding principle against the recognition of foreign confiscations."

[The Appellate Body agreed with the Panel that the differential treatment of non-U.S. nationals could be considered less favorable treatment, and then turned to the Panel's analysis of possible offsets.] As the Panel rightly noted, in *US—1916 Act*, we stated that a distinction should be made between legislation that mandates WTO-inconsistent behaviour, and legislation that gives rise to executive authority that can be exercised with discretion. We quoted with approval there the following statement of the panel in *US—Tobacco*:

> . . . panels had consistently ruled that legislation which mandated action inconsistent with the General Agreement could be challenged as such, whereas legislation which merely gave the discretion to the *executive authority* of a contracting party to act inconsistently with the General Agreement could not be challenged as such; only the actual application of such legislation inconsistent with the General Agreement could be subject to challenge.

Thus, where discretionary authority is vested in the executive branch of a WTO Member, it cannot be assumed that the WTO Member will fail to implement its obligations under the WTO Agreement in good faith. Relying on these rulings, and interpreting them correctly, the Panel concluded that it could not assume that OFAC would exercise its discretionary executive authority inconsistently with the obligations of the United States under the WTO Agreement. Here, too, we agree.

But here, the Panel stopped. We are of the view that, having reached the conclusion it did with respect to the offsetting effect of OFAC practice, the Panel should not have stopped but should have gone on and considered the argument made by the European Communities about the "extra hurdle" faced by non-United States successors-in-interest. For this reason, we do so now.

We note, as did the Panel, the report of the panel in [*United States— Section 337 of the Tariff Act of 1930*].[188] That panel reasoned that "the mere fact that imported products are subject under Section 337 to legal provisions that are different from those applying to products of national origin is in itself not conclusive in establishing inconsistency with Article III:4."

That panel stated further that:

> [I]t would follow . . . that any unfavourable elements of treatment of imported products could be offset by more favourable elements of treatment, provided that the results, as shown in past cases, have not been less favourable. *[E]lements of less and more favourable treatment could thus only be offset against each other to the extent that they always would arise in the same cases and necessarily would have an offsetting influence on the other.* (emphasis added)

And that panel, importantly for our purposes, concluded that:

> . . . while the likelihood of having to defend imported products in two fora is small, the existence of the possibility is inherently less favourable than being faced with having to conduct a defence in only one of those fora.

We agree with this approach and consider it to be particularly relevant to this appeal. It is not disputed that Section 515.201 of the CACR imposes a limitation—a "hurdle"—on both successors-in-interest who are United States nationals and successors-in-interest who are not. It is also not disputed that Section 211(a)(2) applies only to successors-in-interest who are *not* United States nationals. It is likewise not disputed that, under Section 211(a)(2), in *every individual situation* where a non-United States successor-in-interest seeks to assert its rights without the express consent of the original owner or its bona fide successor-in-interest, the United States

---

188 Panel Report, US—Section 337, [Panel Report Adopted 7 November 1989, BISD 36S/345]. Central to that dispute was a situation where the proceedings that were applicable to imported products alleged to infringe United States patents were different in a number of respects from those applicable before a federal district court when a product of foreign origin was challenged on the grounds of patent infringement.

courts are required not to recognize, enforce or otherwise validate any assertion of rights. We emphasize that this situation exists under the statute *on its face*, and that, therefore, unlike the situation with respect to the granting of a special licence to United States successors-in-interest by OFAC, this situation assumes no action by OFAC or by any other agency of the United States Government.

The United States may be right that the likelihood of having to overcome the hurdles of both Section 515.201 of Title 31 CFR and Section 211(a)(2) may, echoing the panel in *US—Section 337*, be *small*. But, again echoing that panel, even the *possibility* that non-United States successors-in-interest face two hurdles is *inherently less favourable* than the undisputed fact that United States successors-in-interest face only one.

Both before the Panel and before us, the United States has submitted that Section 211 is a statutory articulation of the longstanding doctrine of non-recognition of foreign confiscation that is recognized in "virtually every jurisdiction". Thus, the United States argues that, in the unlikely event that a United States national did somehow succeed in getting a specific licence from OFAC, this longstanding doctrine would be applied by United States courts to prevent such a national from enforcing its rights as a successor-in-interest. The United States argues, therefore, that the prohibition imposed by Section 211(a)(2) with respect to non-United States successors-in-interest would also be applied to United States successors-in-interest. We are not persuaded by this argument.

The United States has not shown, as required under the national treatment obligation, that, in every individual case, the courts of the United States would not validate the assertion of rights by a United States successor-in-interest. Moreover, even if there is, as the United States argues, a *likelihood* that United States courts would not enforce rights asserted by a United States successor-in-interest, the fact remains, nevertheless, that non-United States successors-in-interest are placed by the measure, on its face, in an inherently less favourable situation than that faced by United States successors-in-interest. And, even if we were to accept the United States argument about the doctrine of non-recognition of foreign confiscation, presumably that doctrine would apply to those who are not nationals of the United States as well as to those who are. Any application of this doctrine would therefore not offset the discrimination in Section 211(a)(2), because it would constitute yet another, separate obstacle faced by nationals and non-nationals alike. Hence, it would not offset the effect of Section 211(a)(2), which applies only to successors-in-interest who are not United States nationals.

Accordingly, we conclude that Section 211(a)(2) imposes an additional obstacle on successors-in-interest who are not nationals of the United States that is not faced by United States successors-in-interest. And, therefore, we conclude that, by applying the "extra hurdle" imposed by Section 211(a)(2) only to non-United States successors-in-interest, the United States violates the national treatment obligation in Article 2(1) of the Paris Convention (1967) and Article 3.1 of the TRIPS Agreement.

For this reason, we reverse the Panel's conclusion . . . that "[b]ecause US nationals are unable to obtain licences so as to become a successor-in-interest and OFAC has not granted any such licence for such purpose . . . Section 211(a)(2) is not inconsistent with Article 3.1 of the TRIPS Agreement and Article 2.1 of the TRIPS Agreement in conjunction with Article 2(1) of the Paris Convention (1967)."

The European Communities also raised claims at the level of successors-in-interest against Section 211(b). With respect to these claims, the Panel concluded that:

> Section 211(b) states that US courts shall not recognize, enforce or validate any assertion of treaty rights by a "designated national or *its successor-in-interest*". The difference between Section 211(a)(2) and Section 211(b) is that the latter contains the additional term "its successor-in-interest" whereas the former just refers to "a designated national". Moreover, the term "its successor-in-interest" as set out in Section 211(b) is not limited to foreign nationals which means that it includes US nationals. This would mean that any transfer of trademarks used in connection with confiscated assets to any national, including US nationals, would be subject to Section 211(b). For these reasons, Section 211(b) does not accord a treatment less favourable to nationals of other Members than it accords to US nationals. (emphasis in original)

We agree with the Panel that Section 211(b) applies to successors-in-interest of *any origin*, including United States nationals and that, consequently, Section 211(b) does not accord less favourable treatment to non-United States nationals than to United States nationals.

Therefore, we uphold the Panel's conclusion . . . that—at the level of successors-in-interest—Section 211(b) is not inconsistent with Article 2.1 of the TRIPS Agreement in conjunction with Article 2(1) of the Paris Convention (1967) and Article 3.1 of the TRIPS Agreement.

We turn now to the European Communities' claims relating to Sections 211(a)(2) and (b) with respect to the other form of discrimination alleged by the European Communities—that of discrimination among *original* owners.

[On this, the Panel had found that neither Section (a)(2) nor (b) accorded a treatment less favourable to foreign original owners than it accords to original owners who are US nationals.]

On appeal, the European Communities argues that the Panel erred in its conclusion about discrimination among original owners. The European Communities maintains that, on their face, both Sections 211(a)(2) and 211(b) violate the national treatment obligation under the TRIPS Agreement and the Paris Convention (1967) because they provide less favourable treatment to Cuban nationals who are original owners than to United States nationals who are original owners. The European Communities supports this position by relying on a particular set of circumstances that exists under the statute that, according to the European Communities, illustrates how Sections 211(a)(2) and (b), on their face, discriminate in favour of United States nationals who are original owners and against Cuban nationals who are original owners. The European Communities believes this situation demonstrates the discriminatory treatment implicit in Sections 211(a)(2) and (b).

Specifically, the European Communities asks us to consider the following particular set of circumstances that exists under the statute. There are two separate owners who acquired rights, either at common law or based on registration, in two separate United States trademarks, before the Cuban confiscation occurred. Each of these two United States trademarks is the same, or substantially similar to, the signs or combination of signs of which a trademark registered in Cuba is composed. That same or similar Cuban trademark was used in connection with a business or assets that were confiscated in Cuba. Neither of the two original owners of the two United States trademarks was the owner of that same or similar trademark that was registered in Cuba. Those two original owners each seek to assert rights in the United States in their two respective United States trademarks. The situation of these two original owners of these two United States trademarks is identical in every relevant respect, but one. That one difference is this: one original owner is a national of Cuba, and the other original owner is a national of the United States.

The European Communities asks us to consider this specific situation involving these two original owners, one from Cuba and one from the United States. The European Communities argues that, on the face of the statute, in this situation, the original owner who is a Cuban national is subject to Sections 211(a)(2) and (b), and the original owner who is a United States national is not. This alone, as the European Communities sees it, is sufficient for us to find that Sections 211(a)(2) and (b) violate the national treatment obligation of the United States.

Like the European Communities, we see this situation as critical to our determination of whether the treatment of original owners under Section 211 is consistent with the national treatment obligation of the United States under Article 2(1) of the Paris Convention (1967) and Article 3.1 of the TRIPS Agreement.

The situation highlighted by the European Communities on appeal exists because Sections 211(a)(2) and (b) apply to "designated nationals". A "designated national" is defined in Section 515.305 of Title 31 CFR as "Cuba and any national thereof including any person who is a specially designated national."[200] Thus, Sections 211(a)(2) and (b) apply to original owners that are Cuban nationals. Original owners that are United States nationals are

[200] The definition also includes successors-in-interest, but the situation discussed here does not involve successors-in-interest. Nor does it involve "specially designated nationals", given that there is no claim that a person is acting for or on behalf of the Cuban government. The term "specially designated national" is defined in Section 515.306 of 31 CFR. . .

not covered by the definition of "designated national" and, thus, are not subject to the limitations of Sections 211(a)(2) and (b).

Thus, in our view, the European Communities is correct on this issue. Sections 211(a)(2) and (b) are discriminatory *on their face*.

We conclude, therefore, that the European Communities has established a prima facie case that Sections 211(a)(2) and (b) discriminate between Cuban nationals and United States nationals, both of whom are original owners of trademarks registered in the United States which are composed of the same or substantially similar signs as a Cuban trademark used in connection with a business or assets that were confiscated in Cuba.

The United States attempts to rebut this argument by the European Communities by maintaining that Sections 211(a)(2) and (b) are not applicable to original owners, regardless of their nationality, because original owners are always in a position to consent expressly to their own assertion of rights under Sections 211(a)(2) and (b). Section 211(a)(2), when read together with Section 211(a)(1), and Section 211(b) do indeed provide an exception for designated nationals who have the express consent of "the original owner of the mark, trade name, or commercial name, or the bona fide successor-in-interest". However, the United States erroneously assumes in its argument on this issue that the Cuban original owner of the United States trademark is necessarily the same person as the original owner of the same or substantially similar Cuban trademark used in connection with a business or assets that were confiscated. This is by no means necessarily the case, as is demonstrated in the specific situation posed by the European Communities. In that situation, the Cuban national who holds the trademark rights in the United States would be unable to use its own consent to avoid the court's denial of any assertion of rights under Sections 211(a)(2) and (b) because it was not the original owner of the same or similar Cuban trademark.

The United States also argues in rebuttal that Section 211(a)(2) does not apply to Cuban nationals in the situation posed by the European Communities because Section 515.527 of the CACR was not in effect when the original owners in this situation obtained their trademark rights in the United States. We note that Section 211(a)(2) refers to the assertion of rights "based on common law rights or registration obtained under such section 515.527". Thus, it is clear from the text of Section 211(a)(2) that the reference to Section 515.527 relates to rights based on registration, and not to common law rights. Indeed, the United States conceded as much in response to our questions at the oral hearing. Thus, this argument may address the discrimination against Cuban nationals who are original owners of trademark rights in the United States *based on registration*. But it does not address the discrimination against Cuban nationals who are original owners of trademark rights in the United States *based on common law*.

For trademark rights based on registration, it is true that, in the situation posed by the European Communities, Section 515.527 of the CACR would not have been in effect when the Cuban original owner obtained its trademark rights in the United States, namely before the Cuban confiscation. However, we recall that Section 515.527 of the CACR applies not only to the registration, but also to the *renewal* of registered trademarks.[204] Although the Cuban national's initial registration, carried out before the Cuban confiscation, would not have been obtained pursuant to Section 515.527, a renewal of such registration would come within the purview of that provision. Hence, Section 211(a)(2) could apply to a Cuban national who registered a United States trademark before confiscation *and renewed it after that date.*

For trademark rights based on common law, the United States contends that the Cuban original owner could not have maintained its rights in the United States trademark because it would not have been able to import the trademarked goods from Cuba and, thus, would not have been able to continue using the trademark "in commerce". Yet, this argument assumes that the Cuban national who owns the trademark in the United States could have imported the trademarked goods *only from Cuba.* We understand that from the European Communities' responses to questioning at the oral hearing, the Cuban holder of common law trademark rights in the United States could import the trademarked goods from a country other than Cuba. The United States did not deny this at the oral hearing. We are, therefore, not persuaded by this argument.

On this point, the United States replied as well that the Cuban original owner could be "unblocked" under the OFAC regulations, an argument that the United States did not make before the Panel or in its written submissions in this appeal. The relevant regulation is Section 515.505 of the CACR, which lists those persons that are "licensed as unblocked nationals" or who may apply to be "unblocked".[207] According to the United States, as an

---

[204] Section 515.527(a)(1) of 31 CFR provides:

Transactions related to the registration and *renewal* in the United States Patent and Trademark Office or the United States Copyright Office of patents, trademarks, and copyrights in which the Government of Cuba or a Cuban national has an interest are authorized. (emphasis added)

[207] Section 515.505 of 31 CFR provides:

(a) The following persons are hereby licensed as unblocked nationals.

(1) Any person resident in, or organized under the laws of a jurisdiction in, the United States or the authorized trade territory who or which has never been a designated national;

(2) Any individual resident in the United States who is not a specially designated national; and

(3) Any corporation, partnership or association that would be a designated national solely because of the interest therein of an individual licensed in paragraph (a) or (b) of this section as an unblocked national.

(b) Individual nationals of a designated country who have taken up residence in the authorized trade territory may apply to the Office of Foreign Assets Control to be specifically licensed as unblocked nationals.

(c) The licensing of any person as an unblocked national shall not suspend the requirements of any section of this chapter relating to the maintenance or production of records.

"unblocked national,"[208] such a Cuban original owner would have the same status as a United States national. Yet, to fulfill the national treatment obligation, less favourable treatment must be offset, and thereby eliminated, in *every* individual situation that exists under a measure. Therefore, for this argument by the United States to succeed, it must hold true for *all* Cuban original owners of United States trademarks, and not merely for *some* of them.

Accordingly, we examine three possible situations to determine whether the discrimination is eliminated in every individual instance that might arise under Section 515.505. The first example involves a Cuban original owner residing in the United States. The second involves a Cuban original owner residing in a country other than the United States or Cuba. The third involves a Cuban original owner residing in Cuba.

According to the United States, a Cuban original owner residing in the United States is, in fact, "unblocked" by Section 515.505(a)(2) of the CACR. We agree with this reading of Section 515.505(a)(2). This eliminates the less favourable treatment of this Cuban original owner. The other examples, however, yield a different result.

A Cuban original owner residing in a country other than the United States or Cuba, for example, in the European Communities, could apply to OFAC to be "specifically licensed as [an] unblocked national[]." This is pursuant to Section 515.505(b) of the CACR, because the United States does not impose sanctions on the European Communities and, therefore, the European Communities would be considered part of the "authorized trade territory" described in Section 515.322 of the CACR.[212] This could eliminate less favourable treatment *in practice*. Yet, the very existence of the additional "hurdle" that is imposed by requiring application to OFAC is, in itself, inherently less favourable. Sections 211(a)(2) and (b) do not apply to United States original owners; no application to OFAC is required. But Cuban original owners residing in the "authorized trade territory" must apply to OFAC. Thus, such Cuban original owners must comply with an administrative requirement that does not apply to United States original owners.[213]

---

[208] An "unblocked national" is defined in Section 515.307 of 31 CFR as:

> Any person licensed pursuant to § 515.505 licensed as an unblocked national shall, while so licensed, be regarded as a person within the United States who is not a national of any designated foreign country: Provided, however, That the licensing of any person as an unblocked national shall not be deemed to suspend in any way the requirements of any section of this chapter relating to reports, or the production of books, documents, and records specified therein.

[212] Section 515.322 of 31 CFR provides:

> § 515.322 Authorized trade territory; member of the authorized trade territory.
>
> (a) The term authorized trade territory includes all countries, including any colony, territory, possession, or protectorate, except those countries subject to sanctions pursuant to this chapter. The term does not include the United States.
>
> (b) The term member of the authorized trade territory shall mean any of the foreign countries or political subdivisions comprising the authorized trade territory.

[213] See Panel Report, US—Section 337, supra, footnote [188], paras. 5.11–5.14.

By virtue alone of having to apply to OFAC, even Cuban original owners that reside in the "authorized trade territory" described in Section 515.332 are treated less favourably than United States original owners. So, in this second situation, the discrimination remains.

A Cuban original owner residing in Cuba is discriminated against as well. Cuba is not part of the "authorized trade territory" because it is subject to sanctions administered by OFAC under the CACR. From our reading of the regulations, it seems to us that a Cuban national who resides in Cuba could not, under any circumstances, be "unblocked" under Sections 515.505(a) or (b) of Title 31 CFR. Nor has the United States suggested otherwise. Thus, in this third situation, the discrimination remains as well.

[The Appellate Body also rejected the United States' argument that Section 515.201 of the CACR offsets any discrimination implicit in Sections 211(a)(2) and (b). Section 515.201 of the CACR sets out a list of transactions with property in which a designated country has an interest that are prohibited, except as specifically authorized by the Secretary of the Treasury, and the United States argued (unsuccessfully) that these included dealings by U.S. nationals with trademarks covered by Section 211. Looking at the language of Section 515.201, the Appellate Body concluded that it would not *in every case* offset the discriminatory treatment imposed by Sections 211(a)(2) and (b).]

Thus, we conclude that Sections 211(a)(2) and (b) are inconsistent with the national treatment obligation of the United States under the Paris Convention (1967) and the TRIPS Agreement at the level of original owners. And, therefore, we reverse the Panel's findings . . .

X. Article 4 of the TRIPS Agreement

Like the national treatment obligation, the obligation to provide most-favoured-nation treatment has long been one of the cornerstones of the world trading system. For more than fifty years, the obligation to provide most-favoured-nation treatment in Article I of the GATT 1994 has been both central and essential to assuring the success of a global rules-based system for trade in goods. Unlike the national treatment principle, there is no provision in the Paris Convention (1967) that establishes a most-favoured-nation obligation with respect to rights in trademarks or other industrial property. However, the framers of the TRIPS Agreement decided to extend the most-favoured-nation obligation to the protection of intellectual property rights covered by that Agreement. As a cornerstone of the world trading system, the most-favoured-nation obligation must be accorded the same significance with respect to intellectual property rights under the TRIPS Agreement that it has long been accorded with respect to trade in goods under the GATT. It is, in a word, fundamental.

Article 4 of the TRIPS Agreement provides, in relevant part:

> With regard to the protection of intellectual property, any advantage, favour, privilege or immunity granted by a Member to the

nationals of any other country shall be accorded immediately and unconditionally to the nationals of all other Members.

. . . .

The European Communities claimed before the Panel that Sections 211(a)(2) and (b) are inconsistent with Article 4 of the TRIPS Agreement.

[The Panel had found that neither Section 211(a)(2) nor Section 211(b) denied Cuban nationals any advantage, favour, privilege or immunity that it accords to other foreign nationals, and thus neither section was inconsistent with Article 4 of the TRIPS Agreement. The European Communities appealed both of these findings of the Panel].

Before proceeding with our analysis, we find it necessary to address the scope of our examination of this issue. In the light of the claim raised by the European Communities, the Panel limited its examination and findings to the particular situation of Cuban confiscations.[220] Neither the European Communities nor the United States has disputed this point on appeal. Therefore, we also restrict our analysis to that particular situation.

We note also that, with respect to the most-favoured-nation obligation, the European Communities has not presented arguments on appeal addressing the Panel's findings with respect to the level of successors-in-interest. Thus, we do not consider this to be before us on appeal, and, therefore, we will limit our discussion to the Panel's findings with respect to the alleged discrimination involving *original* owners.

The allegations submitted by the European Communities on most-favoured-nation treatment of original owners are similar to those described in the previous section on national treatment. As it did with respect to national treatment, the European Communities supports its claim under Article 4 of the TRIPS Agreement by focusing on a particular set of circumstances that exists under the statute, on its face, involving original owners.

Like the situation posed by the European Communities earlier, the one set forth in the most-favoured-nation treatment involves two separate owners who acquired rights, either at common law or based on registration, in two separate United States trademarks, before the Cuban confiscation

---

[220] In para. 8.143, the Panel explained the parties' position on this issue as follows:

In response to the question as to whether Article 4 of the TRIPS Agreement allows a Member to have a certain policy applicable to confiscations of trademarks in one Member on the condition that all WTO Member nationals are treated similarly or whether Article 4 requires that a similar policy be applied to confiscations of trademarks in all other Members, the European Communities states that the most-favoured-nation treatment flowing from Article 4 attaches to persons and not to situations. The European Communities argues, therefore, that Article 4 requires that all nationals of other Members be treated similarly in respect of a certain event. In response to the same question, the United States submitted that because the European Communities is alleging a violation of the most-favoured-nation principle based on the first situation described by the Panel, there is no need to examine the question of whether Article 4 applies to the second situation.

occurred. Each of these two United States trademarks is the same, or substantially similar to, signs or a combination of signs of which a trademark registered in Cuba is composed. That same or similar Cuban trademark was used in connection with a business or assets that were confiscated in Cuba. Neither of the two original owners of the two United States trademarks was the owner of that same or similar trademark that was registered in Cuba. Those two original owners each now seek to assert rights in the United States in their two respective United States trademarks. The situation of these two original owners of these two United States trademarks is identical in every relevant respect, but one. That one difference is this: one original owner is a national of Cuba, and the other original owner is a national of a country other than Cuba or the United States. We will refer, for the sake of convenience, to this other original owner as "a non-Cuban foreign national".

Pointing to this particular situation, the European Communities argues that, on the face of the statute, the original owner who is a Cuban national is subject to Sections 211(a)(2) and (b), and the original owner who is a non-Cuban foreign national is not. This alone, as the European Communities sees it, is sufficient for us to find that Sections 211(a)(2) and (b) violate the most-favoured-nation obligation of the United States.

We agree with the European Communities that the situation it describes on appeal is within the scope of the statute *on its face*. As we explained earlier, the term "designated national" as defined in Section 515.305 of 31 CFR and Section 211(d)(1) includes non-Cuban foreign nationals only when they are successors-in-interest to Cuba or a Cuban national.[222] Non-Cuban foreign nationals who are original owners are not covered by the definition of "designated national" and are thereby not subject to Sections 211(a)(2) and (b).

Therefore, here too, as with national treatment, the European Communities has established a prima facie case that Sections 211(a)(2) and (b) are discriminatory on their face, as between a Cuban national and a non-Cuban foreign national both of whom are original owners of United States trademarks composed of the same or substantially similar signs as a trademark used in connection with a business or assets that were confiscated in Cuba.

As it did in respect of the national treatment claim, the United States attempts to rebut the European Communities' most-favoured-nation claim with arguments intended to demonstrate that Sections 211(a)(2) and (b) do not apply to a Cuban national who is an original owner of a United States trademark. The United States arguments on this claim are the same as their arguments on national treatment. We have already addressed these arguments. And, as these United States arguments have not changed, our conclusions have not changed either. . . .

. . . .

---

[222] The situation discussed here does not involve successors-in-interest.

We, therefore, reverse the Panel's findings . . . to the extent that they concern the treatment of original owners, and find, in this respect, that Section 211(a)(2) and Section 211(b) are inconsistent with Article 4 of the TRIPS Agreement.

XI. Article 8 of the Paris Convention (1967)—Trade Names

We turn, lastly, to the issue of whether trade names are covered by the TRIPS Agreement.

Article 8 of the Paris Convention (1967) provides:

> A trade name shall be protected in all the countries of the Union without the obligation of filing or registration, whether or not it forms part of a trademark.

There is no question that trade names are covered by the Paris Convention (1967). The question before us is whether trade names are also covered by the TRIPS Agreement. On this, the Panel found:

> *[W]e conclude that the categories of intellectual property covered by the TRIPS Agreement are those referred to in Article 1.2.* Article 8 of the Paris Convention (1967) is relevant as part of the TRIPS Agreement to the extent that it may affect the protection of the categories of intellectual property covered by the Agreement. As *trade names are not a category of intellectual property covered by the TRIPS Agreement*, Members do not have obligations under the TRIPS Agreement to provide protection to trade names. (emphasis added)

As a consequence of this conclusion, the Panel limited its finding on the inconsistency of Section 211(a)(2) with Article 42 of the TRIPS Agreement to trademarks. Also as a consequence of this conclusion, the Panel found that Sections 211(a)(2) and (b) are not inconsistent with Article 2.1 of the TRIPS Agreement in conjunction with Article 8 of the Paris Convention (1967). However, we do not find a similarly clear limitation in the Panel's findings with respect to Articles 3.1 and 4 of the TRIPS Agreement.

The European Communities asks us to reverse the Panel's finding that trade names are not covered in the TRIPS Agreement. . . .

The United States agrees with the European Communities that the Panel erred in finding that the TRIPS Agreement contains no obligations with respect to trade names.

On this issue, we begin with a review of the Panel's analysis of whether trade names are covered by the TRIPS Agreement. The Panel looked first to Article 1.2 of the TRIPS Agreement, which provides:

> For the purposes of this Agreement, the term "intellectual property" refers to all categories of intellectual property that are the subject of Sections 1 through 7 of Part II.

The Panel reasoned that:

> Sections 1 through 7 of Part II of the TRIPS Agreement deal with
> *the following categories of intellectual property*: copyright and
> related rights; trademarks; geographical indications; industrial
> designs; patents; layout-designs (topographies) of integrated circuits;
> and protection of undisclosed information. The categories of related
> rights covered by Article 14 are protection of performers, producers
> of phonograms and broadcasting organizations. (emphasis added).

The Panel assumed that "[c]ategories of protectable subject matters not
dealt within Sections 1 to 7 of Part II of the TRIPS Agreement are not
included in the definition of 'intellectual property' in Article 1.2" and
observed that "Sections 1 to 7 of Part II do not contain any reference to
trade names". The Panel referred to the interpretive principles found in
Article 31 of the Vienna Convention, and drew the following conclusion:

> We interpret the terms "intellectual property" and "intellectual
> property rights" with reference to the definition of "intellectual
> property" in Article 1.2 of the TRIPS Agreement. The textual
> reading of Article 1.2 is that it establishes an inclusive definition
> and this is confirmed by the words "all categories"; the word "all"
> indicates that this is an exhaustive list.

Having thus determined provisionally that trade names are not covered
in the TRIPS Agreement, the Panel then addressed the meaning to be given
to Article 2.1 of the TRIPS Agreement, which provides as follows:

> In respect of Parts II, III and IV of this Agreement, Members shall
> comply with Articles 1 through 12, and Article 19, of the Paris
> Convention (1967).

As we pointed out earlier, Article 8 of the Paris Convention (1967)
specifically requires trade name protection.

However, the Panel interpreted the words "in respect of" in Article 2.1
as limiting the incorporation of the provisions of the Paris Convention
(1967), including Article 8, to Parts II, III and IV of the TRIPS Agreement.
The Panel reasoned as follows:

> The second subclause of Article 2.1 obliges Members to comply with
> the provisions of the Paris Convention (1967) which are identified
> in that provision. However, the second subclause is conditioned by
> the first subclause: Members shall comply with the obligations "*[i]n
> respect of* Parts II, III and IV of this Agreement". As the ordinary
> meaning of the term "in respect of" is in "relation [to], connection
> [with], reference [to]" and it refers to Parts II, III and IV explicitly,
> we consider that Members have to comply with Articles 1 through
> 12 and 19 of the Paris Convention (1967) "in respect" of what is
> covered by those parts of the TRIPS Agreement identified therein,
> namely copyright and related rights; trademarks; geographical indi-
> cations; industrial designs; patents; layout-designs (topographies)

of integrated circuits; and protection of undisclosed information. (underlining added, footnotes omitted)

Relying on Article 32 of the Vienna Convention, the Panel also reviewed the negotiating history of Articles 1.2 and 2.1 of the TRIPS Agreement and concluded that this history confirmed its interpretation of the scope of the TRIPS Agreement.

We disagree with the Panel's reasoning and with the Panel's conclusion on the scope of the TRIPS Agreement as it relates to trade names.

To explain, we turn first to the Panel's interpretation of Article 1.2 of the TRIPS Agreement. . . .

The Panel interpreted the phrase "'intellectual property' refers to all categories of intellectual property that are the *subject* of Sections 1 through 7 of Part II" (emphasis added) as if that phrase read "intellectual property means those categories of intellectual property appearing in the *titles* of Sections 1 through 7 of Part II." To our mind, the Panel's interpretation ignores the plain words of Article 1.2, for it fails to take into account that the phrase "the subject of Sections 1 through 7 of Part II" deals not only with the categories of intellectual property indicated in each section *title*, but with other *subjects* as well. For example, in Section 5 of Part II, entitled "Patents", Article 27(3)(b) provides that Members have the option of protecting inventions of plant varieties by sui generis rights (such as breeder's rights) instead of through patents. Under the Panel's theory, such sui generis rights would not be covered by the TRIPS Agreement. The option provided by Article 27(3)(b) would be read out of the TRIPS Agreement.

Moreover, we do not believe that the Panel's interpretation of Article 1.2 can be reconciled with the plain words of Article 2.1. Article 2.1 explicitly incorporates Article 8 of the Paris Convention (1967) into the TRIPS Agreement.

The Panel was of the view that the words "in respect of" in Article 2.1 have the effect of "conditioning" Members' obligations under the Articles of the Paris Convention (1967) incorporated into the TRIPS Agreement, with the result that trade names are not covered. We disagree.

Article 8 of the Paris Convention (1967) covers only the protection of trade names; Article 8 has no other subject. If the intention of the negotiators had been to exclude trade names from protection, there would have been no purpose whatsoever in including Article 8 in the list of Paris Convention (1967) provisions that were specifically incorporated into the TRIPS Agreement. To adopt the Panel's approach would be to deprive Article 8 of the Paris Convention (1967), as incorporated into the TRIPS Agreement by virtue of Article 2.1 of that Agreement, of any and all meaning and effect. As we have stated previously:

> One of the corollaries of the "general rule of interpretation" in the Vienna Convention is that interpretation must give meaning and effect to all the terms of a treaty. An interpreter is not free to adopt

a reading that would result in reducing whole clauses or paragraphs of a treaty to redundancy or inutility.[244]

. . . .

Thus, in our view, the Panel's interpretation of Articles 1.2 and 2.1 of the TRIPS Agreement is contrary to the ordinary meaning of the terms of those provisions and is, therefore, not in accordance with the customary rules of interpretation prescribed in Article 31 of the Vienna Convention.[247] Moreover, we do not believe that the negotiating history confirms, within the meaning of Article 32 of the Vienna Convention, the Panel's interpretation of Articles 1.2 and 2.1.

For all these reasons, we reverse the Panel's finding . . . that trade names are not covered under the TRIPS Agreement and find that WTO Members do have an obligation under the TRIPS Agreement to provide protection to trade names.

. . . .

Findings and conclusions

. . . .

The Appellate Body *recommends* that the DSB request the United States to bring its measure, found in this Report and in the Panel Report as modified by this Report to be inconsistent with the TRIPS Agreement, into conformity with its obligations under that Agreement.

. . . .

––––––––––

NOTES AND QUESTIONS

(1) **Reciprocity.** As Professor Reichman notes, in the few years before the conclusion of the TRIPS Agreement, several nations had enacted new rights that they claimed were not subject to the national treatment obligations of the Paris and Berne Conventions because the rights were of a kind not covered by those conventions. Instead, these countries, such as the United States with respect to semi-conductor chip protection, the United Kingdom as regards unregistered design protection, and the EU with respect to *sui generis* database protection, conditioned the protection of foreign authors, creators or designers on reciprocal protection being afforded their authors in the country from which the foreign national came. Why was there a flurry of reciprocity-based rights in the years preceding the conclusion of TRIPS? Are there advantages to conditioning new forms of intellectual property protection on reciprocal protection?

––

[244] Appellate Body Report, US—Gasoline, (1996) [cit]. . .
[247] *See* Article 3.2 of the DSU.

(2) *Section 211*: **National Treatment**. What are the doctrinal devices by which the Appellate Body assesses whether Section 211 is in compliance with Article 3 of TRIPS? National treatment might, in some respects, be described as an equal protection clause of international intellectual property law. *See* Graeme B. Dinwoodie, *The Development and Incorporation of International Norms in the Formation of Copyright Law*, 62 OHIO ST. L.J. 733, 738 (2001). To what standard of equality of treatment is the Appellate Body in *Section 211* holding U.S. law? Formal equality? Substantive equality? Which is the most appropriate standard of equality by which to judge national compliance with international law? Would a U.S. law discriminating against its own (U.S.) nationals in the acquisition and enforcement of intellectual property rights violate Article 3 of TRIPS?

(3) *Section 211*: **MFN**. Part of the methodology employed by the Appellate Body in *Section 211* (at the request of the European Union) was to evaluate how the provisions in question might differently impact two hypothetical trademark owners. Compare the hypothetical considered by the Appellate Body in its national treatment discussion and that considered during its MFN discussion. How are they different? Why are they different? To what extent, consistent with its MFN obligations under Article 4 of TRIPS, may the United States apply disabling provisions like Section 211 to trademarks confiscated by the Cuban government without doing so with respect to trademarks confiscated by other WTO countries in similar circumstances?

(4) **MFN in Intellectual Property Law.** What does the incorporation of MFN obligations, which previously had no place in intellectual property treaties, do to the dynamic of international intellectual property relations? What objectives are MFN obligations intended to achieve with respect to intellectual property law?

(5) **Remedial Amendment of U.S. Law?** As we will discuss more fully in Chapter 5, *infra*, the United States is now obliged to amend its law to comply with TRIPS or face sanctions or penalties for its failure to do so. What amendments to Section 211 or the related regulations (other than blanket repeal) would bring U.S. law into compliance with Articles 3–4 of TRIPS?

(6) **The Scope of TRIPS (I): The Meaning of "Intellectual Property."** Determining the scope of the MFN and national treatment provisions of the TRIPS Agreement involves interpretation of the term "intellectual property" as defined in Article 1(2) of TRIPS. How broad an interpretation of the term "intellectual property" has the Appellate Body offered in *Section 211*? Has the Appellate Body read the term "as broadly defining certain modalities of protection," to use Professor Reichman's phrase? Might the analysis suggested by Professor Koumantos, *supra* § 1.02, be of assistance in giving meaning to the term "intellectual property"? If the term was interpreted consistent with the notion discussed by Professor Koumantos, would the EU be able to condition the *sui generis* database rights offered under its 1996 Database Directive on reciprocity? In its 1993 Term Directive, the EU conditioned the extended term of copyright protection (life of

the author plus seventy years) for non-EU authors on reciprocity, citing the so-called rule of the shorter term in Article 7(8) of the Berne Convention. Why could it do this even after TRIPS?

(7) **The Scope of TRIPS (II): Incorporation of the Paris Convention in TRIPS**. What is the significance of the phrase "in respect of Parts II, III, and IV of this Agreement," in Article 2(1) of the TRIPS Agreement? *Cf.* TRIPS Agreement art. 9(1) (requiring member countries to comply with certain provisions of the Berne Convention).

(8) **The Role of the Broader GATT Agreement and General International Economic Law.** The incorporation in the TRIPS Agreement of minimum standards for the protection of intellectual property was based in part upon the assertion that inadequate protection of intellectual property in some GATT member states had trade-distorting effects and there was a need for a level playing field. Some scholars have argued that provisions such as Article XX(d) of the GATT provide a broader context for TRIPS and, rejecting the notion of "fair trade" as a new standard of international economic law, have suggested that "national welfare" (particularly in developing countries) continues to be a ground for legitimate discrimination which states may invoke in interpreting specific WTO agreements, such as TRIPS. *See* Edward A. Laing, *Equal Access/Non-discrimination and Legitimate Discrimination in International Economic Law*, 14 Wis. Int'l L.J. 246 (1996).

MURRAY v. BRITISH BROADCASTING CORP.
81 F.3d 287 (2d Cir. 1996)

Winter, Circuit Judge:

Dominic Murray, a British national, appeals from Judge Stanton's dismissal of his complaint based on the doctrine of *forum non conveniens*. The action was brought against the British Broadcasting Corporation ("the BBC"), a corporation organized under the laws of the United Kingdom, and BBC Lionheart Television International ("Lionheart"), a Delaware corporation and wholly-owned subsidiary of the BBC. It asserted claims based on copyright infringement under both United States and English law, false designation of origin, and unfair competition. Murray's principal arguments on appeal are that *forum non conveniens* was misapplied either because the district court should have granted greater deference to his choice of forum or because a contingent fee arrangement is not available in the United Kingdom for this kind of litigation. Alternatively, Murray contends that the district court abused its discretion in weighing the various factors applicable under *forum non conveniens* doctrine. We affirm.

Background

Murray is a self-employed designer and manufacturer of costumes and props in London, England. In July 1992, the BBC engaged Murray to produce a disguise costume for Noel Edmonds, the host of a BBC television program styled "Noel's House Party." The costume, named Mr. Blobby, was to be worn by Edmonds in order to surprise celebrity guests on the program. The British public began identifying Mr. Blobby as a character rather than a costume. As a consequence, the Mr. Blobby costume, now worn by an actor instead of Mr. Edmonds, has become an unexpected success and has been put to a wider use. In 1993, the BBC began authorizing and licensing products bearing the likeness of Mr. Blobby in the United Kingdom. According to Murray, he consulted with English counsel at that time concerning an action for infringement of his copyright in the Mr. Blobby costume. He allegedly declined to pursue his claim because he could neither pay the 100,000 to 200,000 pounds necessary to bring his case to trial nor post the security necessary to obtain a loan for that amount. In June 1994, the defendants brought Mr. Blobby to New York for his American debut at the International Licensing and Merchandising Conference and Exposition and began actively marketing Mr. Blobby in the United States. Shortly thereafter, Murray obtained American counsel under a contingent fee arrangement. This action ensued. Although it appears that no Mr. Blobby products have yet been produced for the American market, Murray has also filed suit against several alleged licensees, which is still pending in the Southern District. As noted, Judge Stanton dismissed the action against the BBC and Lionheart on the ground of *forum non conveniens,* [cit], and Murray brought this appeal.

DISCUSSION

1. Deference to Murray's Choice of Forum

The doctrine of *forum non conveniens* permits a court to "resist imposition upon its jurisdiction even when jurisdiction is authorized by the letter of a general venue statute," [cit], if dismissal would "best serve the convenience of the parties and the ends of justice." [cit]. There is ordinarily a strong presumption in favor of the plaintiff's choice of forum. [cit]. Where a foreign plaintiff is concerned, however, its choice of forum is entitled to less deference. [cit]. The Supreme Court has emphasized that this rule is not based on a desire to disadvantage foreign plaintiffs but rather on a realistic prediction concerning the ultimate convenience of the forum . . .

Murray quarrels with neither the rule concerning foreign plaintiffs nor the reason underlying it. Instead, he argues that his choice of an American forum must, as a matter of law, be accorded the deference given domestic plaintiffs because of the Berne Convention for the Protection of Literary and Artistic Works, to which both the United States and the United Kingdom are signatories. This is a matter of law that we review *de novo.*

The Convention provides in pertinent part that "the extent of protection, *as well as the means of redress afforded to the author to protect his rights,* shall be governed exclusively by the laws of the country where protection is claimed." Berne Convention for the Protection of Literary and Artistic

Works, Paris Text, July 24, 1971, Art. 5(2), . . . Under the Berne Convention, Murray argues, he is deemed to be in the shoes of an American plaintiff and entitled to greater deference in his choice of forum than the district court believed. The principle set out in Article 5, paragraph 2 of the Berne Convention is one of "national treatment," [cit], a choice-of-law rule mandating that the applicable law be the copyright law of the country in which the infringement occurred, not that of the country of which the author is a citizen or in which the work was first published. [cit]. Murray argues, in essence, that the principle of national treatment contained in the Berne Convention mandates procedural opportunities identical to those accorded American plaintiffs alleging copyright infringement. We disagree.

Murray relies on Irish Nat'l Ins. Co. v. Aer Lingus Teoranta, 739 F.2d 90 (2d Cir. 1984), in which we held that the Treaty of Friendship, Commerce and Navigation between the United States and Ireland required the application of the same *forum non conveniens* standards to the Irish plaintiff as a court would have applied to a United States citizen. *Id.* at 91-92. However, we do not agree that *Aer Lingus* applies in the instant matter. The Treaty of Friendship, Commerce and Navigation between the United States and Ireland provided for "national treatment with respect to . . . having access to the courts of justice." *Id.* at 91 (internal quotation marks and citation omitted). In contrast, the national treatment provision of the Berne Convention contains no such language. We are confident that the inclusion of the quoted language in the Treaty with Ireland was not superfluous, and its omission in the Berne Convention was no oversight. When drafters of international agreements seek to provide equal access to national courts, the long-established practice is to do so explicitly. The United States first concluded a treaty with such a provision in 1775, [cit], and explicit "access to courts" clauses appear regularly in treaties to which the United States is a signatory. Indeed, over a dozen treaties have included such language since 1990.

History and practice thus teach that a principle of equal access must be explicitly adopted. In the absence of such an explicit provision in the Berne Convention, we cannot construe a simple declaration of "national treatment" to imply such a principle and to extend *Aer Lingus* and cases following it to this case. [cit].

. . . .

2. Existence of an Alternative Forum

When addressing a motion to dismiss for *forum non conveniens*, a court must determine whether an alternative forum is available, because application of the doctrine "presupposes at least two forums in which the defendant is amenable to process." [cit]. The requirement of an alternative forum is ordinarily satisfied if the defendant is amenable to process in another jurisdiction, except in "rare circumstances" when "the remedy offered by the other forum is clearly unsatisfactory." The BBC can obviously be sued in the United Kingdom. Murray argues, however, that he is financially unable to litigate this dispute in England because a contingent-fee arrangement is not permitted in this kind of case. In his view, this professed inability to bring suit renders the English forum unavailable as a matter of law. We review this legal issue *de novo* but disagree with Murray.

[The Court recognized a division of authority on whether financial hardships facing a plaintiff in an alternative forum as a result of the absence of contingent fee arrangements may cause a forum to be deemed unavailable, but followed the majority rule that treated this as one factor to be considered in the balancing of interests performed *after* the determination of whether an alternative forum is available.]

3. The Balancing of Interests

. . . .

Murray argues that two public interest factors weigh strongly in favor of permitting his American action to go forward. First, he argues that American copyright law will apply to his copyright infringement claims arising in the United States, militating in favor of an American forum. Murray argues second that the district court erroneously failed to acknowledge that the United States has localized interests in this controversy: the "obvious interest in securing compliance with this nation's laws by citizens of foreign nations who have dealings within this jurisdiction," London Film Productions Ltd. v. Intercontinental Communications, Inc. 580 F. Supp. 47, 49 (S.D.N.Y. 1984), and an interest in whether Mr. Blobby merchandise will be available for sale in the United States. Once again, we disagree.

We are, quite frankly, at a loss to see how this lawsuit has any but the most attenuated American connection. The central issue in dispute concerns the circumstances surrounding the creation of Mr. Blobby. Once that dispute is resolved, the right to exploit the character will be quickly resolved. The crux of the matter, therefore, involves a dispute between British citizens over events that took place exclusively in the United Kingdom. Moreover, it appears that much of the dispute over the creation of Mr. Blobby implicates contract law. British law governs those issues. The United States thus has virtually no interest in resolving the truly disputed issues.

The Berne Convention's national treatment principle insures that no matter where Murray brings his claim, United States copyright law would apply to exploitation of the character in this country. We therefore see little chance that the United States' interest in the application of its laws would be ill-served by a lawsuit in an English forum. Murray makes a great deal of the need to bring additional litigation in the United States to enforce his copyright if this matter is dismissed in favor of an English forum. However, he has offered no reason why his action against the American licensees of Mr. Blobby, currently pending in the Southern District of New York, may not be placed on the suspense calendar pending a resolution of the truly disputed issues in the English courts. Again, once those issues are resolved, everything else will fall into place.

Finally, we note that the forum in which actual infringement of Murray's putative copyright has occurred is not the United States but England. It appears that no Mr. Blobby products have yet been produced for the American market. In virtually all respects, the connection of this case to the United States is as tenuous as its connection to the United Kingdom is strong. We therefore hold that the district court did not abuse its discretion in finding that the public interest factors militated in favor of dismissal.

[The Court also concluded that the district court had properly balanced the private interest factors, and that the financial difficulties Murray may encounter in litigating in England are not sufficiently severe to tip the private interest inquiry in Murray's favor.] We note first that the unavailability of contingent fee arrangements in England is of little weight in the present matter. The availability of such arrangements in the United States is based on a policy decision regarding the assertion of rights in American courts where the parties or the claims have some tangible connection with this country. The decision to permit contingent fee arrangements was not designed to suck foreign parties disputing foreign claims over foreign events into American courts. There is, therefore, no American policy regarding contingent fees that weighs in favor of resolving the underlying dispute over the rights to Mr. Blobby in an American court.

. . . .

We affirm.

———————

NOTES AND QUESTIONS

(1) **National Treatment and Territoriality.** The principle of national treatment is in many respects a corollary of the principle of territoriality: the legality of conduct occurring in the United States will be determined by U.S. law, and the legality of conduct occurring in the United Kingdom will be determined by U.K. law. National treatment simply mandates that U.K. authors bringing a copyright action in the United States will be entitled to the same treatment as would a U.S. author, and that a U.S. author suing for copyright infringement in the United Kingdom will receive the same protection as would a British author.

(2) **National Treatment in Procedural Enforcement Rights.** Did Mr. Murray receive national treatment? Why should the ability to enforce a copyright not be an essential part of the national treatment principle?

Chapter 4

International Treaties and Agreements

§ 4.01   Beginnings of International Patent Cooperation

ERICH KAUFER, THE ECONOMICS OF THE
PATENT SYSTEM 8–10 (1989) *

. . . .

In the German-speaking parts of Europe, monopoly privileges had a varied history. Empress Maria Theresa of Austria was unsympathetic, refusing to grant privileges because she found them *"hoechst schaedlich"* (highly detrimental). Her adversary, Frederick of Prussia, adopted a more receptive policy, granting numerous monopoly privileges for the introduction of new arts. Yet in Austria as in Prussia, monopoly privileges had been established in many trades as the nineteenth century dawned. There, as in the western European lands, they were widely disliked as misuses of royal prerogative.

This association between patents and monopoly privileges gave birth to an energetic anti-patent movement. The seeds were sown by the Napoleonic reordering of the German territories. Some territories in the Rhine area adopted the French patent law of 1791. The territories of southern Germany gave up the practice of privileged grants. But soon "polytechnical associations" were founded, lobbying for the introduction of patent laws and, especially in Bavaria and Wuerttemberg, for tariff protection. By 1825, both kingdoms had laws granting patents on inventions that were new to the kingdom.

Tension rose as Prussia began to dominate policy among the German territories. In 1806, after its defeat by Napoleon, Prussia instituted reforms under which a new kind of civil servant, nourished inter alia on the ideas of Adam Smith, gained power. The Prussian government pushed for free trade among the German territories, and as remnants of mercantilist policy, patents were seen as a barrier to free trade. By 1862, all tariffs had been abolished inside Germany. In that same year, a free trade treaty with France marked the high point of the free trade movement's influence. The Prussian government argued concurrently that all patent laws in the German territories should be abolished

A similarly strong anti-patent movement led to the repeal of the Dutch patent law in 1869. In 1872, the British House of Lords accepted a

---

substantial revision of existing patent law. Between 1849 and 1863, the Swiss parliament rejected four petitions to introduce a patent law.

However, strong counter-forces were also in motion. Prussia was an agrarian state at the beginning of the 19th century. Between 1850 and 1870, the German territories, especially the Prussian ones, were industrializing rapidly. Industrial leaders like the Siemens brothers, one working in Berlin and the other in London, organized pro-patent support groups. Second, world exhibitions emerged, and participation in them became a matter of national prestige. Germany received its first genuine recognition as an industrial nation at the Paris exhibition of 1867. Potential American participants refused to participate in the Vienna exhibition of 1873 unless the German-nations agreed to provide provisional patent protection on the American inventions put on display. Third, the free trade movement in Prussia proved to have shallow roots. Since Austria under the Habsburg monarchy had adopted a strongly protectionist development policy, the creation of a German free trade area was a political tactic used by Prussia for excluding Austria from the German union. Once this goal was achieved, the free trade movement was supported less vigorously. Fourth, at the 1873 Vienna exhibition, a patent congress proposed to introduce into national patent laws strict compulsory licensing principles. To the extent that the proposal was accepted, it undermined the objection that patents were mere mercantilist monopoly privileges. Fifth and finally, the year 1873 marked the onset of a worldwide depression, which in turn precipitated a movement away from free trade and toward protectionism. Tariffs and patents now appeared to be important protectionist instruments.

With these changes, the anti-patent tide ebbed. In 1874, the British government backed off from the drastic patent reform proposal already approved by the House of Lords. In 1877, the German Reich adopted a patent law.

Switzerland played a wavering but pivotal role in the new patent law developments. Patent laws were rejected by popular referenda in Switzerland in 1866 and 1882. Nevertheless, Switzerland participated actively in drafting the Paris Convention, signed in 1883 by Belgium, Brazil, France, Guatemala, Italy, the Netherlands, Portugal, Spain, El Salvador, and Serbia as well as Switzerland. The Convention created mechanisms for worldwide patent grant coordination. Although it had no patent system of its own, Switzerland was charged with administering and supervising the Paris Convention. In accepting this role, the Swiss government agreed to initiate a domestic patent system as soon as possible. Meanwhile, Swiss public opinion was changing, in part because one of the largest Swiss industries, the watch industry, was experiencing intense competition from imitators. In July 1887, a Swiss patent statute was overwhelmingly approved in a referendum. However, because the newly emerging Swiss chemical industry still found it advantageous to imitate the technology of its more advanced German rivals, the Swiss law limited patentability to mechanical inventions only. This prompted the German Reich to threaten Switzerland with retaliatory tariffs. In 1907 Switzerland backed off, extending coverage under its patent law to chemical process inventions (but not product inventions).

———

EMERSON STRINGHAM, PATENTS AND GEBRAUCHMUSTER IN INTERNATIONAL LAW 36 (1934)

A Union of German Engineers 6th meeting in Braunschweig, 1863 urged the adoption of a German patent law. However, there was serious opposition to patents in the trading states of the German Zollverein. The Zollverein Treaty of 1842 made this anti-patent stance explicit. Conformably with Article III of this treaty, the parties pledged themselves not to grant patents under which the inventor would obtain the exclusive right: to import the patented object; to sell; to distribute, or finally to utilize. The patentees were permitted to prohibit only the manufacture of the object in the country concerned or the industrial use of machines, tools, or manufacturing processes. The basic tendency of all these provisions is obvious. A patentee possessed the exclusive right of producing the object in his own country but he was not permitted to break through the domestic customs boundary either directly by prohibiting import, or indirectly by prosecuting those who carried on trade with imported patented goods. . . . [P]atent law reflects the economic polarity of nationalism seeking to exclude foreign competition and internationalism seeking to enter foreign markets.

———

QUESTIONS

Is the right to exclude foreigners from a national market more important than the right of nationals to sell in foreign markets? To what extent are national patents today seen as a barrier to free trade, in league with tariffs? (The question of exhaustion of rights will be discussed *infra* Chapter 7 in connection with parallel importation of patented goods.)

§ 4.02   The Development of International Patent Treaties

The United States first extended patent protection to foreigners in 1800. *See Pennock v. Dialogue*, 27 U.S. 1 (1829). Under the French patent law of 1791 as revised in 1844, the printing of a patent in the United States or another country automatically destroyed novelty in France. So by seeking patent protection in one country, an inventor jeopardized his chances for gaining protection in other countries, such as France, upon publication of the first filing. European states other than Germany established patent laws in the middle years of the nineteenth century as a lure to attract foreign technologies: Spain (1826), Portugal (1837), Austria (1852), Belgium (1854), Italy (1859). Switzerland never had a patent law until 1887. Holland, a trading state, established a patent law by statute in 1817, but abolished it in 1869. Sweden's law of 1859 was limited to nationals. The 1854 Belgian patent act is still in force.

Historical events in the 1870s impelled the industrializing nations of Europe and the United States toward harmonization of patent laws. What emerged from the discussions during that decade became the foundation of the modern international patent system as we know it.

[A] The Making of the Paris Convention: The Congress of Vienna of 1873

In view of the great diversity of existing laws on the subject of patents for inventions, and the changes in the present international commercial relations, it is urgently important that the government seek, at the earliest possible date, to achieve an international accord on the protection of industrial property (patents for invention).

From the voeux of the Washington Conference of 1873.

HEINRICH KRONSTEIN & IRENE TILL, A REEVALUATION OF THE INTERNATIONAL PATENT CONVENTION *
12 Law and Contemporary Problems, 765, 766–76 (1947)

The United States entered the [Paris] Union in 1887; Germany, the last industrial power to join, did so on May 10, 1901. As often happens in the history of treaties the actual decisions were reached before the first country signed. The creative period of the Union was between 1872 and 1881. During this period the negotiations on the international patent convention were the battlefield for three opposing philosophies: (1) the anti-patent movement, aimed at the destruction of the patent system; (2) recognition of patents as private property; (3) the recognition of patents as an instrument of public policy. Certainly the issue of patents versus no-patents had to be disposed of first. The fight on this point marked the first battle between the United States and the newly organized Germany of Bismarck.

The initial invitation for an international conference on patent rights came from the Austrian Government in 1872. The invitation specifically stated, however, that the suggestion came from the United States:

[F]ollowing a suggestion of the Government of the United States of America, the General Direction of the Universal Exposition intends to unite with the Exposition an International Congress, which shall discuss the question of patent right; should this discussion, as may be foreseen, induce a vote in favor of Patent protection,

---

* Copyright 1947 by Law and Contemporary Problems. Reprinted with permission.

it will then be the task of this Congress, on the basis of the experience of various countries and the materials collected, to proceed to a declaration of fundamental principles for an International Reform of Patent Legislation.

American leadership in the conference was eagerly anticipated by the United States Commissioner of Patents. He wrote to the Secretary of the Interior on May 29, 1873:

I regard the patent congress to be held at Vienna of the very greatest importance and the world looks to this government for the presentation of matters for consideration and discussion. If the American system can be properly presented before that Congress, discreetly and cautiously sustained with facts and figures, I feel confident that the best results can be expected.

The very fact of American parentage elevated the prestige of the conference. The proposal for international patent protection did not come from the semi-feudal country of Austria, conspicuously lacking in industrial development; it came from the United States, already at the forefront industrially and with the strongest patent system in the world.

The invitation stated the issue between the patent and the anti-patent forces in forthright manner:

There exists today an antipatent movement which since 1860 has extended too far and the causes of which movement bear, in part at least, too much upon views which are generally acknowledged by the economical progress of our age, to justify at this time as hitherto a partial solution of that problem. The complete abolition of all Patents for inventions, such is the motto of this movement; Patent protection, the maintenance and improvement of the existing Patent law, if possible in simple form, and by international agreement: such is the watchword of the other. The present condition of Patent legislation in the most enlightened and progressive countries shows on which side the majority stands; with the exception of Switzerland and with her, Holland, which recently abolished her Patent law, the legislation of all the other Industrial States today recognizes the protection of Patents as a necessity.

Germany, as the leader of the anti-patent movement, is not mentioned in the invitation, reference being made only to Holland and Switzerland. There is no doubt, however, that it was the larger country which the organizers of the conference really had in mind. As early as 1868 Bismarck, as Chancellor of the North German Federation, had gone on record as hostile to any form of patent protection. On May 10, 1872, the German Parliament discussed, for the first time in the history of the German Reich, the patent problem. There the position of Bismarck was made even clearer. His representative announced that it would not be undesirable "if the Parliament would use the opportunity of the discussion to express itself in favor of the full abolition of patent protection;" in Bismarck's opinion, the example of Holland deserved to be copied. However, it was pointed out to the Parliament that public opinion in Germany might be unprepared for the step:

> [S]ince only people who have a private interest in patent protection can express their views in public . . . The Society of German Engineers has repeatedly and actively come out in favor of patent protection. However, not all engineers share this opinion; only considerations for influential interests prevent them from expressing their opinion in public.

Thus, in the summer of 1872, the issue was joined. The organizers of the conference were fully aware that, in a competitive business economy, the world could not live half with patents and half without patents. The invitation to the conference sets forth the interdependence among national patent systems in the following classical statement:

> We live no longer in the day of Industrial action, which is strictly confined and is removed from foreign competition, and where slow communication prevents or delays the utilization of inventions. We live at a time of liberal Customs policy; Steam and Electricity have newly united once isolated seats of industry in a way undreamt of; and the mutual exchange of goods shows today a magnitude which a generation ago one could not have imagined. Under such altered relations the Patent granted for an invention in one country becomes in fact a restriction unprofitable and obstructive, if the same invention without limitation or increase in price, becomes in an adjoining country common property. The artisan who in the one country must work with the auxiliary material there patented and therefore dearer in price, will suffer an essential injury as soon as the same material is produced in the other country, not only without restriction, but with a damaging competition. Moreover a continuance of the hitherto antagonistic views and measures would scarcely conduce to the preservation of general harmony; and if, for example, Patent protection were maintained in one country, so as to attract thereby skilled operatives from another, then the danger of disturbance of the International industrial balance might readily be apprehended. Such and similar inconveniences can only be met by the common action of all civilized States, disposed to the maintenance of Patent protection.

The American delegation to the Vienna conference was an able one. The Assistant Commissioner of Patents, J. M. Thatcher, headed the group; his experience and knowledge of the United States patent system gave him a leading role in the negotiations. Unlike many American delegations to international conferences, it was also well prepared. M. D. Leggett, Commissioner of Patents, recommended that our representative should: . . . Present and explain the American Patent System, calling special attention to:

1. The justice and expedience of granting patents for new and useful inventions to *original inventors*, and to such only.

2. The importance of thorough preliminary Official examination to determine the questions of novelty.

3. The influence of our Patent System upon the industrial interests of the country.

4. The liberal spirit of our Patent Laws towards the citizens of other countries.

In addition, he should press as a matter of justice between nations, that:

1. Mere importers should not receive patents.

2. That patents granted in one country to citizens of another, should not be subject to such restrictions as to time and place of manufacture, as to render such patents comparatively worthless.

He of course should be instructed to make no concessions that can be interpreted as abandoning any of the essential features of our system.

Thatcher's own report indicates the tenor of the conference. He said:

It was the general, I may say universally expressed, opinion in the congress at Vienna that in order to secure the advancement of the mechanic arts in their own countries and to prevent the emigration of their most skilled artisans, it was necessary to secure a reform in European patent legislation.

Count Andrassy, the premier of the Austrian Government, put it in a very few words during an interview with the permanent committee when he said:

I look to England and I look to America, and I find that they are the foremost countries of the world in manufactures. I find also, upon examining their laws, that they have the best patent systems in the world.

Putting these two facts together, I conclude that the one is dependent upon the other, and therefore I am in favor of a thorough reorganization and revision of the patent laws of Austria.

The Vienna conference made this general attitude manifest in its set of resolutions. It declared that the existence of a patent law was a requirement "of all civilized nations;" and foresaw "great injury . . . inflicted upon countries which have no rational patent laws by the native inventive talent emigrating to more congenial countries where their labor is legally protected." The conference endorsed the "English, American, and Belgian patent laws, and the draft of a patent law prepared for Germany by the society of German engineers" (Bismarck's opponents!). One small bone was thrown to the opponents of an air-tight patent system. A recommendation provided:

It is advisable to establish legal rules, according to which the patentee may be induced, in cases in which the public interest should require it, to allow the use of his invention to all suitable applicants, for an adequate compensation.

Later this resolution was described by one of its drafters as mere propaganda against the enemies of patents.

Thus the Vienna conference was an outstanding American victory, won by a purposeful policy. It is an anticlimax to read in the interdepartmental correspondence that at the last moment the State Department lacked sufficient funds to send an American representative unless he could personally assume a substantial share of the cost of the trip.

Bismarck immediately found himself confronted with a combined attack from within and without Germany. The Society of German Engineers was already hard at work; and now it had the added prestige of powerful support from abroad. Bismarck was forced to retreat. In 1876 he called a committee of experts to study the patent situation. In February, 1877, he submitted a patent bill to Parliament. The eminent Charles Lyon-Cacn made the following observations on this development:

> A complete understanding of this important bill depends on an understanding of the principles which motivate the government. The government has never admitted that the institution of patents has anything to do with its ideas of justice. The government does not even seem to be convinced that the patent system actually favors the progress of industry. It suggested the passing of the bill only because Germany cannot stand isolated in the middle of all great nations which have patent statutes. In fact, the government in its memorandum explaining the new step stated: "Germany, resolved to suppress the patent system, could effectively take steps to this end only if other countries were expected to follow. This is, however, more than doubtful; and such a step would certainly result in the complete isolation of Germany for many years".

III.

The American victory in the issue of patent *versus* no-patent, decisive as it was, merely transferred the battlefront to the next stage. This was the issue of patents as private property rights as against patents as instrument of public policy. The impending struggle was foreseen in the American-Austrian discussions of 1872. The American Government opened the dispute by complaining against the Austrian principle providing for forfeiture of patent rights if local manufacturing were not begun within one year from the grant of the patent. Here was a clear statement of the issue. John Jay, then American Ambassador in Vienna, pointed out to the Austrian Minister for Foreign Affairs on March 17, 1872:

> It has been suggested that the differences in the statutes of different countries, in regard to patents, may be generally traced to a difference in the general view taken of the character and position

of the patentee; whether he is looked upon as a monopolist who owes all his rights to exceptional law, and who must be jealously watched and severely restricted; or whether he is regarded as a public benefactor, who is to be tenderly and kindly treated. The legislation of Congress has inclined more and more to the latter view; and, while adopting, as the true principle, that the inventor and public are both to be treated rationally, justly, and impartially, its tendency has been to give more and more liberally encouragement and assistance to useful inventors.

John Jay frankly assured Count Andrassy that the President would "cordially embrace this opportunity of cementing the friendship of the two countries and of advancing their common interests by a generous and harmonious policy"—if only Austria would modify its patent law in conformity with the United States statute and would agree to full reciprocity in matters of patents between the two countries.

This American view toward patents was novel. It stemmed from an actual faith that, in a competitive economy, patents under the control of private owners would not be subjected to abuse.[2]

The files of the United States Patent Office contain a constant reiteration of this theme; they reveal an absolute faith in the beneficent effects of an uncontrolled patent system. It was precisely this freedom, it was believed, which accounted for the rapid technological advance in the United States.[3]

---

[2] Here and there some doubts were raised in the faith. At a Senate patent hearing in 1877, Senator Wasleigh said bluntly, "While a man has a right to put his horse into his own barn, and not use it himself, he has no right to lock up his invention and let nobody use it. It is his duty to let his invention go out to the world." The reply of A.H.Walker, patent attorney, is a statement of the dominant American position:

"He has no such duty with reference to the period of his monopoly at all. The only duty he has is to spread the description of the invention on the records of the Patent Office, so that *after* the monopoly has expired, whether it be in fourteen, or seventeen, or twenty-one years, it will be free to the world. He has no duty publish that invention, or introduce it during the life of the monopoly; and if he chooses to let it die as useless, there is no law or reason why he shall not be permitted to do so. . . . As I understand the theory of the law, it is his *absolute* property during the life of the monopoly and is *not* qualified. Indeed, that is the language of the Constitution itself, viz., that the right is exclusive. . . ." Arguments before the Committee on Patents of the U.S. Senate and House of Representatives, Misc. Doc. No. 50, 45th Cong., 2d Sess. 36 (1878).

[3] At the 1877 patent hearing, J.J.Storrow, patent attorney, testified: "Sir William Thomson went home from our Centennial Exhibition, and just as he got home he appeared before the British Association, before the section of steam-engineering, of which he is the president, and, in giving them an account of what he had seen in this country, he called their attention very sharply to the effect of patent laws on the improvement of labor-saving machinery. He told them that unless the countries of Europe speedily amended their patent laws, and unless they amended them in a contrary direction to the bill pending in Parliament, they must understand that they would lose their manufacturing supremacy and that America would take it from them". . . . Storrow goes on to quote approvingly the remarks of Hulse, English judge of textile machinery at the Centennial: "As regards extent of invention and ingenuity, the United States was far ahead of other nations . . . The extraordinary extent of ingenuity and invention existing in the United States, and manifested throughout the exhibition, I attribute to the natural aptitude of the people, fostered and stimulated by an admirable patent law and system, and to the appreciation of inventions by the people generally." Arguments before the Committee on Patents, Misc. Doc. No. 50, 45th Cong., 2d Sess. 318 (1878).

In consequence, the Patent Office violently opposed any kind of governmental interference—whether against foreign inventors in this country or American inventors abroad. At every opportunity in the correspondence of the patent commissioners with foreign patent offices—through State Department channels or in direct negotiation—the view is developed that only international cooperation and mutual recognition of private property in patents can serve the final aim of the highest technological advance everywhere. The constant reiteration of this gospel by the most highly industrialized country in the world was bound to have an enormous effect.

But such an approach was in direct conflict with established tradition abroad. The American philosophy was genuinely new. True, the speeches of the French Revolution were aflame with this doctrine; Mirabeau exultantly speaks of inventions and patents as private property equal to any other form of private property. But, in fact, the French never drew the logical conclusion from these theories. The patent statute of France after the Revolution provided that patents should be forfeited in the event that patented goods were imported into France. Such a provision was a clear denial of the private property aspect of a patent, and made patents an instrument of public policy to bring manufacturing plants into France. This law still existed at the time of the Vienna conference.

The English patent statute of 1623 had the same purpose. . . . Obviously, the American view expressed in John Jay's letter had nothing in common with the traditional European approach. The question for the Germans—once they had abandoned their original hostility to the patent system—was which view they would adopt. Quite naturally they turned to the early English position. They were newcomers in the industrial hierarchy; they had all of the anti-monopolistic attitudes of the upstart competitor. They immediately adopted the position that patents should not be granted as a matter of right to every inventor, but should be permitted only in those fields in which the public interest justified the grant. Nor were they prepared to look upon patents as private property, to be granted to outsiders without limitation. Patents were a qualified right, subject to governmental interference in the interest of the nation.

Bismarck's committee of experts meeting in 1876 was fully dominated by this older view. One of its members was founder of the Siemens Combine. He was already concerned about the possibility that American Edison and British Thomson-Houston would take out many patents in Germany—before the German firms could develop their own research. He said bluntly:

> You might consider a rule that patentees are bound to grant licenses as an interference with the right of the inventor; but such a rule is absolutely necessary. The interests of [German] industries require that licenses be made available as a matter of right. Today industry is developing rapidly; and as a result monopolization of inventions and abuse of patent rights will inevitably expose large segments of industry to serious injury. The government must

protect industry against these dangers. From abroad another danger may arise. Inventive work is far more developed in England, United States and France than in Germany. Up to the present the number of patents taken out in Germany by foreigners has been small because the scope of protection given to the inventor has been insufficient. New legislation will lead to a substantial increase of foreign patentees. We shall experience a wave of foreign—particularly American—patent applications. These patents will not be taken out in order to protect industrial plants established or to be established in Germany; they will be taken out to monopolize production abroad. These articles will be imported into this country.

Such a danger must be met. It is not enough to provide that foreign patentees be required to submit "evidence" that they have established a plant in Germany. Such evidence may be mere "shadow"; they can merely keep a small domestic production going to maintain their patents. The French have an effective weapon—a rule that patents shall be forfeited if an inventor imports or permits others to import patented goods. However, the French method is inconvenient to trade interests, and would meet serious objection here. The requirement of actual manufacture under the patent would be excellent if the patentee were forced to show production in such quantities that domestic needs are actually met.

The same end can best be achieved by requiring that licenses be granted. The administration of this plan may be difficult. But the administrative agencies and the courts should be able to meet the difficulties and to come to a modus vivendi. Royalties should be based on the importance of the inventions. . . .

Siemens ended with the proposal that licenses of right should be made available at the end of the fifth year of patent protection. He felt that any other arrangement would be inconsistent with the public interest.

This same meeting was attended by one of the founders of the Hoechst Farbwerke, predecessor of I. G. Farben. Bruening took the position that the entire chemical industry should lie outside of patent protection. He said:

In the chemical industry the most harmful effects of patents are made clearly evident. Patents in France and England prevented the development of new chemical branches such as the manufacturing of aniline and alizarin dyes. Invention in chemical technology consists largely in an idea, and the practical exploitation of this idea usually involves enormous difficulties. In England and France patents for the manufacturing of aniline and alizarin dyes have been issued to the inventors who have not succeeded in the effective exploitation of their invention. In those countries monopolistic organizations came into existence which could not themselves produce and their major function was to prevent the development of other plants. In Germany, however, the chemical industry was able to expand because no patent protection prevented the free play of competition.

In the meantime the American view of patents as private property came into popularity in other countries. Between 1873, the year of the Vienna conference, and 1878, the year of the Paris convention, the American view prevailed in all the following formula was submitted at the Paris meeting:

> The right of inventors and industrial creators in their own work or the right of the industrialists in their trademarks is a property right which has its basis in natural law. The law enacted by each nation does not create these rights but only regulates them.

The Swiss delegation joined issue by offering a counter motion:

> The rights of the inventor and creative worker are a creation of equitable and useful principles of the law of each nation which should reconcile this right of the inventor, based on the grant of a temporary monopoly, with the rights of society.

The Swiss motion was voted down and the "property" motion won, though the clause "which has its basis in natural law" was eliminated.

Once an international convention declared inventions and patents a type of private property, it was only logical to grant to the "owners" of such property equal protection under the law, whatever their nationality might be. In the philosophy prevailing at the end of the nineteenth century, no principle was more sacred than the mutual protection of the vested interests of private property. Once patents were recognized as a type of private property there was no possible justification for the continuance of the forfeiture penalty for importation of patented goods or for the harsh rules respecting working clauses. The French system broke down almost immediately, and the working clauses gradually fell into disuse. The priority rule made its obsequious entry as a simple convenience for the property owner.

Germany continued to remain outside of the convention during the Eighties and mid-Nineties. In that country the scope of the patent grant was limited in the interest of encouraging further invention, and patents were subjected to compulsory licensing. But in 1897, at the Brussels convention, Germany appeared and prepared the way for her retreat. One of her major concerns was the elimination of the working clause. To this end she won the ardent support of the United States.

In 1901 Germany joined the Union. In a short time she became, along with the United States, the most ardent defender of the Union. In the later conferences the two countries worked together effectively to strengthen the protections accorded the patentee. In fact, the International Patent Convention can now almost be referred to as an American-German patent alliance.

NOTES AND QUESTIONS

(1) **The Forfeiture Principle.** The Congress of Vienna of 1873, at which the French government was not represented, adopted the principle of preliminary examination and the policy of no forfeiture for failure to work the invention within a country. This was countered by the French at the Paris Congress of 1878 which adopted the principle of forfeiture for nonworking of the invention within and eliminated preliminary examination. This development led to a deadlock between the parties on most substantive provisions in the negotiations leading up to the eventual signing of the Paris Convention in 1883. What remained was virtually all procedural: the national treatment provision of Article 2 and the right of priority of Article 4, with the provisions on forfeiture, requirements to work the patent within any country where patent protection was sought forming the next stage of international negotiations. The history of Article 5 will be discussed below.

(2) **National Treatment or Reciprocity.** At the time of the Paris Convention, Switzerland participated actively although it did not have and had never had a patent law. Under the principles of national treatment enshrined in Article 1, Switzerland was not required to protect inventions by patents even though Swiss inventors would enjoy patent protection in other countries of the union which did provide patent protection. Is this fair? Efficient? Patent laws were rejected by popular referenda in Switzerland in 1866 and 1882. When Switzerland agreed to administer and supervise the Paris Convention, it also agreed to enact a patent law. Such a law passed overwhelmingly in 1887 (by referendum) with the support of the Swiss watch industry, but chemical processes were excluded until 1907, when the law was changed due to threats of tariff retaliation from Germany, where the chemical industry was strong. (The examination of inventions in the watch industry arts is still treated as a special case under Swiss law.) Does this example indicate the strength of national treatment or its opposite, reciprocity, as the basis for international recognition of rights?

(3) **International Public Policy?** Putting the question another way, to what extent is an international agreement providing patent protection for foreign nationals a question of reciprocal national self-interest and to what extent is it international public policy? Is it a "compact between the individual countries party to it with reciprocal rights and obligations, or an instrument seeking to regulate interests, claims, and demands pressing upon the national and international level?" 1 STEPHEN P. LADAS, PATENTS, TRADEMARKS AND RELATED RIGHTS: NATIONAL AND INTERNATIONAL PROTECTION 12 (1975).

(4) **The Inventor as Patent Applicant.** At the Washington Patent Conference of 1874, the U.S. position was that "only the inventor himself, or his legal representative, should be entitled to a patent." At the same time, "the applicant in German law was not required to be himself the inventor, patents were granted without any question of authorship to the first comer."

STRINGHAM, *supra*, at 53, 144. Is this an ideological or a practical distinction? This will be discussed further below in the context of Article 4*ter* of the Paris Convention.

[B] The Paris Convention of 1883 and the Right of Priority

Notwithstanding false starts and setbacks during the decade-long course of deliberations leading to the signing of the Paris Convention in 1883, its legacy has been an unmitigated success. Article 1 created the Paris Union, the deliberative body of the convention. As noted above, although it had no patent system of its own, Switzerland was charged with administering and supervising the Paris Convention and agreed to initiate a domestic patent system as soon as possible. The ultimate successor of that administration, WIPO, became a specialized agency within the United Nations Organization system in 1974. That event ushered in a new period in international intellectual property law, as the post-colonial states of Africa and Asia became participants in what had up until then been a club of developed nations.

Articles 2 (national treatment) and 4 (right of priority) of the Paris Convention form the bedrock of the international patent system. The right of priority includes priority of invention in the U.S. first-to-invent system and priority of application in the first-to-file system employed in the rest of the world. Friction between the first to invent system and the first to file system over the right of priority must be dealt with to explore how inventors from first to file countries are treated in a first to invent system and vice versa. The principles of national treatment and right of priority are inseparable.

The first to file system is simpler because it eliminates the need for costly interference proceedings. According to Article 4(3) of the Strasbourg Convention of 1963, and EPC Article 54(3), an unpublished patent application is viewed as part of the prior art for purposes of determining novelty of an invention in a later filed application. This is necessitated by the very logic of a first-to-file patent system. There are two main motivations behind the first-to-file systems both of which are based upon economic efficiency. First, there is the incentive of the "race to the Patent Office," which encourages inventors to disclose their inventions to the public earlier rather than later. In the first-to-file system, patent applications are generally published after eighteen months, and competitors are blessed with relatively inexpensive and timely access to patent information. A second motive is to increase certainty as to patent ownership and thereby decrease legal transaction costs, since interference proceedings are eliminated. The motives behind the U.S. first-to-invent system are more complex, and relate to what are genuinely perceived to be the venerable traditions and exceptionalism of the U.S. patent system.

A key development in the early establishment of international patent law was the adoption in 1883 of the principle of "convention priority" in Article

4 of the Paris Convention. Under this principle, the date of a patent application in one member state is accepted as the date for establishing priority of invention for that applicant in any of the other member states where a counterpart application is filed within a period of months (originally six, and now twelve) in the second country. A certain amount of friction has arisen between the United States, with its first-to-invent system, and countries which have a first-to-file system, because the fundamental differences between the two systems are difficult to reconcile.

---

35 U.S.C. § 102. CONDITIONS FOR PATENTABILITY; NOVELTY (1994)

A person shall be entitled to a patent unless—

. . . .

(e) the invention was described in a patent granted on an application for patent by another filed in the United States before the invention thereof by the applicant for patent, or

. . . .

(g) before the applicant's invention thereof the invention was made in this country by another who had not abandoned, suppressed, or concealed it. In determining priority of invention there shall be considered not only the respective dates of conception and reduction to practice of the invention, but also the reasonable diligence of one who was first to conceive and last to reduce to practice, from a time prior to conception by the other.

PARIS CONVENTION, ARTICLE 4 (1883)

A. (1) Any person who has duly applied for a patent . . . in one of the countries of the Union, or his legal representative or assignee, shall enjoy *for the purposes of registration in other countries* a right of priority during the periods hereinafter stated.

(2) Any filing having the value of a formal national filing by virtue of the internal law of each country of the Union or of international treaties concluded among several countries of the Union shall be recognized as giving rise to a right of priority.

B. Consequently, subsequent filing in one of the other countries of the Union before the expiration of these Periods *shall not be invalidated through any acts accomplished in the interval, as, for instance, by another filing,* by publication of the invention or the working thereof, by the sale of copies of the design or model, or by use of the trade mark, and these facts cannot give rise to any right of third parties or any personal possession. The rights acquired by third parties before the day of the first application on which priority is based shall be reserved by the internal legislation of each country of the Union. [emphasis added]

. . . .

APPLICATION OF HANS HILMER
359 F.2d 859 (CCPA 1966)

[Habicht first won an interference over Hilmer in which he was held to have a right of priority on a single count (a "count" refers to subject matter corresponding to a claim) as of the date of his original Swiss application on January 24, 1957. Hilmer had filed his original application in Germany on July 31, 1957. Then Habicht filed his U.S. counterpart application on January 23, 1958. Finally, Hilmer filed his U.S. counterpart application on July 25, 1958. Habicht's disclosure included additional subject matter which Hilmer disclosed and claimed. The examiner rejected Hilmer's application as obvious by combining the Habicht disclosure with another reference. The Patent Office Board of Appeals affirmed, and held that Habicht's disclosure had effect as prior art as of his foreign filing date in Switzerland, under 35 U.S.C. § 119, which is entitled 'Benefit of Earlier Filing Date in Foreign Countries: Right of Priority'. The Court of Customs and Patent Appeals reversed, holding that Section 119 only deals with "right of priority" and does not confer status as "prior art", and so does not provide for the use of the entire contents of a U.S. patent application which matures into a patent as a reference effective as of its convention priority date for the purpose of defeating another U.S. patent under 35 U.S.C. Section 102(e).]

RICH, JUDGE. . . . A patent may be 'entitled' to a foreign filing date for some purposes and not for others, just as a patent may be 'used' in two ways. A patent owner uses his patent as a legal right to exclude others, granted to him under 35 U.S.C. § 154. Others, wholly unrelated to the patentee, use a patent, not as a legal right, but simply as evidence of prior invention or prior art, i.e., as a 'reference.' This is not an exercise of the patent right. This is how the Patent Office is 'using' the Habicht patent. These are totally different things, governed by different law, founded on different theories, and developed through different histories. . . . [T]he board said:

> The Examiner insists, however, that the effective date of the Habicht patent is January 24, 1957, the date of an application filed in Switzerland which is claimed by Habicht under 35 USC § 119. Appellants have not overcome this earlier date of Habicht. The issue is hence presented of whether the foreign priority date of a United States patent can be used as the effective filing date of the patent

when it is used as a reference (and this is the second statement of the issue by the board.) Our conclusion is that the priority date governs.

. . . .

This is the decision alleged to be in error. We think it was error. . . . While it may be that the world is shrinking and the very concept of 'foreign' should be abolished for the good of mankind, this is not a constitution we are expounding but specific statutes enacted to accomplish specific purposes, the meaning of which should stay put, absent intervening Congressional modifications, for well-understood reasons. . . . The board's conclusion is that the foreign priority date of a U.S. patent is its effective date as a reference. . . . [T]he board's statement is:

> Our conclusion is arrived at simply by considering sections 102(e) and the first paragraph of section 119 of the statute together. . .
>
> Section 119 refers to two applications for the same invention stemming from the same inventor, one a first application filed in a foreign country and the other a later application filed in the United States. . . . Section 119 provides that under the specified circumstances, and subject to the requirements of the second paragraph which are not in question here, the second application, filed in the United States, 'shall have the same effect' as it would have if filed in the United States on the date on which the application was filed in the foreign country. This language is plain; it gives the application the status of an application filed in the United States on a particular date. Section 102(e) provides that a patent may not be obtained if the invention was described in a patent granted on an application for patent by another filed in the United States before the invention thereof by the applicant. This paragraph makes the filing date of a U.S. patent (note the omission of 'in the United States') the effective date as a reference. It refers to an application filed in the United States and since section 119 provides that the application shall have the same effect as if filed in this country on a particular date, these two provisions must be read together and the filing date of the foreign application becomes the effective date of the United States reference patent.

This is so plausible that one's impulse is to say "Q.E.D." We find the reasoning at fault, however, and the interpretation untenable. To discuss it we must have section 119 before us, insofar as applicable:

> § 119. Benefit of earlier filing date in foreign country; right of priority. An application for patent for an invention filed in this country by any person who has, or whose legal representatives or assigns have, previously regularly filed an application for a patent for the same invention in a foreign country which affords similar privileges in the case of applications filed in the United States or to citizens of the United States, *shall have the same effect* as the

same application would have if filed in this country on the date on which the application for patent for the same invention was first filed in such foreign country, if the application in this country is filed within twelve months from the earliest date on which such foreign application was filed; *but* no patent shall be granted on any application for patent for an invention which had been patented or described in a printed publication in any country *more than one year before the date of the actual filing* of the application in this country, or which had been in public use or on sale in this country more than one year prior to such filing.

No application for patent shall be entitled *to his right of priority* unless (here follows the requirement for filing certain papers in the Patent Office and claiming priority not in question here, as the board held) * * *.[Emphasis ours]

The board's construction is based on the idea that the language of the statute is plain, that it means what it says, and that what it says is that the application filed abroad is to have the *same effect* as though it were filed here— *for all purposes*. We can reverse the statement to say that the actual U.S. application is to have the same effect as though it were filed in the U.S. on the day when the foreign application was filed, the whole thing being a question of effective date. We take it either way because it makes no difference here.

Before getting into history, we note first that there is in the very words of the statute a refutation of this literalism. It says 'shall have the same effect' and it then says 'but' for several situations it shall *not* have the same effect, namely, it does not enjoy the foreign date with respect to any of the patent-defeating provisions based on publication or patenting anywhere in the world or public use or being on sale in this country *more than one year before the date of actual filing in this country*.

As to the other statute involved, we point out that the words of section 102(e), which the board 'simply' reads together with section 119, also seem plain. Perhaps they mean precisely what *they* say in specifying, as an express patent-defeating provision, an application by another describing the invention but only as of the date it is *'filed in the United States.'*

The great logical flaw we see in the board's reasoning is in its premise (or is it an a priori conclusion?) that 'these two provisions must be read together.' Doing so, it says [Section] 119 in effect destroys the plain meaning of 102(e) but the board will not indulge the reverse construction in which the plain words of 102(e) limit the apparent meaning of 119. We see no reason for reading these two provisions together and the board has stated none. We believe, with the dissenting board member, that [Sections] 119 and 102(e) deal with unrelated concepts and further that the historical origins of the two sections show neither was intended to affect the other, wherefore they should not be read together in violation of the most basic rule of statutory construction, the 'master rule,' of carrying out the legislative intent. . . .

SECTION 119

We shall now take up the history and purpose of section 119. The board opinion devotes the equivalent of four pages in the printed record to a scholarly and detailed review of the history of section 119 with all of which we agree, except for the interwoven conclusions as to its meaning as it bears on the effective date of a U.S. patent used as a reference.

The board shows that the predecessor statute (R.S. 4887), containing the words 'shall have the same force and effect,' was enacted March 3, 1903 (32 Stat. 1225). Theodore Roosevelt signed it into law. The bill was drafted and proposed by a Commission created by Act of Congress in 1898 (30 Stat. 431) to study the effect of the Convention of Paris for the Protection of Industrial Property of 20th March 1883, which was under revision at Brussels even as the Commission deliberated, the revision being adopted at Brussels on 14th December 1900. (It was last revised at Lisbon on 31st October 1958.) The Commission made a report November 27, 1900, printed in 1902, entitled 'Report of the Commissioners Appointed to Revise the Laws Relating to Patents, Trademarks, and Trade Names, with Reference to Existing Conventions and Treaties,' which is fairly descriptive of its purpose. The section entitled 'The Revision of the Patent Law,' which we have read, extends from page 6 to page 39. It begins by saying (p. 6):

> We have found it desirable in considering the question of revision of the patent law to first consider what changes in the law are needed to give full force and effect to the treaty obligations which the United States has undertaken touching the protection of inventions made by the subjects or citizens of certain foreign countries.

Under the heading 'Priority Under the Convention,' it says: The second provision of the Convention to be noticed, and one which may be of very great advantage to those of our citizens who desire to secure patents in foreign countries for their inventions, is that contained in article 4, and relates to the so called 'delay of priority,' or 'period of priority.'

It then explained that in most countries no valid patent can be obtained if before the application is filed, the invention has been described in a printed publication, either in the country of application or even, as in the case of France and six other countries, in any country; that the same was true as to public use of the invention; and that the convention gives applicants in member countries a period (then 7 months, soon extended to 12) in which they can file applications in other countries after the filing in their own country and obtain valid patents notwithstanding publication or use in the interval and before the filing of the foreign application. This, it explained, is the 'delay of priority.' In plain English, it was the right of an applicant to have the foreign application treated at law as prior to the intervening publication or public use, though in fact it was not, by giving a right to that applicant to delay filing in the foreign country, instead of filing simultaneously with the home application, yet have it treated as though filed on the date of the home application. This is what today we call simply 'Convention priority,' or just 'priority.' The foreign filing date is the 'convention date' or the 'priority date.' This priority right was a protection to one who was trying to obtain patents in foreign countries, the protection being against patent-defeating provisions of national laws based on events intervening between the time of filing at home and filing abroad. Under the heading 'Recapitulation of Advantages Secured by the Convention,' the Commission said, so far as relevant here:

> The advantages to our citizens in the matter of patents directly afforded by the convention may be thus recapitulated.
>
> First. The enjoyment in foreign countries of equal rights with subjects or citizens of those countries.
>
> Second. The 'delay of priority' of seven months within which to file applications abroad after filing in this country.
>
> Third. The privilege of introducing articles embodying the invention manufactured in this country into foreign countries to a certain extent without thereby causing the forfeiture of the patents taken out there.

Note the emphasis repeatedly placed in the Commission Report on advantages to United States citizens. It was felt we should do what was necessary to comply with the reciprocity provisions to enjoy the benefits of the convention for our own citizens. It was also believed that by reason of Opinions of Attorneys General, Vol. 19, 273, 'the International Convention, in so far as the agreements therein contained are not in accordance with the present laws of the United States, is without force and effect; that it is not self-executing, but requires legislation to render it effective . . . and . . . it is our opinion that such legislation should be adopted. . . .' (Report p.19.) Specific to the question here, the Commission Report says:

> We are, therefore, of the opinion that an amendment to the law should be made, providing that the foreign application shall have, in case an application is filed in this country by the applicant abroad within the specified period, the same effect as if filed here on the day it was filed abroad.

The board thinks this 'shows the intention of the Commissioners' to create 'a status of (an application) having been filed in the U.S. for all purpose. . . .' In the context of this case, that means for the purpose of using a U.S. patent, obtained with a claim of priority, as a prior art patent to defeat the right of a third party to a patent on subject matter which does not patentably distinguish from anything that happens to be disclosed in such patent—or at least from anything disclosed 'relevant to the (there) claimed invention,' depending on which recent board opinion one looks at. We have read every word of the Commission Report looking for any suggestion of such a concept and have found none. All the board found was the above quotation. We deem it wholly inadequate as a basis for finding an intent to create a 'status' for an application—to say nothing of the patent granted thereon—'for all purposes.' There are other factors to consider which negative any such legislative intent.

There is another sentence in the Commission Report we should consider. . . . It called attention to the fact that in most foreign countries the patent is granted to the first to apply and said:

> The Convention has created an exception to the rule and made an application in any State of the Union for the Protection of Industrial Property of the same effect as an application in the country where an application is subsequently made within the time specified as a period of priority.

This couples very nicely with the wording of the first recommendation for a change in U.S. laws on page 27 where it was said:

> First. The application for a patent filed within seven [extended to 12] months of the filing of an application for a patent for the same invention in any foreign country which is a party to the International Convention should be given the same force as regards the question of priority that it would have if filed on the date on which the foreign application was filed.

The Commission, page 36, recommended proposed legislation, which is, in substance, the amendment to R.S. 4887 which was passed and is, with no change in substance, what we have today in section 119. The proposed bill in the Commission Report was entitled 'A Bill to give effect to treaty stipulations relating to letters patent for inventions.' The Act passed was entitled 'An Act To effectuate the provisions of the additional act of the international convention for the protection of industrial property.' Throughout, the same phrase has always appeared, 'shall have the same force and effect,' until it was simplified in the 1952 codification to 'shall have the same effect.' This change was mere modernization in legislative drafting. The Revisers Note to the section says: 'The first paragraph is the same as the present law with changes in language.' The Federico Commentary on the 1952 Act, 35 U.S.C.A., says (p. 29):

> This so-called right of priority was provided for in the second paragraph of R.S. 4887 which is the basis for the first paragraph of section 119 of this title. . . . (he here states the 4 conditions for obtaining the right) . . . The new statute made no changes in these conditions of the corresponding part of the old statute except to revise the language slightly. . . .

We need not guess what Congress has since believed to be the meaning of the disputed words in section 119, for it has spoken clearly. World wars interfere with normal commerce in industrial property. The one-year period of priority being too short for people in 'enemy' countries, we had after World War I a Nolan Act (41 Stat. 1313, Mar. 3, 1921) and after World War II a Boykin Act. Foreign countries had reciprocal acts. One purpose was to extend the period of priority. House Report No. 1498, January 28, 1946, by Mr. Boykin, accompanied H.R. 5223 which became Public Law 690 of the 79th Cong., 2d Sess., Aug. 8, 1946, 60 Stat. 940. Section 1 of the bill, the report says, was to extend 'the so-called period of priority,' which then existed under R.S. 4887. On p. 3 the report says:

> In this connection, it may be observed that the portion of the statute which provides that the filing of a foreign application—shall have the same force and effect as the same application would have if filed in this country on the date on which the application for patent for the same invention, discovery, or design was first filed in such foreign country—is intended to mean 'shall have the same force and effect,' etc., insofar as applicant's right to a patent is concerned. This statutory provision has no bearing upon the right of another party to a patent except in the case of an interference where the two parties are claiming the same patentable invention.

U.S. Code Congressional Service 1946, p. 1493.

We emphasize none of those words because we wish to emphasize them all. We cannot readily imagine a clearer, more definitive statement as to the legislature's own view of the words 'same effect,' which now appear in section 119. This statement flatly contradicts the board's views. The board does not mention it. . . .

For the foregoing reasons, we are clearly of the opinion that section 119 is not to be read as anything more than it was originally intended to be by its drafters, the Commission appointed under the 1898 Act of Congress, namely, a revision of our statutes to provide for a right of priority in conformity with the International Convention, for the benefit of United States citizens, by creating the necessary reciprocity with foreign members of the then Paris Union.

The board has mentioned that it was not limited in its terms to that treaty, which is true, so that it also functions relative to other treaties and reciprocal laws. We are unable to deduce from this any intent to affect the date as of which U.S. reference patents are effective. Nor can we do so by reason of another 'deviation' from the Convention the board finds in section 4887 (now 119) as to the protection of third parties.

SECTION 102(e)

[The Court then discusses the rule established in Alexander Milburn Co. v. Davis-Bournonville Co., 270 U.S. 390 (1926) and its enactment into 35 USC Section 102(e), concerning prior art which was not publicly known at the time of a patent application—so-called "secret prior art."]

We need not go into the reasoning of the *Milburn* case, which has its weaknesses, because all that matters is the rule of law it established: That a complete description of an invention in a U.S. patent application, filed before the date of invention of another, if it matures into a patent, may be used to show that that other was not the first inventor. This was a patent-defeating, judge-made rule and now is section 102(e). The rule has been expanded somewhat subsequent to 1926 so that the reference patent may be used as of its U.S. filing date as a general prior art reference. . . .

What has always been pointed out in attacks on the *Milburn* rule, or in attempts to limit it, is that it uses, as prior knowledge, information which was secret at the time as of which it is used—the contents of U.S. patent applications which are preserved in secrecy, generally speaking, 35 U.S.C. § 122. This is true, and we think there is some validity to the argument that that which is secret should be in a different category from knowledge which is public. Nevertheless we have the rule. However, we are not disposed to extend that rule, which applies to the date of filing applications in the United States, the actual filing date when the disclosure is on deposit in the U.S. Patent Office and on its way, in due course, to publication in an issued patent.

The board's new view, as expressed in this case . . . has the practical potential effect of pushing back the date of the unpublished, secret disclosures, which ultimately have effect as prior art references in the form of U.S. patents, by the full one-year priority period of section 119. We think the *Milburn* rule, as codified in section 102(e), goes far enough in that direction. We see no valid reason to go further, certainly no compelling reason.

We have seen that section 119 originated in 1903 and that its purpose was to grant protective priority rights so that the United States might be a participating member in the International Convention by giving reciprocal priority rights to foreign applicants with respect to the obtaining of patents. We have also seen that section 102(e) was the codification of a court-developed patent-defeating rule based on a statutory requirement that an applicant's invention must not have been previously known by others in this country. We see no such relation between these two rules of law as requires them to be read together and it is our view that section 119 should not be so read with 102(e) as to modify the express limitation of the latter to applications 'filed in the United States.' . . .

Section 102(e) was a codification of the *Milburn* doctrine. The *Milburn* case accorded a U.S. patent effect as a reference as of its U.S. filing date and stated that the policy of the statute on domestic inventions 'cannot be applied to foreign affairs.' No foreign date was involved in the case. The codifying statute specifies that the date as of which the patent has effect is the date of filing 'in the United States.'

R.S. 4887, predecessor of section 119, was in effect from 1903 to 1952 when it was incorporated unchanged in the present statutes. An examination of the legislative history of that statute fails to reveal a scintilla of evidence that it was ever intended to give 'status' to an application or to serve as a patent-defeating provision except insofar as the application, or patent issuing thereon, becomes involved in a priority contest. The *Milburn* rule, under which U.S. patents are used as prior art references for all matter disclosed in them as of their U.S. filing dates has been consistently and continuously applied since its inception in 1926, if not earlier under lower court decisions, by the United States Patent Office, the agency charged with the administration of the patent system, in accordance with the view . . . that R.S. 4887, and later section 119, does not make a U.S. patent effective as a reference as of a foreign priority date to which it may be entitled. . . . [S]ection 119 does not affect the express provision of 102(e) as to filing 'in the United States' and the decision of the board that the Swiss filing date of Habicht is the effective date of his U.S. patent as a reference must be reversed.

[The Court remanded the case for the Board to clarify its position on two remaining claims in the application, the validity of which had not been previously decided. The Board rejected them as obvious based on Habicht's foreign filing under 35 U.S.C. §§ 102(g), 119, and 104. The CCPA again reversed (In re Hilmer, 424 F.2d 1108 (CCPA 1970), *"Hilmer II"*), holding that the "subject matter" of Habicht's claim was prior art, if at all, as of the application's U.S. filing date, and could not be cited as prior art against Hilmer.]

PATENT COOPERATION TREATY, ARTICLE 64(4)

(a) Any State whose national law provides for prior art effect of its patents as from a date before publication, but does not equate for prior art purposes the priority date claimed under the Paris Convention for the Protection of Industrial Property to the actual filing date in that State, may declare that the filing outside that State of an international application designating that State is not equated to an actual filing in that State for prior art purposes.

(b) Any State making a declaration under subparagraph (a) shall to that extent not be bound by the provisions of Article 11(3).

(c) Any State making a declaration under subparagraph (a) shall, at the same time, state in writing the date from which, and the conditions under which, the prior art effect of any international application designating that State becomes effective in that State. This statement may be modified at any time by notification addressed to the Director General.

NOTES AND QUESTIONS

(1) **The Function of Patent Specification and Claims.** How different is the function of the specification from that of the claims of a patent application for determining novelty and obviousness? Article 54(3) EPC states that the content of prior filed European patent applications which are later published shall be considered as comprised in the state of the art. But Article 56 adds, "If the state of the art also includes documents within

the meaning of Article 54, paragraph 3, these documents are not to be considered in deciding whether there has been an inventive step." Prior to 1977, only the claims of a British patent application were used to determine novelty of a later filed application. The European Patent Office (and the British Patent Act of 1977) uses the whole contents of an application for purposes of determining the novelty (but not obviousness) of a later filed application. According to the *Hilmer* rule, contents of a prior filed U.S. application affect determinations both of novelty and of obviousness. Do differences between the first-to-file and the first-to-invent systems account for all the differences in approach and effect?

(2) **Must the "True" Inventor Be First?** Is the *Hilmer* case about novelty and nonobviousness or about priority? In most of the world, priority means priority of *application* by a *true* inventor or her assigns—not priority of *invention* by a true and *first* inventor. Is the question merely one of how to define the word "first"?

(3) **The "Last in Time" Rule.** The *Hilmer* court states that the *Milburn* rule "has its weaknesses." Is the *Hilmer* court primarily determined to limit the scope of section 119's treatment of foreign applicants or the scope of section 102(e)'s secret prior art effect? Does your answer affect whether the United States is in compliance with its treaty obligations? Should the court have reconciled its interpretation of section 119 in light of the Restatement's formula for treaty interpretation? Under section 115 of the Restatement, an act of Congress supersedes a provision of an international agreement as law of the United States "if the purpose of the act to supersede the earlier rule or provision is clear or if the act and the earlier rule or provision cannot be fairly reconciled." RESTATEMENT (THIRD) OF THE LAW, FOREIGN RELA- TIONS LAW OF THE UNITED STATES § 115 (1987). Is section 102(e) clearly irreconcilable with Article 4? Does the codification of the *Milburn* Rule in 35 U.S.C. § 102(e) in 1952 supercede the effect of Paris Convention Article 4 in U.S. law? Or can the two be reconciled?

(4) **What Result?** G filed an application in Germany on January 3, 1998, disclosing W and X, and disclosing Y as known related technology. On February 3, 1998, A files an application in the U.S. disclosing and claiming X, Y, and Z. On March 3, 1998 G files in the U.S., claiming W and X. Assume that Z is obvious if, but only if, W, X, or Y constitute prior art and that W is obvious if, but only if, Z constitutes prior art. In an interference proceeding in the U.S. between G and A, what are their respective rights? *See* Donald W. Chisum, *Foreign Activity and Patentability under U.S. Law*, 11 I.I.C. 26, 39 (1980).

(5) **Whittling Down *Hilmer*.** A series of amendments to U.S. patent laws during the 1990s relate to the *Hilmer* doctrine. Until 1994, Section 104 of the Patent Act did not allow parties outside the United States located in what were to become WTO countries to prove dates of invention taking place outside the U.S. in U.S. Patent Office interference proceedings or in the courts. Under Section 104, so the reasoning went, U.S. law did not discriminate against foreign *inventors* (which would be a violation of

national treatment under the Paris Convention), but against foreign *inventions* (i.e., foreign inventors could always prove their dates of invention if they desired to, simply by choosing to carry out their acts of invention and reduction to practice in the United States). Section 104 was amended in 1994 to allow proof of date of invention in any WTO country, with the intent of bringing the U.S. into compliance with its article 27.1 TRIPS obligation not to discriminate as to the place of invention. Another provision of the 1994 Uruguay Round Agreements Act established a domestic priority system allowing for the filing of a provisional patent application requiring neither a claim nor an oath or declaration. *See generally* Charles A. Eldering et al., *Comparative Analysis Of Provisional Patent Applications Under US And UK Law,* 79 J. PAT. OFF. SOC'Y 791 (1997). Further relevant amendments were made to the Patent Act in 1999, providing for publication of most U.S. applications eighteen months from their first priority date and amending of Section 102(e) to recognize the prior art effect of a published U.S. national application, or a PCT application, in the English language and designating the United States, as of its filing date wherever in the PCT Member States. However, the 1999 amendment of Section 102(g) "preserves the *Hilmer* doctrine . . . by precluding Section 104 prior invention showings outside the US from constituting prior art, except in the context of an interference." Richard Neifeld, *Analysis of the New Patent Laws Enacted November 29, 1999,* 82 J. PAT. OFF. SOC'Y 181, 189 (2000).

(6) **Continuing *Hilmer* Controversy.** Scholarship on the controversy over the *Hilmer* doctrine could fill an entire book. For some interesting illustrative viewpoints, see Kate H. Murashige, *The Hilmer Doctrine, Self-Collision, Novelty and the Definition of Prior Art,* 26 J. MARSHALL. L. REV. 549 (1993); C. Douglas Thomas, *Secret Prior Art— Get Your Priorities Straight!,* HARV. J.L. & TECH. 147 (1996); Harold C. Wegner, *TRIPS Boomerang— Obligations For Domestic Reform,* 29 VAND. J. TRANSNAT'L L. 535 (1996); R.B. Brody, *U.S. Treaty Law, The Paris Convention,* 35 U.S.C. § 119; 53 J. PAT. OFF. SOC'Y 194 (1971). More recently, the question of U.S. compliance with the TRIPS Agreement has been questioned as a result, among other things, of the Hilmer doctrine. *See* Lauren A. Degnan, *Does U.S. Patent Law Comply with TRIPS Articles 3 and 27 With Respect to the Treatment of Inventive Activity?,* 78 J. PAT. OFF. SOC'Y 108 (1996); Todd R. Miller, *Inventions Made in U.S.A.: Foreign 'Equality' Under Applicable International Treaties,* 27 I.I.C. 587 (1996). New proposals in WIPO for changing the definitions of prior art and novelty in the context of substantive harmonization of patent law will be discussed below.

§ 4.03   Substantive Principles in the Paris Convention: Exploitation of the Patented Invention and the Scope of the Right to Exclude

PARIS CONVENTION, ARTICLE 5 (1883)

The introduction by the patentee into countries where the patent has been granted, of articles manufactured in any other of the States of the Union shall not entail forfeiture. The patentee, however, shall be subject to the obligation of working his patent conformably to the laws of the country into which he has introduced the patented articles.

———

After the Paris Union was formed in 1883, much of the subsequent patent deliberations of its members revolved around the important issue of the scope of the patent right vis-a-vis the rights of third parties, touching again and again on the question of whether a patent is primarily a personal property right or an instrument of public policy. A Conference of Revision was held in Rome in 1886 to discuss Article 5, on the question of forfeiture of the patent right. France insisted that Article 5 should be amended to allow forfeiture of a patent for importing a patented product into a country where there was patent protection. Conversely, Belgium insisted that there be no forfeiture of a patent whatsoever—even where the patent had not been not worked within the country. Attempts to harmonize patent classification were rejected. Article 5 on exploitation of the patent was a prime source of contention for over a half-century, until the Lisbon Conference of 1958. Whether forfeiture of a patent constitutes expropriation, whether compulsory licensing or working requirements unduly hinder the rights of the patentee remain hotly debated questions even today. The history of Article 5 from its original articulation set out above to its final formulation just below is discussed in the next reading.

———

PARIS CONVENTION, ARTICLE 5 (LISBON ACT 1958)

A.—(1) The importation by the patentee into the country the patent has been granted of articles manufactured in any of the countries of the Union shall not entail forfeiture of the patent.

(2) Each country of the Union shall have the right to take legislative measures providing for the grant of compulsory licences to prevent the abuses which might result from the exclusive rights conferred by the patent, for example, failure to work.

(3) Forfeiture of the patent shall not be prescribed except in cases where the grant of compulsory licences would not have been sufficient to prevent such abuses. No proceeding for the forfeiture or revocation of a patent may be instituted before the expiration of two years from the grant of the first compulsory license.

(4) An application for a compulsory licence may not be made on the ground of failure to work or insufficient working before the expiration of a period of four years from the date of filing of the patent application or three years from the date of the grant of the patent, whichever period last expires; it shall be refused if the patentee justifies his inaction by legitimate reasons. Such a compulsory licence shall be non-exclusive and shall not be transferable, even in the form of the grant of a sub-licence, except with that part of the enterprise or goodwill using such licence.

(5) The foregoing provisions shall be applicable, *mutatis mutandis* to utility models.

B.—The protection of industrial designs shall not, under any circumstance, be liable to any forfeiture either by reason of failure to work or by reason of the importation of articles corresponding to those which are protected.

. . .

D.—No indication or mention of the patent, of the utility modes of the registration of the trademark, or of the deposit of the industrial design shall be required upon the product as a condition of recognition of the right to protection.

REVISION CONFERENCES[*]
Excerpted from ULF ANDERFELT, INTERNATIONAL PATENT-LEGISLATION AND DEVELOPING COUNTRIES 72–92 (1971)

[T]he following examination of the evolution of the Convention will deal exclusively with the rules concerning the exploitation of patents. Such rules are contained in Article 5 and prescribe the limits of the extent to which national laws may require patentees to exploit their inventions, and the types of sanctions allowed to enforce such requirements. Although certain other rules of the Convention, such as those that define the administrative measures that a country may impose on foreigners and rules concerning the right of third parties, may have a certain economic impact, the measures concerning the exploitation of patented inventions allowed under the Convention remain by far the most important features of the Convention in terms of their economic significance.

The texts of the first two revision conferences are of little interest since neither of them was ratified. The principal question at the first of these two, held in Rome in 1886, was the continuation of the efforts against compulsory working requirements. When discussion on this point was resumed at the second conference, held in Madrid in 1890, the suggestion was made that compulsory licensing be substituted for compulsory working as the most equitable method of conciliating the interests of individuals and those of society.

1. THE REVISION CONFERENCE OF BRUSSELS, 1897–1900

At this conference the Belgian proposal, made in 1880, for a total ban on revocation for non-working when a patent was being worked in one member country, was repeated, but it was again rejected, this time by a majority of the delegates. The Bureau, taking note of the difficulties created by the unanimity rule, which had led to the non-ratification of two previous revision texts, for the first time (as far as patents are concerned) introduced a proposal for the creation of a restricted union to which countries could adhere, which agreed to adopt a rule by which the sanction of revocation for non-working would be replaced by compulsory licensing. The general opinion, however, was not in favor of restricted unions in patent matters. As no agreement could be reached on any of the major proposals when the conference met in 1897, and in order not to have to close the conference without any tangible results, it was adjourned for the time being. Three years later, Belgium, having in the meantime conferred with the governments of some countries, which had opposed some amendments in 1897, recalled the conference and agreements were reached on several points.

The Bureau, having dropped its proposal for a restricted union, now suggested a clause prohibiting the revocation of a patent for non-working before the lapse of three years from the date of application, with the further qualification that revocation would only be allowed in cases in which the patentee could not justify his inaction. Unsuccessful efforts to license was suggested as justification. Though agreement on this last point could not be reached, the clause as such was accepted, leaving it to each country to decide what constituted justification.

The insertion of this clause may raise two questions: could other sanctions be used before the end of the three-year period, and could revocation be used as a sanction at any time in cases in which the patentee misused his monopoly power other than by non-working? . . . [A] later revision conference (The Hague, 1925) introduced the concept of "abuse" of the patentee's monopoly power. . . .

Despite the fact that the principle of unanimity in theory gives an equally important voice to each member, it is obvious that economically more powerful States can wield considerable influence at times. This was shown in a particular form at the Brussels conference. Both Germany and Austria, neither of which was yet a member, had made it clearly known that, while they were prepared to join the Union, their adherence depended on the adoption of certain amendments, of which the limitation of the sanction of revocation was the most important. From the deliberations it is evident that the decisions taken were strongly influenced by the desirability to accommodate these countries.

2. THE REVISION CONFERENCE OF WASHINGTON OF 1911

In view of the strong opposition of many countries to the abolition of revocation, the Bureau now proposed the following addition to Article 5: while the sanction of revocation should in principle be replaced by compulsory licensing, each country should retain the right to demand that consumers be adequately supplied, and that licenses be given on reasonable terms if asked for, at the risk of revocation; the use of this power should, however, be limited to cases in which parties immediately concerned, *i.e.,* consumers and producers, had complained of not being able to either buy goods or obtain licenses; and the three-year rule limiting the use of revocation should be retained in any case. The Bureau proposal also contained the suggestion that countries, not willing to accept the new proposal, should be able to continue applying the existing provisions.

This latter suggestion would have introduced what is known as the "reservation system," which had been adopted for instance by the Berne Union. As had been the case at Brussels when the suggestion of a restricted union was made, now also a strong opposition against splitting the unity of the rules of the Convention manifested itself.

In their counter-proposals, several countries rejected the Bureau's proposal, which largely substituted compulsory licensing for compulsory working, on the grounds that their national laws were not in agreement with such a provision. The British proposal is particularly interesting in view of the fact that Britain had been a co-sponsor in 1880 of the Belgian proposal to abolish the sanction of revocation for nonworking completely. The British change of mind on this point was due to the introduction of compulsory working in a Patent Act amendment in 1907.

The Bureau, in proposing the new Article 5, evidently had in mind the new English patent law. Referring to new circumstances which had appeared in some countries since the Brussels Conference, the Bureau said that, in order to avoid a regression from the progress already achieved, new provisions tending to conciliate the "legitimate rights" of inventors and the "requirements of public interest" might be desirable. Though reference to "public interest" has always been invoked, both to defend and reject proposed changes, the Bureau, for the abovementioned reason, seems to have gone further in stressing the public interest at Washington than at any other conference, even with due consideration for the second point mentioned below. The new proposal concerning Article 5 was based on the following ideas according to the Bureau: (1) is necessary to give the industry of every country the possibility of utilizing any invention on a footing of equality with all other countries protecting that invention; (2) any intentional bias must be prevented from operating either in favor of the inventor against the public interest or against the inventor in favor of any particular interest; and (3) certain countries apparently wish to retain the faculty to take the necessary measures assuring the introduction either of new industries likely to benefit their economies or of products demanded by their consumers. It must of course be recognized that, though in general the interests of society and of individual patentees, as far as working provisions are concerned, are supposed to be in opposition, this may not always be so. Besides the opinion that there are no differences between the two groups of interests, this seems to be the case particularly of large industrial countries with a large or major portion of their patent grants given to its own nationals, and whose nationals hold significant numbers of patents in other countries.

A German proposal to the Conference suggested the substitution of compulsory licensing for revocation as a sanction for non-working, to be used after the three-year period. A number of countries opposed the proposal—Austria, France, Great Britain, the Netherlands and Spain. The position of France is particularly interesting. Far from basing itself on the principles of "inherent rights of inventors," the French rejection of this proposal stated, in fact, that the working obligation had its rationale in the economic necessity of feeding the national industry of the patent-granting country with the discoveries and inventions there patented. . . .

After the German proposal was rejected, the general opinion was in favor of retaining the *status quo*. Thus, at the Washington Conference no change was made that affected the manner in which a patentee could be obliged to exploit his patent by national law. On the whole, only minor changes concerning patents were agreed upon.

3. THE REVISION CONFERENCE OF THE HAGUE 1925

At this conference the contents of Article 5 were changed in the following respects: in paragraph 2 the essential change was the substitution of the concept of "abuses which might result from the exclusive rights conferred by the patent" for that of "non-working;" a paragraph 3 was inserted, in which the idea of compulsory licenses was introduced for the first time. The paragraph stated that measures to prevent abuses "shall not entail forfeiture unless the grant of compulsory licenses is insufficient to prevent such abuses;" and finally a fourth paragraph was created essentially containing the second part of paragraph 2 of the Washington text, but with the following changes: the three-year period would start from the date of the patent grant rather than from the filing date of the patent application, and the patentee could exonerate himself by proving "the existence of legitimate excuses" rather than "by justifying his inaction." . . .

The proposal of the Bureau suggested the deletion of compulsory working provisions, replacing them with provisions for compulsory licenses after the three-year period, in countries that wanted to prevent an invention from not being worked locally. The Bureau motivated this proposal with the fact that membership was now considerable and that the maintenance of compulsory working clauses in all but one of the Member States (the exception being the United States) was not rational, since if the patentee does not work his invention in a country it is generally because he can work it more profitably in another country, in which case the consumer will pay less.

Later the Bureau added the following particular argument (which has been echoed by several authors commenting on this conference):

> The obligation for the foreign patentee to manufacture in the country may lead to the establishment of a foreign industry towards which the local manufacturers would not be favorable.

Although this latter argument must be seen in the context of the climate of strong economic nationalism that reigned after the First World War, it is of interest today in the case of developing countries whose very objective it is to attract foreign investment in industrial manufacturing.

Several countries objected to the suggestion to abolish any working requirements completely, which was raised this time by the United States. Spain, opposing the proposal, observed that if the abolishment of any working requirement may be favorable to the large, industrialized countries, assuring them complete control of export markets, such a measure would prejudice the interests of less industrialized countries by transforming the patent monopoly into a trading monopoly inimical to the development of local industry.

Three countries (Japan, Poland and Yugoslavia) were also opposed to the abolition of the sanction of revocation for non-working and proposed the maintenance of the *status quo*. All three countries gave essentially the same arguments. . . . The most significant argument, considering that these countries were then comparable to the developing countries of today [was] that compulsory licenses were not always a reliable remedy because of the difficulties of finding local licensees. . . .

A compromise proposal, introduced by Great Britain and the United States, was adopted and became paragraphs two, three and four of Article 5. The sanction of revocation was maintained but was not to be used unless "the grant of compulsory licenses is insufficient to prevent such abuses" [Article 5 (3)]. Diverging opinions have been expressed on the problem of whether an actual grant of a compulsory license had to precede revocation, or whether direct revocation could take place (still only after three years), if a compulsory license was considered insufficient. . . .

There is one interpretation that can be effectively defended[:] . . . each country is free to decide, given their economic and social conditions, whether the granting of compulsory licenses will be insufficient, and whether therefore only a revocation will effectively eliminate abuses of the patent monopoly.

The important innovation at the Hague, in the text of Article 5, is the substitution of the concept of "the abuses which might result from the exclusive rights conferred by the patent" for that of "non-working." The concept of "abuse of monopoly power" was introduced by the Anglo-American compromise proposal and was clearly inspired by the British Patent Act. The phrase "for example, failure to work" was inserted at the request of one delegation, in order to make it clear that non-working might constitute such an abuse. As far as non-exploitation is concerned, the new text has been interpreted to mean that such inaction in itself is not liable to sanctions, and sanctions are allowed only if it is considered an abuse of the patentee's monopoly power. . . .

Although prior to 1925, the Convention text had only dealt with non-working, this did not mean that other actions by a patentee deemed harmful by society could not have been subject to sanctions by virtue of a national law. The only plausible explanation for the fact that the Convention text treated only sanctions against non-working is that it did not regulate other abuses, leaving the Union countries free to legislate on the matter. From what has been suggested above, with reference to the Brussels Conference, on the non-applicability of the three-year grace period to sanctions for causes other than non-working, and, moreover, taking into consideration the British proposal during the Washington Conference to expressly make non-working the only case in which the period was applicable, the obvious conclusion seems to be that the introduction of the concept of "abuse of monopoly power" was, in fact, a further curtailment of society's right to control the use made of the monopoly power that a patent gives its holder.

The third and final modification of Article 5 changed the starting date of the three-year period from that of the patent application to that of the patent grant. It appears that there was little opposition to this change. It meant a substantially greater protection for the patentee against sanctions especially in countries that used the examination system.

Of the three changes introduced in Article 5 at the Hague, the introduction of the concept of compulsory licenses would certainly have the most long term influence, even though initially it may have had less practical value. The appearance of the concept of "abuse of monopoly power," which now included among other causes the only previously, regulated cause for sanction—non-working—must be considered a gain for the patentee, as must also the third change prolonging the period during which sanctions could not be taken. . . .

4. THE REVISION CONFERENCE OF LONDON 1934

At this conference only paragraph 4 was amended, but the change was important. Whereas the text of paragraph 4 in its earlier version contained the expression "the patent may not be subjected to such measures before the expiration of three years," the new text provided that "an application for a compulsory license may not be made before the expiration of three years." A second sentence was added, reading: "No proceedings for the forfeiture or revocation of a patent may be instituted before the expiration of two years from the grant of the first compulsory license."

The Bureau suggested one change of Article 5. The proposed amendment, aimed at the abolition of the sanction of revocation for non-working, would mean a revision of paragraph 3. The draft amendment for a new paragraph 3 read: "These measures may foresee *the compulsory license as a sanction for non-working but not the revocation of the patent grant*." The Bureau after affirming that according to the Hague text, the countries that had opposed the abolition of revocation, fearing that the importation of patented products would retard their industrial development, were still free to maintain that compulsory licenses were not sufficient to avert the disadvantages of non-working, nevertheless maintained that it was difficult to admit that an abuse of the monopoly power exists, when the patentee is prepared "to satisfy all needs of the local market." Although one may take issue with the assertion that the patentee is prepared to satisfy all needs of the local market—in a monopoly market the meaning of satisfaction of consumers is by definition far removed from the general significance of that term—as well as his professed readiness to license, there is another fundamental consideration that may invalidate the statement. As several countries observed at the Hague and would do again at this conference, the sanction of compulsory licenses may not be effective because of the difficulty to find licensees. . . .

Three counter-proposals submitted by Member States are of particular interest. A Mexican suggestion for a new paragraph 3 would keep compulsory licensing but not the sanction of revocation. Instead a country would be able to sanction non-working with a "reasonable reduction" of the duration of the patent. The Polish delegation proposed an amendment of the existing paragraph 3 containing the rule, that non-working should not be considered an abuse in the case where the demand of the local market did not justify local production. . . .

The Czechoslovakian delegation, in a general commentary on the Bureau proposals, declared, that the changes suggested were evidently based on "the desire to satisfy the multiple claims of modern international commerce," and that it was certain, "that the proposals of the Bureau were likely to considerably improve the position of patentee internationally." Nevertheless, it continued:

> One must not lose sight of the fact that this improvement entails a weakening of the economic position of nationals to the advantage of foreigners. Given the proportion that exists between the manufacturing and trade of small countries such as Czechoslovakia, on the one hand, and foreign competition, on the other hand, it is to be feared that the advantages will far from compensate for the disadvantages to the national economy, if the Bureau programme was adopted.

The Czech delegation then declared that already the changes brought about at the Hague had come to lie heavily on the Czechoslovakian manufacturers and merchants. Therefore their government had to examine the Bureau proposal with the utmost care and oppose any reform, which might bring further disadvantages to its nationals. . . .

A compromise proposal was worked out that left paragraph 3 unchanged and introduced a revision of paragraph 4, according to which the sanction of revocation would be kept, but under the condition that it could be invoked only two years after a compulsory license had been granted. . . .

Even though the only textual change in Article 5 at the London Conference appeared in its fourth paragraph, it also had repercussions on the preceding paragraph. Whereas the third paragraph in its Hague version only constituted an affirmation of a theoretical principle, described as a "moral commitment," that revocation should not be resorted to unless a compulsory license was insufficient, the London version of paragraph 3, in virtue of the second sentence of paragraph 4, constituted a "unionist rule," *i.e.*, compulsory for all its members. . . .

5. THE REVISION CONFERENCE OF LISBON 1958

The revision of Article 5 at Lisbon left only its first paragraph unchanged. Paragraph 2, which recognized the right of Member States to take the necessary legislative measures to prevent abuses, now stated that this right was limited to taking measures "providing for the grant of compulsory licenses." In the first part of paragraph 3, the words "is insufficient", indicating the cases in which revocation was allowed, were replaced by "would not have been sufficient." The former second sentence of the fourth paragraph was inserted as a new, second part of paragraph 3. In the new paragraph 4, the introductory words "In any case" were deleted. Furthermore, the application of "grace" periods, during which no compulsory licenses could be granted, was expressly limited to cases of non-working or insufficient working. A certain adjustment concerning the length of such periods was made. Finally a new phrase was added stating that compulsory licenses should be nonexclusive and non-transferable. . . .

How is one to interpret Article 5A as it emerged from the Lisbon revision Conference? Paragraph 2 raises no problem. From the text itself it is clear that the sanction of compulsory license has been made the primary sanction. This is equally clear from the proposals submitted to the Conference and opinions expressed during it. Paragraph 3, however . . . raises the question of whether and to what extent the principle of the previous paragraph is attenuated. The drafting committee evidently intended to limit the possibility of revoking patents to cases in which a compulsory license had, in fact, proved itself insufficient. [. . . T]he final wording of this paragraph appears to lead to the possible interpretation that, in fact, it constitutes a concession to the interests of those countries, that maintained steadfastly during the Conference that the threat of compulsory licenses was often insufficient to avoid abuses or to remedy them. As paragraph 4 expressly limits itself to cases of non-working and insufficient working, this interpretation of paragraph 3 would mean that a country, upon judging that a compulsory license would not be sufficient to prevent or rectify a certain abuse of the monopoly power of the patentee, could directly declare a patent forfeited in all cases save those regulated specifically by paragraph 4. No author commenting on the Lisbon text has, however, mentioned such an interpretation.

As for paragraph 4 two changes are evident. The first is that the only abuses now benefitting from a "grace" period before compulsory licenses may be imposed are non-working or insufficient working, whereas earlier all abuses, and, according to the interpretation of some countries, even grounds other than abuses by the patentee, such as cases involving particular public interests, were subject to the provisions of paragraph 4. Thus, there is one tangible change in favor of the interests of society. The second change amounted to a possible prolongation of the grace period. Though its effect was only to benefit patentees in countries that had pre-examination systems, it confirms the contention that the period of effective protection for the patentee might be not only the specified period but also the time between the application for and the granting of a patent.

NOTES AND QUESTIONS

(1) **Working Requirements and Economic Efficiency.** The United States has never had a working requirement in connection with its patent law. Germany had a working requirement until 1911 but did not use it other than for the purpose of making reciprocal agreements with other nations. A British authority has observed that "the U.S. has always, by geography and economic position, been able to remain aloof from this sort of requirement." WILLIAM CORNISH, INTELLECTUAL PROPERTY: PATENTS, COPYRIGHT, TRADE MARKS AND ALLIED RIGHTS 72 n.51 (2d ed. 1989). Is there anything more than geography and economy to the American position? With regard to the British addition of compulsory licensing in section 15 of the 1905 Patents Act, Cornish continues:

> As in seventeenth century England, any country which offers patents to foreigners will want the invention to be exploited to the advantage of its own economy. It may indeed take measures to make the patent more than a cover protecting the import of foreign-made goods. If it has a domestic industry that competes with the foreign patentee there may be a particular cause for jealousy. This certainly was the motiv[ating] force behind the introduction into the British system of provisions allowing the grant of compulsory licences on the ground that the invention was not being worked domestically: the success of the German and Swiss chemical industries in the late nineteenth century was built to a substantial degree

on the holding of key patents. The French originally went even further, making revocation of the patent the penalty for importing patented articles from abroad; lifting this draconian sanction was made a precondition of membership in the Paris Convention. Article 5A(1). The majority of patenting countries now have some form of compulsory working requirement, which the Paris Convention allows to be sanctioned by compulsory licensing once three years have elapsed from grant; and by revocation if compulsory licensing fails after two years to produce the required result. Provisions of this kind in national law are not only offensive to notions of international comity supposedly underlying the Convention; they are also economically unsound in any case where efficiencies of scale demand production in one place for international markets.

(2) **The Lever of Reciprocity.** In the face of threats from the United States to follow the British example of 1905, in 1909 Germany signed a reciprocal treaty with the United States exempting U.S. patent owners from the German patent law's working requirements. 36 Stat. L. 2178. The German working requirement (section 11) was itself repealed in 1911, and an amendment substituting compulsory licensing was added. By 1914, Germany supplied ninety percent of U.S. dyestuffs and the U.S. industry consisted largely of small assembly plants operating on German intermediates. The treaty has been called "one-sided" since the United States never had such requirements in its patent law. EMERSON STRINGHAM, PATENTS AND GEBRAUCHMUSTER in INTERNATIONAL LAW 110–11 (1934).

(3) **The Consensus Rule.** The successive Conferences of Revision mentioned by Anderfelt were held pursuant to Article 14 of the Paris Convention, which states that:

> The present convention shall be submitted to periodical revisions with a view to the introduction of amendments calculated to improve the system of the Union. . . . For this purpose, conferences shall be had successively in one of the contracting countries between the delegates of the said countries.

A consensus rule that requires unanimity of the parties for any amendments to the Convention was present from the very beginnings of the Paris Union. A modification of the unanimity requirement was proposed by Mexico at the London Conference in 1934, but it did not succeed. The consensus rule, which still exists in the Paris Assembly today, has been pivotal in shaping the character and tone of the International Bureau's efforts to introduce improvements into the Paris Convention throughout the various revisions and the nature of the changes which have been made in the treaty text. At the same time, as noted by Anderfelt, the economically more powerful states can wield considerable influence during deliberations. How do powerful states wield their influence in international fora, consistent with the principles of equality which underpin the international legal system?

(4) **Does Elimination of Local Working Requirements Favor Local Industry?** The International Bureau's discussion of the Hague Revision of 1925 notes the argument that "[t]he obligation for the foreign patentee to manufacture in the country may lead to the establishment of a foreign industry towards which the local manufacturers would not be favorable." Does the overtly protectionist argument against working requirements for foreign patentees in favor of local manufacturers comport with the realities of foreign investment practices? Stringham observed that prior to World War I, "as a general rule Germans did not establish enterprises in the United States due to the absence of measures about compulsory licensing." STRINGHAM, *supra*, at 110–11, esp. 176ff. Compare the discussion of compulsory licensing in studies such as Robert M. Sherwood, *The TRIPS Agreement: Implications For Developing Countries*, 37 IDEA 491, 496 (1997), with reference to "non-robust systems," "trade-enhancing systems" such as TRIPS, and "investment-stimulating systems," described in Edwin Mansfield, *Intellectual Property, Technology, and Economic Growth*, 64 ECONOMIC IMPACT 12 (1988) (measuring private rates of investment) and Joseph Straus, *Implications of the TRIPS Agreement in the Field of Patent Law*, in FROM GATT TO TRIPS: THE AGREEMENT ON TRADE-RELATED ASPECTS of INTELLECTUAL PROPERTY RIGHTS 160, 202–08 (1996). Are there valid justifications for the views of opponents of foreign investment in developing countries?

(5) **Enforcement of the Paris Convention.** At the Hague Conference of 1925, the United States proposed to switch to a reciprocity system for non-compliance by other states. "Among the general principles, the American delegates proposed an amendment which would have permitted reprisals as between member countries, the objective of the American delegates being to force concessions in the matter of compulsory working and annual taxes." The proposal was withdrawn as being "contrary to the principles of the union." STRINGHAM, *supra*, at 85.

(6) **Inventors Rights.** Another provision added in London in 1934 was the right of the inventor to be named (Article 4*ter*), proposed by Italy and Holland. The right of the inventor to see his name figure in the patent, even when taken by a third party, was adopted, but another proposal regarding remuneration due to an employee or a salaried worker for his invention, which had first been urged by the International Bureau of Labor (now the ILO) in 1929, was rejected. Although such rights are powerful, for example, in modern German patent law; in the United States, employee inventors generally have no rights in their inventions if they reasonably relate to the activities of the employer. Is the right of an inventor to be named in the patent a "moral right"? Should firms be required to compensate their employees for assigning their inventions?

(7) **Intervening Rights and Prior User Rights.** The question of intervening rights was also an important one in the period in question. As originally stated in 1883, Article 4 provided that: "Any one who shall have regularly deposited an application for a patent of invention . . . in one of

the contracting States, shall enjoy for the purpose of making the deposit in the other States, and *under reserve of the rights of third parties* ["*sous reserve des droits de tiers*"], a right of priority during the periods hereinafter determined." A Dutch delegate thought the better expression would have been "*except for rights which had already been legitimately acquired by third parties*" ["*sauf les droits qui seraient deja acquis légitimement par les tiers.*"] *See* 1 STEPHEN P. LADAS, PATENTS, TRADEMARKS AND RELATED RIGHTS: NATIONAL AND INTERNATIONAL PROTECTION 499 (1975). The language was not fixed until the London Conference, where the reservation of right of personal possession of an invention [*Vorbenutzungsrecht*] after the priority date was suppressed by the addition of Article 4(B) of the convention. Thenceforward, no prior user rights could arise during the period of priority, while the rights acquired by third parties before the first application, serving as the basis of the right of priority, continued to be regulated according to the internal legislation of each country. Prior user rights have been a part of Canada's patent law since 1849. *See* Gregor Binkley, *Prior User Rights and The Canadian Patent Act*, 18 C.I.P.R. 207 (2001). Binkley states that the earliest reported Canadian case, *Fowell v. Chown* (1894), 25 O.R. 71, was a rejection of the U.S. Supreme Court's reasoning in its decision in *McClurg v. Kingsland*, 1 Howard 201 (1843), which held that prior use necessarily invalidated a patent. Prior user rights were not part of U.S. patent law until the American Inventors' Improvement Act of 1999 (now codified at 35 U.S.C. § 273) created a defense to infringement for a method only commercially used for doing or conducting business.

(8) **Abuse of Patent Rights.** Is Anderfelt persuasive about the need for states to have some semblance of the power of revocation of a patent to make the sanction of a compulsory license effective? Is the specter of patent owners in large economically powerful countries abusing the patent monopoly to create a "trading monopoly" with all manufacturing in the home market a real one? We will pursue the topic further in the discussion of parallel imports and exhaustion of right in Chapter 7.

(9) **Ratchet Effect?** The United States was apparently very pleased with the outcome of the London Conference of 1934:

> Commissioner Coe stated categorically in 1935 that "while the international convention for the protection of industrial property was revised in a number of points, those revisions invariably approached the American law; and every other country in the world belonging to this convention, or practically every other one, yielded its own domestic law in favor of what is apparently regarded as the superior patent laws of the United States.

Hearings before the Committee on Patents on H.R. 4523 Pt. I, 74th Cong. 1st. Sess. 1067, 1068 (1935). The 1990s have sometimes been called the Golden Age of the patent system by American judges and scholars. To what extent can the trend in international patent negotiations over the past century be seen to have been one favoring stronger and stronger patent protection?

§ 4.04   Harmonization of Patent Law

The following readings cover the first real contemporary attempts at international harmonization of substantive patent law beginning in the mid-1980s with negotiations (1) in the WIPO on a "Treaty Supplementing the Paris Convention as Far as Patents are Concerned" and (2) in the GATT on minimum standards of substantive patent law, which were ultimately incorporated into the TRIPS Agreement. Following the failure to conclude a treaty on substantive patent harmonization within WIPO in June 1991, discussed in the readings, the focus of attention shifted to the WTO. Negotiations in WIPO continued on the much more modest task of harmonization of procedure. The TRIPS Agreement came into effect at the beginning of 1995, giving the industrialized countries much of what they had sought from developing nations. Harmonization of patent application procedure culminated in the signing of the WIPO Patent Law Treaty ("PLT") in June, 2000. New negotiations toward a Substantive Patent Law Treaty ("SPLT") are ongoing.

[A]   The Substantive Patent Law Treaty [SPLT]

LEE J. SCHROEDER, THE HARMONIZATION OF PATENT LAWS *
C567 ALI-ABA 473, 473–78 (1990)

INTRODUCTION

Several efforts to harmonize the patent laws of the various countries of the world, including the United States, are presently underway. The most comprehensive effort is taking place within [WIPO] . . . The focus of that effort is to develop a treaty which will harmonize the patent laws of the countries or groups of countries adhering to that treaty.

A second and related effort is the on-going attempt to internationally address the trade-related aspects of intellectual property and raise the levels of intellectual property protection including patent protection. This effort is taking place within the . . . Uruguay round of trade talks under the [GATT]. . . . The two activities are interrelated in that some elements of patent law under discussion in the WIPO exercise are also under discussion in the GATT exercise.

THE WIPO EFFORT

The effort to develop a treaty to harmonize the patent laws of different countries began in 1984 with the convening of several meetings by WIPO to study the availability of a grace period for overcoming the public disclosure of an invention before the filing a patent application. If a

---

* Copyright 1990, Lee J. Schroeder; American Law Institute. Reprinted with permission.

publication disclosing an invention occurs within a grace period prior to the filing of a patent application, the applicant may still be awarded a patent for that invention. The matter of a grace period offering applicants up to 12 months before the filing of a patent application during which the applicant can overcome his own disclosure of the invention or the disclosure of a third party is well-known in the United States. But such a grace period is not a part of the patent laws of most other countries of the world. The U.S. participants at these first meetings sought to have the concept of a grace period accepted by the many countries that do not have a grace period or have a very limited grace period.

The grace period meetings were quite contentious and agreement was only obtained to further study the matter. The grace period topic was next considered along with two other topics in a 1985 WIPO meeting of a committee of experts to harmonize provisions in laws for the protection of inventions. The two additional topics were the requirements to be met in a patent application to obtain a filing date and the requirements for naming an inventor. Over the next five years, some eight additional meetings of the WIPO committee of experts were held and further new topics were introduced and discussed, so that by the time of a meeting this past June, the draft treaty which has evolved consists of some 37 articles and eight rules. . . .

. . . A diplomatic conference is now scheduled for June 3–28, 1991. As the draft treaty has many provisions which have the potential to require changes to U.S. law should the United States adhere to the treaty, I will briefly discuss some of those provisions. . . .

THE MORE CONTROVERSIAL PROVISIONS

Patent Awarded to First to File: Article 13

Probably the most controversial change to the U.S. patent law that would be required by the draft treaty is to award patents to the inventor that first files an application and not the first person that invents, as with our present system.

The first-to-file system is the system followed by the entire world other than for the United States and the Philippines which follow the first-to-invent approach. Canada had a first-to-invent system until the beginning of this year and legislation is now being considered by the Philippines to change to a first-to-file system.

Opponents in the U.S. of the first-to-file system argue that the first-to-file system would greatly increase the number of applications filed in the United States and the applications would be of a poor quality. The opponents of the first-to-file system also argue that the first-to-file system would be unconstitutional, lacks fairness in that a second inventor who has invented later in time might get the patent and that the first-to-file system favors the large corporation over the individual inventor or the small business.

On the other hand, those who advocate that our first-to-invent system should be replaced by a first-to-file system note that the first-to-file system brings with it a degree of certainty, and that the first-to-invent system advantage of being able to show that one person is the first to invent is a very costly procedure out of the reach of most but very large corporations. Furthermore, even the very large corporations often do not engage in first inventor or interference contests, but instead negotiate cross-licensing arrangements.

While our present system to show that one is a first inventor is costly in terms of money, those that advocate the first-to-file system point to the unfortunate loss of time that is built into the first-to-invent system, because inventors are not under the time pressure to move more quickly as under a first-to-file system. They argue that the first-to-invent system served the United States well when the United States had an isolated economy or had a wide-based technological lead, but unfortunately at present the United States has to worry about the technological advances of others, and those others are not moving slowly as they do not have the luxury of time and being able to rely on an earlier date of invention. First-to-invent is wonderful if all you have to worry about is others inventing in the United States, which is now the situation in fewer and fewer technological fields.

Another argument that those that advocate the first-to-file system for the United States is that the majority of filers in the United States are already operating with such a system. This includes the applicants of almost half of the applications that originate from abroad, and most of the applicants filing for U.S. corporations, as they also file the same applications abroad.

Both sides of the debate attempt to refute the arguments offered by the other side. The opponents of the first-to-file system point to the historical record of the United States having a first-to-invent system for over 150 years and the fact that the concept of a first-to-file system for the United States was thoroughly reviewed following the proposal in the 1966 report of the President's Commission to study the U.S. patent system. It is interesting to note that in Congressional hearings on bills before the Congress resulting from the 1966 President's Commission report, a change to first-to-file was opposed by the various patent bar groups and a number of industry groups but was supported by some inventor groups and small business groups.

Grace Period: Article 12

While the issue of first-to-file versus first-to-invent may be the most controversial, or at least the issue that is receiving the most attention, there are other issues that are equally, and quite possibly, more important that are part of the harmonization effort. Of particular interest is the grace period which was mentioned earlier. At present in the United States one has the opportunity to swear behind any publication that takes place in the year immediately before the filing of a patent application. If a researcher publishes his or her work and then six months later decides to file a patent application, his or her own publication would not be a bar to obtaining a patent in the United States.

Furthermore, the publications of others within a year of the filing date of the application also would not be a bar in the United States if the inventor can swear to a date of invention earlier than the date of the publication.

While a grace period is well-known in the United States, it is not found in the patent laws of many other countries. Researchers or inventors in the United States who publish before filing, give up their patent rights in much of the rest of the world as their own publications will be cited against them in their attempt to obtain foreign patents. What the draft treaty now contains is a provision which will provide a grace period for the persons who publish their works prior to filing patent applications.

The grace period provision now under consideration in the draft treaty gives persons who publish their inventions prior to the time a patent application is filed, rights only over the publication by the inventor or by another who obtained information regarding the invention either directly or indirectly from the inventor. It does not given an inventor any protection against the independent activity and publication by another prior to the filing of the inventor's application. The grace period which is provided in the draft treaty is a grace period on which the prudent inventor should not ordinarily rely. However, the provision will be available to excuse the uninformed individuals that unfortunately publish their inventions prior to the time their patent applications are filed from the adverse effect of their own publications.

Early Publication of a Patent Application: Article 15

A third provision that is often held by many of the other countries to the negotiations to be a necessary element to accompany first-to-file and the grace period is the provision calling for publication of the patent application 18 months after the application is filed. In recent negotiations, the United States has attempted, without much success, to have this provision be optional with any country. In the most recent meeting, the United States proposed that a country could optionally publish by 24 months. This would permit the United States to rely on its patents as a publication for most of the applications. The concept of publication optionally at 24 months was accepted by others at least to the extent that it will be included as an option in the text which will go forward to the diplomatic conference.

Advocates of a mandatory early publication of patent applications for the United States argue that this would give the U.S. public the information in foreign origin applications sooner and such information would be published in English. It is their belief that at present only large corporations with extensive information networks have the resources to obtain and translate all the 18-month publications from around the world. It would also give the U.S. public earlier information about the earlier notice of some U.S.-origin applications. Opponents of a mandatory early publication requirement argue that an inventor should not be faced with a publication of his application if patent protection is not obtainable. If an adverse indication regarding patentability was received early enough in the process, the applicant could withdraw the application before it is published and preserve any trade secrets. However, such an early and definite indication may not always be possible even with the 18-month average pendency of applications in the United States unless the optional 24-month publication regime would be available.

OTHER SIGNIFICANT PROVISIONS

Reversal of Burden of Proof for Patented Processes: Article 24

A draft treaty provision provides for the reversal of the burden of proof under certain circumstances in regard to the products of allegedly infringed patented processes. The criteria for the reversal of the burden is still under discussion. Some of the countries wish to limit the availability of the reversal to situations where the product is new whereas others including the United States are seeking to have other criteria. The developing countries prefer to have no provision on the matter.

RECENT LIMITATIONS BY THE DEVELOPING COUNTRIES

While most of the discussions that have taken place in earlier meetings involved North/North discussions, *i.e.*, discussions among the developed countries, this changed dramatically in the [June 1990] session. In that meeting some 25 developing countries introduced a series of proposals into the discussions. One of the proposals of the developing countries permits numerous exceptions to the patenting of all technologies as now called for by Article 10 Alternative A of the draft treaty. The developing countries proposal essentially permits any country to patent or not patent any technology, as it wishes. Other developing country proposals call for no patent term requirement, no obligation regarding the reversal of the burden of proof for certain infringement proceedings and a weak provision regarding rights conferred by a patent. Several new topics have also been proposed by the developing countries, but have not as yet been discussed. One proposal obliges the rights holder to make a "best mode" disclosure, to work the invention and "in respect of license contracts and contracts assigning patents, to refrain from engaging in abusive, restrictive or anticompetitive practices adversely affecting the transfer of technology." Another proposal ensures the compliance of the rights holder with these obligations by authorizing any country to take appropriate measures including the grant of non-voluntary licenses and the revocation or forfeiture of the patent.

THE GATT EFFORT

The new round of trade talks under the GATT began in 1986 and are scheduled to be concluded in December 1990. . . .

Among the patent topics proposed by the United States and others and under discussion in the GATT [TRIPS] talks, are patentable subject matter, a minimum patent term, minimum rights conferred by patents, and enforcement of those rights. An obligation to have a first-to-file patent system has also been called for by others. The developing countries have also introduced proposals in the GATT discussions similar to those they introduced in WIPO setting forth obligations of patent holders and authorizing countries to take remedial measures to ensure compliance with those obligations.

THE IMPACT OF GATT ON WIPO EFFORTS

While the various countries in the patent law harmonization discussions are each attempting to preserve as much of their [sic] existing patent law as possible, the final decisions which will be taken on some of the patent law harmonization topics may depend on the results of the discussion of like topics in the new round of [GATT] trade talks . . . A final determination by the GATT negotiations is expected by December 7, 1990. That determination will undoubtedly heavily influence the WIPO results for the overlapping patent topics. If the GATT successfully concludes the present round of talks and intellectual property and patents is part of the results, those results will dictate the nature of the related provisions in the WIPO draft treaty.

FUTURE WIPO EFFORTS

In a WIPO committee of experts meeting from October 29 to November 9, 1990, Articles 18 to 37 of the draft treaty will be discussed. These discussions will include most of the developing countries proposals. From these discussions and the discussions which took place in June on Articles 1 to 17, WIPO will develop a basic proposal for the diplomatic conference to consider. The basic proposal will contain alternatives for a number of the more contentious topics. The Government of the Netherlands has extended an invitation to host the diplomatic conference and the diplomatic conference will be held in The Hague from June 3 to 28, 1991. Fortunately, this is after the conclusion of the GATT talks.

OUTLOOK

What is the outlook for the United States? Conclusion of a GATT agreement which includes intellectual property and patents in particular is possible and it will dictate some of the patent provisions of a patent law harmonization treaty. The United States is being faced with an ever-increasingly more powerful and united Europe and a somewhat more strident and organized group of developing countries. The United States must carefully consider the value of patent law harmonization, now or in the very near future, not only for our rights holders but also for the future technological, economic and industrial well-being of this country. Clearly, harmonization of the patent laws of the world could serve the interests of the United States and clearly, some sort of patent law harmonization treaty is possible. What is not clear is what has to be in the final treaty in order to obtain sufficient support in the United States for adherence to the treaty and the passage of the necessary implementing legislation. What we hope to achieve in the treaty as concluded are provisions which on balance will be acceptable to most U.S. interests.

. . . .

INTERVENTION OF H.F. MANBECK
(HEAD, UNITED STATES DELEGATION)
Records of the First Part of the Diplomatic Conference for the Conclusion of a Treaty Supplementing The Paris Convention as Far as Patents Are Concerned, Nineteenth Meeting, Main Committee I, The Hague (June 19, 1991)

Mr. MANBECK (United States of America) . . . expressed the hope that all present understood and believed that the United States would like to see the development of a successful harmonization treaty which would simplify and expedite the obtaining of patent protection around the world and strengthen the protection once granted. During the series of meetings of the Committee of Experts that preceded the Diplomatic Conference, a draft treaty evolved that required changes in the laws of all countries in the interests of harmonization, yet allowed countries to optionally maintain certain aspects of their existing national or regional patent laws. The United States was being asked to make a number of changes in its laws. The changes included, apart from first-to-file, mandatory publication of applications, a patent term measured from the filing date, the right to prevent importation of patented products, elimination of the *Hilmer* rule concerning the effective date of foreign-origin United States patents, to mention a few. It was that draft treaty that had been considered by the various interest groups in the United States and supported by some and objected to by others. Some of the support had been conditioned on the inclusion of certain features, as had been heard from some United States interest groups, and some of the objections were limited to certain provisions, namely, of course, first-to-file.

What now faced the United States negotiators during the interval between the sessions of the Diplomatic Conference was the task of convincing its various interest groups and the United States Congress that the present package was still of overall benefit to the United States' interests. That would be difficult to do because the text that had evolved during the first session of the Diplomatic Conference represented a shift away from United States interests.

He stated that his Delegation understood the disappointment of many participants regarding its request to amend Article 9 in order to maximize its chances of participation in the final version of the treaty. It had heard them and understood that they wanted it to reconsider its position and to seek a consensus that would allow it to move to a first-to-file system. He hoped they would understand when he told them that, based on the direction of negotiations during those past three weeks, the interested circles in the United States might never get to the point of approving first-to-file because they might well lose interest and enthusiasm while evaluating the many changes the Treaty would presently require in the law of the United States of America, coupled with the loss of the strengthening improvements sought by the Delegation of the United States of America in the basic proposal. If the United States had to make major changes in its law, and obtain no improvements in the laws of others, it was not realistic to think that a treaty along such lines could be approved in the United States.

He turned then to some of the specific problems that had been created for the United States at the Conference. First, it would be particularly difficult for its various interest groups to understand and agree to a provision in the treaty which would require the United States to consider oral disclosures anywhere in the world as prior art. He did not believe his Delegation could explain satisfactorily to its Congress that it would be required to issue patents on inventions which differed only in obvious details from the disclosures contained in earlier-filed United States patent applications—imposing confusion on the U.S. public in the name of reducing so-called secret prior art. It would be precluded from its present practice of always including the inventor's name on patent documents. It would be required to accept changes in its claim practice regarding multiple dependent claims even though no one at the Conference could cite a compelling example of the need to have that type of practice.

Not only was the United States being asked to make those changes to its law, but it was now facing the possibility that a number of improvements it had sought in the protection of inventions in other countries would not be realized. One of the major improvements it thought the Treaty would provide was an effective Article regarding the time limits for promptly completing examination. Although that Article had not been deleted, it noted that a majority of the government delegations present spoke against it. Without some discipline on time limits, there would be no guarantee in the Treaty of obtaining a meaningful term of patent protection. Likewise, the requirement to provide applicants with the ability to file by referring to earlier applications had been made optional. Its interested circles would not like that. The elimination of self-collision seemed not to be achievable based on the discussion on that topic. His Delegation simply did not understand why. Prior user rights were also a difficult subject, new to it, and as to which it trusted a suitable compromise would be achieved.

It was his hope that in the interval between the sessions careful consideration would be given to accommodating the interests of all countries, and particularly those of the United States, so that a significant number of countries, such as his, that would be required to make fundamental changes to their law. would have sufficient reasons to conclude that, overall, the Treaty would be beneficial and warranted adherence. His Delegation would work to satisfy the needs of other delegations and hoped that it could do so, but it would certainly not be successful unless others could likewise agree to satisfy its needs. . . .

[B]   The New WIPO Patent Law Treaty [PLT] and Substantive Patent Law Treaty [SPLT]

Unwilling to admit failure, and after the successful conclusion of TRIPS, WIPO subsequently revived the Patent Law Treaty talks with scope limited to the harmonization of procedures and formalities of patent applications. Those negotiations led to the successful completion at a diplomatic conference on June 2, 2000, of a new Patent Law Treaty ("PLT") that was signed by forty-three states and regional patent offices, including the United States and the EPO. The PLT harmonization provisions agreed to at the Diplomatic Conference were concerned solely with the form of the application since the United States maintained that it was not in a position to discuss further substantive patent law in any form whatsoever. Recently, however, the U.S. has shifted its position on discussing substantive international harmonization of patent law—even to include ultimately discussing what is now called the "first-inventor-to-file" principle in exchange for the adoption of a grace period in Europe once again. The next reading indicates the current scope of those discussions. The PLT will be treated at greater length in Chapter 6 in the context of the multinational acquisition of industrial property rights.

SUGGESTIONS FOR THE FURTHER DEVELOPMENT OF INTERNATIONAL PATENT LAW
WIPO Standing Committee on the Law of Patents
Fourth Session, Geneva, November 6–10, 2000
WIPO Document No. SCP/4/2 September 25, 2000

I. *Introduction*

During the 1998-1999 biennium, the Standing Committee on the Law of Patents (SCP) devoted its time to the negotiation and finalization of the Patent Law Treaty (PLT), which was adopted at the Diplomatic Conference for the Adoption of the PLT, held in Geneva from May 11 to June 2, 2000. Concerning the future work of the SCP, during its earlier sessions as well as at the PLT Diplomatic Conference, a considerable number of delegations and representatives have expressed their wish to consider issues related to further harmonization of substantive requirements of patent law after the conclusion of the PLT. The present document contains suggestions for issues related to further harmonization of patent laws for consideration by the SCP at its fourth session (the first time the SCP will meet during the 2000-2001 biennium), and at its future sessions.

II. *Issues related to further harmonization for consideration by the SCP*

A number of delegations and representatives had expressed the position . . . that discussions concerning further harmonization, in particular harmonization of substantive issues of patent law, should be resumed as soon as possible after the conclusion of the Diplomatic Conference. In this context, it may be noted that, at its third meeting held on May 4 and 5, 2000, the Industry Advisory Commission of WIPO adopted a Resolution calling for "work, in the medium term, on a treaty on the harmonization of substantive patent law, with a view to facilitating greater mutual recognition of search and examination results by patent offices." In addition, the Policy Advisory Commission of WIPO made several recommendations at its meeting of June 15, 2000, among which one reads as follows: "that efforts should be made towards further substantive harmonization in the field of industrial property law, in particular, patent law."

It should be noted that the Patent Cooperation Treaty (PCT), which has established a system for the filing of international patent applications having the same effect as national applications filed in each of the PCT Contracting States designated in the international application, contains a number of principles of substantive patent law applicable to the international phase provided under the PCT. However, it may also be noted that PCT Article 27(5) allows a Contracting State to apply any substantive conditions of patentability as it desires during the national phase.

In response to international calls for harmonization of national and regional patent laws, negotiations had started, as early as 1985, on a draft Treaty Supplementing the Paris Convention as far as Patents are Concerned (hereafter referred to as "draft Patent Harmonization Treaty 1991"), which was discussed at the first part of a Diplomatic Conference in 1991, but never concluded. The draft Patent Harmonization Treaty of 1991 included substantive as well as formal aspects of patent law. Some of its provisions, for instance those on patentable subject matter, rights conferred, term of protection and reversal of burden of proof for process patents, were incorporated into the Agreement on Trade-Related Aspects of Intellectual Property Rights (TRIPS Agreement), concluded in 1994. Nevertheless, a number of issues in respect of national and regional patent law have neither been addressed by the TRIPS Agreement, nor by any other worldwide international treaty on patent law, in particular not by the recently adopted PLT, which covers only patent formalities. . . .

The need for further patent harmonization beyond the PLT arises mainly from the fact that the costs of obtaining broad patent protection on an international level have become extremely high. The objective of further harmonization should therefore be to lower costs. This goal can, however, only be envisaged if a number of basic legal principles underlying the grant of patents are harmonized.

In view of the present situation and the objective mentioned above, the International Bureau suggests that at least the following basic issues underlying the grant of patents, which are of particular importance to the further development of the international patent system, could be included in the discussions of the SCP: the definitions of prior art, novelty, inventive step (non-obviousness) and industrial applicability (utility); sufficiency of disclosure; and the structure and interpretation of claims.

In order to facilitate discussions of the SCP concerning the desirability and feasibility of further harmonizing patent law, each of the six mentioned issues are described below by (1) explaining the basic issue, [and] (2) giving examples of the present status of laws and practices between different systems showing the existence of, or need for further, harmonization[]. . . .

A. *Prior art*

The basic issue. Prior art is generally understood to constitute the body of knowledge which was available to the public before the filing date or, if priority is claimed, before the priority date, of a patent application. Identifying the relevant prior art is one of the cornerstones of patent examination, since such prior art will be evaluated during examination to determine the patentability of the invention concerned. It is by comparing the invention for which protection is sought with the prior art that novelty and inventive step (non-obviousness) of the invention are established. Furthermore, prior art will, after the grant of a patent, be determining in order to evaluate the validity or invalidity of the patent.

Some of the issues to be considered in the context of prior art include, in particular, notions such as "availability to the public," "person skilled in the art," and "means of making available to the public." Further items to be considered are, in particular, issues such as non-prejudicial disclosures, the grace period, or the question of applications filed earlier than, but published after, the date of filing of the application concerned.

Status of harmonization. The PCT states in Rules 33.1 and 64 what the relevant prior art for the purposes of the international search and international preliminary examination under PCT Articles 15(2) and 33(2) and (3) shall consist of. However, the definition of the term "prior art," as well as its use in patent practice, still varies widely in different patent laws. Such divergences do, obviously, have different consequences with regard to the examination of patent applications in different countries, which may, ultimately, lead to the grant of a patent in certain countries, while in others, for the same invention, no patent will be granted, or the patent may be invalidated after grant. The following examples may illustrate some of the existing differences:

(a) In certain countries, prior art is constituted by everything that has been made available to the public anywhere in the world by any means before the filing or priority date of the application. On the other hand, in other countries, non-written disclosures, such as oral disclosures, or use outside their jurisdiction, do not form part of the prior art, and thus do not constitute a bar to patentability.

(b) While certain patent systems require a concrete disclosure for complying with the standard of "availability to the public," others provide that the theoretical possibility of having access to the information is sufficient.

(c) The law of certain countries provides for a general grace period, during which the invention may be disclosed without its patentability being affected, while other countries provide only for a grace period limited to certain specific cases. Another category of countries provides only for non-prejudicial disclosures in the cases of certain international exhibitions and evident abuse in respect of the applicant. In this context, it may be mentioned that Article 11 of the Paris Convention for the Protection of Industrial Property (Paris Convention) requires the countries of the Paris Union to grant temporary protection to inventions shown at certain international exhibitions.

(d) Applications, which have been filed before, but were published only after, the filing of the application under consideration, are considered in a different way in different countries as far as prior art is concerned. . . .

B. *Novelty*

The basic issue. The requirement of novelty is one of the essential and universally recognized conditions of patentability. According to this principle, an invention shall be considered to be new if it is not comprised in the prior art. Novelty therefore results from the comparison between the existing prior art at the date of filing (or the date of priority) and the claimed invention. The underlying reason for the requirement of novelty is that nothing should be withdrawn from public use that already belongs to the public domain.

Status of harmonization. For the purposes of PCT international preliminary examination (but not necessarily of the national phase), the novelty requirement is contained in Article 33(2) of the PCT, which states that an invention shall be considered novel if it is not anticipated by the prior art as defined in the Regulations. For the purposes of novelty, the relevant description of prior art is contained in PCT Rule 64. This shows how closely the novelty requirement is linked to the notion of prior art, since anything which forms part of the prior art would, in principle, destroy the novelty of the invention. In light of the important divergences identified in the definition and application of the term "prior art" as described above, it is evident that the requirement of novelty is also defined and applied in different ways throughout the world.

Besides this close link to the prior art, there are further issues, which are closely related to the discussion on novelty: for instance, which kind of use should destroy the novelty of an invention. Such divergences may lead to the recognition of the novelty of the invention in certain countries, but not in others. The following examples may illustrate some of the existing differences:

(a) In principle, all of the differences mentioned above, in respect of the definition of prior art have a bearing on novelty, i.e., the definition of prior art itself, the requirements relating to the disclosure of the invention, the existence and nature of a grace period, if any, etc.

(b) Public use of the invention anywhere in the world destroys novelty in certain patent systems, while in others, this consequence depends on the place of use. According to certain laws, even non-public use may be prejudicial to novelty, while in others, non-public use could never lead to the destruction of novelty. . . .

C. *Inventive step (non-obviousness)*

The basic issue. The term inventive step (or inventive activity), called non-obviousness in some countries, is, like novelty, one of the fundamental requirements of patentability. It is, in principle, widely recognized throughout different patent systems. An invention is considered to involve an inventive step or to be non-obvious if, compared to the prior art, it is not obvious to a person skilled in the art. Thus, while the criteria of novelty is fulfilled as soon as there is any kind of difference between the claimed invention and the prior art, inventive step is only found if there is a certain qualitative difference between the prior art and the invention. This may not be the case if the claimed invention would, at the date of filing or of priority, have been obvious for a person skilled in the art.

In a similar way as it is the case with regard to novelty, inventive step or non-obviousness is examined in comparison to the existing prior art at the date of filing or of priority of the application in question. Therefore, any difference between patent systems with regard to the definition of prior art will influence the result of any examination of inventive step or non-obviousness. Beyond this rather obvious conclusion, however, there are further divergences in the application of that term, the most important of which are summarized below.

Status of harmonization. For the purposes of PCT international preliminary examination (but not necessarily of the national phase), the inventive step requirement is contained in Article 33(3) of the PCT, which states that an invention shall be considered to involve an inventive step if, having regard to the prior art as defined in the Regulations, it is not, at the prescribed relevant date, obvious to a person skilled in the art. The relevant description of prior art is contained in PCT Rule 64. Nevertheless, as stated above, the examination of inventive step varies considerably in different systems depending on how prior art is defined. Some specific differences are outlined below:

(a) Not only the definition of the term inventive step as such, but also its practical application vary considerably. For example, certain systems apply the so-called "problem and solution" approach, comprising (1) the determination of the closest prior art, (2) the establishment of the technical problem to be solved, and (3) establishing whether, considering the technical problem and the closest prior art, the invention would be obvious to the person skilled in the art. Other systems have developed different methods for the examination of inventive activity.

(b) The notion of a person skilled in the art is not defined in the same way in all patent systems: sometimes, that term means a person with thorough knowledge of the relevant technical field (without necessarily being a specialist), while in other cases, the person skilled in the art may be close to a layman.

(c) While certain systems consider the contents of previously filed applications to destroy novelty and inventive step of a later filed application, others consider these contents only in respect of novelty, but not when assessing the requirement of inventive step.

(d) In certain systems, for the determination of inventive step, different items of prior art may be combined together, if such combination would have been obvious to the person skilled in the art.

D. *Industrial applicability (utility)*

The basic issue. "Industrial applicability" or "utility" in certain countries is the third widely recognized requirement of patentability. Its objective is to exclude from patentability inventions, which have no utility in any field of industry, which do not achieve the objective, claimed by the invention (e.g., *perpetuum mobile*) or which may only be used for private purposes.

Status of harmonization. For the purposes of PCT international preliminary examination (but not necessarily of the national phase), the requirement of "industrial applicability" is contained in PCT Article 33(4), which states that an invention shall be considered industrially applicable if, according to its nature, it can be made or used in any kind of industry. The said provision further states that the term "industry" is to be understood in its broadest sense, as in the Paris Convention. In addition, it may be mentioned that certain systems use the term "utility" rather than "industrial applicability." However, these terms do not have exactly the same meaning:

(a) In those systems which use the term "industrial applicability," it means in general that the invention must be able to be used in any kind of industry, whereby the term "industry" has to be understood in a broad sense, including agriculture.

(b) The term "utility," on the other hand, is a somewhat more complex notion, according to which it may be examined, in particular, whether an invention is able to do something, whether it works to solve the problem it is supposed to solve, and whether it has some social benefit.

E. *Sufficiency of disclosure*

The basic issue. The disclosure of the invention to the public is considered to be the counterpart for receiving the exclusive right conferred by a patent. The disclosure allows the public to know the most recent technical developments and to freely use the technical teaching after the expiration of the patent (or if the patent is not granted). Adequate disclosure is therefore an important obligation of the applicant.

In principle, where the invention is not, or is not sufficiently, disclosed, no patent may be granted, or a granted patent may be invalidated. As a general principle, and notwithstanding the further explanations . . . below, an invention is disclosed if it can be carried out by a person skilled in the art as fully claimed based on the patent specification, without need for any additional inventiveness. Furthermore, the disclosure must be such that it shows the way to safely and repeatedly achieve the claimed result. Thus, a causal link between the claimed elements and the alleged technical result must exist.

The disclosure does not need to be in the description or in the claims only, but may result from the whole patent specification, and in some cases also from teachings in the prior art. But what needs to be disclosed is the invention, and the invention is defined by the claims. This leads, at least in many legal systems, to the conclusion that the claims must be supported by the description.

One particular case related to the disclosure of the invention is the issue of broad claims. in certain cases, the claims are drafted so broadly that the invention cannot, even by using other parts of the specification, such as the description or the drawings, be carried out by the person skilled in the art. This occurs more frequently in particular fields, for example, chemistry and biotechnology. Patents may be invalidated, or at least partly invalidated, if the breadth of the claims exceeds the disclosure in the specification.

Status of harmonization Article 5 and Rule 5.1(a) of the PCT state the following:

Article 5: The Description

The description shall disclose the invention in a manner sufficiently clear and complete for the invention to be carried out by a person skilled in the art.

Rule 5: The Description

5.1 *Manner of the Description*

(a) The description shall first state the title of the invention as appearing in the request and shall:

(i) specify the technical field to which the invention relates;

(ii) indicate the background art which, as far as known to the applicant, can be regarded as useful for the understanding, searching and examination of the invention, and, preferably, cite the documents reflecting such art;

(iii) disclose the invention, as claimed, in such terms that the technical problem (even if not expressly stated as such) and its solution can be understood, and state the advantageous effects, if any, of the invention with reference to the background art;

(iv) briefly describe the figures in the drawings, if any;

(v) set forth at least the best mode contemplated by the applicant for carrying out the invention claimed; this shall be done in terms of examples, where appropriate, and with reference to the drawings, if any; where the national law of the designated State does not require the description of the best mode but is satisfied with the description of any mode (whether it is the best contemplated or not), failure to describe the best mode contemplated shall have no effect in that State;

(vi) indicate explicitly, when it is not obvious from the description or nature of the invention, the way in which the invention is capable of exploitation in industry and the way in which it can be made and used, or, if it can only be used, the way in which it can be used; the term "industry" is to be understood in its broadest sense as in the Paris Convention for the Protection of Industrial Property.

The main divergence in the definition and application of the disclosure requirement is that certain patent systems request a disclosure allowing a person skilled in the art to carry out the invention, while other systems require the application to disclose the best mode known to the inventor to carry out the invention.

F. Drafting and interpretation of claims

The basic issue. The claims define the invention, and thus the scope of protection of the patent. They are therefore the heart of the patent. This is true in particular after the grant of the patent, since others may not commercially use what is covered by the claims, but may use any other information contained in the specification. It is therefore particularly important that claims contain all the important features of the claimed invention. The claims form the basis for the examination as to the patentability of the invention. In addition, they may be affected by partial renunciation or invalidity of the patent, and they are relevant for the question of unity of invention. They also play a role when defining the contents of two inventions in the case of dependency or priority contests under the first to invent system, and when assessing the identity of inventions in the framework of the prohibition of double patenting.

When talking about claims, there are two different aspects to take into consideration: firstly, the drafting of the claims, and secondly the interpretation of the claims.

Status of harmonization. Article 6 of the PCT states the following:

Article 6: The Claims

The claim or claims shall define the matter for which protection is sought. Claims shall be clear and concise. They shall be fully supported by the description.

In addition, PCT Rule 6 contains, in particular, indications on the manner of claiming, on the numbering of claims, as well as further details. In the context of claims, it may be mentioned that PCT Rule 13 deals with the issue of unity of invention.

Nevertheless, both the drafting and the interpretation of claims diverge significantly in different legal systems, which may lead to different scopes of protection for the same invention, and to different results in the case of invalidity determinations. Some of these differences are described below.

Drafting of claims

(a) Certain systems require that only the *technical* features of the invention be contained in the claims, but not other features, such as economical or other elements. This is not the case for all patent systems. It has to be noted, however, that not all systems require an invention to have a technical character.

(b) While certain patent systems require a two-part form of the claims (the first part containing the designation of the subject matter belonging to the prior art, the second part being the characterizing part indicating the new technical features for which protection is claimed), other systems do not require this kind of structure, so that the prior art basis does not always appear in the claims.

(c) Certain patent laws allow for a plurality of closely related independent claims reflecting a single inventive concept to be contained in the same application ("unity of invention"), while according to other laws, the respective provisions are applied in a very narrow manner.

(d) While certain legal systems allow for different categories of claims, such as for instance product, process or apparatus claim, to be included in the same application, other patent systems have restrictions in this respect.

(e) Certain patent systems provide for restrictions on the dependency of sub-claims, which lead to a high number of dependent claims and, in certain offices, to high costs due to additional fees to be paid for each claim in excess of a certain number.

(f) Certain systems allow the lack of support of the claims by the description to be a ground for rejection or invalidation of the patent.

Interpretation of claims

(a) In most patent systems, the literal text of the claims forms the basis for the determination of the scope of protection of the patent. However, while certain systems do not allow an interpretation of the claims to go much beyond their wording, others have developed a broad way of interpreting the claims.

(b) In certain systems the claims have to be interpreted in an objective manner, while in others, what the inventor subjectively had intended to say is taken into consideration.

(c) In certain patent systems, only the description and the drawings may be used in order to interpret the claims. In other systems, further—or additional— means of interpreting the claims may be allowed.

(d) While certain legal systems provide that equivalents are covered by the claims, other legal systems do not provide for equivalents. In many systems, the doctrine of equivalents has been developed by case law, and is not to be found in statutory law. Systems vary widely as to the scope of equivalents applied.

(e) The possibilities to amend the claims during examination, as well as after the grant of the patent, vary considerably in different systems.

IV. *Conclusion*

In view of the above, the SCP is invited to note and consider the suggested issues related to the further development of international patent law. The SCP is invited, in particular, to express its guidance to the International Bureau as to whether and to what extent the mentioned issues should be included in the future work of the SCP.

———————

NOTES AND QUESTIONS

(1) **The "Balanced Package": First-to-File and Grace Period.** Part of the "balanced package" sought by the United States in exchange for abandoning its first-to-invent system was a worldwide grace period. This initiative was vigorously supported by inventor communities in many countries, including Germany. Germany had a grace period in its patent law until the entry into force of the Strasbourg Unification Convention. *See* Heinz Bardehle, *The WIPO Harmonization Treaty and the Grace Period*, 30 IND. PROP. 372 (1991). In June, 1999, the Intergovernmental Conference of the members of the EPO began explorations of the possibility of instituting a grace period in Europe. A summary of those discussions and arguments (both pro and con) can be found at www.epo.co.at/news/headlns/2000_07_25_e.htm.

(2) **Bilateral Measures.** In January 1994, the U.S. Secretary of Commerce announced that negotiations toward substantive harmonization of patent law had collapsed, and the U.S. Commissioner of Patents announced that the USPTO had reached an agreement with the Japanese Patent Office

to support eighteen-month publication of patent applications in the United States in exchange for removal of post-grant opposition proceedings in Japan and permission to file applications in the JPO in English. Both announcements were made on the same day. Publication of most U.S. patent applications at eighteen months from filing became part of U.S. law in 1999. *See* 35 U.S.C. § 122(b).

(3) **Success for Developed Countries in TRIPS.** While the June 1990 revolt by twenty-five developing countries, referenced in Commissioner Manbeck's intervention, triggered the U.S. response, the primary reason for the failure of the PLT negotiations in 1991 was the inability of the United States to abandon its first-to-invent system. Two years later, the United States got the real prize that it wanted from the developing countries in the form of Article 27 of the TRIPS Agreement which states that "patents shall be available for any inventions, whether products or processes, in all fields of technology, provided that they are new, involve an inventive step and are capable of industrial application. Subject to paragraph 4 of Article 65, paragraph 8 of Article 70 and paragraph 3 of this Article, patents shall be available and patent rights enjoyable without discrimination as to the place of invention, the field of technology and whether products are imported or locally produced." The history of TRIPS as set forth in the *Canada-Pharmaceuticals* decision excerpted in the following section refers to those negotiations.

(4) **Prior Art Effect of Prior Applications.** Article 11(3) of the Patent Cooperation Treaty (1970) provides that an international application shall have the effect of a regular national application in each designated state as of its international filing date. The International Federation of Intellectual Property Attorneys [FICPI], which includes patent attorneys from over 70 countries, has noted that under the SCP proposal, published patent applications would constitute prior art with global effect as of their filing dates for the purposes of novelty. At its Executive Committee meeting in September, 2001, the FICPI drafted a resolution in support of the idea that "the prior art effect of a prior application from its filing date should be limited to the jurisdiction in which the prior application was made," and urged "that an international patent application should not have prior art effect as a prior application in a designated state unless the requirements of Articles 22(1) or 39(1)(a) PCT for that designated state have been completed." The resolution acknowledged that the underlying purpose of the "whole contents" treatment of prior applications as prior art in first-to-file patent systems with early publication was to avoid patents being granted to different applicants for the same invention in the same jurisdiction and that "it is economically undesirable to deny the grants of parallel patents for the same invention to different applicants in different jurisdictions." But it added that "before publication of a prior application, a different applicant cannot have gained knowledge of the invention from the prior application." Is the FICPI proposal better international public policy than the SCP proposal? Is it more fair? If so, to whom?

[C]   The TRIPS Agreement

J.H. REICHMAN, UNIVERSAL MINIMUM STANDARDS OF INTELLECTUAL PROPERTY PROTECTION UNDER THE TRIPS COMPONENT OF THE WTO AGREEMENT[*]
29 Int. Lawyer 345, 351–58 (1995)

In the course of multilateral negotiations to revise the Paris Convention that preceded the Uruguay Round, the developed countries sought to elevate its rudimentary standards concerning patentable inventions while the developing countries demanded preferential measures that would have weakened even the preexisting obligations that states owed foreign inventors under their domestic laws. The TRIPS Agreement breaks this impasse and fills many of the gaps in the international patent system with uniform minimum standards of protection that reflect the practices of the developed countries. The TRIPS Agreement also establishes new rules governing permissible limitations on the foreign patentee's scope of protection, and these rules reflect compromise efforts by both sides to balance private and public interests.

1. Normative Structure

The developed countries scored major achievements in elevating and harmonizing minimum standards of patent protection, especially with regard to basic criteria of eligibility and duration, which the Paris Convention had not addressed. The following provisions are noteworthy:

(1) Member states may not exclude any field of technology from patentability as a whole, and they may not discriminate as to the place of invention when rights are granted.

(2) The domestic patent laws (including that of the United States) must provide a uniform term of twenty years of protection from the filing date, such protection must depend on uniform conditions of eligibility, and specified exclusive rights must be granted.

(3) The patentee's bundle of exclusive rights must include the right to supply the market with imports of the patented products.

(4) Logically, the obligation to work patents locally under article 5A of the Paris Convention appears overridden by the right to supply imports, at least in principle.

These achievements build on standards previously established by the Paris Convention, such as the rights of priority, which even WTO members who do not adhere to this Convention must now respect. Single countries may deviate from these universal patent-law standards only to the extent that they benefit from longer or shorter periods of transitional relief, which

---

vary with the beneficiary's status as either a "developing country" or a "least-developed country (LDC)."

For example, developing countries may postpone implementing most of the required standards for a period of at least five years, and even ten years with respect to fields of technology previously excluded under their domestic patent laws. LDCs obtain a reprieve for ten years, while a showing of hardship may qualify them for further delays and other concessions. Nevertheless, a pipeline provision, clarified at the last minute, safeguards existing pharmaceutical and agrochemical patents, which, if otherwise eligible, must obtain at least five years of exclusive marketing rights even in those developing countries that did not previously grant patents in these fields.

Because inventors in developed countries are eventually entitled to obtain and enforce patents everywhere, competitive pressures in developing countries ought to shift from subject matter exclusions of patentability to scope of protection issues bearing on single patents, as occurs in developed countries. Firms in developing countries may thus exploit disclosed information in order to work around the claimed inventions as well as any unpatented know-how they fairly obtain, whether disclosed or not. The lack of international standards defining the doctrine of equivalents affords additional room in which to maneuver. Arguably, states may also apply a broad experimental use exception so long as the rights holders are notified.

The extent to which developing countries will themselves benefit from stronger patent systems—as distinct from compensatory market access—depends in part on the willingness of firms in developed countries either to increase direct investments in developing countries or to license more of their advanced technology to local firms. Moreover, familiarization with the benefits of the patent system could stimulate greater investment in domestic research and development and should encourage the private sector to develop its own intellectual property. Nevertheless, the value of a patent system to developing countries remains controversial, and single developing countries could suffer hardship because of a growing dependence on foreign patents with few countervailing benefits. In such a case, one must acknowledge the achievements of the developing-country negotiators, who have built numerous safeguards and escape hatches into the TRIPS Agreement.

2. Limits of the Patentee's Exclusive Rights.

Article 30 of the TRIPS Agreement declares that states should tolerate only "limited exceptions to the exclusive rights" that article 28 confers. But other articles permit exceptions to the exclusive rights when needed "to protect public health and nutrition, and to promote the public interest in sectors of vital importance" to economic development; to prevent "abuse of intellectual property rights," including the imposition of unreasonable commercial terms; and to counteract unreasonable trade restraints and practices that "adversely affect the international transfer of technology."

Governments may also attempt to invoke language in article 7 that envisions the effective transfer and dissemination of technology among member countries and the maintenance of social and economic welfare as further grounds for regulatory action limiting grants of exclusive rights in appropriate circumstances. These and other articles thus preserve, and may even expand, preexisting grounds for limiting a patentee's exclusive rights under article 5A of the Paris Convention, which some developed-country delegations had hoped to abrogate.

a. Compulsory Licenses in General.

The standard form of remedial action remains compulsory licensing, as it was under article 5A of the Paris Convention, subject to important refinements and conditions that article 31 of the TRIPS Agreement attempts to introduce. In principle, both the public-interest exception and measures to prevent abuse, respectively stipulated in articles 8(1) and 8(2) of the TRIPS Agreement, could justify resort to compulsory licensing. In the past, however, arguments about the meaning of "abuse" engendered considerable controversy. A few developed countries, notably the United States, limited the concept to anticompetitive practices bordering on antitrust violations. Most other countries—and a leading commentator— considered the doctrine of abuse applicable if a patentee fails to work the patent locally in due course or "refuses to grant licenses on reasonable terms and thereby hampers industrial development, or does not supply the national market with sufficient quantities of the patented product, or demands excessive prices for such products."

The TRIPS Agreement merges this broader concept of abuse with the public-interest exception for purposes of compulsory licensing under article 31. However, considerable effort has been made to discredit the nonworking of foreign patents locally as a sufficient basis for triggering such licenses. The TRIPS Agreement then subjects all nonexclusive compulsory licenses sounding in any of the bases established by articles 8(1) and 8(2) to the conditions of article 31.

So long as the grounds for triggering a nonexclusive compulsory license are rooted in the broad notion of "abuse" under article 8(1), say, because of public-interest considerations or because the patentee refused to authorize the desired use "on reasonable commercial terms and conditions," article 31 requires the would-be licensee to seek a negotiated license from the right holder, and failing this, to pay equitable compensation. The victorious licensee could not normally export the products resulting from use of the patent under such a compulsory license. Nor could the licensee exclude the foreign patentee from subsequently working the patent locally—in direct competition with the former—once the latter had rectified any grievances that might have justified issuance of a compulsory license in the first place.

In contrast, a complainant who seeks a compulsory license under article 8(2) to rectify abuse of a patent in the narrow, technical sense familiar from

United States law will remain exempt from both the duty to negotiate and restrictions on exports, provided that some judicial or administrative authority deems the patentee's conduct anticompetitive. In such a case, "the need to correct anticompetitive practices may be taken into account in determining the amount of remuneration" the patentee will receive.

The sole exception to the compulsory licensing scheme available under article 31 is for patented "semi-conductor technology." Article 31(c), as revised at the last minute, now limits the granting of compulsory licenses for "other use" of such technology to instances of "public non commercial use" or to situations in which the compulsory license obviates judicially determined "anticompetitive practices." Whether unpatented semiconductor layout designs subject to integrated circuit laws are also immunized from compulsory licenses for "other use" remains to be clarified, as discussed below. In any event, these provisions make it harder for interested parties in developing countries to start up local semiconductor industries by persuading their governments to seize foreign semiconductor technologies in the name of overriding public interest.

On balance, Article 31 helps to insulate foreign patentees from confiscatory practices that earlier proposals to reform Article 5A of the Paris Convention appeared to tolerate, while it affords the developing countries broad grounds for curbing conduct that seriously compromises their national development strategies. Apart from semiconductor technologies, the requirement that would-be compulsory licensees negotiate seriously with rights holders to obtain exclusive licenses on reasonable terms should increase the pressure on foreign patentees to accommodate pricing and other strategies to local market conditions. This, in turn, should lessen the need for governments to seek compulsory licensing in the first instance.

b. New Dimensions of the Public-Interest Exception.

Beyond traditional notions of "public interest" and "abuse," the TRIPS Agreement introduces new and more expansive concepts whose outer limits have yet to be delineated at the international level. In particular, article 7 stresses the "promotion of technological innovation and . . . the transfer and dissemination of technology . . . in a manner conducive to social and economic welfare." Article 8(1) expands potential public-interest exceptions to sectors other than public health and nutrition that are "of vital importance to . . . socio-economic and technological development," and article 8(2) seeks to ensure "the international transfer of technology." In addition, article 66 underscores the LDCs' "need for flexibility to create a viable technological base," and it must be read in conjunction with the other provisions favoring this group of countries.

All these provisions arm developing and least-developed countries with legal grounds for maintaining a considerable degree of domestic control over intellectual property policies in a post TRIPS environment, including the imposition of compulsory licenses within article 31 of the TRIPS Agreement and article 5A of the Paris Convention. While the meaning of any particular clause must emerge from evolving state practice, taken together they clearly sanction public-interest exceptions of importance to the developing countries while rejecting the more extreme measures these countries proposed during the Paris Revision process. Eventually, specific public-interest safeguards essential to national economic development will have to be worked out on a case-by case basis, in order to deal with particular complaints about the socially harmful effects of technological dependency that are not offset by enhanced market access, and the resulting compromises are likely to give both sides less than they want.

TRIPS AGREEMENT

Article 2(1)

In respect of Parts II, III and IV of this Agreement, Members shall comply with Articles 1-12 and 19 of the Paris Convention (1967).

Article 27(1)

Patentable Subject Matter

[P]atents shall be available and patent rights enjoyable without discrimination as to . . . the field of technology. . . .

Article 28(1)

Rights Conferred

A patent shall confer on its owner the following exclusive rights:

(a) where the subject matter of a patent is a product, to prevent third parties not having the owner's consent from the acts of: making, using, offering for sale, selling, or importing for these purposes that product;

(b) where the subject matter of a patent is a process, to prevent third parties not having the owner's consent from the act of using the process, and from the acts of: using, offering for sale, selling, or importing for these purposes at least the product obtained directly by that process.

Article 30

Exceptions to Rights Conferred

Members may provide limited exceptions to the exclusive rights conferred by a patent, provided that such exceptions do not unreasonably conflict with a normal exploitation of the patent and do not unreasonably prejudice the legitimate interests of the patent owner, taking account of the legitimate interests of third parties.

Article 31

Other Use Without Authorization of the Right Holder

Where the law of a Member allows for other use of the subject matter of a patent without the authorization of the right holder, including use by the government or third parties authorized by the government, the following provisions shall be respected:

(a) authorization of such use shall be considered on its individual merits;

(b) such use may only be permitted if, prior to such use, the proposed user has made efforts to obtain authorization from the right holder on reasonable commercial terms and conditions and that such efforts have not been successful within a reasonable period of time. This requirement may be waived by a Member in the case of a national emergency or other circumstances of extreme urgency or in cases of public non-commercial use. In situations of national emergency or other circumstances of extreme urgency, the right holder shall, nevertheless, be notified as soon as reasonably practicable. In the case of public non-commercial use, where the government or contractor, without making a patent search, knows or has demonstrable grounds to know that a valid patent is or will be used by or for the government, the right holder shall be informed promptly;

(c) the scope and duration of such use shall be limited to the purpose for which it was authorized, and in the case of semi-conductor technology shall only be for public non-commercial use or to remedy a practice determined after judicial or administrative process to be anti-competitive.

(d) such use shall be non-exclusive;

(e) such use shall be non-assignable, except with that part of the enterprise or goodwill which enjoys such use;

(f) any such use shall be authorized predominantly for the supply of the domestic market of the Member authorizing such use;

(g) authorization for such use shall be liable, subject to adequate protection of the legitimate interests of the persons so authorized, to be terminated if and when the circumstances which led to it cease to exist and are unlikely to recur. The competent authority shall have the authority to review, upon motivated request, the continued existence of these circumstances;

(h) the right holder shall be paid adequate remuneration in the circumstances of each case, taking into account the economic value of the authorization;

(i) the legal validity of any decision relating to the authorization of such use shall be subject to judicial review or other independent review by a distinct higher authority in that Member;

(j) any decision relating to the remuneration provided in respect of such use shall be subject to judicial review or other independent review by a distinct higher authority in that Member;

(k) Members are not obliged to apply the conditions set forth in sub-paragraphs (b) and (f) above where such use is permitted to remedy a practice determined after judicial or administrative process to be anti-competitive. The need to correct anti-competitive practices may be taken into account in determining the amount of remuneration in such cases. Competent authorities shall have the authority to refuse termination of authorization if and when the conditions which led to such authorization are likely to recur;

(l) where such use is authorized to permit the exploitation of a patent ("the second patent") which cannot be exploited without infringing another patent ("the first patent"), the following additional conditions shall apply:

(i) the invention claimed in the second patent shall involve an important technical advance of considerable economic significance in relation to the invention claimed in the first patent;

(ii) the owner of the first patent shall be entitled to a cross-licence on reasonable terms to use the invention claimed in the second patent; and

(iii) the use authorized in respect of the first patent shall be non-assignable except with the assignment of the second patent.

Article 32

Revocation/Forfeiture

An opportunity for judicial review of any decision to revoke or forfeit a patent shall be available.

Article 33

Term of Protection

The term of protection available shall not end before the expiration of a period of twenty years counted from the filing date.

———

DECLARATION ON THE TRIPS AGREEMENT AND PUBLIC HEALTH
Adopted on 14 November 2001, WT/MIN(01)/DEC/2 (Nov. 20, 2001)

1. We recognize the gravity of the public health problems afflicting many developing and least-developed countries, especially those resulting from HIV/AIDS, tuberculosis, malaria and other epidemics.

2. We stress the need for the WTO Agreement on Trade-Related Aspects of Intellectual Property Rights (TRIPS Agreement) to be part of the wider national and international action to address these problems.

3. We recognize that intellectual property protection is important for the development of new medicines. We also recognize the concerns about its effects on prices.

4. We agree that the TRIPS Agreement does not and should not prevent members from taking measures to protect public health. Accordingly, while reiterating our commitment to the TRIPS Agreement, we affirm that the Agreement can and should be interpreted and implemented in a manner supportive of WTO members' right to protect public health and, in particular, to promote access to medicines for all. In this connection, we reaffirm the right of WTO members to use, to the full, the provisions in the TRIPS Agreement, which provide flexibility for this purpose.

5. Accordingly and in the light of paragraph 4 above, while maintaining our commitments in the TRIPS Agreement, we recognize that these flexibilities include:

a. In applying the customary rules of interpretation of public international law, each provision of the TRIPS Agreement shall be read in the light of the object and purpose of the Agreement as expressed, in particular, in its objectives and principles.

b. Each member has the right to grant compulsory licences and the freedom to determine the grounds upon which such licences are granted.

c. Each member has the right to determine what constitutes a national emergency or other circumstances of extreme urgency, it being understood that public health crises, including those relating to HIV/AIDS, tuberculosis, malaria and other epidemics, can represent a national emergency or other circumstances of extreme urgency.

d. The effect of the provisions in the TRIPS Agreement that are relevant to the exhaustion of intellectual property rights is to leave each member free to establish its own regime for such exhaustion without challenge, subject to the MFN and national treatment provisions of Articles 3 and 4.

6. We recognize that WTO members with insufficient or no manufacturing capacities in the pharmaceutical sector could face difficulties in making effective use of compulsory licensing under the TRIPS Agreement. We instruct the Council for TRIPS to find an expeditious solution to this problem and to report to the General Council before the end of 2002.

7. We reaffirm the commitment of developed-country members to provide incentives to their enterprises and institutions to promote and encourage technology transfer to least-developed country members pursuant to Article 66.2. We also agree that the least-developed country members will not be obliged, with respect to pharmaceutical products, to implement or apply Sections 5 and 7 of Part II of the TRIPS Agreement or to enforce rights provided for under these Sections until 1 January 2016, without prejudice to the right of least-developed country members to seek other extensions of the transition periods as provided for in Article 66.1 of the TRIPS Agreement. We instruct the Council for TRIPS to take the necessary action to give effect to this pursuant to Article 66.1 of the TRIPS Agreement.

Notes and Questions

(1) **Patent Policy in Developing Countries.** It is sometimes suggested that developing countries benefit directly by strengthening their patent systems. *See* Edmund W. Kitch, *The Patent Policy of Developing Countries*, 13 UCLA Pac. Basin L.J. 166 (1995). There is considerable opposition to this view from some writers in developing countries, such as Argentina, who assert that strong patents lead not to more investment or inventiveness in developing countries but rather to more wealth transfer from the developing to the developed countries. *See, e.g.*, Carlos Maria Correa, *Intellectual Property Rights and Foreign Direct Investment*, (ECOSOC ST/CTC/SER.A/24 1993). A more strident rhetoric, by an academic writer opining that the TRIPS Agreement is "amoral," is found in Michelle McGrath, *The Patent Provisions in TRIPS: Protecting Reasonable Remuneration for Services Rendered—or the Latest Development in Western Colonialism*, 18 Eur. Intell. Prop. Rev. 398 (1996). The terms of the North-South intellectual property debate as posed by the developing nations in the early days of the Uruguay Round were straightforward and simple: "How can the developing nations in the South get the best access to technological innovations made *elsewhere*—that is, in the developed countries of the North?" Intellectual property protection was deemed an issue for the developed world not the developing one. Submissions made by Brazil and India, among others, at the beginning of the Uruguay round reflected the following sentiments:

• rigid IP protection impedes access to latest technological innovations, and therefore restricts the participation of developing countries in international trade;

• "abusive use" of IPRs distorts international trade;

• what is "trade-related" about intellectual property rights is the restrictive and anticompetitive behavior of the owners of intellectual property and not the behavior of commercial interests in developing countries or that of their governments;

• patent systems can have adverse effects in critical sectors such as food production, poverty alleviation, health care and disease prevention, and have a dampening effect on the promotion of R&D in developing countries and in improving their technological capabilities;

• systems for the protection of IPRs are by nature monopolistic and sovereign nations should be free to attune their own systems of intellectual property protection to their own needs and conditions.

(2) **IP and IPRs.** What is the difference in usage between the terms "intellectual property" ("IP") and "intellectual property *rights*" ("IPRs")? In the context of international trade law, the latter term is common. The reverse is true in the international intellectual property community. According to one commentator:

> Characterizing patent protections as a kind of intellectual property "right" was a first step in setting the terms of debate. This characterization is of course not novel; patents, trademarks, and copyrights have long been viewed as intellectual property rights. This is evidenced, in part, by the common reference to intellectual property rights by the acronym "IPR." Nor is the characterization, from a legal standpoint, startling or at all surprising. Lawyers commonly understand that the holders of government-authorized powers have "rights," without attaching any particular moral force to the term. In the debate over international patent policy, however, the use of the term "right" exercised an important influence. As a preliminary matter, it is important to recognize that while "rights" may be commonplace in legal discourse, the allocation or recognition of a right may nonetheless privilege certain actions or relations. Characterizing something as a right tends to immunize it from challenge both in practice and in the realm of ideas. To transgress a right is to "violate" it, to commit a wrong. To define something as a right is to remove it, more or less, from political challenge. Even if it is not considered a "natural" right; in moral terms, a right is supposed to be somewhat inviolate.

> While rights talk may have the general effect in legal discourse of elevating the defined conduct or relationship above politics, that effect was particularly strong in the case of patent policy. The vociferous insistence of industry and the U.S. government assumed a moral character This was an especially notable accomplishment in light of the intangible nature of intellectual property. Additionally, intellectual property is more obviously a creation of the state than other sorts of property. Hence it intuitively enjoys less of a moral right than other property claims. At the practical level, one does not receive a patent until an invention is certified by the state as new, useful, and nonobvious. This makes it unusually clear that the state could choose not to grant the right at all. At the conceptual level, patent rights evaporate after a set period. Governments may grant patents for longer or shorter periods, on conditions, or not at

all. The characterization of an inventor or producer's intellectual property interest as a "right" works to obscure the contingent nature of the patent.

Robert Weissman, *A Long, Strange TRIPS: The Pharmaceutical Industry Drive to Harmonize Global Intellectual Property Rules, and the Remaining WTO Legal Alternatives Available to Third World Countries*, 17 U. PA. J. INT'L ECON. L. 1069, 1086–87 (1996). Is the author correct that the nature of a patent is merely contingent? Does the term "IPRs" frame the debate in a way different than the term "IP" does—particularly with regard to the identity of the owner? Or is this a distinction without a difference? Are "rights" created by statutes? *See generally* R. NOZICK, ANARCHY, STATE AND UTOPIA (1974); Ned Miltenberg, *The Revolutionary Right to a Remedy*, TRIAL 48–52 (March 1988).

(3) **Refocusing TRIPS.** The U.S. position at the start of the Uruguay Round leading to the eventual adoption of the TRIPS Agreement is set forth in a 1987 General Accounting Office report entitled *International Trade: Strengthening Worldwide Protection of Intellectual Property Rights*, GAO/NSIAD-87-65; *see also* OTA, *Disseminating Information: Evolution of a Concept*, 64 ECON. IMPACT 18 (1988). The entire focus of the report is on foreign piracy of U.S. intellectual property. There is no mention of compulsory licensing allowed to member states under Article 5 of the Paris Convention as part of the U.S. agenda. For an interesting discussion of the history of the shift in the U.S. position, see generally MICHAEL P. RYAN, KNOWLEDGE DIPLOMACY (1998).

(4) **How Often are Compulsory Licenses Used?** An excellent survey of compulsory licensing policies and of compulsory licensing provisions worldwide just prior to the enactment of the TRIPS Agreement in 1995 may be found in Gianna Julian-Arnold, *International Compulsory Licensing: The Rationales and the Reality*, 33 IDEA 349 (1993). Rarely are such provisions exercised. It has been noted that, for example, in Australia, there have been only two applications ever for a compulsory license, and both were rejected. *See* THOMAS A. MANDEVILLE, UNDERSTANDING NOVELTY: INFORMATION, TECHNOLOGICAL CHANGE AND THE PATENT SYSTEM 24 (1996).

(5) **Limiting Exclusive Rights.** It has been asserted that Article 30 of TRIPS allows a state to establish working requirements. Would such a course of action be consistent with Article 5 of the Paris Convention as incorporated by Article 3 of TRIPS? What about price controls? Can a developing country use the lever of price controls to achieve what it cannot through compulsory licensing? *See* Weissman, *supra*, at 1111–23; *see also* Richard P. Rozek & Ruth Berkowitz, *The Effects of Patent Protection on the Prices of Pharmaceutical Products—Is Intellectual Property Protection Raising the Drug Bill in Developing Countries?*, 1 J. WORLD INTELL. PROP. 179 (1998); Thomas G. Field, Jr., *Pharmaceuticals and Intellectual Property: Meeting Needs Throughout the World*, 31 IDEA 3 (1990).

(6) **Have the Developing Countries Turned the TRIPS Table?** The recent AIDS epidemic has set the stage for a dramatic coda to a century

of negotiations concerning the right of states to set working requirements for foreign patentees. After six months of failed consultations, on January 8, 2001, the USTR filed a request for a WTO panel to address Brazil's refusal to amend Article 68 of its industrial property law of 1996, contending that the law was inconsistent with Brazil's obligations under Articles 27.1 and 28 of TRIPS. *See* WT/DS199/3 (Jan. 9, 2001). The United States stated:

> The [TRIPS] Agreement prohibits discrimination regarding the availability of patents and the enjoyment of patent rights on the basis of whether products are imported or locally produced. This obligation prohibits Members of the [WTO] from requiring 'local working.' i.e., local production of the patented invention as a condition for enjoying exclusive patent rights. Article 68 of Brazil's 1996 industrial property law . . . , however, imposes a 'local working' requirement which stipulates that a patent shall be subject to compulsory licensing if the subject matter of the patent is not 'worked' in the territory of Brazil. Specifically, a compulsory license shall be granted on a patent if the patented product is not manufactured in Brazil or if the patent process is not used in Brazil. In addition, if a patent owner chooses to exploit the patent through importation rather than 'local working,' then Article 68 will allow others to import either the patented product or the product obtained from the patented process.

Brazil quickly countered with a request at the WTO for consultations with the U.S., charging that Chapter 18 of the U.S. patent law violates the TRIPS agreement. (That chapter requires certain firms with title to U.S. government-funded inventions to manufacture "substantially in the United States" unless the requirement is waived. *See* 35 U.S.C. § 204; WT/DS224/1, Feb. 7, 2001. www.ipo.org/2001/IPcourts/Brazil.pdf). Shortly thereafter, the non-governmental organization "Doctors Without Borders" announced in Mumbai (Bombay) India that it intended to buy anti-AIDS drugs from the Indian company Cipla, Ltd. to distribute without charge in developing countries. On March 13, new U.S. Trade Representative Robert Zoellick was quoted as voicing concern over a potential backlash against the drug industry for aggressively asserting patent rights in the face of the HIV/AIDS crisis. While emphasizing his support for intellectual property, he said, "If [the pharmaceutical companies] don't get ahead of this issue [the HIV/AIDS issue], the hostility that generates could put at risk the whole intellectual property rights system." Paul Blustein, *Getting Out in Front on Trade: New U.S. Trade Representative Adds "Values" to His Globalization Plan*, WASH. POST, March 13, 2001, at E1. The next day, Bristol-Myers-Squibb said that it would not use patent rights to stop generic drug makers from selling low-cost versions of one of its HIV/AIDS drugs in Africa, and that it would sell the drug in Africa at below cost. Two weeks later, on March 29, 2001, Merck & Co. Inc. pledged to Brazil to cut the price of two AIDS-fighting drugs in a bid to prevent Brazil from producing its own versions of the patented drugs.

(7) **Compulsory Licensing and AIDS.** The history of how pharmaceutical companies holding patents on AIDS medicines have dealt with the AIDS crisis in Africa is interesting for what it reveals about the interface between international law and international politics. In 1997, South Africa amended its Medicines and Related Substances Control Act No. 101 of 1965, adding Section 15C as follows:

> The minister may prescribe conditions for the supply of more affordable medicines in certain circumstances so as to protect the health of the public, and in particular may—
>
> (a) notwithstanding anything to the contrary contained in the Patents Act, 1978 (Act No. 57 of 1978), determine that the rights with regard to any medicine under a patent granted in the Republic shall not extend to acts in respect of such medicine which has been put onto the market by the owner of the medicine, or with his or her consent;
>
> (b) prescribe the conditions on which any medicine which is identical in composition, meets the same quality standard and is intended to have the same proprietary name as that of another medicine already registered in the Republic, but which is imported by a person other than the person who is the holder of the registration certificate of the medicine already registered and which originates from any site of manufacture of the original manufacturer as approved by the council in the prescribed manner, may be imported:
>
> (c) prescribe the registration procedure for, as well as the use of, the medicine referred to in paragraph (b).

On October 21, 1998, the United States enacted Public Law 105-277, "An Act Making omnibus consolidated and emergency appropriations for the fiscal year ending September 30, 1999, and for other purposes." Included was the following provision:

> Provided further, That none of the funds appropriated under this heading may be made available or assistance for the central Government of the Republic of South Africa, until the Secretary of State reports in writing to the appropriate committees of the Congress on the steps being taken by the United States Government to work with the Government of the Republic of South Africa to negotiate the repeal, suspension, or termination of section 15(c) of South Africa's Medicines and Related Substances Control Amendment Act No. 90 of 1997.

Subsequently, thirty-nine pharmaceutical companies brought suit in a South African court to have Section 15(c) declared unconstitutional, and in late 2000, GlaxoWellcome sent cease and desist letters to generic drug manufacturers over imports of its patented retrovirals lamivudine and zidovudine into Africa. In January 2001, the Pharmaceutical Research and Manufacturers of America petitioned USTR for listing of South Africa on a Section 301 watch list. *See infra* § 5.02[A] (discussing Section 301).

In February, 2001, Joseph Papovich, the assistant U.S. Trade Representative for intellectual property rights, stated that President George Bush was "not considering a change in the present flexible policy" on compulsory licensing of drugs by AIDS-stricken countries. The February 22, 2001 *New York Times* reported that "the U.S. will not seek sanctions against poor countries overwhelmed by the AIDS epidemic that try to force down the price of patented anti-AIDS drugs by legalizing the importation or manufacture of generic versions. The administration, . . . will not try to punish such countries even if American drug makers complain or American patent laws are being broken—as long as the country adheres to the rules agreed under World Trade Organization treaties."

Six weeks later, in early April 2001, the drug companies withdrew their suit. (Stock prices plummeted the next day.) South Africa allegedly has represented to the companies (and to the United States) that it will comply with its TRIPS obligations. Does Section 15(c) refer only to AIDS drugs? If the law is not amended, is South Africa TRIPS-compliant? By settling the case, have the pharmaceutical companies agreed not to challenge compulsory licensing of other medications, should it occur? Prozac? Viagra? *See Settlement Does Little Harm To Drug Firms; Lawsuit: Dropping South Africa AIDS Case Has More Symbolic Than Practical Weight, But It Could Embolden Other Countries*, L.A. TIMES, Apr. 21, 2001. On April 5, 2001, the African countries of the WTO secured WTO approval to consider the relationship of intellectual property protection and access to medicine at the June 2001 meeting of the TRIPS Council. In response, the United States stated that it is "committed to fighting the HIV/AIDS epidemic, but expressed concern that intellectual property rights protection is seen as a barrier to that effort."

(8) **Article 31(f) and the Article 28 Right to Import.** Article 31(f) of the TRIPS Agreement states that "where the law of a Member allows for other use of the subject matter of a patent without the authorization of the right holder . . . any such use shall be authorized predominantly for the supply of the domestic market of the Member authorizing such use." Article 28 grants the owner the exclusive right of importing. Suppose Burkina-Faso decides that a compulsory license is necessary for a pharmaceutical product, but there is no local licensee capable of supplying the market. Does Article 31(f) allow the state to "authorize" a manufacturer in India to supply Burkina-Faso's domestic market?

(9) **Impact of Doha Ministerial Declaration on TRIPS and Public Health.** According to the United Nations, more than 25 million Africans now have HIV or AIDS. In eight African countries, more than 15 percent of the adult population is now infected with the virus, and the United Nations predicts that one-third of all Africans may eventually be infected. In the context of HIV/AIDS, access to medicines is more than just the cost of drugs. There are six subtypes or "clades" of HIV-2. Retrovirals used in the developed countries have only been tested in HIV-2 subtype B. None have been tested for HIV-1. The health delivery regimen consists of 20 pills

a day which must be taken with meals. Public health officials warn that if the medicines are not taken according to the prescribed regimen, resistance will increase, as has happened with antibiotics. The regimen has serious side effects. The medicines must also be kept refrigerated.

To what extent is the Doha Declaration on TRIPS and Health a political document and to what extent is it a legal one? According to the Director-General of the International Federation of Pharmaceutical Manufacturers Associations, "the final text of the declaration maintains the current legal provisions of TRIPS." Can the United States, after Doha, assert a claim against a country such as South Africa for failure to negotiate with a drug company prior to the grant of a compulsory license? What about parallel imports, the treatment of which was excluded from the TRIPS Agreement by Article 6? Can the United States exert pressure on South Africa, outside of the obligations of the WTO, not to allow parallel imports from India? *See, e.g.*, Frederic M. Abbott, *The TRIPS-Legality Of Measures Taken To Address Public Health Crises: A Synopsis*, 7-SPG WIDENER L. SYMP. J. 71, 77 (2001); R. Scott Rogers, *WTO Weakens IP Protections for Pharmaceuticals, Slightly*, CORP. LEGAL TIMES INT'L 8 (Jan. 2002).

The Doha Round of the WTO is sometimes termed the "Development Round." Is it now "payback time" for the developing nations who thought that they ceded so much on intellectual property during the Uruguay Round? Does it appear that the parties to the new negotiations intend to build *upon* the TRIPS Agreement, or to *undermine* it?

CANADA—PATENT PROTECTION OF PHARMACEUTICAL PRODUCTS
Doc. WT/DS114/R (WTO Dispute Settlement Panel, Mar. 17, 2000)

II. Factual Aspects

[Section 55.2 of Canada's Patent Act excluded from liability for infringement for making, using, or selling a patented product or using a patented process "solely for uses reasonably related to the development and submission of information required under any law of Canada, a province or a country other than Canada that regulates the manufacture, construction, use or sale of any product" or "during the applicable period provided for by the regulations, for the manufacture and storage of articles intended for sale after the date on which the term of the patent expires." It also provided that the Governor in Council "may make regulations for the purposes of subsection (2), but any period provided for by the regulations must terminate immediately preceding the date on which the term of the patent expires."]

The regulatory review procedure [for new drugs] is time consuming. It may take from one to two-and-a-half years to complete. However, prior to this period, a generic manufacturer will have spent from two to four years in the development of its regulatory submission. Thus, the overall time required for a generic manufacturer to develop its submission and to complete the regulatory review process ranges from three to six-and-a-half years. After the development of its regulatory submission, the generic manufacturer will file an Abbreviated New Drug Submission ("ANDS") with Health Canada. The generic manufacturer files an ANDS because, typically, it is relying on comparative studies to a drug product that has proven to be safe and effective. An innovator, on the other hand, would file a New Drug Submission, since it must provide full pre-clinical and clinical data to establish the safety and efficacy of the drug in question. For an innovator, it takes approximately eight to 12 years to develop a drug and receive regulatory approval, which takes place during the 20-year patent term. The resulting period of market exclusivity under the current Canadian Patent Act varies from drug to drug. Estimated averages, at the time that the Act came into force, range from eight to ten years, according to the Pharmaceutical Manufacturers Association of Canada (PMAC), or 12 to 14 years, according to the Canadian Drug Manufacturers Association (CDMA).

. . . .

III. Findings and Recommendations Requested by the Parties

The European Communities and their member States requested the Panel to make the following rulings, findings and recommendations: . . .

That Canada, by allowing manufacturing and stockpiling of pharmaceutical products without the consent of the patent holder during the six months immediately prior to the expiration of the 20-year patent term by virtue of the provisions of Section 55.2(2) and 55.2(3) of the Patent Act together with the Manufacturing and Storage of Patented Medicines Regulations, violated its obligations under Article 28.1 together with Article 33 of the TRIPS Agreement.

That Canada, by treating patent holders in the field of pharmaceutical inventions by virtue of these provisions less favourably than inventions in all other fields of technology, violated its obligations under Article 27.1 of the TRIPS Agreement requiring patents to be available and patent rights enjoyable without discrimination as to the field of technology.

That the provisions of Section 55.2(1) concerning activities related to the development and submission of information required to obtain marketing approval for pharmaceutical products carried out without the consent of the patent holder violated the provisions of Article 28.1 of the TRIPS Agreement.

That Canada, by treating patent holders in the field of pharmaceutical inventions by virtue of these provisions less favourably than inventions in all other fields of technology, violated its obligations under Article 27.1 of the TRIPS Agreement requiring patents to be available and patent rights enjoyable without discrimination as to the field of technology.

That the violations referred to above constituted prima facie nullification or impairment under Article 64.1 of the TRIPS Agreement, Article XXIII of GATT 1994 and Article 3.8 of the DSU.

That the DSB request Canada to bring its domestic legislation into conformity with its obligations under the TRIPS Agreement.

Canada requested the Panel to reject the complaints of the European Communities and their member States on the basis of the following findings:

Section 55.2(1) and 55.2(2) of the Patent Act conform with Canada's obligations under the TRIPS Agreement, because:

(a) Each of these provisions is a "limited exception" to the exclusive rights conferred by a patent within the meaning of Article 30 of the TRIPS Agreement;

(b) Neither of these provisions discriminates, within the meaning of Article 27 of the TRIPS Agreement, as to the field of technology in which any relevant invention occurs or has occurred, because: the prohibition in Article 27.1 against discrimination on the basis of field of technology does not apply to allowable limited exceptions, or, if the Panel were to find Article 27.1 applicable, because: the limited exceptions of Section 55.2(1) and 55.2(2) are not expressly related to any particular field of technology;

(c) Neither of these provisions reduces the minimum term of protection referred to in Article 33 of the TRIPS Agreement to a term that is less than that minimum.

IV. Arguments of the Parties

A. European Communities

. . . .

The European Communities and their member States argued that, by allowing manufacturing and stockpiling of pharmaceutical products under Sections 55.2(2) and (3) of the Patent Act together with the Manufacturing and Storage of Patented Medicines Regulations during the six months immediately prior to the expiration of the 20-year patent term, Canada breached its obligations under Articles 28.1 and 33 of the TRIPS Agreement. The following points were advanced in support of this argument:

* Canadian law allowed all the acts referred to in Article 28.1(a) of the TRIPS Agreement, if a product patent was concerned, and Article 28.1(b) of the Agreement, if a process patent was concerned, with the sole exception

of the act of selling to a distributor or consumer without the consent of the patent owner from six months before the expiry of the 20-year patent term. In other words Canada only provided for 19 years and six months of the minimum patent protection as mandated by Articles 28.1 and 33 of the TRIPS Agreement.

* In practical terms this meant that anybody in Canada was allowed to perform the acts of making, constructing and using of the invention during the last six months of the patent term without the authorization of the patent holder. This possibility was automatic for anybody in Canada, i.e. no particular authorization had to be applied for and eventually granted by a Canadian authority. The faculty was entirely unqualified in terms of the extent and volume of the use and no royalty fees whatsoever had to be paid to the patent holder nor did the latter have any right to be informed of such unauthorized use of his invention. Both product and process patents were subject to this denial of protection.

* To the best of the knowledge of the European Communities and their member States, Canada was the only country in the world—industrialized or developing—which allowed manufacturing and stockpiling of products covered by a patent during the term of such a patent. Canada itself recognized that, at least in the United States and the member States of the European Communities, such a possibility did not exist.

The European Communities and their member States argued that, by treating patent holders in the field of pharmaceutical inventions less favourably than inventions in all other fields of technology, Canada infringed its obligations contained in Article 27.1 of the TRIPS Agreement. The following points were advanced in support of this argument:

* The Canadian patent legislation, which under Section 55.2(2) and 55.2(3) together with the Manufacturing and Storage of Patented Medicines Regulations practically speaking provided only for a 19-year term of patent protection, applied exclusively to product and process patents for inventions in the field of pharmaceutical products. During the legislative process, other fields of technology were not even considered and no draft legislation to extend the scope of these provisions to other or all fields of technology was, according to the information available to the European Communities and their Member States, presently pending in the Canadian legislature. In this context, it was also noteworthy that Section 55.2(2) of the Canadian Patent Act was, taken in isolation, an inoperative provision and created only legal effects through the promulgation of the Manufacturing and Storage of Patented Medicines Regulations. This Regulation was expressly limited to "patented medicines" and could not apply to any other product.

* Thus, the Canadian legislation discriminated against pharmaceutical inventions by treating them less favourably than inventions in all other fields of technology and therefore Canada violated its obligations under Article 27.1 of the TRIPS Agreement.

The European Communities and their member States argued that Section 55.2(1) of the Canadian Patent Act allowed all activities related to the development and submission of information required to obtain marketing approval for pharmaceutical products carried out by a third party without the consent of the patent holder at any time during the patent term, notwithstanding the exclusive rights stipulated in Article 28.1 of the TRIPS Agreement. These activities were completely unlimited in quantity and extent and included the acts of offering for sale and selling, at least insofar as any manufacturer of the patented product or process could invoke this right, if only the final purchaser of the product had the intention to use the product for "[] uses reasonably related to the development and submission of information required under the law of Canada, a province or a country other than Canada that regulates the manufacture, construction, use or sale of any product". Therefore, Section 55.2(1) of the Canadian Patent Act had to be considered to be incompatible with the provisions of Article 28.1(a) and (b) of the TRIPS Agreement. The following points were advanced in support of this argument:

* The permissible activities under Section 55.2(1) of the Canadian Patent Act were not limited in time. In other words, they might be performed without the consent of the right holder at any point in time during the 20-year patent term.

* Section 55.2(1) of the Patent Act took away all the rights a patent granted its owner, i.e. making, constructing, using (this included importing) and selling, and did not stipulate any quantitative limits for these activities. The only limitation set out by the law consisted in the objective of these activities, i.e. they must be "reasonably related to the development and submission of information" required for obtaining marketing approval anywhere in the world.

* The requirements for obtaining marketing approval for pharmaceutical products in industrialized countries were similar and broadly focused on three criteria: safety, quality and efficacy of the product. Thus, the documentation required by the national drug administrations contained information on the composition, manufacture, quality control and stability of the product. This included also in Canada proof that a full production line was viable and could involve full batch testing, which in turn required the production of significant quantities of the product protected by a patent. The non-clinical testing information that was required related to the pharmacological effects of the product in relation to the proposed use in humans and to the toxicological effects of the product on the organism and in different organs. The clinical test data which had to be compiled constituted by far the most important part of the marketing approval activities as far as time, resources and costs were concerned. It was typically subdivided into three phases starting out from tests in small doses administered to a small number of patients (phase I) to the use of the product in wide-ranging comparative studies involving large numbers of patients which could go into tens of thousands for some indications (phases II and III).

* It was also noteworthy that Section 55.2(1) of the Canadian Patent Act did not only allow all the activities mentioned in the text to be carried out by somebody who had himself the intention to use the substances for preparing his application for marketing approval, but allowed such activities as manufacturing, importing and selling for anybody, if only the results of these activities were eventually intended to be used by somebody else for his application to a marketing approval authority in any country of the world. Here it was important to understand that, while research-based pharmaceutical companies did generally produce the active pharmaceutical ingredients in-house, many—in particular small and medium-sized—copy (generic) producers sourced the active ingredients from independent manufacturers domestically or from abroad. The reason for this was linked to the fact that the production of the active ingredients was often highly capital intensive and once the equipment was in place and running, huge quantities could be manufactured by a very small staff in a short period of time.

* The interplay and cumulation of all these possibilities led to a situation that very significant quantities of the products protected by a patent could be manufactured, imported and sold without the consent of the patent holder at any time during the patent term.

* There existed no provisions under the laws of the EC member States which would allow a party to carry out the activities referred to in Section 55.2(1) of the Canadian Patent Act without the consent of the patent owner.

The European Communities and their member States argued that, by allowing all the activities referred to . . . above related to the development and submission of information required to obtain marketing approval for pharmaceutical products and carried out by a third party without the consent of the patent holder at any time during the patent term, Canada treated holders of pharmaceutical patents less favourably than holders of patents in all other fields of technology and thus violated its obligations under Article 27.1 of the TRIPS Agreement. The following points were advanced in support of this argument:

* It was true that Section 55.2(1) of the Canadian Patent Act did not mention expressly pharmaceuticals or medicines, but referred to cases where "Canada, a province or a country other than Canada [] regulates the manufacture, construction, use or sale of any product"; it was in effect only applied to pharmaceutical products. This was not astonishing because the considerations in relation to the formulation and adoption of Bill C-91, of which Section 55.2(1) of the Patent Act formed a pivotal part, were exclusively concerned with the treatment of pharmaceutical products.

* While the text of the law read as if this provision would apply to all fields of technology, it did in practice only apply to pharmaceuticals. This became apparent from the legislative history of this provision, where in the discussions—to the extent that reports were available to the European Communities and their member States—other areas of technology were not even mentioned. The Canadian authorities had confirmed in the formal consultations under the DSU that this provision was applied only to pharmaceuticals. This was particularly interesting in a situation where for

many other categories of products "the development and submission of information [is] required under any law of Canada, a province or a country other than Canada that regulates the manufacture, construction, use or sale of (such) products". The product categories meeting this condition included agricultural chemical products, certain foodstuffs, motor vehicles, aircraft, ships and many more.

* While the manufacture, construction, use or sale of a great plethora of products were, under the laws of Canada, its provinces or any other country, subject to regulations, Section 55.2(1) of the Patent Act did not apply to these other fields of products; in none of these areas did Section 55.2(1) of the Patent Act apply. This was confirmed by Canada in the formal consultations under the DSU.

The European Communities and their member States advanced the following information about the historical developments in Canada as well as a comparison between the situation in Canada before and after the introduction of Bill C-91 and the Manufacturing and Storage of Patented Medicines Regulations in 1993, taking the view that the curtailment of patent rights for pharmaceuticals as pursued by Canada was incompatible with the patent provisions of the TRIPS Agreement independently of whether it was presented as a compulsory licence, as under the pre-C-91 system or as "exceptions" under the C-91 system itself:

* Patent protection in Canada had been in place for many decades and also inventions in the field of pharmaceuticals had been patentable under the ordinary conditions. As early as 1923, Canada modified the patent protection for pharmaceuticals by introducing a regime of compulsory licences for pharmaceuticals. Compulsory licences allowed a third party without the authorization of the owner of the patent to make, use or sell patented pharmaceuticals. The compulsory licence could be granted at any time during the patent term. The patentee was entitled to the payment of royalties by the beneficiary of the compulsory licence.

* Because the granting of the compulsory licences was subject to the requirement that the active ingredients used in the pharmaceutical product be produced in Canada, few compulsory licences were effectively granted at the time, since it was difficult to obtain Canadian-made active ingredients.

* In 1969, the requirement to produce the active ingredient in Canada was dropped having as a consequence that numerous compulsory licences were granted thereafter. The licensing fee amounted generally to 4 per cent of the sales price of the products produced under the compulsory licence, which often covered several patents.

* In 1987, the Canadian Patent Act was further amended by replacing the previous term of protection of 17 years from the time the patent was granted by one of 20 years from the time the patent application was filed. This amendment entered into force in 1989. Under this new regime, compulsory licences continued to be available but were limited in time. Such

compulsory licences could be obtained after the patented product had been on the Canadian market for seven years, if the licensee intended to produce in Canada, or ten years if he intended to import the active ingredient. These amendments had as practical effect that the patent holder was guaranteed at least seven years (ten years if the holder of the compulsory licence did not intend to produce or source locally) of patent protection.

* Canada further modified its patent laws by the Patent Act Amendment Act, 1992 (Bill C-91), which entered into force in February 1993. While inventions in the area of pharmaceuticals were under the pre-C-91 patent regime only patentable as process patents (or so-called 'product-by-process patents'), product patents for pharmaceutical inventions were only introduced by C-91 in 1993. The major modification consisted of the elimination of the existing compulsory licensing system for pharmaceuticals and the introduction of exceptions to the patent rights of the holder of a patent in the area of pharmaceuticals which were at issue in the present case. In order to understand the motivation of the Canadian authorities one had to look at the historic situation in 1991 and 1992 as far as international rulemaking on intellectual property issues to which Canada was a party was concerned.

* In December 1991, the then Director-General of the General Agreement on Tariffs and Trade, Arthur Dunkel, had compiled a Draft Final Act for the conclusion of the Uruguay Round negotiations, which also contained a text of the draft Agreement on Trade-Related Aspects of Intellectual Property Rights (TRIPS).[27] The text of the TRIPS Agreement as contained

---

[27] The EC provided the following short negotiating history of the TRIPS Agreement:

"At the Ministerial Conference which launched the Uruguay Round of Multilateral Trade Negotiations at Punta del Este, Uruguay in September 1986, TRIPS was included into the negotiation agenda as one of the so-called new topics. Multilateral rulemaking in the IPR area was so far dominated by the World Intellectual Property Organisation (WIPO) which administers or co-administers practically all important conventions in this area. There existed at the outset fundamental divergencies between industrialized countries, who wished to achieve a comprehensive coverage of all intellectual property rights and developing countries (LDCs) who wanted to limit work to a Code against trade in counterfeit goods. During the negotiating process the view of those who pursued a comprehensive approach prevailed. This had as a consequence that practically all existing IPRs were included in TRIPs. To start with the principles of national treatment and most favoured nation treatment (the latter being a novelty in the area of IPRs) were stipulated. The most important WIPO conventions (the Paris Convention covering industrial property rights and the Berne Convention covering copyright as well as the Washington Treaty for the protection of semiconductor topographies) were included by reference, also to make these conventions subject to an efficient dispute settlement system. Over and above the level provided for under the provisions of these conventions the substantive levels of protection were set at the level prevailing in the mid 1980s in the industrialized countries. Furthermore extensive rules for the enforcement of the substantive IPR standards were sought for, which constituted an absolute novelty for international IPR rulemaking. The Dunkel text on TRIPS of December 1991 to which reference was made under point 19 above, became almost verbatim part of the Final Act adopted at the Marrakech Ministerial Conference in April 1994 which successfully concluded the Uruguay Round Negotiations. The substantive provisions for the protection of patents are contained in Section 5 of Part II, i.e. Articles 27 to 34 of the TRIPS Agreement. Article 27.1 TRIPS sets out the principle that patents have to be available in all fields of technology if the general conditions

in the so-called Dunkel text was informally agreed by all parties to the negotiations and became practically verbatim part of the Agreement finally adopted in 1994 in Marrakesh. The TRIPS Agreement contained in Article 31 detailed provisions on "Use Without the Authorization of the Right Holder". It was certain that the Canadian regime on compulsory licences for pharmaceutical products existing in the pre-C-91 system would have been incompatible with Article 31 of the TRIPS Agreement. This had been expressly admitted by the Canadian Government.

* While the Uruguay Round negotiations were somewhat in limbo in 1991/1992, the negotiations on a North American Free Trade Agreement (NAFTA) between Canada, Mexico and the United States of America were concluded in 1992 and the agreement was signed at the end of 1992. NAFTA contained in Chapter Seventeen extensive disciplines on the protection of intellectual property rights. The provisions of Chapter Seventeen were largely based on, and in many instances were a verbatim reproduction of, the provisions of the then draft TRIPS Agreement. [29] Article 31 of the TRIPS Agreement was reproduced almost identically in Article 1709(10) of NAFTA. Thus, the Canadian compulsory licensing system for pharmaceuticals in the pre-C-91 system would also have been incompatible with Canada's obligations under NAFTA, in particular its Article 1709(10). This conclusion had been expressly stated by the Canadian Government.

* In order to fully appreciate the Canadian 'philosophy' for patent protection in the area of pharmaceutical products, it was important to

---

for the grant of a patent are met. This is of fundamental importance because many countries, in particular developing countries, had not made—and some still today do not make—available patents for specific areas of technology, notably pharmaceuticals, agrochemicals or foodstuffs. Article 27.2 and 27.3 TRIPS give the option to exclude a number of well defined subject matter from patentability, which is largely derived from modern pieces of IPR legislation as the European Patent Convention (EPC) (compare in particular Article 53 EPC). Article 28 TRIPS describes in detail the rights, which are conferred on a patent owner once the patent has been granted. Article 29 TRIPS stipulates the duties which a patent applicant has to meet and Article 30 TRIPS addresses exceptions to rights conferred which WTO members may provide. Article 31 TRIPS deals primarily with what is generally termed as compulsory licences and sets out detailed rules for the grant of such licences. Article 32 TRIPS addresses revocation and forfeiture and Article 33 TRIPS mandates a minimum term of protection for patents of 20 years from filing. Finally, Article 34 TRIPS establishes rules for process patents and provides in particular for a reversal of the burden of proof in an infringement procedure. While transitional periods for the benefit of LDCs (including—under certain conditions-so-called economies in transition) and least developed countries (LLDCs) are still running, all industrialized country members of the WTO had to comply fully with all the obligations flowing from the TRIPS Agreement as of 1 January 1996 (see Articles 65 and 66 TRIPS). Thus Canada's obligations vis-a-vis the EC and their Member States had to be met fully as of 1 January 1996." The EC also referred to Gervais, "The TRIPS Agreement: Drafting History and Analysis", London 1998, pages 3 to 28.

[29] Reference was made to Dr. Herz, who was part of the Canadian TRIPS and NAFTA negotiating team, who had written: " . . . with respect to IPRs, NAFTA closely tracks the language of the 1991 Dunkel Draft of the TRIPS negotiating text. Therefore, NAFTA's chapter 17: Intellectual property and TRIPS generally are textually close enough to ensure that interpretations in the meaning of the one would be directly relevant to the elucidation of the other. IP related findings of eventual NAFTA panels may, therefore, powerfully influence TRIPS interpretation and vice-versa." (Canada-US L.J. Vol. 23, (1997), at p. 281).

understand the interplay between pharmaceutical research, patenting of inventions and granting of marketing approval for medicinal products. From the moment an application for a pharmaceutical product or process patent was filed until the resulting pharmaceutical product could be effectively marketed it took on average between eight and 12 years. This period of eight to 12 years was necessary for product development which included important periods for pre-clinical and clinical testing. Subsequent to the testing activities, the submissions for the marketing approval authority had to be prepared and the latter had to process the submitted information. This meant in practical terms that, under the present patent law provisions of Canada, a holder of a pharmaceutical patent enjoyed an effective patent term of eight to 12 years in which he could claim exclusivity on the market and it was during this period that all R&D costs had to be depreciated on sales. Under the pre-C-91 system, compulsory licences were automatically granted to all Canadian operators who wanted to copy the invention after the patented pharmaceutical product had been on the Canadian market for at least seven years (or ten years if the active ingredients for the generic product were imported). Furthermore, a period of at least two-and-a-half years for obtaining marketing approval in Canada for the copy product had to be taken into consideration because, under the previous Canadian patent law, producers of copy products could only start to generate pre-marketing approval testing activities once the compulsory licence had been granted. For the holder of the patent for the original product this system provided for a period of effective market exclusivity from nine-and-a-half years to 12 years. This also had as a consequence that the effective market exclusivity for the patent holder went in certain cases beyond the end of the 20-year patent term. To put it in a nutshell, the economic situation in terms of effective market exclusivity for the holder of the patent under the old 1989 to 1993 system, which granted on average 11 years, was indeed very similar to the C-91 system from 1994, which granted on average a market exclusivity for the patent holder of ten years.

The European Communities and their member States, in support of their claims, also advanced information of the economic losses suffered by their pharmaceutical industry from the effects of Sections 55.2(1) and 55.2(2) of the Patent Act together with the Manufacturing and Storage of Patented Medicines Regulations. The European research-based pharmaceutical industry (EFPIA) had made an analysis of its alleged losses suffered in Canada, which exceeded the amount of C$ 100 million per year. This analysis was based on the conservative assumption that, while the operation of the provisions referred to above would allow copy manufacturers to market the product immediately upon patent expiry, in the absence of these provisions effective marketing would only be possible at the earliest two years after patent term expiry. The extrapolation was based on sales of the top 100 original pharmaceutical products sold in Canada between 1995 and 1997.

In respect of Article 30 of the TRIPS Agreement, the European Communities and their member States initially took the position that, while Canada, during the formal consultations under the DSU, had invoked Article 30 of the TRIPS Agreement to justify the measures at issue, it had done so in a rather summary and rudimentary manner. Therefore, the EC limited itself in its first written submission in this regard to stating that their view was that the Canadian measures could not be justified under Article 30, because the conditions set out in this provision were not met: the curtailment of patent rights under Canadian legislation did not constitute "limited exceptions to the exclusive rights conferred by a patent". Furthermore, the exceptions unreasonably conflicted with a normal exploitation of a patent and unreasonably prejudiced the legitimate interests of the patent owner, taking account of the legitimate interests of third parties. In any event, a violation of Article 27.1 of the TRIPS Agreement could not be justified under Article 30.

B. Canada

Canada, in response, requested the Panel to dismiss the complaint of the European Communities and their member States, submitting that:

(1) Canada's exceptions to the exclusive rights conferred by a patent were "limited exceptions" within the meaning of Article 30 of the TRIPS Agreement, because they: did not conflict in any mode or manner with the "normal exploitation" of a patent; they did not prejudice, or if they did, they did not "unreasonably prejudice" the "legitimate interests" of a patentee taking account of the "legitimate interests" of third parties; and the third party interests that the exceptions took account of were "legitimate interests" of relevant third parties.

(2)(a) the prohibition in Article 27.1 of the TRIPS Agreement against discrimination on the basis of field of technology did not apply to allowable limited exceptions;

(2)(b) in any event, Canada's limited exceptions to the exclusive rights conferred by a patent did not discriminate as to the field of technology in which an invention occurred, because they related to products that were subject to laws regulating the manufacture, construction, use or sale of a product and were not expressly related to any particular field of technology; and

(3) as regards Article 33 of the TRIPS Agreement, Canada's limited exceptions to the exclusive rights conferred by a patent did not reduce the term of protection accorded to a patent, because they did nothing to impair a patentee's right to exploit its patent for the full term of protection by working the patent for its private commercial advantage.

Canada argued that the essential question in these proceedings was whether the provisions of Section 55.2(1) and 55.2(2) were "limited exceptions to the exclusive rights conferred by a patent", within the meaning of Article 30 of the TRIPS Agreement. According to Canada, these two measures:

(a) were "limited exceptions" within the meaning of Article 30, since they allowed patent owners complete freedom to exploit their rights throughout the full term of patent protection, leaving the monopoly of commercial exploitation and the exclusivity of economic benefits unimpaired for the life of the patent;

(b) did not conflict with a normal exploitation of a patent or prejudice the legitimate interests of the patent owner, since they only affected the patent owner's commercial exploitation after the patent had expired;

(c) in any event, took into account Canada's national interest in measures conducive to social welfare and the achievement of a balance between rights and obligations, both of which were recognized objectives in Article 7 of the TRIPS Agreement; and

(d) in particular, as required by Article 30, took account of the legitimate interests of third parties, in that:

* they allowed potential competitors to compete freely with the patentee after the patent expired, consistent with the policy of full competition underlying the requirement of Article 29 that, in return for the grant of patent protection, patentees must disclose their inventions to the public; the provision of Article 33 that the exclusive rights be conferred for a specified term only; and the authorization in Article 40 of national measures to prevent abuse of intellectual property rights having an adverse effect on competition; and

* they sought to protect public health—a value recognized in Article 8.1 of the TRIPS Agreement—through promoting access to cost-effective generic medicines following patent expiry and, in this connection, they took into account the legitimate interests of individuals, private insurers and public sector entities that financed health care in maintaining access to affordable medicines.

According to Canada, Article 30 allowed uses that did not unreasonably conflict with a normal exploitation of the patent or unreasonably prejudice the legitimate interests of the patent owner, taking account of the legitimate interests of third parties. Canada submitted that Article 30 therefore authorized measures that limited exclusive rights, provided that no commercial exploitation—i.e. sales—took place during the patent term. Any other interpretation would:

* ignore the existence of the word "unreasonably" in Article 30 and, thereby, the fact that conflicts with normal exploitation and prejudice to the patent owner's interests were allowed;

* disregard the public policy principles inherent in Articles 29 and 33, which encouraged free and open competition with the patent owner immediately upon expiry of the patent; and

* as a consequence, where regulatory review delayed the entry of competing products on the market, promote the practice of enforcing patent rights within the patent term so as to extend the monopoly of the patent owner

beyond the term, a policy which the European Communities and their member States had sought to have included in the Agreement, but which had not been so included, i.e. as the European Communities and their member States made plain in their first written submission, they sought to win through litigation the windfall period of protection that they could not secure by negotiation.

Canada further referred to the interpretative rule set out in Article 31 of the Vienna Convention on the Law of Treaties and argued that the terms of any international treaty, including the TRIPS Agreement, were to be interpreted in good faith in accordance with their ordinary meaning in their context and in light of the object and purpose of the treaty. When the exception provisions in Part II of the TRIPS Agreement were interpreted in accordance with this rule, it became apparent that Article 30 provided a general and flexible authority for Members to adopt measures that balanced the interests of patent owners with the interests of others, as Article 7 of the Agreement expressly stated was an objective of the TRIPS Agreement.

* The language of Article 30 was markedly different from other provisions, which allowed exceptions to treaty rights. For example, GATT 1994, Article XX, required—as in paragraph(b)—that the exception measures be necessary to protect human health, and it contained additional restrictions in its chapeau portion. No similar restrictions were required under Article 30. Similarly, Article 13 of the TRIPS Agreement (and Article 9(2) of the Berne Convention for the Protection of Literary and Artistic Works (1971), upon which Article 13 was modelled), did not allow conflict with a normal exploitation of the work.

* Thus, the TRIPS Agreement contemplated that Members might, in implementing their obligations within their legal systems, adopt measures which, like those in issue here, introduced limited exceptions to the exclusive rights conferred by a patent and confined the patent monopoly to the specific term for which it was granted, in the interests of promoting full competition in regulated-product markets after the expiry of that term and of realizing the cost-saving benefits that competition in those markets (particularly the health care products market) conferred on society. The TRIPS Agreement did not contemplate that these important societal interests should be overridden by an alleged right of patentees to exploit time-consuming regulatory review system—which were neither designed nor intended to protect intellectual property rights—in order to extend the term of patent protection and to gain a windfall monopoly.

* Equally, the TRIPS Agreement did not contemplate that these important societal interests should be overridden by the anti-discrimination requirement of its Article 27.1. This provision was not intended to require "across-the-board" derogations from patent rights. That would only defeat the purpose of Article 30 of permitting exceptions that were "limited", and would compel the application of exceptions where they were not needed. Instead, since Article 27.1 did not purport to define the "patent rights" that

it required to be made available and enjoyable without discrimination, those rights were the ones enumerated in Article 28.1 of the Agreement, subject to any exception that might be made under Article 30. This interpretation gave effect to the language of Article 27.1 in its context rather than in isolation, and achieved the balance contemplated by Article 7 as an objective of the TRIPS Agreement.

Object, Purpose and Meaning

In order to answer the essential question in these proceedings, i.e. whether the challenged measures were "limited exceptions" within the meaning of Article 30, Canada argued that the language of Article 30 must be interpreted according to the rules of interpretation contained in the Vienna Convention on the Law of Treaties. Article 31, paragraph 1, of that Convention set out the basic principle that "[a] treaty shall be interpreted in good faith in accordance with the ordinary meaning to be given to the terms of the treaty in their context and in the light of its object and purpose". Article 31, paragraph 2, of the Vienna Convention went on to specify that the context in which treaty terms were to be read included, among other things, the preamble to the treaty. Canada advanced the following points as being important to bear in mind in seeking to ascertain the scope of Article 30:

* The first recital in the Preamble of the TRIPS Agreement stated that Members were "[d]esiring to reduce distortions and impediments to international trade, and taking into account the need to promote effective and adequate protection of intellectual property rights, and *to ensure that measures and procedures to enforce intellectual property rights do not themselves become barriers to legitimate trade*" (emphasis added by Canada). The Preamble thus evidenced Members' understanding that protection for intellectual property rights should not go beyond what was "effective and adequate", since any greater level of security would imperil other important interests.

* That basic understanding was expanded upon in Article 7 of the Agreement, where its objectives were stated. Article 7 made it clear that intellectual property rights were not conferred in a vacuum, and that the TRIPS Agreement therefore did not aim to achieve a degree of protection for those rights which would unduly prejudice the vital public interest in social and economic welfare or the rights of others. Article 7 provided that "[t]he protection and enforcement of intellectual property rights should contribute to the promotion of technological innovation and to the transfer and dissemination of technology, to the mutual advantage of producers and users of technological knowledge and in a manner conducive to *social and economic welfare*, and to *a balance of rights and obligations*" (emphasis added by Canada).

* When Article 30 was read in context, it could be seen that it reflected the recognition and agreement of Members that the full application of all

Article 28 rights at all times and in all circumstances would be inconsistent with the "balanced" objectives of the TRIPS Agreement. Unlike provisions such as Articles 31 and 40, which permitted measures that curtailed the rights of patent holders only where specified conditions were met, Article 30 granted Members the discretion to limit the full application of patent rights in light of the particular circumstances that prevailed in their respective jurisdictions, when balance was required and when social and economic welfare had to be considered. The existence of such a discretion was consistent with the provision of Article 1.1 that Members should be free to determine the appropriate method of implementing the provisions of the TRIPS Agreement, which provisions of course included Articles 7 and 30 as well as Articles 27, 28 and 33.

* The provision of this discretion, in the interests of achieving an appropriate balance in each of the national legal systems, reflected Members' desire to ensure that the limitations on the scope of patent rights that existed within—or were contemplated for—their own intellectual property laws at the time the Agreement was being negotiated would be taken into account.

* During the Uruguay Round, an adequate exception provision had been an integral part of the negotiations. Proposals, particularly for exceptions to patent rights, had been made by many Members.

* Although agreeing on the need for safeguard provisions, the negotiators could not agree on the specific circumstances that would merit protection, and had chosen the broad criteria-based text that now appeared as Article 30. Article 30 was not limited to any particular circumstance. It was not limited by reference to any particular purpose or policy objective. It was not limited to any particular type of exception. It was not limited by reference to an exhaustive list of eligible exceptions. Nor was it limited by reference to an illustrative, but non-exhaustive list of special cases justifying an exception.

* More particularly, Article 30 did not require a Member invoking its application to prove that its measure was not a disguised restriction on international trade, unlike the chapeau of GATT 1994, Article XX. Similarly, Article 30 did not require a Member to prove that its measure was the least trade-restrictive possible, unlike Article 2.2 of the Agreement on Technical Barriers to Trade and Article 5.6 of the Agreement on the Application of Sanitary and Phytosanitary Measures. Neither did it require a Member to prove that its measure was necessary for any particular purpose, such as "to protect human, animal or plant life or health", as in paragraph (b) of GATT 1994, Article XX. In addition, unlike Article 2.2 of the Agreement on Technical Barriers to Trade, there was nothing in Article 30 even requiring that a Member's measure fulfil a particular objective or take account of the risks that non-fulfilment would create.

* Article 30 also differed significantly from the other exceptions of the TRIPS Agreement itself. Article 13 (copyright) stipulated that "Members shall confine limitations or exceptions to exclusive rights to *certain special*

cases which do not conflict with a normal exploitation of the work and do not unreasonably prejudice the legitimate interests of the right holder". Article 17 (trademarks) provided that "Members may provide limited exceptions to the rights conferred by a trademark, *such as fair use of descriptive terms,* provided that such exceptions take account of the legitimate interests of the owner of the trademark and of third parties" (emphases added).

* By way of contrast, Article 30 was not confined to certain special cases or fair use, and it did allow conflict with a normal exploitation of the patent, provided that the conflict was not unreasonable. In other words, unlike the other provisions referred to above, there was nothing in Article 30 indicating a limited or special application.

* The extent or scope of the exceptions authorized by Article 30 were only restricted by the requirements that:

(a) they must be "limited";

(b) they must not "unreasonably conflict with a normal exploitation of the patent [. . .] taking account of the legitimate interests of third parties"; and

(c) they must not "[. . .] unreasonably prejudice the legitimate interests of the patent owner, taking account of the legitimate interests of third parties".

Canada argued that the exceptions created by subsections 55.2(1) and (2) of its Patent Act met each of the above requirements, for the following reasons.

(i) Section 55.2(1) and 55.2(2) created limited exceptions

* Canada's measures were "limited" within the ordinary meaning of that word. The early working exception was restricted to the narrow circumstance where a third party made, constructed, used or sold a patented invention solely for purposes reasonably related to regulatory review. The stockpiling exception could only be used by the person who had relied on the first exception, and was limited to the last six months of the relevant patent. Neither measure affected commercial sales by the patent holder during the term or any other economic benefit of a patent, such as the profit that could be earned through licensing royalties or the sale of the right.

* Subsection 55.2(1) permitted a third party to use a patented invention without infringement liability only where the third party made, constructed, used or sold a patented invention solely for uses of the invention that were reasonably related to the development and submission of information required under any law that regulated the manufacture, construction, use or sale of a product to which the invention related. (The reference to selling the invention was necessitated by the fact that a generic drug manufacturer had to usually purchase the active ingredient for its product from a fine chemical producer. Other technical "transfers" made in the course of a regulatory review submission would include administration of the drug to test subjects and use of an outside laboratory for priority testing.)

* The contention by the European Communities and their member States that the activities excepted from infringement liability were unlimited in time, quantity and extent, could not be reconciled with the unequivocal wording that Canada's Parliament had used. In particular, the allegations that "very significant quantities of the products protected by a patent" could be manufactured, imported and sold, and that "only the final purchaser of the product" need have the intention to use it for the purposes of a regulatory submission, were at complete variance with the clear requirement that "any person" who engaged in the activities must do so "solely" for uses connected with the development of a regulatory submission. Every other use of a patented invention would be exposed to infringement liability. Significantly, the EC did not explain how this plain language could be misconstrued in the manner for which it contended, and did not refer to any rule of statutory interpretation in support of its position.

* Subsection 55.2(2) permitted only the third party who made, constructed, used or sold a patented invention, in the manner contemplated by subsection 55.2(1), to make, construct or use the invention without infringement liability during the last six months of the patent term only for the purposes of the manufacture and storage of articles intended for sale after the date on which the term of the patent expired.

* The attack of the European Communities and their member States on this exception again adopted an interpretation of the language which was not supported by the plain meaning of the words used. The EU alleged that the stockpiling provision could be relied upon by"anybody in Canada." Manifestly, that was not so. Subsection 55.2(2) was expressly limited in its application to a person who had engaged in the activities specified in subsection 55.2(1), i.e. a person who had developed information for the purposes of a regulatory submission. Nothing in the language of subsection 55.2(2) lent any support to the allegation that it had a broader application, and the EC offered no explanation at all for interpreting it that way.

* While limiting the right to bring infringement proceedings in the narrow circumstances described in subsections 55.2(1) and 55.2(2), the excepting measures did not otherwise curtail any of the exclusive rights enjoyed by the patent owner. The right holder continued, throughout the full term of protection, to possess the right to bring infringement proceedings to restrain others from any acts of making, using, offering for sale, selling or importing the patented subject-matter outside the restricted scope of the exceptions under Section 55.2. The unsubstantiated allegation that widespread infringing activities could occur during the patent term did not respect the ordinary meaning of the words actually used in the exceptions.

* In fact, all of the effects which the European Communities and their member States complained about occurred after the term of protection had expired. The extension of market exclusivity which was lost because generic manufacturers were permitted to make regulatory submissions during the term was of course a post-expiry phenomenon. So too were the lost profits that a patent owner would otherwise have realized during that extended period. These effects were simply the practical consequences of legislation designed to ensure that lower-cost competitive products, particularly drug products, reached the market as soon as possible after patent expiry. They were purely commercial concepts, not violations of intellectual property law rights which the TRIPS Agreement either recognized or sought to counteract. The attempt of the European Communities and their member States to equate Canada's present regime with its previous compulsory licensing system failed to acknowledge that all of the principal effects of compulsory licensing were felt during the term of patent protection. A compulsory licensee was permitted to work a patented invention in full competition with the patent owner. That was plainly not the case under the challenged measures, since they prohibited all commercial sales until after patent expiry.

* Additionally, the suggestion of the European Communities and their member States that the period of market exclusivity for the patent holder was about the same under the limited exceptions regime as it was under the former compulsory licensing system was based on a wrong assumption. The pre-Bill C-91 law permitted a compulsory licence to be issued at any time. However, that law went on to provide that such licences would only become effective to permit otherwise infringing activities linked to "sale for consumption in Canada" after the patented product had been on the Canadian market for seven to ten years. The EC was wrong in thinking that this law prevented holders of compulsory licences from undertaking the kinds of activities now envisaged by subsections 55.2(1) and 55.2(2) before the period of suspension had expired, and that the patentee's period of exclusivity was effectively extended. The Supreme Court of Canada had earlier held that such activities were covered by the experimental use defence.

* In any event, even if the respective periods of market exclusivity were about the same, that result would be of no significance in these proceedings. Compulsory licensing was an approach to cost containment adopted by Canada which was fully consistent with the then-existing international rules respecting intellectual property law. When it appeared that those rules would be adjusted by the TRIPS Agreement, Canada moved to amend its domestic legislation, in order to be consistent with the new obligations. Even if conformity with the new obligations resulted in about the same period of market exclusivity as was produced by conformity with the previous rules, that would simply be a coincidence, not a matter of any consequence under the TRIPS Agreement. Again, the effective period of market exclusivity cited by the EU was a purely commercial concept, not an intellectual property law right or concept which the TRIPS Agreement recognized.

(ii) Section 55.2(1) and 55.2(2) did not conflict with a normal exploitation of the patent

* The exclusive rights conferred by a patent were normally exploited by "working" the patent for commercial gain. Typically, this would involve the patentee engaging in any combination of the following activities: using the patent to manufacture and sell the product as a monopolist; licensing the right to use the invention to others in return for the payment of royalty or other compensation; and selling either a part or the whole of its property right in the invention and its patent. None of these activities was impaired or prevented by the limited exceptions created by subsections 55.2(1) and 55.2(2). The patentee retained the full, unfettered and exclusive right to work the patent for commercial reward during the full term of protection whether by exercising: the unimpaired exclusive right to manufacture and sell the product; the unimpaired exclusive right to license the right to use the invention to others in return for the payment of valuable consideration; and the unimpaired exclusive right to sell, in whole or in part, its property right in the invention and patent. Therefore, at no time during the term of protection, did either exception conflict in any mode or manner with a normal exploitation of the patent.

* Where there was no conflict, "unreasonableness" was not at issue.

(iii) Section 55.2(1) and 55.2(2) did not prejudice the legitimate interests of the patent owner

* The legitimate interests of a patent owner must, by definition, be interests that related to the rights and duties that the patent laws conferred or imposed, as the case might be, on persons who had developed or subsequently acquired a patentable invention. In other words, legitimate interests arose from the status of being a patent holder, not from the more general status of being a business person or a manufacturer. Thus, in return for disclosing an invention to the public and obtaining the grant of a patent, a patent holder had a legitimate interest in exploiting and enforcing for the duration of the term of protection the exclusive right to "work" the patent as a monopolist and to earn the economic returns that rewarded inventive activity and investment. After the term of protection expired, however, the interest in exploiting the invention could no longer be that of a monopolist. Instead, the interest was reduced to: (a) the right to compete on the open market; (b) any trademark interest in the brand name, which subsisted after patent expiry; (c) any right to prevent "passing off" at common law; and (d) any copyright interest in materials describing the product. None of these interests pertained to patent protection and none was affected by Canada's limited exceptions.

* Since the exceptions created by subsections 55.2(1) and 55.2(2) did not conflict with the normal exploitation of the patent during the term of protection, they did nothing to prejudice the legitimate interest of the patent owner in respect of the right to exploit the patent for the full duration of its term of protection. Similarly, since they did not impair a patentee's right to bring infringement proceedings at any time during the term of protection to restrain others from making any commercial sale of the patented invention, they did nothing to prejudice the patent owner's

legitimate interest in prohibiting commercial exploitation during the term of protection.

* The interest that a patentee could have in restraining, during the term of protection, the activities that were sheltered from infringement liability by subsections 55.2(1) and 55.2(2) involved exploiting regulatory review laws which delayed the market entry of competitor products subject to those laws, in order to extend the patentee's monopoly beyond the term of protection specified by the patent law. As was apparent from their submission, it was that windfall period of protection that the European Communities and their member States asserted here. Such gratuitous distortion of the competitive market could not be said to be a legitimate interest. That interest could not be said to be legitimate, because by treaty and domestic law prescription, patents only conferred exclusive rights for a specified term. When the prescribed term expired, so did the exclusive rights. Accordingly, and notwithstanding the private economic advantage that would be obtained by doing so, a patentee could have no legitimate interest deriving from patent law in exercising its exclusive use and enforcement rights within the term of protection to achieve, through exploitation of regulatory review laws, a de facto extension of that term of protection beyond the prescribed period, thereby unilaterally altering the bargain between the patentee and society. In this respect, the interests of a patentee of a pharmaceutical invention could be no different from those of patentees in other fields of technology.

(iv) Section 55.2(1) and 55.2(2) took account of the legitimate interests of third parties

* If, however, a patentee's "normal exploitation" involved more than working the patent for commercial gain, or if the patentee's "legitimate interest" included exercising its exclusive rights during the term so as to extend the term unilaterally beyond the period specified by statute, neither the exploitation nor the interest was affected unreasonably by the disputed measures, "taking "account of the legitimate interests of third parties".

* In this context, "third parties" had to be a reference to those who were adverse in interest to the patent owner. Persons not adverse in interest, such as licensees, were already covered by the protection that was extended to the patent owner. Consequently, "third parties" had to mean all those who, not having a property interest in the patent, had an interest in the availability, consumption, cost or production of regulated products that were subject to the protection of a patent. Thus "third parties" included society at large, individual and institutional consumers of such regulated products and would-be competitor producers of those products. In the particular case of pharmaceutical products, the "third parties" included the individual users of Canada's health care system and the public and private sector entities that paid for it.

* This reading of Article 30 was the one that gave proper effect to its terms in the context in which they were found. The TRIPS Agreement as a whole was framed so as to achieve balance between competing interests,

and to ensure that the assertion of patent rights did not prevent the realization of other important societal objectives. As stated in the first recital of its Preamble and in the objectives endorsed by its Article 7, the TRIPS Agreement was not intended to promote patent rights at the expense of legitimate trade, social and economic welfare, and the rights of others. In order to achieve the desired balance, these latter interests had been recognized in the reference in Article 30 to "third parties".

 * The interests of these third parties were that the exclusive rights granted to patentees for a specified term of protection would be extinguished on the expiry of that term and that competitive conditions would thereafter govern the operation of the previously monopolized market for the regulated products at issue. The interest in the reinstatement of competition was not merely a "legitimate interest", it was a right which derived from the first principles of patent law. As stated in a report to Congress by the United States House of Representatives Committee on Energy and Commerce: "[T]he Constitution empowers Congress to grant exclusive rights to an inventor for a limited time. That limited time should be a definite time and, thereafter, immediate competition should be encouraged."

 * Third parties therefore had an undeniably legitimate interest in measures which ensured that patent rights were not exercisable in a manner that effectively extended the term of protection sanctioned by statute, thereby giving the former patentee a gratuitous monopoly and restraining trade unreasonably in the post-expiry market.

 * In this regard, it was significant that Articles 8.2 and 40 acknowledged that Members could invoke measures to control the abuse of patent rights by curtailing, whether by compulsory licence or revocation, the patent right for some or all of the remainder of its term of protection. Where such measures could be taken consistently with the Agreement to control the exercise of intellectual property rights that had an abusive or anti-competitive effect during the term specified for their protection, then a fortiori similar measures, which did not conflict with a normal exploitation of the patent, could also be taken consistently with the Agreement to prevent the anti-competitive effects of the patent after its term of protection had expired.

 * The legitimacy of the third party interest in the adoption of measures like those enacted by Section 55.2 to counteract the post-expiry monopoly for regulated products was particularly pronounced in the cases of both users and payers of health care products. Public health was a value whose importance was recognized as a matter of principle in Article 8.1 of the TRIPS Agreement. Accordingly, the exercise of exclusive rights in respect of regulated health care products during the term of protection to extend the patentee's monopoly into the post-expiry market was of particular concern in the pharmaceutical products sector: "It is generally accepted that the scope and duration of the patent monopoly must be limited, because monopolies are inherently economically inefficient. A monopolist profits by

reducing output below competitive levels and correspondingly raising the price, causing a 'deadweight loss' to society. In the pharmaceutical context, outside the patent term, a monopoly would mean that the quantity of drugs available to society would be less than optimal, due to sales at prices considerably higher than marginal cost."

* The cost of health care was a major concern for all WTO Member countries. A significant component of health care costs was the expense of drug therapies. Most Members, including both parties to this dispute, had taken positive measures to contain those costs, including direct price controls and incentives to encourage the use of generic drugs. The latter were particularly relevant here, since the creation of sophisticated and technical review requirements had meant that the only way to ensure a supply of generic drugs in the market as soon after patent expiry as possible was through an exception to the patent monopoly for purposes related solely to the development of information required to obtain marketing authorization for competitive versions of a patented product.

* The use of generic medicines resulted in important economies for the public health care system, and so contributed to its viability and the protection of public health. In view of this, it was not surprising that Members had pursued a wide variety of measures to promote the use of generic drug products: "The actual level of growth of the generic market is becoming increasingly influenced by regulatory measures being introduced by governments and other payers for health care aimed either at forcing or encouraging the increased use of generic products. These measures have been introduced in response to the rising costs of health care in the major markets."

* Measures that sought to control the costs of the health care system and to ensure access to needed drug therapies were obviously conducive to social welfare. As such, they could properly be adopted by Members pursuant to Article 30, as a means of achieving the balance contemplated by Article 7. In the post-expiry market, the interests of consumers and payers in ensuring access to less costly generic drugs were legitimate and important, while a patentee's interest in extending the period of monopoly was not one that was recognized in the TRIPS Agreement, let alone sanctioned as legitimate.

* The legitimacy of measures to promote the use of generic drug products as means of protecting public health was endorsed by the World Health Organization (WHO). In its resolution scheduled for adoption in May 1999, in connection with its Revised Drug Strategy, the WHO encouraged its members "to explore and review their options under relevant international agreements, including trade agreements, to safeguard access to essential drugs". The WHO's Revised Drug Strategy also called for the use of generic drugs as a necessary means for ensuring a supply of essential drugs for individuals in all member states: "Drug supply is certainly one component of an essential drug policy whose economic advantages have been most studied. Generic drug programmes are today probably the most relevant

economic strategy for drug supply. The most important economic feature of generic drugs is that, *unlike the situation with named brands, they allow for competition among producers of a given drug.*" (emphasis added by Canada).

  * Thus, society at large and individual and institutional consumers of the health care system had an undeniably legitimate, indeed essential, interest in assuring the availability of competitively priced generic medicines as soon after patent expiry as possible. Canada's measures served that interest, and in doing so complied with the fundamental objectives, referred to in the TRIPS Agreement, of promoting social welfare and achieving balance between rights and obligations, while protecting the legitimate interests of intellectual property rights holders.

Canada argued that, firstly, Article 33, read in its context, was clearly limited to defining the longevity of a patent right and did not define the right itself, advancing the following points:

  * Patent rights were defined by Article 28, subject of course to any exceptions that might be authorized by Article 30. Thus, to the extent that Article 33 had any bearing on the existence or content of a right, it was subject to the provisions of Articles 28 and 30 of the Agreement.

  * Accordingly if, pursuant to the authority of Article 30, the scope of a right under Article 28 was restricted in a manner that could be said to reduce the minimum term of protection, Article 33 could not operate to negate the restriction and restore the right to its original or ordinary scope. It could not operate in that fashion, because the result produced would plainly be absurd.

  * If Article 33 could negate an exception under Article 30, then the national laws of all Members which contained exceptions that curtailed, in whole or in part, the scope of a right under Article 28 and thereby limited its enjoyment for the whole or a part of the term of protection, would reduce the term by the degree of curtailment and so contravene or not be consistent with the obligation imposed by Article 33.

Canada then argued that, in any event, neither subsection 55.2(1) nor subsection 55.2(2) of the Patent Act reduced the minimum term of protection referred to in Article 33 of the TRIPS Agreement to a term that was less than that minimum. According to Canada, subsections 55.2(1) and 55.2(2) created limited exceptions which did not conflict with the normal exploitation of a patent so as to reduce the term of protection accorded to the patent. Referring to its arguments as to why the provisions in question created "limited exceptions" within the meaning of Article 30 of the TRIPS Agreement, it drew attention to the following points:

  * A patentee whose rights might be affected by the application of the limited exceptions retained the full, unfettered and exclusive right to work the patent for commercial reward during the full term of protection, whether the "working" involved the monopolistic manufacture and sale of the product; the licensing of the right of use to others for valuable consideration; or the sale, in whole or part, of the property right in the patent.

* Similarly, a patentee affected by the limited exceptions continued, throughout the full term of protection, to possess the right to bring infringement proceedings to restrain others from any commercial sale of the patented invention.

* Furthermore, in addition to retaining the rights to work and to restrain, where a person who had used an invention in the manner contemplated by the exceptions sought marketing authorization for a pharmaceutical product during the term of protection on the basis of an allegation that the person would not infringe the product or product-by-process patent, the patentee could bring a summary proceeding under the Patented Medicines (Notice of Compliance) Regulations to challenge that allegation and, where successful, prohibit the issuance of the marketing authorization until the expiry of the patent.

* Where a patentee could bring such proceedings to prevent the issuance of a marketing approval certificate until the expiry, at the conclusion of the full term of protection, of its patent, it could not be tenably argued that the limited exceptions created by subsections 55.2(1) and 55.2(2) of the Patent Act reduced the term of protection to a term shorter than the term prescribed by Article 33.

. . . .

VII. Findings

. . . .

C. Principles of Interpretation

The legal issues in this dispute primarily involve differences over interpretation of the key TRIPS provisions invoked by the parties, chiefly Articles 27.1, 30 and 33. The rules that govern the interpretation of WTO agreements are the rules of treaty interpretation stated in Articles 31 and 32 of the Vienna Convention. The starting point is the rule of Article 31(1) which states:

> A treaty is to be interpreted in good faith in accordance with the ordinary meaning to be given to the terms of the treaty in their context and in the light of its object and purpose.

The parties have submitted arguments on each of these elements, as well as further arguments based on subsequent practice by certain WTO Members, thus relying on Article 31(3)(b), which reads in relevant part as follows:

> There shall be taken into account, together with the context: (a) [];
> (b) any subsequent practice in the application of the treaty which establishes the agreement of the parties regarding its interpretation."

The parties have also advanced arguments based on the negotiating history of the TRIPS provisions in dispute. Negotiating history falls within the category of "Supplementary Means of Interpretation" and is governed by the rule of Article 32 of the Vienna Convention, which provides as follows:

> Recourse may be had to supplementary means of interpretation, including the preparatory work of the treaty and the circumstances of its conclusion, in order to confirm the meaning resulting from the application of Article 31, or to determine the meaning when the interpretation according to Article 31:
>
> (a) leaves the meaning ambiguous or obscure; or
>
> (b) leads to a result which is manifestly absurd or unreasonable.

. . . .

D. Burden of Proof

[I]n the present case, it was the Panel's view that the EC bears the burden to present evidence and argument sufficient to establish a prima facie case that Canada has violated Articles 27.1, 28.1 and 33 of the TRIPS Agreement. It would be up to Canada to advance sufficient argument and evidence to rebut such a prima facie case. Canada has, for all practical purposes, conceded the violation of Article 28, because it has resorted to the exception of Article 30 of the TRIPS Agreement in this case. Since Article 30 is an exception to the obligations of the TRIPS Agreement, it would be up to Canada to demonstrate that the provisions of Sections 55.2(1) and 55.2(2) comply with the criteria laid down in Article 30. It is on this basis that the Panel approached the analysis of the claims submitted to it.

E. Section 55.2(2) (The Stockpiling Exception)

The Panel began by considering the claims of violation concerning Section 55.2(2), the so-called stockpiling provision. It began by considering the EC claim that this measure was in violation of Article 28.1 of the TRIPS Agreement, and Canada's defence that the measure was an exception authorized by Article 30 of the Agreement.

. . . .

Both parties agreed upon the basic structure of Article 30. Article 30 establishes three criteria that must be met in order to qualify for an exception: (1) the exception must be "limited"; (2) the exception must not "unreasonably conflict with normal exploitation of the patent"; (3) the exception must not "unreasonably prejudice the legitimate interests of the patent owner, taking account of the legitimate interests of third parties". The three conditions are cumulative, each being a separate and independent requirement that must be satisfied. Failure to comply with any one of the three conditions results in the Article 30 exception being disallowed.

The three conditions must, of course, be interpreted in relation to each other. Each of the three must be presumed to mean something different from the other two, or else there would be redundancy. Normally, the order of listing can be read to suggest that an exception that complies with the first condition can nevertheless violate the second or third, and that one which complies with the first and second can still violate the third. The syntax of Article 30 supports the conclusion that an exception may be "limited" and yet fail to satisfy one or both of the other two conditions. The ordering further suggests that an exception that does not "unreasonably conflict with normal exploitation" could nonetheless "unreasonably prejudice the legitimate interests of the patent owner".

. . . .

In the Panel's view, Article 30's very existence amounts to a recognition that the definition of patent rights contained in Article 28 would need certain adjustments. On the other hand, the three limiting conditions attached to Article 30 testify strongly that the negotiators of the Agreement did not intend Article 30 to bring about what would be equivalent to a renegotiation of the basic balance of the Agreement. Obviously, the exact scope of Article 30's authority will depend on the specific meaning given to its limiting conditions. The words of those conditions must be examined with particular care on this point. Both the goals and the limitations stated in Articles 7 and 8.1 must obviously be borne in mind when doing so as well as those of other provisions of the TRIPS Agreement which indicate its object and purposes.

Canada asserted that the word "limited" should be interpreted according to the conventional dictionary definition, such as "confined within definite limits", or "restricted in scope, extent, amount". Canada argued that the stockpiling exception in Section 55.2(2) is restricted in scope because it has only a limited impact on a patent owner's rights. The stockpiling exception, Canada noted, does not affect the patent owner's right to an exclusive market for "commercial" sales during the patent term, since the product that is manufactured and stockpiled during the final six months of the term cannot be sold in competition with the patent owner until the patent expires. By "commercial sales", Canada clearly meant sales to the ultimate consumer, because it acknowledged that sales of patented ingredients to producers engaged in authorized stockpiling is permitted. Thus, Canada was arguing that an exception is "limited" as long as the exclusive right to sell to the ultimate consumer during the term of the patent is preserved. In addition, Canada also claimed that the exception is further limited by the six-month duration of the exception, and by the fact that it can be used only by persons that have made, constructed or used the invention under Section 55.2(1).

The EC interpreted the word "limited" to connote a narrow exception, one that could be described by words such as "narrow, small, minor, insignificant or restricted". The EC measured the "limited" quality of the proposed exception by reference to its impact on the exclusionary rights granted to the patent owner under Article 28.1. Applying that measure, the EC contended that the stockpiling exception is not "limited" because it takes away three of the five Article 28.1 rights -the rights to exclude "making", "using" and "importing". The EC argued that the impairment of three out of five basic rights is in itself extensive enough to be considered "not limited". The EC further contended that limitation of the exception to the last six months of the patent term does not constitute a limited impairment of rights when six months is taken as a percentage of the 20-year patent term, and especially not when taken as a percentage of the actual eight to 12-year period of effective market exclusivity enjoyed by most patented pharmaceuticals. In addition, the EC noted, there was no limitation on the quantities that could be produced during this period, nor any limitation on the markets in which such products could be sold. Finally, the EC pointed out that no royalty fees are due for such production, and that the patent holder does not even have a right to be informed of the use of the patent.

In considering how to approach the parties' conflicting positions regarding the meaning of the term "limited exceptions", the Panel was aware that the text of Article 30 has antecedents in the text of Article 9(2) of the Berne Convention. However, the words "limited exceptions" in Article 30 of the TRIPS Agreement are different from the corresponding words in Article 9(2) of the Berne Convention, which reads "in certain special cases". The Panel examined the documented negotiating history of TRIPS Article 30 with respect to the reasons why negotiators may have chosen to use the term "limited exceptions" in place of "in special circumstances". The negotiating records show only that the term "limited exceptions" was employed very early in the drafting process, well before the decision to adopt a text modelled on Berne Article 9(2), but do not indicate why it was retained in the later draft texts modelled on Berne Article 9(2).

The Panel agreed with the EC that, as used in this context, the word "limited" has a narrower connotation than the rather broad definitions cited by Canada. Although the word itself can have both broad and narrow definitions, the narrower being indicated by examples such as "a mail train taking only a limited number of passengers", the narrower definition is the more appropriate when the word "limited" is used as part of the phrase "limited exceptions". The word "exception" by itself connotes a limited derogation, one that does not undercut the body of rules from which it is made. When a treaty uses the term "limited exceptions", the word "limited" must be given a meaning separate from the limitation implicit in the word "exception" itself. The term "limited exceptions" must therefore be read to connote a narrow exception—one which makes only a small diminution of the rights in question.

The Panel agreed with the EC interpretation that "limited" is to be measured by the extent to which the exclusive rights of the patent owner have been curtailed. The full text of Article 30 refers to "limited exceptions to the exclusive rights conferred by a patent". In the absence of other indications, the Panel concluded that it would be justified in reading the text literally, focusing on the extent to which legal rights have been curtailed, rather than the size or extent of the economic impact. In support of this conclusion, the Panel noted that the following two conditions of Article 30 ask more particularly about the economic impact of the exception, and provide two sets of standards by which such impact may be judged. The term "limited exceptions" is the only one of the three conditions in Article 30 under which the extent of the curtailment of rights as such is dealt with.

In the Panel's view, the question of whether the stockpiling exception is a "limited" exception turns on the extent to which the patent owner's rights to exclude "making" and "using" the patented product have been curtailed. The right to exclude "making" and "using" provides protection, additional to that provided by the right to exclude sale, during the entire term of the patent by cutting off the supply of competing goods at the source and by preventing use of such products however obtained. With no limitations at all upon the quantity of production, the stockpiling exception removes that protection entirely during the last six months of the patent term, without regard to what other, subsequent, consequences it might have. By this effect alone, the stockpiling exception can be said to abrogate such rights entirely during the time it is in effect.

In view of Canada's emphasis on preserving commercial benefits before the expiration of the patent, the Panel also considered whether the market advantage gained by the patent owner in the months after expiration of the patent could also be considered a purpose of the patent owner's rights to exclude "making" and "using" during the term of the patent. In both theory and practice, the Panel concluded that such additional market benefits were within the purpose of these rights. In theory, the rights of the patent owner are generally viewed as a right to prevent competitive commercial activity by others, and manufacturing for commercial sale is a quintessential competitive commercial activity, whose character is not altered by a mere delay in the commercial reward. In practical terms, it must be recognized that enforcement of the right to exclude "making" and "using" during the patent term will necessarily give all patent owners, for all products, a short period of extended market exclusivity after the patent expires. The repeated enactment of such exclusionary rights with knowledge of their universal market effects can only be understood as an affirmation of the purpose to produce those market effects.

For both these reasons, the Panel concluded that the stockpiling exception of Section 55.2(2) constitutes a substantial curtailment of the exclusionary rights required to be granted to patent owners under Article 28.1 of the TRIPS Agreement. Without seeking to define exactly what level of curtailment would be disqualifying, it was clear to the Panel that an exception which results in a substantial curtailment of this dimension cannot be considered a "limited exceptions" within the meaning of Article 30 of the Agreement.

Neither of the two "limitations" upon the scope of the measure are sufficient to alter this conclusion. First, the fact that the exception can only be used by those persons who have utilized the regulatory review exception of Section 55.2(1) does limit the scope of the exception both to those persons and to products requiring regulatory approval. In regard to the limitation to such persons, the Panel considered this was not a real limitation since only persons who satisfy regulatory requirements would be entitled to market the product. In regard to the limitation to such products, the Panel considered that the fact that an exception does not apply at all to other products in no way changes its effect with regard to the criteria of Article 30. Each exception must be evaluated with regard to its impact on each affected patent, independently. Second, the fact that the exception applied only to the last six months of the patent term obviously does reduce its impact on all affected patented products, but the Panel agreed with the EC that six months was a commercially significant period of time, especially since there were no limits at all on the volume of production allowed, or the market destination of such production.

Having concluded that the exception in Section 55.2(2) of the Canadian Patent Act does not satisfy the first condition of Article 30 of the TRIPS Agreement, the Panel therefore concluded that Section 55.2(2) is inconsistent with Canada's obligations under Article 28.1 of the Agreement. This conclusion, in turn, made it unnecessary to consider any of the other claims of inconsistency raised by the European Communities. Accordingly, the Panel did not consider the claims of inconsistency under the second and third conditions of Article 30, the claim of inconsistency with TRIPS Article 27.1, and the claim of inconsistency with Article 33.

. . . .

F. Section 55.2(1) (The Regulatory Review Exception)

[The panel concluded that Canada's regulatory review exception is a "limited exceptions" within the meaning of TRIPS Article 30.]

The second condition of Article 30 prohibits exceptions that "unreasonably conflict with a normal exploitation of the patent". Canada took the position that "exploitation" of the patent involves the extraction of commercial value from the patent by "working" the patent, either by selling the product in a market from which competitors are excluded, or by licensing others to do so, or by selling the patent rights outright. The European Communities also defined "exploitation" by referring to the same three ways of "working" a patent. The parties differed primarily on their interpretation of the term "normal".

. . . .

The normal practice of exploitation by patent owners, as with owners of any other intellectual property right, is to exclude all forms of competition that could detract significantly from the economic returns anticipated from a patent's grant of market exclusivity. The specific forms of patent exploitation are not static, of course, for to be effective exploitation must adapt to changing forms of competition due to technological development and the evolution of marketing practices. Protection of all normal exploitation practices is a key element of the policy reflected in all patent laws. Patent laws establish a carefully defined period of market exclusivity as an inducement to innovation, and the policy of those laws cannot be achieved unless patent owners are permitted to take effective advantage of that inducement once it has been defined.

Canada has raised the argument that market exclusivity occurring after the 20-year patent term expires should not be regarded as "normal". The Panel was unable to accept that as a categorical proposition. Some of the basic rights granted to all patent owners, and routinely exercised by all patent owners, will typically produce a certain period of market exclusivity after the expiration of a patent. For example, the separate right to prevent "making" the patented product during the term of the patent often prevents competitors from building an inventory needed to enter the market immediately upon expiration of a patent. There is nothing abnormal about that more or less brief period of market exclusivity after the patent has expired.

The Panel considered that Canada was on firmer ground, however, in arguing that the additional period of de facto market exclusivity created by using patent rights to preclude submissions for regulatory authorization should not be considered "normal". The additional period of market exclusivity in this situation is not a natural or normal consequence of enforcing patent rights. It is an unintended consequence of the conjunction of the patent laws with product regulatory laws, where the combination of patent rights with the time demands of the regulatory process gives a greater than normal period of market exclusivity to the enforcement of certain patent rights. It is likewise a form of exploitation that most patent owners do not in fact employ. For the vast majority of patented products, there is no marketing regulation of the kind covered by Section 55.2(1), and thus there is no possibility to extend patent exclusivity by delaying the marketing approval process for competitors.

[The panel found that the regulatory review exception did not conflict with the "normal" exploitation of patents within the meaning of Article 30.]

The third condition of Article 30 is the requirement that the proposed exception must not "unreasonably prejudice the legitimate interests of the patent owner, taking into account the legitimate interests of third parties". Although Canada, as the party asserting the exception provided for in Article 30, bears the burden of proving compliance with the conditions of that exception, the order of proof is complicated by the fact that the condition involves proving a negative. One cannot demonstrate that no legitimate interest of the patent owner has been prejudiced until one knows what claims of legitimate interest can be made. Likewise, the weight of legitimate third party interests cannot be fully appraised until the legitimacy and weight of the patent owner's legitimate interests, if any, are defined. Accordingly, without disturbing the ultimate burden of proof, the Panel chose to analyse the issues presented by the third condition of Article 30 according to the logical sequence in which those issues became defined.

. . . .

To make sense of the term "legitimate interests" in this context, that term must be defined in the way that it is often used in legal discourse—as a normative claim calling for protection of interests that are "justifiable" in the sense that they are supported by relevant public policies or other social norms. This is the sense of the word that often appears in statements such as "X has no legitimate interest in being able to do Y". We may take as an illustration one of the most widely adopted Article 30-type exceptions in national patent laws—the exception under which use of the patented product for scientific experimentation, during the term of the patent and without consent, is not an infringement. It is often argued that this exception is based on the notion that a key public policy purpose underlying patent laws is to facilitate the dissemination and advancement of technical knowledge and that allowing the patent owner to prevent experimental use during the term of the patent would frustrate part of the purpose of the requirement that the nature of the invention be disclosed to the public. To the contrary, the argument concludes, under the policy of the patent laws, both society and the scientist have a "legitimate interest" in using the patent disclosure to support the advance of science and technology. While the Panel draws no conclusion about the correctness of any such national exceptions in terms of Article 30 of the TRIPS Agreement, it does adopt the general meaning of the term "legitimate interests" contained in legal analysis of this type.

. . . .

The negotiating history of the TRIPS Agreement itself casts no further illumination on the meaning of the term "legitimate interests", but the negotiating history of Article 9(2) of the Berne Convention, from which the text of the third condition was clearly drawn, does tend to affirm the Panel's interpretation of that term. With regard to the TRIPS negotiations them-selves, the meaning of several important drafting changes turns out to be equivocal upon closer examination. The negotiating records of the TRIPS Agreement itself show that the first drafts of the provision that was to become Article 30 contemplated authorizing "limited exceptions" that would be defined by an illustrative list of exceptions—private use, scientific use, prior use, a traditional exception for pharmacists, and the like. Eventually, this illustrative list approach was abandoned in favour of a more general authorization following the outlines of the present Article 30. The negotiat-ing records of the TRIPS Agreement give no explanation of the reason for this decision.

The text of the present, more general version of Article 30 of the TRIPS Agreement was obviously based on the text of Article 9(2) of the Berne Convention. Berne Article 9(2) deals with exceptions to the copyright holder's right to exclude reproduction of its copyrighted work without permission. The text of Article 9(2) is as follows:

> It shall be a matter for legislation in the countries of the Union to permit the reproduction of [literary and artistic] works in certain special cases, provided that such reproduction does not conflict with a normal exploitation of the work and does not unreasonably prejudice the legitimate interests of the author.

The text of Berne Article 9(2) was not adopted into Article 30 of the TRIPS Agreement without change. Whereas the final condition in Berne Article 9(2) ("legitimate interests") simply refers to the legitimate interests of the author, the TRIPS negotiators added in Article 30 the instruction that account must be taken of "the legitimate interests of third parties". Absent further explanation in the records of the TRIPS negotiations, however, the Panel was not able to attach a substantive meaning to this change other than what is already obvious in the text itself, namely that the reference to the "legitimate interests of third parties" makes sense only if the term "legitimate interests" is construed as a concept broader than legal interests.

. . . .

In sum, after consideration of the ordinary meaning of the term "legitimate interests", as it is used in Article 30, the Panel was unable to accept the EC's interpretation of that term as referring to legal interests pursuant to Article 28.1. Accordingly, the Panel was unable to accept the primary EC argument with regard to the third condition of Article 30. It found that the EC argument based solely on the patent owner's legal rights pursuant to Article 28.1, without reference to any more particular normative claims of interest, did not raise a relevant claim of non-compliance with the third condition of Article 30.

After reaching the previous conclusion concerning the EC's primary argument under the "legitimate interests" condition of Article 30, the Panel then directed its attention to another line of argument raised in statements made by the EC and by one third party. This second line of argument called attention to the fact that patent owners whose innovative products are subject to marketing approval requirements suffer a loss of economic benefits to the extent that delays in obtaining government approval prevent them from marketing their product during a substantial part of the patent term. According to information supplied by Canada, regulatory approval of new pharmaceuticals usually does not occur until approximately eight to 12 years after the patent application has been filed, due to the time needed to complete development of the product and the time needed to comply with the regulatory procedure itself. The result in the case of pharmaceuticals, therefore, is that the innovative producer is in fact able to market its patented product in only the remaining eight to 12 years of the 20-year patent term, thus receiving an effective period of market exclusivity that is only 40–60 per cent of the period of exclusivity normally envisaged in a 20-year patent term. The EC argued that patent owners who suffer a reduction of effective market exclusivity from such delays should be entitled to impose the same type of delay in connection with corresponding regulatory requirements upon the market entry of competing products. According to the EC,

> [T]here exists no reason why the research based pharmaceutical enterprise is obliged to accept the economic consequence of patent term erosion because of marketing approval requirements which reduce their effective term of protection to 12-8 years while the copy producer should be entirely compensated for the economic consequence of the need of marketing approval for his generic product, and at the expense of the inventor and patent holder.
>
> . . . .

The type of normative claim put forward by the EC has been affirmed by a number of governments that have enacted de jure extensions of the patent term, primarily in the case of pharmaceutical products, to compensate for the de facto diminution of the normal period of market exclusivity due to delays in obtaining marketing approval. According to the information submitted to the Panel, such extensions have been enacted by the European Communities, Switzerland, the United States, Japan, Australia and Israel. The EC and Switzerland have done so while at the same time allowing patent owners to continue to use their exclusionary rights to gain an additional, de facto extension of market exclusivity by preventing competitors from applying for regulatory approval during the term of the patent. The other countries that have enacted de jure patent term extensions have also, either by legislation or by judicial decision, created a regulatory review exception similar to Section 55.2(1), thereby eliminating the possibility of an additional de facto extension of market exclusivity.

. . . .

This positive response to the claim for compensatory adjustment has not been universal, however. In addition to Canada, several countries have adopted, or are in the process of adopting, regulatory review exceptions similar to Section 55.2(1) of the Canadian Patent Act, thereby removing the de facto extension of market exclusivity, but these countries have not enacted, and are not planning to enact, any de jure extensions of the patent term for producers adversely affected by delayed marketing approval. When regulatory review exceptions are enacted in this manner, they represent a decision not to restore any of the period of market exclusivity due to lost delays in obtaining marketing approval. Taken as a whole, these government decisions may represent either disagreement with the normative claim made by the EC in this proceeding, or they may simply represent a conclusion that such claims are outweighed by other equally legitimate interests.

On balance, the Panel concluded that the interest claimed on behalf of patent owners whose effective period of market exclusivity had been reduced by delays in marketing approval was neither so compelling nor so widely recognized that it could be regarded as a "legitimate interest" within the meaning of Article 30 of the TRIPS Agreement. Notwithstanding the number of governments that had responded positively to that claimed interest by granting compensatory patent term extensions, the issue itself was of relatively recent standing, and the community of governments was obviously still divided over the merits of such claims. Moreover, the Panel believed that it was significant that concerns about regulatory review exceptions in general, although well known at the time of the TRIPS negotiations, were apparently not clear enough, or compelling enough, to make their way explicitly into the recorded agenda of the TRIPS negotiations. The Panel believed that Article 30's "legitimate interests" concept should not be used to decide, through adjudication, a normative policy issue that is still obviously a matter of unresolved political debate.

Consequently, having considered the two claims of "legitimate interest" put forward by the EC, and having found that neither of these claimed interests can be considered "legitimate interests" within the meaning of the third condition of Article 30 of the TRIPS Agreement, the Panel concluded that Canada had demonstrated to the Panel's satisfaction that Section 55.2(1) of Canada's Patent Act did not prejudice "legitimate interests" of affected patent owners within the meaning of Article 30.

Having reviewed the conformity of Section 55.2(1) with each of the three conditions for an exception under Article 30 of the TRIPS Agreement, the Panel concluded that Section 55.2(1) does satisfy all three conditions of Article 30, and thus is not inconsistent with Canada's obligations under Article 28.1 of the TRIPS Agreement.

[The Panel concluded that the anti-discrimination rule of Article 27.1 does apply to exceptions of the kind authorized by Article 30.]

We turn, accordingly, to the question of whether Section 55.2(1) of the Canadian Patent Act discriminates as to fields of technology.

. . . .

With regard to the issue of de jure discrimination, the Panel concluded that the European Communities had not presented sufficient evidence to raise the issue in the face of Canada's formal declaration that the exception of Section 55.2(1) was not limited to pharmaceutical products. Absent other evidence, the words of the statute compelled the Panel to accept Canada's assurance that the exception was legally available to every product that was subject to marketing approval requirements. In reaching this conclusion, the Panel took note that its legal finding of conformity on this point was based on a finding as to the meaning of the Canadian law that was in turn based on Canada's representations as to the meaning of that law, and that this finding of conformity would no longer be warranted if, and to the extent that, Canada's representations as to the meaning of that law were to prove wrong.

. . . .

In sum, the Panel found that the evidence in record before it did not raise a plausible claim of discrimination under Article 27.1 of the TRIPS

Agreement. It was not proved that the legal scope of Section 55.2(1) was limited to pharmaceutical products, as would normally be required to raise a claim of de jure discrimination. Likewise, it was not proved that the adverse effects of Section 55.2(1) were limited to the pharmaceutical industry, or that the objective indications of purpose demonstrated a purpose to impose disadvantages on pharmaceutical patents in particular, as is often required to raise a claim of de facto discrimination. Having found that the record did not raise any of these basic elements of a discrimination claim, the Panel was able to find that Section 55.2(1) is not inconsistent with Canada's obligations under Article 27.1 of the TRIPS Agreement. Because the record did not present issues requiring any more precise interpretation of the term "discrimination" in Article 27.1, none was made.

VIII. Conclusions

In light of the findings above, the Panel has concluded as follows:

(1) Section 55.2(1) of Canada's Patent Act is not inconsistent with Canada's obligations under Article 27.1 and Article 28.1 of the TRIPS Agreement.

(2) Section 55.2(2) of Canada's Patent Act is not consistent with the requirements of Article 28.1 of the TRIPS Agreement.

Accordingly, the Panel recommends that the Dispute Settlement Body request that Canada bring Section 55.2(2) into conformity with Canada's obligations under the TRIPS Agreement.

NOTES AND QUESTIONS

(1) **WTO Adjudication.** The Canada-Pharmaceuticals panel report holds that Article 30's "legitimate interests" concept "should not be used to decide, through adjudication, a normative policy issue that is still obviously a matter of unresolved political debate." What does this say about the nature of the WTO panel/Appellate Body system? We will return to this issue *infra* Chapter 5.

(2) **Scope of TRIPS Article 33.** On May 5, 2000, the WTO published another panel report on Canada's patent law, upon a request of the United States. *See Canada-Term of Patent Protection*, WT/DS170/R (WTO DSB Panel, May 5, 2000). The panel agreed with the United States that Canada's failure to grant a term of at least twenty years from filing on patent applications filed under the Canadian Patent Act prior to 1989 was a violation of its obligation under Article 33 to provide a term of not less than twenty years from filing and its obligation under Article 70.2 to provide protection to "all subject matter existing at the date of application of [TRIPS]." In the course of its decision, the panel stated:

Interpretation of Article 33 as a minimum standard for the expiry of the available term of protection ("minimum standard") is also borne out by Article 1.1 of the TRIPS Agreement which forms part of the context of Article 33. Article 1.1 provides: "Members shall give effect to the provisions of this Agreement. Members may, but shall not be obliged to, implement in their law more extensive protection than is required by this Agreement, provided that such protection does not contravene the provisions of this Agreement."

Article 1.1 confirms that the TRIPS Agreement is a minimum standards agreement in respect of intellectual property rights. The textual reading of Article 1.1 suggests that Members are to "give effect" to, inter alia, Article 33 which obligates Members to make available a term of protection for patents that does not end before 20 years from the date of filing.

By making available a term of protection that runs 17 years from the date of grant for those patents that were filed before 1 October 1989, Section 45 of Canada's Patent Act, on its face, does not meet the minimum standard of Article 33 in all cases. This is confirmed by the figures presented by Canada which show that there were still extant, as of 1 January 2000, approximately 66,936 Old Act patents, representing approximately 40 per cent of the total 169,966 Old Act patents, that would expire before 20 years from the date of filing.

¶¶ 6.86–87.

Canada appealed the panel's adverse decision to the Appellate Body in June, 2000, arguing that according to Article 70.1, the TRIPS Agreement did not give rise to obligations in respect of patents granted under the old law because such patent grants were "acts" which occurred before the date of application of the Agreement. The Appellate Body affirmed in a decision published on September 18, 2000 (WT/DS170/AB/R). Distinguishing between " 'acts' and the 'rights' created by those 'acts' " (paras. 56–60), it stated that "[a] contrary interpretation would seriously erode the scope of the other provisions of Article 70, especially the explicit provisions of Article 70.2." The Appellate Body found that its interpretation of Article 70 did not amount to a retroactive application of the TRIPS Agreement, and was in conformity with the non-retroactivity principles codified in Article 28 of the Vienna Convention on the Law of Treaties. It went on to summarily affirm the panel's interpretation of Articles 33 and 70.2, and recommended that the DSB request Canada to bring Section 45 into conformity with its obligations under TRIPS. Canada amended its Patent Act in July 2001 to comply with the WTO ruling, one month before the deadline set by the WTO.

(3) **Tactical Considerations.** Are industrialized states such as EC or the U.S. likely to bring cases against developing nations for failures similar to Canada's? If so, are such states likely to comply with an unfavorable

ruling? The predicted and actual alignment of parties in WTO proceedings is discussed *infra* § 5.03[A].

(4) **Viability of "TRIPS-plus" Noncompliance Sanctions.** Has "TRIPS-plus" become defunct as a basis for Special 301 proceedings concerning patent protection in developing countries? *See infra* § 5.02 (discussing Special 301). The United States at one time asserted that countries could still be subject to Special 301 proceedings even if they were in compliance with the compulsory licensing provisions found in Article 31 of TRIPS. However, in January 2001, USTR Ambassador Barshevsky announced that, in engaging the other countries of the western hemisphere in FTAA negotiations, the U.S. would limit its response to circumstances in which FTAA countries use a patented product or process, or allow third parties to do so, without the patent holder's consent. Where FTAA countries provide for such use, it must adhere to the requirements applicable to compulsory licensing set out in Article 31 of the TRIPS Agreement and Article 5A(4) of the Paris Convention (and, impliedly, no higher.) The U.S. proposal also stated that it will no longer challenge generic pharmaceutical or agricultural chemical manufacturers for making, using or selling a patented product or process to obtain government marketing approval during the term of the patent so that they can compete with the patent owner soon after the patent expires. Under the U.S. proposal, FTAA countries would agree that so long as the patent remains valid the product or process may be made, used, or sold in their country by competitors only to meet marketing approval requirements. *See* www.ustr.gov/regions/whemisphere/intel.html. It makes no mention of the ongoing dispute in the WTO with Brazil over working requirement and compulsory licensing provisions set forth in the Brazilian patent law.

§ 4.05   Sui Generis Protection of Plants

FREE DISTRIBUTION VERSUS CONTROLLED CULTIVATION

As early as 1556, Spain's Council of the Indies (convened in Madrid) passed legislation making it illegal for foreigners to explore for plants in Spain's New World possessions. During the seventeenth and eighteenth centuries, botanical gardens were established in many European metropolitan states, the most famous being the British Empire collection of plants at Kew Gardens outside London. Such botanical gardens were established to develop systematic collections of plants for study, development, distribution, and commercialization throughout the colonial empires. Plant specimens were not distributed except in connection with the establishment of plantations within the British colonies controlled from London. A mere 100 plants were introduced to Great Britain during the sixteenth century. That figure rose to 1,000 in the seventeenth and 9,000 in the eighteenth centuries. A memorable example was Captain Bligh's mission on the Bounty to bring back breadfruit plants from Tahiti for plantations in the British West Indies.

Common staples from the Americas such as maize, potatoes, squash, tomatoes, peanuts, beans, and sunflowers were transferred to the eastern hemisphere. But equally, if not more, important were strategic plants requiring tropical empires such as spices, sugar, bananas, coffee, tea, rubber, and indigo. The Darjeeling tea industry was started in Calcutta with plants shipped on British ships from Shanghai. The rubber plantations of southeast Asia were built on propagations from disease-free rubber trees spirited out of northeast Brazil in 1876. Within a few years, Brazil's share of rubber exports plummeted from 100% to 5% while the British share rose from 0 to 75 %. Northeast Brazil became a depressed area and remains so to this day. Similarly, expensive cinchona exports from the Andes, used to extract quinine for malaria treatment, dropped 75% in a three-year period in the 1880s as production began on British colonial plantations in labor-rich Asia.

Control of plant production within the European empires emanated from control of the physical plants themselves. "The U.S. government made no effort to limit or control the dissemination of the plants it collected. In fact, the aim was to spread seeds widely and encourage the expansion and adaptation of American agriculture." CARY FOWLER, UNNATURAL SELECTION: TECHNOLOGY, POLITICS AND PLANT EVOLUTION xvii (1994). (Much of the following discussion is based on Fowler's account.)

Plant collection did not begin in earnest in the United States until Henry Ellsworth, a large landowner, became the first commissioner of patents in 1836. Ellsworth established a seed collection and distribution program at the Patent Office in 1839. The Shaker colonies of the northeast U.S. had been the first to develop seed packets for distribution. That function was taken over by the U.S. Patent Office in 1849 and later transferred to the Department of Agriculture.

In the late nineteenth century, over one-third of the budget of the U.S. Department of Agriculture was devoted to seed collection and distribution. The structure of American farming after the Civil War was quite different from that in the colonial empires and the ante-bellum South. American farms were small. Farmers were seed savers because of a lack of commercially reliable sources. That changed between 1860 and 1920. Commercial seed companies began to develop new seeds, and it became more economical for farmers to purchase new varieties produced by the commercial companies than to breed their own varieties.

LEGAL PROTECTION FOR NURSERIES PRODUCING ORNAMENTAL PLANTS AND FRUIT TREES

The United States Congress passed the Plant Patent Act of 1930 at the behest not of commercial seed companies but of commercial nurseries. In the United States, the plant patent statute (35 U.S.C. §§ 161–164) protects asexually reproduced plants commercially propagated through cuttings (clones) or grafts as opposed to seeds. Whereas plant breeders (seed companies) can be thought of as inventors, nurserymen are more properly described as discoverers. Practically all varieties of fruits are the result of chance discoveries and there is no "scientific" breeding of new varieties. In contrast to farmers, for whom the starting material is the same as the final product, the commercial nurseries do not compete with their customers because it is more cost effective for orchards and gardeners to buy stock than to raise it. The grant of the plant patent is the right to exclude others from asexually reproducing the plant or selling or using the plant so reproduced. 35 U.S.C. § 163.

The scope of protection for plant patents is very limited. Plant patent law covers fruits and flowers such as roses but specifically excepts potatoes and Jerusalem artichokes from coverage as well as all seed-propagated plants. Tuber-propagated plants alone among asexually reproduced plants are propagated by the same part of the plant that is sold as food. When the Plant Patent Act was passed, it was thought to have been politically inexpedient to include products which were staple foods such as corn, wheat, rice, and potatoes.

LEGAL PROTECTION FOR SEEDS (PLANT VARIETIES)

Plant breeding for uniformity was still rudimentary in the 1930s, so there was neither much pressure for patent protection nor ability to meet patent uniformity standards. The Netherlands adopted its Breeder's Ordinance in 1941, which provided a limited exclusive right for breeders of agriculturally important species to market the first generation of certified seed and a broader right to market propagating material. Corporate breeding programs began in earnest in the 1950s. Scientific plant breeding uses the principles of Mendelian genetics through sexual reproduction to produce consistent characteristics (desirable traits) which were not achieved by a blending of the characteristics of the parents as had been previously thought but by isolating them. When two closely related variations are crossed, there is produced a generation of inbreds which display what had been a recessive trait. The inbreds are then recrossed producing a hybrid which has the strength of the starting generation and displaying what had been a beneficial recessive trait in a ratio of 1:3. The breeder can place a "technological lock" (sometimes called "nature's patent") on the improved strain because only inbreds breed true, whereas hybrids do not. Therefore, breeding companies which sell the hybrid seeds but strictly control access to the inbreds thereby maintain the hybrid as a trade secret. Once the inbreds have been identified and preserved, the resultant hybrid is stable and will always have the same consistent traits. The customers of seed companies (the farmers) can own the seed they purchase, but the seed produced does not constitute breeding material.

THE UPOV CONVENTION

There developed a split between seed companies (particularly seed corn producers) which pursued research into hybrids and non-breeding seed companies which did not. Pressure from research-oriented seed companies investing in hybrid research grew toward recognition of "plant breeder's rights," protecting them from generic seed companies which did not. The Union for the Protection of New Varieties of Plants (*"Union pour la Protection des Obtentions Végétales"* ["UPOV"]) was drafted at the international Convention of the same name and adopted by member nations on December 2, 1961 at a diplomatic conference in Paris. The treaty made the various breeder's rights laws of the signatories subject to the principle of national treatment and provided a definition of "variety" to apply "to any cultivar, clone, line, stock or hybrid which is capable of cultivation" (Article 2) as long as it is "clearly distinguishable by one or more important characteristics from any other variety whose existence is a matter of common knowledge at the time when protection is applied for." The variety also had to be capable of precise description and be given a denomination by which it would be known which was not proprietary. The position of secretary-general of the union is held by the director-general of WIPO.

Nine years after the first international convention of UPOV, in 1970, the United States adopted the Plant Variety Protection Act, ("PVPA"). (7 U.S.C. §§ 2321 *et. seq.*) Like the UPOV Convention, the PVPA does not provide patent-like protection. It is a registration system which issues a Certificate of Plant Variety Protection to the breeder of any novel variety of sexually reproduced plant. The certificate holder has the exclusive right to sell or reproduce the plant, or to use it to produce (as distinguished from develop) a hybrid or different variety, extending for a period of eighteen years from the date of issue. Both of these *sui generis* forms of protection prevented other companies from multiplying and reselling registered varieties. Protection is provided for the varieties themselves—not the genes which determine their traits, and under the 1978 Act, breeders are free to use protected varieties to produce new varieties. Six vegetables were omitted from coverage (carrots, celery, cucumbers, okra, peppers and tomatoes) due to opposition not from farmers but from large food processors, such as the Campbell Soup Company, which develop and consume their own varieties of those crops and traditionally benefit from publicly and privately available germplasm stocks.

The UPOV Convention was amended in 1972, 1978, and 1991. The U.S. joined the 1978 version of the convention in 1981. By 1973, U.S. farm exports came to exceed chemicals and consumer goods in value. Viewed biologically, both laws provided protection for varieties, that is, for certain combinations of genes. The genes themselves were not made patentable. Breeders are left free to use patented varieties (with unpatented genes) to produce new combinations of genes and new patentable varieties. Furthermore, farmers retained the "right" to save his or her protected seed for replanting (or for resale, if the farmer was not principally in the business of reselling protected varieties).

Under the 1978 Act, a breeder is entitled to protection even if the variety for which protection is sought is a naturally occurring plant. Under the 1991

Act, discovery of a naturally occurring plant is not sufficient. The breeder must have somehow developed the variety in order to secure protection. Article 5(3) of the 1978 Act allowed other breeders to use a protected variety for creating new varieties without authorization.

Conditions for grant were tightened and the scope of the breeder's rights were extended significantly under the 1991 UPOV Act. To receive protection, a variety must meet the requirements of novelty, distinctness, uniformity, and stability. Extension of the scope of the right includes requiring authorization for any multiplication for production. The "farmer's right" to store and plant seed was replaced by a "farmer's privilege" requiring authorization of the breeder. The exception for experimentation and creation of other varieties was narrowed to eliminate use to create a variety which is an essential derivation of the protected variety. (Article 15) It was thought that modern biotechnology allows such close manipulation of genes that there was increasing likelihood for minor variations to be exploited as loopholes to protection of the variety—so-called "cosmetic breeding." The accession of Bulgaria and the Russian Federation on March 24, 1998 triggered the entry into force of the 1991 Act on April 24, 1998. As of that date, there were thirty-seven members of the Union and seven signatories of the 1991 text. (Bulgaria, Denmark, Germany, Israel, Netherlands, Russian Federation, and Sweden.)

Critics of plant breeder's rights complain of the growing separation between the farmer and the tools of farming. Farmers dependent on commercial seed producers for ever more efficient and pesticide/herbicide compatible hybrids no longer retain their old seed varieties.

> The explosion of diversity which had been ignited by seed collection and distribution programs and by immigration was wiped out as farmers ceased saving their own seed. Irrespective of the quality of these varieties relative to purchased seed, the farmer lost a measure of self-reliance in the process. And some portion of the germplasm itself, with all of its adaptation to different American environments, pests, diseases, and cultures became extinct, never again to be seen or used by a farmer or professional plant breeder.

FOWLER, *supra* at 118. "Genetic erosion" is an unintended consequence of modern plant breeding. To the extent that a breeder produces a successful variety, it may displace genetic material needed for future breeding programs.

Advocates of UPOV's system of breeder's rights point out that by the year 2020, the world population may reach 8 billion with 83 % living in developing countries. As productive farmland shrinks in the wake of urbanization, there is no option but to produce more food on less land. It becomes clear that the relevance of the small farmer is fading and the world is moving toward food production by agribusiness. *See, e.g.*, www.upov.int/eng/newplant/needvar.htm. The relevance of *sui generis* protection for plants where utility patent protection is allowed for the underlying genetic material is open to question in developed countries. However, American companies are supportive of the United States entering the 1991 Act for purposes of achieving national treatment in those countries which choose to use a *sui generis* system. Under the TRIPS Agreement, Article 27(3)(b), WTO members must provide either patent protection or sui generis protection for plants.

. . . .

CONVENTION FOR THE PROTECTION OF PLANTS
S. Treaty Doc. No. 104-17, Signed October 25, 1991
Read the first time in the Senate September 5, 1995

LETTER OF SUBMITTAL

DEPARTMENT OF STATE
Washington, May 10, 1995.

The PRESIDENT,
The White House.

I have the honor to submit to you [the 1991 Act of the UPOV Convention]. I recommend that the 1991 Act of the UPOV Convention be transmitted to the Senate for its advice and consent to ratification, subject to a reservation under Article 35(2) of the 1991 Act, which allows states party to the 1978 Act to retain their present patent systems for certain varieties of plants.

. . . .

Member States of the Convention constitute the International Union for the Protection of New Varieties of Plants (the UPOV Union), whose objective is to promote the protection of the rights of plant breeders in new plant varieties.

. . . .

Several considerations prompted the member States to revise the Convention at a Diplomatic Conference held in Geneva, Switzerland in March of 1991. Those considerations were: 1) recognition that the protection offered to breeders under previous Acts of the Convention was not adequate; 2) the need for the Convention to reflect technological changes in the breeding of new plant varieties; and 3) the need to clarify certain provisions of the 1978 Act.

Ten member States of UPOV signed the 1991 Act at the conclusion of the Conference. The 1991 Act remained open for signature by UPOV member States until March 31, 1991, by which time 16 States, including the United States, had signed the Convention.

. . . In the United States, implementing legislation was enacted as Public Law 103-349, on October 6, 1994.

The main aim of the Convention is to promote the protection of the rights of the breeder in new plant varieties. In that regard, the Convention not only requires member States to provide protection for new varieties of plants, but also contains explicit and detailed rules on the conditions and arrangements for granting protection. Further, it prescribes the scope of protection, including possible restrictions and exceptions thereto, establishes, with some limitations, the principle of national treatment for plant breeders from other member States, and provides for a right of priority.

The Convention, as revised by the 1991 Act, would afford additional protection to plant breeders, as follows:

First, the 1991 Act requires Contracting Parties, after certain transitional periods, to protect varieties of all genera and species of the plant kingdom.

Second, the 1991 Act redefines a breeder's right to cover, among other things, the production of a variety's propagating material by others for any purpose. The 1991 Act also expressly permits member States to exclude from the reach of the breeder's right, the practice of farmers to save seed.

Third, the 1991 Act extends breeders' rights to include harvested material of the protected variety.

Fourth, the 1991 Act puts an end to the common practice, permitted by the present Convention, of using protected varieties to derive and freely commercialize other varieties that, although differing to some degree, maintain the essential characteristics of the initial variety.

Finally, the 1991 Act is silent regarding the title of protection under which a breeder's right may be granted. This would afford member States the freedom to provide protection for plant varieties through patents and sui generis breeders' rights, thus affording them greater flexibility in determining how to protect new plant varieties most effectively.

These and other features of the 1991 Act would enhance the protection afforded to breeders of new plant varieties not only in the United States, but also in those future member States where patent protection for plant varieties is not now obtainable, and in present member States where protection of plant breeders' rights is either weak or unavailable for a significant number of plant species and genera.

. . . .

Prompt ratification of the 1991 Act of the UPOV Convention will demonstrate the United States commitment to effective protection for intellectual property in the area of new plant variety development. Ratification of this Convention is consistent, therefore, with United States foreign policy of encouraging other countries to provide adequate and effective protection for intellectual property generally, and for new plant varieties in particular.

I recommend, therefore, that the 1991 Act of the UPOV Convention be transmitted to the Senate as soon as possible for its advice and consent to ratification, subject to a reservation under Article 35(2), which allows parties to the 1978 Act to retain their present plant patent systems for certain varieties of plants.

Respectfully submitted,

PETER TARNOFF

TRIPS AGREEMENT, ARTICLE 27

1. Subject to the provisions of paragraphs 2 and 3 below, patents shall be available for any inventions, whether products or processes, in all fields of technology, provided that they are new, involve an inventive step and are capable of industrial application. Subject to paragraph 4 of Article 65, paragraph 8 of Article 70 and paragraph 3 of this Article, patents shall be available and patent rights enjoyable without discrimination as to the place of invention, the field of technology and whether products are imported or locally produced.

. . . .

3. Members may also exclude from patentability:

. . . .

(b) plants and animals other than microorganisms, and essentially biological processes for the production of plants or animals other than non-biological and microbiological processes. However, Members shall provide for the protection of plant varieties either by patents or by an effective sui generis system or by any combination thereof. The provisions of this sub-paragraph shall be reviewed four years after the entry into force of the Agreement Establishing the WTO.

NOTES AND QUESTIONS

(1) **Patent Rights and Breeders Rights.** The scope of patentable subject matter for biotechnology expands, what is the role of "breeder's rights?" The chief patent counsel of a multinational agribusiness company stated to your editor that his company rarely uses the PVPA registration system, but strongly supports U.S. entry into the 1991 UPOV Convention. Why?

(2) **Legal Protection and Financial Investment.** A 1988 report of the Office of Technology Assessment noted substantial increases in private investment in agricultural research following the *Chakrabarty* decision. The same study also notes that investment shifted toward research on major crops such as corn and soybeans, and away from research on minor crops

at the same time that the USDA abandoned its role in seed and plant variety development and genetic erosion concerns grow. Is the policy trade-off worth the risks? *See* OFFICE OF TECHNOLOGY ASSESSMENT, NEW DEVELOPMENTS IN BIOTECHNOLOGY: PATENTING LIFE 75–81, Doc. No. Y3.T22/2:2B52/4/V.5/pt.3/agric.

(3) **1991 UPOV.** A good summary of the 1991 amendments to the UPOV Convention can be found in Barry Greengrass, *The 1991 Act of the UPOV Convention*, 12 EUR. INTELL. PROP REV. 466 (1991).

(4) **Plant Patents as Copyright-Like Protection.** The U.S. Plant Patent Act protects only against copying and not against independent discovery or invention. *See* David Bennett Bernstein, *Is a Plant Patent a Form of Copyright?*, 25 IDEA 31 (1985).

(5) **What Does The Term "Sui Generis" Mean in TRIPS Article 27(3)((b)?** Could a developing country adopt the text of the 1978 UPOV Convention, no longer open for accession, as a form of sui generis protection for plants. Changes are underway in developing countries regarding the protection of plant varieties, in compliance with Article 27 of the TRIPS Agreement. Not all parties are pleased at the prospect of India's decision to grant sui generis protection to plant varieties. *See* Biswajit Dhar & Sachin Chaturvedi, *Introducing Plant Breeders' Rights in India—A Critical Evaluation of the Proposed Legislation*, 1 J. WORLD INTEL. PROP. 245 (1998).

(6) **TRIPS and the CBD.** The OECD Committee for Scientific and Technological Policy released a report in 1996 summarizing the genetic resource issue and explaining how the new international context created by the Convention on Biological Diversity ("CBD") and the TRIPS agreement might influence the exploitation of genetic resources. *See Intellectual Property, Technology Transfer and Genetic Resources—An OECD Survey of Current Practices and Policies* (OECD, 1996), *available at* www.oecd.org/dsti/biotech/. The United States signed the CBD on June 3, 1993, but ratification by the Senate is unlikely in the near future.

(7) **Concerns in Developing Countries.** According to a *Statement from Peoples' Movements & NGOs in Southeast Asia to the World Trade Organization* dated May 1998 and published by the Filipino Farmer/Scientist Partnership for Development:

> Rice is life in Southeast and other parts of Asia. It has been the cornerstone of our food, our languages, our cultures—in short, our life for thousands of years. Over the centuries, farming communities throughout the region have developed, nurtured and conserved over a hundred thousand distinct varieties of rice to suit different tastes and needs.
>
> The Green Revolution spearheaded by the International Rice Research Institute ("IRRI") in the 1960s resulted the loss of this diversity from farmers' fields and the spread of wholly unsustainable farming systems which require high energy inputs such as pesticides, fertilizers, so-called 'high-yielding' seeds, irrigation

systems and supervised credit schemes. In this process, farmers lost control of their own seeds, their own knowledge and their own self-confidence. Today, people are struggling throughout the region to rebuild more sustainable agriculture systems hinged on farmers' control of genetic resources and local knowledge.

In the past, the whole cycle of the rice economy was under the control of farmers themselves, from production through distribution. Today, global corporations are taking over the rice sector. With the expansion of industrial farming, global corporations—and their local subsidiaries established their predominance in the rice sector through research programs, interference in policy-making, and their exports of farm machinery, pesticides and fertilizers. Now, through the use of genetic engineering, they are increasing their control over our rice cultures. The kinds of rice that we are promised through this technology threaten the environment and public health. For example, herbicide tolerant rice will lead to increased pesticide use. Rice incorporating Bacillus thuringiensis genes will disrupt ecological balances. Both of these are unsafe for consumers and will lead to allergic reactions, increased antibiotic resistance and other health hazards. New hybrids—such as those based on the so-called "Terminator Technology"—will force farmers to buy rice seed every planting season from transnational corporations.

The extension of the patent system through the [TRIPS Agreement] gives global corporations the right to claim monopoly ownership over rice—and life itself. Companies in the industrialized world have already started to claim intellectual property rights on rice. A derivative of IR-8, IRRI's "miracle rice", was monopolised through IPR in the United States already in the 1980s. Recently, RiceTec, a company in Texas, has taken out a patent on basmati rice. This is biopiracy against India and Pakistan. The same company and many others in the US are now marketing what they label as Jasmine rice. This is not only intellectual and cultural theft, it also directly threatens farm communities in Southeast Asia. Jasmine rice comes from Thailand, where it is grown today by over five million resource-poor farmers who are trying to develop ecological alternatives for Jasmine ice production and marketing.

MASIPAG at *masipag@mozcom.com*. Are these claims legitimate? The issues will be explored further below in the discussion of the European Directive on Biotechnological Inventions. We will also return to these issues in Chapter 8.

§ 4.06 Regional Harmonization: the European Union

Regional harmonization of patent law and of exploitation of patent rights is most highly developed in the context of European integration. The following two readings discuss the 1996 European Regulation on Technology Licensing and the 1998 European Directive on the Legal Protection of

Biotechnological Inventions. The European Patent System will be discussed at greater length in Chapter 6 in the context of the multinational acquisition of patent rights.

BRYAN HARRIS, TECHNOLOGY LICENSING IN THE EUROPEAN UNION *
38 IDEA 139 (1997)

I. THE PROHIBITION OF RESTRICTIVE AGREEMENTS

Intellectual property law creates monopolies; antitrust law condemns them. The reconciliation of these two bodies of law presents endless difficulties for both judges and lawmakers. This article examines the recent efforts of the legislators of the European Union to balance these opposing interests through the enactment of a coherent set of rules on certain categories of technology transfer agreements. These rules are known as the Commission Regulation on the Application of Article 85(3) of the Treaty establishing the European Community to Certain Categories of Technology Transfer Agreements.[1]

We begin by exploring how the antitrust or competition rules are applied in the European Union. Article 85(1) of the Treaty establishing the European Community (the EC Treaty)[2] prohibits agreements between undertakings which may affect trade between member states and which have as their object or effect the prevention, restriction, or distortion of trade. However, under Article 85(3) of the EC Treaty, the provisions of Article 85(1) may be declared inapplicable in the case of agreements or categories of agreements between undertakings when certain conditions are fulfilled. A declaration of inapplicability is made by the Commission of the European Communities and the arrangements for exempting categories of agreements, as distinct from individual or specific agreements, take the form of so-called "block exemption" regulations. In other words, an agreement such as a technology transfer license may or may not restrict competition, and if such an agreement does restrict competition, it may or may not qualify for exemption. These are matters on which the Commission rules,[3] and from which there is a right of appeal to the Court of Justice of the European Communities (or, since 1988, to the Court of First Instance). The establishment of a block exemption for patent licenses took many years to achieve and the establishment of such an exemption for know-how licenses took even longer. Patent licenses, know-how licenses, and licenses with mixed

---

* Copyright 1997, Bryan Harris.

[1] The regulation of 31 January 1996, on the Application of Article 85(3) of the TREATY ESTABLISHING THE EUROPEAN COMMUNITY, to Certain Categories of Technology Transfer Agreements, 1996 O.J. (L 31) 2. [hereinafter "the Regulation"].

[2] TREATY ESTABLISHING THE EUROPEAN COMMUNITY, Feb. 7, 1992, 1 C.M.L.R. 573 (1992) *incorporating changes made by* TREATY ON EUROPEAN UNION, Feb. 7, 1992 O.J. © 224) 1 (1992), [1992] 1 C.M.L.R. 719 (1992).

[3] EC Treaty art. 155.

elements, including those that contain clauses on trademark and copyright licensing, are currently covered by the new block exemption regulation on Technology Transfer Agreements.

II. EXEMPTION OF CATEGORIES OF AGREEMENTS ("BLOCK EXEMPTIONS")

Before discussing the content of Commission Regulation 240/96, it is helpful to explain how a block exemption regulation eases the burden on licensors, licensees, and their advisers. Without block exemptions, only individual exemptions can be granted by the Commission under Article 85(3) of the EC Treaty, and the process of obtaining an individual exemption can be slow and hazardous. The process tends to be slow because of the large backlog of individual cases being investigated at any given time by the Commission. The process tends to be hazardous because its quasi-judicial character allows for objections by third parties, hearings, and even the interjection of political considerations.[4] By contrast, a block exemption is essentially automatic. If a licensing agreement satisfies the terms of the block exemption regulation, no further formalities need be followed. The parties save time and trouble, and the Commission does not become bogged down in individual proceedings.

The New Technology Licensing Regulation

The Regulation seeks to: (1) combine the earlier regulations on patent licensing and know-how licensing into a single regulation, (2) allow for a certain amount of overlap between industrial property rights, and (3) simplify the previous law. Whether the third objective is being achieved remains to be seen. Although industrial interests have generally welcomed the Regulation, there is some skepticism.

In combining patent and know-how licensing in a single regulation, the Commission has created three categories of license agreements: "pure" patent licensing agreements, "pure" know-how licensing agreements, and "mixed" agreements that, according to the Commission, are playing an increasingly important role in the transfer of technology. Both pure and mixed agreements may contain provisions for licensing other intellectual property rights, such as trademarks, design rights, copyright, and software protection. These provisions are covered by the regulation to the extent that they contribute to the licensing of technology and are only ancillary provisions. However, the regulation does not cover what may be described in antitrust parlance as "horizontal" agreements.

Over the years, block exemption regulations have tended to conform to a fairly recognizable pattern. Essentially, the scheme of the Regulation is as follows: Article 1(1) declares that Article 85(1) of the EC Treaty—the

---

4 Council Regulation 17/62/EEC, art. 19, 1962 O.J. (L 13), *see generally,* Commission Regulation 99/63/EEC, 1963 O.J. (L 127).

prohibition on restrictive agreements—shall not apply to certain categories of agreements that include one or more of the obligations set out in the Article. In other words, Article 1 both defines the agreements in question and exempts them. Article 2(1) allows the exemption to apply to agreements notwithstanding the presence of certain clauses that are generally not restrictive of competition and which are set out in the Article. Article 2 is intended to clarify the status of certain provisions that may appear restrictive but are regarded by the Commission as acceptable. Article 3 lists the circumstances, including the presence of certain clauses in an agreement, that will ensure that the licensing agreement does not qualify for exemption under the regulation. Finally, the Regulation contains Articles providing for exclusions, special cases, and the withdrawal of exemption in certain circumstances.[16]

Definition and Exemption: Article 1

Following the pattern noted above, Article 1 of the regulation defines the agreements and exempts them.[17] The definition has three parts: (1) the broad description of the types of agreements concerned, (2) the condition that only two undertakings are party to the agreement, and (3) the list of obligations, the inclusion of one or more of which brings the agreement within the scope of the regulation.

The types of agreements concerned are pure patent or know-how licensing agreements and mixed patent and know-how licensing agreements. These agreements include those that contain ancillary provisions relating to intellectual property rights other than patents or know-how. The limitation to agreements to which only two undertakings are a party has been mentioned. However, it should be noted that the case law of the Court of Justice of the European Communities has much to say on what constitutes an undertaking. It may be a person or a company (a natural or legal person, in continental law) and may include a variety of entities, including public bodies if, in this context, they are carrying out an economic function.

There are eight qualifying obligations:

1. an obligation on the licensor not to license other undertakings to exploit a licensed technology in a licensed territory;

2. an obligation on the licensor not to exploit a licensed technology in a licensed territory;

3. an obligation on the licensee not to exploit a licensed technology in a territory of the licensor within the common market [sole license];

4. an obligation on the licensee not to manufacture or use a licensed product, or use a licensed process in territories within the common market that are licensed to other licensees;

---

[16] *See* Council Regulation 19/65/EEC, 1965-1966 O.J. Spec. Ed. 36 (block exemption regulations are made by the Commission under powers delegated by the Council).

[17] Article 1 is explained and justified by Recitals 10 and 12–16. Recitals are essential to the regulation, under Article 190 of the EC Treaty, and may be cited in proceedings.

5. an obligation on the licensee not to pursue an active policy of putting a licensed product on the market in territories within the common market that are licensed to other licensees, and in particular not to engage in advertising specifically aimed at those territories or to establish any branch or maintain any distribution depot there;

6. an obligation on the licensee not to put a licensed product on the market in territories licensed to other licensees within the common market in response to unsolicited orders;

7. an obligation on the licensee to use only the licensor's trademark or trade dress to distinguish a licensed product during the term of the agreement, provided the licensee is not prevented from identifying itself as the manufacturer of the licensed products; and

8. an obligation on the licensee to limit production of a licensed product to the quantities required in manufacturing the licensee's products and to sell the licensed product only as an integral part of or a replacement part for the licensee's own products or otherwise in connection with the sale of these products, provided that such quantities are freely determined by the licensee.

The rules are concerned with the question of territoriality, not purely for reasons of competition. This is because one of the main objects of the EC Treaty was to create a single market without barriers to interstate trade. If intellectual property rights are given absolute territorial protection in the member states, the principle of free movement of goods throughout the Community would be jeopardized. In any event, the Court of Justice ruled in 1982 that absolute territorial protection could not be exempted, and the original block exemption regulation on patent licensing agreements was drafted with the Court's ruling in mind.[21]

Permitted Clauses: Article 2

Article 2 deals with permitted clauses in agreements covered by the regulation. There is an oddity in the wording of Article 2, which provides that the exemption applies to agreements "notwithstanding" the presence of the clauses listed in the Article. This gives the impression that the clauses are accepted on sufferance. But Article 2 goes on to describe the clauses as ones "which are not generally restrictive of competition." This suggests that the list is there simply *ex abundanti cautela* (from an abundance of caution), but the Article is clearly more important than a simple declaration of what is not regarded as objectionable.

As a guide to patentees and their legal advisers on the clauses that are permitted in technology transfer licensing agreements, the following list from Article 2 is invaluable:

---

[21] Case 258/78, Nungesser v. Commission, 1982 E.C.R. 2015 (1983) (sometimes referred to as the *Maize Seed* case).

1. an obligation on the licensee not to divulge the know-how communicated by the licensor (the licensee may be held to this obligation after the agreement has expired);

2. an obligation on the licensee not to grant sublicenses or to assign the license;

3. an obligation on the licensee not to exploit licensed know-how or patents after termination of an agreement as long as the know-how is still secret or the patents are still in force;

4. an obligation on the licensee to grant to the licensor a license in respect of improvements to or new applications of the licensed technology, provided that: (a) in the case of severable improvements, such a license is not exclusive, so that the licensee is free to use the improvements or to license them to third parties, insofar as such licensing does not involve disclosure of the know-how communicated by the licensor that is still secret; and (b) the licensor undertakes to grant an exclusive or non-exclusive license of improvements to the licensee;

5. an obligation on the licensee to observe minimum quality specifications, including technical specifications, for a licensed product or to procure goods or services from an undertaking designated by the licensor, insofar as these quality specifications, products or services are necessary for a technically proper exploitation of the licensed technology, or for ensuring that the product of the licensee conforms to the minimum quality specifications that are applicable to the licensor and other licensees, and to allow the licensor to carry out related checks;

6. an obligation to inform the licensor of misappropriation of know-how, infringement of licensed patents, or to take or assist the licensor in instituting legal action against such misappropriation or infringement;

7. an obligation on the licensee to continue paying royalties: (a) until the end of the agreement in the amounts, for the periods, and according to the methods freely determined by the parties, in the event of the know-how becoming publicly known other than by action of the licensor, without prejudice to the payment of any additional damages in the event of the know-how becoming publicly known by the action of the licensee in breach of the agreement; or (b) over a period going beyond the duration of the licensed patents, in order to facilitate payment;

8. an obligation on the licensee to restrict exploitation of the licensed technology to one or more technical fields of application covered by the licensed technology or to one or more product markets;

9. an obligation on the licensee to pay a minimum royalty, to produce a minimum quantity of a licensed product, or to carry out a minimum number of operations exploiting the licensed technology;

10. an obligation on the licensor to grant to the licensee any more favorable terms that the licensor may grant to another undertaking after the agreement is entered into;

11. an obligation on the licensee to mark a licensed product with an indication of the licensor's name or of the licensed patent;

12. an obligation on the licensee not to use the licensor's technology to construct facilities for third parties (this is without prejudice to the right of the licensee to increase the capacity of its own facilities or to set up additional facilities for use on normal commercial terms, including the payment of additional royalties);

13. an obligation on the licensee to supply only a limited quantity of a licensed product to a particular customer, where the license was granted so that the customer might have a second source of supply inside the licensed territory (this provision shall also apply where the customer is the licensee and the license that was granted in order to provide a second source of supply provides that the customer is to manufacture the licensed products itself or have them manufactured by a subcontractor);

14. a reservation by the licensor of the right to exercise the rights conferred by a patent to oppose the exploitation of the technology by the licensee outside the licensed territory;

15. a reservation by the licensor of the right to terminate the agreement if the licensee contests the secret or substantial nature of licensed know-how or challenges the validity of licensed patents within the common market belonging to the licensor or undertakings connected with it;

16. a reservation by the licensor of the right to terminate a patent license agreement if the licensee raises the claim that such a patent is not necessary;[22]

17. an obligation on the licensee to use best efforts to manufacture and market a licensed product; and

18. a reservation by the licensor of the right to terminate the exclusivity granted to the licensee and to stop licensing improvements to licensee when the licensee enters into competition within the common market with the licensor, with undertakings connected with the licensor or with other undertakings in respect of research and development, production, use or distribution of competing products, and to require the licensee to prove that the licensed know-how is not being used for the production of products and the provision of services other than those licensed.

As the opening words of Article 2 suggest, there are occasions when the clauses listed above are restrictive of competition. In these circumstances, they are exempted, even if they are not accompanied by any of the obligations exempted by Article 1. The rationale is that when clauses are

---

[22] If a licensee claims that a patent is not necessary, perhaps because the substantial part of the design or process is in the public domain, or covered by know-how, the licensor of that patent may terminate the licensing agreement. This right to terminate the licensing agreement is not considered to be restrictive of competition. If it turns out that the licensee is wrong in claiming that the patent is unnecessary, he may expose himself to patent infringement proceedings. Also in this case, the licensor or other party pursuing infringement proceedings, would not be in breach of the rules on competition.

acceptable and not restrictive of competition, they fall squarely within Article 2. However, when clauses are restrictive of competition but are nevertheless acceptable, they are more in the nature of qualifying clauses typical of those listed in Article 1. Clauses similar to those listed in Article 2 but having a more limited scope are also exempted on the same terms.

Exemption Not Applied: Article 3

Article 2 is referred to by some lawyers as the "white list," while Article 3 is known as the "black list." Articles 1 and 2 pave the way for exemption, whereas Article 3 sets out the circumstances where no exemption applies. The circumstances covered by Article 3 are those in which:

1. one party is restricted in the determination of prices, components of prices, or discounts for the licensed products;

2. one party is restricted from competing within the common market with the other party, with undertakings connected with the other party or with other undertakings in respect of research and development, production, use, or distribution of competing products;[23]

3. one or both of the parties are required, without any objectively justified reason, to: (a) refuse to meet orders from users or resellers in their respective territories who would market products in other territories within the common market, or (b) make it difficult for users or resellers to obtain the products from other resellers within the common market, and in particular to exercise intellectual property rights or take measures so as to prevent users or resellers from obtaining outside products, or from putting on the market, in the licensed territory, products which have been lawfully put on the market, within the common market, by the licensor or with the licensor's consent, or (c) do so as a result of a concerted practice between them;

4. the parties were already competing manufacturers before the grant of the license and one of them is restricted, within the same technical field of use or within the same product market, as to the customers it may serve, in particular by being prohibited from supplying certain classes of users, employing certain forms of distribution, or with the aim of sharing customers, using certain types of packaging for the products

5. the quality of the licensed products one party may manufacture or sell, or the number of operations exploiting a licensed technology the party may carry out, are subject to limitations;

6. the licensee is obliged to assign, in whole or in part, to the licensor, rights to improvements to or new applications of a licensed technology; or

7. the licensor is prohibited (whether in separate agreements or through automatic extension of an agreement's initial duration for a period exceeding the length in Article 1(2) and (3)) from licensing other undertakings to exploit a licensed technology in the licensed territory, or from exploiting

---

[23] This is without prejudice to the last two clauses contained in the "white list."

a licensed technology in the other party's territory, or other licensees' territories.

Heading this list is the question of price-fixing, which is anathema to the Commission. There are few cases in which the Commission or Court has approved price restrictions. It is not surprising that the inclusion of a clause on price restriction rules out the chance that the agreement will be covered by the block exemption regulation. Nor is it surprising that the inclusion of a non-competition clause should have the same effect. A refusal-to-supply clause is subject to an objectively justified reason, but field-of-use restrictions are viewed more strictly. As for improvements in a licensed technology, the Commission has always tended to support the rights of the licensee as against those of the licensor.[31] Clauses favoring the licensor, by way of an obligation to assign rights to improvements, take the agreement out of the scope of the exemption.

The Opposition Procedure

It does not require a great feat of imagination to conceive of agreements which nearly comply with the terms of the Regulation, but fall just outside its scope because they contain obligations restrictive of competition that are not explicitly covered by Articles 1 and 2, and not expressly ruled out under Article 3. Under Article 4, these agreements are subject to an opposition procedure. The Commission must be notified of the agreements, but unless the Commission formally opposes exemption within a period of four months, the agreements will be "automatically" exempted. If an agreement is opposed, it is open to the parties either to show that the conditions of Article 85(3) of the EC Treaty are satisfied, or to amend the agreement in such a way as to persuade the Commission that the conditions of Article 85(3) are satisfied.

Exclusions

Article 5 of the Regulation specifies the types of agreements excluded from the scope of the regulation because of the circumstances in which these agreements are made. Broadly, these are horizontal agreements involving the pooling of technologies, the activities of joint ventures, reciprocal licensing and the like. There are provisions in this Article for *de minimis* principles to apply, so that some agreements of these types may be automatically exempted. For example, if the products and services covered by the agreement do not account for more than a given share of the market, the agreement is exempted from the regulation.

---

[31] There is a certain amount of case law on pricing, non-competition clauses, refusal-to-supply, field-of-use restrictions, and improvements in technology, but for the most part this case law antedates the 1984 and 1989 regulations. In recent years the Commission has tended to apply somewhat different, and perhaps more pragmatic, principles to its handling of the cases in this field. For these reasons, the case law is not quoted extensively, and, indeed, readers are advised to cite them with considerable caution, given the changed circumstances.

Circumstances Similar to Exclusive Licensing

Given the similarity between sales and exclusive licensing, and the danger that the requirements of the Regulation might be avoided by presenting exclusive licenses as assignments, Article 6 applies the exemption to agreements concerning the assignment and acquisition of patents or know-how where the risk associated with exploitation remains with the assignor. Article 6 also applies to licensing agreements where the licensor is not the holder of a patent or know-how but is authorized by the holder to grant the license (as in the case of sublicenses) and to licensing agreements in which the parties' rights or obligations are assumed by connected undertakings.

Withdrawal of the Benefit of the Regulation

Where the Commission finds that an agreement exempted by the Regulation nevertheless has certain effects which are incompatible with the conditions laid down in Article 85(3), the Commission may withdraw the benefit of the Regulation. These are factual, economic effects of actual circumstances which may vitiate an otherwise acceptable agreement. Article 6, which sets out these circumstances in general terms, also refers to four specific circumstances that are likely to persuade the Commission to withdraw the benefit of the Regulation. One refers to cases in which the effect of the agreement is to prevent a licensed product from being exposed, in a licensed territory, to effective competition from identical goods or services, or from goods or services considered by users as interchangeable in view of their characteristics, price, and intended use. This condition is especially apt to occur where the licensee's market share exceeds forty percent. Originally, the Commission wanted to make the forty percent market share a basic test of whether the Regulation should apply to certain agreements at all, but this was vigorously opposed, so the Commission had to make do with a reference to market share in subsidiary provisions of the regulation. Nevertheless, the inclusion of this provision in the withdrawal Article is a warning to parties to technology licensing agreements that the Commission, impressed by the ability of some powerful operators to manipulate the market by means of licensing agreements, will in certain cases pay close attention to market shares and the potential domination of the market.

Definitions

Most of the remaining provisions of the Regulation are concerned with definitions. Article 8, for example, includes a number of rights related to patents. Thus, patent applications, utility models, applications for registration of utility models, topographies of semi-conductor products, *certificats d'utilité* and *certificats d'addition* under French law, as well as applications for those certificates, supplementary protection certificates, and plant breeders' certificates, are all deemed to be patents for the purposes of the regulation.

Of the seventeen definitions set out in Article 10 of the Regulation, those concerned with the meaning of "know-how" are among the most important. Under the Article, "know-how" itself means a body of technical information that is secret, substantial and identified in any appropriate form. "Secret" means that a know-how package in the precise configuration and assembly of its components is not generally known or easily accessible. It is not limited to the narrow sense that each individual component of the know-how should be totally unknown or unobtainable outside the licensor's business. "Substantial" means that know-how includes information that must be useful, *i.e.*, can reasonably be expected at the date of conclusion of the agreement to be capable of improving the competitive position of the licensee. For example, know-how could enable the licensee to enter a new market or provide an advantage in competition. "Identified" is defined as the manner in which the know-how is described or recorded, to make it possible to verify that it satisfies the criteria of secrecy and substantiality, and to ensure that the licensee is not unduly restricted in exploiting the technology. To be identified, know-how can either be set out in the licensing agreement, in a separate document, or recorded in any other appropriate form, no later than shortly after the know-how is transferred, provided that the separate document or other record can be made available if the need arises.

Article 10 also defines the terms "necessary patents" and "parallel patents," which appear in paragraphs (2) and (3) of Article 1, that govern the periods to which an exemption applies. "Necessary patents" are those in which the patent is necessary for utilizing a licensed technology where, in the absence of such license, the realization of the licensed technology would not be possible, or would be possible only to a lesser extent, or in more difficult or costly conditions. Such patents must therefore be of technical, legal or economic interest to the licensee. "Parallel patents," on the other hand, are patents that, in spite of the absence of national rule unification concerning industrial property, protect the same invention in various Member States.

Miscellaneous Provisions

Article 9 provides for confidentiality.[41] Article 11 provides for the expiration of the earlier Commission Regulations 2349/84 on patents, and 556/89 on know-how. Article 12 provides for review of The Regulation. Article 13 provides that the Regulation is in force from April 1, 1996, to March 31, 2006.

---

[41] This provision adds to the general requirement of confidentiality contained in EC TREATY art. 214.

Comment

Given the complexity of the subject, the hostility of industrial interests to earlier drafts of the regulation, the difficulty of reconciling the need to restrict licenses to the extent required to make investment worthwhile,[42] and the need to ensure that restrictions are consistent with competitive trade, the Commission has done an unenviable task well. Many more patent licensing and other technology licensing agreements will be covered by the automatic exemption implicit in the Regulation. This is largely due to the broadening of the base of the Regulation. Relatively few patent licenses have proven to be "pure" patent licenses. Many agreements in the past had failed to fit into a precise mold.

Industrial interests still have some reservations about the Regulation—specifically about the market share principle. A great deal depends on how far the Commission takes advantage of the opposition procedure, and of the right to withdraw the benefit of the Regulation. In other words, we shall have to wait and see how well The Regulation operates in practice. This may be hard to judge, since the very nature of automatic exemption under the block exemption regulation is that it is invisible.[43] The Commission may have to publicly assess the application of The Regulation, probably in its annual reports on competition policy. The first of these assessments will be awaited with interest.

———

NOTES AND QUESTIONS

(1) **Scope of Exemption.** The Technology Transfer Block Exemption covers pure or mixed patent and know-how licenses, with licensing of other intellectual property rights included to the extent that they are ancillary to the patent and know-how licensing. But what does "ancillary" mean? Is a complex hybrid license which includes patents, copyrights, trademarks, and know-how, one in which the other rights are ancillary to the technology covered by patents and know-how? Moreover, the Exemption only covers licenses entered into between two undertakings. Software licenses which cover a chain of rights are not included. Nor are pooling arrangements for patents such as those in the automobile and aircraft manufacturing industries. Aren't such arrangements susceptible to anti-competitive effects? *See, e.g., Zenith Radio Corp. v. Hazeltine Research, Inc.,* 395 U.S. 100, 114 (1969). If so, is this a problem?

(2) **Review of the Block Exemption.** In December 2001, the European Commission published an Evaluation Report on the Block Exemption soliciting comments. *See* europa.eu.int/comm/competition/antitrust/technology_transfer/en.pdf. The Report inquires as to whether the scope of

---

[42] The investment factor influenced the Court of Justice in *Nungesser,* 1982 E.C.R. at 2015.

[43] As the cases covered by the regulation do not have to be tracked, the Commission has no statistics of the numbers of agreements automatically exempted.

the Regulation should be broadened to cover copyright, designs and trade-marks. It questions whether the "form-based legalistic" approach of the Exemption Regulation really determines whether a particular practice is anti-competitive. This critique generally follows a trend in the EC toward the adoption of a more economics-based approach to block exemptions. *See* Robert Lane, *Current Developments: EC Law III: Competition*, 50 INT'L. COMP. L.Q. 702, 707 (2001).

EUROPEAN UNION BIOTECHNOLOGY DIRECTIVE

Unlike the Commission Regulation discussed above, issued in accordance with ex-Article 235 (now Article 308) of the EC Treaty, European Community directives seeking approximation of national laws are intended to be more responsive to national cultural variations. *See supra* § 3.03[C][3] (discussing EU legislative instruments). An example is the directive on the legal protection of biotechnological inventions. Following a 1985 European Commission White Paper calling for approximation of intellectual property laws to complete the internal market, a draft directive containing guidelines for biotechnology inventions was proposed by the European Commission in 1988. The Commission noted that revolutionary changes in biotechnology, unforeseen when the European Patent Convention (with its exclusions from patentability) was drafted, had taken place. This 1988 draft directive was vehemently opposed by members of the Green parties in the European Parliament. A modified proposal incorporating provisions on ethics, farmers' "privilege," and compulsory licensing was issued in late 1992. After six years of political give-and-take between the Council, Commission, and Parliament, the revised Directive below was promulgated in early 1998. In the recitals of its preamble, the Directive makes findings concerning the increasingly important role biotechnological invention play in the Community's industrial development. It notes that research and development require a considerable amount of high-risk investment and therefore only adequate legal protection can make it profitable, but that concepts in national laws based upon the EPC and UPOV conventions had created uncertainty regarding the protection of biotechnological and certain micro-biological inventions in Europe. As eventually adopted, the directive attempts at a political compromise between environmental and animal rights activists on the one hand, and proponents of a U.S.-style system with very narrow exceptions to the general rule that "anything under the sun made by man" is patentable. As of December 2000, the Biotechnology Directive had been implemented into the national law in Denmark, Finland, Ireland, and the United Kingdom. A draft law was adopted in October 2000 by the German cabinet, for presentation in the German Parliament in 2001.

CONVENTION ON THE GRANT OF EUROPEAN PATENTS (EUROPEAN PATENT CONVENTION)
13 I.L.M. 271 (1974), as revised November 2000

Article 53

European patents shall not be granted in respect of

(a) inventions the publication or exploitation of which would be contrary to "ordre public" or morality, provided that the exploitation shall not be deemed to be so contrary merely because it is prohibited by law or regulation in some or all of the Contracting States;

(b) plant or animal varieties or essentially biological processes for the production of plants or animals; this provision does not apply to microbiological processes or the products thereof.

(c) methods for treatment of the human or animal body by surgery or therapy and diagnostic methods practised on the human or animal body; these provisions shall not apply to products, in particular substances or compositions, for use in any of these methods. *

DIRECTIVE OF THE EUROPEAN PARLIAMENT AND OF THE COUNCIL ON THE LEGAL PROTECTION OF BIOTECHNOLOGICAL INVENTIONS
1998 OJ (L213) 13 (July 30, 1998)

The European Parliament and the Council of the European Union,

Having regard to the Treaty establishing the European Community, and in particular Article 100a thereof,

Having regard to the proposal from the Commission,

Having regard to the Opinion of the Economic and Social Committee,

Acting in accordance with the procedure laid down in Article 189b of the Treaty,

. . . .

(13) Whereas the Community's legal framework for the protection of biotechnological inventions can be limited to laying down certain principles as they apply to the patentability of biological material as such, such principles being intended in particular to determine the difference between inventions and discoveries with regard to the patentability of certain elements of human origin, to the scope of protection conferred by a patent on a biotechnological invention, to the right to use a deposit mechanism in addition to written descriptions and lastly to the option of obtaining non-exclusive compulsory licences in respect of interdependence between plant varieties and inventions, and conversely;

---

* [Ed. Note: Article 53(c) EPC was formerly Article 52(4) EPC].

(14) Whereas a patent for invention does not authorize the holder to implement that invention, but merely entitles him to prohibit third parties from exploiting it for industrial and commercial purposes; whereas, consequently, substantive patent law cannot serve to replace or render superfluous national, European or international law which may impose restrictions or prohibitions or which concerns the monitoring of research and of the use or commercialization of its results, notably from the point of view of the requirements of public health, safety, environmental protection, animal welfare, the preservation of genetic diversity and compliance with certain ethical standards;

(15) Whereas no prohibition or exclusion exists in national or European patent law (Munich Convention) which precludes a priori the patentability of biological matter;

(16a) Whereas the discussion on the patentability of sequences or partial sequences of sequences of genes is controversial; whereas, according to this Directive, the granting of a patent for inventions which concerns such sequences or partial sequences require the same criteria to be applied as in all other areas of technology;

(16b) Whereas a mere sequence of DNA segments without indication of a biological function does not contain a technical teaching and is therefore not a patentable invention;

(16c) Whereas a sequence or partial sequence can be the subject of a patentable invention when all the necessary conditions for a patent are satisfied: novelty, level of invention and industrial application;

(16d) Whereas for the criterion of industrial application to be complied with, the genetic sequence or partial sequence and thus also the protein for which a DNA sequence code must be determined; whereas for sequences which overlap, each sequence will be considered as an independent sequence in patent law terms;

(16e) Whereas the requirements for disclosure of the industrial application of the sequences or partial sequences do not differ from those in other areas of technology; whereas at least an industrial application must be actually disclosed in the patent application;

(16f) Whereas the free and informed consent of the person from whose body material is taken is required in order for an application to be made for a patent in respect of the use of that material;

(16g) Whereas this Directive in no way affects the basis of current patent law, according to which a patent may be granted for any new application of a patented product; . . . .

(31) Whereas a plant grouping which is characterized by a particular gene (and not its whole genome) is not covered by the protection of new varieties and is therefore not excluded from patentability even if it comprises new varieties of plants;

. . . .

(36) Whereas the TRIPS Agreement provides for the possibility that members of the World Trade Organisation may exclude from patentability inventions, the prevention within their territory of the commercial exploitation of which is necessary to protect ordre public or morality, including to protect human, animal or plant life or health or to avoid serious prejudice to the environment, provided that such exclusion is not made merely because the exploitation is prohibited by their law;

(37) Whereas the principle whereby inventions must be excluded from patentability where their commercial exploitation offends against ordre public or morality must also be stressed in this Directive;

. . . .

(40) Whereas there is a consensus within the Community that interventions in the human germ line and the cloning of human beings offends against ordre public and morality; whereas it is therefore important to exclude unequivocally from patentability processes for modifying the germ line genetic identity of human beings and processes for cloning human beings;

. . . .

(43) Whereas pursuant to Article F(2) of the Treaty on European Union, the Union is to respect fundamental rights, as guaranteed by the European Convention for the Protection of Human Rights and Fundamental Freedoms signed in Rome on 4 November 1950 and as they result from the constitutional traditions common to the Member States, as general principles of Community law;

. . . .

(55) Whereas following Decision 93/626/EEC (7) the Community is party to the Convention on Biological Diversity of 5 June 1992; whereas, in this regard, Member States must give particular weight to Articles 3 and 8(j), the second sentence of Article 16(2) and Article 16(5) of the Convention when bringing into force the laws, regulations and administrative provisions necessary to comply with this Directive;

(56) Whereas the Third Conference of the Parties to the Biodiversity Convention, which took place in November 1996, noted in Decision III/17 that 'further work is required to help develop a common appreciation of the relationship between intellectual property rights and the relevant provisions of the TRIPS Agreement and the Convention on Biological Diversity, in particular on issues relating to technology transfer and conservation and sustainable use of biological diversity and the fair and equitable sharing of benefits arising out of the use of genetic resources, including the protection of knowledge, innovations and practices of indigenous and local communities embodying traditional lifestyles relevant for the conservation and sustainable use of biological diversity,

HAVE ADOPTED THIS DIRECTIVE:

CHAPTER I. Patentability

Article 1

1. Member States shall protect biotechnological inventions under national patent law. They shall, if necessary, adjust their national patent law to take account of the provisions of this Directive. . . .

Article 2

1. For the purposes of this Directive,

(a) "biological material" means any material containing genetic information and capable of reproducing itself or being reproduced in a biological system;

(b) "microbiological process" means any process involving or performed upon or resulting in microbiological material.

2. A process for the production of plants or animals is essentially biological if it consists entirely of natural phenomena such as crossing or selection.

3. The concept of "plant variety" is defined by Article 5 of Regulation (EC) No 2100/94.

Article 3

1. For the purposes of this Directive, inventions which are new, which involve an inventive step and which are susceptible of industrial application shall be patentable even if they concern a product consisting of or containing biological material or a process by means of which biological material is produced, processed or used.

2. Biological material which is isolated from its natural environment or produced by means of a technical process may be the subject of an invention even if it previously occurred in nature.

Article 4

1. The following shall not be patentable;

(a) plant and animal varieties;

(b) essentially biological processes for the production of plants or animals.

2. Inventions which concern plants or animals shall be patentable if the technical feasibility of the invention is not confined to a particular plant or animal variety.

3. Paragraph 1(b) shall be without prejudice to the patentability of inventions which concern a microbiological or other technical process or a product obtained by means of such a process.

Article 5

1. The human body, at the various stages of its formation and development, and the simple discovery of one of its elements, including the sequence or partial sequence of a gene, cannot constitute patentable inventions.

2. An element isolated from the human body or otherwise produced by means of a technical process, including the sequence or partial sequence of a gene, may constitute a patentable invention, even if the structure of that element is identical to that of a natural element.

3. The industrial application of a sequenced or a partial sequence of a gene must be disclosed in the patent application.

Article 6

1. Inventions shall be considered unpatentable where their commercial exploitation would be contrary to ordre public or morality; however, exploitation shall not be deemed to be so contrary merely because it is prohibited by law or regulation.

2. On the basis of paragraph 1, the following, in particular, shall be considered unpatentable:

(a) processes for cloning human beings;

(b) processes for modifying the germ line genetic identity of human beings;

(c) uses of human embryos for industrial or commercial purposes;

(d) processes for modifying the genetic identity of animals which are likely to cause them suffering without any substantial medical benefit to man or animal, and also animals resulting from such processes.

Article 7

The Commission's European Group on Ethics in Science and New Technologies evaluates all ethical aspects of biotechnology.

NOTES AND QUESTIONS

(1) **Regulation or Directive.** Consider the purpose of the EU legislative instruments. *See supra* § 3.03[C][3]. Why do you think that the regulation process was chosen for technology transfer but not for biotechnological inventions?

(2) **EPC Article 53(c) and Directive Article 3.** "The new proposal draws a clear distinction between inventions and discoveries and does not include the famous word 'as such.'" Dominique Vandergheynst, *The New*

Proposal for a Directive on the Legal Protection of Biotechnological Inventions, in BIOTECHNOLOGY, PATENTS AND MORALITY 175 (Sterckx ed., 1997). Does the directive simplify the issues for a future European national court attempting in a subsequent case to interpret those articles? Or must we (and they) wait for national legislation. Proposals to have the EU accede to the European Patent Convention and thereby give it a voice in EPO activities are under consideration. The European Commission issued its proposed Council Regulation on the Community Patent on August 1, 2000. The Community patent will be discussed in Chapter 6 in the context of regional mechanisms for the acquisition of patent rights.

(3) **Patenting Life Forms and Food Security.** Opponents of patents on life forms in Europe state that as a consequence of legal recognition of patent rights, farmers will become dependent on multinational corporations, breeders will not be able to breed, consumers will pay higher prices for food and medicine, public research will be undermined, European producers will become further concentrated, genetic diversity will be eroded, private corporations will control the food supply, Third World farmers will lose the initiative to conserve old varieties, animals will be exposed to increased suffering, and respect for human rights, for nature, and for life itself will be eroded. *See* Luc Vankrunkelsven, *The Case For and Against the Patenting of Biotechnological Inventions*, in BIOTECHNOLOGY, PATENTS AND MORALITY 216–18 (Sterckx ed., 1997). Does the directive address any of these concerns? Or does it merely paper over them? The Netherlands resisted implementation of the Directive, arguing that it had been improperly adopted, but the European Court of Justice recently rejected that argument. *See Kingdom of the Netherlands v. European Parliament and Council EU*, Case-377/98, dismissing the Dutch reasons for intransigence, O.J. C 331 (ECJ 2001).

(4) **Cross-Sectoral Developments.** Recital 56 refers to the Third Conference of the Parties of the Convention on Biological Diversity, which was held in Buenos Aires in November 1996. The report of that conference in turn refers to discussions that are taking place in the Committee on Trade and Environment of the WTO regarding the relationship between the Convention on Biological Diversity and the TRIPS Agreement, a subject discussed *infra* § 8.03. *See* Provisional Agenda of the Third Meeting, UNEP/CBD/COP/3/22 22 (Sept. 1996) and the Advance Report entitled: *The Convention on Biological Diversity and the Agreement on Trade-Related Intellectual Property Rights (TRIPS): Relationships And Synergies*, UNEP/CBD/COP/3/23 (Oct. 5, 1996). Do references to international environmental, biodiversity, and trade agreements in recitals of European directives create direct obligations on the member states, regardless of whether they are signatories of the referenced treaties? The international economic issues surrounding the patenting of biotechnological inventions are discussed in William H. Lesser, *International Treaties and Other Legal and Economic Issues Relating to the Ownership and Use of Genetic Resources*, in GLOBAL GENETIC RESOURCES: ACCESS, OWNERSHIP, AND INTELLECTUAL PROPERTY RIGHTS (K. Elaine Hoagland ed., 1997).

(5) **Potential Impact of the Biotechnology Directive.** For a preliminary assessment of the biotechnology directive, see *Patenting Biotech Inventions—The European Directive*, 1 J. OF BIOLAW & BUS. 24–27 (Summer 1998); Giuseppe Sena, *Directive on Biotechnological Inventions: Patentability of Discoveries*, 30 I.I.C. 731 (1999).

§ 4.07 Trade Secrets

[A] History

THE FIRST SUCCESSFUL FACTORY *
Excerpted from MITCHELL WILSON, AMERICAN SCIENCE AND INVENTION: A PICTORIAL HISTORY 84–86 (New York 1954)

The first true factory in America was not a native product. Before Samuel Slater opened his mill in Pawtucket, there were many shops which employed a number of hands; but a factory is more than many people working together under the same roof. The American factory, as Eli Whitney designed it, was the third step taken in a changing attitude towards the manufacture of goods.

Until the late eighteenth century, the form of the factory, or manufactory, was simply an enlargement of the way in which a single artisan made every part himself. When he received more orders than he himself could fill, he took in a helper who learned first by doing the simplest tasks, and then in turn reached the stage where he too was able to make the entire article by himself. In some cases, where very many men were employed, it was natural that certain workers would be given only those tasks at which they excelled, and the finished product would then be the result of several men's handiwork.

This was the method of work in shops from the times of antiquity, and it was not changed until late in the eighteenth century, when the division of labor became a conscious process. There could be no machinery developed to make the separate parts of a product until the artisan himself was aware that there *were* separate steps to be performed. Whitney's "American System of Manufacture" therefore could not be applied until this division of labor had taken place.

The English factory system, popularly identified with the cotton mills, was based on this rationalization of labor. The separate steps of carding, roving. spinning. and weaving were assigned to different groups of individuals all working under the same roof, and [Sir Richard] Arkwright was the first man to drive the primitive spinning wheels and looms by drive belts from a water wheel. Even this simple step was so revolutionary that the "water loom"—and a powered loom—became a magical phrase.

---

* Copyright 1954, Simon & Schuster, Inc. Reprinted with permission.

After the Revolution, many attempts were made to introduce factory methods in the new republic. The first cotton mill in Massachusetts was built in Beverly in 1787, but in three years it was ready to close. The factories generally failed because the machinery was inadequate, and because Americans preferred English importations. Various states offered bounties and rewards to encourage manufacture, but every effort failed. To import machinery from England was impossible because the British government refused to allow any of its new inventions to leave the country. The American states advertised their bounties in English newspapers to entice English workmen to emigrate; but that too was against the law. England was determined to keep its technological knowledge to itself.

One such advertisement by the Pennsylvania Legislature appeared in Derbyshire. It was read by young Samuel Slater, just finishing his apprenticeship. He had worked for Jedediah Strutt, a partner of Arkwright, and Slater had learned how to use and repair every machine in the factory. He asked Strutt to tell him what his future might be if he remained where he was. Strutt told him to work hard and save his money and he would get his just rewards.

He knew exactly what risks he was running by trying to leave the country. He was careful to avoid taking any sketches of machinery and he did not even tell his mother and brothers of his plans. He went to London, got his passage, and just as the vessel was preparing to leave, he wrote to his family, telling them where he was going.

In 1789 he landed in Philadelphia where he made inquiries about the true situation in the republic. He was told that a mill had recently been completed in Providence by Moses Brown, the famous Quaker merchant [and patron of Brown University], and that Brown was desperately looking for a manager. Slater wrote to Brown, telling him his background and applying for the position.

Moses Brown replied at once and made this handsome offer to Slater: if he could work the machinery they had on hand, all the profits of the business less the cost and interest on the machinery were to go to Slater along with the credit as well as the advantages of perfecting the first water mill in America. In other words' Brown was willing to give the factory to Slater. There is no other record of a man applying for a job by letter and getting the entire plant by return mail.

2. British Know-how In Pawtucket

When Slater went to Pawtucket with Brown to inspect the machines, his rosy dreams wilted. "These will not do," he protested. "They are good for nothing in their present condition. Nor could they be made to answer."

He proposed to make a clean start and build the series of machines which were known as the "Arkwright Patent." He had brought no drawings but he had memorized the designs of the machines invented by Crompton and Hargreaves as well as Arkwright.

Most American machinists were inadequate; the only metal articles being made were scythes, anchors, horse-shoes, nails, and cannon shot. Fortunately, a Nantucket Quaker named Oziel Wilkinson then lived with his family in Pawtucket. Wilkinson was a blacksmith who had made spades and shovels in quantity for turnpike building. He had been the first to make cold-rolled nails. Slater boarded with them, and Wilkinson was willing to help. Without him, Slater would have been helpless. . . .

On December 21, 1790, the little factory began to produce, but business was feeble. When seventy-two spindles were working and the plant had been operating for twenty months, the preference for English yarn left them with several thousand pounds that could not be moved at any price. Not until a loom was added did American cotton begin to find a market. Ten years after Slater landed in America, Almy, Brown and Slater were doing sufficiently well to open a second factory. Scores of imitators followed, but Slater kept well in the lead, and eventually the firm established mills in New Hampshire and Massachusetts, despite the growing competition from innovators.

Drawing on his English training, Slater staffed his factory with children from four to ten years old. The machines were simple, and the parents were delighted to have their children doing something useful in pleasant surroundings. He measured his break with the English tradition by the good food and humane treatment given his hands. In England, the working children were ill-fed, beaten, driven to early drunkenness and degradation. In a time when American children were put to work around the term as soon as they could walk, the Slater factory system was very highly rated.

Slater neither invented anything, nor improved what he brought here; but he was the first in this country to set up a system of manufacture in which the successive steps of the skilled artisan were broken down into such simple components that a group of children could outproduce the finest craftsman. It was the one system ideally suited to a country that was to be plagued by a shortage of skilled manpower for another seventy-five years. No one saw any discrepancy between such a system and the American goal of enhancing the dignity and human value of the individual. The American factory fed, clothed, and equipped men for the fight against the hostile universe; and the factory system was actually considered to be a victory for the American creed of freedom.

. . . .

[B] Modern International Agreements for the Protection of Trade Secrets

The first international agreement containing any explicit provisions for the protection of trade secrets was the North American Free Trade Agreement, signed by the United States on December 8, 1993. The following year (to the day) the legislation implementing the TRIPS Agreement, which contained similar provisions on the protection of "undisclosed information, *see* art. 39, was passed by the U.S. Congress.

ADRIAN OTTEN & HANNU WAGER, COMPLIANCE WITH TRIPS: THE EMERGING WORLD VIEW*
29 Vand. J. Trans'l L. 391 (1996)

The TRIPS Agreement contains a section that, for the first time in international public law, explicitly requires undisclosed information (trade secrets or know-how) to benefit from protection. The protection must apply to information that is secret, that has commercial value because it is secret, and that has been subject to reasonable steps to keep it secret. The Agreement does not require undisclosed information to be treated as a form of property, but it does require that a person lawfully in control of such information have the ability to prevent it from being disclosed to, acquired by, or used by others without his or her consent in a manner contrary to honest commercial practices. The Agreement also contains provisions on undisclosed test data and other data whose submission is required by governments as a condition of approving the marketing of pharmaceutical or agricultural chemical products that use new chemical entities. In such a situation, the member state concerned must protect the data against unfair commercial use.

NORTH AMERICAN FREE TRADE AGREEMENT
Article 1711: Trade Secrets

1. Each Party shall provide the legal means for any person to prevent trade secrets from being disclosed to, acquired by, or used by others without the consent of the person lawfully in control of the information in a manner contrary to honest commercial practices, in so far as:

(a) the information is secret in the sense that it is not, as a body or in the precise configuration and assembly of its components, generally known among or readily accessible to persons that normally deal with the kind of information in question;

(b) the information has actual or potential commercial value because it is secret; and

(c) the person lawfully in control of the information has taken reasonable steps under the circumstances to keep it secret.

2. A Party may require that to qualify for protection a trade secret must be evidenced in documents, electronic or magnetic means, optical discs, microfilms, films or other similar instruments.

3. No Party may limit the duration of protection for trade secrets, so long as the conditions in paragraph 1 exist.

4. No Party may discourage or impede the voluntary licensing of trade secrets by imposing excessive or discriminatory conditions on such licenses, or conditions that dilute the value of the trade secrets.

---

5. If a Party requires, as a condition for approving the marketing of pharmaceutical or agricultural chemical products that utilize new chemical entities, the submission of undisclosed test or other data necessary to determine whether the use of such products is safe and effective, the Party shall protect against disclosure of the data of persons making such submissions, where the origination of such data involves considerable effort, except where the disclosure is necessary to protect the public or unless steps are taken to ensure that the data is protected against unfair commercial use.

6. Each Party shall provide that for data subject to paragraph 5 that are submitted to the Party after the date of entry into force of this Agreement, no person other than the person that submitted them may, without the latter's permission, rely on such data in support of an application for product approval during a reasonable period of time after their submission. For this purpose, a reasonable period shall normally mean not less than five years from the date on which the Party granted approval to the person that produced the data for approval to market its product, taking account of the nature of the data and the person's efforts and expenditures in producing them. Subject to this provision, there shall be no limitation on any Party to implement abbreviated approval procedures for such products on the basis of bioequivalence and bioavailability studies.

7. Where a Party relies upon a marketing approval granted by another Party, the reasonable period of exclusive use of the data submitted in connection with obtaining the approval relied upon shall commence with the date of the first marketing approval relied upon.

. . . .

[C] Regional Agreements: Europe

BLOCK EXEMPTION ON TECHNOLOGY TRANSFER AGREEMENTS: TRADE SECRETS AND KNOW-HOW
EU Competition Bulletin, OJ L 31, 9.2.1996

. . . .

1.3.40. Commission Regulation (EC) No 240/96 on the application of Article 85(3) of the Treaty to certain categories of technology transfer agreements.

Adopted by the Commission on 31 January. The Regulation, which enters into force on 1 April, simplifies and makes more flexible the rules applicable to licensing agreements, thus helping to promote the spread of new technologies within the European Union.

Article 10

For purposes of this Regulation:

(1) 'know-how' means a body of technical information that is secret, substantial and identified in any appropriate form;

(2) 'secret' means that the know-how package as a body or in the precise configuration and assembly of its components is not generally known or easily accessible, so that part of its value consists in the lead which the licensee gains when it is communicated to him; it is not limited to the narrow sense that each individual component of the know-how should be totally unknown or unobtainable outside the licensor's business;

(3) 'substantial' means that the know-how includes information which must be useful, *i.e.* can reasonably be expected at the date of conclusion of the agreement to be capable of improving the competitive position of the licensee, for example by helping him to enter a new market or giving him an advantage in competition with other manufacturers or providers of services who do not have access to the licensed secret know-how or other comparable secret know-how;

(4) 'identified' means that the know-how is described or recorded in such a manner as to make it possible to verify that it satisfies the criteria of secrecy and substantiality and to ensure that the licensee is not unduly restricted in his exploitation of how own technology, to be identified the know-how can either be set out in the licence agreement or in a separate document or recorded in any other appropriate form at the latest when the know-how is transferred or shortly thereafter, provided that the separate document or other record can be made available if the need arises;

. . . .

NOTES AND QUESTIONS

(1) **Trade Secrets in NAFTA and TRIPS.** The NAFTA was the first international agreement to include the protection of trade secrets. The TRIPS Agreement, although negotiated before, was finalized after the NAFTA. *See* Laurinda L. Hicks & James R. Holbein, *Convergence of National Intellectual Property Norms in International Trading Agreements*, 12 AM. U. J. INT'L L. & POL'Y 769, 796 (1997).

(2) **Article 1711 as "TRIPS Plus."** A significant benefit for pharmaceutical and agrochemical patent owners under NAFTA is preventing generic companies from having access to expensively-produced test data submitted to governments in abbreviated new drug applications ("ANDAs").

> [I]n terms of substantive obligations, NAFTA adds a number of significant TRIPS-plus features. For trade secrets, both TRIPS and NAFTA require confidentiality for undisclosed test data submitted to governments for approving the marketing of pharmaceutical or agricultural-chemical products that utilize new chemical entities. However, NAFTA goes further by also requiring non-reliance. For normally at least five years, NAFTA Parties are not to rely on the first applicant's confidential test data to approve a second

applicant's request for approval to market a generic copy of the first applicant's product.

Allen Z. Hertz, *NAFTA Revisited: Shaping the Trident: Intellectual Property Under NAFTA, Investment Protection Agreements and the World Trade Organization*, 23 CAN.-U.S. L.J. 261, 282 (1996).

(3) **Article 10*bis* of the Paris Convention.** Are the undisclosed information provisions of TRIPS and NAFTA different from the unfair competition principles of Article 10*bis* of the Paris Convention? Or are they, as a recent article asserts, fundamentally identical. *See* Carlos Correa, *Intellectual Property Rights in Latin America: Is There Still Room for Differentiation?*, 29 N.Y.U. J. INT'L L. & POL. 109, 132 (1997).

(4) **Criminalization of Trade Secret Misappropriation.** Article 61 of TRIPS mandates criminal procedures only for willful trademark counterfeiting or copyright piracy on a commercial scale but not for deliberate trade secret misappropriation or "economic espionage." Trade secret misappropriation amounting to economic espionage was criminalized in the United States by the Economic Espionage Act of 1996 (discussed above in Chapter Two). *See* 18 U.S.C. § 1831. The Act provides for prison sentences of up to fifteen years. In January 2001, the Computer Crimes and Intellectual Property Section (CCIPS) of the U.S. Department of Justice published a manual on prosecuting intellectual property crimes (also on the DOJ website at www.cybercrime.gov) reporting recent economic espionage cases, indictments, arrests, prosecutions, convictions, fines and sentences. The number of such cases seems to be growing. What is the likelihood that criminal sanctions for trade secret misappropriation (or economic espionage) will become more widespread, and perhaps become part of an international agreement in the near future? For an excellent summary of EEA cases, see Chris Carr, Jack Morton and Jerry Furniss, *The Economic Espionage Act: Bear Trap or Mousetrap*, 8 TEX. INT. PROP. L.J. 159 (2000).

(5) **"Do as We Say, Not as We Did."** The beginnings of the American industrial revolution were built on the uncompensated transfer of Arkwright's trade secrets and patented technology from England to the United States. What should be the response of the United States to contemporary "developing countries" who accuse the United States of preaching what it did not practice? *See* Dru Brenner-Beck, *Do As I Say, Not As I Did*, 11 UCLA PAC. BASIN L. J. 84 (1992).

§ 4.08 Industrial Designs

Unlike patents, copyrights, or trademarks, the regulation of design protection at the international level is quite minimal. Because designs are potentially protectable in some countries not only under a design code proper, but also under other forms of intellectual property, provisions are scattered throughout a variety of intellectual property treaties without significant concentration in any one. In this Section, we review those provisions that do exist in multilateral treaties, including in the regional context (such as the EU) where greater and more substantial progress has occurred of late. Treaties establishing mechanisms for obtaining design rights on a multinational basis—principally the Hague Agreement—are dealt with separately *infra* §§ 6.02 and 6.04.

[A] Multilateral Agreements

ANNETTE KUR, TRIPS AND DESIGN PROTECTION[*]
in FROM GATT TO TRIPS: THE AGREEMENT ON TRADE-RELATED ASPECTS OF INTELLECTUAL PROPERTY RIGHTS 141, 144-56 (Beier & Schricker eds. 1996)

II. INTERNATIONAL DESIGN PROTECTION BEFORE TRIPS

1. Paris Convention

Industrial designs are included among the objects of industrial property protection covered by Art. 1(2) of the Paris Convention. Pursuant to Art. 5*quinquies* of this Convention all countries of the Union are obliged to grant protection to industrial designs and models. Yet this not interpreted so as to mean that protection must be granted on the basis of *sui generis* legislation; it is sufficient that it is accorded by other means-typically under copyright law or as protection against unfair competition.

[Article 5B] prohibits . . . rights in industrial designs or models [from being] declared forfeited as a result of either failure to work or importation of corresponding products.[18] In contrast, such a prohibition does not exist in relation to compulsory licenses. . . .

. . . .

2. Revised Berne Convention (RBC)

As a result of the hybrid nature of design protection, the relevant regulations cannot be found in the Paris Convention alone, rather, they are also anchored in copyright conventions-here, however, not under the category of industrial designs and models, but under that of applied art. This category of works protected by copyright has been included in . . . Article 2(1) RBC since 1908 (Berlin). Furthermore, during the Brussels conference (1948) an attempt was made to establish as a matter of principle that works of applied art should not be excluded from copyright protection *per se,* even where they are used industrially; yet these efforts failed in the face of opposition inter alia from Italy and the United Kingdom. Instead, it was established that each national legislature was free to

---

[18] In contrast, such a possibility does exist regarding utility models and patents in accordance with Art. 5A of the Paris Convention.

determine whether, and to what extent, utilitarian objects may obtain protection on the basis of copyright law. Where the national legislature grants protection to works of applied art, a minimum 25-year term of protection is obligatory by virtue of Art. 7(4) RBC.

The substantive reciprocity clause of Art. 2(7) RBC also stems from the absence of an internationally effective obligation to grant copyright protection to industrially utilized designs: where a member of the Berne Union grants copyright protection to works of its nationals in addition to specific design protection,[25] this protection must only be extended to the works of foreigners who are nationals of another Berne Union country if it would also be possible to claim copyright protection for the same work in such foreigners' country of origin. This clause was of practical significance, for example, in relations between Italy (which practically excludes copyright protection for products that are eligible for design protection) and France (where designs enjoy supplementary full copyright protection on the basis of the "unité de l'art" doctrine). . . .

3. Universal Copyright Convention (UCC)

In contrast to the RBC, the text of the Universal Copyright Convention does not contain an explicit reference to works of applied art within the context of its (non-exclusive) catalogue of protected works. However, it may be inferred from Art. IV(3) of the UCC that this Convention proceeds from the possibility of granting copyright protection to such works: according to this provision the term of protection for works of applied art must run for at least 10 years.

4. Agreement of The Hague Concerning Industrial Designs

Although the possibility of pure copyright protection for designs is not excluded by international law and is still practised in a number of countries, the large majority of countries grants design protection primarily on the basis of specific legislation that normally requires entry in the register or deposit of the design as a prerequisite of protection. For these states the Agreement of The Hague offers the possibility of a central deposit of the design at the WIPO in Geneva and thus-subject to the eligibility of the design for protection under national law-of obtaining protection in all or selected contracting states. [The Hague Agreement is discussed in detail *infra* § 6.02].

---

[25] Where specific design protection does not exist in a certain country (*e.g.* in Greece), but where copyright law constitutes the only possibility of obtaining protection, foreign designs shall enjoy protection under copyright law even where this possibility is excluded under the law of the country of origin of the design at issue.

III. Provisions of the TRIPS Agreement Relevant to Design Law

1. Copyright

. . . .

Apart from [the obligation to comply with the provisions of the Paris and Berne Conventions], the copyright regulations in Part II, Section 1 of the TRIPS Agreement do not contain any statement on the protection of industrially utilized works of applied art. The TRIPS text therefore does not give rise to any new developments regarding the copyright protection of designs . . . The Members are not prevented from granting protection to such works on the exclusive basis of specific design protection legislation, excluding completely a cumulative claim to copyright protection. To an even lesser degree are they prevented from making copyright protection for works of applied art dependent upon extremely strict requirements, whether with regard to the artistic qualification of the work [e.g., in Germany], to its "separability" from the utilitarian object in which it is embodied [e.g., U.S. or Italian law], or to the number of permissible copies of the work, etc. [e.g., U.K. or Irish law].

2. Specific Design Protection

(a) Basis of the Right

Specific provisions on the protection of industrial designs and models are contained in Part II, Section 4 (Arts. 25 and 26) of the TRIPS Agreement. They represent a very brief regulation of the issue. The provisions leave open the question as to how the right to a design shall come into existence, in particular whether this can only take place by means of registration or also through use of the design.

Where the right is obtained by means of registration, the regulations of Article 62 must be respected. The necessary formalities must be kept at a reasonable level (Art. 62(1)); moreover, . . . the grant or registration of the right [must be] possible within a reasonable period of time (Art. 62(2)). The spirit of this provision conflicts to a certain extent with the procedures of registration of design rights in the US and Japan. [I]n these countries registration does not take place until after sometimes lengthy examinations, which, especially with regard to designs with a short life-span, can entail the risk of a total depreciation in the value of the rights granted.

. . . .

(c) Individual Provisions

* Art. 25(1), first/second sentences (subject-matter of protection, requirements for protection)

The text of Art. 25(1) obliges the Members to protect independently created designs, insofar as they fulfill the prerequisites of novelty or originality. This provision does not define the term design nor [the types of product whose design is covered by the provisions], thus leaving scope for individual national definitions.

As a matter of principle, the wording of Art. 25(1), first sentence, requires subjective novelty of the design (it must be 'independently created'); it is only in this case that the international obligation to protect industrial designs takes effect. In addition to the requirement of independent creation, [44] novelty and originality are mentioned as principal requirements for protection. It is argued that by listing these protection criteria in alternative form (" . . . that are new or original"), the negotiating parties intended to make clear that as a matter of principle [Members] should be prohibited [from imposing] cumulative requirements (*i.e.* "new *and* original"). This was intended to ensure that the threshold for protection is not raised to an exceedingly high level by TRIPS Members. [47] It seems doubtful however whether the manner in which this intent was expressed in Art. 25(1) will be sufficient to encompass the underlying objectives. According to Art. 25(1), second sentence, it is still possible for Members to deny protection if the design does not differ *significantly* from what was known previously; and the application of this criterion can in practice amount to a rather high threshold for protection. Moreover, the wording of the second sentence allows the Member countries to continue dividing the assessment of protectability into two "logical steps": namely to assess whether a given design is already known (assessment of novelty) and subsequently to ask whether a sufficient difference from the relevant comparative material can be established (assessment of originality/individual character). The only consequence of Art. 25(1), first sentence, if any, will therefore be that in future these two steps will have to be covered by a single term-be it "novelty" or "originality."

Other issues have been left undecided: for example whether an absolute or in any respect (timewise, geographical, [51] or with reference to the knowledge of the participating expert circles) relative meaning of the term novelty shall be applied. Finally, as mentioned above, it is left to the discretion of the national legislature whether a strict or rather generous standard will apply as regards the threshold for acquiring protection: whilst by adding the word "significantly" it is clarified that a high threshold would also comply with Art. 25(1), the provision on the other hand does not contain anything that would prevent national legislatures from coming very close to a requirement of mere subjective novelty.

---

[44] This means that in this case the criterion of "originality" is not automatically identical to that of "independently created," as is otherwise frequently the case in the Anglo-American use of language.

[47] [This seems] to date back to an early Japanese contribution, [cit], dated November 23, 1987, where the proposal to stipulate both novelty and originality as cumulative criteria for protection was motivated by references to patent law, claiming that since design rights conferred principally the same protection as patents, equally restrictive criteria should apply in both fields.

[51] In that only publications within the domestic territory may be taken into account; *e.g.* in the UK, Australia, Canada, etc. . . .

The wording of Art. 25(1) does pose a special problem for US law, in which the patent law criterion of non-obviousness is applied as the protection requirement for industrial designs. In this respect, in the literature reference is made to footnote 5 concerning Art. 27(1) of the TRIPS Agreement, where, with respect to patentability, it is stated explicitly that a Member country may interpret the term "inventive step" in the sense of "non-obvious." Owing to the fact that such a reference is missing in Art. 25, which regulates the protection requirements for designs, it is concluded that in future in US law only novelty or originality, yet not non-obviousness, may be required as protection criteria in design law.[54]

* Art. 25(1), third sentence (exclusion from protection of functionally dictated designs)

The principle that design protection, being restricted to the exterior appearance of products, necessarily meets its limits where it would lead to protection of technical ideas, . . . is generally accepted and applies to most design laws-whether in the form of explicit regulation or as a principle developed in case law. However, the practical interpretation of this principle is subject to considerable variations.

In its broadest form, this principle is applied in order to limit design protection to those utilitarian objects the "raison d'être" of which essentially lies in pleasing the observer's eye, *e.g.* to fabric designs, jewel[]ry, decorative articles, etc. This means that articles where the functional purpose obviously prevails and which are not primarily purchased according to optical aspects, *e.g.* tools, kitchen appliances, office items, etc., are excluded from protection. A more flexible alternative to this point of view [excludes from protection] not whole product groups, but only such designs . . . that represent an improvement in functionality-*e.g.* that render a pair of scissors easier to manage or improve the user friendliness of office machines, etc. [But] this approach ignores the fact that good product design means combining form and function in an optimal manner, . . . and results in the exclusion from protection of particularly successful designs.

Having recognized this fundamental contradiction, some legislatures consequently limited the exclusion from protection to those rare cases in which the designer had no other option at his or her disposal in order to achieve a certain function-for only in these exceptional cases would protection of the design necessarily lead to protection of the technical idea, contradicting the inherent function of design protection.

Yet this narrow, modern way of viewing the matter is not laid down as an internationally valid standard in Art. 25(1), third sentence of the TRIPS Agreement. The possibility of excluding "designs dictated essentially by technical or functional considerations" means that the national legislatures

---

[54] Reichman, 1993 FORDHAM INTELL. PROP., MEDIA & ENT. L. J. 171, 245 (1993); however, the US legislature has not adopted this argument.

may continue to restrict design protection to products or design elements that essentially serve a decorative purpose.[57]

It remains questionable whether Art. 25(1), third sentence, constitutes a final regulation of any possible exclusionary clauses, or whether the national legislatures will still have a broader scope for regulation in this respect. . . . The issue could . . . affect rules which, for systematic[58] or economic[59] reasons exclude certain product categories from protection,[60] or which establish other special requirements regarding the eligibility for design protection (for example the requirement that the design must be visible in the course of use in accordance with the purpose of the protected item,[61] or that products may not be protected as designs if they are not distributed separately . . .).[62]

A strictly literal interpretation of Art. 25(1), third sentence, could in fact lead to the conclusion that the TRIPS Members are not entitled to exclude designs for reasons other than their functionality. However, in view of the rather vague character of this provision, this conclusion appears somewhat questionable; in particular, it can hardly be assumed that there was a serious intention to declare unlawful the exclusion from protection of "immoral" designs, an exclusion that is anchored in most of the design laws throughout the world. The strict wording and the (presumable) intention of the rule thus do not tally.

. . . .

* Art. 25(2) (Special conditions for protection of textile designs)

Art. 25(2) obliges all members of the TRIPS Agreement to pay particular consideration to the special requirements of the textile industry. This rule

---

[57] A so-called must-fit-exception is doubtlessly also permissible pursuant to art. 25(1), third sentence, as provided for in UK law [cit] and in art. 9 of the proposal for a Community Design Regulation. . . .

[58] *E.g.* the exclusion of computer programs and semi-conductor products contained in Art. 3(b) of the proposal for a Community Design Regulation, based on the assumption that otherwise undesirable overlaps with the EU Directives concerning this subject matter would arise. . .

[59] In particular in the case of rules directed towards excluding spare parts from design protection, such as the must-match rule in UK law. [cit]. The South African Design Act of 1993 is similar, excluding 'spare parts' from registration as functional designs (in contrast to which they may still claim protection as aesthetic designs subject to fulfillment of the prerequisites).

[60] *E.g.*, the US proposal for a *sui generis* design law, presented in the House of Representatives concurrently to the GATT negotiations, in 1991, H.R. 1790: according to Sec. 1002 of this proposal designs for "motor vehicle glass, including windshields and side and rear vision glass" should be excluded from protection.

[61] Following a recommendation of the European Parliament, the amended texts for the proposals for a Community Design Regulation and Directive stipulate the visibility of the design during ordinary use. The same effect results from the US requirement of "ornamentality."

[62] *See, e.g., In re Ford Motor Co. Ltd.'s Design Application*, [1994] R.P.C. 545 (Ch. D. 1994).

was motivated by the specific, frequently lamented problems of this branch of industry: as a rule textile designs are developed in large numbers and are subject to extremely rapid changes that often take place from one season to the next. The effectiveness of traditional design protection founded upon entry in the register and publication therefore seems questionable for reasons of time and costs. At the same time, however, the textile industry relies on effective protection, because in this branch of industry in particular, deliberate and mass copying of new designs poses a grave problem.

Specific regulations aimed at reducing the registration procedure and costs for short-lived designs that are developed in large numbers are already anchored in numerous national design laws. [F]or example, . . . rules allow the combination of a larger number of designs in one single registration (multiple applications) and the possibility of deferring publication, with the result that the costs of publication of the design can be saved [for] a . . . brief period (which in the ideal case corresponds to the life-span of a fashionable design). A further possibility, even more advantageous for the textile industry, is the possibility of acquiring informal protection, whether on the basis of design law provided for in the proposal for a Community Design Regulation or on the basis of other laws.

Article 25(2) obliges the Members of the TRIPS Agreement to make available (at least) one of the workable possibilities of obtaining simplified, less expensive protection. The members are free to choose between fulfilling this obligation within the framework of either design or copyright regulations.

German design law already complies with the obligation under Art. 25(2) of the TRIPS Agreement by offering both multiple application (Section 7(9) Design Act) and deferred publication (Section 8b Design Act); the same applies to most of the other European states. Moreover, a real improvement in the protection of short-lived textile designs will result from the proposed Community Design Regulation, which provides for three-year protection for non-registered designs.

In principle, the design laws of the US and Japan do not offer any possibility of providing inexpensive and (considerably) faster protection for textile designs. However, in the US the possibility exists of obtaining copyright protection for two-dimensional textile designs; the criterion of separability, otherwise applied strictly, is not [as severe] with regard to [protection of] two-dimensional designs.[63] In contrast, in Japan no alleviation is provided with respect to the copyright protection of two-dimensional designs. In practice, there is the possibility of claiming protection against slavish imitation on the basis of the amended law against unfair competition. As Art. 25(2) explicitly mentions design and copyright protection only, this hardly appears to meet the requirements of the TRIPS Agreement.

---

[63] Problems regarding the compatibility of US law with art. 25(2), TRIPS Agreement, remain with respect to three-dimensional forms (shapes of clothing etc.). . . .

* Art. 26(1) (Contents of Protection)

Article 26(1) lists the rights . . . to which design right owners are entitled. According to this list the manufacture, sale or importation of articles "bearing or embodying a design" are [to be] prohibited, if the design "is a copy, or substantially a copy" and "when such acts are undertaken for commercial purposes." In contrast to copyright law, for example, from the outset acts undertaken in the private sphere are not considered infringements. The [use] of the term "copy" means that . . . it will also be possible to restrict design protection to those cases in which the infringer was familiar with the previously existing design, in analogy to copyright law. On the other hand, Art. 26(1) does not preclude more far-reaching regulations with a true monopoly effect, such as are contained in most design laws throughout the world.

* Art. 26(2) (Exceptions from design protection)

According to Art. 26(2) the TRIPS Members are permitted to provide limited exceptions to the protection of industrial designs or models, inasfar as these do not unreasonably conflict with the normal exploitation of *the designs* and do not unreasonably prejudice the legitimate interests of the design owners, whereby the legitimate interests of third parties must also be taken into account.

The wording of this provision, corresponding to similar provisions in other parts of the TRIPS Agreement,[70] is basically consistent with Art. 9(2) of the Revised Berne Convention.[71] [T]he general permission of reproduction for private use of protected works is based upon this provision. In the case of design protection such an explicit exemption is not required, because infringement as referred to in Art. 26(1) only covers acts that are undertaken for commercial purposes.

Examples of exceptions that do not fall within the private sphere, but which must doubtlessly be deemed permissible according to Art. 26(2), are, for example, the display of the design for experimental or educational purposes; the . . . use of the design as equipment on a vehicle etc. that enters the territory of the country of protection temporarily; the importation of parts for the purpose of repairing such vehicles; and the carrying out of such a repair. . .

In addition, compulsory licenses or other rules allowing use of protected designs at reasonable conditions must also be considered to conform with TRIPS. Such regulations are not *per se* irreconcilable with the legitimate interests of the proprietor of the design, nor are they declared unlawful in either the Paris Convention or in the TRIPS Agreement itself, although

---

[70] *E.g.* for patent law (Art. 30) and trademark law (Art. 17).

[71] However, Art. 9(2), Revised Berne Convention, is confined to reproduction; in addition, there is no reference to the "legitimate interests of third parties."

proposals to this effect were submitted and discussed during the negotiations.[73]

NOTES AND QUESTIONS

(1) **Priority Rights**. Article 4(C)(1) of the Paris Convention establishes a six month priority period to facilitate the serial acquisition of design rights on a multinational basis. These are expressly implemented in U.S. design protection systems. *See* Patent Act, 35 U.S.C. § 172 (six month priority available for design patent applicant); Vessel Hull Design Protection Act, 17 U.S.C. § 1311 (same for vessel hull design right owner).

(2) **Notice Requirements**. Under Article 5(D) of the Paris Convention design protection may not be conditioned upon notice. If the United States were to implement its Paris Convention and TRIPS obligations by constructing a broad-based design regime based upon the Vessel Hull Design Protection Act, would the current notice provisions, *see* 17 U.S.C. §§ 1306-1307 (content of notice and effect of omission of notice), require amendment? *Cf.* 17 U.S.C. § 405 (effect of omission of copyright notice); Berne Convention art. 5(2) (enjoyment and exercise of protected rights shall not be subject to any formality). *See* Pierre Maugué, *The International Protection of Industrial Designs under the International Conventions,* 19 U. BALT. L. REV. 393, 394 (1989) (discussing effect of Article 5(D)).

(3) **U.S. Compliance.** The United States adopted the position that the industrial design provisions of TRIPS did not require the amendment of U.S. law. Does the United States comply with TRIPS obligations with respect to industrial designs? If not, in what respects is U.S. law deficient? Does TRIPS require the enactment of a *sui generis* design law? *See* Uma Suthersanen, *Breaking Down the Intellectual Property Barriers,* 2 INTELL. PROP. Q 267, 275 (1998) (answering in the affirmative); Kur, *supra,* at 149 (expressing doubt about such an interpretation). If not (and if, therefore, the United States can rely on its design patent protection to comply with TRIPS), does the United States need to modify any of the particular provisions of the design patent statute? Do you agree with Dr. Kur's relatively minimalist interpretation of the obligations imposed by Article 25(1) of TRIPS? *See* J. H. Reichman, *Universal Minimum Standards of Intellectual Property Protection under the TRIPS Component of the WTO Agreement,* 29 INT. LAW. 345, 376 (1995).

(4) **Exclusions**. Dr. Kur suggests that the third sentence of Article 25(1), permitting members to exclude protection for designs that are "dictated essentially by technical or functional considerations," does not constitute

---

[73] Proposals to declare the compulsory licensing of industrial designs unlawful were submitted by the following delegations: Switzerland, Austria, Hong Kong. The US proposal suggested subjecting compulsory licenses for industrial designs to the same requirements as patents. . . .

what she calls "a final regulation of any possible exclusionary clauses," meaning that that provision does not constitute the only ground upon which a group of designs can be excluded from the universe of protected subject matter. How does that provision interact with Article 26(2), which sets out a standard that any exceptions to protection must meet?

(5) **Term.** Under Article 26(3) of TRIPS, protection must endure for at least ten years, which may have been of some influence in selecting the length of protection for protection under the U.S. Vessel Hull Design Protection Act. *See* 17 U.S.C. §§ 1300 et seq.

(6) **Cumulation.** During the TRIPS negotiations, the Swiss delegation proposed a clause in the design provisions that would have required design protection to be offered independently of copyright or other forms of protection. Would there have been advantages to such an approach? What difficulties would this have engendered?

CASE NO. 4 Ob 95/91
Austrian Supreme Court, Nov. 5, 1991
25 I.I.C. 126 (1994)

The architect Le Corbusier, who died in 1965, designed from 1928-1929 a series of models for furniture that are classed as being in the Bauhaus style. These models, designed in collaboration with the architect's assistants Charlotte Perriand and Pierre Jeanneret, include an infinitely adjustable lounge chair that was manufactured by the Atelier Thonet, Paris, in a number of variations. . . .

On November 26, 1987, the plaintiff, a joint stock company under Italian law, renewed the agreement it had concluded with the Le Corbusier Trust as heir and holder of Le Corbusier's copyright and as representative of Charlotte Perriand and of Pierre Jeanneret's heir, concerning the manufacture and sale of furniture by Le Corbusier, Charlotte Perriand and Pierre Jeanneret. This agreement granted the plaintiff the exclusive worldwide right to manufacture and sell Le Corbusier furniture, including the infinitely adjustable lounge chair (referred to in the agreement as "LC 4"). The plaintiff has manufactured and distributed a nickel-plated steel version of the LC 4 chair since 1974. . . .

The defendant is engaged in the furniture trade in Klagenfurt. In the period from 1988 to 1990 it took delivery from "Danish Rattan AS," Denmark, of a total of seven chairs. . . Some of these were then resold to retailers in Austria, whereby the defendant used a catalogue published by Danish Rattan AS, which contained [several] illustrations of . . . chairs [that were similar to the LC4 and the 1928 prototype of the infinitely adjustable lounge chair.]

. . . .

[The] plaintiff requests an interlocutory injunction enjoining the defendant from offering and selling an imitation of the Le Corbusier lounge chair, claiming that it enjoyed the exclusive and worldwide right to exploit the models of Le Corbusier and his assistants, which rights thus included the Republic of Austria. The infinitely adjustable lounge chair was a work of applied art and thus entitled to copyright protection. This world-famous chair was not based upon the work of another artist. Its individuality was to be found above all in the three-part division in the line forming the sitting and reclining surface, the prominent neck-rest cylinder, and the semicircular support structure contrasting with the broken line of the reclining surface. By selling the imitations of these chairs, the defendant had infringed the plaintiff's exploitation rights. If the infinitely adjustable lounge chair did not enjoy copyright protection, the defendant's activity was in breach of Section 1, Act Against Unfair Competition.

. . . .

FROM THE OPINION:

The [lower court] rightly applied Austrian law to the questions whether the infinitely adjustable lounge chair was a work to which copyright protection applied and whether the chairs distributed by the defendant and manufactured by Danish Rattan AS amounted to a plagiarism of these chairs. If the chair created abroad was (also) issued at the same time in Austria (although no findings were made on this point) within the meaning of Section 9(2) of the Copyright Act, then it is entitled to copyright protection by virtue of Section 95; if on the other hand it was created by a foreign author and issued abroad, then according to Section 96 of the Copyright Act its protection derives from international treaties or on the basis of reciprocity.

Since the architect Le Corbusier was a French national, and the chair he and his assistants designed was manufactured by the French Atelier Thonet in 1928, it can be assumed that the chair was issued in Union countries of the Berne Convention for the Protection of Literary and Artistic Works, of which Austria is also a member. Both countries are also contracting states of the Universal Copyright Convention, whereby the relationship between them is governed by the Paris version of the Berne Convention and of the Universal Copyright Convention. In countries that are Union countries of the Revised Berne Convention and contracting states of the Universal Copyright Convention, protection under the Revised Berne Convention takes priority (Art. XVII(1) of the Universal Copyright Convention (Paris)). "Convention works" of the Berne Convention-*i.e.,* works originating in one of the Union countries (Art. 5(4) of the Berne Convention (Paris))-are entitled to exclusive protection under the Convention in the countries of the Union. Article 5(1) of the Berne Convention (Paris) grants the same protection to authors from a country of the Union as is granted to works by a national. Copyright protection, which in Austria is also granted to works of applied art [cit] also extends to the scope of application of the Berne Convention; Austria has not availed itself of the possibility of restricting the protection of works of applied art. Works of applied art have also enjoyed copyright protection in the country of origin, France, since the Law of 1902, and this irrespective of whether they are also protected by virtue of the Law on Designs and Models. [cit]. Hence works of applied art from France are also entitled to copyright protection in Austria (Art. 2(7) Berne Convention (Paris Act)).

As this Court held in its decision, *Markt-Stahl-Stuht* [cit], the intention of the work, *i.e.* the purpose for which it has been created, is irrelevant for the question of copyright protection. Artistic works that fulfill the requirements of creativity and creativity in a work (individuality) of Section 1(1) of the Copyright Act can claim copyright protection and design protection. The border between copyright protection (artistic protection) and model protection must not, however, be set too low. On the contrary, there must be a considerable "aesthetic excess" or a corresponding artistic creativity. Similarly one and the same utility object can enjoy both artistic protection and patent or utility model protection simultaneously.

According to the literature and case law, a product of the human intellect is an individual intellectual creation (a "work") within the meaning of Section 1 of the Copyright Act if it is the result of creative intellectual activity and if the uniqueness distinguishing it from other works is derived from the personality of its author. The latter should find expression in such a way that it imposes upon the work the mark of uniqueness and its provenance from the author. In other words the work should be given form by the innermost essence of intellectual creativity. In the field of works of art, [cit], this form must be conceptually linked with a certain degree of originality. Here, a certain creativity in a work is necessary, an idea that has been given a form that bears the mark of the author's personal individuality, or at least is distinguishable by virtue of a personal touch from other products of a similar kind. [cit]. Works belonging to an artistic style whose intention is to derive the aesthetic shapes of utility objects exclusively from their purpose, avoiding any decorative additions ("functional form"), could have an aesthetic effect, but are not necessarily protected as works of art as a result. If an artistic movement deliberately rejects all non-functionally determined elements of design, thus by its very nature having less scope for design at its disposal than other artistic styles, *i.e.* permitting less of the author's individuality to enter into the work, then the protection to which it is entitled is also correspondingly diminished. [cit].

In the same decision, this Court also held that novel technical solutions are not entitled to copyright protection. In the case of a combination of technology and art in one work, examination must be made of the extent to which the design elements used are determined by technical factors and to what extent they have been selected for reasons of form, taste, beauty, or aesthetics. Nor is the choice of a geometrical shape alone sufficient to justify recognition as a work of art, since the geometrical shape of itself is in the public domain. Nor, likewise, can an artistic style be eligible for copyright protection in its own right.

According to the decisions referred to above, this question must be answered on the basis of the conditions applying at the time the work was created. Subsequent developments, on the other hand, must be ignored, since otherwise creations whose remarkable artistic uniqueness provided the stimulus for a large number of similar products would lose their protection within a short time.

. . . .

Despite its functional purpose, the chair designed by Le Corbusier and his assistants in 1928 contains an abundance of details that impose upon it the mark of uniqueness. Mention should be made here above all of the particular contrast between the broken line formed by the sitting and reclining surface and the arc-shaped supporting structure that serves both as contact element to the base and to enable infinite adjustment. It is not apparent that the chair only makes use of known features, or that its form is the necessary result of the technical function of the individual elements. In addition, the design of the head and foot of the chair also reveals traits of individuality; these latter shapes are neither determined by the purpose of the chair, nor made up of elements of a particular artistic style. All of these individual characteristics can be seen in the illustration of the prototype submitted in evidence; it is not obvious why this should not amount to evidence of the required creativity in a work. There is no indication that the [1928] "prototype" . . . is only a reproduction of "some possibly" original model. Nor does the fact that a number of variations of the chair were created have any consequence upon its creativity in a work. Furthermore the defendant has failed to present any concrete argument why the chair should be the mere result of ergonomic principles and a technical idea. Nor has the defendant stated which work served as a model for the architect Le Corbusier: the lounge chair designed by Ludwig Mies van der Rohe merely incorporates the three-part division of the sitting and reclining surface; Le Corbusier's lounge chair, with its infinitely variable adjustment, is completely different in the execution of the details. Nor has the defendant claimed that the van der Rohe chair was created before that of Le Corbusier. Thus the defendant has failed to fulfil his burden of proof to establish the contrary. In the absence of sufficient concrete claims and suitable counter-evidence, it must therefore be assumed in the hearing on the interlocutory injunction that the lounge chair was created independently by Le Corbusier and his assistants and that its shape is neither determined by a technical principle or by the chair's function, nor is it part of the public domain.

. . . All the chairs illustrated in the catalog used by the defendant incorporate the characteristic features of the infinitely adjustable lounge chair. . . . Hence the plaintiff has sufficiently established that these chairs amount to an infringement of his exploitation rights. . . .

_____

NOTES AND QUESTIONS

(1) **Article 2(7) of the Berne Convention**. Article 2(7) effectively enables countries offering designs protection under both copyright and *sui generis* design laws to condition copyright protection for foreign nationals' works of applied art on substantive reciprocity. But how is satisfaction of that condition to be assessed? It is quite clear that France-the leading adherent to the unity of art philosophy-offers copyright protection that meets the reciprocity standard. But what if an Austrian national seeks protection in French courts for a design first issued in Austria: would Article 2(7) oblige France to provide protection? *See* SAM RICKETSON, THE BERNE CONVENTION FOR THE PROTECTION OF LITERARY AND ARTISTIC WORKS 1886-1986, at 278-79 (1986) (discussing when copyright protection can be denied); *cf.* Kur, *supra,* at 146 (suggesting that the reciprocity provision is important between Italy and France because Italy "practically excludes" copyright protection for designs).

(2) **Reciprocity After TRIPS.** Does Article 2(7) of the Berne Convention-which derogates from the principle of national treatment-remain operative after TRIPS? *See* TRIPS art. 3(1). Should it? What does it now achieve? When negotiated at the Brussels Revision Conference in 1948, Article 2(7) embodied a compromise negotiated largely by European countries to accommodate their disparate approaches to copyright protection for designs; in particular, Italy and the United Kingdom held firm against the French position that works of applied art should be fully brought within the Berne Convention regardless of whether the works were industrially applied designs. *See* RICKETSON, *supra,* at 276-78. Yet, although Article 2(7) now formally governs relations of most Berne members, the very countries of Europe who generated the provision have now been compelled to repeal the application of Article 2(7) because of the *Phil Collins* decision. *See infra* Chapter 4. The early Commission drafts of the design directive discussed below, prompted by the same policy objectives as the *Phil Collins* decision, would have reached the same result legislatively. *See* Proposed Design Regulation art. 100(3); Proposed Design Directive art. 18(2). Thus, even if TRIPS permits continued application of the substantive reciprocity requirement, should Article 2(7) be changed? If so, in what way?

(3) **Standard of Originality.** How does the standard applied by the Austrian court to determine originality measure against recent international articulations of copyright originality? Does that provide the basis for international agreement on protection of applied art? If not, what obstacles remain?

(4) **The Universal Copyright Convention.** Why were the provisions of the Universal Copyright Convention inapplicable in this case? *See* Universal Copyright Convention art. XVII; RICKETSON, *supra,* at 854-55. Why might the rules under Austrian law applicable to the protectability of the *Le Corbusier* chair be affected by whether the "chair was issued at the same time in Austria" as abroad?

[B]   Regional Agreements

THE EUROPEAN UNION*

In 1993, the European Commission proposed two new legislative instruments that would dramatically revise design protection within the EU. The wide divergence in the means by which EU member states currently protect designs generates additional expense and complications for the producer seeking to obtain protection for its design throughout those countries. The Commission was moved to act by the concern that this expense created significant barriers to the market entry of small or medium sized firms, and threatened the competitiveness of European industry. In addition, however, the Commission recognized-as it had before in proposing trademark reform-that territorial (national) intellectual property rights threaten to disrupt the workings of a common market and interfere with the free movement of goods. Accordingly, the Commission proposed a regulation that would create unitary EU-wide design rights, consisting of a three-year unregistered design right and a registered right that could, with appropriate filings, endure for twenty-five years. The regulation was adopted in December 2001, *see* Council Regulation (EC) No. 6/2002 of 12 December 2001 on Community Designs, O.J. L 003 (January 5, 2002), and is discussed in greater detail *infra* § 6.04.

Although the centrepiece of the proposals was the regulation creating EU-wide rights, the Commission concluded that there was no justification for wholly preempting national design protection. Indeed, even if the Commission wished to replace national forms of protection with the Community level regime, member states could not immediately dismantle their local systems because of pre-existing rights acquired under those systems. Thus the proposed regulation was supplemented by a harmonization directive, containing provisions substantially identical to the regulation, that would harmonize the registered design laws of the member states with each other and with the substantive provisions of the EU-wide system of protection. The co-existence of national and community level systems mirrors the approach the Commission adopted in addressing reform of trademark law. An amended version of the directive was enacted in 1998. *See* Directive 98/71/EC of the European Parliament and of the Council of 13 October 1998 on The Legal Protection of Design, O.J. L 289 (Oct. 28, 1998).

The legislative instruments in combination address three different rights: The Registered Community Design Right and the Unregistered Community Design Right created by the regulation, both of which will exist at the community level and provide unitary protection throughout the union; and the registered design rights that must exist under the laws of each member state once the member state implements the provisions of the directive. The

---

* This analysis is based upon a more lengthy (and earlier) consideration of the proposals in Graeme B. Dinwoodie, *Federalized Functionalism: The Future of Design Protection in the European Union*, 24 AM. INTELL. PROP. L. ASS'N Q.J. 611 (1996).

basic principles underlying the regulation and the directive are the same and govern all three of these types of rights. *See generally* EUROPEAN DESIGN PROTECTION: COMMENTARY TO DIRECTIVE AND REGULATION PROPOSALS (Mario Franzosi ed., 1996).

The scope of the directive is less ambitious than the regulation: it seeks to harmonize national registered design laws, *see* Directive art. 2, but it neither requires member states to introduce unregistered design right protection at the national level, nor obliges the United Kingdom to make amendments to its existing unregistered design law. Moreover, whereas the regulation addresses the entire range of issues pertinent to a self-standing system of design protection, the directive harmonizes only the core elements of existing systems and leaves many issues to the member states. For example, article 14 of the proposed regulation provides that where a design has been developed by an employee in the execution of his duties or following instructions given by his employer the community rights in that design will vest in the employer. In contrast, the directive makes no provision on this question, leaving the allocation of national rights between employer and employee to national law.

For the purpose of the Design Directive, design is defined as "the appearance of the whole or a part of a product resulting from the features of, in particular, the lines, contours, colours, shape, texture and/or materials of the product itself and/or its ornamentation." Art. 1(a). The most important aspect of the definition of design, however, is what it does *not* include: it contains no reference to the aesthetic or functional nature of the design. This is arguably the most important contribution that these proposals make to the advancement of design protection laws. In repudiating the functional/aesthetic dichotomy, the Commission boldly has grasped the nettle of functionalism, which must be done if the problem of design protection is to be resolved. The United Kingdom had addressed this issue in 1988 in the enactment of its unregistered design legislation-which protected aesthetic and functional designs alike-but U.K. law does still distinguish between aesthetic and functional designs in that functional designs cannot obtain registered protection because of that system's "eye-appeal" requirement. The directive goes further and requires the registered design laws of member states to protect the external appearance of a product whether that appearance is pure decoration, has no aesthetic content, or is a combination of functional and aesthetic elements. There is no intention to restrict these new protections to designs that appeal to the eye. Instead of confining protection by restricting the universe of protectable subject-matter, the directive instead requires the registered design laws of member states to circumscribe protection through application of prescribed thresholds and exclusions.

The thresholds to community design protection follow a common structural model: a two-step test that assesses (1) whether the design is different from other designs, and (2) whether the development of the design beyond prior designs involves more than minimal creativity on the part of the designer. More specifically, to obtain protection, a design must be new, and have individual character. *See* art. 3(2). Novelty consists of no identical design or immaterially different design having previously been made available to the public as of the date of the filing of the application. *See* art. 4. The novelty standard is universal, not local, and no time limit will restrict the designs that might be regarded as prior art. *See* art. 6. The Commission intends that novelty for design purposes be a much less difficult standard than the patent requirement of the same name, and one of the principal drafters of the proposals has characterized the novelty standard demanded under the design proposals as one of "false novelty."

To avoid providing protection to designs that differ only in small details from a prior design, a supplementary threshold is contemplated by the proposals. A design will be protected only if it possesses "individual character." This will be the concept that truly sets the outside parameters of *prima facie* protection. A design shall "be considered to have an individual character if the overall impression it produces on the informed user differs from the overall impression produced on such a user by any design which has [previously] been made available to the public." Art. 5. All explanations of the concept tendered by the Commission suggest the clear intent to bring within the scope of protection incremental improvements upon prior designs: such designs arguably possess individual character if they *are* different, even if that difference might have been an obvious one to develop. Individual character does not connote a flash of genius; it simply requires the noticeable and non-trivial development of designs beyond what has gone before. The Commission clearly wished to ensure that adaptations of existing designs are protected by the new design right.

Although the "individual character" standard is somewhat vague, the legislation explicitly mandates consideration of the degree of freedom that the designer enjoyed in developing the design. That is to say, in a crowded field a smaller advance from prior designs will more easily warrant the conclusion of individual character. *See* art. 5(2). Of course, the scope of protection that such designs receive will be correspondingly limited; if there is little room for exceptional creativity on the part of the first designer, he cannot be heard to complain if the same restrictions compel a later designer to create a design that bears a resemblance to his in some respect. *See* art. 9(2).

In a system that broadly envisages the protection of functional designs on conditions that intentionally do not approach those required of applicants for utility patents, the exclusions from protection assume paramount importance. Protecting the appearance of a functional design clearly raises the possibility of incidentally affecting the ability of others to practice that function. Without the caution that this should impel, and the exclusions it justifies, there exists the *potential* that this form of protection might be anticompetitive and offer overbroad protection to functional items. Thus, any designs that are "solely dictated by the technical function [of the product]" are excluded from protection by Article 7(1) of the directive.

Similar exclusions are found in many design laws through the world. The Commission argued that if the design is dictated by the function of the product, the creative choices exercised by the designer are necessarily minimized (or even non-existent). Such an exclusion might also be justified, however, by recognition of the countervailing competitive concerns that are implicated by the protection of functional designs on standards less demanding than those imposed by patent law.

Courts that have considered this question have struggled with whether the term "dictated" is causative or mandatory (*i.e.,* whether the term connotes that functional concerns explain the design or necessitate the design). Although this provision is an essential bulwark against design rights for functional designs circumventing the rigors of the utility patent system, it must not be construed too broadly (*i.e.,* as merely causative). The mere fact that a design is influenced by functional considerations should not disqualify it from protection. Otherwise, the innovation of these proposals-the elimination of the threshold distinction between aesthetics and function-will prove illusory and functionalist design will remain excluded from protection.

Another interpretation of this provision, that flows from viewing the term "dictated" as meaning "mandated," would focus on whether any alternative designs exist: if they do, the design is not solely dictated by the technical function of the product. Such a test has analogues in many intellectual property regimes, including U.S. trade dress law, U.S. design patent law, U.S. copyright law and in the "multiplicity of forms" test found in French copyright and designs patent law. If the test calls simply for a determination of whether there are *any* other designs, however, there remains a danger that the *few* designs that will enable the product to function may be depleted by the successive grant of design rights in those respective possibilities to a small number of producers.

A more flexible interpretation might consider whether there are a sufficient number of designs to permit competition or, in the philosophy of the Commission, to require more than minimal creative choices on the part of the designer. This reading of Article 7(1) would avoid the problem of "design depletion," a concern implicitly recognized by Lord Morris when the House of Lords interpreted broadly the exclusion of designs "dictated solely by function" from U.K. registered design protection. *See* Amp v. Utilux, [1972] R.P.C. 103, 114 (noting that if provision required consideration only of whether alternative shapes existed "the designer could register a separate design in respect of each different shape"). A less mathematical approach has also been adopted by courts in other countries of the European Union already incorporating this exclusion in their design laws. And further parallels can be drawn to judicial interpretation of the idea/expression dichotomy in copyright law, to which the Commission expressly likens this exclusion. Where there is only one way of expressing the idea, that expression will be treated as having merged with the idea and will be unprotectable by copyright. Courts have, however, interpreted that concept broadly and have denied protection where the expression is one of only a limited number of ways of expressing the idea. The EU design legislation would benefit from a similar breadth of interpretation. Thus, although mere functional influences should not result in the denial of protection, nor should the mere availability of a single other alternative be sufficient to ensure protection. That might cause oligopolies rather than monopolies, but the competitive harm would be little different.

The EU proposals contain two additional exclusions from protection that bear confusingly similar popular labels (which were taken from the 1988 U.K. reforms): "must-fit" and "must-match." The must-fit exclusion deals with mechanical synchronicity, while the must-match provision deals with visual synchronicity. Article 7(2) of the Directive creates an exclusion for mechanical interconnections, that is:

> [F]eatures of appearance of a product which must necessarily be reproduced in their exact form and dimensions in order to permit the product in which the design is incorporated or to which it is applied to be mechanically connected or placed in, around or against another product so that either product may perform its function.

The exclusion of interconnections reveals the continuing conviction of the Commission that interoperability and standardization will enhance the competitive environment. As the Commission's *Green Paper* explained:

> Consumers should, for example, be able to replace a vacuum cleaner hose of a given make by another hose which fits into the vacuum cleaner. In principle, the design of the vacuum cleaner hoses qualifies for design protection just as does the design of the vacuum cleaner itself. To ensure interoperability and competition in the spare parts aftermarket in respect of a wide range of household articles, motor vehicles, consumer electronics etc., it appears advisable to exclude from protection those features of a design which would have to be reproduced necessarily in their exact form and dimensions in order for the component part to fit into the complex product for which it is intended.

GREEN PAPER ON THE LEGAL PROTECTION OF INDUSTRIAL DESIGN, WORKING DOCUMENT OF THE SERVICES OF THE COMMISSION, ¶ 5.4.10.1 (1991).

The most rancorous part of the EU design debate concerned what came to be known as the "repair clause." *See* art. 14. This clause addressed the scope of protection for the design of certain spare parts, so-called "must-match" designs, *i.e.*, designs where "the product incorporating the design or to which the design is applied is a component part of a complex product upon whose appearance the protected design is dependent." Amended Proposed Directive art. 14. Must-match designs involve visual, rather than mechanical, correlation. The most commonly cited example of a must-match design, which has also occasioned the greatest controversy, is the design of car body panels. The initial approach of the Commission was to place a limit of three years (from first marketing of the product) on the right of the design owner to stop third parties manufacturing and selling must-match parts for the purpose of repairing the complex product (e.g., the car) so as to restore its original appearance. Opposition to *any* period of exclusive rights was fierce, however, and the Commission accepted that a lesser scope of protection might be appropriate. In the first amended proposal, the Commission settled on a remuneration right for the design owner as against such third parties. That alternative did not, however, attract the support of the qualified majority of member states necessary to enact the directive.

The Council then adopted a common position in which it abandoned efforts at (apparently impossible-to-reach) compromise and mandated no special provision for spare parts. Instead, the limit of provision on spare parts was the imposition of an obligation upon the Commission, five years after implementation of the directive, to prepare an analysis of the effect of the directive on competition. Finally, after a conciliation procedure among Council, the Parliament and the Commission, the directive was passed with a compromise "standstill plus" provision. Article 14 of the enacted directive provides that:

> Until such time as amendments to this Directive are adopted on a proposal from the Commission [as contemplated within 4 years by Article 18], member states shall maintain in force their existing legal provisions relating to the use of the design of a component part used for the purpose of the repair of a complex product so as to restore its original appearance and shall introduce changes to those provisions only if the purpose is to liberalize the market for such parts [*i.e.,* reduce protection].

In the interim, even before the directive was implemented (triggering the Commission's obligation to produce an analysis of the effect of the directive on the spare parts market) the Commission initiated a consultation exercise among interested parties (car parts manufacturers and insurance companies) in the hope of reaching a voluntary resolution of the dispute.

Like most registered design laws, registration will confer upon the holder the exclusive right to use the design and to prevent the unauthorized third party use of the design or designs that do not produce "on the informed user a different overall impression." Arts. 9, 12. Registered designs may, by timely application, receive protection of this patent-like nature for up to twenty-five years. *See* art. 10. The concerns of industry regarding the costs and delay of design registration have largely been addressed in the regulation, where unregistered rights will be available and community-level registered rights will be granted after a relatively cursory examination. Accordingly, the directive does not compel member states (such as the United Kingdom) to dismantle any system of substantive examination used under their registered design laws.

The provisions in the initial draft of the directive *requiring* member states to provide full cumulation with copyright has undergone significant revision during the legislative process. Despite the Commission's reluctance to tackle broad-based copyright harmonization, the initial proposals provided that member states would not be permitted to deny copyright on the basis that the functional elements of the designs were not separable from the artistic elements or that the design had been applied industrially to a certain number of articles. *See* Proposed Directive art. 18. These provisions were aimed at Italy and the United Kingdom, both of which effectively exclude functional designs from copyright protection. Italy excludes designs from copyright by application of the rule of separability, and the United Kingdom now achieves the same by a combination of rules that focus on the industrial application of a design to articles of fifty or more. *See* Italian Copyright Law of April 22, 1941, *amended by* Decree No. 195, January 8, 1979, art. 2(4); Copyright, Designs & Patents Act, 1988, §§ 51-53, 236.

The Commission expressly and forcefully rejected the number of products to which the design is applied as of any relevance in determining the availability of protection. In the enacted directive, however, the Commission has agreed not to force Italy or the United Kingdom to surrender these exclusionary provisions. *See* Directive art. 17 ("The extent to which, and the conditions under which, [copyright] protection is conferred, including the level of originality required, shall be determined by each member state."). That is to say, while formally the Commission has insisted on mandatory cumulation of protection under copyright law, it has made no attempt to harmonize generally the conditions under which designs are accorded protection under the copyright code in each member state. Accordingly, the wide variances in copyright laws will continue to plague producers seeking protection throughout the European Union.

NOTES AND QUESTIONS

(1) **Definition of "Design".** The definition of design in the Design Directive includes both two-and three-dimensional design. The U.K. statute, on which to some extent the EU legislation was patterned, makes some distinction between two-and three-dimensional designs. *See, e.g.,* Copyright, Designs & Patents Act, 1988 § 213(3)(c) (surface decoration can be protected only as *registered* design). Similarly, although not explicit, in the United States, two-dimensional designs are more apt to receive copyright protection than three-dimensional designs. Are there reasons to treat two- and three-dimensional designs differently?

(2) **Protection of Functional Designs.** Why is it important that the EU proposals make no distinction between aesthetic and functional designs? What dangers does the inclusion of functional designs generate? Are the benefits received from their inclusion in the directive worth the costs or risks? How might those costs or risks be controlled or minimized? One writer has suggested that the definition of "design" in the directive-and, in particular, the use of the term "appearance"-defeats the Commission's stated objective of protecting modern functionalist industrial design. *See*

Uma Suthersanen, *Breaking Down the Intellectual Property Barriers,* 2 INTELL. PROP. Q 267, 274-75 (1998); *cf.* 2 STEPHEN P. LADAS, PATENTS, TRADEMARKS AND RELATED RIGHTS 869 (1975) (suggesting broader conception of "appearance"). Review the definition of "design" in Article 1(a): What types of designs are excluded by the limitations built into the definition? Does it by its terms offer protection to functionalist design?

(3) **Software and Hybrids.** The community design regime will not protect the design of computer software; the Commission is relying instead on the Software Directive to delineate the scope of protection available to those works. *See* Design Directive art. 1(b). Professor Reichman has argued that the problems that face industrial design and those that confront software possess sufficient similarities as to warrant treatment by a common regime of intellectual property protection rather than a set of separately tailored laws. *See* J.H. Reichman, *Legal Hybrids Between the Patent and Copyright Paradigms,* 94 COLUM. L. REV. 2432, 2511-19 (1994) (describing common problems of industrial designs and software in receiving appropriate protection under patent and copyright paradigms); *see also* Pamela Samuelson, et. al., *A Manifesto Concerning the Legal Protection of Computer Programs,* 94 COLUM. L. REV. 2308, 2356-57 (1994) (noting parallels). What are the merits and problems of such an approach?

(4) **The Threshold for Protection**. The Commission considered basing protection upon a threshold of originality (the subjective notion of the design being original to the designer, and not copied, regardless of objective similarity to other designs). What arguments might have supported adoption of such a threshold? Why you think that the Commission rejected that threshold? The Commission could also have adopted a modified copyright originality threshold, such as found in the Vessel Hull Design Protection Act, 17 U.S.C. §§ 1301(b), 1302(a)(2), the Semiconductor Chip Protection Act of 1984, 17 U.S.C. §§ 902(b) (1994) (protecting mask works that are original and that are not staple, commonplace, or familiar in the semiconductor industry), and in the U.K.'s unregistered design code. *See* Copyright, Designs & Patents Act, 1988, §§ 213(1), 213(4) (providing unregistered design protection to designs that are "original" and not "commonplace in the design field in question at the time of its creation"). What are the advantages of each respective approach? What difficulties might arise from adopting a new threshold falling between the relatively well-understood thresholds of patent and copyright? In light of the diverse approaches to protectability in member states prior to the enactment of the directive, what institutional forces might help establish common understanding of these terms in practice? The courts might embrace certain conceptual approaches that would help. *See* Dinwoodie, *supra,* at 662 (arguing for affirmative endorsement of link between degree of differential required to escape infringement and that required to demonstrate individual character).

(5) **Prior Art.** The prior art to be considered in the analysis of individual character and novelty is determined universally. In its *Green Paper,* the Commission had suggested that "a test of universal objective novelty cannot

be fulfilled and therefore should not be imposed." Why not? Why might a universal standard be inappropriate for designs? What dangers flow from the reversal of that policy? *See* Design Directive art. 6(1) (adding a "safeguard clause" introduced by the European Parliament that excludes from prior art disclosures that "could not reasonably have become known in the normal course of business to the circles specialized in the sector concerned operating within the Community" at the date of the application.).

(6) **Reliance on Competition Law.** One response to the threat of anticompetitive consequences flowing from the protection of functional designs is to fall back on principles of competition law to deal with any specific instances in which the grant or the enforcement of rights is anticompetitive. *See* Friedreich-Karl Beier, *Protection for Spare Parts in the Proposals for a European Design Law,* 25 I.I.C. 840, 842 (1994); Audrey Horton, *European Design Law and the Spare Parts Dilemma: The Proposed Regulation and Directive,* 16 EUR. INTELL. PROP. REV. 51, 54 (1994). Instead, the Commission sought to address the competitive concerns directly in the construction of the design regime through the use of carefully tailored exceptions. (The outcome of the spare parts debate suggests that they were not entirely successful). Which approach is preferable? Why? *See* Dinwoodie, *supra,* at 665-69.

(7) **Must-Match Exclusions.** Essential mechanical designs will, to a large extent, be caught by the must-fit exception or by the specific exclusion of so-called "under the hood" designs. *See* Directive art. 3(3). Why should the protection of must-match designs — designs where "the product incorporating the design or to which the design is applied is a component part of a complex product upon whose appearance the protected design is dependent" — be restricted? Consider the prototypical case of car body panels. *See* Bernhard Posner, *The Proposed EC Industrial Design Directive and Regulation: An Update and Analysis,* 2 INT'L INTELL. PROP. L. & POL. at 46-10 (1998); *see also British Leyland Motor Corp. v. Armstrong Patents Co.,* [1986] 1 All E.R. 850, 864 (1986) (Lord Templeman) (noting that if copyright gives exclusive rights in spare parts for cars "the purchaser of a BL car sells his soul to the company store"). Are there any costs to allowing free copying of the design of spare parts? What does the term "complex product," with respect to which the must-match provision and its permission to copy in order to supply the repair market applies, mean? *See* Directive art. 1(c). What products other than cars might be encompassed by this term? And what makes a design "dependent upon the appearance" of the complex product? *See* Dietrich C. Ohlgart, *Commentary in* EUROPEAN DESIGN PROTECTION, *supra,* at 154-55 (rehearsing different interpretations of "dependent"); *see also* Jeremy J. Phillips, *Commentary, in* EUROPEAN DESIGN PROTECTION, *supra,* at 164 (suggesting that "[i]n respect of a motor vehicle, the door panels would be covered [by the spare parts provision] but not such non-integral or possibly ornamental accessories for cars as wing mirrors or steering wheels").

(8) **TRIPS Compliance.** Did the earlier versions of the Design Directive's must-match provision-otherwise called the "repair clause"-comply

with TRIPS? Recall that the initial proposal would have required member states, after three years of protection, to permit third parties to manufacture and sell certain protected parts of complex products (so-called "must-match" parts) for repair purposes. The amended proposal made the repair clause right immediately exercisable, but only upon payment of fair and reasonable remuneration to the design owner. Would either of these approaches-which may yet be the basis of an amended directive when the Commission reports in four years, and which may be adopted in design legislation pending elsewhere, including the United States-be a violation of TRIPS? *See* TRIPS art. 26(2) (permissible exceptions); art. 26(3) (requiring minimum of ten years protection); *see also* Annette Kur, *TRIPS and Design Protection, in* FROM GATT TO TRIPS: THE AGREEMENT ON TRADE-RELATED ASPECTS OF INTELLECTUAL PROPERTY RIGHTS 141, 157-59 (Beier & Schricker eds., 1996) (arguing that repair clause proposals were consistent with TRIPS). If you believe that either of these approaches would violate TRIPS, what does that mean for the U.K. design law, which absolutely excludes protection for "must-match" parts and thus bars causes of action even against direct competitors of the original manufacturer?

(9) **Cumulation**. The directive does not regulate the cumulation of rights under member states' copyright, unfair competition, unregistered design, utility model and other laws. Article 16 permits member states to grant protection under any of these alternative regimes. (The only mandatory provision is Article 17, which purports to require cumulative copyright protection; but this provision is rendered meaningless because member states may determine the extent of such protection and the conditions upon which it is available.) What are the consequences of the Commission's reluctance to regulate (and, in particular, limit) cumulative protection? *See* Dinwoodie, *supra,* at 710-19.

To augment the plethora of possible (and different) protections, the Commission has also proposed a directive harmonizing the utility model laws in the EU. *See* Proposal for a European Parliament and Council Directive Approximating the Legal Arrangements for the Protection of Inventions By Utility Model, COM(97)691 final, O.J. C 36 (Mar. 2, 1998); Amended Proposal for a European Parliament and Council Directive Approximating the Legal Arrangements for the Protection of Inventions by Utility Model, COM(1999) 309 final/2 (July 12, 1999). Utility model laws are a form of registered (but unexamined) industrial property that confer exclusive rights (normally for a shorter term than patent) on technical inventions that do not display the level of inventiveness required for patent protection. In addition to harmonizing existing national utility model provisions, the directive would require the enactment of utility model laws in countries (such as the United Kingdom, Sweden and Luxembourg) where such laws do not currently exist. The directive would require member states to accord ten years of utility model protection to subpatentable functional inventions, and its interaction with design protection for functional designs is not clear. *Cf.* Opinion of the Economic and Social Committee on the Green Paper: The Protection of Utility Models in the Single Market, O.J. C 174/6,

¶ 5.2.1 (June 17, 1996) (suggesting that the Commission had not in its initial *Green Paper* taken sufficient account of the relationship between utility model protection and the protection of functional designs under the unregistered design scheme); Green Paper on the Protection of Utility Models in the Single Market, COM(95)370 final at 2 n.7 (distinguishing subject matter of design rights from the technical invention, which can be protected by utility model laws, on basis that design rights accorded protection to "the outward form of an object . . . "). For a thorough and insightful analysis, both of the EU proposals and utility model protection generally, see Mark D. Janis, *Second Tier Patent Protection,* 40 HARV. INT'L L. J. 151 (1999).

(10) **Implementation**. The design directive was to be implemented by October 28, 2001, but on July 1, 2002, the Commission was forced to send reasoned opinions requesting prompt implementation to ten member states that had not yet implemented the directive.

Chapter 5

DISPUTES BETWEEN STATES

In this Chapter, we discuss the different means by which state to state disputes regarding international intellectual property law may be resolved. The conclusion of the TRIPS Agreement, and the incorporation of TRIPS within the WTO dispute settlement system, has revolutionized this subject. There were, however, disputes between states regarding appropriate levels of international intellectual property protection prior to the TRIPS Agreement. We start this Chapter with a brief consideration of how disputes were handled before TRIPS, and continue with discussion of the unilateral trade measures (adopted primarily by the United States) that might be seen as a transitional stage on the road to TRIPS. These materials not only place the TRIPS Agreement in historical perspective, but remain relevant because resort to these alternative means of resolving disputes provides the backdrop against which any rejection or revision of TRIPS and/or WTO dispute settlement will take place. The materials also raise in stark relief issues concerning the relationship between developed and developing countries that the conclusion of the TRIPS Agreement may temporarily obscure, but which we fully expect to occupy much of the post-TRIPS debate.

§ 5.01   Dispute Resolution in WIPO-Administered Treaties

Both of the leading pre-TRIPS multilateral intellectual property conventions, the Paris Convention and the Berne Convention, made provision for the submission of disputes to the International Court of Justice. *See* Berne Convention art. 33(1); Paris Convention art. 28(1). This mechanism was never used. Moreover, no state invoked the doctrine of retaliation and retorsion under public international law, as a state could have done if it believed another country was in violation of its treaty obligations. *See* J.H. Reichman, *Enforcing the Enforcement Procedures of the TRIPS Agreement*, 37 VA. J. INT'L L. 335, 339 n.17 (1997). Why do you think that neither the express mechanism of the International Court of Justice referral nor the general remedies of public international intellectual property law were used?

WIPO has also sought to create intellectual property-specific dispute resolution mechanisms. In particular, prior to the conclusion of TRIPS it convened a Committee of Experts to consider a proposed Dispute Resolution Treaty. Although the Committee of Experts continued to meet post-TRIPS, the accommodation of the Paris and Berne Conventions within the TRIPS/WTO dispute settlement mechanism has made this proposed treaty a lesser priority and it is barely an active issue at WIPO. What relevance might it still have? If you were in charge of setting priorities at WIPO, where would the conclusion of such a treaty fit on your list? Reconsider this question after reading the materials on WTO Dispute Resolution.

§ 5.02   Unilateral Trade Measures

[A]   The United States: Special 301

KIM NEWBY, THE EFFECTIVENESS OF SPECIAL 301 IN CREATING LONG TERM COPYRIGHT PROTECTION FOR U.S. COMPANIES OVERSEAS [*]
21 SYRACUSE J. INT'L L. & COM. 29, 32-62(1995)

III. THE DEVELOPMENT OF SPECIAL 301

In 1974, the United States enacted the Trade Act of 1974 which provides for action to be taken against those trading partners of the U.S. that engage in "unfair competition."[25] Title III of the Act, "Relief From Unfair Trade Practices," expands the ability of the United States to counter offensive trade practices by including, among other sections, Chapter 1, § 301, "Responses to certain trade practices of foreign governments."

Section 301 provided the President with broad authority to retaliate against both unreasonable as well as unjustifiable import restrictions that affect U.S. commerce. . . . Retaliatory measures could include the suspension of trade benefits or the imposition of duties or other import restrictions on the products of the offending foreign country. [§ 301(a)].

The enacting of § 301 was seen as a direct result of Congressional dissatisfaction with the manner in which U.S. trade was being protected under GATT. Trade deficits in the United States were growing and the U.S. economy appeared to be suffering at the expense of the growth of other nations. The Legislative History is instructive in this regard. The History states that:

---

[*] Copyright 1995, Kim Newby; Syracuse Journal of International Law and Commerce. Reprinted with kind permission. Ms. Newby practices technology law in Boston, Massachusetts.

[25] Trade Act of 1974, Pub. L. No. 93-618 § 2, 88 Stat. 1978 (1975), Statement of General Purposes sets out that: The purposes of this Act are, through trade agreements affording mutual benefits—(1) to foster the economic growth of and full employment in the United States and to strengthen economic relations between the United States and foreign countries through open and nondiscriminatory world trade; (2) to harmonize, reduce, and eliminate barriers to trade on a basis which assures substantially equivalent competitive opportunities for the commerce of the United States; (3) to establish fairness and equity in international trading relations, including reform of the General Agreement on Tariffs and Trade; (4) to provide adequate procedures to safeguard American industry and labor against unfair or injurious import competition, and to assist industries, firms, workers, and communities to adjust to changes in international trade flows; (5) to open up market opportunities for United States commerce in nonmarket economies; and (6) to provide fair and reasonable access to products of less developed countries in the United States markets.

The President ought to be able to act or threaten to act under section 301, whether or not such action would be entirely consistent with the General Agreement on Tariffs and Trade. Many GATT articles . . . are either inappropriate in today's economic world or are being observed more often in the breach, to the detriment of the United States. . . . Congress is not urging that the United States undertake wanton or reckless retaliatory action under section 301 in total disdain of applicable international agreements. However, the Committee felt it was necessary to make it clear that the President could act to protect U.S. economic interests whether or not such action was consistent with the articles of an outmoded international agreement initiated by the Executive 25 years ago and never approved by Congress. [30]

Still unhappy with the growing budget deficits, Congress in 1988 enacted the Omnibus Trade and Competitiveness Act. Among the measures taken in this comprehensive trade legislation was an expansion of section 301 powers. The new § 301 takes the power of determining which countries to investigate and retaliate against out of the hands of the President and puts it into the hands of the United States Trade Representative ("USTR"). [33] The revised § 301 also imposes strict time limits within which the USTR must act once an offending country is cited; previously no strict time limits were imposed. The corollary to this is that the USTR has no discretion to act once a country is cited; such action is mandatory. [O]ther amendments to § 301 caused significant controversy among U.S. trading partners. . . . [including] "Special 301." [36]

. . . .

Special 301 . . . addresses only the protection of U.S. intellectual property. . . . [It] requires that the USTR prepare an annual list of countries that allow the most flagrant violations of protection for U.S. intellectual property. The process of determining and naming these countries, along with a credible threat of retaliation against them, is the heart of Special 301. . . .

IV. How Special 301 Works

A. Determination of Problem Countries

Each year by a specified time, [37] the USTR must identify countries that deny effective protection of intellectual property or equitable market access to United States persons who rely upon intellectual property protection.

---

[30] S. Rep. No. 1298, 93d Cong., 2d Sess. (1974), *reprinted in* 1974 U.S.C.C.A.N. 7186, 7304.

[33] The Office of the United States Trade Representative (USTR) was established in 1982 under 19 U.S.C. § 2171. The USTR is an office within the Executive Office of the President. The USTR is responsible for conducting international trade negotiations. [cit].

[36] 19 U.S.C. §§ 2411–2420 (1988).

[37] Generally, by April 30 of each year.

In addition, those countries that the USTR determines to be "Priority Foreign Countries" must be identified and reported in the Federal Register.

A Priority Foreign Country is a country: (1) that has the most "onerous or egregious" practices that deny protection or equitable market access; (2) whose practices have the "greatest adverse impact," either actual or potential, on the relevant U.S. products; or (3) that is not engaging in good faith negotiations to provide effective protection of intellectual property rights. [19 U.S.C. § 2242 (b)(1).]

In order to make the determination of which countries' practices cause that country to rise to the level of Priority Foreign Country status, the USTR has a number of sources upon which to rely. The statute explicitly provides that the USTR shall confer with the Register of Copyrights, the Commissioner of Patents and Trademarks, and other "appropriate officers of the Federal government," in identifying Priority Foreign Countries. [19 U.S.C. § 2242 (b)(2)(A).] The USTR also must consider any sources that may be available to the USTR and such information as may be submitted to the USTR by interested persons.[41] Congressional hearings to discuss Special 301 are a good source of this information. During these hearings, Congress discusses the successes of Special 301 with the USTR and industry representatives. In addition, testimony is given as to which countries are the most problematic for certain industries with regard to intellectual property protection.[43]

The USTR determines that a country is denying adequate and effective protection of intellectual property rights if non-citizens of that country are denied adequate and effective means under the law to "secure, exercise, and enforce rights" related to intellectual property. [19 U.S.C. § 2242(d)(2).] A foreign country is deemed to deny fair and equitable market access if that country denies domestic market access to a product protected by copyright, patent or trademark and such denial is through laws or practices that violate provisions of international law or international agreements, or that constitute discriminatory non-tariff trade barriers. [19 U.S.C. § 2242(d)(3).]

Each year the USTR also identifies and publishes "priority watch list" and "watch list" countries. These lists are not required by statute, but the publishing of these lower level watch lists alerts countries that their practices are being monitored by the USTR. As such, these lists provide a significant deterrent on their own.

---

[41] The definition of an interested person "includes, but is not limited to, domestic firms and workers, representatives of consumer interests, United States product exporters, and any industrial user of any goods or services that may be affected" by actions taken under section 301. 19 U.S.C. § 2411(d)(9).

[43] In the 1993 Congressional hearings, for example, Nintendo of America and Cone Mills Corp. (textile manufacturer) as well as the U.S. Trademark Association, the Recording Industry of America, the International Intellectual Property Alliance, the Business Software Alliance, and the Pharmaceutical Manufacturers Association, all submitted testimony, among others.

B. The Investigation

Once identified as a Priority Foreign Country, within thirty days the USTR must initiate an "investigation" against that country and its offending practices. [19 U.S.C. § 2412(b)(2)(A).] The only time that an investigation is not required in such situations is when the USTR determines that initiation of the investigation "would be detrimental to United States economic interests." [19 U.S.C. § 2412(b)(2)(A).] Any decision not to initiate an investigation, however, must be fully documented in a report to Congress. Such report must include the reasons for this decision and the U.S. interests that would be adversely affected by the investigation. [19 U.S.C. § 2412(b)(2)(C).]

[I]t is important to remember that even without the mandatory listing of Priority Foreign Countries under Special 301, Section 301 requires that an investigation be commenced against any country whenever the USTR determines that (1) the rights of the U.S. under trade agreements are being denied; or (2) any policy or practice of a foreign country denies U.S. benefits that it is entitled to under trade agreements, or is unjustifiable and burdens or restricts U.S. commerce. [19 U.S.C. § 2411(a)(1).] Unjustifiable or unreasonable policies or practices explicitly include any act, policy or practice that denies national or most-favored-nation treatment, denies the rights of establishment, or denies adequate and effective protection of intellectual property rights. [19 U.S.C. § 2411(d)(3)(B), (d)(4)(B).]

Under Section 301, an investigation shall be commenced either upon the independent decision of the USTR or upon the receipt of a petition by an interested party that the USTR decides to act upon. The decision to act upon any submitted petition must be made within forty-five days after the date of the USTR's receipt of such petition. [19 U.S.C. § 2412(a)(2).]

In either 301 action, however, once an investigation has been initiated, the USTR is required to request consultations with the foreign country to discuss the offending practices and a resolution of the situation. [19 U.S.C. § 2413(a)(1).] For matters involving the violation of a bilateral or multilateral trade agreement, the USTR must request that the formal dispute mechanism of the agreement involved be invoked if the two countries are not able to come to an agreement acceptable to the U.S. within a specified period of time. [19 U.S.C. § 2413(a)(2).] If no formal bilateral or multilateral agreement is involved, the USTR must conduct its investigation, consultations, and negotiations within a period of six months in most cases. This deadline may be extended to nine months if the USTR sees "substantial progress" in the Priority Foreign Country's drafting or implementing of measures that will provide effective protection of intellectual property rights. [19 U.S.C. § 2414(a)(3)(B).] On the basis of the consultations and negotiations conducted within the statutory deadlines, the USTR must make a final determination. The determination made by the USTR must be published in the Federal Register together with a description of the facts upon which the determination, either to proceed further or drop the matter, was made. [19 U.S.C. § 2414(c).] If the USTR finds that the violations that spawned the investigation do in fact exist and if no substantial progress has been taken by the Priority Foreign Country within the period of investigation, then the USTR must take action. [19 U.S.C. § 2411(a)(1).] This action generally must be taken within thirty days of the date of determination. [19 U.S.C. § 2415(a)(1).]

C. Taking Responsive Action

The Trade Representative has broad discretionary authority in deciding what actions to take against a Priority Foreign Country. The three main tools that the USTR may invoke are the suspension of trade benefits, the imposition of duties or other import restrictions, and the entering into of binding agreements committing the country either to stop the offending practices or provide the U.S. with compensatory trade benefits. [19 U.S.C. § 2411(c)(1).] The office of the USTR may choose to focus its actions on the entire Priority Foreign Country, or on particular goods or economic sectors of that country. The fact that not all of that country's goods or sectors of its economy are involved in the particular offending practice complained of does not preclude the USTR from targeting the entire country. [19 U.S.C. § 2411(c).] The USTR must, however, ensure that any action taken to eliminate a practice is imposed to affect the Priority Foreign Country in an amount that is "equivalent in value to the burden or restriction imposed by that country on United States commerce." [19 U.S.C. § 2411(a)(3).]

Once a measure is chosen, the USTR must monitor the implementation of the measure and any progress the country takes to change its practices to conform to U.S. requests. During monitoring, if the USTR determines that the Priority Foreign Country is not implementing a 301-imposed measure or agreement, the USTR may take further action as authorized in the act. [19 U.S.C. § 2416(b).] Conversely, if during the monitoring process the Priority Foreign Country removes the offending practices or if the burden on U.S. commerce begins to outweigh the benefits of the measures taken against the Priority Foreign Country, then the USTR may modify or terminate any action taken under 301. [19 U.S.C. § 2417.]

Although once the USTR identifies a Priority Foreign Country mandatory action against that country generally is required, action need not be taken in two situations. The first is when an arbitration committee (under GATT or bilateral agreement dispute resolution committees) determines that the practices complained of do not impair benefits to the U.S. under any trade agreement or do not violate rights of the United States. [19 U.S.C. § 2411(a)(2)(A).] The second situation is when the USTR finds one of the following: (1) that the country has taken or has agreed to take measures to eliminate the offending practices; (2) it is not possible for the country to take such measures, but compensatory trade benefits will be provided to the U.S.; (3) action against the country would have an adverse effect on the U.S. economy out of proportion to the benefits that would be achieved; or (4) action against the country would cause serious harm to the national security of the United States. [19 U.S.C. § 2411(a)(2)(B).] In these two situations, the USTR has the discretion to decide whether to take action or not.

V. Special 301 in Action

. . . .

B. China

China began its Special 301 journey in 1991 when it was one of the first three countries to be named a Priority Foreign Country.[80] Failure to provide adequate patent protection and a marked lack of copyright protection for U.S. works, especially computer software programs, were the driving reasons behind putting China on this list.

Lengthy negotiations between the United States and China resulted in a comprehensive Memorandum of Understanding ("MOU"). This MOU was signed on January 17, 1992, just hours before U.S. retaliatory measures were to be implemented. Articles 1 and 2 of the MOU relate to patent rights. Article 3 sets out the steps China will take to implement an effective, world-standard copyright protection regime. These steps include acceding to the Berne Convention, acceding to the Geneva Convention (protection of phonograms), updating the Chinese copyright law to meet requirements of these two conventions, and, particularly, clarifying the rights of distribution that [apply] to all works and sound recordings, including rental rights and the rights of first sale. In addition, China agreed that by the time that China accede[d] to the Berne Convention, China [would] protect computer programs as literary works under the Berne Convention. Article 4 protects trade secrets as provided for under the Paris Convention for Protection of Industrial Property. Article 5 states that both Governments will provide effective measures to prevent infringement of intellectual property rights within their borders and yet in doing so "shall avoid creating obstacles to legitimate trade." Article 6 relates to consultations between the parties, and Article 7 states that as of the date that the MOU is signed, the U.S. will revoke China's designation as a Priority Foreign Country under the Special 301 provisions.

During the 1992 Senate hearings on Special 301, Senator Max Baucus (Mont.) called this result with China "the most important Special 301 victory to date." He stated of the process: "[U.S. trade negotiators] combined hard negotiations, solid deadlines and the credible threat of retaliation to reach this agreement. . . In the end, they were able to convince China to agree to a regime of intellectual property protection that is in some ways superior to what we were able to win in the draft GATT agreement." In 1992, China was one of eighteen Watch List countries, the lowest level of priority named by the USTR. The signing of an agreement with a country,

---

[80] Up until this time, Special 301 had been used to name countries on the two Watch Lists only. In 1991 the Bush administration identified China, India and Thailand as the first Special 301 Priority Foreign Countries. [cit].

however, is usually not enough. As stated in the 1993 Senate hearings by the General Counsel of the office of the USTR:

> The 1992 Memorandum of Understanding on intellectual property that was entered into with China, represented an enormous amount of progress with respect to the intellectual property regime of China. Now it will not be self-executing. What I tried to do in my testimony is to say that once other countries have adopted laws, we have to make sure that these laws are real.[87]

During those same hearings, there were calls to put China on the Priority Watch List because of non-transparent rules and regulations.

China was upgraded from the Watch List to a Priority Watch List on November 30, 1993, and was designated as a Priority Foreign Country in 1994. The reasons for this stem from continued lack of enforcement of the measures that Beijing has implemented absent satisfactory progress in enforcement measures. The Chinese were upset at this turn of events and viewed it as a betrayal after they had worked to comply with unilateral U.S. demands.

The USTR's actions towards China in late 1994 and early 1995 showed a marked increase in the level of aggressiveness in pursuit of Special 301 goals. The United States threatened 301-allowed trade sanctions on more than one billion dollars worth of Chinese products as punishment for Chinese lack of enforcement of their intellectual property laws.[91] After the U.S. announced its intention, the Chinese threatened retaliatory measures as a response to such trade sanctions.[92] The result was a threatened trade war which ended with a last-minute (actually, past dead-line) agreement. In the agreement, the Chinese continue pledges to crack down on piracy and improve enforcement of existing laws. Although this may be seen as at least a short-term victory for U.S. industry, it remains to be seen if substantive changes will result. One clear consequence, however, is the sharpening of Chinese attitudes towards the United States. Chinese anger

---

[87] Special 301 and the Fight Against Trade Piracy: Hearing Before the Subcomm. on International Trade of the Comm. on Finance, 103d Cong., 1st Sess. 19 (1993). . .

[91] . . . The Chinese, however, have not only beefed up their intellectual property regulatory regime, but also have increased penalties for violators. As of July of 1994, it is a criminal offense to violate a copyright in China (although punishment is only for those who have knowledge that they are violating another's copyright). [cit]. Even before that, however, the Chinese would occasionally come down hard on serious violators of intellectual property rights. In January of 1994, for example, an approximately $25,000 fine was levied on a Chinese computer copyright infringer, [cit], and in 1993 one man was sentenced to death for charges related to the selling of counterfeit brand-name cigarettes. [cit].

Even with all this, however, the Business Software Alliance estimates that software piracy in China costs U.S. industry $322 million each year and states that there is a 94% software piracy rate in that country. [cit].

[92] Threats to block imports of U.S. records, cigarettes, alcoholic beverages, televisions shows, and movies were made by Chinese officials and the Chinese Ministry of Foreign Economic Trade and Economic Cooperation stated that it would refuse to consider requests from U.S. companies to establish subsidiaries in China. *U.S. & China Spar Over Piracy*, NEWSBYTES NEWS NETWORK, Jan. 3, 1995.

and frustration is not just aimed at what they perceive as U.S. meddling in internal Chinese affairs, but also at the lack of [patience] the U.S. trade negotiators have shown. Li Changxu, head of the China United Intellectual Property Investigation Center stated "It's like building a house. You can have the house structure all set up, very beautiful. But then, you need electricity and water pipes. That takes more time."[93] Similar sentiments came from Gao Linghan, Deputy Director of the National Copyright Administration of China: "Give us five years to end this problem. If we can solve these problems in five years, then I think we will have done a good job."

. . . .

VI. How Special 301 is Effective in Developing Copyright Protection Overseas

It is obvious from the above that Special 301 actions grab the targeted country's attention. Being cited on one of the USTR lists and the credible threat of retaliation behind the Special 301 process compel countries to work with the USTR to arrive at a position sufficient, at least, to ward off retaliatory actions. Without the pressure of Special 301 actions against them, Taiwan, China, and Thailand most likely would not have taken steps to strengthen their copyright regimes in the manner that they did from 1989 to the present.

One indication of success is that in 1993 it was reported that from the start of the anti-piracy drive in Thailand as a result of U.S. pressure, there has been a 30% increase in sales of legal cassettes there. Likewise, a statement last Spring by the head of the WIPO commended China on the swift progress that country has made in the realm of developing a copyright protection system. As WIPO director-general Arpad Bogsch stated, China has gone from no system just fifteen years ago to one of the most advanced countries in the developing world in this regard. Many of the measures cited as evidence of this progress were measures implemented as a result of U.S. Special 301 pressure.

Another example of Special 301 successes includes the Indonesian government involvement in a Business Software Alliance[107] raid on printers in Indonesia. The raids resulted in the confiscation of more than 17,000 illegally printed computer software manuals. As described by one who was involved in the raid: "It was an extraordinarily difficult operation—we had been working for a long time gathering enough information and evidence

---

[93] Marcus W. Brauchli & Joseph Kahn, *China Moves Against Piracy As U.S. Trade Battle Looms*, Asian Wall St. J., Jan. 6–7, 1995, at 1.

[107] The Business Software Alliance ("BSA") is a U.S. industry group dedicated to protecting the property and rights of member industries. Member companies account for over 70% of the U.S. prepackaged software market. Members include Aldus Corp., Apple Computer, Autodesk, Borland International, GO Corp., Lotus Development, Microsoft, Novell, and WordPerfect. BSA has been very active and visible in countries that BSA feels do not adequately protect its members' products.

to persuade the authorities to help and get search warrants, . . . This time the Indonesian Government was involved in helping us to break the ring and we're confident we'll achieve a favourable result." The reason for the cooperation was that the USTR was hinting at upgrading Indonesia on the Special 301 lists.

In order to justify the unilateral action that Special 301 imposes, the actions may simply be seen as "damages" for breach of an implied trade contract. Trading with the United States on favorable, most-favored-nation terms is a privilege, not a right.[111] If . . . U.S. copyright owners are not being adequately protected in foreign markets, it is only right to rectify the situation, so the justification may go. As one music industry member put it, "[Special 301] has a very simple predicate, that nations who want to trade with us on favorable terms have an obligation to grant us access to their markets and further, to ensure that the products of American ingenuity and creativity are not pirated or counterfeited."

The USTR and supporters of 301 actions further justify this unilateral bullying by insisting that the United States is not the only party that benefits from these actions. One BSA official recognized the role that Special 301 played in Taiwan's recent copyright regime developments, but he also stated that "[the Taiwanese] are developing their own software industry and, while it's fledgling, they're beginning to understand the frustrations of being ripped off." Further, General Counsel at the office of the USTR had this to say about developing countries in general and developments in Mexico in particular:

> If you look around the world, there are some developing nations that have been quite forthcoming in terms of intellectual property protection. Sometimes, as in the example of Mexico, this is in part because their leadership recognizes the advantages to them as a country. They will advance more rapidly if they create a climate where intellectual property is protected. This is a point you made earlier with respect to Thailand. We are obviously pursuing our intellectual property interests because they matter a great deal to our companies and our jobs here and to our industrial and techno-logical strength, but frankly, it is in the interest of these other countries to upgrade their intellectual property as well. It will strengthen their economy.

---

[111] This may not be as obvious as it sounds. The base tariff rate for goods imported into the United States was developed under the Tariff Act of 1930 and is commonly called the Smoot-Hawley tariff rate. These rates are very high and, in fact, are considered to be one of the triggering events to the self-interested policies that led to the collapse of the world economy in the 1930s. The great majority of products imported into the U.S., however, are imported under the Most Favored Nation rates. These rates are considerably lower and are amended to reflect latest trade agreement rates. As for the General System of Preferences ("GSP") benefits, at present over 100 countries receive these preferential tariff rates. Other preferential status rates that the United States has employed include Caribbean Basin Initiative, NAFTA, and Israeli Free Trade Agreements. Therefore, the "privilege" is extended to most countries.

It may be more likely, however, that Mexico was trying desperately to meet the demands of the United States in order to have the [NAFTA] passed through the U.S. Congress. In general, it may be said that each country will eventually find it in its best interest to adopt an effective copyright protection scheme; the United States is making sure that targeted countries find adopting such a scheme in their best interests sooner than might otherwise occur.

There are theoretical bases for this justifying that both the U.S. and the targeted countries benefit. In a 1990 law review article funded by the Pharmaceutical Manufacturers Association, two researchers used regression analysis and other statistical models to show how the level of economic development of a nation corresponds with the level of patent protection afforded by that country.[116] The theory postulates that with effective intellectual property protection a country is able to attract technology into its own economy. The new technology will spread through the country and eventually, through the incentives intellectual property protection provides, local industries will develop. If there is no protection, there is no incentive to develop new technologies or products and "technological backwardness will result."

Although the statistical correlation shown by the analysis in this article may be compelling and . . . may be accurate with regard to some of the countries cited in the article, for example Bulgaria or Poland, . . . it cannot be extended too broadly and certainly cannot be analogized outside the field of patent protection. For example, Germany, with some of the highest rates of computer software piracy is simultaneously one of the world's most developed economies. In addition Taiwan and Thailand, with annual growth rates of 9% and 8% respectively, are consistently cited among the world's worst pirates of intellectual property and appear to be outside the scope of the analysis. Finally, the article cannot explain how the United States' high level of piracy fits in. As General Counsel of the office of the USTR stated in 1992, " . . . In dollar volume, there may be as much intellectual property piracy here in the United States as there is around the world, largely because we have such a large market." The type of analysis found in this law review article may be used in statements by the USTR and President when discussing the possibility of sanctions, and also used by the Congress to justify supporting such actions. One significant problem with such analysis is that it ignores development patterns that may differ from that followed by the United States and other Western, industrialized countries.

In general, it may be true that the long-term benefits of a strong intellectual property regime in a developing country will help stimulate innovation in research and development and production processes. Such developments may lead to a more highly skilled labor force and encourage other nations to invest in and transfer technology to that country. In

---

[116] Richard T. Rapp & Richard P. Rozer, *Benefits and Costs of Intellectual Property Protection in Developing Countries*, 24 J. WORLD TRADE 75 (1990).

addition, the benefits in quality to consumers of protected, genuine products may in some instances outweigh the benefits of accessibility to poor quality, inexpensive pirated products. These determinations of the scope, pace, and direction of development, however, are for the governments of each individual country to make.

VII. How Special 301 is Inappropriate for Developing Copyright Protection Overseas

[S]pecial 301 has been evolving with the "Priority Watch Lists" and "Watch Lists" in addition to the "Priority Foreign Country" listing, and with "out-of-cycle" reviews that may now take place so that the USTR need not wait until one specified date each year to cite the most egregious violators of U.S. intellectual property rights. In enacting this unilateral trade tool, however, the United States ignores the situation and society behind the violations.

Once a country is entered onto a Special 301 list, that country's government enters into negotiations with the United States for the sole purpose of removing the threat of retaliatory sanctions against that country. It is unlikely that within a developing country itself there is a strong lobby to demand or even support increased protection of copyrightable property. Until the government of a country has the political power and will to strengthen its copyright regimes, little will change; until a country itself decides that it is worth the scarce resources of the government to make a stand on increased copyright protection, changes will be incremental and mainly formalistic. Changes in targeted countries often will be just sufficient to prevent the United States from retaliating. And after the threat of retaliation has passed, it is possible that little will be done in the way of follow up—that is until the U.S. returns the next year to complain. This can be seen in the examples of Taiwan, China and Thailand noted above. Each year these countries work to provide the U.S. with indications of progress, but progress has been incremental and even where it has taken place enforcement measures are not commensurate with the improved legislation.

A. The Response of the Developing Countries

Developing countries in particular resent the United States determining what statutory regimes are in that country's best interest. Such countries see the forcing of U.S. copyright regimes upon them as a new form of colonialism. In addition, it is often simply not practical for a developing country to adopt a developed country's standards in such areas. Developing countries generally understand that a strong, western-style copyright regime will eat up resources in the instituting, monitoring and enforcing of such a system. Without access to copied products and processes, both private and public resources must be garnered to finance the research and development necessary to license or replicate expensive methods already developed in other nations. This problem may be particularly acute in the area of education, where access to books, software, and computers is crucial to raise living standards, yet prohibitively expensive within developing countries. The added restrictions on access to technology and products that strong copyright protection regimes impose are considered an unnecessary constraint to development. It is a struggle for a developing country's government to balance imposing such a regime to cater to U.S. demands (and avoid the threat of retaliation) and providing necessary resources to the population.

B. The Response of the Rest of the World

The developing countries are not alone in expressing anger with Special 301 measures. Most of the United States trading partners, both developing countries and industrialized countries, have protested against the unilateral nature of Special 301. The main complaint raised against the United States with regard to Special 301 is that such unilateral measures destroy attempts to maintain a balanced world trading system developed through multilateral negotiations. By adding parties with various positions, multilateral negotiations provide countries in a less strong position support for their views. On the other hand, the United States, with its strong bargaining position, has a perceived unfair advantage when pursuing bilateral negotiations with less developed nations, as it does when it commences a Special 301 action.[126]

India, Japan, France, and Brazil are among the most consistent and vocal opponents of Special 301. Brazil has been adamant in pursuing international condemnation against the United States for perceived violations of GATT agreements by using Special 301. Brazil has filed complaints with GATT authorities stating that Special 301 actions violate U.S. responsibilities under GATT.

On the other hand, the French have been pressing for a European equivalent of Section 301. . . .

It is, in fact, precisely to guard against such escalation of self-interested actions by nations that the multilateral GATT with its "most favored nation" concept was initiated. When the United States pursues unilateral measures and coerces bilateral negotiations under the threat of sanctions, GATT is undermined. The U.S. has consistently been a supporter of GATT and by ignoring GATT most favored nation treatment and dispute resolution mechanisms, the U.S. sends a message that GATT need not be adhered to. It will be difficult for the United States to persuade other nations to enter into further GATT negotiations and abide by GATT provisions if the U.S. is viewed as a flagrant violator of GATT. As one commentator put it, the United States must recognize that its actions are "norm creating" and that the U.S. should encourage behavior that all nations will find acceptable

---

[126] George Y. Gonzalez, *An Analysis of the Legal Implications of the Intellectual Property Provisions of the North American Free Trade Agreement*, 34 HARV. INT'L L.J. 305, 314 (1993).

for years to come.[129] The United States may not always be among the world's top trading powers, and it would be in the long-term interest of the U.S. to strive (while it is still on top) to develop an international trade regime that takes more into consideration than the current cries of big business lobbyists. This strategy will benefit the U.S. not only today by developing better relations with our trade partners, but also in the future when the U.S. may require the benefits of a more understanding world trade regime.

. . . .

D. An Undermining of U.S. Long-Term Interests

. . . It would be more wise, for the interest of the United States in the future and the harmony of the international trading order now, if the U.S. would consider working with, instead of against, its trading partners to come to mutually acceptable resolutions to trade disagreements.

A world where each country is looking out only for its best interests, even if to the detriment of its allies (a return to the pre-World War II "beggar-thy-neighbor policies" which led in large part to the disintegration of the world economies in the early part of this century) would lead to any particular individual country being worse off. Such activity may further encourage the development of regional trade blocs, where countries could again work to reduce trade barriers among themselves.

Worries of retaliation, or at least a backlash, for Special 301 actions are now a reality in U.S.-China trade relations. Even with the Special 301 tool at its disposal, the U.S. record industry had been hesitant to request action in China. With the assistance of overseas (primarily Hong Kong and Taiwan) equipment and capital, piracy of cassettes, and now CDs, is rampant in China. With the rise of disposable income in China, the demand for music has become enormous (the record market estimate for 1994 is $1 billion). The potential market for U.S. industry is great, both for the marketing of Chinese artists (there are more than 200 record companies in China) and the ever-popular American singers. For this reason, record industry officials had been trying to work with the Chinese both to gain market access and reduce piracy. Now that 301 threats have been made, however, the Chinese may be a long time in welcoming U.S. inroads into this booming consumer market.

[Moreover, Senator Hatch has explained], Chinese retaliation would most likely cost U.S. industries and consumers money in higher tariffs imposed by China, and while U.S. companies would be shut out of the Chinese market due to high costs, tariffs, or outright restrictions, companies from other nations would take their place in China. Finally, he estimated that if the U.S. enters into such a trade war with China, there would be little

---

[129] Jonathan C. Carlson, *Law and Leadership in the Global Schoolyard*, 75 Iowa L. Rev. 877, 886 (1990).

incentive for the Chinese to protect the American technology and intellectual property that would remain in China.

One final interesting argument against Special 301 actions is that they will hurt the United States by actually causing targeted countries to become more competitive. As one Columbia University economist stated, such countries "will be a little more original and a little more creative" and, thus, end up beating the U.S. at our own game. Such an argument is short-sighted, at best, but raises the type of concern that argues against forcing change where change is not yet primed to occur.

. . . .

VIII. ALTERNATIVE SOLUTIONS TO U.S. COPYRIGHT CONCERNS

. . . .

B. Resolving Problems in Non GATT-Member Countries

[Newby argued that, with respect to nations that are not members of GATT, mostly developing or non-market economies, the United States should strive for a more long-term, mutually acceptable solution than Special 301.] There are two main ways in which to do this. One is through government and government-sponsored measures. The other is through private business measures, with businesses either acting individually or through alliances of companies and industries.

Government activities could involve the governments of the industrially and technologically developed nations contributing to programs that assist nations that want to strengthen their domestic protection of copyrights. Such programs might discuss developing or strengthening copyright legislation and the development of effective enforcement measures. . . Tight economies in developed countries, however, undoubtedly will limit the time and resources that those countries will be willing to devote to other nations' development.

Private measures involve nothing more basic than U.S. companies working within the countries in which they are having problems. To achieve the most effective and long-term protection in these countries, U.S. owners of copyrights should increase efforts to create the proper climate for protection.

For the time that Levi Strauss was there, it was very successful in China by working directly with the entities involved, both infringers and local authorities.[151] By cultivating relationships and addressing the problem directly, Levi Strauss created a long-term framework in which to resolve infringement problems. Such a strategy, however, requires devotion to a market and insights beyond a short-term gain. In addition, this strategy

---

[151] Levi Strauss decided to leave the China market in late 1993, stating that it was opposed to the use of prison and other "slave" labor in China.

can only be practicable with a company and a product strong enough to withstand potential infringement when first entering the market.

Likewise, in Thailand, U.S. companies that experience copying of videos and software could work with the major distributors of such goods to ensure that genuine, quality goods are available at a reasonable price. By working directly with corporate purchasers and distributors, U.S. companies can be sure to understand local needs while creating a support network to report and help counter piracy activities. . .

Although there are examples of companies being willing to engage in such activities, it is more realistic to expect such action to be taken by a consortium or alliance of interested companies. The Business Software Alliance provides an example of the core interested companies in the U.S. computer software industry pouring money and time into engaging investigators and attorneys to police the world. Resources may be more beneficially allocated to working with governments to meet their local needs as well as targeting U.S. alliance member concerns. Although this may sound altruistic, it is actually good business sense that considers long-term development and benefits over short-term gains.

One model may be the Taiwanese Information Product Anti-Piracy Union. The union is aimed at intensifying crackdowns on counterfeit computer products and will be patterned after the Business Software Alliance. At present, more than thirty Taiwanese computer software manufacturers have joined the new union. BSA has even agreed to sponsor seminars on software management and other activities promoting protection over piracy. In addition, BSA has offered incentives to encourage Taiwan residents to inform the Alliance of instances of software piracy.

What happens when non-GATT countries still do not cooperate? . . . In deciding what action to take against the country in response to repeated infringing activities, public (global) policy would suggest that the U.S. look at what property is being infringed. Property protected by copyright is as valuable as that protected by trademark or patents, but it may be useful to distinguish between these properties for reasons of public safety and the advancement of a developing country's education and general welfare.

Although many developing countries do not extend patent protection to pharmaceuticals, by enforcing its patent rights on these and other products abroad, the United States ensures that safe, quality products are being distributed to consumers. The strong protection of trademarks abroad likewise ensures the distribution of genuine products to consumers. The false marking of auto parts, electrical appliances, sports equipment, and a range of other products leads consumers to a false sense of safety. Often shoddy, knock-off goods can result in serious health and safety concerns for end-users. In addition, a country cannot claim that the selling of knock-off goods (for example, leather goods, clothing, and jewelry) is economic activity that develops the country. Although such sales may generate enormous profits for pirates and may even increase tourism to a particular country, these industries do little to advance the economy technologically.

The United States would be justified in taking unilateral retaliatory actions against such dangerous and predatory practices in non-GATT member countries.

Copyright infringement may be viewed differently. The goods copied may certainly be used to generate profits for pirates, but the ready accessibility of low cost books and software in the economy is of great importance to a nation's overall development. By denying such access with strict copyright protection laws, U.S. companies may be gaining some otherwise "lost" sales, but the harm and retardation on economic advancement may outweigh such speculative, pecuniary gains. By enforcing copyright laws for U.S. companies with trade sanctions and loss of trade privileges, this will further slow the process of development.

More importantly for U.S. businesses, however, copyrighted software and books that are prohibitively costly will not be used by the general population and so a market demand for these items will be slow in developing. The quickest way for a U.S. company to create a long-term demand is to work with the local government and education officials to develop a program of cheap access immediately that will lead to greater profits later on. One example of this would involve a company, or group of companies, working with local educational facilities to develop a program that will use donated or reduced-cost computers and software, but that [commits] that facility to continue using that company's products, to be paid for after the initial period, for a contracted period of time.

Even with copyright infringement, however, the United States should distinguish between goods used for domestic consumption and those exported for profit. There is no reason to allow countries to export goods based upon U.S. products. Not only does such export activity more clearly reduce potential U.S. sales, it also does little to assist the country in its independent development. The United States should make clear, ideally through multilateral cooperation, that such exporting of pirated goods is not acceptable.

IX. Conclusion

. . . .

At the point when the U.S. desires to pursue a retaliatory action against offending nations, the U.S. should pursue measures sanctioned by the world community, such as a WTO-imposed TRIPS remedy. This way the U.S. can pursue remedies fully without violating trade agreements, and the targeted country will have the spotlight of the world trading community upon it if it does not comply with WTO-imposed measures.

On the private side, U.S. companies must take responsibility for their entrance into a country because their actions in a country, particularly a developing country, often affect the economy of that country and also the way in which the citizens of that country view the United States. . .

By developing a coherent policy that is consistent and based upon both demands at home and understanding of the situation in many countries abroad, the U.S. can implement its policies with more respect and effectiveness in the world community. In a time of growing trade tensions and increasing regionalism, the United States can best insure its long-term competitiveness in the world economy by pursuing less bullying tactics and working within, not against, other nations to create an integrated world economy.

WILLIAM P. ALFORD, HOW THEORY DOES—AND DOES NOT—MATTER: AMERICAN APPROACHES TO INTELLECTUAL PROPERTY LAW IN EAST ASIA *
13 UCLA Pac. Basin L.J. 8, 12-24 (1994)

II. Neglect and Discovery

. . . .

[I]ntellectual property issues came to prominence in our public life [in part] because of the link forged between them and the growth of our trade deficit during the mid-1980s. To be sure, the United States had begun to experience trade problems from the days of the Vietnam War. They continued to grow, especially vis-à-vis Japan, irrespective of steps we took. What was to change in the 1980s, however, was the assertion by intellectual property producing industries—later picked up by the government—that the unlawful appropriation by others of our intellectual property could in important measure explain our burgeoning trade deficit. If only those making unauthorized use of our intellectual property would instead pay retail price for it, so this thinking went, the revenues so generated would in effect wipe out much of our deficit.

[T]his thinking had a certain allure. Yet, attractive though it may have been, it was premised on a somewhat faulty assumption: namely, that if precluded from making unauthorized copies, alleged infringers would certainly purchase the item at its full retail price, rather than, for example, negotiating a discount, purchasing cheaper alternatives, developing their own surrogates, or simply forgoing it altogether. Proponents of the notion that intellectual property leakage is a central factor in explaining our trade deficit seemed not to understand how unlikely a citizen of the People's Republic of China (P.R.C.) earning fifty dollars a month would be to fork out more than a month's salary to buy even such an outstanding work as Melville Nimmer and Paul Geller's treatise on worldwide copyright. And they slighted the fact that any responsible effort to balance the books would need to take account of the foreign intellectual property that we Americans historically have used without authorization.[20]

---

[20] American piracy is discussed in Albert J. Clark, the Movement for International Copyright in Nineteenth Century America (1960).

Despite its many limitations, however, this vision of reality had a great deal of appeal in government and media circles. For one thing, it was most seemingly cogent in the very parts of the world—East Asia and especially Japan—where we were experiencing many of our largest deficits. For another, it spoke to some of our less attractive, subconscious fears, offering a possible explanation of why people with traditions different from our own—who some here considered less creative and capable than ourselves— were besting us at our own game. And, neatly enough, it did all this by turning one of our greatest vulnerabilities, our seemingly unquenchable thirst for imported goods, into a weapon—namely access to our market— that we could then use against the very people who had purloined our intellectual property, all of whom needed to sell their wares here.

This link between intellectual property and trade, especially concerning East Asia, soon became more than just rhetorical. Indeed, by the mid-to late 1980s, it had become an important element of our public policy. [So the United States created Special 301 and] on the multilateral front . . . the United States demanded that the Uruguay Round of the GATT produce a code authorizing trade sanctions in response to intellectual property violations. The United States championed this cause even though many of our trading partners argued that such a step both diminished the authority of existing international bodies in this area—such as the World Intellectual Property Organization and the United Nations Economic, Social and Cultural Organization—and took GATT off in wholly new directions that were not necessarily consistent with its basic purposes and premises.

If anything, this attention to intellectual property in our public arena has become even more conspicuous in recent years. First the Bush administration and now the Clinton administration elevated it into one of the central objectives of American foreign policy generally, and particularly concerning East Asia. . . . [W]hile he was Secretary of State, James Baker informed the leadership of the P.R.C. that there were three issues of equal importance that would determine the fate of U.S.-P.R.C. relations: the spread of weapons of mass destruction, human rights, and trade—of which protection for American intellectual property headed the list. Much the same message has been since reaffirmed by the Clinton administration.

I like Mickey Mouse as much as the next red-blooded American—indeed, I hope that I can convince the Stanford University Press to have him adorn the cover of my book. However, there is something somehow out of whack about putting the little rodent up there with nuclear war and torture. . . .

III. WHAT THEORY DOES—AND DOES NOT—TELL US

Interestingly, the link forged in the public arena between intellectual property and East Asia by and large has not found a counterpart in academe in this country or elsewhere in the West. With very few exceptions—of whom Dennis Karjala[27] and Charles McManis[28] are among the most

---

[27] *See, e.g.*, Dennis S. Karjala, *Copyright, Computer Software and the New Protectionism*, 28 JURIMETRICS J. 33 (1987).

notable—American scholars, whether in law or other fields, have simply not paid much heed to this topic.

This notwithstanding, I believe that the principal schools of [intellectual property] thought . . . can be of help in our effort to understand more about intellectual property in East Asia and about U.S. interaction therewith, even if it is in most instances more in a heuristic, rather than definitive, fashion. . . . Let me turn first to economic analysis. . . One is hard put to look at intellectual property in East Asia without recognizing the importance of economic considerations. To put it in its starkest terms, for example, those nations in East Asia that are the least developed economically are generally those that accord the least protection to intellectual property, while those that are highly developed economically are, for the most part, the most faithful adherents to something approaching international standards of protection.

Having guided us to this level of insight, however, there are many more particular, but highly significant, questions that economic analysis leaves unanswered, at least to the extent it has been applied to this field of inquiry. Let me pose one or two, perhaps in overly simplistic form, to make my point. I begin with perhaps one of the starkest: is respect for intellectual property rights the result of economic development, a principal cause thereof, or both? If it is the result of economic development, how, for example, does one explain the virtually total absence of any concept of such rights in Tang Dynasty (618–906) and Song Dynasty (960–1279) China—for a goodly portion of which China was the world's most economically developed and technologically advanced nation? Our examples need not be only historical. How, for instance, does one explain the ongoing problems that many foreign firms and even some small and middle-sized Japanese enterprises claim to experience in securing their rights in Japan, although it has one of the world's most developed economies?

If, on the other hand, respect for intellectual property rights is most noteworthy as a stimulus,[31] what are we to make of the possibility that Japan, and now China, are flourishing economically because at particular stages of their economic development they liberally made unauthorized use of foreign technology? Indeed, much the same point might be made regarding the United States a century ago. And what are we to make of the fact that Hong Kong, Korea, and Taiwan are far more vibrant economically than Great Britain, Portugal, and Ireland even though ideas of intellectual property rights are far more deeply entrenched, and means of protecting them are far better established, in the latter rather the former group

---

[28] *See, e.g.*, Charles McManis, *International Protection for Semiconductor Chip Designs and the Standard of Judicial Review of Presidential Proclamations Issued Pursuant to the Semiconductor Chip Protection Act of 1984*, 22 GEO. WASH. J. INT'L L. & ECON. 331 (1988).

[31] This view is suggested by the work of Richard Adelstein and Steven Peretz—whose work might be seen as an elaboration of North and Thomas on the indispensability of clear property rights to economic development. *See* Richard P. Adelstein and Steven I. Peretz, *The Competition of Technologies and the Market for Ideas: Copyright and Fair Use—An Evolutionary Perspective*, 5 INT'L REV. L. & ECON. 209 (1985).

of nations? Nor need our data in this regard all be modern. We should not forget that it was East Asia—first Korea and then China—that gave the world the printing press and yet neither has done much with copyright until quite recently.

But as interesting as these matters may be, there are even more fundamental issues raised as we think of applying tools of economic analysis. In casting economic considerations—and at their heart, property rights—in a central role, are we not assuming that the definitions and attributes of property rights are uniform world-wide? Is that a wholly warranted assumption? Research on Chinese legal history and recent developments in the P.R.C. suggest that we not rush to judgment here. This is so particularly if we break property into its constituent elements, rather than treat it as an undifferentiated whole that one either has or lacks. And it is even more so if we pause to consider how the availability of remedies and the willingness to invoke them—which are two different things—shape rights in very real and important ways. Indeed, scholars of such different orientations as Critical Legal Studies theorist James Boyle and the historian of Chinese science Nathan Sivin at least implicitly raise the suggestion that far from being universal, it is the ideas of ownership embedded in modern Western intellectual property that are the historical aberrations, and that these ideas have achieved the currency they now enjoy internationally as much because they are backed by great economic might as because of their appeal to our common sense or their innate conceptual force.

Although holding very different views than proponents of economic analysis as to what motivates behavior, scholars who seek to understand intellectual property in more philosophical terms also, at least implicitly, share a basic belief not only in universals—as opposed to more culturally specific factors—but in universals comprised principally of rights. Their ideas are certainly useful in helping us appreciate the link between intellectual property and other rights—and particularly political rights. Copyright in the Anglo-American world originated with the granting of a royal monopoly by the British Throne to the London Stationers Company in return for the latter's suppression of controversial texts. Nonetheless, it appears that, as was the case with the correlation between economic development and respect for intellectual property rights, so too, one finds that the greater a nation's commitment to the overall rights of its populace, the more likely it is to have serious protection for intellectual property. In a way, it would be hard for this to be otherwise—for societies that sharply constrain their citizens' rights are likely to tolerate far less in the way of private expressive activity, and, in any event, the value of whatever property rights these societies may provide is likely to diminish sharply in the absence of mechanisms for their vindication.

But as with connections between economic development and intellectual property rights, scholarly approaches to intellectual property rights grounded in rights theory leave many questions unanswered, especially as we look to East Asia. If there is a link between political and intellectual property rights, why, for example, is it that problems of piracy have become greater in the P.R.C. as the country has become freer politically and economically? And why is it that today there are probably more instances of infringement in South Korea than in the North? There may well be answers to such questions consistent with a rights-oriented approach, but those working in this field have yet to address such questions. And, as was the case with economic analysis, there are the more basic—and I think more difficult to answer—questions as to how proponents of a vision of society grounded in notions of inalienable rights account for countries in which this type of thinking has only lately taken hold, and then not necessarily in precisely the same ways it has in the West.

At first blush, the deconstructionists would seem to have escaped some of the problems of a universalist posture that arguably afflict both economic-and rights-focused approaches. In seeking to show ways in which ideas of copyright are not absolute or preordained, but contingent upon particular historical circumstances, they too make a valuable contribution. Their work makes less inexplicable the fact that Tang China could reach and stay at the pinnacle of the world economically, politically, technologically, and militarily for more than a century without anything resembling intellectual property rights. And although not focused on contemporary U.S.-East Asian relations as such, the abiding lessons of the Critical Legal Studies movement about the linkage of power and legality are instructive as to why intellectual property issues are so prominent on the American diplomatic agenda and why so many East Asian jurisdictions now are adopting such law.

Caution is, however, no less warranted with regard to the deconstructionists than any of the other schools I have been examining. For one thing, notwithstanding their attacks upon Eurocentrism, their work is almost exclusively grounded in the historical experience of Western Europe and the United States. This foundation is then treated, essentially without qualification, as if it were common for all humankind.[39] But if our modern Western conception of authorship is, as Woodmansee, Rose, and others suggest, so clearly a product of Romantic conceptions of individual genius, what are we to make of authorship in East Asian societies which did not experience the Enlightenment, at least directly? How does one account for images of the author, whether in historical times or at present? Are such scholars being sufficiently careful not to project themselves—or an idealized statement of their hopes for their own society—on East Asia? In short, until deconstructionists move beyond a rhetoric of inclusiveness and begin to take other societies more seriously, it may not be unfair to ask whether their vision of the contingent nature of authorship and its concomitant critique of copyright tells us as much about the historical circumstances of a part

---

[39] The implications of this problem are treated at greater length in William P. Alford, *The Inscrutable Occidental: Roberto Unger's Uses and Abuses of the Chinese Past*, 64 TEX. L. REV. 915 (1986) and William P. Alford, *On the Limits of "Grand Theory" in Comparative Law*, 61 WASH. L. REV. 945 (1986).

of today's professorate as it does about the birth of notions of intellectual property rights.

. . . .

IV. OF MICKEY (MOUSE AND KANTOR) AND GOOFY

If each of the schools of thought I have briefly sketched above has shortcomings, each, nonetheless, gets us much further than the thinking embodied in U.S. governmental policy toward these issues. . . .

American policy has proceeded on the underlying assumption that a society's commitment to intellectual property protection is not contingent on its level of economic development, commitment to basic rights, or even particular historical circumstances. Rather, it is essentially a question of will. That is, if governments are so inclined or can be sufficiently pressured if they are not so inclined, adherence to something approximating an international standard of intellectual property protection will be relatively forthcoming.

As flawed as this vision is, it seems to me that one cannot dismiss it out of hand as one seeks to understand intellectual property in East Asia. The history of the West's relations with East Asia over the past century and a half is replete with examples of the impact of might, even when it has not made right. And one would be disingenuous when assessing intellectual property developments in the ROC and Korea—and even in Japan and the P.R.C.—to ignore the impact of threats to limit access to the American market.

Once again, however, caution is warranted. [Both the USTR and their counterparts in the P.R.C.] display an extraordinary faith in formal legality and a corresponding inattention to what motivates behavior. Each, in their own way, even if only for political effect, vests enormous significance in the mere articulation of new rules—as if promulgating new intellectual property laws and exhortations to follow them from Beijing were tantamount to changing the way in which people in the provinces conduct themselves on a daily basis.[42] Indeed, in my more perverse moments, I am tempted to write an article entitled "Why China Has Too Much Law—And Too Little Legality."

The folly in believing that the rapid-fire issuance of an elaborate web of formal new rules on intellectual property, brought about chiefly through external pressure, will swiftly transform long-standing attitudes and practices comes into sharper focus if we consider recent Chinese trends. A good case can be made that since the United States began to apply considerable pressure to the P.R.C. on this front, infringement of American

---

[42] Of late, in its dealings with the P.R.C., the USTR has begun to emphasize enforcement—but again with the assumption that Beijing has the capacity readily to control economic activity in Guangdong and other distant areas. The fallacy of that assumption is discussed in William P. Alford, *Underestimating a Complex China*, CHI. TRIB., May 24, 1994, at 23.

copyrighted and trademarked items has at least held steady, if not increased significantly. However, in fairness, it should be noted that the reasons for this may have as much to do with the P.R.C.'s liberalization—which has been substantial with respect to markets and more modest politically—as with U.S. policy as such. . . .

But the real deficiencies of vision in U.S. policy are not those of . . . the policy's inability to deliver promised results. They are even more fundamental, lying in this policy's utter failure honestly and carefully to think through what might engender a genuine and sustained respect for intellectual property or any other type of rights in China—or, for that matter, anywhere else. The effort to foster serious, widespread, long-term adherence to something approximating an international level of protection for intellectual property, after all, entails significant transformations in a people's attitudes toward intellectual creation, toward property, toward rights, toward the vindication of such rights through formal legal action, toward government, and so forth. Without apologizing for indifference or deception on the Chinese side, how can we realistically expect that such attitudes will change overnight or that the institutions needed to nurture and support them will suddenly emerge, particularly if there is any truth to suggestions that adherence to intellectual property is correlated either to economic development or political openness or is shaped by culture. Even in our own society, which is economically mature, politically open, and born of the very culture that gave the concept of intellectual property to the world, respect for such rights was a long time in coming and is still far from being universal. Indeed, as Dennis Karjala suggests, there remain very real and legitimate disagreements amongst us as to how to balance protection for intellectual property with the access to data needed to spur further innovation and ensure the citizenry's full participation in our democratic polity.

These, however, are not the only costs to an American policy that consists of little more than crude threats and to the psychology that underlies it. Our policy on intellectual property toward China, or other parts of East Asia, does not occur in a vacuum. The tactics we have been using—and even celebrating—resonate all too much of a past in which the United States and other foreign powers undertook many an act having a great impact on the nations of East Asia in the name of making the world safe for our concerns, including intellectual property. Some such measures were no doubt of value to all involved, but others were of questionable morality and limited efficacy. Without suggesting history will necessarily repeat itself, it might not be a bad idea for our policy makers to look at why earlier foreign efforts at the turn of the century and again in the 1920s and the 1940s through the 1980s to press Chinese society to adopt an idealized version of intellectual property law were failures.

If our policy makers had a better appreciation of the historical context of their actions, they might not only be more tactically adept, but they might also more fully comprehend the depth of bitterness that recent U.S.

measures evoke and therefore better understand the impact of our intellectual property policy on broader relations between our nation and those of East Asia. To make this point is not to subscribe to a victimization theory that seeks to excuse any and all Chinese actions today because of what may have happened a century ago. Instead, it is to urge that we take full heed of the impact of what we are doing. To give but one example, when I spoke on U.S.-ROC intellectual property negotiations at National Taiwan University in 1991, the topic prompted an extraordinary reaction: senior government officials cried publicly in frustration at the humiliation they believed they had experienced at the hands of U.S. negotiators, and serious lawyers and scholars castigated prominent Chinese attorneys who assisted U.S. interests as traitors to Taiwan (*Taijian*).[45]

Clearly, our government's determination to place so much emphasis on intellectual property issues and so readily to resort to pressure to achieve objectives in this area limits what it can expect to achieve in other crucial dimensions of our relations—particularly when dealing with a nation as powerful as the P.R.C. It was saddening to see the Bush administration—which staunchly resisted efforts to address strongly human rights problems in China on the grounds that we should not be interfering in their sovereign affairs—threatening the Chinese with almost one billion dollars of punitive tariffs, opposition to the P.R.C.'s GATT bid, and an end to most favored nation (MFN) status if they did not agree to revise their intellectual property law to our satisfaction and on a schedule essentially of our liking. Much the same point can be made regarding the present administration. . . .

V. Conclusion

. . . .

[In applying the major scholarly approaches toward intellectual property to the East Asian situation,] I do hope . . . that we will remain vigilant as to the basic terms we use and take nothing for granted. . . . When we mention property, we should be mindful of which of its many attributes or constituent elements we are speaking. When we endeavor to explain a phenomenon by reference to culture, let us not take it as a static monolith throughout East Asia, but instead realize its immense variety over time, across national boundaries, and among different people within any country. When we speak of interests, whose interests are we concerned with and at what cost to those of others? And when we refer to intellectual property law, do we mean formal doctrine or the manner in which the law plays itself out in society—and if the latter, how are we to measure it?

. . . .

---

[45] The standard Chinese phrase for traitor, *hanjian*, literally means "traitor to the Chinese." The cited adaptation suggests the deep fissures that course through the ROC and its legal profession.

NOTES AND QUESTIONS

(1) **The Purposes of Special 301.** Review the purposes of the Trade Act of 1974 set out in footnote 25 of the Newby article. To what extent do you think those stated purposes accurately reflect what Congress was seeking to achieve in 1988? *See* Robert Burrell, *A Case Study in Cultural Imperialism: The Imposition of Copyright on China by the West*, 3 PERSP. IN INTELL. PROP. 195, 213 (1998) (discussing broader political concerns). Have the steps taken under Special 301 furthered those purposes? To what extent are the purposes of the Trade Act consistent with the stated purposes of TRIPS? *See* United States—Sections 301–310 of the Trade Act of 1974, WT/DS152/R (WTO Panel Report, Dec. 22, 1999). To what extent are they consistent with the purposes of intellectual property law?

(2) **Assessing the Success of Special 301**. Special 301 was in part a response to the inadequacies of the GATT pre-1994. It may therefore have accelerated the conceptual shift to enforceable minimum standards found in the TRIPS Agreement. Viewed in that light, can Special 301 be hailed as an unqualified success? Newby complains that progress in developing countries acting under pressure from the United States has been "incremental." Is this a fair criticism?

(3) **The Demands Made of China.** Review the demands made of China in 1991. To what extent can these demands be characterized as demands to comply with applicable international intellectual property standards at the time? In what ways did they go beyond that? If the United States was not asking China to adhere to extant standards of international intellectual property law, what was it asking? Was that appropriate or justified?

(4) **Cultural Imperialism.** Some scholars have described aggressive unilateral trade measures such as Special 301 as "cultural imperialism" when applied to countries such as China. *See* Burrell, *supra*, at 195. What is it about Special 301 that arguably permits its characterization as "imperialistic"? Is cultural domination of developing countries by the developed countries of the West more likely with or without intellectual property protection? Does the answer vary as between different forms of intellectual property? Is the dynamic of cultural subordination, which makes some European countries fear international laws that facilitate the expansion of American pop culture, different as between two developed countries?

(5) **Commonality of Values?** China had a vibrant commercial publishing industry for popular works of fiction, drama, and religious tracts at least from the end of the ninth century. This industry regularly received official patronage and commissions, and suffered the attendant injuries from economic competitors. Consider the following:

> In the work Fangyu Shenglan (A [Grand Tour] of the Territories) compiled by Zhu Mu of the Song Dynasty (960–1279), there [is] placed after the compiler's preface a "Notice Issued by the Viceroy of Zhejiang [province]" which says that the book is the result of the

compiler's "assiduous labour of a lifetime and cannot be compared with the plagiarisms by others," [and] whereas "there are recently people in the book market hankering after gains, who are incapable of compiling works based on their own views but devote their efforts to reprinting," [therefore] "a public notice is hereby issued jointly by the viceroy of Zhejiang and the governor of East Zhejiang prohibiting reprinting activities; and if anyone reprints the work for profit, Zhu has the right to "report the act, track down the offender, destroy the plates and enforce the ban, so as to stop acts of piracy."

Zheng Chengsi, *Further on Copyright Protection in Ancient China*, CHINA PATENTS & TRADEMARKS Q. 62, 63 (Oct. 1996). Note particularly the references to "plagiarism" (*piaoqie*) and "piracy" (*fankan zhihuan*—literally "harmful reprints"). Might stopping others from reprinting books for profit or other forms of "free riding" be more universal than cultural critics suggest? *See also* Graziella M. Sarno, Comment, *Viet Nam or Bust: Why Trademark Pirates Are Leaving China for Better Opportunities in Viet Nam*, 14 DICK. J. INT'L L. 291 (1996).

(6) **Arguments on Both Sides.** Was the Chinese Government justifiably irked with the impatience of the United States negotiators in 1995? If you had been negotiating on behalf of the Chinese Government, how might you have best conveyed the sentiment that it takes time to bring an intellectual property system into compliance with international standards? *Cf.* Burrell, *supra*, at 207-08 (discussing development of the Universal Copyright Convention). If you had been negotiating on behalf of the U.S. Trade Representative, how might you have approached the task of persuading the Chinese negotiators that providing the intellectual property protection sought by the United States was in China's best interests? Does the instrumentalist nature of U.S. intellectual property protection make it harder to assert the inherent propriety of enhanced intellectual property protection? Are there other explanations of intellectual property that might offer more persuasive justifications? (And are those other explanations of intellectual property persuasive?)

(7) **Expediting Change.** Newby writes that "[i]n general, it may be said that each country will eventually find it in its best interest to adopt an effective copyright protection scheme; the United States is making sure that targeted countries find adopting such a scheme in their best interests sooner than might otherwise occur." Newby, *supra*, at 49. What are the costs and benefits of ensuring that "targeted countries find adopting such a scheme in their best interests sooner than might otherwise occur"? If the date at which it would have been in a country's best interests to reach a mature system of patent protection was twenty years hence, what is the effect of altering "incentives" such that it implements that system immediately? Does this ensure (or at least assist) that country in capturing the benefits of patent protection twenty years earlier than would otherwise have been the case?

(8) **Cause and Effect.** How does one answer Professor Alford's question: is respect for intellectual property rights the result of economic development, a principal cause thereof, or both? To what extent can intellectual property laws dictate cultural attitudes? Professor Alford cites examples of economically and technologically advanced societies operating without intellectual property rights. Are those examples compelling ? Can one explain those examples? Do we have to be able to explain those examples before acting as the USTR has acted?

(9) **Later Developments in U.S.-China Relations**. The debate between the United States and China regarding the latter's protection of intellectual property did not end with the February 25, 1995, agreement. On May 15, 1996, based on monitoring of the agreement's implementation carried out under section 306(a) of the Trade Act, the USTR expressed dissatisfaction with implementation of the agreement and proposed yet again to impose prohibitive tariffs on imports of certain products from China. This crisis was resolved with another agreement on June 17, 1996. In its 1999 Annual Report, the USTR concluded that:

> China now has a functioning system capable of protecting intellectual property rights. China has made progress on software end-user piracy including the recent issuance of a State Council directive to all government ministries mandating that only legitimate software be used in government and quasi-government agencies. Enforcement of intellectual property rights has become part of China's nationwide anti-crime campaign; the Chinese police and court system have become involved in combating IPR piracy. The production of pirated copyrighted works has dropped dramatically.

OFFICE OF THE UNITED STATES TRADE REPRESENTATIVE, RESULTS OF SPECIAL 301 ANNUAL REVIEW (Apr. 30, 1999). The report also noted, however, that "retail piracy and counterfeit goods remain widespread in China. And that the structure of IPR administration and enforcement in China remains opaque. Enforcement at the provincial level is sporadic. Corruption remains a problem and convictions only occasionally result in jail time." *Id.* For a recent discussion of American foreign intellectual property policy toward China, see Peter K. Yu, *From Pirates to Partners: Protecting Intellectual Property in China in the Twenty-First Century*, 50 AM. U. L. REV. 131 (2001).

(10) **Imposition of Law**. To what extent can the use by the United States of Special 301 powers be described as "imposing foreign law" on other countries? In what circumstances might such "imposition" be justified? In what circumstances might it be wise as a matter of U.S. policy? Might there be circumstances where use of Special 301 might be justified but not wise?

(11) **Respect for Difference.** To what extent should the United States take into account "development patterns that may differ from that followed by the United States and other Western, industrialized countries" in requiring the enactment of intellectual property protection? How should those differences be balanced against the claims of U.S. industries that they

are suffering huge losses as a result of piracy? How do you balance respect for the sovereignty of other nations with the protection of domestic industries? Can that analysis be performed in the abstract? What do you think of Newby's alternative suggestions for addressing perceived inadequacies in intellectual property protection? Would these be more effective than use of Special 301? Would they be more appropriate? Is Newby correct that certain inadequacies in intellectual property protection warrant greater immediate attention than others? What should those priorities be?

(12) **Individual Rights and Intellectual Property**. If there is, as Alford suggests, a connection between respect for intellectual property and respect for individual rights generally, should that affect the policy of the United States toward countries that are perceived as offering inadequate intellectual property protection? If so, how should that affect the conduct of international intellectual property relations? How should the United States respond to news that Chinese citizens have been executed for counterfeiting? In what ways, and by emphasizing which priorities, could U.S. international intellectual property policy accommodate both goals? Can Special 301 measures against China be justified as supportive of human rights? Will greater respect for human rights bring greater protection of intellectual property, or will enhanced protection for intellectual property lead to greater respect for human rights? What is the connection between the two?

(13) **Changes in Chinese Intellectual Property Laws.** What is the significance of the statement by former WIPO director-general Arpad Bogsch that "China has gone from no system just fifteen years ago to one of the most advanced countries in the developing world"? What does Dr. Bogsch mean by "no system" and "one of the most advanced"? What does that change portend for the long-term health of intellectual property protection in China?

(14) **Culturally Contingent Discussions.** How does one avoid infusing this discussion with a culturally-contingent set of values regarding individual ownership, the roots of creativity, or the relevance of free information? Can one? If not, should we abandon the endeavor?

(15) **China and the WTO.** In November 1999, the United States and China reached a trade agreement designed to facilitate China's entry into the WTO. China agreed to a wide-ranging set of market access reforms in return for the establishment of permanent normal trade relations ("PNTR"). But, under U.S. law, PNTR, formerly called most favored nation status, is dependent upon congressional approval of the agreement. Congress passed the necessary legislation in 2000. After other WTO member countries also negotiated agreements relating to terms of entry with China, these bilateral agreements were encompassed within a multinational agreement and China was finally admitted into the WTO in late 2001. The entry of new members requires a vote in favor by two-thirds of current WTO members. *See* WTO Agreement art. XII(2).

The U.S.-China agreement was welcomed by free traders not only for the liberalization of Chinese markets that it mandates, but also for its potential to effect significant political change in China. In what ways might membership of the WTO cause political liberalization? Does this suggest a broader basis upon which to ground support for enhanced intellectual property protection? Will WTO obligations drive the creation of the legal infrastructure and cultural mindset necessary not only to comply with the WTO Agreement but also to accord greater respect for human rights, as the Clinton administration argued? Which aspects of Chinese society will be most challenged by the involvement of the WTO in China's national affairs? Which aspects will provide the greatest challenge for the WTO?

NOTE: SPECIAL 301 AFTER TRIPS

As will be discussed in greater detail below, failure to comply with obligations of international intellectual property law may now be pursued (post-TRIPS) by complaining countries before the WTO dispute settlement body. This did not, however, result in the termination of the Special 301 process. Indeed, section 314(c) of the Uruguay Round Agreements Act, which implemented the GATT Agreement, amended the Trade Act to provide expressly that a failure to provide adequate and effective protection of intellectual property could still trigger Special 301 measures "notwithstanding the fact the foreign country may be in compliance with the specific obligations of the TRIPS Agreement." Trade Act, § 301(d)(3). Thus, the U.S. Trade Representative continues to exercise Special 301 powers, and continues to publish a report on April 30 of each year identifying countries that deny adequate and effective enforcement of intellectual property rights. *See, e.g.*, Notice of Office of the United States Trade Representative, 65 Fed. Reg. 26652 (May 8, 2000). The Special 301 Report builds upon the National Trade Estimate Report on Foreign Trade Barriers, which is published annually by the USTR on March 30 and which produces frenetic activity in Washington.

A short excerpt from the 2000 Special 301 Report follows. A full copy of the report, as well as a summary of all cases initiated under Section 301, and their outcome can be found on the homepage of the USTR at www.ustr.gov/reports/301report/act301.htm. Since the conclusion of TRIPS, the Special 301 process has become one of the means by which the USTR identifies issues that it might ultimately pursue before the WTO Dispute Settlement Body. We will return to a discussion of the interaction between Special 301 and the TRIPS dispute settlement process after a more detailed analysis of the latter.

OFFICE OF THE UNITED STATES TRADE REPRESENTATIVE RESULTS OF SPECIAL 301 ANNUAL REVIEW (April 28, 2000)

United States Trade Representative Charlene Barshefsky today announced the results of the 2000 "Special 301" annual review which examined in detail the adequacy and effectiveness of intellectual property protection in over 70 countries. . .

2000 SPECIAL 301 DECISIONS

Under the Special 301 provisions of the Trade Act of 1974, as amended, Ambassador Barshefsky today identified 59 trading partners that deny adequate and effective protection of intellectual property or deny fair and equitable market access to United States artists and industries that rely upon intellectual property protection.

In today's action, the United States Trade Representative identified Ukraine for potential Priority Foreign Country designation on August 1, 2000. Ambassador Barshefsky stated that the United States has worked with Ukrainian officials over the past several years in an effort to reduce alarming levels of copyright piracy and to improve Ukraine's overall intellectual property regime. Regrettably, according to estimates from our copyright industry, Ukraine is the single largest source of pirate CDs in the Central and East European region. The U.S. Government currently is engaged with the Government of Ukraine in an intense effort to resolve this problem. At this juncture, the United States considers its interests to be best served by continuing these efforts over the next few months. However, Ukraine will be identified as a Priority Foreign Country if it fails to make substantial progress toward eliminating pirate optical media production prior to August 1, 2000.

Copyright piracy in Ukraine is extensive and enforcement is severely lacking, resulting in increasing unauthorized production and export of CDs and CD-ROMs. . . . In addition, a number of Ukraine's intellectual property laws . . . fall short of compliance with the minimum standards set out in the TRIPS Agreement and the 1992 U.S.-Ukraine bilateral trade agreement. . .

Ambassador Barshefsky again designated Paraguay and China for "Section 306 monitoring" to ensure both countries comply with the commitments made to the United States under bilateral intellectual property agreements. Special concern was expressed that Paraguay's efforts have not been sufficient in recent months, and further consultations will be scheduled.

Ambassador Barshefsky also announced placement of 16 trading partners on the "Priority Watch List": Argentina, the Dominican Republic, Egypt, the European Union, Greece, Guatemala, India, Israel, Italy, Korea, Malaysia, Peru, Poland, Russia, Turkey, and Ukraine. She also placed 39 trading partners on the "Watch List." . . .

Finally, Ambassador Barshefsky noted that while she was not listing El Salvador or the West Bank and Gaza, USTR will conduct out-of-cycle reviews of each in September and December 2000, respectively. The review of El Salvador will assess the government's efforts to improve enforcement procedures and to promote the use of authorized software in all government ministries. The review of the West Bank and Gaza will assess its progress toward implementation of promised enforcement actions against pirate CD manufacturers.

INTELLECTUAL PROPERTY AND HEALTH POLICY

On December 1, 1999, President Clinton announced that the United States is committed to helping developing countries gain access to essential medicines, including those for HIV/AIDS. . . .

. . . When a foreign government expresses concern that U.S. trade law related to intellectual property protection significantly impedes its ability to address a health crisis in that country, USTR will seek and give full weight to the advice of the Department of Health and Human Services (HHS) regarding the health considerations involved. This process will permit the application of U.S. trade-related intellectual property law to remain sufficiently flexible to react to public health crises brought to the attention of USTR. It will also ensure that the minimum standards of the TRIPS Agreement are respected. [For the first time, HHS participated actively as a member of the Special 301 Trade Policy Staff Sub-Committee that is charged with developing the Special 301 recommendations.]

. . . .

IMPLEMENTATION OF THE WTO TRIPS AGREEMENT

. . . .

While developed countries are already required to fully implement TRIPS, developing countries were given a five year transition period—until January 1, 2000—to implement most of the Agreement's provisions. Ensuring that developing countries are in full compliance with the Agreement now that this transition period has come to an end is one of this Administration's highest priorities with respect to intellectual property rights. With respect to least developed developing countries, and with respect to the protection of pharmaceuticals and agriculture chemicals in certain developing countries, an even longer transition was provided.

Substantial progress has been made over the past year by developing countries toward full implementation of their TRIPS obligations. The United States has worked diligently to assist countries in meeting this goal through consultations and bilateral technical assistance.

. . . .

Progress continues by many countries toward more effective enforcement against piracy and counterfeiting, though there are notable exceptions

highlighted in this report. This is an ongoing effort which USTR is addressing in a number of ways, including pressing for government software
legalization decrees and controls on optical media production.

. . . .

Government Use of Software

In October 1998, Vice President Gore announced a new Executive Order
directing U.S. Government agencies to maintain appropriate, effective
procedures to ensure legitimate use of software. . .

[L]ast year, China, Colombia, Jordan, Paraguay, and the Philippines issued decrees mandating the use of only authorized software by government
ministries. This year Colombia, Macau, Lebanon, and Taiwan have each
issued similar decrees. Ambassador Barshefsky noted her pleasure that
these governments have recognized the importance of setting an example
in this area. . . .

WTO Dispute Settlement

As in previous years, Ambassador Barshefsky is using the annual Special
301 announcement as a vehicle to announce the launch of WTO dispute
settlement proceedings against countries that have not met their TRIPS
obligations. A priority of this year's Special 301 review is the proper and
timely implementation of the WTO TRIPS Agreement, particularly developing country implementation which was required as of January 1, 2000 for
most obligations.

In December 1999, USTR initiated an out-of-cycle review of developing
countries' progress toward implementing their TRIPS obligations. This
review was conducted in tandem with this year's Special 301 review. In
conducting the review, it was determined that the vast majority of developing countries have made a serious effort to comply with their TRIPS
obligations, though further progress in the area of enforcement is particularly needed. The United States will continue to work with developing
countries that are in the process of finalizing their implementation of the
Agreement and expects further progress in the very near future to complete
this process. However, in those instances where additional progress is not
likely in the near term, or where we have been unable to resolve concerns
through bilateral consultation, USTR is pursuing U.S. rights through WTO
dispute settlement proceedings.

Specifically, Ambassador Barshefsky today announced the initiation of
WTO dispute settlement proceedings against Argentina and Brazil, and
that we will take the next step in our dispute with Denmark and request
the establishment of a WTO panel unless progress is made imminently.

Argentina

Argentina has failed to grant exclusive marketing rights for pharmaceuticals, despite being obliged to do so under the TRIPS Agreement, since

Argentina does not provide patent protection for such products. In addition, Argentina fails to protect confidential test data submitted to government regulatory authorities for pharmaceuticals and agricultural chemicals. Other deficiencies in Argentina's patent law include the denial of certain exclusive rights for patents, such as the protection of products produced by patented processes and the right of importation; the failure to provide prompt and effective provisional measures to address patent infringement; and the exclusion of micro-organisms from patentability. Many of these deficiencies relate to concerns regarding Argentina's compliance with the TRIPS Agreement obligations that applied to Argentina as of January 1, 2000. As such, these claims are being added to the already on-going dispute settlement case against Argentina announced in last year's Special 301 report.

Brazil

Brazil's patent law imposes a "local working" requirement as a condition for enjoyment of exclusive patent rights. This requirement can only be satisfied by local production, and not importation, of the patented product. This appears inconsistent with Brazil's obligations under Article 27 of the WTO TRIPS Agreement . . . Brazil has stated repeatedly that it disagrees with this interpretation of the TRIPS Agreement. In order to resolve this longstanding difference in views over this issue, as well as to address the concern that other countries may cite the Brazilian "local working" requirement as a justification for proposing similar legislation, the United States is now requesting WTO consultations with Brazil to pursue this single-issue case.

. . . .

Potential Dispute Settlement Cases

In addition to the above, there are a number of other WTO Members that likewise appear not to be in compliance with their TRIPS obligations, and which we are still considering as possible future dispute settlement cases. . . We will continue to consult in the coming months with all these countries in an effort to encourage them to resolve outstanding TRIPS compliance concerns as soon as possible. We will also gather data on these countries' enforcement of their TRIPS obligations and assess the best cases for further action if consultations prove unsuccessful.

COUNTRY BY COUNTRY DESCRIPTION

Section 306 Monitoring

China: China is currently engaged in completing the first major revision to its overall [intellectual property rights (IPR)] regime since our bilateral IPR agreements were concluded in 1992 and 1995. China has agreed in the context of the negotiations on accession to the World Trade Organization to implement the TRIPS Agreement without recourse to any transition period. In the meantime, ensuring effective implementation of our bilateral agreements remains an important effort. While the production of pirated copyrighted works has dropped dramatically since 1996, imports of pirated products remain a concern. U.S. companies report that retail piracy and counterfeit goods remain widespread in China, in part because of the inadequacy of deterrent sanctions, including lack of criminal penalties. The structure of IPR administration and enforcement in China still remains too opaque. Enforcement at the provincial level is sporadic, but steps in Guangdong province to increase sanctions against piracy and counterfeiting were a positive development. In addition, four Chinese enforcement authorities have joined together to act against optical media, including DVD, pirates. Most recently, in March 2000, the State Press and Publication Administration, the National Copyright Administration of China, the Ministry of Public Security, and the State Administration of Industry and Commerce issued an urgent joint circular to urge every provincial, regional and municipal government authority to launch a special campaign against DVD piracy in China. End-user piracy of business software (particularly in companies), trademark infringement, and problems in obtaining administrative protection for pharmaceuticals are persistent problems. . . .

Paraguay: On January 16, 1998, Paraguay was identified as a Priority Foreign Country (PFC) . . . In November 1998, the U.S. Government and the Government of Paraguay signed a Memorandum of Understanding (MOU) on the Protection of Intellectual Property. While Paraguay initially made progress toward fulfil[l]ment of its obligations under the MOU, more recently progress has stalled. Last year, the Government of Paraguay, in coordination with industry, seized and destroyed two multi-million dollar pirate CD factories and made several important reforms to its legal regime for the protection of intellectual property. However, Paraguay continues to be a regional center for piracy, especially of optical media, as well as for counterfeiting, and continues to serve as a transshipment point for an alarming volume of infringing products from Asia to the larger markets bordering Paraguay, particularly Brazil. In addition, Paraguay has failed to implement its obligation under the WTO TRIPS Agreement and the bilateral MOU to enact a modern patent law, among other reforms . . . Failure to aggressively prosecute known pirates, such as one high-profile case in which a pirate was twice released on bail despite substantial evidence, is a worrisome sign that further progress toward correcting Paraguay's role as a haven for piracy and counterfeiting is threatened. Therefore, the United States has requested consultations under the MOU which will be held in the coming months. If further results are not forthcoming, the United States may consider other options for resolving concerns regarding protection for intellectual property in Paraguay.

Priority Watch List

Argentina: . . . In contrast to the lack of protection in other areas, Argentina's copyright regime has continued to improve over the past two years with Argentina's enactment of legislation in 1999 to ratify the WIPO Copyright Treaty and Performance and Phonograms Treaty. Regrettably, enforcement against copyright piracy and trademark counterfeiting remains significantly below TRIPS standards.

Dominican Republic: The Dominican Republic has failed to correct deficiencies in its legal framework to meet its obligations under the TRIPS Agreement. Draft copyright legislation would be a major improvement over current law. However, draft patent legislation does not appear to meet TRIPS Agreement standards. The U.S. looks to the Government of the Dominican Republic to pass TRIPS-consistent legislation in both areas in conformance with its international commitments. We will continue to consult informally with the Government of the Dominican Republic in an effort to encourage it to resolve outstanding TRIPS compliance concerns as soon as possible in the coming months. Lax enforcement also remains a problem. . . In response to a petition from the copyright industry, USTR is reviewing the eligibility status of the Dominican Republic under the Generalized System of Preferences (GSP) program.

Egypt: Egypt's intellectual property laws do not comply fully with the TRIPS Agreement. The copyright law remains deficient in the area of protection for pre-existing sound recordings. Egypt's patent law does not provide protection for pharmaceutical and agricultural chemical products and contains other provisions that do not comply with TRIPS Agreement obligations. The government has drafted a new patent law, but had announced previously that it intends to avail itself of the full transition period for product patent protection, i.e., until January 1, 2005. Although the Government of Egypt recently adopted a decree nominally designed to comply with the TRIPS Agreement obligation to provide exclusive marketing rights for pharmaceutical and agricultural products, the adequacy of the decree remains untested. Egypt is considering a revision of its trademark law to meet TRIPS Agreement standards, but the existing trademark law is not enforced strenuously and the courts have only limited experience in adjudicating infringement cases. Although raids have increased, enforcement on the whole remains lax and therefore copyright piracy and trademark infringement remain unchecked. We will continue to consult informally with the Government of Egypt in an effort to encourage it to resolve outstanding TRIPS compliance concerns as soon as possible in the coming months.

The European Union: In 1999, the United States initiated WTO dispute settlement proceedings against the European Union regarding its regulation concerning geographical indications for foodstuffs and agricultural products. Concerns have been expressed that this regulation denies national treatment and does not adequately protect pre-existing trademarks. The EU continues to deny national treatment to U.S. intellectual property right holders in other areas as well. For example, the reciprocity requirement in the data base directive continues to be of concern. Restrictions in certain member states also deny market access opportunities for U.S. right holders. The Administration has made several efforts to address other intellectual property issues of concern to the United States in the context of the U.S.-EU TransAtlantic Economic Partnership—those efforts have produced little result to date, though the United States remains hopeful of progress in these areas.

Greece: In 1998, USTR announced the initiation of WTO dispute settlement consultations with Greece and the European Union regarding the high rates of television piracy in Greece. During the course of these consultations, the Government of Greece has taken steps toward addressing this problem, including the passage of additional legislation and the closure of a number of television stations which continued to broadcast programing without authorization. However, Greece has yet to provide assurances that it would implement its new enforcement procedure in a strong and consistent manner, and to take steps to improve the handling of intellectual property cases in the court system for the purposes of resolving this dispute. . . .

Guatemala: Guatemala's Criminal Procedures Code requires that all criminal enforcement be brought as "private actions", making criminal penalties difficult to obtain in cases of copyright infringement. Piracy, including by government agencies, is widespread, and the Government of Guatemala has failed to take effective enforcement action. . . .

India: India continues to lack adequate and effective patent protection, failing to comply with the obligations of the TRIPS Agreement in a number of areas, especially with regard to local working requirements, patentable subject matter and exclusive patent rights, term of protection, and protection for test data. Although not required to do so under the TRIPS Agreement until 2005, India has yet to provide patent protection for pharmaceutical and agricultural chemical products. Patent legislation has been drafted but not yet passed. While India's copyright law is generally compliant with the TRIPS Agreement, amendments passed in 1999 undermine TRIPS requirements concerning protection for computer programs. In addition, enforcement against piracy, especially cable piracy, remains a growing concern for U.S. copyright industries, as well as enforcement against imports of pirated products coming from Southeast Asia, for the most part Malaysia. . . .

Israel: The Knesset enacted TRIPS omnibus legislation in December 1999 covering a number of areas, including patents, trademarks and copyright. In the last six months, the Government of Israel has allocated additional resources, including hiring new policemen for intellectual property enforcement and funding new prosecutors, to combat widespread copyright infringement. However, we remain very concerned about the unacceptably high rate of piracy of all forms of optical media in Israel. Israel remains a key distribution hub in a multi-country network (including Eastern Europe and Russia) for pirated optical media product, much of which is still manufactured in Israel. We urge the Government of Israel to expedite its ongoing review of CD plant controls, including mandatory use of source identification codes, and to implement quickly effective controls. Other concerns with Israel's intellectual property regime include possible TRIPS deficiencies such as failure to protect adequately confidential test data and to provide criminal penalties for unauthorized end-user copying of computer software. . . .

Italy: Despite five years of effort, the Government of Italy has failed to enact anti-piracy legislation that includes TRIPS-consistent penalties sufficient to provide an effective deterrent to piracy and counterfeiting . . . Italy's failure to pass this important legislation is of particular concern because it has some of the lowest criminal penalties in Europe and one of the highest rates of piracy. Piracy and counterfeiting of American intellectual property in Italy continue to be relatively widespread practices, particularly with regard to piracy of video, sound recordings, computer software, books, and video games. As a result of Italy's continued failure to enact this anti-piracy legislation, USTR will conduct an out-of-cycle review of Italy in September of this year. . . .

Korea: Korea is being elevated to the Priority Watch List this year because of a number of longstanding issues, concerns about enforcement, and new issues relating to recent amendments to Korean copyright laws. Despite numerous U.S. attempts, including at the highest levels, and in a variety of fora, several longstanding issues remain unresolved. . . The United States. . . has ongoing concerns about the consistency, transparency, and effectiveness of Korean enforcement efforts, particularly with regard to piracy of U.S. computer software and books. . . .

Malaysia: Over the past year, Malaysia has focused its efforts on legislation intended to strengthen IPR enforcement against piracy. These priority measures include . . . enactment of a law necessary to implement a comprehensive regime regulating the production of optical disks. . . Malaysia also continues to work closely with U.S. companies to deter unlicen[s]ed use of software by end-users. However, there is a substantial backlog of IPR cases in the Malaysia courts, and when penalties are imposed they are often insufficient to deter future or repeat offenses. While the number of raids initiated by government authorities increased during 1999, more needs to be done to address general nationwide enforcement. . . .

Peru: The Government of Peru has put in place an ambitious plan to strengthen IPR enforcement during 2000. We are encouraged by the initial steps already taken by the government to implement the plan by bolstering its inter-agency coordination and by collaborating more actively with key private sector interests. . . U.S. industry continues to express concern about decisions by the [courts] that are not adequate to deter piracy. We look forward to seeing more complete results from these efforts by late 2000. With respect to patents, the provisions of the revised Andean Community Decision 344 have not yet been brought into conformity with the TRIPS Agreement. We will continue to consult informally with Andean Community governments in an effort to encourage them to resolve the outstanding TRIPS compliance concerns as soon as possible in the coming months.

Poland: Poland has not yet brought its copyright regime into line with its obligations under the TRIPS Agreement. . . The parliament has made significant progress in preparing amendments to the Copyright Law that would provide for the TRIPS-mandated 50-year retroactive protection of sound recordings and would clarify the point of attachment for sound recordings. We urge the Government of Poland to pass these amendments quickly. The amendments would significantly strengthen Poland's regime for the protection of intellectual property, and passage would trigger a review of Poland's Special 301 status. With respect to enforcement, prosecutors and judicial authorities have not vigorously protected intellectual property rights. . .

Russia: A number of the intellectual property laws, especially the patent, copyright and data protection laws, and the enforcement regime of the Russian Federation do not comply with the TRIPS Agreement or the intellectual property provisions of the U.S.-Russian Federation bilateral trade agreement signed in 1991. Despite a significant number of police raids, and commendable official efforts to improve the enforcement climate, criminal enforcement of intellectual property rights remains minimal in Russia. . . Russia's ineffective criminal enforcement system and the lack of any border control not only have allowed the domestic market to become saturated by Ukrainian and Asian-origin pirate products, but have also resulted in the development of Russia into a major transit country for counterfeit products destined for European markets.

Turkey: To date, Turkey has not yet addressed all of the benchmarks set out in the 1997 review. Remaining work needs to be done to enhance Turkey's copyright regime to include copyright protection for pre-existing works and sound recordings and ex parte and injunctive relief, and to include deterrent penalties and jail terms. Passage of amendments to the copyright law to address these concerns is anticipated in the near future, and we urge expeditious legislative action. . . .

. . . .

Watch List

Armenia: Armenia has several remaining steps to take to fulfill its intellectual property commitments under the 1992 U.S.-Armenia Trade Agreement and to make its intellectual property regime consistent with the TRIPS Agreement. . . In addition, we are concerned about weak enforcement of intellectual property rights in Armenia. Although new criminal penalties for intellectual property violations have been adopted, there have been no convictions under the new law and police authority to commence criminal copyright cases is unclear. Further, Armenia's Customs Code does not provide the proper authority to seize material at the border as required by the TRIPS Agreement. If not addressed, ineffective border enforcement could cause Armenia to become a target for illegal optical media producers, a problem that other countries of the region have faced.

. . . .

Bolivia: Bolivia has made some progress this past year with the long-awaited appointment of a director to the National Intellectual Property Service (SENAPI), created by President Banzer in 1997. SENAPI officials appear to be making a good faith effort to train personnel and acquire the resources needed to strengthen the institution. However, SENAPI continues to be seriously underfunded, lacks trained technical personnel, and has no mechanism to enforce intellectual property protections. Overall, enforcement of intellectual property protection in Bolivia remains weak. Software piracy continues to flourish unabated and counterfeit products are produced in Bolivia and imported into the country with impunity, despite efforts by a new national customs service to control contraband at Bolivia's borders and ports of entry. . . .

Brazil: Brazil made substantial progress on an April 1998 commitment to process pipeline applications in an expedited manner, and it has significantly increased the rate at which it processes regular patent applications. . . . Progress has not been sufficient on Brazil's commitment to increase effective enforcement actions, from raids through judicial decisions, against intellectual property infringement; the rate of CD piracy in Brazil continues to worsen. . . .

Canada: A WTO dispute settlement panel recently confirmed that Canada's patent law fails to grant a full twenty-year patent term to certain patents as required by the TRIPS Agreement. In 1999, Ambassador Barshefsky announced initiation of WTO dispute settlement proceedings to address this situation. The United States looks to the Government of Canada to comply swiftly with the panel's ruling and bring its patent regime into compliance with Canada's international obligations before further losses are suffered by patent owners in Canada. In 1997, the Government of Canada adopted amendments to its copyright law that discriminate against the interests of some U.S. copyright holders. Canada has established a right of remuneration for the public performance of sound recordings and performances. It also has established a levy on blank audio recording media, the revenues from which are intended to compensate performers and producers for the performance and unauthorized home-taping of their works in Canada. The United States remains extremely concerned that U.S. performers and record producers are denied national treatment with respect to both these provisions and also that the remuneration right for public performances does not give producers and performers exclusive rights over on-demand and interactive uses. We will closely monitor their implementation and any future reform of Canada's copyright laws. More recently, U.S. industry has expressed concern over specific deficiencies in Canada's enforcement against piracy and counterfeiting, particularly at the border. . . .

Chile: While generally strong, Chile's intellectual property laws are not yet consistent with its obligations under the WTO TRIPS Agreement which came into force on January 1, 2000. . . Inadequate enforcement against

piracy and counterfeiting remains a serious concern, as does the large backlog of pending patent applications. We look to the Government of Chile to
eliminate the backlog of patent applications and to bring its legal regime
into compliance with TRIPS without further delay.

. . . .

Costa Rica: Costa Rica has made significant efforts to improve its legal
framework for the protection of intellectual property. The Government of
Costa Rica passed seven laws at the end of 1999 in an effort to bring its
regime into compliance with its obligations under the TRIPS Agreement,
including a provision to extend patent protection terms to TRIPS levels.
However, a number of problems remain on the enforcement side, particularly with respect to criminal prosecutions, as evidenced by continued high
levels of piracy. The U.S. looks to the Government of Costa Rica to build
on its recent progress by taking adequate and effective enforcement actions.

Czech Republic: The Czech Republic has enacted patent, trademark,
customs, and criminal and civil code amendments to bring its intellectual
property rights regime in line with TRIPS Agreement obligations. . . However, the Czech Republic still does not explicitly provide for
ex parte search and seizure authority in civil proceedings, and alternative
measures in the Civil Procedure Code do not appear to be adequate. In
addition, despite relatively good cooperation with police and customs
officials, enforcement problems with prosecutors and courts remain pervasive throughout all sectors of the copyright industry. As a result, piracy
of audiovisual, software, sound recording, book and optical media products
continues to be a serious problem in the Czech Republic. We will continue
to consult informally with the Czech Republic in the coming months in an
effort to encourage it to resolve outstanding TRIPS compliance concerns,
including enforcement, as soon as possible.

Denmark: The United States initiated WTO dispute settlement proceedings against Denmark in 1997 as a result of Denmark's failure to implement
its obligations under the TRIPS Agreement requiring provisional remedies,
including ex parte procedures in civil enforcement proceedings. Courts must
be granted the ability to order unannounced raids in appropriate cases to
determine whether infringement is taking place and to preserve evidence
of infringements, as well as the ability to order that allegedly infringing
activities be stopped pending the outcome of a civil infringement case. This
type of enforcement remedy is particularly important to the enforcement
efforts of the software industry. After numerous consultations with the
United States, the Government of Denmark established a Special Legislative Committee to consider the issue and determine the need for amendments to Danish law. The Committee is currently in the process of drafting
the necessary legislation, but this process is significantly behind schedule.
Therefore, USTR will take the next step in our dispute with Denmark and
request the establishment of a WTO panel unless progress is made
imminently.

. . . .

Hungary: Hungary has enacted copyright, patent, trademark, and criminal and civil code amendments to brings its intellectual property rights regime in line with its obligations under the TRIPS Agreement and its obligations to the United States and the European Union. However, questions remain whether sufficient legal authority exists as required by the TRIPS Agreement for civil ex parte search procedures. . . . With respect to enforcement, despite good cooperation with the police, video and cable television piracy is widespread, and local television and cable companies regularly transmit programs without authorization. Prosecutors and judicial authorities have generally not dealt with piracy cases in an expeditious manner or imposed deterrent level fines and jail sentences. . . .

Indonesia: . . . Draft legislation in the areas of trade secrets, industrial design and integrated circuits, as well as amendments to existing patent, trademark and copyright laws, was prepared to meet the January 1, 2000 deadline for compliance with the TRIPS Agreement. While the Indonesian Parliament did not act on these proposals prior to that deadline, the legislation was resubmitted to Parliament in February 2000. Police raids were stepped up, but optical media piracy remains rampant and effective enforcement continues to be hindered by corruption and a non-transparent legal and judicial system. . . .

Ireland: It has been over five years since the WTO TRIPS Agreement came into force and the Government of Ireland has yet to implement a fully TRIPS-consistent copyright law. Three years ago, the United States initiated dispute settlement proceedings to address our concern over this situation. After numerous consultations with the United States, Ireland committed to enact comprehensive copyright reform legislation by December 1, 1998, and agreed to pass a separate bill, on an expedited basis, to address two particularly pressing enforcement issues. Consistent with this agreement, Ireland enacted legislation in June 1998 raising criminal penalties for copyright infringement and addressing other enforcement issues. However, Ireland's commitment to enact comprehensive copyright legislation has not been met. We understand recent progress has been made toward finalizing this legislation and expect it will be enacted by parliament before its summer recess. The U.S. Government remains hopeful that Ireland will take the steps necessary to complete the legislative process in the very near future, but will feel compelled to consider other options in the face of any further delay.

. . . .

Latvia: Although Latvia has made progress in improving its intellectual property rights regime since it became a member of the WTO in February 1999, there is still much room for improvement. Latvian law does not allow for civil ex parte searches. . . Although pirate optical media production currently is not a problem, there exists a pervasive transshipment problem in Latvia, not only in optical media but in other copyrighted products as well, with much of Latvia's pirated business software flowing over the border from Russia.

Lebanon: The new copyright law provides a firm basis for copyright protection for U.S. works and sound recordings. However, the law contains exemptions that are not consistent with international standards, and there has been little enforcement against piracy. End-user piracy of computer software is pervasive among large companies, banks, trading companies, and most government ministries. In addition, optical media production facilities are reportedly being set up, with the potential for Lebanon to become an exporter of pirated product. . . . Concerns also remain that health authorities are registering unauthorized copies of patented pharmaceuticals. We look to Lebanon to take swift action to address these concerns.
  . . . .

Macau: Over the past six months, Macau has made reasonable progress in attacking the piracy problems that led to its placement on the Special 301 Priority Watch List. . . . Over the next several months, we look to Macau to organize a new customs department, incorporating elements of both the Macau Economic Services Department and the Marine Police. . . . Macau's courts have implemented a special expedited prosecution system that allows a suspect to be brought immediately to trial. We now look to Macau to vigorously prosecute those responsible for piracy. . . .
  . . . .

Oman: As part of its efforts to accede to the WTO, Oman is currently working with WTO Members to amend its current copyright law to comply with the provisions of the TRIPS Agreement. Although Oman has started to take steps to combat software piracy, no action has been taken to date against end-users of unauthorized computer software. . . .

Pakistan: Pakistan's regime for protection of intellectual property does not yet comply with the obligations of the TRIPS Agreement. The Government of Pakistan has undertaken the task of rewriting legislation in the areas of copyrights, patents, and trademarks, but this work appears to have been hampered by lack of a central coordinating authority. . . .

The Philippines: The Philippines has been inconsistent in its nationwide enforcement efforts which rarely result in the imposition of deterrent penalties. . . . It is . . . unclear whether existing law provides right holders an ex parte search and seizure remedy as required by TRIPS Article 50, which is a major priority for the United States. . . . We are also concerned about ineffective enforcement against cable television piracy, and about the persistence of unacceptably high levels of piracy of U.S. textbooks and other publications. In reaction to increased reports about the proliferation of infringing optical disc production in the Philippines, the United States strongly urges the Philippine Government to adopt an effective regulatory system to combat this problem. . . .

Qatar: Despite isolated enforcement actions, Qatar has not yet pursued sustained and deterrent enforcement against end-users of unauthorized computer software, including government entities and against retail shops selling pirated software. . . .

Romania: Although Romania has joined the Berne Convention and the Geneva Phonograms Convention, and is a signatory of the WIPO treaties, it has yet to ratify the treaties or pass legislation necessary to implement them. Criminal enforcement against copyright piracy and trademark counterfeiting (especially of U.S. distilled spirits) continues to be lax, resulting in troubling levels of infringements against imported products and growing domestic production of pirated goods. . . .

Saudi Arabia: As part of its effort to accede to the WTO, Saudi Arabia is currently working with WTO Members to revise its intellectual property laws, including patent and copyright laws, to bring them into conformity with the TRIPS Agreement. . . While the government has been working with the U.S. copyright-based industries to conduct some raids, overall enforcement is not carried out with sufficient regularity and is not accompanied by the appropriate level of publicity and sentences to reduce the level of piracy. . . .

Singapore: Overall piracy rates in Singapore decreased slightly during 1999, while the number of police-organized raids increased. . . . The United States urges Singapore to continue its anti-piracy consumer education campaign and to reassess the existing "self-help" approach to intellectual property enforcement which shifts to right owners the primary burden and expense of investigating and prosecuting infringement. . . . Further, we remain concerned about insufficient efforts at the border to stop the inflow and transshipment of infringing articles through Singapore.

Spain: . . . Government enforcement activities have increased substantially in recent years with exemplary cooperation from Spanish police. However, recent court decisions have called into question the adequacy of protection for well-known trademarks. . . . The slow pace of both civil and criminal court proceedings and lack of sufficient criminal penalties is thought to have diluted the impact of the increased raids in certain areas.

. . . .

Taiwan: Taiwan has had mixed results on intellectual property during the last year. On the positive side, top level support within the Ministry of Economic Affairs has finally resulted in the establishment of an effective Intellectual Property Office. This office has been well staffed with energetic people. . . . On the negative side, responsibility for intellectual property matters is still badly fragmented among different agencies. Repeated U.S. Government requests for action to improve access to the judicial system in infringements cases, to enforce existing source identification code regulations, and to adopt an effective chip marking system have been rebuffed. Taiwan is now among the world's largest producers of optical media. Toleration of extremely lax procedures in enforcing intellectual property rights in this area is out of step with Taiwan's increasing role as an originator of intellectual property.

. . . .

Thailand: Thailand's . . . intellectual property courts are imposing criminal penalties; however, these are often not sufficient to deter infringement and are often suspended pending appeal. Thai prosecutors remain unwilling to charge infringers for violations of customs and revenue laws, in addition to intellectual property infringement. Moreover, the periodic disappearance from police custody of critical evidence of copyright and trademark infringement continues to hamper prosecution. . . . The government.. needs to do more to address increasing levels of optical media piracy in Thailand. In this regard, the United States will monitor closely ongoing efforts to enact legislation necessary to implement a comprehensive regulatory regime to control optical media production. We also urge Thailand to address the inability of enforcement authorities to conduct raids outside business hours; this deficiency has become a significant liability to the effectiveness of the government's efforts to strengthen intellectual property enforcement.

. . . .

Uruguay: Reform of outdated patent and copyright legislation has been underway in Uruguay for a number of years. The Uruguayan Congress enacted the patent bill in September 1999, but the new law contains several problematic areas, including omission of protection for confidential test data, overly broad compulsory licensing provisions, failure to address exclusive marketing rights, and international exhaustion of patent rights. We urge the Government of Uruguay to enact TRIPS-consistent copyright legislation and to amend the new patent law to bring it into full compliance with TRIPS Agreement obligations. . .

. . . .

Vietnam: The Government is still in the formative stages of drafting, enacting and enforcing intellectual property laws. . . . On December 27, 1998, the bilateral copyright agreement between the United States and Vietnam entered into force, following the issuance of implementing regulations by Vietnam. The agreement grants U.S. works copyright protection in Vietnam for the first time. We look to the Government of Vietnam to enforce its new copyright regime vigorously to reduce piracy levels measurably, and to take steps to ensure that all government offices use only legitimate software. We also expect the Government of Vietnam to address intellectual property rights issues in the contexts of negotiations on a bilateral trade agreement and its accession to the WTO.

QUESTIONS

This edited version of the April 28, 2000 announcement by the USTR provides a representative sample of the comments included by the trade representative with respect to different countries. From the report's summary of areas of concern, can you detect the current priorities of the USTR (in addition to those explicitly acknowledged)? Do you agree with these priorities? To some extent, these annual reports reflect concerns expressed by intellectual property trade associations. *See, e.g.*, Letter from Eric Smith, President, International Intellectual Property Alliance, to Joseph Papovich, Assistant USTR for Intellectual Property, in Response to Request For Submissions Regarding Identification of Countries Under Section 182 of the Trade Act (Special 301), February 16, 1999 (reporting views of coalition of seven trade associations representing segments of U.S. copyright industries and suggesting specific Special 301 categorization of 58 countries), *reprinted in* 46 J. COPR. SOC'Y 99 (1999). Is any apparent area of concern an inappropriate subject of comment by the United States? To what standards does the USTR appear to be holding other countries? Are these standards appropriate? Identify the different means by which and the different fora in which the USTR is seeking to achieve its objectives? Do the responses being sought by the United States from other countries appear consistent with the nature of international intellectual property relations?

[B] European Union Trade Barrier Regulation

As suggested in the Newby article *supra*, the EU has responded some-what in kind to the review aspects of the Special 301 device by enacting a Trade Barrier Regulation. *See* Council Regulation (EC) No. 3286/94 laying down community procedures in the field of the common commercial policy in order to ensure the exercise of the community's right under international trade rules, in particular those established under the auspices of the World Trade Organization, O.J. 1994 L 349/71 of 31 December 1994, as amended by Council Regulation (EC) No. 356/95, O.J. 1995 L 41/3 of 23 February 1995. Under this regulation, individual companies may file a complaint with the European Commission if their trade opportunities in third-country markets are restricted by foreign trade barriers (such as inadequate intellectual property protection). The Trade Barrier Regulation replaces the similar, but weaker and thus little used, mechanism established in 1984 by the New Commercial Policy Instrument ("NCPI"). *See* David Rose, *The EU Trade Barrier Regulation: An Effective Instrument for Promoting Global Harmonisation of Intellectual Property Rights*, 21 EUR. INTELL. PROP. REV. 313 (1999). The NCPI had not specifically addressed inadequacies in intellectual property (although it was used in matters of intellectual property), and had given the Commission very limited powers to deal with third countries. The Trade Barrier Regulation remedies those weaknesses. Complaints alleging third country obstacles to trade may be filed with the Commission either by a community industry or a community enterprise. After consultation with member states (by the vehicle of an advisory com-mittee), the Commission decides whether there is evidence of a basis upon which to conduct an examination of the third country practices. The examination procedure includes an information gathering process that is not unlike that used by the USTR, involving broad solicitation of input from interested parties. The examination procedure takes between five to seven months, and results in the submission of a report by the Commission to the advisory committee of member states' representatives. The Commission may terminate the proceedings if further action is not in the community's interest, may suspend proceedings pending resolution of the matter with the country concerned, or may take retaliatory trade measures. Article 12(2) of the Trade Barrier Regulation requires that where international obligations require the Commission to address the dispute through a particular dispute settlement process, that process must be followed prior to the imposition of retaliatory measures. For a thorough explanation of the Trade Barrier Regulation and its use thus far, *see id.* In its first four years, the Commission ruled on eight complaints. Several of the referrals have led to the initiation of the WTO dispute settlement mechanism by the EU. The use of the Trade Barrier Regulation mechanism is likely to increase as the WTO dispute settlement process develops further.

§ 5.03 Multilateral Trade Measures: WTO Dispute Settlement

[A] An Introduction to the System

The conclusion of TRIPS in 1994 dramatically altered the nature of international intellectual property law. Most significantly, international obligations imposed upon countries are now backed up by real, effective enforcement mechanisms. But the newness of this enforcement system raises many first-impression issues for international intellectual property law (and, indeed, for the GATT system). In a groundbreaking article published before any complaints alleging violations of TRIPS were filed, Professors Rochelle Dreyfuss and Andreas Lowenfeld of New York University School of Law provided an insightful combined trade/intellectual property perspective on these issues. The Dreyfuss/Lowenfeld analysis is built around five hypothetical cases, which serve superbly to highlight many of these first impression issues. Excerpts from the article follow. After each of the hypothetical cases analyzed by Dreyfuss and Lowenfeld, we have inserted notes and questions. These notes and questions not only probe the analysis offered by Dreyfuss and Lowenfeld, but also reflect observations based upon cases actually filed or decided and scholarly commentary authored since the article's publication. It is perhaps a testament to the value of this article that we use the Dreyfuss/Lowenfeld article discussing hypothetical cases as the basis for our discussion of actual cases. (As of March 1, 2002, seven panel reports have been issued on complaints regarding TRIPS compliance, and three of those reports were appealed, resulting in three reports by the Appellate Body: India—Patent Protection for Pharmaceutical and Agricultural Chemical Products, *infra* page 542; Canada—Term of Patent Protection, *supra* page 375; United States—Section 211 Omnibus Appropriations Act of 1998, *supra* page 274).

First, however, David Palmeter has succinctly described the basic dispute resolution procedure and the background to the 1994 GATT Agreement, which gave rise to the World Trade Organization on January 1, 1995. An excerpt from that description precedes our case discussion.

DAVID PALMETER, NATIONAL SOVEREIGNTY AND THE WORLD TRADE ORGANIZATION[*]

2 J. WORLD INTELL. PROP. 77, 78–81 (1999)

III. Background

GATT was a multilateral trade agreement that grew out of the aftermath of World War II. In its 47 years of existence, GATT served as the forum for eight rounds of tariff-cutting negotiations . . . GATT was a complex agreement, but it was based on three core 'constitutional' Articles, which remain fundamental in the WTO. In fact, the 1947 GATT has been brought into the WTO word for word, where it is now part of 'GATT 1994.' . . .

The first core constitutional provision of GATT, set out in Article I, is 'most favoured-nation' treatment, which is an unusual way of saying 'normal' treatment. It means that each GATT party, and now each WTO member, receives the same tariff treatment as the 'most favoured' Party or Member—in other words, they are treated the same. Any favour granted to one is granted to all. The second principle, set out in Article II, is tariff-binding. This is simply a promise not to raise tariffs above agreed levels. The third principle, set out in Article III, is 'national treatment'. It means that once foreign goods have entered the national market of another Member, once the bound tariff is paid and import formalities are completed, foreign goods will be treated the same as domestic goods for tax and all other regulatory purposes.

[GATT] was less than a year old when its first dispute arose . . . The Chairman of the meeting at which the complaint was made ruled that the [tax on imports levied by one state were a violation of GATT] . . . This is how dispute settlement began, with a simple ruling from the Chair in 1948. . . . Over time, the complexity of the questions increased, and the chair began to refer them to working parties comprised of the disputants and any others interested in the issue. Eventually, this evolved into a system of panels composed of delegates from parties not involved in the dispute who heard arguments from the disputants. Still later, non-delegates, usually academics and retired government officials, began serving as panelists from time to time.

. . . .

One characteristic of this system reflected its origin as a multi-party agreement: the requirement that concurrence of the entire membership was necessary for any action, including the adoption of dispute settlement reports. Nothing in GATT gave the Chair the authority to decide that question in 1948. Canada's Dana Wilgress simply was in the chair when the question was raised and he ruled. Any party, most particularly the party he ruled against, could have objected. But no-one did, and that was the key to the GATT dispute settlement.

---

[*] This article was originally published in the January 1999 issue of the Journal of World Intellectual Property (Vol. 2 No. 1) and is reproduced by permission of the publisher.

Reports of working parties and, later of panels were brought before the entire membership. Objection—usually by the losing party—was enough to prevent their adoption. Dissatisfaction with the system, primarily by the United States, led to the adoption of the WTO's Understanding on Rules and Procedures Governing the Settlement of Disputes—the DSU.

IV. WTO Dispute Settlement

The move from GATT to the WTO very much reflects a move away from a diplomatic approach to solving problems toward a juridical approach. Brazil's ambassador to the WTO, Celso Lafer, has used the term "thickening of legality" to describe the change. Vestiges of the diplomatic remain in dispute settlement . . . and at times these have provided ammunition for critics of the WTO.

Formal dispute settlement begins with a request for consultations from the complaining party to a potential defendant. . . [I]n many instances extensive discussions between the governments concerned will already have occurred well before a request for formal consultations is made. Frequently, a decision to request consultations in reality is a decision to start the formal process.

If consultations do not produce a solution, the complaining party may request the Dispute Settlement Body—the DSB—to establish a panel. The WTO Secretariat presents the names of possible panelists to the parties. These names are drawn from a list of qualified individuals maintained by the Secretariat, [which] includes names provided by [WTO] Members. If the parties cannot agree on three names, either party eventually may ask the Director-General to name the panel. This has happened on occasion, although Members generally prefer to avoid it as too unpredictable.

After panelists are agreed upon or are named by the Director-General, the process begins. The parties submit written briefs and meet with the panel, and then repeat the process with rebuttal briefs and a second meeting. The panel subsequently presents an interim report to the parties on which they may comment and point out errors. . . .

The panel gives whatever consideration it deems appropriate to the comments of the parties on the interim report, and then issues its final report first to the parties and, about two weeks later, to the entire membership. In theory, the interim report is confidential; it is intended to give the parties the chance to settle the case before the report is made public. But leaks to the press of the results of interim reports are notorious . . . On at least one occasion, however, the [process] has worked [as hoped]. In a dispute between Canada and the European Communities, the parties settled after they received the final report but before it was made public.

. . . .

Once a panel report has been issued—by being circulated to all the Members of the WTO, at which time it is also released to the public—it will be adopted unless it is appealed or unless there is a consensus not to adopt. Since it is highly unlikely that the winning party would join a consensus not to adopt a decision in a case it just won, adoption is all but automatic.

This is just the opposite of the GATT system where decisions were not adopted unless there was a consensus to do so, consensus [requiring] agreement of the losing party. While the losing party agreed to adopt GATT reports in about 90% of the cases, a number of reports in important cases were blocked and others were adopted only after several years. Change in this system of blockage and delay was an important negotiating goal of the United States in the Uruguay Round. . .

The right to appeal from a panel decision is another extremely important innovation of the Uruguay Round. There was no appeal in the GATT. The Uruguay Round negotiators believed, however, that with the new system of near automatic adoption of reports, appellate review was necessary. The Appellate Body, a semi-permanent group of seven members, three of whom serve on a particular case, was the result. . . . .

NOTES AND QUESTIONS

(1) **Adjudication versus Negotiation**. Which aspects of the system described by David Palmeter reflect the shift toward adjudication rather than diplomatic negotiation? Which aspects retain the "vestiges of the diplomatic"? As you read the excerpt from Dreyfuss and Lowenfeld that follows, consider which approaches or analyses suggested by the authors reflect the different models. In the context of private dispute resolution, we have witnessed over the last few years a trend from adjudication of disputes to mediation of disputes. Why did countries agree to move in the other direction—from negotiated resolutions to adjudicated decisions—in the Uruguay Round in 1994? Why does the WTO dispute settlement process retain *any* aspects of the diplomatic model?

(2) **Transparency**. The United States and the EU have expressed concerns about the transparency of the WTO dispute settlement process. Parties' submissions to the panel are kept confidential by states, *see* DSU art. 18(2), and the meetings between the parties and the panel members are closed to the public. The United States and the EU have argued that documents should be available to the public and that hearings should be open to the public. Would this be advisable? What benefits would it provide? Why do you think that some countries, particularly developing countries, have been more leery of opening up the process? *See The Review of the WTO's Dispute Settlement Understanding: Which Way?*, 1 J. WORLD INTELL. PROP. 447, 459 (1998) (comments of John Kingery); Kim Van der Borght,

The Review of the WTO Understanding on Dispute Settlement: Some Reflections on the Current Debate, 14 Am. U. Int'l L. Rev. 1223, 1228 (1999).

———

Article XXIII GATT (1994)
Nullification or Impairment

1. If any contracting party should consider that any benefit accruing to it directly or indirectly under this Agreement is being nullified or impaired or that the attainment of any objective of the Agreement is being impeded as the result of

(a) the failure of another contracting party to carry out its obligations under this Agreement, or

(b) the application by another contracting party of any measure, whether or not it conflicts with the provisions of this Agreement, or

(c) the existence of any other situation, the contracting party may, with a view to the satisfactory adjustment of the matter, make written representations or proposals to the other contracting party or parties which it considers to be concerned. Any contracting party thus approached shall give sympathetic consideration to the representations or proposals made to it.

2. If no satisfactory adjustment is effected between the contracting parties concerned within a reasonable time, or if the difficulty is of the type described in paragraph 1 (c) of this Article, the matter may be referred to the Contracting Parties. The Contracting Parties shall promptly investigate any matter so referred to them and shall make appropriate recommendations to the contracting parties which they consider to be concerned, or give a ruling on the matter, as appropriate. The Contracting Parties may consult with contracting parties, with the Economic and Social Council of the United Nations and with any appropriate inter-governmental organization in cases where they consider such consultation necessary. If the Contracting Parties consider that the circumstances are serious enough to justify such action, they may authorize a contracting party or parties to suspend the application to any other contracting party or parties of such concessions or other obligations under this Agreement as they determine to be appropriate in the circumstances. If the application to any contracting party of any concession or other obligation is in fact suspended, that contracting party shall then be free, not later than sixty days after such action is taken, to give written notice to the Executive Secretary to the Contracting Parties of its intention to withdraw from this Agreement and such withdrawal shall take effect upon the sixtieth day following the day on which such notice is received by him.

THE WTO DISPUTE SETTLEMENT PROCESS: A FLOWCHART

www.wto.org/wto/about/dispute2.html

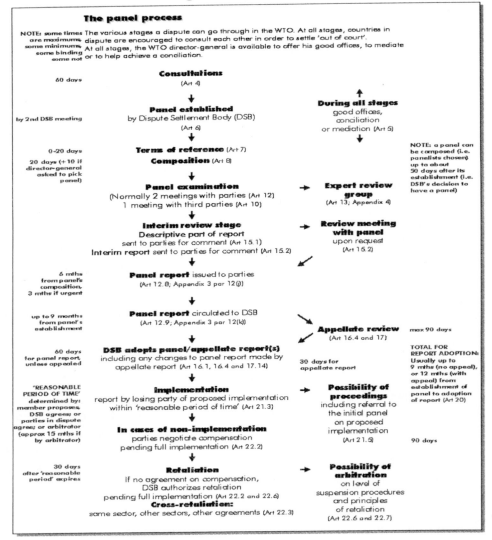

The panel process

NOTE: some times are maximums, some minimums, some binding, some not

The various stages a dispute can go through in the WTO. At all stages, countries in dispute are encouraged to consult each other in order to settle 'out of court'. At all stages, the WTO director-general is available to offer his good offices, to mediate or to help achieve a conciliation.

60 days

Consultations (Art 4)

by 2nd DSB meeting

Panel established
by Dispute Settlement Body (DSB)
(Art 6)

During all stages
good offices,
conciliation
or mediation (Art 5)

0-20 days

20 days (+ 10 if director-general asked to pick panel)

Terms of reference (Art 7)
Composition (Art 8)

NOTE: a panel can be composed (i.e. panelists chosen) up to about 90 days after its establishment (i.e. DSB's decision to have a panel)

Panel examination
(Normally 2 meetings with parties (Art 12)
1 meeting with third parties (Art 10)

Expert review group
(Art 13; Appendix 4)

Interim review stage
Descriptive part of report
sent to parties for comment (Art 15.1)
Interim report sent to parties for comment (Art 15.2)

Review meeting with panel
upon request
(Art 15.2)

6 mths from panel's composition, 3 mths if urgent

Panel report issued to parties
(Art 12.8; Appendix 3 par 12(j))

up to 9 months from panel's establishment

Panel report circulated to DSB
(Art 12.9; Appendix 3 par 12(k))

Appellate review
(Art 16.4 and 17)

max 90 days

60 days for panel report, unless appealed

DSB adopts panel/appellate report(s)
including any changes to panel report made by appellate report (Art 16.1, 16.4 and 17.14)

30 days for appellate report

TOTAL FOR REPORT ADOPTION: Usually up to 9 mths (no appeal), or 12 mths (with appeal) from establishment of panel to adoption of report (Art 20)

'REASONABLE PERIOD OF TIME' determined by: member proposes, DSB agrees; or parties in dispute agree; or arbitrator (approx 15 mths if by arbitrator)

Implementation
report by losing party of proposed implementation within 'reasonable period of time' (Art 21.3)

Possibility of proceedings
including referral to the initial panel on proposed implementation
(Art 21.5)

In cases of non-implementation
parties negotiate compensation pending full implementation (Art 22.2)

90 days

30 days after 'reasonable period' expires

Retaliation
If no agreement on compensation, DSB authorizes retaliation pending full implementation (Art 22.2 and 22.6)
Cross-retaliation:
same sector, other sectors, other agreements (Art 22.3)

Possibility of arbitration
on level of suspension procedures and principles of retaliation
(Art 22.6 and 22.7)

ROCHELLE COOPER DREYFUSS AND ANDREAS F. LOWENFELD, TWO ACHIEVEMENTS OF THE URUGUAY ROUND: PUTTING TRIPS AND DISPUTE SETTLEMENT TOGETHER [*]
37 VA. J. INT'L L. 275–97 (1997)

Introduction

In many ways, completion of the Uruguay Round was a miracle, a package deal with so large an agenda that no state or group of states, and no professional community, could fully grasp the significance of everything that was finally subsumed within the new General Agreement on Tariffs and Trade (GATT). The United States, for instance, was allied with the larger developing countries on agriculture, with the European Community on the other side; but on intellectual property, the United States was, roughly speaking, allied with the European Community, and it was the developing countries that were on the other—or perhaps, better, on another—side. Add in investment issues, services, government procurement, and the traditional trade issues—subsidies, dumping, and safeguards—and the shifting conditions and interests were something like a kaleidoscope.

There were two major breakthroughs in the Uruguay Round. The one that seems to have been the most surprising to the participants was agreement on a strict and binding system of dispute settlement and enforcement. . .

The second significant achievement concerned intellectual property, previously the province of bilateral and multilateral agreements that generally lacked enforcement provisions. The incorporation of an Agreement on Trade-Related Aspects of Intellectual Property Rights (TRIPS) into the GATT means that member states will, for the first time, have a place to resolve disputes concerning the recognition of copyright, patent, trademark, and related rights. Moreover, because every member must now accept all the agreements negotiated during the Uruguay Round, TRIPS signals the entry of many new states into the intellectual property community.

As salutary as these developments are, they raise important questions. While the enforcement system of the new WTO was probably one of the most attractive features of the GATT to the intellectual property community, the architects of the Understanding on Dispute Settlement[2] were thinking more about curing the perceived shortcomings of the prior GATT dispute settlement mechanism—about how to handle disputes concerning measures enforced by states on imports or exports of goods—than they were

---

[*] Copyright 1997, Rochelle Cooper Dreyfuss and Andreas F. Lowenfeld.

[2] Understanding on Rules and Procedures Governing the Settlement of Disputes, art. 3.8, Apr. 15, 1994, Marrakesh Agreement Establishing the World Trade Organization [hereinafter WTO Agreement], Annex 2, Legal Instruments—Results of the Uruguay Round vol. 31, 33 I.L.M. 112 (1994) [hereinafter DSU].

about the TRIPS Agreement. They apparently gave little thought to such issues as the differences between rights in intellectual property and other forms of property, between tangible and intangible goods, between disputes that arise among countries and among firms, and between disputes that arise as a result of judicial, as contrasted with legislative, decision-making.

. . . .

Under prior GATT practice, the parties' duties were often clarified through diplomatic negotiations or dispute resolution that avoided legalistic interpretation of the terms of the Agreement. But the GATT/WTO system is now clearly more adjudicatory than in the past, as well as richer than ever before in the subjects on which member states have come together. To cope with the new and expanded law of international trade, the GATT/WTO system has created an elaborate Understanding on Dispute Settlement (DSU). The DSU provides for a Dispute Settlement Board (DSB), made up of representatives of all the member states but with a separate chairman and secretariat, a standing Appellate Body, to be discussed hereafter, and dispute panels to be established ad hoc on the basis of carefully drafted criteria.

The obligations contained in the TRIPS Agreement are somewhat different than those in the GATT. Of the TRIPS Agreement's three core commitments—national treatment, most-favored-nation treatment, and minimum standards—only the first two are obligations derived from pre-Uruguay Round versions of the General Agreement. Indeed, since they are the only provisions that address conditions that make it more difficult for foreigners, relative to domestic producers, to extract profits, they are the only ones that deal with direct obstacles to trade. In contrast to the traditional GATT provisions, the minimum standards propounded by the TRIPS Agreement are based on the Berne and Paris Conventions, treaties that are principally aimed at promoting innovation by curbing practices deemed to constitute free riding. Free riding is always a problem to those who invest in innovation. However, because a country's refusal to protect against copyists leaves all innovators operating within that country on something of an equal footing, the absence of intellectual property protection is not a direct barrier to international trade.[10]

This difference in focus between TRIPS and the remainder of the GATT means that participants in disputes involving intellectual property will be moving in largely uncharted waters. They will probably not receive much guidance from the case law that developed during the resolution of prior GATT disputes. Article 3.1 of the Understanding on Dispute Settlement acknowledges formal adherence to rules and procedures followed under

[10] In one scenario, innovations could flow more readily across state lines in the absence of intellectual property protection: competitive markets produce more goods at cheaper prices, making works available in markets that could not afford to pay the monopoly rents associated with exclusive rights. In the opposite scenario, innovations flow through investment and licensing, which is made more likely by the existence of intellectual property protection in the receiving country.

GATT 1947; the issues that arise under the TRIPS Agreement, however, may be too novel to make former practices helpful to dispute resolution.

Moreover, the vocabulary of intellectual property and the vocabulary of the GATT sit in uneasy contrast. For instance, consider the terms "competitive" and "protective." For the intellectual property community, pro-competitive measures are those that promote innovation by maximizing the public's ability to utilize intellectual products already a part of the storehouse of knowledge.

Patents, copyrights, trademarks, and trade secrets limit public access. They are, therefore, considered anti-competitive. Within the GATT/WTO system as it has emerged from the Uruguay Round, the thinking is reversed. The TRIPS Agreement, intended mainly to promote global competition, treats patents, copyrights, trademarks, and trade secrets as pro-competitive. Similarly, the GATT disfavors protectionism—a word the intellectual property community has long used to describe precisely the copyright, patent, trademark, and trade secret policies that the TRIPS Agreement mandates.[12]

These differences may turn out to be mere semantics. But in both the world of diplomacy and the world of reasoned decision making, words have persuasive power. More important, these words represent issues that for the intellectual property community are, in many cases, acutely controversial. Intellectual property regimes were initially to be integrated by the World Intellectual Property Organization (WIPO). For many years, that effort was stalled in part because its members could not agree on issues such as whether (and when) consumer welfare is enhanced by sacrificing competition to protect profits in creative efforts. The Uruguay Round succeeded where WIPO failed for a variety of reasons. One of the reasons, it seems, was that the architects of the TRIPS Agreement used words—and a concept of minimum standards—that allowed each state to read into the Agreement what it wished to see.[14]

---

[12] It is not insignificant that one of the places where negotiations over the TRIPS Agreement in the Uruguay Round broke down was over the issue of parallel imports. Doctrines that deem authorized sales in one trading region to exhaust intellectual property interests in other regions have the advantage of facilitating the movement of goods. Thus, an exhaustion doctrine would be in the spirit of the remainder of the free trade provisions of the GATT. At the same time, however, these doctrines limit rights holders' ability to extract maximum profits from their intellectual products by granting distinct territorial licenses to different users. Thus, exhaustion doctrines discourage innovation and are somewhat contrary to the spirit of TRIPS. Exhaustion, then, is one issue that could have forced the drafters of TRIPS to consider the inconsistency between free trade and intellectual property protection. Instead, they provided in article 6 that "nothing in this Agreement shall be used to address the issue of the exhaustion of intellectual property rights." TRIPS Agreement art. 6; [cit].

[Ed. Note: Exhaustion is addressed *infra* Chapter 7.]

[14] For example, [Gail] Evans [has] note[d] that the Punta del Este Declaration described the TRIPS negotiating group's mandate as aimed at reducing "distortions and impediments to international trade," quoting Ministerial Declaration on the Uruguay Round, Sept. 20, 1986, GATT B.I.S.D. (33d Supp.) at 25–26 (1986). "Trade distortion" was interpreted by the United States as loss of comparative advantage through failure to enforce intellectual property rights. The same term was interpreted by India as foreign government intervention in the market place in the name of protecting intellectual property rights. . .

One may hope that the persons who administer the Understanding on Dispute Settlement will have both the authority and the expertise to clarify the meaning of the many agreements making up the WTO system. But neither the DSU, nor the TRIPS Agreement, nor the Berne or Paris Conventions, provide guidance on how minimum standards—rather than actual or optimal standards—will work in conjunction with an adjudicatory dispute resolution system that is backed with enforcement procedures. Success will depend on how well the GATT/WTO system addresses the differences between intellectual property and other trade matters. With these perspectives in mind, we examine the jurisprudential issues that the decision makers operating under the DSU will encounter—questions concerning the source of the law to be applied; the scope of Appellate Body review; and the deference that should be paid to the decisions of other rulemaking authorities, including national courts and administrative agencies. Because our focus is on actual dispute resolution, we have framed our discussion of these matters around a series of hypothetical cases, built upon the substantive issues of major concern to the intellectual property community.

I. Threshold and Subject Matter Issues

It is impossible to predict exactly how complaints involving the TRIPS minimum standards will evolve. Formally, disputes will always be between member states—not between intellectual property producers and consumers. There will be continuing issues on how states will choose which practices to challenge, which cases to use as vehicles for these challenges, and which states to sue. However, because the thrust of the TRIPS initiative was to induce developing countries to move toward effective protection of intellectual property, one may expect that much of the WTO litigation in this area will be between developed countries as complainants and developing countries as respondents.

Moreover, although some of the complaints will surely concern clear breaches—such as failure to sufficiently prevent trademark and copyright piracy, or refusals to protect particular technologies, such as health-related inventions—we expect that many complaints will not be so straightforward. Our expectation stems from the nuanced nature of intellectual property laws. Because these laws are structured so that a country can, at any given point in its intellectual history, achieve what it regards as an appropriate balance between the proprietary interests of producers and the access needs of consumers, they are difficult to draft. Clear cases are unlikely because newcomers to the intellectual property community have little choice but to base their laws on those of developed countries. But literal conformity to the TRIPS Agreement does not tell the entire story: a state intent on preserving access can use the flexibility of the law to strip intellectual property holders of any meaningful protection. These are the cases that we envision, and we expect that they will be difficult to decide.

For example, intellectual property law creates an important distinction between the utilization of ideas and the ideas themselves. Utilizations (expressions for copyright law, applications for patent law) are protectable subject matter, but the ideas themselves cannot be protected. A parallel line is drawn at the enforcement stage, where only certain uses are considered to be infringements. These distinctions are important and generally observed because they assure that the storehouse of knowledge can grow. End-uses are protected, but the building blocks of knowledge are released to all potential innovators. By providing assurance that information essential to progress remains available to all users, these distinctions make it less risky for states not previously party to the international intellectual property conventions to take the step of joining and conforming to the TRIPS Agreement. At the same time, however, the distinctions between ideas and applications may provide a way to avoid complying with the obligations of the TRIPS Agreement. Legislation can appear to be conforming, but lack all bite. Thus, it is almost inevitable that disputes will arise over the question whether a state that has adopted conforming legislation has nonetheless failed to provide meaningful protection to innovators.

One other important, though little understood, aspect of GATT dispute settlement needs to be mentioned here before we consider the first of our cases. The Understanding on Dispute Settlement contemplates several different types of disputes. Under article XXIII(1) of the GATT, retained without change from the 1947 version, the dispute resolution process can be utilized both when a member state asserts that a benefit accruing to it under the Agreement is nullified or impaired by a measure taken by another member state (a violation complaint), or when a member state asserts that any objective of the Agreement is being impeded as the result of any measure applied by another member state, whether or not it conflicts with the Agreement (a nonviolation complaint). Complaints involving failure to carry out obligations—violation complaints—are relatively easy to bring, because such breaches are presumed to cause harm. [DSU art. 3.8]. Indeed, in the half-century history of the GATT, violation complaints have been by far the most common complaints filed. Complaints alleging that countries have undertaken activities or experienced events that have resulted in frustrating the objectives of the Agreement even when not in breach of it (that is, nonviolation complaints) have been rare, in substantial part because in such cases the burden of proving a causal relation between the challenged measure and the alleged injury rests on the complaining party. Moreover, the complaining party must demonstrate not only that it suffered a trade injury as a result of the challenged measure but that it was justified in relying on the nonoccurrence of that measure or event. . . Because the burdens of persuasion and proof are different in violation and nonviolation complaints, a threshold issue for a dispute panel may well be how to characterize a particular complaint.

Perhaps because of the difficulty in resolving nonviolation complaints in respect of an agreement in which all the premises are new, or perhaps out of concern that vulnerability to nonviolation complaints would put too much pressure on developing countries faced with the political problem of passing conforming legislation, the TRIPS Agreement provides a five-year moratorium for nonviolation complaints.[19] Nevertheless, we begin our series of cases with this fundamental question, to illustrate the complexity of fitting together the GATT, the DSU, and the TRIPS Agreement.

Case I

Macrohard is the creator of a computer program that is protected in Xandia, its home country, and elsewhere. It discovers that this program is being sold without authorization in Patria. Macrohard sues the sellers for infringement in Patria, but loses. Patria has not enacted patent protection for programs. Although Patria has enacted copyright protection, the Patrian court holds that Macrohard's program is no more than a principle, system, or method of operation, and so is excluded from protection. Macrohard contends that Patria is engaging in a pattern of nonenforcement; that what it is actually doing is refusing to provide any intellectual property protection for programs, in violation of the TRIPS Agreement. It prevails upon Xandia to bring a complaint to the WTO. After consultation fails to result in a resolution of Xandia's complaint, a panel is formed to consider the allegations.

A. Violation or Nonviolation Complaint

If Patria had failed to enact any protection for computer programs, the assertion by Xandia that Patria had violated article 10 of the TRIPS Agreement would be easily established. Patria has, however, met the literal requirement of article 10, by providing in its legislation that computer programs may be subject to copyright; its court has simply found Macrohard's program to be nonprotectable subject matter. Thus, Patria argues to the dispute panel that it has carried out its obligations; court decisions such as Macrohard are, at most, measures that impede the attainment of an objective of the Agreement. Is this, then, a violation or a nonviolation complaint? . . .

How should the characterization question be resolved? The preliminary question, choice of law, is easily answered: since characterizing the complaint is an issue only because of the terms of the TRIPS Agreement and the GATT, GATT law applies. But what should this law be? If it is necessary to characterize the complaint in order to determine whether the moratorium applies, the issue should be determined by investigating the reasons for the moratorium. Apparently its purpose was to give the Council for

---

[19] Article 64(2) of the TRIPS Agreement provides that subparagraphs 1(b) and 1(c) of article XXIII of the GATT 1994, the non-violation provisions, "shall not apply to the settlement of disputes under this Agreement for a period of five years from the date of entry into force of the WTO Agreement." This special moratorium is applicable to all member states, and is independent of the grace periods available to developing countries or countries in transition to market economies.

TRIPS, which was provided for in the Agreement establishing the World Trade Organization, time to "examine the scope and modalities for nonviolation complaints;" accordingly, then, doubts on characterization should be resolved in favor of Patria. Subject matter issues are among the most difficult of all intellectual property issues. Allowing the parties' understanding of TRIPS to mature before these questions are answered makes considerable sense. But if such a first case is decided as we suggest, it will be important to explain the reasoning with care—not always possible in a collegial body—so that it does not become a precedent for later cases, where, as we discuss below, the priorities and values will be different.

The other reason for characterizing this complaint as a violation or nonviolation complaint is to determine whether Xandia must, as a threshold issue, demonstrate reliance and injury. In this context, one might conclude that doubts should be resolved in favor of Xandia, the complaining party.

Threshold requirements determine the availability of relief. Given that dispute resolution is a primary way in which the TRIPS Agreement will be enforced, the threshold for bringing an action should not be so high as to imperil the success of the enterprise. If we are right in predicting that many complaints will be based on allegations that the flexible features of intellectual property law are systematically misinterpreted to avoid the commitments embodied in the TRIPS Agreement, it is important that the decision makers are able to reach these interpretive questions. And if the experience of countries with well-developed intellectual property law is any indication, DSU panels will need to reach the issue many times before parties achieve a genuine understanding of all its parameters. Thus, at least after the moratorium, it seems that such complaints should be characterized as violation-type complaints.

Characterizing this complaint as a violation complaint would have the additional advantage of avoiding serious questions as to what constitutes an adequate demonstration of reliance and injury. In other parts of the WTO system, treating violation and nonviolation complaints differently makes considerable sense. Breach of a GATT obligation is itself a serious matter; thus, it is efficient for panels to presume that a nullification or impairment has occurred when a party has breached. The effect of other actions or situations is not so clear, and so it is reasonable to require the complainant to establish that harm of the sort that GATT is meant to prevent has occurred. But while prior custom and practice should certainly act as precedent for deciding issues such as the burden of proof in TRIPS disputes,[26] attention also needs to be paid to the differences between intellectual property and the other sorts of goods (and services) encompassed by the WTO system. In Case I, for example, it is the firm, rather than the complaining state, that would have the task of showing reliance. A firm such as Macrohard may have made its decision to invest in producing a major new computer program in small increments, over time, long before the dispute in Patria arose, and in response to other technological changes,

---

[26] *See* DSU arts. 3.1, 26.1

as well as to various factors in the economy and in its own industry. Thus, it would probably be very difficult for Macrohard (or any other member of the computer industry) to establish that any specific decision was made in express reliance on protection in Patria. Accordingly, if the TRIPS Agreement is to be successful in encouraging investment in innovation, it would be wise not to impose a severe burden of showing reliance in TRIPS cases. Indeed, given that intellectual property law is based on the premise that innovation is spurred by the promise of protection, a strong argument could be made that reliance should be presumed. To fit such a standard into the GATT/WTO system, however, would require receptiveness to treating borderline cases as violation, not nonviolation, complaints.

Much the same can be said about demonstrating injury. As with reliance, this issue should be determined under the law of the GATT. But, as with reliance, the GATT precedents may not fit intellectual property disputes. Traditional GATT disputes have focused on loss of trading opportunities by the claimant exporting country by reason of restraints imposed by the respondent importing country; in contrast, the failure by a respondent state to enact or enforce intellectual property protection will never directly interfere with trade. In our Case I, Patria is not preventing Macrohard from selling its products in Patria. Macrohard can fully participate in the market so long as it is willing to sell its program at the competitive price. And if, as seems likely, Macrohard earned back its investment in countries where computer programs are more fully protected, Xandia might well not even be able to demonstrate that Macrohard's incentives to be innovative were harmed.

To be sure, Xandia might be able to show that Macrohard earned less from sales in Patria, both in volume and in price markup, than it would have earned had Patria been in full compliance with Xandia's vision of the TRIPS Agreement, and less than it earned in other states with similar markets. Should such a showing be required before Xandia would be allowed to prevail in its complaint? Or is such a standard too high to achieve the objectives of the Agreement? In domestic copyright cases in the United States, for example, where a showing of injury is required, it often is presumed. The thinking is that the lack of promised exclusivity distorts the market. Once the market is distorted, it is difficult to reconstruct the effect of copying or to evaluate the extent to which the creator was harmed. The law establishes a presumption of injury in order to make sure that infringement is adequately deterred. By the same reasoning, adequate enforcement of the TRIPS Agreement may require either relaxing the standard for demonstrating injury in nonviolation complaints, or treating cases such as Case I as involving a violation complaint.

B. Compliance with TRIPS Article 10

The above analysis leads inevitably to the next question: Is Patria meeting its international obligations, as set out in the TRIPS Agreement? Since it has enacted a copyright law covering computer programs, Patria's obligation under article 10 of the TRIPS Agreement seems to be met, at least prima facie. Patria's patent law does not cover programs. That omission may be inconsistent with article 27(1), which states that, subject to stated exceptions (not including computer programs), patents shall be available "in all fields of technology." If a panel is asked to resolve this inconsistency, it should construe the TRIPS Agreement in accordance with the guidance given by the DSU.

Article 3.2 of the DSU refers to "customary rules of interpretation of public international law," a vague guidepost that may or may not include the negotiating history of the TRIPS Agreement and scrutiny of the domestic laws of the members as they existed when the TRIPS Agreement entered into force.[29] We would urge that both the negotiating history and the concerns and practices of the proponents of the TRIPS Agreement be taken into account in answering the question, along with the less controversial resort to the "ordinary meaning" of the terms of a treaty in the light of the treaty's object and purpose.[30]

Thus, the question whether article 27 of the TRIPS Agreement requires protection for programs should be addressed, first, by noting that it is a general provision. Article 10, on the other hand, is specifically addressed to computer programs and should take priority as the lex specialis. Second, the negotiating history of the TRIPS Agreement indicates that the developed countries were concerned about the inadequacy of the then-extant international intellectual property treaties on the issue of computer programs.[31] The dispute over the extent to which programs should be protected persisted throughout the early years of the Uruguay Round. The record shows that the discussion was limited to the question of considering computer programs as "literary works" for the purpose of extending copyright protection,[32] and that the outcome was a provision expressly requiring only copyright protection. The inference would seem to be clear that the TRIPS Agreement should not be interpreted to require patent protection as well.

As to the domestic practices of member states, we submit that these are relevant not because they apply of their own force, but because they shed light on two significant issues: the understanding of the parties when the

---

[29] *Compare* Vienna Convention on the Law of Treaties, opened for signature May 23, 1969, arts. 31–32, 1155 U.N.T.S. 331, 8 I.L.M. 679 (1969) [hereinafter Vienna Convention] which lists the preparatory work of a treaty and the circumstances of its conclusion as "supplementary means of interpretation," *with* RESTATEMENT (THIRD) OF THE FOREIGN RELATIONS LAW OF THE UNITED STATES § 325 cmt. e (1986), which, reflecting the American practice, is more receptive to using negotiating history and other surrounding circumstances as aids to interpretation of international agreements.

[30] Vienna Convention, *supra* note 29, art. 31(1).

[31] [*Cf.*] 1 THE GATT URUGUAY ROUND: A NEGOTIATING HISTORY (1986-1992) 2246 (Terence P. Stewart ed., 1993) [hereinafter NEGOTIATING HISTORY], noting that several contracting parties were dissatisfied with various aspects of then-extant international intellectual property treaties. . . .

[32] *See* 1 NEGOTIATING HISTORY, *supra* note 31, at 2290–91.

Agreement was signed, and the practicalities of requiring compliance with the interpretation put forth by Xandia. Here, experience supports the conclusion that Patria is not required to enact patent protection for programs. The parties were not thinking along the lines of protecting programs with patents. Although patents on programs have been issued in the United States, the experience during the time of the Uruguay Round was that the sophistication required to examine patents and determine whether they have been infringed outstripped the abilities of both the Patent Office and the courts. Given that the United States has long enjoyed more technological resources than are available to many of the other parties, it seems sound to conclude that article 10 in the copyright chapter of the TRIPS Agreement was intended to be the sole source of protection for computer programs, and that it should be understood as implicitly rejecting a requirement that parties provide patent protection to computer programs. [36]

If, then, the focus is on copyright, and not on patent, the next question is whether Patria's decision in the Macrohard case is inconsistent with the requirement of article 10 that "[c]omputer programs, whether in source or object code, shall be protected as literary works under the Berne Convention." This is likely to be the most difficult issue in the case. Countries that have already provided copyright protection for programs have had a hard time differentiating between unprotectable programming ideas and protectable expression. . . .

C. Lawmaking at the Frontier

One might think that the WTO dispute resolution mechanism, with access to the advice of experts from around the world, would be the ideal way to resolve difficult, high-stakes open questions such as this one. Moreover, the existence of a standing Appellate Body provides a capacity for finding the "best" rules of law for the global economy. If the DSU works as many hope, then these "best" rules might be accepted into the domestic laws of the parties (or at least, into the laws of those parties where the question has not yet been fully answered), leading ultimately to genuine global harmonization.

However, lawmaking in the process of adjudication, a familiar concept to those raised in the common law, is formally circumscribed by the admonition, stated twice in the Understanding on Dispute Settlement, that rulings of the DSB "cannot add to or diminish the rights and obligations

---

[36] *See generally* J.H. Reichman, *The Know-How Gap in the TRIPS Agreement: Why Software Fared Badly, and What Are the Solutions*, 17 HASTINGS COMM. & ENT. L.J. 763, 768 (1995) [hereinafter Reichman, Know-How Gap], noting that there was general reluctance to grant patents on programs in all the developed countries. The United States relented first. After that, patents on software were issued in Japan and European Union countries, but considerable ambivalence on the question remains. Professor Reichman would regard it as incompatible with the TRIPS Agreement for a member state to refuse to permit an inventor to even argue that a particular program met the standards for patent protection. *Id.* at 769.

provided in the covered agreements."[40] While this statement will surely acquire considerable gloss if the intent to make dispute resolution more adjudicative becomes a reality, the GATT's history of conciliation and diplomacy is likely to exert some influence on how disputes are resolved. Thus, at least in its early stages, dispute resolution in the WTO may not be characterized by the sort of give-and-take likely to produce the "best" rule of law.

Furthermore, the limited role permitted to third parties, which requires the third party to have an existing trade interest in the controversy in question, may well distort the decision making process viewed at long range.[41] It is well recognized that creating intellectual property requires a considerable level of sophistication. It is somewhat less recognized—but nonetheless true—that in many areas, even copying requires a measure of technical capacity. Thus, it is likely that all the early disputes in areas such as computer copyright infringement will be among states that have some degree of technological expertise; states with less capability will not be respondents or complainants; nor will they be able to show the "substantial trade interest" necessary to support intervention. The members that participate in dispute resolution will not, therefore, be representative of the entire membership of the WTO. Since disputants will surely argue for the rules that work best for them, the early years of the Agreement are not likely to produce "best" rules when judged from the point of view of the WTO membership as a whole or from the perspective of the global economy. And, unlike adjudication within many of the parties' national courts, there is no legislative check or balance on dispute resolution in the WTO.

To be sure, the TRIPS Agreement also creates a Council for TRIPS, which is charged with the duty to "monitor the operation of this Agreement." Though the intent of the drafters does not appear to have been to create the Council as a rule-enunciating body, it is possible that the system will evolve in a way that will allow the Council to use the occasion of disputes to consider and articulate "best" rules.[43] But, until some body in the WTO— the panels, the Appellate Body, or the Council—develops a capacity to give

---

[40] DSU arts. 3.2, 19.2. The concern about lawmaking by WTO panels is not confined to states in the civil law tradition. *See, e.g.,* U.S. Uruguay Round Agreements Act § 102 (a)(1), 19 U.S.C. § 3512 (a)(1), which provides:

> No provision of any of the Uruguay Round Agreements, *nor the application of any such provision to any person or circumstance,* that is inconsistent with any law of the United States shall have effect. (emphasis added).

[41] Third parties are entitled to participate both in the consultation process that precedes formal adjudication, DSU art. 4.11, and in the actual proceedings before panels, *id.* art. 10. They may also participate in a limited way in appeal proceedings. *Id.* art. 17.4. In each context, however, it is understood that third parties must have an actual and current trade interest in the dispute, and participation in the appeal proceeding appears to be limited to members that have participated in the proceeding before the panel.

[43] *See also* Reichman, *Know-How Gap, supra* note 36, at 773, who suggests that as consensus emerges on particular issues among member states, the topics should be set down for review pursuant to the terms of article 71 of the Agreement.

generally applicable interpretations of the law, disputes will need to be resolved under some other source of law.

One obvious source is the World Intellectual Property Organization. As the administrator of the Madrid Arrangement, and especially the Berne and Paris Conventions, WIPO has a special claim to a role in articulating international intellectual property norms. Its practice of appointing informal groups of experts to consider disputes under the treaties it administers provides, at least in theory, a mechanism for finding best rules. Besides, drawing on WIPO resonates well with the negotiating history of the TRIPS Agreement: the Uruguay Round would not have produced TRIPS had not the administrators of WIPO participated in the identification of generally accepted international norms. The TRIPS Agreement itself contemplates (in article 68) that the Council will consult with WIPO and "shall seek to establish . . . appropriate arrangements for cooperation with bodies of that Organization." We view this provision as a mandate to the TRIPS Council—and to the GATT/WTO system as a whole—to keep up with developments in intellectual property law. Thus, drawing on developments within WIPO seems to be an attractive solution, at least in the early period of the WTO when both the DSU and the TRIPS Agreement are still to some extent in experimental stages, and probably in the long run as well.

The problem with this suggestion is that while it is in harmony with WIPO's aspirations, it fails to take into account WIPO's past performance. WIPO has tended to operate through coordinated group voting rather than through genuine consensus building. For at least the last fifteen years, politicization of deliberations in WIPO has interfered with its lawmaking efforts. Indeed, one principal reason that intellectual property wound up in the WTO was that WIPO had become unable to keep its treaties responsive to the needs of the innovation community. Another reason for the embrace of intellectual property by the WTO is, of course, that only the WTO, as it emerged from the Uruguay Round, has an effective enforcement mechanism. If this mechanism produces a substantial body of decisions at the frontier of intellectual property law, it will inevitably exert an influence over developments within WIPO. . .

It may seem attractive, at least until the transition period is over, or until an arrangement for coordination with WIPO develops, for panels working on a difficult question to consult the laws of developed countries. If a good solution to the problem of, say, drawing the line between ideas and expressions in computer program cases has been found, a panel could adopt such a solution in an international context. The member states would, under this approach, function as laboratories—much as states or provinces do in a federal system. Once one jurisdiction finds a position that appears to work over time, the GATT/WTO system would provide a mechanism for internationalizing that rule.[54] As attractive as this option may seem,

---

[54] For a somewhat different approach, see Reichman, *Know-How Gap, supra* note 36, at 773, who suggests that a panel could take judicial notice of an emerging consensus among member states.

however, we would urge the same caution that we suggested with respect to case-by-case adjudication. The risk of looking to early solutions of national authorities is that predominant attention would be given to the states with the most-developed and sophisticated technology, whose priorities may not be the same as for all members of the WTO.

More fundamentally, we are skeptical that there will always be a "best" rule for every problem that will arise under the TRIPS Agreement. Promoting innovation requires that care be taken not to raise the cost of knowledge to so high a level that it impedes further inventiveness. How that problem is best solved can depend on a country's intellectual and industrial development, its culture, and the types of creative work in which its citizens are engaged. Thus, the nature (and advantage) of a minimum standards regime is that where there is no "best" rule that will work in every economy, each country can tailor the law to its own needs. In short, in areas such as those presented by Case I, where the issue involves that balance between users and producers, drawing the rules from solutions worked out elsewhere—particularly in highly developed economies—may be inappropriate.

D. Deciding Case I

Coming back to Case I, the preceding discussion leads us to urge that a panel begin by according a degree of deference to Patria's own decision in the Macrohard case. Assuming the courts of Patria have made a careful evaluation of the controversy free from improper influences or discrimination by nationality, a WTO panel ought to be reluctant to condemn the result reached by those courts. The panel might inquire whether the Macrohard case was an exception or reflected a pattern of decisions by Patrian authorities that ought to be judged by the TRIPS/WTO dispute settlement mechanism. If a policy concerning protection of computer programs emerged, the panel should inquire (1) whether Patria was furthering a goal shared by countries that protect computer programs (in this case, releasing ideas, as contrasted with applications, into the public domain); and (2) whether Patria's announced law or policy (here, its law differentiating between ideas and copyrightable expression) is recognized elsewhere. If both these inquiries result in affirmative answers, the panel should operate on a presumption that Patria's law and announced policy conform to its treaty obligations. The burden would then shift to Xandia to show the practice is inconsistent with its announced policy by failing to protect the innovations it purports to protect. Xandia might seek to demonstrate that Patria's programming cases lack justification, or that the relevant officials of Patria had disclosed an intent either to avoid the provisions of article 10 of the TRIPS Agreement or to discriminate against foreign holders of programming copyrights.

In the final analysis, a combined approach may be the best way to effectuate the concept of minimum standards. Deference to WIPO when there is an international norm on which member states have agreed would allow the WTO to assume the enforcement role long missing from the Berne and Paris Conventions. In the absence of such a norm, deference to each state's own law is appropriate, on the theory that lack of consensus is an indication that there is no "best rule" and that different economies and cultures require different rules.[57]

NOTES AND QUESTIONS

(1) **Early TRIPS Litigation**. Dreyfuss and Lowenfeld predicted that much WTO TRIPS litigation would involve complaints by developed countries against developing countries. This prediction has been borne out in part. In the first six years, twenty-four TRIPS dispute resolution proceedings were initiated (concerning eighteen discrete matters), comprising almost ten per cent of all cases initiated before the WTO to this point. *See* Dara Williams, *Developing TRIPS Jurisprudence: The First Six Years and Beyond*, 4 J. WORLD INTELL. PROP. 177, 179 (2001) (providing a chart of all twenty-four proceedings and their nature and disposition). A continually updated summary of the status of WTO proceedings generally (not limited to TRIPS matters) can be found at www.wto.org/english/tratop_e/dispu_e/stplay_e.doc. The position as of February 2001, can be summarized as follows:

> Resolutions have been reached in 11 of the 24 disputes; five have been the subject of mutually agreed solutions following bilateral consultations under Article 4 [of the DSU], and in six cases panels have been established and panel reports subsequently adopted by the DSB. Two of the panel reports were appealed. Panels have been established in two more cases . . . The other 11 disputes are the subject of bilateral consultations. . . . The complainants in all but one dispute to date have been developed countries, with the United States initiating two thirds (16), the EC one quarter (6) and Canada one dispute. In February 2001, Brazil became the first developing country to initiate a TRIPS dispute with its request for consultations with the United States. Developed countries have also been the respondent in a majority of cases, with only seven of the 24 disputes (29%) involving complaints against developing countries.

Williams, *supra,* at 177–78. Why does this record from 1995–2001 depart in part from the developed/developing country alignment that Dreyfuss and Lowenfeld predicted? Are there any reasons why this alignment is likely to change? In what ways might the alignment of complaining and defending

---

57 This approach is in agreement with the views of Steven P. Croley & John H. Jackson, *WTO Dispute Procedures, Standard of Review, and Deference to National Governments*, 90 AM. J. INT'L L. 193 (1996). Croley and Jackson urge deference to national outcomes on the theory that this will best promote voluntary compliance and multilateral consensus. They also suggest that the variety in cultural values of the parties, the lack of fact-finding resources by panels, and other shortcomings in international procedure argue against panel activism. *Id.* at 211–13.

members affect either the success of TRIPS or the content of international intellectual property law?

(2) **Initiation of Complaints.** How would Macrohard have successfully "prevailed upon" Xandia to bring an action against Patria? In what ways will the need of private firms to "prevail upon" their governments to bring actions shape the content of international intellectual property law? Can Xandia (or Macrohard) really complain that Patria is engaging in a pattern of nonenforcement based upon this single adverse judicial decision? This is an aspect of trade relations that TRIPS brings to the fore. Should Macrohard be obliged to exhaust its remedies (or at least its judicial remedies) in Patria before bringing the action before the WTO? To what extent should WTO complaints be built upon single judicial decisions? Or should a failure by the Xandian legislature to address unsatisfactory judicial decisions be the triggering event?

(3) **Interpretive Approaches**. What does the obligation in Article 10 of TRIPS to protect computer programs "as literary works" mean? No country has applied its traditional copyright law to computer programs without some adjustment for the particularities of software; so it would appear unlikely that the drafters intended for there to be no form of special tailoring for software. How do we interpret its meaning in international law?

(a) *Relevance of Minimum Standards*. As Dreyfuss and Lowenfeld note, the TRIPS Agreement embodies minimum standards, not optimal standards. How should that affect interpretive devices and considerations that domestic courts might employ in resolving cutting-edge issues? Should Xandia and Patria be able to argue over whether treating the Macrohard program as nothing more than a "method of operation" results systemically in the most efficient and pro-competitive balance between producers and second comer innovators? Can and should WTO panels reach the issue of what is an appropriate exclusion of "methods of operation"? *Cf. Lotus Dev. Corp. v. Borland Int'l Inc.*, 49 F.3d 807 (1st Cir. 1995) (denying protection to menu command hierarchy of spreadsheet program), *aff'd by an equally div. court*, 516 U.S. 233 (1996). Can this answer be resolved as a question of textual interpretation, rather than as a question of optimal competitive balance? *See id.* (Boudin J., concurring).

(b) *Relevance of Article 3(2) DSU*. Article 3(2) provides that rulings of the DSB "cannot add to or diminish the rights and obligations provided in the covered agreements." How should this affect the way in which we interpret the TRIPS Agreement? (Article 9(2) of TRIPS provides simply that copyright protection shall not extend to methods of operation, without further elaboration.) Are there any domestic approaches to statutory interpretation that Article 3(2) would appear to embody? Is it possible for panels to heed this instruction? Can panels engage in "gap-filling" consistent with the above-quoted language from Article 3(2) of the DSU? Can panels "provide security and predictability to the multilateral trading system," DSU art. 3(2), without gap-filling? Petro Mavroidis has argued that "when you discuss a multilateral agreement between one hundred and thirty-two members of different development, different culture, different everything, the end product can only be at a level of generality that it invites interpretation by definition." *The WTO Appellate Body: The First Four Years*, 1 J. WORLD INTELL. PROP. 425, 434 (1999). Do you agree? How should the interpretation of the TRIPS Agreement by WTO panels be affected by the fact that language was intentionally used in TRIPS "that allowed each state to read into the Agreement what it wished to see"?

(c) *Customary Rules of Interpretation*. Article 3(2) of the DSU also affirms that dispute settlement is intended to "preserve the rights and obligations of members under the covered agreements, and to clarify the existing provisions of those agreements in accordance with customary rules of interpretation of public international law." These rules of interpretation are found in the Vienna Convention on the Law of Treaties, *see supra* § 3.01, and thus permit reference in much of the copyright context to the Berne Convention and state practice thereunder, in addition to the negotiating history of TRIPS referenced by Dreyfuss and Lowenfeld. *Cf.* Laurence R. Helfer, *Adjudicating Copyright Claims under the TRIPS Agreement: The Case for a European Human Rights Analogy*, 39 HARV. INT'L L.J. 357, 431 (1998) (suggesting that panels should rely on emergent state practice where there is concordant state practice in all four developmental categories). To what extent did the panel in *Canada-Pharmaceutical Patents*, *supra* § 4.04, use national patents laws to support its construction of Article 30? Is that consistent with the Dreyfuss and Lowenfeld analysis?

(d) *"Berne in TRIPS."* Reference to "the Berne Convention" and state practice thereunder is not, however, as simple it sounds. Neil Netanel has helpfully phrased the dilemma as whether there is a difference between "Berne qua Berne" and "Berne in TRIPS". He concludes that "state practice under Berne should indeed be the fundamental starting point for interpreting Berne in TRIPS, although the Berne provisions that are incorporated into TRIPS will necessarily be colored by TRIPS's state practice and overall object and purpose as well." Neil W. Netanel, *The Next Round: The Impact of the WIPO Copyright Treaty on TRIPS Dispute Settlement*, 37 VA. J. INT'L L. 441, 447 (1997); *see also* TRIPS arts. 7–8. In what ways other than "tincturing" the provisions of Berne with a "trade hue," as Netanel puts it, might the provisions of TRIPS affect the interpretation of the Berne Convention? *See* Vienna Convention art. 31(3). The decision to bring the Berne Convention within the GATT framework could have been achieved in a number of ways, including: repeating the text of the Berne Convention verbatim in the text of TRIPS, requiring all WTO members to adhere to the Berne Convention, or incorporating the terms of the convention by reference. What is the significance of the parties choosing the last of these three options? How would WTO panel interpretation of Berne provisions be affected by the choice made by the drafters? *See* Netanel, *supra*, at 452–53.

(e) *Other Sources*. Netanel has also argued that:

the international law of freedom of expression should require a WTO dispute panel to balance the TRIPS objective of rigorous intellectual property protection with the need for breathing space for public access to and creative reformulations of existing cultural expression. In particular, the dispute panel should accord considerable deference to an allegedly noncompliant member state's own interpretation of TRIPS where that interpretation reflects such free speech concerns.

Id. at 448; *see also* Helfer, *supra*, at 433. Which provision of the Vienna Convention authorizes resort to this source? Netanel argues that an international standard of free expression *permits* member countries to provide certain free expression-based exceptions to copyright, and is relatively less assertive as to whether it requires member countries to create such exceptions. If an "international law of freedom of expression" is relevant to interpreting the scope of TRIPS, why does it not *mandate* free expression-based exceptions? What is the content of the "international law of freedom of expression"? *See* Universal Declaration of Human Rights art. 19. Are WTO panels competent to consider questions of the appropriate international norms of free expression? Is it possible to address questions of copyright without some regard for free expression values?

(f) *Interpretive Focus.* Do you agree with the different sources—TRIPS negotiating history, domestic laws, developments in WIPO—to which Dreyfuss and Lowenfeld turned for guidance? What should be the focus of the interpretive process required to decide Case I between Xandia and Patria? That is, what precisely is a WTO panel trying to decide when confronted with Case I? Does the reasoning behind Dreyfuss and Lowenfeld's suggested resolution of Case I reflect that focus? If there are other considerations or criteria underlying their conclusion, what are they? Are they appropriate or necessary? Is the focus of the Dreyfuss/Lowenfeld interpretive process the same as that exhibited by the panel in *Canada-Patent Pharmaceutical Patents, supra* § 4.04?

Scholars in the United States have noted the parallel between domestic judicial interpretation of statutes and treaties. Which devices of statutory interpretation do you think should have, and should not have, application in interpreting treaties? Does this vary whether the interpretation is by courts construing their effect in domestic law or international panels construing their meaning as part of international law? What other jurisprudential tools would be appropriate in this context? In what ways might an activist DSB be of greater concern than an activist domestic court? *See The Review of the WTO's Dispute Settlement Understanding: Which Way?*, 1 J. WORLD INTELL. PROP. 447, 464–65 (1998) (comments of Thomas Cottier); Graeme B. Dinwoodie, *A New Copyright Order: Why National Courts Should Create Global Norms*, 149 U. PA. L. REV. 469, 570–71 (2000) (discussing the different status of national and international law).

Larry Helfer has argued that in developing a methodological approach to TRIPS disputes, WTO panels could learn from and build upon the experiences of the European Court of Human Rights. *See* Helfer, *supra*. He bases this suggestion upon systemic or structural similarities between the two bodies: (1) interpretation of minimum standards of international obligation; (2) national discretion as to the means of implementing international obligations in national law; (3) historical divergence in national approaches to the subject matter; and (4) risks of non-compliance with rulings of the relevant tribunal. Helfer concludes that these structural characteristics make an analogy to the European Court of Human Rights (which is not part of the EU system) more persuasive than seeking to learn from the European Court of Justice. The European Court of Human Rights adjudicates claims brought by citizens of thirty European countries against their governments under the European Convention on Human Rights. In light of your reading of EU materials, which aspects of the EU system and the role of the ECJ support Helfer's conclusion? (In what ways is the WTO system different from the EU system? In what ways is it similar?) Helfer's argument would suggest that WTO panels refrain from the teleological mode of interpretation adopted by the ECJ, and instead rely on far less dynamic forms of interpretation.

(4) **Third Party Involvement.** Dreyfuss and Lowenfeld note that the limited role permitted to third parties "may well distort the decision making process viewed at long range." In what ways might this occur? In *United States-Import Prohibition of Certain Shrimp and Shrimp Products*, the Appellate Body interpreted DSU article 13 as permitting panels to accept amicus briefs and other submissions by interested persons other than governments. *See* Report of Appellate Body, WT/DS58/AB/R, ¶ 110 (Oct. 12, 1998). Is this appropriate? Is it meaningful or appropriate absent other moves toward a more open and inclusive process? Would it assist panels in making the determinations that they are instructed to make?

(5) **Nonviolation Complaints.** Because Xandia's claim was filed before January 1, 2000, Patria sought to take advantage of the five year moratorium on nonviolation proceedings. *See* TRIPS art. 64. What are the arguments for and against the use of nonviolation complaints? *See* ERNST-ULRICH PETERSMANN, THE GATT/WTO DISPUTE SETTLEMENT SYSTEM: INTERNATIONAL LAW, INTERNATIONAL ORGANIZATIONS AND DISPUTE SETTLEMENT 173 (1997) (arguing against the use of nonviolation complaints in TRIPS cases). If Patria, because it grants copyright protection to computer programs, has not violated a defined obligation of TRIPS, does that not mean that the countries have retained sovereignty beyond that issue?

(a) *Moratorium.* Even if the arguments in favor of nonviolation complaints are persuasive, are there arguments for extending the moratorium? Several countries have argued for the temporary extension of this moratorium; others have suggested eliminating the possibility of nonviolation actions. The status of the moratorium is currently being debated in the TRIPS Council. At the March 2000 TRIPS Council meeting, several countries suggested that the moratorium should remain in effect until new provisions on the "scope and modalities" of nonviolation complaints are agreed upon as contemplated by the TRIPS Agreement. The United States favored ending the moratorium, and took the position that the moratorium had automatically expired on January 1, 2000. (But the United States indicated that it is not preparing non-violation cases for the near future, and would for the moment restrict TRIPS complaints to violation cases. Indeed, at the Doha Ministerial Conference, WTO members agreed that they would not initiate nonviolation TRIPS complaints pending further discussion regarding the scope and modalities of such complaints. *See* Decision on Implementation-Related Issues and Concerns, art. 11, WTO Doc. No. WT/MIN(01)/17 (Nov. 20, 2001).)

(b) *Characterization of the Complaint.* Dreyfuss and Lowenfeld suggest that characterization of a complaint as a violation or nonviolation complaint should depend upon whether the reason for the characterization is the application of the moratorium (which would favor classification as nonviolation) or the requirements in nonviolation cases of demonstrating reliance and injury (which would favor classification as a violation complaint). Accepting the persuasiveness of that distinction, if the moratorium on nonviolation complaints is extended, and the action by Xandia was brought after January 1, 2000, which approach to characterization should a panel adopt? Is there an alternative approach to characterization that should be used in that context?

(c) *Elements of a Nonviolation Complaint.* Dreyfuss and Lowenfeld suggest that if the Xandian action were classified as a nonviolation complaint, then it should be the firm rather than the complaining state that would have the task of showing reliance. Why? What is different about nonviolation complaints that might be reflected in and effectuated by a "reliance" requirement? In light of that, how might you frame a reliance requirement other than requiring Macrohard to establish that a specific decision to invest was made in express reliance on protection in Patria?

(d) *Interpretive Approaches in a Nonviolation Case.* If the panel in Case I had classified the Xandian complaint as a nonviolation complaint, would the panel be required to adopt a different interpretive approach than that developed in deciding the matter as a violation complaint? *See* Joel P. Trachtman, *The Domain of WTO Dispute Resolution*, 40 HARV. INT'L L.J. 333, 370 (1999) (arguing that the nonviolation concept "serves as an invitation to construction, or a catch all, to limit defection by WTO members through the use of avenues of defection with respect to which they have accepted no positive commitment"). Trachtman characterizes nonviolation decisions as involving "construction" rather than "interpretation" of the treaty. In what ways are those two processes different? *See id.* at 339. Is dynamic interpretation and gap-filling more or less appropriate in adjudicating nonviolation complaints?

The panel in a non-TRIPS case, Japan—Measures Affecting Consumer Photographic Film and Paper, WT/DS44/R (98-0886) (WTO Panel, Mar. 31, 1998), has interpreted the scope of nonviolation complaints narrowly to require that the challenged measures could not have been reasonably anticipated at the time of the treaty negotiation. What effect would a similarly strict interpretation of the scope of nonviolation actions under TRIPS have on the future conduct of intellectual property treaty negotiation?

INDIA—PATENT PROTECTION FOR PHARMACEUTICAL AND AGRICULTURAL CHEMICAL PRODUCTS
WT/DS50/AB/R (WTO App. Body, Dec. 19, 1997)

. . . .

. . . The dispute that gives rise to this case represents the first time the TRIPS Agreement has been submitted to the scrutiny of the WTO Dispute Settlement system. . . .

IV. The *TRIPS Agreement*

. . . .

. . . With respect to patent protection for pharmaceutical and agricultural chemical products, certain specific obligations are found in Articles 70.8 and 70.9 of the TRIPS Agreement. The interpretation of these specific obligations is the subject of this dispute. Our task is to address the legal issues arising from this dispute that are raised in this appeal.

. . . .

V. Interpretation of the *TRIPS Agreement*

[In seeking to identify the principles of international law to apply, the panel had first referred to the "disciplines formed under GATT 1947 (the so-called GATT *acquis*)" for the principle that the legitimate expectations of the members regarding the conditions of competition must be protected, including, as adapted for the context of the TRIPS Agreement, "the competitive relationship between a Member's own nationals and those of other Members." Although the Appellate Body affirmed the relevance of the GATT *acquis* to the WTO system, the Appellate Body declared that the panel had erred in its interpretation of the GATT *acquis*. In particular, the Appellate Body found that the doctrine of protecting reasonable expectations had developed in the context of nonviolation complaints under the GATT. But this case involved a violation complaint, and thus the panel erred in concluding that the principle of legitimate expectations must be taken into account in interpreting the provisions of TRIPS. The Appellate Body noted that, under Article 64, whether nonviolation complaints should be available for disputes under the TRIPS Agreement remained to be determined by the TRIPS Council pursuant to Article 64(3) of the TRIPS Agreement, and was not a matter to be resolved through interpretation by panels or the Appellate Body.]

In addition to relying on the GATT *acquis*, the Panel relies also on the customary rules of interpretation of public international law as a basis for the interpretative principle it offers for the TRIPS Agreement. Specifically, the Panel relies on Article 31 of the Vienna Convention, which provides in part:

> 1. A treaty shall be interpreted in good faith in accordance with the ordinary meaning to be given to the terms of the treaty in their context and in the light of its object and purpose.

With this customary rule of interpretation in mind, the Panel stated that:

> In our view, good faith interpretation requires the protection of legitimate expectations derived from the protection of intellectual property rights provided for in the Agreement.

The Panel misunderstands the concept of legitimate expectations in the context of customary rules of interpretation of public international law. The legitimate expectations of the parties to a treaty are reflected in the language of the treaty itself. The duty of a treaty interpreter is to examine the words of the treaty to determine the intentions of the parties. This should be done in accordance with the principles of treaty interpretation set out in Article 31 of the Vienna Convention. But these principles of interpretation neither require nor condone the imputation into a treaty of words that are not there or the importation into a treaty of concepts that were not intended.

In *United States—Standards for Reformulated and Conventional Gasoline*, we set out the proper approach to be applied in interpreting the *WTO Agreement* in accordance with the rules in Article 31 of the *Vienna Convention*. These rules must be respected and applied in interpreting the *TRIPS Agreement* or any other covered agreement. The panel in this case has created its own interpretative principle, which is consistent with neither the customary rules of interpretation of public international law nor established GATT/WTO practice. Both panels and the Appellate Body must be guided by the rules of treaty interpretation set out in the *Vienna Convention*, and must not add to or diminish rights and obligations provided in the *WTO Agreement*.

This conclusion is dictated by two separate and very specific provisions of the DSU. Article 3.2 of the DSU provides that the dispute settlement system of the WTO:

> . . . serves to preserve the rights and obligations of the Members under the covered agreements, and to clarify the existing provisions of those agreements in accordance with customary rules of interpretation of public international law. Recommendations and rulings of the DSB cannot add to or diminish the rights and obligations provided in the covered agreements.

Furthermore, Article 19.2 of the DSU provides:

In accordance with paragraph 2 of Article 3, in their findings and recommendations, the panel and Appellate Body cannot add to or diminish the rights and obligations provided in the covered agreements.

These provisions speak for themselves. Unquestionably, both panels and the Appellate Body are bound by them.

For these reasons, we do not agree with the Panel that the legitimate expectations of Members and private rights holders concerning conditions of competition must always be taken into account in interpreting the TRIPS Agreement.

VI. *Article 70.8*

Article 70.8 states:

Where a Member [as permitted under the grace periods afforded developing countries by Article 65] does not make available as of the date of entry into force of the WTO Agreement patent protection for pharmaceutical and agricultural chemical products commensurate with its obligations under Article 27, that Member shall:

   (a)   notwithstanding the provisions of Part VI, provide as from the date of entry into force of the WTO Agreement a means by which applications for patents for such inventions can be filed;

   (b)   apply to these applications, as of the date of application of this Agreement, the criteria for patentability as laid down in this Agreement as if those criteria were being applied on the date of filing in that Member or, where priority is available and claimed, the priority date of the application; and

   (c)   provide patent protection in accordance with this Agreement as from the grant of the patent and for the remainder of the patent term, counted from the filing date in accordance with Article 33 of this Agreement, for those of these applications that meet the criteria for protection referred to in subparagraph (b).

With respect to Article 70.8(a), the Panel found that:

. . . Article 70.8(a) requires the Members in question to establish a means that not only appropriately allows for the entitlement to file mailbox applications and the allocation of filing and priority dates to them, but also provides a sound legal basis to preserve novelty and priority as of those dates, so as to eliminate any reasonable doubts regarding whether mailbox applications and eventual patents based on them could be rejected or invalidated because, at the filing or priority date, the matter for which protection was sought was unpatentable in the country in question.

In India's view, the obligations in Article 70.8(a) are met by a developing country Member where it establishes a mailbox for receiving, dating and storing patent applications for pharmaceutical and agricultural chemical products in a manner that properly allots filing and priority dates to those applications in accordance with paragraphs (b) and (c) of Article 70.8. India asserts that the Panel established an additional obligation "to create legal certainty that the patent applications and the eventual patents based on them will not be rejected or invalidated in the future". This, India argues, is a legal error by the Panel.

The introductory clause to Article 70.8 provides that it applies "[w]here a Member does not make available as of the date of entry into force of the WTO Agreement patent protection for pharmaceutical and agricultural chemical products commensurate with its obligations under Article 27 . . . " of the *TRIPS Agreement*. Article 27 requires that patents be made available "for any inventions, whether products or processes, in all fields of technology", subject to certain exceptions. However, pursuant to paragraphs 1, 2 and 4 of Article 65, a developing country Member may delay providing product patent protection in areas of technology not protectable in its territory on the general date of application of the *TRIPS Agreement* for that Member until 1 January 2005. Article 70.8 relates specifically and exclusively to situations where a Member does not provide, as of 1 January 1995, patent protection for pharmaceutical and agricultural chemical products.

By its terms, Article 70.8(a) applies "notwithstanding the provisions of Part VI" of the *TRIPS Agreement*. Part VI of the *TRIPS Agreement*, consisting of Articles 65, 66 and 67, allows for certain "transitional arrangements" in the application of certain provisions of the *TRIPS Agreement*. These "transitional arrangements," which allow a Member to delay the application of some of the obligations in the *TRIPS Agreement* for certain specified periods, do not apply to Article 70.8. Thus, although there are "transitional arrangements" which allow developing country Members, in particular, more time to implement certain of their obligations under the *TRIPS Agreement*, no such "transitional arrangements" exist for the obligations in Article 70.8.

Article 70.8(a) imposes an obligation on Members to provide "a means" by which mailbox applications can be filed "from the date of entry into force of the WTO Agreement." Thus, this obligation has been in force since 1 January 1995. The issue before us in this appeal is not whether this obligation exists or whether this obligation is now in force. Clearly, it exists, and, equally clearly, it is in force now. The issue before us in this appeal is: what precisely is the "means" for filing mailbox applications that is contemplated and required by Article 70.8(a)? To answer this question, we must interpret the terms of Article 70.8(a).

We agree with the Panel that "[t]he analysis of the ordinary meaning of these terms alone does not lead to a definitive interpretation as to what sort of 'means' is required by this subparagraph." Therefore, in accordance with the general rules of treaty interpretation set out in Article 31 of the *Vienna Convention*, to discern the meaning of the terms in Article 70.8(a), we must also read this provision in its context, and in light of the object and purpose of the *TRIPS Agreement*.

Paragraphs (b) and (c) of Article 70.8 constitute part of the context for interpreting Article 70.8(a). Paragraphs (b) and (c) of Article 70.8 require that the "means" provided by a Member under Article 70.8(a) must allow the filing of applications for patents for pharmaceutical and agricultural chemical products from 1 January 1995 and preserve the dates of filing and priority of those applications, so that the criteria for patentability may be applied as of those dates, and so that the patent protection eventually granted is dated back to the filing date. In this respect, we agree with the Panel that,

> . . . in order to prevent the loss of the novelty of an invention . . . filing and priority dates need to have a sound legal basis if the provisions of Article 70.8 are to fulfil their purpose. Moreover, if available, a filing must entitle the applicant to claim priority on the basis of an earlier filing in respect of the claimed invention over applications with subsequent filing or priority dates. Without legally sound filing and priority dates, the mechanism to be established on the basis of Article 70.8 will be rendered inoperational.

On this, the Panel is clearly correct. The Panel's interpretation here is consistent also with the object and purpose of the *TRIPS Agreement*. The Agreement takes into account, *inter alia*, "the need to promote effective and adequate protection of intellectual property rights." We believe the Panel was correct in finding that the "means" that the Member concerned is obliged to provide under Article 70.8(a) must allow for "the entitlement to file mailbox applications and the allocation of filing and priority dates to them." Furthermore, the Panel was correct in finding that the "means" established under Article 70.8(a) must also provide "a sound legal basis to preserve novelty and priority as of those dates." These findings flow inescapably from the necessary operation of paragraphs (b) and (c) of Article 70.8.

However, we do *not* agree with the Panel that Article 70.8(a) requires a Member to establish a means "so as to eliminate any reasonable doubts regarding whether mailbox applications and eventual patents based on them could be rejected or invalidated because, at the filing or priority date, the matter for which protection was sought was unpatentable in the country in question." India is *entitled*, by the "transitional arrangements" in paragraphs 1, 2 and 4 of Article 65, to delay application of Article 27 for patents for pharmaceutical and agricultural chemical products until 1 January 2005. In our view, India is obliged, by Article 70.8(a), to provide a legal mechanism for the filing of mailbox applications that provides a sound legal basis to preserve both the novelty of the inventions and the priority of the applications as of the relevant filing and priority dates. No more.

But what constitutes such a sound legal basis in Indian law? To answer this question, we must recall first an important general rule in the *TRIPS Agreement*. Article 1.1 of the *TRIPS Agreement* states, in pertinent part:

> . . . members shall be free to determine the appropriate method of implementing the provisions of this Agreement within their own legal system and practice.

Members, therefore, are free to determine how best to meet their obligations under the *TRIPS Agreement* within the context of their own legal systems. And, as a Member, India is "free to determine the appropriate method of implementing" its obligations under the *TRIPS Agreement* within the context of its own legal system.

India insists that it has done that. India contends that it has established, through "administrative instructions," a "means" consistent with Article 70.8(a) of the *TRIPS Agreement*. According to India, these "administrative instructions" establish a mechanism that provides a sound legal basis to preserve the novelty of the inventions and the priority of the applications as of the relevant filing and priority dates consistent with Article 70.8(a) of the *TRIPS Agreement*. According to India, pursuant to these "administrative instructions," the Patent Office has been directed to store applications for patents for pharmaceutical and agricultural chemical products separately for future action pursuant to Article 70.8, and the Controller General of Patents Designs and Trademarks ("the Controller") has been instructed not to refer them to an examiner until 1 January 2005. According to India, these "administrative instructions "are legally valid in Indian law, as they are reflected in the Minister's Statement to Parliament of 2 August 1996. And, according to India:

> There is . . . *absolute certainty* that India can, when patents are due in accordance with subparagraphs (b) and (c) of Article 70.8, decide to grant such patents on the basis of the applications currently submitted and determine the novelty and priority of the inventions in accordance with the date of these applications. (emphasis added)

India has not provided any text of these "administrative instructions" either to the Panel or to us.

Whatever their substance or their import, these "administrative instructions" were not the initial "means" chosen by the Government of India to meet India's obligations under Article 70.8(a) of the *TRIPS Agreement*. The Government of India's initial preference for establishing a "means" for filing mailbox applications under Article 70.8(a) was the Patents (Amendment) Ordinance (the "Ordinance"), promulgated by the President of India on 31 December 1994 pursuant to Article 123 of India's Constitution. Article 123 enables the President to promulgate an ordinance when Parliament is not in session, and when the President is satisfied "that circumstances exist which render it necessary for him to take immediate action." India notified the Ordinance to the Council for TRIPS, pursuant to Article 63.2 of the

TRIPS Agreement, on 6 March 1995. In accordance with the terms of Article 123 of India's Constitution, the Ordinance expired on 26 March 1995, six weeks after the reassembly of Parliament. This was followed by an unsuccessful effort to enact the Patents (Amendment) Bill 1995 to implement the contents of the Ordinance on a permanent basis. This Bill was introduced in the Lok Sabha (Lower House) in March 1995. After being passed by the Lok Sabha, it was referred to a Select Committee of the Rajya Sabha (Upper House) for examination and report. However, the Bill was subsequently not enacted due to the dissolution of Parliament on 10 May 1996. From these actions, it is apparent that the Government of India initially considered the enactment of amending legislation to be necessary in order to implement its obligations under Article 70.8(a). However, India maintains that the "administrative instructions" issued in April 1995 effectively continued the mailbox system established by the Ordinance, thus obviating the need for a formal amendment to the Patents Act or for a new notification to the Council for TRIPS.

With respect to India's "administrative instructions," the Panel found that "the current administrative practice creates a certain degree of legal insecurity in that it requires Indian officials to ignore certain mandatory provisions of the Patents Act"; and that "even if Patent Office officials do not examine and reject mailbox applications, a competitor might seek a judicial order to do so in order to obtain rejection of a patent claim."

India asserts that the Panel erred in its treatment of India's municipal law because municipal law is a fact that must be established before an international tribunal by the party relying on it. In India's view, the Panel did not assess the Indian law as a fact to be established by the United States, but rather as a law to be interpreted by the Panel. India argues that the Panel should have given India the benefit of the doubt as to the status of its mailbox system under Indian domestic law. India claims, furthermore, that the Panel should have sought guidance from India on matters relating to the interpretation of Indian law.

In public international law, an international tribunal may treat municipal law in several ways.[52] Municipal law may serve as evidence of facts and may provide evidence of state practice. However, municipal law may also constitute evidence of compliance or non-compliance with international obligations. For example, in *Certain German Interests in Polish Upper Silesia*, the Permanent Court of International Justice observed:

> It might be asked whether a difficulty does not arise from the fact that the Court would have to deal with the Polish law of July 14th, 1920. This, however, does not appear to be the case. From the standpoint of International Law and of the Court which is its organ, municipal laws are merely facts which express the will and constitute the activities of States, in the same manner as do legal

---

[52] *See*, for example, I. Brownlie, Principles of Public International Law, 4th ed. (Clarendon Press, 1990), pp. 40–42.

decisions and administrative measures. *The Court is certainly not called upon to interpret the Polish law as such; but there is nothing to prevent the Court's giving judgment on the question whether or not, in applying that law, Poland is acting in conformity with its obligations towards Germany under the Geneva Convention.*[53] (emphasis added)

In this case, the Panel was simply performing its task in determining whether India's "administrative instructions" for receiving mailbox applications were in conformity with India's obligations under Article 70.8(a) of the *TRIPS Agreement*. It is clear that an examination of the relevant aspects of Indian municipal law and, in particular, the relevant provisions of the Patents Act as they relate to the "administrative instructions," is essential to determining whether India has complied with its obligations under Article 70.8(a). There was simply no way for the Panel to make this determination without engaging in an examination of Indian law. But, as in the case cited above before the Permanent Court of International Justice, in this case the Panel was not interpreting Indian law "as such;" rather, the Panel was examining Indian law solely for the purpose of determining whether India had met its obligations under the *TRIPS Agreement*. To say that the Panel should have done otherwise would be to say that only India can assess whether Indian law is consistent with India's obligations under the *WTO Agreement*. This, clearly, cannot be so.

Previous GATT/WTO panels also have conducted a detailed examination of the domestic law of a Member in assessing the conformity of that domestic law with the relevant GATT/WTO obligations. For example, in *United States—Section 337 of the Tariff Act of 1930*, the panel conducted a detailed examination of the relevant United States legislation and practice, including the remedies available under Section 337 as well as the differences between patent-based Section 337 proceedings and federal district court proceedings, in order to determine whether Section 337 was inconsistent with Article III:4 of the GATT 1947. This seems to us to be a comparable case.

And, just as it was necessary for the Panel in this case to seek a detailed understanding of the operation of the Patents Act as it relates to the "administrative instructions" in order to assess whether India had complied with Article 70.8(a), so, too, is it necessary for us in this appeal to review the Panel's examination of the same Indian domestic law.

To do so, we must look at the specific provisions of the Patents Act. Section 5(a) of the Patents Act provides that substances "intended for use, or capable of being used, as food or as medicine or drug" are not patentable. "When the complete specification has been led in respect of an application for a patent", section 12(1) *requires* the Controller to refer that application and that specification to an examiner. Moreover, section 15(2) of the Patents Act states that the Controller "shall refuse" an application in respect of a

---

[53] [1926], PCIJ Rep., Series A, No. 7, p. 19.

substance that is not patentable. We agree with the Panel that these provisions of the Patents Act are mandatory. And, like the Panel, we are not persuaded that India's "administrative instructions" would prevail over the contradictory mandatory provisions of the Patents Act. We note also that, in issuing these "administrative instructions," the Government of India did not avail itself of the provisions of section 159 of the Patents Act, which allows the Central Government "to make rules for carrying out the provisions of [the] Act" or section 160 of the Patents Act, which requires that such rules be laid before each House of the Indian Parliament. We are told by India that such rule-making was not required for the "administrative instructions" at issue here. But this, too, seems to be inconsistent with the mandatory provisions of the Patents Act.

We are not persuaded by India's explanation of these seeming contradictions. Accordingly, we are not persuaded that India's "administrative instructions" would survive a legal challenge under the Patents Act. And, consequently, we are not persuaded that India's "administrative instructions" provide a sound legal basis to preserve novelty of inventions and priority of applications as of the relevant filing and priority dates.

For these reasons, we agree with the Panel's conclusion that India's "administrative instructions" for receiving mailbox applications are inconsistent with Article 70.8(a) of the *TRIPS Agreement*. . . .

NOTES AND QUESTIONS

(1) **The Role of Legitimate Expectations**. Why did the Appellate Body find that the panel had misapplied Article 31 of the Vienna Convention? In what way, according to the Appellate Body, are "legitimate expectations" relevant to interpretation of the TRIPS Agreement? For a detailed discussion of the panel and Appellate Body reports, see Matthijs Geuze & Hannu Wager, *WTO Dispute Settlement Practice Relating to the TRIPS Agreement*, J. INT'L ECON. L. 347, 365–67 (1999) (summarizing arguments); J.H. Reichman, *Securing Compliance with the TRIPS Agreement after U.S. v. India*, J. INT'L ECON. L. 585, 592 (1998).

(2) **The Argument for Circumspection.** The Appellate Body report notes, circumspectly, that "principles of interpretation neither require nor condone the imputation into a treaty of words that are not there or the importation into a treaty of concepts that were not intended." Does this answer the dilemmas posed above regarding interpretive approaches? Indian commentators viewed the Appellate Body decision in *United States-India* as preferable to the panel decision because they believe it adhered more closely to the TRIPS Agreement that was negotiated. Jayashree Watal went so far as to say that the Appellate Body decision "restores some of the faith that we had lost in the WTO." *The WTO Appellate Body: The First Four Years*, 1 J. WORLD INTELL. PROP. 425, 432 (1999) (comments of

Jayashree Watal). Does this observation affect how you think the TRIPS Agreement should be interpreted? Did the panel in *Canada-Pharmaceutical Patents, supra* § 4.04, display the circumspection demanded by the Appellate Body in *United States-India?*

In order to fulfil the objectives of the dispute settlement process, to which values must the Appellate Body adhere most faithfully? Are these values different from those that should motivate the TRIPS Council? If so, why? Joel Trachtman has noted that in the *Shrimp-Turtle* case, the WTO Appellate Body "refined its interpretive tools by rejecting a strict 'original intent' interpretation . . . in favor of a more dynamic interpretation to fit modern circumstances. In doing so, it aggregated substantial power to itself, both to engage in balancing and to 'modernize' the interpretation of Article XX [of the GATT]." Joel P. Trachtman, *The Domain of WTO Dispute Resolution*, 40 HARV. INT'L L.J. 333, 364 (1999). How would the extension of that interpretive philosophy to TRIPS disputes affect the development of international intellectual property law? In what ways would the decision by WTO panels to adopt a dynamic gap-filling methodology or a minimalist textualist methodology affect the future conduct of international intellectual property relations? *See* Paul Edward Geller, *Intellectual Property in the Global Marketplace: Impact of TRIPS Dispute Settlement*, 29 INT. LAW. 99, 113 (1995).

(3) **United States—India: Lessons for Doha?** According to Abbott:

> Article 31 of the TRIPS Agreement establishes the conditions under which WTO Members may grant compulsory licenses. . . . The AB [in United States—India] indicated that the rules of treaty interpretation outlined in Article 31 of the Vienna Convention on the Law of Treaties apply, and that panels and the AB would begin by examining the express terms of the TRIPS Agreement, giving them their ordinary meaning in their context, and in light of the object and purpose of the agreement. The performance of the parties would be evidence of its intended meaning. Under the Vienna Convention, reference to negotiating history is only used to confirm results derived from analysis of the express text or to aid when express text yields ambiguous results. A central point of the AB's decision in the *India-Mailbox Case* was that the "legitimate expectations" of Members and private patent holders in Members is not the basis for interpreting the Agreement. What the pharmaceutical sector in the United States and Europe hoped or expected the Agreement to mean is not relevant to the treaty interpreter. The meaning of the Agreement is to be derived from the language agreed upon by the Members.

Frederick M. Abbott, *The TRIPS-Legality of Measures Taken to Address Public Health Crises: A Synopsis*, 7-SPG WIDENER L. SYMP. J. 71, 77 (2001). What lessons does the *United States—India* report of the Appellate Body offer for the debate concerning access to medicines?

(4) **Stare Decisis.** The panel in *EU v. India* indicated that it did not feel bound by the reports of the panel or the Appellate Body in *United States v. India*. *See EU v. India*, Panel Report, WT/DS79/R (Aug. 24, 1998). Why not? Should it have? *See* Adrian T. Chua, *Precedent and Principles of WTO Panel Jurisprudence*, 2 BERK. J. INT'L L. 171, 172–74 (1998). Does failure to apply principles of stare decisis undermine the purposes of the WTO adjudicative system? *Cf.* DSU art. 3.2. Would the adoption of a system of binding precedent have generated other unfavorable consequences? What lesser presumptions might the panel in *EU v. India* have considered even if it did not feel formally bound by the precedent of *United States v. India*? *See EU v. India*, Panel Report, WT/DS79/R (discussing EU's prima facie case). In large part, the position adopted by the *EU-India* panel merely reflected the practice of pre-WTO GATT panels. In what way does the nature of the new WTO proceedings (as opposed to the prior GATT practice described in the Dreyfuss and Lowenfeld article) support, or undermine, the development of a system of binding precedent? Could it be argued that earlier panel reports adopted by the DSB are part of "subsequent practice in the application of the treaty" under Article 31(3)(b) of the Vienna Convention on the Law of Treaties and thus part of the "customary rules of interpretation of public international law" under Article 3.2 of the DSU? *See Japan—Taxes on Alcoholic Beverages*, Appellate Body Report, Nov. 1, 1996, WT/DS8/AB/R, WT/DS10/AB/R, WT/DS11/AB/R (discussing whether the adoption of a panel report should be treated as subsequent practice, defined by the Appellate Body as "a 'concordant, common and consistent' sequence of acts or pronouncements sufficient to establish a discernible intent implying the parties' agreement regarding its interpretation"); *see also* Chua, *supra* at 183–85 (arguing that panel reports might constitute binding precedent in certain circumstances notwithstanding *Japan-Alcoholic Beverages*). In what ways are the considerations supporting characterization as subsequent practice under international law inconsistent with those considerations that would support treating panel reports as "binding precedent" in the sense that that term is used in common law jurisdictions adjudicating disputes between private parties? What does this tell you about the nature of public international law?

(5) **The GATT** *acquis.* The term "GATT acquis" has been adopted by the Appellate Body as a useful term by which to describe the pre-existing body of GATT practices and understandings. The term *acquis communautaire* is commonly found in the case law of the European Court of Justice. There, it means the "whole body of rules, principles, agreements, declarations, resolutions, opinions, objectives and practices concerning the European Communities . . . whether or not binding in law, which has developed since their establishment and which has been accepted by the Community . . . as governing their activities." Mary Footer, *The Role of Consensus in GATT/WTO Decision-Making*, 17 Nw. J. INT'L L. BUS. 653 (1996–1997).

[B] The Scope of Intellectual Property Protection in the WTO

DREYFUSS AND LOWENFELD, CASE II:
THE SCOPE OF PROTECTION *
37 Va. J. Int'l L. 275, 297–307

In many ways, limitations on the subject matter entitled to protection provide rather coarse control over the balance between public access and private incentives. By fencing off entire fields from protection, such limitations make intellectual property law unavailable as a source of encouragement for whole industries. Moreover, they skew the decisions that individual innovators make about where to invest their resources. Ironically, industries devoted to subject matter that is considered too socially important to protect can wind up being underfunded. For this reason, it makes sense for states to be generous on the question of subject matter protectability, and then to safeguard the public's interest in access in more finely tuned ways. For example, a state may tighten the scope of what it considers infringement—adjusting the degree of similarity for finding infringement of copyrights, and the degree of equivalence needed for finding infringement of patents. [54]

For the TRIPS Agreement, the ability to fine tune raises the danger that a member state could use these measures in the way we previously discussed for coarse tuning: to appear to comply with the Agreement while really sidestepping its obligations. As to that issue, what we have said previously applies here as well. In this section, we discuss the role of the GATT/WTO system in considering the more subtle question of whether the particular balance that a state strikes is permissible under the TRIPS Agreement.

Case II

Monastery Labs developed a new pharmaceutical for treating Sallyheimer disease. The drug, a complex organic compound bound to magnesium, is patented both in Monastery's home country, Xandia, and in Patria, a developing country that has adopted patent legislation conforming to the TRIPS Agreement. A Patrian pharmaceutical company sells the same complex compound, except that its product substitutes manganese for magnesium. Monastery Labs sued the Patrian company in Patria, but lost. The court found (1) that before Monastery Labs invented this compound, it was common knowledge that Sallyheimer sufferers had a problem with metals, so this compound was not inventive enough to qualify for protection; and (2) that Monastery's patent described "alkaline

---

* Copyright 1997, Rochelle Cooper Dreyfuss and Andreas F. Lowenfeld.

[54] For simplicity, the text considers only these alternatives. What is said here, however, applies to other fine-tuning provisions, such as the fair use defense in copyright law or the experimental use defense in patent law.

earth metal bonds" and manganese is not an alkaline earth metal, with the result that the Patrian company's product does not infringe Monastery's patent. Monastery prevailed upon the government of Xandia to bring a complaint to the WTO. Again, after consultation, the dispute was referred to a panel for resolution.

The complaint alleges that Patria violated article 27(1) of the TRIPS Agreement by requiring an inventive leap rather than an "inventive step." Further, the complaint asserts that Patria permitted infringement of Monastery's valid patent, thereby violating article 28(1)(a) by failing to prevent others from using Monastery's insight without its authorization. Patria, in its answering papers, contends that its courts applied settled principles of Patrian patent law, without discriminating by nationality, on the basis that an applicant for monopoly protection has a heavy burden of establishing both nonobviousness[55] and infringement.

A. Alternative Approaches

It is not clear, at the outset, how a WTO panel should resolve this controversy. Case II demonstrates how differently two countries could administer intellectual property laws that ostensibly comply with the TRIPS Agreement. At one time, a court in the United States, for instance, might have handled this case as follows: if it found that the identification of a metals problem was part of the art existing prior to Monastery's invention, it might consider using magnesium compounds "obvious to try." It would then ascertain how many metal-delivery systems there are. If there are many, it could hold Monastery's discovery patentable on the theory that the ordinary artisan would not have found this one easily. The inquiry on infringement would be, in a sense, the reverse: the court would inquire whether it would be obvious to the ordinary artisan to substitute manganese for magnesium—a question that in another context the U.S. Supreme Court has already answered in the affirmative. Accordingly, under the doctrine of equivalents as applied in the United States, Monastery's patent would be considered to be infringed.

One could easily imagine that Patria could take a very different approach. If it is a developing or least-developed country, the transition provisions in the TRIPS Agreement give it a grace period before it is required to extend patent protection to such products.[63] A decision to enact legislation concerning pharmaceuticals without such delay could well indicate that Patria is trying to promote indigenous research and development. A research and

---

[55] A footnote to article 27(1) of the TRIPS Agreement states: "For the purposes of this Article, the term[] 'inventive step' . . . may be deemed by a Member to be synonymous with the term[] 'nonobvious'."

[63] For developing countries, there is a four-year grace period. TRIPS Agreement art. 65(2). For countries that had not previously enacted legislation to protect pharmaceuticals, there is an additional five-year grace period. *Id.* art. 65(4). Least-developed countries may have ten years from the date of application of the substantive provisions of the Agreement to fully comply with these provisions. *Id.* art. 66(1).

development industry, however, requires a technologically trained labor force. One way to encourage the creation of such a resource might be by teaching unskilled labor to work in laboratories. That strategy, in turn, would require that there be meaningful work for this labor force to do. Finding alternatives to expensive foreign medicines certainly seems like an attractive objective. Thus, it might make sense for Patria to reject the "obvious to try" doctrine and argue that in developed countries patent protection is needed in this context to motivate someone to engage in the labor-intensive effort of finding the right choice among many, but that in Patria, where a cheap labor force is looking for work, trudging through obvious alternatives requires no particular encouragement. In other words, supra-competitive profits should be reserved to those who confer genuinely unique and major social benefits by denying a separate patent to the sort of advance over prior art that Monastery's invention represents. Alternatively, Patria could allow its work force to train on Monastery's invention by deciding that any rights that Monastery wishes to assert must be expressly claimed in the patent document. That would release variations for domestic research-ers to find. In short, whether these arguments are after-the-fact rationaliza-tions or actually describe Patria's motivation, the challenged failure to grant Monastery the same protection it receives in the home country is not an obvious or clear violation of the TRIPS Agreement.[65]

B. Special Treatment for Developing Countries

If this dispute were brought during the transition period allowed to developing and least-developed countries, Patria might argue that since it was not yet required to offer patent protection to Monastery, Xandia should not be heard to complain that Patria offers less protection than Xandia finds ideal. To evaluate this position, two issues must be decided: first, whether Patria is a country that can avail itself of the special benefits offered to developing economies, and second, the exact scope of these special benefits.

. . . .

Assuming that Patria qualifies as a developing country, the next question is how much leeway it should be given on that account. One might conclude that the transition provisions are exclusive and that once a country moves out of the transition period (voluntarily or under the pressure of time lim-its), it is expected to conform its laws in every respect to the norms of the developed world. There are, however, significant reasons to refrain from taking so hard a line. It is important to remember that the impact of the TRIPS Agreement on the developing world was not comprehensively considered at the time the Agreement was drafted. The principal negotia-tors were almost uniformly interested in strengthening the international

---

[65] The basic Paris Convention does not guarantee to patent holders in one state patent protection in other member states, but leaves the issues of patentability and infringement to each member state's laws. Paris Convention, art. 2(1). The question here raised is how far this deference to lex fori is changed by the WTO system—the TRIPS Agreement in combination with the DSU.

intellectual property regime. And because the GATT/WTO system requires its members to accept all the principal agreements negotiated in the Uruguay Round, there was no practical way for any country, including Patria, to stay outside the TRIPS Agreement.

Now that there is time to be more reflective, we should recognize that as far as developing countries are concerned, the TRIPS Agreement could have a substantially different impact from the remainder of the WTO agreements. One effect is obvious: the cost to member states of enforcing intellectual property rights is formidable. Monitoring is expensive, the obligation to destroy infringing materials entails high social costs, and countries with weak civil justice systems must spend the money to create them. All of this is in addition to the cost of setting up copyright, trademark, and patent offices and staffing them with trained personnel.

Even after these costs are borne, the TRIPS Agreement may present a significant problem to developing countries. Experience shows that in other economic sectors, comparative advantage tends to shift over time. As each party has (more or less) an equal opportunity to acquire an advantage in any economic sector, each trade barrier that is lowered is either a current benefit or a potential benefit. In contrast, it can be argued that a technologically undeveloped country that agrees to the TRIPS Agreement is handicapping itself. Instead of following the strategy (which many developed countries once pursued) of absorbing the world's knowledge base and coming up to technological speed before protecting foreign intellectual property, a country that enters into the TRIPS Agreement at this stage, before it has a creative community in place, may well raise the costs of acquiring the knowledge it needs. The TRIPS Agreement might, therefore, improve the *incentives* for a developing country's citizens to become innovative, but put the *cost* of becoming innovative out of reach. The opposite argument, which prevailed in the Uruguay Round (though one can debate how much choice the developing countries had at the end) is that by providing secure protection for intellectual property, a member state can remain in the mainstream of technological progress, while denying protection might leave it on the sidelines of innovation[69] . . . [T]hese considerations suggest that unless the TRIPS Agreement is sympathetically interpreted to safeguard public access, it could wind up preventing certain member states from ever becoming players in the intellectual property sector.[76]

---

[69] An interesting illustration of this debate was recently provided by Martin J. Adelman & Sonia Baldia, *Prospects and Limits of the Patent Provision in the TRIPS Agreement: The Case of India*, 29 VAND. J. TRANSNAT'L L. 507, 525–33 (1996). The authors draw the conclusion from India's large infrastructure in pharmaceutical production, coupled with its past failure to contribute innovations in the pharmaceutical field, that strong intellectual property protection has always been in India's interest. In contrast, J.H. Reichman uses the same data to argue that free-riding is a way for a developing economy to accumulate the skills and capital necessary to become innovative. J.H. Reichman, *Compliance with the TRIPS Agreement: Introduction to a Scholarly Debate*, 29 VAND. J. TRANSNAT'L L. 363, 381 (1996).

[76] *See also* article 8.10 of the DSU, which calls for at least one member of a panel to be chosen from a developing state if the controversy concerns such a state; *id*. art. 21.7, which requires that the impact on the economy of developing countries be taken into account in the panel's recommendations. Article 24 calls for additional consideration and restraint on the part of complaining parties in disputes with least-developed member states.

C. Deferring to Patria

All of this goes to argue that on the substantive side, Patria's decision ought to be given considerable deference. Allowing Patrians to make variations on Monastery's drug without incurring the costs of infringement is one way to develop the skills Patria needs if it is ever to see advantages from joining the TRIPS Agreement. Accordingly, whereas in Case I we suggested that deference to Patria's own decisions may properly depend on whether Patria was taking positions consistent with policies of states with demonstrated commitments to intellectual property, in Case II it would probably be wise for a WTO panel—at least with respect to developing countries—to defer even in circumstances where Patria's decisions look quite atypical.

Even if Patria were not a developing country, the better course might well be to make it nearly impossible to prevail before the WTO on a complaint involving fine-tuning, except on an additional showing of violation of the non-discrimination provisions—national treatment and most-favored-nation treatment. Although the TRIPS Agreement is drafted as a set of standards for the protection of innovators, there are two sides to every innovation coin: the greater the protection granted to the innovator, the less is the public's access to the products of intellectual activity. To the extent that DSU panels are instructed not to "diminish rights or obligations," they should be equally careful not to diminish the rights that users of innovative efforts have in particular countries.[80] Again, this is the core difference between a minimum standard and an optimum or harmonized rule: a minimum standard allows each member state to create a law that is suited to the needs of its own creative community; an "optimum" rule would, in contrast, require each state to adopt a single law, whether it was right for its economy or not. The drafters of the TRIPS Agreement chose minimum standards, just as the drafters of the Berne and Paris Convention did. We agree with that choice because we believe that it best promotes innovation.[81]

Further, disputes involving fine-tuning can be quite different from cases where the respondent is charged with a clear failure to protect innovative works. The failure to protect intellectual products often results in counterfeiting. In Case I, for example, Patria was countenancing sales of pirated programs. The campaign against counterfeiting was the original incentive

---

[80] *[S]ee also* article 7 of the TRIPS Agreement, which states that the Agreement's objective is to:

> contribute to the promotion of technological innovation and to the transfer and dissemination of technology, to *the mutual advantage of producers and users* of technological knowledge and in a manner conducive to social and economic welfare, and to a *balance* of rights and obligations. (emphasis added).

[81] We note that Judith Bello, *Some Practical Observations About WTO Settlement of Intellectual Property Disputes*, 37 Va. J. Int'l L., suggests that in taking this view, we are "fabricating" rights or "usurp[ing]" the role of negotiators. However, it is evident to us that any definition of an intellectual property right implies some right for users, and that the TRIPS Agreement, like the Berne and Paris Conventions, reflects this perspective.

for the Uruguay Round to become engaged in the field of intellectual property, and so it makes sense to entertain claims that a country is systematically failing to protect subject matter. Of course, to the extent that Case II was decided on the ground of no infringement, there was no counterfeiting. Patria's laws permitted a product very similar to the protected product to go on the market. However, creating that product required considerable investment. Since the Patrian defendants did not get a free ride, it is unlikely that they could price Monastery out of the Patria (or world) market. Indeed, Monastery's product remains attractive to any Sallyheimer sufferer intent on purchasing the "real thing."[84]

Other issues of fine-tuning—for instance the scope of the fair use defense in copyright—call, in our judgment, for a similar approach in the WTO. The United States, for example, permits certain unauthorized uses of copyrighted materials for socially worthy purposes, so long as the "potential market for or value" of the work is not unduly sacrificed. The TRIPS Agreement countenances exceptions to protection, but only for "special cases which do not conflict with a normal exploitation of the work and do not unreasonably prejudice the legitimate interests of the right holder."[86] Whether these provisions are consistent with one another is not at all clear. Yet, it seems to us that panels ought to tread lightly in this area. Indeed, member states ought to resist pressures from their constituents to bring complaints involving such issues to the WTO. The extent to which fair use is considered necessary depends on fundamental national values such as the importance and extent of free speech, on artistic traditions, and on aesthetic sensibilities.[88] Setting a worldwide standard on this issue would, therefore, reduce flexibility and produce a kind of cultural homogenization that might either induce noncompliance or turn the world into a much less stimulating environment.

In the final analysis, the way to handle complaints about fine-tuning may be the same in all cases. There ought to be a presumption that these issues are for individual member states, with intervention by the international

---

[84] If the case were decided by the Patrian court on the ground that Monastery's invention was obvious, then counterfeiting is a possibility. If Xandia can show a persistent unwillingness to recognize any pharmaceutical inventions as inventive enough to merit protection, the case would resemble Case I. If there is no element of persistence, then Patria's decision represents a determination that not much of an investment was needed to create the invention. That determination is some indication that this is not a case where countenancing competitive sales would significantly reduce the incentive to innovate.

[86] TRIPS Agreement art. 13 (with respect to copyright); *id*. art. 30 (with respect to patents).

[88] *See, e.g.*, Marci A. Hamilton, *Art Speech*, 49 VAND. L. REV. 73, 86–96 (1996). Many of these same points can be made with respect to cultural questions raised in the GATT system for the first time by the TRIPS Agreement. For example, may a member state erect a barrier to services when the services in question are performances and the country is concerned that the importing country's culture will drown out its own? May a member state permit unauthorized utilization of trademarks if it believes that trademarks are among the few symbols that many of its citizens can read? May a member give adapters greater leeway with copyrighted works when adaptation is needed to make the works effectively available to the domestic audience? One wonders how these questions would be addressed in the context of membership by China in the WTO, . . .

community only on the basis of a showing of a pattern of discrimination or failure to grant protection without defensible reasons.

NOTES AND QUESTIONS

(1) **Developing Countries.** Developing countries such as Patria in Case II have been given some preferential treatment by way of transitional provisions delaying the application of the TRIPS Agreement. (And the Doha Ministerial Conference further extended some of the deadlines for least-developed countries with respect to obligations regarding pharmaceutical patents.) Moreover, Article 67 of the TRIPS Agreement calls on developed country members, on request and on mutually agreed terms, to lend assistance (meaning both financial and technical) to developing country members. Professor Reichman has argued that "by shifting international intellectual property protection to the framework of multilateral trade negotiations, developed countries have implicitly acknowledged that compensation has become the new master principle." J.H. Reichman, *Universal Minimum Standards of Intellectual Property Protection under the TRIPS Component of the WTO Agreement*, 29 INT. LAW. 345, 384–85 (1995). In particular, Professor Reichman suggests that developing countries under pressure to enact higher standards of protection may present "counterclaims for the higher social costs that such standards would entail." *Id.* What are the costs to which Professor Reichman refers and to what extent would the measures included in TRIPS to assist developing countries affect the viability of such claims?

(2) **Articles 7–8 of TRIPS.** If Patria sought to support its argument of compliance by reference to the purpose of the agreement, in what way could it make use of Article 7 of TRIPS, which provides that the

> protection and enforcement of intellectual property rights should contribute to the promotion of technological innovation and to the transfer and dissemination of technology, to the mutual advantage of producers and users of technological knowledge and in a manner conducive to social and economic welfare, and to a balance of rights and obligations?

Do the arguments for Patria advanced by Dreyfuss and Lowenfeld find support in Article 7? Article 8(1) permits countries to adopt measures to "promote the public interest in sectors of vital importance to their socio-economic and technological development, provided that such measures are consistent with the provisions of this Agreement." To what extent could Patria rely on this provision to support its case? What are the limits of Article 8(1)? If a panel were to adopt a purposive interpretation of the agreement, would the purpose of the GATT/WTO be the relevant purpose? The purpose of TRIPS? *Cf. United States—Import Prohibition of Certain*

Shrimp and Shrimp Products, AB-1998-4, WT/DS58/AB/R (98-3899) (Appellate Body, Oct. 12, 1998) (using "purposes" in manner different from panel). To what extent did the panel in *Canada-Pharmaceutical Patents*, *supra* § 4.04, make use of Articles 7–8 in assessing the Canadian law in question?

(3) **Deference to Member Countries.** Dreyfuss and Lowenfeld conclude that in Case II a panel should display some deference to the ways in which Patria has implemented its TRIPS obligations, but base deference on a different rationale than Case I. What is the range of arguments for a WTO panel to exhibit deference to member countries? Why and in what circumstances do U.S. domestic courts accord deference to actions of administrative or legislative bodies? Are these reasons the same? *See The Review of the WTO's Dispute Settlement Understanding: Which Way?*, 1 J. WORLD INTELL. PROP. 447, 456 (1998) (comments of David Palmeter).

(4) **Fine-Tuning: Exceptions.** Dreyfuss and Lowenfeld characterize Case II as a case involving "fine-tuning." They are surely correct that such cases are particularly apt cases for deference to national determinations. Intellectual property law contains a series of fine-tuning devices; in particular, fine-tuning is often achieved through statutory exceptions to infringement. Is there a danger in articulating a rule of deference in all instances of "fine-tuning"? Certain fine-tuning devices may be subject to more explicit provisions of TRIPS. For example, Article 30 of TRIPS imposes specific constraints on the types of exceptions that can be imposed upon a patent owner's rights. To what extent might the arguments of deference advanced by Dreyfuss and Lowenfeld in discussing Case II between Xandia and Patria have been of assistance to Canada in *Canada-Pharmaceutical Patents*? Did the WTO panel in that case show deference to Canada consistent with the approach suggested by Dreyfuss and Lowenfeld?

DREYFUSS AND LOWENFELD, CASE III: VIOLATION OF ANTITRUST LAWS, PATENT MISUSE, AND COMPULSORY LICENSING *
37 VA. J INT'L L. 275, 307–16

Cases I and II were concerned with the problem of insuring that intellectual property protection does not undermine its own goals by interfering with or unduly raising the costs of innovation. Intellectual property law holds another risk—abuse of the market power created by exclusivity. For example, intellectual property licenses have been used to disguise cartel arrangements, to use power in one market as leverage for dominating another market, and to inhibit the incentive to innovate. Such effects are generally sought to be controlled through the concept of intellectual property misuse and through invocation of competition or antitrust laws. The negotiators of the Uruguay Round did not place competition law on their agenda . . . The TRIPS Agreement does, however, explicitly permit

---

* Copyright 1997, Rochelle Cooper Dreyfuss and Andreas F. Lowenfeld.

members to adopt appropriate measures to control abuse of intellectual property rights,[95] and provides certain guidelines as to the form that these measures might take.[96] Article 40(3) seeks to facilitate the effort to prevent the abuse of intellectual property rights by requiring each member state to consult on request with other members concerning alleged violations of the requesting member's competition law by intellectual property owners domiciled in the requested member state. As in other areas, the TRIPS Agreement lays down a floor; how far states can circumscribe intellectual property rights in the name of furthering competition is not fully delineated.

Case III

Bilker Metals, a Xandian company, is the world's largest producer of molten metals. It holds many important patents on molten metal technology. In 1996, the government of Patria filed a complaint in a Patrian court against Bilker, alleging that certain of its licensing practices limited the worldwide competitive opportunities of Patrian molten metal producers and chilled their incentives to innovate. Specifically, the complaint alleged that Bilker committed a per se violation of Patria's antitrust laws by requiring its licensees to accept licenses of both patents and know-how (a package license) for a period extending beyond the terms of the patents, and to undertake to assign to Bilker rights in any improvements made by the licensee (a grant back-provision). Further, the government of Patria alleged that Bilker was refusing to license the copyrights in its computerized servicing protocols. Because these protocols were the only cost-effective way to service the equipment needed to practice Bilker's inventions, the refusal amounted to a tie-in of equipment, patents, and servicing. If not an antitrust violation, Patria charged, the tie-in was a misuse of Bilker's copyrights that would render them unenforceable in litigation.

Following extensive litigation, the Patrian court entered a decree enjoining Bilker from enforcing its grant-back and package-licensing provisions, and from utilizing its copyrights as servicing restrictions, anywhere in the world. Moreover, Bilker was ordered to grant worldwide licenses to Patrian firms for certain of its patented technologies at a reasonable royalty. After the Patrian court entered its decree, Xandia filed a complaint with the WTO. Under Xandian law, package licensing and grant backs are considered competition problems only when the technology being licensed has no reasonable substitutes and the patentee has substantial market power. Moreover, Xandia does not recognize the concept of copyright misuse; copyright holders are allowed absolute discretion over licensing decisions. Xandia's complaint asserts that the judgment of the Patrian court amounted to a compulsory license that violates article 31 of the TRIPS Agreement concerning the conditions of compulsory licenses, frustrates the objectives of the TRIPS Agreement

---

[95] *See* TRIPS Agreement arts. 8(2), 40(2).

[96] *See, e.g., id.* arts. 31, 40.

set out in article 7, and undermines the principles of article 8(2), which permit only "appropriate measures" to prevent abuse of intellectual property rights.

A. Tensions Between TRIPS, Trade Law, and Antitrust

Case III illustrates the problems we noted in the Introduction concerning the differing goals of trade law and intellectual property law. When competition law is included, the problems become even harder to sort out. On the one hand, the Patrian judgment in Case III could be said to encourage innovation: freed of grant-back obligations, Patrian molten metal producers have the incentive to improve on Bilker's technology. The judgment could also be said to promote trade in that it allows Bilker's competitors to sell molten metals and related technology on a worldwide basis. Moreover, the prohibition against tie-ins and package licensing could further the objective of the TRIPS Agreement to employ technological innovation "in a manner conducive to social and economic welfare," in that it may lower the worldwide cost of using Bilker's technology both during the term that the intellectual property rights are in force and after they expire.

On the other hand, the judgment also might have significant anti-innovation, competition, and welfare consequences. Patria's position on licensing could substantially restrict the manner in which innovators can capture the social benefits bestowed by their innovations, and reduce their capacity to coordinate developments in their fields. To the extent these restraints are imposed as per se rules—with no investigation of their competitive effect and no opportunity for Bilker to justify its practices—they diminish the incentive to innovate without evidence that they enhance competition.

Nor is it necessarily true that the Patrian approach will improve the conditions of trade. Although the judgment frees all Patrian producers to do business all over the world, not every market is large enough and stable enough to attract investors. In less-developed countries, the efficiencies produced by cooperative and coordinated decision making are sometimes needed to pool all the capital and technical capacity that is available. Without violating some of the competition norms of developed nations, these economies may have considerable difficulty in modernizing. Similarly, underdeveloped economies sometimes use the promise of exclusivity to encourage technology transfers; under the Bilker decree, exclusive rights are not available because Bilker is apparently required by the Patrian judgment to license any Patrian firm that asks.[100] Finally, package licenses can be good for poor economies. Sometimes, extending royalty payments beyond the terms of the relevant intellectual property rights functions as

---

[100] We say "apparently" because there is doubt that a Patrian court could order Bilker to give a license for activity in Tertia contrary to the laws of that country. *See, e.g.*, RESTATEMENT (THIRD) OF THE FOREIGN RELATIONS LAW OF THE UNITED STATES § 403(2)(g) and Reporter's Note 3 (1986).

a loan: the initial cost of licensing is lowered because part of the payment is deferred to later years (when the licensee is better able to afford them). As long as there are suitable substitutes for the licensed technology, package licensing can both promote trade and enhance welfare.

Tensions such as these help to explain why the architects of the Uruguay Round did not wade too deeply into the muddy waters of competition law. Appreciating these tensions does not, however, make dispute resolution easier. In this case, developing countries may seek to intervene; consultations among participants might then enable the DSB to find a method for dealing with Bilker's business practices in a manner that optimizes world trade and research in molten metals. Should the parties fail to reach an agreement, however, it is very difficult to see how a panel would go about resolving this dispute.

The only specific guidelines provided by TRIPS are the fourteen conditions that article 31 places on compulsory licensing. Certain of these conditions were met by Patria: the case was considered on an individualized basis, the rights holder was involved, and the disposition was subject to judicial review. [TRIPS, arts. 31(a), (b), (i) and (j)]. However, the scope and duration of the judgment is quite broad and includes conditions that affect rights outside of Patria. Such a disposition is permissible, [TRIPS arts. 31(c), (k)], and the Agreement states that grant-back conditions and coercive package licensing are practices that members may by legislation specify as abusive. [TRIPS art. 40(2)]. It is not clear, however, whether measures to control such practices may be implemented by Patria in the absence of "judicial or administrative process" [TRIPS art. 31(k)] evaluating evidence that the challenged practices actually produced abusive effects.[107] A WTO panel might here look for precedents from GATT dispute settlement practice; but that practice was not uniform, and in any event might not be regarded as applicable.

B. Resolving the Tensions: Some Suggestions

That the intellectual property/competition interface would raise difficult questions was not lost on those who commented on the TRIPS Agreement at the time it went into force. In an early article, our colleague, Professor Eleanor Fox, suggested a way to deal with at least some of the problems that will arise. She noted that, at the time that the TRIPS Agreement came into force, the European Community and the United States took widely divergent positions on this issue. In effect, their laws staked out two ends of a spectrum, with the United States taking the pro-intellectual property side, and the European Community more oriented towards competition.[109]

---

[107] Article 40(2), for example, speaks of "practices or conditions that may *in particular cases constitute* an abuse of intellectual property rights" (emphasis added). *See also id.* art. 31(a), which specifies that compulsory licenses cannot be authorized without considering the individual merits of the situation; *cf.* Ernst-Ulrich Petersmann, *International Competition Rules for the GATT-MTO World Trade and Legal System*, J. WORLD TRADE, Dec. 1993, at 35, 59 (1993), who interprets this clause to require case-by-case analysis.

[109] *See* [Eleanor M. Fox, *Trade, Competition and Intellectual Property—TRIPS and its Anti-*

She then suggested a principle of preference whereby any antitrust enforcement action by a member state that fell within this spectrum should be considered presumptively valid under the TRIPS Agreement.

It seems to us that such an approach could run counter to the consensus that emerged from the Uruguay Round, where member states agreed to uphold minimum standards of intellectual property law, but did not make substantive decisions regarding competition law: such disparate treatment could be interpreted to mean that in close cases, innovation policy must trump competition policy in all member states. Thus, we do not believe that a principle of deference to U.S. or European Community competition law (or something in between) should be read into the TRIPS Agreement. We do, however, think that Professor Fox offers an attractive approach for interpreting what the minimum standards of the TRIPS Agreement mean by abuse. Thus we would accept her suggestion to compare Patria's law and implementing decree with the laws of the European Community and the United States: if Patria's measures are consistent with those laws (particularly if the practice challenged by Bilker would violate the law of both jurisdictions and the remedy imposed by Patria would be consistent with both their laws), they should be upheld by a WTO panel unless expressly prohibited by the TRIPS Agreement. However, if, for instance, Patria required Bilker to issue a compulsory royalty-free license for its patented products, such an order would be inconsistent with article 31(h) of the TRIPS Agreement, regardless of U.S. or European Community law, and a challenge to the order by Xandia should be upheld by the DSU panel.[111]

Nor does Professor Fox purport to address all of the problems raised by cases such as Case III. She does not provide a method for considering measures that fall outside the EC/U.S. competition-law spectrum. Such situations are easy to imagine. The competition law of the United States and the European Community may well not be appropriate for developing countries and member states in transition to market economies. States that, prior to TRIPS, lacked intellectual property protection did not have rights that could be abused, nonmarket economies had no need for antitrust laws,

---

trust Counterparts, 29 VAND. J. TRANS. L. 481, 487–88 (1996)], who cites as examples the questions whether patentees may charge excessive prices, refuse all licensees, divide territories, or require grantbacks from licensees—all issues that had arisen in both the United States and the European Community at the time the TRIPS Agreement entered into force. All the cited practices appear to be valid under U.S. law, but to violate EC law.

[111] Article 31 of the TRIPS Agreement provides:

Where the law of a Member allows for other use of the subject matter of a patent without the authorization of the right holder, . . . the following provisions shall be respected:

. . . .

(h) the right holder shall be paid adequate remuneration in the circumstances of each case, taking into account the economic value of the authorization[.]

Under paragraph (k), some other conditions are not obligatory when a compulsory license is imposed to remedy a practice determined after judicial or administrative process to be anticompetitive. Paragraph (h) is not among the conditions that may be avoided in such case.

and many developing countries still have not reached a stage where competition policy is of major concern. Once such countries begin to implement their obligations under the TRIPS Agreement by enacting intellectual property law, antitrust rules are likely to follow. However, it is not necessarily the case that any of the antitrust regimes extant at the time of the Uruguay Round will meet their needs. As we have noted, some countries may consider themselves better off sacrificing a little competition in order to attract investment in infrastructure. Conversely, a country that is trying to find technological opportunities for an emerging work force may be justified in being less tolerant of tie-ins that limit the growth of niche industries such as servicing. Even if competition law does not become a major item on the agenda of the WTO, we conclude that the relation between competition law and intellectual property law merits further study, possibly in connection with the review of the TRIPS Agreement that is due in five years' time. We would not expect this rethinking to take place in the course of a dispute settlement proceeding.

C. Deciding Case III

How, then, after this lengthy excursion, should a dispute panel decide whether the disposition by the Patrian court in the Bilker case is consistent with the TRIPS Agreement? Given the lack of consensus on the correct balance between antitrust and intellectual property law, and given what we said in connection with Case II about not second-guessing domestic decisions regarding fine-tuning, it is tempting to start with a presumption that Patria's decision in Bilker should be sustained. Indeed, the approach of article 31 of the TRIPS Agreement is to defer to the decisions of competent national authorities. There are problems with a presumption of deference, however. Competition cases are likely to have more of an impact on rights holders than the sorts of questions raised in connection with Case II. In contrast to fine-tuning mechanisms, the decision to hold an intellectual property right unenforceable permits wholesale copying. In Case III, for example, the judgment of the Patrian court would permit anyone wishing to enter the service business to copy Bilker's servicing protocol programs; in other cases, the decision to hold a patent right unenforceable would allow anyone to enter into competition with the patentee. Indeed, such a decision may allow a product to be sold in any country that has a worldwide exhaustion doctrine.[113] Deciding the issue simply on the basis of deference to national law therefore seems inappropriate.

One approach to evaluating the validity of the decree would be for the dispute panel to examine the extent to which the Patrian court inquired

---

[113] As pointed out in note 12, article 6 of the TRIPS Agreement specifically provides that the Agreement should not be interpreted to address the issue of exhaustion. Usually, exhaustion is found when the product is sold under the authority of the intellectual property holder. Thus, whether the statement in the text is true in a given country will depend on whether the sale of a product in a country that refuses to enforce the intellectual property right is deemed to be a sale under the rights holder's 'authority.'

into the facts of the case and then to examine whether the court analyzed these facts in a manner that would plausibly identify practices abusive to its economy. If the court has acted on the sort of facts that, say, the U.S. Justice Department uses when it proposes a consent decree, then, subject to two caveats, its actions should be considered valid. The first caveat concerns the impact of a decree on countries of very different economic development from the one that issued the decree. . . [T]he panel should supplement Patria's fact-finding with information about the effect of the decree on different economies. Deference would be accorded to Patria's decision only to the extent that its decree affects the economies of states similarly situated to Patria.

The second caveat concerns Patria's per se rules regarding package licensing and tie-ins. It is not clear that the TRIPS Agreement tolerates broad orders based on per se views of particular licensing practices, that is, practices regarded as so bad (such as price-fixing, for instance) that inquiry into the reason for the practice is neither required nor permitted. Per se judgments are not necessarily alien to WTO dispute settlement: Article 3.8 of the Understanding on Dispute Settlement states that when there is an infringement by a member state of the obligations assumed under a covered agreement, the action is considered prima facie to constitute nullification or impairment. But Case III involves only a charge of violation by a Xandian company of the law of Patria, and a response that the challenged conduct is protected by the TRIPS Agreement or that the remedy imposed by Patria exceeds what is permissible under that Agreement.

It seems to us that before pronouncing on Case III, the panel should afford both sides the opportunity to present facts and economic analysis. If this is sound, Bilker ought to have the opportunity to defend its practices in the Patrian court, and to contend to that court that the TRIPS Agreement protects its practices or limits the remedies that may be imposed by Patria. If Bilker has not previously been given such opportunity, the panel should rule that Patria has not complied with the TRIPS Agreement, and should recommend that the case be reopened in that country.

NOTES AND QUESTIONS

(1) **Judicial Analysis of Competition Law**. Dreyfuss and Lowenfeld conclude that "the relation between competition law and intellectual property law merits further study, [but we] would not expect this rethinking to take place in the course of a dispute settlement proceeding." Why not? Patent and copyright misuse doctrines were developed by U.S. courts to mediate the abuse of intellectual property rights. Aside from the language of Article 3(2) of the DSU (and is that more of a constraint here than elsewhere?) are there institutional considerations that might make it

inappropriate for WTO panels to engage in "lawmaking" in the way that we might expect of domestic courts?

(2) **(Non-Intellectual Property) Sources of Guidance.** Where should a panel look when the topic before them has only rarely (if ever) been addressed by the sources that we considered in our analysis of Case I? Is the extent of reference to national competition approaches suggested by Professor Fox appropriate? Should panels be able to look to broader international law principles (for example, in bilateral or multilateral competition law agreements)? By doing so, are panels exceeding their jurisdiction? Remember that competition law is not covered by the GATT. If the panel could apply only "WTO law," what does that say about the value of the panels as a mechanism of international relations? Is it possible for them to decide intellectual property disputes under TRIPS without looking beyond TRIPS? What are the consequences of broadening the perspective of panel members? What are the consequences of confining their perspective? How would you respond to an argument by Patria that it was complying with provisions of a multinational or bilateral competition law agreement? What would be the appropriate forum to litigate an issue if provisions of other agreements were raised by the parties? The International Court of Justice? Could those fora address WTO-related issues? *See* DSU art. 23. *Compare* Joel P. Trachtman, *The Domain of WTO Dispute Resolution*, 40 HARV. INT'L L.J. 333, 342–44 (1999)(discussing scope of reference to non-WTO international law), *with* David Palmeter & Petros C. Mavroidis, *The WTO Legal System: Sources of Law*, 92 AM. J. INT'L L. 398, 399 (1998) and Thomas J. Schoenbaum, *WTO Dispute Settlement: Praise and Suggestions for Reform*, 47 INT'L & COMP. L.Q. 647, 653 (1998). What if two or more countries established a supranational panel to adjudicate competition law issues? *Cf.* BRIAN F. HAVEL, IN SEARCH OF OPEN SKIES: LAW AND POLICY FOR A NEW ERA IN INTERNATIONAL AVIATION (1997) (proposing such a body for international airline competition relations). Should the WTO panel stay the case before it?

(3) **Revisiting Deference.** Why are Dreyfuss and Lowenfeld apparently less reluctant to show deference to Patria here? Can their reasoning be reconciled with the approach to deference shown in Cases I and II? Does a less deferential attitude to Patria's activity trouble you where the issue before the panel was one on which there was minimal guidance in TRIPS?

[C]   The Appellate Body

DREYFUSS AND LOWENFELD, CASE IV:
THE APPELLATE PROCESS *
37 VA. J. INT'L L. 275, 316–24

One of the major innovations in the Uruguay Round was agreement that decisions of dispute panels were to be treated like judgments—that is, that

---

they could not be blocked by the losing party or even by a majority vote of the membership of the WTO. Once that decision had been taken, it became necessary to provide for some type of review, both to correct errors that might be made by an ad hoc panel and to give participants dissatisfied with the outcome a second chance to be heard. The solution, in keeping with the preference for the judicial over the diplomatic model for dispute settlement, was creation of a standing Appellate Body, made up of seven persons drawn from different constituencies included in the WTO.[114] The Appellate Body is supposed to complete its work in sixty days from the date of the appeal (ninety days for exceptionally difficult cases), and appeals are to be "limited to issues of law covered in the panel report and legal interpretations developed by the panel." [DSU arts. 17.7, 17.6.]

Distinguishing legal from factual questions for purposes of jurisdiction is, of course, a common problem in all legal systems. The fact/law distinction is particularly troublesome in the context of patent controversies, where resolution of issues of novelty, prior art, and scope of inventions is dependent both on determinations of fact and on interpretation of imprecise legal standards. For our purposes, however, we illustrate the problem in an apparently easier context—concerning the right to register a trademark.

Case IV

Koka Kola, Ltd., a Xandian company, has registered its mark, KOKA KOLA, for carbonated beverages (soda pop) in Xandia and in most of the world. As a result of Koka Kola's sponsorship of every Olympic Games since World War II, it had every reason to believe that the mark was familiar everywhere. Nonetheless, when it sought registration in Patria, its application was denied, on the ground that the same mark had recently been registered by a Patrian who was in the process of starting a company to manufacture and distribute his version of Koka Kola soda pop. When Koka Kola was unsuccessful in having the other registration canceled, it persuaded the government of Xandia to bring a complaint in the WTO.

According to Xandia's complaint, Koka Kola is a well-known mark for soda pop and Patria's refusal to register it violated article 16(2) of the TRIPS Agreement. A dispute panel was convened. Xandia submitted consumer surveys showing that substantial numbers of Patrian soda pop consumers recognized the mark and that an even higher percentage of consumers in larger markets recognized it. Upon consideration of these surveys and after seeing evidence that since 1980, all telecasts of the Olympic Games could be received on television sets in Patria, the panel determined that the mark was well-enough-known within the meaning

---

114 *See* DSU arts. 17 & 18. . . Members of the Appellate Body are elected for four-year terms and may be reelected once, except that three of the members first appointed, selected by lot, will have an initial term of two years, so that the entire membership will never be changed over at once. Any given appeal is heard by three of the seven members of the Appellate Body serving in rotation, without reference to their nationality.

of the TRIPS Agreement to qualify for the special protection offered by TRIPS article 16(2). Patria appeals to the Appellate Body, pursuant to article 16 of the DSU.

A. Jurisdiction to Hear the Appeal: The Fact/Law Distinction

Xandia might well contend that there is only one issue in this case—whether the Koka Kola mark for soda pop is well-known—and that any lay person would say that this is a question of fact. Thus, Xandia could argue that there is no basis for reviewing the panel report in the Appellate Body. Or, more subtly, Xandia might argue that given the relationship between the resolution of the appeal and the application of article 16(2) of the TRIPS Agreement, the issue sought to be put before the Appellate Body is a mixed question of law and fact, and that resolution of mixed questions is also beyond the mandate of the Appellate Body.

It is important to recognize in this context that the fact/law distinction is jurisdictional. Whether the Appellate Body may hear the appeal depends on an interpretation of the Understanding on Dispute Settlement and the covered Agreement in question, and cannot be decided according to the law of any particular member state. Given the reasons for creation of the Appellate Body and the limited time available for completion of its assignment, our view is that respondent parties in the appeal process—typically (as in Case IV) the party that prevailed before the panel—should be discouraged from raising challenges to the jurisdiction of the Appellate Body; further, if such a challenge is raised, the Appellate Body should be very reluctant to dismiss an appeal over an issue of jurisdiction. Findings of particular facts made by the panel can be accepted. For instance, in Case IV the Appellate Body need not make an independent inquiry into the broadcast history of the Olympic Games or their reception in Patria. It can satisfy itself that the information submitted to the Panel was reliable, or, if differing information was submitted, that the panel made a rational choice as to which version to accept. But as to the ultimate issue—whether Patria complied with the criterion in the TRIPS Agreement regarding knowledge of the mark in the relevant sector of the public—the Appellate Body should make its own decision, free, we would urge, from any debate about whether the decision is based on "fact" or on "law."

[In Case IV] . . . , if the Appellate Body declined to take jurisdiction of the appeal, it would, in effect, exclude itself from participating in the elucidation of one of the most important provisions in the TRIPS Agreement—the provision that enables producers to develop and maintain a worldwide marketing strategy without fear of "trademark pirates" to hold them up. If a panel can address the issue, it must be that the Appellate Body can and should do so as well.

It is instructive in this context to contrast the TRIPS Agreement with the Agreement on Dumping and Antidumping Measures,[119] also concluded

---

[119] The formal name of this Agreement . . . is the Agreement on Implementation of Article VI of the General Agreement on Tariffs and Trade 1994, Apr. 15, 1994, WTO Agreement, Annex 1A.

as an obligatory part of the Uruguay Round package [and subject to WTO dispute settlement review. Under article 17.6 of the Antidumping Agreement, however, if the panel finds that (i) the establishment of the facts by the national authority of the importing country that has imposed antidumping duties on the product of another country was proper, and the evaluation was unbiased and objective, then that evaluation shall not be overturned by the panel even if it would have reached a different conclusion, and (ii) a relevant provision of the Agreement admits of more than one permissible interpretation, the panel shall find the authorities' measure to be in conformity with the Agreement if it rests upon one of those permissible interpretations.]

This provision was inserted upon the insistence of the United States, which feared that international panels unsympathetic to the provisions on dumping generally and in particular to the hard-to-confirm findings on causation of injury might hold antidumping measures ordered by the U.S. Department of Commerce and the U.S. International Trade Commission to be inconsistent with the international understanding.[120] The last-minute solution, for what the United States delegates said was a "deal breaker," was to accord an extra degree of deference to national authorities—for dumping cases only. If Patria considers that a panel convened to review its antidumping measure has exceeded the limitations of article 17.6, such a contention could, it seems clear, be made the subject of an appeal to the Appellate Body. The Appellate Body would not be authorized to examine the underlying issues of price comparison and causation of injury (the "fact issues"), but would be limited to determining whether or not the panel had exceeded the limitations imposed by article 17.6.

No provision comparable to article 17.6 of the Antidumping Agreement appears in the TRIPS Agreement,[121] and we believe that none should be read into it either by panels or by the Appellate Body, in the guise of making rulings on "jurisdiction" or distinguishing "fact" from "law." The ultimate issue—whether denominated "fact," "law," or "mixed,"—should be considered (if a party so desires) at two levels, first by the ad hoc panel that assembles the record, hears the parties, and makes an initial determination, and second by the standing Appellate Body, that considers, for instance, how the Koka Kola case fits in with other intellectual property cases and with the jurisprudence of the GATT/WTO system generally.

---

[120] A pattern along these lines had developed in cases brought under chapter 19 of the Canada-United States Free Trade Agreement, cheered by some but condemned by others. For an early account, see Andreas F. Lowenfeld, *Binational Dispute Settlement Under Chapter 19 of the Canada-United States Free Trade Agreement: An Interim Appraisal*, 24 N.Y.U. J. INTL L. & POL. 269 (1991).

[121] Indeed, it is reported that when the suggestion was made that a single (deferential) standard should be made applicable to all WTO panels reviewing national administrative decisions, the proposal was "greeted with fury" by U.S. intellectual property interests, which did not wish to give to other countries' patent and copyright authorities the deference which the U.S. Trade Representative sought for American antidumping decisions. See Gary N. Horlick & Eleanor C. Shea, *The World Trade Organization Antidumping Agreement*, J. WORLD TRADE, Feb. 1995, at 5, 31.

B. The Role of the Appellate Body

The problems in Case IV—which seemed to be the easy case—do not quite disappear even after the decision is made to consider the ultimate issue one of law. TRIPS article 16(2) calls for inquiry into "the knowledge of the trademark in the relevant sector of the public, including knowledge in the Member concerned which has been obtained as a result of the promotion of the trademark." Here, then, are several sub-issues: How much knowledge is necessary for the mark to be considered well known: must a majority of the relevant public recognize it, or is a substantial minority enough? What is the relevant sector: soda pop drinkers or all beverage consumers? What is considered promotion of the trademark in the member state: is Koka Kola considered to have promoted the mark in Patria by reason of buying air time on an event that could be picked up on television receivers in Patria, or must it have advertised on actual local broadcasts? Even after it is determined that the ultimate issue—the strength of the mark—is a question of law, the issue of characterizing these penultimate questions remains.

Once again, the line between fact and law can only be drawn by reference to the underlying principles to which the adjudicatory system is dedicated, that is, by considering why line drawing is needed under the circumstances. For example, in domestic intellectual property cases in the United States, controversies, such as over the strength of a trademark, that require resolution of a series of penultimate questions are often handled by considering those questions to be ones of fact and the ultimate question one of law. In this way, the opportunity to appeal the outcome of the controversy is preserved, yet the litigants' respect for the trial court as the primary forum for dispute resolution is maintained.[122]

Such allocation of authority may, however, not be generally suitable to disputes under the TRIPS Agreement, where the policy interests can be very different. Dispute panels are chosen in a manner designed to promote considerable respect from the parties. Panel members are selected by the Director General of the WTO, in consultation with the Chairman and counsel of the DSB, from a roster of persons who have served in their own governments, often as judges, or in other capacities in the GATT. [DSU art. 8]. Some are academic experts in the issues raised by the dispute. However, because the panels are chosen for a particular case, there is no assurance that members of a panel will have the same commitment to long-term consistency that is expected from the members of the Appellate Body.[124] Accordingly, one might conclude that less deference is owed to panel decisions than is accorded to court decisions in the United States.

---

[122] *See, e.g.*, Graham v. John Deere Co., 383 U.S. 1 (1966), where the Court held that in a patent case the ultimate issue of nonobviousness consists of four questions: What is in the prior art?; What is the difference between the applicant's invention and the prior art?; What does a person with ordinary skill in the art know?; Could such a person fill the gap? The first three are issues of fact, the last is deemed to be an issue of law.

[124] In the past, the Secretariat has endeavored to fill the role of supplying the sense of continuity, and it may be expected to continue to do so in the future.

On the other hand, at least one, and possibly all members of a panel in a dispute focused on the TRIPS Agreement may be expected to be experts in intellectual property, whereas it is highly unlikely that any member of the Appellate Body possesses comparable knowledge or experience.[125] Thus, it may well be desirable for the Appellate Body to give greater deference to legal decisions of a panel in intellectual property disputes than it would in disputes about, say, export subsidies or import safeguards—and also more deference than a national appellate court would give to a trial court. Indeed, the role of the Appellate Body, as we see it, is not primarily to articulate intellectual property norms in the international economy, but to oversee the work of dispute panels with an eye to the general principles of open markets and nondiscrimination embodied in the GATT/WTO system. In fact, as noted earlier, it is the Council for TRIPS that is charged with monitoring the operation of the Agreement and cooperating with WIPO in setting international norms. The Appellate Body, then, is not the only, or even necessarily the best, source of authoritative articulation of intellectual property norms.

We do suggest, however, that where system-wide rules are desirable, the provision in the DSU concerning "issues of law" should receive broad scope when applied to the TRIPS Agreement; where it is permissible for members to maintain legal regimes that differ from one another, the need for uniform interpretation of the TRIPS Agreement by the Appellate Body is less compelling, and it is "questions of fact" that should be interpreted generously.

As the TRIPS Agreement is written, members have considerable discretion to maintain their own intellectual property regimes. Article 1(1) provides:

> . . . Members *may, but shall not be obliged to*, implement in their law more extensive protection than is required by this Agreement, provided that such protection does not contravene the provisions of this Agreement. *Members shall be free to determine the appropriate method* of implementing the provisions of this Agreement within their own legal system and practice. (emphasis added)

Thus, where the panel has deferred to the respondent state's national authorities, the inclination (not to say presumption) of the Appellate Body ought to be to defer as well. In contrast, a contention by Patria that a panel has acted inconsistently with article 1 in ruling against a practice that does not clearly violate the TRIPS Agreement should be heard and determined by the Appellate Body. In such cases, the proper role for the Appellate Body is to monitor whether panels have been too interventionist, a question of judgment that does not fit easily into the "law" or "fact" classification.

---

[125] Of the first seven members of the Appellate Body, two are (or were) professors of law (but not intellectual property law), one was a justice of his country's Supreme Court, two were career diplomats, one was a professor of economics, and one (the U.S. member) is a practicing attorney and former member of Congress.

One might be tempted to conclude from this discussion that the Appellate Body needs wide authority only in disputes such as those illustrated by Case I, where the question was what the minimum standards require. A review of our other cases demonstrates that this is only sometimes true. It may be true for cases in the category of Case II, where the differing circumstances of member states require that they be allowed to make differing adjustments between the rights of innovation producers and innovation users. The application of the doctrine of equivalents in patent law, for example, should probably be left to interpretation by each member state, subject to intervention by the WTO only upon a showing of discrimination. But the fact that member states have discretion under the TRIPS Agreement to implement their own legal regimes is not necessarily conclusive of the proper role of the WTO panel or the Appellate Body. For instance, Case III, the antitrust case, raised the question of the permissible extraterritorial effect of decisions of a national authority. On that issue, as in Case IV, neither the panel nor the Appellate Authority should defer to the national authority. It is up to the international authority to step in, to declare, for example, whether it is permissible for member states to order worldwide relief for antitrust violations or intellectual property misuse, and if so, whether they may do so on the basis of per se rules, without permitting justification through market-by-market analysis. Furthermore, if the Appellate Body determines that per se rules are objectionable, it will need to have a role in deciding such fact-sounding issues as when an entity occupies a "dominant position," when a technology has suitable substitutes, and how to define separate markets.

In the end, we can offer only discussion of the problem, not hard rules. The Appellate Body is not a Supreme Court, but part of a process not yet tested, which will include the evolution of norm-setting in WIPO, the activity of the Council on TRIPS, and the progress made among the parties in developing a shared understanding of the not always consistent values of intellectual property and competition.

UNITED STATES—SECTION 211 OMNIBUS APPROPRIATIONS ACT OF 1998 ("HAVANA CLUB")
Report of the Appellate Body, WT/DS176/AB/R (WTO 2002)

[The European Communities and the United States appealed from certain issues of law and legal interpretations in the Panel Report, *United States—Section 211 Omnibus Appropriations Act of 1998* (the "Panel Report"). The text and explanation of the challenged measure, Section 211 of the United States Omnibus Appropriations Act of 1998 ("Section 211"), and the relevant Cuban Assets Control Regulations (the "CACR"), which are administered by the Office of Foreign Assets Control ("OFAC"), are set out in the excerpt *supra* § 2.06.]

IV. Preliminary Matters

A. The Scope of Appellate Review

We begin by addressing a preliminary question that is central to our disposition of the specific issues raised in this appeal. This question is the scope of appellate review in this appeal.

With respect to the scope of appellate review, the United States argues that we are bound on appeal by the Panel's conclusions about the meaning of the measure at issue. The United States submits that a panel's review of a Member's domestic law is, in any dispute, a question of fact, and that, therefore, the European Communities' allegations, in this dispute, about the Panel's appreciation of the meaning of the terms of Section 211 are questions of fact. The United States points to our mandate under Article 17.6 of the [Dispute Settlement Understanding (DSU)], which limits appeals to "issues of law covered in the panel report and legal interpretations developed by the panel.". . . . The United States reminds us as well of Article 11 of the DSU, which obliges a panel to "make an objective assessment of the matter before it, including an objective assessment of the facts of the case". Although the United States acknowledges that the question whether a panel has made such an objective assessment of the facts is indeed a legal question, the United States insists that, for such a question to fall within the scope of appellate review, it must be properly raised on appeal. The United States emphasizes that the European Communities has not made a claim under Article 11 of the DSU in this appeal. From this, the United States concludes that the findings of the Panel on the meaning of Section 211 are not within the scope of this appeal.

The European Communities argues that we are in no way bound on appeal by the Panel's characterization of the meaning of Section 211. The European Communities sees this as a "question of law" that is fully within the scope of appellate review under the DSU. The European Communities contends that the findings of the Panel in relation to Section 211 are based, *inter alia*, on an erroneous reading of Section 211 itself. The European Communities argues further that these erroneous findings are based on erroneous interpretations of the relevant provisions of the *TRIPS Agreement* and of the relevant provisions of the Paris Convention (1967) that have been incorporated by reference into the *TRIPS Agreement*. The European Communities insists that the Appellate Body is empowered to review the result of a panel's examination of a WTO Member's domestic law for the purpose of ascertaining its consistency with the [WTO Agreement]. At the oral hearing, the European Communities explained that understanding what is the measure that is the subject of the dispute is a question of law and, if the subject of a dispute is simply a provision of a domestic law which is being attacked as such, then understanding that measure correctly is a question of law.

In addressing the scope of appellate review in this case, we begin by recalling our ruling in [EC Measures Concerning Meat and Meat products (Hormones) (Appellate Body 1998)] (*EC—Hormones*) that:

The consistency or inconsistency of a given fact or set of facts with the requirements of a given treaty provision is . . . a legal characterization issue. It is a legal question.

We believe that our ruling in *India—Patent Protection for Pharmaceutical and Agricultural Chemical Products* ("*India—Patents (US)*") is of even greater relevance. We stated there, in relevant part, that:

> In public international law, an international tribunal may treat municipal law in several ways. Municipal law may serve as evidence of facts and may provide evidence of state practice. However, municipal law may also constitute evidence of compliance or noncompliance with international obligations. . . . (footnote omitted)

> It is clear that an examination of the relevant aspects of Indian municipal law and, in particular, the relevant provisions of the Patents Act as they relate to the "administrative instructions", is essential to determining whether India has complied with its obligations under Article 70.8(a). There was simply no way for the Panel to make this determination without engaging in an examination of Indian law. But, as in the case cited above before the Permanent Court of International Justice, in this case, the Panel was not interpreting Indian law "as such"; rather, the Panel was examining Indian law solely for the purpose of determining whether India had met its obligations under the *TRIPS Agreement*. . . .

> And, just as it was necessary for the Panel in this case to seek a detailed understanding of the operation of the Patents Act as it relates to the "administrative instructions" in order to assess whether India had complied with Article 70.8(a), *so, too, it is necessary for us in this appeal to review the Panel's examination of the same Indian domestic law*. (emphasis added)

Our rulings in these previous appeals are clear: the municipal law of WTO Members may serve not only as evidence of facts, but also as evidence of compliance or non-compliance with international obligations. Under the DSU, a panel may examine the municipal law of a WTO Member for the purpose of determining whether that Member has complied with its obligations under the *WTO Agreement*. Such an assessment is a legal characterization by a panel. And, therefore, a panel's assessment of municipal law as to its consistency with WTO obligations is subject to appellate review under Article 17.6 of the DSU.

To address the legal issues raised in this appeal, we must, therefore, necessarily examine the Panel's interpretation of the meaning of Section 211 under United States law. An assessment of the consistency of Section 211 with the Articles of the *TRIPS Agreement* and of the Paris Convention (1967) that have been invoked by the European Communities necessarily requires a review of the Panel's examination of the meaning of Section 211. Likewise, that assessment necessarily requires a review also of the Panel's examination of the meaning of both the CACR and the Lanham Act, to the extent that they are relevant for assessing the meaning of Section 211. This is an interpretation of the meaning of Section 211 solely for the purpose of determining whether the United States has fulfilled its obligations under the *TRIPS Agreement*. The meaning given by the Panel to Section 211 is, thus, clearly within the scope of our review as set out in Article 17.6 of the DSU.

. . . .

XI. Article 8 of the Paris Convention (1967)—Trade Names

[The Appellate Body reversed the Panel's finding that trade names are not covered under the TRIPS Agreement and found that WTO Members do have an obligation under the TRIPS Agreement to provide protection to trade names.]

Having reversed the Panel's finding, we consider next whether we should complete the legal analysis with respect to the application of Section 211 to trade names and to the consistency of Section 211 with Article 2.1 of the TRIPS Agreement in conjunction with Article 8 of the Paris Convention (1967), with Article 2.1 of the TRIPS Agreement in conjunction with Article 2(1) of the Paris Convention (1967) and Article 3.1 of the TRIPS Agreement, with Article 4 of the TRIPS Agreement, and with Article 42 of the TRIPS Agreement.

In the past, we have completed the analysis where there were sufficient factual findings in the panel report or undisputed facts in the panel record to enable us to do so and we have not completed the analysis where there were not. In one instance, we declined to complete the analysis with respect to a "novel" issue that had not been argued in sufficient detail before the panel.

In this appeal, the European Communities argues that we should complete the analysis, while the United States contends that we should not do so because, in its view, there are insufficient factual findings by the Panel about trade name protection under United States law for us to do so. . . .

We believe that there are sufficient undisputed facts in the Panel record regarding trade name protection to enable us to complete the analysis . . .

. . . .

On the basis of:

    *   the fact that Sections 211(a)(2) and (b) do not distinguish on their face between trade marks and trade names;

    *   the participants' approach in submitting the same arguments and using the same analyses regarding trade name and trademark protection, suggesting that the obligations regarding protection of one are no different from those regarding protection of the other;

    *   the information in the Panel record about the participants' interpretation of Article 8 of the Paris Convention (1967); and

    *   the information in the Panel record about trade name protection under United States law;

we conclude that the Panel record contains sufficient factual findings and facts undisputed between the participants to permit us to complete the analysis. . . .

  . . . .

NOTES AND QUESTIONS

(1) **Composition of Panels and the Appellate Body.** The creation of the Appellate Body was intended not only as a check on panel decisions but also, by virtue of its standing nature, to bring some consistency and uniformity to the development of WTO law. At present, the three members of the Appellate Body who hear a case have been chosen without regard for whether a member is from a country appearing before the body. Thus, American nationals on the Appellate Body have sat on cases involving the United States. This contrasts with the panel stage of the proceedings, where nationals of participating countries generally do not sit. *See* DSU art. 8(3) (nationals of parties should not be appointed to a panel unless the parties agree); *cf. id.* art. 8(10) (allowing developing countries litigating against a developed country to request that at least one of the panelists before whom they appear will be from a developing country). What effect might the recusal of nationals on panels have on the development of WTO law? The EU has proposed that the panel composition be determined like the Appellate Body. Would you support such a change? *See The WTO Appellate Body: The First Four Years,* 1 J. WORLD INTELL. PROP. 425, 428 (1998) (comments of Edwin Vermulst). Or should the practices of the Appellate Body composition be conformed to those used in composing the members of the panel? *See id.* at 431 (comments of Guiguo Wang). One commentator has suggested that the question of balance transcends nationality, and that the panels evince a distinctly Western cultural approach to law. *See id.* (comments of Jacques Bourgeois). How might that be avoided? Can it be avoided?

The EU has also proposed that the ad hoc panels be replaced by a standing body, not unlike the Appellate Body, comprised of between 15–24 members. On the basis of a rotation mechanism, the Panel Body would itself form a chamber of three to deal with each new case as it arose. *See* Kim Van der Borght, *The Review of the WTO Understanding on Dispute Settlement: Some Reflections on the Current Debate,* 14 AM. U. INT'L L. REV. 1223, 1240 (1999) (quoting EU proposal). What are the advantages of each approach? *See The Review of the WTO's Dispute Settlement Understanding: Which Way?,* 1 J. WORLD INTELL. PROP. 447, 449 (1998) (comments of Prof. Brigitte Stern); *id.* at 460 (comments of John Kingery) (describing such a

change as a "major step" that would "change the nature of dispute settlement quite a bit"); *id.* at 468–69 (comments of Geoffrey Hartwell).
Jayashree Watal has commented that "the WTO is so political that it is
not possible for the Appellate Body . . . to be really too activist . . . without
facing criticism from the members. In this sense, the WTO is very different
from any other international organization in the field of public international
law." *The WTO Appellate Body: The First Four Years, supra,* at 436. In what
way is the WTO "so political"? Would a change to a standing body of
panelists reduce or increase the political nature of the process?

(2) **Remand Authority**. Dreyfuss and Lowenfeld suggested above that
in order to decide Case III, the panel might have to supplement Patria's
fact-finding with information about the effect of the decree on different
economies. If the panel failed to engage in that fact-finding, and the Appellate Body finds those facts necessary as a matter of law to decide whether
the Patrian court's order complies with TRIPS, what should the Appellate
Body do? The DSU failed to provide the Appellate Body with the right to
remand the case to the panel. *See* David Palmeter, *National Sovereignty
and the World Trade Organization,* 2 J. WORLD INTELL. PROP. 77, 85 (1999).
Absent such a right, what options does the Appellate Body have? *See* United
States—Import Prohibition of Certain Shrimp and Shrimp Products, AB-
1998-4, WT/DS58/AB/R (98-3899) ¶ 123 (Appellate Body, Oct. 12, 1998).
Can the Appellate Body simply declare that it is remanding a case even
absent express authority in the DSU? If you were a member of the Appellate
Body would you vote to create a remand power judicially? What other
procedural or institutional changes would be required for a remand procedure to work? *See The Review of the WTO's Dispute Settlement Understanding: Which Way?, supra* at 454 (comments of Thomas Cottier).

(3) **The Fact/Law Distinction**. Does the Dreyfuss-Lowenfeld suggestion
on how to interpret the law/fact distinction—with an eye to the proper role
of the Appellate Body—contain a substantive bias? Is it one that is
appropriate? In what way (if any) are the circumstances in which, or
reasons for which, Dreyfuss and Lowenfeld might encourage the Appellate
Body to defer to the panel the same as those that they invoked in support
of panel deference to member countries?

In *India—Patent Protection for Pharmaceutical and Agricultural Chemical Products,* Panel Report, WT/DS50/R (WTO Panel, Sept. 5, 1997), *aff'd,*
WT/DS50/AB/R (WTO App. Body, Dec. 19, 1997) [hereinafter *United States-
India*], India sought to make use of the fact/law distinction before the panel
(and the Appellate Body) but in a much more traditional manner, quite
different from the use of that distinction envisaged by Dreyfuss and
Lowenfeld. India sought to classify Indian law as a question of fact in order
to oblige the United States to prove Indian law as part of its case. *Cf. Walton
v. Arabian Am. Oil Co.,* 233 F.2d 541 (2d Cir. 1956) (traditional approach
to proving foreign law in private litigation in U.S. courts). Are India's arguments persuasive? In what ways could the panel have "sought guidance
from India on matters relating to the interpretation of Indian law" as India

alternatively suggested? *See United States-India*, Appellate Body Report, ¶ 64.

(4) **Deciding Case IV.** If the Appellate Body were to decide Case IV, how would it determine the meaning of "well-known mark" in Article 16 of TRIPS? To what extent should a panel determining Patria's compliance with Article 16 look to the non-binding resolution on the protection of well known marks adopted by the joint meeting of the General Assembly of WIPO and the Assembly of the Paris Union in September 1999? (At the September 1999 Assembly, Asian and African nations insisted on the removal of references in the preamble to TRIPS, arguing that such a reference may cause WTO dispute panels to interpret the recommendation as binding.)

[D]   Enforcement

DREYFUSS AND LOWENFELD, CASE V: ENFORCEMENT[*]
37 Va. J. Int'l L. 275, 324–32 (1997)

Two key enforcement issues are likely to confront the WTO in the intellectual property area. The first concerns enforcement by member states of the intellectual property rights that they have recognized, at least on paper. The second issue, not limited to intellectual property controversies, concerns enforcement of member states' obligations, once these have been determined by the dispute settlement process. Our last case directly raises the first issue, and could well raise the second one also.

Case V

This case is a continuation of Case IV. Xandia, having taken up the case of Koka Kola, has prevailed before a panel established under the DSU. The panel's decision has been upheld by the Appellate Body, and the Report of the Appellate Body has been adopted by the DSB. According to article 21 of the Understanding on Dispute Settlement, Patria is supposed to inform a meeting of the DSB within thirty days of its intention in respect of implementation of the recommendations and rulings of the DSB. In this case, the ruling was that Koka Kola's trademark was widely recognized in Patria, and the recommendation was that the relevant Patrian authority cancel the registration of the local rival and approve the registration of the mark by the multinational company based in Xandia. If necessary, the Patrian authority was to seek an injunction or comparable remedy against infringement. The ruling was upheld by the Appellate Body.

Patria, however, states that it is not in a position to comply with the recommendation and ruling, because its domestic law does not permit the measures recommended by the panel. Alternatively, Patria contends

---

[*] Copyright 1997, Rochelle Cooper Dreyfuss and Andreas F. Lowenfeld.

that its prosecutors have considerable discretion in allocating their resources, and putting a stop to trademark infringement is not a high priority.

A. Competing Priorities

In addressing Patria's defense of lack of resources or competing priorities, a WTO panel or the Appellate Body will need to come to grips with an interesting ambivalence reflected in article 41, the General Obligations article of the TRIPS Agreement. Paragraph 1 of article 41 states that "[m]embers *shall ensure* that enforcement procedures . . . are available under their law so as to permit effective action against any act of infringement of intellectual property rights . . . including expeditious remedies . . . and remedies which constitute a deterrent to further infringements." Paragraph 5 of the same article, however, states that "[n]othing in this Part creates any obligation with respect to the distribution of resources as between enforcement of intellectual property rights and the enforcement of law in general."

If Patria's concern is really the allocation of limited resources, the problem may be addressed by a recommendation of the Panel that the period of compliance be stretched out—for instance until completion of the next session of the legislature—and (if Patria is a developing country) that financial and technical resources be made available to Patria under article 67 of the TRIPS Agreement.

B. Patterns of Nonenforcement

A pattern of nonenforcement by Patria, coupled with an allegation by Xandia that Patria had the resources to carry out its obligations, would be difficult to establish, and certainly could not be established in the first case. Possibly, Xandia could show that repeated efforts to bring infringement proceedings in Patria had led to no effective results. An assertion by Xandia that bringing such proceedings would be fruitless would, we expect, not be sufficient to lead to a determination that Patria was in violation of article 41(1). But if a pattern of non-enforcement by Patria of its laws were established, we believe that a panel could find a violation, and if no improvement were apparent, the controversy could be moved into the compliance stage, as discussed below.[133]

---

[133] The problem of nonenforcement of laws supposed to protect internationally recognized rights is not limited to intellectual property. It became a major issue, for instance, in the negotiation of the North American Free Trade Agreement, and particularly of the so-called side agreements on environmental cooperation and labor cooperation forced through by the Clinton administration after the principal agreement had been completed during President Bush's term. Those side agreements address a concern that a treaty partner (read Mexico) would place acceptable standards on its books but not enforce them; the solution, if it can be called that, was to establish a joint commission, to which nongovernmental as well as governmental organizations could make submissions, which could lead to a process of consultation, arbitration, reports, monetary penalties, and ultimately suspension of benefits under the Free Trade Agreement.

We think that the government of Xandia should hesitate before bringing Case V before the WTO dispute system. A better way to encourage enforcement of intellectual property rights—whether before or after litigation, as illustrated by the preceding cases—may be outside of the dispute resolution system. In many instances, we expect, intellectual property holders could serve their own cause by helping infringers find ways to utilize the investment they have sunk into infringing activities. In Case V, for example, Koka Kola may gain more by licensing to the so-called Patrian "trademark pirate" than by fighting him through to the end under the WTO system. With licensing, his plant would be utilized and Patrian workers would be employed; yet, Koka Kola could protect its marks by regulating the output for quality and quantity. If the relationship became valuable enough to the licensee, the impulse to cheat—for instance by exporting outside the territory covered by the license—might be reduced more than it could ever be controlled by a Patrian police force.[134]

C. Enforcing the Decisions of the Panel or Appellate Body

In the past, that is, under the GATT prior to completion of the Uruguay Round, Patria might have been able to block adoption of the panel report; even if it did not do so, it might have been able to fend off "suspension of equivalent concessions" by Xandia, because such a step required approval of a majority of the Contracting Parties, and retaliation was generally disfavored. The architects of the [DSU] sought to put teeth into the system, with an elaborate (but as yet untried) set of steps applicable if the preferred dispute settlement process breaks down.

First, if Patria cannot comply immediately, it will have a reasonable period of time to do so. Determination of what is a "reasonable period" is subject to approval by the DSB or to an agreement with Xandia within forty-five days of adoption of the Report, or—if no agreement is reached—to binding arbitration. The arbitration is to be held within ninety days of issuance of the Report and is limited to the issue of the "reasonable period" for compliance.[135]

Next, the DSU makes provision for disagreement between the parties over whether a corrective measure proposed by the respondent party is consistent with the GATT or the covered agreement. That question is also to be referred to impartial decision making—not by the arbitrator but by a panel, if possible the panel that heard the original dispute. [DSU art. 21.5] It is hard to imagine how there could be disagreement over implementing

---

[134] On the other hand, it is worth pointing out that disputes about the enforcement of intellectual property rights have been major impediments to admission into the World Trade Organization for states that have persistently failed to enforce such rights, notably China and Taiwan.

[135] All of the above is set out in article 21 of the DSU. Article 21.4 indicates that the "reasonable period" shall not exceed 15 months from the date of establishment of the panel, which would leave 90 days from completion of the appellate process in normal cases, with more time to be added on if either the panel or the Appellate Body asked for additional time.

the ruling in the Koka Kola case, but in other cases, including other intellectual property cases, a proposed corrective measure might well give rise to continuing controversy.[137]

Third, if all else fails, two more possibilities are set out in the DSU. If Patria fails within the "reasonable period" to carry out the recommendation to terminate or modify the practice found to be inconsistent with the Agreement, it may negotiate with Xandia for mutually acceptable compensation. The term is not defined in the DSU, but it seems to mean some offer by Patria of trade interest to Xandia.[138] If no agreement on compensation is reached within twenty days of the expiration of the "reasonable period," Xandia, the prevailing party, may, upon authorization of the DSB, retaliate against Patria by suspending the application to Patria (this time on a discriminatory basis) of concessions or other obligations. [DSU art. 22.2]. Suspension of a concession or other obligation is subject to authorization by the DSB, but article 22.6 of the Understanding on Dispute Settlement provides that the DSB shall grant the authorization within thirty days of the expiry of the "reasonable period," unless it decides by consensus to reject the request.[140]

What kind of suspension might be authorized? Considering that retaliation is generally disfavored in the GATT/WTO system—because it means that not one but two distortions to normal trade will prevail—the Understanding on Dispute Settlement contains surprisingly detailed provisions in answer to this question. [DSU arts. 22.3-6, 22.8] The general principle is that the complaining party should first seek to suspend concessions or other obligations with respect to the same sector(s) as that in which the panel or Appellate Body has found a violation. If that is not practicable, the complaining party may seek to suspend concessions or other obligations in other sectors under the same agreement—in our case the TRIPS Agreement. If that is still not practicable, the complaining party may suspend concessions or other obligations under another covered agreement. Retaliation is not punishment. Article 22.4 of the DSU states clearly what has been understood in the GATT since its origins: "The level of the suspension of concessions or other obligations authorized by the DSB shall be equivalent to the level of nullification or impairment."

---

[137] For instance, in the case about protection for computer programs, Patria might issue a regulation or adopt legislation that went part way, but not completely, to protecting the innovative aspects of computer programs, or that seemed to grant adequate protection but provided such slight punishment for infringement as to lead Xandia to complain that no real deterrence was involved. Of course, even in Koka Kola, if the panel recommendation included legislative reform or revised resource allocation, renewed controversy might arise about the adequacy of implementation by Patria.

[138] Though the DSU does not say so, it seems clear that any offer by Patria in this context must be granted on a most-favored-nation basis, because it would not fit into any of the permitted exceptions to that most fundamental principle of the GATT/WTO system.

[140] If the respondent party, Patria in our example, objects to the level of the suspension proposed or claims that the suspension is not consistent with the principles discussed hereafter, the DSU makes provision for still another arbitration, to be completed within 60 days of the expiry of the 'reasonable period.'

Should Xandia now propose to refuse to recognize trademarks owned by nationals and companies of Patria? Or trademarks on soft drinks? On all food products, or all products sold in grocery stores? We worry about all proposals of this kind. Any form of trade retaliation brings with it a substantial measure of injustice, because it nearly always affects persons that have had no prior involvement in the controversy. We suspect that the adverse effects of retaliation—trade distortion and injustice—could be more severe if implemented in a tit-for-tat last act in an intellectual property dispute than in the traditional fields of exchange of goods.

For example, consider a Xandian factory tooled to manufacture high-quality merchandise under license from a Patrian company. The factory may have been very expensive to build, and it may well employ a large and expensive workforce. If Xandia retaliates by refusing to recognize the Patrian company's trademark, it may be that the price of the output will have to be lowered because of confusing use of the mark in Xandia. At that point, it may no longer be profitable to keep the factory in operation. Retaliation will, in short, have idled an expensive assembly line, hurting both Xandian enterprises and Xandian workers, with some loss also to the Patrian firm whose royalty income is reduced, but with no gain for the original injured party, Koka Kola.

Perhaps more significant, retaliation of this kind could have an adverse effect on consumers and on the market place. Trademark law, after all, is partly geared to consumer protection. Unambiguous signals denoting particular goods allow consumers to make informed purchasing choices. Without effective signals, search costs increase. When they do, the unseen hand of the marketplace begins to allocate resources inefficiently. Even after the retaliation is withdrawn, these effects could persist. Having lost the ability to control their marks and send clear messages to their customers, producers will have difficulty notifying consumers that the meaning of the mark has been restored.

An alternative might be for Xandia to announce that its retaliation would take the form of a refusal to register new trademarks originating in Patria. Continuing to enforce old marks would preserve the reliance interests of those who owned or licensed marks in Xandia at the time the retaliation took effect. However, the refusal to register new marks might also lead to confusion among consumers and distortions of the market. Xandian consumers traveling abroad or receiving signals on television or the internet would be exposed to the way that marks are used outside Xandia, and consumers outside Xandia might well be exposed to the unauthorized usages permitted inside Xandia. Indeed, the whole problem of Case IV arose because of the significance of trans-border exposure, recognized in article 16(2) of the TRIPS Agreement. Allowing Xandia to refuse to recognize marks that are new to Xandia will not, therefore, contain the possibility of confusion in a meaningful way. On the one hand, this means that despite the apparently limited nature of the retaliation, it could have a large enough impact on Patrian business to inspire Patria to conform its behavior to the requirements of the TRIPS Agreement. On the other hand, however, the impact of even this narrow action could be unacceptably high, for there is no way to prevent dislocations in other markets. As in Case III, administration of the TRIPS Agreement needs to be sensitive to extraterritorial effects of intraterritorial actions.

Given that any retaliation focusing on trademarks is unattractive, the next-favored retaliatory measure would be cross-agreement, that is, still within the field of intellectual property governed by the TRIPS Agreement, but addressed to patents or copyrights, rather than to trademarks. Refusal to enforce or register patents and copyrights originating in Patria, however, would raise many of the same issues of expropriation that are raised by canceling or refusing to register trademarks. Although the danger of confusing consumers would not be present, the problem of frustrating the reliance interests of rights holders and licensees would exist at least equally. Moreover, there might well be an extraterritorial effect if products could be exported from Xandia into countries that recognize a doctrine of worldwide exhaustion of copyright and patent rights.

It may be that cross-sectoral retaliation would be the most attractive alternative for Xandia, as in the action taken in 1988 by the United States against Brazil under the famous Section 301, when the Reagan administration imposed 100% tariffs on imports of microwave ovens, quality writing paper, and a number of other products from Brazil, in retaliation for that country's refusal to grant patent protection for pharmaceutical products.[144]

The difficulty in fashioning an appropriate form of retaliation is not a reason to disparage either the TRIPS Agreement or the Understanding on Dispute Settlement. The whole thrust of the WTO dispute settlement regime is that retaliation should never take place. Retaliation should be considered a pain to Patria and Xandia so severe that both member states would be induced to reach agreement before it came to this last of the seven steps provided in the DSU. That the reciprocal pain comes more quickly in the intellectual property area may be attributable to the fact that in contrast to goods, which can be only in one place at one time, intellectual property, being intangible, travels in many directions and can come to rest in many places at once. The moral we draw is that the initial steps in the dispute settlement process, that is the work of the panels and the Appellate Body, should be carried on with great care in the intellectual property area—*terra incognita* for the GATT/WTO system—with attention not only to the outcome of a given case but to the persuasiveness of the reasoning and explanations, for the parties and for the wider interests at stake.

---

144 *See* Proclamation No. 5885, 53 Fed. Reg. 41,551 (1988). Brazil called for creation of a GATT panel to rule on whether the U.S. action was legal under GATT, and a panel was in fact convened, but the President of Brazil announced that he would seek legislation to provide patent protection for pharmaceuticals, and the U.S. sanctions were withdrawn before the panel could issue a ruling.

NOTES AND QUESTIONS

(1) **The Nature of TRIPS's Effective Enforcement Provisions.** Most of the early complaints focused on violations of substantive, relatively delineated TRIPS obligations, but as the system matures one might expect an increasing number of complaints to focus on measures for the enforcement of intellectual property rights. This would reflect a parallel progression in the focus of the United States Trade Representative's efforts under Special 301 against, for example, the People's Republic of China. And it would exploit one of the TRIPS Agreement's other novel contributions to international intellectual property law, namely, attention to measures provided by states to ensure the effective enforcement of intellectual property rights. *See generally* J.H. Reichman, *Enforcing the Enforcement Procedures of the TRIPS Agreement*, 37 VA. J. INT'L L. 335 (1997). But the language used by the TRIPS Agreement to define members' obligations relating to enforcement is that of broad principles or standards rather than carefully delineated rules. One would therefore expect these standards to prove less fertile ground for complainants in a system where the text of the DSU admonishes against panel activism and explicitly allows member states discretion as to how to implement international obligations in national law. Yet, complaints addressing enforcement measures have already been filed and resolved. *See* Matthijs Geuze & Hannu Wager, *WTO Dispute Settlement Practice Relating to the TRIPS Agreement*, J. INT'L ECON. L. 347, 381 (1999) (discussing proceedings brought against Sweden by the United States for failure to make provisional measures available in civil actions involving intellectual property rights); *see also id.* at 381 (discussing pending consultations between the United States and Denmark regarding the latter's compliance with Article 50). Why might the drafters have used broader, more indeterminate language in the agreement (especially when addressing enforcement of rights)? What advantages might accrue from the use of more vague language? How might that affect the way that dispute settlement panels should interpret such language? *See* Joel P. Trachtman, *The Domain of WTO Dispute Resolution*, 40 HARV. INT'L L. J. 333, 346–47 (1999). Trachtman suggests that the "decision between rules and standards is not a decision between more international law and less international law. While rules may be developed by tribunals, the decision is often an institutional choice between adjudicators and legislators. This observation depends upon the perception that tribunals applying standards legislate, even when they purport not to do so." *Id*. Are you persuaded by this argument? What does it mean for who controls the future direction of international intellectual property law? Why might you prefer adjudicators over legislators, or vice versa?

(2) **Article 41(5).** In Case V, the DSB recommendation was that the relevant "Patrian authority cancel the registration of the local rival and approve the registration of the mark by the multinational company based in Xandia. If necessary, the Patrian authority was to seek an injunction or comparable remedy against infringement." Which of Patria's responses—inconsistent domestic law, or prosecutorial discretion—is most persuasive,

and why? Which, if either, implicates the allocation of limited resources such as to trigger reliance upon Article 41(5)?

UNITED STATES—SECTION 211 OMNIBUS APPROPRIATIONS ACT OF 1998 ("HAVANA CLUB")
Report of the Appellate Body, WT/DS176/AB/R (WTO 2002)

[The European Communities and the United States appealed from certain issues of law and legal interpretations in the Panel Report, *United States—Section 211 Omnibus Appropriations Act of 1998* (the "Panel Report"). The text and explanation of the challenged measure, Section 211 of the United States Omnibus Appropriations Act of 1998 ("Section 211"), and the relevant Cuban Assets Control Regulations (the "CACR"), which are administered by the Office of Foreign Assets Control ("OFAC"), are set out in the excerpt *supra* § 3.06.]

VIII. Article 42 of the TRIPS Agreement

Both the United States and the European Communities appeal the Panel's findings on Article 42 of the TRIPS Agreement. The United States appeals the conclusion of the Panel that Section 211(a)(2) violates Article 42 of the TRIPS Agreement. The European Communities appeals the Panel's finding that "it has not been proved that Section 211(b) is inconsistent with Article 42 of the TRIPS Agreement".

We begin our analysis with the text of Article 42 of the TRIPS Agreement, which provides:

Fair and Equitable Procedures

Members shall make available to the right holders [footnote 11] civil judicial procedures concerning the enforcement of any intellectual property right covered by this Agreement. Defendants shall have the right to written notice which is timely and contains sufficient detail, including the basis of the claims. Parties shall be allowed to be represented by independent legal counsel, and procedures shall not impose overly burdensome requirements concerning mandatory personal appearances. *All parties to such procedures shall be duly entitled to substantiate their claims and to present all relevant evidence.* The procedure shall provide a means to identify and protect confidential information, unless this would be contrary to existing constitutional requirements. (emphasis added)

Footnote 11: For the purpose of this Part, the term "right holder" includes federations and associations having legal standing to assert such rights.

Article 42 forms part of Part III on "Enforcement of Intellectual Property Rights". Part III has broad coverage. It applies to all intellectual property rights covered by the TRIPS Agreement. According to Article 1.2 of the TRIPS Agreement, the term "intellectual property" refers to "all categories of intellectual property that are the subject of Sections 1 through 7 of Part II" of that Agreement.

Section 1 of Part III lays out "General Obligations" of Members. According to Article 41.1 of Section 1, Members are required to ensure that enforcement procedures as specified in Part III are available under their domestic law "so as to permit effective action against any act of infringement of intellectual property rights covered by [the TRIPS] Agreement". These enforcement procedures must include expeditious remedies to prevent infringements and remedies which constitute a deterrent to further infringements. At the same time, these procedures must be applied in such a manner as to avoid the creation of barriers to legitimate trade and to provide safeguards against their abuse. These procedures provide for an internationally-agreed minimum standard which Members are bound to implement in their domestic legislation.

Section 2 of Part III is entitled "Civil and Administrative Procedures and Remedies". Article 42 deals with enforcement action in judicial proceedings, and contains detailed requirements which ensure that "civil judicial procedures" are "fair and equitable". Like Section 1 of Part III, Section 2 introduces an international minimum standard which Members are bound to implement in their domestic legislation.

Before the Panel, the European Communities claimed that Sections 211(a)(2) and (b) are inconsistent with Article 42 of the TRIPS Agreement because they "expressly deny[] the availability of [United States] courts to enforce the rights targeted" by Section 211.

The United States contended before the Panel that Sections 211(a)(2) and (b) do not violate Article 42 because nothing in the measure precludes a person asserting ownership rights in the trademark from having access to civil judicial procedures and a full opportunity "to substantiate [its] claim" to ownership and "to present all relevant evidence."

On Section 211(a)(2), the Panel found:

> We note the US argument that Section 211(a)(2) does not affect the availability of judicial procedures to any party to assert a right to a trademark. However, given the clear wording of Section 211(a)(2) which provides that "[n]o U.S. court shall recognize, enforce or otherwise validate any assertion of rights" in certain circumstances, we fail to see how a right holder would be able effectively to assert its rights under these circumstances. While Section 211(a)(2) would not appear to prevent a right holder from initiating civil judicial procedures, its wording indicates that the right holder is not entitled to effective procedures as the court is ab initio not permitted to recognize its assertion of rights if the conditions of Section 211(a)(2) are met. In other words, the right holder is effectively prevented from having a chance to substantiate its claim, a chance

to which a right holder is clearly entitled under Article 42, because effective civil judicial procedures mean procedures with the possibility of an outcome which is not pre-empted a priori by legislation. (footnote omitted)

. . . .

[G]iven that Section 211(a)(2) limits, under certain circumstances, right holders' effective access to and, hence, the availability of civil judicial procedures, we find that Section 211(a)(2) is inconsistent with Article 42 of the TRIPS Agreement.

On Section 211(b), the Panel concluded:

We note that it is plausible that similar concerns mentioned in respect of Section 211(a)(2) might arise in connection with Section 211(b). However, as we noted above, the European Communities did not explain the meaning of various terms contained in Sections 44(b) and (e) even though Article 211(b) explicitly refers to "treaty rights . . . under sections 44(b) or (e)". Therefore, for the reasons set out [above] it has not been proved that Section 211(b) is inconsistent with Article 42 of the TRIPS Agreement.

On appeal, the United States submits that a court would refuse to recognize, enforce or otherwise validate a designated national's assertion of rights under Sections 211(a)(2) or (b) only after making a number of findings.[145] According to the United States, these provisions do not constitute legislation that a priori pre-empts a positive outcome of an assertion of rights by a designated national. Rather, the United States maintains that it is only *after* effective civil judicial procedures have been made available that a court would refuse to recognize, enforce or validate an assertion of rights by a designated national. The United States emphasizes that, in any event, Article 42 does not create obligations with respect to a person who is not the holder of an intellectual property right covered by the TRIPS Agreement. On this basis, the United States argues that Article 42 does not require judicial authorities to provide enforcement procedures once a finding is made that the claimant does not hold any intellectual property right to enforce. Accordingly, the United States concludes that Sections 211(a)(2) and (b) cannot possibly deny enforcement rights guaranteed under Article 42 to a person who is not the legitimate owner of a trademark under United States law.

In contrast, the European Communities emphasizes on appeal that Article 42 entitles parties to more than mere access to civil judicial procedures, which it concedes the United States courts would provide when

---

[145] The United States mentions, for example, the following: whether the trademark at issue was used in connection with a certain business or assets; whether the business or assets were confiscated; whether adequate and effective compensation was paid to the original owner; whether the person claiming ownership is a designated national or a successor-in-interest; whether the original owner expressly consents to the use of that trademark by the claimant. . . .

applying Sections 211(a)(2) and (b). For the European Communities, Article 42 is violated unless domestic civil judicial procedures enable a plaintiff to pursue *all* issues or claims that arise and to present *all* relevant evidence in the context of the enforcement of an intellectual property right covered by the TRIPS Agreement. In the view of the European Communities, Sections 211(a)(2) and (b) each limit the issues of possible litigation to the elements referred to in those Sections,[147] while excluding from judicial inquiry other issues that are typically relevant in trademark-related litigation and regulated by, inter alia, the Lanham Act.[148] On this reasoning, the European Communities alleges that both Sections 211(a)(2) and (b) are inconsistent with Article 42.

In making their respective arguments about the consistency or inconsistency of Sections 211(a)(2) and (b) with Article 42, the participants referred mainly to the first and fourth sentences of that provision. The first sentence of Article 42 requires "Members [to] make available to right holders civil judicial procedures concerning the enforcement of any intellectual property right covered by [the TRIPS] Agreement." The fourth sentence of Article 42 provides that "[a]ll parties to such procedures shall be duly entitled to substantiate their claims and to present all relevant evidence."

The first sentence of Article 42 requires Members to make certain civil judicial procedures "available" to right holders. Making something *available* means making it "obtainable", putting it "within one's reach" and "at one's disposal" in a way that has sufficient force or efficacy.[149] We agree with the Panel that the ordinary meaning of the term "make available" suggests that "right holders" are entitled under Article 42 to have *access* to civil judicial procedures that are effective in bringing about the enforcement of their rights covered by the Agreement.

Article 42, first sentence, does not define what the term "civil judicial procedures" in that sentence encompasses. The TRIPS Agreement thus reserves, subject to the procedural minimum standards set out in that Agreement, a degree of discretion to Members on this, taking into account "differences in national legal systems."[151] Indeed, no Member's national system of civil judicial procedures will be identical to that of another Member.

Pursuant to the first sentence of Article 42, civil judicial procedures must be made available to "right holders" of intellectual property rights covered

---

[147] These issues include: whether the original owner or bona fide successor-in-interest has expressly consented; whether a trademark which is composed of the same or substantially similar signs as a trademark which was used in connection with a business or assets that were confiscated; whether an uncompensated confiscation of a business or asset took place in Cuba. United States' other appellant's submission, para. 18.

[148] These are issues such as use of the trademark; alleged deficiency of a registration; identity or similarity of signs in general; class of goods or services covered by the trademark; existence and scope of a licence. European Communities' appellee's submission, para. 22.

[149] The New Shorter Oxford English Dictionary, Vol. I, p. 154.

[151] Recital 2(c) of the Preamble to the TRIPS Agreement.

by the TRIPS Agreement so as to enable them to protect those rights against infringement. The United States seems to suggest that access to those rights may be limited to the *owner* of a trademark under United States law. The Panel defined the term "right holders" as persons who have the legal capacity to assert rights.[153] We agree with the Panel that the term "right holders" as used in Article 42 is not limited to persons who have been established as owners of trademarks. Where the TRIPS Agreement confers rights exclusively on "owners" of a right, it does so in express terms, such as in Article 16.1, which refers to the "owner of a registered trademark". By contrast, the term "right holders" within the meaning of Article 42 also includes persons who claim to have legal standing to assert rights. This interpretation is also borne out by the fourth sentence of Article 42, which refers to "parties". Civil judicial procedures would not be fair and equitable if access to courts were not given to both complainants and defendants who purport to be owners of an intellectual property right.

In this respect, the Panel stated:

> As we have already noted, in the United States, the registration of a trademark confers a *prima facie* presumption of the registrant's ownership of the registered trademark. This means that, in the United States, the holder of a registration is deemed to be the owner unless otherwise proven. A person who enjoys the presumption of being the owner of a trademark under US law must be entitled to a level of protection of its rights that meets the US obligations under the TRIPS Agreement, including Article 42. Consequently, in our interpretation, this presumptive owner must have access to civil judicial procedures that are effective in terms of bringing about the enforcement of its rights *until the moment that there is a determination by the court that it is, in fact, not the owner of the trademark that it has registered* or that there is some other disqualifying ground which is compatible with international obligations. (emphasis added)

For the reasons we have stated, we agree with the Panel that the "right holders" to whom Members must make the procedural rights of Article 42 available include trademark registrants who are presumptive owners under United States law. In our view, these procedural rights extend as well to all other "right holders".

WTO Members must also guarantee to all "parties" the right to "substantiate their claims", as required by the fourth sentence of Article 42. The use of the words "their claims" suggests that, under Article 42, the choice of which claims or how many issues to raise in civil judicial procedures is left to each party. The use of the word "substantiate" implies that litigants

---

[153] Panel Report, para. 8.98. In its reasoning, the Panel relied on footnote 11 to Article 42. The footnote states that "the term 'right holder' includes federations and associations having legal standing to assert such rights." At the oral hearing, both participants submitted that footnote 11 does not resolve the issue on which they disagree in respect of Article 42, and submitted further that, in their view, that footnote was irrelevant to this dispute.

have the right to do more than simply initiate claims; Members must duly entitle all litigants to "give substance" to, or "give good grounds" for, their claims in order to prove the truth of a charge, and to demonstrate or verify it by evidence.[155]

Litigants are also entitled under the fourth sentence of Article 42 to "present all relevant evidence" in such procedures. These words indicate that parties have the right to file "all relevant evidence" in support of their claims with the courts.

From all this, we understand that the rights which Article 42 obliges Members to make available to right holders are *procedural* in nature. These *procedural* rights guarantee an international minimum standard for nationals of other Members within the meaning of Article 1.3 of the TRIPS Agreement.

With this understanding, we turn now to the measure before us and examine whether Sections 211(a)(2) and (b) are consistent with the procedural requirements set out in the first and fourth sentences of Article 42. . . .

The United States submitted at the oral hearing that the procedural provisions of the Lanham Act and of the United States Federal Rules of Civil Procedure apply and guarantee "fair and equitable . . . civil judicial procedures" in respect of Section 211. The European Communities agreed. Accordingly, the participants agree that designated nationals and successors-in-interest have access to civil judicial procedures. At the oral hearing, the European Communities also agreed that the Federal Rules of Evidence are applicable in such proceedings. It is, therefore, our understanding that both participants agree that designated nationals and successors-in-interest have—to the same extent, and in the same way, as any claimant and defendant—the rights provided under the Federal Rules of Civil Procedure and the Federal Rules of Evidence. These rights are the rights to "substantiate their claims" and "present all relevant evidence" with respect to all elements mentioned in Sections 211(a)(2) and (b). We also understand both participants to agree that Sections 211(a)(2) and (b) do not require or authorize a United States court to reject a claim by a designated national or successor-in-interest as inadmissible or unfounded without having applied fully the Federal Rules of Civil Procedure and the Federal Rules of Evidence. The European Communities has not claimed that either the Federal Rules of Civil Procedure or the Federal Rules of Evidence do not comply with the obligation in Article 42.

We further understand the European Communities to acknowledge that, in a situation where the recognition of an intellectual property right depends on the fulfilment of cumulative substantive conditions, the failure to meet a single one of those substantive conditions (such as ownership of a disputed trademark) would prevent a court from recognizing that right. At the oral hearing, the European Communities also conceded that a court

---

[155] The New Shorter Oxford English Dictionary, Vol. II, p. 3124.

may, in such a situation, abstain from ruling on all the other substantive conditions that may be relevant (for example, on the distinctiveness of the trademark, or on the existence of an infringement).

However, unlike the United States, the European Communities believes that, under Article 42, the decision whether or not to abstain from ruling on substantive conditions or requirements other than those mentioned in Sections 211(a)(2) and (b) must be left to the discretion of the courts. According to the European Communities, a statute must not limit the discretion of the courts by directing the courts to examine certain substantive requirements before, and to the exclusion of, other substantive requirements. As we understand it, the European Communities argues that, in requiring the courts to examine the circumstances they address as a matter of priority, and to the exclusion of other issues typically arising in trademark-related litigation, Sections 211(a)(2) and (b) interfere with the discretion of the courts.

In our view, a conclusion by a court on the basis of Section 211, after applying the Federal Rules of Civil Procedure and the Federal Rules of Evidence, that an enforcement proceeding has failed to establish ownership—a requirement of substantive law—with the result that it is impossible for the court to rule in favour of that claimant's or that defendant's claim to a trademark right, does not constitute a violation of Article 42. There is nothing in the *procedural* obligations of Article 42 that prevents a Member, in such a situation, from legislating whether or not its courts must examine *each and every* requirement of substantive law at issue before making a ruling.

With this in mind, we turn to the alleged inconsistency of Section 211(a)(2) with Article 42. Section 211(a)(2) does not prohibit courts from giving right holders access to fair and equitable civil judicial procedures and the opportunity to substantiate their claims and to present all relevant evidence. Rather, Section 211(a)(2) only requires the United States courts not recognize, enforce or otherwise validate any assertion of rights by designated nationals or successors-in-interest who have been determined, after applying United States Federal Rules of Civil Procedure and Federal Rules of Evidence, not to own the trademarks referred to in Section 211(a)(2). As we have said, Section 211(a)(2) deals with the substance of ownership. Therefore, we do not believe that Section 211(a)(2) denies the *procedural* rights that are guaranteed by Article 42.

For this reason, we conclude that Section 211(a)(2) on its face is not inconsistent with the requirements of Article 42 of the TRIPS Agreement.

[For the same reasons, the Appellate Body concluded that "Section 211(b) on its face is not inconsistent with the requirements of Article 42 of the TRIPS Agreement."]

And, for all these reasons, we find that Sections 211(a)(2) and (b) *on their face* are not inconsistent with the requirements of Article 42 of the TRIPS Agreement. Therefore, we reverse the Panel's finding on Section 211(a)(2) . . . and uphold its finding on Section 211(b) . . .

Finally, we emphasize that the European Communities has challenged Sections 211(a)(2) and (b) on their face. The European Communities has not challenged the application of Sections 211(a)(2) and (b) in particular instances by United States courts. Accordingly, our conclusions that Sections 211(a)(2) and (b) are not inconsistent with Article 42 relate to that measure on its face. We do not rule on whether a particular United States court has, or has not, violated the requirements of Article 42 in applying Sections 211(a)(2) and (b) in any particular case.

. . . .

NOTES AND QUESTIONS

(1) **Responsibility for Devising Remedial Measures.** In the *United States-India* case, the United States tendered to the panel a suggested form by which India should comply with its obligations. But the panel declined to set out in any great detail the means by which India should bring itself into compliance with TRIPS. In what ways is a detailed recommendation of remedies inconsistent with the philosophy underlying the TRIPS Agreement? *See* TRIPS Agreement art. 1(1); *cf.* DSU art. 19.

(2) **Effect of Settlement.** What would have been the effect of a settlement between Xandia and Patria regarding the allocation of a more limited enforcement than Xandia would regard as ideal? *See* DSU art. 3(6) (requiring notification). Are settlements to be encouraged? Do settlements have any disadvantages? *See The Review of the WTO's Dispute Settlement Understanding: Which Way?*, 1 J. WORLD INTELL. PROP. 447, 462–67 (1998) (discussing different arguments).

(3) **Scope of Remedy.** After the panel report had been issued in *United States-India* (but before the Appellate Body upheld the panel's report) the EU filed an identical complaint to that filed (and successfully prosecuted) by the United States. *See* India—Patent Protection for Pharmaceutical and Agricultural Chemical Products—Request for Consultations by the European Communities, WT/DS79/1 (WTO Dispute Settlement Body, May 6, 1997). The EU made that filing because remedies under the DSU are available only to WTO members acting with the authorization of the Dispute Settlement Body (which in turn requires panel and Appellate Body reports to act). Does this make sense? Should such apparently duplicative filings be encouraged? Should they be barred? (India had argued that the EU had lost the right to submit its own case to the WTO.) More fundamentally, are these filings duplicative? What procedural devices that you have seen in other adjudicative models might be considered to eliminate or reduce duplication? *See* DSU arts. 9–10. To what extent are these devices inappropriate because of the different character and purpose of WTO proceedings? *See* Geuze & Wager, *supra* at 357–58 (discussing conduct of EU-India proceeding).

(4) **Private Party Losses.** The panel in *United States—India* suggested that, although India had discretion under Article 1(1) of TRIPS as to the means of implementing its obligations, it should take into account the interests of persons who would have filed patent applications since 1994 had India offered an appropriate (TRIPS-compliant) mechanism for doing so. *See United States—India*, Panel Report, WT/DS50/R, ¶¶ 8.2, 7.66. *Compare Notification by Pakistan to the Dispute Settlement Body*, IP/N/1/PAK1 (WTO Dispute Settlement Body, Mar. 5, 1997) (providing details of ordinance issued by Pakistan to settle the same dispute with the United States). But an intellectual property owner cannot bring an action against a member state for losses sustained as a result of the failure of that member state to implement its TRIPS obligations. In contrast, under EU law, private citizens are entitled to damages from member states that fail timely to implement EU directives. *See Francovich v. Italy*, [1993] 2 CMLR 66 (E.C.J. 1991); *see also R v. Secretary of State for Transport, ex parte Factortame*, [1990] 3 CMLR 1 (E.C.J. 1990) (granting injunction against enforcement of U.K. statute that was in violation of EU law). Why the difference? See the comments of Professor Abbott in Note (3) following *United States–India* above.

(5) **Monitoring Compliance.** In *United States-India*, the parties agreed that India would have fifteen months in which to implement the DSB recommendations. The EU and India then agreed to a shorter implementation time frame, resulting in an implementation date that matched that required by the *United States-India* agreement. India has since promulgated ordinances amending its law. The United States has, however, followed up with a request for consultation with India regarding whether the ordinance established a system of exclusive marketing rights that complied with the requirements of Article 70. How should the United States proceed if it remains unsatisfied with the content of the ordinance? *See* DSU art. 21(5); *see also The Review of the WTO's Dispute Settlement Understanding: Which Way?*, *supra* at 461 (comments of John Kingery) (noting that the EU and the United States are in disagreement over the meaning of Articles 21(5) and 22).

(6) **Cross-Sectoral Retaliation.** Dreyfuss and Lowenfeld illustrate the dilemma faced by Xandia in Case V in trying to fashion effective retaliatory measures within the intellectual property sector that did not cause more harm than good. It is perhaps unsurprising, therefore, that cross-sectoral retaliation was frequently touted by U.S. representatives as one of the primary advantages of addressing inadequate intellectual property protection within trade law mechanisms and institutions (whether through Special 301 or the WTO). In which circumstances does cross-sectoral retaliation provide the most significant advantage over traditional intra-intellectual property law measures? Can it be argued that non-intellectual property based retaliation is not only more effective in certain circumstances, but may also be most appropriate? Is retaliation in the form of refusal to recognize the intellectual property rights of parties from the violating country a permissible form of retaliation? Even if it is permissible,

what limits on its use would you recommend? Are there some types of intellectual property disputes where it would be particularly inadvisable to recommend this form of suspension? Developing countries have argued that retaliation is not an effective enforcement mechanism for them and wish to develop alternative enforcement vehicles (such as the award of monetary damages). *See* Kim Van der Borght, *The Review of the WTO Understanding on Dispute Settlement: Some Reflections on the Current Debate*, 14 AM. U. INT'L L. REV. 1223, 1232 (1999). Why might a prevailing developing country be unhappy with retaliation as its only form of relief?

The possibility of cross-sectoral retaliation theoretically works in both directions. But the following arbitrators' opinion suggests that some of the difficulties that might persuade Xandia to look outside the TRIPS Agreement for relief in Case V might also caution against authorizing suspension of TRIPS obligations as retaliation for non-TRIPS GATT violations.

EUROPEAN COMMUNITIES—REGIME FOR THE IMPORTATION, SALE AND DISTRIBUTION OF BANANAS—RECOURSE TO ARBITRATION BY THE EUROPEAN COMMUNITIES UNDER ARTICLE 22.6 OF THE DSU
(Decision by the Arbitrators, March 24, 2000)

[The EC banana regime was found to be inconsistent with Articles I and XIII of GATT and Articles II and XVII of the General Agreement on Trade In Services (GATS). The original panel was reconvened, pursuant to Article 21.5 of the DSU, upon request by Ecuador, and its report was adopted by the DSB. There were no findings of violations under the TRIPS Agreement in the report of the reconvened panel. On 8 November 1999, Ecuador requested authorization by the DSB to suspend concessions or other obligations under the TRIPS Agreement, the GATS and GATT 1994 in an amount of US$450 million. Ecuador submitted that withdrawal of concessions in the goods sector was not practicable or effective. The EU requested arbitration pursuant to Article 22.6 of the DSU, arguing (i) that the amount of suspension of concessions or other obligations requested by Ecuador was excessive since it has suffered far less nullification or impairment than alleged; and (ii) that Ecuador had not followed the principles and procedures set forth in Article 22.3 of the DSU in suspending concessions or other obligations across sectors and agreements. The DSB referred the matters to arbitration in accordance with Article 22.6 of the DSU. The arbitrators were the members of the original panel. After resolving various procedural issues and stressing the "basic rationale" that "the suspension of concessions or other obligations across sectors or across agreements (beyond those sectors or agreements under which a panel or the Appellate Body has found violations) remains the exception," the Arbitrators considered Ecuador's request for suspension of other obligations under the TRIPS Agreement, pursuant to subparagraph (c) of Article 22.3, as obligations which it intends to suspend across sectors and agreements.]

I. REMARKS ON THE SUSPENSION OF TRIPS OBLIGATIONS

A.   The Scope of the Suspension to Be Authorized under the TRIPS Agreement

We recall that Article 19 of the DSU provides that "the panel or the Appellate Body may suggest ways in which the Member concerned could implement the recommendations". While Article 19 does not explicitly mention arbitration proceedings under Article 22, in our view, there is nothing in the DSU that would preclude Arbitrators, acting pursuant to Article 22.6, from making suggestions on how to implement their decision. Given that this case is the first one involving subparagraphs (b)–(e) of Article 22.3 and the first one concerning the suspension of TRIPS obligations, we believe that it is particularly appropriate to set out our views on the suspension of TRIPS obligations. We also note that Ecuador has expressed its interest in hearing our views on these issues.

We first note that Article 1.3 of the TRIPS Agreement defines in general the reach of the TRIPS Agreement:

> Members shall accord the treatment provided for in this Agreement to the nationals of other Members. In respect of the *relevant intellectual property right*, the nationals of other Members shall be understood as those *natural or legal persons* that would meet the criteria for eligibility for protection provided for in the Paris Convention (1967), the Berne Convention (1971), the Rome Convention and the Treaty on Intellectual Property in Respect of Integrated Circuits, were all Members of the WTO members of those conventions . . . (emphasis added, footnotes omitted).

Thus, an authorization by the DSB of the request for suspension vis-à-vis the European Communities would permit Ecuador to suspend the treatment provided for in the TRIPS provisions in question with respect to nationals within the meaning of Article 1.3 of those 13 EC member States[41] which the request for suspension by Ecuador refers to.

. . . .

[E]cuador's request for the suspension of TRIPS obligations refers to Article 14 of Section 1 of the TRIPS Agreement on "Copyright and related rights" as well as Section 3 on "Geographical indications" and Section 4 on "Industrial designs".

In respect of the protection of *performers, producers of phonograms* (sound recordings) and *broadcasting organisations* within the meaning of Article 14 of the TRIPS Agreement, criteria for eligibility for protection of persons are defined in the Rome Convention. In this respect, it is important to point out that, in the case of suspension of obligations under Article 14, as requested by Ecuador, there may be different right holders of the different rights related to phonograms and that these right holders do not

---

[41] Ecuador's request for suspension under Article 22.2 excludes Denmark and the Netherlands.

necessarily all have the nationality, within the meaning of Article 1.3 of the TRIPS Agreement, of one of those 13 member States in question, even if the phonogram concerned has been produced in one of those member States. The performer having rights to a phonogram under Article 14 may be a non-national of these 13 member States, but the producer of the phonogram may be a national of those member States. Such complicated situations will have to be carefully considered by Ecuador in implementing the suspension of TRIPS obligations, if authorized by the DSB, so as not to adversely affect right holders who cannot be regarded as nationals of those 13 EC member States.

In respect of the criteria for eligibility for the protection of *industrial designs*, the Paris Convention is relevant.

The legal protection of *geographical indications* is enjoyed by "interested parties" within the meaning of Articles 22.2 and 23.1 of the TRIPS Agreement. Article 22.1 of the TRIPS Agreement creates a clear link between a region, locality or territory and a protectable geographical indication. This implies that the suspension of protection of geographical indications would concern parties interested in geographical indications which identify a good as originating in the territory of one of the respective 13 EC member States, or a region or locality in that territory.

It should be emphasized that in its relation to all other WTO Members and the natural or legal persons that are their nationals, Ecuador continues to be bound by its obligations under the TRIPS Agreement and that all these WTO Members continue to be entitled to exercise their rights under the DSU with respect to Ecuador.

B.   The Suspension of TRIPS Obligations and the Relation with the Conventions Administered by World Intellectual Property Organisation (WIPO)

The parties disagree on whether Article 2.2 of the TRIPS Agreement prevents or permits the suspension of TRIPS obligations which have a relation to the Paris Convention, Berne Convention, the Rome Convention or the IPIC Treaty. Article 2.2 provides:

Nothing in Parts I to IV of this Agreement shall derogate from existing obligations that Members have to each other under the Paris Convention, the Berne Convention, the Rome Convention and the Treaty on Intellectual Property Rights in Respect of Integrated Circuits.

This provision can be understood to refer to the obligations that the contracting parties of the Paris, Berne and Rome Conventions and the IPIC Treaty, who are also WTO Members, have between themselves under these four treaties. This would mean that, by virtue of the conclusion of the WTO Agreement, e.g. Berne Union members cannot derogate from existing obligations between each other under the Berne Convention. For example, the fact that Article 9.1 of the TRIPS Agreement incorporates into that Agreement Articles 1-21 of the Berne Convention with the exception of

Article 6*bis* does not mean that Berne Union members would henceforth be exonerated from this obligation to guarantee moral rights under the Berne Convention.

In any event, Article 2.2 only refers to Parts I to IV of the TRIPS Agreement, while the provisions on "Dispute Prevention and Settlement" are embodied in Part V. This Part of the TRIPS Agreement contains, inter alia, Article 64.1 which provides that the DSU applies to disputes under the TRIPS Agreement unless otherwise specifically provided therein. . . However, nothing in Article 64 or other Articles of the TRIPS Agreement provides specifically that Article 22 of the DSU does not apply to the TRIPS Agreement.

We further note that subparagraphs (f)(iii) and (g)(iii) of Article 22.3 of the DSU[46] explicitly define that Sections of the TRIPS Agreement are "sectors", and that the TRIPS Agreement is an "agreement", in respect of which the suspension of TRIPS obligations may be sought, pursuant to subparagraphs (b–c) of Article 22.3, by a complaining party and authorized by the DSB. Provided that Ecuador's request for the suspension of certain TRIPS obligations is consistent with all the requirements of Article 22 of the DSU, including paragraphs 3 and 4 thereof, neither Article 2.2 read in context with Article 64 of the TRIPS Agreement, nor any other provision of the WTO agreements indicate that an authorization by the DSB of that request would in theory be prohibited under WTO law.

It is not within our jurisdiction as Arbitrators, acting pursuant to Article 22.6 of the DSU, to pass judgment on whether Ecuador, by suspending, once authorized by the DSB, certain TRIPS obligations, would act inconsistently with its international obligations arising from treaties other than the agreements covered by the WTO (e.g. the Paris, Berne and Rome Conventions which Ecuador has ratified). It is, if at all, entirely for Ecuador and the other parties to such treaties to consider whether a specific form chosen by Ecuador for implementing such suspension of certain TRIPS obligations gives rise to difficulties in legal or practical terms under such treaties.

  C. The Effect on Third-country WTO Members of the Suspension of Certain TRIPS Obligations by Ecuador with Respect to the European Communities

It is evident that an authorization by the DSB for Ecuador to suspend certain TRIPS obligations would concern Ecuador only. Such authorization does not exonerate any other WTO Member from abiding by its WTO obligations, including those under the TRIPS Agreement.

---

[46] Article 22.3(f) of the DSU: "for purposes of this paragraph, 'sector' means:

(iii) with respect to trade-related intellectual property rights, each of the categories of intellectual property rights covered in Section 1, or Section 2, or Section 3, or Section 4, or Section 5, or Section 6, or Section 7 of Part II, or the obligations under Part III, or Part IV of the Agreement on TRIPS;"

Article 22.3(g) of the DSU: "for purposes of this paragraph, 'agreement' means:

(iii) with respect to intellectual property rights, the Agreement on TRIPS."

The obligations of other WTO Members include those in respect of action against imports of goods which involve other infringements of intellectual property rights. In this context, Article 51 in Section 4 on "Special Requirements Related to Border Measures", contained in Part III of the TRIPS Agreement, provides that "Members shall . . . adopt procedures to enable a right holder who has valid grounds for suspecting that the importation of counterfeit trade or pirated copyright goods may take place", to request customs authorities to suspend release into free circulation of such goods. According to footnote 14 to Article 51, "pirated copyright goods" include copies made without the consent of the right holder or person duly authorized by the right holder in the country of production, where the making of that copy would have constituted an infringement of a copyright or a related right under the law of the country of importation.

We note that, as a result of an authorization by the DSB of Ecuador's request to suspend Article 14 of the TRIPS Agreement, phonograms would be produced in Ecuador consistent with WTO law. However, such phonograms would still be copies made without the consent of the right holder or a person duly authorized by the right holder in the country of production. Pursuant to footnote 13 to Article 51, WTO Members are under no obligation to apply procedures concerning "special requirements related to border measures" to imports of goods put on the market in another country by or with the consent of the right holder. However, with respect to phonograms produced in Ecuador without the consent of the right holder, but consistent with an authorization by the DSB under Article 22.7 of the DSU, the obligations of Article 51 of the TRIPS Agreement to apply such procedures would remain in force for all WTO Members.

Distortions in third-country markets could be avoided if Ecuador would suspend the intellectual property rights in question only for the purposes of supply destined for the domestic market. An authorization of a suspension requested by Ecuador does of course not entitle other WTO Members to derogate from any of their obligations under the TRIPS Agreement. Consequently, such DSB authorization to Ecuador cannot be construed by other WTO Members to reduce their obligations under Part III of the TRIPS Agreement in regard to imports entering their customs territories.

D.   The Suspension of TRIPS Obligations and Interference with Private Rights

We are conscious that the requested suspension of certain TRIPS obligations ultimately interferes with private rights owned by natural or legal persons. These persons are highly unlikely to have any connection with the ongoing failure of the European Communities to fully comply with the DSB rulings in the proceeding under Article 21.5 of the DSU in Bananas III between Ecuador and the European Communities. The same logic holds true for the suspension of concessions or other obligations under the GATT (or other agreements in Annex 1A) and the GATS as well. However, the interference with private property rights of individuals or companies may be perceived as more far-reaching under the TRIPS Agreement, given the

potentially unlimited possibility to copy phonograms or use other intellectual property rights. In contrast, producers of goods and service suppliers
which are affected by the suspension of concessions or other obligations
under the GATT or the GATS may stop exporting to the Member imposing
such suspension.

We are aware that the implementation of the suspension of certain TRIPS
obligations may give rise to legal difficulties or conflicts within the domestic
legal system of the Member so authorized (and perhaps even of the
Member(s) affected by such suspension). The resolution of such difficulties
is of course a matter entirely within the prerogatives of the Member
requesting authorization. Obviously, the degree of such difficulties is likely
to depend on the means chosen by Ecuador for implementing the suspension
of certain TRIPS obligations in relation to the 13 EC member States.

E. Concluding Observations on the Suspension of TRIPS Obligations

[The Arbitrators read their mandate under Article 22(6)–(7) of the DSU
with respect to comparing the level of impairment suffered with the level
of suspension of concessions proposed, as limited to estimating Ecuador's
losses (in actual and potential trade and trade opportunities) in Ecuadorean
bananas and distribution services by suppliers of Ecuadorean origin.] However, in the light of the provisions of Article 19.1 of the DSU referred to
above, we wish to make some remarks on Ecuador's intentions on how to
implement the suspension of certain TRIPS obligations, if authorized by
the DSB.

We note with approval that, in implementing the suspension of certain
TRIPS obligations at a level not exceeding the level authorized by the DSB,
Ecuador intends to account not only for the actual impact of the suspension
of intellectual property rights currently used subject to the authorization
by the right holder and subject to the payment of remuneration. The
mechanisms described in detail below reflect Ecuador's intention to consider also the potential impact of such suspension in terms of the additional
use of the intellectual property rights in question. Such use may be expected
to increase as a result of the fact that the DSB's authorization would allow
using such intellectual property rights without payment of remuneration
to EC right holders and without their authorization, provided that prices
for the products incorporating the intellectual property rights concerned
decrease.

More specifically, we note that in its response to questions by the
Arbitrators, Ecuador submits that it never had the intention to simply
abolish all rules on "related rights" and to put all EC produced phonograms
in the public domain which it could arguably do only if it had requested
suspension of Article 9 of the TRIPS Agreement, too. If Ecuador were authorized by the DSB to suspend the application of "related rights" under Article
14 vis-à-vis the European Communities, it would consider installing a
system whereby companies or individuals established in Ecuador could

obtain an authorization from the Ecuadorean government to apply the suspension of concessions derived from Article 14 of the TRIPS Agreement within the Ecuadorean territory. This authorization would be granted through a licensing system which limits the suspension of concessions in terms of quantity, value and time. The Ecuadorian government would reserve its right to revoke these licences at any time. Each reproduction of a sound recording under this licensing scheme would correspond to a "suspension value" equivalent to the "related right value" of a new, commercially most interesting sound recording. For that purpose, Ecuador would use the average "related right value" of sound recordings in Europe as estimated by the International Federation of the Phonographic Industry (IFPI). A certain proportion of this value would represent the performer's share and another, larger part would represent the producer's share. If the level of suspension thus calculated were to risk reaching (together with authorized suspension in other sectors and/or under other agreements, if any) the level of nullification and impairment suffered by Ecuador, the authorization scheme would be stopped. Ecuador believes that the chances that this would happen are very close to nil.

Regarding geographical indications, Ecuador notes that the analysis should be different from the analysis with regard to Article 14 of the TRIPS Agreement. The non-respect of "related rights" on a sound recording results in a product that is identical in all respects to the product that is put on the market with the authorization of the "related rights" holder. The CD that would be produced under Ecuador's licensing scheme would be cheaper than a CD produced with the authorization and remuneration of the "related rights" holder, and the former would become a substitute for the latter. For products identified by a geographical indication that would be clearly different. For these products it is only possible to make use of the geographical indication, which is different from reproducing the original product. However, the use of geographical indications could be licensed in similar terms as explained for sound recordings above. Licences could be granted for a determined product and a determined value, quantity and time. The licences would be granted for the exclusive use of the holder of the licence and the Ecuadorean government would reserve its rights to revoke these licences at any time. The test for determining the level of suspension would be the extent to which protected EC products would be replaced by non-protected products from other sources.

With respect to industrial designs, Ecuador envisages a similar licensing system as described above even though it considers that the economic effect of suspending the protection of industrial designs would be limited.

In our view, the mechanisms envisaged by Ecuador for implementing the suspension of certain sections of the TRIPS Agreement, if authorized by the DSB, would take account of many of our remarks made in the preceding sections.

Finally, we recall that, according to Article 22.8 of the DSU, an authorization by the DSB of a request for the suspension of concessions or other obligations is in principle a temporary action, pending the removal of the WTO-inconsistent measure at issue, a solution remedying the nullification or impairment of benefits, or a mutually satisfactory solution. Given this temporary nature of the suspension of concessions or other obligations, economic actors in Ecuador should be fully aware of the temporary nature of the suspension of certain TRIPS obligations so as to minimise the risk of them entering into investments and activities which might not prove viable in the longer term.

. . . .

[The Arbitrators concluded that (i) Ecuador's request had not followed, albeit to a limited extent, the principles and procedures set forth in Article 22.3, especially regarding the suspension of concessions under the GATT with respect to goods destined for final consumption, and that (ii) the level of suspension requested by Ecuador exceeded the level of nullification and impairment suffered by it as a result of the EC's failure to bring the EC banana import regime into compliance with WTO law within the reasonable period of time foreseen for that purpose. Accordingly, the Arbitrators suggested to Ecuador that it submit another request to the DSB for authorization of suspension of concessions or other obligations consistent with the panel's conclusions. The panel then set out its calculations from which Ecuador could determine an appropriate suggestion. In particular, it suggested that Ecuador may request, pursuant to paragraph 7 of Article 22, and obtain authorization by the DSB to suspend concessions or other obligations of a level not exceeding US$201.6 million per year which the Arbitrators estimated to be equivalent within the meaning of Article 22.4 to the level of nullification and impairment suffered by Ecuador as a result of the WTO-inconsistent aspects of the EC import regime for bananas. The arbitrators commented that Ecuador may request, pursuant to subparagraph (a) of Article 22.3, and obtain authorization by the DSB to suspend concessions or other obligations under the GATT concerning certain categories of goods in respect of which suspension of concessions is effective and practicable, and to suspend commitments under the GATS with respect to "wholesale trade services" in the principal sector of distribution services.]

To the extent that suspension requested under the GATT and the GATS . . . is insufficient to reach the level of nullification and impairment indicated [above], Ecuador may request, pursuant to subparagraph (c) of Article 22.3, and obtain authorization by the DSB to suspend its obligations under the TRIPS Agreement with respect to the . . . sectors of that Agreement [listed in its request]. . . .

We recall the general principle set forth in subparagraph (a) of Article 22.3 that the complaining party should first seek to suspend concessions or other obligations with respect to the same sectors as those in which the panel or Appellate Body has found a violation or other nullification or impairment. In this respect, we recall that, according to the report in the proceeding between Ecuador and the European Communities under Article 21.5, the GATT and the sector of distribution services under the GATS are those sectors within the meaning of subparagraph (f) of Article 22.3 in which violations were found by the reconvened panel. More specifically, we recall that the reconvened panel in the above-mentioned proceeding under Article 21.5 found the revised EC banana regime, inter alia, to be inconsistent with Articles I and XIII of GATT.

. . . .

We have made extensive remarks above on the suspension of obligations under the TRIPS Agreement and in particular concerning the legal and practical difficulties arising in this context. Given the difficulties and the specific circumstances of this case which involves a developing country Member, it could be that Ecuador may find itself in a situation where it is not realistic or possible for it to implement the suspension authorized by the DSB for the full amount of the level of nullification and impairment estimated by us in all of the sectors and/or under all agreements mentioned above combined. The present text of the DSU does not offer a solution for such an eventuality. Article 22.8 of the DSU merely provides that the suspension of concessions or other obligations is temporary and shall only be applied until the WTO-inconsistent measure in question has been removed, or the Member that must implement recommendations or rulings provides a solution to the nullification or impairment of benefits, or a mutually satisfactory solution is reached. We trust that in this eventuality the parties to this dispute will find a mutually satisfactory solution.

NOTES AND QUESTIONS

(1) **Suspension of TRIPS Obligations and Other Treaties.** The arbitrators suggest that they do not have jurisdiction to determine whether the suspension of certain TRIPS obligations by Ecuador, even if authorized by the DSB, might violate obligations arising from other treaties not covered by the WTO. If the EU sought to pursue the argument that Ecuador's actions in such circumstances violated other international obligations, where would the EU initiate proceedings? If you were counsel for Ecuador, how would you respond? If this did give rise to a violation of those other treaties, what does this suggest about the incorporation of intellectual property within the multilateral trade dispute settlement system?

(2) **Enforceable Standards and National Sovereignty.** Some U.S. critics of the WTO system have complained that the possibility of retaliation against the United States upon receipt of adverse DSB determinations represents a loss of U.S. sovereignty. Is that true? If the WTO system, and the TRIPS Agreement, were not in place, how might other countries respond to perceived inadequacies in U.S. intellectual property protection? To what extent has national sovereignty been surrendered and by whom? *See* David Palmeter, *National Sovereignty and the World Trade Organization*, 2 J. WORLD INTELL. PROP. 77, 89–91 (1999).

(3) **Effect of Binding Dispute Settlement**. What are the different ways in which national authorities might react to an adverse decision of the WTO Dispute Settlement Body? In what ways might the binding, legalistic nature of such decisions help or hurt domestic national debates about intellectual property? *See* Daniel A. Farber & Robert E. Hudec, *Free Trade and the Regulatory State: A GATT's Eye View of the Dormant Commerce Clause*, 47 VAND. L. REV. 1401, 1405–06, 1445 (1994) (suggesting helpful effects). In what ways might the possibility of binding WTO dispute settlement affect national authorities addressing issues with potential TRIPS implications?

Would it have been better to strengthen the jurisdiction and enforcement powers of the International Court of Justice rather than to assign international intellectual property law to WTO panels? *See* Joel P. Trachtman, *The Domain of WTO Dispute Resolution*, 40 HARV. INT'L L.J. 333, 376 (1999) ("How can a WTO dispute resolution decision ignore other international law? On the other hand, how can the WTO dispute resolution process purport to interpret and apply non-WTO international law?"). To what extent has the fate of international intellectual property law been assigned to WTO panels?

(4) **The Importance of the DSU.** Throughout Chapter 4, we raised questions regarding whether various national laws (real and supposed) would be in compliance with TRIPS. Review those questions, and consider whether your answers would have been different had you taken into account the detailed provisions of the DSU? If so, what does this tell you about the DSU and the purpose of the WTO dispute settlement process? Might it be appropriate for your analysis of the national law in the abstract to be different from your analysis in the context of the WTO dispute settlement process? If so, why?

[E] Ministerial Review of the Dispute Settlement Understanding

Members have submitted comments and suggested reforms of the system as part of a planned review of the DSU. The review was scheduled to be completed within four years of the establishment of the WTO, *see Decision on the Application and Review of the Understanding on Rules and Procedures Governing the Settlement of Disputes*, 33 I.L.M. 1125, 1159 (1994), but has been extended because of the volume of proposals. As noted above, both the United States and the European Union have urged greater transparency (principally, open hearings and removal of restrictions on publication of the parties' submission) and the EU has proposed reforming the panel composition in the image of the Appellate Body. *See* Kim Van der Borght, *The Review of the WTO Understanding on Dispute Settlement: Some Reflections on the Current Debate*, 14 AM. U. INT'L L. REV. 1223, 1238–41 (1999). For a general discussion of some possible reforms, see Robert E. Hudec, *The New WTO Dispute Settlement Procedure: An Overview of the First Three Years*, 8 MINN. J. GLOBAL TRADE 1 (1999). The cloak of secrecy is pervasive at present. Indeed, the panel in *United States-Section 110(5) of the U.S. Copyright Act,* commented adversely on the confidentiality of information that "did not assist" the panel in discharging its duty to make findings that would best enable the DSB to perform its dispute settlement functions. *See id.* at nn.194, 211.

The European Commission has also suggested that the DSU be amended to include clearer statements about the role of pre-complaint consultations. Before a dispute panel is constituted, the party alleging a violation must request consultations with the putative defendant. Only upon the expiry of sixty days without the conclusion of an agreement between the parties can a complaint be filed with the WTO. *See* DSU art. 4.7. What should be the role of consultations? *See* DSU arts. 3–4. Do they fit in the WTO process? *See* David Palmeter, *National Sovereignty and the World Trade Organization,* 2 J. WORLD INTELL. PROP. 77, 80 (1999). Many disputes concerning TRIPS compliance have been resolved by bilateral consultations between the members concerned without recourse to formal dispute settlement proceedings. And, indeed, even where formal dispute settlement proceedings are initiated, discussions between the parties are encouraged throughout the process with a view to reaching a mutually acceptable solution. *Cf.* DSU art. 3(7) (reciting the philosophy of mutually acceptable solutions). If a member country displayed a derisory attitude toward its obligation to consult with another country, would you support that conduct being raised before a WTO panel? What would be the basis upon which the issue could be raised, and what would be the relief that a panel could grant? The European Commission's proposals would amend the DSU to (1) require that the request for consultations outline the complainant's case unambiguously; (2) confirm that the legal claims made before the panel must have been raised during consultations; (3) make clear that statements made during consultations cannot be used before the panel; and (4) permit the parties to seek written answers from each other. *See The Review of the WTO's Dispute Settlement Understanding: Which Way?,* 1 J. WORLD INTELL. PROP. 447, 448 (1998) (comments of Prof. Brigitte Stern); Van der Borght, *supra,* at 1235–38). Would you support these changes, and why? *Cf.* DSU art. 6(2). In what ways is the current role of consultations different from private court-based litigation?

In what other ways is the model of state to state litigation before the WTO different from other adjudicatory models? Consider in particular the differences between the WTO process and: (1) other state to state forms of dispute resolution, and (2) private litigation models. Can you explain those differences? How do they affect the ability of the WTO dispute resolution process to achieve its objectives? Should the shift be taken further toward juridicization of the process, and in what ways? What would be the costs and benefits of furthering this shift? *See The Review of the WTO's Dispute Settlement Understanding: Which Way?,* 1 J. WORLD INTELL. PROP. 447, 462 (1998) (comments of John Kingery); *id.* at 472 (comments of Thomas Cottier). That is, how would a highly adjudicatory system change the nature of international intellectual property dispute resolution (and possibly international intellectual property law)? Would the costs and benefits fall disproportionately on one group or another?

In addition to a desire for enforcement mechanisms other than retaliation, developing countries have sought increased funding for and access to legal expertise necessary to prosecute and defend actions. The DSU currently provides developing countries with legal assistance from the WTO Secretariat, *see* DSU art. 27(2), and proposals from developing countries focus on enlarging the Secretariat to increase that assistance. One such proposal suggests creating a Permanent Defense Counsel to assist developing countries in proceedings brought against them. *See* Van der Borght, *supra*, at 1230–32.

[F] The Relationship Between WTO Dispute Settlement and Special 301

The Special 301 mechanisms were introduced by Congress in 1988 largely as a result of the ineffectiveness of the pre-1994 GATT system. Does the WTO system, between periodic TRIPS Council review and binding dispute settlement with effective enforcement, make the Special 301 mechanism unnecessary? Congress did not appear to think so. Section 314(c) of the Uruguay Round Agreements Act, which implemented the GATT Agreement, amended the Trade Act to provide that a failure to provide adequate and effective protection of intellectual property could still trigger Special 301 measures "notwithstanding the fact the foreign country may be in compliance with the specific obligations of the TRIPS Agreement." Trade Act § 301(d)(3).

OFFICE OF THE UNITED STATES TRADE REPRESENTATIVE RESULTS OF SPECIAL 301 ANNUAL REVIEW (April 30, 1999)

Previously-Filed WTO TRIPS Cases

Over the past year, significant results have been achieved in several of the dispute settlement cases previously announced by Ambassador Barshefsky. In 1997, Ambassador Barshefsky announced initiation of WTO dispute settlement proceedings against Sweden, Ireland and Denmark. In 1998, Ambassador Barshefsky initiated dispute settlement proceedings against Greece and the European Union concerning rampant television piracy in Greece and their failure to comply with the enforcement provisions of the TRIPS Agreement.

On November 25, 1999, Sweden passed legislation amending its intellectual property laws to provide provisional remedies in civil enforcement proceedings. This type of remedy is particularly important for enforcement efforts in the software industry. On December 2, 1998, the United States and Sweden formally notified the WTO that they had reached a mutually satisfactory resolution to the U.S. complaint.

The cases against Ireland, Denmark, Greece and the EU are still pending, although progress has been achieved over the past year. In February 1998, Ireland committed to accelerate its work on a new comprehensive copyright law, and in July 1998 passed expedited legislation addressing two pressing enforcement issues. Denmark is presently considering options for amending its law to strengthen provisional remedies available to intellectual property right holders. In Greece, the rate of television piracy declined in 1998, and in September, Greece enacted legislation that provides an additional administrative enforcement procedure against copyright infringement by television stations. Ambassador Barshefsky stated, "We urge the Government of Greece to implement its new enforcement procedure in a strong and consistent manner, and to take steps to improve the handling of intellectual property cases in the court system in order to resolve this dispute."

Ambassador Barshefsky also expressed satisfaction today with the recent conclusion of the United States' dispute settlement proceedings against India. In December 1997, the WTO Appellate Body upheld a panel ruling in favor of the United States in this case involving patent protection for pharmaceuticals and agricultural chemicals. India's deadline for compliance was April 19, 1999. Earlier this year, the Government of India promulgated a temporary ordinance to meet its obligations, and then last month, it enacted permanent legislation entitled the Patents (Amendment) Act 1999. Through these mechanisms, the Government of India has established a mechanism for the filing of so-called "mailbox" patent applications, and a system for granting exclusive marketing rights for pharmaceutical and agricultural chemical products. The United States has expressed serious concerns regarding certain features of the new Indian law regarding exclusive marketing rights; however, in light of the discretionary nature of some of the problematic provisions of the new law, as well as the significant steps that India has taken or pledged to take to mitigate the impact of others, the USTR has concluded that no further action is appropriate at this time. Should any of the problematic provisions in the Indian law be invoked to the detriment of U.S. right holders in the future, the United States retains its rights to take further action.

United States—Sections 301–310 of The Trade Act of 1974, WT/DS152/R (WTO DSB Panel Report, Dec. 22, 1999). The EU requested consultations with the United States under Article XXII:1 of GATT and subsequently requested the establishment of a panel concerning the effect of the Section 301 process instituted by the Trade Act of 1974 (not Special 301). In its panel request, the EU claimed that a number of the procedures followed by the United States under the Trade Act (such as certain time limits and obligations upon the USTR to act) violated several provisions of the DSU and GATT, including *inter alia* the obligation of the United

States under Article 23.2 DSU not to make determinations concerning the acts of other member states "except through recourse to dispute settlement in accordance with the rules and procedures of [the DSU]" and to "obtain DSB authorization" prior to suspending concessions or other obligations. The EU argued that Section 301 created an unacceptable "sword of Damocles effect" and jeopardized the security and predictability of international trade. The United States responded that "the U.S. Administration has carved out WTO covered situations from the general application of the Trade Act, . . . inter alia, through a Statement of Administrative Action ("SAA") submitted by the President to, and approved by, Congress." Under the SAA so approved "it is the expectation of the Congress that future administrations would observe and apply the [undertakings given in the SAA]". One of these undertakings was to "base any section 301 determination that there has been a violation or denial of US rights on the panel or Appellate Body findings adopted by the DSB."

In a report issued on December 22, 1999, the Panel agreed with the United States, finding that the language of the Trade Act, especially when taken along with the SAA, allows the existence of multilateral dispute resolution proceedings to be taken into account under the Section 301 procedure, and allows for determinations by the USTR to be postponed until after the exhaustion of DSU proceedings. The panel found that:

> [T]he statutory language of Section 304 constitutes a serious threat that [Section 304] determinations contrary to Article 23.2(a) may be taken and, in the circumstances of this case, is *prima facie* inconsistent with Article 23.2(a) read in the light of Article 23.1. We then found, however, that this threat had been removed by the aggregate effect of SAA and the U.S. statements before this Panel in a way that also removes the *prima facie* inconsistency and fulfils the guarantees incumbent on the US under Article 23. In the analogy . . . , the sign 'No Trespassing—Trespassers may be shot on sight' was construed by us as going against the mutual promise made among the neighbors always and exclusively to have recourse to the police and the courts of law in any case of alleged trespassing. Continuing with that analogy, we would find in this case that the farmer has added to the original sign which was erected for all to read another line stating: 'In case of trespass by neighbours, however, immediate recourse to the police and the courts of law will be made.' We would hold—as we did in this case—that with this addition the agreement has been respected.

Id. ¶ 7.131.

NOTES AND QUESTIONS

(1) **Special 301 and "TRIPS-Plus."** What is the purpose of retaining Special 301? Is it appropriate? Is it prudent policy? Is it hurting or helping

the appropriate development of international intellectual property law? Is it hurting or helping U.S. interests? What would be the consequences of the United States pursuing measures under Special 301 where a panel has held the other country in question to be in compliance with TRIPS? Could this be used by the United States to circumvent the moratorium on nonviolation complaints? Could it be used to require other countries to implement standards that the United States was unable to include in the agreement during negotiations? Are there any circumstances where this may be more appropriate?

(2) **Special 301 in a Multilateral Context**. To what extent do the procedures pursued through Special 301 mesh with or interfere with the mechanisms established by the TRIPS Agreement? To what extent would the USTR's unilateral actions against China in 1994–95 be available if China joined the WTO and the United States now pursued its claims through the WTO mechanisms? To what extent were the priorities of the United States with respect to China reflected in the priorities of the TRIPS Agreement? (Compare the summary of U.S.-China agreements in the Newby article with the important provisions of TRIPS.) Compare the suggestions made earlier in this Chapter by Newby regarding alternative means of dealing with inadequate intellectual property protection with the forms of assistance to developing countries contemplated by TRIPS. To what extent have the views of Newby been reflected in the TRIPS system, whether in the dispute resolution procedure or other aspects of the WTO or TRIPS system?

(3) **Special 301 and WTO Obligations**. The ability of member states to enforce international intellectual property obligations of other states through the WTO process is hailed as one of the most significant achievements of TRIPS. But countries are also obliged "not to make a determination that a violation [of TRIPS] has occurred except in accordance with [the DSU] procedures and not to retaliate except in accordance with authorization from the WTO's Dispute Settlement Body." Matthijs Geuze & Hannu Wager, *WTO Dispute Settlement Practice Relating to the TRIPS Agreement*, J. INT'L ECON. L. 347 (1999). Does current U.S. practice under Special 301 comply with the letter or spirit of this concomitant obligation regarding the exclusivity of the WTO system? Does current EU practice comply with the same obligation?

(4) **The U.S. Record in the WTO.** The United States has pursued several complaints before the WTO in addition to those referenced in the excerpt from the 1999 USTR Annual Report; the United States has now initiated sixteen proceedings. Several of these have been referenced throughout this book, most notably the successful proceedings brought against India and the recent successful complaint against Canada regarding patent term. The United States has been the respondent in four cases.

§ 5.04   WIPO/WTO Relations in the Era of WTO Dispute Settlement

[A]   The WIPO-WTO Agreement

The incorporation of international intellectual property law within the GATT/WTO system threatened (perhaps destroyed) the primacy of the WIPO in international intellectual property relations. Yet, although the TRIPS exercise was in part motivated by dissatisfaction with the ability of the WIPO-based system to develop and enforce international standards of intellectual property protection, the expertise of the WIPO was important in concluding the TRIPS Agreement. And the TRIPS Agreement expressly contemplates a continuing role for WIPO, both in the context of WTO dispute settlement, *see* TRIPS art. 68, and in the periodic reviews of TRIPS implementation for which the TRIPS Council is responsible under Article 71. Although WIPO is not permitted to provide interpretations of the conventions that it administers, WIPO may (upon the request of a WTO panel) be able to supply information regarding such matters as the negotiating history of a WIPO-administered convention. And WIPO offers significant assistance to countries involved in drafting, revising, or implementing their intellectual property laws in such a way as to be TRIPS-compliant. For a discussion of the institutional relationship between WIPO and the WTO going forward, see Frederick M. Abbott, *The Future of the Multilateral Trading System in the Context of TRIPS*, 20 HAST. INT'L & COMP. L. REV. 661 (1997).

In December 1995, the two institutions signed a cooperation agreement formalizing their relations on an ongoing basis. *See Agreement Between World Intellectual Property Organization and the World Trade Organization*, Dec. 22, 1995, 35 I.L.M. 754. Under this agreement, WTO members and nationals of WTO members are entitled to copies of laws and regulations, and copies of translations thereof, that exist in WIPO's collection, and access to any computerized database of such laws, on the same terms as apply to the member states of WIPO and to nationals of the member states of WIPO. *See* art. 2. Similar benefits are accorded the WTO Secretariat and the Council for TRIPS in order that they can carry out their responsibilities under the TRIPS Agreement. *See, e.g.*, TRIPS art. 68. In return, the WTO Secretariat undertook to transmit to the International Bureau of WIPO, free of charge, a copy of the laws and regulations received by the WTO Secretariat from WTO members under Article 63.2 of the TRIPS Agreement.

WIPO also agreed to make available to developing country WTO members which are not member states of WIPO the same assistance for translation of laws and regulations for the purposes of Article 63.2 of the TRIPS Agreement, the same legal-technical assistance relating to the TRIPS Agreement, and the same technical cooperation, as it makes available to members of WIPO which are developing countries. The Agreements also affirmed more generally that the International Bureau of the WIPO and the WTO Secretariat will enhance cooperation in their legal-technical assistance and technical cooperation activities relating to the TRIPS Agreement for developing countries.

[B] The Use of Post-TRIPS WIPO Treaties and TRIPS Council Developments in WTO Dispute Settlement Proceedings

Despite the conclusion of the TRIPS Agreement, WIPO has continued in its role as a primary vehicle for drafting, revision and conclusion of international intellectual property treaties. As suggested by Dreyfuss and Lowenfeld, WTO panels will almost certainly refer to developments in WIPO to assist in the interpretation of TRIPS. But what is the basis upon which they can do so, and what influence will such developments have? The issue was touched upon briefly by the panel in *United States—Section 110(5) of the U.S. Copyright Act*, where the United States had invoked the language of the WIPO Copyright Treaty to support its interpretation of the Berne Convention minor exceptions doctrine.

At first glance, the WIPO Copyright Treaty would not appear to have any application in the TRIPS environment, or with respect to interpretation of the Berne Convention. *See* WIPO Copyright Treaty art. 1 ("This Treaty shall not have any connection with treaties other than the Berne Convention, nor shall it prejudice any rights and obligations under any other treaties.") The panel was apparently not distracted by that provision and clearly took notice of the provisions in the WIPO Copyright Treaty. A short excerpt from the opinion follows.

UNITED STATES—SECTION 110(5) OF THE U.S. COPYRIGHT ACT
Report of the Panel (WTO DSB, June 15, 2000), WT/DS160/R

[In interpreting the scope of permissible exceptions to copyright under the TRIPS Agreement, the panel was called upon to interpret the scope of the so-called "minor exceptions" doctrine (which, although not expressly set forth in any treaty text, was understood to permit certain exceptions to copyright). Article 9(2) of the Berne Convention and Article 13 of the TRIPS Agreement each contains similar provisions regarding permissible exceptions to copyright. In particular, each provision subjects any such exceptions to a three-step test. Article 10 of the WIPO Copyright Treaty, adopted in 1996, contains a similar test. The panel addressed the relevance of the WIPO Copyright Treaty to its interpretation of the TRIPS Agreement, which was concluded in 1994.]

Subsequent developments

The United States argues that Article 10 of the WIPO Copyright Treaty ("WCT"), adopted at a Diplomatic Conference on 20 December 1996 organized under the auspices of WIPO, reflects the standard set forth in Article

13 of the TRIPS Agreement. Paragraph (1) of that Article provides a standard for permissible limitations and exceptions to the rights granted to authors under the WCT, while paragraph (2) extends this standard to the application of the provisions of the Berne Convention (1971). In the view of the United States, it becomes clear from the Agreed Statement concerning Article 10 of the WCT that the signatories of the WCT, which include the European Communities and its member States and the United States, commonly recognized the minor exceptions doctrine. In support of its view, the United States also points out that Article 10 of the WCT is based on Article 12 of the Basic Proposal for the 1996 Diplomatic Conference. The commentary in the Basic Proposal explains that the TRIPS Agreement already enunciates the standard of that Article for limitations and exceptions in Article 13 of the TRIPS Agreement, and further states that "[n]o limitation, not even those that belong in the category of minor reservations, may exceed the limits set by the three-steps test".

The European Communities argues that the WCT has to date been ratified by only a small number of contracting parties and has not yet reached the threshold of thirty ratifications necessary for its entry into force.

We note that the subsequent developments just mentioned do not constitute a subsequent treaty on the same subject-matter within the meaning of Article 30, or subsequent agreements on the interpretation of a treaty, or subsequent practice within the meaning of Article 31(3). Thus such subsequent developments may be of rather limited relevance in the light of the general rules of interpretation as embodied in the Vienna Convention. However, in our view, the wording of the WCT, and in particular of the Agreed Statement thereto, nonetheless supports, as far as the Berne Convention is concerned, that the Berne Union members are permitted to provide minor exceptions to the rights provided under Articles 11 and 11*bis* of the Paris Act of 1971, and certain other rights. It appears that the objective was not to disallow the provision of such minor exceptions by WCT parties, but rather to make their application subject to the "three step test" contained in Article 10(2) of the WCT.

[W]e [have] discussed . . . the need to interpret the Berne Convention and the TRIPS Agreement in a way that reconciles the texts of these two treaties and avoids a conflict between them, given that they form the overall framework for multilateral copyright protection. The same principle should also apply to the relationship between the TRIPS Agreement and the WCT. The WCT is designed to be compatible with this framework, incorporating or using much of the language of the Berne Convention and the TRIPS Agreement. The WCT was unanimously concluded at a diplomatic conference organized under the auspices of WIPO in December 1996, one year after the WTO Agreement entered into force, in which 127 countries participated. Most of these countries were also participants in the TRIPS negotiations and are Members of the WTO. For these reasons, it is relevant to seek contextual guidance also in the WCT when developing interpretations that avoid conflicts within this overall framework, except where these treaties explicitly contain different obligations.

NOTES AND QUESTIONS

(1) **The Current Relevance of the WCT**. The panel accepted that the WCT constituted neither a subsequent agreement nor practice within the meaning of Article 31(3) of the Vienna Convention. How is the WCT relevant and what weight was it afforded by the panel? Was this appropriate? *See* Graeme B. Dinwoodie, *The Development and Incorporation of International Norms in the Formation of Copyright Law*, 62 OHIO STATE L.J. 733, 773–75 (2001) (noting the relationship between the panel's use of the WCT and the dynamic development of international copyright law)

(2) **WCT as Subsequent Agreement and State Practice.** Neil Netanel has offered a thoughtful analysis of how the WTO dispute settlement process might be infused by consideration of recent international copyright law developments, and in particular the WIPO Copyright Treaty. *See* Neil W. Netanel, *The Next Round: The Impact of the WIPO Copyright Treaty on TRIPS Dispute Settlement*, 37 VA. J. INT'L L. 441, 464–75 (1997). Netanel suggests that the WCT and the accompanying Agreed Statements may constitute subsequent agreement and state practice under both Berne and TRIPS, and thus be relevant to a WTO panel's interpretation of TRIPS. (This will, Netanel concedes, depend upon a variety of considerations such as how many WTO members adhere to the WCT and the practice of WCT parties in implementing those obligations.) Netanel's resort to the WCT in interpreting TRIPS is in large part filtered through the WCT's relevance to the interpretation of the Berne Convention. Under which interpretive provision of the Vienna Convention would the WCT be relevant to an interpretation of a *Berne* provision? What about the Agreed Statements? The WCT is declared to be a "special agreement" under Berne. *See* WCT art. 1(1). How does that affect the use of the WCT in interpreting the Berne Convention before a WTO panel? *See* Berne Convention art. 20.

Even if the WCT is relevant to the meaning of the Berne Convention *qua* Berne, is it relevant to what Netanel calls the "Berne Convention in TRIPS"? It is not obvious that it must be because, although the Berne Convention *qua* Berne is clearly relevant to the Berne Convention in TRIPS, the WCT was concluded after the TRIPS Agreement was finalized. TRIPS imposed an obligation to comply with Berne as it was understood at the time of TRIPS; as yet, TRIPS does not require member countries to comply with the WCT. Netanel acknowledges this argument but suggests that because of the closeness in time between the conclusion of TRIPS and the WCT, the WCT and Agreed Statements retain probative value as indications of the parties' understanding of Berne at the time of TRIPS. *See* Netanel, *supra* at 471. Are you persuaded by the logic of Netanel's argument? *See also* TRIPS art. 68. If it is correct, does it support his further conclusion that panels could temper what he describes as the "maximalist" purpose of TRIPS with consideration of the "more balanced" WCT and Agreed Statements? That is, are there any limits on the ways in which the WCT can affect panel interpretation of TRIPS?

If the WCT and Agreed Statements were relevant to TRIPS interpretation only indirectly through the Berne Convention, this would limit their relevance to Berne-derived provisions, and thus (Netanel argues) prevents their consideration in construing independent provisions such as Article 13 of TRIPS. Does Netanel give too little force to his "indirect effect" argument in reaching this conclusion? How might the WCT and Agreed Statements still be relevant to an interpretation of Article 13 of TRIPS (other than as used by the panel in *Section 110(5)*)? If Netanel is correct about the limits of his "indirect effect" argument, might the WCT and Agreed Statements be directly relevant to the interpretation of TRIPS? Despite Article 1(1) of the WCT, which disclaims any connection to any treaty other than Berne, Netanel argues that the Agreed Statements (which include no corresponding disclaimer but include references to their concordance with TRIPS) may be relevant as subsequent agreements under Article 31 of the Vienna Convention. Does this mean that the Agreed Statements will be accorded more weight in interpretation than the WCT itself? (Netanel ultimately argues that the WCT and Agreed Statements would both be directly relevant as indications of subsequent state practice.)

Netanel highlights the significance of permitting resort to the WCT by considering whether a hypothetical application of the U.S. fair use doctrine permissible under the Berne Convention would also be permissible under Article 13 of TRIPS.[*] Can the meaning of Article 13 be textually determined? If not, one has to ask where else panels would look for guidance. *See* Paul Edward Geller, *Intellectual Property in the Global Marketplace: Impact of TRIPS Dispute Settlement*, 29 INT. LAW. 99, 112–13 (1995). Netanel suggests that a WTO panel should make reference not only to the negotiating history of Article 13—which suggests that Article 13 is a compromise between the repetition of the Berne Convention and the United States' efforts to implement a market failure based notion of fair use—and the trade context of the TRIPS Agreement, but also on the WCT (Article 10(2), which repeats Article 13 of TRIPS) and its accompanying Agreed Statements. He concludes that "seen in light of the Agreed Statements and the Copyright Treaty's 'public interest' preamble, Copyright Treaty article 10(2) and TRIPS Article 13 are meant simply as short-hand descriptions of the multivalent limitations and exceptions to copyright owner rights that are permissible under the Berne Convention. . . ."

Thus, under this argument, post-TRIPS international agreements, both regional and global (and both true minimum standards instruments and

---

[*] Netanel based his particular hypothetical upon a set of facts that fell within the "quotation" exemption provided by Article 10(1) of the Berne Convention.

optimal harmonization instruments), might be subsumed within the TRIPS/
WTO system, and thus made enforceable as the highest statements of public
international intellectual property law, in a variety of ways. They may be
accommodated in part through the dispute settlement mechanism. For
example, as higher standards become international norms through these
other agreements, failure by some countries to implement those standards
might be seen as distortions of trade in the same manner as were inadequacies in protection in 1994. Nonviolation complaints may provide a vehicle
for the expansion of the literal text to accommodate new (probably higher)
standards. Or, as Netanel suggests, those multinational agreements might
be used to affect the interpretation of state practice relevant (under the
Vienna Convention) to the interpretation of TRIPS.

(3) **Relevance of TRIPS Council Developments.** The TRIPS Council
(established by Article 69) is authorized by Article 71 to "undertake reviews
in the light of any new developments which might warrant modification
or amendment of the Agreement." How should the availability of Article
71 reviews affect a WTO dispute settlement panel's use of post-TRIPS
developments in either of these two manners? In other areas, commentators
have noted the complementary roles of the dispute settlement process and
"the more political legislative process." *See, e.g.*, Trachtman, *supra* at 365
(discussing interaction between Committee on Trade and the Environment
and panel decision in *Shrimp-Turtle* case).

In *United States-India*, India sought to rely on the fact that notifications
relating to the implementation of Article 70.9 had been made to the TRIPS
Council and no laws implementing the obligation in the manner sought by
the United States had been enacted by the countries concerned (i.e., those
that could avail themselves of the benefits of the transitional provisions).
See United States v. India, Panel Report WT/DS50/R, ¶ 4.27; *see also*
Matthijs Geuze & Hannu Wager, *WTO Dispute Settlement Practice Relating
to the TRIPS Agreement*, J. INT'L ECON. L. 347, 375 (1999) (discussing issues
raised in the TRIPS Council prior to filing of an action in *EC v. Canada*,
WT/DS/114). What weight should have been given to this fact? (Six months
before the United States initiated proceedings against India for failure to
comply with Articles 70(8) and 70(9) it also requested consultations with
Pakistan on the same issue and followed up with a request to establish a
dispute settlement panel. The parties reached a mutually acceptable
solution, which obviated the need for formal dispute resolution
proceedings.)

[C] The Future of a WIPO Dispute Resolution Treaty?

Does the continued negotiation and revision of treaties within WIPO
frustrate the objectives of the TRIPS Agreement? Why did countries decide
to negotiate the WCT within the confines of WIPO rather than seek to
amend TRIPS through the TRIPS amendment processes? *See* Frederick M.
Abbott, *The Future of the Multilateral Trading System in the Context of
TRIPS*, 20 HAST. INT'L & COMP. L. REV. 661, 667–70 (1997) (describing the

amendment process). Should we encourage countries to act only within a single forum? If a concurrent process of treaty negotiation is to occur within WIPO, is it important to conclude a dispute resolution treaty for disputes concerning such treaties, or are WIPO treaties intended to serve merely as adjuncts to the TRIPS/WTO process? Thus, reconsider the question we asked at the beginning of this Chapter: What relevance might a WIPO Dispute Resolution Treaty have? Professor Fred Abbott has suggested several reasons for pursuing such a treaty, including that

> the creation of a dispute settlement forum outside the WTO may permit states to resolve IPR-related disputes in an environment that is less politically charged than the WTO . . . States may find it useful to be able to submit IPR-related disputes to neutral dispute settlement without the threat of trade sanctions looming against losing parties.

Id. at 672. If Abbott is correct, what does this say about the WTO dispute settlement process? Do you agree with his assessment? What issues would the existence of concurrent dispute settlement processes raise? *Cf.* DSU art. 23.

Where would the greatest support for a WIPO-based dispute settlement process come? The developing countries, who perceive more favorable treatment within WIPO, might be expected to support a shift in focus from the WTO to WIPO. But Abbott notes that "a striking aspect [of the WIPO Dispute Resolution Treaty] negotiations . . . is that they are being pursued with considerable vigor by many of the same OECD governments that moved the international IPRs center of gravity from WIPO into the WTO." *Id.* at 672. Why might such countries be interested in a WIPO dispute resolution process? (The United States is a notable exception, having displayed no enthusiasm for the WIPO Dispute Settlement Treaty.)

From what you have read, what roles in the international intellectual property process should be allocated to the WTO and which should be assigned to the WIPO? (Ask yourself what are the strengths and weaknesses of each institution?) Are there any that should be assigned to both institutions (or to neither)? *See* Abbott, *supra* at 678–82 (suggesting an allocation of institutional responsibilities). Bearing that in mind, how would you assign judicial competence between WTO dispute settlement and any WIPO dispute settlement process? Abbott has proposed the creation of an Inter-Institutional IPRs and Trade Governing Council, comprised of members from the WTO TRIPS Council and the WIPO governing bodies, which would, among other things, propose a "proper dispute settlement forum of first instance if a conflict between the parties arises." *Id.* at 679–80.

§ 5.05 NAFTA Dispute Resolution

The NAFTA Agreement, signed one year before the TRIPS Agreement, contemplates that disputes be submitted to NAFTA dispute settlement panels. Chapter 20 of the NAFTA provides a means for resolving disputes among the NAFTA governments over the application and interpretation of the NAFTA. The process involves consultation (typically for thirty days) between the parties, an attempt at mediation and conciliation (also typically thirty days) before the "Free Trade Commission," submission of the dispute to an arbitral panel, and implementation of the panel report (with failure to do so giving rise to a right to suspend equivalent benefits). The "Free Trade Commission," which consists of the trade ministers from the three NAFTA governments, oversees the implementation of the agreement and the resolution of disputes. The agreement also creates a NAFTA secretariat to provide assistance to the NAFTA Free Trade Commission and to the panels established under chapter 20. Once a party has taken dispute settlement under chapter 20 to the stage of placing the matter before the Commission, the member country is precluded from seeking parallel action under the WTO. *See* NAFTA art. 2005(6). The process is no more transparent than the WTO process. One scholar has noted that:

> the Chapter 20 panel process is intended to remain confidential between the parties, reflecting an almost obsessive concern for secrecy on the part of the governments. Thus, the Rules of Procedure must and do provide that 'the panel's hearings, deliberations, and initial report, and all written submissions to and communications with the panel shall be confidential'.

David Gantz, *Dispute Settlement under the NAFTA and the WTO: Choice of Forum Opportunities and Risks for the NAFTA Parties*, 14 Am. Univ. J. Int'l L. 1025, 1043 (1999). Unlike the WTO, there is no appeal from panel reports.

As of yet, there have been no intellectual property disputes decided by a NAFTA panel. In what circumstances might a NAFTA panel be the appropriate forum for settlement of an intellectual property dispute?

PART IV

ACQUISITION AND ENFORCEMENT OF RIGHTS INTERNATIONALLY

Chapter 6

MECHANISMS FOR THE ACQUISITION OF PATENT AND DESIGN RIGHTS

As economic globalization quickens, the need for producers to obtain industrial property rights on a multinational basis becomes more pressing. The Paris Convention offers only limited assistance to U.S. applicants in this regard. It provides post-application grace periods in which a U.S. applicant can file an application in a Paris Union country and receive the priority of its U.S. application date. However, to secure registered rights in those other countries, the U.S. applicant must file and pursue a separate application in each country in which a registration is sought. In this Chapter, we consider mechanisms that provide greater assistance in securing rights on a multinational basis. At the global level, these mechanisms have primarily involved the centralized filing of an application in pursuit of several national registrations. At the regional level, however, there have been more ambitious efforts to facilitate multinational protection. These efforts, which are being considered most fully in the EU, involve systems that begin to move industrial property law—in differing ways, and to a differing extent—beyond purely national rights.

§ 6.01 Global Patent Registration Agreements

[A] Introduction: Early Visions of a Global Patent

A consistent distinguishing feature of the national patent laws of European countries from the very beginnings of the industrial revolution has been the international thrust of the policies behind them. In Chapter 2, for example, we examined the English Statute of Monopolies, the goal of which was to provide incentives to introduce foreign technology into that country. In high contrast to this, the American patent system from its earliest days to the present has placed its emphasis on creating incentives for inventors within the United States, although foreigners were (almost!) always welcome to participate. Earlier in the twentieth century, developing and some developed countries resisted pressures to give up their compulsory licensing regimes in the belief that such systems created incentives for the substitution of cheaper domestic products for expensive imported technology. (As we saw in Chapter 4, Article 31 of the TRIPS Agreement has since placed significant limits on the discretion of states to impose compulsory licensing.) While no nation or culture holds a monopoly on creativity or innovative initiative, real differences in national character and culture drive the engines of technological and economic development policy, including patent policy, in various countries. These differences have had a chilling effect on the development of a world patent system in the past and continue to do so today.

The ideal of a world patent system is not new. Efforts to create an international patent system, begun in Vienna in 1874, were renewed in earnest after World War I. But as we have seen, variations in the patent systems and the philosophies which underpin them, both between the industrialized and the developing countries and among the industrialized countries themselves, have not yet been reduced beyond the minimalist standardization of the TRIPS Agreement, much less eradicated. The current uniqueness of the American first-to-invent system and the stubborn unwillingness of the United States to change it aside, serious questions remain as to whether conditions for the grant of patents in the various jurisdictions or standards for their enforceability are likely to be harmonized. One authority, observing the British patent law and its harmonization with the European Patent System over the last twenty years, notes that "the resulting edifice is byzantine in complexity." Real difficulties and seemingly insurmountable obstacles have been encountered in attempts at harmonizing substantive patent law internationally, as seen, for example, with the 1991 Patent Law Treaty negotiations mentioned in Chapter 4. The continuing disarray among national courts interpreting the supposedly harmonized patent law of the regional European Patent Convention is discussed in Chapter 7.

But camouflaged by this apparent disharmony and disarray, international patent lawyers and patent office officials in both national offices and international organizations continue to work diligently to simplify and rationalize the complexity and attendant expense entailed in filing patent applications internationally. The pressures to reduce patent costs are felt most by the biggest users of the international patent system—primarily multinational corporations—but in the global economy of the twenty-first century, innovators great and small will likely be affected.

Yet, notwithstanding the fact that states have not been able to come to agreement about substantive harmonization of patent laws, they continue to be spurred to move toward agreement about procedure. The more limited PLT, concluded in June, 2000 is a testament to this. In this section, we examine early ideas about how to create a world patent in the period between the two World Wars. Next, we observe the major efforts to bring the vision of a worldwide patent granting process to fruition, from the establishment of the Patent Cooperation Treaty [PCT] regime in the 1960s to the Twenty-first Century. As we proceed, we may reflect on the extent to which, if at all, procedural simplification and unification have paved the way to substantive harmonization and how the vision of a global system for the protection of patents has evolved over the course of the twentieth century.

SCOTT H. LILLY, INTERNATIONAL USE OF PATENT SEARCHES[*]

1 J. Pat. Off. Soc'y 268–69 (1919)

The Director of the Canadian Patent Office, in an address before the employees of the United States Patent Office, expressed the wish that his office might have the benefit of searches as to novelty made in the United States. He stated that the great majority of applications filed in Canada are filed in substantially the same form in the United States, and in these cases one search as to novelty should be sufficient, and that the one search could be more efficiently made in the United States, where the facilities for search are better.

That wish might be realized if the Canadian office would forward to the United States each application filed, for a report on its novelty. Where a corresponding application had been filed in the United States the report would require little but the copying of the citations made as a result of the previous search, and in other cases the report could be kept available for a subsequently filed application, so that in the majority of cases little extra work would be entailed in preparing such reports. It should be easy to set a price for such reports, which would be much less than the cost to Canada of making searches as to novelty and still would more than cover the cost of the extra work of preparing the reports, so that the arrangement would be mutually advantageous.

Making searches in two offices where they could be confined to one, not only duplicates the work of searching such applications as are presented in duplicate, but it duplicates the cost of providing facilities for searching and lessens the efficient division of labor amongst searchers. Probably a greater proportion of the applications in the Canadian Patent Office than in any other are duplicated in the United States; but it seems worthy of investigation whether, considering both work and plant, it could not be made profitable for the United States to report as to novelty not only to Canada but to England and her other colonies having patent systems.

Now, when the full efficiency of every man is needed and cooperation in other lines between Great Britain and the United States is being extended, should be an auspicious time for inaugurating cooperative searches as to novelty.

After returning from South America, former Commissioner Moore related that a number of representatives of South American countries had expressed their appreciation of the advantages of a patent system, indicating that their countries appreciated the difficulties arising from the grant of patents without search as to novelty and the great cost of a plant in which such searches could be made with any reliability. If the opportunity were properly presented, South American countries might gladly avail themselves of reports as to novelty made by the United States.

---

[*] Copyright 1919.

The more countries use one office for novelty reports the cheaper can [such reports] be made. With many countries using the reports of one office a report as to one invention may be used not only twice but many times, so that the cost for each use of the report is reduced.

Our facilities for searching are far from perfect. Making greater use of the facilities we have would make increased expenditures in perfecting them more reasonable to everyone, not excepting Congress, so that increased use should make it possible for the work to be done with less cost for each application and with greater reliability.

The logical first step seems to be to learn as nearly as possible the proportion of Canadian applications duplicated in the United States and in what respects, if any, the information as to novelty desired by Canada differs from that required in our system. Then an estimate of cost could be made and a definite offer presented to Canada. The logical ultimate goal would seem to be, not only a pan-English speaking and pan-American office, but a highly perfected plant and force justly maintaining itself as the authority on novelty for the whole world.

LE BREVET INTERNATIONAL
Chimie et Industrie, Dec. 1922, at 1332–36
Abstracted in 5 J. PAT. OFF. SOC'Y 342–344 (1923)

Since the question of an international patent seems not to admit of salutation at present, it has been suggested that efforts be made to take a first step which will bring nearer the goal which it is desired to reach. A proceeding is proposed, which would permit attainment of a single registration by limiting to three the number of patents which the inventor would need to take out for protection in all the countries.

In examining the different legislation, the countries could be divided into three general classes:

1. Those which grant patents without any preliminary examination; language of Latin origin.

2. Those which grant patents after a perfunctory examination; English language (with the exception of the United States).

3. Those which grant patents only after thorough examination; language of Germanic origin.

Considering these facts, it is thought that three groups of nations might be formed, each of which could grant a patent valid in all the nations belonging to that group.

Perhaps the objection will be made that in the various participating countries diminution of receipts will result. Since the multiplicity of formalities to be fulfilled now [in order] to get protection in several countries and the [accompanying] great expense prevent the great majority of inventors from protecting their inventions in foreign countries, is it not logical to predict that by simplifying the formalities and reducing the expenses, a very large number of inventors will be led to apply for patents in one or the other of the three groups, if not in all? We believe that, far from diminishing receipts, on the contrary a surplus will be recorded in which the various countries will share in a proportion to be determined for each of them. Perhaps this proportion will not be as difficult to determine as could be supposed. Why not ask each country to contribute to expenses as has been done for the International Bureau at Berne, afterwards sharing the receipts under the same conditions?

The unification of legislation would, it appears, not be difficult, even though limited to the principal nations, but it seems that a concentration for the creation of three patents as above suggested might be achieved without too much difficulty. Most of the countries by making only slight modifications to their own legislation could be classed in one or the other of the three groups.

. . . .

ENRICO LUZZATO, ABOUT INTERNATIONAL PROTECTION OF INVENTIONS[*]
4 Revista 583–588 (1931)

The present system of international protection of inventions is far from being perfect, so much the more when compared with the system of protection of other branches of industrial property, notwithstanding that inventions are really the most important branch of industrial property.

Indeed inventions do not enjoy the wide protection granted to copyright and cannot even be protected by means of a single international registration as is possible for trade marks since the creation of the international office of Bern for the protection of industrial property. On the contrary, for inventions it is necessary to file a separate application for patent in every country and to submit to all the formalities and provisions demanded by domestic laws.

If we examine what are the advantages granted by international conventions to inventors, we notice that these are: the right of priority (that is to say the term of 12 months for filing the patent in foreign countries), the right of independence of patents, [and] the limitation of the obligation of working in comparison with the provisions of national laws.

Therefore, an inventor who wishes to have his invention protected in all countries adhering to the international convention is obliged to file a separate application translated into the language of each country, [including] drawings etc., in every country in which the protection is desired, and this altho[ugh] there is an international union. Of course this entails heavy expense and trouble for the inventor.

Is it possible to improve this position and to obtain . . . better international protection of the rights of the inventor?

---

[*] Reprinted with permission.

Three different ways can be taken into consideration.

1.   By making national laws uniform,

2.   By the creation of an international patent,

3.   By admitting an international filing of applications for patents.

The first system appears to be impossible not so much on account of the differences among the various legislations as on other grounds.

I am of the opinion that there is no essential difference among the various national laws; on the contrary they are on the whole similar and those who hold a different opinion are mistaken.

I believe that if it were possible to ascertain how many patents granted in an important country (for example Great Britain) have been refused in another country (for example Germany) it would come to light that the patents not granted are few.

And if it were possible to know how many of these patents have remained in force after being granted, it would appear that [there are] very few . . . cases in which an invention has been granted protection in a country adhering to the union and has been refused protection in another. These cases are really exceptional and depend on special circumstances rather than on essential differences among the principles of the various laws.

This shows that the real invention is generally protected in the whole world altho[ugh] in different forms and ways, while what cannot be patented is generally no invention in the true sense.

However, altho[ugh] the substance of national laws is on the whole the same, this is not sufficient to achieve uniformity, however relative, in the necessary formalities for the granting of a patent. This happens because the laws on patents and the provisions relating thereto are not isolated and independent but are connected with the fundamental laws of the states and are influenced by them; they are subject to the systems adopted in the various states for the practical application of laws, and these systems vary according to the mentality and traditions of every country.

It has often been said . . . that these different manners of applying the law are only the consequence of different social and economic conditions and of different interests on the part of every country. But this is not [the whole story.]

At first sight it appears to be so, but it is more appearance than reality. [There are] very few . . . provisions of the law which have been enacted only on account of special national interests; [moreover, such] provisions are merely the result of a temporary situation. The difference among the laws depends really on the fact that some theoretical and old conceptions had survived [from] when the law was enacted, that there are some provisions which are bound up with the traditional procedure and are still applied only by custom; and it is very difficult to change all these legal traditions and customs.

I will give the following instance regarding Italy. This country, together with Hungary, has been the last to oppose the abolition *of the reservation of the right of third parties*, in connection with priority right. This attitude of Italy, in whatever way it is interpreted, ought to correspond to an interest, and an important one, of the country, considering that Italy not only wants to keep in force this right of third parties but maintains this attitude; notwithstanding the contrary opinion of nearly all the countries adhering to the union. Now, the opposition has really no practical grounds and depends only on . . . theoretical prejudices. The evident demonstration of this consists in the fact that we do not know what interest Italy has, to maintain this provision. There has never been in the past 20 years a law suit regarding the right of third parties and this provision has never been applied outside of the courts.

I have mentioned this only in order to show one of the aspects of the difficult problem of the unification of laws and I am obliged to conclude that unfortunately there are apparent and real reasons (which may be only of form but cannot be eliminated owing to the different mentality of nations and the different formation of the laws) that make it impossible to unify the laws on patents today and in [the] future for a period which cannot be fixed; this holds true even tho[ugh] the differences may be merely formal, but cannot be eliminated owing to [the] different mentality of nations and [the] different formation of laws.

The second possible system would be the creation of an international patent but such a creation is still more difficult than the unification of the laws. Indeed creating an international patent is equivalent to the unification of laws, at least regarding the issuance of patents, because all countries that would admit an international patent would be also obliged to have the same system for issuing it.

Indeed . . . litigations following the granting of the patent might be decided by the courts of the different countries and according to national laws, but it would be absolutely necessary in order to make an international patent possible that in granting a patent all countries follow a uniform system and uniform criteria, however different from the system and criteria adopted in other countries. Which could be this system?

Would it be necessary to have a preliminary examination of patents? And should an examination be established and accepted by all countries? Of what country would be the examiners and which form would be chosen among the many different forms adopted today in the various countries?

I think that no great substantial difference exists in the different countries regarding the granting of patents, but there is on the contrary a great difference in the procedure, that is to say in the form of the application, in the way the rights of the inventor must be identified and established in connection with the rights of others etc. Therefore [while] it is perhaps possible to accept one of the systems now applied, it is certainly impossible to follow many systems at the same time, and mix together various criteria which are too different.

If a board of persons of different countries [were to] judge on the validity of patents, it would be a tower of Babel; the same would happen if we should adopt for one industrial branch the criteria adopted in one country and different criteria for another. Therefore an international patent is impossible at present.

Another possible system would be the international registration of patents. In this case we should apply to inventions a system which is already applied for trade marks with good results. The Madrid arrangement for the international registration of trade marks does not invalidate the laws of the different countries. It only makes it possible to register the trade mark at the international office in Bern through the patent office of the country of origin, and the registration at the international office is valid for all contracting countries.

It would be necessary to have at the international office a special branch for filing the patent applications, and this filing would have an international validity. The international office, on [its] part, should inform (as [it does] for trade marks) the different countries of the filing, and these countries then ought to inform the office whether they accept this filing or not. This would be sufficient to free the inventor from the very numerous formalities which are now necessary for filing a patent in all countries. I think that an accord could be reached on this system if there were not the difficult[ies] arising from the examination of the patent.

Of course, if the filing of the application is refused in the countries where there is the examination of patents, the same procedure would begin which now takes place after the direct filing in the country and in this case the inventor would be obliged to appoint a representative, etc. as he is obliged to do now.

This trouble cannot be at present avoided, but it would be a great advantage to be able to get rid of many formalities and several separate applications by means of a unique application in the country of origin, together with the application for transmission to the international office.

In this manner the inventor could obtain a patent in a short time in all countries, and only alterations of form would perhaps be required in the countries where there is no examination of the patent, and after the examination in the others.

The only real difficulty is caused by the differen[t] . . . manner of establishing in the various countries what is the invention and its contents, with the consequence of making the patent applications and the claims quite different in the various countries.

This is today a very serious question; indeed, the drafting of applications and claims in order to have the greatest possible protection . . . has become a true profession with an artistic touch in it and is followed by eminent specialists. However, I think that this difficulty could be overcome. It would perhaps be possible to establish by means of an international conference some rules for rendering the patent applications suitable to the laws of the different countries so as to have an application generally acceptable everywhere.

Indeed it would be sufficient to establish some basis which would render the application acceptable to the mentality of the different patent office officials so that the procedure of examination would follow in the ordinary course.

This may seem to be a minor result, but in reality it would be a great forward step for the inventor who has so many difficulties to contend with; moreover we cannot hope to obtain at present more than this and it is useless to lose time inventing unworkable theories.

[B] Realizing the Vision of a Global Patent: The Strasbourg Agreement Concerning the International Patent Classification [IPC] (1971), the Budapest Deposit Treaty of 1977, and the Patent Cooperation Treaty [PCT] (1970)

THE STRASBOURG CONVENTION AND PATENT CLASSIFICATION

The two pillars of the existing international mechanism for protection of patents are the Strasbourg Agreement Concerning the International Patent Classification [IPC] and the Patent Cooperation Treaty [PCT]. (The IPC should not be confused with the Strasbourg Convention of 1963 harmonizing certain points of patent law, discussed below in § 6.03, which was the foundation of the European Patent Convention.)

The IPC was signed in 1971 and establishes the international patent classification system of approximately 67,000 alphanumeric categories. (It is found at Number 51 of the "Internationally Agreed Upon Numbers for Identification of Data" [INID Numbers] on the first page of the patent document.) There are currently 41 member states including all the EPC countries, the U.S., Canada, Australia, China and Japan. According to Article 3 of the IPC Agreement, the purpose of the Agreement is solely administrative. Classification is important both for searching prior art and for assigning applications to examiners examining patents. The United States continues to use the U.S. Patent Classification System (*see* MPEP 902.01) as its principal system of classification and the IPC as a subsidiary system, as is allowed under Article 4(2) of the IPC. The U.S. system is primarily a classification by structure while the IPC system is based primarily on function. Until such time as the U.S. adopts the IPC as its principal classification system, disparities between the search results of a U.S. search and an IPC search are likely to continue. More recently, the IPC as a search tool is gradually being superceded by electronic online search tools. The EPO uses the EPOQUE system, the Japanese Patent Office [JPO] uses what is called the F-term system, and the United States uses the Automated Patent System [APS]. (Efforts toward the development of common ground rules [CGRS] for searching patents between the USPTO, EPO, and JPO are discussed further below.)

THE BUDAPEST TREATY

The Budapest Treaty on the International Recognition of the Deposit of Microorganisms for the Purposes of Patent Procedure was signed in 1977. The Budapest Union member states must allow or require the deposit of microorganisms in order to meet the enablement requirement of the patent specification for inventions involving cell lines; and Budapest member states which meet certain standards may be designated as international depositories. There are 53 member states as of July 15, 2002, including the United States.

THE PATENT COOPERATION TREATY

The PCT was signed in Washington in December 1970 and entered into force on January 1, 1978 for the United States. It provides for a system of coordinated international search, possibility of a preliminary (and advisory) patentability examination, and a single international application designating the PCT countries selected by the applicant. The PCT application is transmitted to national offices of the elected contracting states for further processing in what is known as the "national phase." In states that have acceded to Chapter II of the PCT (including the U.S.) a non-binding Preliminary Examination may be conducted based upon very general criteria set forth in PCT Article 33 and Rule 64. The PCT leads to a bundle of patents which may differ in scope. A significant advantage of the PCT process is that translations on parallel applications may be postponed until after at least a prior art search has been carried out and the results made available, and in some cases for as long as 30 months. The PCT is merely a filing procedure and does not create an international patent. In 1979, 2,625 international applications were received by the International Bureau. The corresponding numbers were 90,946 in 2000 and 103,927 in 2001. The average number of designations per application was 6.66 in 1979 and 107 in 2001.

The PCT, its Rules of Procedure, and implementing legislation in the United States are discussed in the reading below, which also discusses the PCT's unique vocabulary as well as some of the advantages (and pitfalls!) which may be encountered in its use.

WORLD INTELLECTUAL PROPERTY ORGANIZATION
PCT APPLICANT'S GUIDE (May 2002)
www.wipo.int/pct/guide/en
(Last visited on 22 May 2002)

WHAT IS THE PCT?

. . . The PCT facilitates the obtaining of protection for inventions where such protection is sought in any or all of the [115] PCT Contracting States. It provides for the filing of one patent application ("the international application"), with effect in several States, instead of filing several separate national and/or regional patent applications. At the present time, an international application may include designations for regional patents in respect of States [of the] African Regional Industrial Property Organization (ARIPO), the Eurasian Patent Convention, the European Patent Convention, and the African Intellectual Property Organization (OAPI). The PCT does not eliminate the necessity of prosecuting the international application in the national phase of processing before the national or regional Offices, but it does facilitate such prosecution in several important respects by virtue of the procedures carried out first on all international applications during the international phase of processing under the PCT. The formalities check, the international search and (optionally) the international preliminary examination carried out during the international phase, as well as the automatic deferral of national processing which is entailed, give the applicant more time and a better basis for deciding whether and in what countries to further pursue the application.

THE "INTERNATIONAL PHASE" AND THE "NATIONAL PHASE" OF THE PCT PROCEDURE

The PCT procedure consists of two main phases. It begins with the filing of an international application and ends (in the case of a favorable outcome for the applicant) with the grant of a number of national and/or regional patents: hence the terms "international phase" and "national phase." (The expression "national phase" is used even if the Office before which it takes place is a regional Office.) The expressions "international phase" and "national phase" are not actually used in the PCT, but they are convenient, short expressions which have become customary and are therefore used in this Guide.

The international phase consists (if completed) of four main steps of which the first three occur automatically and the last is optional for the applicant. The first three steps consist of the filing of the international application by the applicant and its processing by the "receiving Office", the establishment of the international search report by one of the "International Searching Authorities", and the publication of the international application together with the international search report as well as their communication by the International Bureau of WIPO (hereinafter referred to as "the International Bureau") to the national (or regional) Offices which the applicant wishes to grant him a patent on the basis of his international application (the so-called "designated Offices").

There is also an optional fourth step, namely the establishment of an international preliminary examination report (which, however, is not published) by one of the "International Preliminary Examining Authorities". . . .

On completion of the international phase, further action is required before and in each of the designated Offices. In particular, the applicant has to pay to those Offices the required national (or regional) fees, furnish them with any translations that are required and appoint a representative (patent agent) where required. There are time limits by which those steps must be taken if the application is to proceed in the national phase. If the steps are not taken within the applicable time limit, the effect of the international application may cease in the designated States concerned. The designated Offices then examine the application and grant or refuse the national (or regional) patent on the basis of their national laws [or regional treaty such as the ARIPO, European, Eurasian, or OAPI Conventions and agreements]. These procedures before the designated Offices constitute what is usually referred to as the "national phase". . . .

It is up to the applicant to decide whether and when to enter the national phase before each designated Office. The international phase continues, for any particular designation, until entry into the national phase before the designated Office concerned or until the expiration of the applicable time limit for entering the national phase before that Office. Since the national phase may be entered before different designated Offices at different times, the international application may simultaneously be in the international phase for some designations and the national phase for others. Where the national phase processing or examination has begun before a particular designated Office, any actions taken on the international application remaining in the international phase have no effect on the proceedings before that Office.

USEFULNESS OF THE PCT FOR APPLICANTS

Use of the PCT saves effort—time, work, money—for any person or firm ("the applicant") seeking protection for an invention in a number of countries. Use of the PCT also helps the applicant to make decisions about the prosecution of the application before the various national Patent Offices in the national phase of processing. The saving arises primarily from the fact that, under the PCT, the applicant files one application—the international application—in one place, in one language and pays one initial set of fees, and that this international application has (subject to certain conditions indicated later) the effect of a national or regional application, which, without the PCT, he would have to file separately for each country or region.

The help to the applicant in the national phase prosecution of the application follows from the "advice" he obtains from the international search report, a report which is established for each international application, according to high, internationally regulated standards, by one of the Patent Offices that are highly experienced in examining patent applications and that have been specially appointed to carry out international searches. 21. Even more explicit advice can be obtained in most cases from the international preliminary examination report, a report which is available from equally experienced Offices which have also been appointed to that effect. Those Offices are listed in Annex E ("International Preliminary Examining Authorities").

By the single act of filing an international application under the PCT, it is possible to secure the very effect that, without the PCT, would require as many filings of separate applications as there are countries or regions in which the applicant seeks protection. The filing of an international application takes place in one of the languages accepted by the Office with which the application is filed; for many applicants that will be the language, or one of the languages, used by the national or regional Patent Office of, or acting for, their country. The international application is filed in a single place; it is generally filed at the national Patent Office of the applicant's country or at a regional Patent Office acting for the applicant's country, or it may be filed direct with the International Bureau in its capacity as a receiving Office under the PCT. There is a prescribed form for the international application. This form must be accepted by all designated Offices for the purposes of the national phase, so that there is no need to comply with a great variety of widely differing formal requirements in the many countries in which protection may be sought. The international fees payable in respect of the filing of an international application may be paid at one time, at one Office and in one currency. The costs and possible complications connected with the payment, on filing, of many fees in many countries, and generally in different currencies, are thus avoided.

Before the applicant goes to the effort and expense of having translations prepared, paying the national or regional fees and appointing agents in the various countries, his views are able to mature to a greater extent than would be possible without the PCT, not only because he has more time, but also because the international search report, alone or preferably together with the international preliminary examination report, constitutes a solid basis on which he can judge his chances of obtaining protection. Any patents subsequently granted on the application by the designated or elected Offices can be relied on by the applicant to a greater extent than would have been the case without the benefit of the international search report and the international preliminary examination report. Moreover, because of the longer time the applicant has for making decisions, he is better placed to assess the technical value and economic interest of patent protection and to select the particular countries in which he desires to continue seeking protection for his invention. As a result, substantial savings can be made in both translation and filing costs for those countries which are no longer of interest to the applicant.

If an international application is filed in a language which is not both a language accepted by the International Searching Authority which is to carry out the international search and a language of publication, it needs to be translated into an appropriate language shortly after filing, but all the translations required by the Offices of or acting for the countries in which the applicant ultimately wishes to obtain protection need to be prepared only much later. Instead of having to be filed within the 12-month priority period, they are generally not required until the expiration of 20 months from the priority date (the time limit is even later for some Offices). ("Priority date" means, where the international application contains a priority claim, the filing date of the application whose priority is claimed, and, where it does not contain such a claim, the filing date of the international application. Where the international application contains two or more priority claims, "priority date" means the filing date of the earliest application whose priority is claimed.)

Fees payable to national or regional Patent Offices similarly become due later than they do without the PCT, and only in the case where the applicant decides to go ahead with the processing of his international application at the national or regional Patent Office. Generally, such national or regional fees must be paid within 20 months from the priority date, but a later time limit applies for some Offices.

Where international preliminary examination may be requested and is requested within a certain time limit, the time limits for filing translations and paying national fees are even longer (by as much as 10 months), generally expiring at the end of 30 months from the priority date (or even later for some Offices).

An international search report which is favorable from the applicant's viewpoint strengthens his position vis-a-vis the various national or regional Patent Offices, and his arguments for the grant of a patent by those Offices are likely to become more convincing. This is even more true in the case of a favorable international preliminary examination report, which contains far more material on which to base an opinion on the chances of obtaining patents than does an international search report.

If the international search report is partly favorable and partly unfavorable, the applicant can modify his claims so as to maintain only those which are likely to result in the grant of a patent. If the international search report is unfavorable, and the applicant consequently decides not to proceed any further, he saves the cost of having the application processed in the various countries. . . .

Regional Patents Via the PCT

Important additional advantages for applicants wishing to protect their inventions in countries party both to any of the various regional patent treaties and to the PCT result from combined use of the PCT system and those regional systems. Not only is the PCT fully compatible with the regional patent systems, but there are possibilities for advantageous combined use of both kinds of system by the applicant, irrespective of the country in which he files. The following paragraphs deal with the combined use of the PCT with the regional patent systems under which patents may be obtained via the PCT, namely, the ARIPO Harare Protocol, the Eurasian Patent Convention, the European Patent Convention and the OAPI Agreement, via the so-called "ARIPO-PCT route," "Eurasian-PCT route," "Euro-PCT route" and "OAPI-PCT route." In the case of the European Patent Convention, it is also possible to obtain patents through combined use of that Convention and the PCT in the States to which a European patent may be extended. . . .

Applicants filing a PCT application and wishing to obtain protection in countries party to any of those regional patent treaties obtain, from their PCT application filed, for example, with the Japan Patent Office or with the United States Patent and Trademark Office, the effect of a simultaneous filing with each regional Office concerned for the purposes of obtaining a regional patent, provided that they state their wish to obtain the regional patent(s) in the PCT request. In such a case, before taking any action outside his country, the applicant can safely wait until the results of the PCT search (and, optionally, of the international preliminary examination) are known and also make full use of the extended period (20 (or 30) months from the priority date, or even later for some Offices) by the end of which a translation of the PCT application, if it was not filed in one of the official languages of the regional Office (see the various National Chapters in Volume II), must be submitted and an agent appointed for the procedure before that Office.

An applicant may file a PCT application with his own national Office as receiving Office, even at the very end of the priority year, and still obtain an immediate automatic filing effect with the regional Office concerned. A further advantage is that, at the time of filing the PCT application, the applicant pays only one designation fee for each regional patent desired, no matter how many States are designated in respect of each of them. The four regional designations which are presently possible cover more than 50 PCT Contracting States. If, on the other hand, he chooses to file separate regional patent applications on the basis of his first application with his national Office, he will, by the end of the priority year, have to comply with all the requirements of each of the regional treaties as to formalities, fees and appointment of agents. . . .

FILING AN INTERNATIONAL APPLICATION

An application is "international" when it is filed under and with reference to the PCT. It is the first step towards obtaining a patent in or for a State party to the PCT: "in" such a State when a national patent is desired; "for" such a State when a regional patent (ARIPO, Eurasian, European or OAPI patent) is desired. Article 2(vii), 3(1).

An international application must be an application for the protection of an invention. The PCT encompasses the filing of applications for patents for inventions, inventors' certificates, utility certificates, utility models, and various kinds of patents and certificates of addition [but] cannot validly be filed for certain other forms of industrial property rights which fall outside the scope of "inventions," such as, for example, purely ornamental designs.

Any international application has two main effects. One of those effects, generally speaking, is the same as that of a national (or regional) application. It occurs on the date accorded as the international filing date. It is produced in or for the "designated States," that is, the States which the applicant, desiring to obtain a patent in or for them, expressly "designates" in his international application. [In the U.S., under 35 U.S.C. Section 364 and 102(e), an international application has prior art effect if it designated the United States and was published in English under PCT Article 21(2)(a)]. Designated States in respect of which international preliminary examination has been demanded by the applicant are called "elected States" in the terminology of the PCT.

The other main effect of an international application is that, normally, no designated Office may process or examine the international application prior to the expiration of 20 months from the priority date, and that any fees due to a designated Office and any translation of the international application to be furnished to a designated Office will have to be paid and furnished, respectively, only by the expiration of that 20-month period. This effect of the international application is normally referred to as the effect of "delaying" the patent examination and granting procedure before the national (or regional) Offices.

If international preliminary examination has been demanded, the delaying effect is, normally, 10 months longer, so that any fees due to an elected Office and any translation of the international application will have to be paid and furnished, respectively, only by the expiration of 30 months from the priority date.

An international application which has been accorded an international filing date is the equivalent of a "regular national filing" within the meaning of the Paris Convention for the Protection of Industrial Property and, consequently, may be invoked as the basis of a priority claim in a national, regional or other international application filed subsequently within the time limit and subject to the conditions provided for in that Convention.

[F]or each Contracting State, the authorities with which its nationals and residents may, as applicants, file international applications. In the terminology of the PCT, these authorities are called "receiving Offices" (because they receive international applications). . . . Where there are several applicants who are not all nationals and/or residents of the same Contracting State, any receiving Office of or acting for a Contracting State of which at least one of the applicants is a resident or national is competent to receive an international application filed by those applicants. Alternatively, at the applicant's option, the international application may be filed with the International Bureau as receiving Office, regardless of the Contracting State of which the applicant is a resident or national. If there are two or more applicants, the international application may be filed with the International Bureau as receiving Office if at least one of the applicants is a resident or national of a Contracting State. . . . Applicants may have a choice between several receiving Offices, for example, where there are two or more applicants whose States of nationality and residence include more than one Contracting State, or where a sole applicant has nationality and/or residence in more than one Contracting State.

Any international application must contain the following elements: request, description, claim or claims, one or more drawings (where drawings are necessary for the understanding of the invention), and abstract. The elements of the international application must be arranged in the following order: request, description, claim(s), abstract, drawing(s) (if any). . . .

The language in which an international application must be filed depends on the receiving Office. . . . If the international application is filed in a language other than Chinese, English, French, German, Japanese, Russian or Spanish (that is, the languages in which international applications may be published), or if the language in which the international application is filed is not accepted by the International Searching Authority which is to carry out the international search, a translation of the international application will need to be furnished for the purposes of international search and/or international publication.

The request must: (a) be made on a printed form (Form PCT/RO/101) to be filled in with the required indications; or (b) be presented as a computer print-out complying with the Administrative Instructions; or (c) be presented in the format of the print-out of the computer generated request prepared using the PCT-EASY software. [The request in English is found at http://www.wipo.int/pct/en/forms/index.htm]

The request contains a petition for the international application to be processed according to the PCT and must also contain certain indications. It must contain the title of the invention. It must identify the applicant, (normally) the inventor, and the agent (if any), and must contain the designation of at least one Contracting State. If the applicant wishes to obtain a regional patent rather than, or in addition to, a national patent in respect of one or more designated States, the request must contain a designation for each regional patent concerned. The request should also contain, where applicable, choices of certain kinds of protection in designated States, a priority claim, an indication of the applicant's choice of competent International Searching Authority and a reference to any relevant earlier international, international-type or other search. The request must be signed. . . .

Any resident or national of a Contracting State may file an international application. Where there are two or more applicants, at least one of them must be a national or a resident of a Contracting State. [The applicant(s) must be the inventor(s) in the United States, but different applicants may be indicated for the various designated States.] . . . [P]ossession of a real and effective industrial or commercial establishment in a Contracting State is considered residence in that State, and a legal entity constituted according to the national law of a Contracting State is considered a national of that State. . . .

[I]n view of the importance of careful preparation of the international application and of its proper processing, it is in any case highly advisable for applicants to use the services of a professional patent attorney or patent agent. Any person who can act as an agent before the Office which acts as receiving Office may be appointed as an agent for any international application filed with that Office. Where the international application is filed with the International Bureau as receiving Office, any person who has the right to practice before the national (or regional) Office of, or acting for, a Contracting State of which the applicant (or, if there are two or more applicants, any of the applicants) is a resident or national may be appointed as agent. An appointed agent who has the right to represent the applicant before the receiving Office is automatically also entitled to act before the International Bureau, the International Searching Authority and the International Preliminary Examining Authority. [Corporate applicants do not need an agent.] . . .

Any international application may contain a declaration claiming the priority of one or more earlier applications filed in or for any country party to the Paris Convention for the Protection of Industrial Property or in or for a member of the World Trade Organization (WTO) that is not party to that Convention. An earlier regional (ARIPO, Eurasian, European or OAPI) application or an earlier international application can also serve as a basis for a priority claim. . . .

The PCT makes no change to the provisions which govern the right of priority and are contained in Article 4 of the Paris Convention for the Protection of Industrial Property; WTO members are required to apply Paris Convention Article 4 in accordance with Article 2.1 of the Agreement on Trade-Related Aspects of Intellectual Property Rights (TRIPS Agreement). Since an international application has the effect in each designated State of a regular national application, it may claim priority from another application, and be used as the basis for a priority claim in a later application, just like any regular national application. So far as PCT procedures are concerned, the priority claim is particularly important because it establishes a priority date for the purposes of computing time limits under the PCT. The validity of a priority claim is not determined during the international phase (although the matter is taken into consideration for the purposes of establishing the international preliminary examination report, if any). . . .

Before the expiration of 16 months from the priority date (or, where the applicant requests early processing pursuant to Article 23(2), before that request is made), a certified copy of the earlier application (whether it is a national, regional or international application) must be submitted by the applicant either to the International Bureau or to the receiving Office (unless it has already been filed with the receiving Office together with the international application). . . .

Where two or more International Searching Authorities are competent to carry out the international search, the applicant must indicate the Authority chosen. . . .

The text of the declaration of inventorship for the purposes of the designation of the United States of America only is pre-printed in Box No. VIII (iv) of the request form since that text must be used as shown in Section 214, no parts may be omitted or presented in an order different from that used in the form. In addition, all of the inventors must be named in that declaration, even if they do not sign the same (copy of the) declaration, and bibliographic data (such as, but not limited to, address of residence and citizenship) must be included for each inventor; the declaration must be signed and dated directly by the inventor(s) unless they have signed in Box No. X of the request; a signature by an appointed agent is not sufficient for this purpose.

The standardized wordings [for Declarations] should always be used, otherwise, the designated Offices are entitled, even though they are not obliged, to require the applicant to furnish a new declaration or further evidence in the national phase. . . .

The international application must be signed. . . . by the applicant, or, where there are two or more applicants, by all of them. . . . The international application may be signed by an agent, but in that case the agent must be appointed as such by the applicant in a separate power of attorney signed by the applicant himself. . . .

The description must disclose the invention in a manner sufficiently clear and complete for it to be carried out by a person skilled in the art. . . . The details required for the disclosure of the invention so that it can be carried out by a person skilled in the art depend on the practice of the national Offices. It is therefore recommended that due account be taken of national practice (for instance in Japan and the United States of America) when the description is drafted. The need to amend the description during the national phase may thus be avoided. [This applies in the U.S.] likewise to the need to indicate the "best mode for carrying out the invention." If at least one of the designated Offices requires the indication of the "best mode" (for instance, the United States Patent and Trademark Office), that best mode must be indicated in the description. . . .

The claim or claims must "define the matter for which protection is sought." Claims must be clear and concise. They must be fully supported by the description. . . . In principle, under the PCT, any dependent claim which refers to more than one other claim ("multiple dependent claim") must refer to such claims in the alternative only, and multiple dependent claims cannot serve as a basis for any other multiple dependent claim. . . .

An international application should be drafted so that the claims relate to only one invention or to a group of inventions so linked as to form a single general inventive concept. . . . Since separate searches and examinations are required for distinctly different inventions, additional fees are required if the international search or international preliminary examination is to cover two or more inventions (or groups of inventions linked as just described). Unity of invention is present only when there is a "technical relationship" among the claimed inventions involving one or more of the same or corresponding "special technical features." The expression "special technical features" means those technical features that define a contribution which each of the claimed inventions, considered as a whole, makes over the prior art. The determination whether a group of inventions is so linked as to form a single inventive concept is made without regard to whether the inventions are claimed in separate claims or as alternatives within a single claim. An initial determination of unity of invention based on the assumption that the claims avoid the prior art will be made before the prior art search but may be reconsidered on the basis of the results of the search. . . .

The international application must contain drawings when they are necessary for the understanding of the invention. Moreover where, without drawings being actually necessary for the understanding of the invention, the nature of the invention admits of illustration by drawings, the applicant may include such drawings and any designated Office may require the applicant to file such drawings during the national phase. . . .

The abstract must consist of a summary of the disclosure as contained in the description, the claims and any drawings. Where applicable, it must also contain the most characteristic chemical formula. The abstract must be as concise as the disclosure permits (preferably 50 to 150 words if it is in English or when translated into English) The abstract should be primarily related to what is new in the art to which the invention pertains. Phrases should not be used which are implicit (for instance, "the invention relates to . . ."). . . .

It is to be noted that there must eventually be three copies of every international application: one is kept by the receiving Office (the "home copy"), one is transmitted by the receiving Office to, and is kept by, the International Bureau (the "record copy"), and one is transmitted by the receiving Office to, and kept by, the International Searching Authority (the "search copy"). . . .

There are three kinds of fee which must be paid in connection with every international application. The "transmittal fee" is fixed by, and accrues to, the receiving Office for the performance of its tasks in connection with the receipt and checking of the international application, and for the transmittal of copies of it to the International Bureau and the International

Searching Authority. The "search fee" is fixed by, and accrues to the benefit of, the International Searching Authority for the carrying out of the international search and the establishment of the international search report. The "international fee" is fixed in the Schedule of Fees annexed to the PCT Regulations and accrues to the International Bureau for the performance of various tasks, including the publication of the international application and the communication of various notifications to the applicant, the receiving Office, the International Searching Authority, the International Preliminary Examining Authority, and the designated and elected Offices. The international fee comprises the "basic fee" and "designation fees." The "basic fee" consists of a fixed amount plus an additional amount for each sheet in the international application in excess of 30 sheets (counting the request but not the fee calculation sheet). . . . As many designation fees are payable as there are specific designations [however] the maximum amount due, however, is five designation fees (effective as of January 1, 2002). All further specific designations for which a designation fee is due are free of charge. . . . All three kinds of fee are payable to the receiving Office with which the international application is filed. The receiving Office then transmits the search fee to the International Searching Authority and the international fee to the International Bureau. . . . An applicant who files an international application is entitled to a reduction in the international fee provided that [the applicant uses the PCT-EASY software as a printout, a diskette and filed with an appropriate receiving office.]. . . .

Processing of the International Application by the Receiving Office

The main procedural steps that any international application goes through at the receiving Office are: (i) the international application and the related fees are received by the receiving Office; (ii) the international application is checked by the receiving Office to determine whether it meets the requirements prescribed by the PCT as to the language, form and contents of international applications (the checks performed by the receiving Office are of a formal nature and do not go into the substance of the invention); (iii) where the checks made by the receiving Office show that the international application does not meet certain requirements as to fees, language, form and contents, that Office invites the applicant to furnish the necessary corrections; (iv) where possibly after correction the checks made by the receiving Office show that the international application meets the requirements prescribed for that purpose by the PCT, an international filing date is accorded to the international application by the receiving Office; [and] (v) copies of the international application, its translation, where applicable, and other related documents are transmitted by the receiving Office to the International Searching Authority and to the International Bureau so that they may carry out the procedural steps for which they are responsible in the further processing of the international application. . . .

The receiving Office must accord an "international filing date" to the international application if it finds that the following conditions are fulfilled: (i) the applicant does not obviously lack, for reasons of residence or nationality, the right to file an international application with the receiving Office; (ii) the international application is in the prescribed language; [and] (iii) the international application contains at least the [necessary as described above] elements. . . . [N]on-payment, incomplete payment or late payment of fees [does not] influence the international filing date. . . . Where the receiving Office accords an international filing date to the international application, it promptly notifies the applicant of that date and of the international application number; where it decides that the international application is not to be treated as an international application. . . . , it promptly notifies the applicant accordingly.

TRANSLATION OF INTERNATIONAL APPLICATIONS

Every receiving Office must accept, for the purpose of filing international applications, at least one language which is both a language of publication and a language accepted by the International Searching Authority, or, if applicable, by at least one of the International Searching Authorities, competent for the international searching of international applications filed with that receiving Office. In addition, any receiving Office may accept one or more other languages for the purpose of filing international applications. The translation of the international application [into an acceptable language] must be furnished to the receiving Office within one month from the date on which the international application was received by that Office.

THE INTERNATIONAL SEARCH PROCEDURE: PROCESSING OF THE INTERNATIONAL APPLICATION BY THE INTERNATIONAL SEARCHING AUTHORITY

The main procedural steps that any international application goes through before the International Searching Authority are the making of the international search, and the preparing of the international search report. Each receiving Office (except the International Bureau as receiving Office) specifies one or more International Searching Authorities as competent to carry out international searches on international applications filed with it. For some receiving Offices, different International Searching Authorities are competent depending on the language in which the international application is filed or, where the international application is filed in a language accepted by the receiving Office but not by the International Searching Authority, translated. . . .

The purpose of the international search is to discover relevant prior art. "Prior art" consists of everything which has been made available to the public anywhere in the world by means of written disclosure (including drawings and other illustrations); it is "relevant" in respect of the international application if it can help determine whether or not the claimed invention is new, whether or not it involves an inventive step (in other words, whether it is or is not obvious), and whether the making available to the public occurred prior to the international filing date. . . . The International Searching Authority must endeavor to discover as much of the relevant prior art as its facilities permit, and it must in any case consult the so-called "minimum documentation." Roughly stated, the latter comprises the published patent documents issued [by France, Germany, Japan,the former Soviet Union and now by the Russian Federation,Switzerland, U.K., U.S. regional patent offices]; published international (PCT) applications; and, from various dates, about 135 technical periodicals. It is emphasized, however, that, where the International Searching Authority has more than the "minimum documentation" at its disposal, it is obliged also to consult that additional documentation to the extent permitted by its facilities.

The International Searching Authority is not required to perform an international search on claims which relate to any of the following subject matter: (i) scientific and mathematical theories, (ii) plant or animal varieties or essentially biological processes for the production of plants and animals, other than microbiological processes and the products of such processes, (iii) schemes, rules or methods of doing business, performing purely mental acts or playing games, (iv) methods for treatment of the human or animal body by surgery or therapy, as well as diagnostic methods, (v) mere presentation of information, and (vi) computer programs to the extent that the Authority is not equipped to search prior art concerning such programs. However, certain International Searching Authorities do, in practice, search these fields to varying extents. . . .

The international search report must be established within three months from the receipt of the search copy by the International Searching Authority or nine months from the priority date, whichever time limit expires later. The international search report contains, among other things, the citation of the documents considered relevant, the classification of the subject matter of the invention (at least according to the International Patent Classification, that being carried out by the International Searching Authority itself) and an indication of the fields searched (those fields being identified by a reference to their classification) as well as any electronic data base searched (including, where practicable, the search terms used). . . . It is important to note that an international search report must not contain any expression of opinion, reasoning, argument or explanation of any kind whatsoever. The International Searching Authority transmits copies of the international search report to the applicant and to the International Bureau on the same day. . . .

INTERNATIONAL PUBLICATION, AMENDMENT OF CLAIMS, AND OTHER
PROCESSING OF THE INTERNATIONAL APPLICATION BY THE
INTERNATIONAL BUREAU

The main procedural steps that any international application goes through at the International Bureau are: (i) the International Bureau monitors the receipt of the record copy of the international application and notifies the fact, and the date of receipt, to the applicant and the authorities concerned; (ii) the applicant may amend the claims of the international application under Article 19 by means of a communication addressed to the International Bureau;(iii) the international application is published by the International Bureau (such publication usually takes place just after the expiration of 18 months from the priority date);(iv) copies of the international application and the international search report pertaining to it are transmitted by the International Bureau to the designated Offices; (v) where a demand for international preliminary examination has been filed, the International Bureau notifies the elected Offices, transmits the international preliminary examination report to them and makes a translation of that report into English (if required by any elected Office).

The record copy of the international application should normally reach the International Bureau before the expiration of 13 months from the priority date. After receiving the record copy, the International Bureau notifies the applicant, the receiving Office and the International Searching Authority (unless it has informed the International Bureau that it wishes not to be so notified) of the fact and of the date of receipt of the record copy. The International Bureau also notifies these facts to each designated Office which has informed the International Bureau that it wishes to receive such a notification prior to the communication sent with the pamphlet at the time of international publication; otherwise the designated Offices will be informed only at the time of that communication.

AMENDMENT OF THE CLAIMS UNDER ARTICLE 19

The applicant is entitled, under Article 19, to one opportunity to amend the claims of the international application in the international phase. (Further opportunities to amend the claims, and also the description and the drawings, are available during the international phase under Article 34 if, and only if, the applicant files a demand for international preliminary examination). Any amendment to the claims under Article 19 must be filed with the International Bureau, and must be in the language in which the international application is published. The opportunity to make amendments under Article 19 is available after the applicant has received the international search report and remains available until the end of 16 months from the priority date or two months after the transmittal (that is, the date of mailing) of that report, whichever expires later. Amendments received by the International Bureau after the time limit are still accepted if they have been received before the technical preparations for international publication have been completed. Amendments to the claims under Article 19 are not allowed where the International Searching Authority has declared, under Article 17(2), that no international search report would be established. Any amendment may be accompanied by a brief statement by the applicant explaining the amendment and indicating any impact it might have on the description and the drawings. Such a statement is published together with the international application itself. The PCT provides that amendments are not to go beyond the disclosure in the international application as filed. This requirement is not directly enforceable during the international phase, but failure to comply with it may have adverse consequences for the applicant during the international preliminary examination and in the national phase. Since any amendments of the claims under Article 19 are published with the international application, such amendment may be useful to the applicant if there is a reason to better define the scope of the claims for the purposes of provisional protection in those designated States whose national law provides for such protection. It is to be noted that, where international preliminary examination takes place, the applicant has the right under Article 34(2)(b) to file amendments to the claims (as well as to the description and the drawings) with the International Preliminary Examining Authority, regardless of whether or not he has filed amendments to the claims under Article 19 with the International Bureau. There is therefore normally no need to amend the claims under Article 19 where a demand for international preliminary examination is filed, unless there is a particular reason related to provisional protection or otherwise for amending the claims before international publication.

INTERNATIONAL PUBLICATION

International applications are published by the International Bureau [unless] (i) the international application is not accorded an international filing date by the receiving Office; (ii) the international application is considered withdrawn before the technical preparations for publication have been completed; (iii) the international application is withdrawn by the applicant before the technical preparations for publication have been completed; (iv) the only designated State, or the only designated State remaining at the time of the completion of the technical preparations for publication, is the United States of America. . . . The technical preparations for publication are generally completed by the 15th day prior to the date of publication. International publication takes place promptly after the expiration of 18 months from the priority date. However, when the applicant asks the International Bureau to publish his international application earlier, the International Bureau does so. . . .

International publication is effected in the form of a pamphlet containing the international application and, if available at the time of publication, the international search report or declaration by the International Searching Authority to the effect that no international search report will be established, and also any amendment, including any statement, under Article 19. . . . On the same date as that on which the pamphlet is published, a corresponding entry is published in the PCT Gazette (a publication of the International Bureau). The PCT Gazette is published in electronic form and in paper form. In the PCT Gazette in electronic form, the entry corresponding to each published international application contains bibliographic data, the title of the invention, the abstract and a characteristic drawing (if any) of the international application; in the PCT Gazette in paper form, each entry contains the bibliographic data and the title of the invention. If the international application is filed in Chinese, English, French, German, Japanese, Russian or Spanish, it is published in the language in which it was filed. Where the language of publication is Chinese, French, German, Japanese, Russian or Spanish, the International Bureau prepares English translations of the title of the invention, the abstract and the international search report and includes the translations in the pamphlet. If the international application is filed in a language which is a language other than Chinese, English, French, German, Japanese, Russian or Spanish and is a language accepted by the International Searching Authority for international search, it is published in English translation only. . . .

Article 29 has the [legal] effect of ensuring, with certain qualifications, that provisional protection is available after the international publication of an international application in the same way as it is after national publication of unexamined national applications.

COMMUNICATION OF COPIES TO THE DESIGNATED OFFICES

[Unless a designated Office requests an earlier copy, but no earlier than one year from the priority date] the International Bureau [first] communicates a copy of the international application in the language in which the international application is published, to each designated Office, except for any Offices which have waived the requirement that they be sent the communication. Where the language in which the international application is published is different from the language in which it was filed, the International Bureau will furnish to any designated Office, upon the request of that Office, a copy of that application in the language in which it was filed. Each designated Office is informed, separately from the communication, about the sending and the date of mailing of the notice to the applicant. The notice must be accepted by all designated Offices as conclusive evidence that the communication has duly taken place on the date specified in the notice. On receiving the notice, the applicant knows that he does not have to send a copy of the international application to any of the designated Offices indicated on it as having been sent the communication. [T]he International Bureau effects the communication of the international application promptly after its international publication. In any case, the International Bureau must effect the communication by the end of the 19th month from the priority date.

INTERNATIONAL PRELIMINARY EXAMINATION UNDER CHAPTER II OF THE PCT

International preliminary examination of an international application may be requested under Chapter II of the PCT to obtain "a preliminary and non-binding opinion on the questions whether the claimed invention appears to be novel, to involve an inventive step (to be non-obvious), and to be industrially applicable". It is carried out by an "International Preliminary Examining Authority" at the request—called "demand"—of the applicant, for use before the "elected" Offices, that is, those designated Offices which may be, and are in fact, elected by the applicant for that purpose. Not every applicant who has the right to file an international application has the right to demand international preliminary examination, and not every designated Office may be elected: the following paragraphs explain who may make a demand and which designated Offices may be elected.

Since the criteria on which the international preliminary examination is based correspond to internationally accepted criteria for patentability, the international preliminary examination report gives the applicant the opportunity to evaluate the chances of obtaining patents in elected Offices before incurring the expense and trouble of entering the national phase. Moreover, the fact that the carrying out of such an examination has been demanded has the result that the national phase in each designated State elected in the demand is normally delayed until the expiration of 30 months from the priority date (longer times apply in some elected Offices), provided that the demand is submitted before the expiration of 19 months from the priority date. There are two conditions which have to be fulfilled for a demand to be submitted. First, the applicant—or, if there are two or more applicants, at least one of them—must be a resident or a national of a Contracting State bound by Chapter II of the PCT. Second, the international application must have been filed with the receiving Office of, or acting for, a Contracting State bound by Chapter II. Any Contracting State which has been designated in the international application and is bound by Chapter II of the PCT may be elected.

The demand must be made separately from the international application, and be submitted directly to an International Preliminary Examining Authority which is competent to carry out international preliminary examination on the international application concerned. Each receiving Office (except the International Bureau as receiving Office) specifies one or more International Preliminary Examining Authorities as competent to carry out international preliminary examination on international applications filed with it. In addition, different International Preliminary Examining Authorities may be competent in relation to an international application depending on the language in which the international application was filed and on which International Searching Authority carried out the international search. Where several International Preliminary Examining Authorities are competent in relation to a particular international application, having regard to which receiving Office the international application was filed with and the language of the international application, the applicant may choose between them. Where the international application is filed with the International Bureau as receiving Office, the competent International Preliminary Examining Authority (or Authorities) is that (or are those) which would have been competent if the international application had been filed with a competent national (or regional) Office as receiving Office. The

International Preliminary Examining Authority or Authorities competent for international applications filed with each national (or regional) Office acting as receiving Office, and the languages accepted for international preliminary examination by each International Preliminary Examining Authority, may be ascertained by consulting Annexes C and E. Finally, within the framework of the respective agreements relating to the functioning of certains Offices as International Preliminary Examining Authorities, these Authorities may provide for limitations of their competence in respect of certain international applications. In practice, the European Patent Office has limited its competence in respect of international applications for which demands are filed on or after 1 March 2002 by applicants who are nationals or residents of [the U.S.] where these applications contain one or more claims relating to certain fields of technology [including business methods, computer programs, and gene sequences].

If a demand is submitted to a receiving Office, an International Searching Authority, [or] an International Preliminary Examining Authority which is not competent for the international preliminary examination of the international application, or the International Bureau, that Office or that Authority or the International Bureau, as the case may be, will mark on it the date of receipt, which will be considered to be the date on which the demand was received on behalf of the competent International Preliminary Examining Authority. . . .

There are no time limits in the PCT before or after which the demand must be submitted. However, in order to secure the full effect of the demand—including the delaying of the national phase until 30 months from the priority date—it must be submitted before the expiration of 19 months from the priority date. Since international preliminary examination will normally not start before the international search report is available, the applicant will normally wish to take cognizance of that report before deciding whether to proceed further on his quest for patent protection. On the other hand, the length of time available for the international preliminary examination depends on the earliest possible submission of the demand after the international search report is available, since the international preliminary examination report must in most cases be established before the expiration of 28 months from the priority date. The more time is available for the international preliminary examination, the better will be the result and quality which can be expected. Therefore, a demand should be filed as soon as possible after the applicant's evaluation of the international search report has shown that it is worthwhile to pursue the international application further. . . .

The completed demand must identify the applicant and the international application to which it relates. . . . The demand contains a petition that the international application be the subject of international preliminary examination. It must indicate at least one elected State from among the States designated in the international application. Where more than one International Preliminary Examining Authority is competent in relation to the international application, the Authority chosen by the applicant, and with which the demand is filed, should be identified. . . .

[T]he applicant is not obliged to be represented by an agent, but he may be, and in most cases it is highly advisable for him to be represented. . . .

The applicant has the right, under Article 34(2)(b), to amend the claims, the description and the drawings before the start of the international preliminary examination and also during the examination, if time permits, until the preparation of the international preliminary examination report. (As far as the claims are concerned, this is in fact the second opportunity to amend them before the international preliminary examination starts; the first opportunity is offered by the possibility of submitting amendments under Article 19 to the International Bureau.). . . . If amendments to the claims have been made under Article 19 prior to the filing of the demand, [a] statement must indicate whether, for the purposes of the international preliminary examination, the applicant wishes the amendments to be taken into account (in which case a copy of the amendments should be filed with the demand) or to be considered as reversed by an amendment under Article 34. . . . The applicant is not precluded from later making amendments, or further amendments, during the course of the international preliminary examination, whatever appears in the statement concerning amendments, and in this sense the statement is not binding on the applicant or the conduct of the international preliminary examination. For example, the applicant may choose to file amendments under Article 34 at a later stage which supersede amendments previously made under Article 19, even though the statement indicates that those previous amendments should be taken into account. However, the information contained in the statement is used by the International Preliminary Examining Authority to determine when, and on what basis, the international preliminary examination is to start. Moreover, amendments or arguments need not be taken into account by the International Preliminary Examining Authority for the purposes of a written opinion or the international preliminary examination report if they are received after the Authority has begun to draw up that opinion or report. Since the time available for international preliminary examination is limited, it is in the applicant's interests to be as definite as possible, at the time of filing the demand, as to what should form the basis of the international preliminary examination. If the applicant intends to file amendments under Article 34 but is not in a position to submit them with the demand, that intention should preferably be mentioned in a letter filed with the demand. . . .

Only Contracting States which are bound by Chapter II of the PCT and which have been designated in the international application can be elected. They are the "eligible States." Additional States may be elected later, provided that they [have been designated.]. . . .

The International Preliminary Examining Authority sends the demand or a copy thereof to the International Bureau. The International Bureau then notifies Offices of their election and informs the applicant that it has done so.

THE INTERNATIONAL PRELIMINARY EXAMINATION

[If the competent International Preliminary Examining Authority is part of the same (national or regional) Office as the competent International Searching Authority, the international preliminary examination may, if the Office wishes and except where the applicant has requested that the international preliminary examination be postponed (see paragraph 380), start at the same time as the international search (often called a "telescoped" procedure since the international search and international preliminary examination partly overlap). Where the statement concerning amendments made in the demand contains an indication that amendments under Article 19 are to be taken into account, the International Preliminary Examining Authority will not start the international preliminary examination before it has received a copy of the amendments concerned. Otherwise,] the International Preliminary Examining Authority starts the international preliminary examination when it is in possession both of the demand and of the international search report or a declaration by the International Searching Authority that no international search report will be established. . . .

The international preliminary examination is based on the claims, the description and the drawings comprised in the international application. Amendments to the claims under Article 19 made before the demand was filed are taken into account unless they are superseded by a subsequent amendment under Article 34 or considered as reversed by an amendment under Article 34. Amendments made after the demand is filed, whether under Article 19 or under Article 34, are also taken into account for the purposes of the international preliminary examination, except that they need not be taken into account for the purposes of a written opinion or the international preliminary examination report if they are received after the International Preliminary Examining Authority has begun to draw up that opinion or report. . . .

The International Preliminary Examining Authority notifies the applicant in a "written opinion" if it considers that (i) the international application relates to subject matter on which it is not required to carry out an international preliminary examination, and decides not to carry out such an examination; (ii) the description, the claims or the drawings are so unclear, or the claims are so inadequately supported by the description, that no meaningful opinion can be formed on the novelty, inventive step (non-obviousness) or industrial applicability of the claimed invention; (iii) the international preliminary examination report should be "negative" in respect of any of the claims because the invention claimed therein does not appear to be novel, does not appear to involve an inventive step (be non-obvious), or does not appear to be industrially applicable; (iv) any amendment goes beyond the disclosure in the international application as filed; (v) the international preliminary examination report should be accompanied by (unfavorable) observations on the clarity of the claims, the description and the drawings, or on the question of the claims being fully supported by the description; (vi) a claim relates to an invention in respect of which no international search report has been established and the International Preliminary Examining Authority has decided not to carry out the international preliminary examination in respect of that claim; (vii) a nucleotide and/or amino acid sequence listing is not available to it in such a form that a meaningful international preliminary examination can be carried out; (viii) the national law applied by the national Office which acts as the International Preliminary Examining Authority does not allow [certain] multiple dependent claims [The] "written opinion" is a notification, issued by the International Preliminary Examining Authority to the applicant, which indicates any comments by the Authority on the matters mentioned [above]. The written opinion must fully state the reasons for it, must invite the applicant to submit a written reply and must fix a time limit for the reply (usually two months, but extendible at the applicant's request—for more details). There may be no written opinion if the Authority has no such comments to make (in which case the Authority will proceed direct to the issuance of the international preliminary examination report). . . .

The applicant may ask for further clarifications from the International Preliminary Examining Authority and may himself give clarifications to it, since the PCT expressly provides that the applicant has a right to communicate orally, by telephone or personally, or in writing with the Authority. More specifically, where the applicant receives a written opinion from the Authority on any of the matters referred to [above], he may respond to that written opinion. The response may consist of amendments and/or arguments. . . . It should be noted that the International Preliminary Examining Authority cannot force the applicant to make any change in the international application. In other words the applicant may disregard any opinion of the said Authority, either wholly or in part. Such an attitude may lead to an unfavorable or less favorable international preliminary examination report, but the applicant may prefer such a report (in the hope that he will overcome, in the national phase, any difficulties that it may cause him) to a change which he does not believe in. . . . As for amendments under Article 19 (see paragraph 301), amendments under Article 34(2)(b) may not go beyond the disclosure in the international application as filed. If the International Preliminary Examining Authority considers that any amendments do not comply with this requirement, it will comment accordingly in any written opinion and in the international preliminary examination report, and the report will be established as if such amendment had not been made.

The International Preliminary Examination Report ["IPER"]

The international preliminary examination report must [usually] be established within 28 months from the priority date The international preliminary examination report contains, among other things, a statement (in the form of a simple "yes" or "no"), in relation to each claim which has been examined, on whether the claim appears to satisfy the criteria of novelty, inventive step (non-obviousness) and industrial applicability. The statement is, where appropriate, accompanied by the citation of relevant documents together with concise explanations pointing out the criteria to which the cited documents are applicable and giving reasons for the International Preliminary Examining Authority's conclusions. . . . Article 35(2) expressly states that "the international preliminary examination report shall not contain any statement on the question whether the claimed invention is or seems to be patentable or unpatentable according to any national law." . . . .

Since the international preliminary examination report contains an opinion on the compliance of the international application with internationally accepted criteria of novelty, inventive step (non-obviousness) and industrial applicability, it provides the applicant with a strong basis on which to evaluate the chances of obtaining patents in the various Offices in the national phase. The additional time before entry into the national phase which is achieved by the use of the international preliminary examination procedure also affords the applicant a greater opportunity of assessing the technical value and commercial prospects of the invention. While the international preliminary examination report is not binding on elected Offices, it carries considerable weight with them, and a favorable international preliminary examination report will assist the prosecution of the application before the elected Offices. An elected Office which is the same national or regional Office as that which carried out the international preliminary examination as International Preliminary Examining Authority under the PCT will generally proceed rapidly to the grant of a patent in the national phase if the international preliminary examination report is favorable to the international application.

CHAPTER IV   ACTS TO BE PERFORMED FOR ENTRY INTO THE NATIONAL PHASE

The following acts must be performed (if applicable): (i) payment of the national fee; (ii) furnishing of a translation, if prescribed; [and others in exceptional cases such as if a copy of the international application has not been communicated to the designated Office under Article 20. Most designated Offices require non-resident applicants to be represented by an agent; others require non-resident applicants to have an address for service in the country for which the Office acts. The National Chapters (Summary) indicate whether an agent must be appointed or whether an address for service is required.The priority document must be submitted during the international phase to the receiving Office or to the International Bureau, and the International Bureau furnishes copies of it to designated Offices that request them. Where the priority document has been submitted in due time during the international phase to the receiving Office or to the International Bureau, no designated Office may require an original priority document (that is, an original certified copy of the earlier application) from the applicant. What may be required, however, is a copy of the priority document, that is, a simple photocopy of the original priority document. . . .

In general, a designated Office may require the applicant to furnish a translation of the priority document only where the validity of the priority claim is relevant to the determination of whether the invention concerned is patentable. However, some designated Offices (which have informed the International Bureau to that effect) require a translation of the priority document in all cases once national processing has started. Where such a requirement exists, it is indicated in the National Chapter (either in the Summary, if the translation must be furnished relatively shortly after entry into the national phase, or elsewhere, if it must be furnished at a later stage during the national phase) together with an indication of the time limit for furnishing the translation. . . .

The PCT leaves each Contracting State free to prescribe such substantive conditions of patentability as it desires. This is particularly true of what constitutes "prior art." However, since the requirements of prior art as defined in the PCT and its Regulations for the purposes of the international phase are generally as strict as, or stricter than, those defined in any national law, the chances of unpleasant surprises by way of previously uncited prior art references being raised during the national phase are substantially reduced. On the other hand, the PCT does not prevent any national law from requiring the applicant to furnish, in the national phase, evidence in respect of any substantive condition of patentability prescribed by that law.

WORLD INTELLECTUAL PROPERTY ORGANIZATION
PCT NEWSLETTER – OCTOBER 2001
MODIFICATION OF THE TIME LIMIT UNDER PCT
ARTICLE 22(1)
http://www.wipo.int/pct/en/
(Last visited on 11 November 2002)

The PCT Assembly decided, with effect from 1 April 2002, to change the time limit under PCT Article 22(1) for performing the acts necessary to enter the national phase from 20 to 30 months from the priority date. As a result, the time limit for national phase entry under PCT Article 22(1) will be the same as that which applies under PCT Article 39(1)(a) (that is, the time limit which applies where the applicant files a demand for international preliminary examination within 19 months from the priority date).

At the moment, at least 80% of international applications are the subject of a demand for international preliminary examination. Experience has shown that a significant proportion of applicants use the international preliminary examination procedure only to delay entry into the national phase. Even though such applicants may not even have any interest in using the international preliminary examination report (IPER), the usual procedures involved in processing the demand and IPER must nevertheless be followed. It is expected that this amendment will help to reduce the ever-increasing workload at the Offices which act as International Preliminary Examining Authorities (IPEAs); it will also greatly benefit applicants who are not particularly interested in the international preliminary examination procedure since they will now be able to enter the national phase at 30 months without having to pay the fees associated with filing the demand. The resulting reduction in the workload of IPEAs will allow them to focus their resources on serving the needs of those applicants who have a genuine desire to take advantage of the substantive benefits offered by the international preliminary examination procedure.

Reduction in the maximum number of designation fees payable

The Assembly decided to amend the Schedule of Fees (annexed to the Regulations under the PCT) to decrease, with effect from 1 January 2002, the maximum number of designation fees payable, from six to five. This will be the fifth consecutive year in which the fee payable for designating States has been reduced.

MANUAL OF PATENT EXAMINING PROCEDURE, § 1840

Matters to be Considered When Choosing an International Searching Authority

Choosing the European Patent Office (EPO) as an International Searching Authority could be advantageous to United States applicants who designate countries for European Regional patent protection in the PCT International applications for the following reasons:

(A) Claims may be amended according to EPO search results before entering the European Office as a designated Office.

(B) The EPO search fee need not be paid upon entering the European Office as a designated Office.

(C) The EPO search results may be available for use in a U.S. priority application.

(D) The EPO international search may be obtained without the need for a European professional representative.

(E) The European Patent Office search could provide the U.S. applicant with the benefit of a European art search (which may be different from the applicant's own or the USPTO's search) before it is necessary to enter the European Patent Office or other designated Offices.

[C]   Quasi-Substantive Harmonization

PATENT COOPERATION TREATY, ARTICLE 27

Nothing in this Treaty and the Regulations is intended to be construed as prescribing anything that would limit the freedom of each Contracting State to prescribe such substantive conditions of patentability as it desires.

UNITY OF INVENTION
PCT APPLICANT'S GUIDE, ¶¶ 113–122 (WIPO 1998)

What is meant by the requirement of "unity of invention"? An international application should be drafted so that the claims relate to only one invention or to a group of inventions so linked as to form a single general inventive concept. This principle is laid down in Rule 13. Observance of this requirement is checked by neither the receiving Office nor the International Bureau, but it is checked by, and is important to the procedure before, the International Searching Authority [cit] and the International Preliminary Examining Authority [cit], and may be relevant in the national phase before the designated and elected Offices. Since separate searches and examinations are required for distinctly different inventions, additional fees are required if the international search or international preliminary examination is to cover two or more inventions (or groups of inventions linked as just described).

How is the requirement of unity of invention satisfied? Unity of invention is present only when there is a "technical relationship" among the claimed inventions involving one or more of the same or corresponding "special technical features." The expression "special technical features" means those technical features that define a contribution which each of the claimed inventions, considered as a whole, makes over the prior art. The determination whether a group of inventions is so linked as to form a single inventive concept is made without regard to whether the inventions are claimed in separate claims or as alternatives within on the assumption that the claims avoid the prior art will be made before the prior art search but may be reconsidered on the basis of the results of the search. Annex B of the Administrative Instructions contains detailed criteria governing the determination whether an international application complies with the requirement of unity of invention under Rule 13. The following paragraphs set out a summary of some of the more important criteria discussed in that Annex. Illustrations of three particular situations are explained in detail below:

    (i)   combinations of different categories of claims (for example—product, process, use, and apparatus or means),

    (ii)   so-called "Markush practice," and

    (iii)   the case of intermediate and final products.

May different categories of claims be combined in an international application? The method for determining unity of invention contained in Rule 13 is construed as permitting, in particular, the inclusion of any one of the following combinations of claims of different categories in the same international application:

    (i) in addition to an independent claim for a given product, an independent claim for a process specially adapted for the manufacture of the said product, and an independent claim for a use of the said product, or

(ii) in addition to an independent claim for a given process, an independent claim for an apparatus or means specifically designed for carrying out the said process, or

(iii) in addition to an independent claim for a given product, an independent claim for a process specially adapted for the manufacture of the said product and an independent claim for an apparatus or means specifically designed for carrying out the said process, it being understood that a process is specially adapted for the manufacture of a product if it inherently results in the product and that an apparatus or means is specifically designed for carrying out a process if the contribution over the prior art of the apparatus or means corresponds to the contribution the process makes over the prior art.

An apparatus or means shall be considered to be "specifically designed for carrying out" a claimed process if the contribution over the prior art of the apparatus or means corresponds to the contribution the process makes over the prior art. Consequently, it would not be sufficient that the apparatus or means is merely capable of being used in carrying out the claimed process.

What is permitted under the "Markush Practice"? Rule 13.2 also governs the "Markush practice" wherein a single claim defines alternatives of an invention—a common drafting practice for inventions in the chemical field. In this special situation, the requirement of a technical interrelationship and the same or corresponding special technical features as defined in Rule 13.2, is considered to be met when the alternatives are of a similar nature.

When the Markush grouping is for alternatives of chemical compounds, they are regarded as being of a similar nature where the following criteria are fulfilled:

(i) all alternatives have a common property or activity, and

(ii)(a) a common structure is present—that is, a significant structural element is shared by all of the alternatives, or

(b) in cases where the common structure cannot be the unifying criteria, all alternatives belong to a recognized class of chemical compounds in the art to which the invention pertains.

When dealing with alternatives, if it can be shown that at least one Markush alternative is not novel over the prior art, the question of unity of invention will be reconsidered by the examiner. Reconsideration does not necessarily imply that an objection of lack of unity will be raised.

Can both intermediate and final products be claimed? The situation involving intermediate and final products is also governed by Rule 13.2. The term "intermediate" is intended to mean intermediate or starting products. Such products have the ability to be used to produce final products through a physical or chemical change in which the intermediate loses its identity. Unity of invention should be considered to be present in the context of intermediate and final products where the following two conditions are fulfilled:

(i) the intermediate and final products have the same essential structural element, in that:

(a) the basic chemical structures of the intermediate and the final products are the same, or

(b) the chemical structures of the two products are technically closely interrelated, the intermediate incorporating an essential structural element into the final product, and

(ii) the intermediate and final products are technically interrelated, this meaning that the final product is manufactured directly from the intermediate or is separated from it by a small number of intermediates all containing the same essential structural element.

Unity of invention may also be considered to be present between intermediate and final products of which the structures are not known—for example, as between an intermediate having a known structure and a final product the structure of which is not known, or as between an intermediate of unknown structure and a final product of unknown structure. In order to satisfy unity in such cases, there must be sufficient evidence to lead one to conclude that the intermediate and final products are technically closely interrelated as, for example, when the intermediate contains the same essential element as the final product or incorporates an essential element into the final product.

An international application which complies with the unity of invention requirements laid down in Rule 13 must be accepted by all the designated and elected Offices, since Article 27(1) does not allow any national law (as defined in Article 2(x)) to require compliance with requirements relating to the contents of the international application different from or additional to those provided for in the PCT.

CATERPILLAR TRACTOR CO. v. COMM'R OF PATENTS AND TRADEMARKS
231 U.S.P.Q. 590 (E.D. Va. 1986)

BRYAN, CHIEF JUDGE.

In this action involving an international patent application the plaintiff attacks, as contrary to a treaty provision, a rule of the Patent and Trademark Office (PTO). The provision and rule relate to "unity of invention," and the practical effect of the PTO's ruling on the plaintiff's application is that the plaintiff will have to file two applications instead of one. The treaty provisions involved are in the Patent Cooperation Treaty (PCT). The matter is before the court on cross motions for summary judgment, both parties agreeing that it is appropriate to resolve the issue presented by such motions.

Rule 13 of the PCT provides, in part:

Rule 13, Unity of Invention

13.1 Requirement

The international application shall relate to one invention only or to a group of inventions so linked as to form a single general inventive concept ("requirement of unity of invention").

13.2 Claims of Different Categories

Rule 13.1 shall be construed as permitting, in particular, either of the following two possibilities:

(i) . . .

(ii) in addition to an independent claim for a given process, the inclusion in the same international application of one independent claim for one apparatus or means specifically designed for carrying out the said process.

The words "specifically designed" are what give rise to the present controversy. The PTO rule, which allegedly is in conflict with the PCT rule, reads as follows:

In addition to a claim for a given process, a claim for one apparatus or means specifically designed for carrying out of the said process, *that is, it cannot be used to practice another materially different process.* 37 CFR § 1.141(b)(2) (emphasis added).

The PTO interprets this regulation to mean: Process and apparatus for its practice can be shown to be distinct inventions, if either or both of the following can be shown: (1) that the process *as claimed* can be practiced by another materially different apparatus or by hand, or (2) that the apparatus *as claimed* can be used to practice another and materially different process. MPEP 806.05(e).

If the rule and interpretation of the PTO conflicts with the PCT, it runs afoul of Article 27 of the PCT which provides in part:

(1) No national law shall require compliance with requirements relating to the form or contents of the international application different from or additional to those which are provided for in this Treaty and the Regulations.

An example, while not completely analogous, may help to illustrate the issue. If the process was the removal of a man's beard from his face, and a safety razor was the apparatus, the PTO rule and interpretation would hold that, because the razor could also be used to scrape paint from a pane of glass it was not "specifically designed" for removal of the beard. It would also hold that because the process could be performed with the use of a straight razor the safety razor was not "specifically designed" for the removal of the beard.[1]

---

[1] The specific application here was much more complicated than the example. Here, the plaintiff sought to apply for an international patent for a process or method of making a toothed segment used in the drive sprocket of the final drive assembly of Caterpillar crawler tractors.

The court finds the added [emphasized] portion of the PTO rule, quoted above, and its interpretation to be contrary to the PCT and thus contrary to law.

Only a lawyer would have a problem with what appears to the court to be the plain language of the PCT. And that plain language refutes the interpretation which the PTO gives the language and which it says is no different from that language. The PTO's position is that its interpretation is the only one which accords the word "specifically" any meaning; and that the interpretation urged by the plaintiff could be accomplished by use only of the word "designed" without the preceding adverb. Perhaps, but it does not follow that the PTO's interpretation of the word "specifically" is the correct one. The PTO's interpretation, as expressed in its opinion, is that "specifically designed" means " . . . that the process and apparatus can only be used with each other." In re Caterpillar Tractor Co., 226 U.S.P.Q. (BNA) 625, 639 (Comm'r. Pat. 1985). In the court's view this is an unreasonable interpretation. . . . The court will therefore grant summary judgment to the plaintiff. The rejection by the PTO of the plaintiff's application is contrary to law.

NOTES AND QUESTIONS

(1) **Substance or Procedure?** Is a single standard for unity of invention a substantive or a procedural harmonization? Is it a condition of patentability? (Ponder whether a patent may be found invalid or nullified for lack of unity of invention, as it may be for lack of novelty or inventive step.) The concept is straightforward. A patent office decides that one patent should cover only one invention, for example, a chemical compound, a process for its preparation, or its use. *See., e.g.,* Jean-Jacques Joly, *Unity of Invention in Europe*, FICPI Paper MC/1.1a www.ficpi.org/ficpi/library/montecarlo99/inventunity.html For U.S. national applications, the term

---

The drive sprocket receives the power of the diesel engine. The toothed segments engage the chain of the track that propels the tractor. Plaintiff's application claimed the invention of a forging process, which included use of a three-part forging die. This process obtained the close tolerances needed on three crucial surfaces of the toothed segment so that no machining of those surfaces was required before mounting on the final drive assembly. Claims 1 to 4 of the application relate to the method of forging a sprocket segment for a track-type vehicle undercarriage; claims 5 through 9 are directed to an apparatus, including the three-part die, for forging the track-type undercarriage sprocket segment to the desired, finished dimension. The PTO here initially ruled that the plaintiff's application did not comply with the requirements of unity of invention under the PCT because the method in claims 1 to 4 could be performed by a two-segment die, in addition to the three-segment die contemplated in the application. PTO's acting group director later found Caterpillar's protest to be unjustified, and upheld the patent examiner's findings. The acting group director also ruled that the apparatus as claimed (i.e., the three-segment die) could be used in a materially different process: a process of making a corrugated member. The Assistant Commissioner upheld the prior PTO decisions, In re Caterpillar Tractor Co., 226 U.S.P.Q. (BNA) 625 (July 22, 1985), and reiterated his position on reconsideration, 228 U.S.P.Q. (BNA) 77 (November 26, 1985).

"restriction practice" is used instead of "unity of invention." *See* MPEP 1893.03(d). If unity of invention is lacking, the applicant may file a divisional application with the same priority date as the parent application. The rules on unity of invention vary widely among the United States, the EPO, and Japan. Different countries have different standards for patentability beyond utility, novelty, inventive step, and disclosure. For example, the United States has a best mode requirement in Section 112, first paragraph. Some countries exclude from patentability inventions which are contrary to morality. *See, e.g.*, EPC art. 53; Japanese Patent Law art. 32. Sometimes this leads to claims that Paris Union states are not in compliance with Article 4 of the Paris Convention.

> Regularly filed, national, non-provisional applications in compliance with the home country's substantive patent law, as well as the benefiting-country's substantive patent law, have . . . suffered unjustly through the retroactive application of unity of invention disclosure standards. The U.S. established this apparent violation of article 4H of the Paris Convention in *Yasuko Kawai v. Metlesics*, 480 F.2d 880, 885–889 (C.C.P.A. 1973). This erroneous precedent has been firmly entrenched in subsequent decisions to the extent that other countries have found it necessary to retaliate with their own decisions (*In re "Allopurinol,"* 1975 GRUR 131 (German Federal Supreme Court)).

Todd R. Miller, *United States Provisional Applications and Paris Convention Priority Rights — The Same Effect*, 37 IDEA 161, 177 (1996). The Japanese Patent Office changed its rule as a response.

There are calls for a universal rule on unity of invention. *See* Samson Helfgott, 17 No. 3 INTELL. PROP. L. NEWSL. 20 (ABA 1999). The United States, among others, continues to resist such measures. Why?

(2) **National Stage Procedures**. For a detailed review of PCT national stage procedures in the United States, see Brian W. Brown, *Patent Cooperation Treaty (PCT) National Stage Commencement and Entry in the United States Of America*, 79 J. PAT. & TM OFF. SOC'Y 296 (1997).

(3) **Markush Practice**. The term "Markush practice" refers to a claim to a genus by enumeration of species, which has been allowed in the United States since the decision in *Ex parte Markush*, 1925 Dec. Comm'r Pat. 126. Intermediates which have unity of invention with regard to their function are allowable under U.S. practice. *See In re Jones*, 74 U.S.P.Q. 149 (1947). Reference to "Markush practice" in the PCT Guide reflects U.S. usage. The rules in the European Patent Office and the Japanese Patent Office are similar to the PCT Rules as well.

(4) **Prior Art Effect of a PCT Application**. Consider a recent scenario. A U.S. Provisional Application was filed on November 15, 1996. On November 15, 1997, a PCT application filed claiming priority to the November 15, 1996 application designating the United States was filed. On May 15, 1999, a PCT application enters the U.S. National stage under section 371. The

effective date of the application for the purpose of prior art effect under section 102(e) is May 15, 1999. A U.S. provisional application was filed on November 15, 1996. On November 15, 1997, a PCT application filed claiming priority to the November 15, 1996 application designating the United States is filed. On May 15, 1999, a continuation of the PCT application is filed under section 365(c). The effective date of the application for the purpose of prior art effect under section 102(e) is November 15, 1996. Why the difference? *See* Allen E. Hoover, *Further Comments on PCT/USA National Phase Applications and Section 102(e)*, 79 J. PAT. & TM. OFF. SOC'Y 643 (1997); *International Patent Applications and the Section 102(e): Dates of Patents Issuing Therefrom*, 80 J. PAT. & TM. OFF. SOC'Y 289 (1998); *see also* Edward P. Heller, *Letter to the Editor*, 79 J. PAT. & TM. OFF. SOC'Y 883 (1997); Richard A. Neifeld & Edward P. Heller III, *The 35 U.S.C. 102(e) Date of a Continuation of an International Application*, 80 J. PAT. & TM. OFF. SOC'Y 71 (1998). Section 102(e) was amended effective November 29, 2000. Under the amended provision, and international application published in the English language will be effective as of its filing date. *See* 35 U.S.C. § 102(e) (Supp. 2001).

(5) **Cooperation Between Patent Offices**. Some, if not many authorities, question the extent to which a Japanese patent examiner will rely on a positive examination report issued by a U.S. examiner, and the value of a PCT examination itself before the national patent offices. Cartiglia notes that there still remains a great deal of national or regional bias with respect to the quality of examination of other patent offices, and ventures that when recognition of the quality of other patent offices becomes more widespread, a positive preliminary examination report will carry more weight. *See* James R. Cartiglia, *The Patent Cooperation Treaty: A Rational Approach to International Patent Filing*, 763 J. PAT. & TM. OFC. SOC'Y 261 fn 65 (1994). Efforts to promote mutual recognition of patent examiners are discussed in the next reading.

(6) **Legal Representation in PCT Procedures**. An American attorney can represent a PCT applicant in proceedings before the European Patent Office when it is acting as ISA and/or IPEA. A European patent attorney need only be retained when the PCT international stage is completed and the application enters the national stage in the EPO. The likelihood that an EPO examining panel will give deference to a favorable search and preliminary examination report by another European examiner is very high, and the EPO frequently grants the patent on the PCT application without further substantive examination. Corporate attorneys employed in U.S. companies may represent the corporation in European patent proceedings even further in the process—all the way to the point where the European patent is submitted to the national patent offices for validation, at which time a local attorney must be engaged. For practical advice, see Joahim Weber, *How to Draft a European Patent Application Based on a US-Style Application*, 23 AIPPI J. (Jan. 1998).

[D] Trilateral And Multilateral Initiatives For The Future

[1] The USPTO/JPO/EPO Trilateral Conference

JOINT PRESS RELEASE: TRILATERAL CONFERENCE NOV. 14, 1997

The European Patent Office (EPO), the United States Patent and Trademark Office (USPTO) and the Japanese Patent Office (JPO), at the Fifteenth Trilateral Conference held in Kyoto on November 13–14, 1997, agreed on the following conclusions:

Kyoto Action Plan

The three offices recognize that the globalization of industry and trade creates the need for a world-wide system for the grant of patents. The advantage of such a system for the users of the patent system would be:

* reduction of costs

* improved quality of granted patents

* improved dissemination of patent information

* reduced processing time in the patent granting procedure

With these objectives in mind, the three offices identify the following lines of action:

1. Trilateral Patent Network. The three offices will develop between them a trilateral network for data exchange concerning administrative and technical patent data. . . .

2. Trilateral Concurrent Search and Examination. The three offices agreed to undertake further steps through collaboration on concurrent searches concerning applications filed in each of the three offices and improving search effectiveness by increased reliance on each others search result for examination purposes. . . .

3. Trilateral Web Site. The three offices will promote the use of the internet to disseminate patent information. They agree to study and prepare the concrete implementation of a trilateral web site concept accessible free of charge . . . [The web site is now established at www.european-patent-office.org/tws/twsindex.htm].

NOTES AND QUESTIONS

(1) **Advantages of the Trilateral Approach**. The USPTO has been working with the EPO and JPO to cooperate in search and examination

of PCT applications ("task-sharing") to reduce workloads, eliminate duplication of efforts, and reduce the costs of the system to the offices themselves and to the users. What are the advantages of a trilateral approach among the European, Japanese, and U.S. Patent Offices over a "multilateral approach" within the PCT system? Given that over eighty percent of all patents filed throughout the world ultimately originate from applicants within the trilateral region, would a trilateral approach lead to the formation of an exclusive club of patent administrators and examiners (and patent attorneys) from these countries?

(2) **Work Reduction Through Task Sharing**. The USPTO internally has a policy of "full faith and credit" providing for mutual recognition of the results of patent searches and examinations between U.S. patent examiners. *See* MPEP § 706.04. What would prevent U.S. examiners from extending its full faith and credit policy to EPO and JPO examiners and vice versa? Are the benefits which would be achieved by mutual recognition of search and examination results worth the risks? What *are* the risks?

(3) **"Insourcing" Legal Representation**. A major stumbling block on the road to a global patent system is the question of legal representation of patent applicants and the extent to which patent attorneys in developing countries would continue to find enough incoming work if patent attorneys in developed countries could represent inventors to acquire patent protection abroad—say, in China or India. Would such a trend lead to improvement or thwart the ultimate goals of a truly international patent system?

(4) **Outsourcing Legal Representation**. PCT Rule 83.1*bis* states that

> Where the International Bureau is the Receiving Office . . . [a]ny person who has the right to practice before the national Office of, or acting for, a Contracting State of which the applicant . . . is a resident or national shall be entitled to practice in respect of the international application before the International Bureau in its capacity as receiving Office.

If a PCT Patent becomes a reality, should the common nationality requirement be dropped? If so, might the "competitive advantage" flow to the private patent bar in less expensive jurisdictions? Would some cost-conscious U.S. patent applicants conceivably choose outsource their business, i.e., choose to be represented by, say, an Indian or Chinese patent attorney before the WIPO "World Patent Office" if the cost of the representation was lower and the resultant quality was virtually the same?

(5) **"The More Things Change . . . "** To what extent do the issues addressed by the IPC, PCT, and Trilateral Conference mirror the challenges contemplated by the early visionaries such as Lilly and Luzzato? Have changes in information technology and international cooperation paved the way toward the development of a global patent or have they no effect?

(6) **Future Developments**. Notwithstanding the collapse of efforts to achieve substantive international harmonization of patent law in the early 1990s, do procedural simplification and unification increase the likelihood

of an global patent to any great extent? Or are the differences in ideology between the goals of the patent systems in different countries make the attainment of a unitary world patent unlikely in the near or distant future? This question will be explored in the next reading.

[2] The Multilateral Approach

REPORT OF THE COMMITTEE OF EXPERTS
ON THE PATENT LAW TREATY
WIPO Doc. PLT/CE/IV/4, Fourth Session, Geneva, June 23 to 27, 1997

I. INTRODUCTION

The Committee of Experts on the Patent Law Treaty . . . held its fourth session in Geneva from June 23 to 27, 1997. [In addition to states that are members of WIPO and/or the Paris Union], representatives of the World Trade Organization (WTO), the European Communities (EC), the European Patent Office (EPO) and the Organization of African Unity (OAU) took part in the session in an observer capacity.

Representatives of the following non-governmental organizations took part in the session in an observer capacity: American Bar Association (ABA), American Intellectual Property Law Association (AIPLA), Asian Patent Attorneys Association (APAA), Brazilian Association of Industrial Property (ABPI), Chartered Institute of Patent Agents (CIPA), Committee of National Institutes of Patent Agents (CNIPA), Compagnie nationale des conseils en propriété industrielle (CNCPI), Confederation of Indian Industry (CII), Federal Chamber of Patent Attorneys (Germany) (FCPA), Federation of German Industry (BDI), Institute of Professional Representatives before the European Patent Office (EPI), International Association for the Protection of Industrial Property (AIPPI), International Federation of Industrial Property Attorneys (FICPI), International League of Competition Law (LIDC), Japan Intellectual Property Association (JIPA), Japan Patent Attorneys Association (JPAA), Korea Patent Attorneys Association (KPAA), Max Planck Institute for Foreign and International Patent, Copyright and Competition Law (MPI), Trade Marks, Patents and Designs Federation (TMPDF), Union of European Practitioners in Industrial Property (UEPIP) and Union of Industrial and Employersí Confederations of Europe (UNICE) (21). . . .

II. GENERAL DECLARATIONS

The Delegation of Germany was in favor of most of the provisions in the draft Treaty, but had the intention of raising a number of matters during the discussions. It further expressed the wish that the preparatory work should be completed at the earliest possible time in order to prepare for a diplomatic conference.

(a) The Delegation of the United States of America declared that, as it had already stated at the first, second and third sessions of the Committee of Experts, it was still not in a position to discuss substantive patent law harmonization. Accordingly, the Delegation considered that the distinction to be made between formal and substantive matters continued to be critically important for the ongoing discussions.

(b) The Delegation said that its concern that the current draft Treaty did not impinge upon substantive matters remained. For example, while the issue of unity of invention was not explicitly included in any of the Articles to be discussed during that week, its alleged implicit inclusion in the form or contents reference in Article 5 raised some concerns for the United States of America and might create an impediment to that country's full participation in the effort to harmonize formal matters. The Delegation recalled that it had consistently raised this concern in preceding sessions of the Committee of Experts and that it had not really heard a reason why unity of invention could not be excepted from the draft Treaty.

(c) The Delegation noted further that, in the course of the last three meetings of the Committee of Experts, there had been an additional shift towards substantive matters. In addition to Article 5, Article 6 dealing with validity of patents and revocation, Article 12 dealing with corrections of mistakes and Article 15 dealing with belated claiming of priority could, in the view of the Delegation, be regarded as moving towards a discussion of substantive matters.

(d) Furthermore, the Delegation continued to question the intent and expected results of the entire work of the Committee of Experts. It appeared that many of the provisions had been drafted in a manner to accommodate all currently existing systems. However, the Delegation was pleased to see that some of the Articles were moving away from that approach, tending to be simpler and not an accommodation for all systems, thereby actually making a harmonization effort. Unfortunately, the remaining Articles which attempted to accommodate all systems were not to promote uniformity, simplification or cost reduction, although those considerations were currently of paramount importance to those seeking patent protection throughout the world.

(e) Additionally, many of the proposed Articles and Rules were unduly complex, difficult and costly for national offices to administer. In addition, the Delegation was still not convinced that the subject matter dealt with by the Committee of Experts was treaty level material. Much of what was addressed in many of the Articles of the draft Treaty dealt with matters that did not rise to a level above regulatory status. The Delegation believed that it would not be prudent to elevate the status of those matters to the level of treaty articles, as the practices involved in those articles would be subject to more frequent changes than it would be possible to accommodate if they were dealt with in the Treaty. . . .

(f) Notwithstanding those comments, however, the Delegation continued to view the harmonization of formalities to be a very laudable goal. The resultant ability to prepare an application in a single format, preferably in electronic form that would be accepted by all offices, a universal acceptance policy in other words, was eagerly sought by the users of its country and would be widely applauded.

(g) A first step on the road to achieving the goal of offering to its users a system in which they could prepare an application in a single format that would be accepted by all offices could simply be the mandated acceptance of a [PCT] compliant filing as a national filing. In that regard the PCT could serve as a model for a system which would enable users to prepare an application in one format that would be acceptable to all offices. A second step would be to recognize the limitations of the current paper-based PCT and to seek improvements in that Treaty and associated rules in order to, among other things, accommodate electronic filing. The Delegation noted that there had been some effort in that direction in meetings that were held as recently as in the week preceding the meeting of the Committee of Experts. The Patent Law Treaty could then be subsumed in the moderniza-tion of the PCT in that a provision for mandating universal application acceptance for national filings, such as Articles 4 and 5, could be added to such a rejuvenated PCT.

(h) A key motivating factor for the Patent Law Treaty was the recognition that no office, when undergoing the complex and costly process of automa-tion, desired to create two electronic systems, one for national and another for international applications. To that end, the Patent Law Treaty and the PCT needed to converge to the greatest extent practicable, so that offices intending to automate would be able to develop a system capable of handling both national and international applications. The Treaty would provide the same benefit to inventors, applicants and owners interacting with the offices through the world, for those customers likewise would greatly prefer to purchase or develop a single automated system for preparing applications suitable for filing as international applications and as national applications throughout the world.

(i) The Delegation of the United States of America then went on to propose a list of Patent Law Treaty principles that it thought were underlying the work of the Committee of Experts. The proposed Articles and Rules should be measured against those principles in order to reduce the number of necessary Articles and Rules. Examples of such principles could include simplicity in procedures since procedures in some of the Articles were becoming extremely complicated; avoidance of costly require-ments that may not always be necessary such as, for example, in regard to translations and certifications; avoidance of the loss of patent rights by allowing late submissions; late revivals and reinstatements; provisions for electronic record management, including legally admissible documents for enforceability and the promotion of standards for electronic prosecution history; mutual recognition of the processing results by different offices; lastly, the creation of a single application, preferably in electronic form, that could be used multiple times by applicants filing in more than one national office.

. . . .

The Delegation of Japan said that, in the information age where documents or money were flowing in an electronic form, electronic processing of patent-related information tended to be more and more adopted. In particular, a flow of patent related documents usually consisted of filing an application with the office, clerical processing within the office, substantive examination, registration and dissemination. Dealing with the information by electronic means, from the input through the output, made processing more easily enhanced, efficiency and improved quality. In this regard, the Delegation considered it to be a step in the right direction that the draft Patent Law Treaty contained positive provisions relating to electronic means of communication. With regard to developments in the near future, due to which modern information technologies would be applied around the world, it hoped that those provisions would be more refined. The Delegation announced its readiness to make a contribution in rule-making in this area and to try, as a pioneer country, to undertake electronic processing from the input to the output. Furthermore, the Delegation said that it supported the idea to introduce user-friendliness into the interfaces between users and the office. It noted, however, that this concept did not work well without a sense of responsibility of the individual users, as well as well-functioning dispute settlement procedures between the parties. Furthermore, the Delegation supported the approach that the Patent Law Treaty provisions be in conformity with PCT provisions where appropriate. It supported this idea in the light of the growing importance of PCT and future harmonization of formalities. While recognizing the importance that harmonization of formalities be successfully concluded, the Delegation said that it continued to stress the significance of harmonizing substantive matters.

The Delegation of Chile expressed its support of the draft Treaty. . . . The Delegation stressed the importance of concluding a Treaty which would provide applicants with simple, flexible procedures at a low processing cost. It welcomed that the draft Treaty referred to the PCT provisions. It also favored the flexibility introduced in the draft Treaty with regard to the possibility of electronic filing in the future. Finally, it expressed its gratitude for WIPO's efforts to harmonize patent law and hoped that this would lead to a simple and user-friendly Treaty.

The Delegation of the Republic of Korea expressed its hope that the efforts to harmonize the patent law requirements at the international level would result in an efficient harmonized treaty. . . . However, the Delegation expressed some concern about the contents of the draft Treaty. First, there seemed to be a provision in the draft Treaty obliging Contracting Parties to accept the electronic filing of applications. The Delegation said that this provision needed further discussions because currently only few countries had the capacity to comply with it. Secondly, some provisions in the draft Treaty seemed to make a single request sufficient even where the changes related to more than one application or patent. In the view of the Delegation, these provisions would make it difficult for the Office of its country to determine the contents of a request with respect to an application or patent for which a separate request had not been furnished. In this connection, the Delegation announced that it would intervene during the discussion and that it would do its best to reach a consensus.

The Delegation of Canada expressed its continued support for the work of the Committee of Experts on the Patent Law Treaty. It said that it would very much prefer to be able to include in the discussions matters of greater substance such as, for example, providing a grace period. It further expressed its hope that it would be possible to resume discussions of substantive patent law harmonization in the not too distant future. In the meantime, however, the Delegation supported the work of the Committee of Experts on the more limited issues that were currently being dealt with since it felt that harmonization, even if only in respect of formalities issues, would still be of significant benefit for patent offices and users of the system. In general, the Delegation of Canada viewed favorably the proposals put forward by the International Bureau for this meeting; however, it was concerned that in some areas the approach taken was becoming overly complex. For example, although it supported the principle of aligning the formal requirements under the Patent Law Treaty and under the PCT, it found the currently proposed link between the Patent Law Treaty and the PCT to be less than completely transparent; admittedly this was due in a large measure to the tremendous complexity of the PCT and the Regulations under the PCT. As another example, although Canada had in the past and continued to strongly favor the inclusion of provisions allowing missed time limits to be remedied under certain conditions, the proposals in Articles 13 and 14 for this purpose appeared to be far too detailed and complex. Referring to the continued development of the Patent Law Treaty, the Delegation of Canada encouraged the International Bureau and the Committee of Experts to try to find approaches to harmonization that, as much as possible, were simple, straightforward and easily understandable.

The Delegation of China expressed its appreciation of contributions which the Japanese Patent Office (JPO), United States Patent and Trademark Office (USPTO) and European Patent Office (EPO) had made within the framework of a meeting of consultants held in February 1997 in Geneva in respect of questions relating to electronic filing and transmission of documents. Furthermore, the Delegation expressed its satisfaction about the fact that the revised documents reflected the results of the last session of the Committee of Experts. It considered Articles 1 to 5 to be much simpler than the former drafts and appreciated the fact that they aimed at being consistent with the PCT. The Delegation believed that all these efforts would guarantee the success of the present meeting, thereby facilitating the early conclusion of the Patent Law Treaty. It expressed its hope for further discussions in the meeting over issues of common concern and, especially, on how to facilitate the operations of the offices while at the same time being user-friendly, as, in the final analysis, the offices and the applicants shared a common interest.

The Delegation of Portugal stressed the importance of concluding a Patent Law Treaty that would contribute to harmonization at the world-wide level. However, it would have preferred a treaty with more substantive provisions. Being aware of the difficulties in that respect, it nevertheless expressed its support for the draft Treaty. It intended to submit observations on various Articles during the deliberations of the Committee of Experts and pointed to the importance of achieving an international treaty that was clear, unambiguous and thus would avoid problems of interpretation after conclusion of the Treaty.

The Delegation of France welcomed the fact that the draft Treaty had been aligned wherever possible with the PCT as had been agreed at the third session of the Committee of Experts. It regretted that it had not always been possible to deal with the harmonization of substantive matters and noted that the issue would be discussed at the forthcoming meeting of the Governing Bodies. It noted that certain provisions, such as Article 15, had an effect on matters of substance and held that clarification as to the scope and field of application of the Treaty would be desirable. Although welcoming the increased flexibility of the rules for the benefit of applicants and of an increased conviviality between applicants and offices, it nevertheless wished that the simplification would be carried out with due account taken of third party rights and that it would not be to the detriment of comprehension of the Treaty provisions.

The Delegation of Switzerland stated that the draft Treaty as submitted contained numerous provisions of considerable usefulness for users and emphasized that as its main objective. It considered that the great majority of the proposed provisions should be included within the Treaty itself and repeated its wish to see the Treaty adopted as rapidly as possible. While acknowledging that the draft Treaty constituted an excellent basis for discussion, it stated its intention to make various observations during the detailed discussions, particularly as regards Articles 13 and 14, which could be simplified.

The Delegation of the United Kingdom declared that the working documents prepared by the International Bureau offered a very effective summary of the position the Committee of Experts had reached in its discussions so far, and noted with satisfaction that a number of the issues which had been raised in previous meetings of the Committee of Experts were dealt with in the documents. The Delegation commended progress so far and felt the present documents would contribute in a very effective manner. In the view of the Delegation, the Committee of Experts was concerned with, on the one hand, deregulation in favor of removing burdens on applicants and, on the other hand, with obviating problems of legal certainty relating to rights obtained when the patent was granted. The Delegation further noted that the International Bureau had made a strong attempt to relate the issues before the Committee of Experts to the changes and the discussions currently being undertaken within the framework of the PCT. However, the relationship between the provisions of the draft

Patent Law Treaty and the Patent Cooperation Treaty would need to be investigated with some care and caution. Furthermore, the Delegation noted with satisfaction that the issue of electronic filing had been placed within the Regulations rather than in an Article in the Treaty. The Delegation announced that it would make further comments at the appropriate time during the discussions and concluded by reiterating that it was seeking effective harmonization on as many issues as it was possible to obtain agreement.

The Delegation of Belgium was favorable on the whole of the draft Treaty and welcomed the efforts undertaken to establish an electronic filing system. It stressed the importance of the link between the draft Treaty and the PCT. As for Article 7(2)(i) relating to mandatory representation for filing translations in the case of regional patents, it considered it useful to link that matter to the question of the certification of translations which was sometimes required. It further wished for various clarifications on the matter of evidence referred to in Articles 5, 8, 9, 10, 11, 12 and 13. The Delegation would like to see a transfer of various provisions in the Treaty to the Regulations. Finally, it stressed the importance of maintaining the one year priority period, which could involve a reservation with regard to Article 15 of the draft Treaty.

The Delegation of Australia stated that it supported the draft Treaty since it avoided unnecessary costs for applicants and reduced the risks for applicants in the various States to loose their rights. The Delegation said that it preferred simple provisions over complex provisions and that it supported any suggestion that went in that direction. Furthermore, it expressed its wish that substantive provisions would be contained in the draft Treaty under consideration.

The Delegation of Indonesia referred to the recommendations made at the third session of the Committee of Experts, in which the need that the format of a national or regional patent application should be in line with the PCT requirements had been clearly stated. In that context, the Delegation informed the meeting that Indonesia had recently ratified the PCT. Its national legislation was currently amended in order to apply the PCT as of September 1997. The Delegation stated that, as a result of the meeting of the Committee of Experts, it would be able to anticipate the features of the regulations and administrative matters to be dealt with by a national office under the PCT.

The Representative of the EPO stated that his organization was more or less content with the present draft of the Patent Law Treaty. He said that aligning the application requirements of the draft Patent Law Treaty with the PCT was an important step forward. This would largely avoid the introduction of additional formality standards, thus facilitating the acceptance of the draft Treaty. Although the EPO would like to see the Treaty to contain more provisions on substance, the Representative said that he believed that the draft before the Committee of Experts was a balanced package and a compromise on which the Committee should go forward.

The Representative of the Japan Intellectual Property Association (JIPA) expressed the support of his Organization for the draft Treaty prepared by the International Bureau. As a user of the patent systems, JIPA welcomed to newly introduced Articles relating to electronic filing because an electronic filing system would reduce a regional disparity between applicants. The Representative declared that the new draft Treaty had become more user friendly since the requirements for an application in the new draft Treaty were fewer than the requirements under the PCT. The Representative of JIPA said that his organization believed that the new draft Treaty covering formalities had a great significance and that it hoped that the Patent Law Treaty covering formalities would be entered into at an early stage. Finally, he said that it was JIPA's position that the discussion of substantive issues of patent law harmonization should be continued.

(a) The Representative of the Japan Patent Attorneys Association (JPAA) identified three aspects of the Patent Law Treaty: first, particular provisions on the Patent Law Treaty; second, provisions on improvement of the PCT; and third, provisions on electronic applications.

(b) As regards the first category, the Representative said that it covered the provisions relating to representation and address for service, extension of a time limit and the belated claiming of priority. The JPAA supported the new Articles providing for an extension of time limits and the belated claiming of priority, since those provisions were minimum requirements. The more flexible approach represented in those provisions was seen to be in favor of the basic principle of sufficient patent protection. As regards representation, the Representative of JPAA referred to the second and third sessions of the Committee of Experts, where JPAA had already stressed the importance of a high quality of a first application. Due to the barrier of language, professional knowledge of practice was considered to be essential in order to obtain sufficient patent protection when an application was filed abroad. The effective cooperation between the national patent offices and the qualified representatives served the maintenance of high quality of application and examination prosecution. From this point of view, Article 7 was acceptable for JPAA.

(c) Concerning the second category of provisions, the Representative said that the PCT had an important function. He expressed JPAA's belief that the PCT was a model of a system which would enable users to prepare an application in a single format. Therefore, maximum improvements in the PCT were considered to be acceptable.

(d) Thirdly, referring to the provisions on electronic applications, the Representative said that his organization had about seven years of experience in filing electronic applications. He considered electronic applications to be very effective for communications between the patent office and patent attorneys. . . .

NOTE: THE WIPO PATENT LAW TREATY [PLT]

Years of diligent work by the experts from national patent offices, WIPO, and interested non-governmental organizations culminated in the signing of the "new" Patent Law Treaty on June 2, 2000 by forty-three states and regional intellectual property offices, including the United States, the EPO, EAPO, and ARIPO. The purposes of the treaty are to streamline national patent filing procedures along the lines of the PCT application, reduce requirements for local representation in routine patent application procedures, and to bring the patent systems of the world into the electronic age.

The treaty is characterized as providing no limitations on states with regard to requirements of substantive patent law. Article 2 PLT. (Recall the position of the United States in the previous reading.) The treaty and its rules apply to national, regional, and PCT applications. Article 3 PLT. An applicant may only be required to submit three items in order to receive a filing date: (1) an indication to the effect that the filing is a patent application,(2) identity of the applicant and means of contact, and (3) what appears facially to be a description. The first two items may be required to be in an official language but the description can be in any language. Article 5 PLT. No patent office may make requirements for the form or contents of an application which exceed the requirements of a PCT application, nor may it require formalities in connection with translations or evidence unless it provides a reason for doing so. Article 6 PLT. A patent office may not require the applicant to appoint a local representative for the purpose of filing the application, mere payment of a fee (including a maintenance fee), or where the regulations otherwise prescribe; nor may it require a separate power of attorney document for more than one application by the same applicant. Article 7 PLT. Any member office may exclude paper filings and require electronic filing of patent applications after June 2, 2005, and if it does so, it must make the requirements for the filing of national applications identical to those for PCT applications. Article 8 PLT. A patent may not be revoked for a non-fraudulent failure to comply with specified formalities, Article 10 PLT, and rights of an applicant or patentee may be reinstated after a finding of due care or unintentionality. Article 12 PLT. Under the Agreed Understandings which accompany the treaty, the International Bureau is tasked to create and build an electronic database ("digital library system") of all priority documents. Finally, the PLT Assembly will meet regularly with the PCT Assembly, and it is contemplated that participation in one or the other of the treaties will facilitate participation in both.

NOTES AND QUESTIONS

(1) **Divergent Priorities**. What are the main concerns of the various delegations? Which states are most supportive of the International Bureau's draft and why? How does the position of the United States delegation differ on issues of substance and why? What kinds of issues does the U.S. delegation view as substantive in this supposedly "procedural" treaty?

(2) **Difficult Issues**. From the standpoint of the July, 1997 report, which kinds of issues are likely to be most easy to resolve, and which are likely to be the most difficult?

(3) **A World Patent?** For an idealized vision of how a "world patent" might look, see Michael A. Meller, *Planning For a Global Patent System*, 12 WORLD INT. PROP. REP. 210 (1998). Consider the possibility of a world patent in ten, twenty, or thirty years. Given the expertise of the International Bureau of WIPO, the fact that it administers the PCT and has become one of the best-funded and best-equipped U.N. agencies thereby, and the fact that it will be the repository of a digital library system of priority documents, how likely is it that the patent part of the WIPO will transmogrify into a "World Patent Office" [WPO] over time? Or should the United States, Europe, and Japan pursue a trilateral office? Would it be in the best interests of patent applicants in the new millennium to have a one stop address for all their patent filing needs? If so, are there any downsides? If not, why stop there? If the United States adopts electronic filing of all patent applications in five years and refuses to accept paper filings anymore, is there any reason not to have all U.S. applications (including PCT and national applications) filed with the International Bureau and close down the USPTO mail room entirely? What about examination? Who will examine a world patent application? Who will represent the applicant for a world patent?

§ 6.02 Global Design Deposit Agreements: The Hague Agreement

The Hague Agreement Concerning the International Deposit of Industrial Designs has been in place for 75 years. It establishes a mechanism, not unlike that of the Madrid Agreement and Protocol for trademarks, by which an applicant may make a single deposit of a design with its country of origin or with WIPO and request protection in any number of countries that are members of the Hague Agreement. The United States is not currently a member of the Hague Union; existing texts of the Hague Agreement, the most recent of which is the 1960 Act (the "Hague Act"), were crafted to cater to countries that do not carry out substantial examination of design registration applications and thus rely essentially on a deposit system. For the last several years, WIPO has been supervising efforts to conclude a revised version (a new "act") of the agreement. This new act has been drafted with a view to persuading other countries (such as the United States, Japan, and the United Kingdom) to join the system, and it was concluded at a diplomatic conference in July, 1999 in Geneva (the "Geneva Act"). In this Section, we consider the basic features of the existing Hague system, and the issues raised by the most recent revision process.

PIERRE MAUGUÉ, THE INTERNATIONAL PROTECTION OF INDUSTRIAL DESIGNS UNDER THE INTERNATIONAL CONVENTIONS*
19 U. BALT. L. REV. 393, 397-400 (1989)

The institution of an international registration of industrial designs was the subject of a wish expressed by the Washington Diplomatic Conference in 1911. It was not until November 6, 1925, however, that the Hague Agreement was adopted. That Agreement, which constitutes a "special agreement" within the meaning of article 19 of the Paris Convention, took force on June 1, 1928, and has been revised several times. Depending on the contracting state, the provisions of substance that currently apply are those of the 1934 and 1960 Acts. This Article focuses on the provisions of the 1960 Act which were finalized by the 1967 Act.

The principle of international deposit of industrial designs arose from the need for simplicity and economy. Its main purpose was to enable protection to be obtained for one or more industrial designs in a number of countries through a single deposit filed with the International Bureau of [WIPO].

Under . . . the Hague Agreement, any person entitled to effect an international deposit may obtain, by means of a single deposit, protection for his industrial designs in a number of countries involving a minimum of formalities and expense. Consequently, the applicant is relieved of the need to make a separate national deposit in each of the countries in which the design requires protection, and avoids the inherent complication of procedures that vary from one country to another. The applicant does not have to submit the required documents in various languages or keep watch on the deadlines for renewal of a whole series of national deposits. Also avoided is the need to pay a series of national fees and agents' fees in varying currencies.

Under the Hague Agreement, the same results can be obtained through a single deposit made with a single office, in one language, on payment of a single set of fees, and in one currency. Presently, there are twenty-one member countries of the Hague Union established by the Hague Agreement.**

Any national of a contracting country can make an international deposit, and an international deposit does not require any prior national deposit.[23] One makes an international deposit directly with the International Bureau of WIPO, through the depositor or his representative on a form provided . . . by the International Bureau. [Alternatively, the international] deposit may be effectuated . . . through the national office of a contracting country, if the law of the country so permits.

---

* Copyright 1989 Pierre Maugué; University of Baltimore Law Review.

** [Ed. Note: As of April 15, 2001, there were twenty-nine members of the Hague Union.]

[23] A "national" is any natural or legal person having the nationality of one of those countries included in the Union or any individual having his domicile, headquarters, or a real and effective industrial or commercial establishment, in one of those countries.

The law of a contracting country also may require, in cases where that country is the state of origin, that the international deposit be made through the national office of that country.[25] Noncompliance with this requirement, however, does not prejudice the effects of the international deposit in the other countries. The international deposit has the same effect in each of the countries for which protection is requested, as if the designs included in the deposit had been deposited directly in that state on the date of the international deposit, subject to the special rules established under the Hague Agreement. This is true particularly in regard to the term of protection.

. . . Any contracting country whose domestic legislation offers the possibility of refusing protection as the result of an *ex officio* administrative examination, or of opposition by a third party, may refuse protection for any industrial design, if it fails to meet the requirements of its domestic law.

Refusal of protection may not, however, extend to the formalities and other administrative acts that are to be considered by each contracting country as having been accomplished at the time the international deposit is recorded at the International Bureau. . . .

The national office of a contracting country must notify the International Bureau and . . . the depositor on the refusal to publish the deposit within six months of the date on which the national office received the periodical bulletin in which the international deposit was published. The depositor has the same remedies against the decision to refuse protection that he would have had if he had deposited the refused design at the national level with the office of the country that refused protection. If the refusal is not noted within the applicable six-month period, the international deposit then achieves the same status as a deposit entered in the national register of each of the countries for which protection has been requested.

International deposits are published by the International Bureau in a monthly periodical called the *International Designs Bulletin*. This publication includes a reproduction of the article or articles in which the deposited designs are to be incorporated. . . .

The depositor may request that publication be deferred for a period not to exceed twelve months from the date of the international deposit or, where appropriate, from the date priority is claimed. The owner of an international deposit enjoys the priority right afforded under article 4 of the Paris Convention, if he claims this right and if the international deposit is made within six months of the first national, regional, or international deposit

---

[25] The state of origin is to be understood as the state party to The Hague Agreement in which the depositor has a real and effective industrial or commercial establishment, or where the depositor has such establishments in more than one state party to the Agreement, the state he has designated in the application or, failing this, the state party to the Agreement in which he has his residence (or headquarters), or failing this, the state party to the Agreement of which he has the nationality.

made in one of the countries party to the Paris Convention, or if he makes a deposit having effect in one of those countries.

An international deposit is made for an initial term of five years, and can be renewed at least once for an additional period of five years for all or part of the designs included in the deposit, or for all or only some of the countries in which it has effect. For those contracting countries whose domestic legislation allows a term of protection greater than ten years for national deposits, an international deposit may be renewed more than once.

In each case, a renewal may be made for an additional period of five years, with effect in each country up to the expiration of the total allowable term of protection for national deposits under that country's domestic legislation. . . .

The working languages for the implementation of the Hague Agreement are English and French. International deposits and any amendment affecting the deposits are entered in the international register and published in English or French. Correspondence between the International Bureau and the depositor is drafted in English or French, depending on the language used in completing the application for the international deposit. . . .

The offices of the contracting countries have no specific tasks in the implementation of the Hague Agreement except in those cases where the domestic or regional legislation of the country permits or requires the international deposit to be effected through them or calls for a novelty examination for deposited designs.

WILLIAM T. FRYER, SEEKING A BENEFITS BALANCE IN THE INDUSTRIAL DESIGN TREATY REVISION (HAGUE AGREEMENT): FIFTH MEETING OF EXPERTS, HELD JUNE 13-16, 1995 [*]
77 J. PAT. & TRAD. OFF. SOC'Y 931, 941-942 (1995)

EU members [participating in the Hague revision process] recognized that the [existing text of the] Hague Agreement was based on design protection systems that did not examine for novelty (non-examination systems). These national systems were characterized by relatively prompt formalities review and publication of the design. Rights were established from the filing date, usually. If there was a novelty question, it was raised by a third party after registration.

The Hague Agreement members have received prompt design protection with only a formality view by WIPO, using a system modeled after their non-examination systems. The first Hague Agreement Act (1934) did not allow for refusal by a member country after WIPO formality review. The

---

[*] Copyright 1995, William T. Fryer. Reprinted with permission. Professor Fryer maintains a web site, fryer.com, which contains a wealth of information regarding international design protection.

1960 Act attempted to accommodate novelty examination countries by allowing a six months refusal period.

Examination countries, in sharp contrast, do not award a design right until completion of an extensive examination, including novelty and adequacy of the design reproduction. This examination process is the reason for the extended time . . . now in the draft treaty for refusal of IDR effect. Even after the first office action which reports the results of a novelty search, the concern for issuing only valid design protection requires that new issues can be raised in subsequent stages before the right is granted. Design protection in examination countries will occur only after two or more years from filing, usually . . . Even with the current U.S. effort to reduce the time it takes to obtain a design patent, it will never be as short a period as the time to obtain a registration in non-examination countries.

. . .

In summary, there are two basic types of design protection systems in the world. The current Hague Agreement members are trying to accommodate examination systems while retaining the benefits of the current Hague Agreement which was set up primarily for non-examination systems. If there is significant flexibility allowed in this integration, the two systems can be interfaced to achieve benefits currently received by Hague Agreement members.

FRANÇOIS CURCHOD, THE REVISION OF THE HAGUE AGREEMENT CONCERNING THE INTERNATIONAL DEPOSIT OF INDUSTRIAL DESIGNS [*]
24 Am. Intell. Prop. L. Ass'n Q.J. 599 (1996)

I. INTRODUCTION

The Program of [WIPO] for the 1996-97 biennium provides that "the International Bureau will prepare, convene and service in 1996 a session of a committee of experts on the preparation of a new treaty on the international registration, with WIPO, of industrial designs." . . .

. . . .

II. THE TWO OBJECTIVES OF THE REVISION

The draft new Act ("the new draft"), which will be discussed by the Committee of Experts in November 1996, has been prepared with two main objectives in mind: first, expanding the geographical scope of the Hague system for the international registration of industrial designs; and, second, making the Hague system a more efficient instrument for obtaining protection for industrial designs in more than one country, especially for the design-intensive industries, and in particular the textile and fashion

---

industries. These two objectives are not always immediately compatible. Expanding the geographical scope requires the accommodation of at least the basic requirements of States whose law requires the examination of applications as to substance. Such an accommodation, in turn, requires, for example, the extension of the time period allowed for the refusal of the effect of an international registration. This extension, in turn, runs contrary to the desire of various industries, particularly those in which product cycles are short, to obtain protection as quickly as possible.

In addressing the first objective of expanded geographical scope, the approach adopted in the drafts considered by the Committee of Experts to date has involved the addition of a further layer to the procedure under the 1960 Act of the Hague Agreement. This further layer would apply only where an applicant seeks protection in a Contracting Party whose law requires the examination of applications as to substance. The adoption of this approach is based on an understanding that the purpose of an international registration treaty, such as the Hague Agreement, is to facilitate, through one centralized procedure, the procurement of protection in all the Contracting Parties rather than to harmonize the legislation of those Contracting Parties. It is to be noted that this approach was contested in previous sessions of the Committee of Experts on the ground that it allows nationals of countries having relatively complicated national systems easy access to design protection in countries having simpler systems (based upon a mere deposit), without any reciprocal concession on the part of the former countries.

III. THE TWO-CHAPTER SYSTEM

The new draft maintains this approach but, in accordance with the discussions that took place during the fifth session of the Committee of Experts, it consists, apart from two introductory provisions, of two Chapters. Chapter I provides for a simple and quick system of protection of industrial designs desired by future Contracting Parties that do not have, or do not intend to maintain, a substantive examination system. Chapter II contains additional requirements, some or all of which would have to be complied with by applicants designating Contracting Parties that have, and intend to maintain, a substantive examination system.

There would be limits, however, placed on the registration requirements for "Chapter II Contracting Parties." . . .

. . . .

IV. OTHER MAIN FEATURES OF THE REVISION

The other main features of the revised system for the international registration of industrial designs under the Hague Agreement envisaged by the new draft are as follows:

. . . .

(3) Subject to any requirements concerning security clearance in the applicable national or regional law, applicants may file an international application, at their option, either directly with the International Bureau or indirectly through the intermediary of the Office of a Contracting Party. The international application would be accorded a filing date, which would be the date of its receipt by the International Bureau, when the international application is filed with the International Bureau. When the international application is filed indirectly, the filing date would be that of its receipt by the intermediary filing Office, provided that the Office transmits the international application to the International Bureau within one month of its receipt by the Office. The revised system does not envisage any role on the part of an intermediary filing Office in checking the formalities of the international application. Rather, the formal examination would be undertaken by the International Bureau in the case of applications filed either directly or indirectly. However, if at the time a Contracting Party becomes bound by the new Act its law requires the review of applications for the purpose of granting security clearance, the Office of such a Contracting Party, when serving as an intermediary filing Office for an international application, would not transmit applications to the International Bureau before the application has first been reviewed for this purpose. In such cases, the period of one month allowed for the transmission of an international application from the intermediary filing Office to the International Bureau may be extended to three months without affecting the filing date. At the request of the Delegation of the United States at the Committee of Experts, a provision was made to allow for an extension of this period up to six months without affecting the filing date, provided that the Office concerned (for all practical purposes, the United States Patent and Trademark Office) notifies both the International Bureau and the applicant that, due to the security clearance, the three-month time limit cannot be respected. If the applicable time limit—one month, three months, or six months, as the case may be—for the transmission of the international application to the International Bureau is not observed, the filing date will be the date on which the International Bureau receives the international application.

(4) In order to accommodate some of the varying requirements of the different national and regional systems for the registration of industrial designs, the revised system envisages three different categories of requirements in an international application:

(a) The first category covers the requirements that all international applications, regardless of which Contracting Parties are designated, must satisfy in order to register in the International Register the industrial design that is the subject of the international application. The requirements in the first category correspond to those requirements which would need to be satisfied in all Contracting Parties in a national (or regional) application for a filing date to be accorded to the national (or regional) application under the law of each of those Contracting Parties.

(b) The second category covers certain additional requirements specified in Chapter II that must be satisfied in an international application when Contracting Parties having those requirements are designated. These additional requirements are limited to those imposed by the Contracting Party, in addition to the requirements in the first category, for the grant of a filing date in a national (or regional) application received by that Party's Office. In addition, these requirements are only applicable with respect to Contracting Parties whose Offices examine applications as to substance and who impose them at the time that they enter into the treaty. In the interest of keeping the international system as simple as possible, the list of those additional requirements is limited in the new Act itself.

(c) The third category covers certain additional requirements that must be satisfied in certain Contracting Party States in order to ensure that the international registration is given the effect of a national (or regional) registration. They are not, however, mandatory requirements for the purposes of the international application. An international registration may be obtained with respect to all Contracting Parties on the basis of an international application that does not satisfy these requirements (assuming, of course, that the requirements of the first and, where appropriate, second categories are satisfied). Rather, the requirements in the third category correspond to requirements under the national (or regional) law of the designated Contracting Parties that must be satisfied, not for the purpose of obtaining a filing date, but for the purpose of the grant of protection. Failure to satisfy any such requirements in the international application may form the basis for a refusal, on the part of the concerned designated Contracting Party, to recognize the effect of the international registration. These additional requirements will be specified in the Regulations under the new Act as optional requirements that the applicant may wish to fulfill in the international application in order to avoid unnecessary refusals from the Offices of Contracting Parties having such requirements.

(5) The date of an international registration would be the filing date of the international application, subject to provisions requiring the postponement of the date of international registration in the case of certain irregularities.

(6) The international application may contain a request for deferment of publication. A flexible system is provided with respect to deferment of publication in order to accommodate differing national (or regional) approaches to deferment. Essentially, where an international application contains a request to defer publication, publication would be deferred for the shortest period of deferment recognized under the applicable laws of all of the designated Contracting Parties. Thus, for example, if two Contracting Parties were designated, and they recognized under their applicable laws deferment of publication for periods of twelve and twenty-four months, respectively, publication of the international application would be deferred for a period of twelve months. In any case, the maximum period of deferment of publication is thirty months. It is also possible that a Contracting Party refuses to recognize deferment of publication under its laws. If

an international application containing a request for deferment of publication designated such a Contracting Party, the applicant would be notified by the International Bureau that deferment of publication would not be possible with respect to that designated Contracting Party. If the applicant did not withdraw the designation of that Contracting Party within a certain time limit, the request for deferment of publication in the international application would be disregarded by the International Bureau.

(7) Designated Contracting Parties may refuse to recognize an international registration. The normal period allowed to communicate a refusal is six months, but may be extended up to thirty months * by a Contracting Party whose Office examines applications as to substance. However, the possible grounds for refusal are limited.

(8) In order to accommodate differing national (or regional) approaches to the stage at which protection commences, Contracting Parties must recognize an international registration as having two different effects, which may commence at different times. First, from the date of international registration, each designated Contracting Party must recognize an international registration as having the same effect, including prior art effect, as a regularly-filed application for the grant of protection. Second, the international registration must be recognized by each designated Contracting Party as having the same effect as a grant of protection under its applicable law as of a date no later than the expiration of the period allowed to communicate a refusal (assuming that a refusal has not been communicated by the concerned Contracting Party).

(9) The provisions on fees contain two features designed to attract wider participation in the revised system:

(a) The first feature is designed to ensure that Contracting Parties whose Offices examine applications as to substance are adequately compensated for the work involved in the examination of an international registration. It allows Contracting Parties to replace the standard designation fee payable to each Contracting Party by an individual designation fee, the amount of which is determined, subject to certain limits, by the Contracting Party.

(b) The second feature is designed to make the revised system attractive to applicants seeking deferment of publication in order, inter alia, to determine whether or not to proceed with the international registration upon the expiration of the deferment period. Only a prescribed portion of the international registration fee must be paid at the time of filing the international application, the balance being payable two months before the expiration of the deferment period.

(10) Each designated Contracting Party must recognize a minimum period of fifteen years, subject to renewal, from the date of international registration to the expiration of the period of protection obtained through

---

* [Ed. Note: In the final version of the Geneva Act, this extended period for refusal was set at twelve months after receipt of the IDR from WIPO. *See* Geneva Regulations, Rule 18].

international registration. Any designated Contracting Party whose applicable law allows for a longer period of protection must recognize the equivalent, longer period of protection.

(11) A saving provision is included to confirm that the new Act would not affect any other equivalent or greater form of protection accorded by the applicable law of a Contracting Party, any protection accorded to works of art or works of applied art by international copyright treaties and conventions, or any protection accorded to industrial designs under [TRIPS].

. . . .

WILLIAM T. FRYER, SEEKING A BENEFITS BALANCE IN THE INDUSTRIAL DESIGN TREATY REVISION (HAGUE AGREEMENT): FIFTH MEETING OF EXPERTS, HELD JUNE 13-16, 1995 *
77 J. Pat. & Trade. Off. Soc'y. 931, 944-946 (1995)

The draft text [considered by the Fifth Meeting of the Committee of Experts in 1995 allowed] a reservation for a member to retain the prior art effect of an IDR as other than from its Paris Convention (Convention) date. [1995 Draft Act art. X.] U.S. law, under the *In re Hilmer* [359 F.2d 859 (C.C.P.A. 1966)] decision, gives a Convention application prior art effect from the U.S. filing date.

It is hard to draw a line between substantive and procedural provisions, but prior art effect is primarily substantive. Since the Hague Agreement revision has the purpose of procedural uniformity, prior art effect should not be a topic for discussion. Each country should have its national law apply. In most of the current Hague Agreement countries prior art effect is from the Convention filing date. Consequently, current members desire to harmonize this important feature.

Prior art effect has been a hotly contested issue in connection with harmonization of utility patent law. It has carried forward to the Hague Agreement revision. Since this issue could not be resolved during the more extensive utility patent negotiations, it is unlikely that Hague Agreement discussions can make any greater progress. The fact that U.S. law on prior art effect applies to utility and design patents makes it even more unlikely that a change can be made only for designs, without resolving beforehand all the utility patent law harmonization issues.

The U.S. has consistently stated at the Hague Agreement meetings that the principle of prior art effective date for U.S. design patents could not be changed. Draft text article X was prepared by WIPO for consideration, to make it clear that the U.S. could retain its current law under *Hilmer* by reservation. In fact article X is not needed, as the revised treaty states that national law will apply and, therefore, prior art effect under current

---

U.S. law would be retained. [1995 Draft Act art. 10.] Article X merely restates this fact and highlights it as a disputed topic. . . .

The concern over U.S. law on prior art effect may not be as serious as some may think. A review of U.S case law suggests that prior art effect of a IDR will be from the WIPO publication date, under 35 U.S.C. § 102(a) for most registrations.[36] For deferred registrations, the question of prior art effect will need to be analyzed further. It appears that when the IDR is sent to the PTO, the date it is received would complete the file and establish the effective U.S. filing date under 35 U.S.C. § 102(e) and the *Hilmer* decision.

While the *Hilmer* law will remain in force, the prior art effective date for an IDR will be earlier. It is not as early as the Convention filing date for prior art effect, but it is closer to a harmonization approach. There is a possible six months gap for the Convention based IDR, but in most situations design filings take place quickly and the practical loss of time for prior art purposes should not be of significance. Non-deferred applications filed directly with WIPO will have about a three months gap until prior art effect under U.S. patent law, the time between filing and IDR publication.

Foreign practitioners have a valid point when they state it is better sometimes to file a national design application directly to receive prior art effect at the earliest time. This step avoids the use of a Convention application and the *Hilmer* restriction, but it does not utilize the convenient centralized filing under the Hague Agreement.

The Patent Cooperation Treaty (PCT) incorporates the *Hilmer* law, and in spite of this fact it has been very successful. An application filed under PCT receives prior art effect on receipt in the PTO of the international application.[37] The fact that PCT use has grown suggests that filing in a centralized design system, like the Hague Agreement, will have sufficient benefit to attract members, even if the *Hilmer* barrier exists.

NOTES AND QUESTIONS

(1) **Structure of the Geneva Act**. The system established by the Final Act signed on July 2, 1999, in Geneva is in substance largely as described by François Curchod three years earlier. (The most significant substantive

------

[36] The Federal Circuit settled, in *In re Carlson*, 983 F.2d 1032 (Fed. Cir. 1992), the issue of whether a third party unpublished foreign design registration was patented prior art under 35 U.S.C. § 102(a). The Federal Circuit followed the holding of *In re Ekenstam*, 256 F.2d 321 (C.C.P.A. 1958). The Federal Circuit held that Section 102(a) required public access to the patent document. Another case taking the same position was *Ex parte Winter*, 144 U.S.P.Q 124 (Pat. and Trademark Off. Bd. of App.). An IDR publication is prior art from its publication date under 35 U.S.C. § 102(a), if prior to the invention date.

[37] 35 U.S.C.A. § 363 (West Supp. 1995); M.P.E.P. § 1895.01(1).

change was the reduction, from thirty months to twelve months, of the extended period for countries with Examining Offices to notify any refusal to register a design.) The act was not, however, neatly divided into two chapters. *Compare* Basic Proposal For The New Act of the Hague Agreement Concerning the International Registration of Industrial Designs (Submitted by Director General, WIPO, Dec. 15, 1998) with Geneva Act of the Hague Agreement Concerning the International Registration of Industrial Designs (July 2, 1999). Although a separate set of provisions was included to address the role of Examining Offices, these are interwoven through the final Agreement. *See, e.g.,* Geneva Act art. 5(2) (setting out additional mandatory content requirements for application designating country with Examining Office); Geneva Regulations, Rule 18 (providing countries with Examining Office longer time in which to notify refusal of registration).

(2) **Place of Deposit.** Article 4(2) of the 1960 Act allowed contracting states to require their nationals seeking to use the Hague Agreement to make an international deposit through their national office rather than directly. The Geneva Act does not allow states to deny use of the direct deposit with WIPO, *see* Notes on the Basic Proposal for the New Act of the Hague Agreement Concerning the International Registration of Industrial Designs (WIPO, Dec. 15, 1998) at 7, although a state may still decline to offer use of its office as an intermediary for indirect deposit. *See* Geneva Act art. 4(1)(b). Why might this change have been made?

(3) **Multiple Design Registration and the Locarno Agreement.** One of the most significant aspects of the Hague Agreement is that, like most of the non-examination countries that comprise the Hague Union, it permits registration of multiple designs in the same classification class under the Locarno Agreement in a single registration. *See* Geneva Act art. 5(4); Geneva Regulations, Rule 7(6) (all products to which the designs in the same international application are to be applied must be in the same class under the Locarno Agreement). In an examination country, such as the United States, multiple design registrations have traditionally not been allowed; under the new Act, such countries may not refuse protection on the ground that the international application includes several designs, except if the designs that are the subject of the same application do not conform to a requirement of "unity of design." *See* Geneva Act art. 13. Why is the possibility of a multiple design registration important? And why have examination systems generally not permitted such registrations? *See* Fryer, *Seeking a Benefits Balance, supra,* at 947.

The Locarno Agreement, signed in 1968, established a classification system for industrial designs. The United States was a party to this treaty at its inception, but later withdrew, and thus U.S. design patents for several years included both the international classification and the U.S. classification. Although a state may adhere to the Hague Agreement without being a member of the Locarno Union, *see* Notes on the Basic Proposal for the New Act of the Hague Agreement Concerning the International Registration of Industrial Designs (WIPO, Dec. 15, 1998) at 5, the multiple design registration provision relies upon the Locarno system, in that only designs that fall within a single International Classification subclass can be included in the application. Geneva Regulations, Rule 7(6). If the United States joins the Hague system, this mandatory reference to the Locarno system might prompt reconsideration of whether to participate in the Locarno Agreement.

(4) **Contents of Hague Application.** In order to obtain a filing date, a Hague application must comply with a series of mandatory content requirements as well as with the specific requirements of the contracting states (so-called "additional mandatory" content requirements) designated as countries in which protection is sought. These additional requirements come from states with an administrative examination of novelty (termed "Examination Offices"). The United States had indicated in negotiations that the only additional requirements from Article 5(2)(b) of the Geneva Act that it will impose are a claim and the name of the creator of the design. Determinations that the application satisfies the requirements of the Hague Agreement as to form and content are to be made by WIPO. Once the IDR is received by the designated countries, it will be examined as would any domestic application. Thus, the United States PTO would subject the IDR to the same examination process as it would a domestic design patent applicant. The grounds for refusal will be determined by U.S. law, with the exception that refusal cannot be based on noncompliance with a requirement relating to the form or content of the international application. *See* Geneva Act art. 12(1). For example, a designated state cannot require applicants to provide a translation of the application into a language that is not required by the agreement. Any notification of refusal to register must be communicated to WIPO within six months, or twelve months in the case of countries (such as the United States) with Examining Offices. *See* Geneva Regulations, Rule 18. What developments in the U.S. design patent application process might cause the PTO to issue a refusal to register? *See* Notes on the Basic Proposal for the New Act of the Hague Agreement Concerning the International Registration of Industrial Designs (WIPO, Dec. 15, 1998) at 16-17.

(5) **Deferred Publication**. One of the most significant issues over the course of the negotiation has been how to handle international design registrations for which the applicant has requested deferral of publication (as the Hague Agreement permits, *see* Geneva Act art. 5(5)). In particular, these registrations impede a proper analysis of prior art in those countries undertaking a full novelty examination. Under the Geneva Act, a copy of a deferred registration will be forwarded to each office designated in the IDR application, but the receiving office will be required to treat it as confidential. Which other parties or interests are threatened by the existence of deferred publication IDRs? *See* Geneva Act art. 10(5)(b) (identifying persons to whom and circumstances in which, subject to confidentiality obligations, the Office may divulge the contents of an IDR requesting deferred publication).

(6) **Hilmer**. The Geneva Act did not expressly address the issue of the *Hilmer* doctrine. Are you persuaded by Professor Fryer's arguments both that the express provision (1995 Draft Article X) was not needed to permit U.S. application of the doctrine, and that the *Hilmer* doctrine has very little effect on parties' rights? *See* Geneva Act art. 14; PTO Notice Inviting Public Comment on Hague Agreement on Industrial Designs, 64 Fed. Reg. 19135, 19138 (Apr. 19, 1999) (suggesting that identically-phrased antecedent of Article 14 conflicted with *Hilmer*); Letter from Margaret Boulware, President, American Intellectual Property Law Association, to PTO, (May 6, 1999) (rejecting PTO interpretation).

(7) **Entry Into Effect.** The Geneva Act will enter into effect three months after six states, including at least three "active design" states (*i.e.*, states that received a prescribed number of design filings in the last set of annual statistics), deposit instruments of ratification. *See* Geneva Act art. 28(2). This provision is based upon Article 63(1) of the Patent Cooperation Treaty. What objectives does it serve: why not simply condition effectiveness upon any six states adhering to the new act? *Cf.* Notes on the Basic Proposal for the New Act of the Hague Agreement Concerning the International Registration of Industrial Designs (WIPO, Dec. 15, 1998) at 34 (listing states that would satisfy conditions for "active design states"). Article 31 makes the standard provision for relations between states party to different acts of the Hague Agreement, essentially mandating the application of the most recent text (1999, 1960 or 1934) to which both states are party. Examine the different variations referenced in Article 31: is there any relationship that is not addressed? *See id.* at 35.

(8) **The Status of the EU.** Both states and certain intergovernmental organizations may become party to the agreement. *See* Geneva Act art. 27(1)(ii). The principal organization that might take advantage of this provision are the EU, when the Community Design Regulation is in place, and the African Intellectual Property Organization ("OAPI"). It is also possible that the African Regional Industrial Property Organization ("ARIPO") might become a party. *See* Notes on the Basic Proposal for the New Act of the Hague Agreement Concerning the International Registration of Industrial Designs (WIPO, Dec. 15, 1998) at 31 (noting possible argument that the 1982 Harare Protocol establishes a system of registration of industrial designs that meets Article 27 standards). As with several recent treaty negotiations, the issue of separate intergovernmental organization (largely, EU) voting rights was a sticking point in concluding the Geneva Act. Eventually, a compromise was agreed. Although the EU may participate in the assembly of the Hague Union in addition to its constituent states, Article 21(4)(b)(ii) provides that

> any Contracting Party that is an intergovernmental organization may vote, in place of its Member States, with a number of votes equal to the number of its Member States which are party to the Act, and that no such intergovernmental organization shall participate in the vote if any one of its Member States exercises its right to vote, and vice-versa.

(9) **Term**. One of the areas where the Hague Agreement has attempted substantive harmonization has been the term of protection. Early versions of the agreement contained minimum and maximum terms; the 1960 text contained a minimum term of ten years. Article 17(3) of the Geneva Act adopts a fifteen-year minimum IDR term, which will be measured from the date of the international registration? Does the U.S. design patent term satisfy this obligation? *See* 35 U.S.C. § 173; Geneva Act art. 10(2) (date of international registration).

(10) **Textile Designs.** Design patents are the primary means for protection of clothing shape (as opposed to two-dimensional patterns) in the United States, and thus the ease of design patent protection impacts TRIPS compliance by the United States regarding special attention to the needs of the textile industry. *See* TRIPS art. 25(2). If you were arguing for U.S. adherence to the Geneva text based upon its capacity to enhance protection for textile designs, which features of the system would you identify as particularly important? *See* Geneva Regulations, Rules 12(2), 16(3), Geneva Act arts. 5(1)(iii), 5(4).

(11) **U.S. Adherence**. The United States has participated vigorously in the negotiation of the Geneva Act (although WIPO officials have noted that the United States also participated in the diplomatic conference leading to the 1960 act). Industry and the intellectual property bar in the United States have been generally supportive of U.S. adherence. Would you support adherence to the new act?

§ 6.03   Regional Patent Registration Agreements

[A]   Europe

[1]   Historical Perspective

Sixty years ago, an observer noted that substantive patent examination tended to be strict in Germany, medium in the United States, liberal in Britain and free and easy in Latin countries. *See* EMERSON STRINGHAM, PATENTS AND GEBRAUCHMUSTER IN INTERNATIONAL LAW 142 (1934). "Britain occupied a mid-way position between Germany, the Netherlands, and Switzerland, on the one hand, vis-à-vis France, Belgium, and Italy on the other. It provided for a limited search and examination together with the possibility of third party opposition on somewhat wider grounds." WILLIAM CORNISH, INTELLECTUAL PROPERTY: PATENTS, COPYRIGHT, TRADE MARKS AND ALLIED RIGHTS 76 (2d ed. 1989). Was there ever to be a common ground? The first den of activity for substantive harmonization of patent law has been on the European continent.

LEONARD J. ROBBINS, THE PROPOSED NEW EUROPEAN PATENT*

5 PAT., TRADE., & COPR. J. OF RESEARCH AND EDUC.,
217–232 (1961)

2. PRIOR PROPOSALS FOR COMMON PATENTS

In 1909, Du Bois-Raymond of Germany first suggested a single world-wide patent. During the First World War, uncompleted steps were taken for common patents in Germany and Austria. In 1919, proposals for a single patent covering the British Commonwealth died in the discussion and conference stage. On November 15, 1920, an Arrangement for an international patent was actually concluded in Paris and was signed by eleven countries. However it never went into practical effect. During the height of the Second World War, from 1941 to 1943, a number of detailed proposals for a single European patent were published in the German periodical *Gewerblicher Rechtsschutz und Urheberrecht* [GRUR]. In 1946, Kucera of Czechoslovakia and in 1949, Longchambon of France offered proposals for the creation of a single European Patent Office. Since 1952, the governments of the Scandinavian countries [considered] the possibilities of a common patent while retaining the national laws and patent offices. . . .

3. PRIOR PROPOSALS FOR HARMONIZATION OF PATENT LAWS

The Treaty of Rome emphasizes the desirability of harmonization of the national laws of the member states in all fields. It is well known that Article 85 of the Treaty is exceedingly vague as regards patents, but it is generally agreed that the general principle of harmonization does apply to patent laws. However, harmonization ha[d] been under consideration long before the Common Market came into being. In fact, the broad idea actually goes back to 1883 when the International Convention for the Protection of Industrial Property was established. Among the numerous countries adhering to the International Convention much conformity has been achieved since then by voluntary amendments of national patent laws, but basic differences still remain.

[In] 1947, the governments of the Benelux countries—Belgium, Holland and Luxembourg—[began] studying the possibility for uniformity of their three patent laws. . . . Also, in 1947, the Benelux countries and France established the Institut International des Brevets (International Patent Institute) at the Hague as a central agency for the novelty examination of patents. The purpose [was] to relieve the burden from national patent offices and avoid duplication of effort. . . . In 1951, Dr. Reimer, the then President of the German Patent Office, proposed a single filing system using national patent offices, with extension to other countries, a centralized novelty examination, and various modifications of national procedures

---

* Copyright 1961, by PTC Research Foundation and Franklin Pierce Law Center. Reprinted with permission.

to take place over a period of years in successive steps. In 1954, three other comparable proposals along generally similar lines were made by Dr. Reimer himself, by Mr. de Haan, President of the Dutch Patent Office, and by Dr. Was, a Dutch patent attorney.

In 1958, the heads of various European patent offices, at a meeting in Vienna produced the "Vienna Plan" for a so-called joint application. In the same year, CNIPA, a committee of European national patent associations, submitted a slightly different but comparable plan.

There [were] still other proposals, all of them, like those previously mentioned, of a non-official or at best semi-official origin, and none of them under the aegis of an official international organization having the political power of action. . . .

The basis of harmonization is the preservation of national patent laws. But in the six countries of the Common Market (and in fact throughout Europe) there are two systems. In the civil law countries, France, Belgium, Luxembourg and Italy, patents are granted on the basis of simple registration by payment of a government fee ("*Sans guarantie du Gouvernement*" as explicitly printed on a French patent). In some of them there is an examination of certain formalities, but this is not of basic interest. The scope of patents in these non-examination countries can only be determined by the courts if the patents are litigated. On the other hand, in Germany and Holland, patent applications are submitted to a rigorous patent office examination for novelty, inventive height and advance in the art, followed by availability for opposition by third parties. In the German and Dutch Patent Offices, the sheep are separated from the goats before grant. There is an inference even if not a presumption of the validity of such patents and they are difficult to upset.

As a result, during the last 100 years or so, separate bodies of case law leave been built up involving widely different attitudes towards interpretation, validity and infringement. . . .

4. The Origin of the New Proposal for European Patents

The management of big technological industry in Europe—that is, industry involved in mass production (so rapidly acquiring U.S. techniques) and particularly the steel and non-ferrous metals industries, the electrical industry and the chemical industry, led or at any rate urged on primarily by German interests—has become impatient with the basic problems, and the complexities of possible compromises involved in harmonization. It considers that some form of political and legal federation of European countries is not too far over the horizon, and when this comes it wants a strong autonomous patent system already in existence. . . . What has happened appears to be as follows.

Starting some time during 1959, the powerful and tightly organized inner group applied pressure at the governmental level and used the already established machinery of the Common Market to introduce a concept which is actually outside the provisions of the Rome Treaty—namely, an autonomous European patent to be established by a new Treaty or Convention and to extend throughout the territories of adhering states.

It is true that the powers of the governing and executive bodies of the Common Market are exceedingly broad. However, it is difficult to find a mandate in the Rome Treaty for creating a new supranational industrial property right. What is to be the status or fate of national patents? Numerous legal commentators have interpreted Article 85 of the Rome Treaty to mean that legitimate uses of national patents are excluded from the rules applying to restrictive business practices. Article 36 has been interpreted as sustaining national sovereignty over patents. Seemingly there is no authority whatever to suppress national patents. In any event, for obvious practical reasons, national patents could not suddenly be abolished. Therefore the new proposal includes the reservation that national patents should remain and coexist indefinitely with European patents. Presumably if and when political federation is achieved many national laws will be superseded by unitary laws. Thus, on this distant day, the proposed Convention for European patents may in fact become the single patent law of the new superstate.

At the end of 1959, the Commission of the Common Market started its machinery moving to put this plan into effect. The Commission is the executive body charged with ensuring the functioning and development of the Common Market.

The Commission controls a Committee of Coordination, which, as a first step in February, 1960, appointed Dr. Haertel, an official of the German Ministry of Justice, to prepare a report on the feasibility of the plan and to make proposals for its implementation.

5. THE HAERTEL REPORT

The lengthy Haertel Report was finished by the fall of 1960. It [was] rumored that much preliminary work had already been done, and that representatives of German industry were consulted. . . .

He first considered three possibilities—

    (a)   A European patent obtained by extending a patent granted in one country to the others;

    (b)   A European patent granted by any of the national patent offices having full examination;

    (c)   A European patent granted by a new European authority under more severe conditions than any national patent.

In view of serious practical objections to the first two possibilities, Haertel considered his mission to be confined to the third possibility of creating an autonomous European patent, which would not be just the sum of national patents, but which would co-exist with the national patents. He emphasized that his task was not harmonization but the creation of a new right.

A.

1. *Extent of Inventions to Be Protected*

(a)   Inventions against public order and good morals not patentable,

(b)   Inventions the exploitation of which would be contrary to specific domestic laws permissible (with reservations),

(c)   Pharmaceutical process patents permissible,

(d)   Independent product protection for chemical and pharmaceutical products questionable, but generally approved,

(e)   Independent protection for food products approved,

(f)   Plant patents—possibly.

2. *Concept Of Novelty*

After a long discussion of limited novelty and absolute novelty, more strict or less strict than existing national concepts, Haertel conclude[d] that the standard of novelty for the European patent should correspond to the most severe national laws.

3. *Technical Progress*

After discussing whether this should lie a requirement at all and analyzing existing national viewpoints, Haertel's conclusion [was] that technical progress—*i.e.* advance in the art—should be a requirement for the European patent but considers that a new European judicial authority rather than the European Patent Office may be necessary for examination of this criterion.

4. *Inventive Height*

Haertel . . . propose[d] that inventive height should be essential for patentability—at the German level or even stricter.

5. *Territorial Coverage*

The European patent must cover all the territory of the countries involved and not be divisible in effect.

6. *Scope of Patent*

This is a long section reviewing problems of deferred examination after grant, full preliminary examination before grant, claims as defining the scope of the patent, nullity and infringement. His conclusion is that these problems should be resolved to provide a strong European patent, else scope of which should not be subject to the uncertainties of litigation in the courts throughout its life. His proposals are given in the following sections.

B. GRANT WITH OR WITHOUT PRELIMINARY EXAMINATION

Haertel consider[d] novelty the most important feature for the European patent. In view of the uncertainty in scope of simple registration patents, an official novelty examination [was] recommended, which industry also agree[d was] the ideal procedure. . . .

C. NULLITY

Since the European patent w[ould] be an autonomous right, it c[ould] not be nullified in any one country only. Nullity requirements are different in the various countries—*erga omnes* in some, *inter partes* in others. Therefore for uniformity a separate European authority will be necessary for nullity proceedings.

D. INFRINGEMENT

At first sight a separate European authority for infringement proceedings appear[ed] the ideal solution for uniformity of decision. But this would [have been] impractical in view of the volume of litigation for a single court. Therefore Haertel propose[d] that proceedings in the first instance should be in the national courts, with appeal to a European authority. . . .

F. CREATION OF EUROPEAN PATENT OFFICE

The problems of administration, permissible languages, and location.

G. USE OF THE HAGUE INSTITUTE

According to its constitution, as established by the treaty setting it up, the Hague Institute would not be suitable as an office for granting patents. However it could be used for making novelty searches, if search and novelty examination are divided, which would then be used by a separate novelty examination organization having the power to grant or validate patents.

H. EUROPEAN JURISDICTION

This discusse[d] the establishment of a new European judicial patent tribunal (as distinguished from a European Patent Office).

I. PERSONAS HAVING THE RIGHT TO BE GRANTED EUROPEAN PATENTS

Proper applicants would be both nationals and *ressortissants* of the adhering States.

. . . .

K. ACCESSION OF THIRD PARTY COUNTRIES

This section merely discusses possibilities. What are to be the limits and requirements? Any country? Countries of the International Convention? Countries in the Council of Europe?

L. VIS-A-VIS THE INTERNATIONAL CONVENTION

Haertel argues that the establishment of a new European patent system would not be in conflict with the provisions of the International Convention.

M. OTHER TREATIES

Haertel assert[ed] that a new independent treaty creating the European patent would merely take its place alongside various other independent treaties such as the Benelux and Euratom Treaties.

He regard[ed] the European patent as a base patent with possibilities of extension to *"associated countries."* He discusses the meaning of true accession to the new European Patent Convention and *"association"* by virtue of Art. 238 of the Rome Treaty.

N. CONCLUSION

The European patent w[ould] definitely require a separate European Patent Office to be created in steps. The new treaty establishing the European patent can be regarded as a *particular arrangement—see* Art. 15 of the [Paris] Convention.

. . . .

7. PROTOCOL OF THE SECRETARIES OF STATES OF THE COMMON MARKET COUNTRIES

At Brussels, in December, 1960, the Secretaries of State of the six Common Market countries placed their stamp of approval on the project in a protocol of which the following is a summary with trademark and design references deleted.

The Secretaries of State have studied the conclusions of the Coordination Committee, and have noted two fundamental principles—

(a) The contemplated simplification and unification in the field of patent rights can only be realized by a new Convention.

(b) The restricted extent of the dispositions in the Rome Treaty concerning industrial property, and the possibility of adhesion by third party countries, implies that this new Convention must exceed the scope of the Rome Treaty and must therefore be submitted to the governments of the individual countries for ratification.

They have also noted that the Coordination Committee proposes on the one hand to harmonize national legislation (notably for chemical, pharmaceutical and food processes and products) and on the other hand to study a Convention for patents. It will prepare common rules and define the functions of the organizations granting these rights.

Concerning general principles, they recognize:

1. The European rights should coexist with national legislation, which will be retained with the reservation of eventual necessary harmonization.

2. The European rights will be autonomous and not a juxtaposition of national rights.

3. The preliminary draft of the Convention will propose independent administrations and jurisdictions.

4. Existing obligations (e.g. the [Paris] Convention) will not be contravened.

5. The new Convention will be open to adherence of third party countries with unanimous approval of member countries.

6. Third party countries could adhere to a part only of the Convention—by association established with each of them.

7. The European patent will be autonomous and granted lay an independent international organization working on else basis of searches made by the Hague Institute. Infringement will lie handled in the national courts and nullity in an international court.

8. Ultimately to facilitate adhesion of third party states to the new European Convention, the President of the Coordination Committee should inform representatives of interested countries concerning tile orientation and advancement of the work of the Committee.

8. THE PRELIMINARY DRAFT OF THE EUROPEAN PATENT CONVENTION [EPC]

A Working Group was then immediately formed comprising representatives of the six Common Market countries. It is significant that the President of this Working Group is Dr. Haertel. It is also significant that the majority of the representatives are officials of the Ministries of Justice or Ministries of Economic Affairs of their respective countries, and that Patent Office officials are a small minority.

The drafting has proceeded very rapidly and very secretly. Several unofficial international groups have endeavoured to secure an entree to the Working Group as consultants or as observers at the sessions of the Group, but without success. There is some purely informal or semi-official contact between the national representatives in the Working Group and "outsiders" in their own countries, and possibly some proposals and criticisms thus filtered in may have some effect on the internal deliberations of the whole Group.

A preliminary draft of the Patent Convention was ready early in 1961. This was complete in broad outline, with some articles fully prepared and others very tentative, including remarks concerning the differences of opinion within the Group. As can well be imagined, the principal bones of contention involved—

(a) The nature of the examination—*i.e.* full preliminary examination before grant or some form of deferred examination. The national representatives in the Group split several ways on this question; there is some indication that the final proposal *may* provide for an initial novelty search for record, and a deferred examination for patentability.

(b) The admission of third party states by so-called "partial adherence" or "association." Apparently only a small minority of the national representatives supported full adherence only. The others favored some form of compromise participation in view of the interpretation of the obligations of the International Convention. . . .

As regards the draft Convention as a whole, many European lawyers privately consider it is basically very impressive and sound—a distillation of the best European concepts and experience. It naturally contains many provisions which are more or less fundamental and standard in the patent laws of all major countries: it contains others which to some extent go beyond or modify the provisions of existing national laws. . . .

9. GENERAL COMMENTS AND SPECULATIONS

. . . .

Ultimately the Convention in final form will be submitted to each of the six countries of the Common Market for ratification; possibly several years from the present time. Thereafter there may be very long delays before regulations are prepared, personnel recruited and the new system is actually operative. The year 1970 is being mentioned among European sources as a target date—though they all say it may be sooner in view of the extraordinary and unexpected vitality of the Common Market generally.

Present predictions are that European patents will be difficult and expensive to obtain if the contemplated high standards for patentability are initiated and maintained. Therefore, they are likely to be confined to inventions of major importance. Furthermore both large and small industry may continue to take out national patents as a form of insurance in the event that they are unable to secure grant of a European patent.

As distinguished from the United States, European countries have always objected to non-use of patents and have employed compulsory licensing and possible revocation as a remedy. A new situation may arise with the European patent, since working in any one of the adhering states may be sufficient to render it free from attack. If in the future most of the other European states should adhere to the new Patent Convention in addition to the original six, then the European patent will indeed become massive and invulnerable.

However, it may still be hedged around with antitrust provisions. In recent years there has been a rapid growth in Europe of anticartel and antimonopoly legislation and control of restrictive business practices. The regulations under Articles 85–89 of the Rome Treaty are now being formulated and are likely to include wide powers to prevent uses of patents for restrictive purposes, which may have correspondingly greater effect on broad European patents than national patents.

10. The Position of the United States

Any state which adheres to the new European patent convention obviously cedes a small amount of sovereignty. It seems unlikely that the U.S. Senate would agree to ratify a Treaty whereby an industrial property right obtained abroad by foreign nationals would extend over U.S. territory, and be subject to litigation in a supra-national court. However it is not at all certain that even the possibility of full adherence would ever be offered to countries outside continental Europe, and in any event unanimous consent of the original six countries of the Common Market would be necessary.

The possibilities of simple association as referred to above are clearly highly interesting. There may be political reasons in Europe for desiring both full adherence and also simple association by third party states, but there may also be very strong opposition from European business, particularly medium and small business, to granting such powerful rights to third party countries on a non-reciprocal basis.

If it is impossible for the United States to become a full adhering member of the European Patent Convention, it would of course still be permissible, as at the present time, for U.S. applicants to obtain national patents. However there might be some disadvantages, particularly when negotiating with European interests if the latter were the only ones able to hold broad European patents. At the same time, operating European subsidiaries of U.S. corporations would apparently be in the position of legitimate *ressortissants* and would be able to obtain European patents. But the ownership would presumably have to remain with such subsidiary, since assignment to the U.S. parent corporation could be regarded as a subterfuge: this would raise numerous policy problems.

If actually the United States could join the European Patent Convention on a simple associate basis, then clearly U.S. applicants would be in substantially the same position as European applicants; there would be strong inducements for obtaining European patents on important inventions, but national patents would still be of interest. . . . It will be interesting to find out if any broad U.S. viewpoint will develop and whether this in turn can have any influence on the future course of events in Europe.

. . . .

NOTE: CONVENTION ON THE UNIFICATION OF CERTAIN POINTS OF SUBSTANTIVE PATENT LAW ON PATENTS FOR INVENTIONS ("STRASBOURG UNIFICATION CONVENTION")

The 'Haertal Draft' of 1962 was followed by the proposal of the Council of Europe in 1963 for a Convention on the Unification of Certain Points of Substantive Patent Law on Patents for Inventions (hereinafter called the "Strasbourg Unification Convention" to distinguish from the "Strasbourg Classification Convention" of 1971). *See* Ind. Prop. 13 (1964). "Patentable inventions" had been defined in the Haertal proposal as follows: "European patents will be granted for new inventions capable of industrial use and resulting from inventive activity." The definitions of patentable invention of Article 1 of the Strasbourg Unification Convention, for exceptions from patentability of Article 2, for "novelty" under Article 4, and for "industrial application" under Article 3 were subsequently incorporated directly into corresponding articles 52, 53, 54, and 57 respectively of the EPC. The definition of "inventive step" of Article 5 of the Strasbourg Convention did not make reference to "a person skilled in the art" (as does Article 54 EPC), nor did it make mandatory the EPC Article 54's provision that the contents of a previously filed European application may be considered part of the state of the art only for purposes of determining the existence of novelty— not for the purposes of determining the existence of an inventive step. Nor was there a requirement that there be an "advance" in the art (what Robbins refers to above as "technical progress") in order for there to be found an inventive step. *See generally* HANS ULLRICH, STANDARDS OF PATENTABILITY FOR EUROPEAN INVENTIONS: SHOULD AN INVENTIVE STEP ADVANCE THE ART? (1977). Ullrich observes that the Strasbourg Convention became the "least common denominator" which influenced the formulation of the law of validity in the EPC and Community Patent Convention [CPC] (see below). But it did not itself enter into force until 1980. Nor did it evoke much comment or opposition at the time of its drafting "due to the necessity of strong departure from law of Switzerland and Germany, where advance in the art has been cherished as an indispensable standard of patentability." *See id.*, at 2. The U.K. set up the Banks Committee in 1967 to study the implications of ratification of the Strasbourg Convention. Subsequent to the proposal of the Strasbourg Convention but prior to its enactment, France abandoned its registration system for patents in favor of a search with examiner commentary in the French Patent Law of 1968. Ullrich also noted that the French "*activité inventive*" in articles 6(2) and 9 of the French Patent Law of 1968 is the non-obviousness standard. The draft of the European Patent Convention appeared in 1965. A flurry of new patent legislation appeared throughout Europe in the decade following the Strasbourg Convention and the first EPC draft, including the Uniform Scandinavian Patents Act of 1968 and the U.K. Patents Act of 1977.

[2]   The European Patent Convention [EPC]

The European Patent Convention ("EPC") was signed on 5 October 1973 in Munich. It created a single granting system under the administration of a new organization, the European Patent Organization ("EPO"), supervised by an Administrative Council consisting of representatives of the member States (usually national patent office officials.). The EPC is a special agreement under the Paris Convention (EPC Preamble) which provides free accessibility and national treatment and right of priority (EPC Articles 87–89) in compliance with Article 4 of the Paris Convention. The EPC qualifies as a regional patent treaty under Article 45 of the Patent Cooperation. An applicant may file a PCT application to obtain a European patent in all the contracting parties, all of whom are also contracting parties of the PCT. (*See* Part X of the EPC for special rules on the PCT). The EPC has been amended only once (Article 63) since it entered into force; and the difficulties in amending the convention have had an impact on further developments.

The EPO is an autonomous and self-supporting intergovernmental organization which is completely independent of the EU. It is recognized as an intergovernmental organization under Article 9 of the Budapest Treaty on the International Recognition of the Deposit of Microorganisms for the Purposes of Patent Procedure. The TRIPS Agreement is not directly binding on the EPO, although the standards of the EPC are in compliance with the patent provisions of TRIPS. The relationship of the EPC to the laws of member States (the "legal framework"), the TRIPS Agreement, and the European Union is explored in the following case.

LENZING AG'S EUROPEAN PATENT (UK)
[1997] R.P.C. 245 (Ch. D. 1996) (UK)

JACOB, J.

INTRODUCTION

An Austrian company, Lenzing AG, apply for a variety of forms of relief arising out of allegations that a European Patent Office Board of Appeal (BoA) mishandled an opposition to their patent and wrongly ordered or, as Lenzing say, purported to order, that it be revoked. They seek judicial review of the BoA's decision and judicial review of the decision of the Comptroller-General of the British Patent Office to mark the U.K. Register of Patents with an entry to the effect that their patent has been revoked. Those are proceedings in the Crown Office of the High Court. By way of alternative attack Lenzing invoke the jurisdiction of the Patents Court to order rectification of the entry in the Register of Patents. Also in the Patents Court Lenzing's principal (but not only) commercial adversaries, Courtaulds Fibres (Holdings) Ltd. and other Courtaulds companies seek an order dismissing Lenzing's claim for infringement . . . on the ground that the patent has been revoked. Lenzing resist that, contending that the revocation of their patent is a nullity. . . .

It is first necessary to explain the legal framework of the problem. Until 1978, a patent for an invention in the U.K. could only be obtained by application to the U.K. Patent Office. The procedures for this were laid down in the Patents Act 1949 and the Rules made pursuant to the rule-making power conferred by the Act. Ultimately any decision adverse to an applicant could be the subject of appeal to the Patents Court. Patents in other countries had to be obtained by applications to the national patent office of each country concerned. This was widely regarded as wasteful. . . .

Accordingly in 1973 a number of European countries entered into the European Patent Convention (EPC). This set up the European Patent Office

(EPO) in Munich. The 1977 [U.K.] Patents Act was passed, as its recital says, "to give effect to certain international conventions" of which the EPC was one. I described the broad effect of the position prevailing after the 1977 Act came into force (mid-1978) in Aumac Limited's Patent ([1995] F.S.R. 501) as follows:

> One can obtain a patent in this country by one of two routes. One can simply apply to the British Patent Office who will process the application and if all goes well grant the patent. One can also or alternatively apply to the EPO. This operates as a central processing patent office for the states parties to the EPC. In making one's application there, one must "designate" the states in which one wants a patent. Once the EPO grants a patent it takes effect in each designated state in the same way as a patent from the national office of that state. A patent granted by the EPO which takes effect here is called a "European patent (UK)." There is provision that one cannot at the same time have a patent granted by a national office and the EPO for the same invention. The EPO patent prevails and the corresponding national patent must be revoked. But this happens only when the EPO grants the patent. Until then one can process an application through the two systems simultaneously. Once the EPO has granted a patent, there is a system of "opposition" (really revocation) which is operated by the EPO whereby it is possible to apply within 9 months of grant to have the EPO patent revoked. If it is, the revocation works for all designated states—a central "knock-out" system.

Lenzing's patent has been knocked out centrally. Can they challenge that . . . at least so far as the U.K. patent is concerned? That is what I have to decide.

The patent concerned is (or was) No 0,356,419. . . . Opposition was entered in the EPO . . . within the 9 month period from grant provided for by Article 89(1) of the EPC. On 6 May 1994 the Opposition Division orally announced its decision, refusing the opposition. It gave its reasons on 4 July 1994. The opponents appealed to the BoA, to which appeals lie pursuant to the provisions of Articles 106–111. . . . The BoA received written submissions. It held an oral hearing. . . . In accordance with its usual practice (. . . often criticized), following an adjournment of an hour or so, it announced its decision. The patent was revoked. . . .

The fact of revocation was recorded. . . . There is no attempt to attack that entry in these proceedings. The decision was duly communicated to the Comptroller-General of Patents who caused an entry to be made in the U.K. register. . . . The communication took the form of the supply of the information on a tape or disc which the Comptroller simply ran to alter the electronically kept Register. He did not purport to exercise his discretion.

Meanwhile proceedings had started in the Patents Court. . . . The revocation of the patent intervened. Courtaulds now apply for the action to be dismissed and for their costs of the action and petition.

Lenzing say that the written reasons for the decision show that there was a serious procedural injustice. In particular they say that the reasons were never put to them, either at the hearing or before, and were not argued by the opponents. . .

Lenzing further say that the decision was irrational or perverse, misunderstanding and misconstruing both the cited prior art and their patent. And they say that the BoA made up its mind in advance of the hearing and that such was admitted by the Chairman of the Board in a conversation with their patent agent. This makes the procedural misfeasance allegations all the more serious: The claim is that the Board knew in advance of the grounds of their proposed decision, yet deliberately kept it back. Lenzing say that if they had known of the point, they could have answered it or offered suitable amendments to their patent to deal with it.

Lenzing say the result of the events which they allege is that the decision of the BoA should be regarded as a nullity. They accept that judicial review will not lie against the impugned decision itself (because of the immunity of the EPO from process) but, they say, that does not prevent a collateral attack. They make that attack in three ways. . . .

THE MAIN ARGUMENT

. . . .

[Lenzing] say that Parliament only requires a European patent (UK) to be treated as revoked if that revocation is in accordance with the EPC. . . . Or, put slightly differently, if a party here . . . seeks to rely upon an order of revocation in the EPO it is open to the patentee to rebut the prima facie conclusion that the patent has been revoked by showing that the tribunal ordering revocation . . . did not act in accordance with the Convention.

. . . .

[So] anyone who consulted the EPO register and said "The patent is gone for all Europe: I need not bother to look at national registers" would be misled. And even more seriously, anyone who in reliance on the revocation as being final has made an investment accordingly (either by way of direct investment in plant or R&D or on the stock market) would be adversely affected.

Lenzing accept that all [of] that follows from their argument. Nonetheless they boldly submit that Parliament did intend that there could be inquiry by way of collateral attack here. . . . Further, they say, it would require very strong language indeed for Parliament to exclude an inquiry into the lawfulness of what was done to deprive a party of a U.K. property right. They say no such language is used here. . . .

It is, I think clear . . . that the "opposition" procedure was and is really regarded so far as the Convention is concerned as part of the grant process. It is somewhat Pickwickian to described a post-grant attack on a patent as "opposition" but the word does convey the notion that one is concerned with the early life of the patent. Hence the fact that the attack must be within 9 months of grant. The founding fathers of the Convention had to choose between an opposition proper . . . and this form of "belated opposition." They chose the latter. We had a similar system. . . . Be that as it may, I think it is indisputable that . . . the contracting States intended that the opposition procedure and result should apply to the European patent as a whole. That is so as a matter of public international law. And that is what the U.K. signed up to in joining the EPC.

Next, say Courtaulds, the activities of the EPO are not . . . justiciable in English courts. It is not open to the English courts to consider whether or not the decision was "in excess" of the powers of the BoA. They say that is so even if the BoA had taken a bribe. . . . Thus, say Courtaulds and the Comptroller, all that Parliament has required . . . is proof that the EPO has . . . revoked a European patent. Once that is shown, then our law automatically treats the European patent . . . as revoked. The Comptroller in making the entry in the register is acting in a purely administrative capacity, just recording what has been done.

I have no doubt that Courtaulds and the Comptroller are right. . . . This country has agreed with . . . the EPC that the final arbiter of revocation under the new legal system is to be the Board of Appeal of the EPO. Other States would be justly entitled to complain if we in this country were to ignore such a final decision. If Lenzing are right, for example, the commercial freedom of action of Akzo-Nobel, a Dutch company, is impeded in this country. That might well concern Holland, the State. Likewise an attack in Germany (and I am told one has been mounted before the constitutional court), if successful, would or might well have the effect of putting Germany in breach of its international obligations. . . .

One can put the matter another way: The EPO has an internal legal system of its own. . . . The position is described succinctly in International Institutional Law (Schermers & Blokker) (3rd rev. ed. 1995 ¶ 1141):

> Unlike private international organisations, public international organisations are not subject to any national law. Thus, they must create their own internal law. The resulting law is an exclusive part of a separate legal order . . . independent of any other legal order. . .

Perhaps recognising the full destructive power . . . of a jurisdiction to permit a collateral attack on all the grounds . . . , Mr. Prescott devised a more limited class of attack. . . . This is the principle that the English court will not recognise and enforce a judgment of a foreign court where the proceedings in that court were in breach of the principles of "natural justice" (. . . "due process" as the Americans call it).

This, I felt, was Mr. Prescott's most attractive argument. Why should the English court . . . have to accept a decision of a BoA reached by unfair means? The answer, which I think is clear, is that it would be contrary to the international treaty even to inquire into the question. . . . The U.K. and the other Member States have agreed . . . that the BoA is the final arbiter of oppositions. It is the agreed EPO equivalent of the House of Lords, Cour de Cassation, or Bundesgerichthof. It is not for national courts to query its doings, whether in a direct or collateral attack.

Mr. Prescott's final main submission was this: that the EPO was different from other international organisations. Unlike, say the Tin Council, it is a body whose decisions take effect in national law. He said (correctly) that those decisions only take effect by virtue of an Act of Parliament. So the EPO should be regarded as a public body constituted by Act of Parliament, rather like any other U.K. decision making tribunal. This is fallacious. The EPO is clearly recognised on the plane of international law. The Patents Act causes its decisions to be recognised here as a matter of national law. But its decisions remain decisions at the international level so it is no business of our courts to go into them. . . .

So the main argument fails. Those who apply for patents in the EPO must accept the results of its findings and its methods of procedure. Whether they can or should be strengthened is a matter for the Administrative Council. . . .

THE TRIPS AGREEMENT

Article 32 [of TRIPS] is commendably short:

Revocation/Forfeiture

An opportunity for judicial review of any decision to revoke or forfeit a patent shall be available.

. . . Does a Board of Appeal provide a means of judicial review?

Lenzing . . . boldly submit that the Boards of Appeal of the EPO do not provide a means of "judicial review". A reader may well have been wondering why I set out so many provisions of the EPC earlier. . . . They are relevant to this point. But . . . it is, I think, telling how our Act and our House of Lords have considered the matter. Both call the Boards of Appeal "a court". The Act does so in its definition section . . . And in Merrell Dow Pharmaceuticals Inc. v. H.N. Norton & Co., Ltd. ([1996] R.P.C. 76, at 82) Lord Hoffmann said of decisions of the EPO:

> These decisions are not strictly binding upon courts in the U.K. but they are of great persuasive authority; first, because they are decisions of expert courts (the Boards of Appeal and Enlarged Board of Appeal of the EPO) involved daily in the administration of the EPC.

I have emphasized Lord Hoffmann's use of the word "court". He could hardly have used that word if he did not think that what the Boards were doing was acting as a court—providing a means of judicial review in any ordinary sense.

Next I turn to the provisions of the EPC. . . . I conclude that the Boards of Appeal do provide judicial review within Article 32 of TRIPS. Although strictly this is a matter purely of international law, I also conclude that there is no doubt whatsoever that the ECJ [European Court of Justice] (which has competence to consider the point) would also so find. . . . That is not to say that the judicial structure and procedures of the EPO could not be strengthened. Some hold the view it needs to be in view of the increasing success and importance of the EPO and of the current delays in opposition procedure. But that is a matter for the Administrative Council and not a matter for national courts to consider.

NOTES AND QUESTIONS

(1) **Determining the Validity of a European Patent.** The EPC as conceived and elaborated in the Haertel Report ended up without any kind of centralized nullity proceeding. This has proved very controversial, since opposition proceedings must be initiated within nine months and revocation proceedings for national patents take place in national courts. The EPC creates a centralized procedure for the filing, prosecution, and grant of a European patent. The opposition applies to the European patent in all the contracting states in which that patent has effect. *See* EPC art. 99(2). Once granted, the European patent becomes a bundle of national patents in the selected countries and European grounds for revocation of a European patent are binding on national authorities. *See* EPC art. 138. The inspiration for the post-grant opposition procedure of the EPC was the "belated oppositions" procedure of the former British Patents Act of 1949. *See* WILLIAM CORNISH, INTELLECTUAL PROPERTY: PATENTS, COPYRIGHT, TRADE MARKS AND ALLIED RIGHTS 135 (3d ed. 1996). Does that fact color the court's attitude as to the wisdom of getting to the merits of the case? (Note the judge's concern as to the practical impact of reviving patent rights which had been revoked, and assessment that the European Court of Justice would have reached the same decision.) The disparities between revocation proceedings in European national courts has been described as a "harlequin's suit." Vito Mangini, *The Legal Framework for Infringement and Revocation Proceedings in Patent Matters in the Contracting States of the European Patent Convention*, 14 IIC 776, 791 (1983). Calls for a unified forum for determining the validity of a European patent are discussed below in connection with proposals for a Community Patent for the European Union, discussed below. Until such time as a Community Patent Appellate Court ("COPAC") is established, is there any likelihood that national court judges could agree to defer to a leading role of the EPO on questions of validity? *See* Jan J. Brinkhof & Marie-Helene D.B. Schutjens, *Revocation of European Patents—A Study of the Statutory Provisions and Legal Practice in the Netherlands and Germany*, 27 IIC 1, 25 (1996). European

patent judges now meet regularly to exchange views on patent law interpretation. *See, e.g.*, Fabienne Gauye Wolhändler et al., *Seventh Symposium of European Patent Judges*, 27 IIC 266 (1996).

(2) **Patents as Property.** What does the court make of the petitioner's "natural justice" argument? Do states who become party to the EPC abdicate their rights to protect their nationals from due process violations? (Note the judge's concern as to the practical impact of reviving patent rights which had been revoked.) Compare the treatment of nationals and corporations seeking restoration of real and moveable property expropriated in former Communist nations such as East Germany and the Soviet Union.

(3) **National Tactics.** The purpose of the EPC was to rationalize procedures for the grant of patents in Europe including substantial examination. According to one observer:

> when the U.S. took the lead in promoting the [PCT] in 1967, France sought refuge in a revival of the EEC plan [of the Haertal Draft of 1962 and the Strasbourg Unification Convention of 1963.] With only the beginnings of an examination system, she found reason to fear the advent of international applications for France which would carry the impress of a PCT search and preliminary examination.

CORNISH, *supra*, at 76.

(4) **Translation and The Scope of Protection**. A European patent can sometimes differ from a national patent in a European country where an applicant chooses also to obtain a national patent. The text of a European patent is used in infringement cases except where a national translated version has a narrower scope of protection. A narrower scope of interpretation of a national patent prevails over the official text of a European patent in infringement proceedings.

(5) **EPO Membership**. The European Patent Organization has twenty-four members as of this book's printing. Of these, fifteen are the current members of the EU; non-EU members are Bulgaria, Czech Republic, Estonia, Slovak Republic, Switzerland, Liechtenstein, Monaco, Turkey and Cyprus. In addition, there are six "extension states" recognizing European patents: Albania, Lithuania, Latvia, former Yugoslav Republic of Macedonia, Slovenia, and Romania. In extension states, only a translation of the claims of a European patent is required to obtain national patent protection. States associated with the EU and committed to applying for accession to membership in the EPO are Hungary and Poland. The two additional states entitled to join under the accession provisions of Article 166 of the EPC without invitation are Iceland and Norway. Robbins's speculation that the U.S. might be invited to become a member of the EPC never materialized.

(6) **Official Language.** The official languages of the European Patent Organization are English, French, and German. *See* EPC art. 14. Natural or legal persons in contracting states where an official language other than the three official languages of the EPO is used may submit an application

in that language, but must submit a translation into one of the EPO official languages for prosecution of the application. EPC Art. 14(2).

(7) **Legal Status of the EPO**. In a 1996 case, *Plants/NOVARTIS*, T 1054/96, the Technical Board stated:

> Not all member states of the European Patent Convention are members of the EU, and the EPO is not an organ of the EU. Nor is the EPO a signatory to TRIPS. To meet their obligations under the EU or under TRIPS it would be sufficient for Contracting States to modify their national patent laws. The Board does not see the possibility of giving the EPC any interpretation different from that it had on signing, merely because of the existence of TRIPs or EU directives. To change the EPC a conference of the Contracting States is necessary pursuant to Article 172 EPC. For the Boards of Appeal to take any other view would be to set up as legislators.

Is the EPO a "rogue institution" under international law? *See* Hans-Rainer Jaenichen, *Recent Developments in the Patenting of Plants at the EPO*, 17 BIOTECH. L. REP. 242 (1998).

(8) **Revisions to the EPC.** The EPC was revised at a diplomatic conference held in November, 2000. The Conference authorized the Administrative Council to adapt the EPC to reflect international treaties and developments in the EU. The conference also streamlined EPO procedures and rearranged some provisions, but refused to make substantive changes in the law regarding biotechnology or computer software. The approved revisions will not come into effect until ratified by all of the parties, which will take several years. *See* www.european-patent-office.org/news/pressrel/2000_11_29_e.htm.

NOTE: ORGANS OF THE EUROPEAN PATENT ORGANIZATION

The organs of the EPO include the European Patent Office ("EPO"). EPC arts. 6, 10. The EPO has its headquarters in Munich, a branch at the Hague, and sub-offices in Berlin and Vienna. EPC Articles 15–20 establish the departments of the EPO, including the Receiving Section and Search Divisions (DG1 in the Hague and Berlin), and the Examining and Opposition Divisions (DG2 in Munich), and the Legal Division (DG5 in Munich), and the Patent Information Center ("EPIDOS") in Vienna. Jurisdiction over the granting of European patents is under the supervision of the Boards of Appeal and Enlarged Board of Appeal (DG3 in Munich). EPC arts. 21–24. An Administrative Council (EPC Articles 26–36) provides overall supervision of the operation of the EPO. EPC art. 4(3). Each contracting state provides one representative to the Council under the direction of the President. EPC art. 10.

The EPC provides for common substantive law for the contracting parties with respect to requirements for patentability, EPC arts. 52–57, and disclosure, EPC art. 83. Each application is examined by three examiners.

Granted European patents are subject to national law of the contracting states. EPC art. 2(2). However, European patents are to be treated by the contracting states in accordance with uniform principles or interpretation. Among the uniform principles is a common set of grounds for opposition, EPC arts. 99, following the grant of a European patent and a common term of the patent (twenty years from the date of filing, EPC art. 63. The rights conferred by the patent are also (at least theoretically) unified, including the extension of the protection for a patented process to products directly obtained by the process, EPC art. 64(2), common scope of protection, EPC art. 69, and that the claims should be interpreted on the basis of the description and the drawings and should be understood neither according to their strict literal meaning only nor should they serve only as a guideline (the protocol to EPC Article 69). According to reliable German and British authority, "[t]he aim has been to achieve a standard mid-way between the severity of the Dutch and the lenience of the Austrian and British approaches: the German standard was thought to be 'about right.'" WILLIAM CORNISH, INTELLECTUAL PROPERTY: PATENTS, COPYRIGHT, TRADE MARKS AND ALLIED RIGHTS 90 n.7 (2d ed. 1989); *see also* J. B. van Bentham & Norman Wallace, *The Problem of Assessing Inventive Step in the European Patent Procedure*, 9 I.I.C. 297, 298 (1978).

Applications may be filed in Munich, the Hague, Berlin, or in the national offices. EPC art. 75. Examination on filing as to formalities, the search report, and publication of the application, including the description, the claims and any drawings as filed, the European search report, and the abstract eighteen months from the date of filing or, if priority has been claimed, as from the date of priority, are all conducted by DG1. EPC arts. 90–93. Substantive examination and opposition procedures, if any, are conducted by DG2. EPC arts. 96, 97, 99ff. Appeal from the Examining Division or the Opposition Division is made to the Boards of Appeal. EPC arts. 21, 106. Validation and revocation are up to the national authorities.

NOTE: FILING A EUROPEAN PATENT APPLICATION

There are four elements required for a filing date: an indication that a European patent is sought; the designation of at least one contracting state; information identifying the applicant; and a description of the invention and at least one claim in an allowable language. EPC art. 80. Applicants having their residence or principal place of business within the contracting states may act themselves or through an employee who need not be a professional representative. EPC art. 133(3). Other applicants must be represented by a professional representative appearing on the EPO roster or a legal practitioner of a contracting state to the extent allowed in the respective state. EPC arts. 133(2), 134. Other formal requirements (which can be remedied later, EPO Rules 26–36) are the request for grant, abstract, EPC art. 85, physical requirements for the specification, EPO Rule 40, and designation of the inventor, EPO Rule 17.

NOTE: THE DECISION TO FILE A EUROPEAN PATENT APPLICATION

There are several oft-stated advantages in filing directly with the EPO. An applicant has to file and prosecute only one application, and potentially undergo but a single opposition and appeal proceeding. The whole procedure, including oppositions and appeals, can be conducted in one language, e.g. English. The European Patent Office conducts reliable searches and responsive examination (albeit slowly).

There are also disadvantages. The major one is the high cost. One half of all the annuities (maintenance fees) collected by the European Patent Office are channeled directly to the national patent offices, which have a conflict of interest in that they are the constituents of the Administrative Council. National patent offices are not accountable for how they spend maintenance fees paid to the European system. Fees have been reduced considerably since July 1997 but remain high—particularly with translation costs of activation in member states. A recent estimate is that a "modest" patent application might cost $15,000 to grant and an additional $15,000 in activation costs, national fees, translation, and local agent's charges for only a few countries. Filing in all member countries requires translation of the entire specification into nine foreign languages. A second considerable disadvantage is the central attack provision illustrated by *Lenzing*'s case—that the applicant is putting all her eggs in one basket. If the Board of Appeals finally decides not to grant a patent then the applicant may have lost patent protection in a few European countries where a national patent (for what it is worth) would have been granted. There have been some difficulties for applicants resulting from the operation of the system as well. EPO search reports are sometimes not available for several years, and some applications are still pending for up to ten years.

Applications for European patents continue to grow in number notwithstanding the expense, and numbered approximately 140,000 in 2001. But associations of users, such as the Union of Industrial and Employers' Confederations of Europe ("UNICE") and the American Intellectual Property Law Association have been vocal in their complaints over costs. Approximately 50 percent of EPO applications in the period 1996-2000 were of European origin, while thirty percent were from the United States. Euro-PCT applications (that is, PCT applications designating the EPO) accounted for sixty-three percent of all EPO applications in 2000.

[3] The Luxembourg ("Community Patent") Convention

The Community Patent Convention ("CPC" or "Luxembourg Convention") was signed in Luxembourg in 1973. Yet to enter into force, it contemplates a unitary patent covering the entire territory of the European Community. It was originally conceived to be the natural outcome of the European patent system. It adopts the same standards of patentability as the EPC but also includes a uniform code for the substantive law of patent infringement. The grant of a Community Patent would require a translation of the entire document into the official language of each of the member states. Six of the twelve states which were members of the European Community at the time of signature of the CPC have ratified it: Denmark, France, Germany, Greece, Luxembourg, and the United Kingdom.

The CPC is distinct from the EU and is not subject to the jurisdiction of such community organs as the Council of Ministers, the European Parliament, or the European Court of Justice. The primary reason it has not yet come into force is that much of European industry is opposed to it, primarily due to the cost of translating patents into all of the languages of the member states, and misgivings over its proposed system for dealing with patent disputes. Unlike the European Patent applicant, who can designate selected European countries in which to activate the patent the Community Patent applicant must seek protection throughout the member states. A proposed Community Patent Appellate Court ("COPAC") would hear appeals from national court proceedings on infringement or revocation of Community Patents; however, it would not hear appeals from decisions to grant or not to grant a patent by the EPO. The 1989 Agreement relating to the Community Patent (the "Luxembourg Agreement"), which solidified the language requirement, has only been ratified by seven of the twelve signatories (Denmark, Germany, France, U.K., Greece, Luxembourg, and the Netherlands). The following reading by a former president of the European Patent Office discusses some of the controversies surrounding the CPC.

J. B. VAN BENTHEM, THE EUROPEAN PATENT SYSTEM AND EUROPEAN INTEGRATION*
24 I.I.C. 435 (1993)

[T]he preparatory work which ultimately led to the two European patent conventions was begun in 1960 by the then six contracting parties to the Treaty of Rome in response to a proposal from the Commission of the European Economic Community. There was nothing surprising about this, as Art. 2 of the Treaty of Rome stipulates that the aim of the Community is to establish a Common Market and to gradually bring about the harmonization of economic policy in the member states. And as you know, industrial property rights are instruments of economic policy in that they promote the use and spread of new technology in the economy. Furthermore, overcoming the problems posed by the fact that each Common Market country has its own national industrial property laws is an important step towards the establishment of a Common Market. This "European Economic Community phase", as Haertel called it in his Commentary, came to an end in 1965 with the production of a complete draft of an EEC patent law, which

---

* Copyright 1993, Max Planck Institute for Foreign and International Patent, Copyright and Competition Law. Reprinted with permission.

not only provided for a centralized grant procedure for unitary European patents, but also a system of law governing them.

Following a break of four years due to political reasons, work on the European patent law was resumed on a new basis in 1969, which caused Haertel to refer to it as "the great European phase." The original draft was divided up into two separate conventions. The first convention was intended to create a centralized European procedure for granting European patents which would have the legal value of a bundle of national patents having the same content. Any European country would be able to participate in this convention, whether or not it was a member of the EEC. It was thus no longer a part of European integration within the EEC, and instead became an autonomous agreement between countries of the Paris Convention, just like the PCT, for example. It led to the Munich Patent Convention of 1973.

The second convention was to remain within the EEC's sphere of economic integration. where it would combine the granted European bundle of patents for the EEC countries into a unitary Community patent, setting out the laws governing Community patents. This became the Luxembourg Community Patent Convention of 1975.

I would now like to turn to two questions. The *first* question is whether, in the light of what we now know, 22 years after the decision was made to split the original convention into two, the development of the European patent system has shown that this decision was right. The second question is whether, in view of subsequent developments, it is still right to have two conventions today. I can only touch upon these questions in the course of this paper, but I feel that it is important for them to be raised.

III.

Starting with the *first* question, which was whether developments have vindicated the decision to create two conventions, I would say that, as far as the Munich Convention is concerned, the answer must be a resounding yes. It should not be forgotten that back in 1969 both the concept of European integration and economic necessity were forces pressing for the creation of a centralized European patent grant procedure. The patent offices of the European states were overloaded, and industry desperately wished to be relieved of the time-consuming business of filing numerous national patent applications for one invention in Europe. It therefore made political and economic sense to agree to allow the EFTA countries of Great Britain, Sweden, Austria and Switzerland to participate in the preparatory work. In this way, in addition to the six EEC states, other European countries which had close economic ties with the six and innovative, patent-oriented industries could be included in this centralized European grant system.

Furthermore, the autonomy of the Munich Convention meant that its coming into force could be made dependent not on unanimous ratification by all EEC states, but on ratification by a minimum of six states, regardless of membership of the EEC. The way in which the Munich Convention has developed, the fact that it came into force only a few years after it was signed, and the steady increase in the number of member states, which reflects the success of the centralized grant procedure, all go to prove that the decision to split the original convention into two was clearly right. Just imagine what would have happened had the convention remained within the EEC and, for example, if Ireland, with its constitutional problems which until recently prevented ratification of the Luxembourg Convention, had been able to delay the coming into force of a centralized European patent grant procedure by many years.

What would the answer to my first question be as far as the Luxembourg Community Patent Convention of 1975 is concerned? Have developments since the Luxembourg Conference shown that the decision to divide the original convention into two was the right one for the Community patent as well? Everyone in our field is familiar with the sad and shameful story of this Convention. After three successive diplomatic conferences to improve it—two in Luxembourg in 1975 and 1989, and another in 1992 (which, incidentally, failed to achieve its aims)—the Convention has yet to be ratified by some of the EEC states 17 years after the first Luxembourg Conference. And there is no telling whether it will ever come into force at all.

The difficulties could be ascribed to internal problems between the member states. First there was the British Government's problem with the settlement of disputes about infringements of the Community patent and about its legal validity. This, it must be said, led to an improved system which for the sake of simplicity I will refer to as COPAC. Then there were constitutional and political problems in Ireland and Denmark which prevented ratification by these two countries. However, that is only one side of the coin.

The other side is that European industry, in a number of EEC countries at least, now has little or no interest in the Community patent. It originally asked for the two conventions not to be introduced at the same time, as it wanted to try out the European patent grant procedure first. However, it has since become so used to the European bundle of patents that it manages very well with it, even within the EC. In addition, the European Court of Justice has in its case law now settled the question of the exhaustion of the rights conferred by national or European patents in such a way that the Common Market cannot be divided up again as a result. There is thus no longer any pressure from this direction either for the introduction of a unitary Community patent. As far as my first question is concerned, I would therefore conclude that the decision to divide the original convention into two was not the right decision for the Community patent. As part of an overall solution to the problem of the European patent system in the EEC, the unitary Community patent could have been established using economic pressure and in the wake of the impetus

towards the establishment of a centralized European patent grant procedure. The split took the wind out of the sails of the Community patent and
left it in the doldrums, where it remains to this day.

IV.

I would now like to turn to my second and much more difficult question:
in the light of the situation today, is it still right to have two separate
conventions?

Let us first of all look at the situation with regard to the Munich Convention. I think it can safely be said that it has been very successful since
coming into force in 1977, for not only has the number of European or Euro-
PCT applications increased to ± 60,000 per year, but the number of
member states has also gone up from 7 to 17.

From an examination of the expansion of the European Patent Organisation, three facts stand out. Firstly, following Ireland's accession, all the EC
states are members of the EPO. Secondly, apart from Liechtenstein and
Monaco, the remaining three member states of the EPO, namely Sweden,
Switzerland and Austria, have applied to join the European Community
and it is unanimously assumed in Community circles that their political
and economic situation will allow accession to be negotiated very quickly.
The member states of the EC would then be identical to those of the EPO.
Thirdly, the countries which acceded to the Munich Patent Convention
later, that is Denmark Spain, Portugal, Greece and Ireland, did not do so
spontaneously, but rather under the constraints of the so-called *"acquis
communautaire,"* in other words as a result of their obligation on entering
the European Community to accept the Community's existing laws, including the Community Patent Convention and, consequently, the Munich
Patent Convention. These later accessions were therefore primarily motivated by European integration within the Community.

Drawing these three strands together, one is forced to ask if the time
has come to give serious consideration to the question of whether the
European patent grant procedure should be brought back into the sphere
of European integration in the EC, where the preparatory work was begun,
and if so, how this should be done. One argument in favor of such a step
would be that it is no longer necessary to have two separate conventions
because the industrialized countries of Europe which were interested in a
centralized European patent grant system and which were previously
divided into two blocks will soon all be members of the EC. There are other
important arguments, too.

Look at the economic situation in the world today. In addition to the EC,
there are two other large economic blocks, the United States and Japan.
In view of the striking economic growth rate in Central Asia, we should
expect the formation in the future of further large economic blocks such
as China and India, which will play an increasing role in technological
innovation and the patent business this will produce. The patent system

as an economic tool is firmly integrated in the political and economic systems of all these large economic blocks except Europe. In the EC, the European patent grant system is governed by an autonomous, independent convention between what will soon be 15 EC countries. The organs of the EC, that is the Commission, the Council and the Parliament, which are determining European integration to an increasing extent, are not responsible for the Convention in any way. In view of the progress of European integration within the EC—and I am thinking in particular of the completion of the single market on 1 January 1993 and the Maastricht Treaty—I feel that this situation is no longer appropriate and indeed is actually rather dangerous.

In a purely co-operative association of European contracting states with no higher, joint structure of political and economic integration, it is all too easy for national interests to override the interests of integration. I would like to illustrate this point with a few examples.

Firstly, let us look at the language problem. As you know, the Munich Convention sensibly stipulates that the European Patent Office should have only three official languages, English, French and German. European patent applications may be submitted and processed in one of these three official languages only. When a patent is granted, the patent specification itself is published in the language of the proceedings only, either English. French or German, together with a translation of the claims in the other two official languages. This regulation not only aids the process of integration and co-operation between the contracting states, but is also very practical. It simplifies the work of the Office and is sufficient for the purposes of what I like to call the patent community, by which I mean anyone involved in patents. Taking its lead from a patent-oriented economy, this patent community has long since adopted an international outlook and has become correspondingly conversant with foreign languages. Patent experts can search patent documentation in the above-mentioned three languages (published European patent applications constitute an essential part of the documentation and are in any case published only in the language of proceedings. That is in one of the three official languages) and can usually manage quite well with a translation of the claims. Moreover, in any assessment of the scope of protection of a patent, the version of the patent specification in the language of the proceedings is used. In the early years of the European patent system, the patent community in a number of the contracting states was quite happy with a system in which European patent specifications did not have to be translated into the language of the country concerned. There were few problems or protests.

Unfortunately, we added Art. 65 to the Munich Convention. This article states that if a European patent specification is not drawn up in one of the official languages of a particular contracting state, then that state may prescribe that the proprietor of the patent shall supply a translation. This provision was politically unavoidable, although there was at the time justifiable hope that the contracting states would, for the reasons I have already mentioned, make sparing use of it. And that is what happened at first, although since then almost all the contracting states have made it a requirement to submit a translation. The reasons for this have less to do with the needs of those using the European patent system than with national political interests and the like.

Let me illustrate the result of this development with reference to the Netherlands. Assuming that 60,000 European and Euro-PCT applications are filed per year, one can expect 70%, or 42,000, granted European patents. Around 60% of these patents are granted for the Netherlands, that is about 25,000 European patents per year. This means that 25,000 translations into Dutch are filed each year with the Dutch Patent Office, where they quietly gather dust and, as can be proved, are rarely consulted. If, as we know from experience, the cost of a translation can be assumed to be around DM 4,000, then we are talking about a figure of ± DM 100 million per year which is added unnecessarily to the cost of European patents in the Netherlands. I suspect that the situation is pretty much the same in other contracting states. It would be interesting to investigate further.

I cannot produce any exact figures for translations in the other 16 member states. but I would estimate the total cost of translations of European patents to be around ± DM 1 billion per year. Because this figure is about the same as the total costs of the European Patent Office, it can be said that national translation requirements double the cost of obtaining a European patent. The European Patent Office came to the same conclusion when it calculated the cost of a European patent with seven designations.

The national interests of the contracting states have thus overridden the interests of the European patent system to such an extent that the system is now in jeopardy. It has gradually become too expensive for a large proportion of small and medium-sized firms, which thus no longer have access to the centralized European patent grant procedure, and all for the sake of interests which, although they may be justifiable culturally, and perhaps even politically, are no longer justifiable in economic terms, because the practical needs of the economy are paramount. In moving the political and cultural problem of language into the sphere of the European patent system, the contracting states have moved it into the economic sphere, where it does not belong. By doing so they have overshot the mark in the matter of retaining their national cultural heritages. The fact that the European patent system is at risk because of this directly affects the subject of European integration within the Community. A further example of the danger of national interests overriding the interests of European integration is provided by the financing of the European Patent Office. Like every other patent office, it earns its income on the one hand from procedural fees and on the other hand from renewal fees for granted patents. The renewal fees for European patents are, however, a bundle of national renewal fees, which has two disadvantages for the European patent system.

The first of these is that the contracting states have a completely free hand in fixing the amount of the renewal fees applying to European and national patents equally. The second disadvantage is that the Administrative Council of the EPO, which consists of delegations from the contracting states, is entitled under Art. 39 EPC to fix the proportion of the renewal fees for the granted European bundle of patents to be remitted to the Office. A minimum percentage is specified in favour of the contracting states, but no minimum is fixed for the Office. This was quite clearly a mistake on our part. Although there is as a result scope for balancing national interests with European interests, in practice a considerable degree of risk is involved, as the present situation shows. Many years ago, the Administrative Council fixed the proportion of the renewal fees to be remitted to the Office at 50%—an understandable decision at a time when both the Office's running costs and the income generated by the renewal fees were quite low. Since then, however, the Office's costs have gone up following an increase in staff resulting from the growth in the number of patent applications, and, with almost 200,000 patents granted, income from renewal fees has also risen.

A review of the financial requirements of the European Patent Office on the one hand and of the contracting states and their national patent offices on the other would appear to be called for. However, the contracting states are apparently not willing to do this because of national financial interests. But if the situation stays as it is, it will have a dual negative effect on the European patent system. Firstly, with regard to the financing of the European Patent Office, the proportion of the Office's costs covered by renewal fees is too small compared with other patent offices, which results in relatively high procedural fees. Secondly, the proportion of the renewal fees for granted European patents received by the contracting states is so high that it far exceeds the amount spent by the national patent offices on administering European patents, and consequently substantial surplus amounts are available for use elsewhere in the national patent system, or even end up in the treasury. The proprietors of European patents thus have not only to pay the costs of the European patent grant system, but also to contribute towards national patent systems or the treasuries of some of the contracting states.

My third example relates to co-operation between the European Patent Office and the national patent offices. The European patent system was not set up to replace the national patent systems, but to operate alongside them, giving applicants the choice between a European and a national patent. This structure was intended both to accommodate the interests of applicants and to bring about a sensible division of work between the European Patent Office and the national patent offices. It was assumed that applicants wishing to obtain protection for their inventions in three or more contracting states would use the European patent system, while the others would continue to use the national patent offices. This has proven to be the case.

However, the number of patent applications filed with some national patent offices has dropped to a level which has gradually prompted the question, nurtured by purely national interests, as to the extent to which the Munich Convention permits searches or examinations relating to European patent applications to be transferred to the national offices of the contracting states. The transfer of such work was possible on a restricted scale under the terms of the Protocol on Centralization. Following the expiry on 31 May 1993 of the limited period within which such work could be transferred under the Protocol, the question now touches the basic substance of the Munich Convention, which centralizes the granting of European patents at the European Patent Office. Such centralization was intended to ensure a uniform standard in European searches and examination, and to promote European integration, because in the EPO, as in other European authorities, men and women of different nationalities are working together with a common responsibility towards Europe. The possible decentralization of the European patent grant procedure is thus not just a question of law or a problem of quality, but a basic question of the shaping of European integration. I believe that under a purely co-operative agreement between contracting states without support from higher political structures for European integration, national interests could once again gain the upper hand.

The three examples I have mentioned reinforce my view, as far as the Munich Convention is concerned, regarding the answer to my second question, namely that—in the light of developments so far—the splitting of the original convention into two is no longer useful.

V.

Let me now ask the same question for the Luxembourg Community Patent Convention. As I have already mentioned, this Convention has a sad history. Seventeen years after the Luxembourg Conference in 1975, it still has not been ratified by some of the EC states. It is doubtful whether it will ever come into force at all. Splitting the original convention into two took the wind out of the sails of the Community patent and left it in the doldrums forever. Indeed, many people probably now quite rightly believe that the disadvantages of the Convention outweigh its advantages. Some of these advantages have been anticipated by developments, for example the case law of the European Court of Justice on the exhaustion of patent rights in the Common Market, and the voluntary harmonization of provisions on the rights conferred by patents undertaken by the contracting states on the basis of the Luxembourg Convention. However, the Convention still has some indisputable advantages, including the fact that it is much simpler to administer a Community patent having uniform renewal fees, and the new provisions dating from 1985 for settling disputes about infringements of Community patents and about their legal validity. These advantages are, however, offset by one significant disadvantage of the new 1989 version of the Convention, and that is the provision on languages in Art. 30 CPC.

According to the 1975 version of the CPC, applicants had to provide a translation of the claims only in all the languages of the Community. However, the transitional regulations allowed any contracting state to require that a translation of the whole specification be submitted in its official language. I wish to make three observations about this. Firstly, the Council of the European Communities was authorized to delete this reservation at a later date. Secondly, the translation could be submitted at any time following the grant of the patent because it was only a condition for the enforceability and not the validity of the patent. Thirdly, it was hoped at the time that, in view of the circumstances, not all the contracting states would make use of this reservation.

Surprisingly, the 1989 Luxembourg Conference then tightened up Art. 30 CPC considerably to make the filing of a translation of the full specification in all the languages of the Community within a specified time limit a prerequisite for the validity of a Community patent. Under these circumstances, applicants have understandably been given the opportunity to obtain a normal European bundle of patents for the designated contracting states instead of a Community patent.

This new ruling on translations dealt the fatal blow to the Community patent. How many applicants would still be interested in a Community patent if they had to pay for a translation of the specification into eight languages, that is into two of the three official languages (English, French and German), plus Spanish, Italian, Danish, Dutch, Portuguese and Greek? That would amount to 8 x 4,000 = DM 32,000 per Community patent. And as new countries join the EC, further languages and costs will be added. It therefore looks as though this provision will make the Community patent so expensive that all potential applicants will avoid it because they can save a considerable amount of money by obtaining European bundles of patents for only those states of economic interest to them.

Ratification of the 1989 Luxembourg Agreement relating to Community Patents would therefore be equivalent to "putting a dead man on the throne." It would be both pointless and dangerous, for once Art. 30 CPC comes into force, it can only be changed unanimously and with the approval of the parliaments of all the member states. It would therefore be better, in my opinion, if ratification of the Luxembourg Agreement continued to be blocked so that the language problem could be reconsidered.

VI.

It would then also be possible to consider whether the two separate conventions should be dispensed with in favor of transferring the entire European patent system to the Community in the form of a new convention or a European Council Regulation. In any case, I think it would be appropriate to raise these ideas at the negotiations for entry into the EC of Switzerland, Austria and Sweden. Combining the two conventions would be good for both. As I have already explained, I feel that the future of the entire European patent system is only safe if it is part of the process of European economic and political integration within the European Community, which is where its real basis is to be found. The efforts of the President of the European Patent Office to bring about closer co-operation with the EC Commission are commendable, but I do not think they are enough in the long term.

Let me illustrate this with reference to the difficulties arising from the language problem. Combining the two conventions would enable a common solution to this problem to be found for both conventions. In view of the difficult political situation regarding languages in the Community, some may doubt that the problem could be solved more easily in the Community itself rather than within the framework of an autonomous European patent convention. In reply, I would say that as far as the Community is concerned, with the pressure towards European integration, we have no choice but to ask whether we want a unitary Community patent for the Common Market with a sensible solution to the language problem which is advantageous to the applicant, or no Community patent at all. As far as an autonomous European Patent Convention is concerned, the question is somewhat different. Will the language problem be solved in such a way as to promote the European patent grant procedure or to promote the endangered national patent grant procedures or other related national interests? In the long term, any solution to the language problem undertaken outside the Community would in my opinion have an uncertain outcome. The same applies to the other problems which have been addressed in this paper.

NOTES AND QUESTIONS

(1) **Decline of National Patents in Europe**. National patent applications in Europe have fallen precipitously with the upsurge in European patent applications. In some states (such as the Netherlands), there is no examination of activated European patents whatsoever and the national office has been reduced to ministerial functions. The former president of the EPO, Dr. Kober, questioned whether anyone could have foreseen the continued existence of national offices at the turn of the century. What purposes do national patent offices serve in a modern Europe? Are there better reasons for maintaining national patent offices in a state such as Ireland (population 3.5 million) or Denmark (population 5.1 million) when a single patent in the United States covers a market of 250 million? One writer has even proposed that the European Union issue a directive *forbidding* member states of the EPC from granting national patents! *See* Clifford Lees, *European Patents: What Is Going On?*, 103 PATENT WORLD 19-24 (July 1998).

(2) **Higher Costs**. The costs of a European patent are much higher than a U.S. counterpart. According to an EPO *Report on the Cost of Patenting*

in Europe, the procedural fees of the EPO (9,900 German marks) are more than three times higher than those of the U.S. Patent and Trademark Office (3,000 German marks) and more than four times higher than those of the Japanese Patent Office (2,200 German marks). Then there are the validation costs of a European patent, i.e. expenditures necessary to validate a patent granted by the EPO in each designated state, including the cost for mandatory translations of the complete patent specification into the official language of each of the designated contracting states and official validation fees of the national patent offices of those states. According to one eminent critic:

> Taking into account that in a European patent on average eight Contracting States are designated, *i.e.* a market volume more or less comparable to that of the United States of America or Japan, the successful European applicant has to spend an average of 36,000 German marks as compared with the 3,000 German marks mentioned in the case of the United States of America or with 2,200 German marks in the case of Japan, but his patent still does not cover the entire Community area. . . . Worse and in terms of Community perspectives difficult to explain and justify are the figures if the annual renewal fees are included in the comparison of the official fees between the USA and the EPC: wherever eight Contracting States are designated, which means that nearly half of the EU Member States are not, the total cost for obtaining and maintaining a patent for its full term is about US $ 120,000 under the EPC, whereas in the US the respective amount is only US $13,000. As it has been pointed out, one must note that the principle of the exhaustion of the patent right applies in the Member States of the Community, thus in order to secure the same market volume in Europe as in the United States—with its national exhaustion— not only an American and Japanese but equally a European patent owner has to spend over ten times more.

Joseph Straus, *The Present State of the Patent System in the European Union As Compared with the Situation in the United States of America and Japan*, 1997 EUR 170.14 EN (1997) (Document of the European Commission).

(3) **Replacing the CPC.** Should the EPC be replaced by a patent law for the EU instead of the CPC? If so, what happens to states such as Switzerland which is not a member of the EU? A Green Paper issued by the European Commission in 1997 and a Judges' Proposal put forward by Judge Jacob of the U.K. Patents Court in July of the same year both press for change. The Green Paper pointed to the high costs of translations for all the member states (ten languages) and uncertainties over consistency of interpretation of patents. *See* Green Paper, *at* europa.eu.int/comm/dg15/ en/intprop/indprop/558.htm; *see also* Richard Tyler, *Combating Europe's Innovation Deficit*, MANAGING INTELL. PROP. 23 (July/Aug. 1997). A recent study of the European situation conducted under the auspices of the

European Commission Directorate-General for Telecommunications, Information Market and Exploitation of Research is highly critical of the status quo, and urges that the European patent law be made subject of a community regulation like the European Trademark System. *See generally* Strauss, *supra.*

[4]   A European Union Patent?

Apace with increasing criticism of the European Patent Convention's bundle of national rights approach and the failure of the Community Patent Convention to garner the slightest interest among European states, the organs of the EU have moved ahead on several fronts. One has been the proposal of an EU-wide patent.

COMMISSION OF THE EUROPEAN UNION, PROPOSAL FOR A COUNCIL REGULATION ON THE COMMUNITY PATENT
Explanatory Memorandum, COM(2000) 412 final (Aug. 1, 2000)

Context

In the European Union, patent protection is currently provided by two systems, neither of which is based on a Community legal instrument: the national patent systems and the European patent system.

The national patent appeared first. In the Member States of the European Community, the national patent has undergone de facto harmonisation. First of all, all the Member States are parties to both the Paris Convention for the Protection of Industrial Property of 20 March 1883 (as last amended on 14 July 1967) and the Agreement of 15 April 1994 on Trade Related Aspects of Intellectual Property Rights (referred to hereinafter as the TRIPS Agreement). Several Member States are also party to the Council of Europe's Convention of 27 November 1963 on the unification of certain elements of patent law.

The idea of the Community patent dates back to the 1960s. At that time, initial thought was given to the creation of a patent system applicable to the nascent European Community in its entirety. However, it quickly became apparent that this approach could not take on more tangible form in a purely Community context. Thus it was that the initiative finally led to the signature on 5 October 1973 of the Convention on the Grant of European Patents(referred to hereinafter as the "Munich Convention"), to which all the Member States gradually acceded.

The Munich Convention is governed by conventional international law and does not form part of the Community legal order. The Munich Convention established a European Patent Organisation, the constituent bodies of which are the European Patent Office (referred to hereinafter as the "Office") and the Administrative Council. It lays down a single procedure for the granting of patents. This task has been assigned to the Office. However, once the European patent has been granted, it becomes a national patent and is subject to the national rules of the contracting States designated in the application. At present, nineteen countries are members of the European Patent Organisation. Apart from the Member States of the European Community, these are Switzerland, Liechtenstein, Monaco, Cyprus and, in the near future, Turkey. What is more, several Central and Eastern European countries [Bulgaria, the Czech Republic, Estonia, Hungary, Poland, Romania, Slovakia and Slovenia] have been invited to accede to the Munich Convention from 1 July 2002 at the earliest.

A second attempt by the EC Member States to create a Community patent led in 1975 to the signing of the Luxembourg Convention on the Community patent (referred to hereinafter as the "Luxembourg Convention"). This Convention was amended by an Agreement concluded in Luxembourg on 15 December 1989 concerning Community patents and including, amongst other things, the Protocol on the Settlement of Litigation concerning the Infringement and Validity of Community Patents.

The Luxembourg Convention is a Community convention. In essence, the Convention would have transformed the national stages in the granting of European patents into a single stage common to the Member States. The Luxembourg Convention never entered into force because the only Member States to ratify it were France, Germany, Greece, Denmark, Luxembourg, the United Kingdom and the Netherlands.

The failure of the Luxembourg Convention has generally been attributed to the costs of the Community patent, chiefly that of translation, and to the judicial system. Under the Convention, a patent had to be translated into every Community language. Interested parties felt that this requirement was excessive. Under the highly complex judicial system, national judges would have been able to declare a Community patent invalid with effect for the entire territory of the Community. This aspect aroused the distrust of interested parties, who considered it to be a major element of legal uncertainty.

Recent Work

Following the failure of the Luxembourg Convention, the Commission's Green Paper on the Community patent and the European patent system, which was part of the follow-up to the First Action Plan for Innovation in Europe, launched a broad discussion on the need to take new initiatives in relation to patents. The Green Paper elicited a large number of opinions from interested parties, the European Parliament and the Economic and Social Committee. In addition, the Commission, together with the Luxembourg Presidency of the Council, held a hearing on 25 and 26 November 1997 open to all users of the patent system. The Commission also staged a meeting of experts from Member States on 26 January 1998.

After this extensive consultation process, the Commission adopted, on 5 February 1999, a Communication on the follow-up to the Green Paper on the Community patent and the patent system in Europe. The aim of this Communication was to announce the various measures and new initiatives which the Commission was planning to take or propose in order to make the patent system attractive for promoting innovation in Europe..The initiative concerning the Community patent was announced and sketched out in broad outline in the Communication dated 5 February 1999. This proposal incorporates most of that broad outline. At the European Council in Lisbon on 23 and 24 March 2000, the Heads of State or Government of the Member States underlined the importance of introducing a Community patent without delay.

Proposal for a Council Regulation

. . . .

This proposal for a Regulation is aimed at creating a new unitary industrial property right, the Community patent. It is essential for eliminating the distortion of competition which may result from the territorial nature of national protection rights; it is also one of the most suitable means of ensuring the free movement of goods protected by patents.

The creation of a Community patent will also enable undertakings to adapt their production and distribution activities to the European dimension. It is considered to be an essential tool if we are to succeed in transforming research results and the new technological and scientific know-how into industrial and commercial success stories—and thereby put an end to the "European paradox" in innovation—while at the same time stimulating private R&D investment, which is currently at a very low level in the European Union compared with the United States and Japan.

The Community patent system will coexist with the national and European patent systems. Inventors will remain free to choose the type of patent protection best suited to their needs.

Legal Basis

. . . [T]he legal basis of the proposal for a Regulation is Article 308 [ex-Article 235] of the EC Treaty. Use of this legal bas[is] is in accordance with what has been done in relation to the Community trade mark and Community designs.

The form chosen for the instrument—a Regulation—is warranted by a number of considerations. The Member States cannot be left with any discretion either to determine the Community law applicable to the Community patent or to decide on the effects and administration of the patent once it has been granted. The unity of the patent could not be guaranteed by less "binding" measures.

Link between the Regulation on the Community Patent and the European Patent Organisation

The main thrust of this proposal is the creation of a "symbiosis" between two systems: that of the Regulation on the Community patent, a European Community instrument, and that of the Munich Convention, a classic international instrument. This means not only that the Regulation on the Community patent will have to be adopted, but also that the Munich Convention and the status of the Office will have to be taken properly into account, that the Community will have to accede to the Munich Convention, and that account must be taken of the scope for ensuring consistency in the future development of the Regulation and the Convention.

The Regulation on the Community Patent

By virtue of the Community's accession to the Munich Convention and the designation of the Community as the territory for which the Community patent can be granted, the provisions of that Convention applying to European patent applications will, in principle, be applicable to applications for Community patents. Even though this text refers to an application for the Community patent, in legal terms such an application will, under the Munich Convention, be an application for a European patent designating the territory of the Community. Only when the patent has been granted by the Office will it become a Community patent under the Regulation. In the light of Community accession to the Munich Convention, it is not necessary for the Regulation to refer to the substantive rules of the Munich Convention and its Implementing Regulations in force on a specific date. In essence, the Regulation is limited to governing the Community patent once granted. The Regulation will also contain specific rules which will depart from the Convention. The Regulation will, for instance, introduce some improvements compared with the European patent as regards the cost of the patent, translations and the system of appeals to courts of law.

The Office and the Munich Convention

As already mentioned, the authority responsible for examining patent applications and granting Community patents will be the Office. However, the Office is not a Community body. It is nevertheless intended that it will grant Community patents by virtue of the Community's accession to the Munich Convention and of a revision of that Convention. The current Munich Convention does not allow the Office to perform these functions. To achieve that, the Convention would have to be amended. Now is an opportune time to act, as the Munich Convention is currently undergoing revision. In accordance with the mandate adopted by the intergovernmental conference of the member states of the European Patent Organisation in Paris on 24 and 25 June 1999, two working parties were set up to carry out the preparatory work for a reform of the patent system in Europe, particularly with a view to reducing the cost and lead time involved in the granting of a patent, and for the harmonisation of litigation relating to the Community patent. It should be borne in mind that the envisaged revision of the Munich Convention will require the Contracting States, including four non-EU countries, to agree to the Convention being amended in such a way as to enable the Office to assume these new functions and make accession by the Community possible. The objective of the proposed Regulation is not to amend the present structure of the European patent system. The Regulation does not provide for the setting-up of new special departments within the Office. Rather, the Office would be charged with specific tasks relating to the Community patent. What is more, it will continue its activities concerning the European patent as an international body independent of the Community. Similarly, the Office will apply to the Community patent the case law which it has developed for the European patent, to the extent that the rules in the Regulation and the Convention are identical.

Community Accession to the Munich Convention

Community accession to the Munich Convention is the essential instrument for achieving the objectives of the Regulation. To this end, the Commission will present to the Council a recommendation for a negotiating mandate. The accession of the Community to the Munich Convention should make it possible to achieve the best possible symbiosis between the European Patent Organisation and the Community. The EC Member States, which already have an obligation to ensure compliance with Community law in matters relating to the legal protection of biotechnological inventions in the international arena, will be required under the proposal concerning the Community patent to coordinate to an even greater extent the opinions which they express within the bodies of the European Patent Organisation, pursuant to Article 10 (ex Article 5) of the EC Treaty.

Consistent and Simultaneous Development of the Regulation on the Community Patent and of the Munich Convention

The Munich Convention is currently undergoing revision, and further amendments may follow. Independently of this work, it is possible that the Regulation will have to be amended in line with future developments in society. In order to guarantee, as far as possible, the consistent and simultaneous development of the Regulation and the Munich Convention, the following factors will have to be taken into account:

— first, amendments to the Munich Convention made prior to the adoption of the Regulation on the Community patent will automatically apply to the Community patent;

— secondly, in order to guarantee that the revision of the Munich Convention moves in the right direction, under Article 10 of the EC Treaty Member States should, after the proposal for a Regulation has been adopted by the Commission, cooperate loyally in the negotiations with the European Patent Organisation with a view to facilitating the realisation of the objectives of the proposal. After the adoption of the Regulation, external jurisdiction over the Community patent shall fall within the exclusive remit of the Community.

— Thirdly, as regards subsequent developments in the framework of the Munich Convention, it will be possible to lay down corresponding rules according to the nature of the changes made, either in the form of an amendment to the Regulation or within the Implementing Regulations which will be adopted via a comitology procedure.

— fourthly, given that Member States currently form a large majority among the Contracting States of the European Patent Organisation, they should be in a position effectively to ensure that revisions made to the Munich Convention do not jeopardise either the integrity of Community law or the desired consistency between the Regulation and the Munich Convention.

The Main Features of the Community Patent

The Community patent must be of a unitary and autonomous nature. It must stem from a body of Community patent law, be affordable, have appropriate language arrangements and meet information requirements, guarantee legal certainty and coexist with existing patent systems. . . .

The Community patent must be unitary in nature. It will produce the same effect throughout the territory of the Community and may be granted, transferred, declared invalid or allowed to lapse only in respect of the whole of the Community. The Community patent must be of an autonomous nature. It shall be subject only to the provisions of the proposed Regulation and to the general principles of Community law. . . . The proposed Regulation introduces specific provisions applicable to Community patents. It is important to note that the Regulation does not set out to depart substantially from the principles embodied in national patent law already in force in the Member States; these have all acceded to the Munich Convention and have, moreover, largely harmonised substantive patent law in accordance with the Luxembourg Convention, even though the latter Convention has never entered into force. The same applies concerning the specific rules of the TRIPS Agreement, which links the Community and the Member States. On this basis, the provisions of the Munich Convention concerning such subjects as conditions of patentability, for example, will be applicable to the Community patent. Thus, in accordance with the provisions of the Munich Convention, Community patents will be granted in respect of inventions, whether products or processes, provided that they are new, involve an inventive step and are capable of industrial application. Similarly, exceptions to patentability will be covered by the Munich Convention. Amendments made to the Convention in the course of the intergovernmental conference currently under way for the revision of the Convention will of course be applicable to the Community patent. By contrast, the effects of the Community patent, once granted, will be governed by the provisions of this Regulation. This applies, for instance, to the limitations of the effects of the Community patent. As regards the use of a patented invention without the patent proprietor's authorisation, the proposed Regulation would incorporate the best practice in force in the Member States: the granting of compulsory licences would thus be possible. Although the Regulation makes no such specific provision, Member States would remain free to take any action necessary for the protection of their essential security interests, in accordance with Article 73 of the TRIPS Agreement.

Affordable Cost of the Community Patent

At present, an average European patent (designating eight Contracting States) costs approximately EUR 30 000. The fees due to the Office for such an average European patent account for approximately 14% of the total cost of the patent. The cost of representation before the Office represents 18% of the total cost. The translations required by the Contracting States account for approximately 39% of the total cost. The renewal fees currently paid to Member States represent something in the order of 29% of the cost of an average European patent (between the fifth and the tenth years). Of this income, 50% accrues to the Office and 50% to the Contracting State concerned. This proposal is aimed at making the Community patent more affordable and more attractive than the present European patent. These aspects depend to a very large extent on the costs associated with translations, procedures, and litigation.

Translation Costs

As far as translation costs are concerned, the comparative table below gives a fairly accurate idea of the probable effect of the recommended solution. The three scenarios are based on the following assumptions: applications comprising an average volume of 20 pages, three pages for the claims, 15 claims. As the texts concerned are of a highly complex and technical nature and relate to new matters and processes, the average output of a translator will probably be in the region of three pages per day. Translation costs are therefore estimated at EUR 250 per day.

Translation costs in three scenarios:

Scenario No. 1: Luxembourg Convention

Complete translation of the patent documents into the ten working languages.

Translation costs: EUR 17,000

Scenario No. 2:

Translation of the patent documents into the three working languages of the Office.

Translation costs: EUR 5,100

Scenario No. 3: Proposed solution

Translation of the patent documents into one of the Office's three working languages and of the claims into the other two.

Translation costs: EUR 2,200

Overall, this comparative assessment shows a significant differential in favour of the solution put forward in this proposal for a Regulation. In terms of translation costs, the planned Community patent will be both more affordable than the patent proposed in the first Luxembourg Convention and more attractive than the European patent.

Fees and Other Procedural Costs

Apart from translation costs, the different fees and costs associated with the granting and renewal of a Community patent should also be taken into account. It is essential that the overall cost of a Community patent should be in the same order of magnitude as that associated with patents granted by the Community's main trading partners, or even be more attractive.

. . . .

The cost of the current European patent is . . . three to five times higher than that of Japanese and US patents.

There is thus an urgent need to remedy this situation, which does not provide any incentive for inventors to apply for a patent in Europe.

Under the proposed Regulation, the Office will examine Community patent applications and grant and administer Community patents. The fees charged by the Office during the examination of a patent application are laid down in the Munich Convention. By contrast, it is planned that the annual renewal fees for patents granted, as well as their amount, will be determined in a Commission Regulation on fees which will be adopted according to the comitology procedure. The Regulation provides that the annual renewal fees must also be paid to the Office.

Language Arrangements—Access to Information

The arrangements concerning translations of the patent are a particularly important aspect in terms of the cost of the Community patent. The cost of translating the patent into all the official languages of the Community would entail a risk of the entire Community patent project foundering, placing as it would too heavy a burden on inventors, above all small and medium-sized enterprises. Such a burden would discourage them from using the Community patent and give them an incentive to seek protection only in certain European countries. With the enlargement of the Union, compulsory translation into all the official languages would have even more negative effects in terms of cost.

To remedy this problem, the proposed Regulation provides that the Community patent, once it is has been granted in one of the procedural languages of the Office and published in that language, with a translation of the claims into the two other procedural languages, will be valid without any other translation. A translation could become necessary in legal proceedings against a suspected infringer. In such a situation, a suspected infringer who has been unable to consult the text of the patent in the official language of the Member State in which he is domiciled, is presumed, until proven otherwise, not to have knowingly infringed the patent. In order to protect a suspected infringer who, in such a situation, has not acted in a deliberate manner, it is provided that the proprietor of the patent will not be able to obtain damages in respect of the period prior to the translation of the patent being notified to the infringer. This system will make for a considerable reduction in translation costs.

The proposed system is regarded as appropriate, primarily because the universal language in the field of patents is, in reality, English. Translations are very rarely consulted. For example, at the Institut National de la Propriété Industrielle, the French national institute of industrial property rights, translations are consulted in only 2% of cases. Moreover, any obligation to translate the patent into all the Community languages would not necessarily guarantee easy access to this information for all economic operators established in the Community.

Incidentally, separate information and assistance systems can be put in place or upgraded in order to help small and medium-sized enterprises, in particular, in searching for information on patent applications and patents published.

Secondly, the proposed system is regarded as providing sufficient protection with respect to a suspected infringer, given that the Regulation's provisions on damages will enable the Community intellectual property court, which will be established to deal with Community patent matter, to take into account all the relevant factors in each individual case.

Moreover, this provision is in line with the work begun in the IGC on the revision of the Munich Convention, particularly that undertaken by the working party on cost reduction, whose remit from the member states of the European Patent Organisation is to put forward proposals for lowering the cost of the European patent. Accordingly, it is also provided that translations of the patent—which will, moreover, be optional for the proprietor—must be filed with the Office rather than with national patent offices in several Member States. This should yield a considerable cost reduction compared with the total cost of an average European patent.

Legal Certainty of the Community Patent: the Judicial System

European undertakings and inventors expect a judicial system that provides maximum legal certainty for the European patent. Only if this is the case can the often considerable research and development costs incurred upstream of the patent be offset. Only a centralised Community court can guarantee without fail unity of law and consistent case law. This relates exclusively to litigation between private parties. Appeals against administrative decisions relating to the Community patent will be governed by the procedures provided for by the Munich Convention. Finally, the link between the proposal for a Regulation and the Intergovernmental Conference on Institutional Reform and the division of responsibilities within the centralised Community court must be pointed out.

The Judicial System in Relation to Litigation between Private Parties

The system adopted in the Luxembourg Convention has not been followed in this proposal. It would have enabled a national court hearing a counter-claim for a declaration of invalidity to declare the Community patent invalid throughout the Community. The solution adopted in this proposal is ambitious: it provides for the creation of a centralised judicial system specialising in patent matters, particularly for the examination of questions concerning validity and infringement of the Community patent. To this end, a "Community Intellectual Property Court" will be established. This court will comprise chambers of first instance and appeal. These two instances, whose jurisdiction will cover the entire Community territory, may deal with questions relating to the actual facts of a case as well as to points of law. They will apply their own rules of procedure, grant provisional measures, determine penalties and award damages. The judgments of the court will be enforceable. Enforcement will be governed by the rules of civil procedure in force in the State in the territory of which it is carried out. The national authorities shall automatically issue an enforcement order in respect of an authentic judgment. It is planned to establish this court by way of an amendment to the EC Treaty currently under discussion in the Intergovernmental Conference on Institutional Reform. The Commission regards the creation of a centralised Community judicial system as being necessary for several reasons: first of all, less ambitious solutions which have been negotiated or sketched out in the past have failed. Inventors would not use the future Community patent without "Community-level" legal certainty. A non-centralised judicial system such as that for European patents, under which, for example, legal actions relating to the validity of a patent have to be instituted separately in all the Contracting States for which the patent has been granted, would be unacceptable for the Community patent. Not only would the management of patent rights under such a system be very costly for the proprietor, but—above all—a non-centralised system would not give proprietors of the Community patent the necessary legal certainty as regards the validity of the patent throughout the territory for which it was granted. Only a centralised judicial system can guarantee unity of law and consistent case law. Moreover, it is necessary to avoid from the outset a situation where a national court with no experience of industrial property matters could decide on the validity or infringement of the Community patent. Due account has also been taken of the need for the centralised court to have all the requisite qualifications in patent matters. The composition of the court should be such as to guarantee that the judges have the necessary qualifications in the field of patents, which can involve the examination of highly technical questions. This is not currently the case at the Court of First Instance of the Court of Justice, which has not had the opportunity to gain experience in patent matters.

The creation of a new centralised judicial system is also necessary in order to address the problem of excessive workload which is affecting both the Court of Justice and the Court of First Instance. For the Community patent, it is essential that questions relating to the validity and infringement of the patent be answered definitively within a period of two years. This time limit takes into account the relatively short duration of the protection offered by the patent, which in principle is 20 years but in reality is much shorter on account of the progressive nature of the annual renewal fees which the proprietor of the patent has to pay and the rapid advance of technology. For these reasons, the interesting alternative of assigning to the Court of First Instance the role of a court of appeal against national court decisions which would have decided on the validity of the patent throughout the Community territory was dropped. The jurisdiction of the centralised court would cover only certain categories of actions. It is essential that it be able to deal at the same time with disputes relating to the infringement and the validity of the patent (for example, actions for a declaration of non-infringement, invalidity proceedings, or counterclaims for invalidity). The reason for this is that defendants in infringement actions almost always make a claim of patent invalidity as a means of defence. Separating the jurisdictions for these two types of action would be conducive neither to the sound administration of justice nor to the efficiency aimed for in this Regulation, given that the factors which the judge has to examine in the two cases are essentially the same. The centralised court should also handle litigation relating to use of the patent in the period between publication of the application and the actual granting of the patent. The same applies to actions relating to the limitation or lapse of the patent. It is essential that the jurisdiction of the centralised court be exclusive. This jurisdiction is based on the validity of the patent in the territory of the Community, as well as on the location of the facts and activities concerned taking place in the Community. The Regulation will have to provide that all other disputes between private parties which do not specifically come under the jurisdiction of the centralised court are to be dealt with by the national courts of the Member States. Such disputes might concern, for example, the right to the patent, the transfer of the patent or contractual licences. For situations where jurisdiction resides with national courts, the Regulation provides that the rules set out in the 1968 Brussels Convention on Jurisdiction and Enforcement of Judgments in Civil and Commercial Matters (the "Brussels Convention") shall, in principle, be applicable. The Regulation will specify the necessary exceptions and adaptations. This Convention will be transformed into a Regulation. It is understood that, for the Member States concerned, the reference to the Brussels Convention is to be deemed a reference to the Implementing Regulations once these have been definitively adopted by the Council. However, whenever an action relates to the validity or infringement of the Community patent, the national court before which the case has been brought will be obliged to decline jurisdiction and declare the action inadmissible. If the validity of the patent is a preliminary issue in a case relating to another subject, e.g. unfair competition, the national court hearing the case will stay the proceedings to enable the parties to resolve the issue of a preliminary nature in an action brought before the centralised court. The national courts remain free to submit a request to the Court of Justice for preliminary rulings on matters falling within their jurisdiction, for example concerning interpretation of Directive 98/44/EC on the legal protection of biotechnological inventions. However, national courts will not, in principle, be authorised to request preliminary rulings concerning the validity of the Community patent on the basis of the Regulation, since they will not have jurisdiction in the matter.

Appeals against Decisions of the Office and of the Commission

The Office's internal opposition and appeal procedures will be applicable to the Community patent. Decisions by the Office will not be subject to appeal before the centralised Community court. This solution has been adopted with a view to retaining for as long as possible the unified treatment of simultaneous application for a Community patent and a European patent. It also avoids burdening the centralised Community court with a proliferation of appeals lodged during the examination procedure and before the Community patent has been granted. The solution is also appropriate from the point of view of the legal status of the Office's Boards of Appeal. A board of appeal has been regarded, in the United Kingdom for example, as being entirely equivalent to a court, to the extent that its decisions were final and based on objective criteria, and the independence of its members was guaranteed by the Munich Convention. Account will also have to be taken of the fact that the validity of a patent granted by the Office may subsequently be the subject of litigation between private parties before the Community intellectual property court under the conditions laid down by the Regulation. At present, however, the solution has the disadvantage of considerably delaying the adoption of a final decision on the validity of the Community patent. This delay is due to the sometimes very long examination periods of the Office's Opposition Division and Boards of Appeal. It would appear, however, that a revision of the Munich Convention on this point could resolve the problem. Moreover, it is clear that judicial review of decisions taken by the Commission falls within the jurisdiction of a Community court. Such jurisdiction is vested in the Court of Justice (Court of First Instance) under Article 230 of the EC Treaty. Examination of appeals relating to decisions taken pursuant to the Regulation on the Community patent will in future often require knowledge in the field of competition law. In particular, these will be appeals against decisions by the Commission concerning compulsory licences and licences of right. The Court of First Instance remains best placed to examine the last-named type of appeal, concerning which it has already gained experience. It is, therefore, not proposed to change the attribution of areas of jurisdiction which reside with the Court of First Instance. This solution is an appropriate means of guaranteeing the consistency of Community case law in this field.

Link between the Proposal for a Regulation and the Intergovernmental Conference on Institutional Reform

It is understood that the Community intellectual property court will be established by way of an amendment to the EC Treaty. Discussions to this effect are currently under way in the Intergovernmental Conference on Institutional Reform. The EC Treaty would then also provide that this court, like the Court of First Instance (Articles 225 and 243 to 245 of the EC Treaty), would adopt its own rules of procedure and order provisional measures, and that its judgments would be enforceable in the Member States in the same way as decisions of the Court of Justice. Relations between the Community courts, including the mechanism for referral in the interest of the law referred to below would also be laid down in the EC Treaty. The Commission has already suggested, in its opinions of 26 January and 1 March 2000, that the Intergovernmental Conference discuss an amendment to the Treaty designed to provide adequate legal certainty in matters of Community intellectual property. Thus, in its Additional Contribution to the Intergovernmental Conference on Institutional Reform, the Commission took the view that, "regarding intellectual property rights under Community law, particularly with the prospect of the Community patent, consideration should be given to establishing a specialised tribunal with jurisdiction in cases concerning patent validity and infringements, in order to secure legal certainty regarding unitary documents having effect throughout the Community and to relieving the Court of Justice and the CFI of all this highly specialised litigation."

Pending the outcome of the negotiations under way in the Intergovernmental Conference, the Commission has therefore introduced, in this proposal for a Regulation, fundamental provisions corresponding to its Contribution. It goes without saying that more detailed provisions will have to be adopted, concerning in particular the rules of procedure applicable by the new Community court. These provisions, as well as the status of the court, will be laid down in subsequent instruments.

Division of Responsibilities within the Centralised Community Court

As already mentioned above, the new court would have jurisdiction in certain situations where jurisdiction would normally have been vested in the Court of First Instance. As already mentioned. . . . , the Court of First

Instance will nevertheless continue to have jurisdiction in respect of decisions taken by the Commission. Appeals against the Court's decisions will be governed by the current provisions of the EC Treaty. As far as the new court is concerned, the planned provisions would not include the possibility of lodging a direct appeal before the Court of Justice against decisions of the chamber of appeal of the Community intellectual property court. Nor is it planned to introduce into the relationship between the new Community court and the Court of Justice a mechanism for requesting preliminary rulings like the one that is a feature of relations between the national courts and the Court of Justice. In spite of this, the proposed system would not affect the role of the Court of Justice as the supreme court of Community law. If the Community intellectual property court had to interpret more general aspects of Community law in the cases it dealt with, the amended EC Treaty would provide scope for the matter subsequently to be brought before the Court of Justice in the interest of the law. This mechanism would make it possible to verify whether or not the interpretation of Community law made by the Community intellectual property court was in conflict with the interpretation handed down by the Court of Justice. The principle and the mechanism for requesting preliminary rulings are similar to those adopted in the 1971 Protocol annexed to the Brussels Convention (Article 4). Accordingly, such a referral can only be made in respect of judgments by the chamber of first instance or the chamber of appeal which have become res judicata. The Registrar of the Court of Justice shall give notice of the request to the Member States and Institutions of the Community; they shall then be entitled, within two months of the notification, to submit statements of case or written observations to the Court. What is more, the interpretation given by the Court of Justice in response to such a request shall not affect the decision which gave rise to the request for interpretation. No fees shall be levied or any costs or expenses awarded in respect of the proceedings. In contrast to the provisions of the said Protocol, the Commission can, as guardian of the EC Treaty, bring an action before the Court of Justice. It goes without saying that, as a Community court, the new court would be subject to the case law of the Court of Justice, whether this related to interpretations in appeals made in the interest of the law or to preliminary rulings issued at the request of national courts in cases coming under their jurisdiction.

Links with Other Patent Systems

The Community patent system will coexist with the national and European patent systems. Inventors will remain free to choose the patent system best suited to their needs. For a Community patent to be granted, the territory of the Community will have to be designated in the application for a European patent. It will not be possible to designate, in an application for a European patent, both the territory of the Community and one or more Member States. However, an applicant will be able to request at the same time a patent for the territory of the Community and a European patent for Switzerland, Cyprus, Monaco or Liechtenstein. It is also provided that, at any time up to the grant of the European patent, a European patent application designating all the Member States of the Community can be converted into a European patent application designating the entire territory of the Community. Similarly, a European patent application which designates the entire territory of the Community may be converted into a European patent designating one or more Member States of the Community. The principle of conversion and the procedures for its application should be the subject of negotiations in the context of the Community's accession to the Munich Convention. Once granted, a Community patent may not be converted into a European patent. Nor will it be possible to convert national patents or a European patent into a Community patent. It will not be possible for one and the same invention belonging to one and the same person to be simultaneously protected by a Community patent and by a European patent designating one or more Member States, or by a national patent granted by a Member State.

Justification for Proposal in Terms of Proportionality and Subsidiarity Principles

What are the objectives of the proposed measure in relation to the obligations incumbent on the Community? The proposal is aimed at improving the operation of the internal market and, in particular, at adapting the manufacture and distribution of patented products to the Community dimension. The proposal is also part of the drive to promote innovation and growth in the European Community. Does the measure satisfy the criteria of subsidiarity? These objectives cannot be attained by the Member States acting alone or collectively and must therefore, by reason of the cross-border impact, be attained at Community level. Are the means deployed at Community level proportional to the objectives? The Court of Justice has ruled that Community intellectual property rights cannot be created by harmonising national legislation. Having regard to the unity of the right, Member States cannot be left with any discretion concerning its implementation. The proposed instrument, a Regulation, is thus confined to the minimum needed for the attainment of these objectives and does not exceed what is necessary for that purpose.

———

NOTES AND QUESTIONS

(1) **Political Progress (or Lack Thereof) in the Council of Ministers**. Progress toward the community patent at the political level of the EU Council has not been forthcoming.

> On 20 December 2001, the EU's Council of Internal Market Ministers meeting in Brussels failed to reach agreement on the

Commission proposal for a Community Patent, despite a new compromise presented by the Belgian Presidency. . . . Internal Market Commissioner Frits Bolkestein stressed to the Council that the Community Patent had to be affordable for companies, since otherwise it would not be used. He also insisted that the Community Patent regime had to be sustainable not only in the current EU of 15 Member States but in the future enlarged EU. Commenting afterwards, Mr. Bolkestein said 'Affordable and easy-to-obtain patents are essential to encourage innovation. Innovation is in turn crucial for job creation and economic growth. The Community Patent is therefore a keystone of our declared efforts to make Europe the most competitive economy in the world in 2010. At the Lisbon Summit, Europe's leaders stated that they wanted the Community Patent by the end of 2001. The Council today has made some progress towards this goal thanks to the sterling efforts of the Belgian Presidency, but has not reached agreement, which is very disappointing. We must have a concrete agreement in time for the Barcelona Summit'.

European Commission, Results of the Internal Market Council Brussels, 20th December 2001 – Community Patent, available at http://www.europa.eu.int/comm/internal_market/en/indprop/patent/imc/12-01res.htm.

(2) **The Proposed Belgian Compromise.**

Under the terms of the final compromise presented by the Belgian Presidency:

● The patent application could be made in any EU official language. In the case of an application made in a language other than the languages used by the European Patent Office (EPO) in Munich (i.e., English, French, German), it would be translated into one of the EPO languages with the translation costs met by the Community Patent system (essentially income derived from patent renewal fees).

● When submitting the application, the applicant would indicate which of the three EPO languages in which the Community Patent should be issued.

● The applicant could ask the national patent offices of non-EPO language Member States and of other Member States with experience of working with the EPO and which need to maintain a critical mass of work (i.e., Austria) to carry out searches.

● An 'enhanced' abstract (more than the very brief normal abstract (i.e. summary) but less than the claims) would be published in all the EU official languages, with the translation costs paid for by the applicant.

● The patent (comprising the description, the claims and the abstract) would be issued in the EPO language chosen by the applicant. If the application was submitted in a non-EPO language, the text of that application would be aligned with the patent issued. In any case, the applicant could request that the claims be translated into his mother (official EU) language.

● The jurisdictional arrangements would be sought in the context of Articles 225a and 229a of the EC Treaty as amended in Nice. The first instance court would be a central court to ensure uniform application of law, but existing courts in the Member States could be used where objective criteria justify this.

The Presidency suggested that the total translation costs for applicants under this compromise would be Euros 3,240. An average European Patent (issued under the 1973 Munich Convention) designates 8 countries and must be translated into 5 languages to be valid in these 8 States, for which the cost relating to translation is Euros 11,500 (38% of total cost).

The Commission supported the proposal by the Presidency under the condition, however, that the jurisdictional arrangements would clearly consist of a centralised Community jurisdiction. The central court could, however, use the infrastructures of existing national courts, where justified by objective criteria.

Only twelve Member States were able to accept the latest Belgian Presidency compromise as a good basis for future work. The proposal will need to be adopted unanimously.

See EU Memo/01/451,[*] at www.europa.eu.int/comm/internal_market/en/ indprop/patent/imc/12-01res.htm. The holdouts against the compromise are Spain, Portugal, and Greece. Is the so-called democratic deficit in Europe blocking the adoption of a Community Patent or forcing it down the throats of the Member States? A Commission Working Document on the Planned Community Patent Jurisdiction was published on 30 August 2002. *See* COM(2002) 480 final.

[B]   Eurasian Patent Convention

JOHN RICHARDS, RECENT PATENT LAW DEVELOPMENTS IN ASIA[**]
7 Fordham Intell. Prop. Media & Ent. L.J. 599 (1997)

Marco Polo's silk route proceeds to the countries that are parties to the Eurasian Convention. The Eurasian Convention became operative on January 1, 1996, and could be designated in PCT applications under code EA since that date. Its present members are: Armenia, Azerbaijan, Belarus, Kazakstan, Kyrgyzstan, the Republic of Moldova, the Russian Federation, Tajikistan, and Turkmenistan. This means that, aside from the Baltic

---

republics, which have oriented themselves towards the European Patent Office, the only former Soviet republics not to have joined the Eurasian Patent Convention are Georgia, Ukraine, and Uzbekistan, although Georgia and Ukraine were both signatories to the original treaty.

The standard for patentability under the Eurasian Convention is the now-standard one of novelty, inventive step, and industrial applicability. However, the treaty establishing the Convention left to the Convention's Administrative Council—which consists of the heads of the national patent offices of the member states—the definitions to be adopted for these features. In fact, it appears that the Russian Patent Office will carry out the search and that worldwide publication, use, or disclosure are as destructive of novelty as is a previously-filed Eurasian patent application. Disclosures by, or deriving from, an applicant or inventor are, however, subject to a six-month grace period from the date of disclosure if an application is filed in the Eurasian Patent Office or, apparently, in another patent office if priority is claimed from it.

Under the Eurasian Convention, a single patent application designating all of the Contracting States is filed in Russian in the central Eurasian Patent Office in Moscow, where the application procedure is similar to that of the European Patent Office. There will, therefore, be an early publication of the application eighteen months from either the Eurasian filing date or the national filing date from which priority is claimed. The applicant must request substantive examination within six months of that publication. Unlike the European Patent Office, however, the Eurasian Convention does not require "completion" of the patent in the various designated countries or filing of a translation of the patent in the languages of the designated non-Russian-speaking countries at the end of the prosecution. Renewal fees for a Eurasian patent will depend on the number of countries in which the patentee wishes to keep the patent in force.

The term of a patent under the Eurasian Convention is twenty years. As with the new Russian law, there will be publication of the application before grant, and a right to compensation for use of the invention during the pendency of the actual patent grant.

An interesting side effect of the use of the European Patent Convention as a model for the Eurasian Convention is the Eurasian Convention's attempt to incorporate a counterpart to the infamous Article 69 of the European Patent Convention and its protocol on the interpretation of claims. Rule 12 of the regulations promulgated under the Eurasian Convention provides that the scope of protection shall be determined by the claims, taking into account each feature, and possibly an equivalent of each feature, of the claims, interpreted in light of the description. Such an interpretation, however, will be not only to elucidate what is unclear or indefinite, but also to determine the true meaning of the claim, which is to be neither its literal meaning nor its general inventive idea.

. . . .

NOTES AND QUESTIONS

(1) **Russian Patent Law**. The break-up of the Soviet Union created complications in the effect of patents granted prior to 1991. A new patent law was adopted by the Russian Federation in 1992. These developments are discussed in John M. Romary & Howard A. Kwon, *Adapting to the Modern World*, 76 MANAGING INTELL. PROP. 27 (1998).

(2) **Eurasian Patent Law as a Model**. What attributes of the Eurasian patent system, if any, might serve as models for an improved European patent? The Eurasian system was the product of the rapid disintegration of the Soviet system and rapid reintegration of the same countries, unlike the European system which has grown steadily in tandem with European integration.

[C] African Intellectual Property Organization [OAPI] and the African Regional Industrial Property Organization [ARIPO]

TSHIMANGA KONGOLO, THE AFRICAN INTELLECTUAL PROPERTY ORGANIZATIONS: THE NECESSITY OF ADOPTING ONE UNIFORM SYSTEM FOR ALL AFRICA [*]
3 J. WORLD INT. PROP. 265 (2000)

I. Introduction

. . . [A]t present in Africa, two major regional organizations dealing with intellectual property matters exist: the African Regional Industrial Property Organization (hereinafter the ARIPO) and the Organisation Africaine de la Propriété Intellectuelle (OAPI). The two Organizations were established after the independence of most African countries. However, it is unfortunate to notice that only a few African countries are members of the ARIPO and the OAPI. It should be mentioned at the outset that the systems of protection provided under these Organizations do not reflect, in a strict sense, the African realities. They are, to some extent, simply the transposition of the so-called international protection system to the regional level, almost without adjustment. In other words, the ARIPO and the OAPI systems are modeled after the Western style of intellectual property protection which does not always correspond and fit to the African realities and environment. Notwithstanding that the Organizations have played a significant role in the harmonization of the intellectual property laws of their Members, it should be pointed out that these Organizations are not without shortcomings. Their systems would be more effective if they would take into consideration African needs, priorities and realities. They should guide African countries for the setting up of a unique African system of protection of intellectual property which would enable the international community to acknowledge the African vision. . . .

II. Overview of the ARIPO and the OAPI

A. The ARIPO

1. The Background of the ARIPO

The ARIPO was previously known as the Industrial Property Organization for English-Speaking Africa (ESARIPO). The idea of developing a regional patent system arose as early as 1972 when representatives of English-speaking African countries attending a seminar on copyrights called on the World Intellectual Property Organization and the United Nations Organization to assist in the establishment of a regional industrial property office for English-speaking Africa. The change in name became necessary when it became open to all Member countries of the Organization of African Unity (OAU). Its headquarters is based in Harare, Zimbabwe. The ARIPO Agreement was adopted at Lusaka, Zambia, in 1976 and supplemented by two Protocols, namely the Protocol on Patents and Industrial Designs within the Framework of the ARIPO, adopted at Harare on 10 December 1982, and the Banjul Protocol on Marks, adopted at Banjul, The Gambia, on 19 November 1993.

2. The Objectives of the ARIPO and its Membership

Article III of the Agreement on the Creation of the ARIPO lays down the objectives of the ARIPO as follows:

(a) to promote the harmonisation and development of the industrial property laws, and matters related thereto, appropriate to the needs of its Members and of the region as a whole;

(b) to foster the establishment of a close relationship between its Members in matters relating to industrial property;

(c) to establish such common services or organs as may be necessary or desirable for the co-ordination, harmonization and development of the industrial property activities affecting its Members;

(d) to establish schemes for the training of staff in the administration of industrial property laws;

(e) to organize conferences, seminars and other meetings on industrial property matters; to promote the exchange of ideas and experience, research and studies relating to industrial property matters;

(f) to promote and evolve a common view and approach of its Members on industrial property matters;

(g) to assist its Members, as appropriate, in the acquisition and development of technology relating to industrial property matters; and

(h) to do all such other things as may be necessary or desirable for the achievement of the objectives.

It is not the purpose of this study to examine whether these objectives have been achieved. What can be said is that this Agreement does not contain any objective which would safeguard, foster or promote African values, traditional knowledge and folklore, or facilitate the recognition, under the international framework, of African traditional components and the African vision as regards the protection Of intellectual property in general, and industrial property in particular. This is unfortunate.

Regarding membership, according to Article IV of the Agreement of the Creation of the ARIPO, membership of the Organization shall be open to the State members of the UN Economic Commission for Africa or the Organization of African Unity. At present, the ARIPO is made up off fourteen members. The number of Members is very small. Several reasons restrain countries from adhering to this Organization. One of the barriers is the language. The official language being only English, it is quite obvious that French-speaking countries would not adhere.

3. The ARIPO Agreement and Protocols

The ARIPO is principally governed by the Agreement on the Creation of the ARIPO and by two Protocols, namely, the Protocol on Patents and Industrial Designs within the Framework of the ARIPO, and the Banjul Protocol on Marks.

Besides the Agreement on the Creation, the two Protocols are accompanied by two Regulations; the main features of the Agreement and Protocols will be highlighted below.

(a) Agreement on the Creation of the ARIPO @@@

This Agreement encompasses sixteen Articles that include objectives, organs and functions, membership status, privileges and immunities, obligations of Members of the Organization, settlement of disputes, amendment, etc. The Organization is composed of three main organs, namely, the Council of Ministers, the Administrative Council and the Secretariat. The Agreement has established a special relationship with the UN Economic Commission for Africa, the Organization of African Unity and the WIPO. The ARIPO may co-operate with Governments of States not members of the Organization and with other organizations, institutions and bodies.

(b) Protocol on Patents and Industrial Designs within the Framework of the ARIPO

This Protocol comprises provisions regarding patents and industrial designs. As regards both patents and industrial designs, the ARIPO is empowered to grant, register and administer such patents and industrial designs on behalf of the Contracting States. According to the ARIPO Regulations for Implementing the Protocol on Patents and Industrial Designs, the ARIPO Office shall maintain a Patents Register and an Industrial Designs Register in which shall be recorded, respectively, all patents granted and all industrial designs registered under the Protocol. Applications for the grant of patents or the registration of industrial designs by the ARIPO Office shall be filed by the authorized representative of the applicant or by the applicant with the industrial property office of a Contracting State. The industrial property office with which the application is filed shall, without delay, transmit that application to the Office of the ARIPO. The application may contain a declaration claiming, in respect of one or several designated States, the priority, as provided for in the Paris Convention, of one or more earlier national, regional or international applications filed by the applicant or his predecessor in title in or for any State party to the Paris Convention. Pursuant to the Regulations, the ARIPO has acknowledged the first-to-file principle.

(i) Patents

Under the ARIPO [agreement], the patentee files a single application and designates any Member country of the Contracting States in which the patent will have validity, unless any Member country makes prior renunciation of the same. The ARIPO Office examines the compliance with formal requirements by the applicant and notifies each designated State when the prescribed requirements are met. Before the expiration of six months from the date of the notification, a designated State may declare that the patent shall have no effect in its territory for the reason that the invention is not patentable in accordance with the provisions of the Protocol, or that the nature of the invention is out of the protected subject-matter as stipulated under the national law of that State.

The ARIPO is designated to be an additional system of protection coexisting with the national patent systems of the member States. Its main purpose is the grant of regional patents having effect in all designated Member countries through a common granting authority, under its own rules and standards of patentability. Under the Protocol of the ARIPO various provisions of substantive patent law are set out, such as conditions for patentability, patent granting procedure, and establishment of an independent patent system. In addition, the ARIPO recommends its Members to adhere to the PCT.

It is set out that on each anniversary of the filing of the application, the ARIPO office shall collect the prescribed annual maintenance fee, part of which shall be distributed among the designated States concerned. The amount of the fee shall depend on the number of States in respect of which the application or patent is maintained. Moreover, a patent granted by the ARIPO Office shall, in each designated State, have the same effect as a patent registered, granted or otherwise having effect under the applicable national law but not beyond the maximum duration provided for under the said law. Under paragraph 11 of Section 3, a patent granted by the ARIPO Office shall, in each designated State, be subject to the provisions of the applicable national law on compulsory licences, forfeiture, or the use of patented inventions in the public interest.

The ARIPO, under its Protocol and Regulations, has provided special norms and rules in respect of patents relating to micro-organisms. . . .

4. The Relationship between the ARIPO and the PCT

The ARIPO recommends that its Members adhere to the Patent Co-operation Treaty. The ARIPO operates almost in the same way as the PCT. It is stipulated in Article 3bis(3) of the Protocol on Patents and Industrial Designs, pertaining to international applications, that the ARIPO Office may act as receiving Office under Article 2(XV) of the PCT in relation to an international application filed by an applicant who is a resident or national of a Contracting State which is also bound by the PCT. From the same perspective, an international application in which a Contracting State which is also bound by the PCT is designated for the purposes of obtaining a patent under the provisions of the Protocol shall be considered to be an application for the grant of a patent under this Protocol. In addition, the provisions of the PCT shall apply to such international application in addition to the provisions of this Protocol and the Regulations under this Protocol; in case of conflict, the provisions of the PCT shall prevail.

B. The Organisation Africaine De La Propriété Intellectuelle

"OAPI" is the commonly used acronym for the African Intellectual Property Organization. The acronym OAPI is derived from the French name of the Organization which is Organisation Africaine de la Propriété Intellectuelle. The OAPI is constituted of French-speaking African countries. It has its headquarters in Yaounde, Cameroon.

This section endeavours to scrutinize the main provisions embodied in the OAPI. Attention will be principally drawn to the following matters:

    1.   The background of the OAPI

    2.   The objectives of the OAPI and its Membership

    3.   OAPI Annexes.

1. The Background of the OAPI

After some of the French colonies gained their independence, they joined hands and created the OAPI. The first Agreement, signed at Libreville on 13 September 1962, was known as the Agreement Relating to the Creation of an African and Malagasy Office of Industrial Property. This Agreement was revised at Bangui on 2 March 1977, and called the Agreement Relating to the Creation of an African Intellectual Property Organization which replaced the African and Malagasy Office of Industrial Property. This revised Agreement is called and known as the Bangui Agreement, and it entered into force on 8 February 1982.

It is meaningful to point out that the Bangui Agreement has been under revision since February 1999 so that it will meet the requirements of the TRIPs Agreement. Substantial amendments to the Agreement, which will enter into force after ten Contracting States ratify it, are attached as an Annex to this article. It should be noted that the Bangui Agreement encompasses nine Annexes which cover, respectively: patents; utility models; trademarks and service marks; industrial designs; trade names and protection against unfair competition; appellations of origin; copyright and the cultural heritage; central body for patent documentation and information Documentation Center.

2. The Objectives of the OAPI and its Membership

The main aim of the OAPI is to have a uniform system of protection of intellectual property rights within the national framework of its Members. The OAPI countries have adopted a uniform system of protection whereby intellectual property rights are granted on their behalf by the Organization. In the same context, the OAPI aims at contributing to the promotion of the protection of literary and artistic property and to the recognition of the cultural and social values of artistic and literary property. For each of the Member States, the OAPI serves both as the national industrial property service within the meaning of Article 12 of the Paris Convention and as the central patent documentation and information body. In other words, the OAPI Office serves as the National Office of its Member States.

According to Article 2 of the Agreement, nationals may claim application for their benefit of the provisions of the Paris Convention for the Protection of Industrial Property, the Berne Convention for the Protection of Literary and Artistic Works and/or the Universal Copyright Convention, as well as the Agreements, additional Acts and closing Protocols which have amended or will amend these Conventions, in cases where such provisions are more favourable than those of the present Agreements and its Annexes in protecting intellectual property rights. Furthermore, under Article 14, in the case of discrepancies between the provisions of the present Agreement and its Annexes and those of the international conventions to which the Member states are party and which are administered by the International Bureau of the WIPO, the latter shall prevail.

Regarding membership, the Bangui Agreement provides that any African State which is not a signatory to the present Agreement but which is party to the Convention Establishing the WIPO, to the Paris Convention and to the Berne Convention and/or the Universal Copyright Convention may apply to accede to the present Agreement. In addition, any State may become an associated Member. The OAPI is constituted of fifteen Member countries. . . .

3. The OAPI Annexes

As mentioned above, each Annex deals with a specific intellectual property category:

Annex I: Patents

. . . .

Under this paragraph, attention will be drawn to the conditions for eligibility and scope of protection, rights conferred, the working of patents and compulsory licences, and enforcement of rights.

(i) Conditions for eligibility and scope of protection

Article 1 (1) of Annex I lays down the conditions of eligibility for patents: the invention shall be new, involve an inventive step and be industrially applicable. Articles 2, 3 and 4 define and specify the extent of each condition for patentability. It should be pointed out that patents are not available for inventions which are contrary to public order or morality. In addition, patents are not available in respect of scientific and mathematical theories, inventions having as their object plant varieties, animal species, essentially biological processes for the breeding of plants or animals, other than micro-biological processes and the products of such processes, schemes, rules or methods for doing business, performing purely mental acts or playing games, methods for treatment of the human or animal body by surgery or therapy, as well as diagnostic methods, straightforward presentation of information, computer programs, and works of an exclusively ornamental nature.

Under this Annex, plant varieties and computer programs are out of the ambit of patent protection. Regarding the former a specific law or sui generis regime would be preferable. As to the latter, the copyright regime would be suitable.

(ii) Rights conferred

Under this Annex, the patentee is entitled to preclude any person from exploiting the patented invention without his consent. He has the exclusive rights, in respect of a product or a process, of making, importing, offering for sale, selling and utilizing the product or process. Further, the patentee may preclude any person from stocking such product for the purposes of offering for sale, selling or utilizing it.

It should be mentioned that the patentee is entitled to assign or license his exclusive rights to another person.

The exclusive rights of the patentee are protected for a period of ten years following the date of the filing of the application. This period can be extended for five years if the patentee proves that his invention is being worked on the territory of one of the Member States at the date of request, or that there are legitimate reasons for failing to so work it. TRIPS, however, requires Members to grant patent protection for twenty years from the filing date of the application.

(iii) Working of patents and compulsory licences

According to Article 6(3), working of patents means the manufacture of a patented article, the application of a patented process or the use, in manufacture, of a patented machine, by effective and serious establishment and on a scale which is adequate and reasonable in the circumstances. In the same line of reasoning, the import of a patented product is not deemed to be the working. It is necessary to state this under this Annex, the prior-use regime has been acknowledged. The date of the filing of an application for a patent, or three years from the date of the grant of a patent, a compulsory licence may be granted on the request of any interested person, principally if the patented invention is not worked in the territory of a Member State at the time the request is made. As stated above, the importation of patented products is not deemed to be a working of a patent. The request for the grant of a compulsory licence shall be made to the civil court of the domicile of the patentee. Further, the Annex has provided the regime of licences of right and ex officio licences.

(iv) Enforcement of rights

Under Annex 1, both civil and criminal remedies are provided in the case of infringement of the patentee's exclusive rights. Nevertheless, no action for infringement of a patented invention is accepted if the patented invention had not been worked five years after the grant of patent. It should be mentioned that what constitutes infringement is the fact of knowingly received, sold, exhibited for sale or introduced on the national territory of one of the Member States one or several infringing objects by any person. . . .

QUESTIONS

Assess the extent to which the OAPI and ARIPO (and Eurasian, *see* above) systems serve the interests of the developing or transition economy countries of their member states. How do the mechanisms established in the Libreville and Lusaka Agreements compare to the European patent system? The number of patent applications filed in the OAPI office in Yaounde has been falling consistently. Can you attribute that to any of the characteristics of the "Libreville system"? National applications filed in the ARIPO office have dwindled as well. Some reasons for this may be due to the economic conditions in these countries. But others may be systemic. Does it make sense to "preserve the activity of [local] practitioners" in fashioning a multilateral system? On the other hand, for example, do you think that proximity of Yaounde practitioners to the OAPI office (or for that matter, the proximity of Munich law firms to the EPO) provides a competitive advantage not enjoyed by law firms, say, in Lome or Ouagadougou (or Helsinki and Copenhagen)? To what extent do the interests of patent practitioners *in fact* affect the way an international patent system is structured? To what extent *should* they?

[D]   Latin America

Patent law reform and regional cooperation between Latin American states is taking place at a rapid pace. Two Central American countries, Guatemala and El Salvador, were among the eleven founding countries of the Paris Convention in 1883, but both denounced the convention shortly thereafter. Of all the countries of Latin America, only ten were members of the Paris Convention by 1994 (Argentina, Barbados, Brazil, Chile, Cuba, Dominican Republic, Haiti, Mexico, Trinidad and Tobago, and Uruguay.) Twenty-four more Latin American states have joined since that time.

Mexico modernized its patent law in 1991 and became a member of the North American Free Trade Agreement in 1994. The patent provisions of the NAFTA generally parallel those of the TRIPS Agreement, with the addition of "pipeline protection" for pharmaceutical and agricultural chemicals. NAFTA art. 1709.4. ("Pipeline protection" offers the holder of an unexpired patent on such products in another NAFTA member state patent protection in Mexico for the unexpired term of the patent in the United States or Canada, as long as the product has not been marketed in Mexico.) Enforcement and validity of Mexican patents are determined in the first instance by the Mexican Institute of Industrial Property ("IMPI").

The five Central American countries (Guatemala, El Salvador, Honduras, Nicaragua, and Costa Rica) signed the Central American Convention for the Protection of Industrial Property in 1968; however, this agreement did not cover patents. It did establish the Central American Permanent Secretariat on Economic Integration ("SEICA"), which began work on a regional covenant for patents in February 1997. That work is ongoing.

On October 21, 1993, the four countries of the Andean Pact (Columbia, Ecuador, Peru, and Venezuela) which are parties to the Cartagena Agreement adopted Decision No. 344, entitled *Common Provisions on Industrial Property. See* INDUS. PROP. (March 1994) Text 1-012. This decision established uniform standards of patentability throughout the Andean Pact countries (now called the "Andean Union"). Among the items still excluded from patentability by Decision No. 344 are inventions relating to pharmaceutical products appearing on the List of Essential Drugs of the World Health Organization. Art. 7(e). Decision No. 344 also established that working requirements for an Andean patent could be met by importation. Art. 38.

The countries of the South American Common Market, MERCOSUR (Brazil, Argentina, Uruguay and Paraguay) recently established an intellectual property commission to study and propose harmonized treatment of intellectual property. The focus of these discussions is not on patents, however, but on trademarks.

Broader discussions have taken place within the framework of the Latin American and Caribbean Forum on Intellectual Property Policies of the Latin American Economic System ("SELA"), which has its permanent secretariat in Caracas, and which has focused its studies on the impact of the TRIPS Agreement on the member countries. UNESCO has been a source of support for the activities of SELA.

[E] Proposed Free Trade Area of the Americas ("FTAA")

Following acceptance of the NAFTA by Canada, Mexico, and the United States in late 1993, and the Andean Pact and MERCOSUR developments mentioned above, focus of attention among trade officials shifted to expanding the depth and scope of international economic relations between a greater number of the countries of the Western Hemisphere, consistent with the obligations of these countries under Article XXIV of the GATT Agreement and Article V of the GATS Agreement. Intellectual property became one of the central issues in negotiating broader multilateral trade cooperation between the United States and a greater number of countries in the South and Central American region. This culminated in negotiations between the United States and a number of other countries in the Western Hemisphere toward closer economic integration through the Free Trade Area of the Americas at a ministerial level meeting in 1995 in Miami. Intellectual property rights were originally one of the key areas for negotiation of the FTAA. One purpose of the FTAA negotiations was to maximize the openness of markets through high levels of compliance with the existing agreements (such as the TRIPS Agreement) regarding intellectual property rights and their creation, maintenance, and protection and eventual adoption of "TRIPS-plus" or even "NAFTA-level-plus" protection of IPRs throughout the Western Hemisphere.

The Miami ministerial meeting also requested progress reports from the Working Group on Smaller Economies to recommend measures, including technical assistance, to facilitate the integration of smaller economies into the FTAA. The Inter-American Development Bank ("IDB") was slated to set up a multilateral investment fund as a principal way of stimulating the development of intellectual property rights in Latin American countries. In December 1995, the Office of the USTR promulgated proposed terms of reference for action by the Working Group on Intellectual Property including the following recommendations:

- [to] create an inventory of intellectual property agreements, treaties, and arrangements that exist in the region, including all international conventions (*e.g.*, Berne, Paris, Geneva Phonograms, WIPO, etc.) to which countries are parties;

- compile in the most efficient manner possible an inventory of intellectual property protection laws, practices, and remedies in the region and, on the basis of this information, identify areas of commonality and make specific recommendations in accordance with the goal of establishing a high and effective level of protection throughout the Hemisphere and of ensuring that standards of protection are not eroded by advances in technology;

• recommend methods to promote understanding of the TRIPS Agreement and recommend measures for the effective and prompt implementation of that Agreement;

• identify measures to eliminate possible restrictions on the market access of intellectual property-related products and services throughout the Hemisphere, including through electronic transmission;

• identify measures to improve the administration of intellectual property rights, such as by facilitating the application for and grant of intellectual property rights;

• identify needs for training and technical assistance, involving both the substantive levels of intellectual property protection and the effective enforcement of intellectual property rights; and

• recommend methods to promote greater public understanding of the nature and importance of intellectual property protection throughout the Hemisphere.

The above proposed terms of reference were presented to the March 1996 Second Ministerial Trade Meeting at Cartagena, Columbia. There, they were revised, under the chairmanship of Honduras, to eliminate the emphasis on market restrictions and administrative improvements which had been central to the U.S. position.

A ministerial meeting was held in Belo Horizonte, Minas Gerais, Brazil in May 1997, where one of the areas under consideration was expanded coordination of intellectual property protection standards within the FTAA. At the Belo Horizonte meeting, in the face of continued inability of the United States to obtain Congressional approval for fast-track authority for U.S. negotiators, Brazil's support for the concept of FTAA as a merger of smaller regional trade agreements, with NAFTA and MERCOSUR as co-equal anchors, grew in popularity. Thus, there appears to be considerable and continued resistance to a pan-American intellectual property system spearheaded by and dominated by the United States—particularly in the area of patent law—and support for Latin American integration in patent matters as a counterbalance to the United States. At the Sixth Ministerial Meeting in April 2001, the headquarters of the FTAA Secretariat was moved to Panama. See www.ftaa-alca.org.

§ 6.04   Regional Design Rights

[A]   The European Union: The Community Design Regulation[1]

In 1991, the European Commission undertook a review of existing design protection within the countries of the EU. This revealed a wide divergence in the means by which individual countries protected designs, generating significant costs for EU producers and erecting barriers to the free movement of goods. Thus, two years later, in order to reduce territorial obstacles to the efficient working of the internal market and to ease the burden on producers seeking separate national design registrations in order to secure Community-wide protection, the Commission proposed a regulation that would create unitary EU-wide *sui generis* design rights. *See* Proposal for a European Parliament and Council Regulation on the Community Design, COM(93)342 final (Dec. 1993). The alternative of harmonizing member states' laws (which had been used in minimizing differences in national protection accorded computer software, databases, and semiconductor topographies) would be inadequate in this context. Harmonization in itself would not preclude the partitioning of markets that territorial protection creates; in contrast, the introduction of a single, autonomous law obviates the problems wrought by territorial protection. And where registered rights are involved, unlike the rights by which databases or software was protected, harmonization would not substantially reduce the costs involved in applying for rights separately in each country. Strategically, the Commission found exclusive reliance on a harmonization directive unappealing because approximation of the many different national systems of copyright and unfair competition under which designs are protected looked infeasible, and the Commission believed that the negotiation of a new instrument "could be developed with greater freedom than change to be introduced in existing legislation. . . . One could hope that member states would look for the most appropriate and advanced solutions when starting from scratch." Accordingly, the cornerstone of the proposals was the creation of federal design rights, to be implemented by the enactment of a regulation. That regulation was adopted in December 2001. *See* Council Regulation (EC) No. 6/2002 of 12 December 2001 on community designs, O.J. (L 003) 1 (Jan. 5, 2002) (the "Design Regulation").

The regulation provides a producer with two separate, but related, EU-wide rights with which to protect its design: a Registered Community Design, obtained by application to the Community Design Office, with an initial term of five years (renewable up to twenty-five years); and an Unregistered Community Design right that endures for a period of three years after the design is made available to the public. Most member states have some form of registered design protection at present—and those that

---

[1] This analysis is based upon a more lengthy (and earlier) consideration of the proposals in Graeme B. Dinwoodie, *Federalized Functionalism: The Future of Design Protection in the European Union*, 24 AM. INTELL. PROP. L. ASS'N Q.J. 611 (1996).

do not (Greece) will be required by the parallel Design Harmonization Directive adopted in 1998 to establish such protection, *see supra* § 3.03[B]—but the introduction of the unregistered right is an innovation, if one that is based largely on a similar right first introduced in the United Kingdom in 1988. The purpose of providing protection without registration is to accommodate industries that develop large numbers of designs, only a few of which are commercially exploited, and whose products are short-lived. For these industries, such as fashion and textiles, almost any registration process will remain an overly expensive, unduly time-consuming and not particularly helpful proposition. The registration *process*, particularly if it involves a substantive examination, ordinarily extends beyond the commercial life of the design. For these industries, some form of automatic short-term protection against unauthorized reproduction is necessary (and, largely, sufficient).

Assertion of rights under the unregistered community design system will not prevent application for a community registered design. The two forms of protection are granted on the same conditions and are subject to the same exclusions; any design that could be registered will be entitled to unregistered design protection. Indeed, one of the benefits that the Commission foresees from this structure is the ability of the producer to test the design in the marketplace with the protection offered by the unregistered design right and, if the design proves successful, within one year (the applicable grace period) to seek registration of that design. The substantive provisions governing eligibility for protection under the regulation—in either unregistered or registered form—are intended to mirror those found in the Harmonization Directive. *See supra* § 3.03[B]. Consequently, a revised version of the initial proposal, incorporating changes made to the directive during its progress through the legislative process, was published for consideration on June 21, 1999. *See* Amended Proposal for a Council Regulation on Community Design, COM(1999)310 final (June 21, 1999). After receiving opinions and proposed amendments from the European Parliament and the Economic and Social Committee, the Commission published a further revised proposal in November 2000. *See* Amended Proposal for a Council Regulation on Community Design, COM(2000)660 final/2 (Nov. 23, 2000) (the "Further Amended Proposed Regulation"). The regulation provides does not seek to resolve the contentious repair clause debate and, pending the expected Commission proposal to amend the directive after analyzing its effect on the spare parts market, so-called must-match parts will be excluded from EU registration. Indeed, the Commission has indicated that it intends to make parallel proposals to amend the spare parts provisions of both the directive and the regulation in 2004.

The primary differences between the registered and unregistered rights relate to the date of commencement of protection, and the term and scope of protection obtained. The unregistered protection subsists upon the design being made available to the public within the EU, while registered protection runs from the date of the filing of an application for registration. *See* Design Regulation arts. 11-12. While the rights conferred by a design registration are in the nature of monopoly rights, the owner of the unregistered community design obtains only the right to prevent unauthorized reproduction. *See id.* art. 19. That is to say, independent creation is a defense in an action for infringement of an unregistered, but not a registered, design. *See* Explanatory Memorandum Accompanying the Amended Proposal for a Council Regulation on Community Design, COM(2000)660 final/2 (Nov. 23, 2000) at 4. The Commission settled on a term of three years for unregistered protection; however, because the conditions for protection do not vary as between registered and unregistered designs, each design protected for three years can, by timely application, receive protection of a patent-like nature for up to twenty-five years. *See* Further Amended Proposed Regulation arts. 12-13.

To accommodate the concerns of industry regarding the costs and delay of design registration, the regulation effected two changes to a full-blown registration system. First, the unregistered design right has been included as an integral part of the solution. Second, the registration system will be a "passive" registration (or deposit) system.[1] The Community Design Office will check applications only for obviously inappropriate subject matter and formal deficiencies. *See* Official Commentary on Proposed Article 48, in Explanatory Memorandum Accompanying the Proposal for a European Parliament and Council Regulation on the Community Design, COM(93) 342 final-COD 463 (Brussels, 3 Dec. 1993). The Community Design Office will be the same institution established to deal with trademark applications under the Trademark Regulation, and the procedural mechanisms thus bear strong similarity to those under which the Trademark Office in Alicante has been working since January 1, 1996. For example, an application for design registration may be filed at the Community Design Office or at the central industrial property office of a member state. *See* Design Regulation art. 35. In most countries of the EU, the registration of the design leads to its publication, and that will generally be the case under the design proposals. Provision is made, however, for the possibility of deferred publication in order to maintain the secrecy of the design.

Over the course of the evolution of these proposals, the abolition of substantive examinations appears to have become a priority in the thinking of the Commission. Ironically, however, although the 1960 text of the Hague Agreement was not tailored to accommodate systems that perform extensive substantive examinations, *see* Hague Agreement Concerning the Deposit of Industrial Designs (Hague text, 1960) art. 8(1) (requiring member countries to issue rejection within six months), the recent revision of that agreement is largely intended to permit the involvement of countries

---

[1] The use of passive registration mirrors the nature of the examination under design laws currently in place in several countries of the European Union. (For example, the registration proceedings in the Benelux countries do not involve substantive examination, nor do those in France, Italy and Spain. The U.K. authorities do examine for substantive compliance with the requirements of their act.)

that subject design registration applications to substantive examination. *See supra* § 6.03.

NOTES AND QUESTIONS

(1) **Scope of Protection**. One of the few distinctions between the registered community design and the unregistered community design right is the scope of protection. In practice, how big a difference does this make, especially if courts assessing infringement of unregistered rights follow copyright jurisprudence and are willing to presume copying from access and probative similarity? Should courts indulge that presumption? Should it be modified when dealing with functional designs, and if so, in what ways? *Cf. Computer Assocs. v. Altai, Inc.*, 982 F.2d 693, 708 (2d Cir. 1992) ("Under [the circumstance that programmers are trying to create the most efficient programs possible], the fact that two programs contain the same efficient structure may as likely lead to an inference of independent creation as it does to one of copying.")

Why did the Commission wish to offer designers patent-like rights upon registration? Would producers' legitimate concerns have been addressed by a lesser scope of rights? *See* Dinwoodie, *supra*, at 701-02. What justifies the broader scope of protection for registered rights? Do those justifications extend to the type of registration envisaged by the proposed regulation? *See id.* at 722 (criticizing the grant of "drive-through monopoly rights"). Should variables other than registration affect the scope of protection granted by intellectual property rights? *See id.* at 655-57 n.123-25 (discussing other linkages); Uma Suthersanen, *Breaking Down the Intellectual Property Barriers*, 2 INTELL. PROP. Q. 267, 289-90 (1998) (linking scope of protection to constraints on the creative process). For example, why does copyright offer a lesser scope of protection than patent? Is the registered nature of patent rights the sole reason?

(2) **Unregistered Rights**. If the Commission wished to create an automatic, short-term protection against unauthorized copying, what options were available to it? Why do you think it chose to introduce the (relatively new) concept of an unregistered design right? What dangers flow from granting industrial property rights without registration? Do these justify insisting upon registration before protection? What are the problems of using a novelty standard for unregistered rights? *See* Lionel Bently & Alan Coulthard, *From the Commonplace to the Interface: Five Cases on Unregistered Design Right*, 19 EUR. INTELL. PROP. REV. 401, 407 (1997) (discussing dangers of novelty standard).

(3) **Institutional Issues**. Authoritative interpretations by the European Court of Justice will, to some extent, assist in establishing a common understanding of the new design protection thresholds. That standardizing influence will, however, only be felt periodically, and in a non-examining

system there will be fewer *administrative* determinations from which to forge a collective sense of these concepts. The primary administrative proceeding in which such a sense could be developed would be actions for declarations of invalidity of the registered community design, for which the Community Design Office will have primary, but not exclusive, jurisdiction. *See* Design Regulation art. 52 (conferring jurisdiction on Community Office), arts. 24(1), 81(c) (conferring jurisdiction on national courts designated as community design courts to adjudicate counterclaims seeking declaration of invalidity of registered community design, and to adjudicate direct actions for declaration of invalidity of unregistered community design). Should the central institutions—the European Court or the Community Design Office—have exclusive jurisdiction in such matters? What benefits would such a change produce? Would it have any costs?

The initial proposal expressly reserved the right of the Commission to challenge a registered community design before the Community Design Office and the European Court of Justice if it believed that the design did not meet the standards of protectability, *see* Proposed Regulation art. 56, and an advisory committee on designs would have been established to assist the Commission in determining whether such action needed to be taken. As the proposal evolved, however, the standing of the Commission (and member states) to bring or appear in invalidity proceedings before the office was removed. *See* Design Regulation art. 52. The explanatory memorandum accompanying the 1999 proposals suggested that such office standing would be neither "appropriate nor opportune," but notes the inherent right of the Commission and member states (under Court of Justice case law) to bring an action before the Court of Justice against any decision by the office, or (under the statute of the Court of Justice) to intervene in any appeal before the Court. *See* Explanatory Memorandum Accompanying Amended Proposal for a Council Regulation on Community Design, COM(1999)310 final (June 21, 1999) at 10.

(4) **Passive Examination**. What is the value of a registration system that foregoes substantive examination and instead triggers the formalities-only search envisaged by the Design Regulation? *See* Report of the Departmental Committee on Industrial Designs (Johnston Committee), Cmnd. 1808 (1962) (U.K.) ¶ 12 (noting that the textile industry relied on the "limited" searches conducted by the Manchester Registry as a "rough and ready test of infringement" that would influence whether the manufacturer exploited the design commercially).

(5) **The Relationship Between National and Community Design Rights.** The continued existence of the varied national forms of design protection might be expected to precipitate the need to referee inevitable conflicts that will occur between community and national rights. The Commission appears to have relied upon the fact that (in most cases) the universal, time-unlimited nature of the novelty and individual character determinations will ensure that protection under the national law of a member state will prevent protection as a Community design, or as a

registered design under the newly-harmonized national laws. One express provision on "conflict resolution" is included in the regulation. Several member states provide the option of maintaining the secrecy of a design registration in various circumstances. Such "unpublished" designs will not destroy the novelty or individual character of any later design seeking protection as a community design because they are not "made available to the public." Yet, the secrecy provisions of national laws would be rendered meaningless if these earlier national registrations were superseded by the community rights. Accordingly, the community rights will be invalid as against the holder of the national registration in the country of that registration, but not as against third parties or in other countries of the union. *See* Design Regulation arts. 25(1)(d), 25(3).

(6) **Treatment of Third Country Designers.** The U.K. government took the position that it could condition *its* unregistered design right on reciprocal protection without violating its obligations under either the Paris or Berne Conventions. *See* CHRISTINE FELLNER, INDUSTRIAL DESIGN LAW 125-26 (1995) (explaining reasoning of the U.K. government). While the TRIPS Agreement retained the exceptions to national treatment found in the Paris and Berne Conventions, *see* art. 3, commentators have suggested that the MFN obligations contained in Article 4 should void such conditions of material reciprocity. *See* J. H. Reichman, *Universal Minimum Standards of Intellectual Property Protection under the TRIPS Component of the WTO Agreement*, 29 INT. LAW. 345, 349 n.27 (1995). Although the spirit of the TRIPS Agreement (and the Paris Convention) would suggest that design rights should be available on a national treatment basis, the Commission's intentions with respect to the conditions under which the proposed unregistered community design right would be available to non-EU producers are not evident from any of its formal communications.

(7) **Legislative Basis of the EU Legislation.** Initially, the Commission grounded the submission of both the directive and the proposed regulation on ex-Article 100a of the EC Treaty, under which enactment requires adoption by a majority of the European Parliament and a qualified majority of the Council of Ministers. After the Commission submitted its design proposals, however, the member states suggested (and the Commission agreed) that the proper legal basis for adoption of the regulation was ex-Article 235 of the E.C. Treaty. Ex-Article 235 (now new Article 308) provides for the consideration of legislation pursuant to the more straightforward "consultation" procedure, which requires unanimous approval by the member states (as represented in Council) but envisages a lesser role for the European Parliament. In particular, legislation can be enacted under Article 308 over the objections of the Parliament. The stated legal basis of the adopted regulation was Article 308.

(8) **Link to the Hague Agreement.** The Commission has indicated an intent to link the community design to the Hague Agreement in much the same way that the community trademark has been linked to the Madrid Protocol. *See* Geneva Act of the Hague Agreement Concerning the International Registration of Industrial Designs art. 27(1)(ii) (July 2, 1999).

(9) **Implementation of the Regulation.** Although the provisions of the regulation regarding the unregistered design right do not require further implementation, and thus came into effect in early 2002, the EU must adopt an implementing regulation to fashion the administrative tools necessary for the registration of designs with the OHIM. The Commission adopted such an implementing regulation in October 2002 (which, in so far as is possible, parallels the implementing regulation governing trademark registration with the OHIM), and this will be discussed with member states in early 2003. At present, it is anticipated that the OHIM will begin registering Community designs in early 2003, with the first official registrations taking effect from April 2003.

[B]   Other Regional Groupings

Like developments in the trademark area, the EU exercise is not the sole example of regional groupings that have moved toward unitary supranational design rights. The EU regulation, if adopted, would frame current debate, but other regions already have unitary design rights. Again, the Benelux has been a leader, introducing the unitary Benelux design right in 1975. Design has, however, always been the poor cousin of international intellectual property laws, and thus there has been less international pressure to develop effective design laws. Accordingly, many of the regional groupings discussed above that have given detailed consideration to regional patents and trademarks, have only tentatively addressed the question of unitary design rights. Whether the revised Hague Agreement gives international design protection new impetus remains to be seen.

Epilogue

The different international agreements discussed in this Chapter all move from national to international forms of protection in slightly different ways: they represent, in short, different degrees of internationalization. Can you place each of the systems instituted on a spectrum from national to international models? What are the elements common to each system; in what ways are they different? Would a single model work for all of the different intellectual property rights? Would the same model work for both regional and global agreements? If not, why not?

Chapter 7

INTERNATIONAL ENFORCEMENT OF
PATENT RIGHTS BY RIGHT HOLDERS

§ 7.01 Remedies Under National Laws

A range of remedies are available for the infringement of intellectual property rights under national laws, including criminal penalties as well as various forms of monetary and equitable or injunctive relief. The nature and extent of these remedies varies from country to country, depending in large part on variations in legal systems. They share common goals, however: to put a stop to the infringement; to make the right holder whole; and to punish infringers and provide meaningful deterrence. The relative mix and effectiveness of civil and criminal actions is different in different countries, depending on such factors as the efficiency and cost of the judicial system and the willingness of the government to initiate prosecutions.

The legislation of most countries typically makes available a combination of some or all of the following civil remedies: actual damages suffered by the right holder; some form of statutory, exemplary or punitive damages; recovery of the infringer's profits; injunctions against continued infringement (both as part of the ultimate judgment in the lawsuit and provisionally, to prevent the infringement from continuing pending the resolution of the lawsuit); seizure of infringing materials and/or the equipment used to make them; and a mechanism for customs agencies to prevent entry into the country of infringing materials.

As to equitable remedies, final injunctions are virtually always available to require the defendant to cease the infringing acts. Most countries also provide some form of provisional relief during the pendency of the lawsuit, with the purpose of preserving the status quo, preventing the accumulation of damage from ongoing infringement, and ensuring that evidence is not destroyed, although the frequency of the use of provisional relief tends to be less in patent than in copyright and trademark cases. Typical of these remedies is the Anton Piller order in the United Kingdom to preserve evidence. Anton Piller orders are also used in trade secret and industrial espionage cases. Courts in some countries may also be authorized to order the seizure or destruction of infringing copies and/or the equipment used to make them. Finally, customs agencies often have authority to seize infringing materials at the border to prevent their importation into the country. The standards and requirements of proof to trigger such government action differ from country to country.

Criminal penalties are available in cases brought by the government, and in some countries, in private actions as well. This is especially true in developing countries such as those in Asia where wilful patent infringement is frequent, but not in the United States. Where criminal penalties do exist, they are generally limited to the more egregious cases of infringement, involving wrongful intent and often some degree of commerciality. The penalties include fines as well as prison terms. There is a tremendous range from country to country in the level of both fines and prison terms, reflecting perceptions of what is sufficient deterrence for such a crime in the conditions prevailing in that particular country.

§ 7.02   National Enforcement Under International Law

It is frequently remarked that the achievement of the TRIPS Agreement was its "enforcement" provisions. This term is, however, often used in two different senses. First, as seen in Chapter 5, the TRIPS Agreement addressed the enforcement of states' international obligations by making compliance an issue that could be subject to the WTO Dispute Settlement procedures. Second, the substantive provisions of the TRIPS Agreement went beyond existing intellectual property conventions by delineating standards to which procedures for private enforcement of domestic intellectual property rights would be measured in Part III of TRIPS. This second set of "enforcement" provisions is covered in this section of Chapter 7. The following reading discusses the importance of the TRIPS Agreement for enforcement of copyright, but the principles are equally applicable to enforcement of patent rights.

ADRIAN OTTEN, THE FUNDAMENTAL IMPORTANCE OF THE TRIPS AGREEMENT FOR A BETTER ENFORCEMENT OF COPYRIGHT[*]
Paper Presented to ALAI Congress (Berlin, June 1999)

One of the major features and innovations of the TRIPS Agreement is that it gives as much attention to the enforcement of intellectual property rights through domestic legal procedures as it does to the substantive standards which should be provided for their protection. A weakness of the pre-existing international law in the area of intellectual property was that it was very largely silent on the issue of enforcement. . . . I will discuss the requirements in the TRIPS Agreement on Members to provide domestic procedures and remedies so that right holders can secure the effective enforcement of their rights.

. . . .

Procedures and Remedies for the Enforcement of Intellectual Property Rights

Part III of the TRIPS Agreement concerns procedures and remedies to be provided at the national level for the enforcement of intellectual property rights. These provisions have two main objectives:

---

* First, to permit effective action against any act of infringement, including expeditious remedies to prevent infringements and remedies which constitute a deterrent to further infringements.

* Second, they aim to avoid the creation of barriers to legitimate trade and to provide for safeguards against the abuse of procedures. This second aspect reflects the underlying concern in the TRIPS Agreement to provide for a balance between the interests of producers and those of users of intellectual property. Provisions which reflect this concern can be found notably in the safeguards that have to be provided in relation to the use of measures of a provisional nature, including border measures, such as in regard to time-limits, the possibility that applicants may be required to lodge a security, etc.

[T]he TRIPS enforcement rules . . . constitute the first international disciplines ever negotiated on domestic enforcement procedures and remedies. Thus, to some extent, we are still in the testing phase. Notably, it remains to be seen how successful were the negotiators in producing a set of rules that is precise enough to be meaningful and, if necessary, justiciable through the WTO dispute settlement mechanism, but yet on the other hand sufficiently general to take into account differences in national legal systems, as was required by the mandate given to the negotiators, as well as to respect judicial discretion.

The rules in the TRIPS Agreement on enforcement are not intended to be revolutionary, nor are they intended to lead to a harmonization of national enforcement systems. Rather, they are a compilation of the basic features of good enforcement procedures and remedies that can be found in the main national legal systems. Moreover, it should be recalled that, like the rest of the TRIPS Agreement, they are minimum standards, in the sense that Members are free to, but not obliged to, implement in their law more extensive protection than that required by the Agreement, provided that, in doing so, they do not contravene the provisions of the Agreement. Most persons who read them will find little that is new or surprising in them. However, many countries have had or will have to make some changes to be fully in conformity, especially, but not only, in the area of special border measures.

Also by way of a general observation concerning the TRIPS enforcement rules, I think it is useful to distinguish within them two types of obligation:

* The first are those which prescribe procedures and remedies that must be provided by each Member in its national legal system. Much of this is set out in terms of the authority that must be available to judges and courts or other competent authorities, such as the customs administration.

* The second type of obligation is what might be described as "performance standards" in relation to the workings of these procedures and practice. For example, they must be such as to permit effective action against infringing activity, expeditious and deterrent remedies and applied in a manner that will avoid the creation of barriers to legitimate trade.

The enforcement provisions of the TRIPS Agreement are divided into five sections. The first of these entitled "General Obligations" relates to all enforcement procedures and remedies. The next two, regarding civil and administrative procedures and remedies and provisional measures, concern the infringement of any intellectual property right covered by the TRIPS Agreement, that is to say the seven categories of intellectual property with which the TRIPS Agreement deals. The last two sections, those relating to border measures and criminal procedures, must apply at least to trademark counterfeiting and copyright piracy, but Members are, of course, free to apply such procedures to other infringing acts as well.

Section 1: General Obligations

This section contains the basic objectives and performance standards to which I have already referred. It also contains some basic rules of due process—that procedures should be fair and equitable, and that decisions should, as a rule, be in writing and reasoned, made available without undue delay and based only on the evidence in respect of which parties are offered the opportunity to be heard. It also provides for rights of review. In addition, it requires that procedures shall not be unnecessarily complicated or costly, or entail unreasonable time limits or unwarranted delays.

A further part of the general obligations section addresses concerns that were raised during the negotiations, particularly by developing countries, about the problems that they would have if they were required to devote disproportionate resources to the enforcement of intellectual property rights. The formulation that was reached after negotiation reads as follows:

> It is understood that this Part does not create any obligation to put in place a judicial system for the enforcement of intellectual property rights distinct from that for the enforcement of law in general, nor does it affect the capacity of Members to enforce their law in general. Nothing in this Part creates any obligation with respect to the distribution of resources as between enforcement of intellectual property rights and the enforcement of law in general.

Section 2: Civil Administrative Procedures and Remedies

This section is essentially concerned with civil judicial procedures but also requires that if civil remedies can be ordered as a result of administrative procedures, such procedures shall conform to principles equivalent in substance to those set forth in the section.

The section firstly fleshes out the concept of fair and equitable procedures in regard to such matters as rights to written notice, rights of representation, rights to present evidence and the protection of confidential information. It also addresses the authority that judges must have to order that evidence be produced by a party, against its will, in appropriate situations. This is, of course, an area where there is a wide difference between the practices of WTO Members, for example the discovery system in the United States and the civil law practices in Continental Europe. Nonetheless, a formulation acceptable to all Members was reached.

Most of the rest of the section specifies the remedies that judges and courts must have the authority to order, including injunctions, damages and, in appropriate situations, forfeiture and disposal outside the channels of commerce of infringing goods as well as materials and implements predominantly used in their production. There is also a provision requiring judicial authorities to be able to order the indemnification of defendants who have been wrongfully enjoined or restrained as a result of abuse of enforcement procedures by a plaintiff.

Section 3: Provisional Measures

Under the TRIPS Agreement, WTO Members must ensure that their judicial authorities have the power to order prompt and effective provisional measures both to prevent an infringement and to preserve relevant evidence in regard to an alleged infringement. In appropriate cases, they must have the authority to do this without prior notice being given to the respondent, in particular where any delay is likely to cause irreparable harm to the right holder or where there is a demonstrable risk of evidence being destroyed.

The question of the availability of provisional measures on an ex parte basis under civil judicial procedures has been the subject of two dispute settlement complaints, both by the United States; one against Denmark and the other against Sweden. This issue appears to be one of particular concern to the computer software industry, given the apparent ease with which evidence of the use of infringing programs can be eradicated if prior notice of search and seizure measures is given. One of these disputes, that concerning Sweden, has led to a bilateral mutually agreed solution. The WTO was informed that, to fulfil its TRIPS obligations, Sweden had amended its intellectual property laws so as to give judicial authorities in Sweden the authority to order provisional measures in the context of civil proceedings involving [intellectual property rights] (IPRs). The legislation provides that if there is reason to believe that a person has taken or is about to take action to infringe IPRs, the court may order a search for infringing materials, documents or other relevant evidence and that this might be done *inaudita altera parte* if there is a risk that materials or documents could be moved, destroyed or altered. The other complaint is still the subject of consultations under the dispute settlement process.

The remaining provisions of the section on provisional measures concern various forms of safeguards to ensure that such measures are not abused or used as barriers to legitimate trade.

Section 4: Special Requirements Related to Border Measures

The basic obligation under this section is that Members must provide a means, whether through administrative or judicial bodies, by which right holders can obtain the assistance of the customs administration to prevent the importation of at least counterfeit trademark goods and pirated copyright goods. For this purpose, counterfeit trademark goods are, in essence, defined as goods involving more flagrant types of copying of trademarks and pirated goods as goods which violate a reproduction right in the area of copyright or related rights. Members are free to apply these procedures to other types of infringing activity, provided they respect the safeguards required, but not obliged to do so. Goods in transit, parallel imports and small quantities of a non-commercial nature do not have to be covered by these procedures.

The requirement in the TRIPS Agreement is to put in place a mechanism which can be initiated by the right holder lodging an application to the competent national authorities. Ex officio action by national authorities is not a requirement, but is envisaged provided the appropriate safeguards are respected.

Section 5: Criminal Procedures

The TRIPS Agreement requires Members to provide criminal procedures and penalties to be applied at least in cases of wilful trademark counterfeiting or copyright piracy on a commercial scale. Remedies must be sufficient to provide a deterrent consistent with the level of penalties applied for crimes of a corresponding gravity. Once again, although it is not a requirement, the Agreement envisages that Members may provide for criminal procedures and penalties to be applied in other cases of infringement of IPRs, in particular where they are committed wilfully and on a commercial scale.

Compliance with the requirements of this section, read in conjunction with the general enforcement obligations of the TRIPS Agreement that I referred to earlier, is the subject of a dispute between the United States on the one hand and Greece and the European Communities on the other. This concerns the availability of effective remedies against copyright infringement in Greece with respect to unauthorized broadcasts of motion pictures and television programmes. This matter is at the consultation phase of the dispute settlement system.

NOTES AND QUESTIONS

(1) **Direct Effect of TRIPS Article 50 in Europe.** The European Court of Justice addressed the question of the direct effect of TRIPS in Case C-149/96, *Portugal v. Council*, 1999 E.C.R. I-8395, a trademark case, where

it held that the provisions of TRIPS do not, as a matter of EU law, create rights upon which individuals may rely directly before national courts. *See id.* at ¶¶ 42–46. And in a recent case, Case C-300/98, *Parfums Christian Dior v. Tuk Consultancy,* 2001 E.T.M.R. 276 (E.C.J. 2000), the Court was asked to confront directly whether Article 50(6) has direct effect such that it could be invoked by litigants in the absence of a corresponding provision in Dutch law. The Court affirmed its holding in *Portugal v. Council,* but emphasized that:

> in a field to which TRIPS applies and in respect of which the Community has already legislated, [national courts] are required by virtue of Community law, when called upon to apply national rules [regarding] provisional measures for the protection of rights falling within such a field, to do so as far as possible in light of the wording and purpose of Article 50 of TRIPS.

Id. at 289. If the field is one in which the Community has not legislated, EU law "neither requires nor forbids" member states from giving direct effect to Article 50(6) and permitting individuals from relying on its terms. *See id.*

(2) **WTO Proceedings With Respect to Enforcement Obligations**. As Adrian Otten notes in his paper, the United States is engaged in consultations with Greece regarding compliance with obligations found in Part III of the TRIPS Agreement. Indeed, of the twenty-four TRIPS complaints initiated thus far, nine have involved (at least in part) compliance with obligations found in Part III of TRIPS. *See also* United States—Section 211 of Omnibus Appropriations Act of 1998 ("Havana Club"), Report of the Appellate Body, WT/DS176/AB/R (WTO 2002), *supra* § 5.03[D].

§ 7.03   Multinational Enforcement Issues

[A]   National Enforcement of a European Patent

EDWARD ARMITAGE, INTERPRETATION OF EUROPEAN PATENTS
(ART. 69 EPC AND THE PROTOCOL ON THE INTERPRETATION)*
14 I.I.C. 811–817 (1983)

1. Introduction

In any patent action the essential questions for the court are: is the patent valid and is it infringed? These questions may be taken separately, by different courts, as in Germany, but they may also be taken by the same

---

* Reprinted with permission of the Max Planck Institute for Foreign and International Patent, Copyright and Competition Law and Wiley-VCH Publishers.

court and have commonly to be considered together in the same action. For both questions, the interpretation of the patent, and more particularly of the patent claims, is of crucial importance.

The role of the claims in a European patent, and the principles governing their interpretation, are set out in Arts. 69 and 84 of the [European Patent Convention] ("EPC") and the Protocol on Interpretation of Art. 69. Before looking more closely at the significance of these provisions, perhaps we should ask: to what extent are they binding on national courts in an action on a European patent in what one might call "the national phase?"

2. The European Patent in the National Phase

Article 2(2) EPC states that the European patent shall, in each of the Contracting States for which it is granted, have the effect of and be subject to the same conditions as a national patent granted by the State, unless otherwise provided in the Convention. Does the Convention provide that Arts. 69 and 84 shall override the corresponding provisions of national law which would otherwise be applied to a European patent as to a national patent? Admittedly there is nothing in the Convention which says so directly and one has to turn to the implications of the main exception to the application of national law, *viz.* Art. 138.

Article 138(1) says, in effect, that the validity of a European patent can be attacked in the national phase (*i.e.* after grant) only on the basis of what one might call "European" grounds, *i.e.* the same grounds on which it was granted. Two of these grounds are particularly relevant:

Ground (a)—that the patent is not patentable under the terms of the substantive law in EPC Arts. 52 to 57.

Ground (d)—that the protection conferred by the European patent has been extended.

In granting the patent, the European Patent Office applies Arts. 52–57 and Art. 123(3) (which corresponds to ground (d) just mentioned) in the context of the other Articles of the Convention. In particular, the effect of the patent claims, in applying Arts. 52–57 and 123(3), is determined by Arts. 69 and 84. Similarly, grounds (a) and (d) in Art. 138 cannot operate in a vacuum but carry with them the provisions of Arts. 69 and 84.

It seems inescapable, therefore, that a court will be bound by Arts. 69 and 84 as regards the validity of a patent. But is it equally bound to interpret claims in accordance with those Articles as regards infringement? Surely this must be so. It would be absurd—some might say a recipe for disaster—to interpret claims on one basis in determining their validity and on a different basis in then deciding whether they are infringed. This argument is particularly telling as regards validity ground (d); this ground is concerned with the extent of protection conferred by the patent which is, of course, exactly what the court is concerned with as regards infringement.

It is assumed, therefore, in what follows that the EPC provisions on interpretation are binding on national courts in European patent actions. What, then, do those provisions amount to?

Effect of Arts. 69(1) and 84 and the Protocol

The first point to note is that Art. 84 states that the claims define the matter for which protection is sought. Thus in deciding what it is that is to be protected against infringement, the court cannot look beyond the claims. But what, then, is to be the extent of that protection? (Here we are talking of technical features of a potential infringement, not the acts—making, using, selling etc.,—which constitute infringement, for which one has to look to national law.) This is where Art. 69(1) comes in. This states that the claims, in addition to defining the protected invention, also determine the extent of that protection. But a court, in applying Art. 69(1), is not forced to adopt the strict literal meaning of the claims. It can do so, of course, taking the claim to mean exactly what it says. But the court has some freedom to depart from the strict wording by virtue of the following:

(a) According to Art. 69(1), it is the "terms" of the claims ("teneur" in French and "Inhalt" in German), not the strict wording, which determines the extent of protection.

(b) Again, according to Art. 69(1), the description and drawings can be used to interpret the claims, so that the words in the claim may have to be given, for consistency with the description, a meaning different from that which they have in common usage.

(c) The flexibility thus afforded by Art. 69 is to be applied in accordance with the Protocol on its interpretation.

To appreciate the significance of all this, it may be useful to have a brief look at the history of those provisions in the Convention.

3. History

It is well known that Art. 69(1) derives from the corresponding provision (Art. 8) of the Strasbourg Convention on the harmonization of substantive patent law. This Article defining the function of the claims was one of the most difficult to agree [upon.] At the time, not all member countries of the Council of Europe had patent claims, properly speaking. In those that had, they were taken to define the invention but only in some (e.g. UK, Sweden and Switzerland) were they also stated to define the scope of the protection afforded by the patent. This reflected two different traditions of claim drafting and interpretation, exemplified by the Federal Republic of Germany and the Netherlands on the one hand and Switzerland and the UK on the other hand.

In German practice, the claims concentrated on defining the inventive step; a claim commonly generalized the invention only slightly; and the court had wide powers of generalizing from the claims in considering potential infringements. In UK practice, the generalization took place almost entirely in the wording of the claims as drafted, the court being prepared to generalize further to only a very limited extent. It was necessary to choose between these systems or to adopt some definable intermediate position.

The drafters of the Convention took a big step by stating that the claims should define "the protection applied for" rather than the "invention." At the same time it was accepted all round that courts should be free to depart from the literal meaning of the claims in the interests of justice either (a) where the claim was at variance with the description or (b) where the literal meaning would involve a quite unreasonable or pointless restriction. To deal with (a), the Swiss law was followed, requiring the description to be used to interpret the claims. To deal with (b) the Convention adopted the by-now familiar formula "the extent of the protection conferred by the patent shall be determined by the terms of the claims." It is important to know that "terms of the claims" and "teneur des revendications" in the French version were adopted deliberately as being somewhat broader than "words".

It was recognized that this still left the danger of this formula being applied either over-restrictively or over-liberally. To avoid this, the Council of Europe Committee recorded of the formula that "it seeks to lay down a principle for interpreting claims which is somewhere between the system in which claims may be interpreted strictly according to the letter and that in which they do not play a decisive part in defining the limits of protection."

So much for the Strasbourg history, which is highly relevant because the Strasbourg formula was adopted unchanged in Art. 69(1) of the EPC. But here a new problem arose over the German language term "Inhalt" corresponding to "terms" and "teneur" (the Strasbourg Convention was in English and French only). It was recognized as decidedly wider in significance than the English and French terms but there was no agreement to narrow the German term to match the English and French or to widen the English and French to match the German. This failure to agree highlighted the danger of subsequent divergent interpretations of the Convention. Eventually, the (admittedly varying) language texts were adopted unchanged on the basis that no one language was dominant and that all three versions have to be recognized as influencing the interpretation, and hence the application, of Art. 69. This was reinforced by the Protocol on Interpretation of Art. 69 which aimed to guard against an extreme interpretation of any one text. The Protocol follows very much the lines of the statement by the Council of Europe Committee, adding the desideratum of combining "a fair protection for the patentee with a reasonable degree of certainty for third parties."

4. Problems for Courts

This, then, is the background against which national courts will have to interpret the claims of European patents. The history shows the fears of the legislators that courts might diverge seriously by continuing to follow the long-standing traditions developed under earlier national laws. And, indeed, it is here that courts are likely to find most difficulty in harmonizing their attitudes.

However, this question of claim interpretation is the one where the courts have the biggest role to play in developing the system of European patent law. The Convention has been able to express only the broad lines and it remains now for court jurisprudence to fill in the details.

Two things are clear: that claims should be interpreted in the light of the patent specification as a whole and that courts are not bound by the literal meaning of the words of the claim. The crucial question is: how far should a court be prepared to stretch a claim beyond that literal meaning in the interests of fairness to the patentee? There seem to be two constraints at least:

> 1. In view of Art. 69(1), it seems that the claims must be assumed to have been broadly drafted in the first place, which perhaps suggests caution in any further broadening.

> 2. The requirement of "a reasonable degree of certainty for third parties" (Protocol) suggests that any stretching of the claim to cover an infringement should be reasonably predictable by a third party.

Could it be said of these constraints that they indicate that a stretched interpretation of a claim should not "do violence" to the language of that claim as read, in the light of a description, by an instructed person of the kind to whom the patent specification is addressed?

Within such constraints, however, "a fair protection for the patentee" (Protocol) suggests that claims may be stretched in interpretation so as to correct forgivable drafting oversight (no draftsman of claims is perfect) or failure to foresee possible variants of the claimed invention (no draftsman is omniscient).

I have concentrated almost entirely on the interpretation of claims in connection with infringement because it is there that the influences of Art. 69 and the Protocol are of supreme importance. I mentioned interpretation of claims in determining their validity only to say that the same principles apply. I should like to add something.

Professor Cornish has also referred to claim interpretation in considering novelty and inventive step and he made the same point when he said of the "invention" to which tests of novelty and inventive step are to be applied:

> I shall assume that the invention consists of anything . . . within the scope of protection sought by the claims of the specification.

I quite agree, but does this mean that in considering novelty and inventive step the EPO and national courts have to speculate as to the full range of manufactures which constitute potential infringement?

I would say most definitely "no." For one thing, it is not a practical proposition. It is one thing to decide that a claim can be stretched to cover an actual case of manufacture by a third party; it is quite another thing to decide what imaginary cases of manufacture the claim might be stretched to cover. More importantly, though, such speculation is unnecessary.

In considering whether a claim is valid in the face of a particular disclosure in the prior art, the Patent Office or court does not need to find that the disclosed manufacture falls within the terms of the claim. It has at its disposal EPC Art. 56. It suffices if it can be seen that what is claimed is an obvious variant of the prior art manufacture.

In practice, therefore, I think that claims can be taken at their face value as regards validity, although even then Art. 69 applies. The Patent Office or court must decide what the face value is, interpreting the "terms", "teneur" or "Inhalt" of the claims in the light of the specification as a whole, including the descriptions and drawings.

5. Recognition of Decisions in Different Countries

Just one more point. What influence does a decision on interpretation of a European patent, made by one national court, have on the courts of other member countries and on the EPO itself? Professor Mangini has rightly said that, strictly speaking, decisions of national courts on infringement or validity are effective only in the country concerned. Dr. Bruchhausen has amplified this, saying that although legal precedents in one Contracting State are not binding on interpretation in another, interpretation in one country should take account of precedents from other countries. I would respectfully agree. It is very much to be hoped that the courts of all member countries will contrive to develop a consistent common jurisprudence, much as the courts of Commonwealth countries have done in the past in applying similar provisions of their respective patent statutes. Decisions, while not binding, have been persuasive.

Consider an example. Identical infringing articles are marketed in France and Italy. The scope of protection of the European patent is the same in France and Italy, being determined by Art. 69. The validity is the same in both countries, being governed by Art. 138. A French court finds that the European patent is valid and infringed by the marketing in France. What influence will that have on the Italian court? Is the Brussels Convention on recognition of judgements applicable? Possibly not, but at least the French decision must be highly persuasive in Italy.

Consistent and harmonious jurisprudence is necessary not only to satisfy the aims of the Convention. It is essential if the EPO is to function smoothly. Dr. Bruchhausen has pointed out that decisions of the EPO on interpretation of the Convention are not paramount, *i.e.* binding on national courts. Indeed, surely the reverse applies? Every national Patent Office has to respect and apply interpretations of the law laid down by the national courts. Similarly the EPO has to be guided by interpretations laid down by the courts of Member States, but it can only be so guided to the extent that there is a consensus among the states. Where there is consensus on a particular point of law, the EPO can apply it firmly and confidently during the patent granting procedure. But if the jurisprudence is inconsistent and divergent, the EPO will be forced into a very cautious attitude, since it ought not to be refusing patents which national courts would find valid.

Of course, for full harmonization in litigation of the European patent in the EEC, and for central guidance for the EPO, we need—as referred to by Professor Mangini—the Community patent plus COPAC. But that is another story.

6. Conclusions

a. Article 69(1) and the Protocol do govern interpretation of European patents in national courts. We may hope that the same will apply to national patents.

b. Article 69(1) and the Protocol will tend to induce applicants to draft broad claims.

c. In deciding how much further to stretch the interpretation of claims, courts will have to bear in mind the presumption of broad drafting by the applicant.

d. It is to be hoped that national courts will treat decisions of other courts on European patents as highly persuasive. To that end, publication of important decisions in translation is most important.

e. Uniformity would be greatly assisted if COPAC were to be created. In the meantime, periodical meetings of judges should be of great value.

f. The European patent system is working well at the patent granting stage. Finally, however, the success of the system is in the hands of the courts.

IMPROVER CORP. AND SICOMMERCE v. REMINGTON PRODS.
CASE NO. 2 U 27/89
Dusseldorf Court of Appeals (Oberlandesgericht) (1991)
(Germany)
Excerpted at 24 I.I.C. 838–845 (1993)

From the Facts:

The plaintiffs accuse the defendant of infringement of European Patent 0101656 (patent in suit, Enclosure 1 or 1a, respectively). This patent is based on an application of July 29, 1983 and was published on November 5, 1986. By decision of the Technical Board of Appeal of the European Patent Office of April 24, 1991, the English language patent was maintained in the granted version, claim 1 of which reads as follows:

An electrically powered depilatory device comprising: a hand held portable housing (2); motor means (4, 4') disposed in said housing; and a helical spring (24) comprising a plurality of adjacent windings arranged to be driven by said motor means in rotational sliding motion relative to skin bearing hair to be removed, said helical spring (24) including an arcuate hair engaging portion arranged to define a convex side whereat the windings are spread apart, and a concave side corresponding thereto whereat the windings are pressed together, the rotational motion of the helical spring (24) producing continuous motion of the windings from a spread apart orientation at the convex side to a pressed together orientation at the concave side and for engagement and plucking of hair from the skin of the subject, whereby the surface velocities of the windings relative to the skin greatly exceeds the surface velocity of the housing relative thereto. . . .

In June 1988, the defendant started distributing an electrically driven depilatory device, placing it into circulation in the Federal Republic of Germany under the designation, "Lady Remington Liberty". This device operates by means of an arcuate roll of rubber-like plastics, the smooth outer surface of which features a plurality of radial, spaced apart cuts which are distributed over the circumference of the roll and penetrate the plastics element partially only. By means of the motor, this roll is driven in a rotational motion about its longitudinal axis, so that the cuts open to form gaps at the convex side, and so that the side walls thereof are firmly pressed together when the cuts rotate to the concave side of the arcuate roll.

The plaintiffs asserted that the rubber roll provided with radial slits and used as hair-engaging element in the disputed depilatory device constitutes an equivalent to the helical spring provided by the invention. . . .

With judgment of December 30, 1988, the district court found against the defendant. . . . Against this judgment, the defendant lodged appeal. . . .

From the Opinion:

The defendant's admissible appeal is not successful on the merits. . . . [T]he district court rightfully found that the disputed embodiment makes use of the teaching of patent claim 1 of the patent in suit, so that, taking into account the following statements, reference may be made to the reasons for decision of the appealed judgment. . . .

[I]t is the object of the teaching of the patent in suit to suggest a motor-driven depilatory device with the described operation, so that efficient hair removal is ensured. In addition, however, the device according to its size, complexity, production costs and convenience of use should be suited for home use in such a way as is already the case for the electrical razor.

The solution according to the patent in suit (claim 1) makes use of the finding which is already revealed by Swiss Patent 268696, *i.e.* that a coil spring is an elastic element which opens gaps on bending at the convex side and closes at the concave side, in a device which operates by motor-driven rotational motion of the windings of the spring, namely by a rotational motion which is quicker than the velocity at which the depilatory device is moved by the user's hand over the areas of the skin to be depilated. The coil spring, therefore, operates in such a way that the gaps of the windings are spread apart in the area provided for admission of the hairs, and that the windings are pressed together by the rotation, so that, relative to any hair introduced, the place taken by it between the adjacent windings is continuously narrowed, the hair is clamped by the walls of the winding facing the hair, and the hair is plucked due to the rotational motion which is quick in relation to the forward movement of the device.

Patent claim 1 describes this solution of the problem of the patent by the following features:

The electrically powered depilatory device comprises

1. a hand held portable housing,

2. motor means positioned in said housing,

3. a helical spring comprising a plurality of adjacent windings,

4. the windings are arranged to be driven by said motor means in rotational sliding motion relative to skin bearing hair to be removed,

5. said spring includes a hair engaging portion which

    a) is arcuate,

    b) defines a convex side whereat the windings are spread apart and

    c) defines a concave side corresponding to said convex side whereat the windings are pressed together,

6. the rotational motion of the spring produces a continuous motion of the windings from a spread apart orientation at the convex side to a pressed together orientation at the concave side and for engagement with the hair and for plucking of hair from the skin of the subject,

7. the surface velocity of the windings relative to the skin greatly exceeds the surface velocity of the housing relative thereto.

The depilatory device, "Lady Remington Liberty," introduced in the German market by the defendant makes use of the teaching of the patent in suit as just explained.

The depilatory device distributed by the defendant fulfills features 1 and 2 literally. Features 3 to 7, however, are not given literally since the disputed embodiment uncontestedly does not feature a helical spring. The disputed embodiment instead has a massive roll-shaped body of a flexible and elastic rubber-like plastic material, featuring radial spaced apart cuts on its circumferential surface. This arcuate and motor-driven rubber roll is, however, a replacement means equivalent to the coil spring of the patent, so that features 3 to 7 of patent claim 1 are given in equivalent form.

First of all, the court . . . has no doubts that the disputed embodiment is identical in effect to a device making use of the wording of claim 1 of the patent in suit. The roll of the disputed embodiment unites a plurality of adjacent elements, namely the areas separated by the cuts (*cf.* feature 3); these areas are arranged to be driven by the motor means in rotational motion relative to skin-bearing hair to be removed (*cf.* feature 4). The roll comprises a hair-engaging portion which is arcuate, defines a convex side whereat the elements are spread apart and a concave side corresponding to the convex side whereat the elements are pressed together (*cf.* feature 5). The rotational motion of the roll produces a continuous motion of the elements from a spread apart orientation at the convex side to a pressed together orientation at the concave side for engagement with the hair and for plucking of hair from the skin of the subject (*cf.* feature 6). The surface velocity of the roll relative to the skin greatly exceeds the surface velocity of the housing relative to the skin (*cf.* feature 7). The disputed embodiment thus achieves that a hair that has reached the spaced apart areas of the roll is approached ever more closely by the walls of these areas as a consequence of the rotational movement, which walls then clamp the hair and pluck it out. With respect to the principle and success of the desired hair removal, which is efficient and suited for home use, the hair undergoes the same treatment as with a device using the wording of the patent in suit. In conjunction with this, reference can also be made to the description of the patent in suit, according to which wedge-shaped slits (gaps) are instrumental for the depilatory effect of the device. For wedge-shaped gaps are also featured by the roll of the disputed embodiment. The fact that these—due to the different orientation and depth of their gaps in comparison with the inclined windings of a common coil spring—may move the hair differently before plucking it, namely bend it first, as to be seen from the private expert opinion, is therefore irrelevant for the question of identical effect. . . .

A difference, however, is constituted by the fact that with a roll comprising cuts, part of the hair to be removed may first reach an area of the roll which does not comprise a cut yet (but only when the roll continues to rotate), while with a "helical spring" there will always be an entry gap for those hairs which do not hit upon the front sides of the windings themselves. Also according to the expert opinion this is, however, not a question of identical effects, but only refers to the efficiency, or, in other words, only to the question of the quantity of hair removed. This has to be left to the decision of the person skilled in the art who designs constructions according to the patent in suit. As to be seen therefrom, patent claim 1 does not give any indication of how thick or thin the windings of the spring and how wide the area of the gaps in the arcuate state has to be, considered individually or as a whole.

Therefore, the efficiency of the device, according to the patent as required, according to the object of the invention, cannot consist in removing a certain number of hairs during one revolution or on the whole, but only in overcoming the drawbacks of the state of the art. In this context, the expert correctly drew attention to the fact that "much" would increase the user's pain, while "fast" would reduce it, thereby characterizing the different efficiencies of, for example, the manually operated device according to the Swiss patent specification already mentioned and the device to be evaluated here.

It is furthermore irrelevant for determining the identical effect that, with the accused embodiment, each cut (be it closed or in the form of a gap that opens or closes to a higher or lower extent) travels around the circumference of the roll on rotation, whereas the cut is stationary when a "helical spring" is used. According to its object, the patent in suit does not deal with introducing hairs into a constantly opened gap. The desired efficient depilatory device which is relatively simple and convenient to use rather results from the fact that with a "helical spring" the gaps automatically close in the process of rotation, and hairs which have entered them are clamped and plucked. Accordingly, it is also irrelevant what else the individual hair will undergo when entering the gap and when being in the gap, and how this will happen, so that it is not a shortcoming of the expert opinion that only schematic drawings were attached and that the details were not examined with a high-speed camera. A peculiar configuration of the disputed embodiment concerning the treatment of a hair in the gap before being clamped and plucked may at best constitute a surplus of a device which otherwise operates in the same way. In this respect, too, the expert correctly only spoke of a secondary question and referred to the fact that this question would not change the fact that the disputed embodiment makes use of an elastic body with slits or gaps in the same way as the teaching according to the patent in suit, and that the hair—as taught—is taken along via the gap walls by means of friction and is finally plucked.

When evaluating the scope of protection of claim 1 of the patent in suit, however, the argument cannot be limited to the identity of effect only. . . . For the purpose of fairly delimiting the actual improvement of the field of technical knowledge achieved by an inventor on the basis of Art. 69(1) EPC and the Protocol on Interpretation, the protected invention will only be considered to be used if a person skilled in the art, on the basis of reflections progressing from the meaning of the patent claims, *i.e.* the invention described therein, could find out, with the help of his professional knowledge at the priority date, the modified means used with the disputed embodiment as a means being identical in effect for solving the problem underlying the invention. . . .

After the expert opinion, the court is convinced that a person skilled in the art—owing to the content of the claims of the patent in suit—was capable of arriving at the disputed embodiment in this sense.

The starting point for this conclusion is that a person skilled in the art will recognize by virtue of his professional knowledge that in the patent—in any case as far as the basic teaching of claim 1 is concerned—it is not a matter of the use of a "helical spring" as such. For, it is—as has already been mentioned initially here and in the prior art by the device according to the Swiss patent—used contrary to its common application . . . or, as the expert also expressed, atypically. . . . The knowledge that, in the patent, the coil spring does not act as a power unit as usual, automatically results in the fact that those criteria of a helical spring are sought in order to determine why it is proposed in the patent. With this, however, a person skilled in the art in the field of interest here, and with the education mentioned by the expert and the skills resulting therefrom, will easily recognize that the coil spring is only proposed for the reason that it is an elastic cylindrical body which may be quickly rotated in the arcuate state and, above all, for the reason that it features—by virtue of its windings and their sides (walls) facing each other and separating the windings— means that stretch the surface of the body to form gaps at the convex side, while at the concave side they result in clamping areas with the help of which the hairs that entered the gaps may be clamped and plucked. In this way, to a person skilled in the art, the instruction of claim 1 of the patent in suit reads in a functional respect: Take a cylinder-shaped elastic element comprising separated walls of areas of material, to the effect that gaps will form on the convex side and clamping areas will form of the concave side if it is bent, and select—according to material and quality—an element that may be rotated at high speed when bent. If evaluated as a whole, the expert based his written opinion on this understanding. In view of the undisputed technical knowledge of the expert, both with respect to the technical field of interest here and with respect to his experience in patent litigation matters, the court does not see any reason not to follow the logic of the expert in that a person skilled in the art will actually understand the teaching of the patent in suit in this way. Moreover, the court's expert also confirmed this on inquiry of the defendant and the court. The basic thesis that a person skilled in the art will not interpret the coil spring as a spring, but as an elastic body with gaps is convincing, as it is obvious that the helical spring is not used as a spring per se, and as its use in accordance with the teaching of the patent in suit—and also, however, with the state of the art to be seen from the Swiss patent specification, for example— requires the abstraction by a person skilled in the art that this spring is an elastic element which opens at the convex side and closes at the concave side when bent, and which is furthermore so stable that it may be driven at relatively high speed. This abstraction therefore was professional knowl- edge in view of the state of the art, and it was rendered obvious by the claims of the patent in suit, respectively, if seen in the light of the description.

However, if the patent in suit conveyed this knowledge, it was also obvious to use a roll with cuts as in the accused embodiment as a hair- plucking element. It could be recognized with the help of professional knowledge that cuts in a cylindrical body would be sufficient, as, according to the above, the only thing that is essential is that the hair must be able to enter between adjacent areas of the body (walls), and that the walls must approach it up to clamping it. As opposed thereto, however, it is recogniz- ably unimportant whether the body be completely hollow, feature a core or be massive, which is why a person skilled in the art could easily think of applying a massive roll with cuts. To produce the arcuate cut hair- plucking element of rubber or rubber-like plastic material could already be considered possible by a person skilled in the art for the reason that the wording of the patent in suit (claim 1) does not stipulate a certain material, but the question of the material is left open to the expert choice of a designing engineer proceeding on the basis of the patent in suit. Rubber-like plastic material is known to be a preferred material in conjunction with the use of an elastic, bendable element. Moreover, it can easily be provided with separating cuts, for which reason there was the possibility of having an element with which—like with a coil spring—areas of material and separations (windings and gaps, which may vary in width depending on the degree of bending or spreading) alternate and with which the requirement of having gaps at the convex side and clamping areas at the concave side could easily be met, not only by means of circumferential cuts of 360 [degrees,] but also by means of cuts of smaller circumference, as in the case of the disputed embodiment. A person skilled in the art would even prefer those shorter cuts since questions of durability and stability of the hair-plucking element had to be taken into consideration, too, in particular in view of its high rotational speed.

. . . From the response of the court's expert to question 11, the court moreover concludes that, in case of the variation forming the disputed embodiment, the problems to be faced with regard to drive and stability would not have been so large as to prevent a person skilled in the art from taking a cut roll made of rubber-like plastic material into consideration and testing it. In view of the fact that questions as to the drive and stability of the hair-plucking element could have resulted above all from the selected material, as is also confirmed by the oral statements made by the court's expert, it has to be pointed out once again that the patent in suit does not exclude rubber-like plastic material, but leaves this choice open. Accordingly, this cannot, at any rate, have been an obstacle to putting the teaching of patent claim 1 into practice, even for a person skilled in the art, and the fact is irrelevant that all the looped shapes which are depicted on the patent specification should not be possible with the roll of the disputed embodiment. On the contrary, equivalence has to be determined with regard to features 3 to 7 of the patent.

At best it could be said that the disputed embodiment, by the selection of the length, depth and number of cuts, or possibly also by the selection of a particularly suited material for the cylinder-shaped, elastic and arcuate hair-plucking element, gains additional advantages, such as, for example, a maximum decrease in pain for the user, since with each rotation fewer hairs are plucked at a time than would be the case with a steel spring with thin windings and—in the arcuate state—wide gaps in relation thereto. This, however, would not change anything about the fact that the disputed embodiment, at any rate according to its genus, is identical in effect to a device according to the patent, and could also, according to its genus, be found as an alternative to a device making use of the teaching of claim 1 of the patent in suit by a person skilled in the art orientating himself to the meaning of the patent claims, with the help of findings available to him due to his professional knowledge. The court also considers, as an indication of this finding, the history of the origin of the disputed embodiment as it is described in the British court decision which has been mentioned several times. The starting point was a device according to the patent with a metal coil spring. It was found that the use of this device was annoying because it plucked too many hairs at a time, but the principle of depilation according to the patent was not criticized. This points to the fact that the designing engineer of the disputed embodiment, having proceeded from the starting point assumed above, must have actually thought about what the "helical spring" really meant in the device presented to him. It further suggests that even though only metal coil springs had been used in the prior art, except for the so-called disk solutions, that fact did not actually represent an obstacle to a deviation therefrom.

Finally, it is also undisputed that it cannot be claimed that the disputed embodiment results in an obvious way from prior art. . . .

IMPROVER CORP v. BESKA B.V AND REMINGTON PRODS. INC.

24 I.I.C. 832–836 (1993) (Court of Appeals (Gerechtshof), The Hague, 1992)

1. To determine the scope of protection of a patent, one must investigate the nature or operation and the function of those features, described in the patent claim, which third parties have replaced by other means in their devices, as well as the function of those features within the complex of other features specified in the claim. Formulating the "essence" of the patented invention would not be sufficiently adequate for all situations.

2. Bearing the state of the art in mind, one must determine to what extent the inventor is, in fairness, entitled to a certain extent of abstraction regarding the features of the patent claim and whether this abstraction is not unreasonable towards third parties. With respect to the last question, one must consider the expectations of the average person skilled in the art in the Netherlands concerning the scope of the patent, which expectations are also based on Dutch court practice.

From the Facts:

The following decision concerns the appeal from the summary proceedings before the president of the District Court of The Hague, Case No. 88/1299. In his judgment of September 16, 1989, the president of the district court enjoined the defendant Remington from infringing European patent 0101656 in the name of Improver, including the granting of some ancillary claims. Subsequent to Remington's appeal, the Court of Appeals of The Hague, in its interlocutory judgment of 29 June 1989, determined that "third parties" as mentioned by the Protocol on Interpretation of Art. 69 of the European Patent Convention would normally be advised by persons skilled in the art and requested the Dutch Patent Office to provide a written opinion on the question of the infringement of the patent. On October 23,

1989, the Opposition Division of the European Patent Office revoked the said patent of Improver. Pursuant to that decision, Remington requested the president of the district court to order Improver to cease and desist from enforcing its judgment of September 16, 1988. On November 13, 1989, although by that time the opinion of the Dutch Patent Office had not yet been issued and the grounds for revoking the patent were not known the president of the district court took into consideration that the Opposition Division of the European Patent Office, contrary to Dutch courts, consisted of three technical examiners. Concerning the question whether the invention of Improver would be obvious to a person skilled in the art, the district court could not deny that the chance of a successful opposition had improved considerably, and was even sufficiently great to order Improver to cease the enforcement of the district court injunction. On November 28, 1989, the Special Division of the Dutch Patent Office issued a written opinion to the court of appeals, affirming the infringement of the said patent by Remington.

From the Opinion:

. . . .

3. Improver's European patent 0101656 was revoked by the Opposition Division of the European Patent Office on October 7, 1989 on the grounds that the subject matter was not based on an inventive step within the meaning of Art. 56 of the European Patent Convention. On April 24, 1991, the Technical Board of Appeal of the European Patent Office overturned the Division's aforementioned decision, determining that the patent was reinstated in the originally patented version.

4. In view of the latter decision, this court believes that there is very little chance, far as the Netherlands is concerned, of the patent being invalidated by a Dutch court, so that this court cannot, in these summary yet protracted proceedings, deny Improver's claims regarding the infringement based on that small chance alone.

5. In respect of the question whether the Remington device falls under the patents. scope of protection, Remington went to great lengths to explain what was. in its view, the "essence" of the patented invention, and subsequently it answered that question negatively.

6. Remington's approach stems from the doctrine that a patent's scope of protection is determined by the "essence" of the patented invention. Under this approach, in order to answer the infringement question, "the" essence of the invention must first be formulated and summarized, which results, as it were, in a new patent claim, against which the defendant's device or operational principle is tested.

7. The drawback of this approach is that in instances where not much more can be said of the patented invention other than that its feature or complex of features "works," one nevertheless attempts to find "the" essence, that may result in far-reaching abstractions, which should not be

a factor when applying Art. 30(2) of the Dutch Patents Act and Art. 69 of the European Patent Convention and the related Protocol. Additionally, in cases where more may be said about the patented invention, it is nevertheless difficult to formulate "the" essence properly once and for all; if an attempt is made, the formulation is likely to be inspired by the specific infringement question and a corresponding choice of the state of the art, against which the invention is tested. The resulting formulation will be either too wide, too limited or otherwise inadequate for (other) cases dealing with an alleged infringement of the same patent. . . .

8. Thus, this court is of the opinion that the question of infringement should not be answered in the manner described in item 6 above. This does not mean that this court believes that any part of -what may be called -the essential aspects of the patented invention should be disregarded, but that one must (i) investigate the nature or operation and the function of the feature which is described in the patent claim and which the third party has replaced in its device or operational principles by another feature which does not correspond with the wording of the patent claim, and (ii) establish the place of (the function of) that feature within the complex of the features specified in the claim. Subsequently, also having regard to the state of the art, it must be determined (a) to what extent the inventor is, in fairness, entitled to a certain measure of abstraction regarding the features described by him, and (b) to what extent this abstraction is not unfair towards third parties who are entitled to base their actions relying on the belief that these actions will not be retroactively prohibited or result in liability for damages.

9. In its opinion, the Special Division of the Dutch Patent Office answered the infringement question more or less in the manner described in item 8, albeit that it did not take (a) and (b) separately. In summation, the Division's opinion stated that a third party -the average skilled person -who takes cognizance of the patent and of Remington's device will conclude that the device embodies an application of the patented invention, on the grounds that the hair-engaging component of the device is a mechanical equivalent of the helical spring specified in the patent claims.

10. In contesting the opinion, Remington failed to realize that the decisive factor is not the general nature, operation and function(s) of a helical spring, or of the hair-engaging component of the Remington device. The issue centers on the specific nature, operation, function and place of these component parts in devices such as the one in dispute. In order for the helical spring and the Remington component to function, it suffices that they are driven by a simple motor; that they are fitted with slits; that they are flexible; and that, consequently, they are capable of efficiently engaging and removing hair. Thus, the helical spring and the aforementioned Remington component must, within the framework of the devices as a whole, be considered in their entirety, as variant versions of each other, each with their own advantages or disadvantages, on the understanding that certain properties of the Remington device may render the device patentable.

11. The hair-engaging part of the Remington device was not state of the art in the field of depilatory devices. Nor is this part obvious to users of

the state-of-the-art helical spring. In those circumstances, the applicant did not fail in its duty to third parties to phrase the patent in such a manner that it would minimize uncertainty, and it is fair that the applicant, who, on the basis of the properties specified in item 10 above, referred to the helical spring as a component part of the device for which a patent application was filed, is also granted protection for a hair-engaging means with the same properties.

12. Whether or not such protection is unfair towards third parties must be determined on the basis of what scope of protection an expert in the Netherlands should expect, on the understanding that this expectation is also based on earlier decisions by the Dutch courts. This inevitable "circle" renders it more difficult to arrive at a uniform "European" scope of protection, but it does not violate the Protocol to Art. 69 of the European Patent Convention.

13. Moreover, the expert opinion of the Special Division gives an indication of what the Division expects to be the view of Dutch experts on the patent's scope of protection. On the basis of this opinion, the obvious mechanical equivalence, the circumstances described in item 11, first sentence, and the fairness mentioned in the second sentence to which third parties should have regard in their expectations, this court is of the opinion that third parties should realize that the concept of a helical spring contained in the patent claims warrants such a measure of abstraction that a device such as the one manufactured by Remington falls within the patent's scope of protection.

14. Remington further argued that the weighing of interests for the purposes of the summary action should result in a denial of Improver's claims. However, considering that the patent has not been revoked despite the opposition and in view of the Special Division's opinion and the fact that the parties have extensively debated the issue and have submitted documents in support of their views, this court believes that there is little chance of the patent being invalidated, or of the lower court hearing the principal action on the merits deciding the issue in a manner other than the court has done above. Thus, this court rejects the above-mentioned arguments.

15. The grounds of appeal do not lead to a nullification of the disputed judgment.

IMPROVER CORP. AND OTHERS v. REMINGTON CONSUMER PRODS. LTD.
1990 F.S.R. 181(Ch. D. 1989) (UK)

HOFFMANN J: This is an action for infringement of a European patent for an electrically powered cosmetic device for removing hair. The commercial embodiment of the plaintiff's invention is called "Epilady" and the defendant's device is called "Smooth & Silky." The defences are, first, that Smooth & Silky does not infringe the claims of the patent and secondly, that the patent is invalid for obviousness and insufficiency. In my judgment the patent in suit is valid but the defendant's device does not infringe. The action is therefore dismissed. (A point taken on the title of some of the plaintiffs to sue therefore does not arise.)

The Invention

Depilation means the removal of hair by the root, as opposed to shaving which leaves the root behind. The advantage of depilation is that the hair takes much longer to regenerate. Various methods have been used in the past for cosmetic depilation, but none was completely satisfactory. An article published in an American marketing journal in 1976 ("Where to look for good product ideas" by Joseph J Montesano in Product Management, August 1976) began as follows:

> If you were seeking a truly new product that meets a genuine consumer need you might start with the women's depilatory market. After many years of looking—ever since ancient Egypt—women still say they have not found the ideal product to remove hair from legs and face.

> Pull it off with a hardened wax? It hurts. Use a chemical that dissolves hair? It has an offensive odour. Electrolysis? You need an expert and it's expensive. Use a razor—even a new idea like the disposables? There are still nicks and scratches—at least some women still think so.

> It's a huge, waiting market, and the company that comes up with a safe, effective product will hit the jackpot . . . Everyone knows the market is there and some in the field have been searching for the key to unlock the treasure. . . .

Epilady was invented by two Israelis in 1982. It consists of a small electric motor in a hand-held plastic housing to which is attached a helical steel spring held by its ends and stiffened by a guide wire to form a loop. The arcuate form of the spring causes the gaps between the windings to open on its convex side but to be pressed together on the concave side. When the spring is held close to the skin and rotated by the motor at about 6,000 revolutions per minute, hairs enter the gaps on its convex side and are gripped between the windings as the rotational movement brings them round to the concave side. The effect is to pluck them out of the skin.

Marketing of Epilady began in June 1986. It was an enormous commercial success. In the first two years over 5.8 million devices were made, generating a gross retail turnover in excess of US $340,000,000.

The Patent in Suit

The patent in suit is European Patent (UK) No. 0101656. It refers by way of prior art to six patents. Four involve manually operated helical springs. In Schubiger (US Patent 2,486,616), Binz (US Patent 1,743,590) and Kerr (US Patent 2,458,911) the windings of the coils are used as multi-jawed tweezers and are either pressed together or allowed to come together to engage the hairs, which are then pulled out by a jerking movement with the device. Fischer (Swiss Patent 268,696) consists of two small helical coils each held in arcuate form by a stiff guide wire. The patent requires the coils to be rolled over the surface of the skin so that the hairs are engaged and gripped by the rotation of the spring in the same way as in the patent in suit. Extraction is performed by a jerky movement but the specification is not clear as to whether this is the same movement over the skin by which the hairs are engaged or a movement away from the skin after the hairs have been gripped. The power-operated inventions are Schnell (US Patent 2,900,661), a device for plucking feathers or hair, which uses a power-driven row of rotating discs on an axle with cams to push the edges of the discs together and grip the feathers or hair, and Daar (US Patent 4,079,741), an earlier patent by one of the inventors of the patent in suit. This is a complicated device—a motorized Schubiger by which a helical spring is reciprocatingly compressed and extended by a cam driven by an electric motor to engage and grip the hairs and at the same time intermittently rotated to extract them.

The basic description of the patent in suit declares that—

> There is thus provided in accordance with an embodiment of the present invention an electrically powered depilatory device including a hand held portable housing, motor apparatus disposed in the housing, and a helical spring composed of a plurality of adjacent windings arranged to be driven by the motor apparatus in rotational sliding motion relative to skin bearing hair to be removed, the helical spring including an arcuate hair engaging portion arranged to define a convex side whereat the windings are spread apart, and a concave side corresponding thereto whereat the windings are pressed together, the rotational motion of the helical spring producing continuous motion of the windings from a spread apart orientation at the convex side to a pressed together orientation at the concave side and for the engagement and plucking of hair from the skin, whereby the surface velocities of the windings relative to the skin greatly exceed the surface velocity of the housing relative thereto.

A preferred embodiment of the invention is said to be one in which the helical spring arcuate hair engaging portion—

> extends along an arc subtending more than 90 degrees and preferably more than 180 degrees, whereby the surface velocities of windings of the helical spring simultaneously include components extending in mutually perpendicular directions, for significantly enhanced hair removal efficiency.

The looped configuration to which this description refers can be seen illustrated in figures 1 and 2 of the patent drawings. Its advantages are further explained as follows:

The looped spring configuration of the present invention is a particular feature thereof in that there are simultaneously present at all times windings of the helical spring whose component of velocity relative to the hair extends in mutually perpendicular directions. The apparatus thus is operative to remove hair oriented in various directions without requiring movement of the housing against the skin in all of these directions.

The description ends, however, with the following general statement, which I shall later refer to as the "equivalents clause:"

It will be evident to those skilled in the art that the invention is not limited to the details of the foregoing illustrative embodiments, and that the present invention may be embodied in other specific forms without departing from the essential attributes thereof, and it is therefore desired that the present embodiments be considered in all respects as illustrative and not restrictive, reference being made to the appended claims, rather than to the foregoing description, *and all variations which come within the meaning and range of equivalency of the claims are therefore intended to be embraced therein.* (Emphasis supplied.)

Claim 1 reads as follows: . . . [same as in the decision of the German court above]. . . .

Smooth & Silky

Smooth & Silky also consists of a small electric motor in a hand held housing but the element attached to the motor and used to extract the hair is not a helical metal spring. Instead it is a cylindrical rod of elastomerised synthetic rubber held by its ends to form an arc subtending about 60 degrees. I shall for convenience call it "the rubber rod." A number of parallel radial slits have been cut into the rubber. The arcuate form of the rod causes the slits to open on its convex side but to be pressed together on the concave side. When the rod is held close to the skin and rapidly rotated by the motor, hairs enter the gaps on its convex side and are gripped between the walls of the slits as the rotational movement brings them round to the concave side. The effect is to pluck them out of the skin.

. . . .

Mr. Gross [the inventor] has been granted a patent in the United States (US 4,726,375). . . .

. . . .

Dr. Laming, a distinguished design engineer called as an expert witness by the defendants, said that Mr. Gross's specification contained nothing which distinguished Smooth & Silky from Epilady by function. The difference lay in their respective forms (Evidence Day 6, p 16A).

Infringement

The question of infringement turns upon a short but undoubtedly difficult point of construction, namely whether the rubber rod is a "helical spring" as that expression is used in the claims of the patent in suit. In the Court of Appeal at the interlocutory injunction stage of this action Dillon LJ said that a more attractive way of putting the question, from the plaintiff's point of view, was to ask whether the rod was a "mechanical equivalent" for a helical spring. But I think with respect, for reasons which I shall explain, that these are different ways of saying the same thing.

The proper approach to the interpretation of patents registered under the Patents Act 1949 was explained by Lord Diplock in Catnic Components Ltd. v. Hill & Smith Ltd., 1982 RPC 183, 242. The language should be given a "purposive" and not necessarily a literal construction. If the issue was whether a feature embodied in an alleged infringement which fell outside the primary, literal or acontextual meaning of a descriptive word or phrase in the claim ("a variant") was nevertheless within its language as properly interpreted, the court should ask itself the following three questions:

(1) Does the variant have a material effect upon the way the invention works? If yes, the variant is outside the claim. If no—

(2) Would this (*i.e.* that the variant had no material effect) have been obvious at the date of publication of the patent to a reader skilled in the art. If no, the variant is outside the claim. If yes—

(3) Would the reader skilled in the art nevertheless have understood from the language of the claim that the patentee intended that strict compliance with the primary meaning was an essential requirement of the invention. If yes, the variant is outside the claim.

On the other hand, a negative answer to the last question would lead to the conclusion that the patentee was intending the word or phrase to have not a literal but a figurative meaning (the figure being a form of synecdoche or metonymy) denoting a class of things which included the variant and the literal meaning, the latter being perhaps the most perfect, best-known or striking example of the class. . . .

In the end, therefore, the question is always whether the alleged infringement is covered by the language of the claim. This, I think, is what Lord Diplock meant in *Catnic* when he said that there was no dichotomy between "textual infringement" and infringement of the "pith and marrow" of the patent and why I respectfully think that Fox LJ put the question with great precision in Anchor Building Products Ltd. v. Redland Roof Tiles Ltd. ((CA), unreported, 23 Nov. 1988) when he said the question was whether the absence of a feature mentioned in the claim was "an immaterial variant which a person skilled in the trade would have regarded as being *within the ambit of the language*" (My emphasis). It is worth noticing that Lord Diplock's first two questions, although they cannot sensibly be answered without reference to the patent, do not primarily involve questions of construction: whether the variant would make a material difference to the way the invention worked and whether this would have been obvious to the skilled reader are questions of fact. The answers are used to provide the factual background against which the specification must be construed. It is the third question which raises the question of construction and Lord Diplock's formulation makes it clear that on this question the answers to the first two questions are not conclusive. Even a purposive construction of the language of the patent may lead to the conclusion that although the variant made no material difference and this would have been obvious at the time, the patentee for some reason was confining his claim to the primary meaning and excluding the variant. If this were not the case, there would be no point in asking the third question at all.

Catnic was a decision on the Patents Act 1949. Section 125 of the Patents Act 1977, which is declared by section 139(7) to be framed to have as nearly as practicable the same effect as Article 69 of the European Patent Convention, says that the invention shall be taken to be that specified in a claim, as interpreted by the description and drawings. Section 125(3) applies to English patents the Protocol on the Interpretation of Article 69 which, if I may paraphrase, says that Article 69 and section 125(1) mean what they say: the scope of the invention must be found in the language of the claims. Extrinsic material such as the description can be used to interpret those claims but cannot provide independent support for a cause of action which the language of the claim, literally or figuratively construed, simply cannot bear. On the other hand, the claims should not be interpreted literally but in a way which "combines a fair protection for the patentee with a reasonable degree of certainty for third parties."

Dillon LJ said in his judgment at the interlocutory stage of this action that Lord Diplock's speech in Catnic indicated the same approach to construction as that laid down by the Protocol. This view has been adopted by the Court of Appeal. . . . I regard it as binding upon me. I must therefore ask Lord Diplock's three questions to ascertain whether "helical spring" should be interpreted to mean a class of bendy, slitty rods of which a close-coiled helical spring in its primary sense is a striking and elegant example but which includes the defendant's rubber rod.

(1) Does the variant have a material effect on the way the invention works?

The answer to this question depends upon the level of generality at which one describes the way the invention works. At one extreme, if one says that the invention works by gripping and pulling hair, there is obviously no difference; the same would be true of a pair of tweezers. At the other extreme, if one says that it works by gripping hairs between metal windings of circular cross-section wound in a continuous spiral around a hollow core, there obviously is a difference. . . .

. . . .

It seems to me that the right approach is to describe the working of the invention at the level of generality with which it is described in the claim of the patent. As I have said, Dr. Laming agreed that there was no difference between the descriptions in Mr. Gross's patent and the patent in suit of the way the inventions worked. The differences lay entirely in the descriptions of the hardware. In my judgment, at the appropriate level of description, the rubber rod works in the same way as the helical spring and the differences I have mentioned, so far as they exist, are not material.

(2) Would it have been obvious to a man skilled in the art that the variant would work in the same way?

. . . .

Dr. Laming and Dr. Sharp, the eminent engineer called as an expert by the plaintiff, agreed that it would have been obvious to the skilled man that the attributes which enabled the helical spring to function in the way described in the specification were that it was capable of rotating, capable of transmitting torque along its length to resist the forces involved in plucking hairs, bendy (to form an arc) and slitty (to entrap hairs by the opening and closing effect of rotation). They also agreed that it would have been obvious that any rod which had these qualities in sufficient degree and did not have other defects such as overheating or falling to bits would in principle work in the same way and that the rubber rod plainly belonged to that class. On this evidence the second question must in my judgment be answered yes. I express no view on whether the rubber rod was also an inventive step.

On the other hand, the evidence shows that although the rubber rod could be used in a device which would function in the way described in claim 1 of the patent in suit, it would work only in a limited number of embodiments. In particular, it could not be used in the loop formation described as the preferred embodiment.

(3) Would the skilled reader nevertheless have understood that the patentee intended to confine his claim to the primary meaning of a helical spring?

This brings one to the question of construction. Since the question is what the skilled reader would have understood, I set out the views of the rival experts.

Dr. Sharpe placed considerable emphasis on what I have called the equivalents clause. He said in his report (Report, page 14):

> it would have been obvious to me that all the inventor wanted a helical spring for was as a convenient rotating bent beam in which slits formed by the adjacent windings would open and close as it rotated. It would then have been equally obvious to me that he could not have intended to exclude equivalents like the [rubber] rod . . . in thinking of equivalents I feel driven by the last paragraph of the specification before the claims [the equivalents clause] to think that the inventor was trying to make me think of equivalents for the helical spring . . . some other element that would do the same job.

Dr. Sharpe said that in the course of his own work he had used a slitted rod instead of a helical spring to serve as a coupling (Report, page 9):

> In my experience it is common practice to replace a close coiled helical spring by a rod with slits in a situation where the rod/spring forms an arc. For example, similar circular cross-section beam/spring forms are commonly used for coupling rotating shafts where the axis of the shafts have angular misalignment. These couplings are commonly "close wound" helical springs or in the form of a rod with saw cut slits arranged in a regular staggered pattern as used in the [Smooth & Silky]. I have used a rod with such saw cut slits as part of a mechanism for positioning micro-electrodes.

He concluded (Report, page 14):

> It would have been quite natural for me to have thought of my recent experience and use of a slitted bendy rod [either] with the slits being discontinuous—the only alternative to their being continuous.

In cross-examination Dr. Sharpe was questioned about the process of reasoning which would have taken him from the helical spring to the rubber rod. He said:

> One would look for equivalence and as an engineer I would know that there are many equivalents for providing torque in a bent condition and one of those is obviously a solid rod of a more flexible material. This is the way couplings are made. That is a common way—a common alternative. I see the step as one which the competent engineer or man in his working shop would, sort of, look through the files in his mind, and out would pop a number of alternatives.
>
> Q. You are viewing this just as a coupling. You are viewing the Epilady spring as a form of coupling.
>
> A. In the sense that one of its primary functions is to transmit torque and that is an important one, then obviously methods for transmitting torque in an arc situation would be the obvious thing to come to mind. The fact that you can then put slits in it is something that we have done readily. I mean, I have done it in my own experience for various reasons and I have also known of hair being caught in these slits.

Later he was asked about the disadvantages of the rubber rod (Transcript, Day 3, p 73).

> Q. And the change from a hollow helical spring with those windings to a solid rubber rod would involve the sort of problems we have been talking about: heat build up, length of the roller and the rest of them, is that not correct?
>
> A. Once you had made the mental step of choosing an alternative that was a rubber rod, then obviously your mind is directed, as a designer,

to the problems that ensue from that, which are indeed [that] the internal damping material is higher, the heat build up etc.

Q. And, thirdly, having decided on your solid rubber rod, you change from some helical slit along the circumference to an array of pairs of slits perpendicular to the axis; is that correct?

A. I think you would put the slits in. It is much easier to put them in at right angles to the axis, it is easier to manufacture it that way, and therefore you just put them in. . . .

Dr. Laming, on the other hand, said that a helical spring was a very specific engineering concept. It meant a bar or wire of uniform cross-section wound into a helix. This definition was also accepted by Dr. Sharpe, although he suggested that the rubber rod could also be regarded as a helical spring in a more literal sense because it was springy and had torque stresses running through it in a helical pattern. I do not think it would occur to the ordinary skilled man to think of the rubber rod as a helical spring. Dr. Laming thought that in the context of the specification the skilled man would also not understand a helical spring to mean a genus of bendy, slitty rods. The references to prior art did not suggest that the function of a helical spring was simply to be a bendy slitty rod. In the patents in which they had been used, they were plainly essential features. Dr. Laming said (Report, paragraphs 7.2, 7.3, 4.2, 7.6):

> My opinion is that there is no way of interpreting the [plaintiff's] specification such that anything other than a helical spring (as defined above) is intended. The simple reason for this is, in my view, that the inventor had in mind what he regarded as a novel use of a familiar and readily available engineering component and saw the nub and center of the invention as that use.

> I have now read the European Patent several times and it is clear that nothing other than a helical spring is referred to. If there were alternatives to a helical spring which the inventor or draftsman of the patent had in mind he did not indicate anywhere that such alternative might be used. This stands in contrast to suggested alternatives with regard to e.g. alternative drive arrangements suggested in Column 6 . . .

> The flexibility conferred on the helical spring by its essential features is obtained for the elastomeric rod by quite other means—by its being made of a material of very low elastic modulus, a material about 30,000 times more flexible than the steel of the spring. The difference of material is inherent in the difference between the two devices: the helical spring, if made of the elastomeric material, would be useless spaghetti; and the arcuate rod made of steel would be an undriveably rigid bar . . .

> If the [plaintiff's] specification contained anywhere such words as "or any other configuration of an elastic member or members

whereby rotation of the member or members causes a spread apart orientation at one position and a pressed together orientation at another position or point in the cycle" then at least one might be led to think about alternatives to the helical spring. Whether I would have thought of an elastomeric rod in such a case is hard to say in hindsight but the likelihood is made less by consideration of the Figures 9-14 which show possible configurations which the patentee had in mind. Except possibly for the first (Fig 9) these configurations could not be adopted by an elastomeric rod without some internal wire guide, and in that case, the friction developed between elastomer and guide would in my opinion be prohibitive.

On this last point Dr. Sharpe agreed.

Dealing with the equivalents clause, Dr. Laming said:

It is true that [in the equivalents clause] reference is made to embodiment 'in other specific forms' and it asks there for reference to be made 'to the appended claims rather than the foregoing description.' But what follows is a series of claims in which the variations are all on such matters as the angle subtended by the arcuate portion (claims 2, 3 and 18), the degree of opening of the windings (claims 5 to 8), various mechanical drive options (claims 13 and 14) and different surface speeds (claims 19 and 20). A constant feature of all the claims is the specification of a helical spring which itself is the only type of element mentioned in the text of the specification and shown in the figures.

In my judgment the difference between the experts depends upon how one construes the equivalents clause. The first part of the clause merely says that the description should not be used to restrict the meaning of the language used in the claims. That is not the question here. What matters is the final words: "and all variations which come within the meaning and range of equivalency of the claims are therefore intended to be embraced therein." If this means: "whatever contrary impression the skilled man may be given by the language of the claims read in the context of the rest of the description, all references in the claims to hardware are deemed to include any other hardware which would in any circumstances function in the same way" then I think Dr. Sharpe must be right. In my judgment, however, the clause does not have so wide an effect. The words I have quoted say that the variation must still come within the meaning of the claims and the reference to "range of equivalency" means in my judgment no more than "don't forget that the claims must be interpreted in accordance with *Catnic* and the Protocol."

Thus interpreted, I do not think that "helical spring" can reasonably be given a wide generic construction and I accept Dr. Laming's reasons for thinking that a skilled man would not understand it in this sense. . . . The rubber rod is not an approximation to a helical spring. It is a different thing which can in limited circumstances work in the same way. Nor can the spring be regarded as an "inessential" or the change from metal spring to rubber rod as a minor variant. . . . It would be obvious that the rubber had problems of hysteresis which might be very difficult to overcome. The plaintiff's inventors had done no work on rubber rods. Certainly the rubber rod cannot be used in the loop configuration which is the plaintiff's preferred embodiment. On the other hand, drafting the claim in wide generic terms to cover alternatives like the rubber rod might be unacceptable to the patent office. I do not think that the hypothetical skilled man is also assumed to be skilled in patent law and he would in my judgment be entitled to think that patentee had good reasons for limiting himself, as he obviously appeared to have done, to a helical coil. To derive a different meaning solely from the equivalents clause would in my view be denying third parties that reasonable degree of certainty to which they are entitled under the Protocol.

The German decisions

The patent in suit is being litigated in a number of countries but the only one in which the action has come to trial is in Germany, where the Landgericht of Dusseldorf found in favor of the plaintiff [affirmed by the Oberlandesgericht above.] This naturally causes me concern because the Landgericht was interpreting the same patent according to the same Protocol and came to a different conclusion. It seems to me that the reason for the difference between me and my colleagues in Dusseldorf is that, having answered what I have labeled as Lord Diplock's first two questions in the same way as I have, they treated those answers as concluding the matter in favor of the plaintiff and did not find it necessary to ask the third question at all. The specification, they said, conveyed to the expert "the understanding that the configuration of the hair engaging portion as helical spring has to be understood functionally" (Translation, p. 15) and that the expert to whom the patent was directed would have "no difficulties in perceiving and understanding this meaning of the teaching of the invention." This does seem to me with respect to be an interpretation closer to treating the language of the claims as a "guideline" than the median course required by the Protocol. I also detect some difference in approach between the Landgericht and the Oberlandesgericht (Court of Appeal) which had previously discharged an interlocutory injunction granted by the Landgericht. The Court of Appeal placed much more emphasis upon the language of the specification. Its view on the primary meaning of a helical spring was as follows:

> A spiral or helical shape is characterized by curved lines such as those showing on the level a spiral and, three-dimensionally, more or less the rising turns of a screw. Nothing else is meant by the theory of the [plaintiff's] patent and this is made clear to a person skilled in the art by the state of the art to which the patent refers and on which its proposition is undoubtedly based. A solid roller-shaped hair-engaging part with vertical incisions at a distance from

each other can therefore at the most constitute an equivalent means of replacement for the helical spring.

The court went on to say that the rubber rod undoubtedly worked in the same way as the helical spring (*i.e.* it answered Lord Diplock's first question in the same way as I have). Although it does not specifically say so, I think it may be assumed that it would have regarded this as equally obvious to anyone skilled in the art. But when dealing with the question whether this would affect the question of construction, *i.e.* whether the skilled man would have regarded the rubber rod as included in the claims of the patent, the Court of Appeal expressed considerable doubt. He could have done so if he had analyzed the function of the spring in the invention and then set about thinking of equivalents to perform the same function. But the court doubted whether—

> the average person skilled in the art thinks in such a theoretical way. This applies particularly to the present case because there appeared to be no need for theorizing in view of the fact that a normal helical spring was known as a perfectly suitable means for plucking.

It may be said that the expert evidence before the Landgericht at the trial was different, but I doubt whether this could have been so. There was no real difference between the views of Dr. Sharpe and Dr. Laming on questions of engineering: the difference lay in the approach to construction, which is really a question of law.

[The court went on to find that the invention was not invalid for obviousness and insufficiency.]

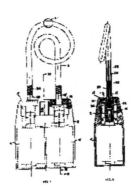

NOTES AND QUESTIONS

(1) **Inter-National Influence?** Armitage says:

> Consider an example. Identical infringing articles are marketed in France and Italy. The scope of protection of the European patent is the same in France and Italy, being determined by Art. 69. The validity is the same in both countries, being governed by Art. 138. A French court finds that the European patent is valid and infringed by the marketing in France. What influence will that have on the Italian court? . . . [A]t least the French decision must be highly persuasive in Italy.

Section 130 of the U.K. Patents Act says that the act is "framed as to have, as nearly as practicable, the same effects in the U.K. as do the corresponding provisions" of the European Patent Convention, the Community Patent Convention, and the Patent Cooperation Treaty, in the territories to which they apply. *See* WILLIAM CORNISH, INTELLECTUAL PROPERTY: PATENTS, COPYRIGHT, TRADE MARKS AND ALLIED RIGHTS 87 (2d ed. 1989). In *Smith Kline v. Harbottle*, Whitford J said:

> it is of the greatest importance that in this jurisdiction we should take note of the decisions of the [European Patent Office] and that, so far as may be possible in all those countries which are now bound by the common interest created by the Convention, an attempt should be made to give the same meaning to relevant provisions, whichever the jurisdiction which is being invoked.

(2) **Divining the Meaning and Scope of the Claims of a European Patent**. A commentator recently observed that:

> Courts in the United Kingdom and Germany have led Europe in analyzing infringement, and the Dutch, Austrians, and Swiss have traditionally followed the direction of German courts. Courts in the United Kingdom have emphasized the actual language of the patent claims, which has resulted in careful, wide-as-possible draftsmanship by counsel[] for the inventors. Courts in Germany, by contrast, have looked for the essence of the claim, going beyond the literal language.

MICHAEL P. RYAN, KNOWLEDGE DIPLOMACY 42 (1998).

Did the Hague Court of Appeals (Gerechtshof) *Improver* decision in 1992 generally follow the "genus" approach of the Oberlandesgericht? The Hague court stated, "this court is of the opinion that third parties should realize that the concept of a helical spring contained in the patent claims warrants such a measure of abstraction that a device such as the one manufactured by Remington falls within the patent's scope of protection." The Gerechtshof also opined, "[w]hether or not such protection is unfair towards third parties must be determined on the basis of what scope of protection an expert in the Netherlands should expect, on the understanding that this expectation is also based on earlier decisions by Dutch courts. This inevitable 'circle' renders it more difficult to arrive at a uniform 'European' scope of protection, but it does not violate the Protocol to Art. 69 of the [EPC]." Is there a lesson in claim draftsmanship to be learned from these cases? Although the November 2000 diplomatic conference revising the EPC did not expressly approve the adoption of the doctrine of equivalents in Europe, it clarified that "for the purposes of determining the extent of protection conferred by a European patent, due account shall be taken of any element which is equivalent to an element specified in a claim." The revisions agreed to at the 2000 revision conference will not come into effect until all the member countries have ratified the revised convention.

(3) **Establishing a European Patent Judiciary**. The European Commission, responding to a 1996 request of the European Council, issued its Green Paper on the Community Patent System in June 1997. *See supra* § 6.03[A][4]. A June 1998 report of the Select Committee on European Communities of the U.K. House of Lords predicts that the Community Patent Convention is a "failure" and is highly unlikely ever to come into force. An important reason for the failure according to the Confederation of British Industries is the "absence of adequate judicial arrangements." Negotiations are ongoing in Europe with a view to establishing an Optional Protocol on the Settlement of Litigation Concerning European Patents within the EPC system. *See* www.european-patent-office.org/news/headlns/2000_08_03_e.htm. Whether there would be a central court, a "roving court" or regional courts, who would serve on a European Patent Judiciary, and whether the new system would replace the national courts or run parallel for an extended period of time, are questions as yet unanswered.

[B]   The Brussels Convention

Historically, U.K. courts (and courts from other British Commonwealth countries) were reluctant to adjudicate claims of foreign intellectual property infringement. Doctrinally, this policy was given effect in both jurisdictional and choice of law rules. As a jurisdictional matter, intellectual property actions were treated as local (rather than transitory) causes of action, to be litigated only where fictionally situated. As a matter of choice of law, foreign intellectual property claims inevitably failed the so-called "double actionability rule." This rule permitted relief for conduct occurring abroad only if it would be actionable under both the law of the forum and the law of the place where the conduct occurred. *See* G.W. Austin, *The Infringement of Foreign Intellectual Property Rights*, 113 LAW QUART. REV. 321 (1997).

Within Europe, the Brussels Convention on Jurisdiction and Enforcement of Judgments in Civil and Commercial Matters (1968) caused a shift in this position. For four decades, this Convention governed civil litigation among EU citizens in national courts of EU states, and its essential principles continue to govern such litigation notwithstanding that since March 2002 some national courts in the EU may formally look to the so-called Brussels Regulation as the source of applicable rules of jurisdiction and judgment recognition. *See infra* page 808 (explaining inter-relationship of the Brussels Convention and the Brussels Regulation after March 2002). The Schlosser Report, one of the two reports (along with the Jenard Report) that represents the authoritative history of the purpose and meaning of the Convention's provisions, emphasized that "in accordance with the general spirit of the 1968 Convention, the fact that foreign law has to be applied, either generally or in a particular case, should not constitute a sufficient reason for a court to decline jurisdiction. Where the courts of several States have jurisdiction, the plaintiff has deliberately been given a right of choice . . . " Thus, the U.K. courts have in recent years, for example, entertained causes of action for infringement of a Dutch copyright in light of the liberal jurisdictional rules found in the Convention. And several European courts (most notably, but not exclusively the Dutch courts) began to use the liberal jurisdictional rules in the Convention to offer cross-border injunctive relief (especially in patent cases). This led in the 1990s to a spate of decisions from the U.K. and Dutch courts seeking to establish the parameters of this form of relief. Before reading two recent cases from the English and Dutch courts, however, consider whether (and why) we should permit courts to adjudicate foreign intellectual property claims. What is the value of cross-border litigation (and relief)? Are there any costs associated with it?

BRUSSELS CONVENTION ON JURISDICTION AND ENFORCEMENT OF JUDGMENTS IN CIVIL AND COMMERCIAL MATTERS (1968)

Article 2

Subject to the provisions of this Convention, persons domiciled in a Contracting State shall, whatever their nationality, be sued in the courts of that State. . . .

Article 5

A person domiciled in a Contracting State may, in another Contracting State, be sued

. . . .

    (3)   In matters relating to tort . . . in the courts for the place where the harmful event occurred.

Article 6

A person domiciled in a Contracting State may also be sued—

    (1)   Where he is one of a number of defendants, in the courts for the place where any one of them is domiciled

Article 16

The following courts shall have exclusive jurisdiction, regardless of domicile

. . . .

    (4)   In proceedings concerned with the registration or validity of patents, trade marks, designs, or other similar rights required to be deposited or registered, the courts of the Contracting State in which the deposit or registration has been applied for, has taken place or is under the terms of an international convention deemed to have taken place

Article 19

Where a court of a Contracting State is seised of a claim which is principally concerned with a matter over which the courts of another Contracting State have exclusive jurisdiction by virtue of Article 16, it shall declare of its own motion that it has no jurisdiction.

Article 24

Application may be made to the courts of a Contracting State for such provisional, including protective, measures as may be available under the law of that State, even if, under this Convention, the courts of another Contracting State have jurisdiction as to the substance of the matter.

FORT DODGE ANIMAL HEALTH LTD v. AKZO NOBEL NV
1998 F.S.R. 222 (Court of Appeal, 1997) (Eng.)

LORD WOOLF M.R.:

. . . The Appellants have petitioned in the English Patents Court to revoke EP (UK) No 0189958 which is owned by the first Respondent, Akzo Nobel NV. The other Respondent, Intervet International BV, is a wholly owned subsidiary of Akzo and claims to have an exclusive licence under the patent.

The Appellants seek to reverse the order of Laddie J of 16 October 1997 which refused to grant relief which, in essence, would have prevented the Respondents from maintaining legal proceedings in the Netherlands for infringement of the United Kingdom patent in respect of acts committed in England. The Appellants contend that such relief is appropriate because the U.K. courts have sole jurisdiction to determine the dispute. They say that is urgent as the proceedings which the Respondents have commenced in the Netherlands, seeking relief both in respect of acts committed in the Netherlands and acts committed in the United Kingdom, are about to be heard. For this reason and to enable the Netherlands courts to know our views we have expedited this appeal.

The Facts

Akzo are a large multinational company domiciled in the Netherlands. They are the owners of the United Kingdom patent and a corresponding Dutch patent. Both patents stem from an application filed at the European Patent Office on 21 January 1986. . . .

There are five Appellants, [all of whom are defendants in the Dutch infringement proceedings and all of whom are part of the American Home Products Group of Companies.] [O]ne of the Appellants is domiciled in the Netherlands. One is domiciled in Australia and the rest in the United Kingdom. [The Dutch domiciliary carried out acts in the Netherlands which are alleged to infringe the Dutch patent; the Australian domiciliary was alleged to have delivered infringing vaccines to other defendants for sale in the United Kingdom and Holland]. It is not alleged that any of the United Kingdom domiciled companies have actively participated in the acts of any company which are alleged to infringe the Dutch patent. What is alleged is that they have carried out acts which are alleged to infringe the United Kingdom patent.

. . . .

On 28 April 1997, Akzo and Intervet commenced proceedings in the Netherlands seeking both preliminary and final relief in respect of alleged acts of infringement of both the Dutch patent and the United Kingdom patent. It is contemplated that, subject to appeal, a decision, at least on interim relief, will be reached after a hearing due to take place on 7 November 1997.

On 22 September 1997 the Appellants petitioned the English Patents Court for revocation of the Akzo United Kingdom patent [on grounds inter alia of lack of novelty and obviousness]. The answer to that petition was due within 21 days. It is likely that if the proceedings are prosecuted by the parties with diligence, it can be determined at first instance in about a year to 18 months time.

The dispute

The Appellants' case on the application before Laddie J and before us is that in the circumstances of this case the only court which has jurisdiction to determine whether the Appellants have infringed the United Kingdom patent is the English Patents Court. That being so, it is said that prosecution of that claim in the Dutch Courts against Appellants domiciled in the United Kingdom is vexatious and should be restrained by injunction. Alternatively, if there be doubt on the question of jurisdiction, guidance should be sought from the European Court of Justice as to the true construction of the relevant Conventions and in the meantime there should be an injunction to protect the Appellants' position. Alternatively, if the Patents Court does not have exclusive jurisdiction by reason of the relevant Conventions, it is nevertheless the appropriate court to decide all issues relating to the United Kingdom patent and therefore the relief sought should be granted.

The Respondents contend that the Dutch courts do have jurisdiction to determine the matters raised in their pleaded case in the Dutch proceedings and in particular to determine whether the Appellants who are domiciled in the United Kingdom are infringing the United Kingdom patent. In any case, the United Kingdom courts have no jurisdiction to grant the relief sought on the present application and should not do so. The correct course is to leave it to the Dutch court to decide whether it has the appropriate jurisdiction.

At the outset we make it clear that we do not believe that consideration of the procedures adopted by the Dutch courts to resolve patent disputes is material to the issue before us nor is it appropriate for the courts of the United Kingdom to voice any opinion upon them. At the heart of the dispute between the parties is whether the English Patents Court has exclusive jurisdiction in respect of the issues concerning the United Kingdom patent. That does not depend upon whether the Respondents are seeking to litigate in the Netherlands as opposed to another State which is a signatory to the Brussels Convention.

One of the purposes of the Brussels and Lugano Conventions was to eliminate disputes as to where actions should be decided and to avoid the need to consider whether one jurisdiction was more appropriate than another. It is therefore necessary to look to those Conventions for a solution.

The Brussels Convention

The Brussels Convention, by section 2 of the Civil Jurisdiction and Judgments Act 1982, has the force of law in the United Kingdom. . . .

We believe that articles 2 and 5(3), subject to the exclusion contained in Article 16, apply to actions in respect of intellectual property rights. Thus an owner of an appropriate right can take proceedings in respect of that right either in the country of domicile of the Defendant or where the infringement takes place. . . .

Mr. Silverleaf QC who appeared for the Appellants submitted that such a conclusion was contrary to the Paris Convention of 1883 as revised, the [TRIPS Agreement], the European Patent Convention and article 222 of the Treaty of Rome. We do not believe that these Conventions or the Treaty are directly concerned with jurisdiction. No doubt it was contemplated, prior to the Brussels Convention, that intellectual property rights, being national rights, would be litigated in the State where the right was registered. Indeed there are cases in this country which so held. Even so, those Conventions and the Treaty are not inconsistent with the provisions of the Brussels Convention which apply to intellectual property rights just as much as to other rights. That we believe to be *acte clair*.

Article 6(1) provides another special jurisdiction in that a Defendant, who is one of a number of Defendants, may be sued in the State where one of them is domiciled. The Article has been interpreted as being an exception to the general rule and is to be treated in such a way as to avoid the principle set out in articles 1 to 5 being called into question. In Kalfelis v. Schroder, Case 189/87 [1988] ECR 5565, the European Court said that there must be a connection between the claim made against the person not domiciled in the State where the litigation is pending and the claim made against the party domiciled in that State. The connection must be of "such a kind that it is expedient to determine those actions together in order to avoid the risk of irreconcilable judgments resulting from separate proceedings."

In the present case there has been no examination of the facts and therefore no concluded view can be reached as to whether there is the necessary connection in respect of some of the Appellants. However, a number of Appellants are only alleged to have infringed the United Kingdom patent and it would appear tenuous to suggest that it was expedient to determine together an action for infringement of a Dutch patent, with which they are not concerned, and a United Kingdom patent with which they are, so as to avoid irreconcilable judgments. They are actions relating to two different national rights. True they stem from the same patent application and similar rules of construction will be applicable, but the rights given by those patents are national rights limited in territory to the State in which they are registered and the ambit of the monopolies will not necessarily be the same as amendment is possible. There is no risk of irreconcilable judgments because a judgment on infringement in the United Kingdom will depend upon a national right having effect only in the United Kingdom. The same applies to a judgment on the Dutch patent.

[Under Article 16(4)] there can be no doubt that all proceedings for revocation of a patent have to be decided by the court of the State where the patent is registered. In this case proceedings for revocation of the United Kingdom patent have to be decided by the English Patents Court. That also applies to proceedings "concerned with the registration or validity of patents." [Based upon language in the Jenard report, the court concluded that Article 16(4) "should be construed as differentiating between actions for infringement and proceedings concerned with validity."]

In the United Kingdom it is possible to have both an action for infringement by a patentee and the equivalent action for a declaration of non-infringement by a person threatened by a patent. Where questions of infringement and validity both arise it is invariably not possible to conclude there is infringement without validity being determined. An extreme example, known as a *Gillette* defence [discussed in Chapter 2's section on novelty *supra*–ed.], is where the alleged infringer's case is that the patent is invalid if the alleged infringing acts fall within the ambit of the claims. That appears to be part of the Appellants' contentions in this case. It follows that the split contemplated in the Jenard Report between actions for infringement and proceedings concerned with validity cannot always be made.

Article 64 of the European Patent Convention states that a European Patent confers on its proprietor the same rights as those of a national patent and that infringement shall be dealt with by national law. In the United Kingdom those rights are defined in section 60 of the Patents Act 1977. They are rights which apply only so long as the patent is in force. In proceedings for infringement, validity of the patent is often disputed and, if the attack on the patent is successful, it will be revoked pursuant to section 72 of the 1977 Act. Such revocation has the effect of revoking the grant of the patent and therefore its registration as a patent, and is the reason for the view held in the United Kingdom that it is not possible to infringe an invalid patent. In many cases the attack on the patent prompts the patentee to seek amendment so as to limit the ambit of his monopoly. In the United Kingdom that is possible under section 75 of the 1977 Act. Any amendment has effect and is deemed always to have had effect from the grant of the patent. [cit].

As article 64 of the European Patent Convention requires the national law to be determinative of what will and what will not amount to infringement, it follows that when there is a bona fide challenge to the validity of a United Kingdom patent, any proceedings for infringement must in English eyes be "concerned with" the validity of the patent. Often, perhaps normally, the issue of validity will be the principal element of the dispute. No conclusion as to the chances of a claim of infringement succeeding can be made until a decision has been reached as to the strength of the allegations of invalidity. No concluded view on infringement can be reached until a decision has been reached as to whether any amendment should be made and the attack on the patent has been rejected.

In the present case the Appellants have raised a substantial attack on the validity of the United Kingdom patent and also intend to rely upon a *Gillette* defence. This is a case therefore in which no conclusion on the infringement can be reached without consideration of the validity of the patent. We believe that for the purposes of Article 19 the claim by the Respondents in respect of acts carried out in the United Kingdom are principally concerned with validity of the United Kingdom patent and therefore by reason of that Article and Article 16 the claim falls within the exclusive jurisdiction of the United Kingdom court.

In our view Laddie J was correct in Coin Controls Ltd. v. Suzo International (UK) Ltd. [1997] 3 All ER 45 when he [noted that although "where there are multiple discrete issues before a court it may be possible to sever one or more claims from another and to decline to accept jurisdiction only over those covered by Article 16, that approach does not apply where infringement and validity of an intellectual property right are concerned because they are so closely interrelated."]

Article 24 relates to provisional, including protective, measures. As explained in the Jenard Report, application may be made to the courts of a Contracting State for such provisional measures as may be available under the internal law of that State. However, the measures must be provisional and, in our view, granted in aid of or as an adjunct to some final determination then in contemplation.

Upon the evidence before this court, provisional relief by way of injunction would not be granted in the United Kingdom to restrain continuance by the Appellants of the acts complained of as infringement because of the delay by the Respondents in taking action. However that delay may or may not be determinative in the eyes of a Dutch court. But that is the court in which Akzo seek provisional relief in respect of acts taking place in the United Kingdom, and it is for that court to determine the effect of the delay.

Mr. Silverleaf accepts that a Dutch court has to apply Dutch law when deciding whether to grant provisional relief pursuant to the jurisdiction conferred by article 24. He submits that the United Kingdom Patents courts has by reason of articles 2, 5 and 16(4) exclusive jurisdiction over the dispute between Akzo and the English domiciled Appellants relating to the United Kingdom patent. It follows, he submits, that provisional relief could only be granted in aid of or as an adjunct to a final determination in the United Kingdom courts. Akzo have not initiated any proceedings in the United Kingdom and have not stated any intention of doing so. It followed that there was no jurisdiction under article 24 to grant provisional relief as sought by Akzo.

Mr. Prescott QC, who appeared for the Respondents, submits that the Dutch court can order provisional relief as an adjunct to Akzo's claim for final relief in the Dutch proceedings. That provisional relief would do justice between the parties pending resolution of the question of validity by the United Kingdom Patents court.

The crucial difference between the submissions of the parties is the effect of Article 16(4). If the United Kingdom courts have exclusive jurisdiction over the dispute concerning the United Kingdom patent, then there is no justification for the Respondents attempting to obtain from the Dutch court even provisional relief as an aid to or an adjunct of the claim for final relief in respect of the United Kingdom patent. It would be vexatious to seek such relief. If our conclusion as to the proper application of Article 16(4) is correct, it follows that article 24 does not provide jurisdiction to grant provisional relief restraining infringement within the United Kingdom as an adjunct to the claim for full relief pleaded in the Dutch proceedings.

The question of relief

We have expressed definite views as to the construction of Articles 16(4) and 24 and their application to the facts. We have also expressed views as to the ambit of article 6. However we accept that a contrary opinion is tenable. The matter is accordingly not "acte clair". The question which view is right is one of considerable importance to the enforcement of intellectual property rights in jurisdictions subject to the Brussels Convention. We believe that it is necessary for the European Court of Justice to consider the construction of those Articles and their application to the facts and therefore it would be right to refer appropriate questions to that Court. That we believe to be the correct course, despite the submission of Mr. Prescott that we did not have jurisdiction to grant any relief and that in any case no reference should be made because it was not necessary. We turn to give our reasons why those submissions should not be accepted.

Mr. Prescott submitted that this court has no jurisdiction to grant an injunction in favour of the United Kingdom domiciled Appellants which would restrain Akzo from maintaining proceedings before the Dutch court in respect of the United Kingdom patent. [We believe that submission is wrong.] The United Kingdom courts have jurisdiction to prevent vexation and oppression by persons subject to their jurisdiction. In particular, the courts are entitled to prevent persons domiciled in this country from being submitted to vexatious or oppressive litigation whether started or to be started in this country or another country. As was stated in the advice of the Privy Council in Société National Industrielle Aerospatiale v. Lee Kui Jak [1987] 1 AC 871 a court can restrain a person from pursuing proceedings in a foreign Court where a remedy is available both in that foreign court and this country, but will only do so if pursuit by the person "would be vexatious or oppressive." Further, since such an order indirectly affects the foreign court, the jurisdiction must be exercised with caution and only if the ends of justice so require. We emphasise that injunctions granted for such purposes are directed against the vexatious party and not the courts of the other jurisdiction.

In the present case we have concluded that the dispute relating to the United Kingdom patent comes, by reason of Article 16(4), within the exclusive jurisdiction of the United Kingdom Patents Court. We have also concluded that the matter is not "acte clair". In those circumstances we do not consider we would be justified in reaching a final conclusion that the pursuit, by Akzo, of the claim in the Dutch courts in respect of the United Kingdom patent would be vexatious. It follows that we are not prepared to grant a final injunction at this time. The reference is necessary in order to decide whether final relief by way of injunction or declaration would be appropriate. We now therefore proceed to consider whether interim relief by way of injunction or otherwise would be appropriate pending the determination of the reference to the European Court.

Despite the fact that the relief would be directed against the Respondents, we have in mind that it would indirectly affect the Dutch court which has not yet considered what action, if any, would be appropriate. We have every confidence that the Dutch court will, when deciding what to do, take into account that this court will be referring to the European Court of Justice questions to elucidate how articles 6, 16(4), 19 and 24 should be applied to the dispute. It will give proper weight to our conclusion that it would be wrong for this court to anticipate the decision of the European Court. It will, we believe, also consider carefully the other views expressed in this judgment and, of course, the submissions of the parties and the facts. That being so we have come to the conclusion that justice does not require that this court should grant any relief at this stage. The nature of the parties' businesses means that it is most unlikely that they will suffer any significant harm pending the decision of the European Court which will not be compensated by the award of damages.

We shall therefore adjourn this appeal pending a judgment of the European Court upon questions to be referred to them. When the views of the European Court are known we shall decide what further relief, if any, is appropriate.

EXPANDABLE GRAFTS P'SHIP v. BOSTON SCIENTIFIC BV
[1999] F.S.R. 352 (Court of Appeal, The Hague) (Neth.)

. . . .

In the originating summons [plaintiffs] EGP claimed interim injunctions "prohibiting each of the defendants individually from infringing European Patent 0335 341 either directly or indirectly, in particular by offering, selling, delivering or at any rate marketing the [allegedly infringing] NIR stents, not only for the Netherlands but also with respect to any direct or indirect infringements in other countries in which the patent applies, with the exception of Germany."

The wording of the summary of claims gives rise to misapprehensions. It makes it appear as if the case concerns one single European Patent which is valid in a number of countries. But this is not the case.

The European Patent in question has been granted for: Austria, Belgium, Switzerland, Germany, Spain, France, Great Britain, Greece, Italy, Liechtenstein, Luxembourg, the Netherlands and Sweden. But there is not one European Patent, one common patent, which is valid in the aggregate territory of all countries for which the patent has been granted. The fact is that according to general and common terminology a European Patent consists of a bundle of national patents, in the present case of national patents which are valid in each of the countries just mentioned. These separate national patents have in common that they have been granted in accordance with the rules of the European Patent Convention (EPC) following one single grant procedure by the European Patent Office at Munich and that after being granted they are governed not only by the national patent laws, which have been harmonised to a considerable extent but are not yet quite identical, but also by a number of provisions of the EPC. *See* EPC, Article 2, paragraph 2, which provides:

> The European Patent shall, in each of the Contracting States for which it is granted, have the effect of and be subject to the same conditions as a national patent granted by that State, unless otherwise provided in this Convention.

and EPC, Article 64, paragraph 1, which provides:

> A European Patent shall subject to the provisions of paragraph 2, confer on its proprietor from the date of publication of the mention of its grant in each Contracting State in respect of which it is granted the same rights as would be conferred by a national patent granted in that State.

EGP are claiming . . . injunctions prohibiting each of the defendants not only from infringing the respective national patents originating from the European Patent granted by the European Patent Office and applicable in the respective countries in which the individual defendant corporations have their respective seats, but also from infringing all other national patents belonging to the bundle of patents in the designated countries.

The Court of Appeal further understands the claims thus, that EGP have not wished to raise the issue of possible infringements of the German patent which belongs to the European bundle. EGP have not maintained the part of their action concerning the infringement of the British patent.

The [defendant] BS corporations which have their seats abroad entered an appearance exclusively for the purpose of taking issue with the jurisdiction of the Dutch courts.

EGP have taken the position that the Dutch courts do have jurisdiction over the actions against the defendants which have their seats in the Netherlands by virtue of Article 2 of the Brussels Convention on Jurisdiction and the Enforcement of Judgements in Civil and Commercial Matters (the Brussels Convention) and that the Dutch courts also have jurisdiction over the actions against the other defendants, "by virtue of the provision with respect to the right to summon foreigners into a Dutch court of Article

6(1) Brussels/Lugano Convention, or at any rate of section 126, subsection 7, Dutch Code of Civil Procedure, and (as far as the interim injunctions are concerned) in conjunction with Art 24 Brussels/Lugano Convention."

International jurisdiction in patent cases is an issue that is under discussion in various countries. In its judgment of October 27, 1997 the London Court of Appeal has referred questions on this issue to the [European] Court of Justice for a preliminary ruling. *See* Fort Dodge Ltd. v. Akzo Nobel NV [1998] F.S.R. 222.

In view of the claims and the countries in which the defendants have their seats, the jurisdiction must be decided according to the Brussels Convention and the Lugano Convention, respectively, on Jurisdiction and the Enforcement of Judgements in Civil and Commercial Matters. The Court of Appeal will first examine whether the jurisdiction of the Dutch courts can be based on Article 6(1) of the Brussels/Lugano Convention. . . .

The Court of Appeal states first of all that in accordance with the principal rule of both Conventions as embodied in Article 2 in conjunction with Article 53, companies and corporations must be sued in the courts for the state in which they have their seats. Article 6(1) contains a special jurisdiction rule.

The literal text of Article 6(1) does not seem to impose any restrictions on the possibilities available to a plaintiff to choose the courts for the desired country by suing defendants from different countries. Thus it would seem as if the plaintiff has as many options as the number of different countries in which the defendants have their seats. This is not the case.

[The court quoted at length from the opinion of the Court of Justice in *Kalfelis* and concluded that] the rule laid down in Article 6(1) therefore applies where the actions brought against the various defendants are related when the proceedings are instituted, that is to say where it is expedient to hear and determine them together in order to avoid the risk of irreconcilable judgments resulting from separate proceedings. It is for the national court to verify in each individual case whether that condition is satisfied.

As appears from paragraph 11 of the judgment of the Court of Justice, the problems under consideration here show a strong affinity to those of Article 22 of the Brussels Convention, which Article deals with connection between actions. In the *Tatry* case, [1994] ECR I-5439, the Court of Justice said at page 5478:

> In order to achieve proper administration of justice, that interpretation must be broad and cover all cases where there is a risk of conflicting decisions even if the judgments can be separately enforced and their legal consequences are not mutually exclusive.

It appears from the above that although this is not expressed in the text of Article 6(1) itself, yet the possibilities of applying this paragraph are certainly subject to restrictions.

Having regard to the reasons stated by the [lower court] for its decision, the question arises whether there is question of related actions as mentioned by the Court of Justice in the *Kalfelis/Schroder* case when in one procedure the proprietor of a European Patent brings an action for, for instance, an injunction prohibiting a defendant domiciled in the Netherlands from infringing the Dutch patent of the European bundle of patents by marketing a certain product in the Netherlands and for an injunction prohibiting a defendant domiciled in France from infringing the French patent of the same European bundle of patents by marketing an identical product in France.

[We are] of the opinion that this question must be answered in the negative. Even if the outcome of the judgments in the Netherlands and in France would differ—which is possible in spite of the application of the same rules of substantive patent law—it cannot be said that the judgments are irreconcilable. The fact is that the national patents out of the European bundle exist independently of each other. It is therefore quite possible for one national patent out of the European bundle to be declared wholly or partially null and void while another is held to be valid. It is moreover not impossible that the scope of protection of one patent turns out to be different from that of the other one. One might say that what the patents originating from a European Patent have in common is, in particular, the past and that, after being granted, each of them lives its own life. It is undeniably true that in a case like the present it is onerous for a patent proprietor who wishes to put a stop to the infringements in the Netherlands and in France, that he is forced to start proceedings in both countries and runs the risk, moreover, that different judgments will be issued regarding the same infringements in the two countries. However, having regard to the pivotal meaning of Article 2 of the Brussels/Lugano Convention and the fact that Article 6(1) forms an exception, the interest of the defendant in being sued in the courts for the country in which he is resident or domiciled must outweigh the inconvenience to the patent proprietor, taking account of the fact that the possibility of different judgments is inherent in the European Patent. [We] comment in this respect that the countries that concluded the EPC must have foreseen this inconvenience to patent proprietors and did not remove it.

If, however, in the example discussed above the Dutch and the French defendants belong to the same group of companies, a different approach may be called for. Where several companies belonging to one group of companies are selling identical products in different national markets, this will have to be considered as one joint action based on a joint business plan. In such case the proper administration of justice calls for the simultaneous hearing and settlement of cases, which is made possible by Article 6(1) of the Brussels/Lugano Convention. This does not mean to say, however, that the plaintiff must have the option of suing all the parties belonging to the group in the courts for the domicile of any one of the companies belonging to the group, at his own choice. In the opinion of the Court of Appeal this would be contrary to the predictableness of the competent court contemplated by the Conventions [cit]. The best way of harmonising the interests which Article 2 and Article 6(1) of the Brussels/Lugano Convention purport to serve is to take the view that in such case, by analogy with the case law concerning the applicability of Article 5(3) of the Brussels Convention [cit], all the actions may only be brought in their entirety in the courts for the domicile of the head office in question which is in charge of the business operations in question and/or from which the business plan originated. The relation between the actions and these courts will be the closest. This solution has the advantage of avoiding jurisdiction being conferred on more than one forum and consequently of reducing the possibilities of forum shopping, which according to Advocate-General Darmon in his advisory opinion in the *Shevill/Presse Alliance* case (paragraphs 57 and 67) is precisely what is contemplated by the Brussels Convention.

The above has the following consequences for the case now before the Court of Appeal.

In the written summary of the argument by Mr. Ebbink in the first instance the following can be read:

> BSC is an American enterprise having offices all over the world. As far as relevant to the present case, the corporate structure of BSC in Europe is as follows.
>
> The European headquarters are located in Paris under the name of BS International BV. BS Paris is charged with the central management of the European offices of BSC. Its duties include the European management, marketing, staff services, communications with and reporting to BSC America etc. The Dutch branch of BS International BV is a small office. The 'centre of activities of the BSC Group outside America', . . . is not in the Netherlands but in Paris. The fact that BS Paris has chosen to be incorporated in the legal form of a Dutch private company (BV) has a fiscal background. The Dutch office of BS International BV serves as a warehouse for the continental European market. In the Netherlands, (Beek, Limburg) the stents are awaiting further distribution.

The activities of the local BS companies among the defendants . . . only include the local marketing and sale of the NIR stents, controlled, as stated before, by BS Paris. The local companies have a high degree of autonomy. They promote the stents in their respective countries or regions, they approach (potential) customers, subsequently order the NIR stents directly from the distributor (the Dutch office of BS International BV) and invoice directly to their customers.

It can be inferred from the above that BS International BV is, as the parties have called it, the spider in the web. All other defendant BS corporations in Europe are controlled from this corporation. All these corporations are acting jointly under the management of BS International BV. In this case the actions for injunctions against infringement may all be brought in their entirety in the courts for the place where BS International BV has its seat.

The parties differ in opinion on the question where BS International has its seat. According to EGP it is the Netherlands, according to BS, France.

The Court of Appeal takes the following position regarding this issue. The second sentence of Article 53 of the Brussels Convention reads as follows:

> In order to determine that seat, the court shall apply its rules of private international law.

Under Dutch private international law a company is held to have its seat at its registered seat. . . . It appears from the extract from the commercial register that the registered seat of BS International is at Maastricht. So BS International BV has its seat in the Netherlands.

Consequently the Dutch courts have jurisdiction over the infringement actions.

The present proceedings are not main proceedings on the merits but interim injunction proceedings. All the grounds stated above relate to the court's jurisdiction in main proceedings on the merits. In the opinion of the Court of Appeal it is the position that in a case in which the Dutch courts have jurisdiction over actions in main proceedings on the merits, the Dutch courts also have jurisdiction over actions brought in interim injunction proceedings.

Yet another complication presents itself in the present case. BS has taken the position that the European Patent at issue in these proceedings was granted wrongfully. Though it is true that BS has not filed an opposition with the Opposition Department of the European Patent Office, it has instituted nullity proceedings in a great number of countries.

According to BS this must result in the Dutch courts no longer having jurisdiction over the infringement actions relating to the foreign patents. BS is relying on Article 16(4) in conjunction with Article 19 of the Brussels/Lugano Convention.

By virtue of Article 16(4) of the Brussels/Lugano Convention, exclusive jurisdiction over actions for the nullification of foreign patents does not vest in the Dutch courts but in the courts for the countries in which the patents in question apply. If a Dutch court should be seised of an action for the nullification of a foreign patent, then by virtue of Article 19, the Dutch court would have to declare of its own motion that it has no jurisdiction.

The actions brought by EGP are infringement actions. With respect to these actions the jurisdiction of the courts does not cease to exist by operation of the law as soon as nullity actions are instituted. For it is the opinion of the Court of Appeal that the jurisdiction issue must be decided on the basis of the claim stated in the summons.

Consequences of the institution of nullity actions for the jurisdiction issue

The institution of nullity actions may have consequences, though, for the hearing of the infringement actions. It is a fact that infringement and nullity are indissolubly linked with each other, since it is impossible to infringe a patent that is null and void. Unless it is immediately clear that a nullity action cannot be deemed to be meant seriously, in the case of main proceedings on the merits the court which is asked to pronounce judgment on the infringement issue will have to adopt a cautious attitude towards the infringement action and in principle will have to stay the infringement proceedings until the foreign court has pronounced judgment on the nullity issue.

Obviously the separate hearing and settlement of the infringement issue and the nullity issue by two different national courts is far from ideal. It would be desirable for the infringement and nullity issues to be decided by the same court. It would also be desirable if the hearing and settlement of actions for infringement and nullity of several patents originating from one European bundle of patents could be concentrated in one court. But this solution is barred by Article 16(4) of the Brussels/Lugano Convention. National courts cannot make the said wishes come true. Amendment of the Conventions seems to be inevitable.

In the opinion of the Court of Appeal the assessment of the interim infringement injunctions claimed in the present proceedings is in fact affected by the nullity actions. This situation calls for at least the same degree of caution.

As will appear in the following, it is not in the least clear right away that the arguments put forward by BS in support of the allegation that the national patents originating from the European Bundle of patents should be declared null and void, must be considered inadequate. The result must be that the Dutch courts will have to refuse the interim injunctions prohibiting infringement of the foreign patents.

Jurisdiction by virtue of Article 24 of the Brussels/Lugano Convention

To the extent that EGP have taken the position that Article 24 of the Brussels/Lugano Convention will avail them, the Court of Appeal cannot subscribe to this view. This Article offers the possibility of imposing provisional or protective measures even in those cases in which the courts of another Contracting State have jurisdiction as to the substance of the matter. The Court of Appeal holds the opinion that in such a case the measures to be imposed can be operative only within the territory of the state of the court. . . . [T]he justification for the said additional jurisdiction lies in the fact that the local courts are in the best position to judge the circumstances on the ground of which the requested measures are to be allowed or refused. It is irreconcilable with this ruling that a Dutch court which has jurisdiction exclusively by virtue of Article 24, should issue regulatory measures having effect abroad.

Jurisdiction by virtue of Dutch Code of Civil Procedure, section 126(7)

Section 126, subsection 7 of the Dutch Code of Civil Procedure cannot apply since the defendants have their seats in countries which are signatories of either the Brussels Convention or the Lugano Convention. The provisions of these Conventions prevail.

Conclusion with regard to the claims for cross-border prohibitive injunctions

The conclusion to be drawn from the above is that though the Dutch courts have jurisdiction over the infringement actions instituted against all the BS corporations that have been summoned, yet the actions for interim injunctions against infringement of the foreign patents must be refused because the likelihood is that the foreign patents will be declared null and void.

Jurisdiction over the claim for an injunction against infringement of the Dutch patent

On the same grounds as are stated above with respect to the jurisdiction over the actions for cross-border prohibitory injunctions, the court has jurisdiction over the action for an injunction against infringement of the Dutch patent.

Consequences of the action for nullity of the Dutch patent

[The Court of Appeals concluded that there was a likelihood that the patent would be declared null and void in the designated countries, and thus the interim injunction against infringement of the Dutch patent was also denied].

NOTES AND QUESTIONS

(1) **Dutch Case Law**. Dutch cross-border injunctions had been the topic of much comment up until April 23, 1998. Indeed, the literature addressing these developments is voluminous. For a good background discussion of the pertinent provisions and case law, see Ian Karet, *Intellectual Property Litigation—Jurisdiction in Europe*, 3 INTELL. PROP. Q. 317 (1998); Jan J. Brinkhof, *Summary Proceedings and Other Provisional Measures in Connection with Patent Infringement*, 26 I.I.C. 762 (1993). The *Expandable*

Grafts court restricted the availability of pan-EU relief by interpreting the requirement of relatedness of claims more strictly and rejecting the argument that sufficient connection may be grounded on the infringement of national patents derived from a common European patent application. For commentary on this more recent case law and the so-called "spider in the web" doctrine developed by the Dutch courts to set the parameters of this jurisdiction, see Charles Gielen, *District Court Refines Case Law on 'Spider in the Web' Doctrine*, 14 WORLD INTELL. PROP. REP. 186 (June 2000).

(2) **Exclusive Jurisdiction**. The exclusive jurisdiction provision in Article 16(4) of the Brussels Convention applies only to registered rights. The registration variable is said to be significant for several reasons, including respect for foreign administrative officials and concerns of institutional competence. First, it is argued that registered rights are more likely directly to implicate decisions of the administrative organs of a state. Courts are generally reluctant to pass on the correctness of the governmental acts of a foreign state. Second, according exclusive jurisdiction to the conferring state on matters implicating validity or nullity of registered rights reflects concern regarding the ability of foreign judges to make judgments regarding the validity of registered rights, which are normally granted only after detailed administrative examination by specially trained national officials. Consider also the following dictum from Mr. Justice Aldous in *Plastus Kreativ AB v. Minnesota Mining and Manufacturing Co.*, [1995] RPC 438 (Eng.), where he explained some of the reasons why he was reluctant to adjudicate foreign patent rights:

> For myself I would not welcome the task of having to decide whether a person had infringed a foreign patent. Although patent actions appear on their face to be disputes between two parties, in reality they also concern the public. A finding of infringement is a finding that a monopoly granted by the state is to be enforced. The result is invariably that the public have to pay higher prices than if the monopoly did not exist. If that be the proper result, then that result should, I believe, come about from a decision of a court situated in the state where the public have to pay the higher prices. One only has to imagine a decision of this court that the German public should pay to a British company substantial sums of money to realise the difficulties that might arise. I believe that, if the local courts are responsible for enforcing and deciding questions of validity and infringement, the conclusions reached are likely to command the respect of the public.

Are any of these arguments persuasive? Are they more persuasive for some forms of intellectual property than others? Are they more persuasive as regards registered rights than unregistered rights (such as copyright)? Could the concerns underlying the exclusive jurisdiction provision be addressed in a manner that permits the full use of the liberal jurisdictional provisions in Articles 2, 5 and 6? For example, could the court hearing the request for cross-border relief refer the question of validity to the national court of the state that granted the registered right?

(3) **The Scope of the Conventions and the Brussels Regulation**. The Brussels Convention governed jurisdiction in the courts of EU states in actions involving European citizens. The parallel Lugano Convention, referenced in *Fort Dodge*, extended the same principles to states in the European Free Trade Association (EFTA). *See* Convention on Jurisdiction and Enforcement of Judgments in Civil and Commercial Matters, Sept. 16, 1988, 1988 O.J. (L 319) 1. The Brussels and Lugano Conventions were incorporated directly into EU law through the enactment of Council Regulation (EC) No. 44/2001 of 22 December 2000 on jurisdiction and the recognition and enforcement of judgments in civil and commercial matters, O.J. (L 12) 1 (Jan. 16, 2001), which came into effect on March 1, 2002. This regulation (the "Brussels Regulation") replaced the Brussels Convention as the formal source of the rules on jurisdiction and recognition of judgments in civil litigation among EU citizens in national courts of most EU member states. (Denmark has, as permitted by the relevant EU treaties, opted not to be governed by the Brussels Regulation, and thus relations between Denmark and other member states continues to be governed by the Brussels Convention.) But the Brussels Regulation carries over most of the essential principles of the Brussels Convention discussed in the cases excerpted above with only minor modification.

(4) **The Role of the European Court of Justice**. The European Court of Justice is accorded jurisdiction to interpret the meaning of the Brussels Convention. *See* Protocol on the Interpretation by the Court of Justice of the Convention of 27 September 1968 on Jurisdiction and Enforcement of Judgments in Civil and Commercial Matters, 1990 O.J. (C189) at 25. (The parties in *Fort Dodge* settled prior to the European Court handing down a decision.) The Court has developed a substantial body of case law on the meaning of the Convention. Notice, however, that the U.K. court decided that certain matters of treaty interpretation were *acte claire* and thus did not require the involvement of the European Court. This doctrine enables national courts to apply allegedly unambiguous interpretations of the Convention and thus to function on a day-to-day basis without the involvement of the European Court.

(5) **Proposed Hague Convention.** A draft convention on jurisdiction and enforcement of foreign judgments has been prepared by the Hague Conference on Private International Law and it is closely modeled upon the Brussels Convention. A two-stage diplomatic conference had been scheduled to discuss the draft; the first session in mid-2001, with the concluding session in early 2002. But negotiations continue to drag on. The draft convention is controversial for a number of reasons not restricted to intellectual property. But the intellectual property provisions have attracted significant attention, both internationally (from WIPO and the WTO) and in the United States (where the State Department, the Copyright Office and the Patent & Trademark Office are each debating what position the United States should adopt). Article 12(4) of the proposed Hague Convention would mirror Article 16(4) of the Brussels Convention, but the precise scope of the provision remains a matter for negotiation. At its narrowest, the exclusion

may be limited to challenges to the validity of registered rights. But some countries have suggested that the exclusive jurisdiction provision should be extended to infringement questions on the theory that the scope of rights (and hence determinations of infringement) is linked to validity; a restrictive approach to one might justify an expansive approach to the other, and vice versa. Would you support such an extended exclusion from the general rules of jurisdiction? What advantages might accrue from applying more liberal jurisdictional rules in multinational patent infringement disputes?

The European Court of Justice has jurisdiction to interpret the meaning of the Brussels Convention. No such court will have a similar role with the Hague Convention. Uniformity will instead be pursued by requiring national courts to interpret the Convention in light of its international character, the need for uniformity, and the case law of other contracting states. *See* Draft Convention art. 38. How will this affect the development of international rules on consolidation of international intellectual property litigation?

(6) **Recent Revival of Cross-Border Relief**. Somewhat against the trend in Dutch jurisprudence, on September 14, 2001, the President of the Brussels court of first instance, relying on the ECJ's 1998 *Van Uden Maritime v. Deco Line* decision, issued a preliminary injunction against a 12-member European consortium on a European patent covering a specially shaped toothbrush. The president held that in order to grant cross-border relief, the required "real connecting link" to the forum was satisfied by the existence of a European patent presumed valid in all the designated countries. *See Belgian Court Issues First Pan-European Patent Injunction*, 15 WIPO REP. 4 (Nov. 2001); *see also* Gretchen Ann Bender, *Clash of the Titans: The Territoriality of Patent Law vs. The European Union*, 40 IDEA 49, 65 (2000).

§ 7.04 Parallel Imports/Gray Goods

Most intellectual property laws have developed the concept of exhaustion of rights (sometimes called the first sale doctrine in copyright law) that in some form is essential to ensure the free alienability of goods. Rights may be exhausted with respect to a particular good when that good is placed on the market by or with the consent of the rights owner. That is to say, the right owner may not assert its intellectual property rights to restrain the free transfer of those goods. Several questions are raised by the exhaustion doctrine, most significantly: (1) what is the geographic scope of exhaustion, i.e., does it matter where the rights owner marketed the goods? (2) are rights exhausted where the goods are placed on the market not by the rights owner but by a company in a form of an economic relationship with the rights owner? and (3) are rights revived, and capable of being asserted, with respect to goods that are placed on the market by the mark owner but then modified or repackaged without the mark owner's consent?

These issues are not new. But in the context of global trade they have assumed heightened significance. The free trade philosophy underpinning our present economic environment, the inclusion of intellectual property law within free trade agreements such as GATT, and the ongoing development of intellectual property laws by a supranational institution (such as the EU) committed to eradicating barriers to the free movement of goods within a multinational territory, has each brought the exhaustion issue to the forefront of current debate. The territorial nature of intellectual property rights clashes with an absolutist vision of free international trade in goods. The exhaustion doctrine mediates to some extent that clash, by determining whether and to what extent a right holder in country A can assert its rights and thus prevent the entry into country A of legitimate goods put on the market in country B. (These goods imported from country B are called "parallel imports" or "gray goods.") In this area, international agreements remain relatively sparse. Thus, after setting out briefly those provisions that exist, we review the approaches to exhaustion adopted in different national and regional jurisdictions, primarily in the United States and the European Union.

[A]   International Treaty Provisions

TRIPS AGREEMENT, ARTICLE 6

For purposes of dispute settlement under this Agreement, subject to the provisions of Articles 3 and 4 above [national treatment and most-favored nation treatment] nothing in this Agreement shall be used to address the issue of exhaustion of intellectual property rights.

DECLARATION ON THE TRIPS AGREEMENT AND PUBLIC HEALTH, ¶¶ 4-5

Adopted at Ministerial Conference of the World Trade Organization,
Doha (Nov. 14, 2001), WTO Doc. No. WT/MIN(01)/DEC/2

4. We agree that the TRIPS Agreement does not and should not prevent Members from taking measures to protect public health. Accordingly, while reiterating our commitment to the TRIPS Agreement, we affirm that the Agreement can and should be interpreted and implemented in a manner supportive of WTO Members' right to protect public health and, in particular, to promote access to medicines for all.

In this connection, we reaffirm the right of WTO Members to use, to the full, the provisions in the TRIPS Agreement, which provide flexibility for this purpose.

5. Accordingly and in light of paragraph 4 above, while maintaining our commitments in the TRIPS Agreement, we recognize that these flexibilities include:

. . . .

(d) The effect of the provisions in the TRIPS Agreement that are relevant to the exhaustion of intellectual property rights is to leave each Member free to establish its own regime for such exhaustion without challenge, subject to the MFN and national treatment provisions of Articles 3 and 4.

PRELIMINARY QUESTION

Before we consider the case law in different jurisdictions, ask yourself whether we should permit intellectual property owners to restrain parallel imports. What legitimate interests of the intellectual property owner are being protected? Do consumers benefit from parallel imports? In all circumstances? If not, what considerations should determine whether parallel imports should be permitted? What changes in global marketing, whether those now occurring or those that might soon occur, might alter the importance of the gray market? How does this affect your analysis of the appropriate approach to parallel importing? Do we need an international law of competition/antitrust to balance the international law of intellectual property?

[B]   Treatment Under U.S. Law

CURTISS AEROPLANE & MOTOR CORP. v. UNITED AIRCRAFT ENGINEERING CORP.
266 F. 71 (2d Cir. 1920)

ROGERS, CIRCUIT JUDGE. This suit is brought under the Patent Laws of the United States for the alleged infringement by defendant of thirteen patents issued by the United States. . . . The defendant is charged with selling and offering for sale in the United States aeroplanes manufactured in Canada pursuant to certain agreements between plaintiff and the British government; the Canadian manufacture having been conducted by a corporation created by that government for that purpose. The total number of claims involved is 80. All the patents involved are for improvements in aeroplanes, and are capable of conjoint use, and are so used by plaintiff and defendant.

The bill of complaint alleges that all of the patents referred to were, by instruments in writing duly executed and recorded in the United States Patent Office, assigned to the plaintiff, and that plaintiff is the sole and exclusive owner of each and all of them. It also alleges that defendant has infringed each and all of said patents by offering for sale, selling, and using within the Southern District of New York, as well as elsewhere within the United States, aeroplanes, each of which embodies the improvements claimed in each and all of said patents. It contains the following statement:

> That the plaintiff, Curtiss Aeroplane & Motor Corporation, has developed at large expense, and produced in large quantities, aeroplanes of a distinctive type known throughout the aeroplane industry and among aviators as the Curtiss JN-4 machine; that such machine and the various parts thereof are embodiments of the several inventions of the letters patent heretofore set forth; that the defendant is now selling in the United States aeroplanes known as Canadian Curtiss or Canadian JN-4 machines, which are copies, in form, appearance, and mechanical details, of plaintiff's JN-4 machine, all in violation of plaintiff's rights under such patents and in an unfair and unlawful manner.

The bill prays an injunction and asks for an account of profits and damages resulting from the infringement which it alleges, and that any damages assessed may be tripled. The court below dismissed the bill for lack of merit, with costs to defendant.

The plaintiff, prior to the beginning of the [First] World War, was engaged in the manufacture of aeroplanes, and as a result of the war its business was greatly extended. In 1916 the plaintiff entered into certain contracts with the British government from which it received some $4,000,000. The contract into which the plaintiff entered with the British government is found in two separate documents: First, the agreement of November 20, 1916, with the annexed schedule, which is a contract of sales; second, the simultaneous agreement of the same date, which is an agreement on the plaintiff's (the seller's) part to promote the manufacture by the British government (the buyer) of the aeroplanes and engines of the type sold. The record contains a third document, dated December 6, 1916. The parties to this document are the Curtiss Aeroplane & Motors, Limited, of the first part, and the Canadian Aeroplanes, Limited, of the second part. The Curtiss Aeroplane & Motors, Limited, is a subsidiary company organized in Canada, in which the plaintiff owned 83 per cent of the outstanding capital stock; and the Canadian Aeroplane, Limited, is a company which the Imperial Munitions Board had caused to be incorporated to take over the plant of the Curtiss Aeroplanes & Motors, Limited.

The document above referred to as a contract of sales was executed on behalf of his Britannic Majesty's Government by J. P. Morgan & Co., agents. That document contains the statement that the British government has contracted to purchase from the plaintiff, and the seller has contracted to manufacture and sell to the buyer, at the price, and subject to the terms and conditions specified, the "seller's JN-4A type aeroplane, each equipped with one seller's OX5 type 90 H.P. engine, spare parts for such aeroplanes, blueprints and such aeroplanes, seller's OX5 type 90 H.P. engine, and spare parts for such engines." It also provides for the sale of a specified number of additional engines and of sets of spare parts of such engines.

The second document of those referred to was executed by his Britannic Majesty's Government, acting by the Imperial Munitions Board of Canada, and it provides in its first clause as follows:

> The seller agrees to cause to be sold and delivered to the buyer within ten (10) days of the date of the fixing of the purchase price therefor, as hereinafter provided, and the buyer agrees to accept and pay for, all of the tools, machinery, drawings, patterns, jigs, etc., of the Canadian company for use in the manufacture of seller's JN-4 aeroplanes, including raw materials and material manufactured and in process of manufacture at said Toronto plants for use in the manufacture of such aeroplanes, the buyer to pay therefor to the Canadian company. . . .

It provides in its third clause as follows:

> The seller agrees that at the option of the buyer it will grant or cause to be granted to the buyer, as part of the consideration moving from the seller to the buyer for this agreement, the exclusive right and license under any and all Canadian patents and applications for Canadian patents now or at any time hereafter owned by the seller or the Canadian company, and any further inventions now or hereafter owned and controlled by them or either of them embodying changes in or improvements of seller's JN-4 type aeroplanes and of seller's type engines, to manufacture such aeroplanes and/or engines within the Dominion of Canada, for sale to or use by the British government or the government of any of its possessions, but not for manufacture, use, or sale otherwise.

The plaintiff alleges that it was not within the contemplation of the parties to the agreements made between plaintiff and the British government, or within plaintiff's intention or by its permission, that the aeroplanes were to be sold or used by the public, or for other than war purposes, or in the United States. These allegations are denied absolutely in an affidavit presented by one who was connected with the Imperial Munitions Board of Canada, which made the contracts, and who was the superintendent of aeronautical supplies; this department being a branch of the Air Ministry in Great Britain and responsible only to the government of Great Britain. His affidavit states that in entering into the contracts made with the plaintiff it was understood that the property manufactured or otherwise acquired by the munitions board should become the absolute property of the board, to be disposed of as it should see fit. This was purely a war organization, and as soon as hostilities ceased the board proceeded to sell off everything controlled by it, including lands, buildings, aeroplanes, motor transports, motorboats, and thousands of patented articles of all kinds, including those complained of by the plaintiff.

It is admitted that the JN-4 aeroplanes which are said to infringe were made in Canada for the British government under the agreements to which reference has been made, and that after the war defendant purchased them from the British government, and, as it appears, is now proceeding to sell them in the United States. It is also admitted that the defendant has announced its intention of establishing warehouses at various parts of the United States, and such warehouses have been established already by it in New York and Chicago, in order that it may supply individuals and companies with the spare parts of air planes of all kinds and descriptions and all standard parts which may be used in their manufacture and development, including the supplying of standard air plane parts for the particular Canadian planes herein involved.

The defendant corporation has a capital of $500,000, and as the record shows, it is in the management of men of character and of excellent business standing. The chief engineer of the Curtiss Aeroplane & Motors Limited, of Canada, states in his affidavit that "their staff of engineers is composed of the leading aeronautical engineers of this country." It was organized on November 22, 1918, which was prior to the signing of the armistice, and was established, it is said, with the idea of organizing an aeronautical engineering and consulting corporation of the highest type. At the time of its incorporation there was no intention of purchasing any of the property of the Imperial Munitions Board of Canada. It appears that after the armistice, and when defendant was first approached on the subject of the purchase of some part of the aeroplane equipment of the British government, which was located in Canada, it declared through its president that it was not interested in any extent whatsoever. In January, 1919, the Imperial Munitions Board sold a number of its machines to the Canadian government, and the remainder of its equipment was sold to F. G. Ericson, a citizen of the United States, at the time a resident of Toronto, Canada. They were purchased by Ericson in his own name, but as a matter of fact he was acting for defendant. He is a member of the Society of Automotive Engineers and a Fellow of the Aeronautical Society of Great Britain, and had been for nine years engaged in the development of aeronautics. In 1915 he was appointed chief engineer of the Curtiss Aeroplane & Motors, Limited, of Canada, and when that concern was taken over by the Canadian Aeroplanes, Limited, he became its chief engineer. Before the sale to Ericson was made he informed the director of aviation of the Imperial Munitions Board what disposition he intended to make of the property upon acquiring it, and that he expected to sell a few of the planes in Canada, but that most of them would be sold for commercial purposes in the United States, and that he expected to establish a depot for such sales in or near Baltimore. With this information in its possession the Imperial Munitions Board made the sale, and made it entirely without restriction of condition, and gave Ericson full right to sell and dispose of the property whenever and wherever he might see fit. It may be remarked in passing that the counsel of the munitions board, who is referred to in one of the affidavits "as one of the most prominent attorneys in Canada," furnished that board with an opinion in which he denied the claims set up by the plaintiff as to the rights which the British government had under the agreements already referred to.

The bill charges no infringement by manufacture, nor does it raise the question when assembling ends and manufacturing begins. It deals with nothing but the right to bring into the United States certain JN-4's which the plaintiff gave permission to make, and in the making of which it aided, and for every one of which it has been compensated. The right to bring these machines into the country is the sole question with which the bill deals.

An aeroplane has been said to be the most mobile article manufactured, and it is not confined by geographical boundaries. It is susceptible of use anywhere in the world. As was said at the argument, aeroplanes were used by the British government, not only in England and Canada, but over the battle fields of Belgium and France, in Egypt, Palestine, Mesopotamia, Northern Russia, South Africa, and indeed wherever hostilities existed. In the very nature of things, and from the language used in the agreements, it is evident that the contracting parties contemplated such widespread use. After this country entered the war, the aviation fields in Texas and in other states were placed at the disposal of the British authorities and were actually used by them as training fields for Canadian aviators. It does not appear in this record whether any of these Canadian JN-4 planes were then brought into the United States for use by Canadian aviators on our aviation fields, who were there undergoing training. If, however, such planes were then brought into the United States, and if they contained the plaintiff's manufactured engines, it would be difficult to believe that any one would seriously contend that their introduction involved any violation of the plaintiff's patents.

The plaintiff and the British government alike understood and intended that the aeroplanes to be manufactured by that government as well as those to be supplied to it by the plaintiff were to become the absolute property of the government, and were to be disposed of as the latter should see fit. The express language of the contract is that the aeroplanes and other articles should "become and be the absolute property of the British government."

The plaintiff, in becoming the owner of the patents in suit, acquired the exclusive privilege of making, using, and vending, and of authorizing others to make, use, and vend the subject-matter of the respective inventions without its permission. Bloomer v. McQuewan, 14 How. 539. The exclusive right of an inventor in his invention was not recognized by the common law, which conferred no such monopoly upon him. The right in the United States rests upon article 1, section 8, of the Constitution, which gives to Congress the power to promote the progress of science and the useful arts by securing for limited times to authors and inventors the exclusive right to their respective writings and discoveries. While a patent is undoubtedly a monopoly it belongs to a class made legal by the constitutional provision referred to.

It is important to determine what right or rights passed to the British government under the agreements which it entered into with the plaintiff. As we have seen, the owner of a patent has three distinct rights, which he can dispose of either together or singly: (1) The right to make the article. (2) The right to use it. (3) The right to sell it. Waterman v. Mackensie, 138 U.S. 252. A grant which does not transfer all these rights is a license. So, also, is the right to make, use, and sell the article for specified purposes only. Gamewell Fire-Alarm Telephone Co. v. Brooklyn (C.C.) 14 Fed. 255; Bogart v. Hinds (C.C.) 25 Fed. 484. *See* 22 Am. & Eng. Encyc. of Law, 430.

That the British government secured the right to manufacture the aeroplanes, and the engines as well, is not open to doubt. In the fourth clause of the agreement of sale the plaintiff bound itself from time to time to furnish the British government all information useful to it "in the building of such aeroplanes and engines, including engineering data, blueprints in detail of such aeroplanes and engines," etc. The sixth clause of that agreement reads as follows:

> The seller agrees that at the request of the buyer from time to time it will send to the plant to be established by the buyer in the Dominion of Canada a competent engineer, familiar with the design, construction, and methods of manufacture of such aeroplanes and/or engines, to assist and advise the buyer in the manufacture thereof. Such engineer shall report his observations and recommendations to the general manager of the plant so to be established by the buyer, or any other person designated by it for that purpose, and shall continue in the exclusive employment of the buyer during its pleasure, receiving compensation from the buyer at a rate not to exceed fifty dollars ($50) per week during the time of such continuous and exclusive employment.

And the seventh clause provides that the British government shall pay "on each such engine manufactured" by it a specified sum, adding:

> "And such exclusive right and license shall be granted only upon the further condition that the buyer shall pay to the seller," etc.

There is much more in the agreements which proves what the plaintiff's intention was respecting the right of the British government to manufacture, but it is not necessary to set it forth herein. It does not in any way restrict or qualify the right of the British government.

That government plainly acquired the right under its license to make. Did it also have the right to use and to vend? The answer to this question depends upon whether the authorization to make was general and unrestricted or subject to qualification and conditions, as to the disposition of the planes by the British government. The agreements will be searched in vain for any restriction of condition as to the right to use or to vend; and in the absence of such restriction we understand the law to be that the British government obtained a full and unqualified right to use and sell the planes and engines, and that this right passed to all subsequent purchasers, and therefore to this defendant. No American or British decision asserting a contrary doctrine is known to us.

The plaintiff relies on certain cases, but an examination shows that they are plainly distinguishable, and do not support the plaintiff's contention. The cases upon which it relies belong to one or the other of two classes: (1) Those in which there has been a sale of a patented article, or a license to manufacture, but accompanied by explicit and unequivocal restrictions as to the time, or place, or manner of using the article so sold or licensed, or as to the ultimate disposal thereof. Dickerson v. Matheson, 57 Fed. 524; Dickerson v. Tinling, 84 Fed. 192; Dickerson v. Sheldon, 98 Fed. 621. (2) Those in which there has been no participation whatever by the owner of the patent, either as a party or as a privy, in the putting out of the article which is alleged to infringe. Boesch v. Graff, 133 U.S. 697; Featherstone v. Ormonde Cycle Co. (C.C.) 53 Fed. 110; Daimler v. Conklin, 170 Fed. 70. And if a patentee retains title to the patented machine, which was not done in this case, he may restrict its manner of use, in the lease or other contract. United States v. United Shoe Machinery Co., 247 U.S. 32, 58. In Chaffee v. Boston Belting Co., 22 How. 217, 223, the Supreme Court said:

> When the patented machine rightfully passes to the hands of the purchaser from the patentee, or from any other person by him authorized to convey it, the machine is no longer within the limits of the monopoly. . . . By a valid sale and purchase, the patented machine becomes the private individual property of the purchaser, and is no longer protected by the laws of the United States. . . .

In Bloomer v. Millinger, 1 Wall. 340, 350, the court said:

> Patentees acquire the exclusive right to make and use, and vend to others to be used, their patented inventions for the period of time specified in the patent; but when they have made and vended to others to be used one or more of the things patented, to that extent they have parted with their exclusive right. They are entitled to but one royalty for a patented machine. and consequently, when a patentee has himself constructed the machine and sold it, or authorized another to construct and sell it, or to construct and use and operate it, and the consideration has been paid to him for the right, he has then to that extent parted with his monopoly, and ceased to have any interest whatever in the machine so sold or so authorized to be constructed and operated.

The purchaser of a patented article from a territorial licensee (one whose rights are limited to a restricted territory) may, unless there is a specific agreement to the contrary, use the article so purchased outside of the territory without interference from the patentee. The article is no longer within the monopoly of the patentee, and the purchaser can use it anywhere. This principle was announced in Adams v. Burke, 17 Wall. 453, 456, where it was said:

> It seems to us that, although the right of Lockhart & Seelye to manufacture, to sell and to use these coffin lids was limited to the circle of 10 miles around Boston, that a purchaser from them of a

single coffin acquired the right to use that coffin for the purpose
for which all coffins are used; that, so far as the use of it was
concerned, the patentee had received his consideration, and it was
no longer within the monopoly of the patent. It would be to ingraft
a limitation upon the right of use not contemplated by the statute,
nor within the reason of the contract to say that it could only be
used within the 10-mile circle.

And see, to the same effect, Hobbie v. Jennison, 149 U.S. 355; Keeler v.
Standard Folding Bed, 157 U.S. In the case last cited the court said:

> Upon the doctrine of these cases we think it follows that one who
> buys patented articles of manufacture from one authorized to sell
> them becomes possessed of an absolute property in such articles,
> unrestricted in time or place. . . . The conclusion reached does not
> deprive a patentee of his just rights, because no article can be
> unfettered from the claim of his monopoly without paying its
> tribute. The inconvenience and annoyance to the public that an
> opposite conclusion would occasion are too obvious to require
> illustration.

If a patentee or his assignee sells a patented article, that article is freed
from the monopoly of any patents which the vendor may possess. If the
thing sold contains inventions of several United States patents owned by
the vendor, the article is freed from each and all of them; and if the vendor
has divided his monopoly into different territorial monopolies, his sale frees
the article from them all. If the vendor's patent monopoly consists of foreign
and domestic patents, the sale frees the article from the monopoly of both
his foreign and his domestic patents, and where there is no restriction in
the contract of sale the purchaser acquires the complete title and full right
to use and sell the article in any and every country. This doctrine was
recognized by Judge Wallace in the Circuit Court for the Southern District
of New York in 1885, in Holiday v. Mattheson, 24 Fed. 185. That case raised
the question whether the owner of a patent in the United States for an
invention, and who had sold the patented article in England without
restrictions or conditions, could treat as an infringer one who had purchased
the article in England of a vendee of the patentee, and could restrain him
from using or selling the article in the United States. In deciding the question adversely Judge Wallace said:

> When the owner sells an article without any reservation respecting
> its use, or the title which is to pass, the purchaser acquires the
> whole right of the vendor in the thing sold, the right to use it, to
> repair it, and to sell it to others; and second purchasers acquire the
> rights of the seller, and may do with the article whatever the first
> purchaser could have lawfully done if he had not parted with it.
> The presumption arising from such a sale is that the vendor intends
> to part with all his rights in the thing sold, and that the purchaser
> is to acquire an unqualified property in it; and it would be inconsis-
> tent with the presumed understanding of the parties to permit the

vendor to retain the power of restricting the purchaser to using the thing bought in a particular way, or in a particular place, for a limited period of time, or from selling his rights to others. It is quite immaterial whether the thing sold is a patented article or not, or whether the vendor is the owner of a patent which gives him a monopoly of its use and sale. If these circumstances happen to concur, the legal effect of the transaction is not changed, unless by the conditions of the bargain the monopoly right is impressed upon the thing purchased; and if the vendor sells without reservation or restriction, he parts with his monopoly so far as it can in any way qualify the rights of the purchaser.

And *see* Morgan Envelope Co. v. Albany Perforated Wrapping Paper Co. (C.C.) 40 Fed. 580.

Counsel for plaintiff relies strongly upon Société Anonyme des Manufactures de Glaces v. Tilgman's Patent Sand Blast Co., L.R. 25 Ch. Div. 7. That case, however, is readily distinguishable in its facts. There were two patents for the same invention, one Belgian and one British. The two patents were owned by the same concern. A third party had purchased the patented article in Belgium, and had then undertaken to import his purchase into England. The owner of the British patent had not manufactured the article, nor sold it, nor in any way authorized the purchaser to bring it into England, and therefore was not estopped from enforcing his rights against the purchaser. The owner of the patent had granted to the Belgian Société Anonyme a mere ordinary license to operate under the Belgian patent, and the court held that, inasmuch as the relationship was that of ordinary licensor and licensee, the Belgian product was not immune from infringement within Great Britain. In the course of his opinion in that case Cotton, L.J., however, said:

When an article is sold without any restriction on the buyer, whether it is manufactured under either one or the other patent, that, in my opinion, as against the vendor gives the purchaser an absolute right to deal with that which he so buys in any way he thinks fit, and of course that includes selling in any country where there is a patent in the possession of and owned by the vendor.

The extract quoted fits the facts of this case. The plaintiff herein as the original vendor gave to the British government, as purchaser, an absolute right to deal with that which it purchased in any way it thought fit, and defendant herein derives its right from that government to bring the aeroplanes into the United States in the manner it did, and the plaintiff is without ground of complaint. As the plaintiff has already been paid for these aeroplanes the full price it asked, it is no longer concerned about the price at which the article is sold, or whether the article is kept in Canada, or in Great Britain, or in the United States. We may summarize our conclusions:

It is admitted that, if the aeroplanes which are alleged to infringe had been built in Canada under a limited license, or under a Canadian patent, and then brought into the United States, infringement would have been made out. But that is not this case.

It appears that the aeroplanes complained of were manufactured under a license from the plaintiff and with the latter's active assistance, and that they contain engines furnished by the plaintiff with the intent that they should be so used.

It appears that the plaintiff has been paid a sum in excess of $4,000,000 for the aeroplanes and engines, which plaintiff sold or agreed might be manufactured.

It appears that the license under which the aeroplanes were manufactured contained no restriction or limitation as to time, or place, or manner of use of the aeroplanes, nor as to the ultimate disposition which might be made of them, and that they were therefore freed from the monopoly of the plaintiff's patents.

The decree appealed from is in all respects affirmed, with the costs of both courts.

SANOFI, S.A. AND AMERICAN HOME PRODUCTS CORP. v. MED-TECH VETERINARIAN PRODS., INC.
565 F. Supp. 931 (D. N.J. 1983)

SAROKIN, DISTRICT JUDGE:

[Sanofi, a French company, owned patents in the United States and in Canada for acepromazine maleate, a tranquilizer and anti-emetic used in the United States for the treatment of animals. Through agreements in 1959 and 1963, Sanofi entered into an agreement with AHP, granting AHP the "exclusive" right to manufacture, sell or use in the U.S. acepromazine maleate and pharmaceutical products containing the substance. In 1981, Medico Industries, Inc., a Kansas company, placed two separate orders with a chemical broker, Flavine International, Inc., of Northvale, New Jersey, for the purchase of the substance in bulk form. Flavine contacted its unaffiliated German counterpart, which purchased the product from one of Sanofi's French subsidiaries. Neither Medico nor Flavine knew of any patent or any license pertaining to the product but the companies through which they purchased the product did, and the French subsidiary sought assurances that the product would not be sold for purchase in the U.S Sanofi and AHP sought an injunction barring the imports.]

. . . Defendants argue that an implied license has arisen here because Sanofi made its sale of the patented product without restrictions. . . . Although defendants are correct in stating that sale of an article exhausts the patentees' monopoly in that article, they are incorrect in applying the rule to the facts of this case. The rule has only been applied where the sale is one which the seller had the authority to make in this country. Compare, Curtiss Aeroplane & Motor Corporation v. United Aircraft Engineering Corporation, 266 F. 71 (2d Cir.1920) (exhaustion doctrine applied where seller abroad had contractual authority to sell in the United States), with, Boesch v. Graff, 133 U.S. 697 (1890) (no exhaustion where seller abroad had no authority to sell in the United States). Sanofi had no authority to sell acepromazine maleate for veterinary purposes in the United States. Although the sale was consummated abroad, this country's patent laws were not implicated until the product was brought into this country. Once the product entered and was sold in the United States for veterinary purposes, it was American Home's interest that was directly affected. Only American Home had the right to sell here for veterinary purposes, not Sanofi. If the court were to hold that Sanofi's sale of the product exhausted the patent, it would be crediting Sanofi with greater rights than the patentee actually had. Sanofi had no right to allow its product to enter this country without the permission of its exclusive licensee. Sanofi could have protected itself by imposing written restrictions upon the sale but chose not to do so. Therefore, Sanofi might be liable to American Home or to defendants for its omissions. In no event, however, would Sanofi's inaction deprive American Home of its rights under the patent. To credit defendants' argument would require this court to conclude that Sanofi could make an unrestricted sale abroad of goods destined for this country without violating the patent laws, yet could not lawfully initiate that same sale within United States borders. Such an anomalous result would discourage the assignment and licensing of patent rights by making those rights less valuable and more susceptible to circumvention through transactions initiated in foreign countries by United States patentees who have previously transferred rights under their patents. Even if the Court were to accept defendants' theory that the sale by Sanofi created an implied license to resell in this country, that license would still be subject to outstanding licenses. Where two licenses conflict, the first prevails, "even though the taker of the second had no notice of the existence of the first.". . . .

Finally, defendants argue that *Curtiss Aeroplane & Motor Corporation*, controls the outcome of this case. In *Curtiss*, plaintiff owned the United States patent rights for certain airplanes. Plaintiff owned 83% of its subsidiary, which entered into a contract to sell the patented planes to the government of Great Britain. The British government subsequently sold some of the planes to a United States citizen who sought to bring the vehicles into this country. Plaintiff brought suit to enjoin the importation.

Critical to the Court's ruling [refusing to issue an injunction] was a finding that in plaintiff's contract with the British Government, it was specifically contemplated that the government could dispose of the planes in any way that it deemed appropriate: The plaintiff and the British government alike understood and intended that the aeroplanes to be manufactured by that government as well as those to be supplied to it by the plaintiff were to become the absolute property of the government, and were to be disposed of as the latter should see fit. . . .

Therefore, unlike here, the seller of the patented merchandise had authority to sell in this country.

It was only because of that circumstance that the court found the sale to be lawful. This case, rather than being controlled by Curtiss, is analogous to Daimler Manufacturing Co. v. Conklin, 170 F. 70 (2d Cir.1909), another Second Circuit opinion. In Daimler, defendant purchased an automobile abroad that contained devices covered by United States patents. The seller had the right to make the sale abroad but had no rights under the United States patents. The court, enjoining the use of the product in this country, found that "the purchaser abroad cannot get any greater right than the patentee from whom he buys." Therefore, because the foreign patentee had no authority to use the product here, the court found that the purchaser also had no such authority. . . .

AN INTERVIEW WITH JUDGE GILES S. RICH
U.S. COURT OF APPEALS FOR THE FEDERAL CIRCUIT
15 ABA-IPL Newsletter 1, 6 (1999)*

Q: While we're on the subject of misnomers, I've heard that you disagree with the reasoning of the so-called "first sale doctrine." What's wrong with the idea that the first authorized sale of a patented product "exhausts" the patentee's right to control the subsequent disposition of that particular item?

Judge Rich: My position is simple: No patent right is involved, and nothing is exhausted. Talking about exhaustion of the patent right is nonsense, and it's about time to stop talking nonsense. To explain, I have to discuss two things: (1) what the patent right is; and (2) what is the meaning of "exhaustion." It is no longer debatable what the patent right is. . . . [T]he Supreme Court told the country in 1852 in Bloomer v. McQuewan that it consists altogether in the right to exclude others—and that is all it is. It is not an ambiguous "exclusive right"; it is a simple right to exclude others. Period.

Now, the premise is that the patentee made and sold the patented invention. That was the so-called "first sale." What did his right to exclude others have to do with those acts? Absolutely nothing. In manufacturing, was he excluding anyone? No. In selling, was he excluding anyone? No. Then he wasn't exercising his patent right, was he? The trouble stems from the old ambiguous statutory definition of the patent right as the "exclusive right to make, use and sell."

Turning to the meaning of "exhaustion," it means the state of being drained or used up completely. It assumes that there is something to be used up. Well, since the patent right is not involved, how could it be used up? It couldn't have been used, even a teeny bit, and it certainly was not exhausted.

But that's not all there is to the analysis. What is this so-called "first sale" of an article on which the seller happens to have a patent? It is a

---

* Reprinted with permission.

simple transfer of ownership—a chattel or personal property—from one person to another. The rights of the buyer are governed by the laws of property or the law of sales or both. And the law of patents has nothing whatever to do with those rights. Any restraints on the new owner have to be made under the law of contracts, and any contractual restrictions are subject to the antitrust laws. So there is neither use nor exhaustion of patent rights.

Conclusion: The term "exhaustion doctrine" is meaningless nonsense. The legal result is OK, but the reasoning is all wrong. The simple fact is that no patent right is involved in the sale of merchandise by the patentee, nothing is exhausted, and the adjective "first" in "first sale" is also without significance. Let's clear up the thinking about this law.

Notes and Questions

(1) **Exhaustion and First Sale.** The *Curtiss* court, in dictum, says that "if the vendor's patent monopoly consists of foreign and domestic patents, the sale frees the article from the monopoly of both his foreign and his domestic patents, and where there is no restriction in the contract of sale the purchaser acquired the complete title and full right to use and sell the article in any and every country." Can the effect of exhaustion be limited by contractual provision? Even with respect to a bona fide third party purchaser without notice? Professor Adelman states that "all legal systems assume that if a sale is unconditional and made *in the territory* covered by the patent, then the product is outside the control of the patent. This is the first sale doctrine. Exhaustion is the opposite of this default rule since it applies the first sale rule regardless of the intention of the parties. As for foreign sales, the default rule may or may not be the same as that applied to domestic sales." Martin J. Adelman, *The Exhaustion Doctrine in American Patent Law*, 6 Proceedings of the Fordham Conference on International Intellectual Property 3 (1998) (emphasis added). The same author asserts that the Federal Circuit eliminated the principle of exhaustion from U.S. patent law in *Mallinckrodt, Inc. v. Medipart, Inc.*, 976 F.2d 700 (Fed. Cir. 1992). Others have found the first sale/exhaustion dichotomy a distinction without a difference. *See* Margreth Barrett, *The United States' Doctrine of Exhaustion: Parallel Imports of Patented Goods*, 27 N. Ky. L. Rev. 911, 918–919 (2000).

(2) ***Bloomer.*** Is the *Curtiss* court in agreement with Judge Rich on the significance of *Bloomer v. McQuewan*? Does 35 U.S.C. § 261, which states that "subject to the provisions of this title, patents shall have the attributes of personal property," clarify whether a patent is a monopoly? Is Judge Rich's view of whether a patent is a negative right necessary to his argument? If so, why? To what extent do divisions of international markets by patent owners by grant of territorial licenses create non-competitive

effects, justifying legal limitations on the freedom of the patentee to contract?

(3) **Reconciling *Curtiss* and *Sanofi*.** The Sanofi court distinguished *Curtiss*, but are these cases distinguishable? Or is the court making a policy argument when it says, "such an anomalous result would discourage the assignment and licensing of patent rights by making those rights less valuable and more susceptible to circumvention through transactions initiated in foreign countries by United States patentees who have previously transferred rights under their patents"?

(4) **Statutory Language.** Is there any significance to the fact that there is an explicit limitation on the rights of a copyright owner upon transfer of a particular copy in Section 109 of the Copyright Act of 1976 and no such limitation on the patentee's right in the Patent Act of 1952? Section 109 limits the first sale doctrine in copyright to "copies lawfully made . . . under this title." Is a copy made in France covered by Section 109? *See Quality King Distributors v. L'Anza Research Int'l Inc.*, 523 U.S. 135 (1998). *A fortiori*, where there is no statutory first sale doctrine, should the courts find one for products covered by a U.S. patent but made abroad under a French patent owned by the U.S. patentee or a related company?

[C]   The European Union

TREATY ESTABLISHING THE EUROPEAN COMMUNITY

Article 28 (ex-Article 30)

Quantitative restrictions on imports and all measures having equivalent effect shall, without prejudice to the following provisions, be prohibited between Member States.

Article 30 (ex-Article 36)

The provisions of Articles 30–34 shall not preclude prohibitions or restrictions on imports . . . justified on grounds of . . . the protection of industrial and commercial property. Such prohibitions or restrictions shall not, however, constitute a means of arbitrary discrimination or a disguised restriction on trade between Member States.

MERCK & CO. INC. v. PRIMECROWN LTD
[1997] F.S.R. 237 (E.C.J. 1997)

[Merck brought an action in the Patents Court in the United Kingdom to restrain parallel imports of pharmaceutical products from states where such products were not patentable, claiming that Primecrown had infringed the patents Merck held in the United Kingdom for certain pharmaceutical products by importing those products from Spain and Portugal and selling them in the United Kingdom. (At the relevant time, Spain and Portugal had joined the community, but had not yet made patent protection available for the products in question and the transitional provisions gave patent holders such as Merck the right to prevent parallel imports until the end of the third year after which Spain and Portugal had made the products patentable.)]

JUDGEMENT

1. By two orders of July 13, 1995, . . . the High Court of Justice of England and Wales, Chancery Division, Patents Court, referred to the Court for a preliminary ruling under Article 177 of the E.C. Treaty questions concerning the interpretation of Article 47 and Article 209 of the Act concerning the Conditions of Accession of the Kingdom of Spain and the Portuguese Republic and the Adjustments to the Treaties ([1985] O.J. L302/23, hereinafter "the Act of Accession") and of Articles 30 and 36 of the E.C. Treaty. . . .

. . . .

3. Merck claims that Primecrown has infringed its United Kingdom patents for a hypertension drug marketed under the trade mark Innovace in the United Kingdom and under the trade mark Renitec elsewhere, for a drug prescribed in prostate treatment, marketed under the trade mark Proscar, and for a glaucoma drug marketed under the trade mark Timoptol. It complains that Primecrown has carried out parallel imports of those products into the United Kingdom. Renitec and Proscar have been imported from Spain whilst Timoptol has been imported from Portugal.

4. Beecham has brought an action against Europharm for infringing its United Kingdom patents covering an antibiotic called Augmentin in the United Kingdom and Augmentine in Spain. Beecham complains that Europharm has imported this product from Spain into the United Kingdom with a view to applying to the competent authorities for an import licence which would allow it to import more of the product.

5. Merck and Beecham consider that they are entitled to oppose parallel imports of a drug for which they hold patents when, as in these cases, those imports come from a Member State where their products are marketed but were not patentable there.

6. Primecrown and Europharm refer, for their part, to the case law of the Court on Articles 30 and 36 of the Treaty and in particular to the principle of the exhaustion of rights, as interpreted by the Court in its judgment in Merck v. Stephar and Exler ([1981] E.C.R. 2063, hereinafter "Merck v. Stephar" or "Merck"). They deduce from Merck v. Stephar that, upon expiry of the transitional periods laid down in Articles 47 and 209 of the Act of Accession, they are entitled to import the products in question from Spain and Portugal where they have been marketed by, or with the consent of, the patent holders.

7. In *Merck v. Stephar*, the Court referred to its case law on Articles 30 and 36 of the Treaty according to which the proprietor of an industrial and commercial property right protected by the legislation of a Member State may not rely on that legislation to oppose the importation of a product which has been lawfully put on the market in another Member State by, or with the consent of, the proprietor of that right himself. The Court held that this case law also applied where the product concerned was put on the market by, or with the consent of, the proprietor in a Member State where the product was not patentable.

. . . .

27. In substance, the High Court is seeking to ascertain whether it is necessary to reconsider the rule in *Merck v. Stephar* or whether, having regard to the specific circumstances mentioned, its scope should be limited.

28. Merck and Beecham consider that there are weighty reasons for departing from the rule in *Merck v. Stephar*. They point out first of all that an important change in the situation has occurred since *Merck*. At the time when the Court gave that judgment, it was the exception rather than the rule for pharmaceutical products to be patentable in Europe. Nowadays, such products are patentable in all the countries of the European Economic Area, with the exception of Iceland. Similarly, the Community institutions have emphasised the importance of patents in the pharmaceutical sector, in particular by the adoption of Council Regulation (E.E.C.) No. 1768/92 of June 18, 1992 concerning the creation of a supplementary protection certificate for medicinal products ([1992] O.J. L182/1). Merck and Beecham then point to the increasingly serious financial consequences of maintaining the rule in *Merck* which, in their view, appreciably reduce the value of patents granted in the Community. Finally, they argue that the specific subject-matter of a patent can be exhausted only if the product in question is marketed with patent protection and that *Merck* is incompatible with the later case law of the Court.

29. It is first necessary to recall the Court's reasoning in *Merck*.

30. In that judgment, the Court referred to its judgment in Case 15/74 Centrafarm v. Sterling Drug [1974] E.C.R. 1147 in which it held, in paragraphs 8 and 9, that as an exception, on grounds of the protection of industrial and commercial property, to one of the fundamental principles of the common market, Article 36 of the Treaty admitted such derogation only in so far as it was justified for the purpose of safeguarding rights constituting the specific subject-matter of that property, which, as regards patents, is, in particular, in order to reward the creative effort of the inventor, to guarantee that the patentee has the exclusive right to use an invention with a view to manufacturing industrial products and putting them into circulation for the first time, either directly or by the grant of licences to third parties, as well as the right to oppose infringements.

31. In paragraphs 9 and 10 of *Merck*, the Court then stated that it followed from the definition of the specific purpose of a patent that the

substance of a patent right lies essentially in according the inventor an exclusive right to put the product on the market for the first time, thereby allowing him a monopoly in exploiting his product and enabling him to obtain the reward for his creative effort without, however, guaranteeing such reward in all circumstances.

32. The Court held, finally, in paragraphs 11 and 13 of *Merck* that it was for the holder of the patent to decide, in the light of all the circumstances, under what conditions he would market his product, including the possibility of marketing it in a Member State where the law did not provide patent protection for the product in question. If he decides to do so, he must then accept the consequences of his choice as regards free movement of the product within the common market, this being a fundamental principle forming part of the legal and economic circumstances which the holder of the patent must take into account in determining how to exercise his exclusive right. Under those conditions, to permit an inventor to invoke a patent held by him in one Member State in order to prevent the importation of the product freely marketed by him in another Member State where that product was not patentable would cause a partitioning of national markets contrary to the aims of the Treaty.

33. For the reasons set out below, the arguments for reconsideration of the rule in *Merck* are not such as to call in question the reasoning on which the Court based that rule.

34. It is true, as Merck and Beecham point out, that it is now the norm for pharmaceutical products to be patentable. However, such a development does not mean that the reasoning underlying the rule in *Merck* is superseded.

35. The same is true in relation to the arguments based, first, on the efforts made by the Community institutions to give enhanced protection to holders of patents for pharmaceutical products and, second, on the consequences of maintaining that rule for research and development by the pharmaceutical industry.

36. There can be no doubt now, any more than at the time when the judgment in *Merck* was given, that if a patentee could prohibit the importation of protected products marketed in another Member State by him or with his consent, he would be able to partition national markets and thereby restrict trade between the Member States. By the same token, if a patentee decides, in the light of all the circumstances, to put a product on the market in a Member State where it is not patentable, he must accept the consequences of his choice as regards the possibility of parallel imports.

37. The arguments put forward in the present cases have not shown that the Court was wrong in its assessment of the balance between the principle of free movement of goods in the Community and the principle of protection of patentees' rights, albeit that, as a result of striking that balance, the right to oppose importation of a product may be exhausted by its being marketed in a Member State where it is not patentable.

38. It is important to remember in this respect that the transitional measures provided for by Articles 47 and 209 of the Act of Accession were adopted in the light of the ruling in *Merck*. Although the Member States considered it necessary to postpone the effects of that ruling for a long period, they provided that, upon expiry of the transitional arrangements, Articles 30 and 36 of the Treaty, as interpreted in *Merck*, should apply in full to trade between Spain and Portugal, on the one hand, and the existing Member States, on the other.

39. Furthermore, the situations addressed by the ruling in *Merck* are set to disappear since pharmaceutical products are now patentable in all the Member States. If, upon accession of new States to the Community, such situations were to recur, the Member States could adopt the measures considered necessary, as was the case when the Kingdom of Spain and the Portuguese Republic acceded to the Community.

. . . .

44. The first question to be considered is whether the rule in *Merck* also applies where the patentee has a legal or ethical obligation to market or to continue to market his product in the exporting State. Here the national court is concerned to know what importance is to be attached to a requirement of that State's legislation or of Community legislation that, once the product has been put on the market in that State, the patentee must supply and continue to supply sufficient quantities to satisfy the needs of domestic patients.

45. The second question is whether the rule in *Merck* applies where the legislation of the exporting State not only grants to its authorities the right, which they exercise, to fix the sale price of the product but also prohibits the sale of the product at any other price. Here the national court is concerned to know whether it is relevant that those authorities have fixed the price of the products at a level such that substantial exports of the product to the Member State of importation are foreseeable.

46. Merck and Beecham maintain in particular that, in the circumstances mentioned in the order for reference, their right to decide freely on the conditions in which they market their products is removed or considerably reduced. In their view, it follows from Pharmon that the rule in *Merck* does not apply in the present cases.

47. As to that, although the imposition of price controls is indeed a factor which may, in certain conditions, distort competition between Member States, that circumstance cannot justify a derogation from the principle of free movement of goods. It is well settled that distortions caused by different price legislation in a Member State must be remedied by measures taken by the Community authorities and not by the adoption by another Member State of measures incompatible with the rules on free movement of goods (see Case 16/74 Winthrop [1974] E.C.R. 1183, para. 17; Joined Cases 55/80 and 57/80 Musik-Vertrieb Membran and K-tel International v. GEMA [1981] E.C.R. 147, para. 24; and Joined Cases C-427/93, C-429/93, and C-436/93Bristol-Myers Squibb and Others [1997] F.S.R. 102, para. 46).

48. The next question which must be examined is how far the rule in *Merck* applies where patentees are legally obliged to market their products in the exporting State.

49. In answering that question it is to be remembered, first, that in *Merck* the Court emphasized the importance of the fact that the patentee had taken his decision to market his product freely and in full knowledge of all relevant circumstances and, second, that it follows from Pharmon that a patentee who is not in a position to decide freely how he will market his products in the exporting State may oppose importation and marketing of those products in the State where the patent is in force.

50. It follows that, where a patentee is legally bound under either national law or Community law to market his products in a Member State, he cannot be deemed, within the meaning of the ruling in *Merck*, to have given his consent to the marketing of the products concerned. He is therefore entitled to oppose importation and marketing of those products in the State where they are protected.

51. It is for the patentee to prove, before the national court from which an order prohibiting imports is sought, that there is a legal obligation to market the product concerned in the exporting State. He must in particular show, for example by reference to decisions of the competent national authorities or courts or of the competent Community authorities, that there is a genuine, existing obligation.

52. According to the information given to the Court in these proceedings and as the Advocate General observes in points 152 and 153 of his Opinion, such obligations can hardly be said to exist in the case of the imports in question.

53. Finally, as regards the argument that ethical obligations may compel patentees to provide supplies of drugs to Member States where they are needed, even if they are not patentable there, such considerations are not, in the absence of any legal obligation, such as to make it possible properly to identify the situations in which the patentee is deprived of his power to decide freely how he will market his product. Such considerations are, at any rate in the present context, difficult to apprehend and distinguish from commercial considerations. Such ethical obligations cannot, therefore, be the basis for derogating from the rule on free movement of goods laid down in *Merck*.

54. In view of the foregoing, the answer to be given to the third question must be that Articles 30 and 36 of the Treaty preclude application of national legislation which grants the holder of a patent for a pharmaceutical product the right to oppose importation by a third party of that product from another Member State in circumstances where the holder first put the product on the market in that State after its accession to the European Community but before the product could be protected by a patent in that State, unless the holder of the patent can prove that he is under a genuine, existing legal obligation to market the product in that Member State.

ORDER

On those grounds, the Court, in answer to the questions submitted to it by the High Court of Justice of England and Wales, Chancery Division, Patents Court, by orders of July 13, 1995, hereby rules:

. . . .

2. Articles 30 and 36 of the E.C. Treaty preclude application of national legislation which grants the holder of a patent for a pharmaceutical product the right to oppose importation by a third party of that product from another Member State in circumstances where the holder first put the product on the market in that State after its accession to the European Community but before the product could be protected by a patent in that State, unless the holder of the patent can prove that he is under a genuine, existing legal obligation to market the product in that Member State.

NOTES AND QUESTIONS

(1) **Consent.** The Court purported to follow its own decision in *Merck v. Stephar* (Case 197/80, [1981] ECR 2063) that where the holder of a patent for a pharmaceutical product sold the product in one member state where patent protection existed, and then marketed the product himself in another member state where there was no patent protection, "he had to accept the consequences of his choice as regards the possibility of parallel imports" and could not rely on his patent rights in the first member state in order to prevent others from importing the product from the second member state and marketing it in the first member state. Is this the same sort of implied consent found by the Second Circuit in *Curtiss*? Under *Merck*, the patent holder could prevent imports if it had a legal obligation to market the product in a state with no patent protection, but not if it were merely ethical obligations which induced the patentee to continue its marketing. Exhaustion of patent rights in the Community is covered in detail in Amiram Benyamini, PATENT INFRINGEMENT IN THE EUROPEAN COMMUNITY Ch. 12 (1993).

(2) **Pharmaceuticals.** In the area of pharmaceuticals, are patent holders "free" to cease marketing a product if they wish to stem the flow of such products to another country? Should they be? Can a company decide not to market a drug in one country to protect its market in another? *See* Maarten Meulenbelt, *Parallel Imports of Medicinal Products: A New Balance?*, 1 J. WORLD INTELL. PROP. 525 (1998).

(3) **. . . And the Purpose of TRIPS.** Recall the Preamble of the TRIPS Agreement. Do high-technology manufacturers (including multinational pharmaceutical companies) enhance global welfare more by intra-brand and inter-brand price competition or by competition in drug research and development? Do expansive policies on patent exhaustion lead to increased

global welfare, or do they merely maximize global trade? *See* Alexander J. Stack, *TRIPS, Patent Exhaustion and Parallel Imports*, 1 J. WORLD INTELL. PROP. 657, 684 (1998).

(4) **Pressure for International Exhaustion.** In *Silhouette v. Hartlauer*, [1998] 2 CMLR 953 (E.C.J.), the ECJ held that the Trademark Directive established a principle of community-wide exhaustion only, and prohibited national laws from following a principle of international exhaustion. After commissioning a study on the economic issues surrounding exhaustion, on May 25, 2000, the Commission indicated that it had decided, *at this stage*, not to propose a change to the approach of community-wide exhaustion in trademark cases. Four member states supported the Commission's decision, while eight indicated regret and emphasized the need for change (the other member states took no position). What are the arguments for international exhaustion? If you were a member of the European Commission, would you recommend a change to international exhaustion? Should that principle be mandated by EU law, or should the question be left up to individual member states? Should a principle of international exhaustion be adopted by the EU absent international agreement? If a member state were free to adopt international exhaustion as its standard, should it?

(5) **EFTA States.** While there is no case law on parallel importation of patented goods from EFTA states, in the trademark case, *Mag Instrument Inc. v. California Trading Co. Norway* (Case E-2/97), [1998] 1 CMLR 331 (EFTA Court 1997), the Fredrikstad City Court in Norway requested an advisory opinion under Article 34 of the agreement between the EFTA states on the establishment of a Surveillance Authority and a Court of Justice. Mag, the owner of the Norwegian registration for the mark "Maglite" for lights, produced Maglite lights in the United States and sold them in Norway through an authorized sole distributor. The defendant, CTC, parallel-imported Maglites bearing the trade marks from the United States into Norway for sale there without Mag's consent. When Mag sought an injunction under the Norwegian Trade Mark Act, CTC argued that Mag's trademark rights had been exhausted when Mag had originally marketed the products in the United States. Mag argued that Article 7(1) of the Trademark Directive, applied to Norway by the EEA, provided for only EEA and not international exhaustion. Article 2(1) of Protocol 28 on Intellectual Property of the EEA deals with "exhaustion of rights." It reads as follows:

> To the extent that exhaustion is dealt with in Community measures or jurisprudence, the Contracting Parties shall provide for such exhaustion of intellectual property rights as laid down in Community law. Without prejudice to future developments of case law, this provision shall be interpreted in accordance with the meaning established in the relevant rulings of the Court of Justice of the European Communities given prior to the signature of the Agreement.

Norwegian law applied a rule of international exhaustion; the Norwegian government argued that to restrict exhaustion to products placed on the market in the EEA would allow for price discrimination, stronger segmentation of the markets and reduced price competition, thereby lessening the efficiency of the economy. The EFTA Court concluded that the issue had not been decided by the European Court of Justice (the case preceded *Silhouette*), and that therefore nothing in the Court of Justice's case law required member states of the community to abandon the principle of international exhaustion. The Court concluded that the principle of international exhaustion was in the interest of free trade and of consumers and was fully in line with the main function of a trade mark, which was to allow consumers to identify with certainty the origin of goods.

[D]   Other Jurisdictions: Japan

BBS KRAFTFAHRZEUG TECHNIK AG v. KABUSHIKI KAISHA RACIMEX
Case No. Heisei 7(wo)1988 (Supreme Court of Japan, 1997)

I

This case was brought by Petitioner against Respondents who engaged in a so-called parallel importation by way of importing and reselling in Japan products manufactured and sold in the Federal Republic of Germany by Petitioner. In this case, Petitioner sought an injunction on importation and sale of products, and damages based on a patent right which Petitioner owns in Japan. The following facts were duly found final by the High Court.

(1) Petitioner owns, in Japan, a patent right entitled "Wheel for Automobile" (filed on October 29, 1983 claiming a priority based on a patent application filed before the European Patent Office on May 27, 1983), published for opposition on January 12, 1990, and granted Patent 1629869 on December 20, 1991. (The patent is hereinafter referred to as the "subject patent" and the invention as the "subject patented invention.")

(2) Petitioner owns a patent right in Germany to cover an invention similar to the subject patented invention. (It was filed on May 27, 1983 before the European Patent Office with Germany and other countries as designated countries. It was given an application number of 83105259.2 and was granted a patent on April 22, 1987.) (This patent is hereinafter referred to as "the corresponding German patent.")

(3) Up until August 1992, Respondent, Jap-Auto Products imported aluminum wheels for automobiles, "BBS/RS," as described in Appendix 1 which was attached to the Decision of the District Court, and aluminum wheels for automobiles, "ROLINZER RSK," as described in Appendix II and sold them to another Respondent, Racimex Japan. Pacimex Japan engaged in the sale of these aluminum wheels at least up until August 1992. It is likely that Respondents would continue their importation and sale. (Hereinafter, the aluminum wheels mentioned here are collectively referred to as the

"subject goods" including both products already sold and those to be sold in the future.)

(4) The subject goods fall within the technical scope of the subject patented invention.

(5) The subject goods were manufactured as the product under the corresponding German patent, and sold by Petitioner in Germany after the German patent became effective.

II.

In the petition to this Court, Respondents argue for what is called international exhaustion. Namely, the effect of the subject patent applicable to subject goods has exhausted because of legitimate distribution by Petitioner of the subject goods in Germany. Therefore, Respondents' importation and sale of the subject goods in Japan does not constitute infringement of the subject patent.

The High Court dismissed the claim filed by Petitioner against Respondents for injunction and damages under the subject patent. The High Court reasoned that Petitioner manufactured and sold the subject goods as products under the corresponding patent in Germany. It was clear that Petitioner was provided an opportunity to secure remuneration for disclosing its invention. There were no admissible facts showing that such opportunity to secure remuneration was legally restricted when the subject goods were distributed. Legitimate distribution in Germany should be deemed to have caused the subject patent to be exhausted with respect to the subject goods.

III.

The High Court decided that Petitioner's claims against Respondents for injunction and damages under the subject patent have no grounds. This Court is agreeable to the conclusion of the High Court decision. Reasons for this Court's agreement are as follows.

1. The Paris Convention . . . as amended in 1979 (hereinafter referred to as the "Paris Convention") provides in Article 4*bis* that:

(1) Patents applied for in the various countries of the Union by nationals of countries of the Union shall be independent of patents obtained for the same invention in other countries, whether members of the Union or not.

(2) The foregoing provision is to be understood in an unrestricted sense, in particular, in the sense that patents applied for during the period of priority are independent, both as regards the grounds for nullity and forfeiture, and as regards their normal duration.

This provision denies the interdependence of patent rights and stipulates that a patent right of each country is independent from others with respect to its grant, changes and surrender. In other words, the existence of a patent right is not affected by the invalidation, forfeiture, expiration, etc. of a patent right in a different country. The question of whether a patentee is allowed to enforce its patent right under certain circumstances is not a matter stipulated in that provision.

Also, the principle of territoriality denotes, in the context of a patent right, that the grant, assignment, validity or the like of a patent right in each country is governed by the law of that country and that the patent right is effective only in the territory of that country.

When a patentee enforces its patent right in Japan, would such fact that a product subject to that patent right was already sold outside Japan by the patentee or the like, affect enforceability of the Japanese patent right? This question is a matter of interpretation of the Japanese Patent Law and is irrelevant to the Paris Convention and the principle of territoriality. It is clear from the foregoing that any interpretation in this respect, whatever interpretation it might be, is not in breach of the provision of Article 4*bis* and the principle of territoriality.

2. A patentee has an exclusive right to commercially exploit its patented invention (*see*, Patent Law, Section 68). In the case of invention of a product, acts of using, assigning or leasing constitute the exploitation of the invention (*see*, Patent Law, Section 2(3)(iii)). If so, acts of a commercial use or resale to a third party by the buyer who obtained products covered by the patent (hereinafter referred to as "patented product") from the patentee or its licensee, or acts of a commercial use or further sale or lease to others by the third party who obtained the patented products from the buyer would appear, on the surface, to constitute the exploitation of a patented invention to cause infringement of the relevant patent. However, in the case of the sale of patented products in Japan by the patentee or its licensee, a relevant patent in Japan should be deemed to have its right exhausted with respect to the product. In that case, the effect of the patent should no longer extend to the acts of use, assignment or lease of the patented product.

This Court bases this interpretation on the following.

(i) The protection of an invention under the patent law has to be achieved in harmony with public interest;

(ii) In general, through the act of a sale, all rights adherent to the goods are transferred to the buyer. The buyer receives all rights which the seller has owned. When a patented product is placed on the market, the buyer enters into a deal with a prerequisite that he would obtain rights to freely use and resell the product as a business. If the sale of a patented product requires approval from the patentee for each transaction, the free flow of products on the market would be interrupted and the smooth distribution of patented products would be disturbed. This would result in adverse affects on the patentee's interests and would be contrary to the purpose of the patent law which aims at encouraging inventions by promoting their protection and utilization so as to contribute to the development of industry. (*See*, Patent Law, Section 1);

(iii) On the other hand, a patentee receives proceeds including reward for disclosing its patented invention when the patentee sells its patented product. When it licenses the patent, it receives royalty payments. It can be said that an opportunity to secure a reward for disclosing its patented invention is guaranteed. Thus, once the patentee or its licensee sells patented products, there is no need to allow the patentee to obtain double profits through the process of distribution.

3. However, this rationale cannot be automatically applicable to the case where a patentee of a Japanese patent has sold its patented products outside Japan, because, in that case, the patentee may not have a patent for the same invention as covered by the Japanese patent (hereinafter referred to as "the counterpart patent"). Even if the patentee owns the counterpart patent, it should be noted that its patent in Japan is separate from its counterpart patent in the country where the sale took place. In light of this fact, the patentee shall be free from any claim about double profits even if the patentee enforces its Japanese patent against the product which is a subject matter of the counterpart patent.

4. Now, the adjustment between the flow of products in international trade and the patentee's right is discussed below. In light of the fact that international trade is being conducted on a tremendously broad and sophisticated basis, it is necessary that freedom of trade including freedom to import should be paid utmost respect when a dealer in Japan imports a patented product marketed in a foreign country to put it in a distribution channel in Japan. Through economic transactions outside Japan, a seller transfers his rights to the product to a buyer. The buyer enters into a deal with the prerequisite recognition that he receives all rights which the seller has owned with respect to the product. In light of the status-quo of international trade in modern society, it is naturally anticipated that the buyer or a third party who purchased a patented product from the buyer can commercially import it into Japan, and commercially use it or resell it to others in Japan, even if the product is sold by the patentee outside Japan. Thus, in the case where the owner of a patent in Japan or a person who can be recognized as an entity identical to the patent owner, sells its patented products outside Japan, a reasonable interpretation is that the patentee should not be allowed to enforce its patent in Japan against the buyer unless the buyer explicitly agrees to exclude Japan from the place of sale or use, and against a third party or subsequent buyers who purchased patented products from the buyer unless a notice of such agreement is clearly placed on the patented products. To be more specific:

(i) As was discussed earlier, it can be naturally anticipated that a patented product sold outside Japan might be imported into Japan. If the product was sold outside Japan without a reservation, it should be construed that the right to control the purchased product was implicitly given to the buyer and its subsequent purchasers without any restriction under the patent in Japan;

(ii) With respect to the right of the patentee, it is permissible for the patentee to reserve the right to enforce its patent in Japan when the patentee sells the product outside Japan. In the case where the buyer explicitly agrees with the patentee to an exclusion of Japan from the place of sale and use of the purchased product, and such exclusion is clearly indicated on the product, the subsequent purchasers will be in a position to learn the product is subject to certain restrictions irrespective of the involvement of other persons in the distribution process. They can fully decide whether or not to buy the patented product, taking into account the presence of such restriction; and

(iii) When the product is sold outside Japan by a subsidiary or an affiliated company which can be regarded as an entity identical to the patentee, such transactions should be deemed as the sale of the patented product by the patentee itself; or

(iv) The buyer of the patented product usually trusts in the free flow of the purchased product. That trust should be well protected. It should not matter whether or not the patentee has a counterpart patent in the country of first sale.

NOTES AND QUESTIONS

(1) **A Question of Municipal Law?** The history of the *BBS* case is detailed in John A. Tessensohn and Shusaku Yamamoto, *The BBS Supreme Court Case — A Cloth too Short for an Obi and too Long for a Tasuki,* 79 J. PAT. TRADE. OFF. SOC'Y 721 (1997). The *BBS* court states that the question of enforcement of a patent right under Japanese law is solely a question of municipal law—not international law of the Paris Convention, at least. Do any international standards apply?

(2) **Article 6 of TRIPS.** Do Article 6 of TRIPS or any provision of the prior GATT provisions place any limitations on a patentee's ability to limit the international distribution of patented goods through license restrictions? Should it, given the fact that all WTO countries are equal parties at the TRIPS table? Does the language of Article 6 TRIPS that *"for the purposes of dispute settlement under this Agreement"* and "nothing *in this Agreement"* shall be used to address the issue of exhaustion imply that there are other principles of international law *not* for the purposes of dispute settlement or *not* in the TRIPS Agreement which address the issue of international exhaustion? According to Professor Abbott:

> Most commentators agree that [Article 6] represents an agreement to disagree among WTO Members on the subject of parallel trade, leaving each Member free to adopt its own policy and rules. However, at least two leading commentators, Thomas Cottier (a TRIPS Uruguay Round negotiator) and Adrian Otten (the Director of the TWO Intellectual Property and Investment Division and Secretary of the GATT TRIPS negotiating group, consider that Article 6 does

not foreclose the application of WTO rules outside the TRIPS Agreement to parallel trade questions.

Frederick M. Abbott, *The TRIPS-Legality of Measures Taken to address Public Health Crises: A Synopsis*, 7 SPG WIDENER L. SYMP. J. 71, 77 (2001). Is international exhaustion a rule of international trade law? Those supporting that view point to Article IX:1 GATT 1994, which provides:

> no prohibitions or restrictions other than duties, taxes or other charges, whether made effective through quotas, import or export licenses or *other measures*, shall be instituted or maintained by any contracting party on the importation of any product of the territory of any other contracting party." [emphasis added]

Professor Abbott adds that "the safeguard in Article XX(d) [of GATT] . . . does not relieve rules restricting parallel imports from inconsistency with Article XI because rules restricting parallel imports are not necessary to protect national IPRs. By definition, parallel import goods are placed on markets with the consent of rights holders." Frederick M. Abbott, *First Report (Final) to the Committee on International Trade Law of the International Law Association on the Subject of Parallel Importation*, 6 PROCEEDINGS OF THE FORDHAM CONFERENCE ON INTERNATIONAL INTELLECTUAL PROPERTY 28 (1998). Assuming that the United States, the EU, and Japan do not permit international exhaustion, are they in violation of their GATT (but not TRIPS) obligations?

PART V

ISSUES IN INTERNATIONAL INTELLECTUAL PROPERTY LAW AND POLICY LOOKING FORWARD

Chapter 8

ISSUES IN INTERNATIONAL INTELLECTUAL PROPERTY LAW AND POLICY LOOKING FORWARD

§ 8.01   Institutional Agendas and Challenges Post-TRIPS

PAUL VANDOREN, THE IMPLEMENTATION OF THE TRIPS AGREEMENT *
2 J. WORLD INTELL. PROP. L. 25 (1999)

I. SOME CONSIDERATIONS RELATING TO THE TRIPS AGREEMENT

. . . .

C. Transitional Periods

Given that the TRIPS Agreement provides a significant number of new obligations, transitional periods were agreed upon to enable WTO members to review and amend their legislation.

Developed country members had a transition period of one year after the date of entry into force of the WTO Agreement, i.e. up until 1 January 1996. Developing country members [had], in general, five years (up until 1 January 2000) and least-developed country members have eleven years (up until 1 January 2006). A member in transition [was] given the possibility of a transition period until the year 2000 if [certain] criteria [were] met.

. . . .

However, all WTO members had to meet the national treatment and most-favoured-nation requirements as of 1 January 1996. In addition, there is the standstill clause, providing that during a transition period, member countries shall not make changes in their legislation or practices which would result in a lesser degree of consistency with the provisions of the TRIPS Agreement.

Experience has shown that, in practice, some . . . members do not wait until the end of the transitional period of which they can avail themselves, to amend their legislation. The world's major trading nations have encouraged . . . members to advance the implementation of their obligations on a voluntary basis, without much success however. . . . In this respect, the

---

* This article was originally published in the January 1999 issue of the Journal of World Intellectual Property (Vol. 2 No. 1) and is reproduced by permission of the publisher.

Directors-General of the [WIPO] and the [WTO] recently took a joint initiative on technical co-operation.

In order to facilitate the implementation of the TRIPS Agreement, in particular by developing and least-developed country members, developed country members shall provide technical and financial co-operation. Such co-operation shall include assistance in the preparation of laws and regulations on the protection and enforcement of intellectual property rights and the prevention of their abuse. It shall also include support for the establishment or reinforcement of domestic offices and agencies, including the training of personnel. The European Community is one of the major providers of technical assistance in this area. . . .

As far as future new WTO members are concerned, the European Community and its major trading partners have requested [that] such countries implement their TRIPS obligations as of the day of their accession, i.e. without a transitional period. This is not unreasonable, given that by then these countries will have known for several years the contents of the TRIPS Agreement and will have had several years to amend their legislation. To this end, the European Community co-operates with countries such as Russia and China.

II. THE TRIPS COUNCIL

A. Review of The Implementing Legislation

An important feature of the WTO is that the monitoring of the operation of the Agreements and, in particular, of members' compliance with their obligations, is done in a systematic way. This is also true for the TRIPS Agreement, which is monitored by the TRIPS Council, to which members are obliged to submit their implementing legislation for examination.

In 1996 and 1997, the implementing legislation of all developed country members was reviewed in four meetings of the TRIPS Council which each lasted for about a week. In addition, the TRIPS Council reviewed the legislation of the following Eastern and Central European countries: Bulgaria, Hungary, the Czech Republic, Romania, Slovakia, Slovenia and Poland. As far as the developing country members are concerned, Korea, Singapore and Hong Kong indicated that they would be open to participate in an advance review. Cyprus also took a similar position. Unfortunately, no agreement on "ground rules" for such a review could be reached in the TRIPS Council.

Overall, the review of the implementing legislation of the above-mentioned countries was clearly interesting, [albeit] time-consuming . . . [T]he exercise was well worth the effort, mainly for the following reasons:

* it raised in a significant way the awareness and understanding of WTO members of the TRIPS obligations;

* it helped to identify shortcomings, and in many cases to remove them (others might be dealt with in the WTO dispute settlement procedure); and

* an important precedent has been set which is likely to serve as the standard for the upcoming review of the legislation of the developing country members as of the year 2000, although some changes concerning the procedures might be necessary.

B. The Built-in Agenda

1. *Geographical Indications*

On the basis of TRIPS, Article 24(2), work in this area has started with the preparation by the WTO Secretariat, with the input of WTO members, of a checklist of questions in relation to the national regimes for the protection and enforcement of geographical indications, to which WTO members have been asked to respond.

Article 23(4) of the TRIPS provides that, in order to facilitate the protection of geographical indications for wines (and spirits), negotiations shall be undertaken in the TRIPS Council on the establishment of a multilateral system of notification and registration. Preliminary work has been undertaken by the WTO Secretariat and preliminary discussions have taken place amongst WTO members.

2. *Patentability*

Article 27(3)(b) of the TRIPS Agreement provides for the review of the provisions of patentability of plants and animals other than microorganisms, and the protection of plant varieties as of 1999. [*See supra* Chapter 4.] With respect to the question of patentability of plants and animals, the Community pharmaceutical and chemical industry generally has a vested interest in this matter. However, progress is likely to depend on more general and politically sensitive considerations such as the question of life forms or traditional knowledge. The [OECD] is also working on this matter. Account also needs to be taken of the fact that the Community recently, and after lengthy debates, adopted the Directive on the legal protection of biotechnological inventions. It is uncertain whether the Community will be in a position to go further than what is provided in this Directive. With respect to the question of the protection of plant varieties, account needs to be taken of developments in the International Union for the Protection of New Varieties of Plants (UPOV).

3. *Review of the Implementation of the TRIPS Agreement*

Article 71(1) provides that the TRIPS Council shall review implementation of the TRIPS Agreement as of 1 January 2000 [and subsequently, every two years]. . . .

4. *Non-Violation Complaints*

Under Article 64(3) of the TRIPS Agreement the TRIPS Council is required to examine, during the period from 1 January 1995 to 1 January 2000, the scope and modalities for "non-violation" complaints, and to submit its recommendations to the Ministerial Conference for approval. Any decision of the Ministerial Conference to approve such recommendations or to extend the five-year period has to be made by consensus. During that five-year period, the rules on "non-violation" do not apply. The Community supports this automatic "re-inclusion" of such complaints into the dispute settlement procedures.

III. Dispute Settlement

The WTO Dispute Settlement system is gradually becoming a major instrument for providing further clarification of the TRIPS Agreement. . . .

. . . .

IV. Need for a TRIPS II?

The Community favours the launching of a comprehensive [new] WTO Round . . . If such a launch takes place, consensus will also be required concerning the subject-matter to be included. The question, therefore, arises: should TRIPS be included?

The TRIPS Agreement was not, of course, intended to be a static instrument but one capable of development. It is obvious that it does not solve all problems in the area of international rules on intellectual property matters and that new problems have emerged, e.g. as a result of new technologies or new ways of communication.

[T]he TRIPS Council will hold a review of the TRIPS Agreement after five years, i.e. as of the year 2000, but is also empowered to review it at any time in the light of any relevant new developments which might warrant modification and amendment (Article 71, paragraph 1). However, the TRIPS Council has no competence to take decisions on these amendments. Generally, amendments to the TRIPS Agreement have to be adopted through a formal acceptance process by all WTO members. In special cases, the TRIPS Agreement provides for a simplified procedure where amendments merely serve the purpose of adjusting higher levels of protection of intellectual property rights (Article 71, paragraph 2).

Apart from the items covered by the built-in agenda mentioned above, the TRIPS Agreement does not address the issues:

> * which were left out of the negotiations in the Uruguay Round, such as the resale right for artists and the question of moral rights in the copyright area; the definition of the "inventive moment" ("first-to-file" or "first-to-invent"), the inclusion of UPOV, improved protection for textile designs and appellations of origin in the industrial rights area;

* where multilateral consensus building, notably in WIPO, made progress only recently, such as protection of copyright and related rights in the Information Society or the introduction of a *sui generis* protection for databases;

* which would further increase the level of protection by expanding beyond what has been agreed upon in the TRIPS Agreement or facilitate the processes of obtaining existing rights, such as the introduction of world-wide patents and trademarks, the extension of the term of patent protection or rules clarifying the protection of trademarks in relation to Internet domain names. In addition, strengthened enforcement mechanisms could add to improving intellectual property right protection.

Consultations with representatives of different categories of right-holders are still ongoing. It is clear, however, that transitional periods already agreed upon during the Uruguay Round negotiations are not negotiable in any new Round.

Notes and Questions

(1) **Speed of Review**. Since the Vandoren article was written, the review by the TRIPS Council of developing countries' legislation has been slow but steady. Delays may cause a short de facto extension of the transitional periods for developing countries. You should now have a keen sense of the role of WIPO in international intellectual property lawmaking. In order to expedite the review process, would it be appropriate for WIPO to offer developing countries assistance in responding to TRIPS Council questions? Would your answer change if WIPO had helped in the drafting of the developing country's legislation?

(2) **Technical Cooperation**. Should there be any limits to the nature and extent of the "technical cooperation" provided by developed countries to the developing countries? What dangers attend this process? What gains does it generate?

(3) **The "Built-in" Agenda**. The TRIPS Council continues to discuss the scope and modalities of nonviolation complaints, but no great progress has been made. In the meantime, countries appear reluctant to test the limits of the concept, and no country has indicated an intent to file a nonviolation complaint in the near future. *See supra* page 540, Note 5 (noting agreement at Doha Ministerial regarding nonviolation complaints).The nonviolation complaint has the potential, however, depending upon how the concept is applied, to affect the future shape of international intellectual property law. *See supra* § 5.03[A].

(4) **The TRIPS II Agenda**. Would you support a "TRIPS II"? If so, based upon your study of international intellectual property law and policy, which

items should be on the agenda? Do you agree with the suggestions made by Paul Vandoren? Other frequently mentioned topics include the protection of traditional knowledge, *see infra* § 8.02, the relationship between intellectual property and biodiversity, *see infra* § 8.03, issues raised by e-commerce, the incorporation of post-TRIPS conventions, as well as the relationship between intellectual property rights and access to health care. *See supra* § 7.04[A].Why should a TRIPS II Agreement not have transitional periods?

(5) **WIPO and the TRIPS Council: Parallel or Competing Tracks?** An example of the delicate interplay between the WIPO-based mechanisms and those of the WTO was seen at the first session of the newly formed WIPO Standing Committee on the Law of Trademarks, Industrial Designs and Geographical Indications in Geneva in July 1998. The question arose whether the committee should give priority to work on the protection of geographical indications. Several delegations suggested that because such work was taking place within the framework of the TRIPS Council, and "in order to avoid unnecessary duplication, the Standing Committee should not deal with the question." Other delegations were of the opinion that the Standing Committee should "give a high priority to work on geographical indications in parallel with the work of WTO in that field." Yet others said that "although WTO's work did not preclude the Standing Committee from dealing with that issue, the two Organizations should draw from each other's experience, and that cooperation between the two Organizations should be pursued." Standing Committee on the Law of Trademarks, Industrial Designs and Geographical Indications, First Session (July 13-17, 1998), Report prepared by the International Bureau ¶¶ 28–29, WIPO Doc. SCT/1/6 (Nov. 5, 1998).

(6) **Other Horizontal Issues.** Are there any other issues that appear to pervade international intellectual property lawmaking, and the resolution of which would facilitate progress on a variety of fronts? Several scholars have bemoaned the poor quality of "harmonized" law. What do they mean by "poor quality"? Do you agree that the process of harmonization is affecting the quality of intellectual property law? In the industrial property context, as registration systems expand their geographic reach, how are we to confront the sensitive issue of the languages used in such systems?

§ 8.02　Genetic Resources, Traditional Knowledge and Folklore

The development of principles relating to genetic resources, traditional knowledge, and folklore is on the agenda of a variety of international intellectual property policymaking institutions. From 1998, WIPO engaged in intensive fact finding regarding traditional knowledge (or "TK"), a process which included dispatching fact-finding missions to different parts of the globe and convening a roundtable on intellectual property rights and traditional knowledge. *See* Report on the Protection of Traditional Knowledge: A Global Intellectual Property Issue, WIPO/IPTK/RT/99/2 (WIPO Oct. 22, 1999); *see also* Michael Blakeney, *What Is Traditional Knowledge? Why Should it Be Protected? Who Should Protect It? For Whom?: Understanding the Value Chain*, WIPO/IPTK/RT/99/3 (Oct. 6, 1999). In September 1999, the WIPO Standing Committee on Patents placed the protection of genetic resources on its agenda. And, although WIPO's work on the protection of folklore goes back to cooperative efforts with UNESCO in 1978, its interest in the topic has intensified in the last few years.

In September 2000, WIPO established the Intergovernmental Committee on Intellectual Property and Genetic Resources, Traditional Knowledge and Folklore (WIPO IGC) to deal with each of these issues. The WIPO IGC met for the first time in April 2001. These issues have also been raised in the TRIPS Council, particularly by the developing countries. For example, in the context of the TRIPS Council's Article 27(3)(b) review, *see supra* § 8.01, developing countries sought to discuss the interaction between TRIPS obligations and biological diversity, as promoted by the Convention on Biological Diversity (CBD). The CBD provides that states have sovereign rights over their genetic resources, which includes the right to regulate access to and sharing the benefits of those genetic resources. A number of developing countries suggested that there was conflict between TRIPS obligations and the provisions of the CBD, to which many WTO countries are signatories. (We deal separately with this issue *infra* § 8.03.)

The greatest momentum on these issues, however, would appear to be within WIPO. The remit of the WIPO IGC covers a broad range of subject matter, as the formal title of the IGC suggests. (The phrase "traditional knowledge" is often used as shorthand for the entire subject matter, however, and we do so also in the following discussion unless otherwise stated.) Developments in the field of traditional knowledge affect a variety of policy areas in addition to intellectual property, such as food and agriculture, human rights (particularly of indigenous peoples), cultural heritage, health, and the environment. Two quite distinct, but related, issues are at the interface between intellectual property law and traditional knowledge. First, to what extent should traditional knowledge be protected as intellectual property and, if so, who should own those rights? Second, to what extent must the rules of intellectual property law be tailored to reflect the sometimes competing demands of traditional knowledge policy? To use a trademark example, should a native tribe that has for centuries used a symbol to assert its distinctive identity as a people be able to claim exclusive (trademark-like) rights to use the symbol? Conversely, and independent of the first question, should the tribe be able to enjoin the adoption of the symbol as a trademark by a third party commercial entity? Similar concerns regarding (i) assertions of ownership and (ii) protection against appropriation by others, are raised with respect to patent-like subject matter (traditional medicines based upon local plants, for example) and copyright-like subject matters (such as traditional music or dances).

In July 2000, WIPO published a draft report for public comment entitled Fact-Finding Missions on Intellectual Property and Traditional Knowledge (1998-1999). A revised report is being prepared presently; an excerpt from the executive summary of the draft report follows below.

FACT-FINDING MISSIONS ON INTELLECTUAL PROPERTY AND TRADITIONAL KNOWLEDGE (1998-1999)
WIPO Draft (For Comment, July 3, 2000)
wipo.int/traditionalknowledge/report/contents.html

. . . .

[IP] is not limited to existing categories such as patents, copyright and trademarks. Indeed, the definition of IP in the Convention Establishing [WIPO] makes it clear that "intellectual property" is a broad concept and can include productions and matter not forming part of the existing categories of intellectual property, provided they result, as the definition states, "from intellectual activity in the industrial, scientific, literary or artistic fields." . . . IP is evolutionary and adaptive. New advances in technology—information technology and biotechnology particularly—and changes in economic, social and cultural conditions require continuous appraisal of the system and at times adjustment and expansion, accompanied often by controversy. For example, the last few decades have seen the recognition of new forms of IP, such as a *sui generis* form of protection for plant varieties (in the 1950s and 1960s), patent protection for biological material, plants and animals (in the 1970s and 1980s), a *sui generis* form of protection for layout designs (topographies) of integrated circuits (1980s), copyright protection for computer software (1980s) and protection for databases and compilations of data (1980s and 1990s). The possible protection of tradition-based innovations and creations by the IP system . . . is a more recently articulated question.

. . . .

The Report seeks to summarize, reflect upon and draw broad conclusions on what may be considered to be the main and most prevalent IP-related needs and expectations expressed to WIPO . . . by TK holders and others with whom WIPO consulted. The main needs and expectations may be summarized as follows:

* The selection of an appropriate term or terms to describe the subject matter for which protection is sought.

* A clear definition or description of what is meant (and not meant) for IP purposes by the term or terms selected.

. . . .

* The prevention of the unauthorized acquisition of IPRs (particularly patents) over TK by documenting and publishing TK as searchable prior art, where so desired by the relevant TK holders.

* An analysis of how prior art is established for purposes of patent examinations in the context of TK.

* Greater awareness-raising of the IP system, particularly among sectors of society and communities unfamiliar with it, such as indigenous and local communities and Governmental offices not directly involved in IP law and administration.

* Greater understanding by the IP community of the perspectives, expectations and needs of TK holders.

* Facilitation of dialogue and contact between TK holders, the private sector, governments, NGOs and other stakeholders to assist in development of modalities for cooperation between them, at community, national, regional and international levels.

* Enhanced participation by the national and regional IP offices and the IP community at large in TK-related processes in which IP issues are raised.

* Study of the relationship between collectivity of TK and IPRs, more particularly testing of options for the collective acquisition, management and enforcement of IPRs by TK holders' associations, including the applicability of collective management of IPRs to TK.

* Study of customary law and informal IP regimes in local and traditional communities, including conclusions relevant for the formal IP system.

* In the shorter term, testing the applicability and use of existing IP tools for TK protection, through practical and technical community-level pilot projects and case studies; and, provision of technical information and training to TK holders and Government officials on possible options under the existing categories of IP for TK protection.

* In the longer term, the possible development of new IP tools to protect TK not protected by existing IP tools, the elaboration of an international framework for TK protection, using *inter alia* the WIPO-UNESCO Model Provisions for National Laws on the Protection of Expressions of Folklore Against Illicit Exploitation and Other Prejudicial Actions, 1982, as a possible foundation, and the development of a *sui generis* system of "community" or "collective" rights to protect TK.

* Facilitating access to the IP system, to enable TK holders to use and enforce rights under the IP system.

* The provision of information, assistance and advice with respect to the enforcement of TK protection.

* The provision of legal/technical assistance with TK documentation, including information and advice on the IP implications of TK documentation.

* The provision of IP advice and assistance in respect of legislation, regulations, guidelines, protocols, agreements (including model terms), policies and processes on access to and benefit-sharing in genetic resources.

* Assistance and training for TK holders in the negotiation, drafting, implementation, and enforcement of contracts.

* The development and testing, with the close involvement of indigenous peoples and local communities, of "best contractual practices," guidelines and model clauses for contracts.

* Awareness-raising on the potential commercial value of TK and the development of tools for the economic valuation of TK.

It is evident that some of the needs and expectations conflict, or reflect competing policy objectives. WIPO has not attempted to mediate the needs or "resolve" conflicts, but rather to report as fully as possible on the information received from [fact-finding mission] informants. WIPO recognises that it cannot address all these needs and a collaborative effort by other relevant organizations and processes would be desirable. The needs as identified pose challenges for the entire IP community—national and regional IP offices, collective management societies, the private sector, NGOs, civil society, consumers, and the international community, including WIPO and its Member States. . . .

. . . .

An efficient IP system that protects TK will promote continued creation and innovation based on that knowledge. IP is not only about conferring property rights. It is also about recognition of and respect for the contributions of human creators. From this perspective, IP has a very important role to play in protecting the dignity of holders of TK and, by recognizing property rights in relation to such knowledge, giving those holders a degree of control of its use by others. The protection of TK also benefits third parties, who are able to enjoy access to protected tradition-based innovation and creation that may not be collected, captured in some media, or find channels of distribution without IP protection.

The [fact-finding missions] have shown the richness and diversity of TK on a global scale, both in terms of its inherent creativity and as potential subject matter for IP protection. . . . There are nevertheless certain conceptual difficulties. However, the fact that existing standards of IP may not be in perfect harmony with elements of TK worthy of protection, should not be seen as an insuperable obstacle. IP has consistently evolved to protect new subject matter, such as software and layout-designs, the emergence of which was unforeseeable even twenty years earlier. Copyright protection has been extended to the digital environment. IP is now moving forward to protect databases. Given its evolutionary and adaptive nature, it is not inconceivable that the IP system might provide effective protection for traditional knowledge.

NOTES AND QUESTIONS

(1) **Needs of Traditional Knowledge Holders**. The draft WIPO report acknowledged difficulties defining "traditional knowledge," and identified

the selection of appropriate terminology as a pressing need. As a working definition, WIPO used the term "traditional knowledge" to refer to:

> Tradition-based literary, artistic, or scientific works; performances; inventions; scientific discoveries; designs; marks, names and symbols; undisclosed information; and, all other tradition-based innovations and creations resulting from intellectual activity in the industrial, scientific, literary or artistic fields. The notion "tradition-based" refers to knowledge systems, creations, innovations and cultural expressions which: have generally been transmitted from generation to generation; are generally regarded as pertaining to a particular people or its territory; have generally been developed in a non-systematic way; and, are constantly evolving in response to a changing environment. Categories of traditional knowledge include: agricultural knowledge; scientific knowledge; technical knowledge; ecological knowledge; medicinal knowledge, including related medicines and remedies; biodiversity-related knowledge; "expressions of folklore" in the form of music, dance, song, handicrafts, designs, stories and artwork; elements of languages, such as names, geographical indications, and symbols; and, movable cultural properties. Excluded from this description of traditional knowledge would be items not resulting from intellectual activity in the industrial, scientific, literary or artistic fields, such as human remains, languages in general, and "heritage" in the broad sense.

Draft WIPO Report, *supra,* at 4. What concerns underlie the "needs" listed by the draft WIPO report? In what ways do some of the needs and expectations of holders of traditional knowledge "conflict or reflect competing policy objectives," as the draft WIPO report suggests? What weight should we give these objectives? Is intellectual property law the appropriate vehicle for pursuit of these objectives?

(2) **Traditional Knowledge as Intellectual Property**. Recall the definition of "intellectual property" tendered by Professor Koumantos in the first excerpt in this book. *See supra* § 1.02. Does traditional knowledge, or some parts of traditional knowledge, fall within his definition? If not, what would that tell us about our notion of "intellectual property" and should we broaden that notion? Is protection of traditional knowledge justified by some theories of intellectual property but not others? Which intellectual property regimes appear most able to accommodate the protection of traditional knowledge?

(3) **International Solutions**. Why might it be important to address such issues internationally? Are these concerns inherently local or national in nature? If not, what has caused them to become international concerns? What prompted the developing countries in particular to raise the question of protection for traditional knowledge in the TRIPS Council? If an international agreement is the solution, what measures might the international intellectual property community adopt? *See* reports of the WIPO

Intergovernmental Committee on Intellectual Property and Genetic Resources, Traditional Knowledge and Folklore at <http://wipo.int/
globalissues/tk/>.

§ 8.03 Intellectual Property and Biological Diversity

COMMITTEE ON TRADE AND THE ENVIRONMENT, THE ENVIRONMENT AND TRIPS
WTO Doc. No. WT/CTE/W/8 (June 8, 1995)

The April 1994 Marrakesh Ministerial Decision on Trade and Environment states that "the Committee on Trade and Environment will consider
the work programme envisaged in the Decision on Trade and Services and
the Environment and the relevant provisions of the Agreement on Trade-
Related Aspects of Intellectual Property Rights as an integral part of its
work." This paper has been prepared in response to the request to the
Secretariat by the Committee for a background document to assist its work
in the latter area.

. . . .

I. PROVISIONS OF THE TRIPS AGREEMENT THAT EXPLICITLY REFER TO THE ENVIRONMENT

Article 27.2 is the only provision in the TRIPS Agreement that makes
an explicit reference to the environment. It states that "Members may
exclude from patentability inventions, the prevention within their territory
of the commercial exploitation of which is necessary to protect ordre public
or morality, including to protect human, animal or plant life or health or
to avoid serious prejudice to the environment, provided that such exclusion
is not made merely because the exploitation is prohibited by their law."
Thus, if it is necessary to ban the commercial exploitation of an invention
in order to avoid serious prejudice to the environment, a WTO Member is
free to refuse a patent for the invention concerned.

II. THE CONVENTION ON BIOLOGICAL DIVERSITY: MAIN ASPECTS AND A BRIEF NEGOTIATING HISTORY

An important concern in the area of environment has been that global
biodiversity (including genetic resources) is being depleted over time and
hence a need to conserve and use it in a sustainable manner has been
emphasized. Biodiversity is valued for maintaining the possibility of
responding to new situations that may arise, for instance, in the area of
agriculture and medicine, and because of its links to the sustainability of
certain ecosystems. The initial response of the international community to
the threat of genetic erosion was to build a network of "gene banks" where
genetic materials, for example, seeds of abandoned varieties, could be stored

and conserved *ex situ*. "*Ex situ* conservation" is defined as the conservation of components of biological diversity outside their natural habitats. However, this method of conservation led to some loss of viability and of characteristics and, over time, the focus has changed towards *in situ*. "*In situ* conservation" is defined as the conservation of ecosystems and natural habitats and the maintenance and recovery of viable populations of species in their natural surroundings and, in the case of domesticated or cultivated species, in the surroundings where they developed their distinctive properties. Therefore, incentives for conserving and sustaining animal and plant biodiversity in the natural habitats have been increasingly emphasized. For example, farmers and local communities are now being encouraged to conserve traditional plant varieties on-farm or *in situ*. *In situ* agro-biodiversity was seen by many to be a result of informal innovations, knowledge and practices of farmers, local communities and indigenous populations, and it was argued that they should get a return on these efforts. Such returns were also seen as important because they would provide incentives to continue to perform the task of preserving biodiversity.

The Convention on Biological Diversity (the Biodiversity Convention) was negotiated under the auspices of the United Nations Environment Programme ("UNEP") and was opened for signature at the United Nations Conference on Environment and Development in 1992. The Convention came into force on 29 December 1993. . . .

The Biodiversity Convention operates at three levels, *i.e.* genes, species, and ecosystems, and extends to all genetic resources, namely, plant, animal and microbial. It affirms that the conservation of biodiversity is "a common concern of humankind," and that States have sovereign rights over the biological resources in their territories. Article 15 recognizes the sovereign rights of States over their natural resources and the preamble reaffirms that "States have sovereign rights over their own biological resources". Article 15.1 states that "[r]ecognizing the sovereign rights of States over their natural resources, the authority to determine access to genetic resources rests with the national governments and is subject to national legislation." The question of ownership (or property rights) is not addressed by the Convention, and is subject to national law. Under the Biodiversity Convention, States are responsible for conserving their biological diversity and for using it in a sustainable manner. Access to a Party's genetic resources must be on mutually agreed terms and on the basis of prior informed consent of the Party providing the resources. Prior informed consent under Article 15 is not an obligation, but an option to be exercised by the Contracting Party providing genetic resources. Article 15.5 states that "[a]ccess to genetic resources shall be subject to prior informed consent of the Contracting Party providing such resources, unless otherwise determined by that Party." The objectives of the Biodiversity Convention are "the conservation of biological diversity, the sustainable use of its components and the fair and equitable sharing of the benefits arising from the use of genetic resources, including by appropriate access to genetic resources and by appropriate transfer of relevant technologies, taking into account all

rights over those resources and to technologies, and by appropriate funding." Article 1 of the Biodiversity Convention. This also reflects a view that
such sharing of benefits would provide incentives for conservation of
biodiversity in the regions where it exists (*i.e.* incentives for *in situ*
conservation).

The Biodiversity Convention provides for sharing research and development activities, benefits from the results of research and development, and
commercial use of these results on mutually agreed terms. Access to or
transfer of technology has to be provided in line with the provisions
mentioned below, and as far as possible and as appropriate, incentives have
to be provided to preserve genetic diversity. Similarly, in order to preserve
and make sustainable use of biodiversity, the Convention provides for
increased encouragement and interaction with regard to information,
research, training, public education and awareness, and technical and
scientific cooperation. With regard to several aspects including, inter alia,
sharing in research and development, in the benefits of the results of
research and development and of the commercial application of these
results, such sharing has to be on mutually agreed terms. *See*, for example,
Articles 15.4, 15.7, 16.2, 16.3, 18.5 and 19.2.

In the negotiation of the Biodiversity Convention, issues related to
intellectual property rights (IPRs) were important in the context of provisions dealing with access to and transfer of technology (Article 16 of the
Convention); in the Biodiversity Convention, the term "technology" includes
biotechnology, and covers technologies that assist further conservation and
sustainable use of genetic resources as well as technologies that do not
cause significant damage to the environment and result from the use of
genetic resources to which access is provided by Contracting Parties.

Relevant features of the Biodiversity Convention

The principles of the Convention are that "States have, in accordance
with the Charter of the United Nations and the principles of international
law, the sovereign right to exploit their own resources pursuant to their
own environmental policies, and the responsibility to ensure that activities
within their jurisdiction or control do not cause damage to the environment
of other States or of areas beyond the limits of national jurisdiction" (Article
3). The role of indigenous and local communities in conserving biodiversity
is recognized in the preamble; the importance of maintaining their knowledge and practices relevant to the conservation of biodiversity and the
sustainable use of its components is also recognized, as is the need to
encourage equitable sharing of benefits derived from the use of their knowledge, innovations and practices (Articles 8(j) and 10(c)). Identification and
monitoring of biodiversity is viewed as an ongoing process involving
development of the capacity of the Parties to fulfil the objectives on a long
term and sustainable basis (Article 7). The Biodiversity Convention provides that, as far as possible and as appropriate, incentives have to be

provided for the conservation and sustainable use of components of bio-diversity (Article 11). In order to preserve and make sustainable use of biodiversity, the Convention provides for increasing encouragement and interaction with regard to information, research, training, public education and awareness, and technical and scientific cooperation (Articles 12, 13, 14, 17 and 18). Article 18.3 provides that the Contracting Parties have to determine at their first meeting how to establish a clearing-house mechanism to promote and facilitate technical and scientific cooperation.

The Biodiversity Convention applies to *in situ* and *ex situ* genetic resources acquired in accordance with the Convention, but not those taken and deposited in gene-banks prior to the Convention's entry into force. It emphasizes *in situ* conservation (Article 8). Article 8 of the Biodiversity Convention calls for measures ranging from the establishment of a system of protected areas to the rehabilitation of degraded ecosystems and recovery of threatened species, the protection of natural habitats and the maintenance of viable populations of species in natural surroundings. *Ex situ* conservation measures are called for principally to complement *in situ* conservation (Article 9). Recognizing the sovereign rights of States over their natural resources, the authority to determine access to genetic resources rests with national governments and is subject to national legislation (Article 15.1). However, each Party to the Biodiversity Convention must endeavour to create conditions to facilitate access to genetic resources for environmentally sound uses by other Parties and must not impose restrictions that run counter to the objectives of the Biodiversity Convention (Article 15.2). Where access to genetic resources is granted, it has to be on mutually agreed terms and be subject to prior informed consent of the Party providing the resources, unless otherwise determined by that Party (Articles 15.4 and 15.5). Genetic resources provided by any Party to the Biodiversity Convention are only those resources that are provided by Parties which are countries of origin of those resources or by Parties that have acquired the genetic resources in accordance with the Convention (Article 15.3). For those Parties providing access to genetic resources, the benefits include possibility of participation in scientific research based on the genetic resource supplied (Articles 15.6). Article 15.6 states that "[e]ach Contracting Party shall endeavor to develop and carry out scientific research based on genetic resources provided by other Contracting Parties with the full participation of, and where possible in, such Contracting Parties," of sharing results of research and development and benefits arising from commercial and other utilization of genetic resources on mutually agreed terms (Article 15.7). Article 15.7 states that "[e]ach Contracting Party shall take legislative, administrative or policy measures, as appropriate, and in accordance with Articles 16 and 19 and, where necessary, through the financial mechanism established by Articles 20 and 21 with the aim of sharing in a fair and equitable way the results of research and development and the benefits arising from the commercial and other utilization of genetic resources with the Contracting Party providing such resources. . . . Article 19.2 states that "[e]ach Contracting Party shall take all practicable measures to promote and advance priority access on a fair and equitable basis by Contracting Parties, especially developing countries, to the results and benefits arising from biotechnologies based upon genetic resources provided by those Contracting Parties. Such access shall be on mutually agreed terms." *See also* Article 8(j), which states that "[e]ach Contracting Party shall, as far as possible, and as appropriate, subject to its national legislation, respect, preserve and maintain knowledge, innovations and practices of indigenous and local communities embodying traditional lifestyles relevant for the conservation and sustainable use of biological diversity and promote their wider application with the approval and involvement of the holders of such knowledge, innovations and practices and encourage the equitable sharing of benefits arising from the utilization of such knowledge, innovations and practices."

Access to and transfer of technology is addressed by Article 16. In order to get an overall perspective on different aspects related to transfer of technology under Articles 16, it is important to also bear in mind certain other provisions in the Biodiversity Convention, for example, Article 12 (research and training), Article 17 (exchange of information), Article 18 (technical and scientific cooperation), and Article 19 (handling of biotechnology and distribution of its benefits). These provisions emphasise both the soft component of technology (such as skills, know-how and design) and the hard component (machinery and equipment, and other tangible inputs). Experience with operation of technology has shown that the soft and hard components have to work in a complementary manner to result in successful transfer of technology. Intellectual property rights are explicitly mentioned in the second, third and fifth paragraphs of Article 16. . . .

Article 19 addresses handling of biotechnology (including biosafety aspects), access to information and research and distribution of benefits of biotechnology. Under Article 20, new and additional financial resources are to be provided to developing countries to enable them to meet the agreed full incremental costs to them of the measures needed to implement the Biodiversity Convention's obligations. The agreement on the composition of these costs is to be bilaterally reached between each developing country Party and the institution chosen to handle the financial mechanism. The mechanism for providing financial resources to developing country Parties is set out in Article 21. The mechanism will operate under the authority of the Conference of the Parties (established under Article 23) to which it will be directly accountable, and funds will be provided on a grant or concessional basis. Article 25 establishes a subsidiary body on scientific, technical and technological advice for timely advice relating to the implementation of the Biodiversity Convention. . . .

Resolution Three of the Nairobi Final Act of the Conference for the Adoption of the Agreed Text of the Convention on Biological Diversity (22 May 1992) identified the need to seek solutions to some unresolved issues, *e.g.* farmers' rights. . . .

III. Relevant Ongoing Work in Other International Organizations

This section reports on certain ongoing work at United Nations Environment Programme, Biodiversity Convention, Consultative Group on International Agricultural Research, Food and Agriculture Organization, World Intellectual Property Organization and UPOV that is relevant for a discussion of environment and TRIPS.

United Nations Environment Programme (UNEP)

In 1993, UNEP's Governing Council approved the creation of two Centres, both based in Japan. The purpose of the Centres is to promote the development and transfer of environmentally-sound technologies, with a particular emphasis on sustainable freshwater management technologies, as well as other environmentally-related technologies. At the Session of UNEP's Governing Council in 1995, governments requested that such Centres include work on developing "modalities for financing endogenous capacity-building of scientific and technology centres, in particular in developing countries and countries with economies in transition."

Consultative Group on International Agricultural Research (CGIAR)

The CGIAR is a consortium of donor and development agencies that supports autonomous research Centres which aim to develop technologies and information relevant to improving the productivity and sustainability of agricultural, forestry and aquatic systems in developing countries. One of the activities of the CGIAR is *ex situ* conservation and use of plant genetic resources. The CGIAR Centres have collected and stored seeds or other reproductive parts of their mandate crops. Each year, more than 120,000 germplasm accessions from the in-trust collections and 500,000 samples of improved material are distributed by the Centres, the large majority to developing countries. The Centres are also involved in research to improve technologies for *in situ* conservation.

Under agreements signed in October 1994, the Centres of the CGIAR that maintain germplasm collections have placed these collections under the auspices of FAO. The agreements contain obligations that the material will be made available to all users, and that the Centres will not claim any property rights on these materials. These conditions will apply also to the material with the users to which it is made available, except for "the repatriation of the germplasm to the country that provided such germplasm."

Food and Agriculture Organization (FAO)

In 1983, the FAO established a Global System for the Conservation and Utilization of Plant Genetic Resources for food and agriculture. The Global

System is being developed and monitored by the intergovernmental Commission on Plant Genetic Resources (CPGR) within the context of the International Undertaking on Plant Genetic Resources, a non-binding agreement that was adopted by the FAO Conference in 1983. The Undertaking recognizes a principle of free access to genetic resources. It includes a provision for an international fund for the conservation and utilization of plant genetic resources. However, compensation was not necessarily to be provided directly to farmers. The fund has not yet become operational. The CPGR is an intergovernmental forum of donors and users of plant genetic resources, technology and funds. Currently 144 countries are formally part of the system. It has negotiated a Code of Conduct for Plant Germplasm Collecting and Transfer which provides guidelines for collecting and transferring plant genetic resources to facilitate access and promote their use and development on an equitable basis. This code of conduct was adopted by the FAO Conference in 1993; a draft Code of Conduct on Biotechnology which includes provisions on IPRs is under development.

The CPGR has also provided a framework for agreements negotiated between various States and institutions, such as the International Agricultural Centres of the Consultative Group on International Agricultural Research. Moreover, in 1989 and 1991, the FAO Conference adopted resolutions on farmers' rights. The role of the farmers in developing plant varieties was recognized at the FAO Conference in 1989, which endorsed a concept of farmers' rights. It was stated that farmers have "rights arising from the past, present and future contributions of farmers in conserving, improving, and making available plant genetic resources [which] allow farmers, their communities, and countries in all regions, to participate fully in the benefits derived, at present and in the future, from the improved use of plant genetic resources, through plant breeding and other scientific methods," (FAO Resolution 5/89) and plant breeders' rights. Plant breeder's right or plant variety protection is an exclusive right granted to the breeder of a new plant variety to exploit his new variety. The nature of these rights can vary depending on the system of protection adopted in this context. See for example the note in Annex 1 to this paper. For more details on plant breeder's rights, *see* International Union for the Protection of New Plant Varieties of Plants (1994), *UPOV National Seminar on the Nature of and Rationale for the Protection of Plant Varieties under the UPOV Convention*, UPOV/ISB/94/1, 10 November 1994.

One of the CPGR's areas of interest relates to IPR over plant varieties, related technologies and farmers' germplasm. During the sessions of the Commission, discussions on these matters have been conducted among member countries since 1983, and following [the 1992 Rio Earth Summit], further discussions are being held on access to plant genetic resources for food and agriculture, access to related technologies, and the realization of farmers' rights. Other matters being discussed by the Commission include the impact of IPRs on the environment, (especially the distinctiveness, uniformity and stability criteria for plant breeders' rights), and a revision of the International Undertaking on Plant Genetic Resources to harmonize it with the Biodiversity Convention (including negotiations on access to plant genetic resources and the realization of farmers' rights). . . .

World Intellectual Property Organization (WIPO)

WIPO offers a range of assistance and services to developing countries. In respect of intellectual property and the environment, two types of assistance are of special interest to developing countries:

(i) the provision of advice and training to governments and public and private sector organizations, and their staff, on negotiations and arrangements relating to the licensing of intellectual property and the management of such property, where such arrangements have an impact on the environment;

(ii) the provision, with the cooperation of some industrialized countries, of technological state-of-the-art search reports covering various categories of technology, including technology relevant to the environment. Those reports, which are provided free, are prepared on the basis of information available from patent documents, of which some 30 million are in existence, held by those industrialized countries. Since the search service started, some 8,000 such search reports have been provided.

International Union for the Protection of New Varieties of Plants (UPOV)

UPOV administers the International Convention for the Protection of New Varieties of Plants, notably the 1978 Act which is presently in force, and the 1991 Act which is yet to enter into force. . . .

UPOV develops test guidelines for the conduct of tests for "distinctness, homogeneity and stability" of plant varieties. This is an ongoing task involving four Technical Working Parties, responsible respectively for test guidelines for individual species for agricultural crops, for fruit crops, for ornamental crops and forest trees, and for vegetables. In addition, there are two special Working Parties.

One studies the application and harmonization of biochemical and molecular techniques in the field of plant variety protection, and the other focuses on the possibility of automation and the harmonization of computer programmes within UPOV with a view to promote the harmonization of the method used by member states in distinguishing between plant varieties.

In order to avoid duplication of tests of varieties for which applications for protection are filed with more than one member State, cooperation in technical examination has been achieved on the basis of agreements between the competent authorities of member States, under which the testing of a given species is effected for a group of member States by one member State, and the purchase by a member State on an ad hoc basis of the result of a test carried out by another member State. The office of

UPOV maintains and updates a list of species for which offers for cooperation in examination have been made.

The Office of the UPOV collects national laws on plant breeders' rights
and prepares translations of them into English. It also provides assistance
in the development of the legal systems in different countries to take
account of the criteria mentioned in the UPOV Convention. . . .

. . . .

V. Provisions of the TRIPS Agreement Relevant to Matters Raised in Discussions in Environmental Fora

While the TRIPS Agreement covers all the main areas of intellectual
property . . . , the intellectual property related issues that have been
raised in the environmental fora concern essentially those IPRs relevant
to technology, in particular patents. . . .

[Several] issues are considered in turn [below]. . . . These points are
addressed without prejudice to whether they are all intellectual property
related or indeed environment related but because they have been raised
in environmental fora by at least some as having an IPR dimension.

(a) Promotion of environmentally-sound technologies

The importance of promoting environmentally-sound technology has been
referred to in many discussions in environmental fora; for example, it is
reflected in Agenda 21 [of the 1992 Rio Earth Summit]. . . . The IPR system provides protection to the results of investment in the development of
new environmentally-friendly technology, thus giving the incentive and the
means to finance such research and development. A combination of a well-
functioning IPR system and appropriate price signals in the market, which
direct research and development effort to environmentally-sound technologies, can play a major role in developing the technologies that will respond
to environmental problems. The TRIPS Agreement will help reinforce this
in a wider range of countries.

The objective of promoting the development of new technology is referred
to in Article 7 of the TRIPS Agreement which says that "the protection and
enforcement of intellectual property rights should contribute to the promotion of technological innovation and to the transfer and dissemination of
technology, to the mutual advantage of producers and users of technological
knowledge and in a manner conducive to social and economic welfare, and
to a balance of rights and obligations."

With this objective in mind, the TRIPS Agreement (Article 27.1) requires
that patents be available for any invention, in all fields of technology,
subject to certain limited exceptions (mainly for inventions in the area of
plants and animals. . . . [M]inimum rights that a patent must confer on
its owner are set out in Article 28. These are subject to a number of
exceptions, some of which are discussed . . . below. . . .

A number of other provisions of the TRIPS Agreement are also of relevance to the promotion of technological innovation. One is Article 39 on the protection of undisclosed information. . . .

(b) Access to and transfer of technology

This issue is addressed in the Biodiversity Convention, in Agenda 21 [of the 1992 Rio Earth Summit] and in a number of other agreements on environmental matters. As indicated above, it is an objective of the TRIPS Agreement to promote not only technological innovation, but also the transfer and dissemination of technology . . . [Article 7].

The objectives of promoting technological innovation and the transfer of technology are usually mutually consistent since right holders are generally more willing to transfer technology voluntarily where a country's IPR system provides effective protection. In addition, the disclosure requirements of the patent system and exceptions to patent rights for experimental use are designed to maximize the degree to which knowledge of new technology becomes publicly available and can be the basis for further technological development. Moreover, the TRIPS Agreement contains some specific requirements on developed country Members to provide incentives for technology transfer to least-developed country Members. . . .

In the event that there is tension between the objectives of promoting technological innovation and the transfer of technology, and with the aim of securing the objectives of Article 7, the TRIPS Agreement contains a number of provisions, in particular on compulsory licensing and control of anti-competitive practices, to establish an appropriate balance between these two objectives, and thus between the interests of producers and users of technological knowledge, conducive to social and economic welfare. . . .

Most technology is in the public domain . . . because protection was never sought in the first place. In order to benefit from patent protection, it is necessary to obtain a separate patent in each jurisdiction and that patent is only valid in that jurisdiction. The extent to which patents are taken out varies greatly from country to country. . . .

When technology, whether patented or not, is in the control of a government, that government is of course free to transfer it on concessional terms if it so wishes.

There is nothing in the TRIPS Agreement that would prevent a government or an international financial mechanism from providing financial assistance to enable the voluntary transfer of privately-held proprietary technology on concessional terms.

. . . [W]here a developing country does not presently give product patent protection in a particular area of technology, the introduction of such protection can be delayed for up to ten years. In respect of pharmaceutical and agricultural chemical products, there are special additional transition provisions that take account of the regulatory delay before such products are approved for marketing (Articles 70.8 and 70.9).

(i) Disclosure

One of the purposes of the patent system is to encourage inventors to disclose new technology rather than attempt to keep it secret, so that new technology can become part of the common pool of knowledge of mankind. Article 29 establishes an obligation on Members to require that patent applicants disclose the invention.

The obligation to disclose has a number of important consequences for the transfer of and access to technology. For the duration of the term of protection, information is readily available about from whom the technology can be obtained; [a]t the end of the patent term, the disclosed invention falls into the public domain and is freely available to all; [and f]urther research and development is facilitated—see next heading.

(ii) Experimental use

Article 30 allows Members to make "limited exceptions" to the rights conferred by a patent, subject to certain conditions.

(iii) Incentives to transfer of technology

As mentioned earlier, the TRIPS Agreement does not stand in the way of governments providing incentives for the transfer of technology. Indeed, Article 66.2 of the TRIPS Agreement requires developed country Members to "provide incentives to enterprises and institutions in their territories for the purpose of promoting and encouraging technology transfer to least-developed country Members in order to enable them to create a sound and viable technological base."

(iv) Compulsory licences, also sometimes referred to as "non-voluntary licences"

The TRIPS Agreement contains a provision allowing a compulsory licence (*i.e.* a licence granted without the agreement of the patent owner) to be granted to an applicant to use a patented invention where the right holder has not been willing to grant a voluntary licence on reasonable commercial terms and conditions within a reasonable period of time, subject to a number of conditions aimed at protecting the legitimate interest of the patent owner. In cases of national emergency or other circumstances of extreme urgency and in cases of public non-commercial use, a Member may waive the requirement to first seek a voluntary licence. The relevant provisions of the TRIPS Agreement are [in] Article 31.

. . . .

(c) Technology that may adversely affect the environment

A concern highlighted in various discussions on environmental matters is the need to curb the adverse effect of certain technology on the environment. In the work on the Biodiversity Convention, in FAO and elsewhere, the issue of control of the release of new biotechnological products into the environment has been prominent. In discussions on plant variety protection and "farmer's rights", concern about the possible effect of uniform new varieties displacing the biodiversity provided by traditional varieties has been expressed by some. Similarly, a long-standing subject of attention in most countries has been the environmental effects of agricultural chemicals, which are generally subject to a testing and approval procedure before being authorized for marketing.

As far as the TRIPS Agreement is concerned, the main point is that it does not affect the right of governments to restrict research or development or the use of technology on the grounds of protecting the environment. A patent gives the right to the patent owner to prevent others from using the protected invention (subject to certain exceptions), but does not guarantee the patent owner the right to exploit the technology in question. . . . In this regard, the provisions of Article 8.1 of the TRIPS Agreement should be noted. . . .

Although . . . the possibility for a government to restrict the use of technology on environmental grounds is not affected by the grant of a patent, it should also be noted that Article 27.2 of the TRIPS Agreement enables a Member to exclude from patentability inventions whose use would seriously prejudice the environment. . . .

Also of relevance to controls on the use of environmentally-prejudicial technology are the provisions of Article 39.3 on the protection of undisclosed test or other data submitted in order to obtain marketing approval for pharmaceutical and agricultural chemical products which utilize new chemical entities. These provisions provide protection to the very considerable investment that frequently has to be made in testing such products to ensure their usefulness and safety, notably for the environment in the case of agricultural chemicals. While one of the forms of protection that should be granted is against disclosure of the information, this does not apply where disclosure is necessary to protect the public or where steps are taken to ensure that the data is protected against unfair commercial use.

(d) Patentability of genetic material/life forms

The extent to which genetic material and life forms should be patentable is an active issue in many contexts—in the judicial, legislative and executive branches of many governments, in commercial circles, and in public opinion. Environmental groups have participated actively in this debate. Concerns that they have raised include the issue of the environmental safety of biotechnological inventions and the possible effect on biodiversity of the uniformization of productive varieties/races. . . . Ethical questions about the patenting of life forms have also been raised as well as economic questions about the effects on users and the distribution of benefits with the suppliers of the underlying genetic material.

The first point to note is that Article 1.1 of the TRIPS Agreement makes it clear that there is no expectation that countries will have identical patent laws: the obligation is to meet the minimum standards of the TRIPS Agreement while being free to grant more extensive protection than is required by the Agreement. The implication of this is that the fact that patents may be granted in response to certain applications in some countries does not necessarily mean that this would be an obligation under the TRIPS Agreement.

Article 27.1 of the TRIPS Agreement establishes the basic criteria for patentability. . . . Thus, the TRIPS Agreement allows each Member to refuse to grant a patent for any claimed invention which does not meet any one of the following criteria: it must be new; it must involve an inventive step or be non-obvious; it must be capable of industrial application or useful (and it must have been adequately disclosed). A country would remain free to refuse a patent for biological or genetic material which has been merely discovered or where the use of it claimed as the subject of the invention was already known.

Even if an application meets the basic tests of patentability, Article 27.3(b) of the TRIPS Agreement allows Members to exclude from patentability certain plant and animal inventions. . . . Even if an invention meets the basic criteria for patentability of Article 27.1 and does not fall within the exceptions allowed under Article 27.3(b), a patent may still be refused under Article 27.2 if the invention is offensive to ordre public or morality, including to human, animal or plant life or health or to avoid serious prejudice to the environment. . . . [T]he main condition attached to the use of this exception to patentability is that the prevention of the commercial exploitation of the invention is necessary to protect ordre public or morality, including to avoid serious prejudice to the environment.

(e) Contribution of countries/communities sources of genetic material

In discussions in fora concerned with environmental matters, such as in the negotiation of the Biodiversity Convention and in the FAO Commission on Plant Genetic Resources, the issue of recognizing the contribution of indigenous peoples and local communities through the provision of traditional knowledge and informal innovation practices has been raised. In the FAO, the concept of "farmer's rights" has been defined as "rights arising from the past, present and future contribution of farmers in conserving, improving and making available plant genetic resources, particularly those in the centres of origin/diversity" (FAO Resolution 5/89). Attention is also given in the Biodiversity Convention to the question of the participation of countries [that are] sources of genetic resources in research activities using such resources and, on mutually agreed terms, in the results and benefits arising from biotechnologies using such genetic resources.

This matter has two aspects. One is the question of the recognition of the intellectual contribution made by indigenous peoples/local communities. The strengthened protection of IPRs worldwide that should flow from the

TRIPS Agreement will help indigenous and local communities benefit from their contributions where the conditions for protection [for existing IPRs] . . . are met. The question of new forms of protection adapted to the particular circumstances of such peoples/local communities was not raised during the TRIPS negotiations.

The second aspect concerns the contribution of countries/communities through the conservation and provision of genetic resources in their natural state. The TRIPS Agreement is silent on the question of the participation of countries/communities in the benefits from the use of technology based on genetic resources originating in their territories. There is also nothing in the TRIPS Agreement that stands in the way of contractual arrangements between countries and companies seeking to use genetic resources from those countries, public transfers of funds or any other mechanism compatible with its provisions.

. . . .

VII. ARTICLE XX OF GATT 1994 AND THE TRIPS AGREEMENT

Article XX of GATT 1994 specifies certain conditions under which a Member is exempted from obligations under other provisions of GATT 1994. Similarly, the TRIPS Agreement has provisions which exempt Members from certain obligations imposed by other provisions of the TRIPS Agreement. For example, Articles 27.2 and 27.3 permit exemption from patenting in specified circumstances or for specified inventions. Article 30 permits certain exemptions to the rights conferred by patents, and Article 31 permits the use of patented technology without authorization of the right holder provided certain conditions are met. . . .

In the Marrakesh Agreement Establishing the World Trade Organization ("WTO Agreement"), there are provisions that regulate conflict between the WTO Agreement and the multilateral trade agreements in its Annexes. *See* Article XVI.3 of the WTO Agreement, between GATT 1994 and other Agreements in Annex 1A. See, for example, the general interpretative note to Annex 1A., and between certain Agreements in Annex 1A (such as Agreement on Technical Barriers to Trade and Agreement on the Application of Sanitary and Phytosanitary Measures. *See* Article 1.5 of the Agreement on Technical Barriers to Trade.). There is no provision regulating conflict between Agreements in Annex 1A and Agreements in Annexes 1B or 1C to the WTO Agreement.

THE CONVENTION ON BIOLOGICAL DIVERSITY AND THE AGREEMENT ON TRADE-RELATED ASPECTS OF INTELLECTUAL PROPERTY RIGHTS (TRIPS): RELATIONSHIPS AND SYNERGIES

Conference of the Parties to the Convention on Biological Diversity

Third meeting, Buenos Aires, Argentina, November 4-15 1996

UNEP/CBD/COP/3/23

1. INTRODUCTION

In response to a request by the second meeting of the Conference of the Parties (COP), this paper reviews synergies and relationships between the Convention on Biological Diversity and the TRIPS Agreement . . . This paper also includes options for the third meeting of the COP to consider in preparing a possible input to the Committee on Trade and Environment (CTE) of the WTO.

The relationships between the TRIPS Agreement and the Convention on Biological Diversity are multifaceted and complex, as are the links between intellectual property rights (IPR) and the Convention. . . . The COP may wish to identify specific topics within this issue area for further work. The CTE of the WTO is discussing the relationship between the TRIPS Agreement and the sustainable development and protection of the environment, which creates a specific opportunity for exploring the relationship between the TRIPS Agreement and the Convention's objectives.

. . . .

2. BACKGROUND

In Decision II/12 on intellectual property rights, the COP asked the Executive Secretary to, inter alia, "[l]iaise with the Secretariat of the World Trade Organization to inform it of the goals and the ongoing work of the Convention on Biological Diversity and to invite the Secretariat of the World Trade Organization to assist in the preparation of a paper for the Conference of the Parties that identifies the synergies and relationship between the objectives of the Convention on Biological Diversity and the TRIPS Agreement".

The COP noted that "[t]his paper could be the basis for consideration by the third meeting of the Conference of the Parties in preparing a possible input for negotiations that are taking place in the Committee on Trade and Environment of the World Trade Organization."

A number of other items on the provisional agenda of the third meeting of the COP are relevant to the relationship between the Convention and the TRIPS Agreement. Most important is Item 14.1, a discussion of the impact of intellectual property rights systems (IPR systems) on the objectives of the Convention. . . . Also relevant is Item 11.1, regarding the implementation of Article 8(j) concerning the knowledge, innovations and practices of indigenous and local communities. . . .

. . . .

4. RELATIONSHIP BETWEEN THE CONVENTION ON BIOLOGICAL DIVERSITY AND THE TRIPS AGREEMENT

Intellectual property rights are important under both the Convention on Biological Diversity and the TRIPS Agreement, but the two agreements approach them from very different perspectives. A large and growing number of countries are both Parties to the Convention and members of the WTO (156 Parties to the Convention on Biological Diversity as of 4 November 1996; 125 members of the WTO as of 23 October 1996). This creates a powerful motivation to develop a mutually supportive relationship and to avoid conflicts. Both the COP and the WTO are beginning to explore the complex interrelationships between IPR and biological diversity. At this stage, the most critical issue for the relationship between the Convention on Biological Diversity and the TRIPS Agreement appears to be whether and how to establish procedures for consultation and cooperation between the bodies associated with the two agreements.

Both the Convention on Biological Diversity and the TRIPS Agreement allow a significant degree of flexibility in national implementation. This suggests that there is potential for complementary and perhaps synergistic implementation. Because both agreements entered into force recently and discussions of the relationships between IPR and biological diversity are preliminary, specific legal or policy mechanisms that would create synergies between the two agreements or their implementing measures have yet to be identified. Nevertheless, some general areas for complementarity have been noted.

For example, mutually agreed-upon terms for access to genetic resources could allocate IPR as part of the benefits to be shared among parties to an agreement on genetic resources . . . Such IPR could be defined under TRIPS-compatible IPR systems.

Another possibility is for the Convention and the TRIPS Agreement to develop procedures for exchanging relevant information. Article 16 of the Convention on Biological Diversity, and possibly others as well, prescribes IPR obligations for the Parties. The implementation of these obligations would likely fall within the scope of the notification requirement found in Article 63 of the TRIPS Agreement. . . . Countries implementing measures that implicate both agreements such as rules requiring patent applications to disclose the country of origin of biological material might report them to the TRIPS Council while at the same time disclosing the same information to the clearing-house mechanism for scientific and technical cooperation established under Article 18(3) of the Convention, or including information regarding the measures in the national reports required under Article 26 of the Convention. It may be useful to note that the WTO and the World Intellectual Property Organization (WIPO) recently concluded an agreement formalizing arrangements for the exchange of information, in particular copies of IPR laws and regulations received by the two organizations.

Other policy and legal proposals involving interrelated implementation of both the Convention on Biological Diversity and the TRIPS Agreement may warrant further examination. One proposal, for example, is to require or encourage disclosure in patent applications of the country and community of origin for genetic resources and informal knowledge used to develop the invention. This has been proposed by a number of commentators (e.g., Gadgil and Devasia 1995; Hendrickx et al. 1994; Gollin 1993). Some evidence suggests that such disclosures are already common practice in filing patent applications. Possible elements of such a requirement, which could help to encourage the implementation of both Article 15 and Article 8(j), are outlined in the Executive Secretary's background paper on Article 8(j). . . .

In spite of the flexibility of the Convention and the TRIPS Agreement, and the potential for synergies, there is still a possibility that conflicts could arise (Downes 1995). For example, national measures to promote technology transfer under Article 16 might raise most-favored nation issues if Convention Parties and non-Parties were treated differently, might raise national-treatment issues if foreign nationals received less favorable treatment, and might raise TRIPS issues if owners of proprietary technology were compelled to license technologies on grounds other than those prescribed in the TRIPS Agreement.

Looking to the provisions of the agreements regarding conflicts, Article 22(1) of the Convention provides that its provisions "shall not affect [a Party's] rights and obligations . . . deriving from any existing international agreement, except where the exercise of those rights and obligations would cause a serious damage or threat to biological diversity." It is not clear how this Article would apply in the case of conflicts with the TRIPS Agreement. The TRIPS Agreement contains no explicit reference to its relationship to the Convention on Biological Diversity or any other environmental agreement.

If WTO members cannot resolve disagreements regarding the implementation of the TRIPS Agreement through consultations, one member may bring a complaint against another for failure to meet its obligations, using the dispute resolution procedures generally applicable for WTO members (Article 64). . . .

If Parties to the Convention have a dispute about its interpretation or application, they may seek solution by negotiation, by the mediation of a third party, by conciliation, or (if they agree to be bound by such a means of dispute settlement) by arbitration or submission of the dispute to the International Court of Justice (Article 27). These procedures have not yet been invoked by a Convention Party. Like the WTO procedures, dispute-resolution procedures for the Convention emphasize avoidance of direct conflict by requiring other steps, such as negotiation.

There are several possible scenarios for conflict. A dispute might arise between countries that are both Convention Parties and WTO members; or between a country that is a Convention Party and a WTO member, and a country that is either a WTO member or a Convention Party. A conflict concerning the two agreements would presumably involve a claim, in a forum associated with one of the instruments, that a country had violated its obligations, countered by a defense that the alleged violation constituted implementation of the other instrument, and was obligated or authorized by it. In such disputes, it is likely that a forum associated with one instrument would need an interpretation of the other agreement. In such a case, it is unclear how a dispute-resolution proceeding would reach such a determination; neither instrument provides for such an eventuality. The absence of a clear mechanism for reconciling perceived differences further emphasizes the value of cooperation to avoid such differences.

. . . .

The CTE's agenda includes ten items. Of these, several are particularly relevant to the subject of this paper. Most important is item 8, "[r]elevant provisions of the Agreement on Trade-Related Aspects of Intellectual Property Rights." Also significant is item 1, "[t]he relationship between provisions of the multilateral trading system and trade measures for environmental purposes, including those pursuant to multilateral environmental agreements". Potentially relevant is item 2, "[t]he relationship between environmental policies relevant to trade and environmental measures with significant trade effects and the provisions of the multilateral trading system." . . . Discussions to date have been preliminary in nature, and have focused on ideas put forward by some delegations on the following issue areas:

(a) the protection of rights to biological resources and measures to ensure the equitable sharing of benefits from patentable products derived from these resources. This has included considerable discussion of protecting the interests of indigenous peoples and enhancing their ability to protect and preserve biological diversity;

(b) methods (such as patent restrictions) for discouraging the development and exploitation of environmentally harmful products. One area of concern has been IPR as to genetically modified organisms, as an ethical as well as an environmental issue; and

(c) the appropriate level of IPR protection, in light of the impact of such protection, on the development of environmentally sound technology (EST), and on access to it and transfer of it. On the one hand, some developing country delegates have called for reforms to TRIPS to facilitate the transfer of EST, while some developed country representatives have argued that IPR are in fact essential to the development of EST and, therefore, to environmental protection. There has also been discussion of the impact of IPR on both developing countries and the environment as applied to technologies that are restricted or otherwise affected by measures pursuant to multilateral environmental agreements.

. . . .

In these discussions, a number of WTO members have highlighted the importance of reconciling TRIPS and its IPR objectives with the CBD objectives of equitable sharing and sustainability. Other delegations do not see any irreconcilability between the two agreements. Some delegations would prefer to limit discussion of the second issue, relating to environmentally harmful products, anticipating that the negotiation of a biosafety protocol to the Convention on Biological Diversity may address many relevant concerns.

. . . .

As discussed above, the TRIPS Council will review Article 27.3(b) of the TRIPS which addresses the exclusion from patentability of plants and animals, the protection of plant varieties, and the right of countries to develop their own system to protect plant varieties in 1999. It is possible that the CTE might study this issue in preparation for the 1999 review.

. . . .

6. OPTIONS FOR FUTURE WORK

In light of the synergies and relationships discussed above, the COP might wish to consider the following options relating to a possible input to the CTE:

(a) Forwarding to the CTE relevant decisions and discussions of the COP contained in the chair's report, as well as this and other relevant papers prepared by the Executive Secretary. Relevant papers might include this study, as well as The Impact of Intellectual Property Rights Systems on the Conservation and Sustainable Use of Biological Diversity and on the Equitable Sharing of Benefits From Its Use: A Preliminary Study, and/or Knowledge, Innovations and Practices of Indigenous and Local Communities: Implementation of Article 8(j).

(b) Commending the CTE and WTO Secretariat for de-restricting and transmitting documents relating to the work of the CTE, inviting the WTO to continue to transmit future relevant documents as they are produced, and requesting the Convention Secretariat to reciprocate by transmitting similar documents to the CTE in the future.

(c) Seeking a role in the deliberations of the CTE, possibly by applying to participate in the CTE as an observer.

(d) Suggesting that Parties that are also WTO members notify the TRIPS Council (pursuant to the notification requirement of Article 63 of the TRIPS Agreement) of those laws and regulations implementing the provisions relating to IPR of Article 16 of the Convention on Biological Diversity. The

COP might also wish to suggest that those Parties simultaneously notify the Secretariat of the Convention so that such measures can be communicated through the clearing-house mechanism.

(e) Exploring additional ways to cooperate with the WTO on exchanging information.

(f) Continuing its exploration of issues relating to IPR by developing informational inputs for the CTE regarding the impact of patenting of genetically modified organisms, including animals and plants and essentially biological processes, in preparation for the 1999 review by the TRIPS Council of Article 27.3(b) of the TRIPS Agreement.

(g) Sending a statement to the WTO CTE. The statement might refer to one or more of the following points:

(i) the large number of countries that are both Parties to the Convention on Biological Diversity and members of the WTO;

(ii) the important interrelationships between the CBD and the WTO agreements, including the TRIPS Agreement; noting that the interrelationships extend beyond TRIPS, although TRIPS is the focus of this statement;

(iii) the international and national processes of implementation now underway for both agreements;

(iv) the significant potential for complementarities in implementing the two agreements, as reflected in the Executive Secretary's report;

(v) the important roles of both institutions in the area of IPR and biological diversity, in cooperation with other relevant international institutions and instruments;

(vi) an invitation to the CTE to present questions to the COP regarding the relationship of IPR and the obligations of the TRIPS Agreement and the Convention's objectives.

(h) The COP might wish to continue exploring the relationships between trade and trade law and policy and the achievement of the objectives of the Convention, possibly with particular attention to Articles of the Convention that appear most closely linked to these relationships, such as articles 5, 7(c), 8(1), or 11. The COP might wish to draw the attention of the CTE to any plans for such work.

NOTES AND QUESTIONS

(1) **Technology and the Environment.** Is there a fundamental clash between technological development and environmental protection in the twenty-first century? *See* Charles R. McManis, *The Interface between International Intellectual Property and Environmental Protection: Biodiversity and Biotechnology,* 76 WASH. U. L. Q. 255 (1998). Are there hopeful

signs in the juxtaposition of biotechnology and biodiversity? For an interesting example of how post-modern authors view the issues of conservation and human development and the juxtaposition of modern and traditional civilizations, see, *e.g.,* VIRGINIA D. NAUSARI, CULTURAL MEMORY AND BIODIVERSITY (1998).

(2) **Section 102(f).** Section 102(f) of the U.S. patent act precludes the award of a patent when the applicant did not invent the subject matter sought to be patented. It has been suggested that patent applications whose claims merely duplicate processes known to indigenous and local communities fail the statutory bar of subsection 102(f) and should be rejected. Section 102(f), which literally says an applicant is entitled to a patent unless "he did not himself invent the subject matter sought to be patented," is sometimes called the "derivation" provision. Section 102(f) has invariably been applied by the courts in situations where the applicant is shown to have acquired the invention from another person, and the party challenging the patent must demonstrate that there was "communication of a complete conception . . . sufficient to enable one of ordinary skill in the art to construct and successfully operate the invention." *Hedgewick v. Akers*, 497 F.2d 905, 908 (C.C.P.A. 1974). But the statute nowhere uses the word "derivation." Should a patent application fail for lack of novelty under 102(f) merely because an indigenous people are shown to have known of the invention and the precise derivation is unknown?

(3) **The Ayahuasca Patent**. On November 3, 1999, the ayahuasca patent granted by the U.S. PTO on a plant considered sacred by some Amazon indigenous peoples was ruled invalid in a reexamination proceeding on the basis that plant specimen sheets in herbarium collections are prior publications because they are publicly available and catalogued. *See Plant Patent's Rejection Highlights Conflict Between Tradition and IP Law*, 1 INTELL. PROP. L. WEEKLY 741 (Nov. 17, 1999).

(4) **Search Obligations**. An applicant for a patent is under no current obligation to conduct a search prior to filing an application. *See American Hoist & Derrick Co. v. Sowa & Sons*, 725 F.2 1350, 1362 (Fed. Cir. 1984). Some scholars have proposed requiring patent applicants to conduct a prior art search of traditional knowledge before filing. At the Diplomatic Conference in Spring 2001 at which the new WIPO Patent Law Treaty [PLT] was concluded, the delegation of Columbia, supported by many developing countries, proposed mandatory identification of the origin of genetic resources as part of the harmonized patent application encapsulated in the PLT. Developed countries have staunchly resisted all attempts to establish such a requirement. WIPO has agreed to provide further study of the issue. Would a new formal requirement such as disclosure of the origin of genetic resources be an additional requirement beyond that which is allowed by Article 27 TRIPS? *See* Nuno Pires de Carvalho, *Requiring Disclosure of the Origin of Genetic Resources and Prior Informed Consent in Patent Applications Without Infringing the TRIPS Agreement: The Problem and the Solution*, 2 WASH. U. J.L. & POL'Y 371 (2000).

Most patent applicants do a search prior to filing an application in any event, given the significant costs of drafting an application and the Section 112 prohibition against adding "new matter" to a disclosure after the filing date. What purposes are served by the present state of the law relieving the applicant of any obligation to search? Wouldn't interests of economy suggest that some sort of search be required of the applicant prior to filing a patent application, particularly given that the applicant is or should be in a better position than the examiner to know where prior art lies?

(5) **The Cord Blood Controversy**. Article 27(2) of TRIPS allows a state to "exclude from patentability inventions, the prevention within their territory of the commercial exploitation of which is necessary to protect ordre public or morality." In early 1999, the European Patent Office revoked a patent covering the use of human blood cells (cord blood) for medical purposes. The patent application, filed in 1989 by the U.S. Company Biocyte, related to the isolation and preservation of fetal and neonatal hematopoietic stem and progenitor cells of the blood. The EPO justified its decision arguing that human blood cannot be placed within the realm of invention. Similarly, the U.S. Patent and Trademark Office has rejected a patent application claiming a part-human "chimera." Is the "appropriation and commodification of a widely held religious system" less offensive to the public policies supposedly upheld by the patent law than patents relating to human beings? Should Congress add explicit exceptions to patentability in the patent law concerning scandalous subject matter, similar to those found in section 2(a) of the Lanham Act?

(6) **UPOV and *Sui Generis* Protection of Plant Varieties**. Recall that under TRIPS Article 27(3)(b), members may also exclude from patentability "plants and animals other than microorganisms, and essentially biological processes for the production of plants or animals other than non-biological and microbiological processes." But it goes on to say, "however, Members shall provide for the protection of plant varieties either by patents or by an effective *sui generis* system or by any combination thereof. The provisions of this sub-paragraph shall be reviewed four years after the entry into force of the Agreement Establishing the WTO." In January 1999, a foreign ministry-level meeting of the sixty-two member Organization of African Unity ("OAU") in Lusaka called for a hold on intellectual property protection of plant varieties until an Africa-wide alternative system to patents has been developed. The proposed system would aim to divide the intellectual property rights of new plant forms between plant breeders and indigenous communities that might have contributed to early varieties in accordance with the "equitable sharing" provisions of the CBD. Two weeks later in Bangui, a meeting of patent office officials from member states of the OAPI countries reached a decision to recommend that the sixteen states collectively adopt the 1991 version of the UPOV convention. Subsequently (according to news reports), Johnson Ekpere, secretary-general of the Scientific, Technical and Research Commission of the OAU, said, "This is a case of the right hand not knowing what the left hand is doing" and described as "unlikely" any attempts to ratify the UPOV convention in an

African parliament. Mzondi Haviland Chirambo, director-general of AR-IPO, agreed, stating that he believes that ARIPO member states are un-likely to follow the lead set by OAPI countries. Does the language of the final sentence of Article 27(3)(b) quoted above suggest that the entire subsection is subject to renegotiation? *See* GENETIC RESOURCES ACTION INT'L [GRAIN], TRIPS VERSUS BIODIVERSITY: WHAT TO DO WITH THE 1999 REVIEW OF ARTICLE 27.3(B), available at www.grain.org/publications/reports/tripsmay99.htm; Philippe Cullet, *Revision of the TRIPS Agreement Concerning the Protection of Plant Varieties: Lessons from India concerning the Development of a* Sui Generis *System*, 2 J. WORLD INTELL. PROP. 617 (1999). If so, are the developing country member states of the WTO still obliged to enact a system for protection of plants now that the TRIPS Agreement has taken effect in those countries?

(7) **Patent Protection and "Biopiracy."** The protection of indigenous knowledge is a key concept of the CBD. *See* CBD art. 8(j). The Coordinating Body for Indigenous Organizations of the Amazon Basin ("COICA"), in its fifth Congress in May of 1997, decided to declare a citizen of the United States, Loren Miller, the *Banisteriopsis* patentee, an "enemy of indigenous people." After that time COICA prohibited his entry into any indigenous territory. In an Open Letter to the U.S. Congress, in April 1998, COICA alleged that as a result:

> the Inter-American Foundation (IAF)—a body of the U.S. govern-ment—has decided to break relations with our organization. In doing so, they have denied any type of collaboration (*sic*) with more than one and a half million indigenous peoples of the Amazon Basin, while we are making an effort to maintain our cultures, as well as, trying to avoid the destruction of the largest rainforest on the planet. . . . COICA will not renounce its legitimate right to defend and preserve the knowledge, practices, innovations and natural resources of the peoples whom we represent. This right has been explicitly recognized in the Treaty of Biological Diversity that was ratified by more than 170 countries. . . . We believe that you the Congressmen/women, should know the fundamental reason which allows your fellow citizens to patent our plants and appropriate our knowledge. There is a lack of ratification by the U.S. Congress of the Treaty of Biological Diversity, and a lack of approval for accurate laws that impede this known worldwide practice of "biopiracy."

Communication from *coica@uio.satnet.net*. The United States signed the CBD on June 4, 1993, but has not ratified it. Assuming that the COICA allegations regarding the IAF are correct, once having signed on (even if not acceding) to the CBD, is the United States obliged under international law not to work against the CBD's objects and purposes by applying such political pressure on indigenous groups? As a rhetorical gesture, is the use of the term "biopiracy" by NGOs against the uncompensated use of indige-nous knowledge in developing countries any different in impact or validity from the use of the term "piracy" by developed countries for counterfeit goods?

(8) **Access to Biodiversity**. For a frank discussion of the issues involving access to biodiversity and intellectual property, see The Greening of Technology Transfer: The Protection of the Environment and of Intellectual Property (William O. Hennessey ed.) (1994), at www.piercelaw.edu/green/contents.htm. *See also* William O. Hennessey, *Sustainable Development Is Win-Win*, 31 LES NOUVELLES 15-19 (Mar. 1996).

TABLE OF CASES

Principal excerpted cases are listed in upper case format and the page number at which the excerpt appears is italicized

Principal excerpted cases are listed in upper case format and the page number at which the excerpt appears is italicized

Principal excerpted cases are listed in upper case format and the page number at which the excerpt appears is italicized

INDEX

[References are to page numbers.]

[References are to page numbers.]

EUROPEAN UNION (EU)—Cont.

Institutions of . . . 239-240

Judicial process . . . 241-243

Legislative instruments . . . 240; 437

Legislative process . . . 240-241

National law and union law, relationship
between . . . 243-244

Parallel imports/gray goods

Consent . . . 830

EFTA states . . . 831-832

Merck & Co. Inc. v. Primecrown Ltd.
(1997) . . . 824-830

Pharmaceuticals . . . 824-831

Treaty provisions . . . 824

Proposal for EU-wide patent . . . 719-735

Purpose . . . 232

Regional agreements . . . 460-466

Software patentability, proposed directive
. . . 114-115

Status . . . 245

Technology licensing, 1996 regulation on
. . . 421-432

Trade barrier regulation . . . 516-517

EXCLUSIVE RIGHTS

TRIPS Agreement . . . 362-363; 371

United States patent laws . . . 153-158

EXHAUSTION OF RIGHTS (See EN-
FORCEMENT)

EXTRATERRITORIAL PROTECTION
(See ENFORCEMENT)

F

FIRST INVENTOR DEFENSE

U. S. patent laws . . . 182

"FIRST SALE DOCTRINE"

General discussion . . . 809-810; 823-824

FIRST-TO-INVENT VS. FIRST-TO-FILE

Harmonization of patent laws . . . 343-346

Novelty and priority of invention . . . . . .
116-117; 128

Paris Convention . . . 316-317

U.S. patent laws . . . 14

FOLKLORE

Generally . . . 846-847

Traditional knowledge, meaning of . . . . .
850-851

WIPO IGC, role of . . . 847

**FOOD AND AGRICULTURE ORGANIZA-
TION (FAO)**

General discussion . . . 857-858

FORFEITURE PRINCIPLE

Congress of Vienna of 1873 . . . 315

Paris Convention (See PARIS CONVEN-
TION)

FORUM NON CONVENIENS

Murray v. British Broadcasting Corp (1996)
. . . 297-301

**FREE TRADE AREA OF THE AMERI-
CAS (FTAA)**

Proposal for . . . 746-747

G

**GENERAL AGREEMENT ON TARIFFS
AND TRADE (GATT)**

Acquis communautaire . . . 552

Dissatisfaction with GATT and enactment of
Special 301 . . . 472-473

Economic law, generally . . . 297

Harmonization of patent laws . . . 347

Impairment . . . 522

Most-favored national treatment . . . 270

Nullification . . . 522

Uruguay Round . . . 10

U.S. patent law and . . . 14

World Intellectual Property Organization
(WIPO) . . . 347

GENETIC RESOURCES

Generally . . . 846-847

Budapest Deposit Treaty of 1977 . . . 630

Convention on Biological Diversity (CBD) and
TRIPS . . . 419; 847

Identification of origin of . . . 872

Patent Law Treaty . . . 872

WIPO IGC . . . 847

GEOGRAPHICAL INDICATIONS

TRIPS Agreement . . . 7

TRIPS Council . . . 846

GERMANY

Anti-patent movement . . . 303-305

Max Planck Society and international journals . . . 63-64

Working requirements . . . 338-339

GLOBALIZATION

EU as model for global union . . . 251

Meaning of . . . 27

Need for international thinking . . . 24-29

Patent registration agreements (See GLOBAL
PATENT REGISTRATION AGREEMENTS)

**GLOBAL PATENT REGISTRATION
AGREEMENTS**

Budapest Deposit Treaty of 1977 . . . 630

[References are to page numbers.]

[References are to page numbers.]

[References are to page numbers.]

[References are to page numbers.]